JOANNE GREENSTEIN.

COLLINS
POCKET
FRENCH
DICTIONARY

COLLINS

POCKET FRENCH DICTIONARY

FRENCH ▶ENGLISH ENGLISH ▶FRENCH

HarperCollins*Publishers*

second edition/deuxième édition 1995

© **HarperCollins Publishers 1995**
© **William Collins Sons & Co. Ltd. 1990**

HarperCollins Publishers
P.O. Box, Glasgow G4 0NB, Great Britain
ISBN 0 00 470396 0

Dictionnaires Le Robert
27, rue de la Glacière, 75013 Paris
ISBN 2 85036398 7

Pierre-Henri Cousin • Lorna Sinclair Knight
Catherine E. Love • Jean-François Allain • Claude Nimmo

contributors to second edition/deuxième édition
Bob Grossmith • Jean-Benoit Ormal-Grenon

editorial staff/secrétariat de rédaction
Val McNulty • Elspeth Anderson

series editor/collection dirigée par
Lorna Sinclair Knight

Dépôt légal: mars 1995
Achevé d'imprimer en mars 1995

Typeset by Morton Word Processing Ltd, Scarborough

Printed in Great Britain by
HarperCollins Manufacturing, Glasgow

INTRODUCTION

We are delighted that you have decided to buy the Collins Pocket French Dictionary, and hope you will enjoy and benefit from using it at home, at school, on holiday or at work.

The innovative use of colour guides you quickly and efficiently to the word you want, and the comprehensive wordlist provides a wealth of modern and idiomatic phrases not normally found in a dictionary this size.

In addition, the supplement provides you with guidance on using the dictionary, along with entertaining ways of improving your dictionary skills.

We hope that you will enjoy using it and that it will significantly enhance your language studies.

COMMENT UTILISER VOTRE DICTIONNAIRE MINI COLLINS

Ce dictionnaire offre une masse d'informations et use de divers formes et tailles de caractères, symboles, abréviations, parenthèses et crochets. Les conventions et symboles utilisés sont expliqués dans les sections qui suivent.

Entrées

Les mots que vous cherchez dans le dictionnaire (les 'entrées') sont classés par ordre alphabétique. Ils sont imprimés en **caractères rouges** pour pouvoir être repérés rapidement. Les deux entrées figurant en haut de page indiquent le premier et le dernier mot qui apparaissent sur la page en question.

Des informations sur l'usage ou sur la forme de certaines entrées sont données entre parenthèses, après la transcription phonétique. Ces indications apparaissent sous forme abrégée et en italiques (ex *(fam)*, *(COMM)*).

Dans les cas appropriés, les mots apparentés aux entrées sont regroupés sous la même entrée (**ronger, rongeur; accept, acceptance**) et apparaissent en caractères rouges, légèrement plus petits que ceux de l'entrée.

Les expressions courantes dans lesquelles apparaît l'entrée sont indiquées par des caractères romains gras (ex **avoir du retard**).

Transcription phonétique

La transcription phonétique de chaque entrée (indiquant sa prononciation) est indiquée entre crochets immédiatement après l'entrée (ex **fumer** [fyme]; **knead** [ni:d]). Une liste de ces symboles figure aux pages x et xi.

Traductions

Les traductions des entrées apparaissent en caractères ordinaires et, lorsque plusieurs sens ou usages coexistent, ces traductions sont séparées par un point-virgule. Vous trouverez souvent entre parenthèses d'autres mots en italiques qui précèdent les traductions. Ces mots fournissent souvent certains des contextes dans lesquels l'entrée est susceptible d'être utilisée (ex **rough** *(voice)* ou *(weather)*) ou offrent des synonymes (ex **rough** *(violent)*).

'Mots-clés'

Une importance particulière est accordée à certains mots français et anglais qui sont considérés comme des "mots-clés" dans chacune des langues. Cela peut être dû à leur utilisation très fréquente ou au fait qu'ils ont divers types d'usages (ex **vouloir, plus; get, that**). Une combinaison de losanges et de chiffres vous aident à distinguer différentes catégories grammaticales et différents sens. D'autres renseignements utiles apparaissent en italiques et entre parenthèses dans la langue de l'utilisateur.

Données grammaticales

Les catégories grammaticales sont données sous forme abrégée et en italiques après la transcription phonétique des entrées (ex *vt, adv, conj*).

Les genres des noms français sont indiqués de la manière suivante: *nm* pour un nom masculin et *nf* pour un nom féminin. Le féminin et le pluriel irréguliers de certains noms sont également indiqués (**directeur, trice; cheval, aux**).

Le masculin et le féminin des adjectifs sont indiqués lorsque ces deux formes sont différentes (ex **noir, e**). Lorsque l'adjectif a un féminin ou un pluriel irrégulier, ces formes sont clairement indiquées (ex **net, nette**). Les pluriels irréguliers des noms, et les formes irréguliers des verbes anglais sont indiqués entre parenthèses, avant la catégorie grammaticale (ex **man** ... (*pl* **men**) *n*; **give** (*pt* **gave**, *pp* **given**) *vt*).

USING YOUR COLLINS POCKET DICTIONARY

A wealth of information is presented in the dictionary, using various typefaces, sizes of type, symbols, abbreviations and brackets. The conventions and symbols used are explained in the following sections.

Headwords

The words you look up in a dictionary — "headwords" — are listed alphabetically. They are printed in **colour** for rapid identification. The two headwords appearing at the top of each page indicate the first and last word dealt with on the page in question.

Information about the usage or form of certain headwords is given in brackets after the phonetic spelling. This usually appears in abbreviated form and in italics (e.g. *(fam)*, *(COMM)*).
Where appropriate, words related to headwords are grouped in the same entry (**ronger, rongeur; accept, acceptance**) in a slightly smaller coloured type than the headword.

Common expressions in which the headword appears are shown in black bold roman type (e.g. **avoir du retard**).

Phonetic spellings

The phonetic spelling of each headword (indicating its pronunciation) is given in square brackets immediately after the headword (e.g. **fumer** [fyme]; **knead** [ni:d]). A list of the phonetic symbols is given on page x.

Translations

Headword translations are given in ordinary type and, where more than one meaning or usage exists, these are separated by a semi-colon. You will often find other words in italics in brackets before the translations. These offer suggested contexts in which the headword might appear (e.g. **rough** *(voice)* or *(weather)*) or provide synonyms (e.g. **rough** *(violent)*).

"Key" words

Special status is given to certain French and English words which are considered as "key" words in each language. They may, for example, occur very frequently or have several types of usage (e.g. **vouloir, plus; get, that**). A combination of lozenges and numbers helps you to distinguish different parts of speech and different meanings. Further helpful information is provided in brackets and in italics in the relevant language for the user.

Grammatical information

Parts of speech are given in abbreviated form in italics after the phonetic spellings of headwords (e.g. *vt, adv, conj*).

Genders of French nouns are indicated as follows: *nm* for a masculine and *nf* for a feminine noun. Feminine and irregular plural forms of nouns are also shown (**directeur, trice; cheval, aux**).

Adjectives are given in both masculine and feminine forms where these forms are different (e.g. **noir, e**). Clear information is provided where adjectives have an irregular feminine or plural form (e.g. **net, nette**).

ABRÉVIATIONS

ABBREVIATIONS

adjectif, locution adjective	**adj**	adjective, adjectival phrase
abréviation	**ab(b)r**	abbreviation
adverbe, locution adverbiale	**adv**	adverb, adverbial phrase
administration	**ADMIN**	administration
agriculture	**AGR**	agriculture
anatomie	**ANAT**	anatomy
architecture	**ARCHIT**	architecture
article défini	**art déf**	definite article
article indéfini	**art indéf**	indefinite article
attribut	**attrib**	predicative
l'automobile	**AUT(O)**	the motor car and motoring
auxiliaire	**aux**	auxiliary
aviation, voyages aériens	**AVIAT**	flying, air travel
biologie	**BIO(L)**	biology
botanique	**BOT**	botany
anglais de Grande-Bretagne	**BRIT**	British English
commerce, finance, banque	**COMM**	commerce, finance, banking
comparatif	**compar**	comparative
informatique	**COMPUT**	computing
conditionnel	**cond**	conditional
chimie	**CHEM**	chemistry
conjonction	**conj**	conjunction
construction	**CONSTR**	building
nom utilisé comme adjectif, ne peut s'employer ni comme attribut, ni après le nom qualifié	**cpd**	compound element: used as an adjective and which cannot follow the noun it qualifies
cuisine, art culinaire	**CULIN**	cookery
article défini	**def art**	definite article
diminutif	**dimin**	diminutive
économie	**ECON**	economics
électricité, électronique	**ELEC**	electricity, electronics
exclamation, interjection	**excl**	exclamation, interjection
féminin	**f**	feminine
langue familière (! emploi vulgaire)	**fam(!)**	informal usage (! very offensive)
emploi figuré	**fig**	figurative use
(verbe anglais) dont la particule est inséparable du verbe	**fus**	(phrasal verb) where the particle cannot be separated from main verb
dans la plupart des sens		in most or all senses
généralement	**gén, gen**	generally
géographie, géologie	**GEO**	geography, geology
géométrie	**GEOM**	geometry
impersonnel	**impers**	impersonal
article indéfini	**indef art**	indefinite article
langue familière (! emploi vulgaire)	**inf(!)**	informal usage (! particularly offensive)
infinitif	**infin**	infinitive
informatique	**INFORM**	computing
invariable	**inv**	invariable

viii

ABRÉVIATIONS

ABBREVIATIONS

irrégulier	**irreg**	irregular
domaine juridique	**JUR**	law
grammaire, linguistique	**LING**	grammar, linguistics
masculin	**m**	masculine
mathématiques, algèbre	**MATH**	mathematics, calculus
médecine	**MÉD, MED**	medical term, medicine
masculin ou féminin, suivant le sexe	**m/f**	either masculine or feminine depending on sex
domaine militaire, armée	**MIL**	military matters
musique	**MUS**	music
nom	**n**	noun
navigation, nautisme	**NAVIG, NAUT**	sailing, navigation
adjectif ou nom numérique	**num**	numeral adjective or noun
	o.s.	oneself
péjoratif	**péj, pej**	derogatory, pejorative
photographie	**PHOT(O)**	photography
physiologie	**PHYSIOL**	physiology
pluriel	**pl**	plural
politique	**POL**	politics
participe passé	**pp**	past participle
préposition	**prép, prep**	preposition
pronom	**pron**	pronoun
psychologie, psychiatrie	**PSYCH**	psychology, psychiatry
temps du passé	**pt**	past tense
quelque chose	**qch**	
quelqu'un	**qn**	
religions, domaine ecclésiastique	**REL**	religions, church service
	sb	somebody
enseignement, système scolaire et universitaire	**SCOL**	schooling, schools and universities
singulier	**sg**	singular
	sth	something
subjonctif	**sub**	subjunctive
sujet (grammatical)	**su(b)j**	(grammatical) subject
superlatif	**superl**	superlative
techniques, technologie	**TECH**	technical term, technology
télécommunications	**TEL**	telecommunications
télévision	**TV**	television
typographie	**TYP(O)**	typography, printing
anglais des USA	**US**	American English
verbe	**vb**	verb
verbe ou groupe verbal à fonction intransitive	**vi**	verb or phrasal verb used intransitively
verbe ou groupe verbal à fonction transitive	**vt**	verb or phrasal verb used transitively
zoologie	**ZOOL**	zoology
marque déposée	**®**	registered trademark
indique une équivalence culturelle	**≈**	introduces a cultural equivalent

TRANSCRIPTION PHONÉTIQUE

Consonnes

Consonants

NB. **p, b, t, d, k, g** sont suivis d'une aspiration en anglais.

NB. **p, b, t, d, k, g** are not aspirated in French.

poupée	p	puppy
bombe	b	baby
tente thermal	t	tent
dinde	d	daddy
coq qui képi	k	cork kiss chord
gag bague	g	gag guess
sale ce nation	s	so rice kiss
zéro rose	z	cousin buzz
tache chat	ʃ	sheep sugar
gilet juge	ʒ	pleasure beige
	tʃ	church
	dʒ	judge general
fer phare	f	farm raffle
valve	v	very rev
	θ	thin maths
	ð	that other
lent salle	l	little ball
rare rentrer	R	
	r	rat rare
maman femme	m	mummy comb
non nonne	n	no ran
agneau vigne	ɲ	
	ŋ	singing bank
hop!	h	hat reheat
yeux paille pied	j	yet
nouer oui	w	wall bewail
huile lui	ɥ	
	x	loch

Divers

Miscellaneous

pour l'anglais: précède le syllabe accentué ` ' `

pour l'anglais: le r final se prononce en liaison devant une voyelle `*`

in French wordlist and transcription: no liaison

PHONETIC TRANSCRIPTION

Voyelles

NB. La mise en équivalence de certains sons n'indique qu'une ressemblance approximative.

Vowels

NB. The pairing of some vowel sounds only indicates approximate equivalence.

ici v*ie* l*y*re	i iː	h*ee*l b*ea*d
	ɪ	h*i*t p*i*ty
jou*er* *été*	e	s*e*t t*e*nt
l*ait* jou*et* m*er*ci	ɛ	
pl*a*t *a*mour	a æ	b*a*t *a*pple
b*a*s p*â*te	ɑ ɑː	*a*fter c*a*r c*a*lm
	ʌ	f*u*n c*ou*sin
l*e* prem*ie*r	ə	*o*ver *a*bove
b*eu*rre p*eu*r	œ	
p*eu* d*eu*x	ø ɜː	*u*rn f*er*n w*or*k
*o*r h*o*mme	ɒ	w*a*sh p*o*t
m*o*t *eau* g*au*che	o ɔː	b*or*n c*or*k
gen*ou* r*ou*e	u ʊ	f*u*ll s*oo*t
	uː	b*oo*n l*ew*d
r*ue* *u*rne	y	

Diphtongues

Diphthongs

	ɪə	b*ee*r t*ie*r
	ɛə	t*ear* f*air* th*ere*
	eɪ	d*a*te pl*ai*ce d*ay*
	aɪ	l*i*fe b*uy* cr*y*
	aʊ	*ow*l f*ou*l n*ow*
	əʊ	l*ow* n*o*
	ɔɪ	b*oi*l b*oy* *oi*ly
	ʊə	p*oor* t*our*

Nasales

Nasal Vowels

mat*in* pl*ein*	ɛ̃
br*un*	œ̃
s*ang* *an* d*ans*	ɑ̃
n*on* p*ont*	ɔ̃

FRANÇAIS - ANGLAIS
FRENCH - ENGLISH

A a

A *abr* = **autoroute**
a *vb voir* **avoir**

à [a] (*à* + *le* = **au**, *à* + *les* = **aux**) *prép* **1** (*endroit, situation*) at, in; **être ~ Paris/au Portugal** to be in Paris/Portugal; **être ~ la maison/~ l'école** to be at home/at school; **~ la campagne** in the country; **c'est ~ 10 km/20 minutes (d'ici)** it's 10 km/20 minutes away
2 (*direction*) to; **aller ~ Paris/au Portugal** to go to Paris/Portugal; **aller ~ la maison/~ l'école** to go home/to school; **~ la campagne** to the country
3 (*temps*): **~ 3 heures/minuit** at 3 o'clock/midnight; **au printemps/mois de juin** in the spring/the month of June
4 (*attribution, appartenance*) to; **le livre est ~ Paul/~ lui/~ nous** this book is Paul's/his/ours; **donner qch ~ qn** to give sth to sb
5 (*moyen*) with; **se chauffer au gaz** to have gas heating; **~ bicyclette** on a *ou* by bicycle; **~ la main/machine** by hand/machine
6 (*provenance*) from; **boire ~ la bouteille** to drink from the bottle
7 (*caractérisation, manière*): **l'homme aux yeux bleus** the man with the blue eyes; **~ la russe** the Russian way
8 (*but, destination*): **tasse ~ café** coffee cup; **maison ~ vendre** house for sale
9 (*rapport, évaluation, distribution*): **100 km/unités ~ l'heure** 100 km/units per *ou* an hour; **payé ~ l'heure** paid by the hour; **cinq ~ six** five to six

abaisser [abese] *vt* to lower, bring down; (*manette*) to pull down; (*fig*) to

debase; to humiliate; **s'~** *vi* to go down; (*fig*) to demean o.s.
abandon [abɑ̃dɔ̃] *nm* abandoning; giving up; withdrawal; **être à l'~** to be in a state of neglect
abandonner [abɑ̃dɔne] *vt* (*personne*) to abandon; (*projet, activité*) to abandon, give up; (*SPORT*) to retire *ou* withdraw from; (*céder*) to surrender; **s'~** *vi* to let o.s. go; **s'~ à** (*paresse, plaisirs*) to give o.s. up to
abasourdir [abazurdir] *vt* to stun, stagger
abat-jour [abaʒur] *nm inv* lampshade
abats [aba] *nmpl* (*de bœuf, porc*) offal *sg*; (*de volaille*) giblets
abattement [abatmɑ̃] *nm* (*déduction*) reduction; **~ fiscal** ≈ tax allowance
abattoir [abatwar] *nm* slaughterhouse
abattre [abatr(ə)] *vt* (*arbre*) to cut down, fell; (*mur, maison*) to pull down; (*avion, personne*) to shoot down; (*animal*) to shoot, kill; (*fig*) to wear out, tire out; to demoralize; **s'~** *vi* to crash down; **s'~ sur** to beat down on; to rain down on
abbaye [abei] *nf* abbey
abbé [abe] *nm* priest; (*d'une abbaye*) abbot
abcès [apsɛ] *nm* abscess
abdiquer [abdike] *vi* to abdicate ♦ *vt* to renounce, give up
abeille [abɛj] *nf* bee
aberrant, e [abɛrɑ̃, -ɑ̃t] *adj* absurd
abêtir [abetir] *vt* to make morons of (*ou* a moron of)
abîme [abim] *nm* abyss, gulf
abîmer [abime] *vt* to spoil, damage; **s'~** *vi* to get spoilt *ou* damaged
ablation [ablɑsjɔ̃] *nf* removal
abois [abwa] *nmpl*: **aux ~** at bay

abolir [abɔliʀ] *vt* to abolish

abondance [abɔ̃dɑ̃s] *nf* abundance; (*richesse*) affluence

abondant, e [abɔ̃dɑ̃, -ɑ̃t] *adj* plentiful, abundant, copious

abonder [abɔ̃de] *vi* to abound, be plentiful; ~ **dans le sens de qn** to concur with sb

abonné, e [abɔne] *nm/f* subscriber; season ticket holder

abonnement [abɔnmɑ̃] *nm* subscription; (*transports, concerts*) season ticket

abonner [abɔne] *vt*: **s'~ à** to subscribe to, take out a subscription to

abord [abɔʀ] *nm*: **être d'un ~ facile** to be approachable; **~s** *nmpl* (*environs*) surroundings; **au premier ~** at first sight, initially; **d'~** first

abordable [abɔʀdabl(ə)] *adj* approachable; reasonably priced

aborder [abɔʀde] *vi* to land ♦ *vt* (*sujet, difficulté*) to tackle; (*personne*) to approach; (*rivage etc*) to reach; (NAVIG: *attaquer*) to board

aboutir [abutiʀ] *vi* (*négociations etc*) to succeed; ~ **à/dans/sur** to end up at/in/on

aboyer [abwaje] *vi* to bark

abrégé [abʀeʒe] *nm* summary

abréger [abʀeʒe] *vt* to shorten

abreuver [abʀœve] *vt* (*fig*): ~ **qn de** to shower ou swamp sb with; **s'~** *vi* to drink; **abreuvoir** *nm* watering place

abréviation [abʀevjasjɔ̃] *nf* abbreviation

abri [abʀi] *nm* shelter; **à l'~** under cover; **à l'~ de** sheltered from; (*fig*) safe from

abricot [abʀiko] *nm* apricot

abriter [abʀite] *vt* to shelter; (*loger*) to accommodate; **s'~** *vt* to shelter, take cover

abroger [abʀɔʒe] *vt* to repeal

abrupt, e [abʀypt] *adj* sheer, steep; (*ton*) abrupt

abrutir [abʀytiʀ] *vt* to daze; to exhaust; to stupefy

absence [apsɑ̃s] *nf* absence; (MÉD) blackout; mental blank

absent, e [apsɑ̃, -ɑ̃t] *adj* absent; (*distrait*: *air*) vacant, faraway ♦ *nm/f* absentee; **absenter**: **s'absenter** *vi* to take time off work; (*sortir*) to leave, go out

absolu, e [apsɔly] *adj* absolute; (*caractère*) rigid, uncompromising; **absolument** *adv* absolutely

absorber [apsɔʀbe] *vt* to absorb; (*gén* MÉD: *manger, boire*) to take

absoudre [apsudʀ(ə)] *vt* to absolve

abstenir [apstəniʀ]: **s'~** *vi* (POL) to abstain; **s'~ de qch/de faire** to refrain from sth/from doing

abstraction [apstʀaksjɔ̃] *nf* abstraction; **faire ~ de** to set ou leave aside

abstrait, e [apstʀɛ, -ɛt] *adj* abstract

absurde [apsyʀd(ə)] *adj* absurd

abus [aby] *nm* abuse; ~ **de confiance** breach of trust

abuser [abyze] *vi* to go too far, overstep the mark ♦ *vt* to deceive, mislead; **s'~** *vi* to be mistaken; ~ **de** to misuse; (*violer, duper*) to take advantage of; **abusif, ive** *adj* exorbitant; excessive; improper

acabit [akabi] *nm*: **de cet ~** of that type

académie [akademi] *nf* academy; (ART: *nu*) nude; (SCOL: *circonscription*) ≈ regional education authority

acajou [akaʒu] *nm* mahogany

acariâtre [akaʀjɑtʀ(ə)] *adj* cantankerous

accablant, e [akablɑ̃, ɑ̃t] *adj* (*témoignage, preuve*) overwhelming

accablement [akabləmɑ̃] *nm* despondency

accabler [akable] *vt* to overwhelm, overcome; (*suj*: *témoignage*) to condemn, damn; ~ **qn d'injures** to heap ou shower abuse on sb

accalmie [akalmi] *nf* lull

accaparer [akapaʀe] *vt* to monopolize; (*suj*: *travail etc*) to take up (all) the time ou attention of

accéder [aksede]: ~ **à** *vt* (*lieu*) to reach; (*fig*) to accede to, attain; (*accorder*: *requête*) to grant, accede to

accélérateur [akseleʀatœʀ] *nm* accelerator

accélération [akseleʀasjɔ̃] *nf* acceleration

accélérer [akseleʀe] *vt* to speed up ♦ *vi* to accelerate

accent [aksɑ̃] *nm* accent; (*inflexions expressives*) tone (of voice); (*PHONÉTIQUE, fig*) stress; **mettre l'~ sur** (*fig*) to stress; **~ aigu/grave** acute/grave accent

accentuer [aksɑ̃tɥe] *vt* (*LING*) to accent; (*fig*) to accentuate, emphasize; **s'~** *vi* to become more marked *ou* pronounced

acceptation [akseptasjɔ̃] *nf* acceptance

accepter [aksepte] *vt* to accept; (*tolérer*): **~ que qn fasse** to agree to sb doing; **~ de faire** to agree to do

accès [aksɛ] *nm* (*à un lieu*) access; (*MÉD*) attack; fit, bout; outbreak ♦ *nmpl* (*routes etc*) means of access, approaches; **d'~ facile** easily accessible; **~ de colère** fit of anger

accessible [aksesibl(ə)] *adj* accessible; (*livre, sujet*): **~ à qn** within the reach of sb; (*sensible*): **~ à** sensitive to

accessoire [akseswar] *adj* secondary; incidental ♦ *nm* accessory; (*THÉÂTRE*) prop

accident [aksidɑ̃] *nm* accident; **par ~** by chance; **~ de la route** road accident; **~ du travail** industrial injury *ou* accident; **accidenté, e** *adj* damaged; injured; (*relief, terrain*) uneven; hilly

acclamer [aklame] *vt* to cheer, acclaim

accolade [akɔlad] *nf* (*amicale*) embrace; (*signe*) brace

accommodant, e [akɔmɔdɑ̃, -ɑ̃t] *adj* accommodating; easy-going

accommoder [akɔmɔde] *vt* (*CULIN*) to prepare; (*points de vue*) to reconcile; **s'~ de** *vt* to put up with; to make do with

accompagnateur, trice [akɔ̃paɲatœr, -tris] *nm/f* (*MUS*) accompanist; (*de voyage: guide*) guide; (: *d'enfants*) accompanying adult; (*de voyage organisé*) courier

accompagner [akɔ̃paɲe] *vt* to accompany, be *ou* go *ou* come with; (*MUS*) to accompany

accompli, e [akɔ̃pli] *adj* accomplished

accomplir [akɔ̃plir] *vt* (*tâche, projet*) to carry out; (*souhait*) to fulfil; **s'~** *vi* to be fulfilled

accord [akɔr] *nm* agreement; (*entre des styles, tons etc*) harmony; (*MUS*) chord; **d'~!** OK!; **se mettre d'~** to come to an agreement; **être d'~** to agree

accordéon [akɔrdeɔ̃] *nm* (*MUS*) accordion

accorder [akɔrde] *vt* (*faveur, délai*) to grant; (*harmoniser*) to match; (*MUS*) to tune; **s'~** *vt* to get on together; to agree

accoster [akɔste] *vt* (*NAVIG*) to draw alongside ♦ *vi* to berth

accotement [akɔtmɑ̃] *nm* verge (*BRIT*), shoulder

accouchement [akuʃmɑ̃] *nm* delivery, (child)birth; labour

accoucher [akuʃe] *vi* to give birth, have a baby; (*être en travail*) to be in labour ♦ *vt* to deliver; **~ d'un garçon** to give birth to a boy

accouder [akude]: **s'~** *vi* to rest one's elbows on/against; **accoudoir** *nm* armrest

accoupler [akuple] *vt* to couple; (*pour la reproduction*) to mate; **s'~** *vt* to mate

accourir [akurir] *vi* to rush *ou* run up

accoutrement [akutrəmɑ̃] (*péj*) *nm* (*tenue*) outfit

accoutumance [akutymɑ̃s] *nf* (*gén*) adaptation; (*MÉD*) addiction

accoutumé, e [akutyme] *adj* (*habituel*) customary, usual

accoutumer [akutyme] *vt*: **s'~ à** to get accustomed *ou* used to

accréditer [akredite] *vt* (*nouvelle*) to substantiate

accroc [akro] *nm* (*déchirure*) tear; (*fig*) hitch, snag

accrochage [akrɔʃaʒ] *nm* (*AUTO*) collision

accrocher [akrɔʃe] *vt* (*suspendre*): **~ qch à** to hang sth (up) on; (*attacher: remorque*): **~ qch à** to hitch sth (up) to; (*heurter*) to catch; to catch on; to hit; (*déchirer*): **~ qch (à)** to catch sth (on); (*MIL*) to engage; (*fig*) to catch, attract; **s'~** (*se disputer*) to have a clash *ou* brush; **s'~ à** (*rester pris à*) to catch on; (*agripper, fig*) to hang on *ou* cling to

accroître [akrwatr(ə)] *vt* to increase; **s'~** *vi* to increase

accroupir [akrupir]: **s'~** *vi* to squat, crouch (down)

accru, e [akʁy] *pp de* **accroître**

accueil [akœj] *nm* welcome; **comité d'~** reception committee

accueillir [akœjiʁ] *vt* to welcome; (*loger*) to accommodate

acculer [akyle] *vt*: **~ qn à** *ou* **contre** to drive sb back against

accumuler [akymyle] *vt* to accumulate, amass; **s'~** *vi* to accumulate; to pile up

accusation [akyzɑsjɔ̃] *nf* (*gén*) accusation; (*JUR*) charge; (*partie*): **l'~** the prosecution; **mettre en ~** to indict

accusé, e [akyze] *nm/f* accused; defendant; **~ de réception** acknowledgement of receipt

accuser [akyze] *vt* to accuse; (*fig*) to emphasize, bring out; to show; **~ qn de** to accuse sb of; (*JUR*) to charge sb with; **~ qch de** (*rendre responsable*) to blame sth for; **~ réception de** to acknowledge receipt of

acerbe [asɛʁb(ə)] *adj* caustic, acid

acéré, e [asere] *adj* sharp

achalandé, e [aʃalɑ̃de] *adj*: **bien ~** well-stocked; well-patronized

acharné, e [aʃaʁne] *adj* (*lutte, adversaire*) fierce, bitter; (*travail*) relentless, unremitting

acharner [aʃaʁne]: **s'~** *vi* to go at fiercely; **s'~ contre** to set o.s. against; to dog; **s'~ à faire** to try doggedly to do; to persist in doing

achat [aʃa] *nm* buying *no pl*; purchase; **faire des ~s** to do some shopping

acheminer [aʃmine] *vt* (*courrier*) to forward, dispatch; (*troupes*) to convey, transport; (*train*) to route; **s'~ vers** to head for

acheter [aʃte] *vt* to buy, purchase; (*soudoyer*) to buy; **~ qch à** (*marchand*) to buy *ou* purchase sth from; (*ami etc: offrir*) to buy sth for; **acheteur, euse** *nm/f* buyer; shopper; (*COMM*) buyer

achever [aʃve] *vt* to complete, finish; (*blessé*) to finish off; **s'~** *vi* to end

acide [asid] *adj* sour, sharp; (*CHIMIE*) acid(ic) ♦ *nm* acid

acier [asje] *nm* steel; **aciérie** *nf* steelworks *sg*

acné [akne] *nf* acne

acolyte [akɔlit] (*péj*) *nm* associate

acompte [akɔ̃t] *nm* deposit; (*versement régulier*) instalment; (*sur somme due*) payment on account

à-côté [akote] *nm* side-issue; (*argent*) extra

à-coup [aku] *nm* (*du moteur*) (hic)cough; (*fig*) jolt; **par ~s** by fits and starts

acoustique [akustik] *nf* (*d'une salle*) acoustics *pl*

acquéreur [akeʁœʁ] *nm* buyer, purchaser

acquérir [akeʁiʁ] *vt* to acquire

acquis, e [aki, -iz] *pp de* **acquérir** ♦ *nm* (accumulated) experience; **être ~ à** (*plan, idée*) to fully agree with; **son aide nous est ~e** we can count on her help

acquit [aki] *vb voir* **acquérir** ♦ *nm* (*quittance*) receipt; **par ~ de conscience** to set one's mind at rest

acquitter [akite] *vt* (*JUR*) to acquit; (*facture*) to pay, settle; **s'~ de** *vt* to discharge, fulfil

âcre [akʁ(ə)] *adj* acrid, pungent

acrobate [akʁɔbat] *nm/f* acrobat

acte [akt(ə)] *nm* act, action; (*THÉÂTRE*) act; **~s** *nmpl* (*compte-rendu*) proceedings; **prendre ~ de** to note, take note of; **faire ~ de candidature** to apply; **faire ~ de présence** to put in an appearance; **~ de naissance** birth certificate

acteur [aktœʁ] *nm* actor

actif, ive [aktif, -iv] *adj* active ♦ *nm* (*COMM*) assets *pl*; (*fig*): **avoir à son ~** to have to one's credit; **population active** working population

action [aksjɔ̃] *nf* (*gén*) action; (*COMM*) share; **une bonne ~** a good deed; **actionnaire** *nm/f* shareholder; **actionner** *vt* to work; to activate; to operate

activer [aktive] *vt* to speed up; **s'~** *vi* to bustle about; to hurry up

activité [aktivite] *nf* activity

actrice [aktʁis] *nf* actress

actualiser [aktɥalize] *vt* to actualize; to bring up to date

actualité [aktɥalite] *nf* (*d'un problème*)

topicality; (*événements*): l'~ current events; les ~s *nfpl* (CINÉMA, TV) the news

actuel, le [aktчεl] *adj* (*présent*) present; (*d'actualité*) topical; **actuellement** *adv* at present; at the present time

acuité [akчite] *nf* acuteness

adaptateur [adaptatœr] *nm* (ÉLEC) adapter

adapter [adapte] *vt* to adapt; **s'~ (à)** (*suj: personne*) to adapt (to); **~ qch à** (*approprier*) to adapt sth to (the fit); **~ qch sur/dans/à** (*fixer*) to fit sth on/into/to

additif [aditif] *nm* additive

addition [adisjɔ̃] *nf* addition; (*au café*) bill; **~ner** [adisjɔne] *vt* to add (up)

adepte [adεpt(ə)] *nm/f* follower

adéquat, e [adekwa, -at] *adj* appropriate, suitable

adhérent, e [aderɑ̃, -ɑ̃t] *nm/f* (*de club*) member

adhérer [adere]: **~ à** *vi* (*coller*) to adhere *ou* stick to; (*se rallier à*) to join; to support; **adhésif, ive** *adj* adhesive, sticky ♦ *nm* adhesive; **adhésion** *nf* joining; membership; support

adieu, x [adjø] *excl* goodbye ♦ *nm* farewell; **dire ~ à qn** to say goodbye *ou* farewell to sb

adjectif [adʒεktif] *nm* adjective

adjoindre [adʒwɛ̃dr(ə)] *vt*: **~ qch à** to attach sth to; to add sth to; **s'~** *vt* (*collaborateur etc*) to take on, appoint; **adjoint, e** *nm/f* assistant; **adjoint au maire** deputy mayor; **directeur adjoint** assistant manager

adjudant [adʒydɑ̃] *nm* (MIL) warrant officer

adjudication [adʒydikasjɔ̃] *nf* sale by auction; (*pour travaux*) invitation to tender (BRIT) *ou* bid (US)

adjuger [adʒyʒe] *vt* (*prix, récompense*) to award; (*lors d'une vente*) to auction (off); **s'~** *vt* to take for o.s.

adjurer [adʒyre] *vt*: **~ qn de faire** to implore *ou* beg sb to do

admettre [admεtr(ə)] *vt* (*laisser entrer*) to admit; (*candidat: SCOL*) to pass; (*tolérer*) to allow, accept; (*reconnaître*) to admit, acknowledge

administrateur, trice [administratœr, -tris] *nm/f* (COMM) director; (ADMIN) administrator; **~ judiciaire** receiver

administration [administrasjɔ̃] *nf* administration; **l'A~** ≈ the Civil Service

administrer [administre] *vt* (*firme*) to manage, run; (*biens, remède, sacrement etc*) to administer

admirable [admirabl(ə)] *adj* admirable, wonderful

admirateur, trice [admiratœr, -tris] *nm/f* admirer

admiration [admirasjɔ̃] *nf* admiration

admirer [admire] *vt* to admire

admis, e *pp de* **admettre**

admissible [admisibl(ə)] *adj* (*candidat*) eligible; (*comportement*) admissible, acceptable

admission [admisjɔ̃] *nf* admission; acknowledgement; **demande d'~** application for membership

adolescence [adɔlesɑ̃s] *nf* adolescence

adolescent, e [adɔlesɑ̃, -ɑ̃t] *nm/f* adolescent, teenager

adonner [adɔne]: **s'~ à** *vt* (*sport*) to devote o.s. to; (*boisson*) to give o.s. over to

adopter [adɔpte] *vt* to adopt; (*projet de loi etc*) to pass; **adoptif, ive** *adj* (*parents*) adoptive; (*fils, patrie*) adopted

adorer [adɔre] *vt* to adore; (REL) to worship

adosser [adɔse] *vt*: **~ qch à** *ou* **contre** to stand sth against; **s'~ à** *ou* **contre** to lean with one's back against

adoucir [adusir] *vt* (*goût, température*) to make milder; (*avec du sucre*) to sweeten; (*peau, voix*) to soften; (*caractère*) to mellow

adresse [adrεs] *nf* (*voir adroit*) skill, dexterity; (*domicile*) address; **à l'~ de** (*pour*) for the benefit of

adresser [adrese] *vt* (*lettre: expédier*) to send; (: *écrire l'adresse sur*) to address; (*injure, compliments*) to address; **s'~ à** (*parler à*) to speak to, address; (*s'informer auprès de*) to go and see; (: *bureau*) to enquire at; (*suj: livre, conseil*) to be aimed at; **~ la parole à** to speak to, address

adroit, e [adʀwa, -wat] *adj* skilful, skilled

adulte [adylt(ə)] *nm/f* adult, grown-up ♦ *adj* (*chien, arbre*) fully-grown, mature; (*attitude*) adult, grown-up

adultère [adyltɛʀ] *nm* (*acte*) adultery

advenir [advəniʀ] *vi* to happen

adverbe [advɛʀb(ə)] *nm* adverb

adversaire [advɛʀsɛʀ] *nm/f* (*SPORT, gén*) opponent, adversary; (*MIL*) adversary, enemy

adverse [advɛʀs(ə)] *adj* opposing

aération [aeʀɑsjɔ̃] *nf* airing; ventilation

aérer [aeʀe] *vt* to air; (*fig*) to lighten

aérien, ne [aeʀjɛ̃, -jɛn] *adj* (*AVIAT*) air *cpd*, aerial; (*câble, métro*) overhead; (*fig*) light

aéro... [aeʀɔ] *préfixe:* **~bic** *nm* aerobics *sg*; **~gare** *nf* airport (buildings); (*en ville*) air terminal; **~glisseur** *nm* hovercraft; **~naval, e** *adj* air and sea *cpd*; **~phagie** [aeʀɔfaʒi] *nf* (*MÉD*) wind, aerophagia (*MÉD*); **~port** *nm* airport; **~porté, e** *adj* airborne, airlifted; **~sol** *nm* aerosol

affable [afabl(ə)] *adj* affable

affaiblir [afebliʀ] *vt* to weaken; **s'~** *vi* to weaken

affaire [afɛʀ] *nf* (*problème, question*) matter; (*criminelle, judiciaire*) case; (*scandaleuse etc*) affair; (*entreprise*) business; (*marché, transaction*) deal; business *no pl*; (*occasion intéressante*) bargain; **~s** *nfpl* (*intérêts publics et privés*) affairs; (*activité commerciale*) business *sg*; (*effets personnels*) things, belongings; **ce sont mes ~s** (*cela me concerne*) that's my business; **ceci fera l'~** this will do (nicely); **avoir ~ à** to be faced with; to be dealing with; **les A~s étrangères** Foreign Affairs; **affairer:** **s'affairer** *vi* to busy o.s., bustle about

affaisser [afese]: **s'~** *vi* (*terrain, immeuble*) to subside, sink; (*personne*) to collapse

affaler [afale]: **s'~** *vi:* **s'~ dans/sur** to collapse *ou* slump into/onto

affamé, e [afame] *adj* starving

affecter [afɛkte] *vt* to affect; (*telle ou telle forme etc*) to take on; **~ qch à** to allocate *ou* allot sth to; **~ qn à** to appoint sb to; (*diplomate*) to post sb to

affectif, ive [afɛktif, -iv] *adj* emotional

affection [afɛksjɔ̃] *nf* affection; (*mal*) ailment; **affectionner** *vt* to be fond of

affectueux, euse [afɛktɥø, -øz] *adj* affectionate

afférent, e [afeʀɑ̃, -ɑ̃t] *adj:* **~ à** pertaining *ou* relating to

affermir [afɛʀmiʀ] *vt* to consolidate, strengthen

affichage [afiʃaʒ] *nm* billposting; (*électronique*) display

affiche [afiʃ] *nf* poster; (*officielle*) notice; (*THÉÂTRE*) bill; **tenir l'~** to run

afficher [afiʃe] *vt* (*affiche*) to put up; (*réunion*) to put up a notice about; (*électroniquement*) to display; (*fig*) to exhibit, display

affilée [afile]: **d'~** *adv* at a stretch

affiler [afile] *vt* to sharpen

affilier [afilje]: **s'~ à** *vt* (*club, société*) to join

affiner [afine] *vt* to refine

affirmatif, ive [afiʀmatif, -iv] *adj* affirmative

affirmation [afiʀmɑsjɔ̃] *nf* assertion

affirmer [afiʀme] *vt* (*prétendre*) to maintain, assert; (*autorité etc*) to assert

affligé, e [afliʒe] *adj* distressed, grieved; **~ de** (*maladie, tare*) afflicted with

affliger [afliʒe] *vt* (*peiner*) to distress, grieve

affluence [aflyɑ̃s] *nf* crowds *pl*; **heures d'~** rush hours; **jours d'~** busiest days

affluent [aflyɑ̃] *nm* tributary

affluer [aflye] *vi* (*secours, biens*) to flood in, pour in; (*sang*) to rush, flow

affolement [afɔlmɑ̃] *nm* panic

affoler [afɔle] *vt* to throw into a panic; **s'~** *vi* to panic

affranchir [afʀɑ̃ʃiʀ] *vt* to put a stamp *ou* stamps on; (*à la machine*) to frank (*BRIT*), meter (*US*); (*fig*) to free, liberate; **affranchissement** *nm* postage

affréter [afʀete] *vt* to charter

affreux, euse [afʀø, -øz] *adj* dreadful, awful

affront [afʁɑ̃] *nm* affront

affrontement [afʁɔ̃tmɑ̃] *nm* clash, confrontation

affronter [afʁɔ̃te] *vt* to confront, face

affubler [afyble] (*péj*) *vt*: ~ **qn de** to rig *ou* deck sb out in; (*surnom*) to attach to sb

affût [afy] *nm*: **à l'~ (de)** (*gibier*) lying in wait (for); (*fig*) on the look-out (for)

affûter [afyte] *vt* to sharpen, grind

afin [afɛ̃]: ~ **que** *conj* so that, in order that; ~ **de faire** in order to do, so as to do

africain, e [afʁikɛ̃, -ɛn] *adj, nm/f* African

Afrique [afʁik] *nf*: **l'~** Africa; **l'~ du Sud** South Africa

agacer [agase] *vt* to pester, tease; (*involontairement*) to irritate

âge [ɑʒ] *nm* age; **quel ~ as-tu?** how old are you?; **prendre de l'~** to be getting on (in years); **l'~ ingrat** the awkward age; **l'~ mûr** maturity; **âgé, e** *adj* old, elderly; **âgé de 10 ans** 10 years old

agence [aʒɑ̃s] *nf* agency, office; (*succursale*) branch; ~ **de voyages** travel agency; ~ **immobilière** estate (*BRIT*) *ou* real estate (*US*) agent's (office); ~ **matrimoniale** marriage bureau

agencer [aʒɑ̃se] *vt* to put together; to arrange, lay out

agenda [aʒɛ̃da] *nm* diary

agenouiller [aʒnuje]: **s'~** *vi* to kneel (down)

agent [aʒɑ̃] *nm* (*aussi*: ~ **de police**) policeman; (*ADMIN*) official, officer; (*fig*: *élément, facteur*) agent; ~ **d'assurances** insurance broker; ~ **de change** stockbroker

agglomération [aglɔmeʁasjɔ̃] *nf* town; built-up area; **l'~ parisienne** the urban area of Paris

aggloméré [aglɔmeʁe] *nm* (*bois*) chipboard; (*pierre*) conglomerate

agglomérer [aglɔmeʁe] *vt* to pile up; (*TECH*: *bois, pierre*) to compress

aggraver [agʁave] *vt* to worsen, aggravate; (*JUR*: *peine*) to increase; **s'~** *vi* to worsen

agile [aʒil] *adj* agile, nimble

agir [aʒiʁ] *vi* to act; **il s'agit de** it's a matter *ou* question of; it is about; (*il importe que*): **il s'agit de faire** we (*ou* you *etc*) must do

agitation [aʒitɑsjɔ̃] *nf* (hustle and) bustle; agitation, excitement; (*politique*) unrest, agitation

agité, e [aʒite] *adj* fidgety, restless; agitated, perturbed; (*mer*) rough

agiter [aʒite] *vt* (*bouteille, chiffon*) to shake; (*bras, mains*) to wave; (*préoccuper, exciter*) to perturb

agneau, x [aɲo] *nm* lamb

agonie [agɔni] *nf* mortal agony, death pangs *pl*; (*fig*) death throes *pl*

agrafe [agʁaf] *nf* (*de vêtement*) hook, fastener; (*de bureau*) staple; **agrafer** *vt* to fasten; to staple; **agrafeuse** *nf* stapler

agraire [agʁɛʁ] *adj* land *cpd*

agrandir [agʁɑ̃diʁ] *vt* to enlarge; (*magasin, domaine*) to extend, enlarge; **s'~** *vi* to be extended; to be enlarged; **agrandissement** *nm* (*PHOTO*) enlargement

agréable [agʁeabl(ə)] *adj* pleasant, nice

agréé, e [agʁee] *adj*: **concessionnaire ~** registered dealer

agréer [agʁee] *vt* (*requête*) to accept; ~ **à** to please, suit; **veuillez ~ ...** (*formule épistolaire*) yours faithfully

agrégation [agʁegɑsjɔ̃] *nf* highest teaching diploma in France; **agrégé, e** *nm/f* holder of the *agrégation*

agrément [agʁemɑ̃] *nm* (*accord*) consent, approval; (*attraits*) charm, attractiveness; (*plaisir*) pleasure

agrémenter [agʁemɑ̃te] *vt* to embellish, adorn

agresser [agʁese] *vt* to attack

agresseur [agʁesœʁ] *nm* aggressor, attacker; (*POL, MIL*) aggressor

agressif, ive [agʁesif, -iv] *adj* aggressive

agricole [agʁikɔl] *adj* agricultural

agriculteur [agʁikyltœʁ] *nm* farmer

agriculture [agʁikyltyʁ] *nf* agriculture; farming

agripper [agʁipe] *vt* to grab, clutch; (*pour arracher*) to snatch, grab; **s'~ à** to cling (on) to, clutch, grip

agrumes [agrym] *nmpl* citrus fruit(s)

aguerrir [ageʀiʀ] *vt* to harden

aguets [agɛ] *nmpl*: **être aux ~** to be on the look out

aguicher [agiʃe] *vt* to entice

ahuri, e [ayʀi] *adj* (*stupéfait*) flabbergasted; (*idiot*) dim-witted

ai *vb voir* **avoir**

aide [ɛd] *nm/f* assistant; carer ♦ *nf* assistance, help; (*secours financier*) aid; **à l'~ de** (*avec*) with the help *ou* aid of; **appeler (qn) à l'~** to call for help (from sb); **~ judiciaire** *nf* legal aid; **~ sociale** *nf* (*assistance*) state aid; **~-mémoire** *nm inv* memoranda pages *pl*; (*key facts*) handbook; **~-soignant, e** *nm/f* auxiliary nurse

aider [ede] *vt* to help; **s'~ de** (*se servir de*) to use, make use of; **~ à qch** (*faciliter*) to help (towards) sth

aie *etc vb voir* **avoir**

aïe [aj] *excl* ouch

aïeul, e [ajœl] *nm/f* grandparent, grandfather(mother); forebear

aïeux [ajø] *nmpl* grandparents; forebears, forefathers

aigle [ɛgl(ə)] *nm* eagle

aigre [ɛgʀ(ə)] *adj* sour, sharp; (*fig*) sharp, cutting; **aigreur** *nf* sourness; sharpness; **aigreurs d'estomac** heartburn *sg*; **aigrir** *vt* (*personne*) to embitter; (*caractère*) to sour

aigu, ë [egy] *adj* (*objet, arête, douleur, intelligence*) sharp; (*son, voix*) high-pitched, shrill; (*note*) high (-pitched)

aiguille [eguij] *nf* needle; (*de montre*) hand; **~ à tricoter** knitting needle

aiguiller [eguije] *vt* (*orienter*) to direct

aiguilleur du ciel [eguijœʀ] *nm* air-traffic controller

aiguillon [eguijɔ̃] *nm* (*d'abeille*) sting; **aiguillonner** *vt* to spur *ou* goad on

aiguiser [egize] *vt* to sharpen; (*fig*) to stimulate; to excite

ail [aj] *nm* garlic

aile [ɛl] *nf* wing; **aileron** *nm* (*de requin*) fin; **ailier** *nm* winger

aille *etc vb voir* **aller**

ailleurs [ajœʀ] *adv* elsewhere, somewhere else; **partout/nulle part ~** everywhere/nowhere else; **d'~** (*du reste*) moreover, besides; **par ~** (*d'autre part*) moreover, furthermore

aimable [ɛmabl(ə)] *adj* kind, nice

aimant [ɛmã] *nm* magnet

aimer [eme] *vt* to love; (*d'amitié, affection, par goût*) to like; (*souhait*): **j'~ais ... I** would like ...; **bien ~ qn/qch** to like sb/sth; **j'aime mieux** *ou* **autant vous dire que** I may as well tell you that; **j'~ais autant y aller maintenant** I'd rather go now; **j'~ais mieux faire** I'd much rather do

aine [ɛn] *nf* groin

aîné, e [ene] *adj* elder, older; (*le plus âgé*) eldest, oldest ♦ *nm/f* oldest child *ou* one, oldest boy *ou* son/girl *ou* daughter; **aînesse** *nf*: **droit d'aînesse** birthright

ainsi [ɛ̃si] *adv* (*de cette façon*) like this, in this way, thus; (*ce faisant*) thus ♦ *conj* thus, so; **~ que** (*comme*) (just) as; (*et aussi*) as well as; **pour ~ dire** so to speak; **et ~ de suite** and so on

air [ɛʀ] *nm* air; (*mélodie*) tune; (*expression*) look, air; **prendre l'~** to get some (fresh) air; (*avion*) to take off; **avoir l'~** (*sembler*) to look, appear; **avoir l'~ de** to look like; **avoir l'~ de faire** to look as though one is doing, appear to be doing; **~bag** [ɛʀbag] *nm* airbag

aire [ɛʀ] *nf* (*zone, fig, MATH*) area

aisance [ɛzɑ̃s] *nf* ease; (*richesse*) affluence

aise [ɛz] *nf* comfort ♦ *adj*: **être bien ~ que** to be delighted that; **être à l'~** *ou* **à son ~** to be comfortable; (*pas embarrassé*) to be at ease; (*financièrement*) to be comfortably off; **se mettre à l'~** to make o.s. comfortable; **être mal à l'~** *ou* **à son ~** to be uncomfortable; to be ill at ease; **en faire à son ~** to do as one likes; **aisé, e** *adj* easy; (*assez riche*) well-to-do, well-off

aisselle [ɛsɛl] *nf* armpit

ait *vb voir* **avoir**

ajonc [aʒɔ̃] *nm* gorse *no pl*

ajourner [aʒuʀne] *vt* (*réunion*) to adjourn; (*décision*) to defer, postpone
ajouter [aʒute] *vt* to add; ~ **foi à** to lend *ou* give credence to
ajusté, e [aʒyste] *adj*: **bien** ~ (*robe etc*) close-fitting
ajuster [aʒyste] *vt* (*régler*) to adjust; (*vêtement*) to alter; (*coup de fusil*) to aim; (*cible*) to aim at; (*TECH, gén: adapter*): ~ **qch à** to fit sth to
alarme [alaʀm(ə)] *nf* alarm; **donner l'**~ to give *ou* raise the alarm; **alarmer** *vt* to alarm; **s'alarmer** *vi* to become alarmed
album [albɔm] *nm* album
albumine [albymin] *nf* albumin; **avoir** *ou* **faire de l'**~ to suffer from albuminuria
alcool [alkɔl] *nm*: **l'**~ alcohol; **un** ~ a spirit, a brandy; ~ **à brûler** methylated spirits (*BRIT*), wood alcohol (*US*); ~ **à 90°** surgical spirit; **alcoolique** *adj, nm/f* alcoholic; **alcoolisé, e** *adj* alcoholic; **alcoolisme** *nm* alcoholism
alco(o)test [alkɔtɛst] *nm* Breathalyser (*BRIT*); (*test*) breath-test
aléas [alea] *nmpl* hazards; **aléatoire** *adj* uncertain; (*INFORM*) random
alentour [alɑ̃tuʀ] *adv* around (about); ~**s** *nmpl* (*environs*) surroundings; **aux** ~**s de** in the vicinity *ou* neighbourhood of, around about; (*temps*) around about
alerte [alɛʀt(ə)] *adj* agile, nimble; brisk, lively ♦ *nf* alert; warning; **alerter** *vt* to alert
algèbre [alʒɛbʀ(ə)] *nf* algebra
Alger [alʒe] *n* Algiers
Algérie [alʒeʀi] *nf*: **l'**~ Algeria; **algérien, ne** *adj, nm/f* Algerian
algue [alg(ə)] *nf* (*gén*) seaweed *no pl*; (*BOT*) alga
alibi [alibi] *nm* alibi
aliéné, e [aljene] *nm/f* insane person, lunatic (*péj*)
aligner [aliɲe] *vt* to align, line up; (*idées, chiffres*) to string together; (*adapter*): ~ **qch sur** to bring sth into alignment with; **s'**~ (*soldats etc*) to line up; **s'**~ **sur** (*POL*) to align o.s. on
aliment [alimɑ̃] *nm* food

alimentation [alimɑ̃tasjɔ̃] *nf* feeding; supplying; (*commerce*) food trade; (*produits*) groceries *pl*; (*régime*) diet; (*INFORM*) feed
alimenter [alimɑ̃te] *vt* to feed; (*TECH*): ~ **(en)** to supply (with); to feed (with); (*fig*) to sustain, keep going
alinéa [alinea] *nm* paragraph
aliter [alite]: **s'**~ *vi* to take to one's bed
allaiter [alete] *vt* to (breast-)feed, nurse; (*suj: animal*) to suckle
allant [alɑ̃] *nm* drive, go
allécher [aleʃe] *vt*: ~ **qn** to make sb's mouth water; to tempt *ou* entice sb
allée [ale] *nf* (*de jardin*) path; (*en ville*) avenue, drive; ~**s et venues** comings and goings
alléger [aleʒe] *vt* (*voiture*) to make lighter; (*chargement*) to lighten; (*souffrance*) to alleviate, soothe
allègre [alɛgʀ(ə)] *adj* lively, cheerful
alléguer [alege] *vt* to put forward (as proof *ou* an excuse)
Allemagne [aləmaɲ] *nf*: **l'**~ Germany; **allemand, e** *adj, nm/f* German ♦ *nm* (*LING*) German
aller [ale] *nm* (*trajet*) outward journey; (*billet: aussi*: ~ **simple**) single (*BRIT*) *ou* one-way (*US*) ticket ♦ *vi* (*gén*) to go; ~ **à** (*convenir*) to suit; (*suj: forme, pointure etc*) to fit; ~ **avec** (*couleurs, style etc*) to go (well) with; **je vais y** ~/**me fâcher** I'm going to go/get angry; ~ **voir** to go and see, go to see; **allez!** come on!; **allons!** come now!; **comment allez-vous?** how are you?; **comment ça va?** how are you?; (*affaires etc*) how are things?; **il va bien/mal** he's well/not well, he's fine/ill; **ça va bien/mal** (*affaires etc*) it's going well/not going well; ~ **mieux** to be better; **cela va sans dire** that goes without saying; **il y va de leur vie** their lives are at stake; **s'en** ~ (*partir*) to be off, go, leave; (*disparaître*) to go away; ~ **(et) retour** return journey (*BRIT*), round trip; (*billet*) return (ticket) (*BRIT*), round trip ticket (*US*)
allergique [alɛʀʒik] *adj*: ~ **à** allergic to
alliage [aljaʒ] *nm* alloy

alliance [aljɑ̃s] *nf* (*MIL, POL*) alliance; (*mariage*) marriage; (*bague*) wedding ring

allier [alje] *vt* (*métaux*) to alloy; (*POL, gén*) to ally; (*fig*) to combine; **s'~** to become allies; to combine

allô [alo] *excl* hullo, hallo

allocation [alɔkasjɔ̃] *nf* allowance; **~ (de) chômage** unemployment benefit; **~ (de) logement** rent allowance; **~s familiales** ≈ child benefit

allocution [alɔkysjɔ̃] *nf* short speech

allonger [alɔ̃ʒe] *vt* to lengthen, make longer; (*étendre: bras, jambe*) to stretch (out); **s'~** *vi* to get longer; (*se coucher*) to lie down, stretch out; **~ le pas** to hasten one's step(s)

allouer [alwe] *vt* to allocate, allot

allumage [alymaʒ] *nm* (*AUTO*) ignition

allume-cigare [alymsigar] *nm inv* cigar lighter

allumer [alyme] *vt* (*lampe, phare, radio*) to put *ou* switch on; (*pièce*) to put *ou* switch the light(s) on in; (*feu*) to light; **s'~** *vi* (*lumière, lampe*) to come *ou* go on

allumette [alymɛt] *nf* match

allure [alyʀ] *nf* (*vitesse*) speed, pace; (*démarche*) walk; (*maintien*) bearing; (*aspect, air*) look; **avoir de l'~** to have style; **à toute ~** at top speed

allusion [alyzjɔ̃] *nf* allusion; (*sous-entendu*) hint; **faire ~ à** to allude *ou* refer to; to hint at

aloi [alwa] *nm*: **de bon ~** of genuine worth *ou* quality

MOT-CLÉ
---

alors [alɔʀ] *adv* **1** (*à ce moment-là*) then, at that time; **il habitait ~ à Paris** he lived in Paris at that time

2 (*par conséquent*) then; **tu as fini? ~ je m'en vais** have you finished? I'm going then; **et ~?** so what?

alors que *conj* **1** (*au moment où*) when, as; **il est arrivé ~ que je partais** he arrived as I was leaving

2 (*pendant que*) while, when; **~ qu'il était à Paris, il a visité ...** while *ou*

when he was in Paris, he visited ...

3 (*tandis que*) whereas, while; **~ son frère travaillait dur, lui se reposait** while his brother was working hard, HE would rest

alouette [alwɛt] *nf* (sky)lark

alourdir [aluʀdiʀ] *vt* to weigh down, make heavy

alpage [alpaʒ] *nm* pasture

Alpes [alp(ə)] *nfpl*: **les ~** the Alps

alphabet [alfabɛ] *nm* alphabet; (*livre*) ABC (book); **alphabétiser** *vt* to teach to read and write; to eliminate illiteracy in

alpinisme [alpinism(ə)] *nm* mountaineering, climbing; **alpiniste** *nm/f* mountaineer, climber

Alsace [alzas] *nf* Alsace; **alsacien, ne** *adj, nm/f* Alsatian

altercation [altɛʀkasjɔ̃] *nf* altercation

altérer [alteʀe] *vt* to falsify; to distort; to debase; to impair

alternateur [altɛʀnatœʀ] *nm* alternator

alternatif, ive [altɛʀnatif, -iv] *adj* alternating; **alternative** *nf* (*choix*) alternative; **alternativement** *adv* alternately

Altesse [altɛs] *nf* Highness

altitude [altityd] *nf* altitude, height

alto [alto] *nm* (*instrument*) viola

altruisme [altʀɥism(ə)] *nm* altruism

aluminium [alyminjɔm] *nm* aluminium (*BRIT*), aluminum (*US*)

amabilité [amabilite] *nf* kindness, amiability

amadouer [amadwe] *vt* to coax, cajole; to mollify, soothe

amaigrir [amegʀiʀ] *vt* to make thin(ner)

amalgame [amalgam] *nm* (*alliage pour les dents*) amalgam

amande [amɑ̃d] *nf* (*de l'amandier*) almond; (*de noyau de fruit*) kernel; **amandier** *nm* almond (tree)

amant [amɑ̃] *nm* lover

amarrer [amaʀe] *vt* (*NAVIG*) to moor; (*gén*) to make fast

amas [amɑ] *nm* heap, pile

amasser [amɑse] *vt* to amass

amateur [amatœʀ] *nm* amateur; **en ~** (*péj*) amateurishly; **~ de musique/sport**

etc music/sport *etc* lover

amazone [amazon] *nf*: **en ~** sidesaddle

ambages [ɑ̄baʒ]: **sans ~** *adv* plainly

ambassade [ɑ̄basad] *nf* embassy; (*mission*): **en ~** on a mission; **ambassadeur, drice** *nm/f* ambassador(dress)

ambiance [ɑ̄bjɑ̄s] *nf* atmosphere

ambiant, e [ɑ̄bjɑ̄, -ɑ̄t] *adj* (*air, milieu*) surrounding; (*température*) ambient

ambigu, ë [ɑ̄bigy] *adj* ambiguous

ambitieux, euse [ɑ̄bisjø, -øz] *adj* ambitious

ambition [ɑ̄bisjɔ̄] *nf* ambition

ambulance [ɑ̄bylɑ̄s] *nf* ambulance; **ambulancier, ière** *nm/f* ambulance man(woman) (*BRIT*), paramedic (*US*)

ambulant, e [ɑ̄bylɑ̄, -ɑ̄t] *adj* travelling, itinerant

âme [ɑm] *nf* soul

améliorer [ameljɔʀe] *vt* to improve; **s'~** *vi* to improve, get better

aménagements [amenaʒmɑ̄] *nmpl* developments; **~ fiscaux** tax adjustments

aménager [amenaʒe] *vt* (*agencer, transformer*) to fit out; to lay out; (: *quartier, territoire*) to develop; (*installer*) to fix up, put in; **ferme aménagée** converted farmhouse

amende [amɑ̄d] *nf* fine; **mettre à l'~** to penalize; **faire ~ honorable** to make amends

amender [amɑ̄de] *vt* (*loi*) to amend; **s'~** *vi* to mend one's ways

amener [amne] *vt* to bring; (*causer*) to bring about; (*baisser: drapeau, voiles*) to strike; **s'~** *vi* to show up (*fam*), turn up

amenuiser [amənɥize]: **s'~** *vi* to grow slimmer, lessen; to dwindle

amer, amère [amɛʀ] *adj* bitter

américain, e [ameʀikɛ̄, -ɛn] *adj, nm/f* American

Amérique [ameʀik] *nf* America; **l'~ centrale/latine** Central/Latin America; **l'~ du Nord/du Sud** North/South America

amerrir [ameʀiʀ] *vi* to land (on the sea)

amertume [amɛʀtym] *nf* bitterness

ameublement [amœbləmɑ̄] *nm* furnish-

ing; (*meubles*) furniture

ameuter [amøte] *vt* (*badauds*) to draw a crowd of; (*peuple*) to rouse

ami, e [ami] *nm/f* friend; (*amant/maîtresse*) boyfriend/girlfriend ♦ *adj*: **pays/groupe ~** friendly country/group; **être ~ de l'ordre** to be a lover of order; **un ~ des arts** a patron of the arts

amiable [amjabl(ə)]: **à l'~** *adv* (*JUR*) out of court; (*gén*) amicably

amiante [amjɑ̄t] *nm* asbestos

amical, e, aux [amikal, -o] *adj* friendly; **amicale** *nf* (*club*) association; **amicalement** *adv* in a friendly way; (*formule épistolaire*) regards

amidon [amidɔ̄] *nm* starch

amincir [amɛ̄siʀ] *vt* (*objet*) to thin (down); **s'~** *vi* to get thinner *ou* slimmer; **~ qn** to make sb thinner *ou* slimmer

amincissant, e *adj*: **régime ~** (slimming) diet; **crème ~e** slenderizing cream

amiral, aux [amiʀal, -o] *nm* admiral

amitié [amitje] *nf* friendship; **prendre en ~** to befriend; **faire** *ou* **présenter ses ~s à qn** to send sb one's best wishes

ammoniac [amɔnjak] *nm*: **(gaz) ~** ammonia

ammoniaque [amɔnjak] *nf* ammonia (water)

amoindrir [amwɛ̄dʀiʀ] *vt* to reduce

amollir [amɔliʀ] *vt* to soften

amonceler [amɔ̄sle] *vt* to pile *ou* heap up; **s'~** *vi* to pile *ou* heap up; (*fig*) to accumulate

amont [amɔ̄]: **en ~** *adv* upstream; (*sur une pente*) uphill

amorce [amɔʀs(ə)] *nf* (*sur un hameçon*) bait; (*explosif*) cap; primer; priming; (*fig: début*) beginning(s), start

amorphe [amɔʀf(ə)] *adj* passive, lifeless

amortir [amɔʀtiʀ] *vt* (*atténuer: choc*) to absorb, cushion; (*bruit, douleur*) to deaden; (*COMM: dette*) to pay off; (: *mise de fonds, matériel*) to write off; **~ un abonnement** to make a season ticket pay (for itself); **amortisseur** *nm* shock absorber

amour [amuʀ] *nm* love; (*liaison*) love affair, love; **faire l'~** to make love; **amouracher**: **s'amouracher de** (*péj*) *vt* to become infatuated with; **amoureux, euse** *adj* (*regard, tempérament*) amorous; (*vie, problèmes*) love *cpd*; (*personne*): **amoureux (de qn)** in love (with sb) ♦ *nmpl* courting couple(s); **amour-propre** *nm* self-esteem, pride

amovible [amɔvibl(ə)] *adj* removable, detachable

ampère [ɑ̃pɛʀ] *nm* amp(ere)

amphithéâtre [ɑ̃fiteatʀ(ə)] *nm* amphitheatre; (*d'université*) lecture hall *ou* theatre

ample [ɑ̃pl(ə)] *adj* (*vêtement*) roomy, ample; (*gestes, mouvement*) broad; (*ressources*) ample; **ampleur** *nf* (*importance*) scale, size; extent

amplificateur [ɑ̃plifikatœʀ] *nm* amplifier

amplifier [ɑ̃plifje] *vt* (*son, oscillation*) to amplify; (*fig*) to expand, increase

ampoule [ɑ̃pul] *nf* (*électrique*) bulb; (*de médicament*) phial; (*aux mains, pieds*) blister

ampoulé, e [ɑ̃pule] (*péj*) *adj* pompous, bombastic

amputer [ɑ̃pyte] *vt* (*MÉD*) to amputate; (*fig*) to cut *ou* reduce drastically

amusant, e [amyzɑ̃, -ɑ̃t] *adj* (*divertissant, spirituel*) entertaining, amusing; (*comique*) funny, amusing

amuse-gueule [amyzgœl] *nm inv* appetizer, snack

amusement [amyzmɑ̃] *nm* amusement; (*jeu etc*) pastime, diversion

amuser [amyze] *vt* (*divertir*) to entertain, amuse; (*égayer, faire rire*) to amuse; (*détourner l'attention de*) to distract; **s'~** *vi* (*jouer*) to amuse o.s., play; (*se divertir*) to enjoy o.s., have fun; (*fig*) to mess around

amygdale [amidal] *nf* tonsil

an [ɑ̃] *nm* year; **le jour de l'~, le premier de l'~, le nouvel ~** New Year's Day

analogique [analɔʒik] *adj* analogical; (*INFORM, montre*) analog

analogue [analɔg] *adj*: **~ (à)** analogous

(to), similar (to)

analphabète [analfabɛt] *nm/f* illiterate

analyse [analiz] *nf* analysis; (*MÉD*) test; **analyser** *vt* to analyse; to test

ananas [anana] *nm* pineapple

anarchie [anaʀʃi] *nf* anarchy

anathème [anatɛm] *nm*: **jeter l'~ sur** to curse

anatomie [anatɔmi] *nf* anatomy

ancêtre [ɑ̃sɛtʀ(ə)] *nm/f* ancestor

anchois [ɑ̃ʃwa] *nm* anchovy

ancien, ne [ɑ̃sjɛ̃, -jɛn] *adj* old; (*de jadis, de l'antiquité*) ancient; (*précédent, ex-*) former, old ♦ *nm/f* (*dans une tribu*) elder; **anciennement** *adv* formerly; **ancienneté** *nf* oldness; antiquity; (*ADMIN*) (length of) service; seniority

ancre [ɑ̃kʀ(ə)] *nf* anchor; **jeter/lever l'~** to cast/weigh anchor; **à l'~** at anchor; **ancrer** [ɑ̃kʀe] *vt* (*CONSTR*: *câble etc*) to anchor; (*fig*) to fix firmly; **s'ancrer** *vi* (*NAVIG*) to (cast) anchor

Andorre [ɑ̃dɔʀ] *nf* Andorra

andouille [ɑ̃duj] *nf* (*CULIN*) sausage made of chitterlings; (*fam*) clot, nit

âne [ɑn] *nm* donkey, ass; (*péj*) dunce

anéantir [aneɑ̃tiʀ] *vt* to annihilate, wipe out; (*fig*) to obliterate, destroy; to overwhelm

anémie [anemi] *nf* anaemia; **anémique** *adj* anaemic

ânerie [ɑnʀi] *nf* stupidity; stupid *ou* idiotic comment *etc*

anesthésie [anɛstezi] *nf* anaesthesia; **faire une ~ locale/générale à qn** to give sb a local/general anaesthetic

ange [ɑ̃ʒ] *nm* angel; **être aux ~s** to be over the moon

angélus [ɑ̃ʒelys] *nm* angelus; evening bells *pl*

angine [ɑ̃ʒin] *nf* throat infection; **~ de poitrine** angina

anglais, e [ɑ̃glɛ, -ɛz] *adj* English ♦ *nm/ f*: **A~, e** Englishman(woman) ♦ *nm* (*LING*) English; **les A~** the English; **filer à l'~e** to take French leave

angle [ɑ̃gl(ə)] *nm* angle; (*coin*) corner; **~ droit** right angle

Angleterre [ɑ̃glətɛʀ] *nf*: **l'~** England

anglo... [ɑ̃glɔ] *préfixe* Anglo-, anglo(-); **~phone** *adj* English-speaking

angoissé, e [ɑ̃gwase] *adj (personne)* full of anxieties *ou* hang-ups *(inf)*

angoisser [ɑ̃gwase] *vt* to harrow, cause anguish to ♦ *vi* to worry, fret

anguille [ɑ̃gij] *nf* eel

anicroche [anikrɔʃ] *nf* hitch, snag

animal, e, aux [animal, -o] *adj, nm* animal

animateur, trice [animatœr, -tris] *nm/f (de télévision)* host; *(de groupe)* leader, organizer

animation [animɑsjɔ̃] *nf (voir animé)* busyness, liveliness; *(CINÉMA: technique)* animation

animé, e [anime] *adj (lieu)* busy, lively; *(conversation, réunion)* lively, animated; *(opposé à in~)* animate

animer [anime] *vt (ville, soirée)* to liven up; *(mettre en mouvement)* to drive

anis [ani] *nm (CULIN)* aniseed; *(BOT)* anise

ankyloser [ɑ̃kiloze]: **s'~** *vi* to get stiff

anneau, x [ano] *nm (de rideau, bague)* ring; *(de chaîne)* link

année [ane] *nf* year

annexe [anɛks(ə)] *adj (problème)* related; *(document)* appended; *(salle)* adjoining ♦ *nf (bâtiment)* annex(e); *(de document, ouvrage)* annex, appendix; *(jointe à une lettre)* enclosure

anniversaire [anivɛrsɛr] *nm* birthday; *(d'un événement, bâtiment)* anniversary

annonce [anɔ̃s] *nf* announcement; *(signe, indice)* sign; *(aussi: ~ publicitaire)* advertisement; **les petites ~s** the classified advertisements, the small ads

annoncer [anɔ̃se] *vt* to announce; *(être le signe de)* to herald; **s'~ bien/difficile** to look promising/difficult; **annonceur, euse** *nm/f (TV, RADIO: speaker)* announcer; *(publicitaire)* advertiser

annuaire [anɥɛr] *nm* yearbook, annual; **~ téléphonique** (telephone) directory, phone book

annuel, le [anɥɛl] *adj* annual, yearly

annuité [anɥite] *nf* annual instalment

annuler [anɥle] *vt (rendez-vous, voyage)* to cancel, call off; *(mariage)* to annul; *(jugement)* to quash *(BRIT)*, repeal *(US)*; *(résultats)* to declare void; *(MATH, PHYSIQUE)* to cancel out

anodin, e [anɔdɛ̃, -in] *adj* harmless; insignificant, trivial

anonyme [anɔnim] *adj* anonymous; *(fig)* impersonal

ANPE *sigle f (= Agence nationale pour l'emploi)* national employment agency

anse [ɑ̃s] *nf (de panier, tasse)* handle; *(GÉO)* cove

antan [ɑ̃tɑ̃]: **d'~** *adj* of long ago

antarctique [ɑ̃tarktik] *adj* Antarctic ♦ *nm*: **l'A~** the Antarctic

antécédents [ɑ̃tesedɑ̃] *nmpl (MÉD etc)* past history *sg*

antenne [ɑ̃tɛn] *nf (de radio)* aerial; *(d'insecte)* antenna, feeler; *(poste avancé)* outpost; *(petite succursale)* sub-branch; **passer à l'~** to go on the air; **prendre l'~** to tune in; **2 heures d'~** 2 hours' broadcasting time

antérieur, e [ɑ̃terjœr] *adj (d'avant)* previous, earlier; *(de devant)* front

anti... [ɑ̃ti] *préfixe* anti...; **~alcoolique** *adj* anti-alcohol; **~atomique** *adj*: **abri ~atomique** fallout shelter; **~biotique** *nm* antibiotic; **~brouillard** *adj*: **phare ~brouillard** fog lamp *(BRIT)* *ou* light *(US)*

anticipation [ɑ̃tisipɑsjɔ̃] *nf*: **livre/film d'~** science fiction book/film

anticipé, e [ɑ̃tisipe] *adj*: **avec mes remerciements ~s** thanking you in advance *ou* anticipation

anticiper [ɑ̃tisipe] *vt (événement, coup)* to anticipate, foresee

anti: ~conceptionnel, le *adj* contraceptive; **~corps** *nm* antibody; **~dote** *nm* antidote

antigel [ɑ̃tiʒɛl] *nm* antifreeze

antihistaminique [ɑ̃tiistaminik] *nm* antihistamine

Antilles [ɑ̃tij] *nfpl*: **les ~** the West Indies

antilope [ɑ̃tilɔp] *nf* antelope

anti: ~mite(s) *adj, nm*: **(produit) ~mite(s)** mothproofer; moth repellent; **~parasite** *adj (RADIO, TV)*: **dispositif ~parasite** suppressor; **~pathique** *adj* unpleasant, disagreeable; **~pelliculaire** *adj* anti-dandruff

antipodes [ɑ̃tipɔd] *nmpl* (*GÉO*): **les** ~ the antipodes; (*fig*): **être aux** ~ **de** to be the opposite extreme of

antiquaire [ɑ̃tikɛʀ] *nm/f* antique dealer

antique [ɑ̃tik] *adj* antique; (*très vieux*) ancient, antiquated

antiquité [ɑ̃tikite] *nf* (*objet*) antique; **l'A~** Antiquity; **magasin d'~s** antique shop

anti: ~**rabique** *adj* rabies *cpd*; ~**rouille** *adj inv* anti-rust *cpd*; **traitement** ~**rouille** rustproofing; ~**sémite** *adj* anti-Semitic; ~**septique** *adj, nm* antiseptic; ~**vol** *adj, nm*: (**dispositif**) ~**vol** anti-theft device

antre [ɑ̃tʀ(ə)] *nm* den, lair

anxieux, euse [ɑ̃ksjø, -øz] *adj* anxious, worried

AOC *sigle f* (= *appellation d'origine contrôlée*) *label guaranteeing the quality of wine*

août [u] *nm* August

apaiser [apeze] *vt* (*colère, douleur*) to soothe; (*faim*) to appease; (*personne*) to calm (down), pacify; **s'~** *vi* (*tempête, bruit*) to die down, subside

apanage [apanaʒ] *nm*: **être l'~ de** to be the privilege *ou* prerogative of

aparté [apaʀte] *nm* (*THÉÂTRE*) aside; (*entretien*) private conversation

apathique [apatik] *adj* apathetic

apatride [apatʀid] *nm/f* stateless person

apercevoir [apɛʀsəvwaʀ] *vt* to see; **s'~ de** *vt* to notice; **s'~ que** to notice that

aperçu [apɛʀsy] *nm* (*vue d'ensemble*) general survey; (*intuition*) insight

apéritif [apeʀitif] *nm* (*boisson*) aperitif; (*réunion*) drinks *pl*

à-peu-près [apøpʀɛ] (*péj*) *nm inv* vague approximation

apeuré, e [apœʀe] *adj* frightened, scared

aphone [afɔn] *adj* voiceless

aphte [aft(ə)] *nm* mouth ulcer

apiculture [apikyltyʀ] *nf* beekeeping, apiculture

apitoyer [apitwaje] *vt* to move to pity; **s'~ (sur)** to feel pity (for)

aplanir [aplaniʀ] *vt* to level; (*fig*) to smooth away, iron out

aplatir [aplatiʀ] *vt* to flatten; **s'~** *vi* to become flatter; to be flattened; (*fig*) to lie flat on the ground

aplomb [aplɔ̃] *nm* (*équilibre*) balance, equilibrium; (*fig*) self-assurance; nerve; **d'~** steady; (*CONSTR*) plumb

apogée [apɔʒe] *nm* (*fig*) peak, apogee

apologie [apɔlɔʒi] *nf* vindication, praise

apostrophe [apɔstʀɔf] *nf* (*signe*) apostrophe

apostropher [apɔstʀɔfe] *vt* (*interpeller*) to shout at, address sharply

apothéose [apɔteoz] *nf* pinnacle (of achievement); (*MUS*) grand finale

apôtre [apotʀ(ə)] *nm* apostle

apparaître [apaʀɛtʀ(ə)] *vi* to appear

apparat [apaʀa] *nm*: **tenue/dîner d'~** ceremonial dress/dinner

appareil [apaʀɛj] *nm* (*outil, machine*) piece of apparatus, device; appliance; (*politique, syndical*) machinery; (*avion*) (aero)plane, aircraft *inv*; (*téléphonique*) phone; (*dentier*) brace (*BRIT*), braces (*US*); **"qui est à l'~?"** "who's speaking?"; **dans le plus simple** ~ in one's birthday suit; **appareiller** [apaʀeje] *vi* (*NAVIG*) to cast off, get under way ♦ *vt* (*assortir*) to match up; **appareil(-photo)** [apaʀɛj(fɔtɔ)] *nm* camera

apparemment [apaʀamɑ̃] *adv* apparently

apparence [apaʀɑ̃s] *nf* appearance

apparent, e [apaʀɑ̃, -ɑ̃t] *adj* visible; obvious; (*superficiel*) apparent

apparenté, e [apaʀɑ̃te] *adj*: ~ **à** related to; (*fig*) similar to

apparition [apaʀisjɔ̃] *nf* appearance; (*surnaturelle*) apparition

appartement [apaʀtəmɑ̃] *nm* flat (*BRIT*), apartment (*US*)

appartenir [apaʀtəniʀ]: ~ **à** *vt* to belong to; **il lui appartient de** it is up to him to, it is his duty to

apparu, e *pp de* **apparaître**

appât [apɑ] *nm* (*PÊCHE*) bait; (*fig*) lure, bait

appauvrir [apovʀiʀ] *vt* to impoverish

appel [apɛl] *nm* call; (*nominal*) roll call; (: SCOL) register; (MIL: *recrutement*) call-up; **faire ~ à** (*invoquer*) to appeal to; (*avoir recours à*) to call on; (*nécessiter*) to call for, require; **faire ~** (JUR) to appeal; **faire l'~** to call the roll; to call the register; **sans ~** (*fig*) final, irrevocable; **~ d'offres** (COMM) invitation to tender; **faire un ~ de phares** to flash one's headlights; **~ (téléphonique)** (tele)phone call

appelé [aple] *nm* (MIL) conscript

appeler [aple] *vt* to call; (*faire venir*: *médecin etc*) to call, send for; (*fig*: *nécessiter*) to call for, demand; **s'~**: **elle s'appelle Gabrielle** her name is Gabrielle, she's called Gabrielle; **comment ça s'appelle?** what is it called?; **être appelé à** (*fig*) to be destined to; **~ qn à comparaître** (JUR) to summon sb to appear; **en ~ à** to appeal to

appendice [apɛdis] *nm* appendix; **appendicite** *nf* appendicitis

appentis [apɑti] *nm* lean-to

appesantir [apzɑtiʀ]: **s'~** *vi* to grow heavier; **s'~ sur** (*fig*) to dwell on

appétissant, e [apetisɑ, -ɑt] *adj* appetizing, mouth-watering

appétit [apeti] *nm* appetite; **bon ~!** enjoy your meal!

applaudir [aplodiʀ] *vt* to applaud ♦ *vi* to applaud, clap; **applaudissements** *nmpl* applause *sg*, clapping *sg*

application [aplikasjɔ] *nf* application

applique [aplik] *nf* wall lamp

appliquer [aplike] *vt* to apply; (*loi*) to enforce; **s'~** *vi* (*élève etc*) to apply o.s.

appoint [apwɛ] *nm* (*extra*) contribution *ou* help; **avoir/faire l'~** (*en payant*) to have/give the right change *ou* money; **chauffage d'~** extra heating

appointements [apwɛtmɑ] *nmpl* salary *sg*

appontement [apɔtmɑ] *nm* landing stage, wharf

apport [apɔʀ] *nm* supply; contribution

apporter [apɔʀte] *vt* to bring

apposer [apoze] *vt* to append; to affix

appréciable [apʀesjabl(ə)] *adj* appreciable

apprécier [apʀesje] *vt* to appreciate; (*évaluer*) to estimate, assess

appréhender [apʀeɑde] *vt* (*craindre*) to dread; (*arrêter*) to apprehend

apprendre [apʀɑdʀ(ə)] *vt* to learn; (*événement, résultats*) to learn of, hear of; **~ qch à qn** (*informer*) to tell sb (of) sth; (*enseigner*) to teach sb sth; **~ à faire qch** to learn to do sth; **~ à qn à faire qch** to teach sb to do sth; **apprenti, e** *nm/f* apprentice; (*fig*) novice, beginner; **apprentissage** *nm* learning; (COMM, SCOL: *période*) apprenticeship

apprêté, e [apʀete] *adj* (*fig*) affected

apprêter [apʀete] *vt* to dress, finish

appris, e *pp de* **apprendre**

apprivoiser [apʀivwaze] *vt* to tame

approbation [apʀɔbasjɔ] *nf* approval

approche [apʀɔʃ] *nf* approaching; approach

approcher [apʀɔʃe] *vi* to approach, come near ♦ *vt* to approach; (*rapprocher*): **~ qch (de qch)** to bring *ou* put sth near (to sth); **s'~ de** to approach, go *ou* come near to; **~ de** to draw near to; (*quantité, moment*) to approach

approfondir [apʀɔfɔdiʀ] *vt* to deepen; (*question*) to go further into

approprié, e [apʀɔpʀije] *adj*: **~ (à)** appropriate (to), suited to

approprier [apʀɔpʀije]: **s'~** *vt* to appropriate, take over

approuver [apʀuve] *vt* to agree with; (*autoriser*: *loi, projet*) to approve, pass; (*trouver louable*) to approve of

approvisionner [apʀɔvizjɔne] *vt* to supply; (*compte bancaire*) to pay funds into; **s'~ en** to stock up with

approximatif, ive [apʀɔksimatif, -iv] *adj* approximate, rough; vague

appui [apɥi] *nm* support; **prendre ~ sur** to lean on; to rest on; **l'~ de la fenêtre** the windowsill, the window ledge; **appui(e)-tête** *nm inv* headrest

appuyer [apɥije] *vt* (*poser*): **~ qch sur/contre** to lean *ou* rest sth on/against; (*soutenir*: *personne, demande*) to support, back (up) ♦ *vi*: **~ sur** (*bouton, frein*) to press, push; (*mot, détail*) to stress, emphasize; (*suj: chose: peser sur*) to rest (heavily) on, press against; **s'~ sur** to lean on; to rely on; **~ à droite** to bear (to the) right

âpre [ɑpʀ(ə)] *adj* acrid, pungent; (*fig*) harsh; bitter; **~ au gain** grasping

après [apʀɛ] *prép* after ♦ *adv* afterwards; **2 heures ~** 2 hours later; **~ qu'il est parti** after he left; **~ avoir fait** after having done; **d'~** (*selon*) according to; **~ coup** after the event, afterwards; **~ tout** (*au fond*) after all; **et (puis) ~?** so what?; **après-demain** *adv* the day after tomorrow; **après-guerre** *nm* post-war years *pl*; **après-midi** *nm ou nf* (*inv*) afternoon

à-propos [apʀopo] *nm* (*d'une remarque*) aptness; **faire preuve d'~** to show presence of mind

apte [apt(ə)] *adj* capable; (*MIL*) fit

aquarelle [akwaʀɛl] *nf* (*tableau*) watercolour; (*genre*) watercolours *pl*

aquarium [akwaʀjɔm] *nm* aquarium

arabe [aʀab] *adj* Arabic; (*désert, cheval*) Arabian; (*nation, peuple*) Arab ♦ *nm/f*: **A~** Arab ♦ *nm* (*LING*) Arabic

Arabie [aʀabi] *nf*: **l'~ (Saoudite)** Saudi Arabia

arachide [aʀaʃid] *nf* (*plante*) groundnut (plant); (*graine*) peanut, groundnut

araignée [aʀeɲe] *nf* spider

arbitraire [aʀbitʀɛʀ] *adj* arbitrary

arbitre [aʀbitʀ(ə)] *nm* (*SPORT*) referee; (: *TENNIS, CRICKET*) umpire; (*fig*) arbiter, judge; (*JUR*) arbitrator; **arbitrer** *vt* to referee; to umpire; to arbitrate

arborer [aʀbɔʀe] *vt* to bear, display

arbre [aʀbʀ(ə)] *nm* tree; (*TECH*) shaft; **~ de transmission** (*AUTO*) driveshaft; **~ généalogique** family tree

arbuste [aʀbyst(ə)] *nm* small shrub

arc [aʀk] *nm* (*arme*) bow; (*GÉOM*) arc; (*ARCHIT*) arch; **en ~ de cercle** semi-circular

arcade [aʀkad] *nf* arch(way); **~s** *nfpl* (*série*) arcade *sg*, arches

arcanes [aʀkan] *nmpl* mysteries

arc-boutant [aʀkbutɑ̃] *nm* flying buttress

arceau, x [aʀso] *nm* (*métallique etc*)

hoop

arc-en-ciel [aʀkɑ̃sjɛl] *nm* rainbow

arche [aʀʃ(ə)] *nf* arch; **~ de Noé** Noah's Ark

archéologie [aʀkeɔlɔʒi] *nf* archeology; **archéologue** *nm/f* arch(a)eologist

archet [aʀʃɛ] *nm* bow

archevêque [aʀʃəvɛk] *nm* archbishop

archipel [aʀʃipɛl] *nm* archipelago

architecte [aʀʃitɛkt(ə)] *nm* architect

architecture [aʀʃitɛktyʀ] *nf* architecture

archive [aʀʃiv] *nf* file; **~s** *nfpl* (*collection*) archives

arctique [aʀktik] *adj* Arctic ♦ *nm*: **l'A~** the Arctic

ardemment [aʀdamɑ̃] *adv* ardently, fervently

ardent, e [aʀdɑ̃, -ɑ̃t] *adj* (*soleil*) blazing; (*fièvre*) raging; (*amour*) ardent, passionate; (*prière*) fervent

ardoise [aʀdwaz] *nf* slate

ardt *abr* = **arrondissement**

ardu, e [aʀdy] *adj* (*travail*) arduous; (*problème*) difficult; (*pente*) steep

arène [aʀɛn] *nf* arena; **~s** *nfpl* (*amphithéâtre*) bull-ring *sg*

arête [aʀɛt] *nf* (*de poisson*) bone; (*d'une montagne*) ridge; (*GÉOM etc*) edge

argent [aʀʒɑ̃] *nm* (*métal*) silver; (*monnaie*) money; **~ de poche** pocket money; **~ liquide** ready money, (ready) cash; **argenterie** *nf* silverware; silver plate

argentin, e [aʀʒɑ̃tɛ̃, -in] *adj* (*son*) silvery; (*d'Argentine*) Argentinian, Argentine

Argentine [aʀʒɑ̃tin] *nf*: **l'~** Argentina, the Argentine

argile [aʀʒil] *nf* clay

argot [aʀgo] *nm* slang; **argotique** *adj* slang *cpd*; slangy

arguer [aʀgɥe]: **~ de** *vt* to put forward as a pretext ou reason

argument [aʀgymɑ̃] *nm* argument

argumentaire [aʀgymɑ̃tɛʀ] *nm* sales leaflet

argumenter [aʀgymɑ̃te] *vi* to argue

argus [aʀgys] *nm* guide to second-hand car etc prices

aristocratique [aʀistɔkʀatik] *adj* aristocratic

arithmétique [aʀitmetik] *adj* arithmetic(al) ♦ *nf* arithmetic

armateur [aʀmatœʀ] *nm* shipowner

armature [aʀmatyʀ] *nf* framework; (*de tente etc*) frame

arme [aʀm(ə)] *nf* weapon; (*section de l'armée*) arm; ~s *nfpl* (*armement*) weapons, arms; (*blason*) (coat of) arms; ~ à feu firearm

armée [aʀme] *nf* army; ~ de l'air Air Force; ~ de terre Army

armement [aʀməmɑ̃] *nm* (*matériel*) arms *pl*, weapons *pl*; (: *d'un pays*) arms *pl*, armament

armer [aʀme] *vt* to arm; (*arme à feu*) to cock; (*appareil-photo*) to wind on; ~ qch de to fit sth with; to reinforce sth with

armistice [aʀmistis] *nm* armistice; l'A~ ≈ Remembrance (BRIT) *ou* Veterans (US) Day

armoire [aʀmwaʀ] *nf* (tall) cupboard; (*penderie*) wardrobe (BRIT), closet (US)

armoiries [aʀmwaʀi] *nfpl* coat *sg* of arms

armure [aʀmyʀ] *nf* armour *no pl*, suit of armour; **armurier** [aʀmyʀje] *nm* gunsmith; armourer

arnaquer [aʀnake] *vt* to swindle

aromates [aʀɔmat] *nmpl* seasoning *sg*, herbs (and spices)

aromathérapie [aʀɔmateʀapi] *nf* aromatherapy

aromatisé, e [aʀɔmatize] *adj* flavoured

arôme [aʀom] *nm* aroma; fragrance

arpenter [aʀpɑ̃te] *vt* (*salle, couloir*) to pace up and down

arpenteur [aʀpɑ̃tœʀ] *nm* surveyor

arqué, e [aʀke] *adj* bandy; arched

arrache-pied [aʀaʃpje]: **d'~** *adv* relentlessly

arracher [aʀaʃe] *vt* to pull out; (*page etc*) to tear off, tear out; (*légumes, herbe*) to pull up; (*bras etc*) to tear off; **s'~** *vt* (*article recherché*) to fight over; ~ qch à qn to snatch sth from sb; (*fig*) to wring sth out of sb

arraisonner [aʀezɔne] *vt* (*bateau*) to board and search

arrangeant, e [aʀɑ̃ʒɑ̃, -ɑ̃t] *adj* accommodating, obliging

arrangement [aʀɑ̃ʒmɑ̃] *nm* agreement, arrangement

arranger [aʀɑ̃ʒe] *vt* (*gén*) to arrange; (*réparer*) to fix, put right; (*régler*) to settle, sort out; (*convenir à*) to suit, be convenient for; **s'~** *vi* (*se mettre d'accord*) to come to an agreement; **je vais m'~** I'll manage; **ça va s'~** it'll sort itself out

arrestation [aʀestasjɔ̃] *nf* arrest

arrêt [aʀɛ] *nm* stopping; (*de bus etc*) stop; (JUR) judgment, decision; **rester** *ou* **tomber en ~ devant** to stop short in front of; **sans ~** non-stop; continually; ~ de mort capital sentence; ~ de travail stoppage (of work)

arrêté [aʀete] *nm* order, decree

arrêter [aʀete] *vt* to stop; (*chauffage etc*) to turn off, switch off; (*fixer: date etc*) to appoint, decide on; (*criminel, suspect*) to arrest; **s'~** *vi* to stop; ~ de faire to stop doing

arrhes [aʀ] *nfpl* deposit *sg*

arrière [aʀjɛʀ] *nm* back; (SPORT) fullback ♦ *adj inv*: **siège/roue** ~ back *ou* rear seat/wheel; **à l'~** behind, at the back; **en** ~ behind; (*regarder*) back, behind; (*tomber, aller*) backwards; **arriéré, e** *adj* (*péj*) backward ♦ *nm* (*d'argent*) arrears *pl*; **~-goût** *nm* aftertaste; **~-grand-mère** *nf* great-grandmother; **~-grand-père** *nm* great-grandfather; **~-pays** *nm inv* hinterland; **~-pensée** *nf* ulterior motive; mental reservation; **~-plan** *nm* background; **~-saison** *nf* late autumn; **~-train** *nm* hindquarters *pl*

arrimer [aʀime] *vt* to stow; to secure

arrivage [aʀivaʒ] *nm* arrival

arrivée [aʀive] *nf* arrival; (*ligne d'~*) finish; ~ d'air air inlet

arriver [aʀive] *vi* to arrive; (*survenir*) to happen, occur; **il arrive à Paris à 8 h** he gets to *ou* arrives in Paris at 8; ~ à (*atteindre*) to reach; ~ à faire qch to succeed in doing sth; **il arrive que** it happens that; **il lui arrive de faire** he sometimes does; **arriviste** *nm/f* go-getter

arrogant, e [aʀɔgɑ̃, -ɑ̃t] *adj* arrogant

arroger [aʀɔʒe]: **s'~** *vt* to assume (without right)

arrondir [aʀɔ̃diʀ] *vt* (*forme, objet*) to round; (*somme*) to round off; **s'~** *vi* to become round(ed)

arrondissement [aʀɔ̃dismɑ̃] *nm* (ADMIN) ≈ district

arroser [aʀoze] *vt* to water; (*victoire*) to celebrate (over a drink); (CULIN) to baste; **arrosoir** *nm* watering can

arsenal, aux [aʀsənal, -o] *nm* (NAVIG) naval dockyard; (MIL) arsenal; (*fig*) gear, paraphernalia

art [aʀ] *nm* art; **~s ménagers** home economics *sg*

artère [aʀtɛʀ] *nf* (ANAT) artery; (*rue*) main road

arthrite [aʀtʀit] *nf* arthritis

artichaut [aʀtiʃo] *nm* artichoke

article [aʀtikl(ə)] *nm* article; (COMM) item, article; **à l'~ de la mort** at the point of death; **~ de fond** (PRESSE) feature article

articulation [aʀtikylasjɔ̃] *nf* articulation; (ANAT) joint

articuler [aʀtikyle] *vt* to articulate

artifice [aʀtifis] *nm* device, trick

artificiel, le [aʀtifisjɛl] *adj* artificial

artificieux, euse [aʀtifisjø, -øz] *adj* guileful, deceitful

artisan [aʀtizɑ̃] *nm* artisan, (self-employed) craftsman; **artisanal, e, aux** *adj* of *ou* made by craftsmen; (*péj*) cottage industry *cpd*, unsophisticated; **artisanat** *nm* arts and crafts *pl*

artiste [aʀtist(ə)] *nm/f* artist; (*de variétés*) entertainer; performer; **artistique** *adj* artistic

as[1] [a] *vb voir* **avoir**

as[2] [as] *nm* ace

ascendance [asɑ̃dɑ̃s] *nf* (*origine*) ancestry

ascendant, e [asɑ̃dɑ̃, -ɑ̃t] *adj* upward ♦ *nm* influence

ascenseur [asɑ̃sœʀ] *nm* lift (BRIT), elevator (US)

ascension [asɑ̃sjɔ̃] *nf* ascent; climb; **l'A~** (REL) the Ascension

aseptiser [asɛptize] *vt* to sterilize; to disinfect

asiatique [azjatik] *adj*, *nm/f* Asiatic, Asian

Asie [azi] *nf*: **l'~** Asia

asile [azil] *nm* (*refuge*) refuge, sanctuary; (POL): **droit d'~** (political) asylum; (*pour malades etc*) home

aspect [aspɛ] *nm* appearance, look; (*fig*) aspect, side; **à l'~ de** at the sight of

asperge [aspɛʀʒ(ə)] *nf* asparagus *no pl*

asperger [aspɛʀʒe] *vt* to spray, sprinkle

aspérité [aspeʀite] *nf* excrescence, protruding bit (of rock *etc*)

asphalte [asfalt(ə)] *nm* asphalt

asphyxier [asfiksje] *vt* to suffocate, asphyxiate; (*fig*) to stifle

aspirateur [aspiʀatœʀ] *nm* vacuum cleaner

aspirer [aspiʀe] *vt* (*air*) to inhale; (*liquide*) to suck (up); (*suj: appareil*) to suck up; **~ à** to aspire to

aspirine [aspiʀin] *nf* aspirin

assagir [asaʒiʀ] *vt* to quieten down; **s'~** *vi* to quieten down, sober down

assaillir [asajiʀ] *vt* to assail, attack

assainir [aseniʀ] *vt* to clean up; to purify

assaisonner [asɛzɔne] *vt* to season

assassin [asasɛ̃] *nm* murderer; assassin; **assassiner** [asasine] *vt* to murder; (*esp* POL) to assassinate

assaut [aso] *nm* assault, attack; **prendre d'~** to storm, assault; **donner l'~** to attack; **faire ~ de** (*rivaliser*) to vie with each other in

assécher [aseʃe] *vt* to drain

assemblée [asɑ̃ble] *nf* (*réunion*) meeting; (*public, assistance*) gathering; assembled people; (POL) assembly

assembler [asɑ̃ble] *vt* (*joindre, monter*) to assemble, put together; (*amasser*) to gather (together), collect (together); **s'~** *vi* to gather

assener [asene] *vt*: **~ un coup à qn** to deal sb a blow

asséner [asene] *vt* = **assener**

assentiment [asɑ̃timɑ̃] *nm* assent, consent; approval

asseoir [aswaʀ] *vt* (*malade, bébé*) to sit up; to sit down; (*autorité, réputation*) to establish; **s'~** *vi* to sit (o.s.) down

assermenté, e [asɛʀmɑ̃te] *adj* sworn, on oath

asservir [asɛʀviʀ] *vt* to subjugate, enslave

assez [ase] *adv* (*suffisamment*) enough, sufficiently; (*passablement*) rather, quite, fairly; **~ de pain/livres** enough *ou* sufficient bread/books; **vous en avez ~?** have you got enough?

assidu, e [asidy] *adj* assiduous, painstaking; regular; **assiduités** *nfpl* assiduous attentions

assied *etc vb voir* **asseoir**

assiéger [asjeʒe] *vt* to besiege

assiérai *etc vb voir* **asseoir**

assiette [asjɛt] *nf* plate; (*contenu*) plate(ful); **~ à dessert** dessert plate; **~ anglaise** assorted cold meats; **~ creuse** (soup) dish, soup plate; **~ de l'impôt** basis of (tax) assessment; **~ plate** (dinner) plate

assigner [asiɲe] *vt*: **~ qch à** (*poste, part, travail*) to assign sth to; (*limites*) to set sth to; (*cause, effet*) to ascribe sth to; **~ qn à** to assign sb to

assimiler [asimile] *vt* to assimilate, absorb; (*comparer*): **~ qch/qn à** to liken *ou* compare sth/sb to; **s'~** *vi* (*s'intégrer*) to be assimilated *ou* absorbed

assis, e [asi, -iz] *pp de* **asseoir** ♦ *adj* sitting (down), seated; **assise** *nf* (*fig*) basis, foundation; **assises** *nfpl* (*JUR*) assizes; (*congrès*) (annual) conference

assistance [asistɑ̃s] *nf* (*public*) audience; (*aide*) assistance

assistant, e [asistɑ̃, -ɑ̃t] *nm/f* assistant; (*d'université*) probationary lecturer; **~e sociale** social worker

assisté, e [asiste] *adj* (*AUTO*) power assisted

assister [asiste] *vt* to assist; **~ à** (*scène, événement*) to witness; (*conférence, séminaire*) to attend, be at; (*spectacle, match*) to be at, see

association [asɔsjasjɔ̃] *nf* association

associé, e [asɔsje] *nm/f* associate; partner

associer [asɔsje] *vt* to associate; **s'~** *vi* to join together ♦ *vt* (*collaborateur*) to take on (as a partner); **s'~ à qn pour faire** to join (forces) with sb to do; **s'~ à** to be combined with; (*opinions, joie de qn*) to share in; **~ qn à** (*profits*) to give sb a share of; (*affaire*) to make sb a partner in; (*joie, triomphe*) to include sb in; **~ qch à** (*joindre, allier*) to combine sth with

assoiffé, e [aswafe] *adj* thirsty

assombrir [asɔ̃bʀiʀ] *vt* to darken; (*fig*) to fill with gloom

assommer [asɔme] *vt* to batter to death; (*étourdir, abrutir*) to knock out; to stun

Assomption [asɔ̃psjɔ̃] *nf*: **l'~** the Assumption

assorti, e [asɔʀti] *adj* matched, matching; (*varié*) assorted; **~ à** matching

assortiment [asɔʀtimɑ̃] *nm* assortment, selection

assortir [asɔʀtiʀ] *vt* to match; **s'~ de** to be accompanied by; **~ qch à** to match sth with; **~ qch de** to accompany sth with

assoupi, e [asupi] *adj* dozing, sleeping; (*fig*) (be)numbed; dulled; stilled

assouplir [asupliʀ] *vt* to make supple; (*fig*) to relax

assourdir [asuʀdiʀ] *vt* (*bruit*) to deaden, muffle; (*suj: bruit*) to deafen

assouvir [asuviʀ] *vt* to satisfy, appease

assujettir [asyʒetiʀ] *vt* to subject

assumer [asyme] *vt* (*fonction, emploi*) to assume, take on

assurance [asyʀɑ̃s] *nf* (*certitude*) assurance; (*confiance en soi*) (self-)confidence; (*contrat*) insurance (policy); (*secteur commercial*) insurance; **~ maladie** health insurance; **~ tous risques** (*AUTO*) comprehensive insurance; **~s sociales** ≈ National Insurance (*BRIT*), ≈ Social Security (*US*); **~-vie** *nf* life assurance *ou* insurance

assuré, e [asyʀe] *adj* (*certain*): **~ de** confident of ♦ *nm/f* insured (person); **assurément** *adv* assuredly, most certainly

assurer [asyʀe] *vt* to insure; (*stabiliser*) to steady; to stabilize; (*victoire etc*) to ensure; (*frontières, pouvoir*) to make secure; (*service, garde*) to provide; to operate; **s'~ (contre)** (*COMM*) to insure o.s. (against); **s'~ de/que** (*vérifier*) to make sure of/that; **s'~ (de)** (*aide de qn*) to secure; ~ **qch à qn** (*garantir*) to secure sth for sb; (*certifier*) to assure sb of sth; ~ **à qn que** to assure sb that; ~ **qn de** to assure sb of

asthme [asm(ə)] *nm* asthma

asticot [astiko] *nm* maggot

astiquer [astike] *vt* to polish, shine

astre [astʀ(ə)] *nm* star

astreignant, e [astʀɛɲɑ̃, -ɑ̃t] *adj* demanding

astreindre [astʀɛ̃dʀ(ə)] *vt*: ~ **qn à qch** to force sth upon sb; ~ **qn à faire** to compel *ou* force sb to do

astrologie [astʀɔlɔʒi] *nf* astrology

astronaute [astʀɔnot] *nm/f* astronaut

astronomie [astʀɔnɔmi] *nf* astronomy

astuce [astys] *nf* shrewdness, astuteness; (*truc*) trick, clever way; (*plaisanterie*) wisecrack; **astucieux, euse** *adj* clever

atelier [atəlje] *nm* workshop; (*de peintre*) studio

athée [ate] *adj* atheistic ♦ *nm/f* atheist

Athènes [atɛn] *n* Athens

athlète [atlɛt] *nm/f* (*SPORT*) athlete; **athlétisme** *nm* athletics *sg*

atlantique [atlɑ̃tik] *adj* Atlantic ♦ *nm*: **l'(océan) A~** the Atlantic (Ocean)

atlas [atlɑs] *nm* atlas

atmosphère [atmɔsfɛʀ] *nf* atmosphere

atome [atom] *nm* atom; **atomique** *adj* atomic, nuclear; (*nombre, masse*) atomic

atomiseur [atɔmizœʀ] *nm* atomizer

atone [aton] *adj* lifeless

atours [atuʀ] *nmpl* attire *sg*, finery *sg*

atout [atu] *nm* trump; (*fig*) asset; trump card

âtre [ɑtʀ(ə)] *nm* hearth

atroce [atʀɔs] *adj* atrocious

attabler [atable]: **s'~** *vi* to sit down at (the) table

attachant, e [ataʃɑ̃, -ɑ̃t] *adj* engaging, lovable, likeable

attache [ataʃ] *nf* clip, fastener; (*fig*) tie

attacher [ataʃe] *vt* to tie up; (*étiquette*) to attach, tie on; (*souliers*) to do up ♦ *vi*

(*poêle, riz*) to stick; **s'~ à** (*par affection*) to become attached to; **s'~ à faire** to endeavour to do; ~ **qch à** to tie *ou* attach sth to

attaque [atak] *nf* attack; (*cérébrale*) stroke; (*d'épilepsie*) fit

attaquer [atake] *vt* to attack; (*en justice*) to bring an action against, sue; (*travail*) to tackle, set about ♦ *vi* to attack

attardé, e [ataʀde] *adj* (*passants*) late; (*enfant*) backward; (*conceptions*) old-fashioned

attarder [ataʀde]: **s'~** *vi* to linger; to stay on

atteindre [atɛ̃dʀ(ə)] *vt* to reach; (*blesser*) to hit; (*émouvoir*) to affect

atteint, e [atɛ̃, -ɛ̃t] *adj* (*MÉD*): **être ~ de** to be suffering from; **atteinte** *nf* attack; **hors d'atteinte** out of reach; **porter atteinte à** to strike a blow at; to undermine

atteler [atle] *vt* (*cheval, bœufs*) to hitch up; (*wagons*) to couple; **s'~ à** (*travail*) to buckle down to

attelle [atɛl] *nf* splint

attenant, e [atnɑ̃, -ɑ̃t] *adj*: ~ **(à)** adjoining

attendant [atɑ̃dɑ̃] *adv*: **en ~** meanwhile, in the meantime

attendre [atɑ̃dʀ(ə)] *vt* (*gén*) to wait for; (*être destiné ou réservé à*) to await, be in store for ♦ *vi* to wait; **s'~ à (ce que)** to expect (that); ~ **un enfant** to be expecting a baby; ~ **de faire/d'être** to wait until one does/is; ~ **que** to wait until; ~ **qch de** to expect sth of; **en attendant** meanwhile, in the meantime; be that as it may

attendrir [atɑ̃dʀiʀ] *vt* to move (to pity); (*viande*) to tenderize

attendu, e [atɑ̃dy] *adj* (*visiteur*) expected; ~ **que** considering that, since

attentat [atɑ̃ta] *nm* assassination attempt; ~ **à la bombe** bomb attack; ~ **à la pudeur** indecent exposure *no pl*; indecent assault *no pl*

attente [atɑ̃t] *nf* wait; (*espérance*) expectation

attenter [atɑ̃te]: ~ **à** *vt* (*liberté*) to violate; ~ **à la vie de qn** to make an attempt on sb's life

attentif, ive [atɑ̃tif, -iv] *adj* (*auditeur*) attentive; (*travail*) scrupulous; careful; ~ **à** mindful of; careful to

attention [atɑ̃sjɔ̃] *nf* attention; (*prévenance*) attention, thoughtfulness *no pl*; **à l'~ de** for the attention of; **faire ~ (à)** to be careful (of); **faire ~ (à ce) que** to be careful *ou* make sure that; ~! careful!, watch out!; **attentionné, e** *adj* thoughtful, considerate

atténuer [atenɥe] *vt* to alleviate, ease; to lessen

atterrer [atere] *vt* to dismay, appal

atterrir [aterir] *vi* to land; **atterrissage** *nm* landing

attestation [atɛstɑsjɔ̃] *nf* certificate

attester [atɛste] *vt* to testify to

attirail [atiraj] *nm* gear; (*péj*) paraphernalia

attirant, e [atirɑ̃, -ɑ̃t] *adj* attractive, appealing

attirer [atire] *vt* to attract; (*appâter*) to lure, entice; ~ **qn dans un coin/vers soi** to draw sb into a corner/towards one; ~ **l'attention de qn (sur)** to attract sb's attention (to); to draw sb's attention (to); **s'~ des ennuis** to bring trouble upon o.s., get into trouble

attiser [atize] *vt* (*feu*) to poke (up)

attitré, e [atitre] *adj* qualified; accredited; appointed

attitude [atityd] *nf* attitude; (*position du corps*) bearing

attouchements [atuʃmɑ̃] *nmpl* touching *sg*; (*sexuels*) fondling *sg*

attraction [atraksjɔ̃] *nf* (*gén*) attraction; (*de cabaret, cirque*) number

attrait [atrɛ] *nm* appeal, attraction; lure

attrape-nigaud [atrapnigo] *nm* con

attraper [atrape] *vt* (*gén*) to catch; (*habitude, amende*) to get, pick up; (*fam: duper*) to con

attrayant, e [atrɛjɑ̃, -ɑ̃t] *adj* attractive

attribuer [atribɥe] *vt* (*prix*) to award; (*rôle, tâche*) to allocate, assign; (*imputer*): ~ **qch à** to attribute sth to; **s'~** *vt*

(*s'approprier*) to claim for o.s.

attribut [atriby] *nm* attribute; (*LING*) complement

attrister [atriste] *vt* to sadden

attroupement [atrupmɑ̃] *nm* crowd, mob

attrouper [atrupe]: **s'~** *vi* to gather

au [o] *prép* +*dét* = **à** +**le**

aubade [obad] *nf* dawn serenade

aubaine [obɛn] *nf* godsend; (*financière*) windfall

aube [ob] *nf* dawn, daybreak; **à l'~** at dawn *ou* daybreak

aubépine [obepin] *nf* hawthorn

auberge [obɛrʒ(ə)] *nf* inn; ~ **de jeunesse** youth hostel

aubergine [obɛrʒin] *nf* aubergine

aubergiste [obɛrʒist(ə)] *nm/f* innkeeper, hotel-keeper

aucun, e [okœ̃, -yn] *dét* no, *tournure négative* +any; (*positif*) any ♦ *pron* none, *tournure négative* +any; any(one); **sans** ~ **doute** without any doubt; **plus qu'~ autre** more than any other; ~ **des deux** neither of the two; ~ **d'entre eux** none of them; **d'~s** (*certains*) some; **aucunement** *adv* in no way, not in the least

audace [odas] *nf* daring, boldness; (*péj*) audacity; **audacieux, euse** *adj* daring, bold

au-delà [odla] *adv* beyond ♦ *nm*: **l'~** the hereafter; ~ **de** beyond

au-dessous [odsu] *adv* underneath; below; ~ **de** under(neath), below; (*limite, somme etc*) below, under; (*dignité, condition*) below

au-dessus [odsy] *adv* above; ~ **de** above

au-devant [odvɑ̃]: ~ **de** *prép*: **aller** ~ (*personne, danger*) to go (out) and meet; (*souhaits de qn*) to anticipate

audience [odjɑ̃s] *nf* audience; (*JUR: séance*) hearing

audimat [odimat] (®) *nm* (*taux d'écoute*) ratings *pl*

audio-visuel, le [odjɔvizɥɛl] *adj* audiovisual

auditeur, trice [oditœr, -tris] *nm/f* listener

audition [odisjɔ̃] *nf* (*ouïe, écoute*) hear-

ing; (*JUR*: *de témoins*) examination; (*MUS.*
THÉÂTRE: *épreuve*) audition
auditoire [oditwar] *nm* audience
auge [oʒ] *nf* trough
augmentation [ɔgmɑ̃tasjɔ̃] *nf*: ~ **(de sa-**
laire) rise (in salary) (*BRIT*), (pay) raise
(*US*)
augmenter [ɔgmɑ̃te] *vt* (*gén*) to increase; (*salaire, prix*) to increase, raise,
put up; (*employé*) to increase the salary
of ♦ *vi* to increase
augure [ɔgyʀ] *nm* soothsayer, oracle; **de**
bon/mauvais ~ of good/ill omen; **augu-**
rer [ɔgyʀe] *vt*: **augurer bien de** to augur
well for
aujourd'hui [oʒuʀdɥi] *adv* today
aumône [ɔmon] *nf inv* alms *sg*; **faire**
l'~ **(à qn)** to give alms (to sb)
aumônier [ɔmonje] *nm* chaplain
auparavant [oparavɑ̃] *adv* before(hand)
auprès [opʀɛ]: ~ **de** *prép* next to, close
to; (*recourir, s'adresser*) to; (*en compa-*
raison de) compared with
auquel [okɛl] *prép* +*pron* = **à** +**lequel**
aurai *etc vb voir* **avoir**
auréole [ɔʀeɔl] *nf* halo; (*tache*) ring
auriculaire [ɔʀikylɛʀ] *nm* little finger
aurons *etc vb voir* **avoir**
aurore [ɔʀɔʀ] *nf* dawn, daybreak
ausculter [ɔskylte] *vt* to sound
aussi [osi] *adv* (*également*) also, too; (*de*
comparaison) as ♦ *conj* therefore, consequently; ~ **fort que** as strong as; **moi** ~
me too; ~ **bien que** (*de même que*) as
well as
aussitôt [osito] *adv* straight away, immediately; ~ **que** as soon as
austère [ɔstɛʀ] *adj* austere; stern
austral, e [ɔstʀal] *adj* southern
Australie [ɔstʀali] *nf*: **l'**~ Australia; **aus-**
tralien, ne *adj, nm/f* Australian
autant [otɑ̃] *adv* so much; (*comparatif*):
~ **(que)** as much (as); (*nombre*) as many
(as); ~ **(de)** so much (*ou* many); as much
(*ou* many); ~ **partir** we (*ou* you *etc*) may
as well leave; ~ **dire que ...** one might
as well say that ...; **pour** ~ for all that;
pour ~ **que** assuming, as long as; **d'**~
plus/mieux (que) all the more/the bet-

ter (since)
autel [otɛl] *nm* altar
auteur [otœʀ] *nm* author
authentique [otɑ̃tik] *adj* authentic,
genuine
auto [oto] *nf* car
auto: ~**biographie** *nf* autobiography;
~**bus** *nm* bus; ~**car** *nm* coach
autochtone [otɔktɔn] *nm/f* native
auto: ~**-collant, e** *adj* self-adhesive; (*en-*
veloppe) self-seal ♦ *nm* sticker; ~**cou-**
chettes *adj*: **train** ~**couchettes** car
sleeper train; ~**cuiseur** *nm* pressure cooker; ~**défense** *nf* self-defence; **groupe**
d'~**défense** vigilante committee; ~**didac-**
te *nm/f* self-taught person; ~**école** *nf*
driving school; ~**gestion** *nf* joint
worker-management control; ~**graphe**
nm autograph
automate [ɔtɔmat] *nm* (*machine*) (automatic) machine
automatique [ɔtɔmatik] *adj* automatic
♦ *nm*: **l'**~ direct dialling; **automatiser** *vt*
to automate
automne [ɔtɔn] *nm* autumn (*BRIT*), fall
(*US*)
automobile [ɔtɔmɔbil] *adj* motor *cpd* ♦
nf (motor) car; **l'**~ motoring; the car industry; **automobiliste** *nm/f* motorist
autonome [ɔtɔnɔm] *adj* autonomous;
autonomie *nf* autonomy; (*POL*) self-
government, autonomy
autopsie [ɔtɔpsi] *nf* post-mortem (examination), autopsy
autoradio [ɔtɔʀadjo] *nm* car radio
autorisation [ɔtɔʀizasjɔ̃] *nf* permission,
authorization; (*papiers*) permit
autorisé, e [ɔtɔʀize] *adj* (*opinion, sour-*
ces) authoritative
autoriser [ɔtɔʀize] *vt* to give permission
for, authorize; (*fig*) to allow (of), sanction
autoritaire [ɔtɔʀitɛʀ] *adj* authoritarian
autorité [ɔtɔʀite] *nf* authority; **faire** ~
to be authoritative
autoroute [ɔtɔʀut] *nf* motorway (*BRIT*),
highway (*US*); ~ **de l'information** (*IN-*
FORM) information superhighway
auto-stop [ɔtɔstɔp] *nm*: **faire de l'**~ to

hitch-hike; **auto-stoppeur, euse** *nm/f* hitch-hiker

autour [otuʀ] *adv* around; **~ de** around; **tout ~** all around

---
MOT-CLÉ
---

autre [otʀ(ə)] *adj* **1** (*différent*) other, different; **je préférerais un ~ verre** I'd prefer another *ou* a different glass
2 (*supplémentaire*) other; **je voudrais un ~ verre d'eau** I'd like another glass of water
3: **~ chose** something else; **~ part** somewhere else; **d'~ part** on the other hand
♦ *pron*: **un ~** another (one); **nous/vous ~s** us/you; **d'~s** others; **l'~** the other (one); **les ~s** the others; (*autrui*) others; **l'un et l'~** both of them; **se détester l'un l'~/les uns les ~s** to hate each other *ou* one another; **d'une semaine à l'~** from one week to the next; (*incessamment*) any week now; **entre ~s** among other things

autrefois [otʀəfwa] *adv* in the past
autrement [otʀəmã] *adv* differently; in another way; (*sinon*) otherwise; **~ dit** in other words
Autriche [otʀiʃ] *nf*: **l'~** Austria; **autrichien, ne** *adj*, *nm/f* Austrian
autruche [otʀyʃ] *nf* ostrich
autrui [otʀɥi] *pron* others
auvent [ovã] *nm* canopy
aux [o] *prép* +*dét* = à +les
auxiliaire [ɔksiljɛʀ] *adj*, *nm/f* auxiliary
auxquelles [okɛl] *prép* +*pron* = à +lesquelles
auxquels [okɛl] *prép* +*pron* = à +lesquels
avachi, e [avaʃi] *adj* limp, flabby
aval [aval] *nm* (*accord*) endorsement, backing; (*GÉO*): **en ~** downstream, downriver; (*sur une pente*) downhill
avalanche [avalɑ̃ʃ] *nf* avalanche
avaler [avale] *vt* to swallow
avance [avãs] *nf* (*de troupes etc*) advance; progress; (*d'argent*) advance; (*opposé à retard*) lead; being ahead of schedule; **~s** *nfpl* (*ouvertures*) overtures;

(*amoureuses*) advances; (**être**) **en ~** (to be) early; (*sur un programme*) (to be) ahead of schedule; **à l'~, d'~** in advance
avancé, e [avãse] *adj* advanced; well on, well under way
avancement [avãsmã] *nm* (*professionnel*) promotion
avancer [avãse] *vi* to move forward, advance; (*projet, travail*) to make progress; (*être en saillie*) to overhang; to jut out; (*montre, réveil*) to be fast; to gain ♦ *vt* to move forward, advance; (*argent*) to advance; (*montre, pendule*) to put forward; **s'~** *vi* to move forward, advance; (*fig*) to commit o.s.; to overhang; to jut out
avant [avã] *prép* before ♦ *adv*: **trop/plus ~** too far/further forward ♦ *adj inv*: **siège/roue ~** front seat/wheel ♦ *nm* (*d'un véhicule, bâtiment*) front; (*SPORT*: *joueur*) forward; **~ qu'il parte/de faire** before he leaves/doing; **~ tout** (*surtout*) above all; **à l'~** (*dans un véhicule*) in (the) front; **en ~** forward(s); **en ~ de** in front of
avantage [avãtaʒ] *nm* advantage; **~s sociaux** fringe benefits; **avantager** *vt* (*favoriser*) to favour; (*embellir*) to flatter; **avantageux, euse** *adj* attractive; attractively priced
avant: **~-bras** *nm inv* forearm; **~-coureur** *adj inv*: **signe ~-coureur** advance indication *ou* sign; **~-dernier, ière** *adj*, *nm/f* next to last, last but one; **~-goût** *nm* foretaste; **~-hier** *adv* the day before yesterday; **~-première** *nf* (*de film*) preview; **~-projet** *nm* (preliminary) draft; **~-propos** *nm* foreword; **~-veille** *nf*; **l'~-veille** two days before
avare [avaʀ] *adj* miserly, avaricious ♦ *nm/f* miser; **~ de** (*compliments etc*) sparing of
avarié, e [avaʀje] *adj* rotting
avaries [avaʀi] *nfpl* (*NAVIG*) damage *sg*
avec [avɛk] *prép* with; (*à l'égard de*) to(wards), with
avenant, e [avnã, -ãt] *adj* pleasant; **à l'~** in keeping
avènement [avɛnmã] *nm* (*d'un roi*) ac-

cession, succession; (*d'un changement*) advent, coming

avenir [avniʀ] *nm* future; **à l'~** in future; **politicien d'~** politician with prospects *ou* a future

Avent [avɑ̃] *nm*: **l'~** Advent

aventure [avɑ̃tyʀ] *nf* adventure; (*amoureuse*) affair; **aventurer: s'aventurer** *vi* to venture; **aventureux, euse** *adj* adventurous, venturesome; (*projet*) risky, chancy

avenue [avny] *nf* avenue

avérer [aveʀe]: **s'~** *vb* +*attrib* to prove (to be)

averse [avɛʀs(ə)] *nf* shower

averti, e [avɛʀti] *adj* (well-)informed

avertir [avɛʀtiʀ] *vt*: **~ qn (de qch/que)** to warn sb (of sth/that); (*renseigner*) to inform sb (of sth/that); **avertissement** *nm* warning; **avertisseur** *nm* horn, siren

aveu, x [avø] *nm* confession

aveugle [avœgl(ə)] *adj* blind; **aveuglément** *adv* blindly; **aveugler** *vt* to blind

aviateur, trice [avjatœʀ, -tʀis] *nm/f* aviator, pilot

aviation [avjɑsjɔ̃] *nf* aviation; (*sport*) flying; (*MIL*) air force

avide [avid] *adj* eager; (*péj*) greedy, grasping

avilir [aviliʀ] *vt* to debase

avion [avjɔ̃] *nm* (aero)plane (*BRIT*), (air)plane (*US*); **aller (quelque part) en ~** to go (somewhere) by plane, fly (somewhere); **par ~** by airmail; **~ à réaction** jet (plane)

aviron [aviʀɔ̃] *nm* oar; (*sport*): **l'~** rowing

avis [avi] *nm* opinion; (*notification*) notice; **changer d'~** to change one's mind; **jusqu'à nouvel ~** until further notice

avisé, e [avize] *adj* sensible, wise

aviser [avize] *vt* (*voir*) to notice, catch sight of; (*informer*): **~ qn de/que** to advise *ou* inform sb of/that ♦ *vi* to think about things, assess the situation; **s'~ de qch/que** to become suddenly aware of sth/that; **s'~ de faire** to take it into one's head to do

avocat, e [avɔka, -at] *nm/f* (*JUR*) barrister (*BRIT*), lawyer ♦ *nm* (*CULIN*) avocado (pear); **~ général** assistant public prosecutor

avoine [avwan] *nf* oats *pl*

MOT-CLÉ

avoir [avwaʀ] *nm* assets *pl*, resources *pl*; (*COMM*) credit
♦ *vt* **1** (*posséder*) to have; **elle a 2 enfants/une belle maison** she has (got) 2 children/a lovely house; **il a les yeux bleus** he has (got) blue eyes
2 (*âge, dimensions*) to be; **il a 3 ans** he is 3 (years old); **le mur a 3 mètres de haut** the wall is 3 metres high; *voir aussi* **faim; peur** *etc*
3 (*fam: duper*) to do, have; **on vous a eu!** you've been done *ou* had!
4: **en ~ contre qn** to have a grudge against sb; **en ~ assez** to be fed up; **j'en ai pour une demi-heure** it'll take me half an hour
♦ *vb aux* **1** to have; **~ mangé/dormi** to have eaten/slept
2 (*avoir +à +infinitif*): **~ à faire qch** to have to do sth; **vous n'avez qu'à lui demander** you only have to ask him
♦ *vb impers* **1**: **il y a** (+ *singulier*) there is; (+ *pluriel*) there are; **qu'y-a-t-il?, qu'est-ce qu'il y a?** what's the matter?, what is it?; **il doit y avoir une explication** there must be an explanation; **il n'y a qu'à ... we** (*ou* you *etc*) will just have to ...
2 (*temporel*): **il y a 10 ans** 10 years ago; **il y a 10 ans/longtemps que je le sais** I've known it for 10 years/a long time; **il y a 10 ans qu'il est arrivé** it's 10 years since he arrived

---

avoisiner [avwazine] *vt* to be near *ou* close to; (*fig*) to border *ou* verge on

avortement [avɔʀtəmɑ̃] *nm* abortion

avorter [avɔʀte] *vi* (*MÉD*) to have an abortion; (*fig*) to fail

avoué, e [avwe] *adj* avowed ♦ *nm* (*JUR*) ≈ solicitor

avouer [avwe] *vt* (*crime, défaut*) to confess (to); ~ **avoir fait/que** to admit *ou* confess to having done/that

avril [avʀil] *nm* April

axe [aks(ə)] *nm* axis; (*de roue etc*) axle; (*fig*) main line; ~ **routier** main road, trunk road; **axer** *vt*: **axer qch sur** to centre sth on

ayons *etc vb voir* **avoir**

azote [azɔt] *nm* nitrogen

B b

babines [babin] *nfpl* chops

babiole [babjɔl] *nf* (*bibelot*) trinket; (*vétille*) trifle

bâbord [bɑbɔʀ] *nm*: **à** *ou* **par ~** to port, on the port side

baby-foot [babifut] *nm* table football

bac [bak] *abr m* = **baccalauréat** ♦ *nm* (*bateau*) ferry; (*récipient*) tub; tray; tank

baccalauréat [bakalɔʀea] *nm* high school diploma

bachelier, ière [baʃəlje, -jɛʀ] *nm/f* *holder of the baccalauréat*

bachoter [baʃɔte] (*fam*) *vi* to cram (for an exam)

bâcler [bɑkle] *vt* to botch (up)

badaud, e [bado, -od] *nm/f* idle onlooker, stroller

badigeonner [badiʒɔne] *vt* to distemper; to colourwash; (*barbouiller*) to daub

badin, e [badɛ̃, -in] *adj* playful

badiner [badine] *vi*: ~ **avec qch** to treat sth lightly

baffe [baf] (*fam*) *nf* slap, clout

bafouer [bafwe] *vt* to deride, ridicule

bafouiller [bafuje] *vi, vt* to stammer

bagage [bagaʒ] *nm*: ~**s** luggage *sg*; ~**s à main** hand-luggage

bagarre [bagaʀ] *nf* fight, brawl; **bagarrer: se bagarrer** *vi* to have a fight *ou* scuffle, fight

bagatelle [bagatɛl] *nf* trifle

bagne [baɲ] *nm* penal colony

bagnole [baɲɔl] (*fam*) *nf* car

bagout [bagu] *nm*: **avoir du ~** to have the gift of the gab

bague [bag] *nf* ring; ~ **de fiançailles** engagement ring; ~ **de serrage** clip

baguette [bagɛt] *nf* stick; (*cuisine chinoise*) chopstick; (*de chef d'orchestre*) baton; (*pain*) stick of (French) bread; ~ **magique** magic wand

baie [bɛ] *nf* (*GÉO*) bay; (*fruit*) berry; ~ (**vitrée**) picture window

baignade [bɛɲad] *nf* bathing

baigner [bɛɲe] *vt* (*bébé*) to bath; **se ~** *vi* to have a swim, go swimming *ou* bathing; **baignoire** *nf* bath(tub)

bail [baj] (*pl* **baux**) *nm* lease

bâiller [bɑje] *vi* to yawn; (*être ouvert*) to gape

bâillon [bɑjɔ̃] *nm* gag; **bâillonner** *vt* to gag

bain [bɛ̃] *nm* bath; **prendre un ~** to have a bath; **se mettre dans le ~** (*fig*) to get into it *ou* things; ~ **de foule** walkabout; ~ **de soleil: prendre un ~ de soleil** to sunbathe; ~**s de mer** sea bathing *sg*; **bain-marie** *nm*: **faire chauffer au bain-marie** (*boîte etc*) to immerse in boiling water

baiser [beze] *nm* kiss ♦ *vt* (*main, front*) to kiss; (*fam!*) to screw (!)

baisse [bɛs] *nf* fall, drop; **"~ sur la viande"** "meat prices down"

baisser [bese] *vt* lower; (*radio, chauffage*) to turn down; (*AUTO: phares*) to dip (*BRIT*), lower (*US*) ♦ *vi* to fall, drop, go down; **se ~** *vi* to bend down

bal [bal] *nm* dance; (*grande soirée*) ball; ~ **costumé** fancy-dress ball

balader [balade] *vt* (*traîner*) to trail round; **se ~** *vi* to go for a walk *ou* stroll, to go for a drive

baladeur [baladœʀ] *nm* personal stereo, Walkman ®

balafre [balafʀ(ə)] *nf* gash, slash; (*cicatrice*) scar

balai [balɛ] *nm* broom, brush; **balai-brosse** *nm* (long-handled) scrubbing brush

balance [balɑ̃s] *nf* scales *pl*; (*de précision*) balance; (*signe*): **la B~** Libra

balancer [balɑ̃se] *vt* to swing; (*lancer*) to fling, chuck; (*renvoyer, jeter*) to chuck out ♦ *vi* to swing; **se ~** *vi* to swing; to rock; to sway; **se ~ de** (*fam*) not to care about; **balancier** *nm* (*de pendule*) pendulum; (*perche*) (balancing) pole; **balançoire** *nf* swing; (*sur pivot*) seesaw

balayer [baleje] *vt* (*feuilles etc*) to sweep up, brush up; (*pièce*) to sweep; (*chasser*) to sweep away; to sweep aside; (*suj: radar*) to scan; **balayeur, euse** *nm/f* roadsweeper; **balayeuse** *nf* (*machine*) roadsweeper

balbutier [balbysje] *vi, vt* to stammer

balcon [balkɔ̃] *nm* balcony; (*THÉÂTRE*) dress circle

baleine [balɛn] *nf* whale; (*de parapluie, corset*) rib; **baleinière** *nf* whaleboat

balise [baliz] *nf* (*NAVIG*) beacon; (*marker*) buoy; (*AVIAT*) runway light, beacon; (*AUTO, SKI*) sign, marker; **baliser** *vt* to mark out (with lights *etc*)

balivernes [balivɛrn(ə)] *nfpl* nonsense *sg*

ballant, e [balɑ̃, -ɑ̃t] *adj* dangling

balle [bal] *nf* (*de fusil*) bullet; (*de sport*) ball; (*paquet*) bale; (*fam: franc*) franc; **~ perdue** stray bullet

ballerine [balrin] *nf* ballet dancer

ballet [balɛ] *nm* ballet

ballon [balɔ̃] *nm* (*de sport*) ball; (*jouet, AVIAT*) balloon; (*de vin*) glass; **~ de football** football

ballot [balo] *nm* bundle; (*péj*) nitwit

ballottage [balotaʒ] *nm* (*POL*) second ballot

ballotter [balote] *vi* to roll around; to toss ♦ *vt* to shake about; to toss

balnéaire [balneɛr] *adj* seaside *cpd*

balourd, e [balur, -urd(ə)] *adj* clumsy ♦ *nm/f* clodhopper

balustrade [balystrad] *nf* railings *pl*, handrail

bambin [bɑ̃bɛ̃] *nm* little child

ban [bɑ̃] *nm* cheer; **~s** *nmpl* (*de mariage*) banns; **mettre au ~ de** to outlaw from

banal, e [banal] *adj* banal, commonplace; (*péj*) trite

banane [banan] *nf* banana

banc [bɑ̃] *nm* seat, bench; (*de poissons*) shoal; **~ d'essai** (*fig*) testing ground; **~**

de sable sandbank

bancaire [bɑ̃kɛr] *adj* banking, bank *cpd*

bancal, e [bɑ̃kal] *adj* wobbly; bow-legged

bandage [bɑ̃daʒ] *nm* bandage

bande [bɑ̃d] *nf* (*de tissu etc*) strip; (*MÉD*) bandage; (*motif*) stripe; (*magnétique etc*) tape; (*groupe*) band; (: *péj*) bunch; **par la ~** in a roundabout way; **faire ~ à part** to keep to o.s.; **~ dessinée** comic strip; **~ sonore** sound track

bandeau, x [bɑ̃do] *nm* headband; (*sur les yeux*) blindfold; (*MÉD*) head bandage

bander [bɑ̃de] *vt* (*blessure*) to bandage; (*muscle*) to tense; **~ les yeux à qn** to blindfold sb

banderole [bɑ̃drɔl] *nf* banner, streamer

bandit [bɑ̃di] *nm* bandit; **banditisme** *nm* violent crime, armed robberies *pl*

bandoulière [bɑ̃duljɛr] *nf*: **en ~** (slung *ou* worn) across the shoulder

banlieue [bɑ̃ljø] *nf* suburbs *pl*; **lignes/quartiers de ~** suburban lines/areas; **trains de ~** commuter trains

bannière [banjɛr] *nf* banner

bannir [banir] *vt* to banish

banque [bɑ̃k] *nf* bank; (*activités*) banking; **~ d'affaires** merchant bank; **banqueroute** [bɑ̃krut] *nf* bankruptcy

banquet [bɑ̃kɛ] *nm* dinner; (*d'apparat*) banquet

banquette [bɑ̃kɛt] *nf* seat

banquier [bɑ̃kje] *nm* banker

banquise [bɑ̃kiz] *nf* ice field

baptême [batɛm] *nm* christening; baptism; **~ de l'air** first flight

baquet [bakɛ] *nm* tub, bucket

bar [bar] *nm* bar

baraque [barak] *nf* shed; (*fam*) house; **~ foraine** fairground stand

baraqué, e [barake] *adj* well-built, hefty

baraquements [barakmɑ̃] *nmpl* (*pour réfugiés, ouvriers*) huts

baratin [baratɛ̃] (*fam*) *nm* smooth talk, patter; **baratiner** *vt* to chat up

barbare [barbar] *adj* barbaric

barbe [barb(ə)] *nf* beard; **quelle ~!** (*fam*) what a drag *ou* bore!; **à la ~ de qn** under sb's nose; **~ à papa** candy-floss

(*BRIT*), cotton candy (*US*)
barbelé [baʁbəle] *nm* barbed wire *no pl*
barboter [baʁbɔte] *vi* to paddle, dabble;
barboteuse [baʁbɔtøz] *nf* rompers *pl*
barbouiller [baʁbuje] *vt* to daub; **avoir
l'estomac barbouillé** to feel queasy
barbu, e [baʁby] *adj* bearded
barda [baʁda] (*fam*) *nm* kit, gear
barder [baʁde] (*fam*) *vi*: **ça va ~** sparks
will fly, things are going to get hot
barème [baʁɛm] *nm* scale; table
baril [baʁil] *nm* barrel; keg
bariolé, e [baʁjɔle] *adj* gaudily-
coloured
baromètre [baʁɔmɛtʁ(ə)] *nm* barometer
baron [baʁɔ̃] *nm* baron; **baronne** *nf*
baroness
baroque [baʁɔk] *adj* (*ART*) baroque; (*fig*)
weird
barque [baʁk(ə)] *nf* small boat
barquette [baʁkɛt] *nf* (*pour repas*) tray;
(*pour fruits*) punnet
barrage [baʁaʒ] *nm* dam; (*sur route*)
roadblock, barricade
barre [baʁ] *nf* bar; (*NAVIG*) helm; (*écrite*)
line, stroke
barreau, x [baʁo] *nm* bar; (*JUR*): **le ~**
the Bar
barrer [baʁe] *vt* (*route etc*) to block;
(*mot*) to cross out; (*chèque*) to cross
(*BRIT*); (*NAVIG*) to steer; **se ~** *vi* (*fam*) to
clear off
barrette [baʁɛt] *nf* (*pour cheveux*)
(hair) slide (*BRIT*) *ou* clip (*US*)
barricader [baʁikade] *vt* to barricade
barrière [baʁjɛʁ] *nf* fence; (*obstacle*)
barrier; (*porte*) gate
barrique [baʁik] *nf* barrel, cask
bas, basse [bɑ, bɑs] *adj* low ♦ *nm* bottom, lower part; (*vêtement*) stocking
♦ *adv* low; (*parler*) softly; **au ~ mot** at
the lowest estimate; **en ~** down below; at
(*ou* to) the bottom; (*dans une maison*)
downstairs; **en ~ de** at the bottom of;
mettre ~ to give birth; **à ~ ...!** down
with ...!; **~ morceaux** *nmpl* (*viande*)
cheap cuts
basané, e [bazane] *adj* tanned, bronzed
bas-côté [bakote] *nm* (*de route*) verge

(*BRIT*), shoulder (*US*)
bascule [baskyl] *nf*: (**jeu de**) **~** seesaw;
(**balance à**) **~** scales *pl*; **fauteuil à ~**
rocking chair
basculer [baskyle] *vi* to fall over, topple
(over); (*benne*) to tip up ♦ *vt* to topple
over; to tip out, tip up
base [bɑz] *nf* base; (*POL*) rank and file;
(*fondement, principe*) basis; **de ~** basic;
à ~ de café *etc* coffee *etc* -based; **~ de
données** database; **baser** *vt* to base; **se
baser sur** *vt* (*preuves*) to base one's argument on
bas-fond [bafɔ̃] *nm* (*NAVIG*) shallow; **~s**
nmpl (*fig*) dregs
basilic [bazilik] *nm* (*CULIN*) basil
basket [basket] *nm* trainer (*BRIT*), sneak-
er (*US*); (*aussi*: ~-*ball*) basketball
basque [bask(ə)] *adj*, *nm/f* Basque
basse [bɑs] *adj voir* **bas** ♦ *nf* (*MUS*) bass;
~-cour *nf* farmyard
bassin [basɛ̃] *nm* (*cuvette*) bowl; (*pièce
d'eau*) pond, pool; (*de fontaine, GÉO*) basin; (*ANAT*) pelvis; (*portuaire*) dock
bassine [basin] *nf* (*ustensile*) basin;
(*contenu*) bowl(ful)
basson [basɔ̃] *nm* bassoon
bas-ventre [bavɑ̃tʁ(ə)] *nm* (lower part
of the) stomach
bat *vb voir* **battre**
bât [bɑ] *nm* packsaddle
bataille [bɑtɑj] *nf* battle; fight
bâtard, e [bɑtaʁ, -aʁd(ə)] *nm/f* illegitimate child, bastard (*pej*)
bateau, x [bato] *nm* boat, ship;
bateau-mouche *nm* passenger pleasure
boat (*on the Seine*)
batelier, ière [batəlje, -jɛʁ] *nm/f* (*de
bac*) ferryman(woman)
bâti, e [bɑti] *adj*: **bien ~** well-built
batifoler [batifɔle] *vi* to frolic about
bâtiment [bɑtimɑ̃] *nm* building; (*NAVIG*)
ship, vessel; (*industrie*) building trade
bâtir [bɑtiʁ] *vt* to build
bâtisse [bɑtis] *nf* building
bâton [bɑtɔ̃] *nm* stick; **à ~s rompus** in-
formally
bats *vb voir* **battre**
battage [bataʒ] *nm* (*publicité*) (hard)

plugging

battant [batɑ̃] *nm* (*de cloche*) clapper; (*de volets*) shutter, flap; (*de porte*) side; (*fig: personne*) fighter; **porte à double ~** double door

battement [batmɑ̃] *nm* (*de cœur*) beat; (*intervalle*) interval (*between classes, trains*); **10 minutes de ~** 10 minutes to spare; **~ de paupières** blinking *no pl* (*of eyelids*)

batterie [batri] *nf* (*MIL, ÉLEC*) battery; (*MUS*) drums *pl*, drum kit; **~ de cuisine** pots and pans *pl*; kitchen utensils *pl*

batteur [batœr] *nm* (*MUS*) drummer; (*appareil*) whisk

battre [batR(ə)] *vt* to beat; (*suj: pluie, vagues*) to beat *ou* lash against; (*blé*) to thresh; (*passer au peigne fin*) to scour ♦ *vi* (*cœur*) to beat; (*volets etc*) to bang, rattle; **se ~** *vi* to fight; **~ la mesure** to beat time; **~ en brèche** to demolish; **~ son plein** to be at its height, be going full swing; **~ des mains** to clap one's hands

battue [baty] *nf* (*chasse*) beat; (*policière etc*) search, hunt

baume [bom] *nm* balm

baux [bo] *nmpl de* **bail**

bavard, e [bavar, -ard(ə)] *adj* (very) talkative; gossipy; **bavarder** *vi* to chatter; (*indiscrètement*) to gossip; to blab

bave [bav] *nf* dribble; (*de chien etc*) slobber; (*d'escargot*) slime; **baver** *vi* to dribble; to slobber; **en baver** (*fam*) to have a hard time (of it); **bavette** *nf* bib; **baveux, euse** *adj* (*omelette*) runny

bavure [bavyr] *nf* smudge; (*fig*) hitch; blunder

bayer [baje] *vi*: **~ aux corneilles** to stand gaping

bazar [bazar] *nm* general store; (*fam*) jumble; **bazarder** (*fam*) *vt* to chuck out

B.C.B.G. *sigle adj* (= *bon chic bon genre*) preppy, smart and trendy

B.C.G. *sigle m* (= *bacille Calmette-Guérin*) BCG

bd. *abr* = **boulevard**

B.D. *sigle f* = **bande dessinée**

béant, e [beɑ̃, -ɑ̃t] *adj* gaping

béat, e [bea, -at] *adj* showing open-eyed wonder; blissful; **béatitude** *nf* bliss

beau (bel), belle [bo, bɛl] (*mpl* ~**x**) *adj* beautiful, lovely; (*homme*) handsome ♦ *adv*: **il fait ~** the weather's fine; **un ~ jour** one (fine) day; **de plus belle** more than ever, even more; **on a ~ essayer** however hard we try; **bel et bien** well and truly; **faire le ~** (*chien*) to sit up and beg

beaucoup [boku] *adv* **1** a lot; **il boit ~** he drinks a lot; **il ne boit pas ~** he doesn't drink much *ou* a lot

2 (*suivi de plus, trop etc*) much, a lot, far; **il est ~ plus grand** he is much *ou* a lot *ou* far taller

3: **~ de** (*nombre*) many, a lot of; (*quantité*) a lot of; **~ d'étudiants/de touristes** a lot of *ou* many students/tourists; **~ de courage** a lot of courage; **il n'a pas ~ d'argent** he hasn't got much *ou* at lot of money

4: **de ~** by far

beau: ~-fils *nm* son-in-law; (*remariage*) stepson; **~-frère** *nm* brother-in-law; **~-père** *nm* father-in-law; (*remariage*) step-father

beauté [bote] *nf* beauty; **de toute ~** beautiful; **en ~** brilliantly

beaux-arts [bozar] *nmpl* fine arts

beaux-parents [boparɑ̃] *nmpl* wife's (*ou* husband's) family, in-laws

bébé [bebe] *nm* baby

bec [bɛk] *nm* beak, bill; (*de récipient*) spout; lip; (*fam*) mouth; **~ de gaz** (street) gaslamp; **~ verseur** pouring lip

bécane [bekan] (*fam*) *nf* bike

bec-de-lièvre [bɛkdəljɛvr(ə)] *nm* harelip

bêche [bɛʃ] *nf* spade; **bêcher** *vt* to dig

bécoter [bekɔte]: **se ~** *vi* to smooch

becqueter [bɛkte] (*fam*) *vt* to eat

bedaine [bədɛn] *nf* paunch

bedonnant, e [bədɔnɑ̃, -ɑ̃t] *adj* pot-bellied

bée [be] *adj*: **bouche** ~ gaping
beffroi [befʀwa] *nm* belfry
bégayer [begeje] *vt, vi* to stammer
bègue [bɛg] *nm/f*: **être** ~ to have a stammer
béguin [begɛ̃] *nm*: **avoir le** ~ **de** *ou* **pour** to have a crush on
beige [bɛʒ] *adj* beige
beignet [bɛɲe] *nm* fritter
bel [bɛl] *adj voir* **beau**
bêler [bele] *vi* to bleat
belette [bəlɛt] *nf* weasel
belge [bɛlʒ(ə)] *adj, nm/f* Belgian
Belgique [bɛlʒik] *nf*: **la** ~ Belgium
bélier [belje] *nm* ram; (*signe*): **le B~** Aries
belle [bɛl] *adj voir* **beau** ♦ *nf* (*SPORT*) decider; ~**-fille** *nf* daughter-in-law; (*remariage*) stepdaughter; ~**-mère** *nf* mother-in-law; stepmother; ~**-sœur** *nf* sister-in-law
belliqueux, euse [belikø, -øz] *adj* aggressive, warlike
belvédère [bɛlvedɛʀ] *nm* panoramic viewpoint (*or small building there*)
bémol [bemɔl] *nm* (*MUS*) flat
bénédiction [benediksjɔ̃] *nf* blessing
bénéfice [benefis] *nm* (*COMM*) profit; (*avantage*) benefit; **bénéficier de** *vt* to enjoy; to benefit by *ou* from; to get, be given; **bénéfique** *adj* beneficial
benêt [bənɛ] *nm* simpleton
bénévole [benevɔl] *adj* voluntary, unpaid
bénin, igne [benɛ̃, -iɲ] *adj* minor, mild; (*tumeur*) benign
bénir [beniʀ] *vt* to bless; **bénit, e** *adj* consecrated; **eau bénite** holy water
benjamin, e [bɛ̃ʒamɛ̃, -in] *nm/f* youngest child
benne [bɛn] *nf* skip; (*de téléphérique*) (cable) car; ~ **basculante** tipper (*BRIT*), dump truck (*US*)
B.E.P.C. *sigle m* = **brevet d'études du premier cycle**
béquille [bekij] *nf* crutch; (*de bicyclette*) stand
berceau, x [bɛʀso] *nm* cradle, crib
bercer [bɛʀse] *vt* to rock, cradle; (*suj:*

musique etc) to lull; ~ **qn de** (*promesses etc*) to delude sb with; **berceuse** *nf* lullaby
béret (basque) [beʀe(bask(ə))] *nm* beret
berge [bɛʀʒ(ə)] *nf* bank
berger, ère [bɛʀʒe, -ɛʀ] *nm/f* shepherd(ess)
berlingot [bɛʀlɛ̃go] *nm* (*emballage*) carton (*pyramid shaped*)
berlue [bɛʀly] *nf*: **j'ai la** ~ I must be seeing things
berner [bɛʀne] *vt* to fool
besogne [bəzɔɲ] *nf* work *no pl*, job
besoin [bəzwɛ̃] *nm* need; (*pauvreté*): **le** ~ need, want; **faire ses** ~**s** to relieve o.s.; **avoir** ~ **de qch/faire qch** to need sth/to do sth; **au** ~ if need be
bestiaux [bɛstjo] *nmpl* cattle
bestiole [bɛstjɔl] *nf* (tiny) creature
bétail [betaj] *nm* livestock, cattle *pl*
bête [bɛt] *nf* animal; (*bestiole*) insect, creature ♦ *adj* stupid, silly; **il cherche la petite** ~ he's being pernickety *ou* overfussy; ~ **noire** pet hate
bêtise [betiz] *nf* stupidity; stupid thing (to say *ou* do)
béton [betɔ̃] *nm* concrete; **(en)** ~ (*alibi, argument*) cast iron; ~ **armé** reinforced concrete; **bétonnière** *nf* cement mixer
betterave [bɛtʀav] *nf* beetroot (*BRIT*), beet (*US*); ~ **sucrière** sugar beet
beugler [bøgle] *vi* to low; (*radio etc*) to blare ♦ *vt* (*chanson*) to bawl out
Beur [bœʀ] *nm/f* person of North African origin living in France
beurre [bœʀ] *nm* butter; **beurrer** *vt* to butter; **beurrier** [bœʀje] *nm* butter dish
beuverie [bœvʀi] *nf* drinking session
bévue [bevy] *nf* blunder
Beyrouth [beʀut] *n* Beirut
bi... [bi] *préfixe* bi..., two-
biais [bjɛ] *nm* (*moyen*) device, expedient; (*aspect*) angle; **en** ~, **de** ~ (*obliquement*) at an angle; (*fig*) indirectly; **biaiser** *vi* (*fig*) to sidestep the issue
bibelot [biblo] *nm* trinket, curio
biberon [bibʀɔ̃] *nm* (feeding) bottle; **nourrir au** ~ to bottle-feed
bible [bibl(ə)] *nf* bible

biblio... *préfixe*: **~bus** *nm* mobile library van; **~phile** *nm/f* booklover; **~thécaire** *nm/f* librarian; **~thèque** *nf* library; *(meuble)* bookcase
bicarbonate [bikaʀbɔnat] *nm*: ~ **(de soude)** bicarbonate of soda
biceps [bisɛps] *nm* biceps
biche [biʃ] *nf* doe
bichonner [biʃɔne] *vt* to groom
bicolore [bikɔlɔʀ] *adj* two-coloured
bicoque [bikɔk] *(péj) nf* shack
bicyclette [bisiklɛt] *nf* bicycle
bide [bid] *nm (fam: ventre)* belly; *(THÉÂTRE)* flop
bidet [bide] *nm* bidet
bidon [bidɔ̃] *nm* can ♦ *adj inv (fam)* phoney
bidonville [bidɔ̃vil] *nm* shanty town
bidule [bidyl] *(fam) nm* thingumajig
bielle [bjɛl] *nf* connecting rod

MOT-CLÉ
---

bien [bjɛ̃] *nm* **1** *(avantage, profit)*: **faire du ~ à qn** to do sb good; **dire du ~ de** to speak well of; **c'est pour son ~** it's for his own good
2 *(possession, patrimoine)* possession, property; **son ~ le plus précieux** his most treasured possession; **avoir du ~** to have property; **~s (de consommation** *etc)* (consumer *etc)* goods
3 *(moral)*: **le ~** good; **distinguer le ~ du mal** to tell good from evil
♦ *adv* **1** *(de façon satisfaisante)* well; **elle travaille/mange ~** she works/eats well; **croyant ~ faire, je/il ...** thinking I/he was doing the right thing, I/he ...; **c'est ~ fait!** it serves him *(ou* her *etc)* right!
2 *(valeur intensive)* quite; ~ **jeune** quite young; ~ **assez** quite enough; ~ **mieux** (very) much better; **j'espère ~ y aller** I do hope to go; **je veux ~ le faire** *(concession)* I'm quite willing to do it; **il faut ~ le faire** it has to be done
3: ~ **du temps/des gens** quite a time/a number of people
♦ *adj inv* **1** *(en bonne forme, à l'aise)*: **je me sens ~** I feel fine; **je ne me sens**

pas ~ I don't feel well; **on est ~ dans ce fauteuil** this chair is very comfortable
2 *(joli, beau)* good-looking; **tu es ~ dans cette robe** you look good in that dress
3 *(satisfaisant)* good; **elle est ~, cette maison/secrétaire** it's a good house/she's a good secretary
4 *(moralement)* right; *(: personne)* good, nice; *(respectable)* respectable; **ce n'est pas ~ de ...** it's not right to ...; **elle est ~, cette femme** she's a nice woman, she's a good sort; **des gens ~s** respectable people
5 *(en bons termes)*: **être ~ avec qn** to be on good terms with sb
♦ *préfixe*: **~-aimé** *adj*, *nm/f* beloved; **~-être** *nm nm* well-being; **~faisance** *nf* charity; **~faisant, e** *adj (chose)* beneficial; **~fait** *nm* act of generosity, benefaction; *(de la science etc)* benefit; **~faiteur, trice** *nm/f* benefactor/benefactress; **~-fondé** *nm* soundness; **~fonds** *nm* property; **~heureux, euse** *adj* happy; *(REL)* blessed, blest; **~ que** *conj* (al)though; ~ **sûr** *adv* certainly

bienséant, e [bjɛ̃seã, -ãt] *adj* seemly
bientôt [bjɛ̃to] *adv* soon; **à ~** see you soon
bienveillant, e [bjɛ̃vɛjã, -ãt] *adj* kindly
bienvenu, e [bjɛ̃vny] *adj* welcome; **bienvenue** *nf*: **souhaiter la bienvenue à** to welcome; **bienvenue à** welcome to
bière [bjɛʀ] *nf (boisson)* beer; *(cercueil)* bier; ~ **(à la) pression** draught beer; ~ **blonde** lager; ~ **brune** brown ale
biffer [bife] *vt* to cross out
bifteck [biftɛk] *nm* steak
bifurquer [bifyʀke] *vi (route)* to fork; *(véhicule)* to turn off
bigarré, e [bigaʀe] *adj* multicoloured; *(disparate)* motley
bigorneau, x [bigɔʀno] *nm* winkle
bigot, e [bigo, -ɔt] *(péj) adj* bigoted
bigoudi [bigudi] *nm* curler
bijou, x [biʒu] *nm* jewel; **bijouterie** *nf* jeweller's (shop); jewellery; **bijoutier, ière** *nm/f* jeweller
bilan [bilã] *nm (COMM)* balance sheet(s);

end of year statement; (*fig*) (net) outcome; (: *de victimes*) toll; **faire le ~ de** to assess; to review; **déposer son ~** to file a bankruptcy statement

bile [bil] *nf* bile; **se faire de la ~** (*fam*) to worry o.s. sick

bilieux, euse [biljø, -jøz] *adj* bilious; (*fig*: *colérique*) testy

bilingue [bilɛ̃g] *adj* bilingual

billard [bijaʀ] *nm* billiards *sg*; billiard table; **c'est du ~** (*fam*) it's a cinch

bille [bij] *nf* (*gén*) ball; (*du jeu de billes*) marble; (*de bois*) log

billet [bijɛ] *nm* (*aussi:* **~ de banque**) (bank)note; (*de cinéma, de bus etc*) ticket; (*courte lettre*) note; **~ circulaire** round-trip ticket

billetterie [bijɛtʀi] *nf* ticket office; (*distributeur*) ticket machine; (*BANQUE*) cash dispenser

billion [biljɔ̃] *nm* billion (*BRIT*), trillion (*US*)

billot [bijo] *nm* block

bimensuel, le [bimɑ̃sɥɛl] *adj* bimonthly

binette [binɛt] *nf* hoe

binocle [binɔkl(ə)] *nm* pince-nez

bio... *préfixe* bio...; **~diversité** *nf* biodiversity; **~éthique** *nf* bioethics *sg*; **~graphie** *nf* biography; **~logie** *nf* biology; **~logique** *adj* biological **~masse** *nf* biomass; **~tope** *nm* biotope

Birmanie [biʀmani] *nf* Burma

bis¹, e [bi, biz] *adj* (*couleur*) greyish brown

bis² [bis] *adv*: **12 bis** 12a *ou* A ♦ *excl*, *nm* encore

bisannuel, le [bizanɥɛl] *adj* biennial

biscornu, e [biskɔʀny] *adj* twisted

biscotte [biskɔt] *nf* (breakfast) rusk

biscuit [biskɥi] *nm* biscuit; sponge cake

bise [biz] *nf* (*baiser*) kiss; (*vent*) North wind

bissextile [bisɛkstil] *adj*: **année ~** leap year

bistouri [bisturi] *nm* lancet

bistro(t) [bistʀo] *nm* bistro, café

bitume [bitym] *nm* asphalt

bizarre [bizaʀ] *adj* strange, odd

blafard, e [blafaʀ, -aʀd(ə)] *adj* wan

blague [blag] *nf* (*propos*) joke; (*farce*) trick; **sans ~!** no kidding!; **~ à tabac** tobacco pouch

blaguer [blage] *vi* to joke ♦ *vt* to tease

blaireau, x [blɛʀo] *nm* (*ZOOL*) badger; (*brosse*) shaving brush

blairer [blɛʀe] (*fam*) *vt*: **je ne peux pas le ~** I can't bear *ou* stand him

blâme [blɑm] *nm* blame; (*sanction*) reprimand

blâmer [blɑme] *vt* to blame

blanc, blanche [blɑ̃, blɑ̃ʃ] *adj* white; (*non imprimé*) blank; (*innocent*) pure ♦ *nm/f* white, white man(woman) ♦ *nm* (*couleur*) white; (*espace non écrit*) blank; (*aussi:* **~ d'œuf**) (egg-)white; (: **~ de poulet**) breast, white meat; (: *vin* **~**) white wine; **~ cassé** off-white; **chèque en ~** blank cheque; **à ~** (*chauffer*) white-hot; (*tirer, charger*) with blanks; **~-bec** *nm* greenhorn; **blanche** *nf* (*MUS*) minim (*BRIT*), half-note (*US*); **blancheur** *nf* whiteness

blanchir [blɑ̃ʃiʀ] *vt* (*gén*) to whiten; (*linge*) to launder; (*CULIN*) to blanch; (*fig*: *disculper*) to clear ♦ *vi* to grow white; (*cheveux*) to go white

blanchisserie *nf* laundry

blason [blazɔ̃] *nm* coat of arms

blazer [blazɛʀ] *nm* blazer

blé [ble] *nm* wheat; **~ noir** (*nm*) buckwheat

bled [blɛd] (*péj*) *nm* hole

blême [blɛm] *adj* pale

blessé, e [blese] *adj* injured ♦ *nm/f* injured person; casualty

blesser [blese] *vt* to injure; (*délibérément*: *MIL etc*) to wound; (*suj: souliers etc, offenser*) to hurt; **se ~** to injure o.s.; **se ~ au pied** *etc* to injure one's foot *etc*

blessure [blesyʀ] *nf* injury; wound

bleu, e [blø] *adj* blue; (*bifteck*) very rare ♦ *nm* (*couleur*) blue; (*novice*) greenhorn; (*contusion*) bruise; (*vêtement: aussi:* **~s**) overalls *pl*; **~ marine** navy blue

bleuet [bløɛ] *nm* cornflower

bleuté, e [bløte] *adj* blue-shaded

blinder [blɛ̃de] *vt* to armour; (*fig*) to

harden

bloc [blɔk] *nm* (*de pierre etc*) block; (*de papier à lettres*) pad; (*ensemble*) group, block; **serré à ~** tightened right down; **en ~** as a whole; wholesale; **~ opératoire** operating *ou* theatre block; **~ sanitaire** toilet block; **blocage** [blɔkaʒ] *nm* blocking; jamming; freezing; (*PSYCH*) hang-up

bloc-notes [blɔknɔt] *nm* note pad

blocus [blɔkys] *nm* blockade

blond, e [blɔ̃, -ɔ̃d] *adj* fair; blond; (*sable, blés*) golden; **~ cendré** ash blond

bloquer [blɔke] *vt* (*passage*) to block; (*pièce mobile*) to jam; (*crédits, compte*) to freeze

blottir [blɔtiʀ]: **se ~** *vi* to huddle up

blouse [bluz] *nf* overall

blouson [bluzɔ̃] *nm* blouson jacket; **~ noir** (*fig*) ≈ rocker

bluff [blœf] *nm* bluff

bluffer [blœfe] *vi* to bluff

bobard [bɔbaʀ] (*fam*) *nm* tall story

bobine [bɔbin] *nf* reel; (*ÉLEC*) coil

bocal, aux [bɔkal, -o] *nm* jar

bock [bɔk] *nm* glass of beer

bœuf [bœf, *pl* bø] *nm* ox, steer; (*CULIN*) beef

bof! [bɔf] (*fam*) *excl* don't care!; (*pas terrible*) nothing special

bohème [bɔɛm] *adj* happy-go-lucky, unconventional; **bohémien, ne** [bɔemjɛ̃, -jɛn] *nm/f* gipsy

boire [bwaʀ] *vt* to drink; (*s'imprégner de*) to soak up; **~ un coup** to have a drink

bois [bwa] *nm* wood; **de ~, en ~** wooden

boisé, e [bwaze] *adj* woody, wooded

boisson [bwasɔ̃] *nf* drink; **pris de ~** drunk, intoxicated

boîte [bwat] *nf* box; (*entreprise*) place, firm; **aliments en ~** canned *ou* tinned (*BRIT*) foods; **~ à gants** glove compartment; **~ aux lettres** letter box; **~ d'allumettes** box of matches; (*vide*) matchbox; **~ (de conserves)** can *ou* tin (*BRIT*) (of food); **~ de nuit** night club; **~ de vitesses** gear box; **~ postale** PO Box

boiter [bwate] *vi* to limp; (*fig*) to wobble;

to be shaky

boîtier [bwatje] *nm* case

bol [bɔl] *nm* bowl; **un ~ d'air** a breath of fresh air; **j'en ai ras le ~** (*fam*) I'm fed up with this

bolide [bɔlid] *nm* racing car; **comme un ~** at top speed, like a rocket

bombance [bɔ̃bɑ̃s] *nf*: **faire ~** to have a feast, revel

bombarder [bɔ̃baʀde] *vt* to bomb; **~ qn de** (*cailloux, lettres*) to bombard sb with; **bombardier** *nm* bomber

bombe [bɔ̃b] *nf* bomb; (*atomiseur*) (aerosol) spray

bomber [bɔ̃be] *vi* to bulge; to camber
♦ *vt*: **~ le torse** to swell out one's chest

MOT-CLÉ

bon, bonne [bɔ̃, bɔn] *adj* **1** (*agréable, satisfaisant*) good; **un ~ repas/restaurant** a good meal/restaurant; **être ~ en maths** to be good at maths

2 (*charitable*): **être ~ (envers)** to be good (to)

3 (*correct*) right; **le ~ numéro/moment** the right number/moment

4 (*souhaits*): **~ anniversaire** happy birthday; **~ voyage** have a good trip; **bonne chance** good luck; **bonne année** happy New Year; **bonne nuit** good night

5 (*approprié*): **~ à/pour** fit to/for

6: **~ enfant** *adj inv* accommodating, easy-going; **bonne femme** (*péj*) woman; **de bonne heure** early; **~ marché** *adj inv* cheap ♦ *adv* cheap; **~ mot** witticism; **~ sens** common sense; **~ vivant** jovial chap; **bonnes œuvres** charitable works, charities

♦ *nm* **1** (*billet*) voucher; (*aussi*: **~ cadeau**) gift voucher; **~ d'essence** petrol coupon; **~ du Trésor** Treasury bond

2: **avoir du ~** to have its good points; **pour de ~** for good

♦ *adv*: **il fait ~** it's *ou* the weather is fine; **sentir ~** to smell good; **tenir ~** to stand firm

♦ *excl* good!; **ah ~?** really?; *voir aussi* **bonne**

bonbon [bɔ̃bɔ̃] *nm* (boiled) sweet

bonbonne [bɔ̃bɔn] *nf* demijohn

bond [bɔ̃] *nm* leap; **faire un ~** to leap in the air

bonde [bɔ̃d] *nf* bunghole

bondé, e [bɔ̃de] *adj* packed (full)

bondir [bɔ̃diʀ] *vi* to leap

bonheur [bɔnœʀ] *nm* happiness; **porter ~ (à qn)** to bring (sb) luck; **au petit ~** haphazardly; **par ~** fortunately

bonhomie [bɔnɔmi] *nf* goodnatured-ness

bonhomme [bɔnɔm] (*pl* **bonshommes**) *nm* fellow; **~ de neige** snowman

bonification [bɔnifikasjɔ̃] *nf* bonus

bonifier [bɔnifje] *vt* to improve

boniment [bɔnimã] *nm* patter *no pl*

bonjour [bɔ̃ʒuʀ] *excl, nm* hello; good morning

bonne [bɔn] *adj voir* **bon ♦** *nf* (*domestique*) maid; **~ à tout faire** general help; **~ d'enfant** nanny; **~ment** *adv*: **tout ~ment** quite simply

bonnet [bɔnɛ] *nm* bonnet, hat; (*de soutien-gorge*) cup; **~ d'âne** dunce's cap; **~ de bain** bathing cap

bonneterie [bɔnɛtʀi] *nf* hosiery

bonshommes [bɔ̃zɔm] *nmpl de* **bonhomme**

bonsoir [bɔ̃swaʀ] *excl* good evening

bonté [bɔ̃te] *nf* kindness *no pl*

bonus [bɔnys] *nm* no-claims bonus

bord [bɔʀ] *nm* (*de table, verre, falaise*) edge; (*de rivière, lac*) bank; (*de route*) side; (**monter**) **à ~** (to go) on board; **jeter par-dessus ~** to throw overboard; **le commandant/les hommes du ~** the ship's master/crew; **au ~ de la mer** at the seaside; **être au ~ des larmes** to be on the verge of tears

bordeaux [bɔʀdo] *nm* Bordeaux (wine) **♦** *adj inv* maroon

bordel [bɔʀdɛl] *nm* brothel; (*fam!*) bloody mess (*!*)

bordelais, e [bɔʀdəlɛ, ɛz] *adj* of *ou* from Bordeaux

border [bɔʀde] *vt* (*être le long de*) to border; to line; (*garnir*): **~ qch de** to line sth with; to trim sth with; (*qn dans son lit*) to tuck up

bordereau, x [bɔʀdəʀo] *nm* slip; statement

bordure [bɔʀdyʀ] *nf* border; **en ~ de** on the edge of

borgne [bɔʀɲ(ə)] *adj* one-eyed

borne [bɔʀn(ə)] *nf* boundary stone; (*aussi*: **~ kilométrique**) kilometre-marker, ≈ milestone; **~s** *nfpl* (*fig*) limits; **dépasser les ~s** to go too far

borné, e [bɔʀne] *adj* narrow; narrow-minded

borner [bɔʀne] *vt* to limit; to confine; **se ~ à faire** to content o.s. with doing; to limit o.s. to doing

Bosnie-Herzégovine [bɔzni-ɛʀtzegɔvin] *nf* Bosnia (and) Herzegovina

bosquet [bɔskɛ] *nm* grove

bosse [bɔs] *nf* (*de terrain etc*) bump; (*enflure*) lump; (*du bossu, du chameau*) hump; **avoir la ~ des maths** *etc* to have a gift for maths *etc*; **il a roulé sa ~** he's been around

bosser [bɔse] (*fam*) *vi* to work; to slave (away)

bossu, e [bɔsy] *nm/f* hunchback

bot [bo] *adj m*: **pied ~** club foot

botanique [bɔtanik] *nf* botany **♦** *adj* botanic(al)

botte [bɔt] *nf* (*soulier*) (high) boot; (*gerbe*): **~ de paille** bundle of straw; **~ de radis** bunch of radishes; **~s de caoutchouc** wellington boots; **botter** [bɔte] *vt* to put boots on; to kick; (*fam*): **ça me botte** I fancy that

bottin [bɔtɛ̃] *nm* directory

bottine [bɔtin] *nf* ankle boot

bouc [buk] *nm* goat; (*barbe*) goatee; **~ émissaire** scapegoat

boucan [bukã] *nm* din, racket

bouche [buʃ] *nf* mouth; **le ~ à ~** the kiss of life; **~ d'égout** manhole; **~ d'incendie** fire hydrant; **~ de métro** métro entrance

bouché, e [buʃe] *adj* (*temps, ciel*) overcast; (*péj: personne*) thick

bouchée [buʃe] *nf* mouthful; **~s à la reine** chicken vol-au-vents

boucher, ère [buʃe, -ɛʀ] *nm/f* butcher

boiling; (*très chaud*) boiling (hot)

bouillie [buji] *nf* gruel; (*de bébé*) cereal; **en ~** (*fig*) crushed

bouillir [bujiʀ] *vi, vt* to boil

bouilloire [bujwaʀ] *nf* kettle

bouillon [bujɔ̃] *nm* (CULIN) stock *no pl*; **bouillonner** [bujɔne] *vi* to bubble; (*fig*) to bubble up; to foam

bouillotte [bujɔt] *nf* hot-water bottle

boulanger, ère [bulɑ̃ʒe, -ɛʀ] *nm/f* baker

boulangerie [bulɑ̃ʒʀi] *nf* bakery

boule [bul] *nf* (*gén*) ball; (*pour jouer*) bowl; (*de machine à écrire*) golf-ball; **se mettre en ~** (*fig: fam*) to fly off the handle, to blow one's top; **~ de neige** snowball

bouleau, x [bulo] *nm* (silver) birch

boulet [bulɛ] *nm* (*aussi*: **~ de canon**) cannonball

boulette [bulɛt] *nf* ball

boulevard [bulvaʀ] *nm* boulevard

bouleversement [bulvɛʀsəmɑ̃] *nm* upheaval

bouleverser [bulvɛʀse] *vt* (*émouvoir*) to overwhelm; (*causer du chagrin*) to distress; (*pays, vie*) to disrupt; (*papiers, objets*) to turn upside down

boulier [bulje] *nm* abacus

boulon [bulɔ̃] *nm* bolt

boulot, te [bulo, -ɔt] *adj* plump, tubby ♦ *nm* (*fam: travail*) work

boum [bum] *nm* bang ♦ *nf* (*fam*) party

bouquet [bukɛ] *nm* (*de fleurs*) bunch (of flowers), bouquet; (*de persil etc*) bunch; (*parfum*) bouquet

bouquin [bukɛ̃] (*fam*) *nm* book; **bouquiner** (*fam*) *vi* to read; to browse around (in a bookshop); **bouquiniste** *nm/f* bookseller

bourbeux, euse [buʀbø, -øz] *adj* muddy

bourbier [buʀbje] *nm* (quag)mire

bourde [buʀd(ə)] *nf* (*erreur*) howler; (*gaffe*) blunder

bourdon [buʀdɔ̃] *nm* bumblebee

bourdonner [buʀdɔne] *vi* to buzz

bourg [buʀ] *nm* small market town

bourgeois, e [buʀʒwa, -waz] *adj* (*péj*) ≈

♦ *vt* (*pour colmater*) to stop up; to fill up; (*obstruer*) to block (up); **se ~** *vi* (*tuyau etc*) to block up, get blocked up; **se ~ le nez** to hold one's nose; **boucherie** [buʃʀi] *nf* butcher's (shop); (*fig*) slaughter

bouche-trou [buʃtʀu] *nm* (*fig*) stop-gap

bouchon [buʃɔ̃] *nm* stopper; (*en liège*) cork; (*fig: embouteillage*) holdup; (PÊCHE) float; **~ doseur** measuring cap

boucle [bukl(ə)] *nf* (*forme, figure*) loop; (*objet*) buckle; **~ (de cheveux)** curl; **~ d'oreilles** earring

bouclé, e [bukle] *adj* curly

boucler [bukle] *vt* (*fermer: ceinture etc*) to fasten; (: *magasin*) to shut; (*terminer*) to finish off; (: *budget*) to balance; (*enfermer*) to shut away; (: *quartier*) to seal off ♦ *vi* to curl

bouclier [buklije] *nm* shield

bouddhiste [budist(ə)] *nm/f* Buddhist

bouder [bude] *vi* to sulk ♦ *vt* to turn one's nose up at; to refuse to have anything to do with

boudin [budɛ̃] *nm* (CULIN) black pudding

boue [bu] *nf* mud

bouée [bwe] *nf* buoy; **~ (de sauvetage)** lifebuoy

boueux, euse [bwø, -øz] *adj* muddy ♦ *nm* refuse collector

bouffe [buf] (*fam*) *nf* grub (*fam*), food

bouffée [bufe] *nf* puff; **~ de fièvre/de honte** flush of fever/shame

bouffer [bufe] (*fam*) *vi* to eat

bouffi, e [bufi] *adj* swollen

bouge [buʒ] *nm* (low) dive; hovel

bougeoir [buʒwaʀ] *nm* candlestick

bougeotte [buʒɔt] *nf*: **avoir la ~** to have the fidgets

bouger [buʒe] *vi* to move; (*dent etc*) to be loose; (*changer*) to alter; (*agir*) to stir ♦ *vt* to move

bougie [buʒi] *nf* candle; (AUTO) spark(ing) plug

bougon, ne [bugɑ̃, -ɔn] *adj* grumpy

bougonner [bugɔne] *vi, vt* to grumble

bouillabaisse [bujabɛs] *nf* type of fish soup

bouillant, e [bujɑ̃, -ɑ̃t] *adj* (*qui bout*)

(upper) middle class; bourgeois; **bour-geoisie** [buRʒwazi] *nf* ≈ upper middle classes *pl*; bourgeoisie
bourgeon [buRʒ3] *nm* bud
Bourgogne [buRɡɔɲ] *nf*: **la ~** Burgundy ♦ *nm*: **b~** burgundy (wine)
bourguignon, ne [buRɡiɲ3, -ɔn] *adj* of *ou* from Burgundy, Burgundian
bourlinguer [buRlɛ̃ɡe] *vi* to knock about a lot, get around a lot
bourrade [buRad] *nf* shove, thump
bourrage [buRaʒ] *nm*: **~ de crâne** brain-washing; (*SCOL*) cramming
bourrasque [buRask(ə)] *nf* squall
bourratif, ive [buRatif] (*fam*) *adj* filling, stodgy (*pej*)
bourré, e [buRe] *adj* (*rempli*): **~ de** crammed full of; (*fam: ivre*) plastered, tanked up (*BRIT*)
bourreau, x [buRo] *nm* executioner; (*fig*) torturer; **~ de travail** workaholic
bourrelet [buRlɛ] *nm* draught excluder; (*de peau*) roll *ou* roll (of flesh)
bourrer [buRe] *vt* (*pipe*) to fill; (*poêle*) to pack; (*valise*) to cram (full)
bourrique [buRik] *nf* (*âne*) ass
bourru, e [buRy] *adj* surly, gruff
bourse [buRs(ə)] *nf* (*subvention*) grant; (*porte-monnaie*) purse; **la B~** the Stock Exchange
boursoufler [buRsufle] *vt* to puff up, bloat
bous *vb voir* **bouillir**
bousculade [buskylad] *nf* rush; crush; **bousculer** [buskyle] *vt* to knock over; to knock into; (*fig*) to push, rush
bouse [buz] *nf* dung *no pl*
boussole [busɔl] *nf* compass
bout [bu] *vb voir* **bouillir** ♦ *nm* bit; (*d'un bâton etc*) tip; (*d'une ficelle, table, rue, période*) end; **au ~ de** at the end of, after; **pousser qn à ~** to push sb to the limit; **venir à ~ de** to manage to finish; **à ~ portant** at point-blank range; **~ filtre** filter tip
boutade [butad] *nf* quip, sally
boute-en-train [butɑ̃tRɛ̃] *nm inv* (*fig*) live wire
bouteille [butɛj] *nf* bottle; (*de gaz bu-tane*) cylinder
boutique [butik] *nf* shop
bouton [but3] *nm* button; (*BOT*) bud; (*sur la peau*) spot; (*de porte*) knob; **~ de manchette** cuff-link; **~ d'or** buttercup; **boutonner** *vt* to button up; **boutonnière** *nf* buttonhole; **bouton-pression** *nm* press stud
bouture [butyR] *nf* cutting
bovins [bɔvɛ̃] *nmpl* cattle *pl*
bowling [bɔliŋ] *nm* (tenpin) bowling; (*salle*) bowling alley
box [bɔks] *nm* lock-up (garage); (*d'écurie*) loose-box
boxe [bɔks(ə)] *nf* boxing
boyau, x [bwajo] *nm* (*galerie*) passage(way); (narrow) gallery; **~x** *nmpl* (*viscères*) entrails, guts
B.P. *abr* = **boîte postale**
bracelet [bRaslɛ] *nm* bracelet; **bracelet-montre** *nm* wristwatch
braconnier [bRakɔnje] *nm* poacher
brader [bRade] *vt* to sell off; **braderie** [bRadRi] *nf* cut-price shop *ou* stall
braguette [bRaɡɛt] *nf* fly *ou* flies *pl* (*BRIT*), zipper (*US*)
brailler [bRaje] *vi* to bawl, yell
braire [bRɛR] *vi* to bray
braise [bRɛz] *nf* embers *pl*
brancard [bRɑ̃kaR] *nm* (*civière*) stretcher; **brancardier** *nm* stretcher-bearer
branchages [bRɑ̃ʃaʒ] *nmpl* boughs
branche [bRɑ̃ʃ] *nf* branch
branché, e [bRɑ̃ʃe] (*fam*) *adj* trendy
brancher [bRɑ̃ʃe] *vt* to connect (up); (*en mettant la prise*) to plug in
branle [bRɑl] *nm*: **donner le ~ à, mettre en ~** to set in motion
branle-bas [bRɑlba] *nm inv* commotion
braquer [bRake] *vi* (*AUTO*) to turn (the wheel) ♦ *vt* (*revolver etc*): **~ qch sur** to aim sth at, point sth at; (*mettre en colère*): **~ qn** to put sb's back up
bras [bRa] *nm* arm ♦ *nmpl* (*fig: travailleurs*) labour *sg*, hands; **à ~ raccourcis** with fists flying; **~ droit** (*fig*) right hand man
brasier [bRazje] *nm* blaze, inferno

bras-le-corps [bʀalkɔʀ]: **à ~** *adv* (a)round the waist

brassard [bʀasaʀ] *nm* armband

brasse [bʀas] *nf* (*nage*) breast-stroke; **~ papillon** butterfly

brassée [bʀase] *nf* armful

brasser [bʀase] *vt* to mix; **~ l'argent/les affaires** to handle a lot of money/ business

brasserie [bʀasʀi] *nf* (*restaurant*) café-restaurant; (*usine*) brewery

brave [bʀav] *adj* (*courageux*) brave; (*bon, gentil*) good, kind

braver [bʀave] *vt* to defy

bravo [bʀavo] *excl* bravo ♦ *nm* cheer

bravoure [bʀavuʀ] *nf* bravery

break [bʀɛk] *nm* (*AUTO*) estate car

brebis [bʀəbi] *nf* ewe; **~ galeuse** black sheep

brèche [bʀɛʃ] *nf* breach, gap; **être sur la ~** (*fig*) to be on the go

bredouille [bʀəduj] *adj* empty-handed

bredouiller [bʀəduje] *vi, vt* to mumble, stammer

bref, brève [bʀɛf, bʀɛv] *adj* short, brief ♦ *adv* in short; **d'un ton ~** sharply, curtly; **en ~** in short, in brief

Brésil [bʀezil] *nm* Brazil

Bretagne [bʀətaɲ] *nf* Brittany

bretelle [bʀətɛl] *nf* (*de fusil etc*) sling; (*de vêtement*) strap; (*d'autoroute*) slip road (*BRIT*), entrance/exit ramp (*US*); **~s** *nfpl* (*pour pantalon*) braces (*BRIT*), suspenders (*US*)

breton, ne [bʀətɔ̃, -ɔn] *adj, nm/f* Breton

breuvage [bʀœvaʒ] *nm* beverage, drink

brève [bʀɛv] *adj voir* **bref**

brevet [bʀəvɛ] *nm* diploma, certificate; **~ d'études du premier cycle** *school certificate (taken at age 16)*; **~ (d'invention)** patent; **breveté, e** *adj* patented; (*diplômé*) qualified

bribes [bʀib] *nfpl* bits, scraps; snatches; **par ~** piecemeal

bricolage [bʀikɔlaʒ] *nm*: **le ~** do-it-yourself

bricole [bʀikɔl] *nf* trifle; small job

bricoler [bʀikɔle] *vi* to do DIY jobs; to

potter about ♦ *vt* to fix up; to tinker with; **bricoleur, euse** *nm/f* handyman(woman), DIY enthusiast

bride [bʀid] *nf* bridle; (*d'un bonnet*) string, tie; **à ~ abattue** flat out, hell for leather; **laisser la ~ sur le cou à** to give free rein to

bridé, e [bʀide] *adj*: **yeux ~s** slit eyes

bridge [bʀidʒ(ə)] *nm* bridge

brièvement [bʀijɛvmɑ̃] *adv* briefly

brigade [bʀigad] *nf* (*POLICE*) squad; (*MIL*) brigade; (*gén*) team

brigadier [bʀigadje] *nm* sergeant

brigandage [bʀigɑ̃daʒ] *nm* robbery

briguer [bʀige] *vt* to aspire to

brillamment [bʀijamɑ̃] *adv* brilliantly

brillant, e [bʀijɑ̃, -ɑ̃t] *adj* brilliant; bright; (*luisant*) shiny, shining ♦ *nm* (*diamant*) brilliant

briller [bʀije] *vi* to shine

brimer [bʀime] *vt* to harass; to bully

brin [bʀɛ̃] *nm* (*de laine, ficelle etc*) strand; (*fig*): **un ~ de** a bit of; **~ d'herbe** blade of grass; **~ de muguet** sprig of lily of the valley

brindille [bʀɛ̃dij] *nf* twig

brio [bʀijo] *nm*: **avec ~** with panache

brioche [bʀijɔʃ] *nf* brioche (bun); (*fam: ventre*) paunch

brique [bʀik] *nf* brick ♦ *adj inv* brick red

briquer [bʀike] *vt* to polish up

briquet [bʀikɛ] *nm* (cigarette) lighter

brise [bʀiz] *nf* breeze

briser [bʀize] *vt* to break; **se ~** *vi* to break

britannique [bʀitanik] *adj* British ♦ *nm/f*: **B~** British person, Briton; **les B~s** the British

brocante [bʀɔkɑ̃t] *nf* junk, second-hand goods *pl*

brocanteur, euse [bʀɔkɑ̃tœʀ, -øz] *nm/f* junkshop owner; junk dealer

broche [bʀɔʃ] *nf* brooch; (*CULIN*) spit; (*MÉD*) pin; **à la ~** spit-roasted

broché, e [bʀɔʃe] *adj* (*livre*) paperbacked

brochet [bʀɔʃɛ] *nm* pike *inv*

brochette [bʀɔʃɛt] *nf* skewer

brochure [bʀɔʃyʀ] *nf* pamphlet, brochure, booklet

broder [bʀɔde] *vt* to embroider ♦ *vi* to embroider the facts; **broderie** *nf* embroidery

broncher [bʀɔ̃ʃe] *vi*: **sans ~** without flinching; without turning a hair

bronches [bʀɔ̃ʃ] *nfpl* bronchial tubes; **bronchite** *nf* bronchitis

bronze [bʀɔ̃z] *nm* bronze

bronzer [bʀɔ̃ze] *vt* to tan ♦ *vi* to get a tan; **se ~** to sunbathe

brosse [bʀɔs] *nf* brush; **coiffé en ~** with a crewcut; **~ à cheveux** hairbrush; **~ à dents** toothbrush; **~ à habits** clothesbrush; **brosser** *vt* (*nettoyer*) to brush; (*fig: tableau etc*) to paint; to draw; **se brosser les dents** to brush one's teeth

brouette [bʀuɛt] *nf* wheelbarrow

brouhaha [bʀuaa] *nm* hubbub

brouillard [bʀujaʀ] *nm* fog

brouille [bʀuj] *nf* quarrel

brouiller [bʀuje] *vt* to mix up; to confuse; (*rendre trouble*) to cloud; (*désunir: amis*) to set at odds; **se ~** *vi* (*vue*) to cloud over; (*détails*) to become confused; (*gens*) to fall out

brouillon, ne [bʀujɔ̃, -ɔn] *adj* disorganized; unmethodical ♦ *nm* draft

broussailles [bʀusaj] *nfpl* undergrowth *sg*; **broussailleux, euse** *adj* bushy

brousse [bʀus] *nf*: **la ~** the bush

brouter [bʀute] *vi* to graze

broutille [bʀutij] *nf* trifle

broyer [bʀwaje] *vt* to crush; **~ du noir** to be down in the dumps

bru [bʀy] *nf* daughter-in-law

brugnon [bʀyɲɔ̃] *nm* (*BOT*) nectarine

bruiner [bʀɥine] *vb impers*: **il bruine** it's drizzling, there's a drizzle

bruire [bʀɥiʀ] *vi* to murmur; to rustle

bruit [bʀɥi] *nm*: **un ~** a noise, a sound; (*fig: rumeur*) a rumour; **le ~** noise; **sans ~** without a sound, noiselessly; **~ de fond** background noise

bruitage [bʀɥitaʒ] *nm* sound effects *pl*

brûlant, e [bʀylɑ̃, -ɑ̃t] *adj* burning; (*liquide*) boiling (hot); (*regard*) fiery

brûlé, e [bʀyle] *adj* (*fig: démasqué*)

blown ♦ *nm*: **odeur de ~** smell of burning

brûle-pourpoint [bʀylpuʀpwɛ̃]: **à ~** *adv* point-blank

brûler [bʀyle] *vt* to burn; (*suj: eau bouillante*) to scald; (*consommer: électricité, essence*) to use; (*feu rouge, signal*) to go through ♦ *vi* to burn; (*jeu*) to be warm; **se ~** to burn o.s.; to scald o.s.; **se ~ la cervelle** to blow one's brains out

brûlure [bʀylyʀ] *nf* (*lésion*) burn; (*sensation*) burning (sensation); **~s d'estomac** heartburn *sg*

brume [bʀym] *nf* mist; **brumisateur** *nm* atomizer

brun, e [bʀœ̃, -yn] *adj* brown; (*cheveux, personne*) dark; **brunir** *vi* to get a tan

brunch [bʀœntʃ] *nm* brunch

brusque [bʀysk(ə)] *adj* abrupt; **brusquer** *vt* to rush

brut, e [bʀyt] *adj* raw, crude, rough; (*COMM*) gross; (*données*) raw; **(pétrole) ~** crude (oil)

brutal, e, aux [bʀytal, -o] *adj* brutal; **brutaliser** *vt* to handle roughly, manhandle

Bruxelles [bʀysɛl] *n* Brussels

bruyamment [bʀɥijamɑ̃] *adv* noisily

bruyant, e [bʀɥijɑ̃, -ɑ̃t] *adj* noisy

bruyère [bʀɥijɛʀ] *nf* heather ⟩

bu, e *pp de* **boire**

buccal, e, aux [bykal, -o] *adj*: **par voie ~e** orally

bûche [byʃ] *nf* log; **prendre une ~** (*fig*) to come a cropper; **~ de Noël** Yule log; **bûcher** [byʃe] *nm* pyre; bonfire ♦ *vi* (*fam*) to swot (*BRIT*), slave (away) ♦ *vt* to swot up (*BRIT*), slave away at; **bûcheron** [byʃʀɔ̃] *nm* woodcutter

budget [bydʒɛ] *nm* budget

buée [bɥe] *nf* (*sur une vitre*) mist; (*de l'haleine*) steam

buffet [byfe] *nm* (*meuble*) sideboard; (*de réception*) buffet; **~ (de gare)** (station) buffet, snack bar

buffle [byfl(ə)] *nm* buffalo

buis [bɥi] *nm* box tree; (*bois*) box(wood)

buisson [bɥisɔ̃] *nm* bush

buissonnière [bɥisɔnjɛʀ] *adj*: **faire**

l'école ~ to skip school
bulbe [bylb(ə)] *nm* (*BOT, ANAT*) bulb; (*coupole*) onion-shaped dome
Bulgarie [bylgaʀi] *nf* Bulgaria
bulle [byl] *nf* bubble
bulletin [byltɛ̃] *nm* (*communiqué, journal*) bulletin; (*papier*) form; (*SCOL*) report; ~ **d'informations** news bulletin; ~ **de salaire** pay-slip; ~ **(de vote)** ballot paper; ~ **météorologique** weather report
bureau, x [byʀo] *nm* (*meuble*) desk; (*pièce, service*) office; ~ **de change** (foreign) exchange office *ou* bureau; ~ **de location** box office; ~ **de poste** post office; ~ **de tabac** tobacconist's (shop); ~ **de vote** polling station; **bureaucratie** *nf* bureaucracy
bureautique [byʀotik] *nf* office automation
burin [byʀɛ̃] *nm* cold chisel; (*ART*) burin
burlesque [byʀlɛsk(ə)] *adj* ridiculous; (*LITTÉRATURE*) burlesque
bus¹ [by] *vb voir* **boire**
bus² [bys] *nm* bus
busqué, e [byske] *adj* (*nez*) hook(ed)
buste [byst(ə)] *nm* (*ANAT*) chest; bust
but [by] *vb voir* **boire** ♦ *nm* (*cible*) target; (*fig*) goal; aim; (*FOOTBALL etc*) goal; **de ~ en blanc** point-blank; **avoir pour ~ de faire** to aim to do; **dans le ~ de** with the intention of
butane [bytan] *nm* butane; Calor gas ®
buté, e [byte] *adj* stubborn, obstinate
buter [byte] *vi*: ~ **contre/sur** to bump into; to stumble against ♦ *vt* to antagonize; **se** ~ *vi* to get obstinate; to dig in one's heels
butin [bytɛ̃] *nm* booty, spoils *pl*; (*d'un vol*) loot
butte [byt] *nf* mound, hillock; **être en** ~ **à** to be exposed to
buvais *etc vb voir* **boire**
buvard [byvaʀ] *nm* blotter
buvette [byvɛt] *nf* bar
buveur, euse [byvœʀ, -øz] *nm/f* drinker

C c

c' [s] *dét voir* **ce**
CA *sigle m* = **chiffre d'affaires**
ça [sa] *pron* (*pour désigner*) this; (: *plus loin*) that; (*comme sujet indéfini*) it; ~ **va?** how are you?; how are things?; (*d'accord?*) OK?, all right?; ~ **alors!** well really!; ~ **fait 10 ans (que)** it's 10 years (since); **c'est** ~ that's right
çà [sa] *adv*: ~ **et là** here and there
cabane [kaban] *nf* hut, cabin
cabaret [kabaʀɛ] *nm* night club
cabas [kaba] *nm* shopping bag
cabillaud [kabijo] *nm* cod *inv*
cabine [kabin] *nf* (*de bateau*) cabin; (*de plage*) (beach) hut; (*de piscine etc*) cubicle; (*de camion, train*) cab; (*d'avion*) cockpit; ~ **d'essayage** fitting room; ~ **spatiale** space capsule; ~ **(téléphonique)** call *ou* (tele)phone box
cabinet [kabinɛ] *nm* (*petite pièce*) closet; (*de médecin*) surgery (*BRIT*), office (*US*); (*de notaire etc*) office; (: *clientèle*) practice; (*POL*) Cabinet; ~**s** *nmpl* (*w.-c.*) toilet *sg*; ~ **d'affaires** business consultants' (bureau), business partnership; ~ **de toilette** toilet; ~ **de travail** study
câble [kɑbl(ə)] *nm* cable
cabrer [kabʀe]: **se** ~ *vi* (*cheval*) to rear up; (*avion*) to nose up; (*fig*) to revolt, rebel
cabriole [kabʀijɔl] *nf* caper; somersault
cacahuète [kakaɥɛt] *nf* peanut
cacao [kakao] *nm* cocoa (powder); (*boisson*) cocoa
cache [kaʃ] *nm* mask, card (for masking) ♦ *nf* hiding place
cache-cache [kaʃkaʃ] *nm*: **jouer à** ~ to play hide-and-seek
cachemire [kaʃmiʀ] *nm* cashmere
cache-nez [kaʃne] *nm inv* scarf, muffler
cacher [kaʃe] *vt* to hide, conceal; **se** ~ *vi* to hide; to be hidden *ou* concealed; ~ **qch à qn** to hide *ou* conceal sth from sb; **il ne s'en cache pas** he makes no secret of it

cachet [kaʃɛ] nm (comprimé) tablet; (sceau: du roi) seal; (: de la poste) postmark; (rétribution) fee; (fig) style, character; **cacheter** vt to seal
cachette [kaʃɛt] nf hiding place; **en ~** on the sly, secretly
cachot [kaʃo] nm dungeon
cachotterie [kaʃɔtʀi] nf: **faire des ~s** to be secretive
cactus [kaktys] nm cactus
cadavre [kadavʀ(ə)] nm corpse, (dead) body
caddie [kadi] nm (supermarket) trolley
caddy nm = **caddie**
cadeau, x [kado] nm present, gift; **faire un ~ à qn** to give sb a present ou gift; **faire ~ de qch à qn** to make a present of sth to sb, give sb sth as a present
cadenas [kadna] nm padlock
cadence [kadɑ̃s] nf (MUS) cadence; (: tempo) rhythm; (de travail etc) rate; **en ~** rhythmically; in time
cadet, te [kadɛ, -ɛt] adj younger; (le plus jeune) youngest ♦ nm/f youngest child ou one, youngest boy ou son/girl ou daughter
cadran [kadʀɑ̃] nm dial; **~ solaire** sundial
cadre [kadʀ(ə)] nm frame; (environnement) surroundings pl; (limites) scope ♦ nm/f (ADMIN) managerial employee, executive; **dans le ~ de** (fig) within the framework ou context of; **rayer qn des ~s** to dismiss sb
cadrer [kadʀe] vi: **~ avec** to tally ou correspond with ♦ vt to centre
caduc, uque [kadyk] adj obsolete; (BOT) deciduous
cafard [kafaʀ] nm cockroach; **avoir le ~** to be down in the dumps
café [kafe] nm coffee; (bistro) café ♦ adj inv coffee(-coloured); **~ au lait** white coffee; **~ noir** black coffee; **~ tabac** tobacconist's or newsagent's serving coffee and spirits; **cafetière** nf (pot) coffee-pot
cafouillage [kafujaʒ] nm shambles sg
cage [kaʒ] nf cage; **~ (des buts)** goal; **~ d'escalier** (stair)well; **~ thoracique** rib cage

cageot [kaʒo] nm crate
cagibi [kaʒibi] nm shed
cagneux, euse [kaɲø, -øz] adj knock-kneed
cagnotte [kaɲɔt] nf kitty
cagoule [kagul] nf cowl; hood; (SKI etc) cagoule
cahier [kaje] nm notebook; **~ de brouillons** roughbook, jotter; **~ d'exercices** exercise book
cahot [kao] nm jolt, bump
caïd [kaid] nm big chief, boss
caille [kɑj] nf quail
cailler [kɑje] vi (lait) to curdle; (sang) to clot
caillot [kɑjo] nm (blood) clot
caillou, x [kɑju] nm (little) stone; **caillouteux, euse** adj stony; pebbly
Caire [kɛʀ] nm: **le ~** Cairo
caisse [kɛs] nf box; (où l'on met la recette) cashbox; till; (où l'on paye) cash desk (BRIT); (de banque) cashier's desk; (TECH) case, casing; **~ d'épargne** savings bank; **~ de retraite** pension fund; **~ enregistreuse** cash register; **caissier, ière** nm/f cashier
cajoler [kaʒɔle] vt to wheedle, coax; to surround with love
cake [kɛk] nm fruit cake
calandre [kalɑ̃dʀ(ə)] nf radiator grill
calanque [kalɑ̃k] nf rocky inlet
calcaire [kalkɛʀ] nm limestone ♦ adj (eau) hard; (GÉO) limestone cpd
calciné, e [kalsine] adj burnt to ashes
calcul [kalkyl] nm calculation; **le ~** (SCOL) arithmetic; **~ (biliaire)** (gall)stone; **~ (rénal)** (kidney) stone; **calculateur** nm calculator; **calculatrice** nf calculator
calculer [kalkyle] vt to calculate, work out; (combiner) to calculate
calculette [kalkylɛt] nf pocket calculator
cale [kal] nf (de bateau) hold; (en bois) wedge; **~ sèche** dry dock
calé, e [kale] (fam) adj clever, bright
caleçon [kalsɔ̃] nm pair of underpants, trunks pl
calembour [kalɑ̃buʀ] nm pun
calendes [kalɑ̃d] nfpl: **renvoyer aux ~**

grecques to postpone indefinitely
calendrier [kalãdʀije] *nm* calendar; (*fig*) timetable
calepin [kalpɛ̃] *nm* notebook
caler [kale] *vt* to wedge; ~ (son moteur/véhicule) to stall (one's engine/vehicle)
calfeutrer [kalføtʀe] *vt* to (make) draughtproof; **se ~** *vi* to make o.s. snug and comfortable
calibre [kalibʀ(ə)] *nm* (d'un fruit) grade; (d'une arme) bore, calibre; (*fig*) calibre
califourchon [kalifuʀʃɔ̃]: **à ~** *adv* astride
câlin, e [kɑlɛ̃, -in] *adj* cuddly, cuddlesome; tender
câliner [kɑline] *vt* to fondle, cuddle
calmant [kalmã] *nm* tranquillizer, sedative; (pour la douleur) painkiller
calme [kalm(ə)] *adj* calm, quiet ♦ *nm* calm(ness), quietness
calmer [kalme] *vt* to calm (down); (douleur, inquiétude) to ease, soothe; **se ~** *vi* to calm down
calomnie [kalɔmni] *nf* slander; (écrite) libel; **calomnier** *vt* to slander; to libel
calorie [kalɔʀi] *nf* calorie
calorifuge [kalɔʀifyʒ] *adj* (heat-)insulating, heat-retaining
calotte [kalɔt] *nf* (coiffure) skullcap; (gifle) slap; **~ glaciaire** (GÉO) icecap
calquer [kalke] *vt* to trace; (*fig*) to copy exactly
calvaire [kalvɛʀ] *nm* (croix) wayside cross, calvary; (souffrances) suffering
calvitie [kalvisi] *nf* baldness
camarade [kamaʀad] *nm/f* friend, pal; (POL) comrade; **camaraderie** *nf* friendship
cambouis [kãbwi] *nm* dirty oil *ou* grease
cambrer [kãbʀe] *vt* to arch
cambriolage [kãbʀijɔlaʒ] *nm* burglary; **cambrioler** [kãbʀijɔle] *vt* to burgle (BRIT), burglarize (US); **cambrioleur, euse** *nm/f* burglar
came [kam] *nf*: **arbre à ~s** camshaft
camelote [kamlɔt] *nf* rubbish, trash, junk
caméra [kameʀa] *nf* (CINÉMA, TV) camera; (d'amateur) cine-camera

caméscope [kameskɔp] *nm* (®) camcorder (®)
camion [kamjɔ̃] *nm* lorry (BRIT), truck; (plus petit, fermé) van; **~ de dépannage** breakdown (BRIT) *ou* tow (US) truck; **camion-citerne** *nm* tanker; **camionnette** *nf* (small) van; **camionneur** *nm* (entrepreneur) haulage contractor (BRIT), trucker (US); (chauffeur) lorry (BRIT) *ou* truck driver; van driver
camisole [kamizɔl] *nf*: **~ (de force)** straitjacket
camomille [kamɔmij] *nf* camomile; (boisson) camomile tea
camoufler [kamufle] *vt* to camouflage; (*fig*) to conceal, cover up
camp [kã] *nm* camp; (*fig*) side
campagnard, e [kãpaɲaʀ, -aʀd(ə)] *adj* country cpd
campagne [kãpaɲ] *nf* country, countryside; (MIL, POL, COMM) campaign; **à la ~** in the country
camper [kãpe] *vi* to camp ♦ *vt* to sketch; **se ~ devant** to plant o.s. in front of; **campeur, euse** *nm/f* camper
camphre [kãfʀ(ə)] *nm* camphor
camping [kãpiŋ] *nm* camping; (terrain de) **~** campsite, camping site; **faire du ~** to go camping
Canada [kanada] *nm*: **le ~** Canada; **canadien, ne** *adj, nm/f* Canadian; **canadienne** *nf* (veste) fur-lined jacket
canaille [kanaj] (péj) *nf* scoundrel
canal, aux [kanal, -o] *nm* canal; (naturel) channel; **canalisation** [kanalizasjɔ̃] *nf* (tuyau) pipe; **canaliser** [kanalize] *vt* to canalize; (*fig*) to channel
canapé [kanape] *nm* settee, sofa
canard [kanaʀ] *nm* duck
canari [kanaʀi] *nm* canary
cancans [kãkã] *nmpl* (malicious) gossip *sg*
cancer [kãsɛʀ] *nm* cancer; (signe): **le C~** Cancer; **~ de la peau** skin cancer
cancre [kãkʀ(ə)] *nm* dunce
candeur [kãdœʀ] *nf* ingenuousness, guilelessness
candidat, e [kãdida, -at] *nm/f* candidate; (à un poste) applicant, candidate; **candidature** *nf* candidature; application;

poser sa **candidature** to submit an application, apply

candide [kɑ̃did] *adj* ingenuous, guileless

cane [kan] *nf* (female) duck

caneton [kantɔ̃] *nm* duckling

canette [kanɛt] *nf* (*de bière*) (flip-top) bottle

canevas [kanva] *nm* (*COUTURE*) canvas

caniche [kaniʃ] *nm* poodle

canicule [kanikyl] *nf* scorching heat

canif [kanif] *nm* penknife, pocket knife

canine [kanin] *nf* canine (tooth)

caniveau, x [kanivo] *nm* gutter

canne [kan] *nf* (walking) stick; **~ à pêche** fishing rod; **~ à sucre** sugar cane

cannelle [kanɛl] *nf* cinnamon

canoë [kanɔe] *nm* canoe; (*sport*) canoeing

canon [kanɔ̃] *nm* (*arme*) gun; (*HISTOIRE*) cannon; (*d'une arme: tube*) barrel; (*fig*) model; (*MUS*) canon; **~ rayé** rifled barrel

canot [kano] *nm* ding(h)y; **~ de sauvetage** lifeboat; **~ pneumatique** inflatable ding(h)y; **canotage** *nm* rowing; **canotier** [kanɔtje] *nm* boater

cantatrice [kɑ̃tatʀis] *nf* (opera) singer

cantine [kɑ̃tin] *nf* canteen

cantique [kɑ̃tik] *nm* hymn

canton [kɑ̃tɔ̃] *nm* *district consisting of several communes*; (*en Suisse*) canton

cantonade [kɑ̃tɔnad]: **à la ~** *adv* to everyone in general; from the rooftops

cantonner [kɑ̃tɔne] *vt* (*MIL*) to quarter, station; **se ~ dans** to confine o.s. to

cantonnier [kɑ̃tɔnje] *nm* roadmender

canular [kanylaʀ] *nm* hoax

caoutchouc [kautʃu] *nm* rubber; **~ mousse** foam rubber

cap [kap] *nm* (*GÉO*) cape; headland; (*fig*) hurdle; watershed; (*NAVIG*): **changer de ~** to change course; **mettre le ~ sur** to head *ou* steer for

C.A.P. *sigle m* (= *Certificat d'aptitude professionnelle*) *vocational training certificate taken at secondary school*

capable [kapablə] *adj* able, capable; **~ de qch/faire** capable of sth/doing

capacité [kapasite] *nf* (*compétence*) ability; (*JUR, contenance*) capacity; **~ (en**

droit) *basic legal qualification*

cape [kap] *nf* cape, cloak; **rire sous ~** to laugh up one's sleeve

C.A.P.E.S. [kapɛs] *sigle m* (= *Certificat d'aptitude pédagogique à l'enseignement secondaire*) *teaching diploma*

capillaire [kapilɛʀ] *adj* (*soins, lotion*) hair *cpd*; (*vaisseau etc*) capillary

capitaine [kapitɛn] *nm* captain

capital, e, aux [kapital, -o] *adj* major; of paramount importance; fundamental ♦ *nm* capital; (*fig*) stock; asset; *voir aussi* **capitaux**; **~ (social)** authorized capital; **capitale** *nf* (*ville*) capital; (*lettre*) capital (letter); **capitaliser** *vt* to amass, build up; **capitalisme** *nm* capitalism; **capitaliste** *adj, nm/f* capitalist; **capitaux** [kapito] *nmpl* (*fonds*) capital *sg*

capitonné, e [kapitɔne] *adj* padded

caporal, aux [kapɔral, -o] *nm* lance corporal

capot [kapo] *nm* (*AUTO*) bonnet (*BRIT*), hood (*US*)

capote [kapɔt] *nf* (*de voiture*) hood (*BRIT*), top (*US*); (*fam*) condom

capoter [kapɔte] *vi* to overturn

câpre [kɑpʀ(ə)] *nf* caper

caprice [kapʀis] *nm* whim, caprice; passing fancy; **capricieux, euse** *adj* capricious; whimsical; temperamental

Capricorne [kapʀikɔʀn] *nm*: **le ~** Capricorn

capsule [kapsyl] *nf* (*de bouteille*) cap; (*BOT etc, spatiale*) capsule

capter [kapte] *vt* (*ondes radio*) to pick up; (*eau*) to harness; (*fig*) to win, capture

captivant, e [kaptivɑ̃, ɑ̃t] *adj* captivating; fascinating

captivité [kaptivite] *nf* captivity

capturer [kaptyʀe] *vt* to capture

capuche [kapyʃ] *nf* hood

capuchon [kapyʃɔ̃] *nm* hood; (*de stylo*) cap, top

capucine [kapysin] *nf* (*BOT*) nasturtium

caquet [kakɛ] *nm*: **rabattre le ~ à qn** to bring sb down a peg or two

caqueter [kakte] *vi* to cackle

car [kaʀ] *nm* coach ♦ *conj* because, for

carabine [karabin] *nf* carbine, rifle

caractère [karaktɛr] *nm* (*gén*) character; **avoir bon/mauvais ~** to be good-/ill-natured; **en ~s gras** in bold type; **en petits ~s** in small print; **~s d'imprimerie** (block) capitals; **caractériel, le** *adj* (of) character ♦ *nm/f* emotionally disturbed child

caractérisé, e [karakterize] *adj*: **c'est une grippe ~e** it is a clear (-cut) case of flu

caractéristique [karakteristik] *adj, nf* characteristic

carafe [karaf] *nf* decanter; carafe

caraïbe [karaib] *adj* Caribbean ♦ *n*: **les C~s** the Caribbean (Islands); **la mer des C~s** the Caribbean Sea

carambolage [karãbɔlaʒ] *nm* multiple crash, pileup

caramel [karamɛl] *nm* (*bonbon*) caramel, toffee; (*substance*) caramel

carapace [karapas] *nf* shell

caravane [karavan] *nf* caravan; **caravaning** *nm* caravanning; (*emplacement*) caravan site

carbone [karbɔn] *nm* carbon; (*feuille*) carbon, sheet of carbon paper; (*double*) carbon (copy); **carbonique** [karbɔnik] *adj*: **neige carbonique** dry ice; **carbonisé, e** [karbɔnize] *adj* charred

carburant [karbyrã] *nm* (motor) fuel

carburateur [karbyratœr] *nm* carburettor

carcan [karkã] *nm* (*fig*) yoke, shackles *pl*

carcasse [karkas] *nf* carcass; (*de véhicule etc*) shell

cardiaque [kardjak] *adj* cardiac, heart *cpd* ♦ *nm/f* heart patient

cardigan [kardigã] *nm* cardigan

cardiologue [kardjɔlɔg] *nm/f* cardiologist, heart specialist

carême [karɛm] *nm*: **le C~** Lent

carence [karãs] *nf* incompetence, inadequacy; (*manque*) deficiency

caresse [karɛs] *nf* caress

caresser [karese] *vt* to caress, fondle; (*fig: projet*) to toy with

cargaison [kargɛzɔ̃] *nf* cargo, freight

cargo [kargo] *nm* cargo boat, freighter

carie [kari] *nf*: **la ~ (dentaire)** tooth decay; **une ~** a bad tooth

carillon [karijɔ̃] *nm* (*d'église*) bells *pl*; (*de pendule*) chimes *pl*; (*de porte*) door chime *ou* bell

carlingue [karlɛ̃g] *nf* cabin

carnassier, ière [karnasje, -jɛr] *adj* carnivorous

carnaval [karnaval] *nm* carnival

carnet [karnɛ] *nm* (*calepin*) notebook; (*de tickets, timbres etc*) book; (*d'école*) school report; (*journal intime*) diary; **~ de chèques** cheque book

carotte [karɔt] *nf* carrot

carpette [karpɛt] *nf* rug

carré, e [kare] *adj* square; (*fig: franc*) straightforward ♦ *nm* (*de terrain, jardin*) patch, plot; (*MATH*) square; **mètre/kilomètre ~** square metre/kilometre

carreau, x [karo] *nm* (*en faïence etc*) (floor) tile; (*wall*) tile; (*de fenêtre*) (window) pane; (*motif*) check, square; (*CARTES: couleur*) diamonds *pl*; (*: carte*) diamond; **tissu à ~x** checked fabric

carrefour [karfur] *nm* crossroads *sg*

carrelage [karlaʒ] *nm* tiling; (tiled) floor

carrelet [karlɛ] *nm* (*poisson*) plaice

carrément [karemã] *adv* straight out, bluntly; completely, altogether

carrière [karjɛr] *nf* (*de roches*) quarry; (*métier*) career; **militaire de ~** professional soldier

carriole [karjɔl] (*péj*) *nf* old cart

carrossable [karɔsabl(ə)] *adj* suitable for (motor) vehicles

carrosse [karɔs] *nm* (horse-drawn) coach

carrosserie [karɔsri] *nf* body, coachwork *no pl*; (*activité, commerce*) coach-building

carrure [karyr] *nf* build; (*fig*) stature, calibre

cartable [kartabl(ə)] *nm* (*d'écolier*) satchel, (school)bag

carte [kart(ə)] *nf* (*de géographie*) map; (*marine, du ciel*) chart; (*de fichier, d'abonnement etc, à jouer*) card; (*au restaurant*) menu; (*aussi: ~ postale*) (post)card; (: ~ **de visite**) (visiting) card; **à la ~** (*au restaurant*) à la carte; **~ bancaire** cash card; **~ de crédit** credit card; **~ d'identité** identity card; **~ de séjour** residence permit; **~ grise** (*AUTO*) ≈ (car) registration book, logbook; **~ routière** road map; **~ téléphonique** phonecard

carter [kaʀtɛʀ] *nm* sump

carton [kaʀtɔ̃] *nm* (*matériau*) cardboard; (*boîte*) (cardboard) box; (*d'invitation*) invitation card; **faire un ~** (*au tir*) to have a go at the rifle range; to score a hit; (: **à dessin**) portfolio; **cartonné, e** *adj* (*livre*) hardback, cased; **carton-pâte** *nm* pasteboard

cartouche [kaʀtuʃ] *nf* cartridge; (*de cigarettes*) carton

cas [kɑ] *nm* case; **faire peu de ~/grand ~ de** to attach little/great importance to; **en aucun ~** on no account; **au ~ où** in case; **en ~ de** in case of, in the event of; **en ~ de besoin** if need be; **en tout ~** in any case, at any rate; **~ de conscience** matter of conscience

casanier, ière [kazanje, -jɛʀ] *adj* stay-at-home

cascade [kaskad] *nf* waterfall, cascade; (*fig*) stream, torrent

cascadeur, euse [kaskadœʀ, -øz] *nm/f* stuntman(girl)

case [kɑz] *nf* (*hutte*) hut; (*compartiment*) compartment; (*pour le courrier*) pigeonhole; (*sur un formulaire, de mots croisés etc*) box

caser [kɑze] *vt* (*trouver de la place pour*) to put (away); to put up; (*fig*) to find a job for; to marry off

caserne [kazɛʀn(ə)] *nf* barracks *pl*

cash [kaʃ] *adv*: **payer ~** to pay cash down

casier [kɑzje] *nm* (*à journaux etc*) rack; (*de bureau*) filing cabinet; (: **à cases**) set of pigeonholes; (*case*) compartment; pigeonhole; (: **à clef**) locker; **~ judiciaire** police record

casino [kazino] *nm* casino

casque [kask(ə)] *nm* helmet; (*chez le coiffeur*) (hair-)drier; (*pour audition*) (head-)phones *pl*, headset

casquette [kaskɛt] *nf* cap

cassant, e [kɑsɑ̃, -ɑ̃t] *adj* brittle; (*fig*) brusque, abrupt

cassation [kɑsasjɔ̃] *nf*: **cour de ~** final court of appeal

casse [kɑs] *nf* (*pour voitures*): **mettre à la ~** to scrap; (*dégâts*): **il y a eu de la ~** there were a lot of breakages; **~-cou** *adj inv* daredevil, reckless; **~-croûte** *nm inv* snack; **~-noisette(s)** *nm inv* nutcrackers *pl*; **~-noix** *nm inv* nutcrackers *pl*; **~-pieds** (*fam*) *adj inv*: **il est ~-pieds** he's a pain in the neck

casser [kɑse] *vt* to break; (*ADMIN: gradé*) to demote; (*JUR*) to quash; **se ~** *vi* to break

casserole [kasʀɔl] *nf* saucepan

casse-tête [kɑstɛt] *nm inv* (*jeu*) brain teaser; (*difficultés*) headache (*fig*)

cassette [kasɛt] *nf* (*bande magnétique*) cassette; (*coffret*) casket

casseur [kɑsœʀ] *nm* hooligan

cassis [kasis] *nm* blackcurrant

cassoulet [kasulɛ] *nm bean and sausage hot-pot*

cassure [kɑsyʀ] *nf* break, crack

castor [kastɔʀ] *nm* beaver

castrer [kastʀe] *vt* (*mâle*) to castrate; (: *cheval*) to geld; (*femelle*) to spay

catalogue [katalɔg] *nm* catalogue

cataloguer [katalɔge] *vt* to catalogue, to list; (*péj*) to put a label on

catalysateur *nm* catalytic convertor

catalyseur [katalizœʀ] *nm* catalyst

catalytique [katalitik] *adj* catalytic

cataplasme [kataplasm(ə)] *nm* poultice

cataracte [kataʀakt(ə)] *nf* cataract

catastrophe [katastʀɔf] *nf* catastrophe, disaster; **catastrophé, e** [katastʀɔfe] (*fam*) *adj* deeply saddened

catch [katʃ] *nm* (all-in) wrestling; **catcheur, euse** *nm/f* (all-in) wrestler

catéchisme [kateʃism(ə)] *nm* catechism

catégorie [kategɔʀi] *nf* category

catégorique [kategɔʀik] *adj* categorical

cathédrale [katedʀal] *nf* cathedral

catholique [katɔlik] *adj, nm/f* (Roman) Catholic; **pas très ~** a bit shady *ou* fishy

catimini [katimini]: **en ~** *adv* on the sly

cauchemar [koʃmar] *nm* nightmare
cause [koz] *nf* cause; (*JUR*) lawsuit, case; **à ~ de** because of, owing to; **pour ~** on account of; owing to; **(et) pour ~** and for (a very) good reason; **être en ~** to be at stake; to be involved; to be in question; **mettre en ~** to implicate; to call into question; **remettre en ~** to challenge; **causer** [koze] *vt* to cause ♦ *vi* to chat, talk; **causerie** [kozri] *nf* talk
caution [kosjɔ̃] *nf* guarantee, security; deposit; (*JUR*) bail (bond); (*fig*) backing, support; **payer la ~ de qn** to stand bail for sb; **libéré sous ~** released on bail; **cautionner** [kosjone] *vt* to guarantee; (*soutenir*) to support
cavalcade [kavalkad] *nf* (*fig*) stampede
cavalier, ière [kavalje, -jɛr] *adj* (*désinvolte*) offhand ♦ *nm/f* rider; (*au bal*) partner ♦ *nm* (*ÉCHECS*) knight; **faire ~ seul** to go it alone
cave [kav] *nf* cellar ♦ *adj*: **yeux ~s** sunken eyes
caveau, x [kavo] *nm* vault
caverne [kavɛrn(ə)] *nf* cave
C.C.P. *sigle m* = **compte chèques postaux**
CD *sigle m* (= *compact disc*) CD
CD-ROM *sigle m* CD-ROM
CE *n abr* (= *Communauté Européenne*) EC

ce, cette [sə, sɛt] (*devant nm* **cet** + *voyelle ou h aspiré; pl* **ces**) *dét* (*proximité*) this; these *pl*; (*non-proximité*) that; those *pl*; **cette maison(-ci/là)** this/that house; **cette nuit** (*qui vient*) tonight; (*passée*) last night
♦ *pron* **1**: **c'est** it's *ou* it is; **c'est un peintre** he's *ou* he is a painter; **ce sont des peintres** they're *ou* they are painters; **c'est le facteur** *etc* (*à la porte*) it's the postman; **qui est-ce?** who is it?; (*en désignant*) who is he/she?; **qu'est-ce?** what is it?
2: **~ qui, ~ que** what; (*chose qui*): **il est bête, ~ qui me chagrine** he's stupid, which saddens me; **tout ~ qui bouge** everything that *ou* which moves; **tout ~ que je sais** all I know; **~ dont j'ai parlé** what I talked about; **~ que c'est grand!** it's so big!; *voir aussi* **-ci**; **est-ce que; n'est-ce pas; c'est-à-dire**

ceci [səsi] *pron* this
cécité [sesite] *nf* blindness
céder [sede] *vt* to give up ♦ *vi* (*pont, barrage*) to give way; (*personne*) to give in; **~ à** to yield to, give in to
CEDEX [sedɛks] *sigle m* (= *courrier d'entreprise à distribution exceptionnelle*) postal service for bulk users
cédille [sedij] *nf* cedilla
cèdre [sɛdr(ə)] *nm* cedar
CEI *abr f* (= *Communauté des États Indépendants*) CIS
ceinture [sɛ̃tyr] *nf* belt; (*taille*) waist; (*fig*) ring; belt; circle; **~ de sécurité** safety *ou* seat belt; **ceinturer** *vt* (*saisir*) to grasp (round the waist)
cela [səla] *pron* that; (*comme sujet indéfini*) it; **quand/où ~?** when/where (was that?)
célèbre [selɛbr(ə)] *adj* famous
célébrer [selebre] *vt* to celebrate; (*louer*) to extol
céleri [sɛlri] *nm*: **~(-rave)** celeriac; **~ (en branche)** celery
célérité [selerite] *nf* speed, swiftness
célibat [seliba] *nm* celibacy; bachelorhood; spinsterhood; **célibataire** [selibatɛr] *adj* single, unmarried
celle(s) [sɛl] *pron voir* **celui**
cellier [selje] *nm* storeroom
cellulaire [selylɛr] *adj*: **voiture** *ou* **fourgon ~** prison *ou* police van
cellule [selyl] *nf* (*gén*) cell
cellulite [selylit] *nf* excess fat, cellulite

celui, celle [səlɥi, sɛl] (*mpl* **ceux**, *fpl* **celles**) *pron* **1**: **~-ci/là, celle-ci/là** this one/that one; **ceux-ci, celles-ci** these (ones); **ceux-là, celles-là** those (ones); **~ de mon frère** my brother's; **~ du salon/du dessous** the one in (*ou* from) the lounge/below

2: ~ **qui bouge** the one which *ou* that moves; (*personne*) the one who moves; ~ **que je vois** the one (which *ou* that) I see; the one (whom) I see; ~ **dont je parle** the one I'm talking about

3 (*valeur indéfinie*): ~ **qui veut** whoever wants

cendre [sɑ̃dʀ(ə)] *nf* ash; ~**s** *nfpl* (*d'un foyer*) ash(es), cinders; (*volcaniques*) ash *sg*; (*d'un défunt*) ashes; **sous la** ~ (*CULIN*) in (the) embers; **cendrier** *nm* ashtray

cène [sɛn] *nf*: **la** ~ (Holy) Communion

censé, e [sɑ̃se] *adj*: **être** ~ **faire** to be supposed to do

censeur [sɑ̃sœʀ] *nm* (*SCOL*) deputy-head (*BRIT*), vice-principal (*US*); (*CINÉMA, POL*) censor

censure [sɑ̃syʀ] *nf* censorship; **censurer** [sɑ̃syʀe] *vt* (*CINÉMA, PRESSE*) to censor; (*POL*) to censure

cent [sɑ̃] *num* a hundred, one hundred; **centaine** *nf*: **une centaine (de)** about a hundred, a hundred or so; **plusieurs centaines (de)** several hundred; **des centaines (de)** hundreds (of); **centenaire** *adj* hundred-year-old ♦ *nm* (*anniversaire*) centenary; **centième** *num* hundredth; **centigrade** *nm* centigrade; **centilitre** *nm* centilitre; **centime** *nm* centime; **centimètre** *nm* centimetre; (*ruban*) tape measure, measuring tape

central, e, aux [sɑ̃tʀal, -o] *adj* central ♦ *nm*: ~ **(téléphonique)** (telephone) exchange; **centrale** *nf* power station

centre [sɑ̃tʀ(ə)] *nm* centre; ~ **commercial** shopping centre; ~ **d'apprentissage** training college; **centre-ville** *nm* town centre, downtown (area) (*US*)

centuple [sɑ̃typl(ə)] *nm*: **le** ~ **de qch** a hundred times sth; **au** ~ a hundredfold

cep [sɛp] *nm* (vine) stock

cèpe [sɛp] *nm* (edible) boletus

cependant [səpɑ̃dɑ̃] *adv* however

céramique [seʀamik] *nf* ceramics *sg*

cercle [sɛʀkl(ə)] *nm* circle; (*objet*) band, hoop; ~ **vicieux** vicious circle

cercueil [sɛʀkœj] *nm* coffin

céréale [seʀeal] *nf* cereal

cérémonie [seʀemɔni] *nf* ceremony; ~**s** *nfpl* (*péj*) fuss *sg*, to-do *sg*

cerf [sɛʀ] *nm* stag

cerfeuil [sɛʀfœj] *nm* chervil

cerf-volant [sɛʀvɔlɑ̃] *nm* kite

cerise [səʀiz] *nf* cherry; **cerisier** *nm* cherry (tree)

cerné, e [sɛʀne] *adj*: **les yeux** ~**s** with dark rings *ou* shadows under the eyes

cerner [sɛʀne] *vt* (*MIL etc*) to surround; (*fig: problème*) to delimit, define

certain, e [sɛʀtɛ̃, -ɛn] *adj* certain ♦ *dét* certain; **d'un** ~ **âge** past one's prime, not so young; **un** ~ **temps** (quite) some time; ~**s** some; **certainement** *adv* (*probablement*) most probably *ou* likely; (*bien sûr*) certainly, of course

certes [sɛʀt(ə)] *adv* admittedly; of course; indeed (yes)

certificat [sɛʀtifika] *nm* certificate

certitude [sɛʀtityd] *nf* certainty

cerveau, x [sɛʀvo] *nm* brain

cervelas [sɛʀvəla] *nm* saveloy

cervelle [sɛʀvɛl] *nf* (*ANAT*) brain

ces [se] *dét voir* **ce**

C.E.S. *sigle m* (= *Collège d'enseignement secondaire*) ≈ (junior) secondary school (*BRIT*)

cesse [sɛs]: **sans** ~ *adv* continually, constantly; continuously; **il n'avait de** ~ **que** he would not rest until

cesser [sese] *vt* to stop ♦ *vi* to stop, cease; ~ **de faire** to stop doing

cessez-le-feu *nm inv* ceasefire

c'est-à-dire [sɛtadiʀ] *adv* that is (to say)

cet, cette [sɛt] *dét voir* **ce**

ceux [sø] *pron* **celui**

CFC *abr* (= *chlorofluorocarbon*) *npl* CFC

C.F.D.T. *sigle f* = **Confédération française démocratique du travail**

C.G.T. *sigle f* = **Confédération générale du travail**

chacun, e [ʃakœ̃, -yn] *pron* each; (*indéfini*) everyone, everybody

chagrin [ʃagʀɛ̃] *nm* grief, sorrow; **chagriner** *vt* to grieve; to bother

chahut [ʃay] *nm* uproar; **chahuter** *vt* to

rag, bait ♦ *vi* to make an uproar

chaîne [ʃɛn] *nf* chain; (*RADIO, TV*: *stations*) channel; **travail à la ~** production line work; **~ (de montage** *ou* **de fabrication)** production *ou* assembly line; **~ (de montagnes)** (mountain) range; **~ (haute-fidélité** *ou* **hi-fi)** hi-fi system; **~ (stéréo)** stereo (system)

chair [ʃɛʀ] *nf* flesh ♦ *adj*: **(couleur) ~** flesh-coloured; **avoir la ~ de poule** to have goosepimples *ou* gooseflesh; **bien en ~** plump, well-padded; **en ~ et en os** in the flesh

chaire [ʃɛʀ] *nf* (*d'église*) pulpit; (*d'université*) chair

chaise [ʃɛz] *nf* chair; **~ longue** deck-chair

châle [ʃɑl] *nm* shawl

chaleur [ʃalœʀ] *nf* heat; (*fig*) warmth; fire, fervour; heat

chaleureux, euse [ʃalœʀø, -øz] *adj* warm

chaloupe [ʃalup] *nf* launch; (*de sauvetage*) lifeboat

chalumeau, x [ʃalymo] *nm* blowlamp, blowtorch

chalutier [ʃalytje] *nm* trawler

chamailler [ʃamaje]: **se ~** *vi* to squabble, bicker

chambouler [ʃɑbule] *vt* to disrupt, turn upside down

chambre [ʃɑbʀ(ə)] *nf* bedroom; (*TECH*) chamber; (*POL*) chamber, house; (*JUR*) court; (*COMM*) chamber, federation; **faire ~ à part** to sleep in separate rooms; **~ à air** (*de pneu*) (inner) tube; **~ à coucher** bedroom; **~ à un lit/deux lits** (*à l'hôtel*) single/twin-bedded room; **~ d'amis** spare *ou* guest room; **~ noire** (*PHOTO*) dark room

chambrer [ʃɑbʀe] *vt* (*vin*) to bring to room temperature

chameau, x [ʃamo] *nm* camel

champ [ʃɑ] *nm* field; **prendre du ~** to draw back; **~ de bataille** battlefield; **~ de courses** racecourse; **~ de tir** rifle range

champagne [ʃɑpaɲ] *nm* champagne

champêtre [ʃɑpɛtʀ(ə)] *adj* country *cpd*, rural

champignon [ʃɑpiɲɔ̃] *nm* mushroom; (*terme générique*) fungus; **~ de Paris** button mushroom

champion, ne [ʃɑpjɔ̃, -jɔn] *adj, nm/f* champion; **championnat** *nm* championship

chance [ʃɑs] *nf*: **la ~** luck; **~s** *nfpl* (*probabilités*) chances; **une ~** a stroke *ou* piece of luck *ou* good fortune; (*occasion*) a lucky break; **avoir de la ~** to be lucky

chanceler [ʃɑsle] *vi* to totter

chancelier [ʃɑsəlje] *nm* (*allemand*) chancellor

chanceux, euse [ʃɑsø, -øz] *adj* lucky

chandail [ʃɑdaj] *nm* (thick) sweater

chandelier [ʃɑdəlje] *nm* candlestick

chandelle [ʃɑdɛl] *nf* (tallow) candle; **dîner aux ~s** candlelight dinner

change [ʃɑʒ] *nm* (*COMM*) exchange

changement [ʃɑʒmɑ] *nm* change; **~ de vitesses** gears *pl*; gear change

changer [ʃɑʒe] *vt* (*modifier*) to change, alter; (*remplacer, COMM, rhabiller*) to change ♦ *vi* to change, alter; **se ~** *vi* to change (o.s.); **~ de** (*remplacer: adresse, nom, voiture etc*) to change one's; (*échanger, alterner: côté, place, train etc*) to change +*npl*; **~ de couleur/direction** to change colour/direction; **~ d'idée** to change one's mind; **~ de vitesse** to change gear

chanson [ʃɑsɔ̃] *nf* song

chant [ʃɑ] *nm* song; (*art vocal*) singing; (*d'église*) hymn; **chantage** [ʃɑtaʒ] *nm* blackmail; **faire du chantage** to use blackmail; **chanter** [ʃɑte] *vt, vi* to sing; **si cela lui chante** (*fam*) if he feels like it; **chanteur, euse** [ʃɑtœʀ, -øz] *nm/f* singer

chantier [ʃɑtje] *nm* (building) site; (*sur une route*) roadworks *pl*; **mettre en ~** to put in hand; **~ naval** shipyard

chantilly [ʃɑtiji] *nf voir* **crème**

chantonner [ʃɑtɔne] *vi, vt* to sing to oneself, hum

chanvre [ʃɑvʀ(ə)] *nm* hemp

chaparder [ʃapaʀde] *vt* to pinch

chapeau, x [ʃapo] *nm* hat; **~ mou** trilby

chapelet [ʃaplɛ] *nm* (*REL*) rosary

chapelle [ʃapɛl] *nf* chapel; ~ **ardente** chapel of rest

chapelure [ʃaplyʀ] *nf* (dried) breadcrumbs *pl*

chapiteau, x [ʃapito] *nm* (*de cirque*) marquee, big top

chapitre [ʃapitʀ(ə)] *nm* chapter; (*fig*) subject, matter

chaque [ʃak] *dét* each, every; (*indéfini*) every

char [ʃaʀ] *nm* (*à foin etc*) cart, waggon; (*de carnaval*) float; ~ (**d'assaut**) tank

charabia [ʃaʀabja] (*péj*) *nm* gibberish

charade [ʃaʀad] *nf* riddle; (*mimée*) charade

charbon [ʃaʀbɔ̃] *nm* coal; ~ **de bois** charcoal

charcuterie [ʃaʀkytʀi] *nf* (*magasin*) pork butcher's shop and delicatessen; (*produits*) cooked pork meats *pl*; **charcutier, ière** *nm/f* pork butcher

chardon [ʃaʀdɔ̃] *nm* thistle

charge [ʃaʀʒ(ə)] *nf* (*fardeau*) load, burden; (*explosif, ÉLEC, MIL, JUR*) charge; (*rôle, mission*) responsibility; ~s *nfpl* (*du loyer*) service charges; **à la ~ de** (*dépendant de*) dependent upon; (*aux frais de*) chargeable to; **j'accepte, à ~ de revanche** I accept, provided I can do the same for you one day; **prendre en ~** to take charge of; (*suj: véhicule*) to take on; (*dépenses*) to take care of; ~s **sociales** social security contributions; **chargement** [ʃaʀʒəma] *nm* (*objets*) load

charger [ʃaʀʒe] *vt* (*voiture, fusil, caméra*) to load; (*batterie*) to charge ♦ *vi* (*MIL etc*) to charge; **se ~ de** *vt* to see to; ~ **qn de (faire) qch** to put sb in charge of (doing) sth

chariot [ʃaʀjo] *nm* trolley; (*charrette*) waggon; (*de machine à écrire*) carriage

charité [ʃaʀite] *nf* charity; **faire la ~ à** to give (something) to

charmant, e [ʃaʀmã, -ãt] *adj* charming

charme [ʃaʀm(ə)] *nm* charm; **charmer** *vt* to charm

charnel, le [ʃaʀnɛl] *adj* carnal

charnière [ʃaʀnjɛʀ] *nf* hinge; (*fig*) turning-point

charnu, e [ʃaʀny] *adj* fleshy

charpente [ʃaʀpɑ̃t] *nf* frame(work); **charpentier** *nm* carpenter

charpie [ʃaʀpi] *nf*: **en ~** (*fig*) in shreds *ou* ribbons

charrette [ʃaʀɛt] *nf* cart

charrier [ʃaʀje] *vt* to carry (along); to cart, carry

charrue [ʃaʀy] *nf* plough (*BRIT*), plow (*US*)

chasse [ʃas] *nf* hunting; (*au fusil*) shooting; (*poursuite*) chase; (*aussi*: ~ **d'eau**) flush; **la ~ est ouverte** the hunting season is open; ~ **gardée** private hunting grounds *pl*; **prendre en ~** to give chase to; **tirer la ~ (d'eau)** to flush the toilet, pull the chain; ~ **à courre** hunting

chassé-croisé [ʃasekʀwaze] *nm* (*fig*) mix-up where people miss each other in turn

chasse-neige [ʃasnɛʒ] *nm inv* snowplough (*BRIT*), snowplow (*US*)

chasser [ʃase] *vt* to hunt; (*expulser*) to chase away *ou* out, drive away *ou* out; **chasseur, euse** *nm/f* hunter ♦ *nm* (*avion*) fighter; **chasseur de têtes** *nm* (*fig*) headhunter

châssis [ʃasi] *nm* (*AUTO*) chassis; (*cadre*) frame; (*de jardin*) cold frame

chat [ʃa] *nm* cat

châtaigne [ʃatɛɲ] *nf* chestnut; **châtaignier** *nm* chestnut (tree)

châtain [ʃatɛ̃] *adj inv* chestnut (brown); chestnut-haired

château, x [ʃato] *nm* castle; ~ **d'eau** water tower; ~ **fort** stronghold, fortified castle

châtier [ʃatje] *vt* to punish; (*fig: style*) to polish; **châtiment** *nm* punishment

chaton [ʃatɔ̃] *nm* (*ZOOL*) kitten

chatouiller [ʃatuje] *vt* to tickle; (*l'odorat, le palais*) to titillate; **chatouilleux, euse** *adj* ticklish; (*fig*) touchy, over-sensitive

chatoyer [ʃatwaje] *vi* to shimmer

châtrer [ʃatʀe] *vt* (*mâle*) to castrate; (: *cheval*) to geld; (*femelle*) to spay

chatte [ʃat] *nf* (she-)cat

chaud, e [ʃo, -od] *adj* (*gén*) warm; (*très*

chaud) hot; (*fig*) hearty; heated; **il fait ~** it's warm; it's hot; **avoir ~** to be warm; to be hot; **ça me tient ~** it keeps me warm; **rester au ~** to stay in the warm
chaudière [ʃodjɛʀ] *nf* boiler
chaudron [ʃodʀɔ̃] *nm* cauldron
chauffage [ʃofaʒ] *nm* heating; **~ central** central heating
chauffard [ʃofaʀ] *nm* (*péj*) reckless driver; hit-and-run driver
chauffe-eau [ʃofo] *nm inv* water-heater
chauffer [ʃofe] *vt* to heat ♦ *vi* to heat up, warm up; (*trop ~: moteur*) to overheat; **se ~** *vi* (*se mettre en train*) to warm up; (*au soleil*) to warm o.s.
chauffeur [ʃofœʀ] *nm* driver; (*privé*) chauffeur
chaume [ʃom] *nm* (*du toit*) thatch
chaumière [ʃomjɛʀ] *nf* (thatched) cottage
chaussée [ʃose] *nf* road(way)
chausse-pied [ʃospje] *nm* shoe-horn
chausser [ʃose] *vt* (*bottes, skis*) to put on; (*enfant*) to put shoes on; **~ du 38/42** to take size 38/42
chaussette [ʃosɛt] *nf* sock
chausson [ʃosɔ̃] *nm* slipper; (*de bébé*) bootee; **~ (aux pommes)** (apple) turnover
chaussure [ʃosyʀ] *nf* shoe; **~s basses** flat shoes; **~s de ski** ski boots
chauve [ʃov] *adj* bald
chauve-souris [ʃovsuʀi] *nf* bat
chauvin, e [ʃovɛ̃, -in] *adj* chauvinistic
chaux [ʃo] *nf* lime; **blanchi à la ~** whitewashed
chavirer [ʃaviʀe] *vi* to capsize
chef [ʃɛf] *nm* head, leader; (*de cuisine*) chef; **en ~** (*MIL etc*) in chief; **~ d'accusation** charge; **~ d'entreprise** company head; **~ d'état** head of state; **~ de file** (*de parti etc*) leader; **~ de gare** station master; **~ d'orchestre** conductor (*BRIT*), director (*US*); **~-d'œuvre** [ʃɛdœvʀ(ə)] *nm* masterpiece; **~-lieu** [ʃɛfljø] *nm* county town
chemin [ʃəmɛ̃] *nm* path; (*itinéraire, direction, trajet*) way; **en ~** on the way; **~ de fer** railway (*BRIT*), railroad (*US*); **par ~**

de fer by rail
cheminée [ʃəmine] *nf* chimney; (*à l'intérieur*) chimney piece, fireplace; (*de bateau*) funnel
cheminement [ʃəminmɑ̃] *nm* progress; course
cheminot [ʃəmino] *nm* railwayman
chemise [ʃəmiz] *nf* shirt; (*dossier*) folder; **~ de nuit** nightdress
chemisier [ʃəmizje] *nm* blouse
chenal, aux [ʃənal, -o] *nm* channel
chêne [ʃɛn] *nm* oak (tree); (*bois*) oak
chenil [ʃənil] *nm* kennels *pl*
chenille [ʃənij] *nf* (*ZOOL*) caterpillar; (*AUTO*) caterpillar track
chèque [ʃɛk] *nm* cheque (*BRIT*), check (*US*); **~ sans provision** bad cheque; **~ de voyage** traveller's cheque; **chéquier** *nm* cheque book
cher, ère [ʃɛʀ] *adj* (*aimé*) dear; (*coûteux*) expensive, dear ♦ *adv*: **cela coûte ~** it's expensive
chercher [ʃɛʀʃe] *vt* to look for; (*gloire etc*) to seek; **aller ~** to go for, go and fetch; **~ à faire** to try to do; **chercheur, euse** [ʃɛʀʃœʀ, -øz] *nm/f* researcher, research worker
chère [ʃɛʀ] *adj voir* **cher** ♦ *nf*: **la bonne ~** good food
chéri, e [ʃeʀi] *adj* beloved, dear; **(mon) ~** darling
chérir [ʃeʀiʀ] *vt* to cherish
cherté [ʃɛʀte] *nf*: **la ~ de la vie** the high cost of living
chétif, ive [ʃetif, -iv] *adj* puny, stunted
cheval, aux [ʃəval, -o] *nm* horse; (*AUTO*): **~ (vapeur)** horsepower *no pl*; **faire du ~** to ride; **à ~** on horseback; **à ~ sur** astride; (*fig*) overlapping; **~ de course** racehorse
chevalet [ʃəvalɛ] *nm* easel
chevalier [ʃəvalje] *nm* knight
chevalière [ʃəvaljɛʀ] *nf* signet ring
chevalin, e [ʃəvalɛ̃, -in] *adj*: **boucherie ~e** horse-meat butcher's
chevaucher [ʃəvoʃe] *vi* (*aussi: se ~*) to overlap (each other) ♦ *vt* to be astride, straddle
chevaux [ʃəvo] *nmpl de* **cheval**

chevelu, e [ʃəvly] *adj* with a good head of hair, hairy (*péj*)

chevelure [ʃəvlyʀ] *nf* hair *no pl*

chevet [ʃəvɛ] *nm*: **au ~ de qn** at sb's bedside; **lampe de ~** bedside lamp

cheveu, x [ʃəvø] *nm* hair; **~x** *nmpl* (*chevelure*) hair *sg*; **avoir les ~x courts** to have short hair

cheville [ʃəvij] *nf* (*ANAT*) ankle; (*de bois*) peg; (*pour une vis*) plug

chèvre [ʃɛvʀ(ə)] *nf* (she-)goat

chevreau, x [ʃəvʀo] *nm* kid

chèvrefeuille [ʃɛvʀəfœj] *nm* honeysuckle

chevreuil [ʃəvʀœj] *nm* roe deer *inv*; (*CULIN*) venison

chevronné, e [ʃəvʀɔne] *adj* seasoned

MOT-CLÉ

---

chez [ʃe] *prép* **1** (*à la demeure de*) at; (: *direction*) to; **~ qn** at/to sb's house *ou* place; **~ moi** at home; (*direction*) home

2 (+*profession*) at; (: *direction*) to; **~ le boulanger/dentiste** at *or* to the baker's/dentist's

3 (*dans le caractère, l'œuvre de*) in; **~ les renards/Racine** in foxes/Racine

---

chez-soi [ʃeswa] *nm inv* home

chic [ʃik] *adj inv* chic, smart; (*généreux*) nice, decent ♦ *nm* stylishness; **~!** great!; **avoir le ~ de** to have the knack of

chicane [ʃikan] *nf* (*querelle*) squabble

chicaner [ʃikane] *vi* (*ergoter*): **~ sur** to quibble about

chiche [ʃiʃ] *adj* niggardly, mean ♦ *excl* (*à un défi*) you're on!

chichi [ʃiʃi] (*fam*) *nm* fuss

chicorée [ʃikɔʀe] *nf* (*café*) chicory; (*salade*) endive

chien [ʃjɛ̃] *nm* dog; **en ~ de fusil** curled up; **~ de garde** guard dog

chiendent [ʃjɛ̃dɑ̃] *nm* couch grass

chienne [ʃjɛn] *nf* dog, bitch

chier [ʃje] (*fam!*) *vi* to crap (*!*)

chiffon [ʃifɔ̃] *nm* (*piece of*) rag; **chiffonner** [ʃifɔne] *vt* to crumple; (*tracasser*) to concern; **chiffonnier** [ʃifɔnje] *nm* rag-and-bone man

chiffre [ʃifʀ(ə)] *nm* (*représentant un nombre*) figure; numeral; (*montant, total*) total, sum; **en ~s ronds** in round figures; **~ d'affaires** turnover; **chiffrer** *vt* (*dépense*) to put a figure to, assess; (*message*) to (en)code, cipher

chignon [ʃiɲɔ̃] *nm* chignon, bun

Chili [ʃili] *nm*: **le ~** Chile

chimie [ʃimi] *nf* chemistry; **chimique** *adj* chemical; **produits chimiques** chemicals

Chine [ʃin] *nf*: **la ~** China

chinois, e [ʃinwa, -waz] *adj, nm/f* Chinese ♦ *nm* (*LING*) Chinese

chiot [ʃjo] *nm* pup(py)

chips [ʃips] *nfpl* crisps (*BRIT*), (potato) chips (*US*)

chiquenaude [ʃiknod] *nf* flick, flip

chirurgical, e, aux [ʃiʀyʀʒikal, -o] *adj* surgical

chirurgie [ʃiʀyʀʒi] *nf* surgery; **~ esthétique** plastic surgery; **chirurgien, ne** *nm/f* surgeon

choc [ʃɔk] *nm* impact; shock; crash; (*moral*) shock; (*affrontement*) clash

chocolat [ʃɔkɔla] *nm* chocolate; (*boisson*) (hot) chocolate; **~ au lait** milk chocolate

chœur [kœʀ] *nm* (*chorale*) choir; (*OPÉRA, THÉÂTRE*) chorus; **en ~** in chorus

choisir [ʃwaziʀ] *vt* to choose, select

choix [ʃwa] *nm* choice, selection; **avoir le ~** to have the choice; **premier ~** (*COMM*) class one; **de ~** choice, selected; **au ~** as you wish

chômage [ʃomaʒ] *nm* unemployment; **mettre au ~** to make redundant, put out of work; **être au ~** to be unemployed *ou* out of work; **chômeur, euse** *nm/f* unemployed person

chope [ʃɔp] *nf* tankard

choquer [ʃɔke] *vt* (*offenser*) to shock; (*commotionner*) to shake (up)

choriste [kɔʀist(ə)] *nm/f* choir member; (*OPÉRA*) chorus member

chorus [kɔʀys] *nm*: **faire ~ (avec)** to voice one's agreement (with)

chose [ʃoz] *nf* thing; **c'est peu de ~** it's nothing (really); it's not much

chou, x [ʃu] *nm* cabbage; **mon petit ~** (my) sweetheart; **~ à la crème** cream bun (*made of choux pastry*)

chouchou, te [ʃuʃu, -ut] *nm/f* (*SCOL*) teacher's pet

choucroute [ʃukʀut] *nf* sauerkraut

chouette [ʃwɛt] *nf* owl ♦ *adj* (*fam*) great, smashing

chou-fleur [ʃuflœʀ] *nm* cauliflower

choyer [ʃwaje] *vt* to cherish; to pamper

chrétien, ne [kʀetjɛ̃, -ɛn] *adj, nm/f* Christian

Christ [kʀist] *nm*: **le ~** Christ; **christianisme** *nm* Christianity

chrome [kʀom] *nm* chromium; **chromé, e** *adj* chromium-plated

chronique [kʀɔnik] *adj* chronic ♦ *nf* (*de journal*) column, page; (*historique*) chronicle; (*RADIO, TV*): **la ~ sportive/théâtrale** the sports/theatre review; **la ~ locale** local news and gossip

chronologique [kʀɔnɔlɔʒik] *adj* chronological

chronomètre [kʀɔnɔmɛtʀ(ə)] *nm* stopwatch; **chronométrer** *vt* to time

chrysanthème [kʀizɑ̃tɛm] *nm* chrysanthemum

C.H.U. *sigle m* (= *centre hospitalier universitaire*) ≈ (teaching) hospital

chuchoter [ʃyʃɔte] *vt, vi* to whisper

chuinter [ʃɥɛ̃te] *vi* to hiss

chut [ʃyt] *excl* sh!

chute [ʃyt] *nf* fall; (*de bois, papier: déchet*) scrap; **faire une ~ (de 10 m)** to fall (10 m); **~ (d'eau)** waterfall; **la ~ des cheveux** hair loss; **~ libre** free fall; **~s de pluie/neige** rain/snowfalls

Chypre [ʃipʀ] Cyprus

-ci [si] *adv voir* **par ♦** *dét*: **ce garçon-ci/-là** this/that boy; **ces femmes-ci/-là** these/those women

ci-après [siapʀɛ] *adv* hereafter

cible [sibl(ə)] *nf* target

ciboulette [sibulɛt] *nf* (small) chive

cicatrice [sikatʀis] *nf* scar

cicatriser [sikatʀize] *vt* to heal

ci-contre [sikɔ̃tʀ(ə)] *adv* opposite

ci-dessous [sidəsu] *adv* below

ci-dessus [sidəsy] *adv* above

cidre [sidʀ(ə)] *nm* cider

Cie *abr* (= *compagnie*) Co.

ciel [sjɛl] *nm* sky; (*REL*) heaven; **cieux** *nmpl* (*littéraire*) sky *sg*, skies; **à ~ ouvert** open-air; (*mine*) opencast

cierge [sjɛʀʒ(ə)] *nm* candle

cieux [sjø] *nmpl de* **ciel**

cigale [sigal] *nf* cicada

cigare [sigaʀ] *nm* cigar

cigarette [sigaʀɛt] *nf* cigarette

ci-gît [siʒi] *adv +vb* here lies

cigogne [sigɔɲ] *nf* stork

ci-inclus, e [siɛ̃kly, -yz] *adj, adv* enclosed

ci-joint, e [siʒwɛ̃, -ɛt] *adj, adv* enclosed

cil [sil] *nm* (eye)lash

cime [sim] *nf* top; (*montagne*) peak

ciment [simɑ̃] *nm* cement; **~ armé** reinforced concrete

cimetière [simtjɛʀ] *nm* cemetery; (*d'église*) churchyard

cinéaste [sineast(ə)] *nm/f* film-maker

cinéma [sinema] *nm* cinema; **cinématographique** *adj* film *cpd*, cinema *cpd*

cinéphile [sinefil] *nm/f* cinema-goer

cinglant, e [sɛ̃glɑ̃, -ɑ̃t] *adj* (*échec*) crushing

cinglé, e [sɛ̃gle] (*fam*) *adj* crazy

cingler [sɛ̃gle] *vt* to lash; (*fig*) to sting

cinq [sɛ̃k] *num* five

cinquantaine [sɛ̃kɑ̃tɛn] *nf*: **une ~ (de)** about fifty; **avoir la ~** (*âge*) to be around fifty

cinquante [sɛ̃kɑ̃t] *num* fifty; **cinquantenaire** *adj, nm/f* fifty-year-old

cinquième [sɛ̃kjɛm] *num* fifth

cintre [sɛ̃tʀ(ə)] *nm* coat-hanger

cintré, e [sɛ̃tʀe] *adj* (*chemise*) fitted

cirage [siʀaʒ] *nm* (shoe) polish

circonflexe [siʀkɔ̃flɛks(ə)] *adj*: **accent ~** circumflex accent

circonscription [siʀkɔ̃skʀipsjɔ̃] *nf* district; **~ électorale** (*d'un député*) constituency

circonscrire [siʀkɔ̃skʀiʀ] *vt* to define, delimit; (*incendie*) to contain

circonstance [siʀkɔ̃stɑ̃s] *nf* circumstance; (*occasion*) occasion

circonvenir [siʀkɔ̃vniʀ] *vt* to circumvent

circuit [siʀkɥi] *nm* (*trajet*) tour, (round) trip; (*ÉLEC, TECH*) circuit

circulaire [siʀkylɛʀ] *adj*, *nf* circular

circulation [siʀkylɑsjɔ̃] *nf* circulation; (*AUTO*): **la ~** (the) traffic

circuler [siʀkyle] *vi* to drive (along); to walk along; (*train etc*) to run; (*sang, devises*) to circulate; **faire ~** (*nouvelle*) to spread (about), circulate; (*badauds*) to move on

cire [siʀ] *nf* wax; **ciré** [siʀe] *nm* oilskin; **cirer** [siʀe] *vt* to wax, polish

cirque [siʀk(ə)] *nm* circus; (*GÉO*) cirque; (*fig*) chaos, bedlam; carry-on

cisaille(s) [sizaj] *nf(pl)* (gardening) shears *pl*

ciseau, x [sizo] *nm:* **~ (à bois)** chisel; **~x** *nmpl* (*paire de ~x*) (pair of) scissors

ciseler [sizle] *vt* to chisel, carve

citadin, e [sitadɛ̃, -in] *nm/f* city dweller

citation [sitasjɔ̃] *nf* (*d'auteur*) quotation; (*JUR*) summons *sg*

cité [site] *nf* town; (*plus grande*) city; **~ universitaire** students' residences *pl*

citer [site] *vt* (*un auteur*) to quote (from); (*nommer*) to name; (*JUR*) to summon

citerne [sitɛʀn(ə)] *nf* tank

citoyen, ne [sitwajɛ̃, -ɛn] *nm/f* citizen

citron [sitʀɔ̃] *nm* lemon; **~ vert** lime; **citronnade** *nf* lemonade; **citronnier** *nm* lemon tree

citrouille [sitʀuj] *nf* pumpkin

civet [sivɛ] *nm* stew

civière [sivjɛʀ] *nf* stretcher

civil, e [sivil] *adj* (*JUR, ADMIN, poli*) civil; (*non militaire*) civilian; **en ~** in civilian clothes; **dans le ~** in civilian life

civilisation [sivilizasjɔ̃] *nf* civilization

civisme [sivism(ə)] *nm* public-spiritedness

clair, e [klɛʀ] *adj* light; (*chambre*) light, bright; (*eau, son, fig*) clear ♦ *adv:* **voir ~** to see clearly; **tirer qch au ~** to clear sth up, clarify sth; **mettre au ~** (*notes etc*) to tidy up; **le plus ~ de son temps** the better part of his time; **~ de lune** *nm* moonlight; **clairement** *adv* clearly

clairière [klɛʀjɛʀ] *nf* clearing

clairon [klɛʀɔ̃] *nm* bugle

claironner [klɛʀɔne] *vt* (*fig*) to trumpet, shout from the rooftops

clairsemé, e [klɛʀsəme] *adj* sparse

clairvoyant, e [klɛʀvwajɑ̃, -ɑ̃t] *adj* perceptive, clear-sighted

clandestin, e [klɑ̃dɛstɛ̃, -in] *adj* clandestine, covert; **passager ~** stowaway

clapier [klapje] *nm* (rabbit) hutch

clapoter [klapɔte] *vi* to lap

claque [klak] *nf* (*gifle*) slap

claquer [klake] *vi* (*drapeau*) to flap; (*porte*) to bang, slam; (*coup de feu*) to ring out ♦ *vt* (*porte*) to slam, bang; (*doigts*) to snap; **se ~ un muscle** to pull *ou* strain a muscle

claquettes [klakɛt] *nfpl* tap-dancing *sg*

clarinette [klaʀinɛt] *nf* clarinet

clarté [klaʀte] *nf* lightness; brightness; (*d'un son, de l'eau*) clearness; (*d'une explication*) clarity

classe [klɑs] *nf* class; (*SCOL: local*) class(room); (*: leçon, élèves*) class; **faire la ~** to be a *ou* the teacher; to teach; **classement** [klɑsmɑ̃] *nm* (*rang: SCOL*) place; (*: SPORT*) placing; (*liste: SCOL*) class list (in order of merit); (*: SPORT*) placings *pl*; **classer** [klɑse] *vt* (*idées, livres*) to classify; (*papiers*) to file; (*candidat, concurrent*) to grade; (*JUR: affaire*) to close; **se classer premier/dernier** to come first/last; (*SPORT*) to finish first/last

classeur [klɑsœʀ] *nm* (*cahier*) file; (*meuble*) filing cabinet

classique [klasik] *adj* classical; (*sobre: coupe etc*) classic(al); (*habituel*) standard, classic

clause [kloz] *nf* clause

claustrer [klostʀe] *vt* to confine

clavecin [klavsɛ̃] *nm* harpsichord

clavicule [klavikyl] *nf* collarbone

clavier [klavje] *nm* keyboard

clé [kle] *nf* key; (*MUS*) clef; (*de mécanicien*) spanner (*BRIT*), wrench (*US*); **prix ~s en main** (*d'une voiture*) on-the-road price; **~ anglaise** (monkey) wrench; **~ de contact** ignition key

clef [kle] *nf* = **clé**

clément, e [klemɑ̃, -ɑ̃t] *adj* (*temps*)

mild; (*indulgent*) lenient

clerc [klɛʀ] *nm*: ~ **de notaire** solicitor's clerk

clergé [klɛʀʒe] *nm* clergy

cliché [kliʃe] *nm* (*PHOTO*) negative; print; (*LING*) cliché

client, e [klijɑ̃, -ɑ̃t] *nm/f* (*acheteur*) customer, client; (*d'hôtel*) guest, patron; (*du docteur*) patient; (*de l'avocat*) client; **clientèle** *nf* (*du magasin*) customers *pl*, clientèle; (*du docteur, de l'avocat*) practice

cligner [kliɲe] *vi*: ~ **des yeux** to blink (one's eyes); ~ **de l'œil** to wink

clignotant [kliɲɔtɑ̃] *nm* (*AUTO*) indicator

clignoter [kliɲɔte] *vi* (*étoiles etc*) to twinkle; (*lumière*) to flash; (: *vaciller*) to flicker

climat [klima] *nm* climate

climatisation [klimatizasjɔ̃] *nf* air conditioning; **climatisé, e** *adj* air-conditioned

clin d'œil [klɛ̃dœj] *nm* wink; **en un** ~ in a flash

clinique [klinik] *nf* nursing home

clinquant, e [klɛ̃kɑ̃, -ɑ̃t] *adj* flashy

cliqueter [klikte] *vi* to clash; to jangle, jingle; to chink

clochard, e [klɔʃaʀ, -aʀd(ə)] *nm/f* tramp

cloche [klɔʃ] *nf* (*d'église*) bell; (*fam*) clot; ~ **à fromage** cheese-cover

cloche-pied [klɔʃpje]: **à** ~ *adv* on one leg, hopping (along)

clocher [klɔʃe] *nm* church tower; (*en pointe*) steeple ♦ *vi* (*fam*) to be ou go wrong; **de** ~ (*péj*) parochial

cloison [klwazɔ̃] *nf* partition (wall)

cloître [klwatʀ(ə)] *nm* cloister

cloîtrer [klwatʀe] *vt*: **se** ~ to shut o.s. up ou away

cloque [klɔk] *nf* blister

clore [klɔʀ] *vt* to close; **clos, e** *adj voir* **maison; huis** ♦ *nm* (enclosed) field

clôture [klotyʀ] *nf* closure; (*barrière*) enclosure; **clôturer** *vt* (*terrain*) to enclose; (*débats*) to close

clou [klu] *nm* nail; (*MÉD*) boil; ~**s** *nmpl* (*passage clouté*) pedestrian crossing; **pneus à** ~**s** studded tyres; **le** ~ **du spectacle** the highlight of the show; ~ **de gi-**

rofle clove; **clouer** *vt* to nail down ou up

clown [klun] *nm* clown

club [klœb] *nm* club

C.N.R.S. *sigle m* = **Centre nationale de la recherche scientifique**

coasser [kɔase] *vi* to croak

cobaye [kɔbaj] *nm* guinea-pig

coca [kɔka] *nm* Coke (®)

cocaïne [kɔkain] *nf* cocaine

cocasse [kɔkas] *adj* comical, funny

coccinelle [kɔksinɛl] *nf* ladybird (*BRIT*), ladybug (*US*)

cocher [kɔʃe] *nm* coachman ♦ *vt* to tick off; (*entailler*) to notch

cochère [kɔʃɛʀ] *adj f*: **porte** ~ carriage entrance

cochon, ne [kɔʃɔ̃, -ɔn] *nm* pig ♦ *adj* (*fam*) dirty, smutty; **cochonnerie** (*fam*) *nf* filth; rubbish, trash

cocktail [kɔktɛl] *nm* cocktail; (*réception*) cocktail party

coco [kɔko] *nm voir* **noix;** (*fam*) bloke

cocorico [kɔkɔʀiko] *excl, nm* cock-a-doodle-do

cocotier [kɔkɔtje] *nm* coconut palm

cocotte [kɔkɔt] *nf* (*en fonte*) casserole; ~ **(minute)** pressure cooker; **ma** ~ (*fam*) sweetie (pie)

cocu [kɔky] *nm* cuckold

code [kɔd] *nm* code ♦ *adj*: **phares** ~**s** dipped lights; **se mettre en** ~**(s)** to dip one's (head)lights; ~ **à barres** bar code; ~ **civil** Common Law; ~ **de la route** highway code; ~ **pénal** penal code; ~ **postal** (*numéro*) post (*BRIT*) ou zip (*US*) code

cœur [kœʀ] *nm* heart; (*CARTES: couleur*) hearts *pl*; (: *carte*) heart; **avoir bon** ~ to be kind-hearted; **avoir mal au** ~ to feel sick; **en avoir le** ~ **net** to be clear in one's own mind (about it); **par** ~ by heart; **de bon** ~ willingly; **cela lui tient à** ~ that's (very) close to his heart

coffre [kɔfʀ(ə)] *nm* (*meuble*) chest; (*d'auto*) boot (*BRIT*), trunk (*US*); **coffre (-fort)** *nm* safe

coffret [kɔfʀɛ] *nm* casket

cognac [kɔɲak] *nm* brandy, cognac

cogner [kɔɲe] *vi* to knock
cohérent, e [kɔerã, -ãt] *adj* coherent, consistent
cohorte [kɔɔʀt(ə)] *nf* troop
cohue [kɔy] *nf* crowd
coi, coite [kwa, kwat] *adj*: **rester ~** to remain silent
coiffe [kwaf] *nf* headdress
coiffé, e [kwafe] *adj*: **bien/mal ~** with tidy/untidy hair; **~ en arrière** with one's hair brushed *ou* combed back
coiffer [kwafe] *vt* (*fig*) to cover, top; **se ~** *vi* to do one's hair; to put on one's hat; **~ qn** to do sb's hair
coiffeur, euse [kwafœʀ, -øz] *nm/f* hairdresser; **coiffeuse** *nf* (*table*) dressing table
coiffure [kwafyʀ] *nf* (*cheveux*) hairstyle, hairdo; (*chapeau*) hat, headgear *no pl*; (*art*): **la ~** hairdressing
coin [kwɛ̃] *nm* corner; (*pour coincer*) wedge; **l'épicerie du ~** the local grocer; **dans le ~** (*aux alentours*) in the area, around about; locally; **au ~ du feu** by the fireside; **regard en ~** sideways glance
coincé, e [kwɛ̃se] *adj* stuck, jammed; (*fig: inhibé*) inhibited, hung up (*fam*)
coincer [kwɛ̃se] *vt* to jam
coïncidence [kɔɛ̃sidãs] *nf* coincidence
coïncider [kɔɛ̃side] *vi* to coincide
col [kɔl] *nm* (*de chemise*) collar; (*encolure, cou*) neck; (*de montagne*) pass; **~ de l'utérus** cervix; **~ roulé** polo-neck
colère [kɔlɛʀ] *nf* anger; **une ~** a fit of anger; (**se mettre**) **en ~** (*to get*) angry; **coléreux, euse** *adj*, **colérique** *adj* quick-tempered, irascible
colifichet [kɔlifiʃe] *nm* trinket
colimaçon [kɔlimasɔ̃] *nm*: **escalier en ~** spiral staircase
colin [kɔlɛ̃] *nm* hake
colique [kɔlik] *nf* diarrhoea; colic (*pains*)
colis [kɔli] *nm* parcel
collaborateur, trice [kɔlabɔʀatœʀ, -tʀis] *nm/f* (*aussi POL*) collaborator; (*d'une revue*) contributor
collaborer [kɔlabɔʀe] *vi* to collaborate; **~ à** to collaborate on; (*revue*) to contribute

to
collant, e [kɔlã, -ãt] *adj* sticky; (*robe etc*) clinging, skintight; (*péj*) clinging ♦ *nm* (*bas*) tights *pl*
collation [kɔlasjɔ̃] *nf* light meal
colle [kɔl] *nf* glue; (*à papiers peints*) (wallpaper) paste; (*devinette*) teaser, riddle; (*SCOL: fam*) detention
collecte [kɔlɛkt(ə)] *nf* collection
collectif, ive [kɔlɛktif, -iv] *adj* collective; (*visite, billet*) group *cpd*
collection [kɔlɛksjɔ̃] *nf* collection; (*ÉDITION*) series; **collectionner** *vt* (*tableaux, timbres*) to collect; **collectionneur, euse** *nm/f* collector
collectivité [kɔlɛktivite] *nf* group; **~s locales** *nfpl* (*ADMIN*) local authorities
collège [kɔlɛʒ] *nm* (*école*) (secondary) school; (*assemblée*) body; **collégien** *nm* schoolboy; **collégienne** *nf* schoolgirl
collègue [kɔlɛg] *nm/f* colleague
coller [kɔle] *vt* (*papier, timbre*) to stick (on); (*affiche*) to stick up; (*enveloppe*) to stick down; (*morceaux*) to stick *ou* glue together; (*fam: mettre, fourrer*) to stick, shove; (*SCOL: fam*) to keep in ♦ *vi* (*être collant*) to be sticky; (*adhérer*) to stick; **~ à** to stick to
collet [kɔlɛ] *nm* (*piège*) snare, noose; (*cou*): **prendre qn au ~** to grab sb by the throat; **~ monté** *adj inv* straightlaced
collier [kɔlje] *nm* (*bijou*) necklace; (*de chien, TECH*) collar; **~ (de barbe)** narrow beard along the line of the jaw
collimateur [kɔlimatœʀ] *nm*: **avoir qn/qch dans le ~** (*fig*) to have sb/sth in one's sights
colline [kɔlin] *nf* hill
collision [kɔlizjɔ̃] *nf* collision, crash; **entrer en ~ (avec)** to collide (with)
colmater [kɔlmate] *vt* (*fuite*) to seal off; (*brèche*) to plug, fill in
colombe [kɔlɔ̃b] *nf* dove
colon [kɔlɔ̃] *nm* settler
colonel [kɔlɔnɛl] *nm* colonel
colonie [kɔlɔni] *nf* colony; **~ (de vacances)** holiday camp (*for children*)
colonne [kɔlɔn] *nf* column; **se mettre**

en ~ par deux to get into twos; **~ (ver-tébrale)** spine, spinal column
colorant [kɔlɔʀɑ̃] *nm* colouring
colorer [kɔlɔʀe] *vt* to colour
colorier [kɔlɔʀje] *vt* to colour (in)
coloris [kɔlɔʀi] *nm* colour, shade
colporter [kɔlpɔʀte] *vt* to hawk, peddle
colza [kɔlza] *nm* rape (seed)
coma [kɔma] *nm* coma
combat [kɔ̃ba] *nm* fight; fighting *no pl*; **~ de boxe** boxing match
combattant [kɔ̃batɑ̃] *nm*: **ancien ~** war veteran
combattre [kɔ̃batʀ(ə)] *vt* to fight; (*épidémie, ignorance*) to combat, fight against
combien [kɔ̃bjɛ̃] *adv* (*quantité*) how much; (*nombre*) how many; (*exclamatif*) how; **~ de** how much; how many; **~ de temps** how long; **~ coûte/pèse ceci?** how much does this cost/weigh?
combinaison [kɔ̃binɛzɔ̃] *nf* combination; (*astuce*) device, scheme; (*de femme*) slip; (*d'aviateur*) flying suit; (*d'homme-grenouille*) wetsuit; (*bleu de travail*) boiler suit (*BRIT*), coveralls *pl* (*US*)
combine [kɔ̃bin] *nf* trick; (*péj*) scheme, fiddle (*BRIT*)
combiné [kɔ̃bine] *nm* (*aussi: ~ téléphonique*) receiver
combiner [kɔ̃bine] *vt* to combine; (*plan, horaire*) to work out, devise
comble [kɔ̃bl(ə)] *adj* (*salle*) packed (full) ♦ *nm* (*du bonheur, plaisir*) height; **~s** *nmpl* (*CONSTR*) attic *sg*, loft *sg*; **c'est le ~!** that beats everything!
combler [kɔ̃ble] *vt* (*trou*) to fill in; (*besoin, lacune*) to fill; (*déficit*) to make good; (*satisfaire*) to fulfil
combustible [kɔ̃bystibl(ə)] *nm* fuel
comédie [kɔmedi] *nf* comedy; (*fig*) play-acting *no pl*; **~ musicale** musical; **comédien, ne** *nm/f* actor(tress)
comestible [kɔmɛstibl(ə)] *adj* edible
comique [kɔmik] *adj* (*drôle*) comical; (*THÉÂTRE*) comic ♦ *nm* (*artiste*) comic, comedian
comité [kɔmite] *nm* committee; **~ d'entreprise** works council

commandant [kɔmɑ̃dɑ̃] *nm* (*gén*) commander, commandant; (*NAVIG, AVIAT*) captain
commande [kɔmɑ̃d] *nf* (*COMM*) order; **~s** *nfpl* (*AVIAT etc*) controls; **sur ~** to order; **~ à distance** remote control
commandement [kɔmɑ̃dmɑ̃] *nm* command; (*REL*) commandment
commander [kɔmɑ̃de] *vt* (*COMM*) to order; (*diriger, ordonner*) to command; **~ à qn de faire** to command *ou* order sb to do
commando [kɔmɑ̃do] *nm* commando (squad)

MOT-CLÉ

---

comme [kɔm] *prép* **1** (*comparaison*) like; **tout ~ son père** just like his father; **fort ~ un bœuf** as strong as an ox; **joli ~ tout** ever so pretty

2 (*manière*) like; **faites-le ~ ça** do it like this, do it this way; **~ ci, ~ ça** so-so, middling

3 (*en tant que*) as a; **donner ~ prix** to give as a prize; **travailler ~ secrétaire** to work as a secretary

♦ *conj* **1** (*ainsi que*) as; **elle écrit ~ elle parle** she writes as she talks; **~ si** as if

2 (*au moment où, alors que*) as; **il est parti ~ j'arrivais** he left as I arrived

3 (*parce que, puisque*) as; **~ il était en retard, il ...** as he was late, he ...

♦ *adv*: **~ il est fort/c'est bon!** he's so strong/it's so good!

---

commémorer [kɔmemɔʀe] *vt* to commemorate
commencement [kɔmɑ̃smɑ̃] *nm* beginning, start, commencement
commencer [kɔmɑ̃se] *vt, vi* to begin, start, commence; **~ à** *ou* **de faire** to begin *ou* start doing
comment [kɔmɑ̃] *adv* how ♦ *nm*: **le ~ et le pourquoi** the whys and wherefores; **~?** (*que dites-vous*) pardon?
commentaire [kɔmɑ̃tɛʀ] *nm* comment; remark
commenter [kɔmɑ̃te] *vt* (*jugement, événement*) to comment (up)on; (*RADIO, TV*:

match, manifestation) to cover

commérages [kɔmeʀaʒ] *nmpl* gossip *sg*

commerçant, e [kɔmɛʀsɑ̃, -ɑ̃t] *nm/f* shopkeeper, trader

commerce [kɔmɛʀs(ə)] *nm* (*activité*) trade, commerce; (*boutique*) business; **vendu dans le ~** sold in the shops; **commercial, e, aux** *adj* commercial, trading; (*péj*) commercial; **les commerciaux** the sales people; **commercialiser** *vt* to market

commère [kɔmɛʀ] *nf* gossip

commettre [kɔmɛtʀ(ə)] *vt* to commit

commis [kɔmi] *nm* (*de magasin*) (shop) assistant; (*de banque*) clerk; **~ voyageur** commercial traveller

commissaire [kɔmisɛʀ] *nm* (*de police*) ≈ (police) superintendent; **~-priseur** *nm* auctioneer

commissariat [kɔmisaʀja] *nm* police station

commission [kɔmisjɔ̃] *nf* (*comité, pourcentage*) commission; (*message*) message; (*course*) errand; **~s** *nfpl* (*achats*) shopping *sg*

commode [kɔmɔd] *adj* (*pratique*) convenient, handy; (*facile*) easy; (*air, personne*) easy-going; (*personne*): **pas ~** awkward (to deal with) ♦ *nf* chest of drawers; **commodité** *nf* convenience

commotion [kɔmosjɔ̃] *nf*: **~ (cérébrale)** concussion; **commotionné, e** *adj* shocked, shaken

commun, e [kɔmœ̃, -yn] *adj* common; (*pièce*) communal, shared; (*réunion, effort*) joint; **cela sort du ~** it's out of the ordinary; **le ~ des mortels** the common run of people; **en ~ (faire)** jointly; **mettre en ~** to pool, share; *voir aussi* **communs**

communauté [kɔmynote] *nf* community; (*JUR*): **régime de la ~** communal estate settlement

commune [kɔmyn] *nf* (*ADMIN*) commune, ≈ district; (: *urbaine*) ≈ borough

communication [kɔmynikasjɔ̃] *nf* communication; **~ (téléphonique)** (telephone) call

communier [kɔmynje] *vi* (*REL*) to re-

ceive communion; (*fig*) to be united; **communion** [kɔmynjɔ̃] *nf* communion

communiquer [kɔmynike] *vt* (*nouvelle, dossier*) to pass on, convey; (*maladie*) to pass on; (*peur etc*) to communicate; (*chaleur, mouvement*) to transmit ♦ *vi* to communicate; **se ~ à** (*se propager*) to spread to

communisme [kɔmynism(ə)] *nm* communism; **communiste** *adj, nm/f* communist

communs [kɔmœ̃] *nmpl* (*bâtiments*) outbuildings

commutateur [kɔmytatœʀ] *nm* (*ÉLEC*) (change-over) switch, commutator

compact, e [kɔ̃pakt] *adj* dense; compact

compagne [kɔ̃paɲ] *nf* companion

compagnie [kɔ̃paɲi] *nf* (*firme, MIL*) company; (*groupe*) gathering; **tenir ~ à qn** to keep sb company; **fausser ~ à qn** to give sb the slip, slip *ou* sneak away from sb; **~ aérienne** airline (company)

compagnon [kɔ̃paɲɔ̃] *nm* companion

comparable [kɔ̃paʀabl(ə)] *adj*: **~ (à)** comparable (to)

comparaison [kɔ̃paʀɛzɔ̃] *nf* comparison

comparaître [kɔ̃paʀɛtʀ(ə)] *vi*: **~ (devant)** to appear (before)

comparer [kɔ̃paʀe] *vt* to compare; **~ qch/qn à** *ou* **et** (*pour choisir*) to compare sth/sb with *ou* and; (*pour établir une similitude*) to compare sth/sb to

comparse [kɔ̃paʀs(ə)] (*péj*) *nm/f* associate, stooge

compartiment [kɔ̃paʀtimɑ̃] *nm* compartment

comparution [kɔ̃paʀysjɔ̃] *nf* appearance

compas [kɔ̃pa] *nm* (*GÉOM*) (pair of) compasses *pl*; (*NAVIG*) compass

compatible [kɔ̃patibl(ə)] *adj* compatible

compatir [kɔ̃patiʀ] *vi*: **~ (à)** to sympathize (with)

compatriote [kɔ̃patʀijɔt] *nm/f* compatriot

compenser [kɔ̃pɑ̃se] *vt* to compensate for, make up for

compère [kɔ̃pɛʀ] *nm* accomplice

compétence [kɔ̃petɑ̃s] *nf* competence

compétent, e [kɔ̃petɑ̃, -ɑ̃t] *adj* (*apte*)

competent, capable

compétition [kɔpetisjɔ̃] *nf* (*gén*) competition; (*SPORT: épreuve*) event; **la ~** competitive sport; **la ~ automobile** motor racing

complainte [kɔ̃plɛ̃t] *nf* lament

complaire [kɔ̃plɛʀ]: **se ~** *vi*: **se ~ dans/parmi** to take pleasure in/in being among

complaisance [kɔ̃plɛzɑ̃s] *nf* kindness; **pavillon de ~** flag of convenience; **complaisant, e** [kɔ̃plɛzɑ̃, -ɑ̃t] *adj* (*aimable*) kind, obliging

complément [kɔ̃plemɑ̃] *nm* complement; remainder; **~ d'information** (*ADMIN*) supplementary *ou* further information; **complémentaire** *adj* complementary; (*additionnel*) supplementary

complet, ète [kɔ̃plɛ, -ɛt] *adj* (*plein: hôtel etc*) full ♦ *nm* (*aussi: ~-veston*) suit; **complètement** *adv* completely; **compléter** *vt* (*porter à la quantité voulue*) to complete; (*augmenter*) to complement, supplement; (*ajouter à*) to add to

complexe [kɔ̃plɛks(ə)] *adj, nm* complex; **complexé, e** *adj* mixed-up, hung-up

complication [kɔ̃plikasjɔ̃] *nf* complexity, intricacy; (*difficulté, ennui*) complication

complice [kɔ̃plis] *nm* accomplice

compliment [kɔ̃plimɑ̃] *nm* (*louange*) compliment; **~s** *nmpl* (*félicitations*) congratulations

compliqué, e [kɔ̃plike] *adj* complicated, complex; (*personne*) complicated

complot [kɔ̃plo] *nm* plot

comportement [kɔ̃pɔʀtəmɑ̃] *nm* behaviour

comporter [kɔ̃pɔʀte] *vt* to consist of, comprise; (*être équipé de*) to have; (*impliquer*) to entail; **se ~** *vi* to behave

composant [kɔ̃pozɑ̃] *nm* component

composante [kɔ̃pozɑ̃t] *nf* component

composé [kɔ̃poze] *nm* compound

composer [kɔ̃poze] *vt* (*musique, texte*) to compose; (*mélange, équipe*) to make up; (*faire partie de*) to make up, form ♦ *vi* (*transiger*) to come to terms; **se ~ de** to be composed of, be made up of; **~**

un numéro to dial a number

compositeur, trice [kɔ̃pozitœʀ, -tʀis] *nm/f* (*MUS*) composer

composition [kɔ̃pozisjɔ̃] *nf* composition; (*SCOL*) test; **de bonne ~** (*accommodant*) easy to deal with

composter [kɔ̃pɔste] *vt* to date-stamp; to punch

compote [kɔ̃pɔt] *nf* stewed fruit *no pl*; **~ de pommes** stewed apples; **compotier** *nm* fruit dish *ou* bowl

compréhensible [kɔ̃pʀeɑ̃sibl(ə)] *adj* comprehensible; (*attitude*) understandable

compréhensif, ive [kɔ̃pʀeɑ̃sif, -iv] *adj* understanding

comprendre [kɔ̃pʀɑ̃dʀ(ə)] *vt* to understand; (*se composer de*) to comprise, consist of

compresse [kɔ̃pʀɛs] *nf* compress

compression [kɔ̃pʀesjɔ̃] *nf* compression; reduction

comprimé [kɔ̃pʀime] *nm* tablet

comprimer [kɔ̃pʀime] *vt* to compress; (*fig: crédit etc*) to reduce, cut down

compris, e [kɔ̃pʀi, -iz] *pp de* **comprendre** ♦ *adj* (*inclus*) included; **~ entre** (*situé*) contained between; **la maison ~e/non ~e, y/non ~ la maison** including/excluding the house; **100 F tout ~** 100 F all inclusive *ou* all-in

compromettre [kɔ̃pʀɔmɛtʀ(ə)] *vt* to compromise

compromis [kɔ̃pʀɔmi] *nm* compromise

comptabilité [kɔ̃tabilite] *nf* (*activité, technique*) accounting, accountancy; (*d'une société: comptes*) accounts *pl*, books *pl*; (: *service*) accounts office

comptable [kɔ̃tabl(ə)] *nm/f* accountant

comptant [kɔ̃tɑ̃] *adv*: **payer ~** to pay cash; **acheter ~** to buy for cash

compte [kɔ̃t] *nm* count, counting; (*total, montant*) count, (right) number; (*bancaire, facture*) account; **~s** *nmpl* (*FINANCE*) accounts, books; (*fig*) explanation *sg*; **en fin de ~** all things considered; **à bon ~** at a favourable price; (*fig*) lightly; **avoir son ~** (: *fam*) to have had it; **pour le ~ de** on behalf of; **pour son propre ~**

for one's own benefit; **tenir ~ de** to take account of; **travailler à son ~** to work for oneself; **rendre ~ (à qn) de qch** to give (sb) an account of sth; *voir aussi* **rendre**; **~ à rebours** countdown; **~ chèques postaux** Post Office account; **~ courant** current account

compte-gouttes [kɔ̃tgut] *nm inv* dropper

compter [kɔ̃te] *vt* to count; (*facturer*) to charge for; (*avoir à son actif, comporter*) to have; (*prévoir*) to plan, (*penser, espérer*): **~ réussir** to expect to succeed ♦ *vi* to count; (*être économe*) to economize; (*figurer*): **~ parmi** to be *ou* rank among; **~ sur** to count (up)on; **~ avec qch/qn** to reckon with *ou* take account of sth/sb; **sans ~ que** besides which

compte rendu [kɔ̃tRɑ̃dy] *nm* account, report; (*de film, livre*) review

compte-tours [kɔ̃ttuR] *nm inv* rev(olution) counter

compteur [kɔ̃tœR] *nm* meter; **~ de vitesse** speedometer

comptine [kɔ̃tin] *nf* nursery rhyme

comptoir [kɔ̃twaR] *nm* (*de magasin*) counter

compulser [kɔ̃pylse] *vt* to consult

comte [kɔ̃t] *nm* count

comtesse [kɔ̃tɛs] *nf* countess

con, ne [kɔ̃, kɔn] (*fam!*) *adj* damned *ou* bloody (*BRIT*) stupid (!)

concéder [kɔ̃sede] *vt* to grant; (*défaite, point*) to concede

concentrer [kɔ̃sɑ̃tRe] *vt* to concentrate; **se ~** *vi* to concentrate

concept [kɔ̃sɛpt] *nm* concept

conception [kɔ̃sɛpsjɔ̃] *nf* conception; (*d'une machine etc*) design; (*d'un problème, de la vie etc*) approach

concerner [kɔ̃sɛRne] *vt* to concern; **en ce qui me concerne** as far as I am concerned

concert [kɔ̃sɛR] *nm* concert; **de ~** in unison; together

concerter [kɔ̃sɛRte] *vt* to devise; **se ~** *vi* (*collaborateurs etc*) to put our (*ou* their *etc*) heads together

concessionnaire [kɔ̃sesjɔnɛR] *nm/f* agent, dealer

concevoir [kɔ̃svwaR] *vt* (*idée, projet*) to conceive (of); (*méthode, plan d'appartement, décoration*) to plan, design; (*enfant*) to conceive; **bien/mal conçu** well-/badly-designed

concierge [kɔ̃sjɛRʒ(ə)] *nm/f* caretaker; (*d'hôtel*) head porter

concile [kɔ̃sil] *nm* council

conciliabules [kɔ̃siljabyl] *nmpl* (private) discussions, confabulations

concilier [kɔ̃silje] *vt* to reconcile; **se ~** *vt* to win over

concitoyen, ne [kɔ̃sitwajɛ̃, -jɛn] *nm/f* fellow citizen

concluant, e [kɔ̃klyɑ̃, -ɑ̃t] *adj* conclusive

conclure [kɔ̃klyR] *vt* to conclude

conclusion [kɔ̃klyzjɔ̃] *nf* conclusion

conçois *etc vb voir* **concevoir**

concombre [kɔ̃kɔ̃bR(ə)] *nm* cucumber

concorder [kɔ̃kɔRde] *vi* to tally, agree

concourir [kɔ̃kuRiR] *vi* (*SPORT*) to compete; **~ à** (*effet etc*) to work towards

concours [kɔ̃kuR] *nm* competition; (*SCOL*) competitive examination; (*assistance*) aid, help; **~ de circonstances** combination of circumstances; **~ hippique** horse show

concret, ète [kɔ̃kRɛ, -ɛt] *adj* concrete

concrétiser [kɔ̃kretize] *vt* (*plan, projet*) to put in concrete form; **se ~** *vi* to materialize

conçu, e [kɔ̃sy] *pp de* **concevoir**

concubinage [kɔ̃kybinaʒ] *nm* (*JUR*) cohabitation

concurrence [kɔ̃kyRɑ̃s] *nf* competition; **jusqu'à ~ de** up to

concurrent, e [kɔ̃kyRɑ̃, -ɑ̃t] *nm/f* (*SPORT, ÉCON etc*) competitor; (*SCOL*) candidate

condamner [kɔ̃dane] *vt* (*blâmer*) to condemn; (*JUR*) to sentence; (*porte, ouverture*) to fill in, block up; (*malade*) to give up (hope for); **~ qn à 2 ans de prison** to sentence sb to 2 years' imprisonment

condensation [kɔ̃dɑ̃sɑsjɔ̃] *nf* condensation

condenser [kɔ̃dɑse] *vt* to condense; **se ~** *vi* to condense

condisciple [kɔ̃disipl(ə)] *nm/f* school fellow, fellow student

condition [kɔ̃disjɔ̃] *nf* condition; **~s** *nfpl* (*tarif, prix*) terms; (*circonstances*) conditions; **sans ~** unconditional ♦ *adv* unconditionally; **à ~ de** *ou* **que** provided that; **conditionnel, le** *adj* conditional ♦ *nm* conditional (tense)

conditionnement [kɑ̃disjɔnmɑ̃] *nm* (*emballage*) packaging

conditionner [kɔ̃disjɔne] *vt* (*déterminer*) to determine; (*COMM: produit*) to package; (*fig: personne*) to condition; **air conditionné** air conditioning

condoléances [kɔ̃dɔleɑs] *nfpl* condolences

conducteur, trice [kɔ̃dyktœʀ, -tʀis] *nm/f* driver ♦ *nm* (*ÉLEC etc*) conductor

conduire [kɔ̃dɥiʀ] *vt* to drive; (*délégation, troupeau*) to lead; **se ~** *vi* to behave; **~ vers/à** to lead towards/to; **~ qn quelque part** to take sb somewhere; to drive sb somewhere

conduite [kɔ̃dɥit] *nf* (*comportement*) behaviour; (*d'eau, de gaz*) pipe; **sous la ~ de** led by; **~ à gauche** left-hand drive; **~ intérieure** saloon (car)

cône [kon] *nm* cone

confection [kɔ̃fɛksjɔ̃] *nf* (*fabrication*) making; (*COUTURE*): **la ~** the clothing industry; **vêtement de ~** ready-to-wear *ou* off-the-peg garment

confectionner [kɔ̃fɛksjɔne] *vt* to make

conférence [kɔ̃feʀɑs] *nf* (*exposé*) lecture; (*pourparlers*) conference; **~ de presse** press conference

confesser [kɔ̃fese] *vt* to confess; **se ~** *vi* (*REL*) to go to confession

confession [kɔ̃fesjɔ̃] *nf* confession; (*culte: catholique etc*) denomination

confiance [kɔ̃fjɑs] *nf* confidence, trust; faith; **avoir ~ en** to have confidence *ou* faith in, trust; **mettre qn en ~** to win sb's trust; **~ en soi** self-confidence

confiant, e [kɔ̃fjɑ̃, -ɑ̃t] *adj* confident; trusting

confidence [kɔ̃fidɑs] *nf* confidence

confidentiel, le [kɔ̃fidɑsjɛl] *adj* confidential

confier [kɔ̃fje] *vt*: **~ à qn** (*objet en dépôt, travail etc*) to entrust to sb; (*secret, pensée*) to confide to sb; **se ~ à qn** to confide in sb

confiné, e [kɔ̃fine] *adj* enclosed; stale

confins [kɔ̃fɛ̃] *nmpl*: **aux ~ de** on the borders of

confirmation [kɔ̃fiʀmasjɔ̃] *nf* confirmation

confirmer [kɔ̃fiʀme] *vt* to confirm

confiserie [kɔ̃fizʀi] *nf* (*magasin*) confectioner's *ou* sweet shop; **~s** *nfpl* (*bonbons*) confectionery *sg*; **confiseur, euse** *nm/f* confectioner

confisquer [kɔ̃fiske] *vt* to confiscate

confit, e [kɔ̃fi, -it] *adj*: **fruits ~s** crystallized fruits ♦ *nm*: **~ d'oie** conserve of goose

confiture [kɔ̃fityʀ] *nf* jam; **~ d'oranges** (orange) marmalade

conflit [kɔ̃fli] *nm* conflict

confondre [kɔ̃fɔ̃dʀ(ə)] *vt* (*jumeaux, faits*) to confuse, mix up; (*témoin, menteur*) to confound; **se ~** *vi* to merge; **se ~ en excuses** to apologize profusely; **confondu, e** [kɔ̃fɔ̃dy] *adj* (*stupéfait*) speechless, overcome

conforme [kɔ̃fɔʀm(ə)] *adj*: **~ à** in accordance with; in keeping with; true to

conformément [kɔ̃fɔʀmemɑ̃] *adv*: **~ à** in accordance with

conformer [kɔ̃fɔʀme] *vt*: **se ~ à** to conform to

conformité [kɔ̃fɔʀmite] *nf*: **en ~ avec** in accordance with, in keeping with

confort [kɔ̃fɔʀ] *nm* comfort; **tout ~** (*COMM*) with all modern conveniences; **confortable** *adj* comfortable

confrère [kɔ̃fʀɛʀ] *nm* colleague; fellow member; **confrérie** *nf* brotherhood

confronter [kɔ̃fʀɔ̃te] *vt* to confront; (*textes*) to compare, collate

confus, e [kɔ̃fy, -yz] *adj* (*vague*) confused; (*embarrassé*) embarrassed

confusion [kɔ̃fyzjɔ̃] *nf* (*voir confus*) confusion; embarrassment; (*voir confondre*) confusion, mixing up

congé [kɔ̃ʒe] *nm* (*vacances*) holiday; **en ~** on holiday; off (work); **semaine de ~** week off; **prendre ~ de qn** to take one's leave of sb; **donner son ~ à** to give in one's notice to; **~ de maladie** sick leave; **~s payés** paid holiday

congédier [kɔ̃ʒedje] *vt* to dismiss

congélateur [kɔ̃ʒelatœr] *nm* freezer, deep freeze

congeler [kɔ̃ʒle] *vt* to freeze

congestion [kɔ̃ʒɛstjɔ̃] *nf* congestion; **~ cérébrale** stroke

congestionner [kɔ̃ʒɛstjɔne] *vt* to congest; (*MÉD*) to flush

congrès [kɔ̃grɛ] *nm* congress

congru, e [kɔ̃gry] *adj*: **la portion ~e** the smallest *ou* meanest share

conifère [kɔnifɛr] *nm* conifer

conjecture [kɑ̃ʒɛktyr] *nf* conjecture

conjoint, e [kɔ̃ʒwɛ̃, -wɛ̃t] *adj* joint ♦ *nm/f* spouse

conjonction [kɔ̃ʒɔ̃ksjɔ̃] *nf* (*LING*) conjunction

conjonctivite [kɔ̃ʒɔ̃ktivit] *nf* conjunctivitis

conjoncture [kɔ̃ʒɔ̃ktyr] *nf* circumstances *pl*; climate

conjugaison [kɔ̃ʒygɛzɔ̃] *nf* (*LING*) conjugation

conjuger [kɔ̃ʒyge] *vt* (*LING*) to conjugate; (*efforts etc*) to combine

conjuration [kɔ̃ʒyrasjɔ̃] *nf* conspiracy

conjurer [kɔ̃ʒyre] *vt* (*sort, maladie*) to avert; (*implorer*) to beseech, entreat

connaissance [kɔnɛsɑ̃s] *nf* (*savoir*) knowledge *no pl*; (*personne connue*) acquaintance; **être sans ~** to be unconscious; **perdre/reprendre ~** to lose/regain consciousness; **à ma/sa ~** to (the best of) my/his knowledge; **avoir ~ de** to be aware of; **prendre ~ de** (*document etc*) to peruse; **en ~ de cause** with full knowledge of the facts

connaître [kɔnɛtr(ə)] *vt* to know; (*éprouver*) to experience; (*avoir*) to have; to enjoy; **~ de nom/vue** to know by name/sight; **ils se sont connus à Genève** they (first) met in Geneva

connecté, e [kɔnɛkte] *adj* on line

connecter [kɔnɛkte] *vt* to connect

connerie [kɔnri] (*fam!*) *nf* stupid thing (to do *ou* say)

connu, e [kɔny] *adj* (*célèbre*) well-known

conquérir [kɔ̃kerir] *vt* to conquer, win; **conquête** *nf* conquest

consacrer [kɔ̃sakre] *vt* (*REL*) to consecrate; (*fig*: *usage etc*) to sanction, establish; (*employer*) to devote, dedicate

conscience [kɔ̃sjɑ̃s] *nf* conscience; **avoir/prendre ~ de** to be/become aware of; **perdre ~** to lose consciousness; **avoir bonne/mauvaise ~** to have a clear/guilty conscience; **consciencieux, euse** *adj* conscientious; **conscient, e** *adj* conscious

conscrit [kɔ̃skri] *nm* conscript

consécutif, ive [kɔ̃sekytif, -iv] *adj* consecutive; **~ à** following upon

conseil [kɔ̃sɛj] *nm* (*avis*) piece of advice, advice *no pl*; (*assemblée*) council; **prendre ~ (auprès de qn)** to take advice (from sb); **~ d'administration** board (of directors); **le ~ des ministres** ≈ the Cabinet

conseiller, ère [kɔ̃seje, kɔ̃sejɛr] *nm/f* adviser ♦ *vt* (*personne*) to advise; (*méthode, action*) to recommend, advise; **~ à qn de** to advise sb to

consentement [kɔ̃sɑ̃tmɑ̃] *nm* consent

consentir [kɔ̃sɑ̃tir] *vt* to agree, consent

conséquence [kɔ̃sekɑ̃s] *nf* consequence; **en ~** (*donc*) consequently; (*de façon appropriée*) accordingly; **ne pas tirer à ~** to be unlikely to have any repercussions

conséquent, e [kɔ̃sekɑ̃, -ɑ̃t] *adj* logical, rational; (*fam*: *important*) substantial; **par ~** consequently

conservateur, trice [kɔ̃sɛrvatœr, -tris] *nm/f* (*POL*) conservative; (*de musée*) curator

conservatoire [kɔ̃sɛrvatwar] *nm* academy; (*ÉCOLOGIE*) conservation area

conserve [kɔ̃sɛrv(ə)] *nf* (*gén pl*) canned *ou* tinned (*BRIT*) food; **en ~** canned, tinned (*BRIT*)

conserver [kɔ̃sɛrve] *vt* (*faculté*) to retain, keep; (*amis, livres*) to keep; (*pré-*

server, aussi CULIN) to preserve

considérable [kɔ̃sideʀabl(ə)] *adj* considerable, significant, extensive

considération [kɔ̃sideʀasjɔ̃] *nf* consideration; (*estime*) esteem

considérer [kɔ̃sideʀe] *vt* to consider; ~ **qch comme** to regard sth as

consigne [kɔ̃siɲ] *nf* (*de gare*) left luggage (office) (BRIT), checkroom (US); (*ordre, instruction*) instructions *pl*; ~ **(automatique)** left-luggage locker; **consigner** [kɔ̃siɲe] *vt* (*note, pensée*) to record; (*punir*) to confine to barracks; to put in detention; (COMM) to put a deposit on

consistant, e [kɔ̃sistɑ̃, -ɑ̃t] *adj* thick; solid

consister [kɔ̃siste] *vi*: ~ **en/dans/à faire** to consist of/in/in doing

consœur [kɔ̃sœʀ] *nf* (lady) colleague; fellow member

consoler [kɔ̃sɔle] *vt* to console

consolider [kɔ̃sɔlide] *vt* to strengthen; (*fig*) to consolidate

consommateur, trice [kɔ̃sɔmatœʀ, -tʀis] *nm/f* (ÉCON) consumer; (*dans un café*) customer

consommation [kɔ̃sɔmasjɔ̃] *nf* (*boisson*) drink; ~ **aux 100 km** (AUTO) (fuel) consumption per 100 km

consommer [kɔ̃sɔme] *vt* (*suj: personne*) to eat *ou* drink, consume; (: *voiture, usine, poêle*) to use, consume ♦ *vi* (*dans un café*) to (have a) drink

consonne [kɔ̃sɔn] *nf* consonant

conspirer [kɔ̃spiʀe] *vi* to conspire

constamment [kɔ̃stamɑ̃] *adv* constantly

constant, e [kɔ̃stɑ̃, -ɑ̃t] *adj* constant; (*personne*) steadfast

constat [kɔ̃sta] *nm* (*d'huissier*) certified report; (*de police*) report; (*affirmation*) statement

constatation [kɔ̃statasjɔ̃] *nf* (*observation*) observed fact, observation; (*affirmation*) statement

constater [kɔ̃state] *vt* (*remarquer*) to note; (ADMIN, JUR: *attester*) to certify; (*dire*) to state

consterner [kɔ̃stɛʀne] *vt* to dismay

constipé, e [kɔ̃stipe] *adj* constipated

constitué, e [kɔ̃stitɥe] *adj*: ~ **de** made up *ou* composed of

constituer [kɔ̃stitɥe] *vt* (*comité, équipe*) to set up; (*dossier, collection*) to put together; (*suj: éléments: composer*) to make up, constitute; (*représenter, être*) to constitute; **se** ~ **prisonnier** to give o.s. up

constitution [kɔ̃stitysjɔ̃] *nf* (*composition*) composition, make-up; (*santé, POL*) constitution

constructeur [kɔ̃stʀyktœʀ] *nm* manufacturer, builder

construction [kɔ̃stʀyksjɔ̃] *nf* construction, building

construire [kɔ̃stʀɥiʀ] *vt* to build, construct

consul [kɔ̃syl] *nm* consul; **consulat** *nm* consulate

consultant [kɔ̃syltɑ̃] *adj, nm* consultant

consultation [kɔ̃syltasjɔ̃] *nf* consultation; ~**s** *nfpl* (POL) talks; **heures de** ~ (MÉD) surgery (BRIT) *ou* office (US) hours

consulter [kɔ̃sylte] *vt* to consult ♦ *vi* (*médecin*) to hold surgery (BRIT), be in (the office) (US)

consumer [kɔ̃syme] *vt* to consume; **se** ~ *vi* to burn

contact [kɔ̃takt] *nm* contact; **au** ~ **de** (*air, peau*) on contact with; (*gens*) through contact with; **mettre/couper le** ~ (AUTO) to switch on/off the ignition; **entrer en** *ou* **prendre** ~ **avec** to get in touch *ou* contact with; **contacter** *vt* to contact, get in touch with

contagieux, euse [kɔ̃taʒjø, -øz] *adj* contagious; infectious

contaminer [kɔ̃tamine] *vt* to contaminate

conte [kɔ̃t] *nm* tale; ~ **de fées** fairy tale

contempler [kɔ̃tɑ̃ple] *vt* to contemplate, gaze at

contemporain, e [kɔ̃tɑ̃pɔʀɛ̃, -ɛn] *adj, nm/f* contemporary

contenance [kɔ̃tnɑ̃s] *nf* (*d'un récipient*) capacity; (*attitude*) bearing, attitude; **perdre** ~ to lose one's composure

conteneur [kɔ̃tnœʀ] *nm* container

contenir [kɔ̃tniʀ] *vt* to contain; (*avoir une capacité de*) to hold

content, e [kɔ̃tɑ̃, -ɑ̃t] *adj* pleased, glad; ~ **de** pleased with; **contenter** *vt* to satisfy, please; **se contenter de** to content o.s. with

contentieux [kɔ̃tɑ̃sjø] *nm* (COMM) litigation; litigation department

contenu [kɔ̃tny] *nm* (*d'un bol*) contents *pl*; (*d'un texte*) content

conter [kɔ̃te] *vt* to recount, relate

contestable [kɔ̃tɛstabl(ə)] *adj* questionable

contestation [kɔ̃tɛstasjɔ̃] *nf* (POL) protest

conteste [kɔ̃tɛst(ə)]: **sans ~** *adv* unquestionably, indisputably

contester [kɔ̃tɛste] *vt* to question, contest ♦ *vi* (POL, *gén*) to protest, rebel (against established authority)

contexte [kɔ̃tɛkst(ə)] *nm* context

contigu, ë [kɔ̃tigy] *adj*: ~ **(à)** adjacent (to)

continent [kɔ̃tinɑ̃] *nm* continent

continu, e [kɔ̃tiny] *adj* continuous; **(courant)** ~ direct current, DC

continuel, le [kɔ̃tinɥɛl] *adj* (*qui se répète*) constant, continual; (*continu*) continuous

continuer [kɔ̃tinɥe] *vt* (*travail, voyage etc*) to continue (with), carry on (with), go on (with); (*prolonger: alignement, rue*) to continue ♦ *vi* (*pluie, vie, bruit*) to continue, go on; (*voyageur*) to go on; ~ **à** *ou* **de faire** to go on *ou* continue doing

contorsionner [kɔ̃tɔʀsjɔne]: **se ~** *vi* to contort o.s., writhe about

contour [kɔ̃tuʀ] *nm* outline, contour

contourner [kɔ̃tuʀne] *vt* to go round

contraceptif, ive [kɔ̃tʀasɛptif, -iv] *adj, nm* contraceptive; **contraception** [kɔ̃tʀasɛpsjɔ̃] *nf* contraception

contracté, e [kɔ̃tʀakte] *adj* tense

contracter [kɔ̃tʀakte] *vt* (*muscle etc*) to tense, contract; (*maladie, dette, obligation*) to contract; (*assurance*) to take out; **se ~** *vi* (*métal, muscles*) to contract

contractuel, le [kɔ̃tʀaktɥɛl] *nm/f*

(*agent*) traffic warden

contradiction [kɔ̃tʀadiksjɔ̃] *nf* contradiction; **contradictoire** *adj* contradictory, conflicting

contraignant, e [kɔ̃tʀɛɲɑ̃, aɑ̃t] *adj* restricting

contraindre *vt*: ~ **qn à faire** to compel sb to do; **contraint, e** [kɔ̃tʀɛ̃, -ɛ̃t] *adj* (*mine, air*) constrained, forced; **contrainte** *nf* constraint

contraire [kɔ̃tʀɛʀ] *adj, nm* opposite; ~ **à** contrary to; **au ~** on the contrary

contrarier [kɔ̃tʀaʀje] *vt* (*personne*) to annoy, bother; (*fig*) to impede; to thwart, frustrate; **contrariété** [kɔ̃tʀaʀjete] *nf* annoyance

contraste [kɔ̃tʀast(ə)] *nm* contrast

contrat [kɔ̃tʀa] *nm* contract; ~ **de travail** employment contract

contravention [kɔ̃tʀavɑ̃sjɔ̃] *nf* (*amende*) fine; (*P.V. pour stationnement interdit*) parking ticket

contre [kɔ̃tʀ(ə)] *prép* against; (*en échange*) (in exchange) for; **par ~** on the other hand

contrebande [kɔ̃tʀəbɑ̃d] *nf* (*trafic*) contraband, smuggling; (*marchandise*) contraband, smuggled goods *pl*; **faire la ~ de** to smuggle

contrebas [kɔ̃tʀəba]: **en ~** *adv* (down) below

contrebasse [kɔ̃tʀəbas] *nf* (double) bass

contre: **~carrer** *vt* to thwart; **~cœur**: **à ~cœur** *adv* (be)grudgingly, reluctantly; **~coup** *nm* repercussions *pl*; **par ~coup** as an indirect consequence; **~dire** *vt* (*personne*) to contradict; (*témoignage, assertion, faits*) to refute

contrée [kɔ̃tʀe] *nf* region; land

contrefaçon [kɔ̃tʀəfasɔ̃] *nf* forgery

contrefaire [kɔ̃tʀəfɛʀ] *vt* (*document, signature*) to forge, counterfeit; (*personne, démarche*) to mimic; (*dénaturer: sa voix etc*) to disguise

contre-indication (*pl* **contre-indications**) *nf* (MÉD) contra-indication

contre-jour [kɔ̃tʀəʒuʀ]: **à ~** *adv* against the sunlight

contremaître [kɔ̃tʀəmɛtʀ(ə)] *nm* foreman

contrepartie [kɔ̃trəparti] *nf* compensation; **en ~** in return

contre-pied [kɔ̃trəpje] *nm*: **prendre le ~ de** to take the opposing view of; to take the opposite course to

contre-plaqué [kɔ̃trəplake] *nm* plywood

contrepoids [kɔ̃trəpwa] *nm* counterweight, counterbalance

contrer [kɔ̃tre] *vt* to counter

contresens [kɔ̃trəsɑ̃s] *nm* misinterpretation; mistranslation; nonsense *no pl*; **à ~** the wrong way

contretemps [kɔ̃trətɑ̃] *nm* hitch; **à ~** (*MUS*) out of time; (*fig*) at an inopportune moment

contrevenir [kɔ̃trəvnir]: **~ à** *vt* to contravene

contribuable [kɔ̃tribɥabl(ə)] *nm/f* taxpayer

contribuer [kɔ̃tribɥe]: **~ à** *vt* to contribute towards; **contribution** *nf* contribution; **contributions directes/indirectes** direct/indirect taxation; **mettre à contribution** to call upon

contrôle [kɔ̃trol] *nm* checking *no pl*, check; supervision; monitoring; (*test*) test, examination; **perdre le ~ de** (*véhicule*) to lose control of; **~ continu** (*SCOL*) continuous assessment; **~ d'identité** identity check; **~ des naissances** birth control

contrôler [kɔ̃trole] *vt* (*vérifier*) to check; (*surveiller*) to supervise; to monitor, control; (*maîtriser*, *COMM: firme*) to control; **contrôleur, euse** *nm/f* (*de train*) (ticket) inspector; (*de bus*) (bus) conductor(tress)

contrordre [kɔ̃trɔrdr(ə)] *nm*: **sauf ~** unless otherwise directed

controversé, e [kɔ̃trɔverse] *adj* (*personnage, question*) controversial

contusion [kɔ̃tyzjɔ̃] *nf* bruise, contusion

convaincre [kɔ̃vɛ̃kr(ə)] *vt*: **~ qn (de qch)** to convince sb (of sth); **~ qn (de faire)** to persuade sb (to do); (*JUR: délit*) to convict sb of

convalescence [kɔ̃valesɑ̃s] *nf* convalescence

convenable [kɔ̃vnabl(ə)] *adj* suitable; (*assez bon, respectable*) decent

convenance [kɔ̃vnɑ̃s] *nf*: **à ma/votre ~** to my/your liking; **~s** *nfpl* (*normes sociales*) proprieties

convenir [kɔ̃vnir] *vi* to be suitable; **~ à** to suit; **il convient de** it is advisable to; (*bienséant*) it is right *ou* proper to; **~ de** (*bien-fondé de qch*) to admit (to), acknowledge; (*date, somme etc*) to agree upon; **~ que** (*admettre*) to admit that; **~ de faire** to agree to do

convention [kɔ̃vɑ̃sjɔ̃] *nf* convention; **~s** *nfpl* (*convenances*) convention *sg*; **~ collective** (*ÉCON*) collective agreement; **conventionné, e** *adj* (*ADMIN*) *applying charges laid down by the state*

convenu, e [kɔ̃vny] *pp de* **convenir** ♦ *adj* agreed

conversation [kɔ̃vɛrsasjɔ̃] *nf* conversation

convertir [kɔ̃vɛrtir] *vt*: **~ qn (à)** to convert sb (to); **se ~ (à)** to be converted (to); **~ qch en** to convert sth into

conviction [kɔ̃viksjɔ̃] *nf* conviction

convienne *etc vb voir* **convenir**

convier [kɔ̃vje] *vt*: **~ qn à** (*dîner etc*) to (cordially) invite sb to

convive [kɔ̃viv] *nm/f* guest (*at table*)

convivial, e [kɔ̃vivjal] *adj* (*INFORM*) user-friendly

convocation [kɔ̃vɔkasjɔ̃] *nf* (*document*) notification to attend; summons *sg*

convoi [kɔ̃vwa] *nm* (*de voitures, prisonniers*) convoy; (*train*) train

convoiter [kɔ̃vwate] *vt* to covet

convoquer [kɔ̃vɔke] *vt* (*assemblée*) to convene; (*subordonné*) to summon; (*candidat*) to ask to attend; **~ qn (à)** (*réunion*) to invite sb (to attend)

convoyeur [kɔ̃vwajœr] *nm* (*NAVIG*) escort ship; **~ de fonds** security guard

coopération [kɔɔperasjɔ̃] *nf* cooperation; (*ADMIN*): **la C~** ≈ Voluntary Service Overseas (*BRIT*), ≈ Peace Corps (*US*)

coopérer [kɔɔpere] *vi*: **~ (à)** to cooperate (in)

coordonner [kɔɔrdɔne] *vt* to coordinate

copain [kɔpɛ̃] *nm* mate, pal

copeau, x [kɔpo] *nm* shaving

copie [kɔpi] *nf* copy; (*SCOL*) script, paper; exercise

copier [kɔpje] *vt, vi* to copy; ~ **sur** to copy from

copieur [kɔpjœʀ] *nm* (photo)copier

copieux, euse [kɔpjø, -øz] *adj* copious

copine [kɔpin] *nf* = **copain**

copropriété [kɔpʀɔpʀijete] *nf* co-ownership, joint ownership

coq [kɔk] *nm* cock, rooster; ~-à-l'âne [kɔkalɑn] *nm inv* abrupt change of subject

coque [kɔk] *nf* (*de noix, mollusque*) shell; (*de bateau*) hull; **à la** ~ (*CULIN*) (soft-)boiled

coquelicot [kɔkliko] *nm* poppy

coqueluche [kɔklyʃ] *nf* whooping-cough

coquet, te [kɔkɛ, -ɛt] *adj* flirtatious; appearance-conscious; pretty

coquetier [kɔktje] *nm* egg-cup

coquillage [kɔkijaʒ] *nm* (*mollusque*) shellfish *inv*; (*coquille*) shell

coquille [kɔkij] *nf* shell; (*TYPO*) misprint; ~ **St Jacques** scallop

coquin, e [kɔkɛ̃, -in] *adj* mischievous, roguish; (*polisson*) naughty

cor [kɔʀ] *nm* (*MUS*) horn; (*MÉD*): ~ **(au pied)** corn; **réclamer à** ~ **et à cri** to clamour for

corail, aux [kɔʀaj, -o] *nm* coral *no pl*

Coran [kɔʀɑ̃] *nm*: **le** ~ **the Koran**

corbeau, x [kɔʀbo] *nm* crow

corbeille [kɔʀbɛj] *nf* basket; ~ **à papier** waste paper basket *ou* bin

corbillard [kɔʀbijaʀ] *nm* hearse

corde [kɔʀd(ə)] *nf* rope; (*de violon, raquette, d'arc*) string; (*ATHLÉTISME, AUTO*): **la** ~ the rails *pl*; **usé jusqu'à la** ~ threadbare; ~ **à linge** washing *ou* clothes line; ~ **à sauter** skipping rope; ~**s vocales** vocal cords; **cordée** [kɔʀde] *nf* (*d'alpinistes*) rope, roped party

cordialement [kɔʀdjalmɑ̃] *adv* (*formule épistolaire*) (kind) regards

cordon [kɔʀdɔ̃] *nm* cord, string; ~ **ombilical** umbilical cord; ~ **sanitaire/de police** sanitary/police cordon

cordonnerie [kɔʀdɔnʀi] *nf* shoe repairer's (shop); **cordonnier** [kɔʀdɔnje] *nm* shoe repairer

Corée [kɔʀe] *nf*: **la** ~ **du Sud/du Nord** South/North Korea

coriace [kɔʀjas] *adj* tough

corne [kɔʀn(ə)] *nf* horn; (*de cerf*) antler

corneille [kɔʀnɛj] *nf* crow

cornemuse [kɔʀnəmyz] *nf* bagpipes *pl*

cornet [kɔʀnɛ] *nm* (paper) cone; (*de glace*) cornet, cone

corniche [kɔʀniʃ] *nf* (*de meuble, neigeuse*) cornice; (*route*) coast road

cornichon [kɔʀniʃɔ̃] *nm* gherkin

Cornouailles [kɔʀnwaj] *nf* Cornwall

corporation [kɔʀpɔʀasjɔ̃] *nf* corporate body

corporel, le [kɔʀpɔʀɛl] *adj* bodily; (*punition*) corporal

corps [kɔʀ] *nm* body; **à son** ~ **défendant** against one's will; **à** ~ **perdu** headlong; **perdu** ~ **et biens** lost with all hands; **prendre** ~ to take shape; ~ **à** ~ *adv* hand-to-hand ♦ *nm* clinch; ~ **de garde** guardroom; **le** ~ **électoral** the electorate; **le** ~ **enseignant** the teaching profession

corpulent, e [kɔʀpylɑ̃, -ɑ̃t] *adj* stout

correct, e [kɔʀɛkt] *adj* correct; (*passable*) adequate

correction [kɔʀɛksjɔ̃] *nf* (*voir corriger*) correction; (*voir correct*) correctness; (*rature, surcharge*) correction, emendation; (*coups*) thrashing

correctionnel, le [kɔʀɛksjɔnɛl] *adj* (*JUR*): **tribunal** ~ ≈ criminal court

correspondance [kɔʀɛspɔ̃dɑ̃s] *nf* correspondence; (*de train, d'avion*) connection; **cours par** ~ correspondence course; **vente par** ~ mail-order business

correspondant, e [kɔʀɛspɔ̃dɑ̃, -ɑ̃t] *nm/f* correspondent; (*TÉL*) person phoning (*ou* being phoned)

correspondre [kɔʀɛspɔ̃dʀ(ə)] *vi* to correspond, tally; ~ **à** to correspond to; ~ **avec qn** to correspond with sb

corrida [kɔʀida] *nf* bullfight

corridor [kɔʀidɔʀ] *nm* corridor

corriger [kɔʀiʒe] *vt* (*devoir*) to correct;

(*punir*) to thrash; ~ **qn de** (*défaut*) to cure sb of

corrompre [kɔʀɔ̃pʀ(ə)] *vt* to corrupt; (*acheter: témoin etc*) to bribe

corruption [kɔʀypsjɔ̃] *nf* corruption; bribery

corsage [kɔʀsaʒ] *nm* bodice; blouse

corse [kɔʀs(ə)] *adj, nm/f* Corsican ♦ *nf*: **la C~** Corsica

corsé, e [kɔʀse] *adj* vigorous; (*vin, goût*) full-flavoured; (*fig*) spicy; tricky

corset [kɔʀsɛ] *nm* corset; bodice

cortège [kɔʀtɛʒ] *nm* procession

corvée [kɔʀve] *nf* chore, drudgery *no pl*

cosmétique [kɔsmetik] *nm* beauty care product

cossu, e [kɔsy] *adj* well-to-do

costaud, e [kɔsto, -od] *adj* strong, sturdy

costume [kɔstym] *nm* (*d'homme*) suit; (*de théâtre*) costume; **costumé, e** *adj* dressed up

cote [kɔt] *nf* (*en Bourse etc*) quotation; quoted value; (*d'un cheval*): **la ~ de** the odds *pl* on; (*d'un candidat etc*) rating; (*sur un croquis*) dimension; ~ **d'alerte** danger *ou* flood level

côte [kot] *nf* (*rivage*) coast(line); (*pente*) slope; (: *sur une route*) hill; (*ANAT*) rib; (*d'un tricot, tissu*) rib, ribbing *no pl*; ~ **à ~** side by side; **la C~ (d'Azur)** the (French) Riviera

côté [kote] *nm* (*gén*) side; (*direction*) way, direction; **de chaque ~ (de)** on each side (of); **de tous les ~s** from all directions; **de quel ~ est-il parti?** which way did he go?; **de ce/de l'autre ~** this/the other way; **du ~ de** (*provenance*) from; (*direction*) towards; (*proximité*) near; **de ~** sideways; on one side; to one side; aside; **laisser/mettre de ~** to leave/put to one side; **à ~** (*right*) nearby; beside; next door; (*d'autre part*) besides; **à ~ de** beside; next to; **être aux ~s de** to be by the side of

coteau, x [kɔto] *nm* hill

côtelette [kotlɛt] *nf* chop

coter [kɔte] *vt* (*en Bourse*) to quote

côtier, ière [kotje, -jɛʀ] *adj* coastal

cotisation [kɔtizasjɔ̃] *nf* subscription, dues *pl*; (*pour une pension*) contributions *pl*

cotiser [kɔtize] *vi*: ~ **(à)** to pay contributions (to); **se** ~ *vi* to club together

coton [kɔtɔ̃] *nm* cotton; ~ **hydrophile** cotton wool (*BRIT*), absorbent cotton (*US*)

côtoyer [kotwaje] *vt* to be close to; to rub shoulders with; to run alongside

cou [ku] *nm* neck

couchant [kuʃɑ̃] *adj*: **soleil ~** setting sun

couche [kuʃ] *nf* (*strate: gén, GÉO*) layer; (*de peinture, vernis*) coat; (*de bébé*) nappy (*BRIT*), diaper (*US*); ~s *nfpl* (*MÉD*) confinement *sg*; ~ **d'ozone** ozone layer; ~s **sociales** social levels *ou* strata

couché, e [kuʃe] *adj* lying down; (*au lit*) in bed

couche-culotte [kuʃkylɔt] *nf* disposable nappy (*BRIT*) *ou* diaper (*US*) and waterproof pants in one

coucher [kuʃe] *nm* (*du soleil*) setting ♦ *vt* (*personne*) to put to bed; (: *loger*) to put up; (*objet*) to lay on its side ♦ *vi* to sleep; **se** ~ *vi* (*pour dormir*) to go to bed; (*pour se reposer*) to lie down; (*soleil*) to set; ~ **de soleil** sunset

couchette [kuʃɛt] *nf* couchette; (*de marin*) bunk

coucou [kuku] *nm* cuckoo

coude [kud] *nm* (*ANAT*) elbow; (*de tuyau, de la route*) bend; ~ **à ~** shoulder to shoulder, side by side

coudre [kudʀ(ə)] *vt* (*bouton*) to sew on; (*robe*) to sew (up) ♦ *vi* to sew

couenne [kwan] *nf* (*de lard*) rind

couette [kwɛt] *nf* duvet, quilt; ~s *nfpl* (*cheveux*) bunches

couffin [kufɛ̃] *nm* Moses basket

couler [kule] *vi* to flow, run; (*fuir: stylo, récipient*) to leak; (*sombrer: bateau*) to sink ♦ *vt* (*cloche, sculpture*) to cast; (*bateau*) to sink; (*fig*) to ruin, bring down

couleur [kulœʀ] *nf* colour (*BRIT*), color (*US*); (*CARTES*) suit; **film/télévision en ~s** colo(u)r film/television

couleuvre [kulœvʀ(ə)] *nf* grass snake

coulisse [kulis] *nf*: ~s *nfpl* (*THÉÂTRE*)

wings; (*fig*): **dans les ~s** behind the scenes; **coulisser** *vi* to slide, run

couloir [kulwaʀ] *nm* corridor, passage; (*de bus*) gangway; (*d'avion*) aisle; (*sur la route*) bus lane; (*SPORT: de piste*) lane; (*GÉO*) gully; **~ aérien/de navigation** air/shipping lane

coup [ku] *nm* (*heurt, choc*) knock; (*affectif*) blow, shock; (*agressif*) blow; (*avec arme à feu*) shot; (*de l'horloge*) chime; stroke; (*SPORT*) stroke; shot; blow; (*fam: fois*) time; **~ de coude** nudge (with the elbow); **~ de tonnerre** clap of thunder; **~ de sonnette** ring of the bell; **~ de crayon** stroke of the pencil; **donner un ~ de balai** to give the floor a sweep; **avoir le ~** (*fig*) to have the knack; **boire un ~** to have a drink; **être dans le ~** to be in on it; **du ~ ... so** (you see) ...; **d'un seul ~** (*subitement*) suddenly; (*à la fois*) at one go; in one blow; **du premier ~** first time; **du même ~** at the same time; **à ~ sûr** definitely, without fail; **~ sur ~** in quick succession; **sur le ~** outright; **sous le ~ de** (*surprise etc*) under the influence of; **~ de chance** stroke of luck; **~ de couteau** stab (of a knife); **~ d'envoi** kick-off; **~ d'essai** first attempt; **~ de feu** shot; **~ de filet** (*POLICE*) haul; **~ de frein** (sharp) braking *no pl*; **~ de main**: **donner un ~ de main à qn** to give sb a (helping) hand; **~ d'œil** glance; **~ de pied** kick; **~ de poing** punch; **~ de soleil** sunburn *no pl*; **~ de téléphone** phone call; **~ de tête** (*fig*) (sudden) impulse; **~ de théâtre** (*fig*) dramatic turn of events; **~ de vent** gust of wind; **en coup de vent** in a tearing hurry; **~ franc** free kick

coupable [kupabl(ə)] *adj* guilty ♦ *nm/f* (*gén*) culprit; (*JUR*) guilty party

coupe [kup] *nf* (*verre*) goblet; (*à fruits*) dish; (*SPORT*) cup; (*de cheveux, de vêtement*) cut; (*graphique, plan*) (cross) section; **être sous la ~ de** to be under the control of

coupe-papier [kuppapje] *nm inv* paper knife

couper [kupe] *vt* to cut; (*retrancher*) to cut (out); (*route, courant*) to cut off; (*appétit*) to take away; (*vin, cidre*) to blend; (*: à table*) to dilute ♦ *vi* to cut; (*prendre un raccourci*) to take a short-cut; **se ~ vi** (*se blesser*) to cut o.s.; **~ la parole à qn** to cut sb short

couple [kupl(ə)] *nm* couple

couplet [kuplɛ] *nm* verse

coupole [kupɔl] *nf* dome; cupola

coupon [kupɔ̃] *nm* (*ticket*) coupon; (*de tissu*) remnant; roll; **~-réponse** *nm* reply coupon

coupure [kupyʀ] *nf* cut; (*billet de banque*) note; (*de journal*) cutting; **~ de courant** power cut

cour [kuʀ] *nf* (*de ferme, jardin*) (court)yard; (*d'immeuble*) back yard; (*JUR, royale*) court; **faire la ~ à qn** to court sb; **~ d'assises** court of assizes; **~ martiale** court-martial

courage [kuʀaʒ] *nm* courage, bravery; **courageux, euse** brave, courageous

couramment [kuʀamɑ̃] *adv* commonly; (*parler*) fluently

courant, e [kuʀɑ̃, -ɑ̃t] *adj* (*fréquent*) common; (*COMM, gén: normal*) standard; (*en cours*) current ♦ *nm* current; (*fig*) movement; trend; **être au ~ (de)** (*fait, nouvelle*) to know (about); **mettre qn au ~ (de)** to tell sb (about); (*nouveau travail etc*) to teach sb the basics (of); **se tenir au ~ (de)** (*techniques etc*) to keep o.s. up-to-date (on); **dans le ~ de** (*pendant*) in the course of; **le 10 ~** (*COMM*) the 10th inst.; **~ d'air** draught; **~ électrique** (electric) current, power

courbature [kuʀbatyʀ] *nf* ache

courbe [kuʀb(ə)] *adj* curved ♦ *nf* curve; **courber** [kuʀbe] *vt* to bend

coureur, euse [kuʀœʀ, -øz] *nm/f* (*SPORT*) runner (*ou* driver); (*péj*) womanizer; manhunter; **~ automobile** racing driver

courge [kuʀʒ(ə)] *nf* (*CULIN*) marrow; **courgette** [kuʀʒɛt] *nf* courgette (*BRIT*), zucchini (*US*)

courir [kuʀiʀ] *vi* to run ♦ *vt* (*SPORT: épreuve*) to compete in; (*risque*) to run; (*danger*) to face; **~ les magasins** to go round the shops; **le bruit court que** the rumour is going round that

couronne [kuʀɔn] *nf* crown; (*de fleurs*) wreath, circlet

courons *etc vb voir* **courir**

courrier [kuʀje] *nm* mail, post; (*lettres à écrire*) letters *pl*; **avion long/moyen ~** long-/medium-haul plane

courroie [kuʀwa] *nf* strap; (*TECH*) belt

courrons *etc vb voir* **courir**

cours [kuʀ] *nm* (*leçon*) lesson; class; (*série de leçons, cheminement*) course; (*écoulement*) flow; (*COMM*) rate; price; **donner libre ~ à** to give free expression to; **avoir ~** (*monnaie*) to be legal tender; (*fig*) to be current; (*SCOL*) to have a class *ou* lecture; **en ~** (*année*) current; (*travaux*) in progress; **en ~ de route** on the way; **au ~ de** in the course of, during; **~ d'eau** waterway; **~ du soir** night school

course [kuʀs(ə)] *nf* running; (*SPORT*: *épreuve*) race; (*d'un taxi, autocar*) journey, trip; (*petite mission*) errand; **~s** *nfpl* (*achats*) shopping *sg*; **faire des ~s** to do some shopping

court, e [kuʀ, kuʀt(ə)] *adj* short ♦ *adv* short ♦ *nm*: **~ (de tennis)** (tennis) court; **tourner ♦** to come to a sudden end; **ça fait ~** that's not very long; **à ~ de** short of; **prendre qn de ~** to catch sb unawares; **tirer à la ~e paille** to draw lots; **~-circuit** *nm* short-circuit

courtier, ère [kuʀtje, -jɛʀ] *nm/f* broker

courtiser [kuʀtize] *vt* to court, woo

courtois, e [kuʀtwa, -waz] *adj* courteous

couru, e [kuʀy] *pp de* **courir ♦** *adj*: **c'est ~** it's a safe bet

cousais *etc vb voir* **coudre**

couscous [kuskus] *nm* couscous

cousin, e [kuzɛ̃, -in] *nm/f* cousin

coussin [kusɛ̃] *nm* cushion

cousu, e [kuzy] *pp de* **coudre**

coût [ku] *nm* cost; **le ~ de la vie** the cost of living

coûtant [kutɑ̃] *adj m*: **au prix ~** at cost price

couteau, x [kuto] *nm* knife; **~ à cran d'arrêt** flick-knife

coûter [kute] *vt, vi* to cost; **combien ça**

coûte? how much is it?, what does it cost?; **coûte que coûte** at all costs; **coûteux, euse** *adj* costly, expensive

coutume [kutym] *nf* custom

couture [kutyʀ] *nf* sewing; dressmaking; (*points*) seam; **couturier** [kutyʀje] *nm* fashion designer; **couturière** [kutyʀjɛʀ] *nf* dressmaker

couvée [kuve] *nf* brood, clutch

couvent [kuvɑ̃] *nm* (*de sœurs*) convent; (*de frères*) monastery

couver [kuve] *vt* to hatch; (*maladie*) to be sickening for ♦ *vi* (*feu*) to smoulder; (*révolte*) to be brewing

couvercle [kuvɛʀkl(ə)] *nm* lid; (*de bombe aérosol etc, qui se visse*) cap, top

couvert, e [kuvɛʀ, -ɛʀt(ə)] *pp de* **couvrir ♦** *adj* (*ciel*) overcast ♦ *nm* place setting; (*place à table*) place; (*au restaurant*) cover charge; **~s** *nmpl* (*ustensiles*) cutlery *sg*; **~ de** covered with *ou* in; **mettre le ~** to lay the table

couverture [kuvɛʀtyʀ] *nf* blanket; (*de bâtiment*) roofing; (*de livre, assurance, fig*) cover; (*presse*) coverage; **~ chauffante** electric blanket

couveuse [kuvøz] *nf* (*de maternité*) incubator

couvre-feu *nm* curfew

couvre-lit *nm* bedspread

couvrir [kuvʀiʀ] *vt* to cover; **se ~** *vi* (*ciel*) to cloud over; (*s'habiller*) to cover up; (*se coiffer*) to put one's hat on

crabe [kʀab] *nm* crab

cracher [kʀaʃe] *vi, vt* to spit

crachin [kʀaʃɛ̃] *nm* drizzle

craie [kʀɛ] *nf* chalk

craindre [kʀɛ̃dʀ(ə)] *vt* to fear, be afraid of; (*être sensible à: chaleur, froid*) to be easily damaged by

crainte [kʀɛ̃t] *nf* fear; **de ~ de/que** for fear of/that; **craintif, ive** *adj* timid

cramoisi, e [kʀamwazi] *adj* crimson

crampe [kʀɑ̃p] *nf* cramp

cramponner [kʀɑ̃pɔne]: **se ~** *vi*: **se ~ (à)** to hang *ou* cling on (to)

cran [kʀɑ̃] *nm* (*entaille*) notch; (*de courroie*) hole; (*courage*) guts *pl*; **~ d'arrêt** safety catch

crâne [kʀɑn] *nm* skull

crâner [kʀɑne] (*fam*) *vi* to show off

crapaud [kʀapo] *nm* toad

crapule [kʀapyl] *nf* villain

craquement [kʀakmɑ̃] *nm* crack, snap; (*du plancher*) creak, creaking *no pl*

craquer [kʀake] *vi* (*bois, plancher*) to creak; (*fil, branche*) to snap; (*couture*) to come apart; (*fig*) to break down ♦ *vt* (*allumette*) to strike

crasse [kʀas] *nf* grime, filth

cravache [kʀavaʃ] *nf* (riding) crop

cravate [kʀavat] *nf* tie

crawl [kʀol] *nm* crawl; **dos** ~é backstroke

crayeux, euse [kʀɛjø, -øz] *adj* chalky

crayon [kʀɛjɔ̃] *nm* pencil; ~ **à bille** ballpoint pen; ~ **de couleur** crayon, colouring pencil; ~ **optique** light pen; **crayon-feutre** [kʀɛjɔ̃føtʀ(ə)] (*pl* **crayons-feutres**) *nm* felt(-tip) pen

créancier, ière [kʀeɑ̃sje, -jɛʀ] *nm/f* creditor

création [kʀeasjɔ̃] *nf* creation

créature [kʀeatyʀ] *nf* creature

crèche [kʀɛʃ] *nf* (*de Noël*) crib; (*garderie*) crèche, day nursery

crédit [kʀedi] *nm* (*gén*) credit; ~s *nmpl* (*fonds*) funds; **payer/acheter à** ~ to pay/buy on credit *ou* on easy terms; **faire** ~ **à qn** to give sb credit; **créditer** *vt*: **créditer un compte (de)** to credit an account (with)

crédule [kʀedyl] *adj* credulous, gullible

créer [kʀee] *vt* to create; (*THÉÂTRE*) to produce (for the first time)

crémaillère [kʀemajɛʀ] *nf* (*RAIL*) rack; **pendre la** ~ to have a house-warming party

crématoire [kʀematwaʀ] *adj*: **four** ~ crematorium

crème [kʀɛm] *nf* cream; (*entremets*) cream dessert ♦ *adj inv* cream (-coloured); **un (café)** ~ ≈ a white coffee; ~ **à raser** shaving cream; ~ **chantilly** whipped cream; ~ **fouettée** = **crème chantilly**; **crémerie** *nf* dairy; **crémeux, euse** *adj* creamy

créneau, x [kʀeno] *nm* (*de fortification*) crenel(le); (*fig*) gap, slot; (*AUTO*): **faire un** ~ to reverse into a parking space (*alongside the kerb*)

crêpe [kʀɛp] *nf* (*galette*) pancake ♦ *nm* (*tissu*) crêpe; **crêpé, e** *adj* (*cheveux*) backcombed; **crêperie** *nf* pancake shop *ou* restaurant

crépir [kʀepiʀ] *vt* to roughcast

crépiter [kʀepite] *vi* to sputter, splutter; to crackle

crépu, e [kʀepy] *adj* frizzy, fuzzy

crépuscule [kʀepyskyl] *nm* twilight, dusk

cresson [kʀesɔ̃] *nm* watercress

crête [kʀɛt] *nf* (*de coq*) comb; (*de vague, montagne*) crest

creuser [kʀøze] *vt* (*trou, tunnel*) to dig; (*sol*) to dig a hole in; (*bois*) to hollow out; (*fig*) to go (deeply) into; **ça creuse** that gives you a real appetite; **se** ~ **(la cervelle)** to rack one's brains

creux, euse [kʀø, -øz] *adj* hollow ♦ *nm* hollow; (*fig: sur graphique etc*) trough; **heures creuses** slack periods; off-peak periods

crevaison [kʀəvɛzɔ̃] *nf* puncture

crevasse [kʀəvas] *nf* (*dans le sol*) crack, fissure; (*de glacier*) crevasse

crevé, e [kʀəve] *adj* (*fatigué*) all in, exhausted

crever [kʀəve] *vt* (*papier*) to tear, break; (*tambour, ballon*) to burst ♦ *vi* (*pneu*) to burst; (*automobiliste*) to have a puncture (*BRIT*) *ou* a flat (tire) (*US*); (*fam*) to die; **cela lui a crevé un œil** it blinded him in one eye

crevette [kʀəvɛt] *nf*: ~ **(rose)** prawn; ~ **grise** shrimp

cri [kʀi] *nm* cry, shout; (*d'animal: spécifique*) cry, call; **c'est le dernier** ~ (*fig*) it's the latest fashion

criant, e [kʀijɑ̃, -ɑ̃t] *adj* (*injustice*) glaring

criard, e [kʀijaʀ, -aʀd(ə)] *adj* (*couleur*) garish, loud; (*voix*) yelling

crible [kʀibl(ə)] *nm* riddle; **passer qch au** ~ (*fig*) to go over sth with a finetooth comb

criblé, e [kʀible] *adj*: ~ **de** riddled with;

(*de dettes*) crippled with

cric [kʀik] *nm* (*AUTO*) jack

crier [kʀije] *vi* (*pour appeler*) to shout, cry (out); (*de peur, de douleur etc*) to scream, yell ♦ *vt* (*ordre, injure*) to shout (out), yell (out)

crime [kʀim] *nm* crime; (*meurtre*) murder; **criminel, le** *nm/f* criminal; murderer

crin [kʀɛ̃] *nm* hair *no pl*; (*fibre*) horsehair; **crinière** [kʀinjɛʀ] *nf* mane

crique [kʀik] *nf* creek, inlet

criquet [kʀikɛ] *nm* locust; grasshopper

crise [kʀiz] *nf* crisis; (*MÉD*) attack; fit; ~ **cardiaque** heart attack; ~ **de foie** bilious attack; ~ **de nerfs** attack of nerves

crisper [kʀispe] *vt* to tense; (*poings*) to clench; **se ~** *vi* to tense; to clench; (*personne*) to get tense

crisser [kʀise] *vi* (*neige*) to crunch; (*pneu*) to screech

cristal, aux [kʀistal, -o] *nm* crystal; **cristallin, e** *adj* crystal-clear

critère [kʀitɛʀ] *nm* criterion

critiquable [kʀitikablə] *adj* open to criticism

critique [kʀitik] *adj* critical ♦ *nm/f* (*de théâtre, musique*) critic ♦ *nf* criticism; (*THÉÂTRE etc*: *article*) review; **critiquer** [kʀitike] *vt* (*dénigrer*) to criticize; (*évaluer, juger*) to assess, examine (critically)

croasser [kʀoase] *vi* to caw

Croatie [kʀɔsl] *nf* Croatia

croc [kʀo] *nm* (*dent*) fang; (*de boucher*) hook

croc-en-jambe [kʀokɑ̃ʒɑ̃b] *nm*: **faire un ~ à qn** to trip sb up

croche [kʀɔʃ] *nf* (*MUS*) quaver (*BRIT*), eighth note (*US*); **~-pied** [kʀɔʃpje] *nm* = **croc-en-jambe**

crochet [kʀɔʃɛ] *nm* hook; (*détour*) detour; (*TRICOT*: *aiguille*) crochet hook; (: *technique*) crochet; **vivre aux ~s de qn** to live *ou* sponge off sb; **crocheter** *vt* (*serrure*) to pick

crochu, e [kʀɔʃy] *adj* hooked; claw-like

crocodile [kʀɔkɔdil] *nm* crocodile

crocus [kʀɔkys] *nm* crocus

croire [kʀwaʀ] *vt* to believe; **se ~ fort** to think one is strong; ~ **que** to believe *ou* think that; ~ **à**, ~ **en** to believe in

croîs *vb voir* **croître**

croisade [kʀwazad] *nf* crusade

croisé, e [kʀwaze] *adj* (*veston*) double-breasted

croisement [kʀwazmɑ̃] *nm* (*carrefour*) crossroads *sg*; (*BIO*) crossing; crossbreed

croiser [kʀwaze] *vt* (*personne, voiture*) to pass; (*route*) to cross, cut across; (*BIO*) to cross ♦ *vi* (*NAVIG*) to cruise; **se ~** *vi* (*personnes, véhicules*) to pass each other; (*routes, lettres*) to cross; (*regards*) to meet; ~ **les jambes/bras** to cross one's legs/fold one's arms

croiseur [kʀwazœʀ] *nm* cruiser (*warship*)

croisière [kʀwazjɛʀ] *nf* cruise; **vitesse de ~** (*AUTO etc*) cruising speed

croissance [kʀwasɑ̃s] *nf* growth

croissant [kʀwasɑ̃] *nm* (*à manger*) croissant; (*motif*) crescent

croître [kʀwatʀ(ə)] *vi* to grow

croix [kʀwa] *nf* cross; **en ~** in the form of a cross; **la C~ Rouge** the Red Cross

croque-monsieur [kʀɔkməsje] *nm inv* toasted ham and cheese sandwich

croquer [kʀɔke] *vt* (*manger*) to crunch; to munch; (*dessiner*) to sketch ♦ *vi* to be crisp *ou* crunchy; **chocolat à ~** plain dessert chocolate

croquis [kʀɔki] *nm* sketch

crosse [kʀɔs] *nf* (*de fusil*) butt; (*de revolver*) grip

crotte [kʀɔt] *nf* droppings *pl*

crotté, e [kʀɔte] *adj* muddy, mucky

crottin [kʀɔtɛ̃] *nm* dung, manure

crouler [kʀule] *vi* (*s'effondrer*) to collapse; (*être délabré*) to be crumbling

croupe [kʀup] *nf* rump; **en ~** pillion

croupir [kʀupiʀ] *vi* to stagnate

croustillant, e [kʀustijɑ̃, -ɑ̃t] *adj* crisp; (*fig*) spicy

croûte [kʀut] *nf* crust; (*du fromage*) rind; (*MÉD*) scab; **en ~** (*CULIN*) in pastry

croûton [kʀutɔ̃] *nm* (*CULIN*) crouton; (*bout du pain*) crust, heel

croyable [kʀwajablə] *adj* credible

croyant, e [kʀwajɑ̃, -ɑ̃t] *nm/f* believer
C.R.S. *sigle fpl* (= *Compagnies républicaines de sécurité*) state security police force ♦ *sigle m* member of the C.R.S.
cru, e [kʀy] *pp de* **croire** ♦ *adj* (*non cuit*) raw; (*lumière, couleur*) harsh; (*paroles, description*) crude ♦ *nm* (*vignoble*) vineyard; (*vin*) wine
crû *pp de* **croître**
cruauté [kʀyote] *nf* cruelty
cruche [kʀyʃ] *nf* pitcher, jug
crucifix [kʀysifi] *nm* crucifix
crucifixion [kʀysifiksjɔ̃] *nf* crucifixion
crudités [kʀydite] *nfpl* (*CULIN*) salads
cruel, le [kʀyɛl] *adj* cruel
crus *etc vb voir* **croire; croître**
crûs *etc vb voir* **croître**
crustacés [kʀystase] *nmpl* shellfish
CSA *sigle f* (= *Conseil supérieur de l'audiovisuel*) French broadcasting regulatory body
CSG *sigle f* (= *contribution sociale généralisée*) supplementary social security contribution in aid of the underprivileged
Cuba [kyba] *nf* Cuba
cube [kyb] *nm* cube; (*jouet*) brick; **mètre ~** cubic metre; **2 au ~** 2 cubed
cueillette [kœjɛt] *nf* picking; (*quantité*) crop, harvest
cueillir [kœjiʀ] *vt* (*fruits, fleurs*) to pick, gather; (*fig*) to catch
cuiller [kɥijɛʀ] *nf* spoon; **~ à café** coffee spoon; (*CULIN*) ≈ teaspoonful; **~ à soupe** soup-spoon; (*CULIN*) ≈ tablespoonful
cuillère [kɥijɛʀ] *nf* = **cuiller**
cuillerée [kɥijʀe] *nf* spoonful
cuir [kɥiʀ] *nm* leather; **~ chevelu** scalp
cuire [kɥiʀ] *vt* (*aliments*) to cook; (*au four*) to bake; (*poterie*) to fire ♦ *vi* to cook; **bien cuit** (*viande*) well done; **trop cuit** overdone
cuisant, e [kɥizɑ̃, -ɑ̃t] *adj* (*douleur*) stinging; (*fig: souvenir, échec*) bitter
cuisine [kɥizin] *nf* (*pièce*) kitchen; (*art culinaire*) cookery, cooking; (*nourriture*) cooking, food; **faire la ~** to cook
cuisiné, e [kɥizine] *adj*: **plat ~** ready-made meal *or* dish; **cuisiner** *vt* to cook;

(*fam*) to grill ♦ *vi* to cook; **cuisinier, ière** *nm/f* cook; **cuisinière** *nf* (*poêle*) cooker
cuisse [kɥis] *nf* thigh; (*CULIN*) leg
cuisson [kɥisɔ̃] *nf* cooking; firing
cuit, e *pp de* **cuire**
cuivre [kɥivʀ(ə)] *nm* copper; **les ~s** (*MUS*) the brass
cul [ky] (*fam!*) *nm* arse (*!*)
culasse [kylas] *nf* (*AUTO*) cylinder-head; (*de fusil*) breech
culbute [kylbyt] *nf* somersault; (*accidentelle*) tumble, fall
culminant, e [kylminɑ̃, -ɑ̃t] *adj*: **point ~** highest point
culminer [kylmine] *vi* to reach its highest point; to tower
culot [kylo] *nm* (*effronterie*) cheek
culotte [kylɔt] *nf* (*de femme*) knickers *pl* (*BRIT*), panties *pl*; **~ de cheval** riding breeches *pl*
culpabilité [kylpabilite] *nf* guilt
culte [kylt(ə)] *nm* (*religion*) religion; (*hommage, vénération*) worship; (*protestant*) service
cultivateur, trice [kyltivatœʀ, -tʀis] *nm/f* farmer
cultivé, e [kyltive] *adj* (*personne*) cultured, cultivated
cultiver [kyltive] *vt* to cultivate; (*légumes*) to grow, cultivate
culture [kyltyʀ] *nf* cultivation; growing; (*connaissances etc*) culture; **~ physique** physical training; **culturisme** *nm* body-building
cumin [kymɛ̃] *nm* cumin; (*carvi*) caraway seeds *pl*
cumuler [kymyle] *vt* (*emplois, honneurs*) to hold concurrently; (*salaires*) to draw concurrently; (*JUR: droits*) to accumulate
cupide [kypid] *adj* greedy, grasping
cure [kyʀ] *nf* (*MÉD*) course of treatment; **n'avoir ~ de** to pay no attention to
curé [kyʀe] *nm* parish priest
cure-dent [kyʀdɑ̃] *nm* toothpick
cure-pipe [kyʀpip] *nm* pipe cleaner
curer [kyʀe] *vt* to clean out
curieux, euse [kyʀjø, -øz] *adj* (*étrange*) strange, curious; (*indiscret*) curious, in-

quisitive ♦ *nmpl* (*badauds*) onlookers;
curiosité *nf* curiosity; (*site*) unusual feature
curriculum vitae [kyʀikylɔmvite] *nm
inv* curriculum vitae
curseur [kyʀsœʀ] *nm* (*INFORM*) cursor
cuti-réaction [kytiʀeaksjɔ̃] *nf* (*MÉD*)
skin-test
cuve [kyv] *nf* vat; (*à mazout etc*) tank;
cuvée [kyve] *nf* vintage
cuvette [kyvɛt] *nf* (*récipient*) bowl, basin; (*GÉO*) basin
C.V. *sigle m* (*AUTO*) = **cheval vapeur**;
(*COMM*) = **curriculum vitae**
cyanure [sjanyʀ] *nm* cyanide
cyclable [siklablə)] *adj:* **piste ~** cycle
track
cycle [sikl(ə)] *nm* cycle
cyclisme [siklism(ə)] *nm* cycling
cycliste [siklist(ə)] *nm/f* cyclist ♦ *adj*
cycle *cpd*; **coureur ~** racing cyclist
cyclomoteur [siklɔmɔtœʀ] *nm* moped
cyclone [siklon] *nm* hurricane
cygne [siɲ] *nm* swan
cylindre [silɛ̃dʀ(ə)] *nm* cylinder; **cylindrée** *nf* (*AUTO*) (cubic) capacity
cymbale [sɛ̃bal] *nf* cymbal
cynique [sinik] *adj* cynical
cystite [sistit] *nf* cystitis

D d

d' [d] *prép voir* **de**
dactylo [daktilo] *nf* (*aussi:* ~*graphe*)
typist; (: ~*graphie*) typing; **dactylographier** *vt* to type (out)
dada [dada] *nm* hobby-horse
daigner [deɲe] *vt* to deign
daim [dɛ̃] *nm* (fallow) deer *inv*; (*peau*)
buckskin; (*imitation*) suede
dalle [dal] *nf* paving stone; slab
daltonien, ne [daltɔnjɛ̃, -jɛn] *adj*
colour-blind
dam [dam] *nm:* **au grand ~ de** much to
the detriment (*ou* annoyance) of
dame [dam] *nf* lady; (*CARTES, ÉCHECS*)
queen; **~s** *nfpl* (*jeu*) draughts *sg* (*BRIT*),
checkers *sg* (*US*)

damner [dɑne] *vt* to damn
dancing [dɑ̃siŋ] *nm* dance hall
Danemark [danmaʀk] *nm* Denmark
danger [dɑ̃ʒe] *nm* danger; **dangereux,
euse** [dɑ̃ʒʀø, -øz] *adj* dangerous
danois, e [danwa, -waz] *adj* Danish
♦ *nm/f:* **D~, e** Dane ♦ *nm* (*LING*) Danish

---MOT-CLÉ---

dans [dɑ̃] *prép* **1** (*position*) in; (*à
l'intérieur de*) inside; **c'est ~ le tiroir/
le salon** it's in the drawer/lounge; **~ la
boîte** in *ou* inside the box; **marcher ~
la ville** to walk about the town
2 (*direction*) into; **elle a couru ~ le salon** she ran into the lounge
3 (*provenance*) out of, from; **je l'ai pris
~ le tiroir/salon** I took it out of *ou*
from the drawer/lounge; **boire ~ un
verre** to drink out of *ou* from a glass
4 (*temps*) in; **~ 2 mois** in 2 months, in 2
months' time
5 (*approximation*) about; **~ les 20 F**
about 20F

danse [dɑ̃s] *nf:* **la ~** dancing; **une ~** a
dance; **danser** *vi, vt* to dance; **danseur,
euse** *nm/f* ballet dancer; (*au bal etc*)
dancer; partner
dard [daʀ] *nm* sting (*organ*)
date [dat] *nf* date; **de longue ~** longstanding; **~ de naissance** date of birth;
~ limite deadline; **dater** *vt, vi* to date;
dater de to date from; **à dater de** (as)
from
datte [dat] *nf* date; **dattier** *nm* date
palm
dauphin [dofɛ̃] *nm* (*ZOOL*) dolphin
davantage [davɑ̃taʒ] *adv* more; (*plus
longtemps*) longer; **~ de** more

---MOT-CLÉ---

de (d') (*de +le =* **du**, *de +les =* **des**)
prép **1** (*appartenance*) of; **le toit ~ la
maison** the roof of the house; **la voiture
d'Elisabeth/~ mes parents** Elizabeth's/my parents' car
2 (*provenance*) from; **il vient ~ Londres** he comes from London; **elle est**

sortie du cinéma she came out of the cinema
3 (*caractérisation, mesure*): **un mur ~ brique/bureau d'acajou** a brick wall/mahogany desk; **un billet ~ 50 F** a 50F note; **une pièce ~ 2 m ~ large** *ou* **large ~ 2 m** a room 2m wide, a 2m-wide room; **un bébé ~ 10 mois** a 10-month-old baby; **12 mois ~ crédit/travail** 12 months' credit/work; **augmenter ~ 10 F** to increase by 10F; **~ 14 à 18** from 14 to 18
♦ **dét 1** (*phrases affirmatives*) some (*souvent omis*); **du vin, ~ l'eau, des pommes** (some) wine, (some) water, (some) apples; **des enfants sont venus** some children came; **pendant des mois** for months
2 (*phrases interrogatives et négatives*) any; **a-t-il du vin?** has he got any wine?; **il n'a pas ~ pommes/d'enfants** he hasn't (got) any apples/children, he has no apples/children

dé [de] *nm* (*à jouer*) die *ou* dice; (*aussi*: ~ **à coudre**) thimble
dealer [dilœʀ] (*fam*) *nm* (drug) pusher
déambuler [deãbyle] *vi* to stroll about
débâcle [debɑkl(ə)] *nf* rout
déballer [debale] *vt* to unpack
débandade [debɑ̃dad] *nf* rout; scattering
débarbouiller [debaʀbuje] *vt* to wash; **se ~** *vi* to wash (one's face)
débarcadère [debaʀkadɛʀ] *nm* wharf
débardeur [debaʀdœʀ] *nm* (*maillot*) tank top
débarquer [debaʀke] *vt* to unload, land ♦ *vi* to disembark; (*fig*) to turn up
débarras [debaʀa] *nm* lumber room; junk cupboard; **bon ~!** good riddance!
débarrasser [debaʀase] *vt* to clear; **se ~ de** to get rid of; **~ qn de** (*vêtements, paquets*) to relieve sb of
débat [deba] *nm* discussion, debate
débattre [debatʀ(ə)] *vt* to discuss, debate; **se ~** *vi* to struggle
débaucher [deboʃe] *vt* (*licencier*) to lay off, dismiss; (*entraîner*) to lead astray, debauch

débile [debil] *adj* weak, feeble; (*fam: idiot*) dim-witted
débit [debi] *nm* (*d'un liquide, fleuve*) flow; (*d'un magasin*) turnover (of goods); (*élocution*) delivery; (*bancaire*) debit; **~ de boissons** drinking establishment; **~ de tabac** tobacconist's; **débiter** *vt* (*compte*) to debit; (*liquide, gaz*) to give out; (*couper: bois, viande*) to cut up; (*péj: paroles etc*) to churn out; **débiteur, trice** *nm/f* debtor ♦ *adj* in debit; (*compte*) debit *cpd*
déblayer [debleje] *vt* to clear
débloquer [deblɔke] *vt* (*frein*) to release; (*prix, crédits*) to free
déboires [debwaʀ] *nmpl* setbacks
déboiser [debwaze] *vt* to deforest
déboîter [debwate] *vt* (*AUTO*) to pull out; **se ~ le genou** *etc* to dislocate one's knee *etc*
débonnaire [debɔnɛʀ] *adj* easy-going, good-natured
débordé, e [debɔʀde] *adj*: **être ~ (de)** (*travail, demandes*) to be snowed under (with)
déborder [debɔʀde] *vi* to overflow; (*lait etc*) to boil over; **~ (de) qch** (*dépasser*) to extend beyond sth
débouché [debuʃe] *nm* (*pour vendre*) outlet; (*perspective d'emploi*) opening
déboucher [debuʃe] *vt* (*évier, tuyau etc*) to unblock; (*bouteille*) to uncork ♦ *vi*: **~ de** to emerge from; **~ sur** to come out onto; to open out onto
débourser [debuʀse] *vt* to pay out
debout [dəbu] *adv*: **être ~** (*personne*) to be standing, stand; (: *levé, éveillé*) to be up; (*chose*) to be upright; **être encore ~** (*fig: en état*) to be still going; **se mettre ~** to stand up; **se tenir ~** to stand; **~!** stand up!; (*du lit*) get up!; **cette histoire ne tient pas ~** this story doesn't hold water
déboutonner [debutɔne] *vt* to undo, unbutton
débraillé, e [debʀaje] *adj* slovenly, untidy
débrancher [debʀɑ̃ʃe] *vt* to disconnect; (*appareil électrique*) to unplug

débrayage [debrɛjaʒ] *nm* (*AUTO*) clutch; **débrayer** [debreje] *vi* (*AUTO*) to declutch; (*cesser le travail*) to stop work

débris [debri] *nm* (*fragment*) fragment ♦ *nmpl* rubbish *sg*; debris *sg*

débrouillard, e [debrujar, -ard(ə)] *adj* smart, resourceful

débrouiller [debruje] *vt* to disentangle, untangle; **se ~** *vi* to manage

débusquer [debyske] *vt* to drive out (from cover)

début [deby] *nm* beginning, start; **~s** *nmpl* (*dans la vie*) beginnings; (*de carrière*) début *sg*

débutant, e [debytã, -ãt] *nm/f* beginner, novice

débuter [debyte] *vi* to begin, start; (*faire ses débuts*) to start out

deçà [dəsa]: **en ~ de** *prép* this side of

décacheter [dekaʃte] *vt* to unseal

décadence [dekadãs] *nf* decadence; decline

décaféiné, e [dekafeine] *adj* decaffeinated

décalage [dekalaʒ] *nm* gap; discrepancy; **~ horaire** time difference (*between time zones*); time-lag

décaler [dekale] *vt* (*dans le temps*: *avancer*) to bring forward; (: *retarder*) to put back; (*changer de position*) to shift forward *ou* back

décalquer [dekalke] *vt* to trace; (*par pression*) to transfer

décamper [dekãpe] *vi* to clear out *ou* off

décaper [dekape] *vt* to strip; (*avec abrasif*) to scour; (*avec papier de verre*) to sand

décapiter [dekapite] *vt* to behead; (*par accident*) to decapitate

décapotable [dekapɔtabl(ə)] *adj* convertible

décapsuler [dekapsyle] *vt* to take the cap *ou* top off; **décapsuleur** *nm* bottle-opener

décédé, e [desede] *adj* deceased

décéder [desede] *vi* to die

déceler [desle] *vt* to discover, detect; to indicate, reveal

décembre [desãbr(ə)] *nm* December

décemment [desamã] *adv* decently

décennie [desni] *nf* decade

décent, e [desã, -ãt] *adj* decent

déception [desɛpsjɔ̃] *nf* disappointment

décerner [deserne] *vt* to award

décès [desɛ] *nm* death, decease

décevoir [desvwar] *vt* to disappoint

déchaîner [deʃene] *vt* to unleash, arouse; **se ~** to be unleashed

déchanter [deʃãte] *vi* to become disillusioned

décharge [deʃarʒ(ə)] *nf* (*dépôt d'ordures*) rubbish tip *ou* dump; (*électrique*) electrical discharge; **à la ~ de** in defence of

décharger [deʃarʒe] *vt* (*marchandise, véhicule*) to unload; (*ÉLEC, faire feu*) to discharge; **~ qn de** (*responsabilité*) to release sb from

décharné, e [deʃarne] *adj* emaciated

déchausser [deʃose] *vt* (*skis*) to take off; **se ~** *vi* to take off one's shoes; (*dent*) to come *ou* work loose

déchéance [deʃeãs] *nf* degeneration; decay, decline; fall

déchet [deʃɛ] *nm* (*de bois, tissu etc*) scrap; (*perte*: *gén COMM*) wastage, waste; **~s** *nmpl* (*ordures*) refuse *sg*, rubbish *sg*

déchiffrer [deʃifre] *vt* to decipher

déchiqueter [deʃikte] *vt* to tear *ou* pull to pieces

déchirant, e [deʃirã, -ãt] *adj* heart-rending

déchirement [deʃirmã] *nm* (*chagrin*) wrench, heartbreak; (*gén pl*: *conflit*) rift, split

déchirer [deʃire] *vt* to tear; (*en morceaux*) to tear up; (*pour ouvrir*) to tear off; (*arracher*) to tear out; (*fig*) to rack; to tear (apart); **se ~** *vi* to tear, rip; **se ~ un muscle** to tear a muscle

déchirure [deʃiryr] *nf* (*accroc*) tear, rip; **~ musculaire** torn muscle

déchoir [deʃwar] *vi* (*personne*) to lower o.s., demean o.s.

déchu, e [deʃy] *adj* fallen; deposed

décidé, e [deside] *adj* (*personne, air*) determined; **c'est ~** it's decided

décidément [desidemɑ̃] *adv* undoubtedly; really

décider [deside] *vt*: ~ **qch** to decide on sth; **se ~ (à faire)** to decide (to do), make up one's mind (to do); **se ~ pour** to decide on *ou* in favour of; ~ **de faire/que** to decide to do/that; ~ **qn (à faire qch)** to persuade sb (to do sth); ~ **de qch** to decide upon sth; (*suj: chose*) to determine sth

décilitre [desilitʀ(ə)] *nm* decilitre

décimal, e, aux [desimal, -o] *adj* decimal; **décimale** *nf* decimal

décimètre [desimɛtʀ(ə)] *nm* decimetre; **double ~** (20 cm) ruler

décisif, ive [desizif, -iv] *adj* decisive

décision [desizjɔ̃] *nf* decision; (*fermeté*) decisiveness, decision

déclaration [deklaʀasjɔ̃] *nf* declaration; registration; (*discours: POL etc*) statement; ~ **(d'impôts)** ≈ tax return; ~ **(de sinistre)** (insurance) claim

déclarer [deklaʀe] *vt* to declare; (*décès, naissance*) to register; **se ~** *vi* (*feu, maladie*) to break out

déclasser [deklɑse] *vt* to relegate; to downgrade; to lower in status

déclencher [deklɑ̃ʃe] *vt* (*mécanisme etc*) to release; (*sonnerie*) to set off, activate; (*attaque, grève*) to launch; (*provoquer*) to trigger off; **se ~** *vi* to release itself; to go off

déclic [deklik] *nm* trigger mechanism; (*bruit*) click

décliner [dekline] *vi* to decline ♦ *vt* (*invitation*) to decline; (*responsabilité*) to refuse to accept; (*nom, adresse*) to state

déclivité [deklivite] *nf* slope, incline

décocher [dekɔʃe] *vt* to throw; to shoot

décoiffer [dekwafe] *vi*: **se ~** to take off one's hat

déçois *etc vb voir* **décevoir**

décollage [dekɔlaʒ] *nm* (*AVIAT*) takeoff

décoller [dekɔle] *vt* to unstick ♦ *vi* (*avion*) to take off; **se ~** *vi* to come unstuck

décolleté, e [dekɔlte] *adj* low-cut; wearing a low-cut dress ♦ *nm* low neck(line); (*bare*) neck and shoulders; (*plongeant*) cleavage

décolorer [dekɔlɔʀe] *vt* (*tissu*) to fade; (*cheveux*) to bleach, lighten; **se ~** *vi* to fade

décombres [dekɔ̃bʀ(ə)] *nmpl* rubble *sg*, debris *sg*

décommander [dekɔmɑ̃de] *vt* to cancel; (*invités*) to put off; **se ~** *vi* to cancel one's appointment *etc*, cry off

décomposé, e [dekɔ̃poze] *adj* (*pourri*) decomposed; (*visage*) haggard, distorted

décompte [dekɔ̃t] *nm* deduction; (*facture*) detailed account

déconcerter [dekɔ̃sɛʀte] *vt* to disconcert, confound

déconfit, e [dekɔ̃fi, -it] *adj* crestfallen; **déconfiture** [dekɔ̃fityʀ] *nf* failure, defeat; collapse, ruin

décongeler [dekɔ̃ʒle] *vt* to thaw

déconner [dekɔne] (*fam*) *vi* to talk rubbish

déconseiller [dekɔ̃seje] *vt*: ~ **qch (à qn)** to advise (sb) against sth

déconsidérer [dekɔ̃sideʀe] *vt* to discredit

décontracté, e [dekɔ̃tʀakte] *adj* relaxed, laid-back (*fam*)

décontracter [dekɔ̃tʀakte] *vt* to relax; **se ~** *vi* to relax

déconvenue [dekɔ̃vny] *nf* disappointment

décor [dekɔʀ] *nm* décor; (*paysage*) scenery; **~s** *nmpl* (*THÉÂTRE*) scenery *sg*, décor *sg*; (*CINÉMA*) set *sg*; **décorateur** [dekɔʀatœʀ] *nm* (interior) decorator; (*CINÉMA*) set designer; **décoration** [dekɔʀasjɔ̃] *nf* decoration; **décorer** [dekɔʀe] *vt* to decorate

décortiquer [dekɔʀtike] *vt* to shell; (*riz*) to hull; (*fig*) to dissect

découcher [dekuʃe] *vi* to spend the night away from home

découdre [dekudʀ(ə)] *vt* to unpick; **se ~** *vi* to come unstitched; **en ~** (*fig*) to fight, do battle

découler [dekule] *vi*: ~ **de** to ensue *ou* follow from

découper [dekupe] *vt* (*papier, tissu etc*) to cut up; (*volaille, viande*) to carve;

(*détacher: manche, article*) to cut out; **se ~ sur** (*ciel, fond*) to stand out against

décourager [dekuraʒe] *vt* to discourage; **se ~** *vi* to lose heart, become discouraged

décousu, e [dekuzy] *adj* unstitched; (*fig*) disjointed, disconnected

découvert, e [dekuvɛʀ, -ɛʀt(ə)] *adj* (*tête*) bare, uncovered; (*lieu*) open, exposed ♦ *nm* (*bancaire*) overdraft; **découverte** *nf* discovery

découvrir [dekuvʀiʀ] *vt* to discover; (*apercevoir*) to see; (*enlever ce qui couvre ou protège*) to uncover; (*montrer, dévoiler*) to reveal; **se ~** *vi* to take off one's hat; to take something off (*au lit*) to uncover o.s.; (*ciel*) to clear

décret [dekʀɛ] *nm* decree; **décréter** *vt* to decree; to order; to declare

décrié, e [dekʀije] *adj* disparaged

décrire [dekʀiʀ] *vt* to describe

décrocher [dekʀɔʃe] *vt* (*dépendre*) to take down; (*téléphone*) to take off the hook; (: *pour répondre*): **~ (le téléphone)** to lift the receiver; (*fig: contrat etc*) to get, land ♦ *vi* to drop out; to switch off

décroître [dekʀwatʀ(ə)] *vi* to decrease, decline

décrypter [dekʀipte] *vt* to decipher

déçu, e [desy] *pp de* **décevoir**

décupler [dekyple] *vt, vi* to increase tenfold

dédaigner [dedɛɲe] *vt* to despise, scorn; (*négliger*) to disregard, spurn

dédaigneux, euse [dedɛɲø, -øz] *adj* scornful, disdainful

dédain [dedɛ̃] *nm* scorn, disdain

dédale [dedal] *nm* maze

dedans [dədɑ̃] *adv* inside; (*pas en plein air*) indoors, inside ♦ *nm* inside; **au ~** on the inside; inside; **en ~** (*vers l'intérieur*) inwards; *voir aussi* **là**

dédicacer [dedikase] *vt*: **~ (à qn)** to sign (for sb), autograph (for sb)

dédier [dedje] *vt* to dedicate

dédire [dediʀ]: **se ~** *vi* to go back on one's word; to retract, recant

dédommager [dedɔmaʒe] *vt*: **~ qn (de)** to compensate sb (for); (*fig*) to repay sb (for)

dédouaner [dedwane] *vt* to clear through customs

dédoubler [deduble] *vt* (*classe, effectifs*) to split (into two); **~ les trains** to run additional trains

déduire [dedɥiʀ] *vt*: **~ qch (de)** (*ôter*) to deduct sth (from); (*conclure*) to deduce *ou* infer sth (from)

déesse [deɛs] *nf* goddess

défaillance [defajɑ̃s] *nf* (*syncope*) blackout; (*fatigue*) (sudden) weakness *no pl*; (*technique*) fault, failure; (*morale etc*) weakness; **~ cardiaque** heart failure

défaillir [defajiʀ] *vi* to faint; to feel faint; (*mémoire etc*) to fail

défaire [defɛʀ] *vt* (*installation*) to take down, dismantle; (*paquet etc, nœud, vêtement*) to undo; **se ~** *vi* to come undone; **se ~ de** (*se débarrasser de*) to get rid of; (*se séparer de*) to part with

défait, e [defɛ, -ɛt] *adj* (*visage*) haggard, ravaged; **défaite** *nf* defeat

défalquer [defalke] *vt* to deduct

défaut [defo] *nm* (*moral*) fault, failing, defect; (*d'étoffe, métal*) fault, flaw, defect; (*manque, carence*): **~ de** lack of; shortage of; **en ~** at fault; in the wrong; **faire ~** (*manquer*) to be lacking; **à ~** failing that; **à ~ de** for lack *ou* want of; **par ~** (*JUR*) in his (*ou* her *etc*) absence

défavorable [defavɔʀabl(ə)] *adj* (*avis, conditions, jury*) unfavourable (*BRIT*), unfavorable (*US*)

défavoriser [defavɔʀize] *vt* to put at a disadvantage

défection [defɛksjɔ̃] *nf* defection, failure to give support *ou* assistance; failure to appear; **faire ~** (*d'un parti etc*) to withdraw one's support, leave

défectueux, euse [defɛktɥø, -øz] *adj* faulty, defective

défendre [defɑ̃dʀ(ə)] *vt* to defend; (*interdire*) to forbid; **se ~** *vi* to defend o.s.; **~ à qn qch/de faire** to forbid sb sth/to do; **il se défend** (*fig*) he can hold his own; **se ~ de/contre** (*se protéger*) to protect o.s. from/against; **se ~ de** (*se garder de*) to refrain from; (*nier*): **se ~ de vouloir** to deny wanting

défense [defãs] *nf* defence; (*d'éléphant etc*) tusk; **"~ de fumer/cracher"** "no smoking/spitting"

déférer [defeʀe] *vt* (*JUR*) to refer; **~ à** (*requête, décision*) to defer to

déferler [defeʀle] *vi* (*vagues*) to break; (*fig*) to surge

défi [defi] *nm* (*provocation*) challenge; (*bravade*) defiance

défiance [defjãs] *nf* mistrust, distrust

déficit [defisit] *nm* (*COMM*) deficit

défier [defje] *vt* (*provoquer*) to challenge; (*fig*) to defy, brave; **se ~ de** (*se méfier de*) to distrust

défigurer [defigyʀe] *vt* to disfigure

défilé [defile] *nm* (*GÉO*) (narrow) gorge *ou* pass; (*soldats*) parade; (*manifestants*) procession, march

défiler [defile] *vi* (*troupes*) to march past; (*sportifs*) to parade; (*manifestants*) to march; (*visiteurs*) to pour, stream; **se ~ vi** (*se dérober*) to slip away, sneak off

définir [definiʀ] *vt* to define

définitif, ive [definitif, -iv] *adj* (*final*) final, definitive; (*pour longtemps*) permanent, definitive; (*sans appel*) final, definite; **définitive** *nf*: **en définitive** eventually; (*somme toute*) when all is said and done

définitivement [definitivmã] *adv* definitively; permanently; definitely

déflagration [deflagʀasjɔ̃] *nf* explosion

défoncer [defɔ̃se] *vt* (*caisse*) to stave in; (*porte*) to smash in *ou* down; (*lit, fauteuil*) to burst (the springs of); (*terrain, route*) to rip *ou* plough up

déformation [defɔʀmasjɔ̃] *nf*: **~ professionnelle** conditioning by one's job

déformer [defɔʀme] *vt* to put out of shape; (*corps*) to deform; (*pensée, fait*) to distort; **se ~ vi** to lose its shape

défouler [defule] **se ~ vi** to unwind, let off steam

défraîchir [defʀeʃiʀ] **se ~ vi** to fade; to become worn

défrayer [defʀeje] *vt*: **~ qn** to pay sb's expenses; **~ la chronique** to be in the news

défricher [defʀiʃe] *vt* to clear (for cultivation)

défroquer [defʀɔke] *vi* (*aussi: se ~*) to give up the cloth

défunt, e [defœ̃, -œ̃t] *adj*: **son ~ père** his late father ♦ *nm/f* deceased

dégagé, e [degaʒe] *adj* clear; (*ton, air*) casual, jaunty

dégagement [degaʒmã] *nm*: **voie de ~** slip road; **itinéraire de ~** alternative route (*to relieve congestion*)

dégager [degaʒe] *vt* (*exhaler*) to give off; (*délivrer*) to free, extricate; (*désencombrer*) to clear; (*isoler: idée, aspect*) to bring out; **se ~ vi** (*odeur*) to be given off; (*passage, ciel*) to clear

dégarnir [degaʀniʀ] *vt* (*vider*) to empty, clear; **se ~ vi** (*tempes, crâne*) to go bald

dégâts [dega] *nmpl* damage *sg*

dégel [deʒɛl] *nm* thaw

dégeler [deʒle] *vt* to thaw (out); (*fig*) to unfreeze ♦ *vi* to thaw (out)

dégénérer [deʒeneʀe] *vi* to degenerate; (*empirer*) to go from bad to worse

dégingandé, e [deʒɛ̃gɑ̃de] *adj* gangling

dégivrer [deʒivʀe] *vt* (*frigo*) to defrost; (*vitres*) to de-ice

déglutir [deglytiʀ] *vt*, *vi* to swallow

dégonflé, e [degɔ̃fle] *adj* (*pneu*) flat

dégonfler [degɔ̃fle] *vt* (*pneu, ballon*) to let down, deflate; **se ~ vi** (*fam*) to chicken out

dégouliner [deguline] *vi* to trickle, drip

dégourdi, e [deguʀdi] *adj* smart, resourceful

dégourdir [deguʀdiʀ] *vt*: **se ~ (les jambes)** to stretch one's legs (*fig*)

dégoût [degu] *nm* disgust, distaste

dégoûtant, e [degutã, -ãt] *adj* disgusting

dégoûté, e [degute] *adj* disgusted; **~ de** sick of

dégoûter [degute] *vt* to disgust; **~ qn de qch** to put sb off sth

dégoutter [degute] *vi* to drip

dégradé [degʀade] *nm* (*PEINTURE*) gradation

dégrader [degʀade] *vt* (*MIL: officier*) to

degrade; (*abîmer*) to damage, deface; **se ~** *vi* (*relations, situation*) to deteriorate

dégrafer [degʀafe] *vt* to unclip, unhook

degré [dəgʀe] *nm* degree; (*d'escalier*) step; **alcool à 90 ~s** surgical spirit

dégressif, ive [degʀesif, -iv] *adj* on a decreasing scale

dégrèvement [degʀɛvmɑ̃] *nm* tax relief

dégringoler [degʀɛ̃gɔle] *vi* to tumble (down)

dégrossir [degʀosiʀ] *vt* (*fig*) to work out roughly; to knock the rough edges off

déguenillé, e [dɛgnije] *adj* ragged, tattered

déguerpir [degɛʀpiʀ] *vi* to clear off

dégueulasse [degœlas] (*fam*) *adj* disgusting

déguisement [degizmɑ̃] *nm* disguise

déguiser [degize] *vt* to disguise; **se ~** *vi* (*se costumer*) to dress up; (*pour tromper*) to disguise o.s.

déguster [degyste] *vt* (*vins*) to taste; (*fromages etc*) to sample; (*savourer*) to enjoy, savour

dehors [dəɔʀ] *adv* outside; (*en plein air*) outdoors ♦ *nm* outside ♦ *nmpl* (*apparences*) appearances; **mettre** *ou* **jeter ~** (*expulser*) to throw out; **au ~** outside; outwardly; **au ~ de** outside; **en ~** (*vers l'extérieur*) outside; outwards; **en ~ de** (*hormis*) apart from

déjà [deʒa] *adv* already; (*auparavant*) before, already

déjeuner [deʒœne] *vi* to (have) lunch; (*le matin*) to have breakfast ♦ *nm* lunch; breakfast

déjouer [deʒwe] *vt* to elude; to foil

delà [dəla] *adv*: **par ~, en ~ (de), au ~ (de)** beyond

délabrer [delɑbʀe]: **se ~** *vi* to fall into decay, become dilapidated

délacer [delase] *vt* to unlace

délai [delɛ] *nm* (*attente*) waiting period; (*sursis*) extension (of time); (*temps accordé*) time limit; **à bref ~** shortly, very soon; at short notice; **dans les ~s** within the time limit

délaisser [delese] *vt* to abandon, desert

délasser [delase] *vt* (*reposer*) to relax;

(*divertir*) to divert, entertain; **se ~** *vi* to relax

délateur, trice [delatœʀ, -tʀis] *nm/f* informer

délavé, e [delave] *adj* faded

délayer [deleje] *vt* (*CULIN*) to mix (with water *etc*); (*peinture*) to thin down

delco [dɛlko] *nm* (*AUTO*) distributor

délecter [delɛkte]: **se ~** *vi* to revel *ou* delight in

délégué, e [delege] *nm/f* delegate; representative

déléguer [delege] *vt* to delegate

délibéré, e [delibeʀe] *adj* (*conscient*) deliberate; (*déterminé*) determined

délibérer [delibeʀe] *vi* to deliberate

délicat, e [delika, -at] *adj* delicate; (*plein de tact*) tactful; (*attentionné*) thoughtful; (*exigeant*) fussy, particular; **procédés peu ~s** unscrupulous methods; **délicatement** *adv* delicately; (*avec douceur*) gently

délice [delis] *nm* delight

délicieux, euse [delisjø, -jøz] *adj* (*au goût*) delicious; (*sensation, impression*) delightful

délimiter [delimite] *vt* to delimit, demarcate; to determine; to define

délinquance [delɛ̃kɑ̃s] *nf* criminality; **délinquant, e** [delɛ̃kɑ̃, -ɑ̃t] *adj, nm/f* delinquent

délirer [deliʀe] *vi* to be delirious; (*fig*) to be raving, be going wild

délit [deli] *nm* (*criminal*) offence; **~ d'initié** (*BOURSE*) insider dealing *ou* trading

délivrer [delivʀe] *vt* (*prisonnier*) to (set) free, release; (*passeport, certificat*) to issue; **~ qn de** (*ennemis*) to deliver *ou* free sb from; (*fig*) to relieve sb of; to rid sb of

déloger [delɔʒe] *vt* (*locataire*) to turn out; (*objet coincé, ennemi*) to dislodge

deltaplane [dɛltaplan] *nm* hang-glider

déluge [delyʒ] *nm* (*biblique*) Flood

déluré, e [delyʀe] *adj* smart, resourceful; (*péj*) forward, pert

demain [dəmɛ̃] *adv* tomorrow

demande [dəmɑ̃d] *nf* (*requête*) request;

(*revendication*) demand; (*ADMIN, formulaire*) application; (*ÉCON*) **la ~** demand; **"~s d'emploi**" "situations wanted"; **~ de poste** job application

demandé, e [dəmɑ̃de] *adj* (*article etc*): **très ~** (very) much in demand

demander [dəmɑ̃de] *vt* to ask for; (*date, heure etc*) to ask; (*nécessiter*) to require, demand; **se ~** to wonder; (*sens purement réfléchi*) to ask o.s.; **~ qch à qn** to ask sb for sth; to ask sb sth; **~ à qn de faire** to ask sb to do; **on vous demande au téléphone** you're wanted on the phone

demandeur, euse [dəmɑ̃dœr, -øz] *nm/f*: **~ d'emploi** job-seeker; (*job*) applicant

démangeaison [demɑ̃ʒɛzɔ̃] *nf* itching

démanger [demɑ̃ʒe] *vi* to itch

démanteler [demɑ̃tle] *vt* to break up; to demolish

démaquillant [demakijɑ̃] *nm* make-up remover

démaquiller [demakije] *vt*: **se ~** to remove one's make-up

démarche [demarʃ(ə)] *nf* (*allure*) gait, walk; (*intervention*) step; approach; (*fig: intellectuelle*) thought processes *pl*; approach; **faire des ~s auprès de qn** to approach sb

démarcheur, euse [demarʃœr, -øz] *nm/f* (*COMM*) door-to-door salesman(woman)

démarquer [demarke] *vt* (*prix*) to mark down; (*joueur*) to stop marking

démarrage [demaraʒ] *nm* start

démarrer [demare] *vi* (*conducteur*) to start (up); (*véhicule*) to move off; (*travaux*) to get moving; **démarreur** *nm* (*AUTO*) starter

démêler [demele] *vt* to untangle

démêlés [demele] *nmpl* problems

déménagement [demenaʒmɑ̃] *nm* move, removal; **camion de ~** removal van

déménager [demenaʒe] *vt* (*meubles*) to (re)move ♦ *vi* to move (house); **déménageur** *nm* removal man; (*entrepreneur*) furniture remover

démener [demne]: **se ~** *vi* to thrash about; (*fig*) to exert o.s.

dément, e [demɑ̃, -ɑ̃t] *adj* (*fou*) mad, crazy; (*fam*) brilliant, fantastic

démentiel, le [demɑ̃sjɛl] *adj* insane

démentir [demɑ̃tir] *vt* to refute; **~ que** to deny that

démerder [demɛrde] (*fam*): **se ~** *vi* to sort things out for o.s.

démesuré, e [deməzyre] *adj* immoderate

démettre [demɛtr(ə)] *vt*: **~ qn de** (*fonction, poste*) to dismiss sb from; **se ~ (de ses fonctions)** to resign (from) one's duties; **se ~ l'épaule** *etc* to dislocate one's shoulder *etc*

demeurant [dəmœrɑ̃]: **au ~** *adv* for all that

demeure [dəmœr] *nf* residence; **mettre qn en ~ de faire** to enjoin *ou* order sb to do; **à ~** permanently

demeurer [dəmœre] *vi* (*habiter*) to live; (*séjourner*) to stay; (*rester*) to remain

demi, e [dəmi] *adj* half ♦ *nm* (*bière*) ≈ half-pint (*0,25 litres*) ♦ *préfixe*: **~...** half-, semi..., demi-; **trois heures/bouteilles et ~es** three and a half hours/bottles, three hours/bottles and a half; **il est 2 heures/midi et ~e** it's half past 2/12; **à ~** half-; **à la ~e** (*heure*) on the half-hour; **~-cercle** *nm* semicircle; **en ~-cercle** *adj* semicircular ♦ *adv* in a half circle; **~-douzaine** *nf* half-dozen, half a dozen; **~-finale** *nf* semifinal; **~-frère** *nm* half-brother; **~-heure** *nf* half-hour, half an hour; **~-journée** *nf* half-day, half a day; **~-litre** *nm* half-litre, half a litre; **~-livre** *nf* half-pound, half a pound; **~-mot** *adv*: **à ~-mot** without having to spell things out; **~-pension** *nf* (*à l'hôtel*) half-board; **~-place** *nf* half-fare

démis, e [demi, -iz] *adj* (*épaule etc*) dislocated

demi: **~-saison** *nf*: **vêtements de ~-saison** spring *ou* autumn clothing; **~-sel** *adj inv* (*beurre, fromage*) slightly salted; **~-sœur** *nf* half-sister

démission [demisjɔ̃] *nf* resignation; **donner sa ~** to give *ou* hand in one's notice; **démissionner** *vi* (*de son poste*) to resign

demi-tarif [dəmitaʀif] *nm* half-price; (*TRANSPORTS*) half-fare

demi-tour [dəmituʀ] *nm* about-turn; **faire** ~ to turn (and go) back; (*AUTO*) to do a U-turn

démocratie [demɔkʀasi] *nf* democracy; **démocratique** [demɔkʀatik] *adj* democratic

démodé, e [demɔde] *adj* old-fashioned

démographique [demɔgʀafik] *adj* demographic, population *cpd*

demoiselle [dəmwazɛl] *nf* (*jeune fille*) young lady; (*célibataire*) single lady, maiden lady; ~ **d'honneur** bridesmaid

démolir [demɔliʀ] *vt* to demolish

démon [demɔ̃] *nm* (*enfant turbulent*) devil, demon; **le D~** the Devil

démonstration [demɔ̃stʀasjɔ̃] *nf* demonstration; (*aérienne, navale*) display

démonté, e [demɔ̃te] *adj* (*fig*) raging, wild

démonter [demɔ̃te] *vt* (*machine etc*) to take down, dismantle; **se** ~ *vi* (*personne*) to lose countenance

démontrer [demɔ̃tʀe] *vt* to demonstrate

démordre [demɔʀdʀ(ə)] *vi*: **ne pas** ~ **de** to refuse to give up, stick to

démouler [demule] *vt* (*gâteau*) to turn out

démuni, e [demyni] *adj* (*sans argent*) impoverished

démunir [demyniʀ] *vt*: ~ **qn de** to deprive sb of; **se** ~ **de** to part with, give up

dénatalité [denatalite] *nf* fall in the birth rate

dénaturer [denatyʀe] *vt* (*goût*) to alter; (*pensée, fait*) to distort

déniaiser [denjeze] *vt*: ~ **qn** to teach sb about life

dénicher [denife] *vt* to unearth; to track *ou* hunt down

dénier [denje] *vt* to deny

dénigrer [denigʀe] *vt* to denigrate, run down

dénivellation [denivelasjɔ̃] *nf* = **dénivellement**

dénivellement [denivɛlmɑ̃] *nm* ramp; dip; difference in level

dénombrer [denɔ̃bʀe] *vt* (*compter*) to count; (*énumérer*) to enumerate, list

dénomination [denɔminasjɔ̃] *nf* designation, appellation

dénommer [denɔme] *vt* to name

dénoncer [denɔ̃se] *vt* to denounce; **se** ~ *vi* to give o.s. up, come forward

dénouement [denumɑ̃] *nm* outcome

dénouer [denwe] *vt* to unknot, undo

dénoyauter [denwajɔte] *vt* to stone

denrée [dɑ̃ʀe] *nf*: ~**s (alimentaires)** foodstuffs

dense [dɑ̃s] *adj* dense

densité [dɑ̃site] *nf* density

dent [dɑ̃] *nf* tooth; **en** ~**s de scie** serrated; jagged; ~ **de lait/sagesse** milk/ wisdom tooth; **dentaire** *adj* dental

dentelé, e [dɑ̃tle] *adj* jagged, indented

dentelle [dɑ̃tɛl] *nf* lace *no pl*

dentier [dɑ̃tje] *nm* denture

dentifrice [dɑ̃tifʀis] *nm* toothpaste

dentiste [dɑ̃tist(ə)] *nm/f* dentist

dénuder [denyde] *vt* to bare

dénué, e [denye] *adj*: ~ **de** devoid of; lacking in; **dénuement** [denymɑ̃] *nm* destitution

déodorant [deɔdɔʀɑ̃] *nm* deodorant

dépannage [depanaʒ] *nm*: **service de** ~ (*AUTO*) breakdown service

dépanner [depane] *vt* (*voiture, télévision*) to fix, repair; (*fig*) to bail out, help out; **dépanneuse** *nf* breakdown lorry (*BRIT*), tow truck (*US*)

dépareillé, e [depaʀeje] *adj* (*collection, service*) incomplete; (*objet*) odd

déparer [depaʀe] *vt* tc spoil, mar

départ [depaʀ] *nm* leaving *no pl*, departure; (*SPORT*) start; (*sur un horaire*) departure; **au** ~ at the start; **à son** ~ when he left

départager [depaʀtaʒe] *vt* to decide between

département [depaʀtəmɑ̃] *nm* department

départir [depaʀtiʀ]: **se** ~ **de** *vt* to abandon, depart from

dépassé, e [depɑse] *adj* superseded, outmoded; (*affolé*) panic-stricken

dépasser [depɑse] *vt* (*véhicule, concurrent*) to overtake; (*endroit*) to pass, go past; *(somme, limite)* to exceed; *(fig: en beauté etc)* to surpass, outshine; *(être en saillie sur)* to jut out above *(ou* in front of)* ♦ *vi (jupon)* to show

dépaysé, e [depeize] *adj* disoriented

dépecer [depəse] *vt* to joint, cut up

dépêche [depɛʃ] *nf* dispatch

dépêcher [depeʃe] *vt* to dispatch; **se ~** *vi* to hurry

dépeindre [depɛ̃dʀ(ə)] *vt* to depict

dépénalisation [depenalizasjɔ̃] *nf* decriminalization

dépendre [depɑ̃dʀ(ə)]: **~ de** *vt* to depend on; *(financièrement etc)* to be dependent on

dépens [depɑ̃] *nmpl*: **aux ~ de** at the expense of

dépense [depɑ̃s] *nf* spending *no pl*, expense, expenditure *no pl*; *(fig)* consumption; expenditure

dépenser [depɑ̃se] *vt* to spend; *(gaz, eau)* to use; *(fig)* to expend, use up; **se ~** *vi (se fatiguer)* to exert o.s.

dépensier, ière [depɑ̃sje, -jɛʀ] *adj*: **il est ~** he's a spendthrift

déperdition [depɛʀdisjɔ̃] *nf* loss

dépérir [depeʀiʀ] *vi* to waste away; to wither

dépêtrer [depetʀe] *vt*: **se ~ de** to extricate o.s. from

dépeupler [depœple] *vt* to depopulate; **se ~** *vi* to be depopulated

dépilatoire [depilatwaʀ] *adj* depilatory, hair-removing

dépister [depiste] *vt* to detect; *(voleur)* to track down; *(poursuivants)* to throw off the scent

dépit [depi] *nm* vexation, frustration; **en ~ de** in spite of; **en ~ du bon sens** contrary to all good sense; **dépité, e** *adj* vexed, frustrated

déplacé, e [deplase] *adj (propos)* out of place, uncalled-for

déplacement [deplasmɑ̃] *nm (voyage)* trip, travelling *no pl*

déplacer [deplase] *vt (table, voiture)* to move, shift; *(employé)* to transfer, move; *(os, vertèbre etc)* to displace; **se ~** *vi* to move; *(voyager)* to travel

déplaire [deplɛʀ] *vi*: **ceci me déplaît** I don't like this, I dislike this; **se ~** *vr*: **se ~ quelque part** to be unhappy somewhere; **déplaisant, e** *adj* disagreeable

dépliant [deplijɑ̃] *nm* leaflet

déplier [deplije] *vt* to unfold

déplorer [deplɔʀe] *vt (regretter)* to deplore

déployer [deplwaje] *vt* to open out, spread; to deploy; to display, exhibit

déporter [depɔʀte] *vt (POL)* to deport; *(dévier)* to carry off course

déposer [depoze] *vt (gén: mettre, poser)* to lay *ou* put down; *(à la banque, à la consigne)* to deposit; *(passager)* to drop (off), set down; *(roi)* to depose; *(ADMIN: faire enregistrer)* to file; to register; *(JUR)*: **~ (contre)** to testify *ou* give evidence (against); **se ~** *vi* to settle; **dépositaire** *nm/f (COMM)* agent

dépôt [depo] *nm (à la banque, sédiment)* deposit; *(entrepôt, réserve)* warehouse, store; *(gare)* depot; *(prison)* cells *pl*

dépotoir [depɔtwaʀ] *nm* dumping ground, rubbish dump

dépouille [depuj] *nf (d'animal)* skin, hide; *(humaine)*: **~ (mortelle)** mortal remains *pl*

dépouillé, e [depuje] *adj (fig)* bare, bald

dépouiller [depuje] *vt (animal)* to skin; *(spolier)* to deprive of one's possessions; *(documents)* to go through, peruse; **~ qn/qch de** to strip sb/sth of; **~ le scrutin** to count the votes

dépourvu, e [depuʀvy] *adj*: **~ de** lacking in, without; **au ~** unprepared

déprécier [depʀesje] *vt* to depreciate; **se ~** *vi* to depreciate

dépression [depʀesjɔ̃] *nf* depression; **~ (nerveuse)** (nervous) breakdown

déprimer [depʀime] *vt* to depress

MOT-CLÉ

---

depuis [dəpɥi] *prép* **1** *(point de départ dans le temps)* since; **il habite Paris ~ 1983/l'an dernier** he has been living in Paris since 1983/last year; **~ quand le**

connaissez-vous? how long have you known him?

2 (*temps écoulé*) for; **il habite Paris ~ 5 ans** he has been living in Paris for 5 years; **je le connais ~ 3 ans** I've known him for 3 years

3 (*lieu*): **il a plu ~ Metz** it's been raining since Metz; **elle a téléphoné ~ Valence** she rang from Valence

4 (*quantité, rang*) from; **~ les plus petits jusqu'aux plus grands** from the youngest to the oldest

♦ *adv* (*temps*) since (then); **je ne lui ai pas parlé ~** I haven't spoken to him since (then)

depuis que *conj* (ever) since; **~ qu'il m'a dit ça** (ever) since he said that to me

député, e [depyte] *nm/f* (*POL*) ≈ Member of Parliament (*BRIT*), ≈ Member of Congress (*US*)

députer [depyte] *vt* to delegate

déraciner [derasine] *vt* to uproot

dérailler [deraje] *vi* (*train*) to be derailed; **faire ~** to derail

déraisonner [derɛzɔne] *vi* to talk nonsense, rave

dérangement [derãʒmã] *nm* (*gêne*) trouble; (*gastrique etc*) disorder; (*mécanique*) breakdown; **en ~** (*téléphone*) out of order

déranger [derãʒe] *vt* (*personne*) to trouble, bother; to disturb; (*projets*) to disrupt, upset; (*objets, vêtements*) to disarrange; **se ~** *vi* to put o.s. out; to (take the trouble to) come *ou* go out; **est-ce que cela vous dérange si ...?** do you mind if ...?

déraper [derape] *vi* (*voiture*) to skid; (*personne, semelles, couteau*) to slip

déréglé, e [deregle] *adj* (*mœurs*) dissolute

déréglementation [dereglǝmãtɑsjɔ̃] *nf* deregulation

dérégler [deregle] *vt* (*mécanisme*) to put out of order; (*estomac*) to upset

dérider [deride] *vt* to brighten up; **se ~** *vi* to brighten up

dérision [derizjɔ̃] *nf*: **tourner en ~** to deride

dérivatif [derivatif] *nm* distraction

dérive [deriv] *nf* (*de dériveur*) centreboard; **aller à la ~** (*NAVIG, fig*) to drift

dérivé, e [derive] *nm* (*TECH*) by-product; **dérivée** *nf* (*MATH*) derivative

dériver [derive] *vt* (*MATH*) to derive; (*cours d'eau etc*) to divert ♦ *vi* (*bateau*) to drift; **~ de** to derive from

dermatologue [dɛrmatɔlɔg] *nm/f* dermatologist

dernier, ière [dɛrnje, -jɛr] *adj* last; (*le plus récent*) latest, last; **lundi/le mois ~** last Monday/month; **du ~ chic** extremely smart; **les ~s honneurs** the last tribute; **en ~** last; **ce ~** the latter; **dernièrement** *adv* recently

dérobé, e [derɔbe] *adj* (*porte*) secret, hidden; **à la ~e** surreptitiously

dérober [derɔbe] *vt* to steal; **se ~** *vi* (*s'esquiver*) to slip away; to shy away; **se ~ sous** (*s'effondrer*) to give way beneath; **se ~ à** (*justice, regards*) to hide from; (*obligation*) to shirk; **~ qch à (la vue de) qn** to conceal *ou* hide sth from sb('s view)

dérogation [derɔgɑsjɔ̃] *nf* (special) dispensation

déroger [derɔʒe]: **~ à** *vt* to go against, depart from

dérouiller [deruje] *vt*: **se ~ les jambes** to stretch one's legs (*fig*)

déroulement [derulmã] *nm* (*d'une opération etc*) progress

dérouler [derule] *vt* (*ficelle*) to unwind; (*papier*) to unroll; **se ~** *vi* (*avoir lieu*) to take place; (*se passer*) to go on; to go (off); to unfold

déroute [derut] *nf* rout; total collapse; **à la ~e**

dérouter [derute] *vt* (*avion, train*) to reroute, divert; (*étonner*) to disconcert, throw (out)

derrière [dɛrjɛr] *adv, prép* behind ♦ *nm* (*d'une maison*) back; (*postérieur*) behind, bottom; **les pattes de ~** the back *ou* hind legs; **par ~** from behind; (*fig*) behind one's back

des [de] *dét voir* **de** ♦ *prép* +*dét* = **de** +*les*

dès [dɛ] *prép* from; ~ **que** as soon as; ~ **son retour** as soon as he was (*ou* is) back; ~ **lors** from then on; ~ **lors que** from the moment (that)

désabusé, e [dezabyze] *adj* disillusioned

désaccord [dezakɔʀ] *nm* disagreement; **désaccordé, e** [dezakɔʀde] *adj* (*MUS*) out of tune

désaffecté, e [dezafɛkte] *adj* disused

désagréable [dezagʀeable(ə)] *adj* unpleasant

désagréger [dezagʀeʒe]: **se** ~ *vi* to disintegrate, break up

désagrément [dezagʀemɑ̃] *nm* annoyance, trouble *no pl*

désaltérer [dezalteʀe] *vt*: **se** ~ to quench one's thirst

désamorcer [dezamɔʀse] *vt* to defuse; to forestall

désapprobateur, trice [dezapʀɔbatœʀ, -tʀis] *adj* disapproving

désapprouver [dezapʀuve] *vt* to disapprove of

désarçonner [dezaʀsɔne] *vt* to unseat, throw; (*fig*) to throw, puzzle

désarmant, e [dezaʀmɑ̃, -ɑ̃t] *adj* disarming

désarroi [dezaʀwa] *nm* disarray

désarticulé, e [dezaʀtikyle] *adj* (*pantin, corps*) dislocated

désastre [dezastʀ(ə)] *nm* disaster

désavantage [dezavɑ̃taʒ] *nm* disadvantage; (*inconvénient*) drawback, disadvantage; **désavantager** *vt* to put at a disadvantage

désavouer [dezavwe] *vt* to disown

désaxé, e [dezakse] *adj* (*fig*) unbalanced

descendre [desɑ̃dʀ(ə)] *vt* (*escalier, montagne*) to go (*ou* come) down; (*valise, paquet*) to take *ou* get down; (*étagère etc*) to lower; (*fam: abattre*) to shoot down ♦ *vi* to go (*ou* come) down; (*passager: s'arrêter*) to get out, alight; ~ **à pied/en voiture** to walk/drive down; ~ **de** (*famille*) to be descended from; ~ **du train** to get out of *ou* get off the train; ~ **d'un arbre** to climb down from a tree; ~ **de cheval** to dismount; ~ **à l'hôtel** to

stay at a hotel

descente [desɑ̃t] *nf* descent, going down; (*chemin*) way down; (*SKI*) downhill (race); **au milieu de la** ~ halfway down; ~ **de lit** bedside rug; ~ **(de police)** (police) raid

description [dɛskʀipsjɔ̃] *nf* description

désemparé, e [dezɑ̃paʀe] *adj* bewildered, distraught

désemparer [dezɑ̃paʀe] *vi*: **sans** ~ without stopping

désemplir [dezɑ̃pliʀ] *vi*: **ne pas** ~ to be always full

déséquilibre [dezekilibʀ(ə)] *nm* (*position*): **en** ~ unsteady; (*fig: des forces, du budget*) imbalance; **déséquilibré, e** [dezekilibʀe] *nm/f* (*PSYCH*) unbalanced person; **déséquilibrer** [dezekilibʀe] *vt* to throw off balance

désert, e [dezɛʀ, -ɛʀt(ə)] *adj* deserted ♦ *nm* desert

déserter [dezɛʀte] *vi*, *vt* to desert

désertique [dezɛʀtik] *adj* desert *cpd*; barren, empty

désespéré, e [dezɛspeʀe] *adj* desperate

désespérer [dezɛspeʀe] *vt* to drive to despair ♦ *vi*: ~ **de** to despair of

désespoir [dezɛspwaʀ] *nm* despair; **en** ~ **de cause** in desperation

déshabillé [dezabije] *nm* négligée

déshabiller [dezabije] *vt* to undress; **se** ~ *vi* to undress (o.s.)

désherbant [dezɛʀbɑ̃] *nm* weed-killer

déshériter [dezeʀite] *vt* to disinherit

déshérités [dezeʀite] *nmpl*: **les** ~ the underprivileged

déshonneur [dezɔnœʀ] *nm* dishonour

déshydraté, e [dezidʀate] *adj* dehydrated

desiderata [deziderata] *nmpl* requirements

désigner [deziɲe] *vt* (*montrer*) to point out, indicate; (*dénommer*) to denote; (*candidat etc*) to name

désinfectant, e [dezɛ̃fɛktɑ̃, -ɑ̃t] *adj, nm* disinfectant; **désinfecter** [dezɛ̃fɛkte] *vt* to disinfect

désintégrer [dezɛ̃tegʀe] *vt* to disintegrate; **se** ~ *vi* to disintegrate

désintéressé, e [dezɛ̃teʀese] *adj* disinterested, unselfish

désintéresser [dezɛ̃teʀese] *vt*: **se ~ (de)** to lose interest (in)

désintoxication [dezɛ̃tɔksikasjɔ̃] *nf*: **faire une cure de ~** to undergo treatment for alcoholism (*ou* drug addiction)

désinvolte [dezɛ̃vɔlt(ə)] *adj* casual, offhand; **désinvolture** *nf* casualness

désir [deziʀ] *nm* wish; (*fort, sensuel*) desire

désirer [deziʀe] *vt* to want, wish for; (*sexuellement*) to desire; **je désire ...** (*formule de politesse*) I would like ...

désister [deziste]: **se ~** *vi* to stand down, withdraw

désobéir [dezɔbeiʀ] *vi*: **~ (à qn/qch)** to disobey (sb/sth); **désobéissant, e** *adj* disobedient

désobligeant, e [dezɔbliʒɑ̃, -ɑ̃t] *adj* disagreeable

désodorisant [dezɔdɔʀizɑ̃] *nm* air freshener, deodorizer

désœuvré, e [dezœvʀe] *adj* idle

désolé, e [dezɔle] *adj* (*paysage*) desolate; **je suis ~** I'm sorry

désoler [dezɔle] *vt* to distress, grieve

désolidariser [desɔlidaʀize] *vt*: **se ~ de** *ou* **d'avec** to dissociate o.s. from

désopilant, e [dezɔpilɑ̃, -ɑ̃t] *adj* hilarious

désordonné, e [dezɔʀdɔne] *adj* untidy

désordre [dezɔʀdʀ(ə)] *nm* disorder(liness), untidiness; (*anarchie*) disorder; **~s** *nmpl* (*POL*) disturbances, disorder *sg*; **en ~** in a mess, untidy

désorienté, e [dezɔʀjɑ̃te] *adj* disorientated

désormais [dezɔʀmɛ] *adv* from now on

désosser [dezɔse] *vt* to bone

desquelles [dekɛl] *prép +pron* = **de +lesquelles**

desquels [dekɛl] *prép +pron* = **de +lesquels**

dessaisir [deseziʀ]: **se ~ de** *vt* to give up, part with

dessaler [desale] *vt* (*eau de mer*) to desalinate; (*CULIN*) to soak

desséché, e [desefe] *adj* dried up

dessécher [desefe] *vt* to dry out, parch; **se ~** *vi* to dry out

dessein [desɛ̃] *nm* design; **à ~** intentionally, deliberately

desserrer [deseʀe] *vt* to loosen; (*frein*) to release

dessert [desɛʀ] *nm* dessert, pudding

desserte [desɛʀt(ə)] *nf* (*table*) side table; (*transport*): **la ~ du village est assurée par autocar** there is a coach service to the village

desservir [desɛʀviʀ] *vt* (*ville, quartier*) to serve; (*nuire à*) to go against, put at a disadvantage; (*débarrasser*): **~ (la table)** to clear the table

dessin [desɛ̃] *nm* (*œuvre, art*) drawing; (*motif*) pattern, design; (*contour*) (out)line; **~ animé** cartoon (film); **~ humoristique** cartoon

dessinateur, trice [desinatœʀ, -tʀis] *nm/f* drawer; (*de bandes dessinées*) cartoonist; (*industriel*) draughtsman(woman) (*BRIT*), draftsman(woman) (*US*)

dessiner [desine] *vt* to draw; (*concevoir*) to design

dessous [dəsu] *adv* underneath, beneath ♦ *nm* underside ♦ *nmpl* (*sous-vêtements*) underwear *sg*; **en ~, par ~** underneath; below; **au-dessous (de)** below; (*peu digne de*) beneath; **avoir le ~** to get the worst of it; **dessous-de-plat** *nm inv* tablemat

dessus [dəsy] *adv* on top; (*collé, écrit*) on it ♦ *nm* top; **en ~** above; **par ~** *adv* over it ♦ *prép* over; **au-~ (de)** above; **avoir le ~** to get the upper hand; **dessus-de-lit** *nm inv* bedspread

destin [dɛstɛ̃] *nm* fate; (*avenir*) destiny

destinataire [dɛstinatɛʀ] *nm/f* (*POSTES*) addressee; (*d'un colis*) consignee

destination [dɛstinasjɔ̃] *nf* (*lieu*) destination; (*usage*) purpose; **à ~ de** bound for, travelling to

destinée [dɛstine] *nf* fate; (*existence, avenir*) destiny

destiner [dɛstine] *vt*: **~ qn à** (*poste, sort*) to destine sb for; **~ qn/qch à** (*prédestiner*) to destine sb/sth to +*verbe*; **~**

qch à qn (*envisager de donner*) to intend sth to have sth; (*adresser*) to intend sth for sb; to aim sth at sb; **être destiné à** (*sort*) to be destined to +*verbe*; (*usage*) to be meant for; (*suj: sort*) to be in store for

destituer [dɛstitɥe] *vt* to depose

désuet, ète [desɥɛ, -ɛt] *adj* outdated, outmoded; **désuétude** *nf*: **tomber en désuétude** to fall into disuse

détachant [detaʃɑ̃] *nm* stain remover

détachement [detafmɑ̃] *nm* detachment

détacher *vt* (*enlever*) to detach, remove; (*délier*) to untie; (*ADMIN*): ~ **qn (auprès de** *ou* **à)** to post sb (to); **se** ~ *vi* (*tomber*) to come off; to come out; (*se défaire*) to come undone; **se** ~ **sur** to stand out against; **se** ~ **de** (*se désintéresser*) to grow away from

détail [detaj] *nm* detail; (*COMM*): **le** ~ retail; **en** ~ in detail; **au** ~ (*COMM*) retail; separately

détaillant [detajɑ̃] *nm* retailer

détailler [detaje] *vt* (*expliquer*) to explain in detail; to detail; (*examiner*) to look over, examine

détartrant [detaʀtʀɑ̃] *nm* scale remover

détecter [detɛkte] *vt* to detect

détective [detɛktiv] *nm* (*policier: en Grande Bretagne*) detective; ~ **(privé)** private detective

déteindre [detɛ̃dʀ(ə)] *vi* (*tissu*) to fade; (*fig*): ~ **sur** to rub off on

dételer [detle] *vt* to unharness

détendre [detɑ̃dʀ(ə)] *vt*: **se** ~ to lose its tension; to relax

détenir [detniʀ] *vt* (*fortune, objet, secret*) to be in possession of; (*prisonnier*) to detain, hold; (*record, pouvoir*) to hold

détente [detɑ̃t] *nf* relaxation; (*d'une arme*) trigger

détention [detɑ̃sjɔ̃] *nf* possession; detention; holding; ~ **préventive** (pre-trial) custody

détenu, e [detny] *nm/f* prisoner

détergent [detɛʀʒɑ̃] *nm* detergent

détériorer [deteʀjɔʀe] *vt* to damage; **se** ~ *vi* to deteriorate

déterminé, e [detɛʀmine] *adj* (*résolu*) determined; (*précis*) specific, definite

déterminer [detɛʀmine] *vt* (*fixer*) to determine; (*décider*): ~ **qn à faire** to decide sb to do

déterrer [detɛʀe] *vt* to dig up

détestable [detɛstabl(ə)] *adj* foul, ghastly; detestable, odious

détester [detɛste] *vt* to hate, detest

détonation [detɔnɑsjɔ̃] *nf* detonation, bang, report (of a gun)

détonner [detɔne] *vi* (*MUS*) to go out of tune; (*fig*) to clash

détour [detuʀ] *nm* detour; (*tournant*) bend, curve; **sans** ~ (*fig*) plainly

détourné, e [detuʀne] *adj* (*moyen*) roundabout

détournement [detuʀnəmɑ̃] *nm*: ~ **d'avion** hijacking; ~ **de mineur** corruption of a minor

détourner [detuʀne] *vt* to divert; (*par la force*) to hijack; (*yeux, tête*) to turn away; (*de l'argent*) to embezzle; **se** ~ *vi* to turn away

détracteur, trice [detʀaktœʀ, -tʀis] *nm/f* disparager, critic

détraquer [detʀake] *vt* to put out of order; (*estomac*) to upset; **se** ~ *vi* to go wrong

détrempé, e [detʀɑ̃pe] *adj* (*sol*) sodden, waterlogged

détresse [detʀɛs] *nf* distress

détriment [detʀimɑ̃] *nm*: **au** ~ **de** to the detriment of

détritus [detʀitys] *nmpl* rubbish *sg*, refuse *sg*

détroit [detʀwa] *nm* strait

détromper [detʀɔ̃pe] *vt* to disabuse

détrôner [detʀone] *vt* to dethrone

détrousser [detʀuse] *vt* to rob

détruire [detʀɥiʀ] *vt* to destroy

dette [dɛt] *nf* debt

D.E.U.G. [døg] *sigle m*

deuil [dœj] *nm* (*perte*) bereavement; (*période*) mourning; (*chagrin*) grief; **être en** ~ to be in mourning

deux [dø] *num* two; **les** ~ both; **ses** ~ **mains** both his hands, his two hands; **deuxième** *num* second; **deuxièmement** *adv* secondly, in the second place;

deux-pièces *nm inv* (*tailleur*) two-piece suit; (*de bain*) two-piece (swimsuit); (*appartement*) two-roomed flat (BRIT) *ou* apartment (US); **deux-roues** *nm inv* two-wheeled vehicle

deux points *nm inv* colon *sg*

devais *etc vb voir* **devoir**

dévaler [devale] *vt* to hurtle down

dévaliser [devalize] *vt* to rob, burgle

dévaloriser [devalɔʀize] *vt* to depreciate; **se ~** *vi* to depreciate

dévaluation [devalɥasjɔ̃] *nf* depreciation; (ÉCON: *mesure*) devaluation

devancer [dəvɑ̃se] *vt* to be ahead of; to get ahead of; to arrive before; (*prévenir*) to anticipate

devant [dəvɑ̃] *adv* in front; (*à distance*: *en avant*) ahead ♦ *prép* in front of; ahead of; (*avec mouvement*: *passer*) past; (*fig*) before, in front of; faced with; in view of ♦ *nm* front; **prendre les ~s** to make the first move; **les pattes de ~** the front legs, the forelegs; **par ~** (*boutonner*) at the front; (*entrer*) the front way; **aller au-~ de qn** to go out to meet sb; **aller au-~ de** (*désirs de qn*) to anticipate

devanture [dəvɑ̃tyʀ] *nf* (*façade*) (shop) front; (*étalage*) display; (shop) window

déveine [devɛn] *nf* rotten luck *no pl*

développement [devlɔpmɑ̃] *nm* development

développer [devlɔpe] *vt* to develop; **se ~** *vi* to develop

devenir [dəvniʀ] *vb +attrib* to become; **~ instituteur** to become a teacher; **que sont-ils devenus?** what has become of them?

dévergondé, e [devɛʀgɔ̃de] *adj* wild, shameless

déverser [devɛʀse] *vt* (*liquide*) to pour (out); (*ordures*) to tip (out); **se ~ dans** (*fleuve, mer*) to flow into

dévêtir [devetiʀ] *vt* to undress; **se ~** *vi* to undress

devez *etc vb voir* **devoir**

déviation [devjasjɔ̃] *nf* deviation; (AUTO) diversion (BRIT), detour (US)

dévider [devide] *vt* to unwind

devienne *etc vb voir* **devenir**

dévier [devje] *vt* (*fleuve, circulation*) to divert; (*coup*) to deflect ♦ *vi* to veer (off course)

devin [dəvɛ̃] *nm* soothsayer, seer

deviner [dəvine] *vt* to guess; (*prévoir*) to foresee; (*apercevoir*) to distinguish; **devinette** [dəvinɛt] *nf* riddle

devins *etc vb voir* **devenir**

devis [dəvi] *nm* estimate, quotation

dévisager [devizaʒe] *vt* to stare at

devise [dəviz] *nf* (*formule*) motto, watchword; (ÉCON: *monnaie*) currency; **~s** *nfpl* (*argent*) currency *sg*

deviser [dəvize] *vi* to converse

dévisser [devise] *vt* to unscrew, undo; **se ~** *vi* to come unscrewed

dévoiler [devwale] *vt* to unveil

devoir [dəvwaʀ] *nm* duty; (SCOL) homework *no pl*; (: *en classe*) exercise ♦ *vt* (*argent, respect*): **~ qch (à qn)** to owe (sb) sth; (*suivi de l'infinitif*: *obligation*): **il doit le faire** he has to do it, he must do it; (: *intention*): **il doit partir demain** he is (due) to leave tomorrow; (: *probabilité*): **il doit être tard** it must be late

dévolu, e [devɔly] *adj*: **~ à** allotted to ♦ *nm*: **jeter son ~ sur** to fix one's choice on

dévorer [devɔʀe] *vt* to devour; (*suj*: *feu, soucis*) to consume

dévot, e [devo, -ɔt] *adj* devout, pious

dévotion [devosjɔ̃] *nf* devoutness; **être à la ~ de qn** to be totally devoted to sb

dévoué, e [devwe] *adj* devoted

dévouer [devwe]: **se ~** *vi* (*se sacrifier*): **se ~ (pour)** to sacrifice o.s. (for); (*se consacrer*): **se ~ à** to devote *ou* dedicate o.s. to

dévoyé, e [devwaje] *adj* delinquent

devrai *etc vb voir* **devoir**

diabète [djabɛt] *nm* diabetes *sg*; **diabétique** *nm/f* diabetic

diable [djɑbl(ə)] *nm* devil

diabolo [djabɔlo] *nm* (*boisson*) lemonade with fruit cordial

diacre [djakʀ(ə)] *nm* deacon

diagnostic [djagnɔstik] *nm* diagnosis *sg*

diagonal, e, aux [djagɔnal, -o] *adj* diagonal; **diagonale** *nf* diagonal; **en diagonale** diagonally; **lire en diagonale** to skim through

diagramme [djagʀam] *nm* chart, graph

dialecte [djalɛkt(ə)] *nm* dialect

dialogue [djalɔg] *nm* dialogue

diamant [djamɑ̃] *nm* diamond; **diamantaire** *nm* diamond dealer

diamètre [djamɛtʀ(ə)] *nm* diameter

diapason [djapazɔ̃] *nm* tuning fork

diaphragme [djafʀagm(ə)] *nm* diaphragm

diaporama [djapɔʀama] *nm* slide show

diapositive [djapozitiv] *nf* transparency, slide

diarrhée [djaʀe] *nf* diarrhoea

dictateur [diktatœʀ] *nm* dictator; **dictature** *nf* dictatorship

dictée [dikte] *nf* dictation

dicter [dikte] *vt* to dictate

dictionnaire [diksjɔnɛʀ] *nm* dictionary

dicton [diktɔ̃] *nm* saying, dictum

dièse [djɛz] *nm* sharp

diesel [djezɛl] *nm* diesel ♦ *adj inv* diesel

diète [djɛt] *nf* (*jeûne*) starvation diet; (*régime*) diet

diététique [djetetik] *adj*: **magasin ~** health food shop

dieu, x [djø] *nm* god; **D~** God; **mon D~!** good heavens!

diffamation [difamasjɔ̃] *nf* slander; (*écrite*) libel

différé [difeʀe] *nm* (*TV*): **en ~** (pre-) recorded

différence [difeʀɑ̃s] *nf* difference; **à la ~ de** unlike; **différencier** [difeʀɑ̃sje] *vt* to differentiate; **différend** [difeʀɑ̃] *nm* difference (of opinion), disagreement

différent, e [difeʀɑ̃, -ɑ̃t] *adj*: **~ (de)** different (from); **~s objets** different *ou* various objects

différer [difeʀe] *vt* to postpone, put off ♦ *vi*: **~ (de)** to differ (from)

difficile [difisil] *adj* difficult; (*exigeant*) hard to please; **difficilement** *adv* with difficulty

difficulté [difikylte] *nf* difficulty; **en ~** (*bateau, alpiniste*) in difficulties

difforme [difɔʀm(ə)] *adj* deformed, misshapen

diffuser [difyze] *vt* (*chaleur, bruit*) to diffuse; (*émission, musique*) to broadcast; (*nouvelle, idée*) to circulate; (*COMM*) to distribute

digérer [diʒeʀe] *vt* to digest; (*fig: accepter*) to stomach, put up with; **digestif** *nm* (after-dinner) liqueur

digne [diɲ] *adj* dignified; **~ de** worthy of; **~ de foi** trustworthy

dignité [diɲite] *nf* dignity

digression [digʀesjɔ̃] *nf* digression

digue [dig] *nf* dike, dyke

dilapider [dilapide] *vt* to squander

dilemme [dilɛm] *nm* dilemma

diligence [diliʒɑ̃s] *nf* stagecoach; (*empressement*) despatch

diluer [dilɥe] *vt* to dilute

diluvien, ne [dilyvjɛ̃, -jɛn] *adj*: **pluie ~ne** torrential rain

dimanche [dimɑ̃ʃ] *nm* Sunday

dimension [dimɑ̃sjɔ̃] *nf* (*grandeur*) size; (*cote, de l'espace*) dimension

diminuer [diminɥe] *vt* to reduce, decrease; (*ardeur etc*) to lessen; (*personne: physiquement*) to undermine; (*dénigrer*) to belittle ♦ *vi* to decrease, diminish; **diminutif** *nm* (*surnom*) pet name; **diminution** *nf* decreasing, diminishing

dinde [dɛ̃d] *nf* turkey

dindon [dɛ̃dɔ̃] *nm* turkey

dîner [dine] *nm* dinner ♦ *vi* to have dinner

dingue [dɛ̃g] (*fam*) *adj* crazy

diplomate [diplɔmat] *adj* diplomatic ♦ *nm* diplomat; (*fig*) diplomatist

diplomatie [diplɔmasi] *nf* diplomacy

diplôme [diplom] *nm* diploma; **diplômé, e** *adj* qualified

dire [diʀ] *nm*: **au ~ de** according to ♦ *vt* to say; (*secret, mensonge*) to tell; **leurs ~s** what they say; **~ l'heure/la vérité** to tell the time/the truth; **~ qch à qn** to tell sb sth; **~ à qn qu'il fasse** *ou* **de faire** to tell sb to do; **on dit que** they say that; **ceci dit** that being said; (*à ces mots*) whereupon; **si cela lui dit**

(*plaire*) if he fancies it; **que dites-vous de** (*penser*) what do you think of; **on dirait que** it looks (*ou* sounds *etc*) as if; **dis/dites (donc)** I say; (*à propos*) by the way

direct, e [dirɛkt] *adj* direct ♦ *nm* (*TV*): **en ~** live; **directement** *adv* directly

directeur, trice [dirɛktœr, -tris] *nm/f* (*d'entreprise*) director; (*de service*) manager(eress); (*d'école*) head (teacher) (*BRIT*), principal (*US*)

direction [dirɛksjɔ̃] *nf* management; conducting; supervision; (*AUTO*) steering; (*sens*) direction; **"toutes ~s"** "all routes"

dirent *vb voir* **dire**

dirigeant, e [diriʒɑ̃, -ɑ̃t] *adj* managerial; ruling ♦ *nm/f* (*d'un parti etc*) leader; (*d'entreprise*) manager

diriger [diriʒe] *vt* (*entreprise*) to manage, run; (*véhicule*) to steer; (*orchestre*) to conduct; (*recherches, travaux*) to supervise; (*braquer: regard, arme*): **~ sur** to point *ou* level at; **se ~** *vi* (*s'orienter*) to find one's way; **se ~ vers** *ou* **sur** to make *ou* head for

dirigisme [diriʒism(ə)] *nm* (*ÉCON*) state intervention, interventionism

dis *etc vb voir* **dire**

discernement [disɛrnəmɑ̃] *nm* (*bon sens*) discernment, judgement

discerner [disɛrne] *vt* to discern, make out

discipline [disiplin] *nf* discipline; **discipliner** *vt* to discipline; to control

discontinu, e [diskɔ̃tiny] *adj* intermittent

discontinuer [diskɔ̃tinɥe] *vi*: **sans ~** without stopping, without a break

disconvenir [diskɔ̃vnir] *vi*: **ne pas ~ de qch/que** not to deny sth/that

discordant, e [diskɔrdɑ̃, -ɑ̃t] *adj* discordant; conflicting

discothèque [diskɔtɛk] *nf* (*disques*) record collection; (: *dans une bibliothèque*) record library; (*boîte de nuit*) disco(thèque)

discourir [diskurir] *vi* to discourse, hold forth

discours [diskur] *nm* speech

discret, ète [diskrɛ, -ɛt] *adj* discreet; (*fig*) unobtrusive; quiet

discrétion [diskresjɔ̃] *nf* discretion; **être à la ~ de qn** to be in sb's hands; **à ~** unlimited; as much as one wants

discrimination [diskriminasjɔ̃] *nf* discrimination; **sans ~** indiscriminately

disculper [diskylpe] *vt* to exonerate

discussion [diskysjɔ̃] *nf* discussion

discutable [diskytabl(ə)] *adj* debatable

discuté, e [diskyte] *adj* controversial

discuter [diskyte] *vt* (*contester*) to question, dispute; (*débattre: prix*) to discuss ♦ *vi* to talk; (*ergoter*) to argue; **~ de** to discuss

dise *etc vb voir* **dire**

disette [dizɛt] *nf* food shortage

diseuse [dizøz] *nf*: **~ de bonne aventure** fortuneteller

disgracieux, euse [disgrasjø, -jøz] *adj* ungainly, awkward

disjoindre [disʒwɛ̃dr(ə)] *vt* to take apart; **se ~** *vi* to come apart

disjoncteur [disʒɔ̃ktœr] *nm* (*ÉLEC*) circuit breaker

disloquer [dislɔke] *vt* (*chaise*) to dismantle; **se ~** *vi* (*parti, empire*) to break up; **se ~ l'épaule** to dislocate one's shoulder

disons *vb voir* **dire**

disparaître [disparɛtr(ə)] *vi* to disappear; (*à la vue*) to vanish, disappear; to be hidden *ou* concealed; (*se perdre: traditions etc*) to die out; **faire ~** to remove; to get rid of

disparition [disparisjɔ̃] *nf* disappearance

disparu, e [dispary] *nm/f* missing person; (*défunt*) dead person, departed (*littér*)

dispensaire [dispɑ̃sɛr] *nm* community clinic

dispenser [dispɑ̃se] *vt* (*donner*) to lavish, bestow; (*exempter*): **~ qn de** to exempt sb from; **se ~ de** *vt* to avoid; to get out of

disperser [dispɛrse] *vt* to scatter; (*fig: son attention*) to dissipate

disponibilité [disponibilite] *nf* (*ADMIN*): **être en ~** to be on leave of absence

disponible [dispɔnibl(ə)] *adj* available

dispos [dispo] *adj m*: **(frais et) ~** fresh (as a daisy)

disposé, e [dispoze] *adj*: **bien/mal ~** (*humeur*) in a good/bad mood; **~ à** (*prêt à*) willing *ou* prepared to

disposer [dispoze] *vt* (*arranger, placer*) to arrange ♦ *vi*: **vous pouvez ~** you may leave; **~ de** to have (at one's disposal); to use; **se ~ à faire** to prepare to do, be about to do

dispositif [dispozitif] *nm* device; (*fig*) system, plan of action; set-up

disposition [dispozisjɔ̃] *nf* (*arrangement*) arrangement, layout; (*humeur*) mood; (*tendance*) tendency; **~s** *nfpl* (*mesures*) steps, measures; (*préparatifs*) arrangements; (*loi, testament*) provisions; (*aptitudes*) bent *sg*, aptitude *sg*; **à la ~ de qn** at sb's disposal

disproportionné, e [dispʀɔpɔʀsjɔne] *adj* disproportionate, out of all proportion

dispute [dispyt] *nf* quarrel, argument

disputer [dispyte] *vt* (*match*) to play; (*combat*) to fight; (*course*) to run, fight; **se ~ vi** to quarrel; **~ qch à qn** to fight with sb over sth

disquaire [diskɛʀ] *nm/f* record dealer

disqualifier [diskalifje] *vt* to disqualify

disque [disk(ə)] *nm* (*MUS*) record; (*forme, pièce*) disc; (*SPORT*) discus; **~ compact** compact disc; **~ d'embrayage** (*AUTO*) clutch plate

disquette [diskɛt] *nf* floppy disk, diskette

disséminer [disemine] *vt* to scatter

disséquer [diseke] *vt* to dissect

dissertation [disɛʀtasjɔ̃] *nf* (*SCOL*) essay

disserter [disɛʀte] *vi*: **~ sur** to discourse upon

dissimuler [disimyle] *vt* to conceal

dissiper [disipe] *vt* to dissipate; (*fortune*) to squander; **se ~ vi** (*brouillard*) to clear, disperse; (*doutes*) to melt away; (*élève*) to become unruly

dissolu, e [disɔly] *adj* dissolute

dissolvant [disɔlvɑ̃] *nm* solvent; **~ (gras)** nail polish remover

dissonant, e [disɔnɑ̃, -ɑ̃t] *adj* discordant

dissoudre [disudʀ(ə)] *vt* to dissolve; **se ~ vi** to dissolve

dissuader [disɥade] *vt*: **~ qn de faire/de qch** to dissuade sb from doing/from sth

dissuasion [disɥazjɔ̃] *nf*: **force de ~** deterrent power

distance [distɑ̃s] *nf* distance; (*fig: écart*) gap; **à ~** at *ou* from a distance; **distancer** *vt* to outdistance

distant, e [distɑ̃, -ɑ̃t] *adj* (*réservé*) distant; **~ de** (*lieu*) far away from

distendre [distɑ̃dʀ(ə)] *vt* to distend; **se ~ vi** to distend

distiller [distile] *vt* to distil; **distillerie** *nf* distillery

distinct, e [distɛ̃(kt), distɛ̃kt(ə)] *adj* distinct; **distinctif, ive** *adj* distinctive

distingué, e [distɛ̃ge] *adj* distinguished

distinguer [distɛ̃ge] *vt* to distinguish

distraction [distʀaksjɔ̃] *nf* (*manque d'attention*) absent-mindedness; (*oubli*) lapse (in concentration); (*détente*) diversion, recreation; (*passe-temps*) distraction, entertainment

distraire [distʀɛʀ] *vt* (*déranger*) to distract; (*divertir*) to entertain, divert; **se ~ vi** to amuse *ou* enjoy o.s.

distrait, e [distʀɛ, -ɛt] *adj* absent-minded

distribuer [distʀibɥe] *vt* to distribute; to hand out; (*CARTES*) to deal (out); (*courrier*) to deliver; **distributeur** *nm* (*COMM*) distributor; (*automatique*) (vending) machine; (: *de billets*) (cash) dispenser; **distribution** *nf* distribution; (*postale*) delivery; (*choix d'acteurs*) casting, cast

dit, e [di, dit] *pp de* **dire** ♦ *adj* (*fixé*): **le jour ~** the arranged day; (*surnommé*): **X, ~ Pierrot** X, known as Pierrot

dites *vb voir* **dire**

divaguer [divage] *vi* to ramble; to rave

divan [divɑ̃] *nm* divan

divers, e [divɛʀ, -ɛʀs(ə)] *adj* (*varié*) diverse, varied; (*différent*) different, various ♦ *dét* (*plusieurs*) various, several; **(frais) ~** sundries, miscellaneous (expenses)

divertir [divɛʀtiʀ] *vt* to amuse, entertain; **se ~** *vi* to amuse *ou* enjoy o.s.

divin, e [divɛ̃, -in] *adj* divine

diviser [divize] *vt* (*gén, MATH*) to divide; (*morceler, subdiviser*) to divide (up), split (up); **division** *nf* division

divorce [divɔʀs(ə)] *nm* divorce; **divorcé, e** *nm/f* divorcee; **divorcer** *vi* to get a divorce, get divorced; **divorcer de** *ou* **d'avec qn** to divorce sb

divulguer [divylge] *vt* to divulge, disclose

dix [dis] *num* ten; **dixième** *num* tenth

dizaine [dizɛn] *nf* (*10*) ten; (*environ 10*): **une ~ (de)** about ten, ten or so

do [do] *nm* (*note*) C; (*en chantant la gamme*) do(h)

dock [dɔk] *nm* dock

docker [dɔkɛʀ] *nm* docker

docte [dɔkt(ə)] *adj* learned

docteur [dɔktœʀ] *nm* doctor

doctorat [dɔktɔʀa] *nm*: **~ (d'Université)** doctorate; **~ d'État** ≈ Ph.D.

doctrine [dɔktʀin] *nf* doctrine

document [dɔkymɑ̃] *nm* document

documentaire [dɔkymɑ̃tɛʀ] *adj, nm* documentary

documentaliste [dɔkymɑ̃talist(ə)] *nm/f* archivist; researcher

documentation [dɔkymɑ̃tɑsjɔ̃] *nf* documentation, literature; (*PRESSE, TV: service*) research

documenter [dɔkymɑ̃te] *vt*: **se ~ (sur)** to gather information (on)

dodeliner [dɔdline] *vi*: **~ de la tête** to nod one's head gently

dodo [dɔdo] *nm*: **aller faire ~** to go to beddy-byes

dodu, e [dɔdy] *adj* plump

dogue [dɔg] *nm* mastiff

doigt [dwa] *nm* finger; **à deux ~s de** within an inch of; **un ~ de lait** a drop of milk; **~ de pied** toe

doigté [dwate] *nm* (*MUS*) fingering; (*fig: habileté*) diplomacy, tact

doit *etc vb voir* **devoir**

doléances [dɔleɑ̃s] *nfpl* complaints; grievances

dollar [dɔlaʀ] *nm* dollar

D.O.M. [deɔɛm, dɔm] *sigle m* = **département d'outre-mer**

domaine [dɔmɛn] *nm* estate, property; (*fig*) domain, field

domestique [dɔmɛstik] *adj* domestic ♦ *nm/f* servant, domestic

domicile [dɔmisil] *nm* home, place of residence; **à ~** at home; **domicilié, e** *adj*: **être domicilié à** to have one's home in *ou* at

dominant, e [dɔminɑ̃, -ɑ̃t] *adj* dominant; predominant

dominateur, trice [dɔminatœʀ, -tʀis] *adj* dominating; domineering

dominer [dɔmine] *vt* to dominate; (*passions etc*) to control, master; (*surpasser*) to outclass, surpass ♦ *vi* to be in the dominant position; **se ~** *vi* to control o.s.

domino [dɔmino] *nm* domino

dommage [dɔmaʒ] *nm* (*préjudice*) harm, injury; (*dégâts, pertes*) damage *no pl*; **c'est ~ de faire/que** it's a shame *ou* pity to do/that; **dommages-intérêts** *nmpl* damages

dompter [dɔ̃te] *vt* to tame; **dompteur, euse** *nm/f* trainer; liontamer

don [dɔ̃] *nm* (*cadeau*) gift; (*charité*) donation; (*aptitude*) gift, talent; **avoir des ~s pour** to have a gift *ou* talent for

donc [dɔ̃k] *conj* therefore, so; (*après une digression*) so, then

donjon [dɔ̃ʒɔ̃] *nm* keep

donné, e [dɔne] *adj* (*convenu*) given; (*pas cher*): **c'est ~** it's a gift; **étant ~ ...** given ...; **donnée** *nf* (*MATH, gén*) datum

donner [dɔne] *vt* to give; (*vieux habits etc*) to give away; (*spectacle*) to put on; (*film*) to show; **~ qch à qn** to give sb sth, give sth to sb; **~ sur** (*suj: fenêtre, chambre*) to look (out) onto; **~ dans** (*piège etc*) to fall into; **se ~ à fond** to give one's all; **s'en ~ à cœur joie** (*fam*) to have a great time

---

MOT-CLÉ

---

dont [dɔ̃] *pron relatif* **1** (*appartenance: objets*) whose, of which; (*appartenance: êtres animés*) whose; **la maison ~ le**

toit est rouge the house the roof of which is red; **l'homme ~ je connais la sœur** the man whose sister I know

2 (*parmi lesquel(le)s*): **2 livres, ~ l'un est ...** 2 books, one of which is ...; **il y avait plusieurs personnes, ~ Gabrielle** there were several people, among them Gabrielle; **10 blessés, ~ 2 grièvement** 10 injured, 2 of them seriously

3 (*complément d'adjectif, de verbe*): **le fils ~ il est si fier** the son he's so proud of; **ce ~ je parle** what I'm talking about

doré, e [dɔʀe] *adj* golden; (*avec dorure*) gilt, gilded

dorénavant [dɔʀenavɑ̃] *adv* henceforth

dorer [dɔʀe] *vt* (*cadre*) to gild; **(faire) ~** (*CULIN*) to brown

dorloter [dɔʀlɔte] *vt* to pamper

dormir [dɔʀmiʀ] *vi* to sleep; (*être endormi*) to be asleep

dortoir [dɔʀtwaʀ] *nm* dormitory

dorure [dɔʀyʀ] *nf* gilding

dos [do] *nm* back; (*de livre*) spine; **"voir au ~"** "see over"; **de ~** from the back

dosage [dozaʒ] *nm* mixture

dose [doz] *nf* dose; **doser** [doze] *vt* to measure out; to mix in the correct proportions; (*fig*) to expend in the right amounts; to strike a balance between

dossard [dosaʀ] *nm* number (*worn by competitor*)

dossier [dosje] *nm* (*renseignements, fichier*) file; (*de chaise*) back; (*PRESSE*) feature

dot [dɔt] *nf* dowry

doter [dɔte] *vt* to equip

douane [dwan] *nf* (*poste, bureau*) customs *pl*; (*taxes*) (customs) duty; **douanier, ière** *adj* customs *cpd* ♦ *nm* customs officer

double [dubl(ə)] *adj, adv* double ♦ *nm* (*2 fois plus*): **le ~ (de)** twice as much (*ou* many) (as); (*autre exemplaire*) duplicate, copy; (*sosie*) double; (*TENNIS*) doubles *sg*; **en ~ (exemplaire)** in duplicate; **faire ~ emploi** to be redundant

doubler [duble] *vt* (*multiplier par 2*) to

double; (*vêtement*) to line; (*dépasser*) to overtake, pass; (*film*) to dub; (*acteur*) to stand in for ♦ *vi* to double

doublure [dublyʀ] *nf* lining; (*CINÉMA*) stand-in

douce [dus] *adj voir* **doux**; **douceâtre** *adj* sickly sweet; **doucement** *adv* gently; slowly; **doucereux, euse** (*péj*) *adj* sugary; **douceur** *nf* softness; sweetness; mildness; gentleness; **douceurs** *nfpl* (*friandises*) sweets

douche [duʃ] *nf* shower; **~s** *nfpl* (*salle*) shower room *sg*; **doucher: se doucher** *vi* to have *ou* take a shower

doudoune [dudun] *nf* padded jacket; boob (*fam*)

doué, e [dwe] *adj* gifted, talented; **~ de** endowed with

douille [duj] *nf* (*ÉLEC*) socket; (*de projectile*) case

douillet, te [dujɛ, -ɛt] *adj* cosy; (*péj*) soft

douleur [dulœʀ] *nf* pain; (*chagrin*) grief, distress; **douloureux, euse** *adj* painful

doute [dut] *nm* doubt; **sans ~** no doubt; (*probablement*) probably

douter [dute] *vt* to doubt; **~ de** (*allié*) to doubt, have (one's) doubts about; (*résultat*) to be doubtful of; **se ~ de qch/que** to suspect sth/that; **je m'en doutais** I suspected as much

douteux, euse [dutø, -øz] *adj* (*incertain*) doubtful; (*discutable*) dubious, questionable; (*péj*) dubious-looking

Douvres [duvʀ(ə)] *n* Dover

doux, douce [du, dus] *adj* (*gén*) soft; (*sucré, agréable*) sweet; (*peu fort: moutarde, clément: climat*) mild; (*pas brusque*) gentle

douzaine [duzɛn] *nf* (*12*) dozen; (*environ 12*): **une ~ (de)** a dozen or so, twelve or so

douze [duz] *num* twelve; **douzième** *num* twelfth

doyen, ne [dwajɛ̃, -ɛn] *nm/f* (*en âge, ancienneté*) most senior member; (*de faculté*) dean

dragée [dʀaʒe] *nf* sugared almond; (*MÉD*) (sugar-coated) pill

dragon [dʀagɔ̃] *nm* dragon
draguer [dʀage] *vt (rivière)* to dredge; to drag; *(fam)* to try to pick up
dramatique [dʀamatik] *adj* dramatic; *(tragique)* tragic ♦ *nf (TV)* (television) drama
dramaturge [dʀamatyʀʒ(ə)] *nm* dramatist, playwright
drame [dʀam] *nm (THÉÂTRE)* drama
drap [dʀa] *nm (de lit)* sheet; *(tissu)* woollen fabric
drapeau, x [dʀapo] *nm* flag; **sous les ~x** with the colours, in the army
dresser [dʀese] *vt (mettre vertical, monter)* to put up, erect; *(fig: liste, bilan, contrat)* to draw up; *(animal)* to train; **se ~** *vi (falaise, obstacle)* to stand; to tower (up); *(personne)* to draw o.s. up; **~ qn contre qn** to set sb against sb; **~ l'oreille** to prick up one's ears
drogue [dʀɔg] *nf* drug; **la ~** drugs *pl*; **drogué, e** *nm/f* drug addict
droguer [dʀɔge] *vt (victime)* to drug; *(malade)* to give drugs to; **se ~** *vi (aux stupéfiants)* to take drugs; *(péj: de médicaments)* to dose o.s. up
droguerie [dʀɔgʀi] *nf* hardware shop
droguiste [dʀɔgist(ə)] *nm* keeper *(ou* owner) of a hardware shop
droit, e [dʀwa, dʀwat] *adj (non courbe)* straight; *(vertical)* upright, straight; *(fig: loyal)* upright, straight(forward); *(opposé à gauche)* right, right-hand ♦ *adv* straight ♦ *nm (prérogative)* right; *(taxe)* duty, tax; *(: d'inscription)* fee; *(JUR):* **le ~** law; **avoir le ~ de** to be allowed to; **avoir ~ à** to be entitled to; **être en ~ de** to have a *ou* the right to; **être dans son ~** to be within one's rights; **à ~e** on the right; *(direction)* (to the) right; **~s d'auteur** royalties; **~s d'inscription** *nmpl* enrolment fee; *(competition)* entry fee; **droite** *nf (POL):* **la droite** the right (wing)
droitier, ière [dʀwatje, -jɛʀ] *nm/f* right-handed person
droits *nmpl voir* **droit**
droiture [dʀwatyʀ] *nf* uprightness, straightness

drôle [dʀol] *adj* funny; **une ~ d'idée** a funny idea; **drôlement** *adv (très)* terribly, awfully
dromadaire [dʀɔmadɛʀ] *nm* dromedary
dru, e [dʀy] *adj (cheveux)* thick, bushy; *(pluie)* heavy
du [dy] *dét voir* **de** ♦ *prép* +*dét* = **de** +**le**
dû, due [dy] *vb voir* **devoir** ♦ *adj (somme)* owing, owed; *(: venant à échéance)* due; *(causé par):* **~ à** due to ♦ *nm* due; *(somme)* dues *pl*
dubitatif, ive [dybitatif, -iv] *adj* doubtful, dubious
duc [dyk] *nm* duke; **duchesse** *nf* duchess
dûment [dymɑ̃] *adv* duly
Dunkerque [dœ̃kɛʀk] *n* Dunkirk
duo [dɥo] *nm (MUS)* duet
dupe [dyp] *nf* dupe ♦ *adj:* **(ne pas) être ~ de** (not) to be taken in by
duplex [dyplɛks] *nm (appartement)* split-level apartment, duplex
duplicata [dyplikata] *nm* duplicate
duquel [dykɛl] *prép* +*pron* = **de** +**lequel**
dur, e [dyʀ] *adj (pierre, siège, travail, problème)* hard; *(lumière, voix, climat)* harsh; *(sévère)* hard, harsh; *(cruel)* hard(-hearted); *(porte, col)* stiff; *(viande)* tough ♦ *adv* hard; **~ d'oreille** hard of hearing
durant [dyʀɑ̃] *prép (au cours de)* during; *(pendant)* for; **des mois ~** for months
durcir [dyʀsiʀ] *vt, vi* to harden; **se ~** *vi* to harden
durée [dyʀe] *nf* length; *(d'une pile etc)* life; *(déroulement: des opérations etc)* duration
durement [dyʀmɑ̃] *adv* harshly
durer [dyʀe] *vi* to last
dureté [dyʀte] *nf* hardness; harshness; stiffness; toughness
durit [dyʀit] ® *nf (car radiator)* hose
dus *etc vb voir* **devoir**
duvet [dyvɛ] *nm* down; *(sac de couchage)* down-filled sleeping bag
dynamique [dinamik] *adj* dynamic

dynamite [dinamit] *nf* dynamite
dynamiter [dinamite] *vt* to (blow up with) dynamite
dynamo [dinamo] *nf* dynamo
dysenterie [disɑ̃tʀi] *nf* dysentery
dyslexie [dislɛksi] *nf* dyslexia, word-blindness

E e

eau, x [o] *nf* water; **~x** *nfpl* (MED) waters; **prendre l'~** to leak, let in water; **tomber à l'~** (*fig*) to fall through; **~ courante** running water; **~ de Cologne** Eau de Cologne; **~ de Javel** bleach; **~ de toilette** toilet water; **~ douce** fresh water; **~ minérale** mineral water; **~ plate** still water; **~ salée** salt water; **eau-de-vie** *nf* brandy; **eau-forte** *nf* etching
ébahi, e [ebai] *adj* dumbfounded
ébattre [ebatʀ(ə)]: **s'~** *vi* to frolic
ébaucher [eboʃe] *vt* to sketch out, outline; **s'~** *vi* to take shape
ébène [ebɛn] *nf* ebony
ébéniste [ebenist(ə)] *nm* cabinetmaker
éberlué, e [ebɛʀlɥe] *adj* astounded
éblouir [ebluiʀ] *vt* to dazzle
éblouissement [ebluismɑ̃] *nm* (*faiblesse*) dizzy turn
éborgner [ebɔʀɲe] *vt*: **~ qn** to blind sb in one eye
éboueur [ebwœʀ] *nm* dustman (*BRIT*), garbageman (*US*)
ébouillanter [ebujɑ̃te] *vt* to scald; (*CULIN*) to blanch
éboulement [ebulmɑ̃] *nm* rock fall
ébouler [ebule]: **s'~** *vi* to crumble, collapse
éboulis [ebuli] *nmpl* fallen rocks
ébouriffé, e [eburife] *adj* tousled
ébranler [ebrɑ̃le] *vt* to shake; (*rendre instable: mur*) to weaken; **s'~** *vi* (*partir*) to move off
ébrécher [ebreʃe] *vt* to chip
ébriété [ebrijete] *nf*: **en état d'~** in a state of intoxication
ébrouer [ebrue]: **s'~** *vi* to shake o.s.; (*souffler*) to snort

ébruiter [ebrɥite] *vt* to spread, disclose
ébullition [ebylisjɔ̃] *nf* boiling point; **en ~** boiling; (*fig*) in an uproar
écaille [ekaj] *nf* (*de poisson*) scale; (*de coquillage*) shell; (*matière*) tortoiseshell;
écailler [ekaje] *vt* (*poisson*) to scale; (*huitre*) to open; **s'ecailler** *vi* to flake *ou* peel (off)
écarlate [ekarlat] *adj* scarlet
écarquiller [ekarkije] *vt*: **~ les yeux** to stare wide-eyed
écart [ekar] *nm* gap; (*embardée*) swerve; sideways leap; (*fig*) departure, deviation; **à l'~** out of the way; **à l'~ de** away from
écarté, e [ekarte] *adj* (*lieu*) out-of-the-way, remote; (*ouvert*): **les jambes ~es** legs apart; **les bras ~s** arms outstretched
écarteler [ekartəle] *vt* to quarter; (*fig*) to tear
écarter [ekarte] *vt* (*séparer*) to move apart, separate; (*éloigner*) to push back, move away; (*ouvrir: bras, jambes*) to spread, open; (: *rideau*) to draw (back); (*éliminer: candidat, possibilité*) to dismiss; **s'~** *vi* to part; to move away; **s'~ de** to wander from
écervelé, e [esɛrvəle] *adj* scatterbrained, featherbrained
échafaud [eʃafo] *nm* scaffold
échafaudage [eʃafodaʒ] *nm* scaffolding
échafauder [eʃafode] *vt* (*plan*) to construct
échalote [eʃalɔt] *nf* shallot
échancrure [eʃɑ̃kryr] *nf* (*de robe*) scoop neckline; (*de côte, arête rocheuse*) indentation
échange [eʃɑ̃ʒ] *nm* exchange; **en ~ de** in exchange *ou* return for
échanger [eʃɑ̃ʒe] *vt*: **~ qch (contre)** to exchange sth (for); **échangeur** *nm* (*AUTO*) interchange
échantillon [eʃɑ̃tijɔ̃] *nm* sample
échappement [eʃapmɑ̃] *nm* (*AUTO*) exhaust
échapper [eʃape]: **~ à** *vt* (*gardien*) to escape (from); (*punition, péril*) to escape; **s'~** *vi* to escape; **~ à qn** (*détail, sens*) to escape sb; (*objet qu'on tient*) to

slip out of sb's hands; **laisser** ~ (*cri etc*) to let out; **l'~ belle** to have a narrow escape

écharde [eʃaʀd(ə)] *nf* splinter (of wood)

écharpe [eʃaʀp(ə)] *nf* scarf; (*de maire*) sash; (*MÉD*) sling

échasse [eʃas] *nf* stilt

échauffer [eʃofe] *vt* (*métal, moteur*) to overheat; (*fig: exciter*) to fire, excite; **s'~** *vi* (*SPORT*) to warm up; (*dans la discussion*) to become heated

échéance [eʃeɑ̃s] *nf* (*d'un paiement: date*) settlement date; (: *somme due*) financial commitment(s); (*fig*) deadline; **à brève/longue** ~ *adj* short-/long-term ♦ *adv* in the short/long run

échéant [eʃeɑ̃]: **le cas** ~ *adv* if the case arises

échec [eʃɛk] *nm* failure; (*ÉCHECS*): ~ **et mat/au roi** checkmate/check; ~**s** *nmpl* (*jeu*) chess *sg*; **tenir en** ~ to hold in check; **faire** ~ **à** to foil *ou* thwart

échelle [eʃɛl] *nf* ladder; (*fig, d'une carte*) scale

échelon [eʃlɔ̃] *nm* (*d'échelle*) rung; (*ADMIN*) grade

échelonner [eʃlɔne] *vt* to space out

échevelé, e [eʃəvle] *adj* tousled, dishevelled; wild, frenzied

échine [eʃin] *nf* backbone, spine

échiquier [eʃikje] *nm* chessboard

écho [eko] *nm* echo; ~**s** *nmpl* (*potins*) gossip *sg*, rumours

échoir [eʃwaʀ] *vi* (*dette*) to fall due; (*délais*) to expire; ~ **à** to fall to

échouer [eʃwe] *vi* to fail; **s'~** *vi* to run aground

échu, e [eʃy] *pp de* **échoir**

éclabousser [eklabuse] *vt* to splash

éclair [eklɛʀ] *nm* (*d'orage*) flash of lightning, lightning *no pl*; (*gâteau*) éclair

éclairage [eklɛʀaʒ] *nm* lighting

éclaircie [eklɛʀsi] *nf* bright interval

éclaircir [eklɛʀsiʀ] *vt* to lighten; (*fig*) to clear up; to clarify; (*CULIN*) to thin (down); **s'~** *vi* (*ciel*) to clear; **s'~ la voix** to clear one's throat; **éclaircissement** *nm* clearing up; clarification

éclairer [eklɛʀe] *vt* (*lieu*) to light (up);

(*personne: avec une lampe etc*) to light the way for; (*fig*) to enlighten; to shed light on ♦ *vi*: ~ **mal/bien** to give a poor/good light; **s'~ à l'électricité** to have electric lighting

éclaireur, euse [eklɛʀœʀ, -øz] *nm/f* (*scout*) (boy) scout/(girl) guide ♦ *nm* (*MIL*) scout

éclat [ekla] *nm* (*de bombe, de verre*) fragment; (*du soleil, d'une couleur etc*) brightness, brilliance; (*d'une cérémonie*) splendour; (*scandale*): **faire un** ~ to cause a commotion; ~**s de voix** shouts; ~ **de rire** *nm* roar of laughter

éclatant, e [eklatɑ̃, -ɑ̃t] *adj* brilliant

éclater [eklate] *vi* (*pneu*) to burst; (*bombe*) to explode; (*guerre, épidémie*) to break out; (*groupe, parti*) to break up; ~ **en sanglots/de rire** to burst out sobbing/laughing

éclipser [eklipse]: **s'~** *vi* to slip away

éclopé, e [eklope] *adj* lame

éclore [eklɔʀ] *vi* (*œuf*) to hatch; (*fleur*) to open (out)

écluse [eklyz] *nf* lock

écœurant, e [ekœʀɑ̃, -ɑ̃t] *adj* (*gâteau etc*) sickly

écœurer [ekœʀe] *vt*: ~ **qn** to make sb feel sick

école [ekɔl] *nf* school; **aller à l'~** to go to school; ~ **normale** teachers' training college; ~ **publique** state school; **écolier, ière** *nm/f* schoolboy/girl

écologie [ekɔlɔʒi] *nf* ecology; environmental studies *pl*

écologique [ekɔlɔʒik] *adj* environment-friendly

éconduire [ekɔ̃dɥiʀ] *vt* to dismiss

économe [ekɔnɔm] *adj* thrifty ♦ *nm/f* (*de lycée etc*) bursar (*BRIT*), treasurer (*US*)

économie [ekɔnɔmi] *nf* economy; (*gain: d'argent, de temps etc*) saving; (*science*) economics *sg*; ~**s** *nfpl* (*pécule*) savings; **économique** *adj* (*avantageux*) economical; (*ÉCON*) economic; **économiser** [ekɔnɔmize] *vt, vi* to save

écoper [ekɔpe] *vi* to bale out; (*fig*) to cop it; ~ (**de**) to get

écorce [ekɔʀs(ə)] *nf* bark; (*de fruit*) peel

écorcher [ekɔʀʃe] *vt* (*animal*) to skin; (*égratigner*) to graze; **écorchure** *nf* graze

écossais, e [ekɔsɛ, -ɛz] *adj* Scottish ♦ *nm/f*: **É~, e** Scot

Écosse [ekɔs] *nf*: **l'~** Scotland

écosser [ekɔse] *vt* to shell

écouler [ekule] *vt* to sell; to dispose of; **s'~** *vi* (*eau*) to flow (out); (*jours, temps*) to pass (by)

écourter [ekuʀte] *vt* to curtail, cut short

écoute [ekut] *nf* (*RADIO. TV*): **temps/heure d'~** listening (*ou* viewing) time/hour; **prendre l'~** to tune in; **rester à l'~ (de)** to stay tuned in (to)

écouter [ekute] *vt* to listen to; **écoutes téléphoniques** phone tapping *sg*; **écouteur** *nm* (*TÉL*) receiver; (*RADIO*) head-phones *pl*, headset

écran [ekʀɑ̃] *nm* screen

écrasant, e [ekʀazɑ̃, -ɑ̃t] *adj* over-whelming

écraser [ekʀaze] *vt* to crush; (*piéton*) to run over; **s'~ (au sol)** to crash; **s'~ contre** to crash into

écrémer [ekʀeme] *vt* to skim

écrevisse [ekʀəvis] *nf* crayfish *inv*

écrier [ekʀije]: **s'~** *vi* to exclaim

écrin [ekʀɛ̃] *nm* case, box

écrire [ekʀiʀ] *vt* to write; **s'~** to write to each other; **ça s'écrit comment?** how is it spelt?; **écrit** *nm* document; (*examen*) written paper; **par écrit** in writing

écriteau, x [ekʀito] *nm* notice, sign

écriture [ekʀityʀ] *nf* writing; (*COMM*) entry; **~s** *nfpl* accounts, books; **l'É~, les É~s** the Scriptures

écrivain [ekʀivɛ̃] *nm* writer

écrou [ekʀu] *nm* nut

écrouer [ekʀue] *vt* to imprison; to remand in custody

écrouler [ekʀule]: **s'~** *vi* to collapse

écru, e [ekʀy] *adj* (*toile*) raw, un-bleached; (*couleur*) off-white, écru

ECU *sigle m* ECU

écueil [ekœj] *nm* reef; (*fig*) pitfall; stumbling block

écuelle [ekɥɛl] *nf* bowl

éculé, e [ekyle] *adj* (*chaussure*) down-at-heel; (*fig: péj*) hackneyed

écume [ekym] *nf* foam; (*CULIN*) scum; **écumer** *vt* (*CULIN*) to skim; (*fig*) to plunder

écureuil [ekyʀœj] *nm* squirrel

écurie [ekyʀi] *nf* stable

écusson [ekysɔ̃] *nm* badge

écuyer, ère [ekɥije, -ɛʀ] *nm/f* rider

eczéma [ɛgzema] *nm* eczema

édenté, e [edɑ̃te] *adj* toothless

E.D.F. *sigle f* (= *Électricité de France*) *national electricity company*

édifice [edifis] *nm* edifice, building

édifier [edifje] *vt* to build, erect; (*fig*) to edify

édit [edi] *nm* edict

éditer [edite] *vt* (*publier*) to publish; (: *disque*) to produce; **éditeur, trice** *nm/f* editor; publisher; **édition** *nf* editing *no pl*; edition; (*industrie du livre*) publishing

édredon [edʀədɔ̃] *nm* eiderdown, comforter (*US*)

éducateur, trice [edykatœʀ, -tʀis] *nm/f* teacher; (*in special school*) instructor

éducatif, ive [edykatif, -iv] *adj* educational

éducation [edykasjɔ̃] *nf* education; (*familiale*) upbringing; (*manières*) (good) manners *pl*; **~ physique** physical education

édulcorer [edylkɔʀe] *vt* to sweeten; (*fig*) to tone down

éduquer [edyke] *vt* to educate; (*élever*) to bring up; (*faculté*) to train

effacé, e [efase] *adj* unassuming

effacer [efase] *vt* to erase, rub out; **s'~** *vi* (*inscription etc*) to wear off; (*pour laisser passer*) to step aside

effarant, e [efaʀɑ̃, -ɑ̃t] *adj* alarming

effarer [efaʀe] *vt* to alarm

effaroucher [efaʀuʃe] *vt* to frighten *ou* scare away; to alarm

effectif, ive [efɛktif, -iv] *adj* real; effective ♦ *nm* (*MIL*) strength; (*SCOL*) (pupil) numbers *pl*; **effectivement** *adv* effectively; (*réellement*) actually, really; (*en effet*) indeed

effectuer [efɛktɥe] *vt* (*opération*) to carry out; (*déplacement, trajet*) to make; (*mouvement*) to execute

efféminé, e [efemine] *adj* effeminate

effervescent, e [efɛrvesã, -ãt] *adj* effervescent; (*fig*) agitated

effet [efɛ] *nm* (*résultat, artifice*) effect; (*impression*) impression; **~s** *nmpl* (*vêtements etc*) things; **faire de l'~** (*médicament, menace*) to have an effect; **en ~** indeed; **~ de serre** greenhouse effect; **gaz à ~ de serre** greenhouse gas

efficace [efikas] *adj* (*personne*) efficient; (*action, médicament*) effective

effilé, e [efile] *adj* slender; sharp; streamlined

effiler [efile] *vt* (*tissu*) to fray

effilocher [efilɔʃe]: **s'~** *vi* to fray

efflanqué, e [eflãke] *adj* emaciated

effleurer [eflœre] *vt* to brush (against); (*sujet*) to touch upon; (*suj: idée, pensée*): **~ qn** to cross sb's mind

effluves [eflyv] *nmpl* exhalation(s)

effondrer [efɔ̃dre]: **s'~** *vi* to collapse

efforcer [efɔrse]: **s'~ de** *vt*: **s'~ de faire** to try hard to do, try hard to

effort [efɔr] *nm* effort

effraction [efraksjɔ̃] *nf*: **s'introduire par ~ dans** to break into

effrayant, e [efrɛjã, -ãt] *adj* frightening

effrayer [efrɛje] *vt* to frighten, scare

effréné, e [efrene] *adj* wild

effriter [efrite]: **s'~** *vi* to crumble

effroi [efrwa] *nm* terror, dread *no pl*

effronté, e [efrɔ̃te] *adj* insolent, brazen

effroyable [efrwajabl(ə)] *adj* horrifying, appalling

effusion [efyzjɔ̃] *nf* effusion; **sans ~ de sang** without bloodshed

égal, e, aux [egal, -o] *adj* equal; (*plan: surface*) even, level; (*constant: vitesse*) steady; (*équitable*) even ♦ *nm/f* equal; **être ~ à** (*prix, nombre*) to be equal to; **ça lui est ~** it's all the same to him; he doesn't mind; **sans ~** matchless, unequalled; **à l'~ de** (*comme*) just like; **d'~ à ~** as equals; **également** *adv* equally; evenly; steadily; (*aussi*) too, as well; **égaler** *vt* to equal; **égaliser** *vt* (*sol, salaires*) to level (out); (*chances*) to equal-

ize ♦ *vi* (*SPORT*) to equalize; **égalité** *nf* equality; evenness; steadiness; (*MATH*) identity; **être à égalité (de points)** to be level

égard [egar] *nm*: **~s** *nmpl* consideration *sg*; **à cet ~** in this respect; **eu ~ à** in view of; **par ~ pour** out of consideration for; **sans ~ pour** without regard for; **à l'~ de** towards; concerning

égarement [egarmã] *nm* distraction; aberration

égarer [egare] *vt* to mislay; (*moralement*) to lead astray; **s'~** *vi* to get lost, lose one's way; (*objet*) to go astray; (*dans une discussion*) to wander

égayer [egeje] *vt* (*personne*) to amuse; to cheer up; (*récit, endroit*) to brighten up, liven up

églantine [eglãtin] *nf* wild *ou* dog rose

église [egliz] *nf* church; **aller à l'~** to go to church

égoïsme [egɔism(ə)] *nm* selfishness; **égoïste** *adj* selfish

égorger [egɔrʒe] *vt* to cut the throat of

égosiller [egozije]: **s'~** *vi* to shout o.s. hoarse

égout [egu] *nm* sewer

égoutter [egute] *vt* (*linge*) to wring out; (*vaisselle*) to drain ♦ *vi* to drip; **s'~** *vi* to drip; **égouttoir** *nm* draining board; (*mobile*) draining rack

égratigner [egratiɲe] *vt* to scratch; **égratignure** *nf* scratch

égrillard, e [egrijar, -ard(ə)] *adj* ribald

Égypte [eʒipt(ə)] *nf*: **l'~** Egypt; **égyptien, ne** *adj, nm/f* Egyptian

eh [e] *excl* hey!; **~ bien** well

éhonté, e [eɔ̃te] *adj* shameless, brazen

éjecter [eʒɛkte] *vt* (*TECH*) to eject; (*fam*) to kick *ou* chuck out

élaborer [elabɔre] *vt* to elaborate; (*projet, stratégie*) to work out; (*rapport*) to draft

élaguer [elage] *vt* to prune

élan [elã] *nm* (*ZOOL*) elk, moose; (*SPORT: avant le saut*) run up; (*d'objet en mouvement*) momentum; (*fig: de tendresse etc*) surge; **prendre de l'~** to gather speed

élancé, e [elɑ̃se] *adj* slender

élancement [elɑ̃smɑ̃] *nm* shooting pain

élancer [elɑ̃se]: **s'~** *vi* to dash, hurl o.s.; (*fig: arbre, clocher*) to soar (upwards)

élargir [elaʀʒiʀ] *vt* to widen; (*vêtement*) to let out; (*JUR*) to release; **s'~** *vi* to widen; (*vêtement*) to stretch

élastique [elastik] *adj* elastic ♦ *nm* (*de bureau*) rubber band; (*pour la couture*) elastic *no pl*

électeur, trice [elɛktœʀ, -tʀis] *nm/f* elector, voter

élection [elɛksjɔ̃] *nf* election

électorat [elɛktɔʀa] *nm* electorate

électricien, ne [elɛktʀisjɛ̃, -jɛn] *nm/f* electrician

électricité [elɛktʀisite] *nf* electricity; **allumer/éteindre l'~** to put on/off the light

électrique [elɛktʀik] *adj* electric(al)

électrochoc [elɛktʀɔʃɔk] *nm* electric shock treatment

électroménager [elɛktʀɔmenaʒe] *adj, nm:* **appareils ~s, l'~** domestic (electrical) appliances

électronique [elɛktʀɔnik] *adj* electronic ♦ *nf* electronics *sg*

électrophone [elɛktʀɔfɔn] *nm* record player

élégant, e [elegɑ̃, -ɑ̃t] *adj* elegant; (*solution*) neat, elegant; (*attitude, procédé*) courteous, civilized

élément [elemɑ̃] *nm* element; (*pièce*) component, part; **élémentaire** *adj* elementary

éléphant [elefɑ̃] *nm* elephant

élevage [elvaʒ] *nm* breeding; (*de bovins*) cattle rearing

élévation [elevasjɔ̃] *nf* (*gén*) elevation; (*voir élever*) raising; (*voir s'élever*) rise

élevé, e [elve] *adj* (*prix, sommet*) high; (*fig: noble*) elevated; **bien/mal ~** well-/ill-mannered

élève [elɛv] *nm/f* pupil

élever [elve] *vt* (*enfant*) to bring up, raise; (*bétail, volaille*) to breed; (*abeilles*) to keep; (*hausser: taux, niveau*) to raise; (*fig: âme, esprit*) to elevate; (*édifier: monument*) to put up,

erect; **s'~** *vi* (*avion, alpiniste*) to go up; (*niveau, température; aussi cri etc*) to rise; (*survenir: difficultés*) to arise; **s'~ à** (*suj: frais, dégâts*) to amount to, add up to; **s'~ contre qch** to rise up against sth; **~ la voix** to raise one's voice; **éleveur, euse** *nm/f* breeder

élimé, e [elime] *adj* threadbare

éliminatoire [eliminatwaʀ] *nf* (*SPORT*) heat

éliminer [elimine] *vt* to eliminate

élire [eliʀ] *vt* to elect

elle [ɛl] *pron* (*sujet*) she; (: *chose*) it; (*complément*) her; it; **~s** they; them; **~-même** herself; itself; **~s-mêmes** themselves; *voir aussi* **il**

élocution [elɔkysjɔ̃] *nf* delivery; **défaut d'~** speech impediment

éloge [elɔʒ] *nm* (*gén no pl*) praise; **élogieux, euse** *adj* laudatory, full of praise

éloigné, e [elwaɲe] *adj* distant, far-off; **éloignement** [elwaɲmɑ̃] *nm* removal; putting off; estrangement; (*fig*) distance

éloigner [elwaɲe] *vt* (*objet*): **~ qch (de)** to move *ou* take sth away (from); (*personne*): **~ qn (de)** to take sb away *ou* remove sb (from); (*échéance*) to put off, postpone; (*soupçons, danger*) to ward off; **s'~ (de)** (*personne*) to go away (from); (*véhicule*) to move away (from); (*affectivement*) to become estranged (from)

élongation [elɔ̃gasjɔ̃] *nf* strained muscle

élu, e [ely] *pp de* **élire** ♦ *nm/f* (*POL*) elected representative

élucubrations [elykybʀasjɔ̃] *nfpl* wild imaginings

éluder [elyde] *vt* to evade

Élysée *nm:* **(le palais de) l'~** the Élysée Palace (*the French president's residence*)

émacié, e [emasje] *adj* emaciated

émail, aux [emaj, -o] *nm* enamel

émaillé, e [emaje] *adj* (*fig*): **~ de** dotted with

émanciper [emɑ̃sipe] *vt* to emancipate; **s'~** *vi* (*fig*) to become emancipated *ou* liberated

émaner [emane]: **~ de** *vt* to come from;

(ADMIN) to proceed from

emballage [ãbalaʒ] nm wrapping; packaging

emballer [ãbale] vt to wrap (up); (dans un carton) to pack (up); (fig: fam) to thrill (to bits); **s'~** vi (moteur) to race; (cheval) to bolt; (fig: personne) to get carried away

embarcadère [ãbaʀkadɛʀ] nm wharf, pier

embarcation [ãbaʀkasjõ] nf (small) boat, (small) craft inv

embardée [ãbaʀde] nf: **faire une ~** to swerve

embarquement [ãbaʀkəmã] nm embarkation; loading; boarding

embarquer [ãbaʀke] vt (personne) to embark; (marchandise) to load; (fam) to cart off; to nick ♦ vi (passager) to board; **s'~** vi to board; **s'~ dans** (affaire, aventure) to embark upon

embarras [ãbaʀa] nm (obstacle) hindrance; (confusion) embarrassment

embarrassant, e [ãbaʀasã, -ãt] adj embarrassing

embarrasser [ãbaʀase] vt (encombrer) to clutter (up); (gêner) to hinder, hamper; (fig) to cause embarrassment to; to put in an awkward position

embauche [ãboʃ] nf hiring; **bureau d'~** labour office; **embaucher** [ãboʃe] vt to take on, hire

embaumer [ãbome] vt to embalm; to fill with its fragrance; **~ la lavande** to be fragrant with (the scent of) lavender

embellie [ãbeli] nf brighter period

embellir [ãbeliʀ] vt to make more attractive; (une histoire) to embellish ♦ vi to grow lovelier ou more attractive

embêtements [ãbɛtmã] nmpl trouble sg

embêter [ãbete] vt to bother; **s'~** vi (s'ennuyer) to be bored

emblée [ãble]: **d'~** adv straightaway

emboîter [ãbwate] vt to fit together; **s'~ (dans)** to fit (into); **~ le pas à qn** to follow in sb's footsteps

embonpoint [ãbõpwɛ̃] nm stoutness

embouchure [ãbuʃyʀ] nf (GÉO) mouth

embourber [ãbuʀbe]: **s'~** vi to get stuck in the mud

embourgeoiser [ãbuʀʒwaze]: **s'~** vi to adopt a middle-class outlook

embouteillage [ãbutejaʒ] nm traffic jam

emboutir [ãbutiʀ] vt (heurter) to crash into, ram

embranchement [ãbʀãʃmã] nm (routier) junction; (classification) branch

embraser [ãbʀaze]: **s'~** vi to flare up

embrasser [ãbʀase] vt to kiss; (sujet, période) to embrace, encompass; (carrière, métier) to enter upon

embrasure [ãbʀazyʀ] nf: **dans l'~ de la porte** in the door(way)

embrayage [ãbʀejaʒ] nm clutch

embrayer [ãbʀeje] vi (AUTO) to let in the clutch

embrigader [ãbʀigade] vt to recruit

embrocher [ãbʀɔʃe] vt to put on a spit

embrouiller [ãbʀuje] vt (fils) to tangle (up); (fiches, idées, personne) to muddle up; **s'~** vi (personne) to get in a muddle

embruns [ãbʀœ̃] nmpl sea spray sg

embûches [ãbyʃ] nfpl pitfalls, traps

embué, e [ãbɥe] adj misted up

embuscade [ãbyskad] nf ambush

éméché, e [emeʃe] adj tipsy, merry

émeraude [emʀod] nf emerald

émerger [emɛʀʒe] vi to emerge; (faire saillie, aussi fig) to stand out

émeri [ɛmʀi] nm: **toile ou papier ~** emery paper

émérite [emeʀit] adj highly skilled

émerveiller [emɛʀveje] vt to fill with wonder; **s'~ de** to marvel at

émetteur, trice [emɛtœʀ, -tʀis] adj transmitting; (poste) ~ transmitter

émettre [emɛtʀ(ə)] vt (son, lumière) to give out, emit; (message etc: RADIO) to transmit; (billet, timbre, emprunt) to issue; (hypothèse, avis) to voice, put forward ♦ vi to broadcast

émeus etc vb voir **émouvoir**

émeute [emøt] nf riot

émietter [emjete] vt to crumble

émigrer [emigʀe] vi to emigrate

éminence [eminãs] nf distinction; (col-

line) knoll, hill; **Son É~** His Eminence; **éminent, e** [eminã, -ãt] *adj* distinguished

émission [emisjɔ̃] *nf* emission; transmission; issue; (*RADIO, TV*) programme, broadcast; **~s** *fpl* emissions

emmagasiner [ãmagazine] *vt* to (put into) store; (*fig*) to store up

emmanchure [ãmãʃyr] *nf* armhole

emmêler [ãmele] *vt* to tangle (up); (*fig*) to muddle up; **s'~** *vi* to get into a tangle

emménager [ãmenaʒe] *vi* to move in; **~ dans** to move into

emmener [ãmne] *vt* to take (with one); (*comme otage, capture*) to take away; **~ qn au cinéma** to take sb to the cinema

emmerder [ãmɛrde] (*fam!*) *vt* to bug, bother; **s'~** *vi* to be bored stiff

emmitoufler [ãmitufle] *vt* to wrap up (warmly)

émoi [emwa] *nm* commotion; (*trouble*) agitation

émonder [emɔ̃de] *vt* to prune

émotif, ive [emɔtif, -iv] *adj* emotional

émotion [emosjɔ̃] *nf* emotion

émousser [emuse] *vt* to blunt; (*fig*) to dull

émouvoir [emuvwar] *vt* (*troubler*) to stir, affect; (*toucher, attendrir*) to move; (*indigner*) to rouse; **s'~** *vi* to be affected; to be moved; to be roused

empailler [ãpaje] *vt* to stuff

empaler [ãpale] *vt* to impale

emparer [ãpare]: **s'~ de** *vt* (*objet*) to seize, grab; (*comme otage, MIL*) to seize; (*suj: peur etc*) to take hold of

empâter [ãpate]: **s'~** *vi* to thicken out

empêchement [ãpɛʃmã] *nm* (*unexpected*) obstacle, hitch

empêcher [ãpeʃe] *vt* to prevent; **~ qn de faire** to prevent *ou* stop sb (from) doing; **il n'empêche que** nevertheless; **il n'a pas pu s'~ de rire** he couldn't help laughing

empereur [ãprœr] *nm* emperor

empeser [ãpəze] *vt* to starch

empester [ãpɛste] *vi* to stink, reek

empêtrer [ãpetre] *vt*: **s'~ dans** (*fils etc*) to get tangled up in

emphase [ãfaz] *nf* pomposity, bombast

empiéter [ãpjete] *vi*: **~ sur** to encroach upon

empiffrer [ãpifre]: **s'~** (*péj*) *vi* to stuff o.s.

empiler [ãpile] *vt* to pile (up)

empire [ãpir] *nm* empire; (*fig*) influence

empirer [ãpire] *vi* to worsen, deteriorate

emplacement [ãplasmã] *nm* site

emplettes [ãplɛt] *nfpl* shopping *sg*

emplir [ãplir] *vt* to fill; **s'~ (de)** to fill (with)

emploi [ãplwa] *nm* use; (*COMM, ÉCON*) employment; (*poste*) job, situation; **~ du temps** timetable, schedule

employé, e [ãplwaje] *nm/f* employee; **~ de bureau** office employee *ou* clerk

employer [ãplwaje] *vt* (*outil, moyen, méthode, mot*) to use; (*ouvrier, main-d'œuvre*) to employ; **s'~ à faire** to apply *ou* devote o.s. to doing; **employeur, euse** *nm/f* employer

empocher [ãpɔʃe] *vt* to pocket

empoigner [ãpwaɲe] *vt* to grab

empoisonner [ãpwazɔne] *vt* to poison; (*empester: air, pièce*) to stink out; (*fam*): **~ qn** to drive sb mad

emporté, e [ãpɔrte] *adj* quick-tempered

emporter [ãpɔrte] *vt* to take (with one); (*en dérobant ou enlevant, emmener: blessés, voyageurs*) to take away; (*entraîner*) to carry away; (*arracher*) to tear off; (*avantage, approbation*) to win; **s'~** *vi* (*de colère*) to lose one's temper; **l'~ (sur)** to get the upper hand (of); (*méthode etc*) to prevail (over); **boissons à ~** take-away drinks

empreint, e [ãprɛ̃, -ɛ̃t] *adj*: **~ de** marked with; tinged with; **empreinte** *nf* (*de pied, main*) print; (*fig*) stamp, mark; **empreinte (digitale)** fingerprint

empressé, e [ãprese] *adj* attentive

empressement [ãprɛsmã] *nm* (*hâte*) eagerness

empresser [ãprese]: **s'~** *vi*: **s'~ auprès de qn** to surround sb with attentions; **s'~ de faire** (*se hâter*) to hasten to do

emprise [ãpriz] *nf* hold, ascendancy

emprisonner [ãprizɔne] *vt* to imprison

emprunt [ɑ̃pʀœ̃] *nm* borrowing *no pl*, loan

emprunté, e [ɑ̃pʀœ̃te] *adj* (*fig*) ill-at-ease, awkward

emprunter [ɑ̃pʀœ̃te] *vt* to borrow; (*itinéraire*) to take, follow; (*style, manière*) to adopt, assume

ému, e [emy] *pp de* **émouvoir** ♦ *adj* excited; touched; moved

émulsion [emylsjɔ̃] *nf* (*cosmétique*) (water-based) lotion

MOT-CLÉ
---

en [ɑ̃] *prép* **1** (*endroit, pays*) in; (*direction*) to; **habiter** ~ **France/ville** to live in France/town; **aller** ~ **France/ville** to go to France/town

2 (*moment, temps*) in; ~ **été/juin** in summer/June

3 (*moyen*) by; ~ **avion/taxi** by plane/taxi

4 (*composition*) made of; **c'est** ~ **verre** it's (made of) glass; **un collier** ~ **argent** a silver necklace

5 (*description, état*): **une femme (habillée)** ~ **rouge** a woman (dressed) in red; **peindre qch** ~ **rouge** to paint sth red; ~ **T/étoile** T/star-shaped; ~ **chemise/chaussettes** in one's shirt sleeves/socks: ~ **soldat** as a soldier; **cassé** ~ **plusieurs morceaux** broken into several pieces; ~ **réparation** being repaired, under repair; ~ **vacances** on holiday; ~ **deuil** in mourning; **le même** ~ **plus grand** the same but *ou* only bigger

6 (*avec gérondif*) while; on; by; ~ **dormant** while sleeping, as one sleeps; ~ **sortant** on going out, as he *etc* went out; **sortir** ~ **courant** to run out

♦ *pron* **1** (*indéfini*): **j'**~ **ai/veux** I have/want some; ~ **as-tu?** have you got any?; **je n'**~ **veux pas** I don't want any; **j'**~ **ai 2** I've got 2; **combien y** ~ **a-t-il?** how many (of them) are there?; **j'**~ **ai assez** I've got enough (of it *ou* them); (*j'en ai marre*) I've had enough

2 (*provenance*) from there; **j'**~ **viens** I've come from there

3 (*cause*): **il** ~ **est malade/perd le som-**
meil he is ill/can't sleep because of it

4 (*complément de nom, d'adjectif, de verbe*): **j'**~ **connais les dangers** I know its *ou* the dangers; **j'**~ **suis fier/ai besoin** I am proud of it/need it

---

E.N.A. [ena] *sigle f* (= *École Nationale d'Administration*) *one of the Grandes Écoles*

encadrer [ɑ̃kɑdʀe] *vt* (*tableau, image*) to frame; (*fig: entourer*) to surround; (*personnel, soldats etc*) to train

encaissé, e [ɑ̃kese] *adj* steep-sided; with steep banks

encaisser [ɑ̃kese] *vt* (*chèque*) to cash; (*argent*) to collect; (*fig: coup, défaite*) to take

encart [ɑ̃kaʀ] *nm* insert

encastrer [ɑ̃kɑstʀe] *vt*: ~ **qch dans** (*mur*) to embed sth in(to); (*boîtier*) to fit sth into

encaustique [ɑ̃kostik] *nf* polish, wax

enceinte [ɑ̃sɛ̃t] *adj f*: ~ **(de 6 mois)** (6 months) pregnant ♦ *nf* (*mur*) wall; (*espace*) enclosure

encens [ɑ̃sɑ̃] *nm* incense

encercler [ɑ̃seʀkle] *vt* to surround

enchaîner [ɑ̃ʃene] *vt* to chain up; (*mouvements, séquences*) to link (together) ♦ *vi* to carry on

enchanté, e [ɑ̃ʃɑ̃te] *adj* delighted; enchanted; ~ **(de faire votre connaissance)** pleased to meet you

enchantement [ɑ̃ʃɑ̃tmɑ̃] *nm* delight; (*magie*) enchantment

enchâsser [ɑ̃ʃɑse] *vt* to set

enchère [ɑ̃ʃɛʀ] *nf* bid; **mettre/vendre aux** ~**s** to put up for (sale by)/sell by auction

enchevêtrer [ɑ̃ʃvetʀe] *vt* to tangle (up)

enclencher [ɑ̃klɑ̃ʃe] *vt* (*mécanisme*) to engage; **s'**~ *vi* to engage

enclin, e [ɑ̃klɛ̃, -in] *adj*: ~ **à** inclined *ou* prone to

enclos [ɑ̃klo] *nm* enclosure

enclume [ɑ̃klym] *nf* anvil

encoche [ɑ̃kɔʃ] *nf* notch

encoignure [ɑ̃kɔɲyʀ] *nf* corner

encolure [ɑ̃kɔlyʀ] *nf* (*tour de cou*) collar

size; (*col, cou*) neck

encombrant, e [ɑ̃kɔ̃brɑ̃, -ɑ̃t] *adj* cumbersome, bulky

encombre [ɑ̃kɔ̃br(ə)]: **sans ~** *adv* without mishap *ou* incident

encombrer [ɑ̃kɔ̃bre] *vt* to clutter (up); (*gêner*) to hamper; **s'~ de** (*bagages etc*) to load *ou* burden o.s. with

encontre [ɑ̃kɔ̃tr(ə)]: **à l'~ de** *prép* against, counter to

---
| MOT-CLÉ |
---

encore [ɑ̃kɔr] *adv* 1 (*continuation*) still; **il y travaille ~** he's still working on it; **pas ~** not yet

2 (*de nouveau*) again; **j'irai ~ demain** I'll go again tomorrow; **~ une fois** (once) again; **~ deux jours** two more days

3 (*intensif*) even, still; **~ plus fort/mieux** even louder/better, louder/better still

4 (*restriction*) even so *ou* then, only; **~ pourrais-je le faire si ...** even so, I might be able to do it if ...; **si ~** if only

encore que *conj* although

---

encourager [ɑ̃kuraʒe] *vt* to encourage

encourir [ɑ̃kurir] *vt* to incur

encrasser [ɑ̃krase] *vt* to clog up; (*AUTO: bougies*) to soot up

encre [ɑ̃kr(ə)] *nf* ink; **~ de Chine** Indian ink; **encrier** *nm* inkwell

encroûter [ɑ̃krute]: **s'~** *vi* (*fig*) to get into a rut, get set in one's ways

encyclopédie [ɑ̃siklɔpedi] *nf* encyclopaedia

endetter [ɑ̃dete] *vt* to get into debt; **s'~** *vi* to get into debt

endiablé, e [ɑ̃djɑble] *adj* furious; boisterous

endiguer [ɑ̃dige] *vt* to dyke (up); (*fig*) to check, hold back

endimancher [ɑ̃dimɑ̃ʃe] *vt*: **s'~** to put on one's Sunday best

endive [ɑ̃div] *nf* chicory *no pl*

endoctriner [ɑ̃dɔktrine] *vt* to indoctrinate

endommager [ɑ̃dɔmaʒe] *vt* to damage

endormi, e [ɑ̃dɔrmi] *adj* asleep

endormir [ɑ̃dɔrmir] *vt* to put to sleep; (*suj: chaleur etc*) to send to sleep; (*MÉD: dent, nerf*) to anaesthetize; (*fig: soupçons*) to allay; **s'~** *vi* to fall asleep, go to sleep

endosser [ɑ̃dose] *vt* (*responsabilité*) to take, shoulder; (*chèque*) to endorse; (*uniforme, tenue*) to put on, don

endroit [ɑ̃drwa] *nm* place; (*opposé à l'envers*) right side; **à l'~** the right way out; the right way up; **à l'~ de** regarding

enduire [ɑ̃dyir] *vt* to coat

enduit [ɑ̃dyi] *nm* coating

endurant, e [ɑ̃dyrɑ̃, -ɑ̃t] *adj* tough, hardy

endurcir [ɑ̃dyrsir] *vt* (*physiquement*) to toughen; (*moralement*) to harden; **s'~** *vi* to become tougher; to become hardened

endurer [ɑ̃dyre] *vt* to endure, bear

énergie [enɛrʒi] *nf* (*PHYSIQUE*) energy; (*TECH*) power; (*morale*) vigour, spirit; **énergique** *adj* energetic; vigorous; (*mesures*) drastic, stringent

énergumène [enɛrgymɛn] *nm* rowdy character *ou* customer

énerver [enɛrve] *vt* to irritate, annoy; **s'~** *vi* to get excited, get worked up

enfance [ɑ̃fɑ̃s] *nf* (*âge*) childhood; (*fig*) infancy; (*enfants*) children *pl*

enfant [ɑ̃fɑ̃] *nm/f* child; **~ de chœur** *nm* (*REL*) altar boy; **enfanter** *vi* to give birth ♦ *vt* to give birth to; **enfantillage** (*péj*) *nm* childish behaviour *no pl*; **enfantin, e** *adj* childlike; child *cpd*

enfer [ɑ̃fɛr] *nm* hell

enfermer [ɑ̃fɛrme] *vt* to shut up; (*à clef, interner*) to lock up

enfiévré, e [ɑ̃fjevre] *adj* (*fig*) feverish

enfiler [ɑ̃file] *vt* (*vêtement*) to slip on, slip into; (*insérer*): **~ qch dans** to stick sth into; (*rue, couloir*) to take; (*perles*) to string; (*aiguille*) to thread

enfin [ɑ̃fɛ̃] *adv* at last; (*en énumérant*) lastly; (*de restriction, résignation*) still; well; (*pour conclure*) in a word

enflammer [ɑ̃flame] *vt* to set fire to; (*MÉD*) to inflame; **s'~** *vi* to catch fire; to become inflamed

enflé, e [ɑ̃fle] *adj* swollen

enfler [ɑ̃fle] *vi* to swell (up)

enfoncer [ɑ̃fɔ̃se] *vt* (*clou*) to drive in; (*faire pénétrer*): ~ **qch dans** to push (*ou* drive) sth into; (*forcer: porte*) to break open; (*: plancher*) to cause to cave in ♦ *vi* (*dans la vase etc*) to sink in; (*sol, surface*) to give way; **s'~** *vi* to sink; **s'~ dans** to sink into; (*forêt, ville*) to disappear into

enfouir [ɑ̃fwiʀ] *vt* (*dans le sol*) to bury; (*dans un tiroir etc*) to tuck away

enfourcher [ɑ̃fuʀʃe] *vt* to mount

enfourner [ɑ̃fuʀne] *vt* to put in the oven

enfreindre [ɑ̃fʀɛ̃dʀ(ə)] *vt* to infringe, break

enfuir [ɑ̃fɥiʀ]: **s'~** *vi* to run away *ou* off

enfumer [ɑ̃fyme] *vt* to smoke out

engageant, e [ɑ̃gaʒɑ̃, -ɑ̃t] *adj* attractive, appealing

engagement [ɑ̃gaʒmɑ̃] *nm* (*promesse, contrat, POL*) commitment; (*MIL: combat*) engagement

engager [ɑ̃gaʒe] *vt* (*embaucher*) to take on, engage; (*commencer*) to start; (*lier*) to bind, commit; (*impliquer, entraîner*) to involve; (*investir*) to invest, lay out; (*faire intervenir*) to engage; (*inciter*) to urge; (*faire pénétrer*) to insert; **s'~** *vi* to hire o.s., get taken on; (*MIL*) to enlist; (*promettre, politiquement*) to commit o.s.; (*débuter*) to start (up); **s'~ à faire** to undertake to do; **s'~ dans** (*rue, passage*) to turn into; (*s'emboîter*) to engage into; (*fig: affaire, discussion*) to enter into, embark on

engelures [ɑ̃ʒlyʀ] *nfpl* chilblains

engendrer [ɑ̃ʒɑ̃dʀe] *vt* to father

engin [ɑ̃ʒɛ̃] *nm* machine; instrument; vehicle; (*AVIAT*) aircraft *inv*; missile

englober [ɑ̃glɔbe] *vt* to include

engloutir [ɑ̃glutiʀ] *vt* to swallow up

engoncé, e [ɑ̃gɔ̃se] *adj*: ~ **dans** cramped in

engorger [ɑ̃gɔʀʒe] *vt* to obstruct, block

engouement [ɑ̃gumɑ̃] *nm* (sudden) passion

engouffrer [ɑ̃gufʀe] *vt* to swallow up, devour; **s'~ dans** to rush into

engourdir [ɑ̃guʀdiʀ] *vt* to numb; (*fig*) to

dull, blunt; **s'~** *vi* to go numb

engrais [ɑ̃gʀɛ] *nm* manure; ~ **(chimique)** (chemical) fertilizer

engraisser [ɑ̃gʀese] *vt* to fatten (up)

engrenage [ɑ̃gʀənaʒ] *nm* gears *pl*, gearing; (*fig*) chain

engueuler [ɑ̃gœle] (*fam*) *vt* to bawl at

enhardir [ɑ̃aʀdiʀ]: **s'~** *vi* to grow bolder

énigme [enigm(ə)] *nf* riddle

enivrer [ɑ̃nivʀe] *vt*: **s'~** to get drunk; **s'~ de** (*fig*) to become intoxicated with

enjambée [ɑ̃ʒɑ̃be] *nf* stride

enjamber [ɑ̃ʒɑ̃be] *vt* to stride over; (*suj: pont etc*) to span, straddle

enjeu, x [ɑ̃ʒø] *nm* stakes *pl*

enjoindre [ɑ̃ʒwɛ̃dʀ(ə)] *vt* to enjoin, order

enjôler [ɑ̃ʒole] *vt* to coax, wheedle

enjoliver [ɑ̃ʒolive] *vt* to embellish; **enjoliveur** [ɑ̃ʒolivœʀ] *nm* (*AUTO*) hub cap

enjoué, e [ɑ̃ʒwe] *adj* playful

enlacer [ɑ̃lase] *vt* (*étreindre*) to embrace, hug

enlaidir [ɑ̃lediʀ] *vt* to make ugly ♦ *vi* to become ugly

enlèvement [ɑ̃lɛvmɑ̃] *nm* (*rapt*) abduction, kidnapping

enlever [ɑ̃lve] *vt* (*ôter: gén*) to remove; (*: vêtement, lunettes*) to take off; (*emporter: ordures etc*) to take away; (*prendre*): ~ **qch à qn** to take sth (away) from sb; (*kidnapper*) to abduct, kidnap; (*obtenir: prix, contrat*) to win

enliser [ɑ̃lize]: **s'~** *vi* to sink, get stuck

enluminure [ɑ̃lyminyʀ] *nf* illumination

enneigé, e [ɑ̃neʒe] *adj* snowy; snowed-up

ennemi, e [ɛnmi] *adj* hostile; (*MIL*) enemy *cpd* ♦ *nm/f* enemy

ennui [ɑ̃nɥi] *nm* (*lassitude*) boredom; (*difficulté*) trouble *no pl*; **avoir des ~s** to have problems; **ennuyer** *vt* to bother; (*lasser*) to bore; **s'ennuyer** *vi* to be bored; **s'ennuyer de** (*regretter*) to miss; **ennuyeux, euse** *adj* boring, tedious; annoying

énoncé [enɔ̃se] *nm* terms *pl*; wording

énoncer [enɔ̃se] *vt* to say, express; (*conditions*) to set out, state

enorgueillir [ɑ̃nɔʀgœjiʀ]: **s'~ de** *vt* to

pride o.s. on; to boast

énorme [enɔʀm(ə)] *adj* enormous, huge; **énormément** *adv* enormously; **enormément de neige/gens** an enormous amount of snow/number of people

enquérir [ɑ̃keʀiʀ]: **s'~ de** *vt* to inquire about

enquête [ɑ̃kɛt] *nf* (*de journaliste, de police*) investigation; (*judiciaire, administrative*) inquiry; (*sondage d'opinion*) survey; **enquêter** *vi* to investigate; to hold an inquiry; to conduct a survey

enquiers *etc vb voir* **enquérir**

enraciné, e [ɑ̃ʀasine] *adj* deep-rooted

enragé, e [ɑ̃ʀaʒe] *adj* (*MÉD*) rabid, with rabies; (*fig*) fanatical

enrageant, e [ɑ̃ʀaʒɑ̃, -ɑ̃t] *adj* infuriating

enrager [ɑ̃ʀaʒe] *vi* to be in a rage

enrayer [ɑ̃ʀeje] *vt* to check, stop; **s'~** *vi* (*arme à feu*) to jam

enregistrement [ɑ̃ʀʒistʀəmɑ̃] *nm* recording; (*ADMIN*) registration; **~ des bagages** (*à l'aéroport*) baggage check-in; **enregistrer** [ɑ̃ʀʒistʀe] *vt* (*MUS etc, remarquer, noter*) to record; (*fig: mémoriser*) to make a mental note of; (*ADMIN*) to register; (*bagages: par train*) to register; (: *à l'aéroport*) to check in

enrhumer [ɑ̃ʀyme]: **s'~** *vi* to catch a cold

enrichir [ɑ̃ʀiʃiʀ] *vt* to make rich(er); (*fig*) to enrich; **s'~** *vi* to get rich(er)

enrober [ɑ̃ʀɔbe] *vt*: **~ qch de** to coat sth with; (*fig*) to wrap sth up in

enrôler [ɑ̃ʀole] *vt* to enlist; **s'~ (dans)** to enlist (in)

enrouer [ɑ̃ʀwe]: **s'~** *vi* to go hoarse

enrouler [ɑ̃ʀule] *vt* (*fil, corde*) to wind (up); **s'~** *vi* to coil up; to wind; **~ qch autour de** to wind sth (a)round

ensanglanté, e [ɑ̃sɑ̃glɑ̃te] *adj* covered with blood

enseignant, e [ɑ̃sɛɲɑ̃, -ɑ̃t] *nm/f* teacher

enseigne [ɑ̃sɛɲ] *nf* sign; **à telle ~ que** so much so that; **~ lumineuse** neon sign

enseignement [ɑ̃sɛɲmɑ̃] *nm* teaching; (*ADMIN*) education

enseigner [ɑ̃sɛɲe] *vt, vi* to teach; **~ qch à qn/à qn que** to teach sb sth/sb that

ensemble [ɑ̃sɑ̃bl(ə)] *adv* together ♦ *nm* (*assemblage, MATH*) set; (*totalité*): **l'~ du/de la** the whole *ou* entire; (*unité, harmonie*) unity; **impression/idée d'~** overall *ou* general impression/idea; **dans l'~** (*en gros*) on the whole

ensemencer [ɑ̃səmɑ̃se] *vt* to sow

ensevelir [ɑ̃səvliʀ] *vt* to bury

ensoleillé, e [ɑ̃sɔleje] *adj* sunny

ensommeillé, e [ɑ̃sɔmeje] *adj* drowsy

ensorceler [ɑ̃sɔʀsəle] *vt* to enchant, bewitch

ensuite [ɑ̃sɥit] *adv* then, next; (*plus tard*) afterwards, later; **~ de quoi** after which

ensuivre [ɑ̃sɥivʀ(ə)]: **s'~** *vi* to follow, ensue

entailler [ɑ̃taje] *vt* to notch; to cut

entamer [ɑ̃tame] *vt* (*pain, bouteille*) to start; (*hostilités, pourparlers*) to open; (*fig: altérer*) to make a dent in; to shake; to damage

entasser [ɑ̃tase] *vt* (*empiler*) to pile up, heap up; (*tenir à l'étroit*) to cram together; **s'~** *vi* to pile up; to cram

entendre [ɑ̃tɑ̃dʀ(ə)] *vt* to hear; (*comprendre*) to understand; (*vouloir dire*) to mean; (*vouloir*): **~ être obéi/que** to mean to be obeyed/that; **s'~** *vi* (*sympathiser*) to get on; (*se mettre d'accord*) to agree; **s'~ à qch/à faire** (*être compétent*) to be good at sth/doing; **j'ai entendu dire que** I've heard (it said) that

entendu, e [ɑ̃tɑ̃dy] *adj* (*réglé*) agreed; (*au courant: air*) knowing; **(c'est) ~** all right, agreed; **c'est ~** (*concession*) all right, granted; **bien ~** of course

entente [ɑ̃tɑ̃t] *nf* understanding; (*accord, traité*) agreement; **à double ~** (*sens*) with a double meaning

entériner [ɑ̃teʀine] *vt* to ratify, confirm

enterrement [ɑ̃teʀmɑ̃] *nm* (*cérémonie*) funeral, burial

enterrer [ɑ̃teʀe] *vt* to bury

entêtant, e [ɑ̃tetɑ̃, -ɑ̃t] *adj* heady

entêté, e [ɑ̃tete] *adj* stubborn

en-tête [ãtɛt] *nm* heading; **papier à ~** headed notepaper

entêter [ãtete]: **s'~** *vi*: **s'~ (à faire)** to persist (in doing)

enthousiasme [ãtuzjasm(ə)] *nm* enthusiasm; **enthousiasmer** *vt* to fill with enthusiasm; **s'enthousiasmer (pour qch)** to get enthusiastic (about sth)

enticher [ãtiʃe]: **s'~ de** *vt* to become infatuated with

entier, ère [ãtje, -jɛʀ] *adj* (*non entamé, en totalité*) whole; (*total, complet*) complete; (*fig: caractère*) unbending ♦ *nm* (MATH) whole; **en ~** totally; in its entirety; **lait ~** full-cream milk; **entièrement** *adv* entirely, wholly

entonner [ãtɔne] *vt* (*chanson*) to strike up

entonnoir [ãtɔnwaʀ] *nm* funnel

entorse [ãtɔʀs(ə)] *nf* (MÉD) sprain; (*fig*): **~ au reglement** infringement of the rule

entortiller [ãtɔʀtije] *vt* (*envelopper*) to wrap; (*enrouler*) to twist, wind; (*duper*) to deceive

entourage [ãtuʀaʒ] *nm* circle; family (circle); entourage; (*ce qui enclôt*) surround

entourer [ãtuʀe] *vt* to surround; (*apporter son soutien à*) to rally round; **~ de** to surround with; (*trait*) to encircle with

entourloupettes [ãtuʀlupɛt] *nfpl* mean tricks

entracte [ãtʀakt(ə)] *nm* interval

entraide [ãtʀɛd] *nf* mutual aid; **s'~r** *vi* to help each other

entrain [ãtʀɛ̃] *nm* spirit; **avec/sans ~** spiritedly/half-heartedly

entraînement [ãtʀɛnmã] *nm* training; (TECH) drive

entraîner [ãtʀene] *vt* (*tirer: wagons*) to pull; (*charrier*) to carry *ou* drag along; (TECH) to drive; (*emmener: personne*) to take (off); (*mener à l'assaut, influencer*) to lead; (SPORT) to train; (*impliquer*) to entail; (*causer*) to lead to, bring about; **s'~** *vi* (SPORT) to train; **s'~ à qch/à faire** (*inciter*) to lead sb to do; **entraîneur, euse** *nm/f* (SPORT) coach, trainer ♦ *nm*

(HIPPISME) trainer; **entraîneuse** *nf* (*de bar*) hostess

entraver [ãtʀave] *vt* (*circulation*) to hold up; (*action, progrès*) to hinder

entre [ãtʀ(ə)] *prép* between; among(st); **l'un d'~ eux/nous** one of them/us; **~ eux** among(st) themselves

entre-: **~bâillé, e** *adj* half-open, ajar; **~choquer: s'~choquer** *vi* to knock *ou* bang together; **~côte** *nf* entrecôte *ou* rib steak; **~couper** *vt*: **~couper qch de** to intersperse sth with; **~croiser: s'~croiser** *vi* to intertwine

entrée [ãtʀe] *nf* entrance; (*accès: au cinéma etc*) admission; (*billet*) (admission) ticket; (CULIN) first course; **d'~** from the outset; **~ en matière** introduction

entrefaites [ãtʀəfɛt]: **sur ces ~** *adv* at this juncture

entrefilet [ãtʀəfilɛ] *nm* paragraph (*short article*)

entrejambes [ãtʀəʒãb] *nm* crotch

entrelacer [ãtʀəlase] *vt* to intertwine

entrelarder [ãtʀəlaʀde] *vt* to lard

entremêler [ãtʀəmele] *vt*: **~ qch de** to (inter)mingle sth with

entremets [ãtʀəmɛ] *nm* (cream) dessert

entremetteur, euse [ãtʀəmɛtœʀ, -øz] *nm/f* go-between

entremise [ãtʀəmiz] *nf* intervention; **par l'~ de** through

entreposer [ãtʀəpoze] *vt* to store, put into storage

entrepôt [ãtʀəpo] *nm* warehouse

entreprenant, e [ãtʀəpʀənã, -ãt] *adj* (*actif*) enterprising; (*trop galant*) forward

entreprendre [ãtʀəpʀãdʀ(ə)] *vt* (*se lancer dans*) to undertake; (*commencer*) to begin *ou* start (upon); (*personne*) to buttonhole; to tackle

entrepreneur [ãtʀəpʀənœʀ] *nm*: **~ (en bâtiment)** (building) contractor

entreprise [ãtʀəpʀiz] *nf* (*société*) firm, concern; (*action*) undertaking, venture

entrer [ãtʀe] *vi* to go (*ou* come) in, enter ♦ *vt* (INFORM) to enter, input; **(faire) ~ qch dans** to get sth into; **~ dans** (*gén*) to enter; (*pièce*) to go (*ou* come) into, enter; (*club*) to join; (*heurter*) to run into; (*être une composante de*) to go into; to form part of; ~ **à l'hôpital** to go into hospital; **faire** ~ (*visiteur*) to show in

entresol [ɑ̃tʀəsɔl] *nm* mezzanine

entre-temps [ɑ̃tʀətɑ̃] *adv* meanwhile

entretenir [ɑ̃tʀətniʀ] *vt* to maintain; (*famille, maîtresse*) to support, keep; **s'~ (de)** to converse (about); ~ **qn (de)** to speak to sb (about)

entretien [ɑ̃tʀətjɛ̃] *nm* maintenance; (*discussion*) discussion, talk; (*audience*) interview

entrevoir [ɑ̃tʀəvwaʀ] *vt* (*à peine*) to make out; (*brièvement*) to catch a glimpse of

entrevue [ɑ̃tʀəvy] *nf* meeting; (*audience*) interview

entrouvert, e [ɑ̃tʀuvɛʀ, -ɛʀt(ə)] *adj* half-open

énumérer [enymeʀe] *vt* to list, enumerate

envahir [ɑ̃vaiʀ] *vt* to invade; (*suj: inquiétude, peur*) to come over; **envahissant, e** (*péj*) *adj* (*personne*) interfering, intrusive

enveloppe [ɑ̃vlɔp] *nf* (*de lettre*) envelope; (*TECH*) casing; outer layer

envelopper [ɑ̃vlɔpe] *vt* to wrap; (*fig*) to envelop, shroud

envenimer [ɑ̃vnime] *vt* to aggravate

envergure [ɑ̃vɛʀgyʀ] *nf* (*fig*) scope; calibre

enverrai *etc vb voir* **envoyer**

envers [ɑ̃vɛʀ] *prép* towards, to ♦ *nm* other side; (*d'une étoffe*) wrong side; **à l'~** upside down; back to front; (*vêtement*) inside out

envie [ɑ̃vi] *nf* (*sentiment*) envy; (*souhait*) desire, wish; **avoir ~ de (faire)** to feel like (doing); (*plus fort*) to want to do); **avoir ~ que** to wish that; **ça lui fait ~** he would like that; **envier** *vt* to envy; **envieux, euse** *adj* envious

environ [ɑ̃viʀɔ̃] *adv*: ~ **3 h/2 km** (around) about 3 o'clock/2 km; *voir aussi* **environs**

environnement [ɑ̃viʀɔnmɑ̃] *nm* environment

environner [ɑ̃viʀɔne] *vt* to surround

environs [ɑ̃viʀɔ̃] *nmpl* surroundings

envisager [ɑ̃vizaʒe] *vt* (*examiner, considérer*) to view, contemplate; (*avoir en vue*) to envisage

envoi [ɑ̃vwa] *nm* (*paquet*) parcel, consignment

envoler [ɑ̃vɔle]: **s'~** *vi* (*oiseau*) to fly away *ou* off; (*avion*) to take off; (*papier, feuille*) to blow away; (*fig*) to vanish (into thin air)

envoûter [ɑ̃vute] *vt* to bewitch

envoyé, e [ɑ̃vwaje] *nm/f* (*POL*) envoy; (*PRESSE*) correspondent

envoyer [ɑ̃vwaje] *vt* to send; (*lancer*) to hurl, throw; ~ **chercher** to send for

épagneul, e [epaɲœl] *nm/f* spaniel

épais, se [epɛ, -ɛs] *adj* thick; **épaisseur** *nf* thickness

épancher [epɑ̃ʃe]: **s'~** *vi* to open one's heart

épanouir [epanwiʀ]: **s'~** *vi* (*fleur*) to bloom, open out; (*visage*) to light up; (*fig*) to blossom; to open up

épargne [epaʀɲ(ə)] *nf* saving

épargner [epaʀɲe] *vt* to save; (*ne pas tuer ou endommager*) to spare ♦ *vi* to save; ~ **qch à qn** to spare sb sth

éparpiller [epaʀpije] *vt* to scatter; (*pour répartir*) to disperse; **s'~** *vi* to scatter; (*fig*) to dissipate one's efforts

épars, e [epaʀ, -aʀs(ə)] *adj* scattered

épatant, e [epatɑ̃, -ɑ̃t] (*fam*) *adj* super

épater [epate] *vt* to amaze; to impress

épaule [epol] *nf* shoulder

épauler [epole] *vt* (*aider*) to back up, support; (*arme*) to raise (to one's shoulder) ♦ *vi* to (take) aim

épaulette [epolɛt] *nf* epaulette; (*rembourrage*) shoulder pad

épave [epav] *nf* wreck

épée [epe] *nf* sword

épeler [eple] *vt* to spell

éperdu, e [epɛʀdy] *adj* distraught, overcome; passionate; frantic

éperon [epʀɔ̃] *nm* spur

épi [epi] *nm* (*de blé, d'orge*) ear

épice [epis] *nf* spice

épicer [epise] *vt* to spice

épicerie [episʀi] *nf* grocer's shop; (*denrées*) groceries *pl*; ~ **fine** delicatessen; **épicier, ière** *nm/f* grocer

épidémie [epidemi] *nf* epidemic

épier [epje] *vt* (*jambes*) to spy on, watch closely; (*occasion*) to look out for

épilepsie [epilɛpsi] *nf* epilepsy

épiler [epile] *vt* (*jambes*) to remove the hair from; (*sourcils*) to pluck

épilogue [epilɔg] *nm* (*fig*) conclusion, dénouement; **épiloguer** [epilɔge] *vi:* **épiloguer sur** to hold forth on

épinards [epinaʀ] *nmpl* spinach *sg*

épine [epin] *nf* thorn, prickle; (*d'oursin etc*) spine; ~ **dorsale** backbone

épingle [epɛ̃gl(ə)] *nf* pin; ~ **de nourrice** safety pin; ~ **de sûreté** *ou* **double** safety pin

épingler [epɛ̃gle] *vt* (*badge, décoration*): ~ **qch sur** to pin sth on(to); (*fam*) to catch, nick

épique [epik] *adj* epic

épisode [epizɔd] *nm* episode; **film/roman à ~s** serial; **épisodique** *adj* occasional

éploré, e [eplɔʀe] *adj* tearful

épluche-légumes [eplyʃlegym] *nm inv* (potato) peeler

éplucher [eplyʃe] *vt* (*fruit, légumes*) to peel; (*fig*) to go over with a fine-tooth comb; **épluchures** *nfpl* peelings

éponge [epɔ̃ʒ] *nf* sponge; **éponger** *vt* (*liquide*) to mop up; (*surface*) to sponge; (*fig: déficit*) to soak up; **s'éponger le front** to mop one's brow

épopée [epɔpe] *nf* epic

époque [epɔk] *nf* (*de l'histoire*) age, era; (*de l'année, la vie*) time; **d'~** (*meuble*) period *cpd*

époumoner [epumɔne]: **s'~** *vi* to shout o.s. hoarse

épouse [epuz] *nf* wife

épouser [epuze] *vt* to marry; (*fig: idées*) to espouse; (: *forme*) to fit

épousseter [epuste] *vt* to dust

époustouflant, e [epustuflɑ̃, -ɑ̃t] *adj* staggering, mind-boggling

épouvantable [epuvɑ̃tabl(ə)] *adj* appalling, dreadful

épouvantail [epuvɑ̃taj] *nm* (*à oiseaux*) scarecrow

épouvante [epuvɑ̃t] *nf* terror; **film d'~** horror film; **épouvanter** *vt* to terrify

époux [epu] *nm* husband ♦ *nmpl* (married) couple

éprendre [epʀɑ̃dʀ(ə)]: **s'~ de** *vt* to fall in love with

épreuve [epʀœv] *nf* (*d'examen*) test; (*malheur, difficulté*) trial, ordeal; (*PHOTO*) print; (*TYPO*) proof; (*SPORT*) event; **à l'~ des balles** bulletproof; **à toute ~** unfailing; **mettre à l'~** to put to the test

épris, e [epri, -iz] *pp de* **éprendre**

éprouver [epʀuve] *vt* (*tester*) to test; (*marquer, faire souffrir*) to afflict, distress; (*ressentir*) to experience

éprouvette [epʀuvɛt] *nf* test tube

épuisé, e [epɥize] *adj* exhausted; (*livre*) out of print; **épuisement** [epɥizmɑ̃] *nm* exhaustion

épuiser [epɥize] *vt* (*fatiguer*) to exhaust, wear *ou* tire out; (*stock, sujet*) to exhaust; **s'~** *vi* to wear *ou* tire o.s. out, exhaust o.s.; (*stock*) to run out

épurer [epyʀe] *vt* (*liquide*) to purify; (*parti etc*) to purge; (*langue, texte*) to refine

équateur [ekwatœʀ] *nm* equator; **(la république de) l'É~** Ecuador

équation [ekwasjɔ̃] *nf* equation

équerre [ekɛʀ] *nf* (*à dessin*) (set) square; (*pour fixer*) brace; **en ~** at right angles; **à l'~, d'~** straight

équilibre [ekilibʀ(ə)] *nm* balance; (*d'une balance*) equilibrium; **garder/perdre l'~** to keep/lose one's balance; **être en ~** to be balanced; **équilibré, e** *adj* (*fig*) well-balanced, stable; **équilibrer** *vt* to balance; **s'équilibrer** *vi* (*poids*) to balance; (*fig: défauts etc*) to balance each other out

équipage [ekipaʒ] *nm* crew

équipe [ekip] *nf* team; (*bande: parfois péj*) bunch

équipé, e [ekipe] *adj:* **bien/mal ~** well-/poorly-equipped

équipée [ekipe] *nf* escapade

équipement [ekipmɑ̃] *nm* equipment; **~s** *nmpl* (*installations*) amenities, facilities

équiper [ekipe] *vt* to equip; (*voiture, cuisine*) to equip, fit out; **~ qn/qch de** to equip sb/sth with

équipier, ière [ekipje, -jɛʀ] *nm/f* team member

équitable [ekitabl(ə)] *adj* fair

équitation [ekitasjɔ̃] *nf* (horse-) riding

équivalent, e [ekivalɑ̃, -ɑ̃t] *adj, nm* equivalent

équivaloir [ekivalwaʀ]: **~ à** *vt* to be equivalent to

équivoque [ekivɔk] *adj* equivocal, ambiguous; (*louche*) dubious

érable [eʀabl(ə)] *nm* maple

érafler [eʀafle] *vt* to scratch; **éraflure** *nf* scratch

éraillé, e [eʀaje] *adj* (*voix*) rasping

ère [ɛʀ] *nf* era; **en l'an 1050 de notre ~** in the year 1050 A.D.

érection [eʀɛksjɔ̃] *nf* erection

éreinter [eʀɛ̃te] *vt* to exhaust, wear out

ériger [eʀiʒe] *vt* (*monument*) to erect

ermite [ɛʀmit] *nm* hermit

éroder [eʀɔde] *vt* to erode

érotique [eʀɔtik] *adj* erotic

errer [eʀe] *vi* to wander

erreur [eʀœʀ] *nf* mistake, error; (*morale*) error; **faire ~** to be mistaken; **par ~** by mistake; **~ judiciaire** miscarriage of justice

érudit, e [eʀydi, -it] *nm/f* scholar

éruption [eʀypsjɔ̃] *nf* eruption; (*MÉD*) rash

es *vb voir* être

ès [ɛs] *prép*: **licencié ~ lettres/sciences** ≈ Bachelor of Arts/Science

escabeau, x [ɛskabo] *nm* (*tabouret*) stool; (*échelle*) stepladder

escadre [ɛskadʀ(ə)] *nf* (*NAVIG*) squadron; (*AVIAT*) wing

escadron [ɛskadʀɔ̃] *nm* squadron

escalade [ɛskalad] *nf* climbing *no pl*; (*POL etc*) escalation

escalader [ɛskalade] *vt* to climb

escale [ɛskal] *nf* (*NAVIG*) call; port of call; (*AVIAT*) stop(over); **faire ~ à** to put in at; to stop over at

escalier [ɛskalje] *nm* stairs *pl*; **dans l'~** *ou* **les ~s** on the stairs; **~ roulant** escalator

escamoter [ɛskamɔte] *vt* (*esquiver*) to get round, evade; (*faire disparaître*) to conjure away

escapade [ɛskapad] *nf*: **faire une ~** to go on a jaunt; to run away *ou* off

escargot [ɛskaʀgo] *nm* snail

escarmouche [ɛskaʀmuʃ] *nf* skirmish

escarpé, e [ɛskaʀpe] *adj* steep

escient [esjɑ̃]*nm*: **à bon ~** advisedly

esclaffer [ɛsklafe]: **s'~** *vi* to guffaw

esclandre [ɛsklɑ̃dʀ(ə)] *nm* scene, fracas

esclavage [ɛsklavaʒ] *nm* slavery

esclave [ɛsklav] *nm/f* slave

escompter [ɛskɔ̃te] *vt* (*COMM*) to discount; (*espérer*) to expect, reckon upon

escorte [ɛskɔʀt(ə)] *nf* escort

escrime [ɛskʀim] *nf* fencing

escrimer [ɛskʀime]: **s'~** *vi*: **s'~ à faire** to wear o.s. out doing

escroc [ɛskʀo] *nm* swindler, conman

escroquer [ɛskʀɔke] *vt*: **~ qn (de qch)/qch (à qn)** to swindle sb (out of sth)/sth (out of sb); **escroquerie** *nf* swindle

espace [ɛspas] *nm* space

espacer [ɛspase] *vt* to space out; **s'~** *vi* (*visites etc*) to become less frequent

espadon [ɛspadɔ̃] *nm* swordfish *inv*

espadrille [ɛspadʀij] *nf* rope-soled sandal

Espagne [ɛspaɲ(ə)] *nf*: **l'~** Spain; **espagnol, e** *adj* Spanish ♦ *nm/f*: **Espagnol, e** Spaniard ♦ *nm* (*LING*) Spanish

espèce [ɛspɛs] *nf* (*BIO, BOT, ZOOL*) species *inv*; (*gén: sorte*) sort, kind, type; (*péj*): **~ de maladroit!** you clumsy oaf!; **~s** *nfpl* (*COMM*) cash *sg*; **en ~** in cash; **en l'~** in the case in point

espérance [ɛspeʀɑ̃s] *nf* hope; **~ de vie** life expectancy

espérer [ɛspeʀe] *vt* to hope for; **j'espère (bien)** I hope so; **~ que/faire** to hope that/to do; **~ en** to trust in

espiègle [ɛspjɛgl(ə)] *adj* mischievous

espion, ne [ɛspjɔ̃, -ɔn] *nm/f* spy

espionnage [ɛspjɔnaʒ] *nm* espionage,

spying

espionner [ɛspjɔne] *vt* to spy (up)on

esplanade [ɛsplanad] *nf* esplanade

espoir [ɛspwaʀ] *nm* hope

esprit [ɛspʀi] *nm* (*pensée, intellect*) mind; (*humour, ironie*) wit; (*mentalité, d'une loi etc, fantôme etc*) spirit; **faire de l'~** to try to be witty; **reprendre ses ~s** to come to; **perdre l'~** to lose one's mind

esquimau, de, x [ɛskimo, -od] *adj, nm/f* Eskimo ♦ *nm* ice lolly (*BRIT*), popsicle (*US*)

esquinter [ɛskɛ̃te] (*fam*) *vt* to mess up

esquisse [ɛskis] *nf* sketch

esquisser [ɛskise] *vt* to sketch; **s'~** *vi* (*amélioration*) to begin to be detectable; **~ un sourire** to give a vague smile

esquiver [ɛskive] *vt* to dodge; **s'~** *vi* to slip away

essai [esɛ] *nm* trying; testing; (*tentative*) attempt, try; (*RUGBY*) try; (*LITTÉRATURE*) essay; **~s** *nmpl* (*AUTO*) trials; **~ gratuit** (*COMM*) free trial; **à l'~** on a trial basis

essaim [esɛ̃] *nm* swarm

essayer [eseje] *vt* (*gén*) to try; (*vêtement, chaussures*) to try (on); (*restaurant, méthode, voiture*) to try (out) ♦ *vi* to try; **~ de faire** to try *ou* attempt to do

essence [esɑ̃s] *nf* (*de voiture*) petrol (*BRIT*), gas(oline) (*US*); (*extrait de plante, PHILOSOPHIE*) essence; (*espèce: d'arbre*) species

essentiel, le [esɑ̃sjɛl] *adj* essential; **c'est l'~** (*ce qui importe*) that's the main thing; **l'~ de** the main part of

essieu, x [esjø] *nm* axle

essor [esɔʀ] *nm* (*de l'économie etc*) rapid expansion

essorer [esɔʀe] *vt* (*en tordant*) to wring (out); (*par la force centrifuge*) to spin-dry; **essoreuse** *nf* mangle, wringer; spin-dryer

essouffler [esufle] *vt* to make breathless; **s'~** *vi* to get out of breath; (*fig*) to run out of steam

essuie-glace [esɥiglas] *nm inv* windscreen (*BRIT*) *ou* windshield (*US*) wiper

essuie-main [esɥimɛ̃] *nm* hand towel

essuyer [esɥije] *vt* to wipe; (*fig: subir*) to suffer; **s'~** *vi* (*après le bain*) to dry o.s.; **~ la vaisselle** to dry up

est[1] [ɛ] *vb voir* **être**

est[2] [ɛst] *nm* east ♦ *adj inv* east; (*région*) east(ern); **à l'~** in the east; (*direction*) to the east, east(wards); **à l'~ de** (to the) east of

estampe [ɛstɑ̃p] *nf* print, engraving

est-ce que [ɛskə] *adv*: **~ c'est cher/ c'était bon?** is it expensive/was it good?; **quand est-ce qu'il part?** when does he leave?, when is he leaving?; *voir aussi* **que**

esthéticienne [ɛstetisjɛn] *nf* beautician

esthétique [ɛstetik] *adj* attractive; aesthetically pleasing

estimation [ɛstimasjɔ̃] *nf* valuation; assessment

estime [ɛstim] *nf* esteem, regard

estimer [ɛstime] *vt* (*respecter*) to esteem; (*expertiser*) to value; (*évaluer*) to assess, estimate; (*penser*): **~ que/être** to consider that/o.s. to be

estival, e, aux [ɛstival, -o] *adj* summer *cpd*

estivant, e [ɛstivɑ̃, -ɑ̃t] *nm/f* (summer) holiday-maker

estomac [ɛstɔma] *nm* stomach

estomaqué, e [ɛstɔmake] *adj* flabbergasted

estomper [ɛstɔ̃pe] *vt* (*fig*) to blur, dim; **s'~** *vi* to soften; to become blurred

estrade [ɛstʀad] *nf* platform, rostrum

estragon [ɛstʀagɔ̃] *nm* tarragon

estropier [ɛstʀɔpje] *vt* to cripple, maim; (*fig*) to twist, distort

et [e] *conj* and; **~ lui?** what about him?; **~ alors!** so what!

étable [etabl(ə)] *nf* cowshed

établi [etabli] *nm* (work)bench

établir [etabliʀ] *vt* (*papiers d'identité, facture*) to make out; (*liste, programme*) to draw up; (*entreprise, camp, gouvernement, artisan*) to set up; (*réputation, usage, fait, culpabilité*) to establish; **s'~** *vi* (*se faire: entente etc*) to be established; **s'~ (à son compte)** to set up in

business; **s'~ à/près de** to settle in/near
établissement [etablismɑ̃] *nm* making
out; drawing up; setting up, establishing;
(*entreprise, institution*) establishment; ~
scolaire school, educational establishment

étage [etaʒ] *nm* (*d'immeuble*) storey,
floor; (*de fusée*) stage; (*GÉO: de culture,
végétation*) level; **à l'~** upstairs; **au
2ème ~** on the 2nd (*BRIT*) *ou* 3rd (*US*)
floor; **de bas ~** low-born

étagère [etaʒɛR] *nf* (*rayon*) shelf; (*meuble*) shelves *pl*

étai [etɛ] *nm* stay, prop

étain [etɛ̃] *nm* tin; (*ORFÈVRERIE*) pewter
no pl

étais *etc vb voir* **être**

étal [etal] *nm* stall

étalage [etalaʒ] *nm* display; display window; **faire ~ de** to show off, parade

étaler [etale] *vt* (*carte, nappe*) to spread
(out); (*peinture, liquide*) to spread;
(*échelonner: paiements, vacances*) to
spread, stagger; (*marchandises*) to display; (*richesses, connaissances*) to parade; **s'~** *vi* (*liquide*) to spread out;
(*fam*) to fall flat on one's face; **s'~ sur**
(*suj: paiements etc*) to be spread out
over

étalon [etalɔ̃] *nm* (*mesure*) standard;
(*cheval*) stallion

étamer [etame] *vt* (*casserole*) to
tin(plate); (*glace*) to silver

étanche [etɑ̃ʃ] *adj* (*récipient*) watertight; (*montre, vêtement*) waterproof

étancher [etɑ̃ʃe] *vt*: ~ **sa soif** to quench
one's thirst

étang [etɑ̃] *nm* pond

étant [etɑ̃] *vb voir* **être; donné**

étape [etap] *nf* stage; (*lieu d'arrivée*)
stopping place; (: *CYCLISME*) staging point;
faire ~ à to stop off at

état [eta] *nm* (*POL, condition*) state;
(*liste*) inventory, statement; **en mauvais
~** in poor condition; **en ~ (de marche)**
in (working) order; **remettre en ~** to repair; **hors d'~** out of order; **être en ~/
hors d'~ de faire** to be in a/in no fit
state to do; **en tout ~ de cause** in any

event; **être dans tous ses ~s** to be in a
state; **faire ~ de** (*alléguer*) to put forward; **en ~ d'arrestation** under arrest;
~ **civil** civil status; ~ **des lieux** inventory of fixtures; **étatiser** *vt* to bring under state control

état-major [etamaʒɔR] *nm* (*MIL*) staff
Etats-Unis [etazyni] *nmpl*: **les ~** the
United States

étau, x [eto] *nm* vice (*BRIT*), vise (*US*)
étayer [eteje] *vt* to prop *ou* shore up
etc. *adv* etc
et c(a)etera [ɛtsetera] *adv* et cetera,
and so on

été [ete] *pp de* **être** ♦ *nm* summer
éteindre [etɛ̃dR(ə)] *vt* (*lampe, lumière,
radio*) to turn *ou* switch off; (*cigarette,
incendie, bougie*) to put out, extinguish;
(*JUR: dette*) to extinguish; **s'~** *vi* to go
out; to go off; (*mourir*) to pass away;
éteint, e *adj* (*fig*) lacklustre, dull; (*volcan*) extinct

étendard [etɑ̃daR] *nm* standard
étendre [etɑ̃dR(ə)] *vt* (*pâte, liquide*) to
spread; (*carte etc*) to spread out; (*linge*)
to hang up; (*bras, jambes, par terre:
blessé*) to stretch out; (*diluer*) to dilute,
thin; (*fig: agrandir*) to extend; **s'~** *vi*
(*augmenter, se propager*) to spread;
(*terrain, forêt etc*) to stretch;
(*s'allonger*) to stretch out; (*se coucher*)
to lie down; (*fig: expliquer*) to elaborate

étendu, e [etɑ̃dy] *adj* extensive; **étendue** *nf* (*d'eau, de sable*) stretch, expanse; (*importance*) extent

éternel, le [etɛRnɛl] *adj* eternal
éterniser [etɛRnize]: **s'~** *vi* to last for
ages; to stay for ages

éternité [etɛRnite] *nf* eternity
éternuer [etɛRnɥe] *vi* to sneeze
êtes *vb voir* **être**
éthique [etik] *adj* ethical
ethnie [ɛtni] *nf* ethnic group
éthylisme [etilism(ə)] *nm* alcoholism
étiez *vb voir* **être**
étinceler [etɛ̃sle] *vi* to sparkle
étincelle [etɛ̃sɛl] *nf* spark
étioler [etjole]: **s'~** *vi* to wilt
étiqueter [etikte] *vt* to label

étiquette [etikɛt] *nf* label; (*protocole*): l'~ etiquette

étirer [etiʀe] *vt* to stretch; **s'~** *vi* (*personne*) to stretch; (*convoi, route*): **s'~ sur** to stretch out over

étoffe [etɔf] *nf* material, fabric

étoffer [etɔfe] *vt* to fill out; **s'etoffer** *vi* to fill out

étoile [etwal] *nf* star; **à la belle ~** in the open; **~ de mer** starfish; **~ filante** shooting star; **étoilé, e** *adj* starry

étole [etɔl] *nf* stole

étonnant, e [etɔnɑ̃, -ɑ̃t] *adj* amazing

étonner [etɔne] *vt* to surprise, amaze; **s'~ que/de** to be amazed that/at; **cela m'~ait (que)** (*j'en doute*) I'd be very surprised (if)

étouffée [etufe]: **à l'~** *adv* (*CULIN*) steamed; braised

étouffer [etufe] *vt* to suffocate; (*bruit*) to muffle; (*scandale*) to hush up ♦ *vi* to suffocate; **s'~** *vi* (*en mangeant etc*) to choke

étourderie [etuʀdəʀi] *nf* heedlessness *no pl*; thoughtless blunder

étourdi, e [etuʀdi] *adj* (*distrait*) scatter-brained, heedless

étourdir [etuʀdiʀ] *vt* (*assommer*) to stun, daze; (*griser*) to make dizzy *ou* giddy; **étourdissement** *nm* dizzy spell

étourneau, x [etuʀno] *nm* starling

étrange [etʀɑ̃ʒ] *adj* strange

étranger, ère [etʀɑ̃ʒe, -ɛʀ] *adj* foreign; (*pas de la famille, non familier*) strange ♦ *nm/f* foreigner; stranger ♦ *nm*: **à l'~** abroad; **de l'~** from abroad; **~ à** (*fig*) unfamiliar to; irrelevant to

étranglement [etʀɑ̃gləmɑ̃] *nm* (*d'une vallée etc*) constriction

étrangler [etʀɑ̃gle] *vt* to strangle; **s'~** *vi* (*en mangeant etc*) to choke

étrave [etʀav] *nf* stem

MOT-CLÉ

être [ɛtʀ(ə)] *nm* being; **~ humain** human being

♦ *vb +attrib* **1** (*état, description*) to be; **il est instituteur** he is *ou* he's a teacher; **vous êtes grand/intelligent/**fatigué you are *ou* you're tall/clever/tired

2 (*+à: appartenir*) to be; **le livre est à Paul** the book is Paul's *ou* belongs to Paul; **c'est à moi/eux** it is *ou* it's mine/theirs

3 (*+de: provenance*): **il est de Paris** he is from Paris; (*: appartenance*): **il est des nôtres** he is one of us

4 (*date*): **nous sommes le 10 janvier** it's the 10th of January (today)

♦ *vi* to be; **je ne serai pas ici demain** I won't be here tomorrow

♦ *vb aux* **1** to have; to be; **~ arrivé/allé** to have arrived/gone; **il est parti** he has left, he has gone

2 (*forme passive*) to be; **~ fait par** to be made by; **il a été promu** he has been promoted

3 (*+à: obligation*): **c'est à réparer** it needs repairing; **c'est à essayer** it should be tried

♦ *vb impers* **1**: **il est** *+adjectif* it is *+adjective*; **il est impossible de le faire** it's impossible to do it

2 (*heure, date*): **il est 10 heures, c'est 10 heures** it is *ou* it's 10 o'clock

3 (*emphatique*): **c'est moi** it's me; **c'est à lui de le faire** it's up to him to do it

étreindre [etʀɛ̃dʀ(ə)] *vt* to clutch, grip; (*amoureusement, amicalement*) to embrace; **s'~** *vi* to embrace

étrenner [etʀene] *vt* to use (*ou* wear) for the first time

étrennes [etʀɛn] *nfpl* Christmas box *sg*

étrier [etʀije] *nm* stirrup

étriller [etʀije] *vt* (*cheval*) to curry; (*fam: battre*) to slaughter (*fig*)

étriqué, e [etʀike] *adj* skimpy

étroit, e [etʀwa, -wat] *adj* narrow; (*vêtement*) tight; (*fig: serré*) close, tight; **à l'~** cramped; **~ d'esprit** narrow-minded

étude [etyd] *nf* studying; (*ouvrage, rapport*) study; (*de notaire: bureau*) office; (*: charge*) practice; (*SCOL: salle de travail*) study room; **~s** *nfpl* (*SCOL*) studies; **être à l'~** (*projet etc*) to be under consideration; **faire des ~s (de droit/ médecine)** to study (law/medicine)

étudiant, e [etydjɑ̃, -ɑ̃t] *nm/f* student

étudié, e [etydje] *adj* (*démarche*) studied; (*système*) carefully designed; (*prix*) keen

étudier [etydje] *vt, vi* to study

étui [etɥi] *nm* case

étuve [etyv] *nf* steamroom

étuvée [etyve]: **à l'~** *adv* braised

eu, eue [y] *pp de* avoir

euh [ø] *excl* er

eurodollar [ørɔdɔlar] *nm* Eurodollar

Europe [ørɔp] *nf*: **l'~** Europe; **européen, ne** *adj, nm/f* European

eurosceptique [ørɔsɛptik] *nm/f* Eurosceptic

eus *etc vb voir* avoir

eux [ø] *pron* (*sujet*) they; (*objet*) them

évacuer [evakɥe] *vt* to evacuate

évader [evade]: **s'~** *vi* to escape

évangile [evɑ̃ʒil] *nm* gospel

évanouir [evanwir]: **s'~** *vi* to faint; (*disparaître*) to vanish, disappear

évanouissement [evanwismɑ̃] *nm* (*syncope*) fainting fit; (*dans un accident*) loss of consciousness

évaporer [evapɔre]: **s'~** *vi* to evaporate

évaser [evaze] *vt* (*tuyau*) to widen, open out; (*jupe, pantalon*) to flare

évasif, ive [evazif, -iv] *adj* evasive

évasion [evazjɔ̃] *nf* escape

évêché [eveʃe] *nm* bishopric; bishop's palace

éveil [evɛj] *nm* awakening; **être en ~** to be alert

éveillé, e [eveje] *adj* awake; (*vif*) alert, sharp

éveiller [eveje] *vt* to (a)waken; **s'~** *vi* to (a)waken; (*fig*) to be aroused

événement [evɛnmɑ̃] *nm* event

éventail [evɑ̃taj] *nm* fan; (*choix*) range

éventaire [evɑ̃tɛr] *nm* stall, stand

éventer [evɑ̃te] *vt* (*secret*) to uncover; **s'~** *vi* (*parfum*) to go stale

éventrer [evɑ̃tre] *vt* to disembowel; (*fig*) to tear *ou* rip open

éventualité [evɑ̃tɥalite] *nf* eventuality; possibility; **dans l'~ de** in the event of

éventuel, le [evɑ̃tɥɛl] *adj* possible; **éventuellement** *adv* possibly

évêque [evɛk] *nm* bishop

évertuer [evertɥe]: **s'~** *vi*: **s'~ à faire** to try very hard to do

éviction [eviksjɔ̃] *nf* ousting; (*de locataire*) eviction

évidemment [evidamɑ̃] *adv* obviously

évidence [evidɑ̃s] *nf* obviousness; obvious fact; **de toute ~** quite obviously *ou* evidently; **en ~** conspicuous; **mettre en ~** to highlight; to bring to the fore; **évident, e** [evidɑ̃, -ɑ̃t] *adj* obvious, evident

évider [evide] *vt* to scoop out

évier [evje] *nm* (kitchen) sink

évincer [evɛ̃se] *vt* to oust

éviter [evite] *vt* to avoid; **~ de faire/que qch ne se passe** to avoid doing/sth happening; **~ qch à qn** to spare sb sth

évolué, e [evɔlɥe] *adj* advanced

évoluer [evɔlɥe] *vi* (*enfant, maladie*) to develop; (*situation, moralement*) to evolve, develop; (*aller et venir: danseur etc*) to move about, circle; **évolution** *nf* development; evolution

évoquer [evɔke] *vt* to call to mind, evoke; (*mentionner*) to mention

ex... [ɛks] *préfixe* ex-

exact, e [ɛgzakt] *adj* (*précis*) exact, accurate, precise; (*correct*) correct; (*ponctuel*) punctual; **l'heure ~e** the right *ou* exact time; **exactement** *adv* exactly, accurately, precisely; correctly; (*c'est cela même*) exactly

ex aequo [ɛgzeko] *adj* equally placed

exagéré, e [ɛgzaʒere] *adj* (*prix etc*) excessive

exagérer [ɛgzaʒere] *vt* to exaggerate ♦ *vi* (*abuser*) to go too far; to overstep the mark; (*déformer les faits*) to exaggerate

exalter [ɛgzalte] *vt* (*enthousiasmer*) to excite, elate; (*glorifier*) to exalt

examen [ɛgzamɛ̃] *nm* examination; (*SCOL*) exam, examination; **à l'~** under consideration; (*COMM*) on approval

examiner [ɛgzamine] *vt* to examine

exaspérant, e [ɛgzasperɑ̃, -ɑ̃t] *adj* exasperating

exaspérer [ɛgzaspeʀe] *vt* to exasperate; to exacerbate

exaucer [ɛgzose] *vt* (*vœu*) to grant

excédent [ɛksedɑ̃] *nm* surplus; **en ~** surplus; **~ de bagages** excess luggage

excéder [ɛksede] *vt* (*dépasser*) to exceed; (*agacer*) to exasperate

excellence [ɛksɛlɑ̃s] *nf* (*titre*) Excellency

excellent, e [ɛksɛlɑ̃, -ɑ̃t] *adj* excellent

excentrique [ɛksɑ̃tʀik] *adj* eccentric; (*quartier*) outlying

excepté, e [ɛksɛpte] *adj, prép*: **les élèves ~s, ~ les élèves** except for the pupils; **~ si** except if

exception [ɛksɛpsjɔ̃] *nf* exception; **à l'~ de** except for, with the exception of; **d'~** (*mesure, loi*) special, exceptional; **exceptionnel, le** *adj* exceptional

excès [ɛksɛ] *nm* surplus ♦ *nmpl* excesses; **à l'~** to excess; **~ de vitesse** speeding *no pl*; **excessif, ive** *adj* excessive

excitant, e [ɛksitɑ̃, -ɑ̃t] *adj* exciting ♦ *nm* stimulant; **excitation** [ɛksitasjɔ̃] *nf* (*état*) excitement

exciter [ɛksite] *vt* to excite; (*suj: café etc*) to stimulate; **s'~** *vi* to get excited

exclamation [ɛksklamasjɔ̃] *nf* exclamation

exclamer [ɛksklame]: **s'~** *vi* to exclaim

exclure [ɛksklyʀ] *vt* (*faire sortir*) to expel; (*ne pas compter*) to exclude, leave out; (*rendre impossible*) to exclude, rule out; **il est exclu que** it's out of the question that ...; **il n'est pas exclu que ...**, it's not impossible that ...; **exclusif, ive** *adj* exclusive; **exclusion** *nf* expulsion; **à l'exclusion de** with the exclusion *ou* exception of; **exclusivité** *nf* (*COMM*) exclusive rights *pl*; **film passant en exclusivité à** film showing only at

excursion [ɛkskyʀsjɔ̃] *nf* (*en autocar*) excursion, trip; (*à pied*) walk, hike

excuse [ɛkskyz] *nf* excuse; **~s** *nfpl* (*regret*) apology *sg*, apologies

excuser [ɛkskyze] *vt* to excuse; **s'~ (de)** to apologize (for); **"excusez-moi"** "I'm sorry"; (*pour attirer l'attention*) "excuse me"

exécrable [ɛgzekʀabl(ə)] *adj* atrocious

exécrer [ɛgzekʀe] *vt* to loathe, abhor

exécuter [ɛgzekyte] *vt* (*prisonnier*) to execute; (*tâche etc*) to execute, carry out; (*MUS: jouer*) to perform, execute; (*INFORM*) to run; **s'~** *vi* to comply; **exécutif, ive** *adj, nm* (*POL*) executive; **exécution** *nf* execution; carrying out; **mettre à exécution** to carry out

exemplaire [ɛgzɑ̃plɛʀ] *nm* copy

exemple [ɛgzɑ̃pl(ə)] *nm* example; **par ~** for instance, for example; **donner l'~** to set an example; **prendre ~ sur** to take as a model; **à l'~ de** just like

exempt, e [ɛgzɑ̃, ɑ̃t] *adj*: **~ de** (*dispensé de*) exempt from; (*sans*) free from

exercer [ɛgzɛʀse] *vt* (*pratiquer*) to exercise, practise; (*prérogative*) to exercise; (*influence, contrôle*) to exert; (*former*) to exercise, train; **s'~** *vi* (*sportif, musicien*) to practise; (*se faire sentir: pression etc*) to be exerted

exercice [ɛgzɛʀsis] *nm* (*tâche, travail*) exercise; **l'~** exercise; (*MIL*) drill; **en ~** (*juge*) in office; (*médecin*) practising

exhaustif, ive [ɛgzostif, -iv] *adj* exhaustive

exhiber [ɛgzibe] *vt* (*montrer: papiers, certificat*) to present, produce; (*péj*) to display, flaunt; **s'~** *vi* to parade; (*suj: exhibitionniste*) to expose o.s.

exhorter [ɛgzɔʀte] *vt* to urge

exigeant, e [ɛgziʒɑ̃, -ɑ̃t] *adj* demanding; (*péj*) hard to please

exigence [ɛgziʒɑ̃s] *nf* demand, requirement

exiger [ɛgziʒe] *vt* to demand, require

exigu, ë [ɛgzigy] *adj* (*lieu*) cramped, tiny

exil [ɛgzil] *nm* exile; **exiler** *vt* to exile; **s'exiler** *vi* to go into exile

existence [ɛgzistɑ̃s] *nf* existence

exister [ɛgziste] *vi* to exist; **il existe un/des** there is a/are (some)

exonérer [ɛgzɔneʀe] *vt*: **~ de** to exempt from

exorbitant, e [ɛgzɔʀbitɑ̃, -ɑ̃t] *adj* (*somme, nombre*) exorbitant

exorbité, e [ɛgzɔʀbite] *adj*: **yeux ~**

bulging eyes

exotique [εgzɔtik] *adj* exotic

expatrier [εkspatrije] *vt*: **s'~** to leave one's country

expectative [εkspεktativ] *nf*: **être dans l'~** to be still waiting

expédient [εkspedjã] (*péj*) *nm* expedient; **vivre d'~s** to live by one's wits

expédier [εkspedje] *vt* (*lettre, paquet*) to send; (*troupes*) to dispatch; (*péj: travail etc*) to dispose of, dispatch; **expéditeur, trice** *nm/f* sender

expédition [εkspedisjɔ̃] *nf* sending; (*scientifique, sportive, MIL*) expedition

expérience [εkspeʀjãs] *nf* (*de la vie*) experience; (*scientifique*) experiment

expérimenté, e [εkspeʀimãte] *adj* experienced

expérimenter [εkspeʀimãte] *vt* to test out, experiment with

expert, e [εkspεʀ, -εʀt(ə)] *adj, nm* expert; **~ en assurances** insurance valuer; **expert-comptable** *nm* ≈ chartered accountant (*BRIT*), ≈ certified public accountant (*US*)

expertise [εkspεʀtiz] *nf* valuation; assessment; valuer's (*ou* assessor's) report; (*JUR*) (forensic) examination

expertiser [εkspεʀtize] *vt* (*objet de valeur*) to value; (*voiture accidentée etc*) to assess damage to

expier [εkspje] *vt* to expiate, atone for

expirer [εkspiʀe] *vi* (*prendre fin, mourir*) to expire; (*respirer*) to breathe out

explicatif, ive [εksplikatif, -iv] *adj* explanatory

explication [εksplikasjɔ̃] *nf* explanation; (*discussion*) discussion; argument; **~ de texte** (*SCOL*) critical analysis

explicite [εksplisit] *adj* explicit

expliquer [εksplike] *vt* to explain; **s'~** to explain (o.s.); (*discuter*) to discuss things; to have it out; **son erreur s'explique** one can understand his mistake

exploit [εksplwa] *nm* exploit, feat

exploitation [εksplwatɑsjɔ̃] *nf* exploitation; running; **~ agricole** farming concern; **exploiter** [εksplwate] *vt* (*mine*) to exploit, work; (*entreprise, ferme*) to run,

operate; (*clients, ouvriers, erreur, don*) to exploit

explorer [εksplɔʀe] *vt* to explore

exploser [εksploze] *vi* to explode, blow up; (*engin explosif*) to go off; (*fig: joie, colère*) to burst out, explode; **explosif, ive** *adj, nm* explosive; **explosion** *nf* explosion

exportateur, trice [εkspɔʀtatœʀ, -tʀis] *adj* export *cpd*, exporting ♦ *nm* exporter

exportation [εkspɔʀtɑsjɔ̃] *nf* exportation; export

exporter [εkspɔʀte] *vt* to export

exposant [εkspozã] *nm* exhibitor

exposé, e [εkspoze] *nm* talk ♦ *adj*: **~ au sud** facing south; **bien ~** well situated

exposer [εkspoze] *vt* (*marchandise*) to display; (*peinture*) to exhibit, show; (*parler de*) to explain, set out; (*mettre en danger, orienter, PHOTO*) to expose; **exposition** *nf* (*manifestation*) exhibition; (*PHOTO*) exposure

exprès¹ [εkspʀε] *adv* (*délibérément*) on purpose; (*spécialement*) specially

exprès², esse [εkspʀεs] *adj* (*ordre, défense*) express, formal ♦ *adj inv* (*PTT*) express ♦ *adv* express

express [εkspʀεs] *adj, nm*: **(café) ~** espresso (coffee); **(train) ~** fast train

expressément [εkspʀesemã] *adv* expressly; specifically

expression [εkspʀesjɔ̃] *nf* expression

exprimer [εkspʀime] *vt* (*sentiment, idée*) to express; (*jus, liquide*) to press out; **s'~** *vi* (*personne*) to express o.s.

exproprier [εkspʀɔpʀije] *vt* to buy up by compulsory purchase, expropriate

expulser [εkspylse] *vt* to expel; (*locataire*) to evict; (*SPORT*) to send off

exquis, e [εkski, -iz] *adj* exquisite; delightful

exsangue [εksãg] *adj* bloodless, drained of blood

extase [εkstaz] *nf* ecstasy; **extasier**: **s'extasier** *vi* to go into raptures over

extension [εkstãsjɔ̃] *nf* (*d'un muscle, ressort*) stretching; (*fig*) extension; expansion

exténuer [ɛkstenɥe] *vt* to exhaust

extérieur, e [ɛksterjœr] *adj* (*porte, mur etc*) outer, outside; (*au dehors: escalier, w.-c*) outside; (*commerce*) foreign; (*influences*) external; (*apparent: calme, gaieté etc*) surface *cpd* ♦ *nm* (*d'une maison, d'un récipient etc*) outside, exterior; (*apparence*) exterior; (*d'un groupe social*): **l'~** the outside world; **à l'~** outside; (*à l'étranger*) abroad; **extérieurement** *adv* on the outside; (*en apparence*) on the surface

exterminer [ɛkstɛrmine] *vt* to exterminate, wipe out

externat [ɛkstɛrna] *nm* day school

externe [ɛkstɛrn(ə)] *adj* external, outer ♦ *nm/f* (*MÉD*) non-resident medical student (*BRIT*), extern (*US*); (*SCOL*) day pupil

extincteur [ɛkstɛ̃ktœr] *nm* (fire) extinguisher

extinction [ɛkstɛ̃ksjɔ̃] *nf*: ~ **de voix** loss of voice

extorquer [ɛkstɔrke] *vt* to extort

extra [ɛkstra] *adj inv* first-rate; top-quality ♦ *nm inv* extra help

extrader [ɛkstrade] *vt* to extradite

extraire [ɛkstrɛr] *vt* to extract; **extrait** *nm* extract

extraordinaire [ɛkstraɔrdinɛr] *adj* extraordinary; (*POL: mesures etc*) special

extravagant, e [ɛkstravagɑ̃, -ɑ̃t] *adj* extravagant; wild

extraverti, e [ɛkstravɛrti] *adj* extrovert

extrême [ɛkstrɛm] *adj, nm* extreme; **extrêmement** *adv* extremely; **extrême-onction** *nf* last rites *pl*; **Extrême-Orient** *nm* Far East

extrémité [ɛkstremite] *nf* end; (*situation*) straits *pl*, plight; (*geste désespéré*) extreme action; **~s** *nfpl* (*pieds et mains*) extremities; **à la dernière ~** on the point of death

exutoire [ɛgzytwar] *nm* outlet, release

F f

F *abr* = **franc**

fa [fa] *nm inv* (*MUS*) F; (*en chantant la gamme*) fa

fable [fabl(ə)] *nf* fable

fabricant [fabrikɑ̃] *nm* manufacturer

fabrication [fabrikasjɔ̃] *nf* manufacture

fabrique [fabrik] *nf* factory

fabriquer [fabrike] *vt* to make; (*industriellement*) to manufacture; (*fig*): **qu'est-ce qu'il fabrique?** what is he doing?

fabulation [fabylasjɔ̃] *nf* fantasizing

fac [fak] (*fam*) *abr f* (*SCOL*) = **faculté**

façade [fasad] *nf* front, façade

face [fas] *nf* face; (*fig: aspect*) side ♦ *adj*: **le côté ~** heads; **perdre la ~** to lose face; **en ~ de** opposite; (*fig*) in front of; **de ~** from the front; **face on**; **~ à** facing; (*fig*) faced with, in the face of; **faire ~ à** to face; **~ à ~** *adv* facing each other ♦ *nm inv* encounter

facétieux, euse [fasesjø, -øz] *adj* mischievous

fâché, e [fɑʃe] *adj* angry; (*désolé*) sorry

fâcher [fɑʃe] *vt* to anger; **se ~** *vi* to get angry; **se ~ avec** (*se brouiller*) to fall out with

fâcheux, euse [fɑʃø, -øz] *adj* unfortunate, regrettable

facile [fasil] *adj* easy; (*accommodant*) easy-going; **facilement** *adv* easily; **facilité** *nf* easiness; (*disposition, don*) aptitude; **facilités** *nfpl* (*possibilités*) facilities; **facilités de paiement** easy terms; **faciliter** *vt* to make easier

façon [fasɔ̃] *nf* (*manière*) way; (*d'une robe etc*) making-up; cut; **~s** *nfpl* (*péj*) fuss *sg*; **de quelle ~?** (in) what way?; **de ~ à/à ce que** so as to/that; **de toute ~** anyway, in any case; **façonner** [fasɔne] *vt* (*fabriquer*) to manufacture; (*travailler: matière*) to shape, fashion; (*fig*) to mould, shape

facteur, trice [faktœr, -tris] *nm/f* postman(woman) (*BRIT*), mailman(woman) (*US*) ♦ *nm* (*MATH, fig: élément*) factor; **~ de pianos** piano maker

factice [faktis] *adj* artificial

faction [faksjɔ̃] *nf* faction; (*MIL*) guard *ou* sentry (duty); watch

facture [faktyr] *nf* (*à payer: gén*) bill;

(: *COMM*) invoice; (*d'un artisan, artiste*) technique, workmanship; **facturer** *vt* to invoice

facultatif, ive [fakyltatif, -iv] *adj* optional; (*arrêt de bus*) request *cpd*

faculté [fakylte] *nf* (*intellectuelle, d'université*) faculty; (*pouvoir, possibilité*) power

fade [fad] *adj* insipid

fagot [faɡo] *nm* bundle of sticks

faible [fɛbl(ə)] *adj* weak; (*voix, lumière, vent*) faint; (*rendement, intensité, revenu etc*) low ♦ *nm* weak point; (*pour quelqu'un*) weakness, soft spot; ~ **d'esprit** feeble-minded; **faiblesse** *nf* weakness; **faiblir** *vi* to weaken; (*lumière*) to dim; (*vent*) to drop

faïence [fajɑ̃s] *nf* earthenware *no pl*; piece of earthenware

faignant, e [fɛɲɑ̃, -ɑ̃t] *nm/f* = **fainéant, e**

faille [faj] *vb voir* **falloir** ♦ *nf* (*GÉO*) fault; (*fig*) flaw, weakness

faillir [fajiʀ] *vi*: **j'ai failli tomber** I almost *ou* very nearly fell

faillite [fajit] *nf* bankruptcy

faim [fɛ̃] *nf* hunger; **avoir ~** to be hungry; **rester sur sa ~** (*aussi fig*) to be left wanting more

fainéant, e [fɛneɑ̃, -ɑ̃t] *nm/f* idler, loafer

MOT-CLÉ

faire [fɛʀ] *vt* **1** (*fabriquer, être l'auteur de*) to make; ~ **du vin/une offre/un film** to make wine/an offer/a film; ~ **du bruit** to make a noise

2 (*effectuer: travail, opération*) to do; **que faites-vous?** (*quel métier etc*) what do you do?; (*quelle activité: au moment de la question*) what are you doing?; ~ **la lessive** to do the washing

3 (*études*) to do; (*sport, musique*) to play; ~ **du droit/du français** to do law/French; ~ **du rugby/piano** to play rugby/the piano

4 (*simuler*): ~ **le malade/l'ignorant** to act the invalid/the fool

5 (*transformer, avoir un effet sur*): ~ **de qn un frustré/avocat** to make sb frustrated/a lawyer; **ça ne me fait rien** (*m'est égal*) I don't care *ou* mind; (*me laisse froid*) it has no effect on me; **ça ne fait rien** it doesn't matter; ~ **que** (*impliquer*) to mean that

6 (*calculs, prix, mesures*): **2 et 2 font 4** 2 and 2 are *ou* make 4; **ça fait 10 m/15 F** it's 10 m/15F; **je vous le fais 10 F** I'll let you have it for 10F

7: **qu'a-t-il fait de sa valise?** what has he done with his case?

8: **ne ~ que: il ne fait que critiquer** (*sans cesse*) all he (ever) does is criticize; (*seulement*) he's only criticizing

9 (*dire*) to say; **vraiment? fit-il** really? he said

10 (*maladie*) to have; ~ **du diabète** to have diabetes *sg*

♦ *vi* **1** (*agir, s'y prendre*) to act, do; **il faut ~ vite** we (*ou* you *etc*) must act quickly; **comment a-t-il fait pour?** how did he manage to?; **faites comme chez vous** make yourself at home

2 (*paraître*) to look; ~ **vieux/démodé** to look old/old-fashioned; **ça fait bien** it looks good

♦ *vb substitut* to do; **ne le casse pas comme je l'ai fait** don't break it as I did; **je peux le voir? - faites!** can I see it? - please do!

♦ *vb impers* **1**: **il fait beau** *etc* the weather is fine *etc*; *voir aussi* **jour; froid** *etc*

2 (*temps écoulé, durée*): **ça fait 2 ans qu'il est parti** it's 2 years since he left; **ça fait 2 ans qu'il y est** he's been there for 2 years

♦ *vb semi-aux* **1**: ~ **+infinitif** (*action directe*) to make; ~ **tomber/bouger qch** to make sth fall/move; ~ **démarrer un moteur/chauffer de l'eau** to start up an engine/heat some water; **cela fait dormir** it makes you sleep; ~ **travailler les enfants** to make the children work *ou* get the children to work

2 (*indirectement, par un intermédiaire*): ~ **réparer qch** to get *ou* have sth repaired; ~ **punir les enfants** to

have the children punished
se faire *vi* **1** (*vin, fromage*) to mature
2: **cela se fait beaucoup/ne se fait pas**
it's done a lot/not done
3: **se ~ +*nom ou pron***: **se ~ une jupe**
to make o.s. a skirt; **se ~ des amis** to
make friends; **se ~ du souci** to worry; **il
ne s'en fait pas** he doesn't worry
4: **se ~ +*adj*** (*devenir*) to be getting old;
(*délibérément*): **se ~ beau** to do o.s. up
5: **se ~ à** (*s'habituer*) to get used to; **je
n'arrive pas à me ~ à la nourriture/
au climat** I can't get used to the food/
climate
6: **se ~ +*infinitif***: **se ~ examiner la
vue/opérer** to have one's eyes tested/
have an operation; **se ~ couper les cheveux** to get one's hair cut; **il va se ~
tuer/punir** he's going to get himself
killed/get (himself) punished; **il s'est
fait aider** he got somebody to help him;
il s'est fait aider par Simon he got
Simon to help him; **se ~ faire un
vêtement** to get a garment made for o.s.
7 (*impersonnel*): **comment se fait-il/
faisait-il que?** how is it/was it that?

faire-part [fɛʀpaʀ] *nm inv* announcement (*of birth, marriage etc*)
faisable [fəzabl(ə)] *adj* feasible
faisan, e [fəzɑ̃, -an] *nm/f* pheasant
faisandé, e [fəzɑ̃de] *adj* high (*bad*)
faisceau, x [fɛso] *nm* (*de lumière etc*)
beam; (*de branches etc*) bundle
faisons [fəzɔ̃] *vb voir* **faire**
fait, e [fɛ, fɛt] *adj* (*mûr: fromage, melon*) ripe ♦ *nm* (*événement*) event, occurrence; (*réalité, donnée*) fact; **c'en est
~ de** that's the end of; **être le ~ de**
(*causé par*) to be the work of; **être au ~
(de)** to be informed (of); **au ~** (*à propos*)
by the way; **en venir au ~** to get to the
point; **de ~** *adj* (*opposé à: de droit*) de
facto ♦ *adv* in fact; **du ~ de ceci/qu'il a
menti** because of/on account of this/
his having lied; **de ce ~** for this reason;
en ~ in fact; **en ~ de repas** by way of a
meal; **prendre ~ et cause pour qn** to
support sb, side with sb; **prendre qn**

sur le ~ to catch sb in the act; **~ divers**
news item; **~s et gestes: les ~s et gestes
de qn** sb's actions *ou* doings
faîte [fɛt] *nm* top; (*fig*) pinnacle, height
faites *vb voir* **faire**
faitout [fɛtu] *nm* = **fait-tout**
fait-tout [fɛtu] *nm inv* stewpot
falaise [falɛz] *nf* cliff
fallacieux, euse [falasjø, -øz] *adj* falla-
cious; deceptive; illusory
falloir [falwaʀ] *vb impers*: **il va ~ 100 F**
we'll (*ou* I'll) need 100 F; **s'en ~**: **il s'en
est fallu de 100 F/5 minutes** we (*ou*
they) were 100 F short/5 minutes late
(*ou* early); **il s'en faut de beaucoup
qu'il soit** he is far from being; **il s'en
est fallu de peu que cela n'arrive** it
very nearly happened; **ou peu s'en faut**
or as good as; **il doit ~ du temps** that
must take time; **il me faudrait 100 F** I
would need 100 F; **il vous faut tourner
à gauche après l'église** you have to
turn left past the church; **nous avons ce
qu'il (nous) faut** we have what we
need; **il faut qu'il parte/a fallu qu'il
parte** (*obligation*) he has to *ou* must
leave/had to leave; **il a fallu le faire** it
had to be done
falsifier [falsifje] *vt* to falsify; to doctor
famé, e [fame] *adj*: **mal ~** disreputable,
of ill repute
famélique [famelik] *adj* half-starved
fameux, euse [famø, -øz] *adj* (*illustre*)
famous; (*bon: repas, plat etc*) first-rate,
first-class; (*valeur intensive*) real, downright
familial, e, aux [familjal, -o] *adj* family
cpd; **familiale** *nf* (*AUTO*) estate car (*BRIT*),
station wagon (*US*)
familiarité [familjaʀite] *nf* informality;
familiarity; **~s** *nfpl* (*privautés*) familiar-
ities
familier, ère [familje, -ɛʀ] *adj* (*connu,
impertinent*) familiar; (*dénotant une
certaine intimité*) informal, friendly;
(*LING*) informal, colloquial ♦ *nm* regular
(visitor)
famille [famij] *nf* family; **il a de la ~ à
Paris** he has relatives in Paris

famine [famin] *nf* famine

fanatique [fanatik] *adj* fanatical ♦ *nm/f* fanatic; **fanatisme** *nm* fanaticism

faner [fane]: **se ~** *vi* to fade

fanfare [fɑ̃far] *nf* (*orchestre*) brass band; (*musique*) fanfare

fanfaron, ne [fɑ̃farɔ̃, -ɔn] *nm/f* braggart

fange [fɑ̃ʒ] *nf* mire

fanion [fanjɔ̃] *nm* pennant

fantaisie [fɑ̃tezi] *nf* (*spontanéité*) fancy, imagination; (*caprice*) whim; extravagance ♦ *adj*: **bijou/pain (de) ~** costume jewellery/fancy bread; **fantaisiste** *adj* (*péj*) unorthodox, eccentric ♦ *nm/f* (*de music-hall*) variety artist *ou* entertainer

fantasme [fɑ̃tasm(ə)] *nm* fantasy

fantasque [fɑ̃task(ə)] *adj* whimsical, capricious; fantastic

fantastique [fɑ̃tastik] *adj* fantastic

fantôme [fɑ̃tom] *nm* ghost, phantom

faon [fɑ̃] *nm* fawn

farce [fars(ə)] *nf* (*viande*) stuffing; (*blague*) (practical) joke; (*THÉÂTRE*) farce; **farcir** *vt* (*viande*) to stuff

fard [far] *nm* make-up

fardeau, x [fardo] *nm* burden

farder [farde] *vt* to make up

farfelu, e [farfəly] *adj* hare-brained

farine [farin] *nf* flour; **farineux, euse** *adj* (*sauce, pomme*) floury ♦ *nmpl* (*aliments*) starchy foods

farouche [faruʃ] *adj* shy, timid; savage, wild; fierce

fart [far(t)] *nm* (ski) wax

fascicule [fasikyl] *nm* volume

fasciner [fasine] *vt* to fascinate

fascisme [faʃism(ə)] *nm* fascism

fasse *etc vb voir* **faire**

faste [fast(ə)] *nm* splendour ♦ *adj*: **c'est un jour ~** it's his (*ou* our *etc*) lucky day

fastidieux, euse [fastidjø, -øz] *adj* tedious, tiresome

fastueux, euse [fastɥø, -øz] *adj* sumptuous, luxurious

fatal, e [fatal] *adj* fatal; (*inévitable*) inevitable; **fatalité** *nf* fate; fateful coincidence; inevitability

fatidique [fatidik] *adj* fateful

fatigant, e [fatigɑ̃, -ɑ̃t] *adj* tiring; (*agaçant*) tiresome

fatigue [fatig] *nf* tiredness, fatigue

fatigué, e [fatige] *adj* tired

fatiguer [fatige] *vt* to tire, make tired; (*TECH*) to put a strain on, strain; (*fig: importuner*) to wear out ♦ *vi* (*moteur*) to labour, strain; **se ~** to get tired; to tire o.s. (out)

fatras [fatra] *nm* jumble, hotchpotch

fatuité [fatɥite] *nf* conceitedness, smugness

faubourg [fobur] *nm* suburb

fauché, e [foʃe] (*fam*) *adj* broke

faucher [foʃe] *vt* (*herbe*) to cut; (*champs, blés*) to reap; (*fig*) to cut down; to mow down

faucille [fosij] *nf* sickle

faucon [fokɔ̃] *nm* falcon, hawk

faudra *vb voir* **falloir**

faufiler [fofile] *vt* to tack, baste; **se ~** *vi*: **se ~ dans** to edge one's way into; **se ~ parmi/entre** to thread one's way among/between

faune [fon] *nf* (*ZOOL*) wildlife, fauna

faussaire [foser] *nm* forger

fausse [fos] *adj voir* **faux**

faussement [fosmɑ̃] *adv* (*accuser*) wrongly, wrongfully; (*croire*) falsely

fausser [fose] *vt* (*objet*) to bend, buckle; (*fig*) to distort

fausseté [foste] *nf* wrongness; falseness

faut *vb voir* **falloir**

faute [fot] *nf* (*erreur*) mistake, error; (*péché, manquement*) misdemeanour; (*FOOTBALL etc*) offence; (*TENNIS*) fault; **c'est de sa/ma ~** it's his/my fault; **être en ~** to be in the wrong; **~ de** (*temps, argent*) for *ou* through lack of; **sans ~** without fail; **~ de frappe** typing error; **~ professionnelle** professional misconduct *no pl*

fauteuil [fotœj] *nm* armchair; **~ d'orchestre** seat in the front stalls; **~ roulant** wheelchair

fauteur [fotœr] *nm*: **~ de troubles** trouble-maker

fautif, ive [fotif, -iv] *adj* (*incorrect*) incorrect, inaccurate; (*responsable*) at fault, in the wrong; guilty

fauve [fov] *nm* wildcat ♦ *adj* (*couleur*) fawn

faux¹ [fo] *nf* scythe

faux², **fausse** [fo, fos] *adj* (*inexact*) wrong; (*piano, voix*) out of tune; (*falsifié*) fake; forged; (*sournois, postiche*) false ♦ *adv* (*MUS*) out of tune ♦ *nm* (*copie*) fake, forgery; (*opposé au vrai*): **le ~** falsehood; **faire ~ bond à qn** to stand sb up; **fausse alerte** false alarm; **fausse couche** miscarriage; **~ frais** *nmpl* extras, incidental expenses; **~ pas** tripping *no pl*; (*fig*) faux pas; **~ témoignage** (*délit*) perjury; **faux-filet** *nm* sirloin; **faux-fuyant** *nm* equivocation; **faux-monnayeur** *nm* counterfeiter, forger

faveur [favœʀ] *nf* favour; **traitement de ~** preferential treatment; **à la ~ de** under cover of; thanks to; **en ~ de** in favour of

favorable [favɔʀabl(ə)] *adj* favourable

favori, **te** [favɔʀi, -it] *adj*, *nm/f* favourite; **~s** *nmpl* (*barbe*) sideboards (*BRIT*), sideburns

favoriser [favɔʀize] *vt* to favour

fax [faks] *nm* fax

fébrile [febʀil] *adj* feverish, febrile

fécond, **e** [fekɔ̃, -ɔ̃d] *adj* fertile; **féconder** *vt* to fertilize; **fécondité** *nf* fertility

fécule [fekyl] *nf* potato flour

féculent [fekylɑ̃] *nm* starchy food

fédéral, **e**, **aux** [federal, -o] *adj* federal

fée [fe] *nf* fairy; **féerie** *nf* enchantment; **féerique** *adj* magical, fairytale *cpd*

feignant, **e** [fɛɲɑ̃, -ɑ̃t] *nm/f* = **fainéant**, **e**

feindre [fɛ̃dʀ(ə)] *vt* to feign ♦ *vi* to dissemble; **~ de faire** to pretend to do

feinte [fɛ̃t] *nf* (*SPORT*) dummy

fêler [fele] *vt* to crack

félicitations [felisitasjɔ̃] *nfpl* congratulations

féliciter [felisite] *vt*: **~ qn (de)** to congratulate sb (on); **se ~ (de)** to congratulate o.s. (on)

félin, **e** [felɛ̃, -in] *adj* feline ♦ *nm* (big) cat

fêlure [felyʀ] *nf* crack

femelle [fəmɛl] *adj*, *nf* female

féminin, **e** [feminɛ̃, -in] *adj* feminine; (*sexe*) female; (*équipe, vêtements etc*) women's ♦ *nm* (*LING*) feminine; **féministe** *adj* feminist

femme [fam] *nf* woman; (*épouse*) wife; **~ au foyer** *nf* housewife; **~ de chambre**, **~ de ménage** cleaning lady

fémur [femyʀ] *nm* femur, thighbone

fendre [fɑ̃dʀ(ə)] *vt* (*couper en deux*) to split; (*fissurer*) to crack; (*fig: traverser*) to cut through; to cleave through; **se ~** *vi* to crack

fenêtre [fənɛtʀ(ə)] *nf* window

fenouil [fənuj] *nm* fennel

fente [fɑ̃t] *nf* (*fissure*) crack; (*de boîte à lettres etc*) slit

féodal, **e**, **aux** [feɔdal, -o] *adj* feudal

fer [fɛʀ] *nm* iron; (*de cheval*) shoe; **~ à cheval** horseshoe; **~ (à repasser)** iron; **~ forgé** wrought iron

ferai *etc vb voir* **faire**

fer-blanc [fɛʀblɑ̃] *nm* tin(plate)

férié, **e** [feʀje] *adj*: **jour ~** public holiday

ferions *etc vb voir* **faire**

ferme [fɛʀm(ə)] *adj* firm ♦ *adv* (*travailler etc*) hard ♦ *nf* (*exploitation*) farm; (*maison*) farmhouse

fermé, **e** [fɛʀme] *adj* closed, shut; (*gaz, eau etc*) off; (*fig: personne*) uncommunicative; (: *milieu*) exclusive

fermenter [fɛʀmɑ̃te] *vi* to ferment

fermer [fɛʀme] *vt* to close, shut; (*cesser l'exploitation de*) to close down, shut down; (*eau, lumière, électricité, robinet*) to put off, turn off; (*aéroport, route*) to close ♦ *vi* to close, shut; to close down, shut down; **se ~** *vi* (*yeux*) to close, shut; (*fleur, blessure*) to close up

fermeté [fɛʀməte] *nf* firmness

fermeture [fɛʀmətyʀ] *nf* closing; shutting; closing *ou* shutting down; putting *ou* turning off; (*dispositif*) catch; fastening, fastener; **~ à glissière** = **fermeture éclair**; **~ éclair** (®) zip (fastener) (*BRIT*), zipper (*US*)

fermier [fɛʀmje] *nm* farmer; **fermière** *nf* woman farmer; farmer's wife

fermoir [fɛʀmwaʀ] *nm* clasp
féroce [feʀɔs] *adj* ferocious, fierce
ferons *vb voir* **faire**
ferraille [feʀɑj] *nf* scrap iron; **mettre à la** ~ to scrap
ferré, e [feʀe] *adj* hobnailed; steel-tipped; (*fam*): ~ **en** well up on, hot at; **ferrer** [feʀe] *vt* (*cheval*) to shoe
ferronnerie [feʀɔnʀi] *nf* ironwork
ferroviaire [feʀɔvjɛʀ] *adj* rail(way) *cpd* (*BRIT*), rail(road) *cpd* (*US*)
ferry(boat) [feʀe(bot)] *nm* ferry
fertile [fɛʀtil] *adj* fertile; ~ **en incidents** eventful, packed with incidents
féru, e [feʀy] *adj*: ~ **de** with a keen interest in
férule [feʀyl] *nf*: **être sous la** ~ **de qn** to be under sb's (iron) rule
fervent, e [fɛʀvɑ̃, -ɑ̃t] *adj* fervent
fesse [fɛs] *nf* buttock; **fessée** *nf* spanking
festin [fɛstɛ̃] *nm* feast
festival [fɛstival] *nm* festival
festoyer [fɛstwaje] *vi* to feast
fêtard [fɛtaʀ] (*péj*) *nm* high liver, merry-maker
fête [fɛt] *nf* (*religieuse*) feast; (*publique*) holiday; (*en famille etc*) celebration; (*kermesse*) fête, fair, festival; (*du nom*) feast day, name day; **faire la** ~ to live it up; **faire** ~ **à qn** to give sb a warm welcome; **les** ~**s (de fin d'année)** the festive season; **la salle/le comité des** ~**s** the village hall/festival committee; ~ **foraine** (fun)fair; **la F**~ **Nationale** the national holiday; **fêter** *vt* to celebrate; (*personne*) to have a celebration for
fétu [fety] *nm*: ~ **de paille** wisp of straw
feu, x [fø] *nm* (*gén*) fire; (*signal lumineux*) light; (*de cuisinière*) ring; (*sensation de brûlure*) burning (sensation) ♦ *adj inv*: **son père** his late father; ~**x** *nmpl* (*éclat, lumière*) fire *sg*; (*AUTO*) (traffic) lights; **au** ~! (*incendie*) fire!; **à** ~ **doux/vif** over a slow/brisk heat; **à petit** ~ (*CULIN*) over a gentle heat; (*fig*) slowly; **faire** ~ to fire; **prendre** ~ to catch fire; **mettre le** ~ **à** to set fire to; **faire du** ~ to make a fire; **avez-vous du** ~? (*pour*

cigarette) have you (got) a light?; ~ **arrière** rear light; ~ **d'artifice** firework; (*spectacle*) fireworks *pl*; ~ **de joie** bonfire; ~ **rouge/vert/orange** red/green/amber (*BRIT*) *ou* yellow (*US*) light; ~**x de brouillard** fog-lamps; ~**x de croisement** dipped (*BRIT*) *ou* dimmed (*US*) headlights; ~**x de position** sidelights; ~**x de route** headlights
feuillage [fœjaʒ] *nm* foliage, leaves *pl*
feuille [fœj] *nf* (*d'arbre*) leaf; (*de papier*) sheet; ~ **d'impôts** tax form; ~ **de maladie** medical expenses claim form; ~ **de paie** pay slip; ~ **de vigne** (*BOT*) vine leaf; (*sur statue*) fig leaf; ~ **volante** loose sheet
feuillet [fœjɛ] *nm* leaf
feuilleté, e [fœjte] *adj* (*CULIN*) flaky; (*verre*) laminated
feuilleter [fœjte] *vt* (*livre*) to leaf through
feuilleton [fœjtɔ̃] *nm* serial
feuillu, e [fœjy] *adj* leafy ♦ *nm* broad-leaved tree
feutre [føtʀ(ə)] *nm* felt; (*chapeau*) felt hat; (*aussi: stylo-*~) felt-tip pen; **feutré, e** *adj* feltlike; (*pas, voix*) muffled
fève [fɛv] *nf* broad bean
février [fevʀije] *nm* February
fi [fi] *excl*: **faire** ~ **de** to snap one's fingers at
fiable [fjabl(ə)] *adj* reliable
fiacre [fjakʀ(ə)] *nm* (hackney) cab *ou* carriage
fiançailles [fjɑ̃saj] *nfpl* engagement *sg*
fiancé, e [fjɑ̃se] *nm/f* fiancé(fiancée) ♦ *adj*: **être** ~ **(à)** to be engaged (to)
fiancer [fjɑ̃se]: **se** ~ *vi* to become engaged
fibre [fibʀ(ə)] *nf* fibre; ~ **de verre** fibreglass, glass fibre
ficeler [fisle] *vt* to tie up
ficelle [fisɛl] *nf* string *no pl*; piece *ou* length of string
fiche [fiʃ] *nf* (*pour fichier*) (index) card; (*formulaire*) form; (*ÉLEC*) plug
ficher [fiʃe] *vt* (*dans un fichier*) to file; (*POLICE*) to put on file; (*planter*) to stick, drive; (*fam*) to do; to give; to stick *ou*

shove; **se ~ de** (*fam*) to make fun of; not to care about; **fiche-(moi) le camp** (*fam*) clear off; **fiche-moi la paix** leave me alone

fichier [fiʃje] *nm* file; card index

fichu, e [fiʃy] *pp de* **ficher** (*fam*) ♦ *adj* (*fam: fini, inutilisable*) bust, done for; (: *intensif*) wretched, darned ♦ *nm* (*foulard*) (head)scarf; **mal ~** (*fam*) feeling lousy; useless

fictif, ive [fiktif, -iv] *adj* fictitious

fiction [fiksjɔ̃] *nf* fiction; (*fait imaginé*) invention

fidèle [fidɛl] *adj* faithful ♦ *nm/f* (*REL*): **les ~s** the faithful *pl*; (*à l'église*) the congregation *sg*

fief [fjɛf] *nm* fief; (*fig*) preserve; stronghold

fier[1] [fje] : **se ~ à** *vt* to trust

fier[2], **fière** [fjɛr] *adj* proud; **fierté** *nf* pride

fièvre [fjɛvʀ(ə)] *nf* fever; **avoir de la ~/ 39 de ~** to have a high temperature/a temperature of 39°C; **fiévreux, euse** *adj* feverish

figer [fiʒe] *vt* to congeal; (*fig: personne*) to freeze, root to the spot; **se ~** *vi* to congeal; to freeze; (*institutions etc*) to become set, stop evolving

figue [fig] *nf* fig; **figuier** *nm* fig tree

figurant, e [figyʀɑ̃, -ɑ̃t] *nm/f* (*THÉÂTRE*) walk-on; (*CINÉMA*) extra

figure [figyʀ] *nf* (*visage*) face; (*image, tracé, forme, personnage*) figure; (*illustration*) picture, diagram; **faire ~ de** to look like

figuré, e [figyʀe] *adj* (*sens*) figurative

figurer [figyʀe] *vi* to appear ♦ *vt* to represent; **se ~ que** to imagine that

fil [fil] *nm* (*brin, fig: d'une histoire*) thread; (*du téléphone*) cable, wire; (*textile de lin*) linen; (*d'un couteau*) edge; **au ~ des années** with the passing of the years; **au ~ de l'eau** with the stream *ou* current; **coup de ~** phone call; **~ à coudre** (sewing) thread; **~ à pêche** fishing line; **~ à plomb** plumbline; **~ de fer** wire; **~ de fer barbelé** barbed wire; **~ électrique** electric wire

filament [filamɑ̃] *nm* (*ÉLEC*) filament; (*de liquide*) trickle, thread

filandreux, euse [filɑ̃dʀø, -øz] *adj* stringy

filasse [filas] *adj inv* white blond

filature [filatyʀ] *nf* (*fabrique*) mill; (*policière*) shadowing *no pl*, tailing *no pl*

file [fil] *nf* line; (*AUTO*) lane; **en ~ indienne** in single file; **à la ~** (*d'affilée*) in succession; **~ (d'attente)** queue (*BRIT*), line (*US*)

filer [file] *vt* (*tissu, toile*) to spin; (*prendre en filature*) to shadow, tail; (*fam: donner*): **~ qch à qn** to slip sb sth ♦ *vi* (*bas, liquide, pâte*) to run; (*aller vite*) to fly past; (*fam: partir*) to make off; **~ doux** to toe the line

filet [filɛ] *nm* net; (*CULIN*) fillet; (*d'eau, de sang*) trickle; **~ (à provisions)** string bag

filiale [filjal] *nf* (*COMM*) subsidiary

filière [filjɛr] *nf*: **passer par la ~** to go through the (administrative) channels; **suivre la ~** (*dans sa carrière*) to work one's way up (through the hierarchy)

filiforme [filifɔʀm(ə)] *adj* spindly; threadlike

filigrane [filigʀan] *nm* (*d'un billet, timbre*) watermark; **en ~** (*fig*) showing just beneath the surface

fille [fij] *nf* girl; (*opposé à fils*) daughter; **vieille ~** old maid; **fillette** *nf* (little) girl

filleul, e [fijœl] *nm/f* godchild, godson/ daughter

film [film] *nm* (*pour photo*) (roll of) film; (*œuvre*) film, picture, movie; (*couche*) film; **~ d'animation** animated film; **~ policier** thriller

filon [filɔ̃] *nm* vein, lode; (*fig*) lucrative line, money spinner

fils [fis] *nm* son; **~ à papa** daddy's boy

filtre [filtʀ(ə)] *nm* filter; **~ à air** (*AUTO*) air filter; **filtrer** *vt* to filter; (*fig: candidats, visiteurs*) to screen ♦ *vi* to filter (through)

fin[1] [fɛ̃] *nf* end; **~s** *nfpl* (*but*) ends; **prendre ~** to come to an end; **mettre ~ à** to put an end to; **à la ~** in the end, eventually; **sans ~** *adj* endless ♦ *adv* endlessly

fin², e [fɛ̃, fin] *adj* (*papier, couche, fil*) thin; (*cheveux, poudre, pointe, visage*) fine; (*taille*) neat, slim; (*esprit, remarque*) subtle; shrewd ♦ *adv* (*moudre, couper*) finely; **un ~ tireur** a crack shot; **avoir la vue/l'ouïe ~e** to have sharp *ou* keen eyes/ears; **vin ~** fine wine; **~ gourmet** gourmet; **~ prêt** quite ready; **~es herbes** mixed herbs

final, e [final] *adj* final ♦ *nm* (*MUS*) finale; **finale** *nf* final; **quarts de finale** quarter finals; **8èmes/16èmes de finale** 2nd/1st round (*in knock-out competition*); **finalement** *adv* finally, in the end; (*après tout*) after all

finance [finɑ̃s] *nf* finance; **~s** *nfpl* (*situation*) finances; (*activités*) finance *sg*; **moyennant ~** for a fee; **financer** *vt* to finance; **financier, ière** *adj* financial

finaud, e [fino, -od] *adj* wily

fine [fin] *nf* (*alcool*) liqueur brandy

finesse [fines] *nf* thinness; fineness; neatness, slimness; subtlety; shrewdness

fini, e [fini] *adj* finished; (*MATH*) finite; (*intensif*) **un menteur ~** a liar through and through ♦ *nm* (*d'un objet manufacturé*) finish

finir [finiʀ] *vt* to finish ♦ *vi* to finish, end; **~ quelque part/par faire** to end up *ou* finish up somewhere/doing; **~ de faire** to finish doing; (*cesser*) to stop doing; **il finit par m'agacer** he's beginning to get on my nerves; **~ en pointe/tragédie** to end in a point/in tragedy; **en ~ avec** to be *ou* have done with; **il va mal ~** he will come to a bad end

finition [finisjɔ̃] *nf* finishing; finish

finlandais, e [fɛ̃lɑ̃dɛ, -ɛz] *adj* Finnish ♦ *nm/f*: **F~, e** Finn

Finlande [fɛ̃lɑ̃d] *nf*: **la ~** Finland

fiole [fjɔl] *nf* phial

fioriture [fjɔʀityʀ] *nf* embellishment, flourish

firme [fiʀm(ə)] *nf* firm

fis *vb voir* **faire**

fisc [fisk] *nm* tax authorities *pl*; **fiscal, e, aux** *adj* tax *cpd*, fiscal; **fiscalité** *nf* tax system; (*charges*) taxation

fissure [fisyʀ] *nf* crack; **fissurer** [fisyʀe] *vt* to crack; **se fissurer** *vi* to crack

fiston [fistɔ̃] (*fam*) *nm* son, lad

fit *vb voir* **faire**

fixation [fiksasjɔ̃] *nf* fixing; fastening; setting; (*de ski*) binding; (*PSYCH*) fixation

fixe [fiks(ə)] *adj* fixed; (*emploi*) steady, regular ♦ *nm* (*salaire*) basic salary; **à heure ~** at a set time; **menu à prix ~** set menu

fixé, e [fikse] *adj*: **être ~ (sur)** (*savoir à quoi s'en tenir*) to have made one's mind (about); to know for certain (about)

fixer [fikse] *vt* (*attacher*): **~ qch (à/sur)** to fix *ou* fasten sth (to/onto); (*déterminer*) to fix, set; (*CHIMIE, PHOTO*) to fix; (*regarder*) to stare at; **se ~** *vi* (*s'établir*) to settle down; **se ~ sur** (*suj: attention*) to focus on

flacon [flakɔ̃] *nm* bottle

flageller [flaʒele] *vt* to flog, scourge

flageoler [flaʒɔle] *vi* (*jambes*) to sag

flageolet [flaʒɔlɛ] *nm* (*MUS*) flageolet; (*CULIN*) dwarf kidney bean

flagrant, e [flagʀɑ̃, -ɑ̃t] *adj* flagrant, blatant; **en ~ délit** in the act

flair [flɛʀ] *nm* sense of smell; (*fig*) intuition; **flairer** *vt* (*humer*) to sniff (at); (*détecter*) to scent

flamand, e [flamɑ̃, -ɑ̃d] *adj* Flemish ♦ *nm* (*LING*) Flemish ♦ *nm/f*: **F~, e** Fleming; **les F~s** the Flemish

flamant [flamɑ̃] *nm* flamingo

flambant [flɑ̃bɑ̃] *adv*: **~ neuf** brand new

flambé, e [flɑ̃be] *adj* (*CULIN*) flambé

flambeau, x [flɑ̃bo] *nm* (flaming) torch

flambée [flɑ̃be] *nf* blaze; (*fig*) flaring-up, explosion

flamber [flɑ̃be] *vi* to blaze (up)

flamboyer [flɑ̃bwaje] *vi* to blaze (up); to flame

flamme [flam] *nf* flame; (*fig*) fire, fervour; **en ~s** on fire, ablaze

flan [flɑ̃] *nm* (*CULIN*) custard tart *ou* pie

flanc [flɑ̃] *nm* side; (*MIL*) flank; **prêter le ~ à** (*fig*) to lay o.s. open to

flancher [flɑ̃ʃe] *vi* to fail, pack up; to quit

flanelle [flanɛl] *nf* flannel

flâner [flɑne] *vi* to stroll; **flânerie** *nf* stroll

flanquer [flɑ̃ke] *vt* to flank; (*fam: mettre*) to chuck, shove; (: *jeter*): ~ **par terre/à la porte** to fling to the ground/ chuck out

flaque [flak] *nf* (*d'eau*) puddle; (*d'huile, de sang etc*) pool

flash [flaʃ] (*pl* **flashes**) *nm* (PHOTO) flash; ~ **(d'information)** newsflash

flasque [flask(ə)] *adj* flabby

flatter [flate] *vt* to flatter; **se ~ de qch** to pride o.s. on sth; **flatterie** *nf* flattery *no pl*; **flatteur, euse** *adj* flattering ♦ *nm/f* flatterer

fléau, x [fleo] *nm* scourge

flèche [flɛʃ] *nf* arrow; (*de clocher*) spire; (*de grue*) jib; **monter en ~** (*fig*) to soar, rocket; **partir en ~** to be off like a shot; **fléchette** *nf* dart; **fléchettes** *nfpl* (*jeu*) darts *sg*

fléchir [fleʃiʀ] *vt* (*corps, genou*) to bend; (*fig*) to sway, weaken ♦ *vi* (*poutre*) to sag, bend; (*fig*) to weaken, flag; to yield

flemmard, e [flemaʀ, -aʀd(ə)] *nm/f* lazybones *sg*, loafer

flétrir [fletʀiʀ] *vt* to wither; **se ~** *vi* to wither

fleur [flœʀ] *nf* flower; (*d'un arbre*) blossom; **en ~** (*arbre*) in blossom; **à ~ de terre** just above the ground

fleurer [flœʀe] *vt*: ~ **la lavande** to have the scent of lavender

fleuri, e [flœʀi] *adj* in flower *ou* bloom; surrounded by flowers; (*fig*) flowery; florid

fleurir [flœʀiʀ] *vi* (*rose*) to flower; (*arbre*) to blossom; (*fig*) to flourish ♦ *vt* (*tombe*) to put flowers on; (*chambre*) to decorate with flowers

fleuriste [flœʀist(ə)] *nm/f* florist

fleuron [flœʀɔ̃] *nm* (*fig*) jewel

fleuve [flœv] *nm* river

flexible [flɛksibl(ə)] *adj* flexible

flexion [flɛksjɔ̃] *nf* flexing, bending

flic [flik] (*fam: péj*) *nm* cop

flipper [flipœʀ] *nm* pinball (machine)

flirter [flœʀte] *vi* to flirt

flocon [flɔkɔ̃] *nm* flake

floraison [flɔʀezɔ̃] *nf* flowering; blossoming; flourishing

flore [flɔʀ] *nf* flora

florissant [flɔʀisɑ̃] *vb voir* **fleurir**

flot [flo] *nm* flood, stream; ~**s** *nmpl* (*de la mer*) waves; **être à ~** (NAVIG) to be afloat; (*fig*) to be on an even keel; **entrer à ~s** to stream *ou* pour in

flotte [flɔt] *nf* (NAVIG) fleet; (*fam*) water; rain

flottement [flɔtmɑ̃] *nm* (*fig*) wavering, hesitation

flotter [flɔte] *vi* to float; (*nuage, odeur*) to drift; (*drapeau*) to fly; (*vêtements*) to hang loose; (*monnaie*) to float ♦ *vt* to float; **faire ~** to float; **flotteur** *nm* float

flou, e [flu] *adj* fuzzy, blurred; (*fig*) woolly, vague

flouer [flue] *vt* to swindle

fluctuation [flyktɥasjɔ̃] *nf* fluctuation

fluet, te [flyɛ, -ɛt] *adj* thin, slight

fluide [flɥid] *adj* fluid; (*circulation etc*) flowing freely ♦ *nm* fluid; (*force*) (mysterious) power

fluor [flyɔʀ] *nm* fluorine

fluorescent, e [flyɔʀesɑ̃, -ɑ̃t] *adj* fluorescent

flûte [flyt] *nf* flute; (*verre*) flute glass; (*pain*) long loaf; ~! drat it!; ~ **à bec** recorder

flux [fly] *nm* incoming tide; (*écoulement*) flow; **le ~ et le reflux** the ebb and flow

FM *sigle f* (= **fréquence modulée**) FM

foc [fɔk] *nm* jib

foi [fwa] *nf* faith; **sous la ~ du serment** under *ou* on oath; **ajouter ~ à** to lend credence to; **digne de ~** reliable; **sur la ~ de** on the word *ou* strength of; **être de bonne/mauvaise ~** to be sincere/ insincere; **ma ~ ...** well ...

foie [fwa] *nm* liver

foin [fwɛ̃] *nm* hay; **faire du ~** (*fig: fam*) to kick up a row

foire [fwaʀ] *nf* fair; (*fête foraine*) (fun) fair; **faire la ~** (*fig: fam*) to whoop it up; ~ **(exposition)** trade fair

fois [fwa] *nf* time; **une/deux ~** once/ twice; **2 ~ 2** 2 times 2; **quatre ~ plus grand (que)** four times as big (as); **une**

~ (*passé*) once; (*futur*) sometime; **une ~ pour toutes** once and for all; **une ~ que** once; **des ~** (*parfois*) sometimes; **à la ~** (*ensemble*) at once

foison [fwazɔ̃] *nf*: **une ~ de** an abundance of; **à ~** in plenty

foisonner [fwazɔne] *vi* to abound

fol [fɔl] *adj voir* **fou**

folâtrer [fɔlɑtʀe] *vi* to frolic (about)

folie [fɔli] *nf* (*d'une décision, d'un acte*) madness, folly; (*état*) madness, insanity; (*acte*) folly; **la ~ des grandeurs** delusions of grandeur; **faire des ~s** (*en dépenses*) to be extravagant

folklorique [fɔlklɔʀik] *adj* folk *cpd*; (*fam*) weird

folle [fɔl] *adj*, *nf voir* **fou**; **follement** *adv* (*très*) madly, wildly

foncé, e [fɔ̃se] *adj* dark

foncer [fɔ̃se] *vi* to go darker; (*fam*: *aller vite*) to tear *ou* belt along; **~ sur** to charge at

foncier, ère [fɔ̃sje, -ɛʀ] *adj* (*honnêteté etc*) basic, fundamental; (*malhonnêteté*) deep-rooted; (*COMM*) real estate *cpd*

fonction [fɔ̃ksjɔ̃] *nf* (*rôle*, MATH, LING) function; (*emploi*, *poste*) post, position; **~s** *nfpl* (*professionnelles*) duties; **entrer en ~** to take up one's post *ou* duties; to take up office; **voiture de ~** company car; **être ~ de** (*dépendre de*) to depend on; **en ~ de** (*par rapport à*) according to; **faire ~ de** to serve as; **la ~ publique** the state *ou* civil (*BRIT*) service; **fonctionnaire** [fɔ̃ksjɔnɛʀ] *nm/f* state employee, local authority employee; (*dans l'administration*) ≈ civil servant; **fonctionner** [fɔ̃ksjɔne] *vi* to work, function; (*entreprise*) to operate, function

fond [fɔ̃] *nm* (*d'un récipient, trou*) bottom; (*d'une salle, scène*) back; (*d'un tableau, décor*) background; (*opposé à la forme*) content; (*SPORT*): **le ~** long distance (running); **sans ~** bottomless; **au ~ de** at the bottom of; at the back of; **à ~** (*connaître, soutenir*) thoroughly; (*appuyer, visser*) right down *ou* home; **à ~** (*de train*) (*fam*) full tilt; **dans le ~, au ~** (*en somme*) basically, really; **de ~ en**

comble from top to bottom; *voir aussi* **fonds**; **~ de teint** (make-up) foundation; **~ sonore** background noise; background music

fondamental, e, aux [fɔ̃damɑ̃tal, -o] *adj* fundamental

fondant, e [fɔ̃dɑ̃, -ɑ̃t] *adj* (*neige*) melting; (*fruit*) that melts in the mouth

fondateur, trice [fɔ̃datœʀ, -tʀis] *nm/f* founder

fondation [fɔ̃dasjɔ̃] *nf* founding; (*établissement*) foundation; **~s** *nfpl* (*d'une maison*) foundations

fondé, e [fɔ̃de] *adj* (*accusation etc*) well-founded ♦ *nm*: **~ de pouvoir** authorized representative; **être ~ à** to have grounds for *ou* good reason to

fondement [fɔ̃dmɑ̃] *nm* (*derrière*) behind; **~s** *nmpl* (*base*) foundations; **sans ~** (*rumeur etc*) groundless, unfounded

fonder [fɔ̃de] *vt* to found; (*fig*) to base; **se ~ sur** (*suj: personne*) to base o.s. on

fonderie [fɔ̃dʀi] *nf* smelting works *sg*

fondre [fɔ̃dʀ(ə)] *vt* (*aussi: faire ~*) to melt; (*dans l'eau*) to dissolve; (*fig*: *mélanger*) to merge, blend ♦ *vi* to melt; to dissolve; (*fig*) to melt away; (*se précipiter*): **~ sur** to swoop down on; **~ en larmes** to burst into tears

fonds [fɔ̃] *nm* (*de bibliothèque*) collection; (*COMM*): **~ (de commerce)** business ♦ *nmpl* (*argent*) funds; **à ~ perdus** with little or no hope of getting the money back

fondu, e [fɔ̃dy] *adj* (*beurre, neige*) melted; (*métal*) molten; **fondue** *nf* (*CULIN*) fondue

font *vb voir* **faire**

fontaine [fɔ̃tɛn] *nf* fountain; (*source*) spring

fonte [fɔ̃t] *nf* melting; (*métal*) cast iron; **la ~ des neiges** (the spring) thaw

foot [fut] (*fam*) *nm* football

football [futbol] *nm* football, soccer; **footballeur** *nm* footballer

footing [futiŋ] *nm* jogging; **faire du ~** to go jogging

for [fɔʀ] *nm*: **dans son ~ intérieur** in one's heart of hearts

forain, e [fɔrɛ̃, -ɛn] *adj* fairground *cpd*
♦ *nm* stallholder; fairground entertainer

forçat [fɔrsa] *nm* convict

force [fɔrs(ə)] *nf* strength; (*puissance:
surnaturelle etc*) power; (*PHYSIQUE,
MÉCANIQUE*) force; **~s** *nfpl* (*physiques*)
strength *sg*; (*MIL*) forces; **à ~ d'insister**
by dint of insisting; as he (*ou* I *etc*) kept
on insisting; **de ~** forcibly, by force; **être
de ~ à faire** to be up to doing; **de première ~** first class; **les ~s de l'ordre** the
police

forcé, e [fɔrse] *adj* forced; unintended;
inevitable

forcément [fɔrsemɑ̃] *adv* necessarily;
inevitably; (*bien sûr*) of course

forcené, e [fɔrsəne] *nm/f* maniac

forcer [fɔrse] *vt* (*porte, serrure, plante*)
to force; (*moteur, voix*) to strain ♦ *vi*
(*SPORT*) to overtax o.s.; **~ la dose** to overdo it; **~ l'allure** to increase the pace; **se
~ (pour faire)** to force o.s. (to do)

forcir [fɔrsir] *vi* (*grossir*) to broaden
out; (*vent*) to freshen

forer [fɔre] *vt* to drill, bore

forestier, ère [fɔrɛstje, -ɛr] *adj* forest
cpd

forêt [fɔrɛ] *nf* forest

forfait [fɔrfɛ] *nm* (*COMM*) fixed *ou* set
price; all-in deal *ou* price; (*crime*) infa-
my; **déclarer ~** to withdraw; **travailler
à ~** to work for a lump sum; **forfaitaire**
adj inclusive; set

forge [fɔrʒ(ə)] *nf* forge, smithy

forger [fɔrʒe] *vt* to forge; (*fig: personnalité*) to form; (: *prétexte*) to contrive,
make up

forgeron [fɔrʒərɔ̃] *nm* (black)smith

formaliser [fɔrmalize]: **se ~** *vi*: **se ~ (de)**
to take offence (at)

formalité [fɔrmalite] *nf* (*ADMIN, JUR*) formality; (*acte sans importance*): **simple
~** mere formality

format [fɔrma] *nm* size

formater [fɔrmate] *vt* (*disque*) to format

formation [fɔrmasjɔ̃] *nf* forming; training; (*MUS*) group; (*MIL, AVIAT, GÉO*) formation; **~ permanente** continuing education; **~ professionnelle** vocational train-

ing

forme [fɔrm(ə)] *nf* (*gén*) form; (*d'un objet*) shape, form; **~s** *nfpl* (*bonnes manières*) proprieties; (*d'une femme*) figure
sg; **en ~ de poire** pear-shaped; **être en
~** (*SPORT etc*) to be on form; **en bonne et
due ~** in due form

formel, le [fɔrmɛl] *adj* (*preuve, décision*) definite, positive; (*logique*) formal;
formellement *adv* (*absolument*) posi-
tively

former [fɔrme] *vt* to form; (*éduquer*) to
train; **se ~** *vi* to form

formidable [fɔrmidabl(ə)] *adj* tremendous

formulaire [fɔrmylɛr] *nm* form

formule [fɔrmyl] *nf* (*gén*) formula; (*formulaire*) form; **~ de politesse** polite
phrase; letter ending

formuler [fɔrmyle] *vt* (*émettre: réponse,
vœux*) to formulate; (*expliciter: sa pensée*) to express

fort, e [fɔr, fɔrt(ə)] *adj* strong; (*intensité, rendement*) high, great; (*corpulent*)
stout; (*doué*) good, able ♦ *adv* (*serrer,
frapper*) hard; (*sonner*) loud(ly); (*beaucoup*) greatly, very much; (*très*) very
♦ *nm* (*édifice*) fort; (*point fort*) strong
point, forte; **se faire ~ de ...** to claim
one can ...; **au plus ~ de** (*au milieu de*)
in the thick of; at the height of; **~e tête**
rebel

fortifiant [fɔrtifjɑ̃] *nm* tonic

fortifier [fɔrtifje] *vt* to strengthen, fortify; (*MIL*) to fortify

fortiori [fɔrtjɔri]: **à ~** *adv* all the more
so

fortuit, e [fɔrtɥi, -it] *adj* fortuitous,
chance *cpd*

fortune [fɔrtyn] *nf* fortune; **faire ~** to
make one's fortune; **de ~** makeshift;
chance *cpd*

fortuné, e [fɔrtyne] *adj* wealthy

fosse [fos] *nf* (*grand trou*) pit; (*tombe*)
grave; **~ (d'orchestre)** (orchestra) pit

fossé [fose] *nm* ditch; (*fig*) gulf, gap

fossette [fosɛt] *nf* dimple

fossile [fosil] *nm* fossil

fossoyeur [foswajœr] *nm* gravedigger

fou (fol), folle [fu, fɔl] *adj* mad; *(déréglé etc)* wild, erratic; *(fam: extrême, très grand)* terrific, tremendous ♦ *nm/f* madman(woman) ♦ *nm (du roi)* jester; **être ~ de** to be mad *ou* crazy about; **avoir le ~ rire** to have the giggles; **faire le ~** to act the fool

foudre [fudʀ(ə)] *nf*: **la ~** lightning

foudroyant, e [fudʀwajɑ̃, -ɑ̃t] *adj* lightning *cpd*, stunning; *(maladie, poison)* violent

foudroyer [fudʀwaje] *vt* to strike down; **être foudroyé** to be struck by lightning; **~ qn du regard** to glare at sb

fouet [fwɛ] *nm* whip; *(CULIN)* whisk; **de plein ~** *(se heurter)* head on; **fouetter** *vt* to whip; to whisk

fougère [fuʒɛʀ] *nf* fern

fougue [fug] *nf* ardour, spirit

fouille [fuj] *nf* search; **~s** *nfpl (archéologiques)* excavations

fouiller [fuje] *vt* to search; *(creuser)* to dig ♦ *vi* to rummage

fouillis [fuji] *nm* jumble, muddle

fouiner [fwine] *(péj) vi*: **~ dans** to nose around *ou* about in

foulard [fulaʀ] *nm* scarf

foule [ful] *nf* crowd; **les ~s** the masses; **la ~** crowds *pl*; **une ~ de** masses of

foulée [fule] *nf* stride

fouler [fule] *vt* to press; *(sol)* to tread upon; **se ~** *vi (fam)* to overexert o.s.; **se ~ la cheville** to sprain one's ankle; **~ aux pieds** to trample underfoot; **foulure** [fulyʀ] *nf* sprain

four [fuʀ] *nm* oven; *(de potier)* kiln; *(THÉÂTRE: échec)* flop

fourbe [fuʀb(ə)] *adj* deceitful

fourbu, e [fuʀby] *adj* exhausted

fourche [fuʀʃ(ə)] *nf* pitchfork; *(de bicyclette)* fork

fourchette [fuʀʃɛt] *nf* fork; *(STATISTIQUE)* bracket, margin

fourgon [fuʀgɔ̃] *nm* van; *(RAIL)* wag(g)on

fourmi [fuʀmi] *nf* ant; **~s** *nfpl (fig)* pins and needles; **fourmilière** *nf* ant-hill

fourmiller [fuʀmije] *vi* to swarm

fournaise [fuʀnɛz] *nf* blaze; *(fig)* furnace, oven

fourneau, x [fuʀno] *nm* stove

fournée [fuʀne] *nf* batch

fourni, e [fuʀni] *adj (barbe, cheveux)* thick; *(magasin)*: **bien ~ (en)** well stocked (with)

fournir [fuʀniʀ] *vt* to supply; *(preuve, exemple)* to provide, supply; *(effort)* to put in; **fournisseur, euse** *nm/f* supplier

fourniture [fuʀnityʀ] *nf* supply(ing); **~s** *nfpl (provisions)* supplies

fourrage [fuʀaʒ] *nm* fodder

fourrager¹, ère [fuʀaʒe, -ɛʀ] *adj* fodder *cpd*

fourrager² *vi*: **~ dans/parmi** *(fouiller)* to rummage through/among

fourré, e [fuʀe] *adj (bonbon etc)* filled; *(manteau etc)* fur-lined ♦ *nm* thicket

fourreau, x [fuʀo] *nm* sheath

fourrer [fuʀe] *(fam) vt* to stick, shove; **se ~ dans/sous** to get into/under

fourre-tout [fuʀtu] *nm inv (sac)* holdall; *(péj)* junk room *(ou* cupboard); *(fig)* rag-bag

fourrière [fuʀjɛʀ] *nf* pound

fourrure [fuʀyʀ] *nf* fur; *(sur l'animal)* coat

fourvoyer [fuʀvwaje]: **se ~** *vi* to go astray, stray

foutre [futʀ(ə)] *(fam!) vt* = **ficher**; **foutu, e** *(fam!) adj* = **fichu, e**

foyer [fwaje] *nm (de cheminée)* hearth; *(famille)* family; *(maison)* home; *(de jeunes etc)* (social) club; hostel; *(salon)* foyer; *(OPTIQUE, PHOTO)* focus *sg*; **lunettes à double ~** bi-focal glasses

fracas [fʀaka] *nm* din; crash; roar

fracasser [fʀakase] *vt* to smash

fraction [fʀaksjɔ̃] *nf* fraction; **fractionner** *vt* to divide (up), split (up)

fracture [fʀaktyʀ] *nf* fracture; **~ du crâne** fractured skull; **fracturer** [fʀaktyʀe] *vt (coffre, serrure)* to break open; *(os, membre)* to fracture

fragile [fʀaʒil] *adj* fragile, delicate; *(fig)* frail; **fragilité** *nf* fragility

fragment [fʀagmɑ̃] *nm (d'un objet)* fragment, piece; *(d'un texte)* passage, extract

fraîche [fʀɛʃ] *adj voir* **frais**; **fraîcheur**

nf coolness; freshness; **fraîchir** *vi* to get cooler; (*vent*) to freshen

frais, fraîche [frɛ, frɛʃ] *adj* fresh; (*froid*) cool ♦ *adv* (*récemment*) newly, fresh(ly) ♦ *nm*: **mettre au ~** to put in a cool place ♦ *nmpl* (*débours*) expenses; (*COMM*) costs; (*facturés*) charges; **il fait ~** it's cool; **servir ~** serve chilled; **prendre le ~** to take a breath of cool air; **faire des ~** to spend; to go to a lot of expense; **faire les ~ de** to bear the brunt of; **~ de scolarité** school fees (*BRIT*), tuition (*US*); **~ généraux** overheads

fraise [frɛz] *nf* strawberry; (*TECH*) countersink (bit); (*de dentiste*) drill; **~ des bois** wild strawberry

framboise [frɑ̃bwaz] *nf* raspberry

franc, franche [frɑ̃, frɑ̃ʃ] *adj* (*personne*) frank, straightforward; (*visage*) open; (*net: refus, couleur*) clear; (: *coupure*) clean; (*intensif*) downright; (*exempt*): **~ de port** postage paid ♦ *adv*: **parler ~** to be frank *ou* candid ♦ *nm* franc

français, e [frɑ̃sɛ, -ɛz] *adj* French ♦ *nm/f*: **F~, e** Frenchman(woman) ♦ *nm* (*LING*) French; **les F~** the French

France [frɑ̃s] *nf*: **la ~** France

franche [frɑ̃ʃ] *adj voir* **franc**; **franchement** *adv* frankly; clearly; (*tout à fait*) downright

franchir [frɑ̃ʃir] *vt* (*obstacle*) to clear, get over; (*seuil, ligne, rivière*) to cross; (*distance*) to cover

franchise [frɑ̃ʃiz] *nf* frankness; (*douanière, d'impôt*) exemption; (*ASSURANCES*) excess

francilien, ne [frɑ̃siljɛ̃, -jɛn] *adj* of *ou* from the Île-de-France region ♦ *nm/f*: **F~, ne** person of *ou* from the Île-de-France region

franciser [frɑ̃size] *vt* to gallicize, Frenchify

franc-maçon [frɑ̃masɔ̃] *nm* freemason

franco [frɑ̃ko] *adv* (*COMM*): **~ (de port)** postage paid

francophone [frɑ̃kɔfɔn] *adj* French-speaking; **francophonie** *nf* French-speaking communities

franc-parler [frɑ̃parle] *nm inv* outspokenness

franc-tireur [frɑ̃tirœr] *nm* (*MIL*) irregular; (*fig*) freelance

frange [frɑ̃ʒ] *nf* fringe

frangipane [frɑ̃ʒipan] *nf* almond paste

franquette [frɑ̃kɛt]: **à la bonne ~** *adv* without any fuss

frappe [frap] *nf* (*de pianiste, machine à écrire*) touch; (*BOXE*) punch

frappé, e [frape] *adj* iced

frapper [frape] *vt* to hit, strike; (*étonner*) to strike; (*monnaie*) to strike, stamp; **se ~** *vi* (*s'inquiéter*) to get worked up; **~ dans ses mains** to clap one's hands; **~ du poing sur** to bang one's fist on; **frappé de stupeur** dumbfounded

frasques [frask(ə)] *nfpl* escapades

fraternel, le [fraternɛl] *adj* brotherly, fraternal

fraternité [fraternite] *nf* brotherhood

fraude [frod] *nf* fraud; (*SCOL*) cheating; **passer qch en ~** to smuggle sth in (*ou* out); **~ fiscale** tax evasion; **frauder** *vi, vt* to cheat; **frauduleux, euse** *adj* fraudulent

frayer [freje] *vt* to open up, clear ♦ *vi* to spawn; (*fréquenter*): **~ avec** to mix with

frayeur [frɛjœr] *nf* fright

fredonner [frədɔne] *vt* to hum

freezer [frizœr] *nm* freezing compartment

frein [frɛ̃] *nm* brake; **~ à main** handbrake; **~s à disques/tambour** disc/drum brakes

freiner [frene] *vi* to brake ♦ *vt* (*progrès etc*) to check

frelaté, e [frəlate] *adj* adulterated; (*fig*) tainted

frêle [frɛl] *adj* frail, fragile

frelon [frəlɔ̃] *nm* hornet

frémir [fremir] *vi* to tremble, shudder; to shiver; to quiver

frêne [frɛn] *nm* ash

frénétique [frenetik] *adj* frenzied, frenetic

fréquemment [frekamɑ̃] *adv* frequently

fréquent, e [frekɑ̃, -ɑ̃t] *adj* frequent

fréquentation [fʀekɑ̃tasjɔ̃] nf frequenting; seeing; ~s nfpl (relations) company sg

fréquenté, e [fʀekɑ̃te] adj: **très ~** (very) busy; **mal ~** patronized by disreputable elements

fréquenter [fʀekɑ̃te] vt (lieu) to frequent; (personne) to see; **se ~** to see each other

frère [fʀɛʀ] nm brother

fresque [fʀɛsk(ə)] nf (ART) fresco

fret [fʀɛ] nm freight

frétiller [fʀetije] vi to wriggle; to quiver; (chien) to wag its tail

fretin [fʀətɛ̃] nm: **menu ~** small fry

friable [fʀijabl(ə)] adj crumbly

friand, e [fʀijɑ̃, -ɑ̃d] adj: **~ de** very fond of

friandise [fʀijɑ̃diz] nf sweet

fric [fʀik] (fam) nm cash, bread

friche [fʀiʃ] : **en ~** adj, adv (lying) fallow

friction [fʀiksjɔ̃] nf (massage) rub, rubdown; (TECH, fig) friction; **frictionner** vt to rub (down); to massage

frigidaire [fʀiʒidɛʀ] (®) nm refrigerator

frigide [fʀiʒid] adj frigid

frigo [fʀigo] nm fridge

frigorifier [fʀigɔʀifje] vt to refrigerate; **frigorifique** adj refrigerating

frileux, euse [fʀilø, -øz] adj sensitive to (the) cold

frimer [fʀime] vi to put on an act

frimousse [fʀimus] nf (sweet) little face

fringale [fʀɛ̃gal] nf: **avoir la ~** to be ravenous

fringant, e [fʀɛ̃gɑ̃, -ɑ̃t] adj dashing

fringues [fʀɛ̃g] (fam) nfpl clothes

fripé, e [fʀipe] adj crumpled

fripon, ne [fʀipɔ̃, -ɔn] adj roguish, mischievous ♦ nm/f rascal, rogue

fripouille [fʀipuj] nf scoundrel

frire [fʀiʀ] vt, vi: **faire ~** to fry

frisé, e [fʀize] adj curly; curly-haired

frisson [fʀisɔ̃] nm shudder, shiver; quiver; **frissonner** vi to shudder, shiver; to quiver

frit, e [fʀi, fʀit] pp de **frire**; **frite** nf: **(pommes) frites** chips (BRIT), French

fries; **friteuse** nf chip pan; **friture** nf (huile) (deep) fat; (plat): **friture (de poissons)** fried fish; (RADIO) crackle

frivole [fʀivɔl] adj frivolous

froid, e [fʀwa, fʀwad] adj, nm cold; **il fait ~** it's cold; **avoir/prendre ~** to be/catch cold; **être en ~ avec** to be on bad terms with; **froidement** adv (accueillir) coldly; (décider) coolly

froisser [fʀwase] vt to crumple (up), crease; (fig) to hurt, offend; **se ~** vi to crumple, crease; to take offence; **se ~ un muscle** to strain a muscle

frôler [fʀole] vt to brush against; (suj: projectile) to skim past; (fig) to come very close to

fromage [fʀɔmaʒ] nm cheese; **~ blanc** soft white cheese; **fromager, ère** nm/f cheese merchant

froment [fʀɔmɑ̃] nm wheat

froncer [fʀɔ̃se] vt to gather; **~ les sourcils** to frown

frondaisons [fʀɔ̃dɛzɔ̃] nfpl foliage sg

fronde [fʀɔ̃d] nf sling; (fig) rebellion, rebelliousness

front [fʀɔ̃] nm forehead, brow; (MIL) front; **de ~** (se heurter) head-on; (rouler) together (i.e. 2 or 3 abreast); (simultanément) at once; **faire ~ à** to face up to; **~ de mer** (sea) front

frontalier, ère [fʀɔ̃talje, -ɛʀ] adj border cpd, frontier cpd ♦ nm/f: **(travailleurs) ~s** commuters from across the border

frontière [fʀɔ̃tjɛʀ] nf frontier, border; (fig) frontier, boundary

fronton [fʀɔ̃tɔ̃] nm pediment

frotter [fʀɔte] vi to rub, scrape ♦ vt to rub; (pour nettoyer) to rub (up); to scrub; **~ une allumette** to strike a match

fructifier [fʀyktifje] vi to yield a profit; **faire ~** to turn to good account

fructueux, euse [fʀyktɥø, -øz] adj fruitful; profitable

fruit [fʀɥi] nm fruit gen no pl; **~s de mer** seafood(s); **~s secs** dried fruit sg; **fruité, e** adj fruity; **fruitier, ère** adj: **arbre fruitier** fruit tree ♦ nm/f fruiterer (BRIT), fruit merchant (US)

fruste [fʀyst(ə)] *adj* unpolished, uncultivated

frustrer [fʀystʀe] *vt* to frustrate

fuel(-oil) [fjul(ɔjl)] *nm* fuel oil; heating oil

fugace [fygas] *adj* fleeting

fugitif, ive [fyʒitif, -iv] *adj* (*lueur, amour*) fleeting; (*prisonnier etc*) fugitive, runaway ♦ *nm/f* fugitive

fugue [fyg] *nf*: **faire une ~** to run away, abscond

fuir [fɥiʀ] *vt* to flee from; (*éviter*) to shun ♦ *vi* to run away; (*gaz, robinet*) to leak

fuite [fɥit] *nf* flight; (*écoulement, divulgation*) leak; **être en ~** to be on the run; **mettre en ~** to put to flight

fulgurant, e [fylgyʀɑ̃, -ɑ̃t] *adj* lightning *cpd*, dazzling

fulminer [fylmine] *vi* to thunder forth

fumé, e [fyme] *adj* (*CULIN*) smoked; (*verre*) tinted

fume-cigarette [fymsigaʀɛt] *nm inv* cigarette holder

fumée [fyme] *nf* smoke

fumer [fyme] *vi* to smoke; (*soupe*) to steam ♦ *vt* to smoke; (*terre, champ*) to manure

fûmes *etc vb voir* **être**

fumet [fyme] *nm* aroma

fumeur, euse [fymœʀ, -øz] *nm/f* smoker

fumeux, euse [fymø, -øz] (*péj*) *adj* woolly, hazy

fumier [fymje] *nm* manure

fumiste [fymist(ə)] *nm/f* (*péj: paresseux*) shirker; (*charlatan*) phoney

fumisterie [fymistəʀi] (*péj*) *nf* fraud, con

funambule [fynɑ̃byl] *nm* tightrope walker

funèbre [fynɛbʀ(ə)] *adj* funeral *cpd*; (*fig*) doleful; funereal

funérailles [fyneʀɑj] *nfpl* funeral *sg*

funeste [fynɛst(ə)] *adj* disastrous; deathly

fur [fyʀ]: **au ~ et à mesure** *adv* as one goes along; **au ~ et à mesure que** as

furet [fyʀe] *nm* ferret

fureter [fyʀte] (*péj*) *vi* to nose about

fureur [fyʀœʀ] *nf* fury; (*passion*): **~ de**

passion for; **faire ~** to be all the rage

furibond, e [fyʀibɔ̃, -ɔ̃d] *adj* furious

furie [fyʀi] *nf* fury; (*femme*) shrew, vixen; **en ~** (*mer*) raging; **furieux, euse** *adj* furious

furoncle [fyʀɔ̃kl(ə)] *nm* boil

furtif, ive [fyʀtif, -iv] *adj* furtive

fus *vb voir* **être**

fusain [fyzɛ̃] *nm* (*ART*) charcoal

fuseau, x [fyzo] *nm* (*pour filer*) spindle; (*pantalon*) (ski) pants; **~ horaire** time zone

fusée [fyze] *nf* rocket; **~ éclairante** flare

fuselé, e [fyzle] *adj* slender; tapering

fuser [fyze] *vi* (*rires etc*) to burst forth

fusible [fyzibl(ə)] *nm* (*ÉLEC: fil*) fuse wire; (: *fiche*) fuse

fusil [fyzi] *nm* (*de guerre, à canon rayé*) rifle, gun; (*de chasse, à canon lisse*) shotgun, gun; **fusillade** *nf* gunfire *no pl*, shooting *no pl*; shooting battle; **fusiller** *vt* to shoot; **fusil-mitrailleur** *nm* machine gun

fusionner [fyzjɔne] *vi* to merge

fustiger [fystiʒe] *vt* to denounce

fut *vb voir* **être**

fût [fy] *vb voir* **être** ♦ *nm* (*tonneau*) barrel, cask

futaie [fyte] *nf* forest, plantation

futé, e [fyte] *adj* crafty

futile [fytil] *adj* futile; frivolous

futur, e [fytyʀ] *adj, nm* future

fuyant, e [fɥijɑ̃, -ɑ̃t] *vb voir* **fuir** ♦ *adj* (*regard etc*) evasive; (*lignes etc*) receding; (*perspective*) vanishing

fuyard, e [fɥijaʀ, -aʀd(ə)] *nm/f* runaway

G g

gabarit [gabaʀi] *nm* (*fig*) size; calibre

gâcher [gɑʃe] *vt* (*gâter*) to spoil, ruin; (*gaspiller*) to waste

gâchette [gɑʃɛt] *nf* trigger

gâchis [gɑʃi] *nm* waste *no pl*

gadoue [gadu] *nf* sludge

gaffe [gaf] *nf* (*instrument*) boat hook; (*erreur*) blunder; **faire ~** (*fam*) to be careful

gage [gaʒ] *nm* (*dans un jeu*) forfeit; (*fig: de fidélité*) token; **~s** *nmpl* (*salaire*) wages; (*garantie*) guarantee *sg*; **mettre en ~** to pawn

gager [gaʒe] *vt* to bet, wager

gageure [gaʒyʀ] *nf*: **c'est une ~** it's attempting the impossible

gagnant, e [gaɲɑ̃, -ɑ̃t] *nm/f* winner

gagne-pain [gaɲpɛ̃] *nm inv* job

gagner [gaɲe] *vt* to win; (*somme d'argent, revenu*) to earn; (*aller vers, atteindre*) to reach; (*envahir*) to overcome; to spread to ♦ *vi* to win; (*fig*) to gain; **~ du temps/de la place** to gain time/save space; **~ sa vie** to earn one's living

gai, e [ɡe] *adj* gay, cheerful; (*un peu ivre*) merry

gaieté [ɡete] *nf* cheerfulness; **de ~ de cœur** with a light heart

gaillard, e [gajaʀ, -aʀd(ə)] *adj* (*grivois*) bawdy, ribald ♦ *nm* (strapping) fellow

gain [ɡɛ̃] *nm* (*revenu*) earnings *pl*; (*bénéfice: gén pl*) profits *pl*; (*au jeu*) winnings *pl*; (*fig: de temps, place*) saving; **avoir ~ de cause** to win the case; (*fig*) to be proved right

gaine [ɡɛn] *nf* (*corset*) girdle; (*fourreau*) sheath

galant, e [galɑ̃, -ɑ̃t] *adj* (*courtois*) courteous, gentlemanly; (*entreprenant*) flirtatious, gallant; (*aventure, poésie*) amorous

galère [galɛʀ] *nf* galley

galérer [galeʀe] (*fam*) *vi* to slog away, work hard

galerie [galʀi] *nf* gallery; (*THÉÂTRE*) circle; (*de voiture*) roof rack; (*fig: spectateurs*) audience; **~ de peinture** (private) art gallery; **~ marchande** shopping arcade

galet [galɛ] *nm* pebble; (*TECH*) wheel

galette [galɛt] *nf* flat cake

Galles [gal] *nfpl*: **le pays de ~** Wales

gallois, e [galwa, -waz] *adj* Welsh ♦ *nm* (*LING*) Welsh ♦ *nm/f*: **G~, e** Welshman(woman)

galon [galɔ̃] *nm* (*MIL*) stripe; (*décoratif*) piece of braid

galop [galo] *nm* gallop

galoper [galɔpe] *vi* to gallop

galopin [galɔpɛ̃] *nm* urchin, ragamuffin

galvauder [galvode] *vt* to debase

gambader [gɑ̃bade] *vi* (*animal, enfant*) to leap about

gamelle [gamɛl] *nf* mess tin; billy can

gamin, e [gamɛ̃, -in] *nm/f* kid ♦ *adj* mischievous, playful

gamme [gam] *nf* (*MUS*) scale; (*fig*) range

gammé, e [game] *adj*: **croix ~e** swastika

gant [gɑ̃] *nm* glove; **~ de toilette** face flannel (*BRIT*), face cloth

garage [gaʀaʒ] *nm* garage; **garagiste** *nm/f* garage owner; garage mechanic

garant, e [gaʀɑ̃, -ɑ̃t] *nm/f* guarantor ♦ *nm* guarantee; **se porter ~ de** to vouch for; to be answerable for

garantie [gaʀɑ̃ti] *nf* guarantee; (*gage*) security, surety; **(bon de) ~** guarantee *ou* warranty slip

garantir [gaʀɑ̃tiʀ] *vt* to guarantee; (*protéger*): **~ de** to protect from

garçon [gaʀsɔ̃] *nm* boy; (*célibataire*) bachelor; (*serveur*): **~ (de café)** waiter; **~ de courses** messenger; **garçonnet** *nm* small boy; **garçonnière** *nf* bachelor flat

garde [gaʀd(ə)] *nm* (*de prisonnier*) guard; (*de domaine etc*) warden; (*soldat, sentinelle*) guardsman ♦ *nf* guarding; looking after; (*soldats, BOXE, ESCRIME*) guard; (*faction*) watch; (*TYPO*) **~** endpaper; flyleaf; **de ~** on duty; **monter la ~** to stand guard; **mettre en ~** to warn; **prendre ~ (à)** to be careful (of); **~ champêtre** *nm* rural policeman; **~ du corps** *nm* bodyguard; **~ des enfants** *nf* (*après divorce*) custody of the children; **~ des Sceaux** *nm* ≈ Lord Chancellor (*BRIT*), ≈ Attorney General (*US*); **~ à vue** *nf* (*JUR*) ≈ police custody; **~-à-vous** *nm*: **être/se mettre au ~-à-vous** to be at/ stand to attention; **~-barrière** *nm/f* level-crossing keeper; **~-boue** *nm inv* mudguard; **~-chasse** *nm* gamekeeper; **~-fou** *nm* railing, parapet; **~-malade** *nf* home nurse; **~-manger** *nm inv* meat safe; pantry, larder

garder [gaʀde] *vt* (*conserver*) to keep;

(*surveiller*: *enfants*) to look after; (: *immeuble, lieu, prisonnier*) to guard; **se ~** *vi* (*aliment*: *se conserver*) to keep; **se ~ de faire** to be careful not to do; **~ le lit/la chambre** to stay in bed/indoors; **pêche/chasse gardée** private fishing/ hunting (ground)

garderie [gaʀdəʀi] *nf* day nursery, crèche

garde-robe [gaʀdəʀɔb] *nf* wardrobe

gardien, ne [gaʀdjɛ̃, -jɛn] *nm/f* (*garde*) guard; (*de prison*) warder; (*de domaine, réserve*) warden; (*de musée etc*) attendant; (*de phare, cimetière*) keeper; (*d'immeuble*) caretaker; (*fig*) guardian; **~ de but** goalkeeper; **~ de la paix** policeman; **~ de nuit** night watchman

gare [gaʀ] *nf* (railway) station, train station (*US*) ♦ *excl* watch out!; **~ routière** bus station

garer [gaʀe] *vt* to park; **se ~** *vi* to park; (*pour laisser passer*) to draw into the side

gargariser [gaʀgaʀize]: **se ~** *vi* to gargle

gargarisme [gaʀgaʀism] *nm* gargling *no pl*; gargle

gargote [gaʀgɔt] *nf* cheap restaurant

gargouille [gaʀguj] *nf* gargoyle

gargouiller [gaʀguje] *vi* to gurgle

garnement [gaʀnəmɑ̃] *nm* rascal, scallywag

garni, e [gaʀni] *adj* (*plat*) served with vegetables (*and chips or rice etc*) ♦ *nm* furnished accommodation *no pl*

garnir [gaʀniʀ] *vt* (*orner*) to decorate; to trim; (*approvisionner*) to fill, stock; (*protéger*) to fit

garnison [gaʀnizɔ̃] *nf* garrison

garniture [gaʀnityʀ] *nf* (*CULIN*) vegetables *pl*; filling; (*décoration*) trimming; (*protection*) fittings *pl*; **~ de frein** brake lining

garrot [gaʀo] *nm* (*MÉD*) tourniquet

gars [ga] *nm* lad; guy

Gascogne [gaskɔɲ] *nf* Gascony; **le golfe de ~** the Bay of Biscay

gas-oil [gazɔjl] *nm* diesel (oil)

gaspiller [gaspije] *vt* to waste

gastronomique [gastʀɔnɔmik] *adj* gastronomic

gâteau, x [gato] *nm* cake; **~ sec** biscuit

gâter [gate] *vt* to spoil; **se ~** *vi* (*dent, fruit*) to go bad; (*temps, situation*) to change for the worse

gâterie [gatʀi] *nf* little treat

gâteux, euse [gatø, -øz] *adj* senile

gauche [goʃ] *adj* left, left-hand; (*maladroit*) awkward, clumsy ♦ *nf* (*POL*) left (wing); **à ~** on the left; (*direction*) (to the) left; **gaucher, ère** *adj* left-handed; **gauchiste** *nm/f* leftist

gaufre [gofʀ] *nf* waffle

gaufrette [gofʀɛt] *nf* wafer

gaulois, e [golwa, -waz] *adj* Gallic; (*grivois*) bawdy ♦ *nm/f*: **G~, e** Gaul

gausser [gose]: **se ~ de** *vt* to deride

gaver [gave] *vt* to force-feed; (*fig*): **~ de** to cram with, fill up with

gaz [gaz] *nm inv* gas

gaze [gaz] *nf* gauze

gazéifié, e [gazeifje] *adj* aerated

gazette [gazɛt] *nf* news sheet

gazeux, euse [gazø, -øz] *adj* gaseous; (*boisson*) fizzy; (*eau*) sparkling

gazoduc [gazɔdyk] *nm* gas pipeline

gazon [gazɔ̃] *nm* (*herbe*) turf; grass; (*pelouse*) lawn

gazouiller [gazuje] *vi* to chirp; (*enfant*) to babble

geai [ʒɛ] *nm* jay

géant, e [ʒeɑ̃, -ɑ̃t] *adj* gigantic, giant; (*COMM*) giant-size ♦ *nm/f* giant

geindre [ʒɛ̃dʀ(ə)] *vi* to groan, moan

gel [ʒɛl] *nm* frost; freezing

gélatine [ʒelatin] *nf* gelatine

gelée [ʒəle] *nf* jelly; (*gel*) frost

geler [ʒəle] *vt, vi* to freeze; **il gèle** it's freezing

gélule [ʒelyl] *nf* (*MÉD*) capsule

gelures [ʒəlyʀ] *nfpl* frostbite *sg*

Gémeaux [ʒemo] *nmpl*: **les ~** Gemini

gémir [ʒemiʀ] *vi* to groan, moan

gemme [ʒɛm] *nf* gem(stone)

gênant, e [ʒɛnɑ̃, -ɑ̃t] *adj* annoying; embarrassing

gencive [ʒɑ̃siv] *nf* gum

gendarme [ʒɑ̃daʀm(ə)] *nm* gendarme; **gendarmerie** *nf* military police force in countryside and small towns; *their po-*

lice station or barracks

gendre [ʒɑ̃dʀ(ə)] *nm* son-in-law

gêne [ʒɛn] *nf* (*à respirer, bouger*) discomfort, difficulty; (*dérangement*) bother, trouble; (*manque d'argent*) financial difficulties *pl ou* straits *pl*; (*confusion*) embarrassment

gêné, e [ʒene] *adj* embarrassed

gêner [ʒene] *vt* (*incommoder*) to bother; (*encombrer*) to hamper; to be in the way; (*embarrasser*): ~ **qn** to make sb feel ill-at-ease; **se** ~ *vi* to put o.s. out

général, e, aux [ʒeneʀal, -o] *adj, nm* general; **en** ~ usually, in general; **générale** *nf*: (*répétition*) **générale** final dress rehearsal; **généralement** *adv* generally

généraliser [ʒeneʀalize] *vt, vi* to generalize; **se** ~ *vi* to become widespread

généraliste [ʒeneʀalist(ə)] *nm/f* general practitioner, G.P.

générateur, trice [ʒeneʀatœʀ, -tʀis] *adj*: ~ **de** which causes

génération [ʒeneʀasjɔ̃] *nf* generation

généreux, euse [ʒeneʀø, -øz] *adj* generous

générique [ʒeneʀik] *nm* (*CINÉMA*) credits *pl*, credit titles *pl*

générosité [ʒeneʀozite] *nf* generosity

genêt [ʒənɛ] *nm* broom *no pl* (*shrub*)

génétique [ʒenetik] *adj* genetic

Genève [ʒənɛv] *n* Geneva

génial, e, aux [ʒenjal, -o] *adj* of genius; (*fam: formidable*) fantastic, brilliant

génie [ʒeni] *nm* genius; (*MIL*): **le** ~ the Engineers *pl*; ~ **civil** civil engineering

genièvre [ʒənjɛvʀ(ə)] *nm* juniper

génisse [ʒenis] *nf* heifer

genou, x [ʒnu] *nm* knee; **à** ~**x** on one's knees; **se mettre à** ~**x** to kneel down

genre [ʒɑ̃ʀ] *nm* kind, type, sort; (*allure*) manner; (*LING*) gender

gens [ʒɑ̃] *nmpl* (*f in some phrases*) people *pl*

gentil, le [ʒɑ̃ti, -ij] *adj* kind; (*enfant: sage*) good; (*endroit etc*) nice; **gentillesse** *nf* kindness; **gentiment** *adv* kindly

géographie [ʒeɔgʀafi] *nf* geography

geôlier [ʒolje] *nm* jailer

géologie [ʒeɔlɔʒi] *nf* geology

géomètre [ʒeɔmɛtʀ(ə)] *nm* (*aussi*: *arpenteur-*~) (land) surveyor

géométrie [ʒeɔmetʀi] *nf* geometry; **géométrique** *adj* geometric

gérance [ʒeʀɑ̃s] *nf* management; **mettre en** ~ to appoint a manager for

géranium [ʒeʀanjɔm] *nm* geranium

gérant, e [ʒeʀɑ̃, -ɑ̃t] *nm/f* manager(eress)

gerbe [ʒɛʀb(ə)] *nf* (*de fleurs*) spray; (*de blé*) sheaf; (*fig*) shower, burst

gercé, e [ʒɛʀse] *adj* chapped

gerçure [ʒɛʀsyʀ] *nf* crack

gérer [ʒeʀe] *vt* to manage

germain, e [ʒɛʀmɛ̃, -ɛn] *adj*: **cousin** ~ first cousin

germe [ʒɛʀm(ə)] *nm* germ; **germer** [ʒɛʀme] *vi* to sprout; to germinate

geste [ʒɛst(ə)] *nm* gesture; move; motion

gestion [ʒɛstjɔ̃] *nf* management

gibecière [ʒibsjɛʀ] *nf* gamebag

gibet [ʒibɛ] *nm* gallows *pl*

gibier [ʒibje] *nm* (*animaux*) game; (*fig*) prey

giboulée [ʒibule] *nf* sudden shower

gicler [ʒikle] *vi* to spurt, squirt

gifle [ʒifl(ə)] *nf* slap (in the face); **gifler** *vt* to slap (in the face)

gigantesque [ʒigɑ̃tɛsk(ə)] *adj* gigantic

gigogne [ʒigɔɲ] *adj*: **lits** ~**s** truckle (*BRIT*) *ou* trundle beds

gigot [ʒigo] *nm* leg (of mutton *ou* lamb)

gigoter [ʒigɔte] *vi* to wriggle (about)

gilet [ʒilɛ] *nm* waistcoat; (*pull*) cardigan; (*de corps*) vest; ~ **de sauvetage** life jacket

gingembre [ʒɛ̃ʒɑ̃bʀ(ə)] *nm* ginger

girafe [ʒiʀaf] *nf* giraffe

giratoire [ʒiʀatwaʀ] *adj*: **sens** ~ roundabout

girofle [ʒiʀɔfl(e)] *nf*: **clou de** ~ clove

girouette [ʒiʀwɛt] *nf* weather vane *ou* cock

gisait *etc vb voir* **gésir**

gisement [ʒizmɑ̃] *nm* deposit

gît *vb voir* **gésir**

gitan, e [ʒitɑ̃, -an] *nm/f* gipsy

gîte [ʒit] *nm* home; shelter; ~ **(rural)**

holiday cottage *ou* apartment

givre [ʒivʀ(ə)] *nm* (hoar) frost

glabre [glabʀ(ə)] *adj* hairless; clean-shaven

glace [glas] *nf* ice; (*crème glacée*) ice cream; (*verre*) sheet of glass; (*miroir*) mirror; (*de voiture*) window

glacé, e [glase] *adj* icy; (*boisson*) iced

glacer [glase] *vt* to freeze; (*boisson*) to chill, ice; (*gâteau*) to ice; (*papier, tissu*) to glaze; (*fig*): ~ **qn** to chill sb; to make sb's blood run cold

glacial, e [glasjal] *adj* icy

glacier [glasje] *nm* (*GÉO*) glacier; (*marchand*) ice-cream maker

glacière [glasjɛʀ] *nf* icebox

glaçon [glasɔ̃] *nm* icicle; (*pour boisson*) ice cube

glaise [glɛz] *nf* clay

gland [glɑ̃] *nm* acorn; (*décoration*) tassel

glande [glɑ̃d] *nf* gland

glaner [glane] *vt, vi* to glean

glapir [glapiʀ] *vi* to yelp

glas [glɑ] *nm* knell, toll

glauque [glok] *adj* dull blue-green

glissant, e [glisɑ̃, -ɑ̃t] *adj* slippery

glissement [glismɑ̃] *nm*: ~ **de terrain** landslide

glisser [glise] *vi* (*avancer*) to glide *ou* slide along; (*coulisser, tomber*) to slide; (*déraper*) to slip; (*être glissant*) to be slippery ♦ *vt* to slip; **se** ~ **dans** to slip into

global, e, aux [glɔbal, -o] *adj* overall

globe [glɔb] *nm* globe

globule [glɔbyl] *nm* (*du sang*) corpuscle

globuleux, euse [glɔbylø, -øz] *adj*: **yeux** ~ protruding eyes

gloire [glwaʀ] *nf* glory; (*mérite*) distinction, credit; (*personne*) celebrity; **glorieux, euse** *adj* glorious

glousser [gluse] *vi* to cluck; (*rire*) to chuckle

glouton, ne [glutɔ̃, -ɔn] *adj* gluttonous

gluant, e [glyɑ̃, -ɑ̃t] *adj* sticky, gummy

glycine [glisin] *nf* wisteria

go [go]: **tout de** ~ *adv* straight out

G.O. *sigle* = **grandes ondes**

gobelet [gɔblɛ] *nm* tumbler; beaker; (*à dés*) cup

gober [gɔbe] *vt* to swallow

godasse [gɔdas] (*fam*) *nf* shoe

godet [gɔdɛ] *nm* pot

goéland [gɔelɑ̃] *nm* (sea)gull

goélette [gɔelɛt] *nf* schooner

goémon [gɔemɔ̃] *nm* wrack

gogo [gogo]: **à** ~ *adv* galore

goguenard, e [gɔɡnaʀ, -aʀd(ə)] *adj* mocking

goinfre [gwɛ̃fʀ(ə)] *nm* glutton

golf [gɔlf] *nm* golf; golf course

golfe [gɔlf(ə)] *nm* gulf; bay

gomme [gɔm] *nf* (*à effacer*) rubber (*BRIT*), eraser; **gommer** *vt* to rub out (*BRIT*), erase

gond [gɔ̃] *nm* hinge; **sortir de ses** ~**s** (*fig*) to fly off the handle

gondoler [gɔ̃dɔle]: **se** ~ *vi* to warp; to buckle

gonflé, e [gɔ̃fle] *adj* swollen; bloated

gonfler [gɔ̃fle] *vt* (*pneu, ballon*) to inflate, blow up; (*nombre, importance*) to inflate ♦ *vi* to swell (up); (*CULIN: pâte*) to rise

gonzesse [gɔ̃zɛs] (*fam*) *nf* chick, bird (*BRIT*)

goret [gɔʀɛ] *nm* piglet

gorge [gɔʀʒ(ə)] *nf* (*ANAT*) throat; (*poitrine*) breast

gorgé, e [gɔʀʒe] *adj*: ~ **de** filled with; (*eau*) saturated with; **gorgée** *nf* mouthful; sip; gulp

gorille [gɔʀij] *nm* gorilla; (*fam*) bodyguard

gosier [gozje] *nm* throat

gosse [gɔs] *nm/f* kid

goudron [gudʀɔ̃] *nm* tar; **goudronner** *vt* to tar(mac) (*BRIT*), asphalt (*US*)

gouffre [gufʀ(ə)] *nm* abyss, gulf

goujat [guʒa] *nm* boor

goulot [gulo] *nm* neck; **boire au** ~ to drink from the bottle

goulu, e [guly] *adj* greedy

gourd, e [guʀ, guʀd(ə)] *adj* numb (with cold)

gourde [guʀd(ə)] *nf* (*récipient*) flask; (*fam*) (clumsy) clot *ou* oaf ♦ *adj* oafish

gourdin [guʀdɛ̃] *nm* club, bludgeon
gourmand, e [guʀmɑ̃, -ɑ̃d] *adj* greedy;
gourmandise *nf* greed; (*bonbon*) sweet
gousse [gus] *nf*: ~ **d'ail** clove of garlic
goût [gu] *nm* taste; **de bon** ~ tasteful;
de mauvais ~ tasteless; **prendre** ~ **à** to
develop a taste *ou* a liking for
goûter [gute] *vt* (*essayer*) to taste; (*apprécier*) to enjoy ♦ *vi* to have (afternoon)
tea ♦ *nm* (afternoon) tea
goutte [gut] *nf* drop; (*MÉD*) gout; (*alcool*)
brandy; **tomber** ~ **à** ~ to drip
goutte-à-goutte [gutagut] *nm* (*MÉD*)
drip
gouttière [gutjɛʀ] *nf* gutter
gouvernail [guvɛʀnaj] *nm* rudder;
(*barre*) helm, tiller
gouvernante [guvɛʀnɑ̃t] *nf* governess
gouverne [guvɛʀn(ə)] *nf*: **pour sa** ~ for
his guidance
gouvernement [guvɛʀnəmɑ̃] *nm* government; **gouvernemental, e, aux** *adj*
government *cpd*; pro-government
gouverner [guvɛʀne] *vt* to govern
grabuge [gʀabyʒ] *nm* mayhem
grâce [gʀɑs] *nf* grace; favour; (*JUR*) pardon; ~s *nfpl* (*REL*) grace *sg*; **faire** ~ **à qn**
de qch to spare sb sth; **rendre** ~(**s**) **à** to
give thanks to; **demander** ~ to beg for
mercy; ~ **à** thanks to; **gracier** *vt* to pardon; **gracieux, euse** *adj* graceful
grade [gʀad] *nm* rank; **monter en** ~ to
be promoted
gradé [gʀade] *nm* officer
gradin [gʀadɛ̃] *nm* tier; step; ~s *nmpl*
(*de stade*) terracing *sg*
graduel, le [gʀadɥɛl] *adj* gradual; progressive
graduer [gʀadɥe] *vt* (*effort etc*) to increase gradually; (*règle, verre*) to graduate
grain [gʀɛ̃] *nm* (*gén*) grain; (*NAVIG*)
squall; ~ **de beauté** beauty spot; ~ **de
café** coffee bean; ~ **de poivre** peppercorn; ~ **de poussière** speck of dust; ~ **de
raisin** grape
graine [gʀɛn] *nf* seed
graissage [gʀesaʒ] *nm* lubrication,
greasing

graisse [gʀɛs] *nf* fat; (*lubrifiant*) grease;
graisser *vt* to lubricate, grease; (*tacher*)
to make greasy
grammaire [gʀamɛʀ] *nf* grammar;
grammatical, e, aux *adj* grammatical
gramme [gʀam] *nm* gramme
grand, e [gʀɑ̃, gʀɑ̃d] *adj* (*haut*) tall;
(*gros, vaste, large*) big, large; (*long*)
long; (*sens abstraits*) great ♦ *adv*: ~
ouvert wide open; **au** ~ **air** in the open
(air); **les** ~**s blessés** the severely injured; ~ **ensemble** housing scheme; ~
magasin department store; ~**e personne**
grown-up; ~**e surface** hypermarket; ~**es
écoles** *prestige* schools of university
level; ~**es lignes** (*RAIL*) main lines; ~**es
vacances** summer holidays; **grand-
chose** *nm/f inv*: **pas grand-chose** not
much; **Grande-Bretagne** *nf* (Great) Britain; **grandeur** *nf* (*dimension*) size; magnitude; (*fig*) greatness; **grandeur nature**
life-size; **grandir** *vi* to grow ♦ *vt*: **grandir qn** (*suj: vêtement, chaussure*) to
make sb look taller; ~**-mère** *nf* grandmother; ~**-messe** *nf* high mass; ~**-peine**:
à ~**-peine** *adv* with difficulty; ~**-père**
nm grandfather; ~**-route** *nf* main road;
~**s-parents** *nmpl* grandparents
grange [gʀɑ̃ʒ] *nf* barn
granit(e) [gʀanit] *nm* granite
graphique [gʀafik] *adj* graphic ♦ *nm*
graph
grappe [gʀap] *nf* cluster; ~ **de raisin**
bunch of grapes
grappiller [gʀapije] *vt* to glean
grappin [gʀapɛ̃] *nm* grapnel; **mettre le**
~ **sur** (*fig*) to get one's claws on
gras, se [gʀɑ, gʀɑs] *adj* (*viande, soupe*)
fatty; (*personne*) fat; (*surface, main*)
greasy; (*plaisanterie*) coarse; (*TYPO*) bold
♦ *nm* (*CULIN*) fat; **faire la** ~**se matinée**
to have a lie-in (*BRIT*), sleep late (*US*);
grassement *adv*: **grassement payé**
handsomely paid; **grassouillet, te** *adj*
podgy, plump
gratifiant, e [gʀatifjɑ̃, -ɑ̃t] *adj* gratifying, rewarding
gratifier [gʀatifje] *vt*: ~ **qn de** to favour
sb with; to reward sb with

gratiné, e [gʀatine] *adj (CULIN)* au gratin
gratis [gʀatis] *adv* free
gratitude [gʀatityd] *nf* gratitude
gratte-ciel [gʀatsjɛl] *nm inv* skyscraper
gratte-papier [gʀatpapje] *(péj) nm inv* penpusher
gratter [gʀate] *vt (frotter)* to scrape; *(enlever)* to scrape off; *(bras, bouton)* to scratch
gratuit, e [gʀatɥi, -ɥit] *adj (entrée, billet)* free; *(fig)* gratuitous
gravats [gʀava] *nmpl* rubble *sg*
grave [gʀav] *adj (maladie, accident)* serious, bad; *(sujet, problème)* serious, grave; *(air)* grave, solemn; *(voix, son)* deep, low-pitched; **gravement** *adv* seriously; gravely
graver [gʀave] *vt* to engrave
gravier [gʀavje] *nm* gravel *no pl*; **gravillons** *nmpl* loose gravel *sg*
gravir [gʀaviʀ] *vt* to climb (up)
gravité [gʀavite] *nf* seriousness; gravity
graviter [gʀavite] *vi* to revolve
gravure [gʀavyʀ] *nf* engraving; *(reproduction)* print; plate
gré [gʀe] *nm*: **à son ~** to his liking; ~s he pleases; **au ~ de** according to, following; **contre le ~ de qn** against sb's will; **de son (plein) ~** of one's own free will; **bon ~ mal ~** like it or not; **de ~ ou de force** whether one likes it or not; **savoir ~ à qn de qch** to be grateful to sb for sth
grec, grecque [gʀɛk] *adj* Greek; *(classique: vases etc)* Grecian ♦ *nm/f* Greek
Grèce [gʀɛs] *nf*: **la ~** Greece
gréement [gʀemɑ̃] *nm* rigging
greffer [gʀefe] *vt (BOT, MÉD: tissu)* to graft; *(MÉD: organe)* to transplant
greffier [gʀefje] *nm* clerk of the court
grêle [gʀɛl] *adj (very) thin* ♦ *nf* hail
grêlé, e [gʀele] *adj* pockmarked
grêler [gʀele] *vb impers*: **il grêle** it's hailing; **grêlon** [gʀelɔ̃] *nm* hailstone
grelot [gʀəlo] *nm* little bell
grelotter [gʀəlɔte] *vi* to shiver
grenade [gʀənad] *nf (explosive)* grenade; *(BOT)* pomegranate
grenat [gʀəna] *adj inv* dark red

grenier [gʀənje] *nm* attic; *(de ferme)* loft
grenouille [gʀənuj] *nf* frog
grès [gʀɛ] *nm* sandstone; *(poterie)* stoneware
grésiller [gʀezije] *vi* to sizzle; *(RADIO)* to crackle
grève [gʀɛv] *nf (d'ouvriers)* strike; *(plage)* shore; **se mettre en/faire ~** to go on/be on strike; **~ de la faim** hunger strike; **~ du zèle** work-to-rule *(BRIT)*, slowdown *(US)*
grever [gʀəve] *vt* to put a strain on
gréviste [gʀevist(ə)] *nm/f* striker
gribouiller [gʀibuje] *vt* to scribble, scrawl
grief [gʀijɛf] *nm* grievance; **faire ~ à qn de** to reproach sb for
grièvement [gʀijɛvmɑ̃] *adv* seriously
griffe [gʀif] *nf* claw; *(fig)* signature
griffer [gʀife] *vt* to scratch
griffonner [gʀifɔne] *vt* to scribble
grignoter [gʀiɲɔte] *vt* to nibble *ou* gnaw at
gril [gʀil] *nm* steak *ou* grill pan
grillade [gʀijad] *nf* grill
grillage [gʀijaʒ] *nm (treillis)* wire netting; wire fencing
grille [gʀij] *nf (clôture)* railings *pl*; *(portail)* (metal) gate; *(d'égout)* (metal) grate; *(fig)* grid
grille-pain [gʀijpɛ̃] *nm inv* toaster
griller [gʀije] *vt (aussi: faire ~: pain)* to toast; *(: viande)* to grill; *(fig: ampoule etc)* to burn out, blow
grillon [gʀijɔ̃] *nm* cricket
grimace [gʀimas] *nf* grimace; *(pour faire rire)*: **faire des ~s** to pull *ou* make faces
grimer [gʀime] *vt* to make up
grimper [gʀɛ̃pe] *vi, vt* to climb
grincer [gʀɛ̃se] *vi (porte, roue)* to grate; *(plancher)* to creak; **~ des dents** to grind one's teeth
grincheux, euse [gʀɛ̃ʃø, -øz] *adj* grumpy
grippe [gʀip] *nf* flu, influenza; **grippé, e** *adj*: **être grippé** to have flu
gris, e [gʀi, gʀiz] *adj* grey; *(ivre)* tipsy; **faire ~e mine** to pull a miserable *ou*

wry face

grisaille [gʀizaj] *nf* greyness, dullness

griser [gʀize] *vt* to intoxicate

grisonner [gʀizɔne] *vi* to be going grey

grisou [gʀizu] *nm* firedamp

grive [gʀiv] *nf* thrush

grivois, e [gʀivwa, -waz] *adj* saucy

Groenland [gʀɔɛnlãd] *nm* Greenland

grogner [gʀɔɲe] *vi* to growl; (*fig*) to grumble

groin [gʀwɛ̃] *nm* snout

grommeler [gʀɔmle] *vi* to mutter to o.s.

gronder [gʀɔ̃de] *vi* to rumble; (*fig: révolte*) to be brewing ♦ *vt* to scold

gros, se [gʀo, gʀos] *adj* big, large; (*obèse*) fat; (*travaux, dégâts*) extensive; (*large: trait, fil*) thick, heavy ♦ *adv*: **risquer/gagner** ~ to risk/win a lot ♦ *nm* (*COMM*): **le** ~ the wholesale business; **prix de** ~ wholesale price; **par** ~ **temps/grosse mer** in rough weather/heavy seas; **le** ~ **de** the main body of, the bulk of; **en** ~ roughly; (*COMM*) wholesale; ~ **lot** jackpot; ~ **mot** coarse word; ~ **œuvre** *nm* (*CONSTR*) shell (of building); ~ **plan** (*PHOTO*) close-up; ~ **sel** cooking salt; ~**se caisse** big drum

groseille [gʀozɛj] *nf*: ~ (**rouge**)/(**blanche**) red/white currant; ~ **à maquereau** gooseberry

grosse [gʀos] *adj voir* **gros**

grossesse [gʀosɛs] *nf* pregnancy

grosseur [gʀosœʀ] *nf* size; fatness; (*tumeur*) lump

grossier, ière [gʀosje, -ɛʀ] *adj* coarse; (*travail*) rough, crude; (*évident: erreur*) gross

grossir [gʀosiʀ] *vi* (*personne*) to put on weight; (*fig*) to grow, get bigger; (*rivière*) to swell ♦ *vt* to increase; to exaggerate; (*au microscope*) to magnify; (*suj: vêtement*): ~ **qn** to make sb look fatter

grossiste [gʀosist(ə)] *nm/f* wholesaler

grosso modo [gʀɔsɔmɔdo] *adv* roughly

grotte [gʀɔt] *nf* cave

grouiller [gʀuje] *vi* to mill about; to swarm about; ~ **de** to be swarming with

groupe [gʀup] *nm* group; **le** ~ **des 7** Group of 7; ~ **sanguin** *nm* blood group;

groupement [gʀupmã] *nm* grouping; group

grouper [gʀupe] *vt* to group; **se** ~ *vi* to get together

grue [gʀy] *nf* crane

grumeaux [gʀymo] *nmpl* lumps

gué [ge] *nm* ford; **passer à** ~ to ford

guenilles [gənij] *nfpl* rags

guenon [gənɔ̃] *nf* female monkey

guépard [gepaʀ] *nm* cheetah

guêpe [gɛp] *nf* wasp

guêpier [gepje] *nm* (*fig*) trap

guère [gɛʀ] *adv* (*avec adjectif, adverbe*): **ne ... ~** hardly; (*avec verbe*): **ne ... ~** *tournure négative* +much; hardly ever; *tournure négative* +(very) long; **il n'y a** ~ **que/de** there's hardly anybody (*ou* anything) but/hardly any

guéridon [geʀidɔ̃] *nm* pedestal table

guérilla [geʀija] *nf* guerrilla warfare

guérir [geʀiʀ] *vt* (*personne, maladie*) to cure; (*membre, plaie*) to heal ♦ *vi* to recover, be cured; to heal; **guérison** *nf* curing; healing; recovery

guérite [geʀit] *nf* sentry box

guerre [gɛʀ] *nf* war; (*méthode*): ~ **atomique** atomic warfare *no pl*; **en** ~ at war; **faire la** ~ **à** to wage war against; **de** ~ **lasse** finally; ~ **d'usure** war of attrition; **guerrier, ière** *adj* warlike ♦ *nm/f* warrior

guet [gɛ] *nm*: **faire le** ~ to be on the watch *ou* look-out

guet-apens [gɛtapã] *nm* ambush

guetter [gete] *vt* (*épier*) to watch (intently); (*attendre*) to watch (out) for; to be lying in wait for

gueule [gœl] *nf* mouth; (*fam*) face; mouth; **ta** ~! (*fam*) shut up!; ~ **de bois** (*fam*) hangover

gueuler [gœle] (*fam*) *vi* to bawl

gui [gi] *nm* mistletoe

guichet [giʃɛ] *nm* (*de bureau, banque*) counter, window; (*d'une porte*) wicket, hatch; **les** ~**s** (*à la gare, au théâtre*) the ticket office *sg*

guide [gid] *nm* guide

guider [gide] *vt* to guide

guidon [gidɔ̃] *nm* handlebars *pl*

guignol [giɲɔl] *nm* ≈ Punch and Judy show; (*fig*) clown

guillemets [gijme] *nmpl*: **entre** ~ in inverted commas

guillotiner [gijɔtine] *vt* to guillotine

guindé, e [gɛ̃de] *adj* stiff, starchy

guirlande [girlɑ̃d] *nf* garland; (*de papier*) paper chain

guise [giz] *nf*: **à votre** ~ as you wish *ou* please; **en** ~ **de** by way of

guitare [gitar] *nf* guitar

gymnase [ʒimnɑz] *nm* gym(nasium)

gymnastique [ʒimnastik] *nf* gymnastics *sg*; (*au réveil etc*) keep-fit exercises *pl*

gynécologie [ʒinekɔlɔʒi] *nf* gynaecology; **gynécologue** *nm/f* gynaecologist

H h

habile [abil] *adj* skilful; (*malin*) clever; **habileté** *nf* skill, skilfulness; cleverness

habilité, e [abilite] *adj*: ~ **à faire** entitled to do, empowered to do

habillé, e [abije] *adj* dressed; (*chic*) dressy; (*TECH*): ~ **de** covered with; encased in

habillement [abijmɑ̃] *nm* clothes *pl*

habiller [abije] *vt* to dress; (*fournir en vêtements*) to clothe; **s'**~ *vi* to dress (o.s.); (*se déguiser, mettre des vêtements chic*) to dress up

habit [abi] *nm* outfit; ~**s** *nmpl* (*vêtements*) clothes; ~ (**de soirée**) tails *pl*; evening dress

habitant, e [abitɑ̃, -ɑ̃t] *nm/f* inhabitant; (*d'une maison*) occupant

habitation [abitasjɔ̃] *nf* living; residence, home; house; ~**s à loyer modéré** low-rent housing *sg*

habiter [abite] *vt* to live in; (*suj: sentiment*) to dwell in ♦ *vi*: ~ **à/dans** to live in *ou* at/in

habitude [abityd] *nf* habit; **avoir l'**~ **de faire** to be in the habit of doing; (*expérience*) to be used to doing; **d'**~ usually; **comme d'**~ as usual

habitué, e [abitye] *nm/f* regular visitor; regular (customer)

habituel, le [abitɥɛl] *adj* usual

habituer [abitɥe] *vt*: ~ **qn à** to get sb used to; **s'**~ **à** to get used to

'hache ['aʃ] *nf* axe

'hacher ['aʃe] *vt* (*viande*) to mince; (*persil*) to chop

'hachis ['aʃi] *nm* mince *no pl*

'hachoir ['aʃwar] *nm* chopper; (*meat*) mincer; chopping board

'hagard, e ['agar, -ard(ə)] *adj* wild, distraught

'haie ['ɛ] *nf* hedge; (*SPORT*) hurdle; (*fig: rang*) line, row

'haillons ['ajɔ̃] *nmpl* rags

'haine ['ɛn] *nf* hatred

'haïr ['air] *vt* to detest, hate

'hâlé, e ['ɑle] *adj* (sun)tanned, sunburnt

haleine [alɛn] *nf* breath; **hors d'**~ out of breath; **tenir en** ~ to hold spellbound; to keep in suspense; **de longue** ~ long-term

'haler ['ale] *vt* to haul in; to tow

'haleter ['alte] *vi* to pant

'hall ['ol] *nm* hall

'halle ['al] *nf* (covered) market; ~**s** *nfpl* (*d'une grande ville*) central food market *sg*

hallucinant, e [alysinɑ̃, -ɑ̃t] *adj* staggering

hallucination [alysinasjɔ̃] *nf* hallucination

'halte ['alt(ə)] *nf* stop, break; stopping place; (*RAIL*) halt ♦ *excl* stop!; **faire** ~ to stop

haltère [altɛr] *nm* dumbbell, barbell; ~**s** *nmpl*: (**poids et**) ~**s** (*activité*) weight lifting *sg*

'hamac ['amak] *nm* hammock

'hamburger ['ɑburgœr] *nm* hamburger

'hameau, x ['amo] *nm* hamlet

hameçon [amsɔ̃] *nm* (fish) hook

'hanche ['ɑ̃ʃ] *nf* hip

handicapé, e ['ɑ̃dikape] *nm/f* physically (*ou* mentally) handicapped person; ~ **moteur** spastic

'hangar ['ɑ̃gar] *nm* shed; (*AVIAT*) hangar

'hanneton ['antɔ̃] *nm* cockchafer

'hanter ['ɑ̃te] *vt* to haunt

'hantise ['ɑ̃tiz] *nf* obsessive fear

'happer ['ape] *vt* to snatch; (*suj: train*

etc) to hit

'haras ['aʀa] *nm* stud farm

'harassant, e ['aʀasɑ̃, -ɑ̃t] *adj* exhausting

'harcèlement ['aʀsɛlmɑ̃] *nm* harassment; ~ **sexuel** sexual harassment

'harceler ['aʀsəle] *vt* (MIL, CHASSE) to harass, harry; (*importuner*) to plague

'hardi, e ['aʀdi] *adj* bold, daring

'hareng ['aʀɑ̃] *nm* herring

'hargne ['aʀɲ(ə)] *nf* aggressiveness

'haricot ['aʀiko] *nm* bean; ~ **blanc** haricot bean; ~ **vert** green bean

harmonica [aʀmɔnika] *nm* mouth organ

harmonie [aʀmɔni] *nf* harmony

'harnacher ['aʀnaʃe] *vt* to harness

'harnais ['aʀnɛ] *nm* harness

'harpe ['aʀp(ə)] *nf* harp

'harponner ['aʀpɔne] *vt* to harpoon; (*fam*) to collar

'hasard ['azaʀ] *nm*: **le ~** chance, fate; **un ~** a coincidence; a stroke of luck; **au ~** aimlessly; at random; haphazardly; **par ~** by chance; **à tout ~** just in case; on the off chance (BRIT); **'hasarder** ['azaʀde] *vt* (*mot*) to venture; (*fortune*) to risk

'hâte ['ɑt] *nf* haste; **à la ~** hurriedly, hastily; **en ~** posthaste, with all possible speed; **avoir ~ de** to be eager *ou* anxious to; **hâter** *vt* to hasten; **se hâter** *vi* to hurry

'hâtif, ive ['ɑtif, -iv] *adj* hurried; hasty; (*légume*) early

'hausse ['os] *nf* rise, increase

'hausser ['ose] *vt* to raise; ~ **les épaules** to shrug (one's shoulders)

'haut, e ['o, 'ot] *adj* high; (*grand*) tall; (*son, voix*) high(-pitched) ♦ *adv* high ♦ *nm* top (part); **de 3 m de ~** 3 m high, 3 m 'in height; **des ~s et des bas** ups and downs; **en ~ lieu** in high places; **à ~e voix, (tout)** ~ aloud, out loud; **du ~ de** from the top of; **de ~ en bas** from top to bottom; downwards; **plus ~** higher up, further up; (*dans un texte*) above; (*parler*) louder; **en ~** up above; at (*ou* to) the top; (*dans une maison*) upstairs; **en ~ de** at the top of

'hautain, e ['otɛ̃, -ɛn] *adj* haughty

'hautbois ['obwa] *nm* oboe

'haut-de-forme ['odfɔʀm(ə)] *nm* top hat

'hauteur ['otœʀ] *nf* height; (*fig*) loftiness; haughtiness; **à la ~ de** (*sur la même ligne*) level with; by; (*fig*) equal to; **à la ~** up to it

'haut-fond ['ofɔ̃] *nm* shallow, shoal

'haut-fourneau ['ofuʀno] *nm* blast *ou* smelting furnace

'haut-le-cœur ['olkœʀ] *nm inv* retch, heave

'haut-parleur ['opaʀlœʀ] *nm* (loud)speaker

'havre ['avʀ(ə)] *nm* haven

'Haye ['ɛ] *n*: **la ~** the Hague

hebdo [ɛbdɔ] (*fam*) *nm* weekly

hebdomadaire [ɛbdɔmadɛʀ] *adj, nm* weekly

héberger [ebɛʀʒe] *vt* to accommodate, lodge; (*réfugiés*) to take in

hébété, e [ebete] *adj* dazed

hébreu, x [ebʀø] *adj m, nm* Hebrew

hécatombe [ekatɔ̃b] *nf* slaughter

hectare [ɛktaʀ] *nm* hectare

'hein ['ɛ̃] *excl* eh?

'hélas ['elas] *excl* alas! ♦ *adv* unfortunately

'héler ['ele] *vt* to hail

hélice [elis] *nf* propeller

hélicoptère [elikɔptɛʀ] *nm* helicopter

helvétique [ɛlvetik] *adj* Swiss

hémicycle [emisikl(ə)] *nm* semicircle; (POL): **l'~** ≈ the benches (of the Commons) (BRIT), ≈ the floor (of the House of Representatives) (US)

hémorragie [emɔʀaʒi] *nf* bleeding *no pl*, haemorrhage

hémorroïdes [emɔʀɔid] *nfpl* piles, haemorrhoids

'hennir ['eniʀ] *vi* to neigh, whinny

herbe [ɛʀb(ə)] *nf* grass; (CULIN, MÉD) herb; **en ~** unripe; (*fig*) budding; **herbicide** *nm* weed-killer; **herboriste** *nm/f* herbalist

'hère ['ɛʀ] *nm*: **pauvre ~** poor wretch

héréditaire [eʀeditɛʀ] *adj* hereditary

'hérisser ['eʀise] *vt*: ~ **qn** (*fig*) to ruffle sb; **se ~** *vi* to bristle, bristle up

'hérisson ['eʀisɔ̃] *nm* hedgehog

héritage [eritaʒ] *nm* inheritance; (*fig*) heritage; legacy

hériter [erite] *vi*: ~ **de qch (de qn)** to inherit sth (from sb); **héritier, ière** *nm/f* heir(ess)

hermétique [ermetik] *adj* airtight; watertight; (*fig*) abstruse; impenetrable

hermine [ermin] *nf* ermine

'**hernie** [ɛrni] *nf* hernia

héroïne [erɔin] *nf* heroine; (*drogue*) heroin

'**héron** [erɔ̃] *nm* heron

'**héros** [ero] *nm* hero

hésitation [ezitasjɔ̃] *nf* hesitation

hésiter [ezite] *vi*: ~ (**à faire**) to hesitate (to do)

hétéroclite [eterɔklit] *adj* heterogeneous; (*objets*) sundry

'**hêtre** [ɛtr(ə)] *nm* beech

heure [œr] *nf* hour; (*SCOL*) period; (*moment*) time; **c'est l'~** it's time; **quelle ~ est-il?** what time is it?; **2 ~s (du matin)** 2 o'clock (in the morning); **être à l'~** to be on time; (*montre*) to be right; **mettre à l'~** to set right; **à toute ~** at any time; **24 ~s sur 24** round the clock, 24 hours a day; **à l'~ qu'il est** at this time (of day); by now; **sur l'~** at once; ~ **de pointe** rush hour; ~**s supplémentaires** overtime *sg*

heureusement [œrøzmɑ̃] *adv* (*par bonheur*) fortunately, luckily

heureux, euse [œrø, -øz] *adj* happy; (*chanceux*) lucky, fortunate; (*judicieux*) felicitous, fortunate

'**heurt** [œr] *nm* (*choc*) collision; ~**s** *nmpl* (*fig*) clashes

'**heurter** [œrte] *vt* (*mur*) to strike, hit; (*personne*) to collide with; (*fig*) to go against, upset; **se ~ à** *vt* to come up against; '**heurtoir** *nm* door knocker

hexagone [ɛgzagɔn] *nm* hexagon; (*la France*) France (*because of its shape*)

hiberner [ibɛrne] *vi* to hibernate

'**hibou, x** [ibu] *nm* owl

'**hideux, euse** [idø, -øz] *adj* hideous

hier [jɛr] *adv* yesterday; **toute la journée d'~** all day yesterday; **toute la matinée d'~** all yesterday morning

'**hiérarchie** [ˈjerarʃi] *nf* hierarchy

hilare [ilar] *adj* mirthful

hippique [ipik] *adj* equestrian, horse *cpd*

hippodrome [ipɔdrom] *nm* racecourse

hippopotame [ipɔpɔtam] *nm* hippopotamus

hirondelle [irɔ̃dɛl] *nf* swallow

hirsute [irsyt] *adj* hairy; shaggy; tousled

'**hisser** [ˈise] *vt* to hoist, haul up

histoire [istwar] *nf* (*science, événements*) history; (*anecdote, récit, mensonge*) story; (*affaire*) business *no pl*; ~**s** *nfpl* (*chichis*) fuss *no pl*; (*ennuis*) trouble *sg*; **historique** *adj* historical; (*important*) historic

hiver [ivɛr] *nm* winter; **hivernal, e, aux** *adj* winter *cpd*; wintry; **hiverner** *vi* to winter

HLM *sigle m/f* = **habitation(s) à loyer modéré**

'**hobby** [ˈɔbi] *nm* hobby

'**hocher** [ˈɔʃe] *vt*: ~ **la tête** to nod; (*signe négatif ou dubitatif*) to shake one's head

'**hochet** [ˈɔʃɛ] *nm* rattle

'**hockey** [ˈɔkɛ] *nm*: ~ (**sur glace/gazon**) (ice/field) hockey

'**hold-up** [ˈɔldœp] *nm inv* hold-up

'**hollandais, e** [ˈɔlɑ̃dɛ, -ez] *adj* Dutch ♦ *nm* (*LING*) Dutch ♦ *nm/f*: **H~, e** Dutchman(woman); **les H~** the Dutch

'**Hollande** [ˈɔlɑ̃d] *nf*: **la ~** Holland

'**homard** [ˈɔmar] *nm* lobster

homéopathique [ɔmeɔpatik] *adj* homoeopathic

homicide [ɔmisid] *nm* murder; ~ **involontaire** manslaughter

hommage [ɔmaʒ] *nm* tribute; ~**s** *nmpl*: **présenter ses ~s** to pay one's respects; **rendre ~ à** to pay tribute *ou* homage to

homme [ɔm] *nm* man; ~ **d'affaires** businessman; ~ **d'État** statesman; ~ **de main** hired man; ~ **de paille** stooge; ~**-grenouille** *nm* frogman

homo: ~**gène** *adj* homogeneous; ~**logue** *nm/f* counterpart, opposite number; ~**logué, e** *adj* (*SPORT*) officially recognized, ratified; (*tarif*) authorized; ~**nyme** *nm*

(*LING*) homonym; (*d'une personne*) namesake; **~sexuel, le** *adj* homosexual

Hongrie [ˈɔ̃gʀi] *nf*: **la ~** Hungary; **'hongrois, e** *adj*, *nm/f* Hungarian

honnête [ɔnɛt] *adj* (*intègre*) honest; (*juste, satisfaisant*) fair; **~ment** *adv* honestly; **~té** *nf* honesty

honneur [ɔnœʀ] *nm* honour; (*mérite*) credit; **en l'~ de** in honour of; (*événement*) on the occasion of; **faire ~ à** (*engagements*) to honour; (*famille*) to be a credit to; (*fig: repas etc*) to do justice to

honorable [ɔnɔʀabl(ə)] *adj* worthy, honourable; (*suffisant*) decent

honoraire [ɔnɔʀɛʀ] *adj* honorary; **professeur ~** professor emeritus; **honoraires** *nmpl* fees *pl*

honorer [ɔnɔʀe] *vt* to honour; (*estimer*) to hold in high regard; (*faire honneur à*) to do credit to; **s'~ de** *vt* to pride o.s. upon; **honorifique** *adj* honorary

honte [ˈɔ̃t] *nf* shame; **avoir ~ de** to be ashamed of; **faire ~ à qn** to make sb (feel) ashamed; **'honteux, euse** *adj* ashamed; (*conduite, acte*) shameful, disgraceful

hôpital, aux [ɔpital, -o] *nm* hospital

hoquet [ˈɔkɛ] *nm*: **avoir le hoquet** to have (the) hiccoughs; **'hoqueter** *vi* to hiccough

horaire [ɔʀɛʀ] *adj* hourly ♦ *nm* timetable, schedule; **~s** *nmpl* (*d'employé*) hours; **~ souple** flexitime

horizon [ɔʀizɔ̃] *nm* horizon; (*paysage*) landscape, view

horizontal, e, aux [ɔʀizɔ̃tal, -o] *adj* horizontal

horloge [ɔʀlɔʒ] *nf* clock; **horloger, ère** *nm/f* watchmaker; clockmaker; **horlogerie** *nf* watch-making; watchmaker's (shop); clockmaker's (shop)

hormis [ˈɔʀmi] *prép* save

horoscope [ɔʀɔskɔp] *nm* horoscope

horreur [ɔʀœʀ] *nf* horror; **avoir ~ de** to loathe *ou* detest; **horrible** *adj* horrible

horripiler [ɔʀipile] *vt* to exasperate

hors [ˈɔʀ] *prép* except (for); **~ de** out of; **~ pair** outstanding; **~ de propos** inopportune; **être ~ de soi** to be beside o.s.;

~ d'usage out of service; **~-bord** *nm inv* speedboat (with outboard motor); **~-concours** *adj* ineligible to compete; **~-d'œuvre** *nm inv* hors d'œuvre; **~-jeu** *nm inv* offside; **~-la-loi** *nm inv* outlaw; **~-taxe** *adj* (*boutique, articles*) duty-free

hospice [ɔspis] *nm* (*de vieillards*) home

hospitalier, ière [ɔspitalje, -jɛʀ] *adj* (*accueillant*) hospitable; (*MÉD: service, centre*) hospital *cpd*

hospitalité [ɔspitalite] *nf* hospitality

hostie [ɔsti] *nf* host (*REL*)

hostile [ɔstil] *adj* hostile; **hostilité** *nf* hostility

hôte [ot] *nm* (*maître de maison*) host; (*invité*) guest

hôtel [otɛl] *nm* hotel; **aller à l'~** to stay in a hotel; **~ de ville** town hall; **~ (particulier)** (*private*) mansion; **hôtelier, ière** *adj* hotel *cpd* ♦ *nm/f* hotelier; **hôtellerie** *nf* hotel business; (*auberge*) inn

hôtesse [otɛs] *nf* hostess; **~ de l'air** air stewardess

hotte [ˈɔt] *nf* (*panier*) basket (*carried on the back*); (*de cheminée*) hood; **~ aspirante** cooker hood

houblon [ˈublɔ̃] *nm* (*BOT*) hop; (*pour la bière*) hops *pl*

houille [ˈuj] *nf* coal; **~ blanche** hydroelectric power

houle [ˈul] *nf* swell

houlette [ˈulɛt] *nf*: **sous la ~ de** under the guidance of

houleux, euse [ˈulø, -øz] *adj* heavy, swelling; (*fig*) stormy, turbulent

houspiller [ˈuspije] *vt* to scold

housse [ˈus] *nf* cover; dust cover; loose *ou* stretch cover

houx [ˈu] *nm* holly

hublot [ˈyblo] *nm* porthole

huche [ˈyʃ] *nf*: **~ à pain** bread bin

huer [ˈɥe] *vt* to boo

huile [ɥil] *nf* oil; **huiler** *vt* to oil; **huileux, euse** *adj* oily

huis [ɥi] *nm*: **à ~ clos** in camera

huissier [ɥisje] *nm* usher; (*JUR*) ≈ bailiff

'huit [ˈɥit] *num* eight; **samedi en ~ a**

week on Saturday; **'huitaine** *nf*: **une huitaine (de jours)** a week or so; **'huitième** *num* eighth

huître [ųitʀ(ə)] *nf* oyster

humain, e [ymɛ̃, -ɛn] *adj* human; (*compatissant*) humane ♦ *nm* human (being); **humanité** *nf* humanity

humble [œ̃bl(ə)] *adj* humble

humecter [ymɛkte] *vt* to dampen

'humer ['yme] *vt* to smell; to inhale

humeur [ymœʀ] *nf* mood; (*tempérament*) temper; (*irritation*) bad temper; **de bonne/mauvaise ~** in a good/bad mood

humide [ymid] *adj* damp; (*main, yeux*) moist; (*climat, chaleur*) humid; (*saison, route*) wet

humilier [ymilje] *vt* to humiliate

humilité [ymilite] *nf* humility, humbleness

humoristique [ymɔʀistik] *adj* humorous; humoristic

humour [ymuʀ] *nm* humour; **avoir de l'~** to have a sense of humour; **~ noir** sick humour

'hurlement ['yʀləmɑ̃] *nm* howling *no pl*, howl, yelling *no pl*, yell

'hurler ['yʀle] *vi* to howl, yell

hurluberlu [yʀlybɛʀly] (*péj*) *nm* crank

'hutte ['yt] *nf* hut

hydratant, e [idʀatɑ̃, -ɑ̃t] *adj* (*crème*) moisturizing

hydrate [idʀat] *nm*: **~s de carbone** carbohydrates

hydraulique [idʀolik] *adj* hydraulic

hydravion [idʀavjɔ̃] *nm* seaplane

hydrogène [idʀɔʒɛn] *nm* hydrogen

hydroglisseur [idʀɔglisœʀ] *nm* hydroplane

hygiénique [iʒjenik] *adj* hygienic

hymne [imn(ə)] *nm* hymn; **~ national** national anthem

hypermarché [ipɛʀmaʀʃe] *nm* hypermarket

hypermétrope [ipɛʀmetʀɔp] *adj* longsighted

hypnotiser [ipnɔtize] *vt* to hypnotize

hypocrite [ipɔkʀit] *adj* hypocritical

hypothèque [ipɔtɛk] *nf* mortgage

hypothèse [ipɔtɛz] *nf* hypothesis

hystérique [isteʀik] *adj* hysterical

I i

iceberg [isbɛʀg] *nm* iceberg

ici [isi] *adv* here; **jusqu'~** as far as this; until now; **d'~ là** by then; in the meantime; **d'~ peu** before long

idéal, e, aux [ideal, -o] *adj* ideal ♦ *nm* ideal; ideals *pl*

idée [ide] *nf* idea; **avoir dans l'~ que** to have an idea that; **~s noires** black *ou* dark thoughts

identifier [idɑ̃tifje] *vt* to identify; **s'~ à** (*héros etc*) to identify with

identique [idɑ̃tik] *adj*: **~ (à)** identical (to)

identité [idɑ̃tite] *nf* identity

idiot, e [idjo, idjɔt] *adj* idiotic ♦ *nm/f* idiot

idole [idɔl] *nf* idol

if [if] *nm* yew

ignare [iɲaʀ] *adj* ignorant

ignoble [iɲɔbl(ə)] *adj* vile

ignorant, e [iɲɔʀɑ̃, -ɑ̃t] *adj* ignorant

ignorer [iɲɔʀe] *vt* (*ne pas connaître*) not to know, be unaware *ou* ignorant of; (*être sans expérience de*: *plaisir, guerre etc*) not to know about, have no experience of; (*bouder*: *personne*) to ignore

il [il] *pron* he; (*animal, chose, en tournure impersonnelle*) it; **~s** they; *voir aussi* **avoir**

île [il] *nf* island; **les ~s anglonormandes** the Channel Islands; **les ~s Britanniques** the British Isles

illégal, e, aux [ilegal, -o] *adj* illegal

illégitime [ileʒitim] *adj* illegitimate

illettré, e [iletʀe] *adj, nm/f* illiterate

illimité, e [ilimite] *adj* unlimited

illisible [ilizibl(ə)] *adj* illegible; (*roman*) unreadable

illumination [ilyminasjɔ̃] *nf* illumination, floodlighting; (*idée*) flash of inspiration

illuminer [ilymine] *vt* to light up; (*monument, rue*: *pour une fête*) to illuminate, floodlight

illusion [ilyzjɔ̃] *nf* illusion; **se faire des ~s** to delude o.s.; **faire ~** to delude *ou* fool people; **illusionniste** *nm/f* conjuror

illustration [ilystʀasjɔ̃] *nf* illustration

illustre [ilystʀ(ə)] *adj* illustrious

illustré, e [ilystʀe] *adj* illustrated ♦ *nm* illustrated magazine; comic

illustrer [ilystʀe] *vt* to illustrate; **s'~** to become famous, win fame

îlot [ilo] *nm* small island, islet; *(de maisons)* block

ils [il] *pron voir* **il**

image [imaʒ] *nf (gén)* picture; *(comparaison, ressemblance, OPTIQUE)* image; **~ de marque** brand image; *(fig)* public image

imagination [imaʒinasjɔ̃] *nf* imagination; *(chimère)* fancy; **avoir de l'~** to be imaginative

imaginer [imaʒine] *vt* to imagine; *(inventer: expédient)* to devise, think up; **s'~** *vt (se figurer: scène etc)* to imagine, picture; **s'~ que** to imagine that

imbécile [ɛ̃besil] *adj* idiotic ♦ *nm/f* idiot

imberbe [ɛ̃bɛʀb(ə)] *adj* beardless

imbiber [ɛ̃bibe] *vt* to moisten, wet; **s'~ de** to become saturated with

imbu, e [ɛ̃by] *adj*: **~ de** full of

imitateur, trice [imitatœʀ, -tʀis] *nm/f (gén)* imitator; *(MUSIC-HALL)* impersonator

imitation [imitasjɔ̃] *nf* imitation; *(sketch)* imitation, impression; impersonation

imiter [imite] *vt* to imitate; *(contrefaire)* to forge; *(ressembler à)* to look like

immaculé, e [imakyle] *adj* spotless; immaculate

immatriculation [imatʀikylasjɔ̃] *nf* registration

immatriculer [imatʀikyle] *vt* to register; **faire/se faire ~** to register

immédiat, e [imedja, -at] *adj* immediate ♦ *nm*: **dans l'~** for the time being; **immédiatement** *adv* immediately

immense [imɑ̃s] *adj* immense

immerger [imɛʀʒe] *vt* to immerse, submerge

immeuble [imœbl(ə)] *nm* building; **~ lo-**

catif block of rented flats *(BRIT)*, rental building *(US)*

immigration [imigʀasjɔ̃] *nf* immigration

immigré, e [imigʀe] *nm/f* immigrant

imminent, e [iminɑ̃, -ɑ̃t] *adj* imminent

immiscer [imise]: **s'~** *vi* to interfere in *ou* with

immobile [imɔbil] *adj* still, motionless; *(fig)* unchanging

immobilier, ière [imɔbilje, -jɛʀ] *adj* property *cpd* ♦ *nm*: **l'~** the property business

immobiliser [imɔbilize] *vt (gén)* to immobilize; *(circulation, véhicule, affaires)* to bring to a standstill; **s'~** *(personne)* to stand still; *(machine, véhicule)* to come to a halt

immonde [imɔ̃d] *adj* foul

immondices [imɔ̃dis] *nmpl* refuse *sg*; filth *sg*

immoral, e, aux [imɔʀal, -o] *adj* immoral

immuable [imɥabl(ə)] *adj* immutable; unchanging

immunisé, e [imynize] *adj*: **~ contre** immune to

immunité [imynite] *nf* immunity

impact [ɛ̃pakt] *nm* impact

impair, e [ɛ̃pɛʀ] *adj* odd ♦ *nm* faux pas, blunder

impardonnable [ɛ̃paʀdɔnabl(ə)] *adj* unpardonable, unforgiving

imparfait, e [ɛ̃paʀfɛ, -ɛt] *adj* imperfect

impartial, e, aux [ɛ̃paʀsjal, -o] *adj* impartial, unbiased

impartir [ɛ̃paʀtiʀ] *vt* to assign; to bestow

impasse [ɛ̃pas] *nf* dead-end, cul-de-sac; *(fig)* deadlock

impassible [ɛ̃pasibl(ə)] *adj* impassive

impatience [ɛ̃pasjɑ̃s] *nf* impatience

impatient, e [ɛ̃pasjɑ̃, -ɑ̃t] *adj* impatient

impayable [ɛ̃pejabl(ə)] *adj (drôle)* priceless

impeccable [ɛ̃pekabl(ə)] *adj* faultless, impeccable; spotlessly clean; impeccably dressed; *(fam)* smashing

impensable [ɛ̃pɑ̃sabl(ə)] *adj* unthinkable; unbelievable

impératif, ive [ɛ̃peʀatif, -iv] *adj* impera-

tive ♦ *nm* (*LING*) imperative; **~s** *nmpl*
(*exigences*) requirements; demands

impératrice [ɛpeʀatʀis] *nf* empress

impérial, e, aux [ɛpeʀjal, -o] *adj* imperial; **impériale** *nf* top deck

impérieux, euse [ɛpeʀjø, -øz] *adj* (*caractère, ton*) imperious; (*obligation, besoin*) pressing, urgent

impérissable [ɛpeʀisabl(ə)] *adj* undying;
imperishable

imperméable [ɛpɛʀmeabl(ə)] *adj* waterproof; (*GÉO*) impermeable; (*fig*): **~ à** impervious à ♦ *nm* raincoat

impertinent, e [ɛpɛʀtinɑ̃, -ɑ̃t] *adj* impertinent

impétueux, euse [ɛpetɥø, -øz] *adj*
fiery

impie [ɛpi] *adj* impious, ungodly

impitoyable [ɛpitwajabl(ə)] *adj* pitiless,
merciless

implanter [ɛplɑ̃te] *vt* (*usine, industrie,
usage*) to establish; (*colons etc*) to settle;
(*idée, préjugé*) to implant

impliquer [ɛplike] *vt* to imply; **~ qn
(dans)** to implicate sb (in)

impoli, e [ɛpɔli] *adj* impolite, rude

importance [ɛpɔʀtɑ̃s] *nf* importance;
sans ~ unimportant

important, e [ɛpɔʀtɑ̃, -ɑ̃t] *adj* important; (*en quantité*) considerable, sizeable; extensive; (*péj: airs, ton*) self-
important ♦ *nm*: **l'~** the important thing

importateur, trice [ɛpɔʀtatœʀ, -tʀis]
nm/f importer

importation [ɛpɔʀtasjɔ̃] *nf* importation;
introduction; (*produit*) import

importer [ɛpɔʀte] *vt* (*COMM*) to import;
(*maladies, plantes*) to introduce ♦ *vi*
(*être important*) to matter; **il importe
qu'il fasse** it is important that he
should do; **peu m'importe** I don't mind;
I don't care; **peu importe (que)** it
doesn't matter (if); *voir aussi* **n'importe**

importun, e [ɛpɔʀtœ̃, -yn] *adj* irksome,
importunate; (*arrivée, visite*) inopportune, ill-timed ♦ *nm* intruder; **importuner** *vt* to bother

imposable [ɛpozabl(e)] *adj* taxable

imposant, e [ɛpozɑ̃, -ɑ̃t] *adj* imposing

imposer [ɛpoze] *vt* (*taxer*) to tax; **s'~**
(*être nécessaire*) to be imperative; (*montrer sa proéminence*) to stand out,
emerge; (*artiste: se faire connaître*) to
win recognition; **~ qch à qn** to impose
sth on sb; **en ~ à** to impress; **imposition**
[ɛpozisjɔ̃] *nf* (*ADMIN*) taxation

impossible [ɛpɔsibl(ə)] *adj* impossible;
il m'est ~ de le faire it is impossible
for me to do it, I can't possibly do it;
faire l'~ to do one's utmost

impôt [ɛpo] *nm* tax; (*taxes*) taxation;
taxes *pl*; **~s** *nmpl* (*contributions*) (income) tax *sg*; **payer 1 000 F d'~s** to pay
1,000 F in tax; **~ foncier** land tax; **~ sur
le chiffre d'affaires** corporation (*BRIT*)
ou corporate (*US*) tax; **~ sur le revenu**
income tax

impotent, e [ɛpɔtɑ̃, -ɑ̃t] *adj* disabled

impraticable [ɛpʀatikabl(ə)] *adj* (*projet*)
impracticable, unworkable; (*piste*) impassable

imprécis, e [ɛpʀesi, -iz] *adj* imprecise

imprégner [ɛpʀeɲe] *vt* (*tissu, tampon*)
to soak, impregnate; (*lieu, air*) to fill;
s'~ de (*fig*) to absorb

imprenable [ɛpʀənabl(ə)] *adj* (*forteresse*) impregnable; **vue ~** unrestricted
view

impression [ɛpʀesjɔ̃] *nf* impression;
(*d'un ouvrage, tissu*) printing; **faire
bonne ~** to make a good impression

impressionnant, e [ɛpʀesjɔnɑ̃, -ɑ̃t] *adj*
impressive; upsetting

impressionner [ɛpʀesjɔne] *vt* (*frapper*)
to impress; (*troubler*) to upset

imprévisible [ɛpʀevizibl(ə)] *adj* unfore-
seeable

imprévoyant, e [ɛpʀevwajɑ̃, -ɑ̃t] *adj*
lacking in foresight; (*en matière
d'argent*) improvident

imprévu, e [ɛpʀevy] *adj* unforeseen, unexpected ♦ *nm* unexpected incident; **en
cas d'~** if anything unexpected happens

imprimante [ɛpʀimɑ̃t] *nf* printer; **~ matricielle** dot-matrix printer

imprimé [ɛpʀime] *nm* (*formulaire*)
printed form; (*POSTES*) printed matter *no
pl*

imprimer [ɛ̃pʀime] *vt* to print; (*empreinte etc*) to imprint; (*publier*) to publish; (*communiquer: mouvement, impulsion*) to impart, transmit; **imprimerie** *nf* printing; (*établissement*) printing works *sg*; **imprimeur** *nm* printer

impromptu, e [ɛ̃pʀɔ̃pty] *adj* impromptu; sudden

impropre [ɛ̃pʀɔpʀ(ə)] *adj* inappropriate; ~ **à** unsuitable for

improviser [ɛ̃pʀɔvize] *vt, vi* to improvise

improviste [ɛ̃pʀɔvist(ə)]: **à l'~** *adv* unexpectedly, without warning

imprudence [ɛ̃pʀydɑ̃s] *nf* carelessness *no pl*; imprudence *no pl*

imprudent, e [ɛ̃pʀydɑ̃, -ɑ̃t] *adj* (*conducteur, geste, action*) careless; (*remarque*) unwise, imprudent; (*projet*) foolhardy

impudent, e [ɛ̃pydɑ̃, -ɑ̃t] *adj* impudent; brazen

impudique [ɛ̃pydik] *adj* shameless

impuissant, e [ɛ̃pɥisɑ̃, -ɑ̃t] *adj* helpless; (*sans effet*) ineffectual; (*sexuellement*) impotent; ~ **à faire** powerless to do

impulsif, ive [ɛ̃pylsif, -iv] *adj* impulsive

impulsion [ɛ̃pylsjɔ̃] *nf* (*ÉLEC, instinct*) impulse; (*élan, influence*) impetus

impunément [ɛ̃pynemɑ̃] *adv* with impunity

imputer [ɛ̃pyte] *vt* (*attribuer*) to ascribe, impute; (*COMM*): ~ **à** *ou* **sur** to charge to

inabordable [inabɔʀdabl(ə)] *adj* (*cher*) prohibitive

inaccessible [inaksesibl(ə)] *adj* inaccessible; unattainable; (*insensible*): ~ **à** impervious to

inachevé, e [inaʃve] *adj* unfinished

inadapté, e [inadapte] *adj* (*gén*): ~ **à** not adapted to, unsuited to; (*PSYCH*) maladjusted

inadmissible [inadmisibl(ə)] *adj* inadmissible

inadvertance [inadvɛʀtɑ̃s]: **par** ~ *adv* inadvertently

inaltérable [inalteʀabl(ə)] *adj* (*matière*) stable; (*fig*) unchanging; ~ **à** unaffected by

inamovible [inamɔvibl(ə)] *adj* fixed; (*JUR*) irremovable

inanimé, e [inanime] *adj* (*matière*) inanimate; (*évanoui*) unconscious; (*sans vie*) lifeless

inanition [inanisjɔ̃] *nf*: **tomber d'~** to faint with hunger (and exhaustion)

inaperçu, e [inapɛʀsy] *adj*: **passer** ~ to go unnoticed

inappréciable [inapʀesjabl(ə)] *adj* (*service*) invaluable

inapte [inapt(ə)] *adj*: ~ **à** incapable of; (*MIL*) unfit for

inattaquable [inatakabl(ə)] *adj* (*texte, preuve*) irrefutable

inattendu, e [inatɑ̃dy] *adj* unexpected

inattentif, ive [inatɑ̃tif, -iv] *adj* inattentive; ~ **à** (*dangers, détails*) heedless of; **inattention** *nf*: **faute d'inattention** careless mistake

inaugurer [inɔgyʀe] *vt* (*monument*) to unveil; (*exposition, usine*) to open; (*fig*) to inaugurate

inavouable [inavwabl(ə)] *adj* shameful; undisclosable

inavoué, e [inavwe] *adj* unavowed

incandescence [ɛ̃kɑ̃desɑ̃s] *nf*: **porter à** ~ to heat white-hot

incapable [ɛ̃kapabl(ə)] *adj* incapable; ~ **de faire** incapable of doing; (*empêché*) unable to do

incapacité [ɛ̃kapasite] *nf* incapability; (*JUR*) incapacity

incarcérer [ɛ̃kaʀseʀe] *vt* to incarcerate, imprison

incarner [ɛ̃kaʀne] *vt* to embody, personify; (*THÉÂTRE*) to play

incartade [ɛ̃kaʀtad] *nf* prank

incassable [ɛ̃kɑsabl(ə)] *adj* unbreakable

incendiaire [ɛ̃sɑ̃djɛʀ] *adj* incendiary; (*fig: discours*) inflammatory ♦ *nm/f* fire-raiser, arsonist

incendie [ɛ̃sɑ̃di] *nm* fire; ~ **criminel** arson *no pl*; ~ **de forêt** forest fire; **incendier** [ɛ̃sɑ̃dje] *vt* (*mettre le feu à*) to set fire to, set alight; (*brûler complètement*) to burn down

incertain, e [ɛ̃sɛʀtɛ̃, -ɛn] *adj* uncertain; (*temps*) uncertain, unsettled; (*imprécis*:

contours) indistinct, blurred; **incertitude** *nf* uncertainty

incessamment [ɛ̃sɛsamɑ̃] *adv* very shortly

incidemment [ɛ̃sidamɑ̃] *adv* in passing

incident [ɛ̃sidɑ̃] *nm* incident; **~ de parcours** minor hitch *ou* setback; **~ technique** technical difficulties *pl*

incinérer [ɛ̃sineʀe] *vt* (*ordures*) to incinerate; (*mort*) to cremate

incisive [ɛ̃siziv] *nf* incisor

inciter [ɛ̃site] *vt*: **~ qn à (faire) qch** to encourage sb to do sth; (*à la révolte etc*) to incite sb to do sth

inclinable [ɛ̃klinabl(ə)] *adj*: **siège à dossier ~** reclining seat

inclinaison [ɛ̃klinɛzɔ̃] *nf* (*déclivité: d'une route etc*) incline; (: *d'un toit*) slope; (*état penché*) tilt

inclination [ɛ̃klinasjɔ̃] *nf*: **~ de (la) tête** nod (of the head); **~ (de buste)** bow

incliner [ɛ̃kline] *vt* (*tête, bouteille*) to tilt ♦ *vi*: **~ qch/à faire** to incline towards sth/doing; **s'~ (devant)** to bow (before); (*céder*) to give in *ou* yield (to); **~ la tête** *ou* **le front** to give a slight bow

inclure [ɛ̃klyʀ] *vt* to include; (*joindre à un envoi*) to enclose; **jusqu'au 10 mars inclus** until 10th March inclusive

incoercible [ɛ̃kɔɛʀsibl(ə)] *adj* uncontrollable

incohérent, e [ɛ̃kɔeʀɑ̃, -ɑ̃t] *adj* inconsistent; incoherent

incollable [ɛ̃kɔlabl(ə)] *adj*: **il est ~** he's got all the answers

incolore [ɛ̃kɔlɔʀ] *adj* colourless

incomber [ɛ̃kɔ̃be]: **~ à** *vt* (*suj: devoirs, responsabilité*) to rest upon; (: *frais, travail*) to be the responsibility of

incommensurable [ɛ̃kɔmɑ̃syʀabl(ə)] *adj* immeasurable

incommode [ɛ̃kɔmɔd] *adj* inconvenient; (*posture, siège*) uncomfortable

incommoder [ɛ̃kɔmɔde] *vt*: **~ qn** to inconvenience sb; (*embarrasser*) to make sb feel uncomfortable

incompétent, e [ɛ̃kɔ̃petɑ̃, -ɑ̃t] *adj* incompetent

incompris, e [ɛ̃kɔ̃pʀi, -iz] *adj* misunderstood

inconcevable [ɛ̃kɔ̃svabl(ə)] *adj* incredible

inconciliable [ɛ̃kɔ̃siljabl(ə)] *adj* irreconcilable

inconditionnel, le [ɛ̃kɔ̃disjɔnɛl] *adj* unconditional; (*partisan*) unquestioning

incongru, e [ɛ̃kɔ̃gʀy] *adj* unseemly

inconnu, e [ɛ̃kɔny] *adj* unknown; new, strange ♦ *nm/f* stranger; unknown person (*ou* artist *etc*) ♦ *nm*: **l'~** the unknown; **inconnue** *nf* unknown

inconsciemment [ɛ̃kɔ̃sjamɑ̃] *adv* unconsciously

inconscient, e [ɛ̃kɔ̃sjɑ̃, -ɑ̃t] *adj* unconscious; (*irréfléchi*) thoughtless, reckless ♦ *nm* (*PSYCH*): **l'~** the unconscious; **~ de** unaware of

inconsidéré, e [ɛ̃kɔ̃sideʀe] *adj* ill-considered

inconsistant, e [ɛ̃kɔ̃sistɑ̃, -ɑ̃t] *adj* flimsy, weak; runny

incontestable [ɛ̃kɔ̃tɛstabl(ə)] *adj* indisputable

incontournable [ɛ̃kɔ̃tuʀnabl(ə)] *adj* unavoidable

inconvenant, e [ɛ̃kɔ̃vnɑ̃, -ɑ̃t] *adj* unseemly, improper

inconvénient [ɛ̃kɔ̃venjɑ̃] *nm* (*d'une situation, d'un projet*) disadvantage, drawback; (*d'un remède, changement etc*) inconvenience; **si vous n'y voyez pas d'~** if you have no objections

incorporer [ɛ̃kɔʀpɔʀe] *vt*: **~ (à)** to mix in (with); (*paragraphe etc*): **~ (dans)** to incorporate (in); (*MIL: appeler*) to recruit, call up

incorrect, e [ɛ̃kɔʀɛkt] *adj* (*impropre, inconvenant*) improper; (*défectueux*) faulty; (*inexact*) incorrect; (*impoli*) impolite; (*déloyal*) underhand

incrédule [ɛ̃kʀedyl] *adj* incredulous; (*REL*) unbelieving

increvable [ɛ̃kʀəvabl(ə)] *(fam)* tireless

incriminer [ɛ̃kʀimine] *vt* (*personne*) to incriminate; (*action, conduite*) to bring under attack; (*bonne foi, honnêteté*) to call into question

incroyable [ɛ̃kʀwajabl(ə)] *adj* incredible; unbelievable

incruster [ɛ̃kʀyste] *vt* (*ART*) to inlay; **s'~** *vi* (*invité*) to take root; (*radiateur etc*) to become coated with fur *ou* scale

inculpé, e [ɛ̃kylpe] *nm/f* accused

inculper [ɛ̃kylpe] *vt*: **~ (de)** to charge (with)

inculquer [ɛ̃kylke] *vt*: **~ qch à** to inculcate sth in *ou* instil sth into

inculte [ɛ̃kylt(ə)] *adj* uncultivated; (*esprit, peuple*) uncultured; (*barbe*) unkempt

Inde [ɛ̃d] *nf*: **l'~** India

indécis, e [ɛ̃desi, -iz] *adj* indecisive; (*perplexe*) undecided

indéfendable [ɛ̃defɑ̃dabl(ə)] *adj* indefensible

indéfini, e [ɛ̃defini] *adj* (*imprécis, incertain*) undefined; (*illimité, LING*) indefinite; **indéfiniment** *adv* indefinitely; **indéfinissable** *adj* indefinable

indélébile [ɛ̃delebil] *adj* indelible

indélicat, e [ɛ̃delika, -at] *adj* tactless; dishonest

indemne [ɛ̃dɛmn(ə)] *adj* unharmed

indemniser [ɛ̃dɛmnize] *vt*: **~ qn (de)** to compensate sb (for)

indemnité [ɛ̃dɛmnite] *nf* (*dédommagement*) compensation *no pl*; (*allocation*) allowance; **~ de licenciement** redundancy payment

indépendamment [ɛ̃depɑ̃damɑ̃] *adv* independently; **~ de** (*abstraction faite de*) irrespective of; (*en plus de*) over and above

indépendance [ɛ̃depɑ̃dɑ̃s] *nf* independence

indépendant, e [ɛ̃depɑ̃dɑ̃, -ɑ̃t] *adj* independent; **~ de** independent of

indescriptible [ɛ̃dɛskʀiptibl(ə)] *adj* indescribable

indétermination [ɛ̃detɛʀminasjɔ̃] *nf* indecision; indecisiveness

indéterminé, e [ɛ̃detɛʀmine] *adj* unspecified; indeterminate

index [ɛ̃dɛks] *nm* (*doigt*) index finger; (*d'un livre etc*) index; **mettre à l'~** to blacklist

indexé, e [ɛ̃dɛkse] *adj* (*ÉCON*): **~ (sur)** index-linked (to)

indicateur [ɛ̃dikatœʀ] *nm* (*POLICE*) informer; (*livre*) guide; directory; (*TECH*) gauge; indicator; **~ des chemins de fer** railway timetable

indicatif, ive [ɛ̃dikatif, -iv] *adj*: **à titre ~** for (your) information ♦ *nm* (*LING*) indicative; (*RADIO*) theme *ou* signature tune; (*TÉL*) dialling code

indication [ɛ̃dikasjɔ̃] *nf* indication; (*renseignement*) information *no pl*; **~s** *nfpl* (*directives*) instructions

indice [ɛ̃dis] *nm* (*marque, signe*) indication, sign; (*POLICE: lors d'une enquête*) clue; (*JUR: présomption*) piece of evidence; (*SCIENCE, ÉCON, TECH*) index

indicible [ɛ̃disibl(ə)] *adj* inexpressible

indien, ne [ɛ̃djɛ̃, -jɛn] *adj*, *nm/f* Indian

indifféremment [ɛ̃diferamɑ̃] *adv* (*sans distinction*) equally (well); indiscriminately

indifférence [ɛ̃diferɑ̃s] *nf* indifference; **indifférent, e** [ɛ̃diferɑ̃, -ɑ̃t] *adj* (*peu intéressé*) indifferent

indigence [ɛ̃diʒɑ̃s] *nf* poverty

indigène [ɛ̃diʒɛn] *adj* native, indigenous; local ♦ *nm/f* native

indigeste [ɛ̃diʒɛst(ə)] *adj* indigestible

indigestion [ɛ̃diʒɛstjɔ̃] *nf* indigestion *no pl*

indigne [ɛ̃diɲ] *adj* unworthy

indigner [ɛ̃diɲe] *vt*: **s'~ (de *ou* contre)** to be indignant (at)

indiqué, e [ɛ̃dike] *adj* (*date, lieu*) given; (*adéquat, conseillé*) suitable

indiquer [ɛ̃dike] *vt* (*désigner*): **~ qch/qn à qn** to point sth/sb out to sb; (*suj: pendule, aiguille*) to show; (: *étiquette, plan*) to show, indicate; (*faire connaître: médecin, restaurant*): **~ qch/qn à qn** to tell sb of sth/sb; (*renseigner sur*) to point out, tell; (*déterminer: date, lieu*) to give, state; (*dénoter*) to indicate, point to

indirect, e [ɛ̃diʀɛkt] *adj* indirect

indiscipline [ɛ̃disiplin] *nf* lack of discipline; **indiscipliné, e** *adj* undisciplined; (*fig*) unmanageable

indiscret, ète [ɛ̃diskʀɛ, -ɛt] *adj* indiscreet
indiscutable [ɛ̃diskytabl(ə)] *adj* indisputable
indispensable [ɛ̃dispɑ̃sabl(ə)] *adj* indispensable; essential
indisposé, e [ɛ̃dispoze] *adj* indisposed
indisposer [ɛ̃dispoze] *vt* (*incommoder*) to upset; (*déplaire à*) to antagonize
indistinct, e [ɛ̃distɛ̃, -ɛ̃kt(ə)] *adj* indistinct; **indistinctement** *adv* (*voir, prononcer*) indistinctly; (*sans distinction*) indiscriminately
individu [ɛ̃dividy] *nm* individual
individuel, le [ɛ̃dividɥɛl] *adj* (*gén*) individual; (*opinion, livret, contrôle, avantages*) personal; **chambre** ~**le** single room; **maison** ~**le** detached house
indolore [ɛ̃dɔlɔʀ] *adj* painless
indomptable [ɛ̃dɔ̃tabl(ə)] *adj* untameable; (*fig*) invincible, indomitable
Indonésie [ɛ̃dɔnezi] *nf* Indonesia
indu, e [ɛ̃dy] *adj*: **à des heures** ~**es** at some ungodly hour
induire [ɛ̃dɥiʀ] *vt*: ~ **qn en erreur** to lead sb astray, mislead sb
indulgent, e [ɛ̃dylʒɑ̃, -ɑ̃t] *adj* (*parent, regard*) indulgent; (*juge, examinateur*) lenient
indûment [ɛ̃dymɑ̃] *adv* wrongfully; without due cause
industrie [ɛ̃dystʀi] *nf* industry; **industriel, le** *adj* industrial ♦ *nm* industrialist; manufacturer
inébranlable [inebʀɑ̃labl(ə)] *adj* (*masse, colonne*) solid; (*personne, certitude, foi*) steadfast, unwavering
inédit, e [inedi, -it] *adj* (*correspondance etc*) hitherto unpublished; (*spectacle, moyen*) novel, original
ineffaçable [inefasabl(ə)] *adj* indelible
inefficace [inefikas] *adj* (*remède, moyen*) ineffective; (*machine, employé*) inefficient
inégal, e, aux [inegal, -o] *adj* unequal; uneven; **inégalable** [inegalabl(e)] *adj* matchless; **inégalé, e** [inegale] *adj* unmatched, unequalled
inerte [inɛʀt(ə)] *adj* lifeless; inert

inestimable [inɛstimabl(e)] *adj* priceless; (*fig: bienfait*) invaluable
inévitable [inevitabl(ə)] *adj* unavoidable; (*fatal, habituel*) inevitable
inexact, e [inɛgzakt] *adj* inaccurate, inexact; unpunctual
in extremis [inɛkstʀemis] *adv* at the last minute ♦ *adj* last-minute
infaillible [ɛ̃fajibl(ə)] *adj* infallible
infâme [ɛ̃fɑm] *adj* vile
infanticide [ɛ̃fɑ̃tisid] *nm/f* child-murderer(eress) ♦ *nm* (*meurtre*) infanticide
infarctus [ɛ̃faʀktys] *nm*: ~ **(du myocarde)** coronary (thrombosis)
infatigable [ɛ̃fatigabl(ə)] *adj* tireless
infect, e [ɛ̃fɛkt] *adj* vile; foul; (*repas, vin*) revolting
infecter [ɛ̃fɛkte] *vt* (*atmosphère, eau*) to contaminate; (*MÉD*) to infect; **s'~** to become infected *ou* septic; **infection** *nf* infection
inférieur, e [ɛ̃feʀjœʀ] *adj* lower; (*en qualité, intelligence*) inferior; ~ **à** (*somme, quantité*) less *ou* smaller than; (*moins bon que*) inferior to
infernal, e, aux [ɛ̃fɛʀnal, -o] *adj* (*chaleur, rythme*) infernal; (*méchanceté, complot*) diabolical
infidèle [ɛ̃fidɛl] *adj* unfaithful
infiltrer [ɛ̃filtʀe]: **s'~** *vi* to penetrate into; (*liquide*) to seep into; (*fig: noyauter*) to infiltrate
infime [ɛ̃fim] *adj* minute, tiny; (*inférieur*) lowly
infini, e [ɛ̃fini] *adj* infinite ♦ *nm* infinity; **à l'~** (*MATH*) to infinity; (*agrandir, varier*) infinitely; (*interminablement*) endlessly; **infinité** *nf*: **une infinité de** an infinite number of
infinitif [ɛ̃finitif] *nm* infinitive
infirme [ɛ̃fiʀm(ə)] *adj* disabled ♦ *nm/f* disabled person; ~ **de guerre** war cripple
infirmerie [ɛ̃fiʀməʀi] *nf* sick bay
infirmier, ière [ɛ̃fiʀmje, -jɛʀ] *nm/f* nurse; **infirmière chef** sister; **infirmière visiteuse** ≈ district nurse
infirmité [ɛ̃fiʀmite] *nf* disability

inflammable [ɛflamabl(ə)] *adj* (in)flammable

inflation [ɛflɑsjɔ̃] *nf* inflation

inflexion [ɛflɛksjɔ̃] *nf* inflexion; ~ **de la tête** slight nod (of the head)

infliger [ɛfliʒe] *vt:* ~ **qch (à qn)** to inflict sth (on sb); (*amende, sanction*) to impose sth (on sb)

influence [ɛflyɑ̃s] *nf* influence; (*d'un médicament*) effect; **influencer** *vt* to influence; **influent, e** *adj* influential

influer [ɛflye]: ~ **sur** *vt* to have an influence upon

informaticien, ne [ɛfɔrmatisjɛ̃, -jɛn] *nm/f* computer scientist

information [ɛfɔrmɑsjɔ̃] *nf* (*renseignement*) piece of information; (*PRESSE, TV: nouvelle*) item of news; (*diffusion de renseignements, INFORM*) information; (*JUR*) inquiry, investigation; ~**s** *nfpl* (*TV*) news *sg*; **voyage d'**~ fact-finding trip

informatique [ɛfɔrmatik] *nf* (*technique*) data processing; (*science*) computer science ♦ *adj* computer *cpd*; **informatiser** *vt* to computerize

informe [ɛfɔrm(ə)] *adj* shapeless

informer [ɛfɔrme] *vt:* ~ **qn (de)** to inform sb (of); **s'**~ **(de/si)** to inquire *ou* find out (about/whether *ou* if)

infortune [ɛfɔrtyn] *nf* misfortune

infraction [ɛfraksjɔ̃] *nf* offence; ~ **à** violation *ou* breach of; **être en** ~ to be in breach of the law

infranchissable [ɛfrɑ̃fisabl(ə)] *adj* impassable; (*fig*) insuperable

infrastructure [ɛfrastryktyr] *nf* (*AVIAT, MIL*) ground installations *pl*; (*ÉCON: touristique etc*) infrastructure

infuser [ɛfyze] *vt, vi* (*thé*) to brew; (*tisane*) to infuse; **infusion** *nf* (*tisane*) herb tea

ingénier [ɛʒenje]: **s'**~ *vi* to strive to do

ingénierie [ɛʒenjəri] *nf* engineering; ~ **génétique** genetic engineering

ingénieur [ɛʒenjœr] *nm* engineer; ~ **du son** sound engineer

ingénieux, euse [ɛʒenjø, -øz] *adj* ingenious, clever

ingénu, e [ɛʒeny] *adj* ingenuous, artless

ingérer [ɛʒere]: **s'**~ *vi* to interfere in

ingrat, e [ɛgra, -at] *adj* (*personne*) ungrateful; (*sol*) poor; (*travail, sujet*) thankless; (*visage*) unprepossessing

ingrédient [ɛgredjɑ̃] *nm* ingredient

ingurgiter [ɛgyrʒite] *vt* to swallow

inhabitable [inabitabl(ə)] *adj* uninhabitable

inhabituel, le [inabitɥɛl] *adj* unusual

inhérent, e [inerɑ̃, -ɑ̃t] *adj:* ~ **à** inherent in

inhibition [inibisjɔ̃] *nf* inhibition

inhumain, e [inymɛ̃, -ɛn] *adj* inhuman

inhumer [inyme] *vt* to inter, bury

inimitié [inimitje] *nf* enmity

initial, e, aux [inisjal, -o] *adj* initial; **initiale** *nf* initial

initiateur, trice [inisjatœr, -tris] *nm/f* initiator; (*d'une mode, technique*) innovator, pioneer

initiative [inisjativ] *nf* initiative

initier [inisje] *vt:* ~ **qn à** to initiate sb into; (*faire découvrir: art, jeu*) to introduce sb to

injecté, e [ɛʒɛkte] *adj:* **yeux** ~**s de sang** bloodshot eyes

injecter [ɛʒɛkte] *vt* to inject; **injection** *nf* injection; **à injection** (*AUTO*) fuel injection *cpd*

injure [ɛʒyr] *nf* insult, abuse *no pl*

injurier [ɛʒyrje] *vt* to insult, abuse; **injurieux, euse** *adj* abusive, insulting

injuste [ɛʒyst(ə)] *adj* unjust, unfair; **injustice** *nf* injustice

inlassable [ɛlasabl(ə)] *adj* tireless

inné, e [ine] *adj* innate, inborn

innocent, e [inɔsɑ̃, -ɑ̃t] *adj* innocent; **innocenter** *vt* to clear, prove innocent

innombrable [inɔ̃brabl(ə)] *adj* innumerable

innommable [inɔmabl(ə)] *adj* unspeakable

innover [inɔve] *vi* to break new ground

inoccupé, e [inɔkype] *adj* unoccupied

inoculer [inɔkyle] *vt* (*volontairement*) to inoculate; (*accidentellement*) to infect

inodore [inɔdɔr] *adj* (*gaz*) odourless; (*fleur*) scentless

inoffensif, ive [inɔfɑ̃sif, -iv] *adj* harmless, innocuous

inondation [inɔdasjɔ̃] *nf* flooding *no pl*; flood; **inonder** [inɔ̃de] *vt* to flood; *(fig)* to inundate, overrun

inopérant, e [inɔperɑ̃, -ɑ̃t] *adj* inoperative, ineffective

inopiné, e [inɔpine] *adj* unexpected, sudden

inopportun, e [inɔpɔrtœ̃, -yn] *adj* ill-timed, untimely; inappropriate

inoubliable [inublijabl(ə)] *adj* unforgettable

inouï, e [inwi] *adj* unheard-of, extraordinary

inox(ydable) [inɔks(idabl(ə))] *adj* stainless

inqualifiable [ɛ̃kalifjabl(ə)] *adj* unspeakable

inquiet, ète [ɛ̃kjɛ, -ɛt] *adj* anxious

inquiétant, e [ɛ̃kjetɑ̃, -ɑ̃t] *adj* worrying, disturbing

inquiéter [ɛ̃kjete] *vt* to worry; *(harceler)* to harass; **s'~** to worry; **s'~ de** to worry about; *(s'enquérir de)* to inquire about

inquiétude [ɛ̃kjetyd] *nf* anxiety

insaisissable [ɛ̃sezisabl(ə)] *adj* elusive

insatisfait, e [ɛ̃satisfɛ, -ɛt] *adj* *(non comblé)* unsatisfied; unfulfilled; *(mécontent)* dissatisfied

inscription [ɛ̃skripsjɔ̃] *nf* inscription; *(voir s'inscrire)* enrolment; registration

inscrire [ɛ̃skrir] *vt* *(marquer: sur son calepin etc)* to note *ou* write down; *(: sur un mur, une affiche etc)* to write; *(: dans la pierre, le métal)* to inscribe; *(mettre: sur une liste, un budget etc)* to put down; **s'~** *(pour une excursion etc)* to put one's name down; **s'~ (à)** *(club, parti)* to join; *(université)* to register *ou* enrol (at); *(examen, concours)* to register (for); **s'~ en faux contre** to challenge; **~ qn à** *(club, parti)* to enrol sb at

insecte [ɛ̃sɛkt(ə)] *nm* insect; **insecticide** *nm* insecticide

insensé, e [ɛ̃sɑ̃se] *adj* mad

insensibiliser [ɛ̃sɑ̃sibilize] *vt* to anaesthetize

insensible [ɛ̃sɑ̃sibl(ə)] *adj* *(nerf, membre)* numb; *(dur, indifférent)* insensitive; *(imperceptible)* imperceptible

insérer [ɛ̃sere] *vt* to insert; **s'~ dans** to fit into; to come within

insigne [ɛ̃siɲ] *nm* *(d'un parti, club)* badge ♦ *adj* distinguished

insignifiant, e [ɛ̃siɲifjɑ̃, -ɑ̃t] *adj* insignificant; trivial

insinuer [ɛ̃sinɥe] *vt* to insinuate, imply; **s'~ dans** *(fig)* to creep into

insister [ɛ̃siste] *vi* to insist; *(s'obstiner)* to keep on; **~ sur** *(détail, note)* to stress

insolation [ɛ̃sɔlasjɔ̃] *nf* *(MÉD)* sunstroke *no pl*

insolent, e [ɛ̃sɔlɑ̃, -ɑ̃t] *adj* insolent

insolite [ɛ̃sɔlit] *adj* strange, unusual

insomnie [ɛ̃sɔmni] *nf* insomnia *no pl*, sleeplessness *no pl*

insondable [ɛ̃sɔ̃dabl(ə)] *adj* unfathomable

insonoriser [ɛ̃sɔnɔrize] *vt* to soundproof

insouciant, e [ɛ̃susjɑ̃, -ɑ̃t] *adj* carefree; *(imprévoyant)* heedless

insoumis, e [ɛ̃sumi, -iz] *adj* *(caractère, enfant)* rebellious, refractory; *(contrée, tribu)* unsubdued

insoupçonnable [ɛ̃supsɔnabl(ə)] *adj* unsuspected; *(personne)* above suspicion

insoupçonné, e [ɛ̃supsɔne] *adj* unsuspected

insoutenable [ɛ̃sutnabl(ə)] *adj* *(argument)* untenable; *(chaleur)* unbearable

inspecter [ɛ̃spɛkte] *vt* to inspect

inspecteur, trice [ɛ̃spɛktœr, -tris] *nm/f* inspector; **~ d'Académie** *(regional)* director of education; **~ des finances** ≈ tax inspector *(BRIT)*, ≈ Internal Revenue Service agent *(US)*

inspection [ɛ̃spɛksjɔ̃] *nf* inspection

inspirer [ɛ̃spire] *vt* *(gén)* to inspire ♦ *vi* *(aspirer)* to breathe in; **s'~ de** *(suj: artiste)* to draw one's inspiration from

instable [ɛ̃stabl(ə)] *adj* *(meuble, équilibre)* unsteady; *(population, temps)* unsettled; *(régime, caractère)* unstable

installation [ɛ̃stalasjɔ̃] *nf* putting in *ou* up; fitting out; settling in; *(appareils etc)* fittings *pl*, installations *pl*; **~s** *nfpl* *(appareils)* equipment; *(équipements)* facilities

installer [ɛstale] *vt* (*loger*): ~ **qn** to get sb settled; (*placer*) to put, place; (*meuble, gaz, électricité*) to put in; (*rideau, étagère, tente*) to put up; (*appartement*) to fit out; **s'~** (*s'établir: artisan, dentiste etc*) to set o.s. up; (*se loger*) to settle (o.s.); (*emménager*) to settle in; (*sur un siège, à un emplacement*) to settle (down); (*fig: maladie, grève*) to take a firm hold

instamment [ɛstamã] *adv* urgently

instance [ɛstɑ̃s] *nf* (ADMIN: *autorité*) authority; ~s *nfpl* (*prières*) entreaties; **affaire en** ~ matter pending; **être en** ~ **de divorce** to be awaiting a divorce

instant [ɛstɑ̃] *nm* moment, instant; **dans un** ~ in a moment; **à l'~** this instant; **à tout** *ou* **chaque** ~ at any moment; constantly; **pour l'~** for the moment, for the time being; **par** ~s at times; **de tous les** ~s perpetual

instantané, e [ɛstɑ̃tane] *adj* (*lait, café*) instant; (*explosion, mort*) instantaneous ♦ *nm* snapshot

instar [ɛstaʀ]: **à l'~ de** *prép* following the example of, like

instaurer [ɛstɔʀe] *vt* to institute

instinct [ɛstɛ̃] *nm* instinct

instituer [ɛstitɥe] *vt* to set up

institut [ɛstity] *nm* institute; ~ **de beauté** beauty salon; **I~ universitaire de technologie** ≈ polytechnic

instituteur, trice [ɛstitytœʀ, -tʀis] *nm/f* (primary school) teacher

institution [ɛstitysjɔ̃] *nf* institution; (*collège*) private school

instruction [ɛstʀyksjɔ̃] *nf* (*enseignement, savoir*) education; (JUR) (preliminary) investigation and hearing; ~s *nfpl* (*ordres, mode d'emploi*) directions, instructions; ~ **civique** civics *sg*

instruire [ɛstʀɥiʀ] *vt* (*élèves*) to teach; (*recrues*) to train; (JUR: *affaire*) to conduct the investigation for; **s'~** to educate o.s.; **instruit, e** *adj* educated

instrument [ɛstʀymɑ̃] *nm* instrument; ~ **à cordes/vent** stringed/wind instrument; ~ **de mesure** measuring instrument; ~ **de musique** musical instrument; ~ **de travail** (working) tool

insu [ɛsy] *nm*: **à l'~ de qn** without sb knowing (it)

insubmersible [ɛsybmɛʀsibl(ə)] *adj* unsinkable

insubordination [ɛsybɔʀdinɑsjɔ̃] *nf* rebelliousness; (MIL) insubordination

insuccès [ɛsyksɛ] *nm* failure

insuffisant, e [ɛsyfizɑ̃, -ɑ̃t] *adj* insufficient; (*élève, travail*) inadequate

insuffler [ɛsyfle] *vt* to blow; to inspire

insulaire [ɛsylɛʀ] *adj* island *cpd*; (*attitude*) insular

insuline [ɛsylin] *nf* insulin

insulte [ɛsylt(ə)] *nf* insult; **insulter** *vt* to insult

insupportable [ɛsypɔʀtabl(ə)] *adj* unbearable

insurger [ɛsyʀʒe]: **s'~** *vi* to rise up *ou* rebel (against)

insurmontable [ɛsyʀmɔ̃tabl(ə)] *adj* (*difficulté*) insuperable; (*aversion*) unconquerable

intact, e [ɛtakt] *adj* intact

intangible [ɛtɑ̃ʒibl(ə)] *adj* intangible; (*principe*) inviolable

intarissable [ɛtaʀisabl(ə)] *adj* inexhaustible

intégral, e, aux [ɛtegʀal, -o] *adj* complete

intégrant, e [ɛtegʀɑ̃, -ɑ̃t] *adj*: **faire partie ~e de** to be an integral part of

intègre [ɛtegʀ(ə)] *adj* upright

intégrer [ɛtegʀe] *vt* to integrate; **s'~ à** *ou* **dans** to become integrated into

intégrisme [ɛtegʀism(e)] *nm* fundamentalism

intellectuel, le [ɛtelɛktɥel] *adj* intellectual ♦ *nm/f* intellectual; (*péj*) highbrow

intelligence [ɛteliʒɑ̃s] *nf* intelligence; (*compréhension*): **l'~ de** the understanding of; (*complicité*): **regard d'~** glance of complicity; (*accord*): **vivre en bonne ~ avec qn** to be on good terms with sb

intelligent, e [ɛteliʒɑ̃, -ɑ̃t] *adj* intelligent

intempéries [ɛtɑ̃peʀi] *nfpl* bad weather *sg*

intempestif, ive [ɛ̃tɑ̃pɛstif, -iv] *adj* untimely

intenable [ɛ̃tnabl(ə)] *adj* (*chaleur*) unbearable

intendant, e [ɛ̃tɑ̃dɑ̃, -ɑ̃t] *nm/f* (*MIL*) quartermaster; (*SCOL*) bursar; (*d'une propriété*) steward

intense [ɛ̃tɑ̃s] *adj* intense; **intensif, ive** *adj* intensive

intenter [ɛ̃tɑ̃te] *vt:* ~ **un procès contre** *ou* **à** to start proceedings against

intention [ɛ̃tɑ̃sjɔ̃] *nf* intention; (*JUR*) intent; **avoir l'~ de faire** to intend to do; **à l'~ de** for; (*renseignement*) for the benefit of; (*film, ouvrage*) aimed at; **à cette** ~ with this aim in view; **intentionné, e** *adj:* **bien intentionné** well-meaning *ou* -intentioned; **mal intentionné** ill-intentioned

interactif, ive [ɛ̃tɛraktif, -iv] *adj* (*COMPUT*) interactive

intercaler [ɛ̃tɛrkale] *vt* to insert

intercepter [ɛ̃tɛrsɛpte] *vt* to intercept; (*lumière, chaleur*) to cut off

interchangeable [ɛ̃tɛrʃɑ̃ʒabl(ə)] *adj* interchangeable

interclasse [ɛ̃tɛrklɑs] *nm* (*SCOL*) break (between classes)

interdiction [ɛ̃tɛrdiksjɔ̃] *nf* ban

interdire [ɛ̃tɛrdir] *vt* to forbid; (*ADMIN*) to ban, prohibit; (: *journal, livre*) to ban; ~ **à qn de faire** to forbid sb to do, prohibit sb from doing; (*suj: empêchement*) to prevent sb from doing

interdit, e [ɛ̃tɛrdi, -it] *adj* (*stupéfait*) taken aback ♦ *nm* prohibition

intéressant, e [ɛ̃terɛsɑ̃, -ɑ̃t] *adj* interesting

intéressé, e [ɛ̃terese] *adj* (*parties*) involved, concerned; (*amitié, motifs*) self-interested

intéresser [ɛ̃terese] *vt* (*captiver*) to interest; (*toucher*) to be of interest to; (*ADMIN: concerner*) to affect, concern; **s'~ à** to be interested in

intérêt [ɛ̃terɛ] *nm* (*aussi COMM*) interest; (*égoïsme*) self-interest; **avoir** ~ **à faire** to do well to do

intérieur, e [ɛ̃terjœr] *adj* (*mur, escalier, poche*) inside; (*commerce, politique*) domestic; (*cour, calme, vie*) inner; (*navigation*) inland ♦ *nm* (*d'une maison, d'un récipient etc*) inside; (*d'un pays, aussi: décor, mobilier*) interior; (*POL*): **l'I~** the Interior; **à l'~ (de)** inside; (*fig*) within

intérim [ɛ̃terim] *nm* interim period; **assurer l'~ (de)** to deputize (for); **par** ~ interim

intérimaire [ɛ̃terimɛr] *nm/f* (*secretaire*) temporary secretary, temp (*BRIT*); (*suppléant*) temporary replacement

intérioriser [ɛ̃terjɔrize] *vt* to internalize

interlocuteur, trice [ɛ̃tɛrlɔkytœr, -tris] *nm/f* speaker; **son** ~ the person he was speaking to

interloquer [ɛ̃tɛrlɔke] *vt* to take aback

intermède [ɛ̃tɛrmɛd] *nm* interlude

intermédiaire [ɛ̃tɛrmedjɛr] *adj* intermediate; middle; half-way ♦ *nm/f* intermediary; (*COMM*) middleman; **sans** ~ directly; **par l'~ de** through

intermittence [ɛ̃tɛrmitɑ̃s] *nf:* **par** ~ sporadically, intermittently

internat [ɛ̃tɛrna] *nm* (*SCOL*) boarding school

international, e, aux [ɛ̃tɛrnasjɔnal, -o] *adj, nm/f* international

interne [ɛ̃tɛrn(ə)] *adj* internal ♦ *nm/f* (*SCOL*) boarder; (*MÉD*) houseman; **interner** [ɛ̃tɛrne] *vt* (*POL*) to intern; (*MÉD*) to confine to a mental institution

interpeller [ɛ̃tɛrpele] *vt* (*appeler*) to call out to; (*apostropher*) to shout at; (*POLICE*) to take in for questioning; (*POL*) to question

interphone [ɛ̃tɛrfɔn] *nm* intercom

interposer [ɛ̃tɛrpoze] *vt* to interpose; **s'~** *vi* to intervene; **par personnes interposées** through a third party

interprète [ɛ̃tɛrprɛt] *nm/f* interpreter; (*porte-parole*) spokesperson

interpréter [ɛ̃tɛrprete] *vt* to interpret

interrogateur, trice [ɛ̃terɔgatœr, -tris] *adj* questioning, inquiring

interrogatif, ive [ɛ̃terɔgatif, -iv] *adj* (*LING*) interrogative

interrogation [ɛ̃terɔgasjɔ̃] *nf* question;

(SCOL) (written ou oral) test

interrogatoire [ɛ̃tɛʀɔgatwaʀ] nm (PO-LICE) questioning no pl; (JUR) cross-examination

interroger [ɛ̃tɛʀɔʒe] vt to question; (IN-FORM) to consult; (SCOL) to test

interrompre [ɛ̃tɛʀɔ̃pʀ(ə)] vt (gén) to interrupt; (travail, voyage) to break off, interrupt; **s'~** to break off

interrupteur [ɛ̃tɛʀyptœʀ] nm switch

interruption [ɛ̃tɛʀypsjɔ̃] nf interruption; (pause) break

interstice [ɛ̃tɛʀstis] nm crack; slit

interurbain [ɛ̃tɛʀyʀbɛ̃] nm (TÉL) long-distance call service ♦ adj long-distance

intervalle [ɛ̃tɛʀval] nm (espace) space; (de temps) interval; **dans l'~** in the meantime

intervenir [ɛ̃tɛʀvəniʀ] vi (gén) to intervene; (survenir) to take place; **~ auprès de qn** to intervene with sb

intervention [ɛ̃tɛʀvɑ̃sjɔ̃] nf intervention; (discours) paper; **~ chirurgicale** (surgical) operation

intervertir [ɛ̃tɛʀvɛʀtiʀ] vt to invert (the order of), reverse

interview [ɛ̃tɛʀvju] nf interview

intestin, e [ɛ̃tɛstɛ̃, -in] adj internal ♦ nm intestine

intime [ɛ̃tim] adj intimate; (vie, journal) private; (conviction) inmost; (dîner, cérémonie) quiet ♦ nm/f close friend

intimer [ɛ̃time] vt (JUR) to notify; **~ à qn l'ordre de faire** to order sb to do

intimider [ɛ̃timide] vt to intimidate

intimité [ɛ̃timite] nf: **dans l'~** in private; (sans formalités) with only a few friends, quietly

intitulé, e [ɛ̃tityle] adj entitled

intolérable [ɛ̃tɔleʀabl(ə)] adj intolerable

intoxication [ɛ̃tɔksikasjɔ̃] nf: **~ alimentaire** food poisoning

intoxiquer [ɛ̃tɔksike] vt to poison; (fig) to brainwash

intraduisible [ɛ̃tʀadɥizibl(ə)] adj untranslatable; (fig) inexpressible

intraitable [ɛ̃tʀɛtabl(ə)] adj inflexible, uncompromising

intransigeant, e [ɛ̃tʀɑ̃ziʒɑ̃, -ɑ̃t] adj in-transigent; (morale) uncompromising

intransitif, ive [ɛ̃tʀɑ̃zitif, -iv] adj (LING) intransitive

intrépide [ɛ̃tʀepid] adj dauntless

intrigue [ɛ̃tʀig] nf (scénario) plot

intriguer [ɛ̃tʀige] vi to scheme ♦ vt to puzzle, intrigue

intrinsèque [ɛ̃tʀɛ̃sɛk] adj intrinsic

introduction [ɛ̃tʀɔdyksjɔ̃] nf introduction

introduire [ɛ̃tʀɔdɥiʀ] vt to introduce; (visiteur) to show in; (aiguille, clef): **~ qch dans** to insert ou introduce sth into; **s'~ dans** to gain entry into; to get o.s. accepted into; (eau, fumée) to get into

introuvable [ɛ̃tʀuvabl(ə)] adj which cannot be found; (COMM) unobtainable

introverti, e [ɛ̃tʀɔvɛʀti] nm/f introvert

intrus, e [ɛ̃tʀy, -yz] nm/f intruder

intrusion [ɛ̃tʀyzjɔ̃] nf intrusion; interference

intuition [ɛ̃tɥisjɔ̃] nf intuition

inusable [inyzabl(ə)] adj hard-wearing

inusité, e [inyzite] adj rarely used

inutile [inytil] adj useless; (superflu) unnecessary; **inutilisable** adj unusable

invalide [ɛ̃valid] adj disabled ♦ nm: **~ de guerre** disabled ex-serviceman

invasion [ɛ̃vazjɔ̃] nf invasion

invectiver [ɛ̃vɛktive] vt to hurl abuse at

invendable [ɛ̃vɑ̃dabl(ə)] adj unsaleable; unmarketable; **invendus** nmpl unsold goods

inventaire [ɛ̃vɑ̃tɛʀ] nm inventory; (COMM: liste) stocklist; (: opération) stocktaking no pl; (fig) survey

inventer [ɛ̃vɑ̃te] vt to invent; (subterfuge) to devise, invent; (histoire, excuse) to make up, invent; **inventeur** nm inventor; **inventif, ive** adj inventive; **invention** nf invention

inverse [ɛ̃vɛʀs(ə)] adj reverse; opposite; inverse ♦ nm inverse, reverse; **dans l'ordre ~** in the reverse order; **en sens ~** in (ou from) the opposite direction; **inversement** adv conversely; **inverser** vt to invert, reverse; (ÉLEC) to reverse

investir [ɛ̃vɛstiʀ] vt to invest; investis-

sement *nm* investment; **investiture** *nf* investiture; (*à une élection*) nomination
invétéré, e [ɛ̃vetere] *adj* (*habitude*) ingrained; (*bavard, buveur*) inveterate
invisible [ɛ̃vizibl(ə)] *adj* invisible
invitation [ɛ̃vitɑsjɔ̃] *nf* invitation
invité, e [ɛ̃vite] *nm/f* guest
inviter [ɛ̃vite] *vt* to invite; ~ **qn à faire** (*suj: chose*) to induce *ou* tempt sb to do
involontaire [ɛ̃vɔlɔ̃tɛr] *adj* (*mouvement*) involuntary; (*insulte*) unintentional; (*complice*) unwitting
invoquer [ɛ̃vɔke] *vt* (*Dieu, muse*) to call upon, invoke; (*prétexte*) to put forward (as an excuse); (*loi, texte*) to refer to
invraisemblable [ɛ̃vrɛsɑ̃blabl(ə)] *adj* unlikely, improbable; incredible
iode [jɔd] *nm* iodine
irai *etc vb voir* **aller**
Irak [irak] *nm* Iraq
Iran [irɑ̃] *nm* Iran
irions *etc vb voir* **aller**
irlandais, e [irlɑ̃dɛ, -ɛz] *adj* Irish ♦ *nm/f*: **I~, e** Irishman(woman); **les I~** the Irish
Irlande [irlɑ̃d] *nf* Ireland; ~ **du Nord** Northern Ireland
ironie [irɔni] *nf* irony; **ironique** *adj* ironical; **ironiser** *vi* to be ironical
irons *etc vb voir* **aller**
irradier [iradje] *vi* to radiate ♦ *vt* (*aliment*) to irradiate
irraisonné, e [irɛzɔne] *adj* irrational, unreasoned
irrationnel, le [irasjɔnɛl] *adj* irrational
irréalisable [irealizabl(ə)] *adj* unrealizable; impracticable
irrécupérable [irekyperabl(ə)] *adj* unreclaimable, beyond repair; (*personne*) beyond redemption
irrécusable [irekyzabl(ə)] *adj* unimpeachable; incontestable
irréductible [iredyktibl(ə)] *adj* indomitable, implacable
irréel, le [ireɛl] *adj* unreal
irréfléchi, e [irefleʃi] *adj* thoughtless
irrégularité [iregylarite] *nf* irregularity; unevenness *no pl*
irrégulier, ière [iregylje, -jɛr] *adj* ir-

regular; uneven; (*élève, athlète*) erratic
irrémédiable [iremedjabl(ə)] *adj* irreparable
irréprochable [ireprɔʃabl(ə)] *adj* irreproachable, beyond reproach; (*tenue*) impeccable
irrésistible [irezistibl(ə)] *adj* irresistible; (*preuve, logique*) compelling
irrespectueux, euse [irɛspɛktɥø, -øz] *adj* disrespectful
irriguer [irige] *vt* to irrigate
irritable [iritabl(ə)] *adj* irritable
irriter [irite] *vt* to irritate
irruption [irypsjɔ̃] *nf* irruption *no pl*; **faire** ~ **dans** to burst into
islamique [islamik] *adj* Islamic; **islamiste** *adj* (*militant*) Islamic; (*mouvement*) Islamic fundamentalist ♦ *nm/f* Islamic fundamentalist
Islande [islɑ̃d] *nf* Iceland
isolant, e [izɔlɑ̃, -ɑ̃t] *adj* insulating; (*insonorisant*) soundproofing
isolation [izɔlɑsjɔ̃] *nf* insulation
isolé, e [izɔle] *adj* isolated; insulated
isoler [izɔle] *vt* to isolate; (*prisonnier*) to put in solitary confinement; (*ville*) to cut off, isolate; (*ÉLEC*) to insulate
isoloir *nm* polling booth
Israël [israɛl] *nm* Israel; **israélien, ne** *adj, nm/f* Israeli; **israélite** *adj* Jewish ♦ *nm/f* Jew(Jewess)
issu, e [isy] *adj*: ~ **de** descended from; (*fig*) stemming from; **issue** *nf* (*ouverture, sortie*) exit; (*solution*) way out, solution; (*dénouement*) outcome; **à l'~e de** at the conclusion *ou* close of; **rue sans** ~**e** dead end
Italie [itali] *nf* Italy; **italien, ne** *adj, nm/f* Italian ♦ *nm* (*LING*) Italian
italique [italik] *nm*: **en** ~ in italics
itinéraire [itinerɛr] *nm* itinerary, route
IUT *sigle m* = **Institut universitaire de technologie**
IVG *sigle f* (= *interruption volontaire de grossesse*) abortion
ivoire [ivwar] *nm* ivory
ivre [ivr(ə)] *adj* drunk; ~ **de** (*colère, bonheur*) wild with; **ivresse** *nf* drunkenness; **ivrogne** *nm/f* drunkard

J j

j' [ʒ] *pron* I
jachère [ʒaʃɛʀ] *nf*: **(être) en ~** (to lie) fallow
jacinthe [ʒasɛ̃t] *nf* hyacinth
jack [ʒak] *nm* jack plug
jadis [ʒadis] *adv* in times past, formerly
jaillir [ʒajiʀ] *vi* (*liquide*) to spurt out; (*fig*) to burst out; to flood out
jais [ʒɛ] *nm* jet; **(d'un noir) de ~** jet-black
jalon [ʒalɔ̃] *nm* range pole; (*fig*) milestone; **jalonner** *vt* to mark out; (*fig*) to mark, punctuate
jalousie [ʒaluzi] *nf* jealousy; (*store*) (Venetian) blind
jaloux, ouse [ʒalu, -uz] *adj* jealous
jamais [ʒamɛ] *adv* never; (*sans négation*) ever; **ne ... ~** never; **à ~** for ever
jambe [ʒɑ̃b] *nf* leg
jambon [ʒɑ̃bɔ̃] *nm* ham
jambonneau, x [ʒɑ̃bɔno] *nm* knuckle of ham
jante [ʒɑ̃t] *nf* (wheel) rim
janvier [ʒɑ̃vje] *nm* January
Japon [ʒapɔ̃] *nm* Japan; **japonais, e** *adj, nm/f* Japanese ♦ *nm* (*LING*) Japanese
japper [ʒape] *vi* to yap, yelp
jaquette [ʒakɛt] *nf* (*de cérémonie*) morning coat; (*de dame*) jacket
jardin [ʒaʀdɛ̃] *nm* garden; **~ d'enfants** nursery school; **jardinage** *nm* gardening; **jardinier, ière** *nm/f* gardener; **jardinière** *nf* (*de fenêtre*) window box
jarre [ʒaʀ] *nf* (earthenware) jar
jarret [ʒaʀɛ] *nm* back of knee, ham; (*CULIN*) knuckle, shin
jarretelle [ʒaʀtɛl] *nf* suspender (*BRIT*), garter (*US*)
jarretière [ʒaʀtjɛʀ] *nf* garter
jaser [ʒaze] *vi* to chatter, prattle; (*indiscrètement*) to gossip
jatte [ʒat] *nf* basin, bowl
jauge [ʒoʒ] *nf* (*instrument*) gauge; **jauger** *vt* (*fig*) to size up

jaune [ʒon] *adj, nm* yellow ♦ *adv* (*fam*): **rire ~** to laugh on the other side of one's face; **~ d'œuf** (egg) yolk; **jaunir** *vi, vt* to turn yellow
jaunisse [ʒonis] *nf* jaundice
Javel [ʒavɛl] *nf voir* **eau**
javelot [ʒavlo] *nm* javelin
J.-C. *sigle* = **Jésus-Christ**
je(j') [ʒ(ə)] *pron* I
jean [dʒin] *nm* jeans *pl*
Jésus-Christ [ʒezykʀi(st)] *n* Jesus Christ; **600 avant/après ~** *ou* **J.-C.** 600 B.C./A.D.
jet¹ [ʒɛ] *nm* (*lancer*) throwing *no pl*, throw; (*jaillissement*) jet; spurt; (*de tuyau*) nozzle; **du premier ~** at the first attempt *or* shot; **~ d'eau** fountain; spray
jet² [dʒɛt] *nm* (*avion*) jet
jetable [ʒətabl(ə)] *adj* disposable
jetée [ʒəte] *nf* jetty; pier
jeter [ʒəte] *vt* (*gén*) to throw; (*se défaire de*) to throw away *ou* out; (*son, lueur etc*) to give out; **se ~ dans** to flow into; **~ qch à qn** to throw sth to sb; (*de façon agressive*) to throw sth at sb; **~ un coup d'œil (à)** to take a look (at); **~ un sort à qn** to cast a spell on sb
jeton [ʒətɔ̃] *nm* (*au jeu*) counter; (*de téléphone*) token
jette *etc vb voir* **jeter**
jeu, x [ʒø] *nm* (*divertissement, TECH*: *d'une pièce*) play; (*TENNIS*: *partie, FOOTBALL etc*: *façon de jouer*) game; (*THÉÂTRE etc*) acting; (*au casino*): **le ~** gambling; (*fonctionnement*) working, interplay; (*série d'objets, jouet*) set; (*CARTES*) hand; **en ~** at stake; at work; **remettre en ~** to throw in; **entrer/mettre en ~** to come/ bring into play; **~ de cartes** pack of cards; **~ d'échecs** chess set; **~ de hasard** game of chance; **~ de mots** pun
jeudi [ʒødi] *nm* Thursday
jeun [ʒœ̃]: **à ~** *adv* on an empty stomach
jeune [ʒœn] *adj* young; **~ fille** girl; **~ homme** young man
jeûne [ʒøn] *nm* fast
jeunesse [ʒœnɛs] *nf* youth; (*aspect*) youthfulness; youngness
joaillerie [ʒoajʀi] *nf* jewel trade; jew-

ellery; **joaillier, ière** *nm/f* jeweller

joie [ʒwa] *nf* joy

joindre [ʒwɛ̃dʀ(ə)] *vt* to join; (*à une lettre*): **~ qch à** to enclose sth with; (*contacter*) to contact, get in touch with; **se ~ à** to join; **~ les mains** to put one's hands together

joint, e [ʒwɛ̃, ʒwɛ̃t] *adj*: **pièce ~e** enclosure ♦ *nm* joint; (*ligne*) join; **~ de culasse** cylinder head gasket; **~ de robinet** washer

joli, e [ʒɔli] *adj* pretty, attractive; **c'est du ~!** (*ironique*) that's very nice!; **c'est bien ~, mais ...** that's all very well but ...

jonc [ʒɔ̃] *nm* (bul)rush

joncher [ʒɔ̃ʃe] *vt* (*suj: choses*) to be strewed on

jonction [ʒɔ̃ksjɔ̃] *nf* joining; (**point de) ~** junction

jongleur, euse [ʒɔ̃glœʀ, -øz] *nm/f* juggler

jonquille [ʒɔ̃kij] *nf* daffodil

Jordanie [ʒɔʀdani] *nf*: **la ~** Jordan

joue [ʒu] *nf* cheek; **mettre en ~** to take aim at

jouer [ʒwe] *vt* to play; (*somme d'argent, réputation*) to stake, wager; (*pièce, rôle*) to perform; (*film*) to show; (*simuler: sentiment*) to affect, feign ♦ *vi* to play; (*THÉÂTRE, CINÉMA*) to act, perform; (*bois, porte: se voiler*) to warp; (*clef, pièce: avoir du jeu*) to be loose; **se ~ de** (*difficultés*) to make light of; to deceive; **~ sur** (*miser*) to gamble on; **~ de** (*MUS*) to play; **~ des coudes** to use one's elbows; **~ à** (*jeu, sport, roulette*) to play; **~ avec** (*risquer*) to gamble with; **~ un tour à qn** to play a trick on sb; **~ serré** to play a close game; **~ de malchance** to be dogged with ill-luck

jouet [ʒwe] *nm* toy; **être le ~ de** (*illusion etc*) to be the victim of

joueur, euse [ʒwœʀ, -øz] *nm/f* player; **être beau ~** to be a good loser

joufflu, e [ʒufly] *adj* chubby-cheeked

joug [ʒu] *nm* yoke

jouir [ʒwiʀ]: **~ de** *vt* to enjoy; **jouissance** *nf* pleasure; (*JUR*) use

joujou [ʒuʒu] (*fam*) *nm* toy

jour [ʒuʀ] *nm* day; (*opposé à la nuit*) day, daytime; (*clarté*) daylight; (*fig: aspect*) light; (*ouverture*) opening; **au ~ le ~** from day to day; **de nos ~s** these days; **il fait ~** it's daylight; **au grand ~** (*fig*) in the open; **mettre au ~** to disclose; **mettre à ~** to update; **donner le ~ à** to give birth to; **voir le ~** to be born; **~ férié** *nm* public holiday

journal, aux [ʒuʀnal, -o] *nm* (news)paper; (*personnel*) journal, diary; **~ de bord** log; **~ parlé/télévisé** radio/television news *sg*

journalier, ière [ʒuʀnalje, -jɛʀ] *adj* daily; (*banal*) everyday

journalisme [ʒuʀnalism(ə)] *nm* journalism; **journaliste** *nm/f* journalist

journée [ʒuʀne] *nf* day; **la ~ continue** the 9 to 5 working day

journellement [ʒuʀnɛlmɑ̃] *adv* daily

joyau, x [ʒwajo] *nm* gem, jewel

joyeux, euse [ʒwajø, -øz] *adj* joyful, merry; **~ Noël!** merry Christmas!; **~ anniversaire!** happy birthday!

jubiler [ʒybile] *vi* to be jubilant, exult

jucher [ʒyʃe] *vt, vi* to perch

judas [ʒyda] *nm* (*trou*) spy-hole

judiciaire [ʒydisjɛʀ] *adj* judicial

judicieux, euse [ʒydisjø, -øz] *adj* judicious

judo [ʒydo] *nm* judo

juge [ʒyʒ] *nm* judge; **~ d'instruction** examining (*BRIT*) *ou* committing (*US*) magistrate; **~ de paix** justice of the peace

jugé [ʒyʒe]: **au ~** *adv* by guesswork

jugement [ʒyʒmɑ̃] *nm* judgment; (*JUR: au pénal*) sentence; (: *au civil*) decision

juger [ʒyʒe] *vt* to judge; **~ qn/qch satisfaisant** to consider sb/sth (to be) satisfactory; **~ bon de faire** to see fit to do; **~ de** to appreciate

juif, ive [ʒɥif, -iv] *adj* Jewish ♦ *nm/f* Jew(Jewess)

juillet [ʒɥije] *nm* July

juin [ʒɥɛ̃] *nm* June

jumeau, elle, x [ʒymo, -ɛl] *adj, nm/f* twin; *voir aussi* **jumelle**

jumeler [ʒymle] *vt* to twin

jumelle [ʒymɛl] *adj, nf voir* **jumeau**; **~s** *nfpl* (*appareil*) binoculars
jument [ʒymɑ̃] *nf* mare
jungle [ʒɔ̃gl(ə)] *nf* jungle
jupe [ʒyp] *nf* skirt
jupon [ʒypɔ̃] *nm* waist slip
juré, e [ʒyʀe] *nm/f* juror
jurer [ʒyʀe] *vt* (*obéissance etc*) to swear, vow ♦ *vi* (*dire des jurons*) to swear, curse; (*dissoner*): **~ (avec)** to clash (with); (*s'engager*): **~ de faire/que** to swear *ou* vow to do/that; (*affirmer*): **~ que** to swear *ou* vouch that; **~ de qch** (*s'en porter garant*) to swear to sth
juridique [ʒyʀidik] *adj* legal
juron [ʒyʀɔ̃] *nm* curse, swearword
jury [ʒyʀi] *nm* jury; board
jus [ʒy] *nm* juice; (*de viande*) gravy, (meat) juice; **~ de fruit** fruit juice
jusque [ʒysk(ə)]: **jusqu'à** *prép* (*endroit*) as far as, (up) to; (*moment*) until, till; (*limite*) up to; **~ sur/dans** up to; (*y compris*) even on/in; **jusqu'à ce que** until; **jusqu'à présent** until now
juste [ʒyst(ə)] *adj* (*équitable*) just, fair; (*légitime*) just, justified; (*exact, vrai*) right; (*étroit, insuffisant*) tight ♦ *adv* right; tight; (*chanter*) in tune; (*seulement*) just; **~ assez/au-dessus** just enough/above; **au ~** exactly; **le ~ milieu** the happy medium; **justement** *adv* rightly; justly; (*précisément*) just, precisely; **justesse** *nf* (*précision*) accuracy; (*d'une remarque*) aptness; (*d'une opinion*) soundness; **de justesse** just
justice [ʒystis] *nf* (*équité*) fairness, justice; (*ADMIN*) justice; **rendre la ~** to dispense justice; **rendre ~ à qn** to do sb justice; **justicier, ière** [ʒystisje, -jɛʀ] *nm/f* judge, righter of wrongs
justificatif, ive [ʒystifikatif, -iv] *adj* (*document*) supporting; **pièce justificative** written proof
justifier [ʒystifje] *vt* to justify; **~ de** to prove
juteux, euse [ʒytø, -øz] *adj* juicy
juvénile [ʒyvenil] *adj* young, youthful

K k

K [ka] *nm* (*INFORM*) K
kaki [kaki] *adj inv* khaki
kangourou [kɑ̃guʀu] *nm* kangaroo
karaté [kaʀate] *nm* karate
karting [kaʀtiŋ] *nm* go-carting, karting
kermesse [kɛʀmɛs] *nf* bazaar, (charity) fête; village fair
kidnapper [kidnape] *vt* to kidnap
kilo [kilo] *nm* = **kilogramme**
kilo: **~gramme** *nm* kilogramme; **~métrage** *nm* number of kilometres travelled, ≈ mileage; **~mètre** *nm* kilometre; **~métrique** *adj* (*distance*) in kilometres
kinésithérapeute [kineziteʀapøt] *nm/f* physiotherapist
kiosque [kjɔsk(ə)] *nm* kiosk, stall
klaxon [klaksɔn] *nm* horn; **klaxonner** *vi, vt* to hoot (*BRIT*), honk (*US*)
km. *abr* = **kilomètre**; **km/h** (= *kilomètres/heure*) ≈ m.p.h.
Ko [kao] *abr* (*INFORM: kilooctet*) K
K.-O. [kao] *adj inv* (knocked) out
kyste [kist(ə)] *nm* cyst

L l

l' [l] *dét voir* **le**
la [la] *dét* **le** ♦ *nm* (*MUS*) A; (*en chantant la gamme*) la
là [la] *adv* there; (*ici*) here; (*dans le temps*) then; **elle n'est pas ~** she isn't here; **c'est ~ que** this is where; **~ où** where; **de ~** (*fig*) hence; **par ~** by that; **tout est ~** that's what it's all about; *voir aussi* **-ci**; **celui**; **là-bas** *adv* there
label [labɛl] *nm* stamp, seal
labeur [labœʀ] *nm* toil *no pl*, toiling *no pl*
labo [labo] *abr m* (= *laboratoire*) lab
laboratoire [labɔʀatwaʀ] *nm* laboratory; **~ de langues** language laboratory
laborieux, euse [labɔʀjø, -øz] *adj* (*tâche*) laborious; **classes laborieuses** working classes

labour [labuʀ] *nm* ploughing *no pl*; **~s** *nmpl* (*champs*) ploughed fields; **cheval de ~** plough- *ou* cart-horse; **bœuf de ~** ox

labourer [labuʀe] *vt* to plough; (*fig*) to make deep gashes *ou* furrows in

labyrinthe [labiʀɛ̃t] *nm* labyrinth, maze

lac [lak] *nm* lake

lacer [lase] *vt* to lace *ou* do up

lacérer [laseʀe] *vt* to tear to shreds

lacet [lase] *nm* (*de chaussure*) lace; (*de route*) sharp bend; (*piège*) snare

lâche [lɑʃ] *adj* (*poltron*) cowardly; (*desserré*) loose, slack ♦ *nm/f* coward

lâcher [lɑʃe] *nm* (*de ballons, oiseaux*) release ♦ *vt* to let go of; (*ce qui tombe, abandonner*) to drop; (*oiseau, animal: libérer*) to release, set free; (*fig: mot, remarque*) to let slip, come out with; (*SPORT: distancer*) to leave behind ♦ *vi* (*fil, amarres*) to break, give way; (*freins*) to fail; **~ les amarres** (*NAVIG*) to cast off (the moorings); **~ les chiens** to unleash the dogs; **~ prise** to let go

lâcheté [lɑʃte] *nf* cowardice; lowness

lacrymogène [lakʀimɔʒɛn] *adj*: **gaz ~** teargas

lacté, e [lakte] *adj* (*produit, régime*) milk *cpd*

lacune [lakyn] *nf* gap

là-dedans [ladədɑ̃] *adv* inside (there), in it; (*fig*) in that

là-dessous [ladsu] *adv* underneath, under there; (*fig*) behind that

là-dessus [ladsy] *adv* on there; (*fig*) at that point; about that

ladite [ladit] *dét voir* **ledit**

lagune [lagyn] *nf* lagoon

là-haut [la'o] *adv* up there

laïc [laik] *adj, nm/f* = **laïque**

laid, e [lɛ, lɛd] *adj* ugly; **laideur** *nf* ugliness *no pl*

lainage [lɛnaʒ] *nm* woollen garment; woollen material

laine [lɛn] *nf* wool

laïque [laik] *adj* lay, civil; (*SCOL*) state *cpd* ♦ *nm/f* layman(woman)

laisse [lɛs] *nf* (*de chien*) lead, leash; **tenir en ~** to keep on a lead *ou* leash

laisser [lese] *vt* to leave ♦ *vb aux*: **~ qn faire** to let sb do; **se ~ aller** to let o.s. go; **laisse-toi faire** let me (*ou* him *etc*) do it; **laisser-aller** *nm* carelessness, slovenliness; **laissez-passer** *nm inv* pass

lait [lɛ] *nm* milk; **frère/sœur de ~** foster brother/sister; **~ condensé/concentré** evaporated/condensed milk; **laiterie** *nf* dairy; **laitier, ière** *adj* dairy *cpd* ♦ *nm/f* milkman(dairywoman)

laiton [lɛtɔ̃] *nm* brass

laitue [lety] *nf* lettuce

laïus [lajys] (*péj*) *nm* spiel

lambeau, x [lɑ̃bo] *nm* scrap; **en ~x** in tatters, tattered

lambris [lɑ̃bʀi] *nm* panelling *no pl*

lame [lam] *nf* blade; (*vague*) wave; (*lamelle*) strip; **~ de fond** ground swell *no pl*; **~ de rasoir** razor blade

lamelle [lamɛl] *nf* thin strip *ou* blade

lamentable [lamɑ̃tabl(ə)] *adj* appalling; pitiful

lamenter [lamɑ̃te]: **se ~** *vi* to moan (over)

lampadaire [lɑ̃padɛʀ] *nm* (*de salon*) standard lamp; (*dans la rue*) street lamp

lampe [lɑ̃p(ə)] *nf* lamp; (*TECH*) valve; **~ à souder** blowlamp; **~ de poche** torch (*BRIT*), flashlight (*US*)

lampion [lɑ̃pjɔ̃] *nm* Chinese lantern

lance [lɑ̃s] *nf* spear; **~ d'incendie** fire hose

lancée [lɑ̃se] *nf*: **être/continuer sur sa ~** to be under way/keep going

lancement [lɑ̃smɑ̃] *nm* launching

lance-pierres [lɑ̃spjɛʀ] *nm inv* catapult

lancer [lɑ̃se] *nm* (*SPORT*) throwing *no pl*, throw ♦ *vt* to throw; (*émettre, projeter*) to throw out, send out; (*produit, fusée, bateau, artiste*) to launch; (*injure*) to hurl, fling; (*proclamation, mandat d'arrêt*) to issue; **se ~** *vi* (*prendre de l'élan*) to build up speed; (*se précipiter*): **se ~ sur** *ou* **contre** to rush at; **se ~ dans** (*discussion*) to launch into; (*aventure*) to embark on; **~ qch à qn** to throw sth to sb; (*de façon agressive*) to throw sth at sb; **~ du poids** *nm* putting the shot

lancinant, e [lɑ̃sinɑ̃, -ɑ̃t] *adj* (*regrets etc*) haunting; (*douleur*) shooting

landau [lɑ̃do] *nm* pram (*BRIT*), baby carriage (*US*)

lande [lɑ̃d] *nf* moor

langage [lɑ̃gaʒ] *nm* language

langer [lɑ̃ʒe] *vt* to change (the nappy (*BRIT*) *ou* diaper (*US*) of)

langouste [lɑ̃gust(ə)] *nf* crayfish *inv*; **langoustine** *nf* Dublin Bay prawn

langue [lɑ̃g] *nf* (*ANAT. CULIN*) tongue; (*LING*) language; **tirer la ~ (à)** to stick out one's tongue (at); **de ~ française** French-speaking; **~ maternelle** native language, mother tongue; **~ verte** slang; **~ vivante** modern language

langueur [lɑ̃gœʀ] *nf* languidness

languir [lɑ̃giʀ] *vi* to languish; (*conversation*) to flag; **faire ~ qn** to keep sb waiting

lanière [lanjɛʀ] *nf* (*de fouet*) lash; (*de valise, bretelle*) strap

lanterne [lɑ̃tɛʀn(ə)] *nf* (*portable*) lantern; (*électrique*) light, lamp; (*de voiture*) (side)light

laper [lape] *vt* to lap up

lapidaire [lapidɛʀ] *adj* stone *cpd*; (*fig*) terse

lapin [lapɛ̃] *nm* rabbit; (*peau*) rabbitskin; (*fourrure*) cony

Laponie [laponi] *nf* Lapland

laps [laps] *nm*: **~ de temps** space of time, time *no pl*

laque [lak] *nf* lacquer; (*brute*) shellac; (*pour cheveux*) hair spray

laquelle [lakɛl] *pron voir* **lequel**

larcin [laʀsɛ̃] *nm* theft

lard [laʀ] *nm* (*graisse*) fat; (*bacon*) (streaky) bacon

lardon [laʀdɔ̃] *nm*: **~s** chopped bacon

large [laʀʒ(ə)] *adj* wide; broad; (*fig*) generous ♦ *adv*: **calculer/voir ~** to allow extra/think big ♦ *nm* (*largeur*): **5 m de ~** 5 m wide *ou* in width; (*mer*): **le ~** the open sea; **au ~ de** off; **d'esprit** broadminded; **largement** *adv* widely; greatly; easily; generously; **largesse** *nf* generosity; **largesses** *nfpl* (*dons*) liberalities;

largeur *nf* (*qu'on mesure*) width; (*impression visuelle*) wideness, width; breadth; broadness

larguer [laʀge] *vt* to drop; **~ les amarres** to cast off (the moorings)

larme [laʀm(ə)] *nf* tear; (*fig*) drop; **en ~s** in tears; **larmoyer** *vi* (*yeux*) to water; (*se plaindre*) to whimper

larvé, e [laʀve] *adj* (*fig*) latent

laryngite [laʀɛ̃ʒit] *nf* laryngitis

las, lasse [lɑ, lɑs] *adj* weary

laser [lazɛʀ] *nm*: **(rayon) ~** laser (beam); **chaîne ~** compact disc (player); **disque ~** compact disc

lasse [lɑs] *adj voir* **las**

lasser [lɑse] *vt* to weary, tire; **se ~ de** *vt* to grow weary *ou* tired of

latéral, e, aux [lateʀal, -o] *adj* side *cpd*, lateral

latin, e [latɛ̃, -in] *adj, nm/f* Latin ♦ *nm* (*LING*) Latin

latitude [latityd] *nf* latitude

latte [lat] *nf* lath, slat; (*de plancher*) board

lauréat, e [lɔʀea, -at] *nm/f* winner

laurier [lɔʀje] *nm* (*BOT*) laurel; (*CULIN*) bay leaves *pl*; **~s** *nmpl* (*fig*) laurels

lavable [lavabl(ə)] *adj* washable

lavabo [lavabo] *nm* washbasin; **~s** *nmpl* (*toilettes*) toilet *sg*

lavage [lavaʒ] *nm* washing *no pl*, wash; **~ de cerveau** brainwashing *no pl*

lavande [lavɑ̃d] *nf* lavender

lave [lav] *nf* lava *no pl*

lave-glace [lavglas] *nm* windscreen (*BRIT*) *ou* windshield (*US*) washer

lave-linge [lavlɛ̃ʒ] *nm inv* washing machine

laver [lave] *vt* to wash; (*tache*) to wash off; **se ~** *vi* to have a wash, wash; **se ~ les mains/dents** to wash one's hands/ clean one's teeth; **~ qn de** (*accusation*) to clear sb of; **laverie** *nf*: **laverie (automatique)** launderette; **lavette** *nf* dish cloth; (*fam*) drip; **laveur, euse** *nm/f* cleaner; **lave-vaisselle** *nm inv* dishwasher; **lavoir** *nm* wash house

laxatif, ive [laksatif, -iv] *adj, nm* laxative

MOT-CLÉ

le (l'), **la** [l(ə)] (*pl* **les**) *art déf* **1** the; ~ **livre/la pomme/l'arbre** the book/the apple/the tree; **les étudiants** the students

2 (*noms abstraits*): ~ **courage/l'amour/la jeunesse** courage/love/ youth

3 (*indiquant la possession*): **se casser la jambe** *etc* to break one's leg *etc*; **levez la main** put your hand up; **avoir les yeux gris/~ nez rouge** to have grey eyes/a red nose

4 (*temps*): ~ **matin/soir** in the morning/ evening; mornings/evenings; ~ **jeudi** *etc* (*d'habitude*) on Thursdays *etc*; (*ce jeudi-là etc*) on (the) Thursday

5 (*distribution, évaluation*) a, an; **10 F** ~ **mètre/kilo** 10F a *ou* per metre/kilo; ~ **tiers/quart de** a third/quarter of

♦ *pron* **1** (*personne: mâle*) him; (: *femelle*) her; (: *pluriel*) them; **je ~/la/les vois** I can see him/her/them

2 (*animal, chose: singulier*) it; (: *pluriel*) them; **je ~** (*ou* **la**) **vois** I can see it; **je les vois** I can see them

3 (*remplaçant une phrase*): **je ne ~ savais pas** I didn't know (about it); **il était riche et ne l'est plus** he was once rich but no longer is

---

lécher [leʃe] *vt* to lick; (*laper: lait, eau*) to lick *ou* lap up; ~ **les vitrines** to go window-shopping

leçon [ləsɔ̃] *nf* lesson; **faire la ~ à** (*fig*) to give a lecture to; **~s de conduite** driving lessons

lecteur, trice [lɛktœʀ, -tʀis] *nm/f* reader; (*d'université*) foreign language assistant ♦ *nm* (*TECH*): ~ **de cassettes** cassette player; ~ **de disque compact** compact disc player; ~ **de disquette** disk drive

lecture [lɛktyʀ] *nf* reading

ledit, ladite [lədi] (*mpl* **lesdits**, *fpl* **lesdites**) *dét* the aforesaid

légal, e, aux [legal, -o] *adj* legal

légende [leʒɑ̃d] *nf* (*mythe*) legend; (*de carte, plan*) key; (*de dessin*) caption

léger, ère [leʒe, -ɛʀ] *adj* light; (*bruit, retard*) slight; (*superficiel*) thoughtless; (*volage*) free and easy; flighty; **à la légère** (*parler, agir*) rashly, thoughtlessly; **légèrement** *adv* lightly; thoughtlessly; slightly

législatif, ive [leʒislatif, -iv] *adj* legislative; **législatives** *nfpl* general election *sg*; **législature** [leʒislatyʀ] *nf* legislature; term (of office)

légitime [leʒitim] *adj* (*JUR*) lawful, legitimate; (*fig*) rightful, legitimate; **en état de ~ défense** in self-defence

legs [lɛg] *nm* legacy

léguer [lege] *vt*: ~ **qch à qn** (*JUR*) to bequeath sth to sb; (*fig*) to hand sth down *ou* pass sth on to sb

légume [legym] *nm* vegetable

lendemain [lɑ̃dmɛ̃] *nm*: **le ~** the next *ou* following day; **le ~ matin/soir** the next *ou* following morning/evening; **le ~ de** the day after; **sans ~** short-lived

lent, e [lɑ̃, lɑ̃t] *adj* slow; **lentement** *adv* slowly; **lenteur** *nf* slowness *no pl*

lentille [lɑ̃tij] *nf* (*OPTIQUE*) lens *sg*; (*CULIN*) lentil

léopard [leɔpaʀ] *nm* leopard

lèpre [lɛpʀ(ə)] *nf* leprosy

MOT-CLÉ

lequel, laquelle [ləkɛl, lakɛl] (*mpl* **lesquels**, *fpl* **lesquelles**; *à* + *lequel* = **auquel**, *de* + *lequel* = **duquel** *etc*) *pron* **1** (*interrogatif*) which, which one

2 (*relatif: personne: sujet*) who; (: *objet, après préposition*) whom; (: *chose*) which

♦ *adj*: **auquel cas** in which case

---

les [le] *dét voir* **le**

lesbienne [lɛsbjɛn] *nf* lesbian

lesdites [ledit] *dét pl voir* **ledit**

lesdits [ledi] *dét pl voir* **ledit**

léser [leze] *vt* to wrong

lésiner [lezine] *vi*: ~ **(sur)** to skimp (on)

lésion [lezjɔ̃] *nf* lesion, damage *no pl*

lesquelles [lekɛl] *pron pl voir* **lequel**

lesquels [lekɛl] *pron pl voir* **lequel**

lessive [lesiv] *nf* (*poudre*) washing pow-

der; (*linge*) washing *no pl*, wash
lessiver [lesive] *vt* to wash
lest [lɛst] *nm* ballast
leste [lɛst(ə)] *adj* sprightly, nimble
lettre [lɛtʀ(ə)] *nf* letter; **~s** *nfpl* (*littérature*) literature *sg*; (*SCOL*) arts (subjects); **à la ~** literally; **en toutes ~s** in full
lettré, e [letʀe] *adj* well-read
leucémie [løsemi] *nf* leukaemia

MOT-CLÉ

---

leur [lœʀ] *adj possessif* their; **~ maison** their house; **~s amis** their friends
♦ *pron* **1** (*objet indirect*) (to) them; **je ~ ai dit la vérité** I told them the truth; **je le ~ ai donné** I gave it to them, I gave them it
2 (*possessif*): **le(la) ~, les ~s** theirs

---

leurre [lœʀ] *nm* (*appât*) lure; (*fig*) delusion; snare
leurrer [lœʀe] *vt* to delude, deceive
leurs [lœʀ] *dét voir* **leur**
levain [ləvɛ̃] *nm* leaven
levé, e [ləve] *adj*: **être ~** to be up
levée [ləve] *nf* (*POSTES*) collection; (*CARTES*) trick; **~ de boucliers** general outcry
lever [ləve] *vt* (*vitre, bras etc*) to raise; (*soulever de terre, supprimer: interdiction, siège*) to lift; (*séance*) to close; (*impôts, armée*) to levy ♦ *vi* to rise ♦ *nm*: **au ~** on getting up; **se ~** *vi* to get up; (*soleil*) to rise; (*jour*) to break; (*brouillard*) to lift; **~ de soleil** sunrise; **~ du jour** daybreak
levier [ləvje] *nm* lever
lèvre [lɛvʀ(ə)] *nf* lip
lévrier [levʀije] *nm* greyhound
levure [ləvyʀ] *nf* yeast; **~ chimique** baking powder
lexique [lɛksik] *nm* vocabulary; lexicon
lézard [lezaʀ] *nm* lizard
lézarde [lezaʀd(ə)] *nf* crack
liaison [ljɛzɔ̃] *nf* (*rapport, lien*) link; (*amoureuse*) affair; (*PHONÉTIQUE*) liaison; **entrer/être en ~ avec** to get/be in contact with
liane [ljan] *nf* creeper
liant, e [ljɑ̃, -ɑ̃t] *adj* sociable

liasse [ljas] *nf* wad, bundle
Liban [libɑ̃] *nm*: **le ~** (the) Lebanon; **libanais, e** *adj, nm/f* Lebanese
libeller [libele] *vt* (*chèque, mandat*): **~ (au nom de)** to make out (to); (*lettre*) to word
libellule [libelyl] *nf* dragonfly
libéral, e, aux [liberal, -o] *adj, nm/f* liberal
libérer [libeʀe] *vt* (*délivrer*) to free, liberate; (: *moralement, PSYCH*) to liberate; (*relâcher, dégager: gaz*) to release; to discharge; **se ~** *vi* (*de rendez-vous*) to get out of previous engagements
liberté [libɛʀte] *nf* freedom; (*loisir*) free time; **~s** *nfpl* (*privautés*) liberties; **mettre/être en ~** to set/be free; **en ~ provisoire/surveillée/conditionnelle** on bail/probation/parole; **~s individuelles** personal freedom *sg*
libraire [libʀɛʀ] *nm/f* bookseller
librairie [libʀeʀi] *nf* bookshop
libre [libʀ(ə)] *adj* free; (*route*) clear; (*place etc*) vacant; empty; not engaged; not taken; (*SCOL*) non-state; **de ~** (*place*) free; **~ de qch/de faire** free from sth/to do; **~ arbitre** free will; **~-échange** *nm* free trade; **~-service** *nm* self-service store
Libye [libi] *nf*: **la ~** Libya
licence [lisɑ̃s] *nf* (*permis*) permit; (*diplôme*) degree; (*liberté*) liberty; licence (*BRIT*), license (*US*); licentiousness; **licencié, e** *nm/f* (*SCOL*): **licencié ès lettres/ en droit** ≈ Bachelor of Arts/Law; (*SPORT*) member of a sports federation
licencier [lisɑ̃sje] *vt* (*renvoyer*) to dismiss; (*débaucher*) to make redundant; to lay off
licite [lisit] *adj* lawful
lie [li] *nf* dregs *pl*, sediment
lié, e [lje] *adj*: **très ~ avec** very friendly with *ou* close to; **~ par** (*serment*) bound by
liège [ljɛʒ] *nm* cork
lien [ljɛ̃] *nm* (*corde, fig: affectif*) bond; (*rapport*) link, connection; **~ de parenté** family tie
lier [lje] *vt* (*attacher*) to tie up; (*joindre*)

to link up; (*fig: unir, engager*) to bind; (*CULIN*) to thicken; **se ~ avec** to make friends with; **~ qch à** to tie *ou* link sth to; **~ conversation avec** to strike up a conversation with

lierre [ljɛʀ] *nm* ivy

liesse [ljɛs] *nf*: **être en ~** to be celebrating *ou* jubilant

lieu, x [ljø] *nm* place; **~x** *nmpl* (*habitation*) premises; (*endroit: d'un accident etc*) scene *sg*; **en ~ sûr** in a safe place; **en premier ~** in the first place; **en dernier ~** lastly; **avoir ~** to take place; **avoir ~ de faire** to have grounds for doing; **tenir ~ de** to take the place of; to serve as; **donner ~ à** to give rise to; **au ~ de** instead of

lieu-dit [ljødi] (*pl* lieux-dits) *nm* locality

lieutenant [ljøtnɑ̃] *nm* lieutenant

lièvre [ljɛvʀ(ə)] *nm* hare

ligament [ligamɑ̃] *nm* ligament

ligne [liɲ] *nf* (*gén*) line; (*TRANSPORTS: liaison*) service; (: *trajet*) route; (*silhouette*) figure; **entrer en ~ de compte** to come into it

lignée [liɲe] *nf* line; lineage; descendants *pl*

ligoter [ligɔte] *vt* to tie up

ligue [lig] *nf* league; **liguer** *vt*: **se liguer contre** (*fig*) to combine against

lilas [lila] *nm* lilac

limace [limas] *nf* slug

limaille [limaj] *nf*: **~ de fer** iron filings *pl*

limande [limɑ̃d] *nf* dab

lime [lim] *nf* file; **~ à ongles** nail file; **limer** *vt* to file

limier [limje] *nm* bloodhound; (*détective*) sleuth

limitation [limitasjɔ̃] *nf*: **~ de vitesse** speed limit

limite [limit] *nf* (*de terrain*) boundary; (*partie ou point extrême*) limit; **vitesse/charge ~** maximum speed/load; **cas ~** borderline case; **date ~** deadline

limiter [limite] *vt* (*restreindre*) to limit, restrict; (*délimiter*) to border

limitrophe [limitʀɔf] *adj* border *cpd*

limoger [limɔʒe] *vt* to dismiss

limon [limɔ̃] *nm* silt

limonade [limɔnad] *nf* lemonade (*BRIT*), (lemon) soda (*US*)

lin [lɛ̃] *nm* flax

linceul [lɛ̃sœl] *nm* shroud

linge [lɛ̃ʒ] *nm* (*serviettes etc*) linen; (*pièce de tissu*) cloth; (*aussi*: **~ de corps**) underwear; (: **~ de toilette**) towels *pl*; (*lessive*) washing

lingerie [lɛ̃ʒʀi] *nf* lingerie, underwear

lingot [lɛ̃go] *nm* ingot

linguistique [lɛ̃gɥistik] *adj* linguistic ♦ *nf* linguistics *sg*

lion, ne [ljɔ̃, ljɔn] *nm/f* lion(lioness); (*signe*): **le L~** Leo; **lionceau, x** *nm* lion cub

liposuccion [liposyksjɔ̃] *nf* liposuction

liqueur [likœʀ] *nf* liqueur

liquide [likid] *adj* liquid ♦ *nm* liquid; (*COMM*): **en ~** in ready money *ou* cash; **liquider** *vt* (*société, biens, témoin gênant*) to liquidate; (*compte, problème*) to settle; (*COMM: articles*) to clear, sell off; **liquidités** [likidite] *nfpl* (*COMM*) liquid assets

lire [liʀ] *nf* (*monnaie*) lira ♦ *vt, vi* to read

lis [lis] *nm* = lys

lisible [lizibl(ə)] *adj* legible

lisière [lizjɛʀ] *nf* (*de forêt*) edge; (*de tissu*) selvage

lisons *vb voir* lire

lisse [lis] *adj* smooth

liste [list(ə)] *nf* list; **faire la ~ de** to list; **~ électorale** electoral roll

listing [listiŋ] *nm* (*INFORM*) printout

lit [li] *nm* (*gén*) bed; **faire son ~** to make one's bed; **aller/se mettre au ~** to go to/get into bed; **~ de camp** campbed; **~ d'enfant** cot (*BRIT*), crib (*US*)

literie [litʀi] *nf* bedding, bedclothes *pl*

litière [litjɛʀ] *nf* litter

litige [litiʒ] *nm* dispute

litre [litʀ(ə)] *nm* litre; (*récipient*) litre measure

littéraire [liteʀɛʀ] *adj* literary

littéral, e, aux [liteʀal, -o] *adj* literal

littérature [liteʀatyʀ] *nf* literature

littoral, aux [litɔʀal, -o] *nm* coast

liturgie [lityrʒi] *nf* liturgy
livide [livid] *adj* livid, pallid
livraison [livrɛzɔ̃] *nf* delivery
livre [livr(ə)] *nm* book ♦ *nf* (*poids, monnaie*) pound; ~ **de bord** logbook; ~ **de poche** paperback (*pocket size*)
livré, e [livre] *adj*: ~ **à soi-même** left to o.s. *ou* one's own devices; **livrée** *nf* livery
livrer [livre] *vt* (*COMM*) to deliver; (*otage, coupable*) to hand over; (*secret, information*) to give away; **se** ~ **à** (*se confier*) to confide in; (*se rendre, s'abandonner*) to give o.s. up to; (*faire: pratiques, actes*) to indulge in; (: *travail*) to engage in; (: *sport*) to practise; (*travail: enquête*) to carry out
livret [livrɛ] *nm* booklet; (*d'opéra*) libretto; ~ **de caisse d'épargne** (savings) bank-book; ~ **de famille** (official) family record book; ~ **scolaire** (school) report book
livreur, euse [livrœr, -øz] *nm/f* delivery boy *ou* man/girl *ou* woman
local, e, aux [lɔkal, -o] *adj* local ♦ *nm* (*salle*) premises *pl*; *voir aussi* **locaux**
localiser [lɔkalize] *vt* (*repérer*) to locate, place; (*limiter*) to confine
localité [lɔkalite] *nf* locality
locataire [lɔkatɛr] *nm/f* tenant; (*de chambre*) lodger
location [lɔkasjɔ̃] *nf* (*par le locataire, le loueur*) renting; (*par le propriétaire*) renting out, letting; (*THÉÂTRE*) booking office; "~ **de voitures**" "car rental"
location-vente [lɔkasjɔ̃vɑ̃t] (*pl* **locations-ventes**) *nf* hire purchase (*BRIT*), instalment plan (*US*)
locaux [lɔko] *nmpl* premises
locomotive [lɔkɔmɔtiv] *nf* locomotive, engine; (*fig*) pacesetter, pacemaker
locution [lɔkysjɔ̃] *nf* phrase
loge [lɔʒ] *nf* (*THÉÂTRE: d'artiste*) dressing room; (: *de spectateurs*) box; (*de concierge, franc-maçon*) lodge
logement [lɔʒmɑ̃] *nm* accommodation *no pl* (*BRIT*), accommodations *pl* (*US*); flat (*BRIT*), apartment (*US*); housing *no pl*
loger [lɔʒe] *vt* to accommodate ♦ *vi* to

live; **se** ~ **dans** (*suj: balle, flèche*) to lodge itself in; **trouver à se** ~ to find accommodation; **logeur, euse** *nm/f* landlord(lady)
logiciel [lɔʒisjɛl] *nm* software
logique [lɔʒik] *adj* logical ♦ *nf* logic
logis [lɔʒi] *nm* home; abode, dwelling
loi [lwa] *nf* law; **faire la** ~ to lay down the law
loin [lwɛ̃] *adv* far; (*dans le temps*) a long way off; a long time ago; **plus** ~ further; ~ **de** far from; **au** ~ far off; **de** ~ from a distance; (*fig: de beaucoup*) by far; **il vient de** ~ he's come a long way
lointain, e [lwɛ̃tɛ̃, -ɛn] *adj* faraway, distant; (*dans le futur, passé*) distant, far-off; (*cause, parent*) remote, distant ♦ *nm*: **dans le** ~ in the distance
loir [lwar] *nm* dormouse
loisir [lwazir] *nm*: **heures de** ~ spare time; ~**s** *nmpl* leisure *sg*; leisure activities; **avoir le** ~ **de faire** to have the time *ou* opportunity to do; **à** ~ at leisure; at one's pleasure
londonien, ne [lɔ̃dɔnjɛ̃, -jɛn] *adj* London *cpd*, of London ♦ *nm/f*: **L~, ne** Londoner
Londres [lɔ̃dr(ə)] *n* London
long, longue [lɔ̃, lɔ̃g] *adj* long ♦ *adv*: **en savoir** ~ to know a great deal ♦ *nm*: **de 3 m de** ~ 3 m long, 3 m in length; **ne pas faire** ~ **feu** not to last long; (**tout**) **le** ~ **de** (all) along; **tout au** ~ **de** (*année, vie*) throughout; **de** ~ **en large** (*marcher*) to and fro, up and down; *voir aussi* **longue**
longer [lɔ̃ʒe] *vt* to go (*ou* walk *ou* drive) along(side); (*suj: mur, route*) to border
longiligne [lɔ̃ʒiliɲ] *adj* long-limbed
longitude [lɔ̃ʒityd] *nf* longitude
longitudinal, e, aux [lɔ̃ʒitydinal, -o] *adj* (*running*) lengthways
longtemps [lɔ̃tɑ̃] *adv* (for) a long time, (for) long; **avant** ~ before long; **pour** *ou* **pendant** ~ for a long time; **mettre** ~ **à faire** to take a long time to do
longue [lɔ̃g] *adj voir* **long** ♦ *nf*: **à la** ~ in the end; **longuement** *adv* for a long time

longueur [lɔ̃gœʀ] *nf* length; ~s *nfpl* (*fig: d'un film etc*) tedious parts; **en ~** lengthwise; **tirer en ~** to drag on; **à ~ de journée** all day long; **~ d'onde** wavelength

longue-vue [lɔ̃gvy] *nf* telescope

lopin [lɔpɛ̃] *nm*: **~ de terre** patch of land

loque [lɔk] *nf* (*personne*) wreck; ~s *nfpl* (*habits*) rags

loquet [lɔkɛ] *nm* latch

lorgner [lɔʀɲe] *vt* to eye; (*fig*) to have one's eye on

lors [lɔʀ]: **~ de** *prép* at the time of; during; **~ même que** even though

lorsque [lɔʀsk(ə)] *conj* when, as

losange [lɔzɑ̃ʒ] *nm* diamond; (*GÉOM*) lozenge

lot [lo] *nm* (*part*) share; (*de loterie*) prize; (*fig: destin*) fate, lot; (*COMM, INFORM*) batch

loterie [lɔtʀi] *nf* lottery; raffle

loti, e [lɔti] *adj*: **bien/mal ~** well-/badly off

lotion [losjɔ̃] *nf* lotion

lotir [lɔtiʀ] *vt* (*terrain*) to divide into plots; to sell by lots; **lotissement** *nm* housing development; plot, lot

loto [lɔto] *nm* lotto; numerical lottery

louable [lwabl(ə)] *adj* commendable

louanges [lwɑ̃ʒ] *nfpl* praise *sg*

loubard [lubaʀ] (*fam*) *nm* lout

louche [luʃ] *adj* shady, fishy, dubious ♦ *nf* ladle

loucher [luʃe] *vi* to squint

louer [lwe] *vt* (*maison: suj: propriétaire*) to let, rent (out); (*: locataire*) to rent; (*voiture etc: entreprise*) to hire out (*BRIT*), rent (out); (*: locataire*) to hire, rent; (*réserver*) to book; (*faire l'éloge de*) to praise; **"à ~"** "to let" (*BRIT*), "for rent" (*US*)

loup [lu] *nm* wolf

loupe [lup] *nf* magnifying glass

louper [lupe] *vt* (*manquer*) to miss

lourd, e [luʀ, luʀd(ə)] *adj, adv* heavy; **~ de** (*conséquences, menaces*) charged with; **lourdaud, e** (*péj*) *adj* clumsy

loutre [lutʀ(ə)] *nf* otter

louveteau, x [luvto] *nm* wolf-cub; (*scout*) cub (scout)

louvoyer [luvwaje] *vi* (*NAVIG*) to tack; (*fig*) to hedge, evade the issue

lover [lɔve]: **se ~** *vi* to coil up

loyal, e, aux [lwajal, -o] *adj* (*fidèle*) loyal, faithful; (*fair-play*) fair; **loyauté** *nf* loyalty, faithfulness; fairness

loyer [lwaje] *nm* rent

lu, e [ly] *pp de* **lire**

lubie [lybi] *nf* whim, craze

lubrifiant [lybʀifjɑ̃] *nm* lubricant

lubrifier [lybʀifje] *vt* to lubricate

lubrique [lybʀik] *adj* lecherous

lucarne [lykaʀn(ə)] *nf* skylight

lucratif, ive [lykʀatif, -iv] *adj* lucrative; profitable; **à but non ~** non profit-making

lueur [lɥœʀ] *nf* (*chatoyante*) glimmer *no pl*; (*métallique, mouillée*) gleam *no pl*; (*rougeoyante, chaude*) glow *no pl*; (*pâle*) (faint) light; (*fig*) glimmer; gleam

luge [lyʒ] *nf* sledge (*BRIT*), sled (*US*)

lugubre [lygybʀ(ə)] *adj* gloomy; dismal

MOT-CLÉ
---

lui [lɥi] *pron* **1** (*objet indirect: mâle*) (to) him; (*: femelle*) (to) her; (*: chose, animal*) (to) it; **je ~ ai parlé** I have spoken to him (*ou* to her); **il ~ a offert un cadeau** he gave him (*ou* her) a present
2 (*après préposition, comparatif: personne*) him; (*: chose, animal*) it; **elle est contente de ~** she is pleased with him; **je la connais mieux que ~** I know her better than he does; I know her better than him
3 (*sujet, forme emphatique*) he; **~, il est à Paris** HE is in Paris
4: **~-même** himself; itself

---

luire [lɥiʀ] *vi* to shine; to glow

lumière [lymjɛʀ] *nf* light; ~s *nfpl* (*d'une personne*) wisdom *sg*; **mettre en ~** (*fig*) to highlight; **~ du jour** daylight

luminaire [lyminɛʀ] *nm* lamp, light

lumineux, euse [lyminø, -øz] *adj* (*émettant de la lumière*) luminous; (*éclairé*) illuminated; (*ciel, couleur*) bright; (*relatif à la lumière: rayon etc*) of light, light *cpd*; (*fig: regard*) radiant

lunaire [lynɛʀ] *adj* lunar, moon *cpd*

lunatique [lynatik] *adj* whimsical, temperamental

lundi [lœdi] *nm* Monday; ~ **de Pâques** Easter Monday

lune [lyn] *nf* moon; ~ **de miel** honeymoon

lunette [lynɛt] *nf:* ~**s** *nfpl* glasses, spectacles; (*protectrices*) goggles; ~ **arrière** (*AUTO*) rear window; ~**s de soleil** sun glasses; ~**s noires** dark glasses

lus *etc vb voir* **lire**

lustre [lystʀ(ə)] *nm* (*de plafond*) chandelier; (*fig: éclat*) lustre

lustrer [lystʀe] *vt* to shine

lut *vb voir* **lire**

luth [lyt] *nm* lute

lutin [lytɛ̃] *nm* imp, goblin

lutte [lyt] *nf* (*conflit*) struggle; (*sport*) wrestling; **lutter** *vi* to fight, struggle

luxe [lyks(ə)] *nm* luxury; **de** ~ luxury *cpd*

Luxembourg [lyksɑ̃buʀ] *nm:* **le** ~ Luxembourg

luxer [lykse] *vt:* **se** ~ **l'épaule** to dislocate one's shoulder

luxueux, euse [lyksɥø, -øz] *adj* luxurious

luxure [lyksyʀ] *nf* lust

lycée [lise] *nm* secondary school; **lycéen, ne** *nm/f* secondary school pupil

lyrique [liʀik] *adj* lyrical; (*OPÉRA*) lyric; **artiste** ~ opera singer

lys [lis] *nm* lily

M m

M *abr* = **Monsieur**

m' [m] *pron voir* **me**

ma [ma] *dét voir* **mon**

macaron [makaʀɔ̃] *nm* (*gâteau*) macaroon; (*insigne*) (round) badge

macaronis [makaʀɔni] *nmpl* macaroni *sg*

macédoine [masedwan] *nf:* ~ **de fruits** fruit salad; ~ **de légumes** *nf* mixed vegetables

macérer [maseʀe] *vi, vt* to macerate;

(*dans du vinaigre*) to pickle

mâcher [mɑʃe] *vt* to chew; **ne pas** ~ **ses mots** not to mince one's words

machin [maʃɛ̃] (*fam*) *nm* thing(umajig)

machinal, e, aux [maʃinal, -o] *adj* mechanical, automatic

machination [maʃinɑsjɔ̃] *nf* scheming, frame-up

machine [maʃin] *nf* machine; (*locomotive*) engine; (*fig: rouages*) machinery; ~ **à écrire** typewriter; ~ **à laver/coudre** washing/sewing machine; ~ **à sous** fruit machine; ~ **à vapeur** steam engine; **machinerie** *nf* machinery, plant; (*d'un navire*) engine room; **machiniste** *nm* (*de bus, métro*) driver

mâchoire [mɑʃwaʀ] *nf* jaw; ~ **de frein** brake shoe

mâchonner [mɑʃɔne] *vt* to chew (at)

maçon [masɔ̃] *nm* bricklayer; builder; **maçonnerie** [masɔnʀi] *nf* (*murs*) brickwork; masonry, stonework; (*activité*) bricklaying; building

maculer [makyle] *vt* to stain

Madame [madam] (*pl* **Mesdames**) *nf:* ~ **X** Mrs X; **occupez-vous de** ~/ **Monsieur/Mademoiselle** please serve this lady/gentleman/(young) lady; **bonjour** ~/**Monsieur/Mademoiselle** good morning; (*ton déférent*) good morning Madam/Sir/Madam; (*le nom est connu*) good morning Mrs/Mr/Miss X; ~/**Monsieur/Mademoiselle!** (*pour appeler*) Madam/Sir/Miss!; ~/**Monsieur/Mademoiselle** (*sur lettre*) Dear Madam/Sir/ Madam; **chère** ~/**cher Monsieur/chère Mademoiselle** Dear Mrs/Mr/Miss X; **Mesdames** Ladies

Mademoiselle [madmwazɛl] (*pl* **Mesdemoiselles**) *nf* Miss; *voir aussi* **Madame**

madère [madɛʀ] *nm* Madeira (wine)

magasin [magazɛ̃] *nm* (*boutique*) shop; (*entrepôt*) warehouse; (*d'une arme*) magazine; **en** ~ (*COMM*) in stock

magazine [magazin] *nm* magazine

magicien, ne [maʒisjɛ̃, -jɛn] *nm/f* magician

magie [maʒi] *nf* magic; **magique** *adj* magic; (*enchanteur*) magical

magistral, e, aux [maʒistʀal, -o] *adj*
(*œuvre, addresse*) masterly; (*ton*)
authoritative; (*ex cathedra*): **enseignement** ~ lecturing, lectures *pl*

magistrat [maʒistʀa] *nm* magistrate

magnétique [maɲetik] *adj* magnetic

magnétiser [maɲetize] *vt* to magnetize;
(*fig*) to mesmerize, hypnotize

magnétophone [maɲetɔfɔn] *nm* tape
recorder; ~ **à cassettes** cassette recorder

magnétoscope [maɲetɔskɔp] *nm*
video-tape recorder

magnifique [maɲifik] *adj* magnificent

magot [mago] *nm* (*argent*) pile (of
money); nest egg

magouille [maguj] *nf* scheming

mai [mɛ] *nm* May

maigre [mɛgʀ(ə)] *adj* (very) thin, skinny; (*viande*) lean; (*fromage*) low-fat; (*végétation*) thin, sparse; (*fig*) poor,
meagre, skimpy ♦ *adv*: **faire** ~ not to
eat meat; **jours** ~**s** days of abstinence,
fish days; **maigreur** *nf* thinness; **maigrir**
vi to get thinner, lose weight

maille [maj] *nf* stitch; **avoir** ~ **à partir
avec qn** to have a brush with sb; ~ **à
l'endroit/à l'envers** plain/purl stitch

maillet [majɛ] *nm* mallet

maillon [majɔ̃] *nm* link

maillot [majo] *nm* (*aussi*: ~ **de corps**)
vest; (*de danseur*) leotard; (*de sportif*)
jersey; ~ **de bain** swimsuit; (*d'homme*)
bathing trunks *pl*

main [mɛ̃] *nf* hand; **à la** ~ in one's hand;
se donner la ~ to hold hands; **donner
ou tendre la** ~ **à qn** to hold out one's
hand to sb; **se serrer la** ~ to shake
hands; **serrer la** ~ **à qn** to shake hands
with sb; **sous la** ~ to ou at hand; **attaque à** ~ **armée** armed attack; **à** ~
droite/gauche to the right/left; **à remettre en** ~**s propres** to be delivered
personally; **de première** ~ (*COMM*: *voiture etc*) second-hand with only one previous owner; **mettre la dernière** ~ **à** to
put the finishing touches to; **se faire/
perdre la** ~ to get one's hand in/lose
one's touch; **avoir qch bien en** ~ to
have (got) the hang of sth

main-d'œuvre [mɛ̃dœvʀ(ə)] *nf* manpower, labour

main-forte [mɛ̃fɔʀt(ə)] *nf*: **prêter** ~ **à qn**
to come to sb's assistance

mainmise [mɛ̃miz] *nf* seizure; (*fig*): ~
sur complete hold on

maint, e [mɛ̃, mɛ̃t] *adj* many a; ~**s**
many; **à** ~**es reprises** time and (time)
again

maintenant [mɛ̃tnɑ̃] *adv* now; (*actuellement*) nowadays

maintenir [mɛ̃tniʀ] *vt* (*retenir, soutenir*)
to support; (*contenir: foule etc*) to hold
back; (*conserver, affirmer*) to maintain;
se ~ *vi* to hold; to keep steady; to persist

maintien [mɛ̃tjɛ̃] *nm* maintaining; (*attitude*) bearing

maire [mɛʀ] *nm* mayor

mairie [meʀi] *nf* (*bâtiment*) town hall;
(*administration*) town council

mais [mɛ] *conj* but; ~ **non!** of course
not!; ~ **enfin** but after all; (*indignation*)
look here!; ~ **encore?** is that all?

maïs [mais] *nm* maize (*BRIT*), corn (*US*)

maison [mɛzɔ̃] *nf* house; (*chez-soi*)
home; (*COMM*) firm ♦ *adj inv* (*CULIN*)
home-made; made by the chef; (*fig*) in-
house, own; **à la** ~ at home; (*direction*)
home; ~ **close** *ou* **de passe** brothel; ~ **de
correction** reformatory; ~ **de repos** con-
valescent home; ~ **de santé** mental
home; ~ **des jeunes** ≈ youth club; ~
mère parent company; **maisonnée** *nf*
household, family; **maisonnette** *nf*
small house, cottage

maître, esse [mɛtʀ(ə), mɛtʀɛs] *nm/f*
master(mistress); (*SCOL*) teacher, school-
master(mistress) ♦ *nm* (*peintre etc*) master; (*titre*): **M**~ Maître, term of address
gen for a barrister ♦ *adj* (*principal, essentiel*) main; **être** ~ **de** (*soi-même, situation*) to be in control of; **une
maîtresse femme** a managing woman; ~
chanteur blackmailer; ~/**maîtresse
d'école** schoolmaster(mistress); ~
d'hôtel (*domestique*) butler; (*d'hôtel*)
head waiter; ~ **nageur** lifeguard;
maîtresse *nf* (*amante*) mistress;
maîtresse de maison hostess; housewife

maîtrise [metʀiz] *nf* (*aussi:* ~ *de soi*) self-control, self-possession; (*habileté*) skill, mastery; (*suprématie*) mastery, command; (*diplôme*) ≈ master's degree

maîtriser [metʀize] *vt* (*cheval, incendie*) to (bring under) control; (*sujet*) to master; (*émotion*) to control, master; **se ~** to control o.s.

majestueux, euse [maʒɛstɥø, -øz] *adj* majestic

majeur, e [maʒœʀ] *adj* (*important*) major; (*JUR*) of age; (*fig*) adult ♦ *nm* (*doigt*) middle finger; **en ~e partie** for the most part

majorer [maʒɔʀe] *vt* to increase

majoritaire [maʒɔʀitɛʀ] *adj* majority *cpd*

majorité [maʒɔʀite] *nf* (*gén*) majority; (*parti*) party in power; **en ~** mainly

majuscule [maʒyskyl] *adj, nf:* **(lettre) ~** capital (letter)

mal [mal, mo] (*pl* **maux**) *nm* (*opposé au bien*) evil; (*tort, dommage*) harm; (*douleur physique*) pain, ache; (*maladie*) illness, sickness *no pl* ♦ *adv* badly ♦ *adj* bad, wrong; **être ~** to be uncomfortable; **être ~ avec qn** to be on bad terms with sb; **être au plus ~** (*malade*) to be at death's door; (*brouillé*) to be at daggers drawn; **il a ~ compris** he misunderstood; **dire/penser du ~ de** to speak/think ill of; **ne voir aucun ~ à** to see no harm in, see nothing wrong in; **craignant ~ faire** fearing he was doing the wrong thing; **faire du ~ à qn** to hurt sb; to harm sb; **se faire ~** to hurt o.s.; **se donner du ~ pour faire qch** to go to a lot of trouble to do sth; **ça fait ~** it hurts; **j'ai ~ au dos** my back hurts; **avoir ~ à la tête/à la gorge/aux dents** to have a headache/a sore throat/toothache; **avoir le ~ du pays** to be homesick; **prendre ~** to be taken ill, feel unwell; *voir aussi* **cœur; maux; ~ de mer** seasickness; **~ en point** *adj inv* in a bad state

malade [malad] *adj* ill, sick; (*poitrine, jambe*) bad; (*plante*) diseased ♦ *nm/f* invalid, sick person; (*à l'hôpital etc*) patient; **tomber ~** to fall ill; **être ~ du cœur** to have heart trouble *ou* a bad heart; **~ mental** mentally sick *ou* ill person

maladie [maladi] *nf* (*spécifique*) disease, illness; (*mauvaise santé*) illness, sickness; **~ d'Alzheimer** Alzheimer's (disease); **maladif, ive** *adj* sickly; (*curiosité, besoin*) pathological

maladresse [maladʀɛs] *nf* clumsiness *no pl*; (*gaffe*) blunder

maladroit, e [maladʀwa, -wat] *adj* clumsy

malaise [malɛz] *nm* (*MÉD*) feeling of faintness; feeling of discomfort; (*fig*) uneasiness, malaise

malaisé, e [maleze] *adj* difficult

malaria [malaʀja] *nf* malaria

malaxer [malakse] *vt* to knead; to mix

malchance [malʃɑ̃s] *nf* misfortune, ill luck *no pl*; **par ~** unfortunately

mâle [mɑl] *adj* (*aussi ÉLEC, TECH*) male; (*viril: voix, traits*) manly ♦ *nm* male

malédiction [malediksjɔ̃] *nf* curse

mal: **~encontreux, euse** *adj* unfortunate, untoward; **~-en-point** *adj inv* in a sorry state; **~entendu** *nm* misunderstanding; **~façon** *nf* fault; **~faisant, e** *adj* evil, harmful; **~faiteur** *nm* lawbreaker, criminal; burglar, thief; **~famé, e** *adj* disreputable

malgache [malgaʃ] *adj, nm/f* Madagascan, Malagasy ♦ *nm* (*LING*) Malagasy

malgré [malgʀe] *prép* in spite of, despite; **~ tout** all the same

malheur [malœʀ] *nm* (*situation*) adversity, misfortune; (*événement*) misfortune; disaster, tragedy; **faire un ~** to be a smash hit; **malheureusement** *adv* unfortunately; **malheureux, euse** *adj* (*triste*) unhappy, miserable; (*infortuné, regrettable*) unfortunate; (*malchanceux*) unlucky; (*insignifiant*) wretched ♦ *nm/f* poor soul; unfortunate creature; **les malheureux** the destitute

malhonnête [malɔnɛt] *adj* dishonest

malice [malis] *nf* mischievousness; (*méchanceté*): **par ~** out of malice *ou* spite; **sans ~** guileless; **malicieux, euse**

adj mischievous

malin, igne [malɛ̃, -iɲ] *adj (futé: f gén: maline)* smart, shrewd; *(MÉD)* malignant

malingre [malɛ̃gʀ(ə)] *adj* puny

malle [mal] *nf* trunk

mallette [malɛt] *nf* (small) suitcase; overnight case; attaché case

malmener [malmənə] *vt* to manhandle; *(fig)* to give a rough handling to

malodorant, e [malɔdɔʀɑ̃, -ɑ̃t] *adj* foul- *ou* ill-smelling

malotru [malɔtʀy] *nm* lout, boor

malpropre [malpʀɔpʀ(ə)] *adj* dirty

malsain, e [malsɛ̃, -ɛn] *adj* unhealthy

malt [malt] *nm* malt

Malte [malt(ə)] *nf* Malta

maltraiter [maltʀete] *vt (brutaliser)* to manhandle, ill-treat

malveillance [malvɛjɑ̃s] *nf (animosité)* ill will; *(intention de nuire)* malevolence; *(JUR)* malicious intent *no pl*

malversation [malvɛʀsasjɔ̃] *nf* embezzlement

maman [mamɑ̃] *nf* mum(my), mother

mamelle [mamɛl] *nf* teat

mamelon [mamlɔ̃] *nm (ANAT)* nipple; *(colline)* knoll, hillock

mamie [mami] *(fam) nf* granny

mammifère [mamifɛʀ] *nm* mammal

manche [mɑ̃ʃ] *nf (de vêtement)* sleeve; *(d'un jeu, tournoi)* round; *(GÉO):* **la M~** the Channel ♦ *nm (d'outil, casserole)* handle; *(de pelle, pioche etc)* shaft; **~ à balai** *nm* broomstick; *(AVIAT, INFORM)* joystick

manchette [mɑ̃ʃɛt] *nf (de chemise)* cuff; *(coup)* forearm blow; *(titre)* headline

manchon [mɑ̃ʃɔ̃] *nm (de fourrure)* muff

manchot [mɑ̃ʃo] *nm* one-armed man; armless man; *(ZOOL)* penguin

mandarine [mɑ̃daʀin] *nf* mandarin (orange), tangerine

mandat [mɑ̃da] *nm (postal)* postal *ou* money order; *(d'un député etc)* mandate; *(procuration)* power of attorney, proxy; *(POLICE)* warrant; **~ d'amener** summons *sg*; **~ d'arrêt** warrant for arrest; **mandataire** *nm/f* representative; proxy

manège [manɛʒ] *nm* riding school; *(à la foire)* roundabout, merry-go-round; *(fig)* game, ploy

manette [manɛt] *nf* lever, tap; **~ de jeu** joystick

mangeable [mɑ̃ʒabl(ə)] *adj* edible, eatable

mangeoire [mɑ̃ʒwaʀ] *nf* trough, manger

manger [mɑ̃ʒe] *vt* to eat; *(ronger: suj: rouille etc)* to eat into *ou* away ♦ *vi* to eat

mangue [mɑ̃g] *nf* mango

maniable [manjabl(ə)] *adj (outil)* handy; *(voiture, voilier)* easy to handle

maniaque [manjak] *adj* finicky, fussy; suffering from a mania ♦ *nm/f* maniac

manie [mani] *nf* mania; *(tic)* odd habit

manier [manje] *vt* to handle

manière [manjɛʀ] *nf (façon)* way, manner; **~s** *nfpl (attitude)* manners; *(chichis)* fuss *sg*; **de ~ à** so as to; **de telle ~ que** in such a way that; **de cette ~** in this way *ou* manner; **d'une certaine ~** in a way; **d'une ~ générale** generally speaking, as a general rule; **de toute ~** in any case

maniéré, e [manjeʀe] *adj* affected

manifestant, e [manifɛstɑ̃, -ɑ̃t] *nm/f* demonstrator

manifestation [manifɛstasjɔ̃] *nf (de joie, mécontentement)* expression, demonstration; *(symptôme)* outward sign; *(fête etc)* event; *(POL)* demonstration

manifeste [manifɛst(ə)] *adj* obvious, evident ♦ *nm* manifesto

manifester [manifɛste] *vt (volonté, intentions)* to show, indicate; *(joie, peur)* to express, show ♦ *vi* to demonstrate; **se ~** *vi (émotion)* to show *ou* express itself; *(difficultés)* to arise; *(symptômes)* to appear; *(témoin etc)* to come forward

manigance [manigɑ̃s] *nf* scheme

manigancer [manigɑ̃se] *vt* to plot

manipuler [manipyle] *vt* to handle; *(fig)* to manipulate

manivelle [manivɛl] *nf* crank

mannequin [mankɛ̃] *nm (COUTURE)* dummy; *(MODE)* model

manœuvre [manœvʀ(ə)] *nf (gén)* manoeuvre *(BRIT)*, maneuver *(US)* ♦ *nm* labourer; **manœuvrer** [manœvre] *vt* to manoeuvre (*BRIT*), maneuver (*US*); (*levier, machine*) to operate ♦ *vi* to manoeuvre

manoir [manwaʀ] *nm* manor *ou* country house

manque [mɑ̃k] *nm* (*insuffisance*): **~ de** lack of; (*vide*) emptiness, gap; (*MÉD*) withdrawal; **~s** *nmpl* (*lacunes*) faults, defects

manqué, e [mɑ̃ke] *adj* failed; **garçon ~** tomboy

manquer [mɑ̃ke] *vi* (*faire défaut*) to be lacking; (*être absent*) to be missing; (*échouer*) to fail ♦ *vt* to miss ♦ *vb impers*: **il (nous) manque encore 100 F** we are still 100 F short; **il manque des pages (au livre)** there are some pages missing (from the book); **il/cela me manque** I miss him/this; **~ à** (*règles etc*) to be in breach of, fail to observe; **~ de** to lack; **il a manqué (de) se tuer** he very nearly got killed

mansarde [mɑ̃saʀd(ə)] *nf* attic

mansuétude [mɑ̃syetyd] *nf* leniency

manteau, x [mɑ̃to] *nm* coat

manucure [manykyʀ] *nf* manicurist

manuel, le [manɥɛl] *adj* manual ♦ *nm* (*ouvrage*) manual, handbook

manufacture [manyfaktyʀ] *nf* factory; **manufacturé, e** [manyfaktyʀe] *adj* manufactured

manuscrit, e [manyskʀi, -it] *adj* handwritten ♦ *nm* manuscript

manutention [manytɑ̃sjɔ̃] *nf* (*COMM*) handling; (*local*) storehouse

mappemonde [mapmɔ̃d] *nf* (*plane*) map of the world; (*sphère*) globe

maquereau, x [makʀo] *nm* (*ZOOL*) mackerel *inv*; (*fam*) pimp

maquette [makɛt] *nf* (*d'un décor, bâtiment, véhicule*) (scale) model; (*d'une page illustrée*) paste-up

maquillage [makijaʒ] *nm* making up; faking; (*crème etc*) make-up

maquiller [makije] *vt* (*personne, visage*) to make up; (*truquer: passeport, statistique*) to fake; (: *voiture volée*) to do over (*respray etc*); **se ~** *vi* to make up (one's face)

maquis [maki] *nm* (*GÉO*) scrub; (*MIL*) maquis, underground fighting *no pl*

maraîcher, ère [maʀeʃe, maʀeʃɛʀ] *adj*: **cultures maraîchères** market gardening *sg* ♦ *nm/f* market gardener; **jardin ~** market garden (*BRIT*), truck farm (*US*)

marais [maʀɛ] *nm* marsh, swamp

marasme [maʀasm(ə)] *nm* stagnation, slump

marathon [maʀatɔ̃] *nm* marathon

marâtre [maʀɑtʀ(ə)] *nf* cruel mother

maraudeur [maʀodœʀ] *nm* prowler

marbre [maʀbʀ(ə)] *nm* (*pierre, statue*) marble; (*d'une table, commode*) marble top; **marbrer** *vt* to mottle, blotch

marc [maʀ] *nm* (*de raisin, pommes*) marc; **~ de café** coffee grounds *pl ou* dregs *pl*

marchand, e [maʀʃɑ̃, -ɑ̃d] *nm/f* shopkeeper, tradesman(woman); (*au marché*) stallholder ♦ *adj*: **prix/valeur ~(e)** market price/value; **~/e de fruits** fruiterer (*BRIT*), fruit seller (*US*); **~/e de journaux** newsagent (*BRIT*), newsdealer (*US*); **~/e de légumes** greengrocer (*BRIT*), produce dealer (*US*); **~/e de quatre saisons** costermonger (*BRIT*), street vendor (selling fresh fruit and vegetables) (*US*)

marchander [maʀʃɑ̃de] *vi* to bargain, haggle

marchandise [maʀʃɑ̃diz] *nf* goods *pl*, merchandise *no pl*

marche [maʀʃ(ə)] *nf* (*d'escalier*) step; (*activité*) walking; (*promenade, trajet, allure*) walk; (*démarche*) walk, gait; (*MIL etc, MUS*) march; (*fonctionnement*) running; (*progression*) progress; course; **ouvrir/fermer la ~** to lead the way/ bring up the rear; **dans le sens de la ~** (*RAIL*) facing the engine; **en ~** (*monter etc*) while the vehicle is moving *ou* in motion; **mettre en ~** to start; **se mettre en ~** (*personne*) to get moving; (*machine*) to start; **~ à suivre** (correct) procedure; (*sur notice*) (step by step) instructions *pl*; **~ arrière** reverse (gear); **faire ~ arrière** to reverse; (*fig*) to backtrack, back-pedal

marché [maʀʃe] *nm* (*lieu, COMM, ÉCON*)

market; (*ville*) trading centre; (*transaction*) bargain, deal; **faire du ~ noir** to buy and sell on the black market; **~ aux puces** flea market; **M~ commun** Common Market

marchepied [maʀʃəpje] *nm* (*RAIL*) step; (*fig*) stepping stone

marcher [maʀʃe] *vi* to walk; (*MIL*) to march; (*aller*: *voiture, train, affaires*) to go; (*prospérer*) to go well; (*fonctionner*) to work, run; (*fam*) to go along, agree; to be taken in; **~ sur** to walk on; (*mettre le pied sur*) to step on *ou* in; (*MIL*) to march upon; **~ dans** (*herbe etc*) to walk in *ou* on; (*flaque*) to step in; **faire ~ qn** to pull sb's leg; to lead sb up the garden path; **marcheur, euse** *nm/f* walker

mardi [maʀdi] *nm* Tuesday; **M~ gras** Shrove Tuesday

mare [maʀ] *nf* pond

marécage [maʀekaʒ] *nm* marsh, swamp

maréchal, aux [maʀeʃal, -o] *nm* marshal

marée [maʀe] *nf* tide; (*poissons*) fresh (sea) fish; **~ haute/basse** high/low tide; **~ montante/descendante** rising/ebb tide

marémotrice [maʀemɔtʀis] *adj f* tidal

margarine [maʀgaʀin] *nf* margarine

marge [maʀʒ(ə)] *nf* margin; **en ~ de** (*fig*) on the fringe of; cut off from; **~ bénéficiaire** profit margin

marguerite [maʀgəʀit] *nf* marguerite, (oxeye) daisy; (*d'imprimante*) daisy-wheel

mari [maʀi] *nm* husband

mariage [maʀjaʒ] *nm* (*union, état, fig*) marriage; (*noce*) wedding; **~ civil/religieux** registry office (*BRIT*) *ou* civil/church wedding

marié, e [maʀje] *adj* married ♦ *nm* (bride)groom; **les ~s** the bride and groom; **les (jeunes) ~s** the newly-weds; **mariée** *nf* bride

marier [maʀje] *vt* to marry; (*fig*) to blend; **se ~ (avec)** to marry

marin, e [maʀɛ̃, -in] *adj* sea *cpd*, marine ♦ *nm* sailor

marine [maʀin] *adj voir* **marin** ♦ *adj inv* navy (blue) ♦ *nm* (*MIL*) marine ♦ *nf* navy; **~ de guerre** navy; **~ marchande** merchant navy

marionnette [maʀjɔnɛt] *nf* puppet

maritime [maʀitim] *adj* sea *cpd*, maritime

mark [maʀk] *nm* mark

marmelade [maʀməlad] *nf* stewed fruit, compote; **~ d'oranges** marmalade

marmite [maʀmit] *nf* (cooking-)pot

marmonner [maʀmɔne] *vt, vi* to mumble, mutter

marmotter [maʀmɔte] *vt* to mumble

Maroc [maʀɔk] *nm*: **le ~** Morocco; **marocain, e** *adj* Moroccan ♦ *nm/f*: **Marocain, e** Moroccan

maroquinerie [maʀɔkinʀi] *nf* leather craft; fine leather goods *pl*

marquant, e [maʀkɑ̃, -ɑ̃t] *adj* outstanding

marque [maʀk(ə)] *nf* mark; (*SPORT, JEU*: *décompte des points*) score; (*COMM*: *de produits*) brand; make; (*de disques*) label; **de ~** (*COMM*) brand-name *cpd*; proprietary; (*fig*) high-class; distinguished; **~ de fabrique** trademark; **~ déposée** registered trademark

marquer [maʀke] *vt* to mark; (*inscrire*) to write down; (*bétail*) to brand; (*SPORT*: *but etc*) to score; (: *joueur*) to mark; (*accentuer*: *taille etc*) to emphasize; (*manifester*: *refus, intérêt*) to show ♦ *vi* (*évènement, personnalité*) to stand out, be outstanding; (*SPORT*) to score; **~ les points** (*tenir la marque*) to keep the score

marqueterie [maʀkətʀi] *nf* inlaid work, marquetry

marquis [maʀki] *nm* marquis *ou* marquess

marquise [maʀkiz] *nf* marchioness; (*auvent*) glass canopy *ou* awning

marraine [maʀɛn] *nf* godmother

marrant, e [maʀɑ̃, -ɑ̃t] (*fam*) *adj* funny

marre [maʀ] (*fam*) *adv*: **en avoir ~ de** to be fed up with

marrer [maʀe]: **se ~** (*fam*) *vi* to have a (good) laugh

marron [maʀɔ̃] *nm* (*fruit*) chestnut ♦ *adj inv* brown; **marronnier** *nm* chestnut (tree)

mars [maʀs] *nm* March

marsouin [maʀswɛ̃] *nm* porpoise

marteau, x [maʀto] *nm* hammer; (*de porte*) knocker; **marteau-piqueur** *nm* pneumatic drill

marteler [maʀtəle] *vt* to hammer

martien, ne [maʀsjɛ̃, -jɛn] *adj* Martian, of *ou* from Mars

martinet [maʀtinɛ] *nm* (*fouet*) small whip; (*ZOOL*) swift

martyr, e [maʀtiʀ] *nm/f* martyr

martyre [maʀtiʀ] *nm* martyrdom; (*fig: sens affaibli*) agony, torture

martyriser [maʀtiʀize] *vt* (*REL*) to martyr; (*fig*) to bully; (*enfant*) to batter, beat

marxiste [maʀksist(ə)] *adj, nm/f* Marxist

masculin, e [maskylɛ̃, -in] *adj* masculine; (*sexe, population*) male; (*équipe, vêtements*) men's; (*viril*) manly ♦ *nm* masculine

masque [mask(ə)] *nm* mask; **masquer** [maske] *vt* (*cacher: paysage, porte*) to hide, conceal; (*dissimuler: vérité, projet*) to mask, obscure

massacre [masakʀ(ə)] *nm* massacre, slaughter; **massacrer** [masakʀe] *vt* to massacre, slaughter; (*fig: texte etc*) to murder

massage [masaʒ] *nm* massage

masse [mas] *nf* mass; (*péj*): **la ~** the masses *pl*; (*ÉLEC*) earth; (*maillet*) sledgehammer; **une ~ de** (*fam*) masses *ou* loads of; **en ~** *adv* (*en bloc*) in bulk; (*en foule*) en masse ♦ *adj* (*exécutions, production*) mass *cpd*

masser [mase] *vt* (*assembler*) to gather; (*pétrir*) to massage; **se ~** *vi* to gather; **masseur, euse** *nm/f* masseur(euse)

massif, ive [masif, -iv] *adj* (*porte*) solid, massive; (*visage*) heavy, large; (*bois, or*) solid; (*dose*) massive; (*déportations etc*) mass *cpd* ♦ *nm* (*montagneux*) massif; (*de fleurs*) clump, bank

massue [masy] *nf* club, bludgeon

mastic [mastik] *nm* (*pour vitres*) putty; (*pour fentes*) filler

mastiquer [mastike] *vt* (*aliment*) to chew, masticate; (*fente*) to fill; (*vitre*) to putty

mat, e [mat] *adj* (*couleur, métal*) mat(t); (*bruit, son*) dull ♦ *adj inv* (*ÉCHECS*): **être ~** to be checkmate

mât [mɑ] *nm* (*NAVIG*) mast; (*poteau*) pole, post

match [matʃ] *nm* match; **faire ~ nul** to draw; **~ aller** first leg; **~ retour** second leg, return match

matelas [matla] *nm* mattress; **~ pneumatique** air bed *ou* mattress

matelassé, e [matlase] *adj* padded; quilted

matelot [matlo] *nm* sailor, seaman

mater [mate] *vt* (*personne*) to bring to heel, subdue; (*révolte*) to put down

matérialiste [mateʀjalist(ə)] *adj* materialistic

matériaux [mateʀjo] *nmpl* material(s)

matériel, le [mateʀjɛl] *adj* material ♦ *nm* equipment *no pl*; (*de camping etc*) gear *no pl*

maternel, le [matɛʀnɛl] *adj* (*amour, geste*) motherly, maternal; (*grand-père, oncle*) maternal; **maternelle** *nf* (*aussi: école maternelle*) (state) nursery school

maternité [matɛʀnite] *nf* (*établissement*) maternity hospital; (*état de mère*) motherhood, maternity; (*grossesse*) pregnancy

mathématique [matematik] *adj* mathematical; **mathématiques** *nfpl* (*science*) mathematics *sg*

matière [matjɛʀ] *nf* (*PHYSIQUE*) matter; (*COMM, TECH*) material, matter *no pl*; (*fig: d'un livre etc*) subject matter, material; (*SCOL*) subject; **en ~ de** as regards; **~s grasses** fat content *sg*; **~s premières** raw materials

matin [matɛ̃] *nm, adv* morning; **du ~ au soir** from morning till night; **de bon** *ou* **grand ~** early in the morning; **matinal, e, aux** *adj* (*toilette, gymnastique*) morning *cpd*; (*de bonne heure*) early; **être matinal** (*personne*) to be up early; to be an early riser

matinée [matine] *nf* morning; (*spectacle*) matinée

matou [matu] *nm* tom(cat)

matraque [matʀak] *nf* club; (*de policier*) truncheon (*BRIT*), billy (*US*)

matricule [matʀikyl] *nf* (*aussi: registre* ~) roll, register ♦ *nm* (*aussi: numéro* ~: *MIL*) regimental number; (: *ADMIN*) reference number

matrimonial, e, aux [matʀimɔnjal, -o] *adj* marital, marriage *cpd*

maudire [modiʀ] *vt* to curse

maudit, e [modi, -it] (*fam*) *adj* (*satané*) blasted, confounded

maugréer [mogʀee] *vi* to grumble

maussade [mosad] *adj* sullen

mauvais, e [mɔvɛ, -ɛz] *adj* bad; (*faux*): **le** ~ **numéro/moment** the wrong number/moment; (*méchant, malveillant*) malicious, spiteful; **il fait** ~ the weather is bad; **la mer est** ~**e** the sea is rough; ~ **plaisant** hoaxer; ~**e herbe** weed; ~**e langue** gossip, scandalmonger (*BRIT*); ~**e passe** difficult situation; bad patch; ~**e tête** rebellious *ou* headstrong customer

maux [mo] *nmpl de* **mal**; ~ **de ventre** stomachache *sg*

maximum [maksimɔm] *adj, nm* maximum; **au** ~ (*le plus possible*) to the full; as much as one can; (*tout au plus*) at the (very) most *ou* maximum

mayonnaise [majɔnɛz] *nf* mayonnaise

mazout [mazut] *nm* (fuel) oil

Me *abr* = **Maître**

me(m') [m(ə)] *pron* me; (*réfléchi*) myself

mec [mɛk] (*fam*) *nm* bloke, guy

mécanicien, ne [mekanisjɛ̃, -jɛn] *nm/f* mechanic; (*RAIL*) (train *ou* engine) driver

mécanique [mekanik] *adj* mechanical ♦ *nf* (*science*) mechanics *sg*; (*technologie*) mechanical engineering; (*mécanisme*) mechanism; engineering; works *pl*; **ennui** ~ engine trouble *no pl*

mécanisme [mekanism(ə)] *nm* mechanism

méchamment [meʃamɑ̃] *adv* nastily, maliciously, spitefully

méchanceté [meʃɑ̃ste] *nf* nastiness, ma-

liciousness; nasty *ou* spiteful *ou* malicious remark (*ou* action)

méchant, e [meʃɑ̃, -ɑ̃t] *adj* nasty, malicious, spiteful; (*enfant: pas sage*) naughty; (*animal*) vicious; (*avant le nom: valeur péjorative*) nasty; miserable; (: *intensive*) terrific

mèche [mɛʃ] *nf* (*de lampe, bougie*) wick; (*d'un explosif*) fuse; (*de vilebrequin, perceuse*) bit; (*de cheveux*) lock; **de** ~ **avec** in league with

mécompte [mekɔ̃t] *nm* miscalculation; (*déception*) disappointment

méconnaissable [mekɔnɛsabl(ə)] *adj* unrecognizable

méconnaître [mekɔnɛtʀ(ə)] *vt* (*ignorer*) to be unaware of; (*mésestimer*) to misjudge

mécontent, e [mekɔ̃tɑ̃, -ɑ̃t] *adj*: ~ (**de**) discontented *ou* dissatisfied *ou* displeased (with); (*contrarié*) annoyed (at); **mécontentement** *nm* dissatisfaction, discontent, displeasure; annoyance

médaille [medaj] *nf* medal

médaillon [medajɔ̃] *nm* (*portrait*) medallion; (*bijou*) locket

médecin [medsɛ̃] *nm* doctor; ~ **légiste** forensic surgeon

médecine [medsin] *nf* medicine; ~ **légale** forensic medicine

média [medja] *nmpl*: **les** ~ the media

médiatique [medjatik] *adj* media *cpd*

médiatisé, e [medjatize] *adj* reported in the media; **ce procès a été très** ~ (*péj*) this trial was turned into a media event

médical, e, aux [medikal, -o] *adj* medical

médicament [medikamɑ̃] *nm* medicine, drug

médiéval, e, aux [medjeval, -o] *adj* medieval

médiocre [medjɔkʀ(ə)] *adj* mediocre, poor

médire [mediʀ] *vi*: ~ **de** to speak ill of; **médisance** *nf* scandalmongering (*BRIT*); piece of scandal *ou* of malicious gossip

méditer [medite] *vt* (*approfondir*) to meditate on, ponder (over); (*combiner*) to meditate ♦ *vi* to meditate

Méditerranée [mediterane] nf: **la (mer)** ~ the Mediterranean (Sea); **méditerranéen, ne** adj, nm/f Mediterranean

méduse [medyz] nf jellyfish

meeting [mitiŋ] nm (POL, SPORT) rally

méfait [mefe] nm (faute) misdemeanour, wrongdoing; ~**s** nmpl (ravages) ravages, damage sg

méfiance [mefjɑ̃s] nf mistrust, distrust; **méfiant, e** [mefjɑ̃, -ɑ̃t] adj mistrustful, distrustful

méfier [mefje]: **se** ~ vi to be wary; to be careful; **se** ~ **de** to mistrust, distrust, be wary of; (faire attention) to be careful about

mégarde [megard(ə)] nf: **par** ~ accidentally; by mistake

mégère [meʒɛr] nf shrew

mégot [mego] nm cigarette end

meilleur, e [mejœr] adj, adv better; (valeur superlative) best ♦ nm: **le** ~ (celui qui ...) the best (one); (ce qui ...) the best; **le** ~ **des deux** the better of the two; **de** ~**e heure** earlier; ~ **marché** cheaper; **meilleure** nf: **la meilleure** the best (one)

mélancolie [melɑ̃kɔli] nf melancholy, gloom; **mélancolique** adj melancholic, melancholy

mélange [melɑ̃ʒ] nm mixture

mélanger [melɑ̃ʒe] vt (substances) to mix; (vins, couleurs) to blend; (mettre en désordre) to mix up, muddle (up)

mélasse [melas] nf treacle, molasses sg

mêlée [mele] nf mêlée, scramble; (RUGBY) scrum(mage)

mêler [mele] vt (substances, odeurs, races) to mix; (embrouiller) to muddle (up), mix up; **se** ~ vi to mix; to mingle; **se** ~ **à** (suj: personne) to join; to mix with; (suj: odeurs etc) to mingle with; **se** ~ **de** (suj: personne) to meddle with, interfere in; ~ **qn à** (affaire) to get sb mixed up ou involved in

mélodie [melɔdi] nf melody

melon [m(ə)lɔ̃] nm (BOT) (honeydew) melon; (aussi: chapeau ~) bowler (hat)

membre [mɑ̃br(ə)] nm (ANAT) limb; (personne, pays, élément) member ♦ adj

member cpd

mémé [meme] (fam) nf granny

MOT-CLÉ
---

même [mɛm] adj **1** (avant le nom) same; **en** ~ **temps** at the same time

2 (après le nom: renforcement): **il est la loyauté** ~ he is loyalty itself; **ce sont ses paroles/celles-là** ~ they are his very words/the very ones

♦ pron: **le(la)** ~ the same one

♦ adv **1** (renforcement): **il n'a** ~ **pas pleuré** he didn't even cry; ~ **lui l'a dit** even HE said it; **ici** ~ at this very place

2: **à** ~: **à** ~ **la bouteille** straight from the bottle; **à** ~ **la peau** next to the skin; **être à** ~ **de faire** to be in a position to do, be able to do

3: ~ **si** to do likewise; **lui de** ~ so does (ou did ou is) he; **de** ~ **que** just as; **il en va de** ~ **pour** the same goes for

---

mémento [memɛ̃to] nm (agenda) appointments diary; (ouvrage) summary

mémoire [memwar] nf memory ♦ nm (ADMIN, JUR) memorandum; (SCOL) dissertation, paper; ~**s** nmpl (souvenirs) memoirs; **à la** ~ **de** to the ou in memory of; **pour** ~ for the record; **de** ~ from memory; ~ **morte/vive** (INFORM) ROM/RAM

menace [mənas] nf threat

menacer [mənase] vt to threaten

ménage [menaʒ] nm (travail) housekeeping, housework; (couple) (married) couple; (famille, ADMIN) household; **faire le** ~ to do the housework

ménagement [menaʒmɑ̃] nm care and attention; ~**s** nmpl (égards) consideration sg, attention sg

ménager, ère [menaʒe, -ɛr] adj household cpd, domestic ♦ vt (traiter) to handle with tact; to treat considerately; (utiliser) to use sparingly; to use with care; (prendre soin de) to take (great) care of, look after; (organiser) to arrange; (installer) to put in; to make; ~ **qch à qn** (réserver) to have sth in store for sb; **ménagère** nf housewife

mendiant, e [mãdjã, -ãt] *nm/f* beggar; **mendier** [mãdje] *vi* to beg ♦ *vt* to beg (for)

mener [məne] *vt* to lead; (*enquête*) to conduct; (*affaires*) to manage ♦ *vi*: ~ (à la marque) to lead, be in the lead; ~ à/dans (*emmener*) to take to/into; ~ qch à terme *ou* à bien to see sth through (to a successful conclusion), complete sth successfully

meneur, euse [mənœʀ, -øz] *nm/f* leader; (*péj*) agitator; ~ **de jeu** host, quizmaster

méningite [menẽʒit] *nf* meningitis *no pl*

ménopause [menopoz] *nf* menopause

menottes [mənɔt] *nfpl* handcuffs

mensonge [mãsɔ̃ʒ] *nm* lie; lying *no pl*; **mensonger, ère** *adj* false

mensualité [mãsɥalite] *nf* monthly payment; monthly salary

mensuel, le [mãsɥɛl] *adj* monthly

mensurations [mãsyʀasjɔ̃] *nfpl* measurements

mentalité [mãtalite] *nf* mentality

menteur, euse [mãtœʀ, -øz] *nm/f* liar

menthe [mãt] *nf* mint

mention [mãsjɔ̃] *nf* (*note*) note, comment; (*SCOL*): ~ **bien** *etc* ≈ grade B *etc* (*ou* upper 2nd class *etc*) pass (*BRIT*), ≈ pass with (high) honors (*US*); **mentionner** *vt* to mention

mentir [mãtiʀ] *vi* to lie; to be lying

menton [mãtɔ̃] *nm* chin

menu, e [məny] *adj* slim, slight; tiny; (*frais, difficulté*) minor ♦ *adv* (*couper, hacher*) very fine ♦ *nm* menu; **par le ~** (*raconter*) in minute detail; ~**e monnaie** small change

menuiserie [mənɥizʀi] *nf* (*travail*) joinery, carpentry; woodwork; (*local*) joiner's workshop; (*ouvrage*) woodwork *no pl*; **menuisier** [mənɥizje] *nm* joiner, carpenter

méprendre [mepʀãdʀ(ə)]: **se** ~ *vi* to be mistaken (about)

mépris [mepʀi] *nm* (*dédain*) contempt, scorn; (*indifférence*): **le** ~ **de** contempt *ou* disregard for; **au** ~ **de** regardless of, in defiance of

méprisable [mepʀizabl(ə)] *adj* contemptible, despicable

méprise [mepʀiz] *nf* mistake, error; misunderstanding

mépriser [mepʀize] *vt* to scorn, despise; (*gloire, danger*) to scorn, spurn

mer [mɛʀ] *nf* sea; (*marée*) tide; **en** ~ at sea; **prendre la** ~ to put out to sea; **en haute** *ou* **pleine** ~ off shore, on the open sea; **la** ~ **du Nord/Rouge** the North/Red Sea

mercantile [mɛʀkãtil] (*péj*) *adj* mercenary

mercenaire [mɛʀsənɛʀ] *nm* mercenary, hired soldier

mercerie [mɛʀsəʀi] *nf* haberdashery (*BRIT*), notions (*US*); haberdasher's shop (*BRIT*), notions store (*US*)

merci [mɛʀsi] *excl* thank you ♦ *nf*: **à** ~ **de qn/qch** at sb's mercy/the mercy of sth; ~ **de** thank you for; **sans** ~ merciless(ly)

mercredi [mɛʀkʀədi] *nm* Wednesday

mercure [mɛʀkyʀ] *nm* mercury

merde [mɛʀd(ə)] (*fam!*) *nf* shit (!) ♦ *excl* (bloody) hell (!)

mère [mɛʀ] *nf* mother; ~ **célibataire** unmarried mother

méridional, e, aux [meʀidjɔnal, -o] *adj* southern ♦ *nm/f* Southerner

meringue [məʀɛ̃g] *nf* meringue

mérite [meʀit] *nm* merit; **le** ~ (**de ceci**) **lui revient** the credit (for this) is his

mériter [meʀite] *vt* to deserve

merlan [mɛʀlã] *nm* whiting

merle [mɛʀl(ə)] *nm* blackbird

merveille [mɛʀvɛj] *nf* marvel, wonder; **faire** ~ to work wonders; **à** ~ perfectly, wonderfully

merveilleux, euse [mɛʀvɛjø, -øz] *adj* marvellous, wonderful

mes [me] *dét voir* **mon**

mésange [mezãʒ] *nf* tit(mouse)

mésaventure [mezavãtyʀ] *nf* misadventure, misfortune

Mesdames [medam] *nfpl de* **Madame**

Mesdemoiselles [medmwazɛl] *nfpl de* **Mademoiselle**

mésentente [mezãtãt] *nf* dissension,

disagreement

mesquin, e [mɛskɛ̃, -in] *adj* mean, petty

message [mesaʒ] *nm* message; **messager, ère** *nm/f* messenger

messe [mɛs] *nf* mass; **aller à la ~** to go to mass; **~ de minuit** midnight mass

Messieurs [mesjø] *nmpl de* **Monsieur**

mesure [məzyʀ] *nf* (*évaluation, dimension*) measurement; (*étalon, récipient, contenu*) measure; (*MUS: cadence*) time, tempo; (: *division*) bar; (*retenue*) moderation; (*disposition*) measure, step; **sur ~** (*costume*) made-to-measure; **à la ~ de** (*fig*) worthy of; on the same scale as; **dans la ~ où** insofar as, inasmuch as; **à ~ que** as; **être en ~ de** to be in a position to

mesurer [məzyʀe] *vt* to measure; (*juger*) to weigh up, assess; (*limiter*) to limit, ration; (*modérer*) to moderate; **se ~ avec** to have a confrontation with; to tackle; **il mesure 1 m 80** he's 1 m 80 tall

met *vb voir* **mettre**

métal, aux [metal, -o] *nm* metal; **métallique** *adj* metallic

météo [meteo] *nf* weather report; ≈ Met Office (*BRIT*); ≈ National Weather Service (*US*)

météorologie [meteɔʀɔlɔʒi] *nf* meteorology

méthode [metɔd] *nf* method; (*livre, ouvrage*) manual, tutor

métier [metje] *nm* (*profession: gén*) job; (: *manuel*) trade; (*artisanal*) craft; (*technique, expérience*) (acquired) skill *ou* technique; (*aussi: ~ à tisser*) (weaving) loom

métis, se [metis] *adj, nm/f* half-caste, half-breed

métisser [metise] *vt* to cross

métrage [metʀaʒ] *nm* (*de tissu*) length, ≈ yardage; (*CINÉMA*) footage, length; **long/moyen/court ~** full-length/medium-length/short film

mètre [mɛtʀ(ə)] *nm* metre; (*règle*) (metre) rule; (*ruban*) tape measure; **métrique** *adj* metric

métro [metʀo] *nm* underground (*BRIT*), subway

métropole [metʀɔpɔl] *nf* (*capitale*) metropolis; (*pays*) home country

mets [mɛ] *nm* dish

metteur [metœʀ] *nm*: **~ en scène** (*THÉÂTRE*) producer; (*CINÉMA*) director; **~ en ondes** producer

---
MOT-CLÉ
---

mettre [mɛtʀ(ə)] *vt* **1** (*placer*) to put; **~ en bouteille/en sac** to bottle/put in bags *ou* sacks; **~ en charge (pour)** to charge (with), indict (for)

2 (*vêtements: revêtir*) to put on; (: *porter*) to wear; **mets ton gilet** put your cardigan on; **je ne mets plus mon manteau** I no longer wear my coat

3 (*faire fonctionner: chauffage, électricité*) to put on; (: *reveil, minuteur*) to set; (*installer: gaz, eau*) to put in, to lay on; **~ en marche** to start up

4 (*consacrer*): **~ du temps à faire qch** to take time to do sth *ou* over sth

5 (*noter, écrire*): to say, put (down); **qu'est-ce qu'il a mis sur la carte?** what did he say *ou* write on the card?; **mettez au pluriel** ... put ... into the plural

6 (*supposer*): **mettons que** ... let's suppose *ou* say that ...

7: **y ~ du sien** to pull one's weight

se mettre *vi* **1** (*se placer*): **vous pouvez vous ~ là** you can sit (*ou* stand) there; **où ça se met?** where does it go?; **se ~ au lit** to get into bed; **se ~ au piano** to sit down at the piano; **se ~ de l'encre sur les doigts** to get ink on one's fingers

2 (*s'habiller*): **se ~ en maillot de bain** to get into *ou* put on a swimsuit; **n'avoir rien à se ~** to have nothing to wear

3: **se ~ à** to begin, start; **se ~ à faire** to begin *ou* start doing *ou* to do; **se ~ au piano** to start learning the piano; **se ~ au travail/à l'étude** to get down to work/one's studies

---

meuble [mœbl(ə)] *nm* piece of furniture; furniture *no pl* ♦ *adj* (*terre*) loose, friable; **meublé** *nm* furnished flatlet (*BRIT*) *ou* room; **meubler** *vt* to furnish; (*fig*): **meubler qch (de)** to fill sth (with)

meugler [møgle] *vi* to low, moo

meule [møl] *nf* (*à broyer*) millstone; (*à aiguiser*) grindstone; (*de foin, blé*) stack; (*de fromage*) round

meunier [mønje] *nm* miller; **meunière** *nf* miller's wife

meure *etc vb voir* **mourir**

meurtre [mœrtr(ə)] *nm* murder; **meurtrier, ière** *adj* (*arme etc*) deadly; (*fureur, instincts*) murderous ♦ *nm/f* murderer(eress); **meurtrière** *nf* (*ouverture*) loophole

meurtrir [mœrtrir] *vt* to bruise; (*fig*) to wound; **meurtrissure** *nf* bruise; (*fig*) scar

meus *etc vb voir* **mouvoir**

meute [møt] *nf* pack

Mexico [mɛksiko] *n* Mexico City

Mexique [mɛksik] *nm:* **le ~** Mexico

Mgr *abr* = **Monseigneur**

mi [mi] *nm* (*MUS*) E; (*en chantant la gamme*) mi ♦ *préfixe:* **~...** half(-); **mid-:** **à la ~-janvier** in mid-January; **à ~-jambes/-corps** (up *ou* down) to the knees/waist; **à ~-hauteur/-pente** halfway up *ou* down/up *ou* down the hill

miauler [mjole] *vi* to mew

miche [miʃ] *nf* round *ou* cob loaf

mi-chemin [miʃmɛ̃]: **à ~** *adv* halfway, midway

mi-clos, e [miklo, -kloz] *adj* half-closed

micro [mikro] *nm* mike, microphone; (*INFORM*) micro

microbe [mikrɔb] *nm* germ, microbe

micro: **~-onde** *nf:* **four à ~-ondes** microwave oven; **~-ordinateur** *nm* microcomputer; **~scope** *nm* microscope

midi [midi] *nm* midday, noon; (*moment du déjeuner*) lunchtime; (*sud*) south; **à ~** at 12 (o'clock) *ou* midday *ou* noon; **en plein ~** (right) in the middle of the day; facing south; **le M~** the South (of France), the Midi

mie [mi] *nf* crumb (of the loaf)

miel [mjɛl] *nm* honey

mien, ne [mjɛ̃, mjɛn] *pron:* **le(la) ~(ne),**

---

les ~(ne)s mine; **les ~s** my family

miette [mjɛt] *nf* (*de pain, gâteau*) crumb; (*fig: de la conversation etc*) scrap; **en ~s** in pieces *ou* bits

---

mieux [mjø] *adv* 1 (*d'une meilleure façon*): **~ (que)** better (than); **elle travaille/mange ~** she works/eats better; **elle va ~** she is better

2 (*de la meilleure façon*) best; **ce que je sais le ~** what I know best; **les livres les ~ faits** the best made books

3: **de ~ en ~** better and better

♦ *adj* 1 (*plus à l'aise, en meilleure forme*) better; **se sentir ~** to feel better

2 (*plus satisfaisant*) better; **c'est ~ ainsi** it's better like this; **c'est ~ des deux** it's the better of the two; **le(la) ~, les ~** the best; **demandez-lui, c'est le ~** ask him, it's the best thing

3 (*plus joli*) better-looking

4: **au ~** at best; **au ~ avec** on the best of terms with; **pour le ~** for the best

♦ *nm* 1 (*progrès*) improvement

2: **de mon/ton ~** as best I/you can (*ou* could); **faire de son ~** to do one's best

---

mièvre [mjɛvr(ə)] *adj* mawkish (*BRIT*), sickly sentimental

mignon, ne [miɲɔ̃, -ɔn] *adj* sweet, cute

migraine [migrɛn] *nf* headache; migraine

mijoter [miʒɔte] *vt* to simmer; (*préparer avec soin*) to cook lovingly; (*affaire, projet*) to plot, cook up ♦ *vi* to simmer

mil [mil] *num* = **mille**

milieu, x [miljø] *nm* (*centre*) middle; (*fig*) middle course *ou* way; happy medium; (*BIO, GÉO*) environment; (*entourage social*) milieu; background; circle; (*pègre*): **le ~** the underworld; **au ~ de** in the middle of; **au beau** *ou* **en plein ~ (de)** right in the middle (of)

militaire [militɛr] *adj* military, army *cpd* ♦ *nm* serviceman

militant, e [militɑ̃, -ɑ̃t] *adj, nm/f* militant

militer [milite] *vi* to be a militant; **~**

pour/contre (*suj: faits, raisons etc*) to militate in favour of/against

mille [mil] *num* a *ou* one thousand ♦ *nm* (*mesure*): ~ **(marin)** nautical mile; **mettre dans le** ~ to hit the bull's-eye; to be bang on target; **millefeuille** *nm* cream *ou* vanilla slice; **millénaire** *nm* millennium ♦ *adj* thousand-year-old; (*fig*) ancient; **mille-pattes** *nm inv* centipede

millésime [milezim] *nm* year; **millésimé, e** *adj* vintage *cpd*

millet [mijɛ] *nm* millet

milliard [miljaʀ] *nm* milliard, thousand million (*BRIT*), billion (*US*); **milliardaire** *nm/f* multimillionaire (*BRIT*), billionaire (*US*)

millier [milje] *nm* thousand; **un** ~ **(de)** a thousand *ou* so, about a thousand; **par** ~**s** in (their) thousands, by the thousand

milligramme [miligram] *nm* milligramme

millimètre [milimɛtʀ(ə)] *nm* millimetre

million [miljɔ̃] *nm* million; **deux** ~**s de** two million; **millionnaire** *nm/f* millionaire

mime [mim] *nm/f* (*acteur*) mime(r) ♦ *nm* (*art*) mime, miming

mimer [mime] *vt* to mime; (*singer*) to mimic, take off

mimique [mimik] *nf* (funny) face; (*signes*) gesticulations *pl*, sign language *no pl*

minable [minabl(ə)] *adj* shabby(-looking); pathetic

mince [mɛ̃s] *adj* thin; (*personne, taille*) slim, slender; (*fig: profit, connaissances*) slight, small, weak ♦ *excl*: ~ **alors!** drat it!, darn it! (*US*); **minceur** *nf* thinness; slimness, slenderness

mine [min] *nf* (*physionomie*) expression, look; (*extérieur*) exterior, appearance; (*de crayon*) lead; (*gisement, exploitation, explosif, fig*) mine; **avoir bonne** ~ (*personne*) to look well; (*ironique*) to look an utter idiot; **avoir mauvaise** ~ to look unwell *ou* poorly; **faire** ~ **de faire** to make a pretence of doing; to make as if to do; ~ **de rien** with a casual air; although you wouldn't think so

miner [mine] *vt* (*saper*) to undermine, erode; (*MIL*) to mine

minerai [minʀɛ] *nm* ore

minéral, e, aux [mineral, -o] *adj, nm* mineral

minéralogique [mineralɔʒik] *adj*: **numéro** ~ registration number

minet, te [minɛ, -ɛt] *nm/f* (*chat*) pussycat; (*péj*) young trendy

mineur, e [minœʀ] *adj* minor ♦ *nm/f* (*JUR*) minor, person under age ♦ *nm* (*travailleur*) miner

miniature [minjatyʀ] *adj, nf* miniature

minibus [minibys] *nm* minibus

mini-cassette [minikasɛt] *nf* cassette (recorder)

minier, ière [minje, -jɛʀ] *adj* mining

mini-jupe [miniʒyp] *nf* mini-skirt

minime [minim] *adj* minor, minimal

minimiser [minimize] *vt* to minimize; (*fig*) to play down

minimum [minimɔm] *adj, nm* minimum; **au** ~ (*au moins*) at the very least

ministère [ministɛʀ] *nm* (*aussi REL*) ministry; (*cabinet*) government; ~ **public** (*JUR*) Prosecution, public prosecutor

ministre [ministʀ(ə)] *nm* (*aussi REL*) minister; ~ **d'État** senior minister

Minitel [minitɛl] ® *nm* videotext terminal and service

minorité [minɔrite] *nf* minority; **être en** ~ to be in the *ou* a minority; **mettre en** ~ (*POL*) to defeat

minoterie [minɔtri] *nf* flour-mill

minuit [minɥi] *nm* midnight

minuscule [minyskyl] *adj* minute, tiny ♦ *nf*: **(lettre)** ~ small letter

minute [minyt] *nf* minute; (*JUR: original*) minute, draft; **à la** ~ (just) this instant; there and then; **minuter** *vt* to time; **minuterie** *nf* time switch

minutieux, euse [minysjø, -øz] *adj* meticulous; minutely detailed

mirabelle [mirabɛl] *nf* (cherry) plum

miracle [miʀakl(ə)] *nm* miracle

mirage [miʀaʒ] *nm* mirage

mire [mir] *nf*: **point de** ~ target; (*fig*) focal point; **ligne de** ~ line of sight

miroir [miʀwaʀ] *nm* mirror

miroiter [miʀwate] *vi* to sparkle, shimmer; **faire** ~ **qch à qn** to paint sth in glowing colours for sb, dangle sth in front of sb's eyes

mis, e [mi, miz] *pp de* **mettre** ♦ *adj*: **bien** ~ well-dressed

mise [miz] *nf* (*argent: au jeu*) stake; (*tenue*) clothing; attire; **être de** ~ to be acceptable *ou* in season; ~ **à feu** blast-off; ~ **au point** (*fig*) clarification; ~ **de fonds** capital outlay; ~ **en examen** charging, indictment; ~ **en plis** set; ~ **en scène** production

miser [mize] *vt* (*enjeu*) to stake, bet; ~ **sur** (*cheval, numéro*) to bet on; (*fig*) to bank *ou* count on

misérable [mizeʀabl(ə)] *adj* (*lamentable, malheureux*) pitiful, wretched; (*pauvre*) poverty-stricken; (*insignifiant, mesquin*) miserable ♦ *nm/f* wretch; (*miséreux*) poor wretch

misère [mizeʀ] *nf* (*extreme*) poverty, destitution; ~**s** *nfpl* (*malheurs*) woes, miseries; (*ennuis*) little troubles; **salaire de** ~ starvation wage

miséricorde [mizeʀikɔʀd(ə)] *nf* mercy, forgiveness

missile [misil] *nm* missile

mission [misjɔ̃] *nf* mission; **partir en** ~ (*ADMIN, POL*) to go on an assignment; **missionnaire** *nm/f* missionary

mit *vb voir* **mettre**

mité, e [mite] *adj* moth-eaten

mi-temps [mitɑ̃] *nf inv* (*SPORT: période*) half; (: *pause*) half-time; **à** ~ part-time

mitigé, e [mitiʒe] *adj* lukewarm; mixed

mitonner [mitɔne] *vt* to cook with loving care; (*fig*) to cook up quietly

mitoyen, ne [mitwajɛ̃, -ɛn] *adj* common, party *cpd*

mitrailler [mitʀaje] *vt* to machine-gun; (*fig*) to pelt, bombard; (: *photographier*) to take shot after shot of; **mitraillette** *nf* submachine gun; **mitrailleuse** *nf* machine gun

mi-voix [mivwa]: **à** ~ *adv* in a low *ou* hushed voice

mixage [miksaʒ] *nm* (*CINÉMA*) (sound) mixing

mixer [miksœʀ] *nm* (food) mixer

mixte [mikst(ə)] *adj* (*gén*) mixed; (*SCOL*) mixed, coeducational; **à usage** ~ dual-purpose

mixture [mikstyʀ] *nf* mixture; (*fig*) concoction

MLF *sigle m* = **Mouvement de Libération de la femme**

Mlle (*pl* **Mlles**) *abr* = **Mademoiselle**

MM *abr* = **Messieurs**

Mme (*pl* **Mmes**) *abr* = **Madame**

Mo *abr* = **métro**

mobile [mɔbil] *adj* mobile; (*pièce de machine*) moving; (*élément de meuble etc*) movable ♦ *nm* (*motif*) motive; (*œuvre d'art*) mobile

mobilier, ière [mɔbilje, -jɛʀ] *adj* (*JUR*) personal ♦ *nm* furniture

mobiliser [mɔbilize] *vt* (*MIL, gén*) to mobilize

moche [mɔʃ] (*fam*) *adj* ugly; rotten

modalité [mɔdalite] *nf* form, mode; ~**s** *nfpl* (*d'un accord etc*) clauses, terms

mode [mɔd] *nf* fashion ♦ *nm* (*manière*) form, mode; **à la** ~ fashionable, in fashion; ~ **d'emploi** directions *pl* (for use)

modèle [mɔdɛl] *adj, nm* model; (*qui pose: de peintre*) sitter; ~ **déposé** registered design; ~ **réduit** small-scale model; **modeler** [mɔdle] *vt* (*ART*) to model, mould; (*suj: vêtement, érosion*) to mould, shape

modem [mɔdɛm] *nm* modem

modéré, e [mɔdeʀe] *adj, nm/f* moderate

modérer [mɔdeʀe] *vt* to moderate; **se** ~ *vi* to restrain o.s.

moderne [mɔdɛʀn(ə)] *adj* modern ♦ *nm* modern style; modern furniture; **moderniser** *vt* to modernize

modeste [mɔdɛst(ə)] *adj* modest; **modestie** *nf* modesty

modifier [mɔdifje] *vt* to modify, alter; **se** ~ *vi* to alter

modique [mɔdik] *adj* modest

modiste [mɔdist(ə)] *nf* milliner

modulation [mɔdylasjɔ̃] *nf*: ~ **de fréquence** frequency modulation

module [mɔdyl] *nm* module

moelle [mwal] *nf* marrow

moelleux, euse [mwalø, -øz] *adj* soft; (*au goût, à l'ouïe*) mellow

moellon [mwalɔ̃] *nm* rubble stone

mœurs [mœʀ] *nfpl* (*conduite*) morals; (*manières*) manners; (*pratiques sociales, mode de vie*) habits

mohair [mɔɛʀ] *nm* mohair

moi [mwa] *pron* me; (*emphatique*): ~, **je** ... for my part, I ...., I myself ...

moignon [mwaɲɔ̃] *nm* stump

moi-même [mwamɛm] *pron* myself; (*emphatique*) I myself

moindre [mwɛ̃dʀ(ə)] *adj* lesser; lower; **le(la) ~, les ~s** the least, the slightest

moine [mwan] *nm* monk, friar

moineau, x [mwano] *nm* sparrow

MOT-CLÉ

moins [mwɛ̃] *adv* **1** (*comparatif*): ~ **(que)** less (than); ~ **grand que** less tall than, not as tall as; ~ **je travaille, mieux je me porte** the less I work, the better I feel

2 (*superlatif*): **le ~** (the) least; **c'est ce que j'aime le ~** it's what I like (the) least; **le(la) ~ doué(e)** the least gifted; **au ~, du ~** at least; **pour le ~** at the very least

3: ~ **de** (*quantité*) less (than); (*nombre*) fewer (than); ~ **de sable/d'eau** less sand/water; ~ **de livres/gens** fewer books/people; ~ **de 2 ans** less than 2 years; ~ **de midi** not yet midday

4: **de** ~, **en** ~: **100 F/3 jours de** ~ 100F/ 3 days less; **3 livres en** ~ 3 books fewer; 3 books too few; **de l'argent en** ~ less money; **le soleil en** ~ but for the sun, minus the sun; **de** ~ **en** ~ less and less

5: **à** ~ **de, à** ~ **que** unless; **à** ~ **de faire** unless we do (*ou* he does *etc*); **à** ~ **que tu ne fasses** unless you do; **à** ~ **d'un accident** barring any accident

♦ *prép*: **4** ~ **2** 4 minus 2; **il est** ~ **5** it's 5 to; **il fait** ~ **5** it's 5 (degrees) below (freezing), it's minus 5

---

mois [mwa] *nm* month; ~ **double** (*COMM*) extra month's salary

moisi [mwazi] *nm* mould, mildew; **odeur de** ~ musty smell

moisir [mwaziʀ] *vi* to go mouldy; (*fig*) to rot; to hang about

moisissure [mwazisyʀ] *nf* mould *nopl*

moisson [mwasɔ̃] *nf* harvest; **moissonner** *vt* to harvest, reap; **moissonneuse** *nf* (*machine*) harvester

moite [mwat] *adj* sweaty, sticky

moitié [mwatje] *nf* half; **la** ~ half; **la** ~ **de** half (of); **la** ~ **du temps/des gens** half the time/the people; **à la** ~ **de** halfway through; **à** ~ (*avant le verbe*) half; (*avant l'adjectif*) half-; **de** ~ by half; ~ ~ half-and-half

mol [mɔl] *adj voir* **mou**

molaire [mɔlɛʀ] *nf* molar

molester [mɔlɛste] *vt* to manhandle, maul (about)

molle [mɔl] *adj voir* **mou**; **mollement** *adv* softly; (*péj*) sluggishly; (*protester*) feebly

mollet [mɔlɛ] *nm* calf ♦ *adj m*: **œuf** ~ soft-boiled egg

molletonné, e [mɔltɔne] *adj* fleece-lined

mollir [mɔliʀ] *vi* to give way; to relent; to go soft

môme [mom] (*fam*) *nm/f* (*enfant*) brat ♦ *nf* (*fille*) chick

moment [mɔmɑ̃] *nm* moment; **ce n'est pas le** ~ this is not the (right) time; **à un certain** ~ at some point; **à un** ~ **donné** at a certain point; **pour un bon** ~ for a good while; **pour le** ~ for the moment, for the time being; **au** ~ **de** at the time of; **au** ~ **où** as; at a time when; **à tout** ~ at any time *ou* moment; constantly, continually; **en ce** ~ at the moment; at present; **sur le** ~ at the time; **par** ~**s** now and then, at times; **du** ~ **où** *ou* **que** seeing that, since; **momentané, e** *adj* temporary, momentary

momie [mɔmi] *nf* mummy

mon, ma [mɔ̃, ma] (*pl* **mes**) *dét* my

Monaco [mɔnako] *nm*: **le** ~ Monaco

monarchie [mɔnaʀʃi] *nf* monarchy

monastère [mɔnastɛʀ] *nm* monastery

monceau, x [mɔ̃so] *nm* heap

mondain, e [mɔ̃dɛ̃, -ɛn] *adj* society *cpd*;

social; fashionable; ~e *nf*: **la M~e, la police ~e** ≈ the vice squad

monde [mɔ̃d] *nm* world; (*haute société*): **le ~** (high) society; (*milieu*): **être du même ~** to move in the same circles; (*gens*): **il y a du ~** (*beaucoup de gens*) there are a lot of people; (*quelques personnes*) there are some people; **beaucoup/peu de ~** many/few people; **le meilleur** *etc* **du ~** the best *etc* in the world *ou* on earth; **mettre au ~** to bring into the world; **pas le moins du ~** not in the least; **se faire un ~ de qch** to make a great deal of fuss about sth; **mondial, e**, *aux adj* (*population*) world *cpd*; (*influence*) world-wide; **mondialement** *adv* throughout the world

monégasque [mɔnegask(ə)] *adj* Monegasque, of *ou* from Monaco

monétaire [mɔnetɛʀ] *adj* monetary

moniteur, trice [mɔnitœʀ, -tʀis] *nm/f* (*SPORT*) instructor(tress); (*de colonie de vacances*) supervisor ♦ *nm* (*écran*) monitor

monnaie [mɔnɛ] *nf* (*pièce*) coin; (*ÉCON, gén: moyen d'échange*) currency; (*petites pièces*): **avoir de la ~** to have (some) change; **faire de la ~** to get (some) change; **avoir/faire la ~ de 20 F** to have change of/get change for 20 F; **rendre à qn la ~ (sur 20 F)** to give sb the change (out of *ou* from 20 F); **monnayer** *vt* to convert into cash; (*talent*) to capitalize on

monologue [mɔnɔlɔg] *nm* monologue, soliloquy; **monologuer** *vi* to soliloquize

monopole [mɔnɔpɔl] *nm* monopoly

monotone [mɔnɔtɔn] *adj* monotonous

monseigneur [mɔ̃sɛɲœʀ] *nm* (*archevêque, évêque*) Your (*ou* His) Grace; (*cardinal*) Your (*ou* His) Eminence

Monsieur [məsjø] (*pl* **Messieurs**) *titre* Mr ♦ *nm* (*homme quelconque*): **un/le m~** a/the gentleman; *voir aussi* **Madame**

monstre [mɔ̃stʀ(ə)] *nm* monster ♦ *adj*: **un travail ~** a fantastic amount of work; an enormous job

mont [mɔ̃] *nm*: **par ~s et par vaux** up hill and down dale; **le M~ Blanc** Mont Blanc

montage [mɔ̃taʒ] *nm* putting up; mounting, setting; assembly; (*PHOTO*) photomontage; (*CINÉMA*) editing

montagnard, e [mɔ̃taɲaʀ, -aʀd(ə)] *adj* mountain *cpd* ♦ *nm/f* mountain-dweller

montagne [mɔ̃taɲ] *nf* (*cime*) mountain; (*région*): **la ~** the mountains *pl*; **~s russes** big dipper *sg*, switchback *sg*; **montagneux, euse** [mɔ̃taɲø, -øz] *adj* mountainous; hilly

montant, e [mɔ̃tɑ̃, -ɑ̃t] *adj* rising; (*robe, corsage*) high-necked ♦ *nm* (*somme, total*) (sum) total, (total) amount; (*de fenêtre*) upright; (*de lit*) post

monte-charge [mɔ̃tʃaʀʒ(ə)] *nm inv* goods lift, hoist

montée [mɔ̃te] *nf* rising, rise; ascent, climb; (*chemin*) way up; (*côte*) hill; **au milieu de la ~** halfway up

monter [mɔ̃te] *vt* (*escalier, côte*) to go (*ou* come) up; (*valise, paquet*) to take (*ou* bring) up; (*cheval*) to mount; (*étagère*) to raise; (*tente, échafaudage*) to put up; (*machine*) to assemble; (*bijou*) to mount, set; (*COUTURE*) to set in; to sew on; (*CINÉMA*) to edit; (*THÉÂTRE*) to put on, stage; (*société etc*) to set up ♦ *vi* to go (*ou* come) up; (*avion etc*) to climb, go up; (*chemin, niveau, température*) to go up, rise; (*passager*) to get on; (*à cheval*): **~ bien/mal** to ride well/badly; **se ~ à** (*frais etc*) to add up to, come to; **~ à pied** to walk up, go up on foot; **~ à bicyclette/en voiture** to cycle/drive up, go up by bicycle/by car; **~ dans le train/l'avion** to get into the train/plane, board the train/plane; **~ sur** to climb up onto; **~ à cheval** to get on *ou* mount a horse

monticule [mɔ̃tikyl] *nm* mound

montre [mɔ̃tʀ(ə)] *nf* watch; **faire ~ de** to show, display; **contre la ~** (*SPORT*) against the clock; **montre-bracelet** *nf* wristwatch

montrer [mɔ̃tʀe] *vt* to show; **~ qch à qn** to show sb sth

monture [mɔ̃tyʀ] *nf* (*bête*) mount; (*d'une bague*) setting; (*de lunettes*) frame

monument [mɔnymɑ̃] *nm* monument; ~ **aux morts** war memorial

moquer [mɔke]: **se ~ de** *vt* to make fun of, laugh at; (*fam: se désintéresser de*) not to care about; (*tromper*): **se ~ de qn** to take sb for a ride

moquette [mɔkɛt] *nf* fitted carpet

moqueur, euse [mɔkœʀ, -øz] *adj* mocking

moral, e, aux [mɔʀal, -o] *adj* moral ♦ *nm* morale; **avoir le ~ à zéro** to be really down; **morale** *nf* (*conduite*) morals *pl*; (*règles*) moral code, ethic; (*valeurs*) moral standards *pl*, morality; (*science*) ethics *sg*, moral philosophy; (*conclusion: d'une fable etc*) moral; **faire la morale à** to lecture, preach at; **moralité** *nf* morality; (*conduite*) morals *pl*; (*conclusion, enseignement*) moral

morceau, x [mɔʀso] *nm* piece, bit; (*d'œuvre*) passage, extract; (*MUS*) piece; (*CULIN: de viande*) cut; **mettre en ~x** to pull to pieces *ou* bits

morceler [mɔʀsəle] *vt* to break up, divide up

mordant, e [mɔʀdɑ̃, -ɑ̃t] *adj* scathing, cutting; biting

mordiller [mɔʀdije] *vt* to nibble at, chew at

mordre [mɔʀdʀ(ə)] *vt* to bite; (*suj: lime, vis*) to bite into ♦ *vi* (*poisson*) to bite; ~ **sur** (*fig*) to go over into, overlap into; ~ **à l'hameçon** to bite, rise to the bait

mordu, e [mɔʀdy] *nm/f*: **un ~ du jazz** a jazz fanatic

morfondre [mɔʀfɔ̃dʀ(ə)]: **se ~** *vi* to mope

morgue [mɔʀg(ə)] *nf* (*arrogance*) haughtiness; (*lieu: de la police*) morgue; (: *à l'hôpital*) mortuary

morne [mɔʀn(ə)] *adj* dismal, dreary

mors [mɔʀ] *nm* bit

morse [mɔʀs(ə)] *nm* (*ZOOL*) walrus; (*TÉL*) Morse (code)

morsure [mɔʀsyʀ] *nf* bite

mort¹ [mɔʀ] *nf* death

mort², e [mɔʀ, mɔʀt(ə)] *pp de* **mourir** ♦ *adj* dead ♦ *nm/f* (*défunt*) dead man(woman); (*victime*): **il y a eu plusieurs ~s** there were several killed ♦ *nm* (*CARTES*) dummy; ~ **ou vif** dead or alive; ~ **de peur/fatigue** frightened to death/dead tired

mortalité [mɔʀtalite] *nf* mortality, death rate

mortel, le [mɔʀtɛl] *adj* (*poison etc*) deadly, lethal; (*accident, blessure*) fatal; (*REL*) mortal; (*fig*) deathly; deadly boring

mortier [mɔʀtje] *nm* (*gén*) mortar

mort-né, e [mɔʀne] *adj* (*enfant*) stillborn

mortuaire [mɔʀtɥɛʀ] *adj* funeral *cpd*

morue [mɔʀy] *nf* (*ZOOL*) cod *inv*

mosaïque [mɔzaik] *nf* (*ART*) mosaic; (*fig*) patchwork

Moscou [mɔsku] *n* Moscow

mosquée [mɔske] *nf* mosque

mot [mo] *nm* word; (*message*) line, note; (*bon mot etc*) saying; sally; ~ **à ~** word for word; ~ **d'ordre** watchword; ~ **de passe** password; ~s **croisés** crossword (puzzle) *sg*

motard [mɔtaʀ] *nm* biker; (*policier*) motorcycle cop

motel [mɔtɛl] *nm* motel

moteur, trice [mɔtœʀ, -tʀis] *adj* (*ANAT, PHYSIOL*) motor; (*TECH*) driving; (*AUTO*): **à 4 roues motrices** 4-wheel drive ♦ *nm* engine, motor; **à ~** power-driven, motor *cpd*

motif [mɔtif] *nm* (*cause*) motive; (*décoratif*) design, pattern, motif; (*d'un tableau*) subject, motif; ~s *nmpl* (*JUR*) grounds *pl*; **sans ~** groundless

motiver [mɔtive] *vt* (*justifier*) to justify, account for; (*ADMIN, JUR, PSYCH*) to motivate

moto [mɔto] *nf* (motor)bike; **motocycliste** *nm/f* motorcyclist

motorisé, e [mɔtɔʀize] *adj* (*troupe*) motorized; (*personne*) having transport *ou* a car

motrice [mɔtʀis] *adj voir* **moteur**

motte [mɔt] *nf*: ~ **de terre** lump of

earth, clod (of earth); ~ **de beurre** lump of butter; ~ **de gazon** turf, sod

mou (mol), molle [mu, mɔl] *adj* soft; (*péj*) flabby; sluggish ♦ *nm* (*abats*) lights *pl*, lungs *pl*; (*de la corde*): **avoir du** ~ to be slack

mouche [muʃ] *nf* fly

moucher [muʃe] *vt* (*enfant*) to blow the nose of; (*chandelle*) to snuff (out); **se** ~ *vi* to blow one's nose

moucheron [muʃʀɔ̃] *nm* midge

moucheté, e [muʃte] *adj* dappled; flecked

mouchoir [muʃwaʀ] *nm* handkerchief, hanky; ~ **en papier** tissue, paper hanky

moudre [mudʀ(ə)] *vt* to grind

moue [mu] *nf* pout; **faire la** ~ to pout; (*fig*) to pull a face

mouette [mwɛt] *nf* (sea)gull

moufle [mufl(ə)] *nf* (*gant*) mitt(en)

mouillé, e [muje] *adj* wet

mouiller [muje] *vt* (*humecter*) to wet, moisten; (*tremper*): ~ **qn/qch** to make sb/sth wet; (*couper, diluer*) to water down; (*mine etc*) to lay (*NAVIG*) to lie *ou* be at anchor; **se** ~ to get wet; (*fam*) to commit o.s.; to get o.s. involved

moule [mul] *nf* mussel ♦ *nm* (*creux, CULIN*) mould; (*modèle plein*) cast; ~ **à gâteaux** *nm* cake tin (*BRIT*) *ou* pan (*US*)

moulent *vb voir* **moudre; mouler**

mouler [mule] *vt* (*suj: vêtement*) to hug, fit round; ~ **qch sur** (*fig*) to model sth on

moulin [mulɛ̃] *nm* mill; ~ **à café/à poivre** coffee/pepper mill; ~ **à légumes** (vegetable) shredder; ~ **à paroles** (*fig*) chatterbox; ~ **à vent** windmill

moulinet [mulinɛ] *nm* (*de treuil*) winch; (*de canne à pêche*) reel; (*mouvement*): **faire des** ~**s avec qch** to whirl sth around

moulinette [mulinɛt] *nf* (vegetable) shredder

moulu, e [muly] *pp de* **moudre**

moulure [mulyʀ] *nf* (*ornement*) moulding

mourant, e [muʀɑ̃, -ɑ̃t] *adj* dying

mourir [muʀiʀ] *vi* to die; (*civilisation*) to

die out; ~ **de froid/faim** to die of exposure/hunger; ~ **de faim/d'ennui** (*fig*) to be starving/be bored to death; ~ **d'envie de faire** to be dying to do

mousse [mus] *nf* (*BOT*) moss; (*écume: sur eau, bière*) froth, foam; (: *shampooing*) lather; (*CULIN*) mousse ♦ *nm* (*NAVIG*) ship's boy; **bas** ~ stretch stockings; ~ **à raser** shaving foam; ~ **carbonique** (fire-fighting) foam

mousseline [muslin] *nf* muslin; chiffon

mousser [muse] *vi* to foam; to lather

mousseux, euse [musø, -øz] *adj* frothy ♦ *nm*: (*vin*) ~ sparkling wine

mousson [musɔ̃] *nf* monsoon

moustache [mustaʃ] *nf* moustache; ~**s** *nfpl* (*du chat*) whiskers *pl*

moustiquaire [mustikɛʀ] *nf* mosquito net (*ou* screen)

moustique [mustik] *nm* mosquito

moutarde [mutaʀd(ə)] *nf* mustard

mouton [mutɔ̃] *nm* (*ZOOL, péj*) sheep *inv*; (*peau*) sheepskin; (*CULIN*) mutton

mouvant, e [muvɑ̃, -ɑ̃t] *adj* unsettled; changing; shifting

mouvement [muvmɑ̃] *nm* (*gén, aussi mécanisme*) movement; (*fig*) activity; impulse; gesture; (*MUS: rythme*) tempo; **en** ~ in motion; on the move; **mouvementé, e** *adj* (*vie, poursuite*) eventful; (*réunion*) turbulent

mouvoir [muvwaʀ] *vt* (*levier, membre*) to move; **se** ~ *vi* to move

moyen, ne [mwajɛ̃, -ɛn] *adj* average; medium; (*tailles, prix*) medium; (*de grandeur moyenne*) medium-sized ♦ *nm* (*façon*) means *sg*, way; ~**s** *nmpl* (*capacités*) means; **au** ~ **de** by means of; **par tous les** ~**s** by every possible means, every possible way; **par ses propres** ~**s** all by oneself; ~ **âge** Middle Ages; ~ **de transport** means of transport

moyennant [mwajenɑ̃] *prép* (*somme*) for; (*service, conditions*) in return for; (*travail, effort*) with

moyenne [mwajɛn] *nf* average; (*MATH*) mean; (*SCOL: à l'examen*) pass mark; (*AUTO*) average speed; **en** ~ on (an) average; ~ **d'âge** average age

Moyen-Orient [mwajɛnɔʀjɑ̃] *nm*: **le ~** the Middle East

moyeu, x [mwajø] *nm* hub

MST *sigle f* (= *maladie sexuellement transmissible*) STD

mû, mue [my] *pp de* **mouvoir**

muer [mɥe] *vi* (*oiseau, mammifère*) to moult; (*serpent*) to slough; (*jeune garçon*): **il mue** his voice is breaking; **se ~ en** to transform into

muet, te [mɥɛ, -ɛt] *adj* dumb; (*fig*): **~ d'admiration** *etc* speechless with admiration *etc*; (*joie, douleur, CINÉMA*) silent; (*carte*) blank mute

mufle [myfl(ə)] *nm* muzzle; (*goujat*) boor

mugir [myʒiʀ] *vi* (*taureau*) to bellow; (*vache*) to low; (*fig*) to howl

muguet [mygɛ] *nm* lily of the valley

mule [myl] *nf* (*ZOOL*) (she-)mule

mulet [mylɛ] *nm* (*ZOOL*) (he-)mule

multiple [myltipl(ə)] *adj* multiple, numerous; (*varié*) many, manifold ♦ *nm* (*MATH*) multiple

multiplex [myltiplɛks] *nm* (*RADIO*) live link-up

multiplication [myltiplikasjɔ̃] *nf* multiplication

multiplier [myltiplije] *vt* to multiply; **se ~** *vi* to multiply; to increase in number

municipal, e, aux [mynisipal, -o] *adj* municipal; town *cpd*; ≈ borough *cpd*

municipalité [mynisipalite] *nf* (*corps municipal*) town council, corporation

munir [myniʀ] *vt*: **~ qn/qch de** to equip sb/sth with

munitions [mynisjɔ̃] *nfpl* ammunition *sg*

mur [myʀ] *nm* wall; **~ du son** sound barrier

mûr, e [myʀ] *adj* ripe; (*personne*) mature

muraille [myʀaj] *nf* (high) wall

mural, e, aux [myʀal, -o] *adj* wall *cpd*; mural

mûre [myʀ] *nf* blackberry; mulberry

murer [myʀe] *vt* (*enclos*) to wall (in); (*porte, issue*) to wall up; (*personne*) to wall up *ou* in

muret [myʀɛ] *nm* low wall

mûrir [myʀiʀ] *vi* (*fruit, blé*) to ripen; (*abcès, furoncle*) to come to a head; (*fig: idée, personne*) to mature ♦ *vt* to ripen; to (make) mature

murmure [myʀmyʀ] *nm* murmur; **~s** *nmpl* (*plaintes*) murmurings, mutterings; **murmurer** *vi* to murmur; (*se plaindre*) to mutter, grumble

muscade [myskad] *nf* (*aussi: noix ~*) nutmeg

muscat [myska] *nm* muscat grape; muscatel (wine)

muscle [myskl(ə)] *nm* muscle; **musclé, e** *adj* muscular; (*fig*) strong-arm

museau, x [myzo] *nm* muzzle

musée [myze] *nm* museum; art gallery

museler [myzle] *vt* to muzzle; **muselière** *nf* muzzle

musette [myzɛt] *nf* (*sac*) lunchbag ♦ *adj inv* (*orchestre etc*) accordion *cpd*

musical, e, aux [myzikal, -o] *adj* musical

music-hall [myzikol] *nm* variety theatre; (*genre*) variety

musicien, ne [myzisjɛ̃, -jɛn] *adj* musical ♦ *nm/f* musician

musique [myzik] *nf* music; (*fanfare*) band; **~ de chambre** chamber music

musulman, e [myzylmɑ̃, -an] *adj, nm/f* Moslem, Muslim

mutation [mytasjɔ̃] *nf* (*ADMIN*) transfer

mutilé, e [mytile] *nm/f* disabled person (*through loss of limbs*)

mutiler [mytile] *vt* to mutilate, maim

mutin, e [mytɛ̃, -in] *adj* (*air, ton*) mischievous, impish ♦ *nm/f* (*MIL, NAVIG*) mutineer

mutinerie [mytinʀi] *nf* mutiny

mutisme [mytism(ə)] *nm* silence

mutuel, le [mytɥɛl] *adj* mutual; **mutuelle** *nf* mutual benefit society

myope [mjɔp] *adj* short-sighted

myosotis [mjozɔtis] *nm* forget-me-not

myrtille [miʀtij] *nf* bilberry

mystère [mistɛʀ] *nm* mystery; **mystérieux, euse** *adj* mysterious

mystifier [mistifje] *vt* to fool; to mystify

mythe [mit] *nm* myth

mythologie [mitɔlɔʒi] *nf* mythology

N n

n' [n] *adv voir* **ne**

nacre [nakʀ(ə)] *nf* mother-of-pearl

nage [naʒ] *nf* swimming; style of swimming, stroke; **traverser/s'éloigner à la ~** to swim across/away; **en ~** bathed in perspiration

nageoire [naʒwaʀ] *nf* fin

nager [naʒe] *vi* to swim; **nageur, euse** *nm/f* swimmer

naguère [nagɛʀ] *adv* formerly

naïf, ïve [naif, naiv] *adj* naïve

nain, e [nɛ̃, nɛn] *nm/f* dwarf

naissance [nɛsɑ̃s] *nf* birth; **donner ~ à** to give birth to; *(fig)* to give rise to

naître [nɛtʀ(ə)] *vi* to be born; *(fig)*: **~ de** to arise from, be born out of; **il est né en 1960** he was born in 1960; **faire ~** *(fig)* to give rise to, arouse

naïve [naiv] *adj voir* **naïf**

nana [nana] *(fam) nf (fille)* chick, bird *(BRIT)*

nantir [nɑ̃tiʀ] *vt*: **~ qn de** to provide sb with; **les nantis** *(péj)* the well-to-do

nappe [nap] *nf* tablecloth; *(fig)* sheet; layer; **napperon** *nm* table-mat

naquit *etc vb voir* **naître**

narcodollars [naʀkodɔlaʀ] *nmpl* drug money *sg*

narguer [naʀge] *vt* to taunt

narine [naʀin] *nf* nostril

narquois, e [naʀkwa, -waz] *adj* derisive, mocking

naseau, x [nazo] *nm* nostril

natal, e [natal] *adj* native

natalité [natalite] *nf* birth rate

natation [natasjɔ̃] *nf* swimming

natif, ive [natif, -iv] *adj* native

nation [nasjɔ̃] *nf* nation

national, e, aux [nasjɔnal, -o] *adj* national; **nationale** *nf*: **(route) nationale** ≈ A road *(BRIT)*, ≈ state highway *(US)*; **nationaliser** *vt* to nationalize; **nationalité** *nf* nationality

natte [nat] *nf (tapis)* mat; *(cheveux)* plait

naturaliser [natyʀalize] *vt* to naturalize

nature [natyʀ] *nf* nature ♦ *adj, adv (CULIN)* plain, without seasoning or sweetening; *(café, thé)* black, without sugar; **payer en ~** to pay in kind; **~ morte** still-life; **naturel, le** *adj (gén, aussi: enfant)* natural ♦ *nm* naturalness; disposition, nature; *(autochtone)* native; **naturellement** *adv* naturally; *(bien sûr)* of course

naufrage [nofʀaʒ] *nm* (ship)wreck; *(fig)* wreck; **faire ~** to be shipwrecked

nauséabond, e [nozeabɔ̃, -ɔ̃d] *adj* foul, nauseous

nausée [noze] *nf* nausea

nautique [notik] *adj* nautical, water *cpd*

nautisme [notism(ə)] *nm* water sports

navet [navɛ] *nm* turnip

navette [navɛt] *nf* shuttle; **faire la ~ (entre)** to go to and fro *ou* shuttle (between)

navigateur [navigatœʀ] *nm (NAVIG)* seafarer, sailor; *(AVIAT)* navigator

navigation [navigasjɔ̃] *nf* navigation, sailing; shipping

naviguer [navige] *vi* to navigate, sail

navire [naviʀ] *nm* ship

navrer [navʀe] *vt* to upset, distress; **je suis navré** I'm so sorry

ne (n') [n(ə)] *adv voir* **pas; plus; jamais** *etc*; *(explétif)* non traduit

né, e [ne] *pp (voir* **naître***)*: **~ en 1960** born in 1960; **~e Scott** née Scott

néanmoins [neɑ̃mwɛ̃] *adv* nevertheless

néant [neɑ̃] *nm* nothingness; **réduire à ~** to bring to nought; *(espoir)* to dash

nécessaire [nesesɛʀ] *adj* necessary ♦ *nm* necessary; *(sac)* kit; **~ de couture** sewing kit; **~ de toilette** toilet bag; **nécessité** *nf* necessity; **nécessiter** *vt* to require; **nécessiteux, euse** *adj* needy

nécrologique [nekʀɔlɔʒik] *adj*: **article ~** obituary; **rubrique ~** obituary column

nectar [nɛktaʀ] *nm (sucré)* nectar; *(boisson) sweetened, diluted fruit juice*

néerlandais, e [neɛʀlɑ̃dɛ, -ɛz] *adj* Dutch

nef [nɛf] *nf (d'église)* nave

néfaste [nefast(ə)] *adj* baneful; ill-fated

négatif, ive [negatif, -iv] *adj* negative
♦ *nm (PHOTO)* negative

négligé, e [negliʒe] *adj (en désordre)*
slovenly ♦ *nm (tenue)* negligee

négligent, e [negliʒɑ̃, -ɑ̃t] *adj* careless;
negligent

négliger [negliʒe] *vt (épouse, jardin)* to
neglect; *(tenue)* to be careless about;
(avis, précautions) to disregard; ~ **de
faire** to fail to do, not bother to do

négoce [negɔs] *nm* trade

négociant [negɔsjɑ̃] *nm* merchant

négociation [negɔsjasjɔ̃] *nf* negotiation

négocier [negɔsje] *vi, vt* to negotiate

nègre [nɛgʁ(ə)] *nm* Negro; ghost (writer)

négresse [negʁɛs] *nf* Negro woman

neige [nɛʒ] *nf* snow; **neiger** *vi* to snow

nénuphar [nenyfaʁ] *nm* water-lily

néon [neɔ̃] *nm* neon

néophyte [neɔfit] *nm/f* novice

néo-zélandais, e [neɔzelɑ̃dɛ, -ɛz] *adj*
New Zealand *cpd* ♦ *nm/f*: **N~, e** New
Zealander

nerf [nɛʁ] *nm* nerve; *(fig)* spirit; stamina; **nerveux, euse** *adj* nervous; *(voiture)* nippy, responsive; *(tendineux)* sinewy; **nervosité** *nf* excitability; state of
agitation; nervousness

nervure [nɛʁvyʁ] *nf* vein

n'est-ce pas [nɛspa] *adv* isn't it?, won't
you? *etc, selon le verbe qui précède*

net, nette [nɛt] *adj (sans équivoque,
distinct)* clear; *(évident)* definite;
(propre) neat, clean; *(COMM: prix, salaire)* net ♦ *adv (refuser)* flatly ♦ *nm*:
mettre au ~ to copy out; **s'arrêter ~** to
stop dead; **nettement** *adv* clearly, distinctly; **netteté** *nf* clearness

nettoyage [nɛtwajaʒ] *nm* cleaning; ~ **à
sec** dry cleaning

nettoyer [nɛtwaje] *vt* to clean; *(fig)* to
clean out

neuf¹ [nœf] *num* nine

neuf², neuve [nœf, nœv] *adj* new ♦ *nm*:
repeindre à ~ to redecorate; **remettre à
~** to do up (as good as new), refurbish

neutre [nøtʁ(ə)] *adj* neutral; *(LING)* neuter ♦ *nm* neuter

neuve [nœv] *adj voir* **neuf²**

neuvième [nœvjɛm] *num* ninth

neveu, x [nəvø] *nm* nephew

névrosé, e [nevʁoze] *adj, nm/f* neurotic

nez [ne] *nm* nose; ~ **à ~ avec** face to
face with; **avoir du ~** to have flair

ni [ni] *conj*: ~ **l'un** ~ **l'autre ne sont**
neither one nor the other are; **il n'a
rien dit** ~ **fait** he hasn't said or done
anything

niais, e [njɛ, -ɛz] *adj* silly, thick

niche [niʃ] *nf (du chien)* kennel; *(de
mur)* recess, niche

nicher [niʃe] *vi* to nest

nid [ni] *nm* nest; ~ **de poule** pothole

nièce [njɛs] *nf* niece

nier [nje] *vt* to deny

nigaud, e [nigo, -od] *nm/f* booby, fool

Nil [nil] *nm*: **le** ~ the Nile

n'importe [nɛ̃pɔʁt(ə)] *adv*: ~ **qui/quoi/
où** anybody/anything/anywhere; ~
quand any time; ~ **quel/quelle** any; ~
lequel/laquelle any (one); ~ **comment**
(sans soin) carelessly

niveau, x [nivo] *nm* level; *(des élèves,
études)* standard; **de** ~ **(avec)** level
(with); **le** ~ **de la mer** sea level; ~ **de
vie** standard of living

niveler [nivle] *vt* to level

NN *abr (= nouvelle norme) revised
standard of hotel classification*

noble [nɔbl(ə)] *adj* noble; **noblesse** *nf*
nobility; *(d'une action etc)* nobleness

noce [nɔs] *nf* wedding; *(gens)* wedding
party *(ou* guests *pl)*; **faire la** ~ *(fam)* to
go on a binge; ~**s d'or/d'argent** golden/
silver wedding

nocif, ive [nɔsif, -iv] *adj* harmful, noxious

noctambule [nɔktɑ̃byl] *nm* night-bird

nocturne [nɔktyʁn(ə)] *adj* nocturnal ♦
nf late-night opening

Noël [nɔɛl] *nm* Christmas

nœud [nø] *nm (de corde, du bois, NAVIG)*
knot; *(ruban)* bow; *(fig: liens)* bond, tie;
~ **papillon** bow tie

noir, e [nwaʁ] *adj* black; *(obscur,
sombre)* dark ♦ *nm/f* black
man(woman), Negro ♦ *nm*: **dans le** ~ in

the dark; **travail au** ~ moonlighting; **noirceur** *nf* blackness; darkness; **noircir** *vt, vi* to blacken; **noire** *nf* (*MUS*) crotchet (*BRIT*), quarter note (*US*)

noisette [nwazɛt] *nf* hazelnut

noix [nwa] *nf* walnut; (*CULIN*): **une ~ de beurre** a knob of butter; ~ **de cajou** cashew nut; ~ **de coco** coconut

nom [nɔ̃] *nm* name; (*LING*) noun; ~ **d'emprunt** assumed name; ~ **de famille** surname; ~ **de jeune fille** maiden name; ~ **déposé** trade name; ~ **propre** proper noun

nombre [nɔ̃bʀ(ə)] *nm* number; **venir en** ~ to come in large numbers; **depuis** ~ **d'années** for many years; **ils sont au** ~ **de 3** there are 3 of them; **au ~ de mes amis** among my friends

nombreux, euse [nɔ̃bʀø, -øz] *adj* many, numerous; (*avec nom sg: foule etc*) large; **peu** ~ few; small

nombril [nɔ̃bʀi] *nm* navel

nommer [nɔme] *vt* (*baptiser, mentionner*) to name; (*qualifier*) to call; (*élire*) to appoint, nominate; **se ~: il se nomme Pascal** his name's Pascal, he's called Pascal

non [nɔ̃] *adv* (*réponse*) no; (*avec loin, sans, seulement*) not; ~ (**pas**) **que** not that; **moi** ~ **plus** neither do I, I don't either

non: ~-alcoolisé, e *adj* non-alcoholic; **~-fumeur** *nm* non-smoker; **~-lieu** *nm*: **il y a eu ~-lieu** the case was dismissed; **~-sens** *nm* absurdity

nord [nɔʀ] *nm* North ♦ *adj* northern; north; **au ~** (*situation*) in the north; (*direction*) to the north; **au ~ de** (*to the*) north of; **nord-est** *nm* North-East; **nord-ouest** *nm* North-West

normal, e, aux [nɔʀmal, -o] *adj* normal; **normale** *nf*: **la normale** the norm, the average; **normalement** *adv* (*en général*) normally; **normaliser** *vt* (*COMM, TECH*) to standardize

normand, e [nɔʀmɑ̃, -ɑ̃d] *adj* of Normandy

Normandie [nɔʀmɑ̃di] *nf* Normandy

norme [nɔʀm(ə)] *nf* norm; (*TECH*) standard

Norvège [nɔʀvɛʒ] *nf* Norway; **norvégien, ne** *adj* Norwegian ♦ *nm/f*: **Norvégien, ne** Norwegian ♦ *nm* (*LING*) Norwegian

nos [no] *dét voir* **notre**

nostalgie [nɔstalʒi] *nf* nostalgia

notable [nɔtabl(ə)] *adj* notable, noteworthy; (*marqué*) noticeable, marked ♦ *nm* prominent citizen

notaire [nɔtɛʀ] *nm* notary; solicitor

notamment [nɔtamɑ̃] *adv* in particular, among others

note [nɔt] *nf* (*écrite, MUS*) note; (*SCOL*) mark (*BRIT*), grade; (*facture*) bill; ~ **de service** memorandum

noté, e [nɔte] *adj*: **être bien/mal** ~ (*employé etc*) to have a good/bad record

noter [nɔte] *vt* (*écrire*) to write down; (*remarquer*) to note, notice

notice [nɔtis] *nf* summary, short article; (*brochure*) leaflet, instruction book

notifier [nɔtifje] *vt*: ~ **qch à qn** to notify sb of sth, notify sth to sb

notion [nɔsjɔ̃] *nf* notion, idea

notoire [nɔtwaʀ] *adj* widely known; (*en mal*) notorious

notre [nɔtʀ(ə), no] (*pl* **nos**) *dét* our

nôtre [notʀ(ə)] *pron*: **le** ~, **la** ~, **les** ~**s** ours ♦ *adj* ours; **les** ~**s** ours; (*alliés etc*) our own people; **soyez des** ~**s** join us

nouer [nwe] *vt* to tie, knot; (*fig: alliance etc*) to strike up

noueux, euse [nwø, -øz] *adj* gnarled

nouilles [nuj] *nfpl* noodles; pasta *sg*

nourrice [nuʀis] *nf* wet-nurse

nourrir [nuʀiʀ] *vt* to feed; (*fig: espoir*) to harbour, nurse; **logé nourri** with board and lodging; **nourrissant, e** *adj* nourishing, nutritious

nourrisson [nuʀisɔ̃] *nm* (unweaned) infant

nourriture [nuʀityʀ] *nf* food

nous [nu] *pron* (*sujet*) we; (*objet*) us; **nous-mêmes** *pron* ourselves

nouveau (nouvel), elle, x [nuvo, -ɛl] *adj* new ♦ *nm/f* new pupil (*ou* employee); **de** ~, **à** ~ again; ~ **venu, nouvelle venue** newcomer; **~-né, e** *nm/f* newborn baby; **nouveauté** *nf* novelty; (COMM) new film (*ou* book *ou* creation *etc*)

nouvel [nuvɛl] *adj voir* **nouveau**; **N~ An** New Year

nouvelle [nuvɛl] *adj voir* **nouveau** ♦ *nf* (piece of) news *sg*; (LITTÉRATURE) short story; **je suis sans ~s de lui** I haven't heard from him; **N~-Calédonie** *nf* New Caledonia; **N~-Zélande** *nf* New Zealand

novembre [nɔvɑ̃bʀ(ə)] *nm* November

novice [nɔvis] *adj* inexperienced

noyade [nwajad] *nf* drowning *no pl*

noyau, x [nwajo] *nm* (*de fruit*) stone; (BIO, PHYSIQUE) nucleus; (ÉLEC, GÉO, *fig*: *centre*) core; **noyauter** *vt* (POL) to infiltrate

noyer [nwaje] *nm* walnut (tree); (*bois*) walnut ♦ *vt* to drown; (*fig*) to flood; to submerge; **se ~** *vi* to be drowned, drown; (*suicide*) to drown o.s.

nu, e [ny] *adj* naked; (*membres*) naked, bare; (*chambre, fil, plaine*) bare ♦ *nm* (ART) nude; **se mettre ~** to strip; **mettre à ~** to bare

nuage [nɥaʒ] *nm* cloud; **nuageux, euse** *adj* cloudy

nuance [nɥɑ̃s] *nf* (*de couleur, sens*) shade; **il y a une ~ (entre)** there's a slight difference (between); **nuancer** *vt* (*opinion*) to bring some reservations *ou* qualifications to

nucléaire [nykleɛʀ] *adj* nuclear

nudiste [nydist(ə)] *nm/f* nudist

nuée [nɥe] *nf*: **une ~ de** a cloud *ou* host *ou* swarm of

nues [ny] *nfpl*: **tomber des ~** to be taken aback; **porter qn aux ~** to praise sb to the skies

nuire [nɥiʀ] *vi* to be harmful; **~ à** to harm, do damage to; **nuisible** *adj* harmful; **animal nuisible** pest

nuit [nɥi] *nf* night; **il fait ~** it's dark; **cette ~** last night; tonight; **~ blanche** sleepless night; **~ de noces** wedding night

nul, nulle [nyl] *adj* (*aucun*) no; (*minime*) nil, non-existent; (*non valable*) null; (*péj*) useless, hopeless ♦ *pron* none, no

one; **match** *ou* **résultat ~** draw; **~le part** nowhere; **nullement** *adv* by no means

numérique [nymeʀik] *adj* numerical

numéro [nymeʀo] *nm* number; (*spectacle*) act, turn; **~ de téléphone** (tele)phone number; **~ vert** *nm* ≈ freefone (®) number (BRIT), ≈ toll-free number (US); **numéroter** *vt* to number

nu-pieds [nypje] *adj inv* barefoot

nuque [nyk] *nf* nape of the neck

nu-tête [nytɛt] *adj inv* bareheaded

nutritif, ive [nytʀitif, -iv] *adj* nutritional; (*aliment*) nutritious

nylon [nilɔ̃] *nm* nylon

O o

oasis [ɔazis] *nf* oasis

obéir [ɔbeiʀ] *vi* to obey; **~ à** to obey; (*suj: moteur, véhicule*) to respond to; **obéissant, e** *adj* obedient

objecter [ɔbʒɛkte] *vt* (*prétexter*) to plead, put forward as an excuse; **~ (à qn) que** to object (to sb) that

objecteur [ɔbʒɛktœʀ] *nm*: **~ de conscience** conscientious objector

objectif, ive [ɔbʒɛktif, -iv] *adj* objective ♦ *nm* (OPTIQUE, PHOTO) lens *sg*, objective; (MIL, *fig*) objective; **~ à focale variable** zoom lens

objection [ɔbʒɛksjɔ̃] *nf* objection

objet [ɔbʒɛ] *nm* object; (*d'une discussion, recherche*) subject; **être** *ou* **faire l'~ de** (*discussion*) to be the subject of; (*soins*) to be given *ou* shown; **sans ~** purposeless; groundless; **~ d'art** objet d'art; **~s personnels** personal items; **~s trouvés** lost property *sg* (BRIT), lost-and-found *sg* (US)

obligation [ɔbligasjɔ̃] *nf* obligation; (COMM) bond, debenture; **obligatoire** *adj* compulsory, obligatory

obligé, e [ɔbliʒe] *adj* (*redevable*): **être très ~ à qn** to be most obliged to sb

obligeance [ɔbliʒɑ̃s] *nf*: **avoir l'~ de ...** to be kind *ou* good enough to ...; **obligeant, e** *adj* obliging; kind

obliger [ɔbliʒe] *vt* (*contraindre*): ~ **qn à faire** to force ou oblige sb to do; (*JUR: engager*) to bind; (*rendre service à*) to oblige; **je suis bien obligé** I have to

oblique [ɔblik] *adj* oblique; **regard ~** sidelong glance; **en ~** diagonally; **obliquer** *vi*: **obliquer vers** to turn off towards

oblitérer [ɔblitere] *vt* (*timbre-poste*) to cancel

obscène [ɔpsɛn] *adj* obscene

obscur, e [ɔpskyʀ] *adj* dark; (*fig*) obscure; lowly; **obscurcir** *vt* to darken; (*fig*) to obscure; **s'obscurcir** *vi* to grow dark; **obscurité** *nf* darkness; **dans l'obscurité** in the dark, in darkness

obséder [ɔpsede] *vt* to obsess, haunt

obsèques [ɔpsɛk] *nfpl* funeral *sg*

observateur, trice [ɔpsɛʀvatœʀ, -tʀis] *adj* observant, perceptive ♦ *nm/f* observer

observation [ɔpsɛʀvasjɔ̃] *nf* observation; (*d'un règlement etc*) observance; (*reproche*) reproof

observatoire [ɔpsɛʀvatwaʀ] *nm* observatory; (*lieu élevé*) observation post, vantage point

observer [ɔpsɛʀve] *vt* (*regarder*) to observe, watch; (*examiner*) to examine; (*scientifiquement, aussi règlement, jeûne etc*) to observe; (*surveiller*) to watch; (*remarquer*) to observe, notice; **faire ~ qch à qn** (*dire*) to point out sth to sb

obstacle [ɔpstakl(ə)] *nm* obstacle; (*ÉQUITATION*) jump, hurdle; **faire ~ à** (*lumière*) to block out; (*projet*) to hinder, put obstacles in the path of

obstiné, e [ɔpstine] *adj* obstinate

obstiner [ɔpstine]: **s'~** *vi* to insist, dig one's heels in; **s'~ à faire** to persist (obstinately) in doing; **s'~ sur qch** to keep working at sth, labour away at sth

obstruer [ɔpstʀye] *vt* to block, obstruct

obtempérer [ɔptɑ̃pere] *vi* to obey

obtenir [ɔptəniʀ] *vt* to obtain, get; (*total, résultat*) to arrive at, reach; to achieve, obtain; ~ **de pouvoir faire** to obtain permission to do; ~ **de qn qu'il fasse** to

get sb to agree to do; **obtention** *nf* obtaining

obturateur [ɔptyʀatœʀ] *nm* (*PHOTO*) shutter

obturer [ɔptyʀe] *vt* to close (up); (*dent*) to fill

obus [ɔby] *nm* shell

occasion [ɔkazjɔ̃] *nf* (*aubaine, possibilité*) opportunity; (*circonstance*) occasion; (*COMM: article non neuf*) secondhand buy; (*: acquisition avantageuse*) bargain; **à plusieurs ~s** on several occasions; **être l'~ de** to occasion, give rise to; **à l'~** sometimes, on occasions; some time; **d'~** secondhand; **occasionnel, le** *adj* (*fortuit*) chance *cpd*; (*non régulier*) occasional; casual

occasionner [ɔkazjɔne] *vt* to cause, bring about; ~ **qch à qn** to cause sb sth

occident [ɔksidɑ̃] *nm*: **l'O~** the West; **occidental, e, aux** *adj* western; (*POL*) Western

occupation [ɔkypasjɔ̃] *nf* occupation

occupé, e [ɔkype] *adj* (*MIL, POL*) occupied; (*personne: affairé, pris*) busy; (*place, sièges*) taken; (*toilettes*) engaged; (*ligne*) engaged (*BRIT*), busy (*US*)

occuper [ɔkype] *vt* to occupy; (*main-d'œuvre*) to employ; **s'~ de** (*être responsable de*) to be in charge of; (*se charger de: affaire*) to take charge of, deal with; (*: clients etc*) to attend to; (*s'intéresser à, pratiquer*) to be involved in; **s'~ (à qch)** to occupy o.s. ou keep o.s. busy (with sth); **ça occupe trop de place** it takes up too much room

occurrence [ɔkyʀɑ̃s] *nf*: **en l'~** in this case

océan [ɔseɑ̃] *nm* ocean; **l'~ Indien** the Indian Ocean

octet [ɔktɛt] *nm* byte

octobre [ɔktɔbʀ(ə)] *nm* October

octroyer [ɔktʀwaje] *vt*: ~ **qch à qn** to grant sth to sb, grant sb sth

oculiste [ɔkylist(ə)] *nm/f* eye specialist

odeur [ɔdœʀ] *nf* smell

odieux, euse [ɔdjø, -øz] *adj* hateful

odorant, e [ɔdɔʀɑ̃, -ɑ̃t] *adj* sweet-smelling, fragrant

odorat [ɔdɔʀa] *nm* (sense of) smell

œil [œj] (*pl* **yeux**) *nm* eye; **à l'~** (*fam*) for free; **à l'~ nu** with the naked eye; **tenir l'~ à l'~** to keep an eye ou a watch on sb; **avoir l'~ à** to keep an eye on; **fermer les yeux (sur)** (*fig*) to turn a blind eye (to)

œillade [œjad] *nf*: **lancer une ~ à qn** to wink at sb, give sb a wink; **faire des ~s à** to make eyes at

œillères [œjɛʀ] *nfpl* blinkers (*BRIT*), blinders (*US*)

œillet [œjɛ] *nm* (*BOT*) carnation

œuf [œf, *pl* ø] *nm* egg; **~ à la coque** *nm* boiled egg; **~ au plat** fried egg; **~ de Pâques** Easter egg; **~ dur** hard-boiled egg; **~s brouillés** scrambled eggs

œuvre [œvʀ(ə)] *nf* (*tâche*) task, undertaking; (*ouvrage achevé, livre, tableau etc*) work; (*ensemble de la production artistique*) works *pl*; (*organisation charitable*) charity ♦ *nm* (*d'un artiste*) works *pl*; (*CONSTR*): **le gros ~** the shell; **être à l'~** to be at work; **mettre en ~** (*moyens*) to make use of; **~ d'art** work of art

offense [ɔfɑ̃s] *nf* insult

offenser [ɔfɑ̃se] *vt* to offend, hurt; (*principes, Dieu*) to offend against; **s'~ de** to take offence at

offert, e [ɔfɛʀ, -ɛʀt(ə)] *pp de* **offrir**

office [ɔfis] *nm* (*charge*) office; (*agence*) bureau, agency; (*REL*) service ♦ *nm ou nf* (*pièce*) pantry; **faire ~ de** to act as; **d'~** automatically; **~ du tourisme** tourist bureau

officiel, le [ɔfisjɛl] *adj, nm/f* official

officier [ɔfisje] *nm* officer ♦ *vi* to officiate; **~ de l'état-civil** registrar

officieux, euse [ɔfisjø, -øz] *adj* unofficial

officinal, e, aux [ɔfisinal, -o] *adj*: **plantes ~es** medicinal plants

officine [ɔfisin] *nf* (*de pharmacie*) dispensary; (*bureau*) office

offrande [ɔfʀɑ̃d] *nf* offering

offre [ɔfʀ(ə)] *nf* offer; (*aux enchères*) bid; (*ADMIN: soumission*) tender; (*ÉCON*): **l'~** supply; **"~s d'emploi"** "situations vacant"; **~ d'emploi** job advertised; **~ publique d'achat** takeover bid

offrir [ɔfʀiʀ] *vt*: **~ (à qn)** to offer (to sb); (*faire cadeau de*) to give (to sb); **s'~** *vi* (*occasion, paysage*) to present itself ♦ *vt* (*vacances, voiture*) to treat o.s. to; **~ (à qn) de faire qch** to offer to do sth (for sb); **~ à boire à qn** to offer sb a drink; **s'~ comme guide/en otage** to offer one's services as (a) guide/offer o.s. as hostage

offusquer [ɔfyske] *vt* to offend

ogive [ɔʒiv] *nf*: **~ nucléaire** nuclear warhead

oie [wa] *nf* (*ZOOL*) goose

oignon [ɔɲɔ̃] *nm* (*BOT, CULIN*) onion; (*de tulipe etc: bulbe*) bulb; (*MÉD*) bunion

oiseau, x [wazo] *nm* bird; **~ de proie** bird of prey

oiseux, euse [wazø, -øz] *adj* pointless; trivial

oisif, ive [wazif, -iv] *adj* idle ♦ *nm/f* (*péj*) man(woman) of leisure

oléoduc [ɔleɔdyk] *nm* (oil) pipeline

olive [ɔliv] *nf* (*BOT*) olive; **olivier** *nm* olive (tree)

OLP *sigle f* = **Organisation de libération de la Palestine**

olympique [ɔlɛ̃pik] *adj* Olympic

ombrage [ɔ̃bʀaʒ] *nm* (*ombre*) (leafy) shade

ombragé, e *adj* shaded, shady

ombrageux, euse *adj* (*cheval*) skittish, nervous; (*personne*) touchy, easily offended

ombre [ɔ̃bʀ(ə)] *nf* (*espace non ensoleillé*) shade; (*~ portée, tache*) shadow; **à l'~** in the shade; **tu me fais de l'~** you're in my light; **ça nous donne de l'~** it gives us (some) shade; **dans l'~** (*fig*) in obscurity; in the dark; **~ à paupières** eyeshadow; **ombrelle** [ɔ̃bʀɛl] *nf* parasol, sunshade

omelette [ɔmlɛt] *nf* omelette

omettre [ɔmɛtʀ(ə)] *vt* to omit, leave out

omnibus [ɔmnibys] *nm* slow ou stopping train

omoplate [ɔmɔplat] *nf* shoulder blade

MOT-CLÉ

on [ɔ̃] *pron* **1** (*indéterminé*) you, one; ~ **peut le faire ainsi** you *ou* one can do it like this, it can be done like this

2 (*quelqu'un*): ~ **les a attaqués** they were attacked; ~ **vous demande au téléphone** there's a phone call for you, you're wanted on the phone

3 (*nous*) we; ~ **va y aller demain** we're going tomorrow

4 (*les gens*) they; **autrefois, ~ croyait ...** they used to believe ...

5: ~ **ne peut plus** *adv*: ~ **ne peut plus stupide** as stupid as can be

---

oncle [ɔ̃kl(ə)] *nm* uncle

onctueux, euse [ɔ̃ktɥø, -øz] *adj* creamy, smooth; (*fig*) smooth, unctuous

onde [ɔ̃d] *nf* (*PHYSIQUE*) wave; **sur les ~s** on the radio; **mettre en ~s** to produce for the radio; **sur ~s courtes** on short wave *sg*; **moyennes/longues ~s** medium/long wave *sg*

ondée [ɔ̃de] *nf* shower

on-dit [ɔ̃di] *nm inv* rumour

ondoyer [ɔ̃dwaje] *vi* to ripple, wave

onduler [ɔ̃dyle] *vi* to undulate; (*cheveux*) to wave

onéreux, euse [ɔneRø, -øz] *adj* costly; **à titre ~** in return for payment

ongle [ɔ̃gl(ə)] *nm* (*ANAT*) nail; **se faire les ~s** to do one's nails

onguent [ɔ̃gɑ̃] *nm* ointment

ont *vb voir* **avoir**

O.N.U. [ɔny] *sigle f* = **Organisation des Nations Unies**

onze [ɔ̃z] *num* eleven; **onzième** *num* eleventh

O.P.A. *sigle f* = **offre publique d'achat**

opaque [ɔpak] *adj* opaque

opéra [ɔpeRa] *nm* opera; (*édifice*) opera house

opérateur, trice [ɔpeRatœR, -tRis] *nm/f* operator; ~ **(de prise de vues)** cameraman

opération [ɔpeRɑsjɔ̃] *nf* operation; (*COMM*) dealing

opératoire [ɔpeRatwaR] *adj* operating;

(*choc etc*) post-operative

opérer [ɔpeRe] *vt* (*MÉD*) to operate on; (*faire, exécuter*) to carry out, make ♦ *vi* (*remède: faire effet*) to act, work; (*procéder*) to proceed; (*MÉD*) to operate; **s'~** *vi* (*avoir lieu*) to occur, take place; **se faire ~** to have an operation

opiner [ɔpine] *vi*: ~ **de la tête** to nod assent

opinion [ɔpinjɔ̃] *nf* opinion; **l'~ (publique)** public opinion

opportun, e [ɔpɔRtœ̃, -yn] *adj* timely, opportune; **en temps ~** at the appropriate time; **opportuniste** [ɔpɔRtynist(ə)] *nm/f* opportunist

opposant, e [ɔpozɑ̃, -ɑ̃t] *adj* opposing; **opposants** *nmpl* opponents

opposé, e [ɔpoze] *adj* (*direction, rive*) opposite; (*faction*) opposing; (*couleurs*) contrasting; (*opinions, intérêts*) conflicting; (*contre*): ~ **à** opposed to, against ♦ *nm*: **l'~** the other *ou* opposite side (*ou* direction); (*contraire*) the opposite; **à l'~** (*fig*) on the other hand; **à l'~ de** on the other *ou* opposite side from; (*fig*) contrary to, unlike

opposer [ɔpoze] *vt* (*personnes, armées, équipes*) to oppose; (*couleurs, termes, tons*) to contrast; **s'~** (*sens réciproque*) to conflict; to clash; to contrast; **s'~ à** (*interdire, empêcher*) to oppose; (*tenir tête à*) to rebel against; ~ **qch à** (*comme obstacle, défense*) to set sth against; (*comme objection*) to put sth forward against

opposition [ɔpozisjɔ̃] *nf* opposition; **par ~ à** as opposed to, in contrast with; **entrer en ~ avec** to come into conflict with; **être en ~ avec** (*idées, conduite*) to be at variance with; **faire ~ à un chèque** to stop a cheque

oppresser [ɔpRese] *vt* to oppress; **oppression** *nf* oppression; (*malaise*) feeling of suffocation

opprimer [ɔpRime] *vt* to oppress; (*liberté, opinion*) to suppress, stifle; (*suj: chaleur etc*) to suffocate, oppress

opter [ɔpte] *vi*: ~ **pour** to opt for; ~ **entre** to choose between

opticien, ne [ɔptisjɛ̃, -ɛn] *nm/f* optician
optimiste [ɔptimist(ə)] *nm/f* optimist
♦ *adj* optimistic
option [ɔpsjɔ̃] *nf* option; **matière à ~** (*SCOL*) optional subject
optique [ɔptik] *adj* (*nerf*) optic; (*verres*) optical ♦ *nf* (*PHOTO*: *lentilles etc*) optics *pl*; (*science, industrie*) optics *sg*; (*fig*: *manière de voir*) perspective
opulent, e [ɔpylɑ̃, -ɑ̃t] *adj* wealthy, opulent; (*formes, poitrine*) ample, generous
or [ɔR] *nm* gold ♦ *conj* now, but; **en ~** gold *cpd*; (*fig*) golden, marvellous
orage [ɔraʒ] *nm* (thunder)storm; **orageux, euse** *adj* stormy
oraison [ɔrɛzɔ̃] *nf* orison, prayer; **~ funèbre** funeral oration
oral, e, aux [ɔral, -o] *adj, nm* oral
orange [ɔrɑ̃ʒ] *nf* orange ♦ *adj inv* orange; **oranger** *nm* orange tree
orateur [ɔratœr] *nm* speaker; orator
orbite [ɔrbit] *nf* (*ANAT*) (eye-)socket; (*PHYSIQUE*) orbit
orchestre [ɔrkɛstr(ə)] *nm* orchestra; (*de jazz, danse*) band; (*places*) stalls *pl* (*BRIT*), orchestra (*US*); **orchestrer** *vt* (*MUS*) to orchestrate; (*fig*) to mount, stage-manage
orchidée [ɔrkide] *nf* orchid
ordinaire [ɔrdinɛr] *adj* ordinary; everyday; standard ♦ *nm* ordinary; (*menus*) everyday fare ♦ *nf* (*essence*) ≈ two-star (petrol) (*BRIT*), ≈ regular gas (*US*); **d'~** usually, normally; **à l'~** usually, ordinarily
ordinateur [ɔrdinatœr] *nm* computer; **~ domestique** home computer; **~ individuel** personal computer
ordonnance [ɔrdɔnɑ̃s] *nf* organization; layout; (*MÉD*) prescription; (*JUR*) order; (*MIL*) orderly, batman (*BRIT*)
ordonné, e [ɔrdɔne] *adj* tidy, orderly; (*MATH*) ordered
ordonner [ɔrdɔne] *vt* (*agencer*) to organize, arrange; (*donner un ordre*): **~ à qn de faire** to order sb to do; (*REL*) to ordain; (*MÉD*) to prescribe
ordre [ɔrdr(ə)] *nm* (*gén*) order; (*propreté et soin*) orderliness, tidiness; (*na-*

ture): **d'~ pratique** of a practical nature; **~s** *nmpl* (*REL*) holy orders; **mettre en ~** to tidy (up), put in order; **à l'~ de qn** payable to sb; **être aux ~s de qn/sous les ~s de qn** to be at sb's disposal/under sb's command; **jusqu'à nouvel ~** until further notice; **dans le même ~ d'idées** in this connection; **donnez-nous un ~ de grandeur** give us some idea as regards size (*ou* the amount); **de premier ~** first-rate; **~ du jour** (*d'une réunion*) agenda; (*MIL*) order of the day; **à l'~ du jour** (*fig*) topical
ordure [ɔrdyr] *nf* filth *no pl*; **~s** *nfpl* (*balayures, déchets*) rubbish *sg*, refuse *sg*; **~s ménagères** household refuse
oreille [ɔrɛj] *nf* (*ANAT*) ear; (*de marmite, tasse*) handle; **avoir de l'~** to have a good ear (for music)
oreiller [ɔrɛje] *nm* pillow
oreillons [ɔrɛjɔ̃] *nmpl* mumps *sg*
ores [ɔr]: **d'~ et déjà** *adv* already
orfèvrerie [ɔrfɛvrəri] *nf* goldsmith's (*ou* silversmith's) trade; (*ouvrage*) gold (*ou* silver) plate
organe [ɔrgan] *nm* organ; (*porte-parole*) representative, mouthpiece
organigramme [ɔrganigram] *nm* organization chart; flow chart
organique [ɔrganik] *adj* organic
organisateur, trice [ɔrganizatœr, -tris] *nm/f* organizer
organisation [ɔrganizasjɔ̃] *nf* organization; **O~ des Nations Unies** United Nations (Organization); **O~ du traité de l'Atlantique Nord** North Atlantic Treaty Organization
organiser [ɔrganize] *vt* to organize; (*mettre sur pied*: *service etc*) to set up; **s'~** to get organized
organisme [ɔrganism(ə)] *nm* (*BIO*) organism; (*corps, ADMIN*) body
organiste [ɔrganist(ə)] *nm/f* organist
orgasme [ɔrgasm(ə)] *nm* orgasm, climax
orge [ɔrʒ(ə)] *nf* barley
orgie [ɔrʒi] *nf* orgy
orgue [ɔrg(ə)] *nm* organ; **~s** *nfpl* (*MUS*) organ *sg*
orgueil [ɔrgœj] *nm* pride; **orgueilleux,**

euse *adj* proud

Orient [ɔrjɑ̃] *nm*: **l'~** the East, the Orient

oriental, e, aux [ɔrjɑ̃tal, -o] *adj* oriental, eastern; (*frontière*) eastern

orientation [ɔrjɑ̃tɑsjɔ̃] *nf* positioning; orientation; (*d'une maison etc*) aspect; (*d'un journal*) leanings *pl*; **avoir le sens de l'~** to have a (good) sense of direction; **~ professionnelle** careers advising; careers advisory service

orienté, e [ɔrjɑ̃te] *adj* (*fig: article, journal*) slanted; **bien/mal ~** (*appartement*) well/badly positioned; **~ au sud** facing south, with a southern aspect

orienter [ɔrjɑ̃te] *vt* (*placer, disposer: pièce mobile*) to adjust, position; (*tourner*) to direct, turn; (*voyageur, touriste, recherches*) to direct; (*fig: élève*) to orientate; **s'~** (*se repérer*) to find one's bearings; **s'~ vers** (*fig*) to turn towards

origan [ɔrigɑ̃] *nm* (*BOT*) oregano

originaire [ɔriʒinɛr] *adj*: **être ~ de** to be a native of

original, e, aux [ɔriʒinal, -o] *adj* original; (*bizarre*) eccentric ♦ *nm/f* eccentric ♦ *nm* (*document etc, ART*) original; (*dactylographie*) top copy

origine [ɔriʒin] *nf* origin; **dès l'~** at *ou* from the outset; **à l'~** originally; **originel, le** *adj* original

O.R.L. *sigle nm/f* = **oto-rhino-laryngologiste**

orme [ɔrm(ə)] *nm* elm

ornement [ɔrnəmɑ̃] *nm* ornament; (*fig*) embellishment, adornment

orner [ɔrne] *vt* to decorate, adorn

ornière [ɔrnjɛr] *nf* rut

orphelin, e [ɔrfəlɛ̃, -in] *adj* orphan(ed) ♦ *nm/f* orphan; **~ de père/mère** fatherless/motherless; **orphelinat** *nm* orphanage

orteil [ɔrtɛj] *nm* toe; **gros ~** big toe

orthographe [ɔrtɔgraf] *nf* spelling; **orthographier** *vt* to spell

orthopédiste [ɔrtɔpedist(ə)] *nm/f* orthopaedic specialist

ortie [ɔrti] *nf* (stinging) nettle

os [ɔs, *pl* o] *nm* bone

osciller [ɔsile] *vi* (*pendule*) to swing; (*au vent etc*) to rock; (*TECH*) to oscillate; (*fig*): **~ entre** to waver *ou* fluctuate between

osé, e [oze] *adj* daring, bold

oseille [ozɛj] *nf* sorrel

oser [oze] *vi, vt* to dare; **~ faire** to dare (to) do

osier [ozje] *nm* willow; **d'~, en ~** wicker(work)

ossature [ɔsatyr] *nf* (*ANAT*) frame, skeletal structure; (*fig*) framework

osseux, euse [ɔsø, -øz] *adj* bony; (*tissu, maladie, greffe*) bone *cpd*

ostensible [ɔstɑ̃sibl(ə)] *adj* conspicuous

otage [ɔtaʒ] *nm* hostage; **prendre qn comme ~** to take sb hostage

O.T.A.N. [ɔtɑ̃] *sigle f* = **Organisation du traité de l'Atlantique Nord**

otarie [ɔtari] *nf* sea-lion

ôter [ote] *vt* to remove; (*soustraire*) to take away; **~ qch à qn** to take sth (away) from sb; **~ qch de** to remove sth from

otite [ɔtit] *nf* ear infection

oto-rhino(-laryngologiste) [ɔtɔrino(larɛ̃gɔlɔʒist(ə))] *nm/f* ear nose and throat specialist

ou [u] *conj* or; **~ ... ~** either ... or; **~ bien** or (else)

MOT-CLÉ

où [u] *pron relatif* **1** (*position, situation*) where, that (*souvent omis*); **la chambre ~ il était** the room (that) he was in, the room where he was; **la ville ~ je l'ai rencontré** the town where I met him; **la pièce d'~ il est sorti** the room he came out of; **le village d'~ je viens** the village I come from; **les villes par ~ il est passé** the towns he went through

2 (*temps, état*) that (*souvent omis*); **le jour ~ il est parti** the day (that) he left; **au prix ~ c'est** at the price it is

♦ *adv* **1** (*interrogation*) where; **~ est-il/va-t-il?** where is he/is he going?; **par ~?** which way?; **d'~ vient que ...?** how come ...?

2 (*position*) where; **je sais ~ il est** I

ouate [wat] *nf* cotton wool (*BRIT*), cotton (*US*); (*bourre*) padding, wadding

oubli [ubli] *nm* (*acte*): l'~ **de** forgetting; (*étourderie*) forgetfulness *no pl*; (*négligence*) omission, oversight; (*absence de souvenirs*) oblivion

oublier [ublije] *vt* (*gén*) to forget; (*ne pas voir: erreurs etc*) to miss; (*ne pas mettre: virgule, nom*) to leave out; (*laisser quelque part: chapeau etc*) to leave behind; **s'~** to forget o.s.

oubliettes [ublijɛt] *nfpl* dungeon *sg*

ouest [wɛst] *nm* west ♦ *adj inv* west; (*région*) western; **à l'~** in the west; (*to the*) west, westwards; **à l'~ de** (*to the*) west of

ouf [uf] *excl* phew!

oui [wi] *adv* yes

ouï-dire [widiʀ]: **par ~** *adv* by hearsay

ouïe [wi] *nf* hearing; **~s** *nfpl* (*de poisson*) gills

ouïr [wiʀ] *vt* to hear; **avoir ouï dire que** to have heard it said that

ouragan [uʀagɑ̃] *nm* hurricane

ourlet [uʀlɛ] *nm* hem

ours [uʀs] *nm* bear; ~ **brun/blanc** brown/polar bear; ~ (**en peluche**) teddy (bear)

oursin [uʀsɛ̃] *nm* sea urchin

ourson [uʀsɔ̃] *nm* (bear-)cub

ouste [ust(ə)] *excl* hop it!

outil [uti] *nm* tool

outiller [utije] *vt* (*ouvrier, usine*) to equip

outrage [utʀaʒ] *nm* insult; **faire subir les derniers ~s à** (*femme*) to ravish; ~ **à la pudeur** indecent conduct *no pl*; **outrager** [utʀaʒe] *vt* to offend gravely

outrance [utʀɑ̃s]: **à ~** *adv* excessively, to excess

outre [utʀ(ə)] *nf* goatskin, water skin ♦ *prép* besides ♦ *adv*: **passer ~ à** to disregard, take no notice of; **en ~** besides, moreover; ~ **que** apart from the fact that; ~ **mesure** immoderately; unduly; **~-Atlantique** *adv* across the Atlantic;

~-Manche *adv* across the Channel; **~-mer** *adj inv* ultramarine; **~-mer** *adv* overseas; **~-passer** *vt* to go beyond, exceed

ouvert, e [uvɛʀ, -ɛʀt(ə)] *pp de* **ouvrir** ♦ *adj* open; (*robinet, gaz etc*) on; **ouvertement** *adv* openly

ouverture [uvɛʀtyʀ] *nf* opening; (*MUS*) overture; (*PHOTO*): ~ (**du diaphragme**) aperture; **~s** *nfpl* (*propositions*) overtures; ~ **d'esprit** open-mindedness

ouvrable [uvʀabl(ə)] *adj*: **jour ~** working day, weekday

ouvrage [uvʀaʒ] *nm* (*tâche, de tricot etc, MIL*) work *no pl*; (*texte, livre*) work

ouvragé, e [uvʀaʒe] *adj* finely embroidered (*ou* worked *ou* carved)

ouvre-boîte(s) [uvʀəbwat] *nm inv* tin (*BRIT*) *ou* can opener

ouvre-bouteille(s) [uvʀəbutɛj] *nm inv* bottle-opener

ouvreuse [uvʀøz] *nf* usherette

ouvrier, ière [uvʀje, -jɛʀ] *nm/f* worker ♦ *adj* working-class; industrial, labour *cpd*; **classe ouvrière** working class

ouvrir [uvʀiʀ] *vt* (*gén*) to open; (*brèche, passage, MÉD: abcès*) to open up; (*commencer l'exploitation de, créer*) to open (up); (*eau, électricité, chauffage, robinet*) to turn on ♦ *vi* to open; to open up; **s'~** *vi* to open; **s'~ à qn** to open one's heart to sb; ~ **l'appétit à qn** to whet sb's appetite

ovaire [ovɛʀ] *nm* ovary

ovale [ɔval] *adj* oval

ovni [ɔvni] *sigle m* (= *objet volant non identifié*) UFO

oxyder [ɔkside]: **s'~** *vi* to become oxidized

oxygène [ɔksiʒɛn] *nm* oxygen; (*fig*): **cure d'~** fresh air cure

oxygéné, e [ɔksiʒene] *adj*: **eau ~e** hydrogen peroxide

P p

pacifique [pasifik] *adj* peaceful ♦ *nm*: **le P~, l'océan P~** the Pacific (Ocean)

pacte [pakt(ə)] *nm* pact, treaty
pactiser [paktize] *vi*: ~ **avec** to come to terms with
pagaie [pagɛ] *nf* paddle
pagaille [pagaj] *nf* mess, shambles *sg*
page [paʒ] *nf* page ♦ *nm* page (boy); **à la ~** (*fig*) up-to-date
paiement [pɛmɑ̃] *nm* payment
païen, ne [pajɛ̃, -jɛn] *adj, nm/f* pagan, heathen
paillard, e [pajaʀ, -aʀd(ə)] *adj* bawdy
paillasson [pajasɔ̃] *nm* doormat
paille [pɑj] *nf* straw; (*défaut*) flaw
paillettes [pajɛt] *nfpl* (*décoratives*) sequins, spangles; **lessive en ~** soapflakes *pl*
pain [pɛ̃] *nm* (*substance*) bread; (*unité*) loaf (of bread); (*morceau*): ~ **de cire** *etc* bar of wax *etc*; ~ **bis/complet** brown/wholemeal (*BRIT*) *ou* wholewheat (*US*) bread; ~ **d'épice** gingerbread; ~ **de mie** sandwich loaf; ~ **de sucre** sugar loaf; ~ **grillé** toast
pair, e [pɛʀ] *adj* (*nombre*) even ♦ *nm* peer; **aller de ~** to go hand in hand *ou* together; **jeune fille au ~** au pair
paire [pɛʀ] *nf* pair
paisible [pezibl(ə)] *adj* peaceful, quiet
paître [pɛtʀ(ə)] *vi* to graze
paix [pɛ] *nf* peace; (*fig*) peacefulness, peace; **faire/avoir la ~** to make/have peace
Pakistan [pakistɑ̃] *nm*: **le ~** Pakistan
palace [palas] *nm* luxury hotel
palais [palɛ] *nm* palace; (*ANAT*) palate
pale [pal] *nf* (*d'hélice, de rame*) blade
pâle [pal] *adj* pale; **bleu ~** pale blue
Palestine [palɛstin] *nf*: **la ~** Palestine
palet [palɛ] *nm* disc; (*HOCKEY*) puck
palette [palɛt] *nf* (*de peintre*) palette; (*produits*) range
pâleur [palœʀ] *nf* paleness
palier [palje] *nm* (*d'escalier*) landing; (*fig*) level, plateau; (*TECH*) bearing; **par ~s** in stages
pâlir [paliʀ] *vi* to turn *ou* go pale; (*couleur*) to fade
palissade [palisad] *nf* fence
palliatif [paljatif] *nm* palliative; (*expé-*

dient) stopgap measure
pallier [palje]: ~ **à** *vt* to offset, make up for
palmarès [palmaʀɛs] *nm* record (of achievements); (*SCOL*) prize list; (*SPORT*) list of winners
palme [palm(ə)] *nf* (*symbole*) palm; (*de plongeur*) flipper; **palmé, e** *adj* (*pattes*) webbed
palmier [palmje] *nm* palm tree
palombe [palɔ̃b] *nf* woodpigeon
pâlot, te [palo, -ɔt] *adj* pale, peaky
palourde [paluʀd(ə)] *nf* clam
palper [palpe] *vt* to feel, finger
palpitant, e [palpitɑ̃, -ɑ̃t] *adj* thrilling
palpiter [palpite] *vi* (*cœur, pouls*) to beat; (: *plus fort*) to pound, throb
paludisme [palydism(ə)] *nm* malaria
pamphlet [pɑ̃flɛ] *nm* lampoon, satirical tract
pamplemousse [pɑ̃pləmus] *nm* grapefruit
pan [pɑ̃] *nm* section, piece ♦ *excl* bang!
panachage [panaʃaʒ] *nm* blend, mix
panache [panaʃ] *nm* plume; (*fig*) spirit, panache
panaché, e [panaʃe] *adj*: **glace ~e** mixed-flavour ice cream; **bière ~e** shandy
pancarte [pɑ̃kaʀt(ə)] *nf* sign, notice; (*dans un défilé*) placard
pancréas [pɑ̃kʀeas] *nm* pancreas
pané, e [pane] *adj* fried in breadcrumbs
panier [panje] *nm* basket; **mettre au ~** to chuck away; ~ **à provisions** shopping basket
panique [panik] *nf, adj* panic; **paniquer** *vi* to panic
panne [pan] *nf* (*d'un mécanisme, moteur*) breakdown; **être/tomber en ~** to have broken down/break down; **être en ~ d'essence** *ou* **sèche** to have run out of petrol (*BRIT*) *ou* gas (*US*); ~ **d'électricité** *ou* **de courant** power *ou* electrical failure
panneau, x [pano] *nm* (*écriteau*) sign, notice; (*de boiserie, de tapisserie etc*) panel; ~ **d'affichage** notice board; ~ **de signalisation** roadsign

panonceau, x [panɔ̃so] *nm* sign
panoplie [panɔpli] *nf (jouet)* outfit; *(d'armes)* display; *(fig)* array
panorama [panɔrama] *nm* panorama
panse [pɑ̃s] *nf* paunch
pansement [pɑ̃smɑ̃] *nm* dressing, bandage; ~ **adhésif** sticking plaster
panser [pɑ̃se] *vt (plaie)* to dress, bandage; *(bras)* to put a dressing on, bandage; *(cheval)* to groom
pantalon [pɑ̃talɔ̃] *nm (aussi: ~s, paire de ~s)* trousers *pl*, pair of trousers; ~ **de ski** ski pants *pl*
pantelant, e [pɑ̃tlɑ̃, -ɑ̃t] *adj* gasping for breath, panting
panthère [pɑ̃tɛr] *nf* panther
pantin [pɑ̃tɛ̃] *nm* jumping jack; *(péj)* puppet
pantois [pɑ̃twa] *adj m*: **rester ~** to be flabbergasted
pantomime [pɑ̃tɔmim] *nf* mime; *(pièce)* mime show
pantoufle [pɑ̃tufl(ə)] *nf* slipper
paon [pɑ̃] *nm* peacock
papa [papa] *nm* dad(dy)
pape [pap] *nm* pope
paperasse [papras] *(péj) nf* bumf *no pl*, papers *pl*; **paperasserie** *(péj) nf* red tape *no pl*; paperwork *no pl*
papeterie [papetri] *nf (usine)* paper mill; *(magasin)* stationer's (shop)
papier [papje] *nm* paper; *(article)* article; ~**s** *nmpl (aussi: ~s d'identité)* (identity) papers; ~ **à lettres** writing paper, notepaper; ~ **buvard** blotting paper; ~ **carbone** carbon paper; ~ **(d')aluminium** aluminium *(BRIT)* ou aluminum *(US)* foil, tinfoil; ~ **de verre** sandpaper; ~ **hygiénique** toilet paper; ~ **journal** newsprint; *(pour emballer)* newspaper; ~ **peint** wallpaper
papillon [papijɔ̃] *nm* butterfly; *(fam: contravention)* (parking) ticket; *(TECH: écrou)* wing nut; ~ **de nuit** moth
papilloter [papijɔte] *vi* to blink, flicker
paquebot [pakbo] *nm* liner
pâquerette [pakrɛt] *nf* daisy
Pâques [pɑk] *nm, nfpl* Easter
paquet [pakɛ] *nm* packet; *(colis)* parcel;

(fig: tas): ~ **de** ou heap of; **paquet-cadeau** *nm* gift-wrapped parcel
par [par] *prép* by; **finir** *etc* ~ to end *etc* with; ~ **amour** out of love; **passer** ~ **Lyon/la côte** to go via ou through Lyons/along by the coast; ~ **la fenêtre** *(jeter, regarder)* out of the window; **3** ~ **jour/personne** 3 a ou per day/head; **2** ~ **2** two at a time; in twos; ~ **ici** this way; *(dans le coin)* round here; ~**-ci**, ~**-là** here and there
parabole [parabɔl] *nf (REL)* parable
parachever [paraʃve] *vt* to perfect
parachute [paraʃyt] *nm* parachute
parachutiste [paraʃytist(ə)] *nm/f* parachutist; *(MIL)* paratrooper
parade [parad] *nf (spectacle, défilé)* parade; *(ESCRIME, BOXE)* parry
paradis [paradi] *nm* heaven, paradise
paradoxe [paradɔks(ə)] *nm* paradox
paraffine [parafin] *nf* paraffin
parages [paraʒ] *nmpl*: **dans les ~ (de)** in the area ou vicinity (of)
paragraphe [paragraf] *nm* paragraph
paraître [parɛtr(ə)] *vb +attrib* to seem, look, appear ♦ *vi* to appear; *(être visible)* to show; *(PRESSE, ÉDITION)* to be published, come out, appear; *(briller)* to show off ♦ *vb impers*: **il paraît que ...** it seems ou appears that ..., they say that ...; **il me paraît que ...** it seems to me that ...
parallèle [paralɛl] *adj* parallel; *(police, marché)* unofficial ♦ *nm (comparaison)*: **faire un ~ entre** to draw a parallel between; *(GÉO)* parallel ♦ *nf* parallel (line)
paralyser [paralize] *vt* to paralyse
paramédical, e, aux [paramedikal] *adj*: **personnel** ~ paramedics *pl*, paramedical workers *pl*
parapet [parapɛ] *nm* parapet
parapher [parafe] *vt* to initial; to sign
paraphrase [parafraz] *nf* paraphrase
parapluie [paraplɥi] *nm* umbrella
parasite [parazit] *nm* parasite; ~**s** *nmpl (TÉL)* interference *sg*
parasol [parasɔl] *nm* parasol, sunshade
paratonnerre [paratɔnɛr] *nm* lightning conductor
paravent [paravɑ̃] *nm* folding screen

parc [park] *nm* (public) park, gardens *pl*; (*de château etc*) grounds *pl*; (*pour le bétail*) pen, enclosure; (*d'enfant*) playpen; (MIL: *entrepôt*) depot; (*ensemble d'unités*) stock; (*de voitures etc*) fleet; ~ **automobile** (*d'un pays*) number of cars on the roads; ~ **(d'attractions) à thème** theme park; ~ **de stationnement** car park

parcelle [parsɛl] *nf* fragment, scrap; (*de terrain*) plot, parcel

parce que [parskə] *conj* because

parchemin [parʃəmɛ̃] *nm* parchment

parc(o)mètre [park(ɔ)mɛtr(ə)] *nm* parking meter

parcourir [parkurir] *vt* (*trajet, distance*) to cover; (*article, livre*) to skim *ou* glance through; (*lieu*) to go all over, travel up and down; (*suj: frisson, vibration*) to run through

parcours [parkur] *nm* (*trajet*) journey; (*itinéraire*) route; (SPORT: *terrain*) course; (: *tour*) round; run; lap

par-dessous [pardəsu] *prép, adv* under(neath)

pardessus [pardəsy] *nm* overcoat

par-dessus [pardəsy] *prép* over (the top of) ♦ *adv* over (the top); ~ **le marché** on top of all that

par-devant [pardəvɑ̃] *prép* in the presence of, before ♦ *adv* at the front; round the front

pardon [pardɔ̃] *nm* forgiveness *no pl* ♦ *excl* sorry!; (*pour interpeller etc*) excuse me!; **demander ~ à qn (de)** to apologize to sb (for); **je vous demande ~** I'm sorry; excuse me

pardonner [pardɔne] *vt* to forgive; ~ **qch à qn** to forgive sb for sth

pare: ~**-balles** *adj inv* bulletproof; ~**-boue** *nm inv* mudguard; ~**-brise** *nm inv* windscreen (BRIT), windshield (US); ~**-chocs** *nm inv* bumper

pareil, le [parɛj] *adj* (*identique*) the same, alike; (*similaire*) similar; (*tel*): **un courage/livre ~** such courage/a book, courage/a book like this; **de ~s livres** such books; **ses ~s** one's fellow men; one's peers; **ne pas avoir son(sa) ~(le)**

to be second to none; ~ **à** the same as; similar to; **sans ~** unparalleled, unequalled

parent, e [parɑ̃, -ɑ̃t] *nm/f*: **un/une ~/e** a relative *ou* relation ♦ *adj*: **être ~ de** to be related to; ~**s** *nmpl* (*père et mère*) parents; **parenté** *nf* (*lien*) relationship

parenthèse [parɑ̃tɛz] *nf* (*ponctuation*) bracket, parenthesis; (MATH) bracket; (*digression*) parenthesis, digression; **ouvrir/fermer la ~** to open/close the brackets; **entre ~s** in brackets; (*fig*) incidentally

parer [pare] *vt* to adorn; (CULIN) to dress, trim; (*éviter*) to ward off

paresse [parɛs] *nf* laziness; **paresseux, euse** *adj* lazy; (*fig*) slow, sluggish

parfaire [parfɛr] *vt* to perfect

parfait, e [parfɛ, -ɛt] *adj* perfect ♦ *nm* (LING) perfect (tense); **parfaitement** *adv* perfectly ♦ *excl* (most) certainly

parfois [parfwa] *adv* sometimes

parfum [parfœ̃] *nm* (*produit*) perfume, scent; (*odeur: de fleur*) scent, fragrance; (: *de tabac, vin*) aroma; (*goût*) flavour; **parfumé, e** *adj* (*fleur, fruit*) fragrant; (*femme*) perfumed; **parfumé au café** coffee-flavoured; **parfumer** *vt* (*suj: odeur, bouquet*) to perfume; (*mouchoir*) to put scent *ou* perfume on; (*crème, gâteau*) to flavour; **parfumerie** *nf* (*commerce*) perfumery; (*produits*) perfumes *pl*; (*boutique*) perfume shop

pari [pari] *nm* bet, wager; (SPORT) bet

paria [parja] *nm* outcast

parier [parje] *vt* to bet

Paris [pari] *n* Paris; **parisien, ne** *adj* Parisian; (GÉO, ADMIN) Paris *cpd* ♦ *nm/f*: **Parisien, ne** Parisian

paritaire [paritɛr] *adj* joint

parjure [parʒyr] *nm* perjury

parking [parkiŋ] *nm* (*lieu*) car park

parlant, e [parlɑ̃, -ɑ̃t] *adj* (*fig*) graphic, vivid; eloquent; (CINÉMA) talking

parlement [parləmɑ̃] *nm* parliament; **parlementaire** *adj* parliamentary ♦ *nm/f* member of parliament

parlementer [parləmɑ̃te] *vi* to negotiate, parley

parler [paʀle] *vi* to speak, talk; *(avouer)* to talk; ~ **(à qn) de** to talk *ou* speak (to sb) about; ~ **le/en français** to speak French/in French; ~ **affaires** to talk business; ~ **en dormant** to talk in one's sleep; **sans ~ de** *(fig)* not to mention, to say nothing of; **tu parles!** you must be joking!

parloir [paʀlwaʀ] *nm (de prison, d'hôpital)* visiting room; *(REL)* parlour

parmi [paʀmi] *prép* among(st)

paroi [paʀwa] *nf* wall; *(cloison)* partition; ~ **rocheuse** rock face

paroisse [paʀwas] *nf* parish

parole [paʀɔl] *nf (faculté)*: **la ~** speech; *(mot, promesse)* word; **~s** *nfpl (MUS)* words, lyrics; **tenir ~** to keep one's word; **prendre la ~** to speak; **demander la ~** to ask for permission to speak; **je le crois sur ~** I'll take his word for it

parquer [paʀke] *vt (voiture, matériel)* to park; *(bestiaux)* to pen (in *ou* up)

parquet [paʀkɛ] *nm* (parquet) floor; *(JUR)*: **le ~** the Public Prosecutor's department

parrain [paʀɛ̃] *nm* godfather; *(d'un nouvel adhérent)* sponsor, proposer

parrainer [paʀene] *vt (suj: entreprise)* to sponsor

pars *vb voir* **partir**

parsemer [paʀsəme] *vt (suj: feuilles, papiers)* to be scattered over; ~ **qch de** to scatter sth with

part [paʀ] *nf (qui revient à qn)* share; *(fraction, partie)* part; *(FINANCE)* (non-voting) share; **prendre ~ à** *(débat etc)* to take part in; *(soucis, douleur de qn)* to share in; **faire ~ de qch à qn** to announce sth to sb, inform sb of sth; **pour ma ~** as for me, as far as I'm concerned; **à ~ entière** full; **de la ~ de** *(au nom de)* on behalf of; *(donné par)* from; **de toute(s) ~(s)** from all sides *ou* quarters; **de ~ et d'autre** on both sides, on either side; **de ~ en ~** right through; **d'une ... d'autre ~** on the one hand ... on the other hand; **à ~** *adv* separately; *(de côté)* aside ♦ *prép* apart from, except for ♦ *adj* exceptional, special; **faire la ~ des**

choses to make allowances

partage [paʀtaʒ] *nm* dividing up; sharing (out) *no pl*, share-out; sharing; **recevoir qch en ~** to receive sth as one's share (*ou* lot)

partager [paʀtaʒe] *vt* to share; *(distribuer, répartir)* to share (out); *(morceler, diviser)* to divide (up); **se ~** *vt (héritage etc)* to share between themselves (*ou* ourselves)

partance [paʀtɑ̃s]: **en ~** *adv* outbound, due to leave; **en ~ pour** (bound) for

partant [paʀtɑ̃] *vb voir* **partir** ♦ *nm (SPORT)* starter; *(HIPPISME)* runner

partenaire [paʀtənɛʀ] *nm/f* partner

parterre [paʀtɛʀ] *nm (de fleurs)* (flower) bed; *(THÉÂTRE)* stalls *pl*

parti [paʀti] *nm (POL)* party; *(décision)* course of action; *(personne à marier)* match; **tirer ~ de** to take advantage of, turn to good account; **prendre le ~ de qn** to stand up for sb, side with sb; **prendre ~ (pour/contre)** to take sides *ou* a stand (for/against); **prendre son ~ de** to come to terms with; ~ **pris** bias

partial, e, aux [paʀsjal, -o] *adj* biased, partial

participant, e [paʀtisipɑ̃, -ɑ̃t] *nm/f* participant; *(à un concours)* entrant

participation [paʀtisipasjɔ̃] *nf* participation; sharing; *(COMM)* interest; **la ~ aux bénéfices** profit-sharing

participe [paʀtisip] *nm* participle

participer [paʀtisipe]: ~ **à** *vt (course, réunion)* to take part in; *(profits etc)* to share in; *(frais etc)* to contribute to; *(chagrin, succès de qn)* to share (in)

particularité [paʀtikylaʀite] *nf* particularity; *(distinctive)* characteristic

particule [paʀtikyl] *nf* particle

particulier, ière [paʀtikylje, -jɛʀ] *adj (personnel, privé)* private; *(spécial)* special, particular; *(caractéristique)* characteristic, distinctive; *(spécifique)* particular ♦ *nm (individu; ADMIN)* private individual; ~ **à** peculiar to; **en ~** *(surtout)* in particular, particularly; *(en privé)* in private; **particulièrement** *adv* particularly

partie [paʀti] *nf* (*gén*) part; (*profession, spécialité*) field, subject; (*JUR etc*: *protagonistes*) party; (*de cartes, tennis etc*) game; **une ~ de campagne/de pêche** an outing in the country/a fishing party *ou* trip; **en ~** partly, in part; **faire ~ de** to belong to; **en ~** to be part of; **prendre qn à ~** to take sb to task; (*malmener*) to set on sb; **en grande ~** largely, in the main; **~ civile** (*JUR*) party claiming damages in a criminal case

partiel, le [paʀsjɛl] *adj* partial ♦ *nm* (*SCOL*) class exam

partir [paʀtiʀ] *vi* (*gén*) to go; (*quitter*) to go, leave; (*s'éloigner*) to go (*ou* drive *etc*) away *ou* off; (*moteur*) to start; **~ de** (*lieu*: *quitter*) to leave; (: *commencer à*) to start from; (*date*) to run *ou* start from; **à ~ de** from

partisan, e [paʀtizɑ̃, -an] *nm/f* partisan ♦ *adj*: **être ~ de qch/de faire** to be in favour of sth/doing

partition [paʀtisjɔ̃] *nf* (*MUS*) score

partout [paʀtu] *adv* everywhere; **~ où il allait** everywhere *ou* wherever he went; **trente ~** (*TENNIS*) thirty all

paru *pp de* **paraître**

parure [paʀyʀ] *nf* (*bijoux etc*) finery *no pl*; jewellery *no pl*; (*assortiment*) set

parution [paʀysjɔ̃] *nf* publication, appearance

parvenir [paʀvəniʀ]: **~ à** *vt* (*atteindre*) to reach; (*réussir*): **~ à faire** to manage to do, succeed in doing; **faire ~ qch à qn** to have sth sent to sb

parvis [paʀvi] *nm* square (*in front of a church*)

pas¹ [pɑ] *nm* (*allure, mesure*) pace; (*démarche*) tread; (*enjambée, DANSE*) step; (*bruit*) (foot)step; (*trace*) footprint; (*TECH*: *de vis, d'écrou*) thread; **~ à ~** step by step; **au ~** at walking pace; **à ~ de loup** stealthily; **faire les cent ~** to pace up and down; **faire les premiers ~** to make the first move; **sur le ~ de la porte** on the doorstep

---

MOT-CLÉ

pas² [pɑ] *adv* **1** (*en corrélation avec*

---

ne, non etc) not; **il ne pleure ~** he does not *ou* doesn't cry; he's not *ou* isn't crying; **il n'a ~ pleuré/ne pleurera ~** he did not *ou* didn't/will not *ou* won't cry; **ils n'ont ~ de voiture/d'enfants** they haven't got a car/any children, they have no car/children; **il m'a dit de ne ~ le faire** he told me not to do it; **non ~ que ...** not that ...

2 (*employé sans ne etc*): **~ moi** not me; not I, I don't (*ou* can't *etc*); **une pomme ~ mûre** an apple which isn't ripe; **~ plus tard qu'hier** only yesterday; **~ du tout** not at all

3: **~ mal** not bad; not badly; **~ mal de** quite a lot of

---

passage [pɑsaʒ] *nm* (*fait de passer*) *voir* **passer**; (*lieu, prix de la traversée, extrait*) passage; (*chemin*) way; **de ~** (*touristes*) passing through; (*amants etc*) casual; **~ à niveau** level crossing; **~ clouté** pedestrian crossing; **"~ interdit"** "no entry"; **"~ protégé"** right of way over secondary road(s) on your right; **~ souterrain** subway (*BRIT*), underpass

passager, ère [pɑsaʒe, -ɛʀ] *adj* passing ♦ *nm/f* passenger; **~ clandestin** stowaway

passant, e [pɑsɑ̃, -ɑ̃t] *adj* (*rue, endroit*) busy ♦ *nm/f* passer-by; **en ~** in passing

passe [pɑs] *nf* (*SPORT, magnétique, NAVIG*) pass ♦ *nm* (*passe-partout*) master *ou* skeleton key; **être en ~ de faire** to be on the way to doing

passé, e [pɑse] *adj* (*événement, temps*) past; (*couleur, tapisserie*) faded ♦ *prép* after ♦ *nm* past; (*LING*) past (tense); **~ de mode** out of fashion; **~ composé** perfect (tense); **~ simple** past historic

passe-: ~-droit *nm* special privilege; **~-montagne** *nm* balaclava; **~-partout** *nm inv* master *ou* skeleton key ♦ *adj inv* all-purpose; **~~** *nm*: **tour de ~-~** trick, sleight of hand *no pl*

passeport [pɑspɔʀ] *nm* passport

passer [pɑse] *vi* (*se rendre, aller*) to go; (*voiture, piétons*: *défiler*) to pass (by), go by; (*faire une halte rapide*: *facteur,* *laitier etc*) to come, call; (: *pour rendre visite*) to call *ou* drop in; (*air, lumière: franchir un obstacle etc*) to get through; (*accusé, projet de loi*): ~ **devant** to come before; (*film, émission*) to be on; (*temps, jours*) to pass, go by; (*couleur, papier*) to fade; (*mode*) to die out; (*douleur*) to pass, go away; (*CARTES*) to pass; (*SCOL*) to go up (to the next class) ♦ *vt* (*frontière, rivière etc*) to cross; (*douane*) to go through; (*examen*) to sit, take; (*visite médicale etc*) to have; (*journée, temps*) to spend; (*donner*): ~ **qch à qn** to pass ou hand sth to sb; (: *to give sb* sth; (*transmettre*): ~ **qch à qn** to pass sth on to sb; (*enfiler: vêtement*) to slip on; (*faire entrer, mettre*): **(faire)** ~ **qch dans/par** to get sth into/through; (*café*) to pour the water on; (*thé, soupe*) to strain; (*film, pièce*) to show, put on; (*disque*) to play, put on; (*marché, accord*) to agree on; (*tolérer*): ~ **qch à qn** to let sb get away with sth; **se** ~ *vi* (*avoir lieu: scène, action*) to take place; (*se dérouler: entretien etc*) to go on; (*s'écouler: semaine etc*) to pass, go by; (*arriver*): **que s'est-il passé?** what happened?; **se** ~ **de** to go ou do without; **se** ~ **les mains sous l'eau/de l'eau sur le visage** to put one's hands under the tap/run water over one's face; ~ **par** to go through; ~ **sur** (*faute, détail inutile*) to pass over; ~ **avant qch/qn** (*fig*) to come before sth/sb; **laisser** ~ (*air, lumière, personne*) to let through; (*occasion*) to let slip, miss; (*erreur*) to overlook; ~ **à la radio/télévision** to be on the radio/on television; ~ **pour riche** to be taken for a rich man; ~ **en seconde**, ~ **la seconde** (*AUTO*) to change into second; ~ **le balai/l'aspirateur** to sweep up/hoover; **je vous passe M. X** (*je vous mets en communication avec lui*) I'm putting you through to Mr X; (*je lui passe l'appareil*) here is Mr X, I'll hand you over to Mr X

passerelle [pɑsʀɛl] *nf* footbridge; (*de navire, avion*) gangway

passe-temps [pɑstɑ̃] *nm inv* pastime

passeur, euse [pɑsœʀ, -øz] *nm/f* smuggler

passible [pasibl(ə)] *adj*: ~ **de** liable to

passif, ive [pasif, -iv] *adj* passive ♦ *nm* (*LING*) passive; (*COMM*) liabilities *pl*

passion [pɑsjɔ̃] *nf* passion; **passionnant, e** *adj* fascinating; **passionné, e** *adj* passionate; impassioned; **passionner** *vt* (*personne*) to fascinate, grip; **se passionner pour** to take an avid interest in; to have a passion for

passoire [pɑswaʀ] *nf* sieve; (*à légumes*) colander; (*à thé*) strainer

pastèque [pastɛk] *nf* watermelon

pasteur [pastœʀ] *nm* (*protestant*) minister, pastor

pastille [pastij] *nf* (*à sucer*) lozenge, pastille; (*de papier etc*) (small) disc

patate [patat] *nf*: ~ **douce** sweet potato

patauger [patoʒe] *vi* (*pour s'amuser*) to splash about; (*avec effort*) to wade about

pâte [pɑt] *nf* (*à tarte*) pastry; (*à pain*) dough; (*à frire*) batter; (*substance molle*) paste; cream; ~**s** *nfpl* (*macaroni etc*) pasta *sg*; ~ **à modeler** modelling clay, Plasticine (®: *BRIT*); ~ **brisée** shortcrust pastry; ~ **d'amandes** almond paste; ~ **de fruits** crystallized fruit *no pl*

pâté [pɑte] *nm* (*charcuterie*) pâté; (*tache*) ink blot; (*de sable*) sandpie; ~ **de maisons** block (of houses); ~ **en croûte** ≈ pork pie

pâtée [pɑte] *nf* mash, feed

patente [patɑ̃t] *nf* (*COMM*) trading licence

paternel, le [patɛʀnɛl] *adj* (*amour, soins*) fatherly; (*ligne, autorité*) paternal

pâteux, euse [pɑtø, -øz] *adj* thick; pasty

pathétique [patetik] *adj* moving

patience [pasjɑ̃s] *nf* patience

patient, e [pasjɑ̃, -ɑ̃t] *adj, nm/f* patient

patienter [pasjɑ̃te] *vi* to wait

patin [patɛ̃] *nm* skate; (*sport*) skating; ~**s (à glace)** (ice) skates; ~**s à roulettes** roller skates

patinage [patinaʒ] *nm* skating

patiner [patine] *vi* to skate; (*embrayage*)

to slip; (*roue, voiture*) to spin; **se ~** *vi* (*meuble, cuir*) to acquire a sheen; **patineur, euse** *nm/f* skater; **patinoire** *nf* skating rink, (ice) rink

pâtir [patiʀ]: **~ de** *vt* to suffer because of

pâtisserie [patisʀi] *nf* (*boutique*) cake shop; (*métier*) confectionery; (*à la maison*) pastry- *ou* cake-making, baking; **~s** *nfpl* (*gâteaux*) pastries, cakes; **pâtissier, ière** *nm/f* pastrycook; confectioner

patois [patwa] *nm* dialect, patois

patrie [patʀi] *nf* homeland

patrimoine [patʀimwan] *nm* inheritance, patrimony; (*culture*) heritage

patriotique [patʀijɔtik] *adj* patriotic

patron, ne [patʀɔ̃, -ɔn] *nm/f* boss; (*REL*) patron saint ♦ *nm* (*COUTURE*) pattern

patronat [patʀɔna] *nm* employers *pl*

patronner [patʀɔne] *vt* to sponsor, support

patrouille [patʀuj] *nf* patrol

patte [pat] *nf* (*jambe*) leg; (*pied: de chien, chat*) paw; (: *d'oiseau*) foot; (*languette*) strap

pâturage [pɑtyʀaʒ] *nm* pasture

pâture [pɑtyʀ] *nf* food

paume [pom] *nf* palm

paumé, e [pome] (*fam*) *nm/f* drop-out

paumer [pome] (*fam*) *vt* to lose

paupière [popjɛʀ] *nf* eyelid

pause [poz] *nf* (*arrêt*) break; (*en parlant, MUS*) pause

pauvre [povʀ(ə)] *adj* poor; **pauvreté** *nf* (*état*) poverty

pavaner [pavane]: **se ~** *vi* to strut about

pavé, e [pave] *adj* paved; cobbled ♦ *nm* (*bloc*) paving stone; cobblestone; (*pavage*) paving

pavillon [pavijɔ̃] *nm* (*de banlieue*) small (detached) house; (*kiosque*) lodge; pavilion; (*drapeau*) flag

pavoiser [pavwaze] *vi* to put out flags; (*fig*) to rejoice, exult

pavot [pavo] *nm* poppy

payant, e [pɛjɑ̃, -ɑ̃t] *adj* (*spectateurs etc*) paying; (*fig: entreprise*) profitable; **c'est ~** you have to pay, there is a charge

paye [pɛj] *nf* pay, wages *pl*

payer [peje] *vt* (*créancier, employé, loyer*) to pay; (*achat, réparations, fig: faute*) to pay for ♦ *vi* to pay; (*métier*) to be well-paid; (*tactique etc*) to pay off; **il me l'a fait ~ 10 F** he charged me 10 F for it; **~ qch à qn** to buy sth for sb, buy sb sth; **cela ne paie pas de mine** it doesn't look much

pays [pei] *nm* country; land; region; village; **du ~** local

paysage [peizaʒ] *nm* landscape

paysan, ne [peizɑ̃, -an] *nm/f* countryman(woman); farmer; (*péj*) peasant ♦ *adj* country *cpd*, farming; farmers'

Pays-Bas [peiba] *nmpl*: **les ~** the Netherlands

PC *nm* (*INFORM*) PC

PDG *sigle m* = **président directeur général**

péage [peaʒ] *nm* toll; (*endroit*) tollgate; **pont à ~** toll bridge

peau, x [po] *nf* skin; **gants de ~** fine leather gloves; **~ de chamois** (*chiffon*) chamois leather, shammy; **Peau-Rouge** *nm/f* Red Indian, redskin

péché [peʃe] *nm* sin

pêche [pɛʃ] *nf* (*sport, activité*) fishing; (*poissons pêchés*) catch; (*fruit*) peach; **~ à la ligne** (*en rivière*) angling

pécher [peʃe] *vi* (*REL*) to sin; (*fig: personne*) to err; (: *chose*) to be flawed

pêcher [peʃe] *nm* peach tree ♦ *vi* to go fishing ♦ *vt* to catch; to fish for

pécheur, eresse [peʃœʀ, peʃʀɛs] *nm/f* sinner

pêcheur [peʃœʀ] *nm* fisherman; angler

pécule [pekyl] *nm* savings *pl*, nest egg

pécuniaire [pekynjɛʀ] *adj* financial

pédagogie [pedagɔʒi] *nf* educational methods *pl*, pedagogy; **pédagogique** *adj* educational

pédale [pedal] *nf* pedal

pédalo [pedalo] *nm* pedal-boat

pédant, e [pedɑ̃, -ɑ̃t] (*péj*) *adj* pedantic

pédestre [pedɛstʀ(ə)] *adj*: **tourisme ~** hiking

pédiatre [pedjatʀ(ə)] *nm/f* paediatrician, child specialist

pédicure [pedikyʀ] *nm/f* chiropodist

pègre [pɛgʀ(ə)] nf underworld

peignais etc vb voir **peindre; peigner**

peigne [pɛɲ] nm comb

peigner [peɲe] vt to comb (the hair of); **se ~** vi to comb one's hair

peignoir [peɲwaʀ] nm dressing gown; **~ de bain** bathrobe

peindre [pɛ̃dʀ(ə)] vt to paint; (fig) to portray, depict

peine [pɛn] nf (affliction) sorrow, sadness no pl; (mal, effort) trouble no pl, effort; (difficulté) difficulty; (punition, châtiment) punishment; (JUR) sentence; **faire de la ~ à qn** to distress ou upset sb; **prendre la ~ de faire** to go to the trouble of doing; **se donner de la ~** to make an effort; **ce n'est pas la ~ de faire** there's no point in doing, it's not worth doing; **à ~** scarcely, hardly, barely; **à ~ ... que** hardly ... than; **défense d'afficher sous ~ d'amende** billposters will be fined; **~ capital ou de mort** capital punishment, death sentence; **peiner** vi to work hard; to struggle; (moteur, voiture) to labour ♦ vt to grieve, sadden

peintre [pɛ̃tʀ(ə)] nm painter; **~ en bâtiment** house painter

peinture [pɛ̃tyʀ] nf painting; (couche de couleur, couleur) paint; (surfaces peintes: aussi: ~s) paintwork; **"~ fraîche"** "wet paint"; **~ mate/brillante** matt/gloss paint

péjoratif, ive [peʒɔʀatif, -iv] adj pejorative, derogatory

pelage [pəlaʒ] nm coat, fur

pêle-mêle [pɛlmɛl] adv higgledy-piggledy

peler [pəle] vt, vi to peel

pèlerin [pɛlʀɛ̃] nm pilgrim

pelle [pɛl] nf shovel; (d'enfant, de terrassier) spade; **~ mécanique** mechanical digger

pellicule [pelikyl] nf film; **~s** nfpl (MÉD) dandruff sg

pelote [pəlɔt] nf (de fil, laine) ball; (d'épingles) pin cushion; **~ basque** pelota

peloton [pəlɔtɔ̃] nm group, squad; (CYCLISME) pack; **~ d'exécution** firing squad

pelotonner [pəlɔtɔne]: **se ~** vi to curl (o.s.) up

pelouse [pəluz] nf lawn

peluche [pəlyʃ] nf: **animal en ~** fluffy animal, soft toy

pelure [pəlyʀ] nf peeling, peel no pl

pénal, e, aux [penal, -o] adj penal

pénalité [penalite] nf penalty

penaud, e [pəno, -od] adj sheepish, contrite

penchant [pɑ̃ʃɑ̃] nm tendency, propensity; liking, fondness

pencher [pɑ̃ʃe] vi to tilt, lean over ♦ vt to tilt; **se ~** vi to lean over; (se baisser) to bend down; **se ~ sur** to bend over; (fig: problème) to look into; **se ~ au dehors** to lean out; **~ pour** to be inclined to favour

pendaison [pɑ̃dɛzɔ̃] nf hanging

pendant [pɑ̃dɑ̃] nm: **faire ~ à** to match; to be the counterpart of ♦ prép during; **~ que** while

pendentif [pɑ̃dɑ̃tif] nm pendant

penderie [pɑ̃dʀi] nf wardrobe

pendre [pɑ̃dʀ(ə)] vt, vi to hang; **se ~ (à)** (se suicider) to hang o.s. (on); **~ à** to hang (down) from; **~ qch à** to hang sth (up) on

pendule [pɑ̃dyl] nf clock ♦ nm pendulum

pénétrer [penetre] vi, vt to penetrate; **~ dans** to enter; (suj: projectile) to penetrate; (: air, eau) to come into, get into

pénible [penibl(ə)] adj (astreignant) hard; (affligeant) painful; (personne, caractère) tiresome; **~ment** adv with difficulty

péniche [peniʃ] nf barge

pénicilline [penisilin] nf penicillin

péninsule [penɛ̃syl] nf peninsula

pénis [penis] nm penis

pénitence [penitɑ̃s] nf (repentir) penitence; (peine) penance

pénitencier [penitɑ̃sje] nm penitentiary

pénombre [penɔ̃bʀ(ə)] nf half-light; darkness

pensée [pɑ̃se] nf thought; (démarche, doctrine) thinking no pl; (BOT) pansy; **en ~** in one's mind

penser [pɑ̃se] *vi* to think ♦ *vt* to think; (*concevoir: problème, machine*) to think out; ~ **à** to think of; (*songer à: ami, vacances*) to think of *ou* about; (*réfléchir à: problème, offre*): ~ **à qch** to think about sth, think sth over; **faire** ~ **à** to remind one of; ~ **faire qch** to be thinking of doing sth, intend to do sth

pensif, ive [pɑ̃sif, -iv] *adj* pensive, thoughtful

pension [pɑ̃sjɔ̃] *nf* (*allocation*) pension; (*prix du logement*) board and lodgings, bed and board; (*maison particulière*) boarding house; (*hôtel*) guesthouse, hotel; (*école*) boarding school; **prendre qn en** ~ to take sb (in) as a lodger; **mettre en** ~ to send to boarding school; ~ **alimentaire** (*d'étudiant*) living allowance; (*de divorcée*) maintenance allowance; alimony; ~ **complète** full board; ~ **de famille** boarding house, guesthouse; **pensionnaire** *nm/f* boarder; guest; **pensionnat** *nm* boarding school

pente [pɑ̃t] *nf* slope; **en** ~ sloping

Pentecôte [pɑ̃tkot] *nf*: **la** ~ Whitsun (*BRIT*), Pentecost

pénurie [penyri] *nf* shortage

pépé [pepe] (*fam*) *nm* grandad

pépin [pepɛ̃] *nm* (*BOT: graine*) pip; (*ennui*) snag, hitch

pépinière [pepinjɛr] *nf* nursery

perçant, e [pɛrsɑ̃, -ɑ̃t] *adj* sharp, keen; piercing, shrill

percée [pɛrse] *nf* (*trouée*) opening; (*MIL, technologique*) breakthrough; (*SPORT*) break

perce-neige [pɛrsənɛʒ] *nf inv* snowdrop

percepteur [pɛrsɛptœr] *nm* tax collector

perception [pɛrsɛpsjɔ̃] *nf* perception; (*d'impôts etc*) collection; (*bureau*) tax office

percer [pɛrse] *vt* to pierce; (*ouverture etc*) to make; (*mystère, énigme*) to penetrate ♦ *vi* to come through; to break through; ~ **une dent** to cut a tooth; **perceuse** *nf* drill

percevoir [pɛrsəvwar] *vt* (*distinguer*) to perceive, detect; (*taxe, impôt*) to collect;

(*revenu, indemnité*) to receive

perche [pɛrʃ(ə)] *nf* (*bâton*) pole

percher [pɛrʃe] *vt, vi* to perch; **se** ~ *vi* to perch; **perchoir** *nm* perch

perçois *etc vb voir* **percevoir**

percolateur [pɛrkɔlatœr] *nm* percolator

perçu, e *pp de* **percevoir**

percussion [pɛrkysjɔ̃] *nf* percussion

percuter [pɛrkyte] *vt* to strike; (*suj: véhicule*) to crash into

perdant, e [pɛrdɑ̃, -ɑ̃t] *nm/f* loser

perdition [pɛrdisjɔ̃] *nf*: **en** ~ (*NAVIG*) in distress; **lieu de** ~ den of vice

perdre [pɛrdr(ə)] *vt* to lose; (*gaspiller: temps, argent*) to waste; (*personne: moralement etc*) to ruin ♦ *vi* to lose; (*sur une vente etc*) to lose out; **se** ~ *vi* (*s'égarer*) to get lost, lose one's way; (*fig*) to go to waste; to disappear, vanish

perdrix [pɛrdri] *nf* partridge

perdu, e [pɛrdy] *pp de* **perdre** ♦ *adj* (*isolé*) out-of-the-way; (*COMM: emballage*) non-returnable; (*malade*): **il est** ~ there's no hope left for him; **à vos moments** ~**s** in your spare time

père [pɛr] *nm* father; ~**s** *nmpl* (*ancêtres*) forefathers; ~ **de famille** father; family man; **le** ~ **Noël** Father Christmas

perfectionné, e [pɛrfɛksjɔne] *adj* sophisticated

perfectionner [pɛrfɛksjɔne] *vt* to improve, perfect

perforatrice [pɛrfɔratris] *nf* (*pour cartes*) card-punch; (*de bureau*) punch

perforer [pɛrfɔre] *vt* to perforate; to punch a hole (*ou* holes) in; (*ticket, bande, carte*) to punch

performant, e [pɛrfɔrmɑ̃, -ɑ̃t] *adj*: **très** ~ high-performance *cpd*

perfusion [pɛrfyzjɔ̃] *nf*: **faire une** ~ **à qn** to put sb on a drip

péril [peril] *nm* peril

périmé, e [perime] *adj* (out)dated; (*ADMIN*) out-of-date, expired

périmètre [perimɛtr(ə)] *nm* perimeter

période [perjɔd] *nf* period; **périodique** *adj* (*phases*) periodic; (*publication*) periodical ♦ *nm* periodical

péripéties [peripesi] *nfpl* events, episodes

périphérique [peʀifeʀik] *adj* (*quartiers*) outlying; (*ANAT, TECH*) peripheral; (*station de radio*) operating from outside France ♦ *nm* (*AUTO*) ring road; (*INFORM*) peripheral

périple [peʀipl(ə)] *nm* journey

périr [peʀiʀ] *vi* to die, perish

périssable [peʀisabl(ə)] *adj* perishable

perle [pɛʀl(ə)] *nf* pearl; (*de plastique, métal, sueur*) bead

perlé, e [pɛʀle] *adj*: **grève ~e** go-slow

perler [pɛʀle] *vi* to form in droplets

permanence [pɛʀmanɑ̃s] *nf* permanence; (*local*) (duty) office; emergency service; **assurer une ~** (*service public, bureaux*) to operate *ou* maintain a basic service; **être de ~** to be on call *ou* duty; **en ~** permanently; continuously

permanent, e [pɛʀmanɑ̃, -ɑ̃t] *adj* permanent; (*spectacle*) continuous; **permanente** *nf* perm

perméable [pɛʀmeabl(ə)] *adj* (*terrain*) permeable; **~ à** (*fig*) receptive *ou* open to

permettre [pɛʀmɛtʀ(ə)] *vt* to allow, permit; **~ à qn de faire/qch** to allow sb to do/sth; **se ~ de faire** to take the liberty of doing; **permettez!** excuse me!

permis [pɛʀmi] *nm* permit, licence; **~ de chasse** hunting permit; **~ (de conduire)** (driving) licence (*BRIT*), (driver's) license (*US*); **~ de construire** planning permission (*BRIT*), building permit (*US*); **~ de séjour** residence permit; **~ de travail** work permit

permission [pɛʀmisjɔ̃] *nf* permission; (*MIL*) leave; **avoir la ~ de faire** to have permission to do; **en ~** on leave

permuter [pɛʀmyte] *vt* to change around, permutate ♦ *vi* to change, swap

Pérou [peʀu] *nm* Peru

perpétuel, le [pɛʀpetɥɛl] *adj* perpetual; (*ADMIN etc*) permanent; for life

perpétuité [pɛʀpetɥite] *nf*: **à ~** *adj, adv* for life; **être condamné à ~** to receive a life sentence

perplexe [pɛʀplɛks(ə)] *adj* perplexed, puzzled

perquisitionner [pɛʀkizisjɔne] *vi* to carry out a search

perron [pɛʀɔ̃] *nm* steps *pl* (*in front of mansion etc*)

perroquet [pɛʀɔke] *nm* parrot

perruche [peʀyʃ] *nf* budgerigar (*BRIT*), budgie (*BRIT*), parakeet (*US*)

perruque [peʀyk] *nf* wig

persan, e [pɛʀsɑ̃, -an] *adj* Persian

persécuter [pɛʀsekyte] *vt* to persecute

persévérer [pɛʀsevere] *vi* to persevere

persiennes [pɛʀsjɛn] *nfpl* (metal) shutters

persiflage [pɛʀsiflaʒ] *nm* mockery *no pl*

persil [pɛʀsi] *nm* parsley

Persique [pɛʀsik] *adj*: **le golfe ~** the (Persian) Gulf

persistant, e [pɛʀsistɑ̃, -ɑ̃t] *adj* persistent; (*feuilles*) evergreen

persister [pɛʀsiste] *vi* to persist; **~ à faire qch** to persist in doing sth

personnage [pɛʀsɔnaʒ] *nm* (*notable*) personality; figure; (*individu*) character, individual; (*THÉÂTRE*) character; (*PEINTURE*) figure

personnalité [pɛʀsɔnalite] *nf* personality; (*personnage*) prominent figure

personne [pɛʀsɔn] *nf* person ♦ *pron* nobody, no one; (*quelqu'un*) anybody, anyone; **~s** *nfpl* (*gens*) people *pl*; **il n'y a ~** there's nobody there, there isn't anybody there; **~ âgée** elderly person; **personnel, le** *adj* personal ♦ *nm* staff, personnel; **personnellement** *adv* personally

perspective [pɛʀspɛktiv] *nf* (*ART*) perspective; (*vue, coup d'œil*) view; (*point de vue*) viewpoint, angle; (*chose escomptée, envisagée*) prospect; **en ~** in prospect

perspicace [pɛʀspikas] *adj* clear-sighted, gifted with (*ou* showing) insight

persuader [pɛʀsɥade] *vt*: **~ qn (de/de faire)** to persuade sb (of/to do)

perte [pɛʀt(ə)] *nf* loss; (*de temps*) waste; (*fig: morale*) ruin; **à ~** (*COMM*) at a loss; **à ~ de vue** as far as the eye can (*ou* could) see; **~ sèche** dead loss; **~s blanches** (vaginal) discharge *sg*

pertinemment [pɛʀtinamɑ̃] *adv* to the point; full well

pertinent, e [pɛʀtinɑ̃, -ɑ̃t] *adj* apt, relevant

perturbation [pɛʀtyʀbasjɔ̃] *nf* disruption; perturbation; ~ **(atmosphérique)** atmospheric disturbance

perturber [pɛʀtyʀbe] *vt* to disrupt; (*PSYCH*) to perturb, disturb

pervers, e [pɛʀvɛʀ, -ɛʀs(ə)] *adj* perverted, depraved; perverse

pervertir [pɛʀvɛʀtiʀ] *vt* to pervert

pesant, e [pəzɑ̃, -ɑ̃t] *adj* heavy; (*fig*) burdensome

pesanteur [pəzɑ̃tœʀ] *nf* gravity

pèse-personne [pɛzpɛʀsɔn] *nm* (bathroom) scales *pl*

peser [pəze] *vt* to weigh ♦ *vi* to be heavy; (*fig*) to carry weight; ~ **sur** (*fig*) to lie heavy on; to influence

pessimiste [pesimist(ə)] *adj* pessimistic ♦ *nm/f* pessimist

peste [pɛst(ə)] *nf* plague

pester [pɛste] *vi*: ~ **contre** to curse

pétale [petal] *nm* petal

pétanque [petɑ̃k] *nf* type *of* bowls

pétarader [petaʀade] *vi* to backfire

pétard [petaʀ] *nm* banger (*BRIT*), firecracker

péter [pete] *vi* (*fam*: *casser*, *sauter*) to burst; to bust; (*fam!*) to fart (!)

pétillant, e [petijɑ̃, -ɑ̃t] *adj* (*eau etc*) sparkling

pétiller [petije] *vi* (*flamme*, *bois*) to crackle; (*mousse*, *champagne*) to bubble; (*yeux*) to sparkle

petit, e [pəti, -it] *adj* (*gén*) small; (*main*, *objet*, *colline*, *en âge*: *enfant*) small, little; (*voyage*) short, little; (*bruit etc*) faint, slight; (*mesquin*) mean; ~s *nmpl* (*d'un animal*) young *pl*; **faire des** ~s to have kittens (*ou* puppies *etc*); **les tout-petits** the little ones, the tiny tots; ~ **à** ~ bit by bit, gradually; ~**(e) ami(e)** boyfriend/girlfriend; ~ **déjeuner** breakfast; ~ **pain** (bread) roll; **les** ~**es annonces** the small ads; ~**s pois** garden peas; ~**-bourgeois** (*f* ~**-bourgeoise**: *péj*) *adj* middle-class; ~**-fille** *nf* granddaughter; ~**-fils** *nm* grandson

pétition [petisjɔ̃] *nf* petition

petits-enfants [pətizɑ̃fɑ̃] *nmpl* grandchildren

petit-suisse [pətisɥis] (*pl* **petits-suisses**) *nm* small individual pot of cream cheese

pétrin [petʀɛ̃] *nm* kneading-trough; (*fig*): **dans le** ~ in a jam *ou* fix

pétrir [petʀiʀ] *vt* to knead

pétrole [petʀɔl] *nm* oil; (*pour lampe*, *réchaud etc*) paraffin (oil); **pétrolier, ière** *adj* oil *cpd* ♦ *nm* oil tanker

┌─────────────┐
│ **MOT-CLÉ** │
└─────────────┘

peu [pø] *adv* **1** (*modifiant verbe*, *adjectif*, *adverbe*): **il boit** ~ he doesn't drink (very) much; **il est** ~ **bavard** he's not very talkative; ~ **avant/après** shortly before/afterwards

2 (*modifiant nom*): ~ **de**: ~ **de gens/ d'arbres** few *ou* not (very) many people/trees; **il a** ~ **d'espoir** he hasn't (got) much hope, he has little hope; **pour** ~ **de temps** for (only) a short while

3: **à** ~ little by little; **à** ~ **près** just about, more or less; **à** ~ **près 10 kg/ 10 F** approximately 10 kg/10F

♦ *nm* **1**: **le** ~ **de gens qui** the few people who; **le** ~ **de sable qui** what little sand, the little sand which

2: **un** ~ a little; **un petit** ~ a little bit; **un** ~ **d'espoir** a little hope

♦ *pron*: ~ **le savent** few know (it); **avant** *ou* **sous** ~ shortly, before long; **de** ~ (only) just

peuple [pœpl(ə)] *nm* people

peupler [pœple] *vt* (*pays*, *région*) to populate; (*étang*) to stock; (*suj*: *hommes*, *poissons*) to inhabit; (*fig*: *imagination*, *rêves*) to fill

peuplier [pøplije] *nm* poplar (tree)

peur [pœʀ] *nf* fear; **avoir** ~ **(de/de faire/que)** to be frightened *ou* afraid (of/of doing/that); **faire** ~ **à** to frighten; **de** ~ **de/que** for fear of/that; **peureux, euse** *adj* fearful, timorous

peut *vb voir* **pouvoir**

peut-être [pøtɛtʀ(ə)] *adv* perhaps,

maybe; ~ **que** perhaps, maybe; ~ **bien qu'il fera/est** he may well do/be

peux *etc vb voir* **pouvoir**

phare [faʀ] *nm* (*en mer*) lighthouse; (*de véhicule*) headlight; **mettre ses ~s** to put on one's headlights; **~s de recul** reversing lights

pharmacie [faʀmasi] *nf* (*magasin*) chemist's (*BRIT*), pharmacy; (*officine*) pharmacy; (*de salle de bain*) medicine cabinet; **pharmacien, ne** *nm/f* pharmacist, chemist (*BRIT*)

phénomène [fenɔmɛn] *nm* phenomenon; (*monstre*) freak

philanthrope [filɑ̃tʀɔp] *nm/f* philanthropist

philatélie [filateli] *nf* philately, stamp collecting

philosophe [filɔzɔf] *nm/f* philosopher ♦ *adj* philosophical

philosophie [filɔzɔfi] *nf* philosophy

phobie [fɔbi] *nf* phobia

phonétique [fɔnetik] *nf* phonetics *sg*

phoque [fɔk] *nm* seal; (*fourrure*) sealskin

phosphorescent, e [fɔsfɔʀesɑ̃, -ɑ̃t] *adj* luminous

photo [fɔto] *nf* photo(graph); **en ~** *ou* **sur une ~** on a photograph; **prendre en ~** to take a photo of; **aimer la/faire de la ~** to like taking/take photos; ~ **d'identité** passport photograph; **~copie** *nf* photocopying; **~copier** *vt* to photocopy; **~copieuse** [fɔtokɔpjøz] *nf* photocopier; **~graphe** *nm/f* photographer; **~graphie** *nf* (*procédé, technique*) photography; (*cliché*) photograph; **~graphier** *vt* to photograph

phrase [fʀɑz] *nf* (*LING*) sentence; (*propos, MUS*) phrase

physicien, ne [fizisjɛ̃, -ɛn] *nm/f* physicist

physionomie [fizjɔnɔmi] *nf* face

physique [fizik] *adj* physical ♦ *nm* physique ♦ *nf* physics *sg*; **au ~** physically; **~ment** *adv* physically

piaffer [pjafe] *vi* to stamp

piailler [pjaje] *vi* to squawk

pianiste [pjanist(ə)] *nm/f* pianist

piano [pjano] *nm* piano

pianoter [pjanɔte] *vi* to tinkle away (at the piano); (*tapoter*): ~ **sur** to drum one's fingers on

pic [pik] *nm* (*instrument*) pick(axe); (*montagne*) peak; (*ZOOL*) woodpecker; **à ~** vertically; (*fig*) just at the right time

pichet [piʃɛ] *nm* jug

picorer [pikɔʀe] *vt* to peck

picoter [pikɔte] *vt* (*suj: oiseau*) to peck ♦ *vi* (*irriter*) to smart, prickle

pie [pi] *nf* magpie; (*fig*) chatterbox

pièce [pjɛs] *nf* (*d'un logement*) room; (*THÉÂTRE*) play; (*de mécanisme, machine*) part; (*de monnaie*) coin; (*COUTURE*) patch; (*document*) document; (*de drap, fragment, de collection*) piece; **dix francs ~** ten francs each; **vendre à la ~** to sell separately; **travailler/payer à la ~** to do piecework/pay piece rate; **un maillot une ~** a one-piece swimsuit; **un deux-pièces cuisine** a two-room(ed) flat (*BRIT*) *ou* apartment (*US*) with kitchen; ~ **à conviction** exhibit; ~ **d'eau** ornamental lake *ou* pond; ~ **d'identité: avez-vous une ~ d'identité?** have you got any (means of) identification?; ~ **montée** tiered cake; **~s détachées** spares, (spare) parts; **~s justificatives** supporting documents

pied [pje] *nm* foot; (*de verre*) stem; (*de table*) leg; (*de lampe*) base; (*plante*) plant; **à ~** on foot; **à ~ sec** without getting one's feet wet; **au ~ de la lettre** literally; **de ~ en cap** from head to foot; **en ~** (*portrait*) full-length; **avoir ~** to be able to touch the bottom, not to be out of one's depth; **avoir le ~ marin** to be a good sailor; **sur ~** (*debout, rétabli*) up and about; **mettre sur ~** (*entreprise*) to set up; **mettre à ~** to dismiss; to lay off; ~ **de vigne** vine

piédestal, aux [pjedɛstal, -o] *nm* pedestal

pied-noir [pjɛnwaʀ] *nm* Algerian-born Frenchman

piège [pjɛʒ] *nm* trap; **prendre au ~** to trap; **piéger** *vt* (*avec une bombe*) to booby-trap; **lettre/voiture piégée** letter-/

car-bomb

pierraille [pjɛʀaj] *nf* loose stones *pl*

pierre [pjɛʀ] *nf* stone; ~ **à briquet** flint; ~ **fine** semiprecious stone; ~ **tombale** tombstone; **pierreries** [pjɛʀʀi] *nfpl* gems, precious stones

piétiner [pjetine] *vi* (*trépigner*) to stamp (one's foot); (*marquer le pas*) to stand about; (*fig*) to be at a standstill ♦ *vt* to trample on

piéton, ne [pjetɔ̃, -ɔn] *nm/f* pedestrian; **piétonnier, ière** *adj*: **rue** *ou* **zone** **piétonnière** pedestrian precinct

pieu, x [pjø] *nm* post; (*pointu*) stake

pieuvre [pjœvʀ(ə)] *nf* octopus

pieux, euse [pjø, -øz] *adj* pious

piffer [pife] (*fam*) *vt*: **je ne peux pas le** ~ I can't stand him

pigeon [piʒɔ̃] *nm* pigeon

piger [piʒe] (*fam*) *vi, vt* to understand

pigiste [piʒist(ə)] *nm/f* freelance(r)

pignon [piɲɔ̃] *nm* (*de mur*) gable; (*d'engrenage*) cog(wheel), gearwheel

pile [pil] *nf* (*tas*) pile; (*ÉLEC*) battery ♦ *adv* (*s'arrêter etc*) dead; **à deux heures** ~ at two on the dot; **jouer à** ~ **ou face** to toss up (for it); ~ **ou face?** heads or tails?

piler [pile] *vt* to crush, pound

pileux, euse [pilø, -øz] *adj*: **système** ~ (body) hair

pilier [pilje] *nm* pillar

piller [pije] *vt* to pillage, plunder, loot

pilon [pilɔ̃] *nm* pestle

pilote [pilɔt] *nm* pilot; (*de char, voiture*) driver ♦ *adj* pilot *cpd*; ~ **de course** racing driver; ~ **de ligne/d'essai/de chasse** airline/test/fighter pilot; **piloter** [pilɔte] *vt* to pilot, fly; to drive

pilule [pilyl] *nf* pill; **prendre la** ~ to be on the pill

piment [pimɑ̃] *nm* (*BOT*) pepper, capsicum; (*fig*) spice, piquancy

pimpant, e [pɛ̃pɑ̃, -ɑ̃t] *adj* spruce

pin [pɛ̃] *nm* pine (tree); (*bois*) pine(wood)

pinard [pinaʀ] (*fam*) *nm* (cheap) wine, plonk (*BRIT*)

pince [pɛ̃s] *nf* (*outil*) pliers *pl*; (*de homard, crabe*) pincer, claw; (*COUTURE*: *pli*) dart; ~ **à épiler** tweezers *pl*; ~ **à linge** clothes peg (*BRIT*) *ou* pin (*US*); ~ **à sucre** sugar tongs *pl*

pincé, e [pɛ̃se] *adj* (*air*) stiff

pinceau, x [pɛ̃so] *nm* (paint)brush

pincée [pɛ̃se] *nf*: **une** ~ **de** a pinch of

pincer [pɛ̃se] *vt* to pinch; (*MUS*: *cordes*) to pluck; (*fam*) to nab

pincettes [pɛ̃sɛt] *nfpl* (*pour le feu*) (fire) tongs

pinède [pinɛd] *nf* pinewood, pine forest

pingouin [pɛ̃gwɛ̃] *nm* penguin

ping-pong [piŋpɔ̃g] (®) *nm* table tennis

pingre [pɛ̃gʀ(ə)] *adj* niggardly

pinson [pɛ̃sɔ̃] *nm* chaffinch

pintade [pɛ̃tad] *nf* guinea-fowl

pioche [pjɔʃ] *nf* pickaxe; **piocher** *vt* to dig up (with a pickaxe)

piolet [pjɔlɛ] *nm* ice axe

pion [pjɔ̃] *nm* (*ÉCHECS*) pawn; (*DAMES*) piece

pionnier [pjɔnje] *nm* pioneer

pipe [pip] *nf* pipe

pipeau, x [pipo] *nm* (reed-)pipe

piquant, e [pikɑ̃, -ɑ̃t] *adj* (*barbe, rosier etc*) prickly; (*saveur, sauce*) hot, pungent; (*fig*) racy; biting ♦ *nm* (*épine*) thorn, prickle; (*fig*) spiciness, spice

pique [pik] *nf* pike; (*fig*) cutting remark ♦ *nm* (*CARTES*: *couleur*) spades *pl*; (: *carte*) spade

pique-nique [piknik] *nm* picnic

piquer [pike] *vt* (*percer*) to prick; (*planter*): ~ **qch dans** to stick sth into; (*MÉD*) to give a jab to; (: *animal blessé etc*) to put to sleep; (*suj*: *insecte, fumée, ortie*) to sting; (: *poivre*) to burn; (: *froid*) to bite; (*COUTURE*) to machine (stitch); (*intérêt etc*) to arouse; (*fam*) to pick up; (: *voler*) to pinch; (: *arrêter*) to nab ♦ *vi* (*avion*) to go into a dive; **se** ~ **de faire** to pride o.s. on doing; ~ **un galop/un cent mètres** to break into a gallop/put on a sprint

piquet [pikɛ] *nm* (*pieu*) post, stake; (*de tente*) peg; ~ **de grève** (strike-)picket; ~ **d'incendie** fire-fighting squad

piqûre [pikyʀ] *nf* (*d'épingle*) prick; (*d'ortie*) sting; (*de moustique*) bite; (*MÉD*) injection, shot (*US*); (*COUTURE*) (straight) stitch; straight stitching; **faire une ~ à qn** to give sb an injection

pirate [piʀat] *nm, adj* pirate; **~ de l'air** hijacker

pire [piʀ] *adj* worse; (*superlatif*): **le(la) ~ ...** the worst ... ♦ *nm*: **le ~ (de)** the worst (of)

pis [pi] *nm* (*de vache*) udder; (*pire*): **le ~** the worst ♦ *adj, adv* worse; **~-aller** *nm inv* stopgap

piscine [pisin] *nf* (swimming) pool; **~ couverte** indoor (swimming) pool

pissenlit [pisɑ̃li] *nm* dandelion

pistache [pistaʃ] *nf* pistachio (nut)

piste [pist(ə)] *nf* (*d'un animal, sentier*) track, trail; (*indice*) lead; (*de stade, de magnétophone*) track; (*de cirque*) ring; (*de danse*) floor; (*de patinage*) rink; (*de ski*) run; (*AVIAT*) runway; **~ cyclable** cycle track

pistolet [pistɔlɛ] *nm* (*arme*) pistol, gun; (*à peinture*) spray gun; **~ à air comprimé** airgun; **~-mitrailleur** *nm* submachine gun

piston [pistɔ̃] *nm* (*TECH*) piston; **pistonner** *vt* (*candidat*) to pull strings for

piteux, euse [pitø, -øz] *adj* pitiful (*avant le nom*), sorry (*avant le nom*)

pitié [pitje] *nf* pity; **faire ~** to inspire pity; **avoir ~ de** (*compassion*) to pity, feel sorry for; (*merci*) to have pity *ou* mercy on

piton [pitɔ̃] *nm* (*clou*) peg; **~ rocheux** rocky outcrop

pitoyable [pitwajabl(ə)] *adj* pitiful

pitre [pitʀ(ə)] *nm* clown; **pitrerie** *nf* tomfoolery *no pl*

pittoresque [pitɔʀɛsk(ə)] *adj* picturesque

pivot [pivo] *nm* pivot; **pivoter** *vi* to swivel; to revolve

P.J. *sigle f* (= *police judiciaire*) ≈ CID (*BRIT*), ≈ FBI (*US*)

placard [plakaʀ] *nm* (*armoire*) cupboard; (*affiche*) poster, notice; **placarder** *vt* (*affiche*) to put up

place [plas] *nf* (*emplacement, situation, classement*) place; (*de ville, village*) square; (*espace libre*) room, space; (*de parking*) space; (*siège: de train, cinéma, voiture*) seat; (*emploi*) job; **en ~** (*mettre*) in its place; **sur ~** on the spot; **faire ~ à** to give way to; **faire de la ~ à** to make room for; **ça prend de la ~** it takes up a lot of room *ou* space; **à la ~ de** in place of, instead of; **il y a 20 ~s assises/debout** there are 20 seats/there is standing room for 20

placement [plasmɑ̃] *nm* placing; (*FINANCE*) investment; **bureau de ~** employment agency

placer [plase] *vt* to place; (*convive, spectateur*) to seat; (*capital, argent*) to place, invest; (*dans la conversation*) to put *ou* get in; **se ~ au premier rang** to go and stand (*ou* sit) in the first row

plafond [plafɔ̃] *nm* ceiling

plafonner [plafɔne] *vi* to reach one's (*ou* a) ceiling

plage [plaʒ] *nf* beach; (*fig*) band, bracket; (*de disque*) track, band; **~ arrière** (*AUTO*) parcel *ou* back shelf

plagiat [plaʒja] *nm* plagiarism

plaider [plede] *vi* (*avocat*) to plead; (*plaignant*) to go to court, litigate ♦ *vt* to plead; **~ pour** (*fig*) to speak for; **plaidoyer** *nm* (*JUR*) speech for the defence; (*fig*) plea

plaie [plɛ] *nf* wound

plaignant, e [plɛɲɑ̃, -ɑ̃t] *nm/f* plaintiff

plaindre [plɛ̃dʀ(ə)] *vt* to pity, feel sorry for; **se ~** *vi* (*gémir*) to moan; (*protester, rouspéter*): **se ~ (à qn) (de)** to complain (to sb) (about); (*souffrir*): **se ~ de** to complain of

plaine [plɛn] *nf* plain

plain-pied [plɛ̃pje] *adv*: **de ~ (avec)** on the same level (as)

plainte [plɛ̃t] *nf* (*gémissement*) moan, groan; (*doléance*) complaint; **porter ~** to lodge a complaint

plaire [plɛʀ] *vi* to be a success, be successful; to please; **~ à**: **cela me plaît** I like it; **se ~ quelque part** to like being somewhere *ou* like it somewhere; **s'il vous plaît** please

plaisance [plɛzɑ̃s] *nf* (*aussi: navigation*

de ~) (pleasure) sailing, yachting

plaisant, e [plɛzɑ̃, -ɑ̃t] *adj* pleasant; (*histoire, anecdote*) amusing

plaisanter [plɛzɑ̃te] *vi* to joke; **plaisanterie** *nf* joke; joking *no pl*

plaise *etc vb voir* **plaire**

plaisir [pleziʀ] *nm* pleasure; **faire ~ à qn** (*délibérément*) to be nice to sb, please sb; (*suj: cadeau, nouvelle etc*): **ceci me fait ~** I'm delighted *ou* very pleased with this; **pour le** *ou* **par ~** for pleasure

plaît *vb voir* **plaire**

plan, e [plɑ̃, -an] *adj* flat ♦ *nm* plan; (*GÉOM*) plane; (*fig*) level, plane; (*CINÉMA*) shot; **au premier/second ~** in the foreground/middle distance; **à l'arrière ~** in the background; **~ d'eau** lake; pond

planche [plɑ̃ʃ] *nf* (*pièce de bois*) plank, (wooden) board; (*illustration*) plate; **les ~s** *nfpl* (*THÉÂTRE*) the stage *sg*, the boards; **~ à repasser** ironing board; **~ à roulettes** skateboard; **~ de salut** (*fig*) sheet anchor

plancher [plɑ̃ʃe] *nm* floor; floorboards *pl*; (*fig*) minimum level ♦ *vi* to work hard

planer [plane] *vi* to glide; **~ sur** (*fig*) to hang over; to hover above

planète [planɛt] *nf* planet

planeur [planœʀ] *nm* glider

planification [planifikasjɔ̃] *nf* (economic) planning

planifier [planifje] *vt* to plan

planning [planiŋ] *nm* programme, schedule; **~ familial** family planning

planque [plɑ̃k] (*fam*) *nf* (*emploi peu fatigant*) cushy (*BRIT*) *ou* easy number; (*cachette*) hiding place

plant [plɑ̃] *nm* seedling, young plant

plante [plɑ̃t] *nf* plant; **~ d'appartement** house *ou* pot plant; **~ du pied** sole (of the foot)

planter [plɑ̃te] *vt* (*plante*) to plant; (*enfoncer*) to hammer *ou* drive in; (*tente*) to put up, pitch; (*fam*) to dump; to ditch; **se ~** (*fam: se tromper*) to get it wrong

plantureux, euse [plɑ̃tyʀø, -øz] *adj* copious, lavish; (*femme*) buxom

plaque [plak] *nf* plate; (*de verglas, d'eczéma*) patch; (*avec inscription*) plaque; **~ chauffante** hotplate; **~ de chocolat** bar of chocolate; **~ (minéralogique** *ou* **d'immatriculation)** number (*BRIT*) *ou* license (*US*) plate; **~ tournante** (*fig*) centre

plaqué, e [plake] *adj*: **~ or/argent** gold-/silver-plated; **~ acajou** veneered in mahogany

plaquer [plake] *vt* (*aplatir*): **~ qch sur** *ou* **contre** to make sth stick *ou* cling to; (*RUGBY*) to bring down; (*fam: laisser tomber*) to drop

plaquette [plakɛt] *nf* (*de chocolat*) bar; (*beurre*) pack(et)

plastic [plastik] *nm* plastic explosive

plastique [plastik] *adj, nm* plastic

plastiquer [plastike] *vt* to blow up (*with a plastic bomb*)

plat, e [pla, -at] *adj* flat; (*cheveux*) straight; (*personne, livre*) dull ♦ *nm* (*récipient, CULIN*) dish; (*d'un repas*): **le premier ~** the first course; **à ~ ventre** face down; **à ~** (*pneu, batterie*) flat; (*personne*) dead beat; **~ cuisiné** pre-cooked meal; **~ de résistance** main course; **~ du jour** dish of the day

platane [platan] *nm* plane tree

plateau, x [plato] *nm* (*support*) tray; (*GÉO*) plateau; (*de tourne-disques*) turntable; (*CINÉMA*) set; **~ à fromages** cheeseboard

plate-bande [platbɑ̃d] *nf* flower bed

plate-forme [platfɔʀm(ə)] *nf* platform; **~ de forage/pétrolière** drilling/oil rig

platine [platin] *nm* platinum ♦ *nf* (*d'un tourne-disque*) turntable

plâtras [plɑtʀa] *nm* rubble *no pl*

plâtre [plɑtʀ(ə)] *nm* (*matériau*) plaster; (*statue*) plaster statue; (*MÉD*) (plaster) cast; **avoir un bras dans le ~** to have an arm in plaster

plein, e [plɛ̃, -ɛn] *adj* full; (*porte, roue*) solid; (*chienne, jument*) big (with young) ♦ *nm*: **faire le ~ (d'essence)** to fill up (with petrol); **à ~es mains** (*ramasser*) in handfuls; (*empoigner*) firmly; **à ~ régime** at maximum revs; (*fig*) full steam; **à ~ temps** full-time; **en ~ air** in the open air; **en ~ soleil** in direct sunlight; **en ~e nuit/rue** in the middle of the night/street; **en ~ jour** in broad daylight; **en ~ sur** right on; **plein-emploi** *nm* full employment

plénitude [plenityd] *nf* fullness

pleurer [plœʀe] *vi* to cry; *(yeux)* to water ♦ *vt* to mourn (for); **~ sur** to lament (over), bemoan

pleurnicher [plœʀniʃe] *vi* to snivel, whine

pleurs [plœʀ] *nmpl*: **en ~** in tears

pleut *vb voir* **pleuvoir**

pleuvoir [pløvwaʀ] *vb impers* to rain ♦ *vi* *(fig)*: **~ (sur)** to shower down (upon); to be showered upon; **il pleut** it's raining

pli [pli] *nm* fold; *(de jupe)* pleat; *(de pantalon)* crease; *(aussi: faux ~)* crease; *(enveloppe)* envelope; *(lettre)* letter; *(CARTES)* trick

pliant, e [plijɑ̃, -ɑ̃t] *adj* folding ♦ *nm* folding stool, campstool

plier [plije] *vt* to fold; *(pour ranger)* to fold up; *(table pliante)* to fold down; *(genou, bras)* to bend ♦ *vi* to bend; *(fig)* to yield; **se ~ à** to submit to

plinthe [plɛ̃t] *nf* skirting board

plisser [plise] *vt* *(rider, chiffonner)* to crease; *(jupe)* to put pleats in

plomb [plɔ̃] *nm* *(métal)* lead; *(d'une cartouche)* (lead) shot; *(PÊCHE)* sinker; *(sceau)* (lead) seal; *(ÉLEC)* fuse; **sans ~** *(essence etc)* unleaded

plombage [plɔ̃baʒ] *nm* *(de dent)* filling

plomber [plɔ̃be] *vt* *(canne, ligne)* to weight (with lead); *(dent)* to fill

plomberie [plɔ̃bʀi] *nf* plumbing

plombier [plɔ̃bje] *nm* plumber

plongeant, e [plɔ̃ʒɑ̃, -ɑ̃t] *adj* *(vue)* from above; *(tir, décolleté)* plunging

plongée [plɔ̃ʒe] *nf* *(SPORT)* diving *no pl*; *(: sans scaphandre)* skin diving

plongeoir [plɔ̃ʒwaʀ] *nm* diving board

plongeon [plɔ̃ʒɔ̃] *nm* dive

plonger [plɔ̃ʒe] *vi* to dive ♦ *vt*: **~ qch dans** to plunge sth into

ployer [plwaje] *vi* to bend ♦ *vi* to sag; to

bend

plu *pp de* **plaire; pleuvoir**

pluie [plɥi] *nf* rain; *(fig)*: **~ de** shower of

plume [plym] *nf* feather; *(pour écrire)* (pen) nib; *(fig)* pen; **plumer** [plyme] *vt* to pluck; **plumier** [plymje] *nm* pencil box

plupart [plypaʀ]: **la ~** *pron* the majority, most (of them); **la ~ des** most, the majority of; **la ~ du temps/d'entre nous** most of the time/of us; **pour la ~** for the most part, mostly

pluriel [plyʀjɛl] *nm* plural

plus¹ [ply] *vb voir* **plaire**

MOT-CLÉ
---

plus² [ply] *adv* **1** *(forme négative)*: **ne ... ~** no more, no longer; **je n'ai ~ d'argent** I've got no more money *ou* no money left; **il ne travaille ~** he's no longer working, he doesn't work any more

2 [ply, plyz + *voyelle*] *(comparatif)* more, ...+er; *(superlatif)*: **le ~** the most, the ...+est; **~ grand/intelligent (que)** bigger/more intelligent (than); **le ~ grand/intelligent** the biggest/most intelligent; **tout au ~** at the very most

3 [plys] *(davantage)* more; **il travaille ~ (que)** he works more (than); **~ il travaille, ~ il est heureux** the more he works, the happier he is; **~ de pain** more bread; **~ de 10 personnes** more than 10 people, over 10 people; **3 heures de ~ que** 3 hours more than; **de ~** what's more, moreover; **3 kilos en ~** 3 kilos more; **en ~ de** in addition to; **de ~ en ~** more and more; **~ ou moins** more or less; **ni ~ ni moins** no more, no less

♦ *prép* [plys]: **4 ~ 2** 4 plus 2

---

plusieurs [plyzjœʀ] *dét, pron* several; **ils sont ~** there are several of them

plus-que-parfait [plyskəpaʀfɛ] *nm* pluperfect, past perfect

plus-value [plyvaly] *nf* appreciation; capital gain; surplus

plut *vb voir* **plaire**

plutôt [plyto] *adv* rather; **je ferais ~ ceci** I'd rather *ou* sooner do this; **fais ~**

comme ça try this way instead, you'd better try this way; **~ que (de) faire** rather than *ou* instead of doing

pluvieux, euse [plyvjø, -øz] *adj* rainy, wet

PMU *sigle m* (= *pari mutuel urbain*) system of betting on horses; (*café*) betting agency

pneu [pnø] *nm* tyre (*BRIT*), tire (*US*)

pneumatique [pnømatik] *nm* tyre (*BRIT*), tire (*US*)

pneumonie [pnømɔni] *nf* pneumonia

poche [pɔʃ] *nf* pocket; (*déformation*): **faire une** *ou* **des ~(s)** to bag; (*sous les yeux*) bag, pouch; **de ~** pocket *cpd*

pocher [pɔʃe] *vt* (*CULIN*) to poach

pochette [pɔʃɛt] *nf* (*de timbres*) wallet, envelope; (*d'aiguilles etc*) case; (*mouchoir*) breast pocket handkerchief; **~ de disque** record sleeve

poêle [pwal] *nm* stove ♦ *nf*: **~ (à frire)** frying pan

poêlon [pwalɔ̃] *nm* casserole

poème [pɔɛm] *nm* poem

poésie [pɔezi] *nf* (*poème*) poem; (*art*): **la ~** poetry

poète [pɔɛt] *nm* poet

poids [pwa] *nm* weight; (*SPORT*) shot; **vendre au ~** to sell by weight; **prendre du ~** to put on weight; **~ lourd** (*camion*) lorry (*BRIT*), truck (*US*)

poignard [pwaɲaʀ] *nm* dagger; **poignarder** *vt* to stab, knife

poigne [pwaɲ] *nf* grip; (*fig*): **à ~** firmhanded

poignée [pwaɲe] *nf* (*de sel etc, fig*) handful; (*de couvercle, porte*) handle; **~ de main** handshake

poignet [pwaɲɛ] *nm* (*ANAT*) wrist; (*de chemise*) cuff

poil [pwal] *nm* (*ANAT*) hair; (*de pinceau, brosse*) bristle; (*de tapis*) strand; (*pelage*) coat; **à ~** (*fam*) starkers; **au ~** (*fam*) hunky-dory; **poilu, e** *adj* hairy

poinçon [pwɛ̃sɔ̃] *nm* awl; bodkin; (*marque*) hallmark; **poinçonner** *vt* to stamp; to hallmark; (*billet*) to punch

poing [pwɛ̃] *nm* fist

point [pwɛ̃] *nm* (*marque, signe*) dot; (: *de ponctuation*) full stop, period (*US*); (*moment, de score etc, fig*: question) point; (*endroit*) spot; (*COUTURE, TRICOT*) stitch ♦ *adv* = **pas**; **faire le ~** (*NAVIG*) to take a bearing; (*fig*) to take stock (of the situation); **en tout ~** in every respect; **sur le ~ de faire** (just) about to do; **à tel ~ que** so much so that; **mettre au ~** (*mécanisme, procédé*) to develop; (*appareil-photo*) to focus; (*affaire*) to settle; **à ~** (*CULIN*) medium; just right; **à ~ (nommé)** just at the right time; **~ (de côté)** stitch (*pain*); **~ d'eau** spring; water point; **~ d'exclamation** exclamation mark; **~ d'interrogation** question mark; **~ de repère** landmark; (*dans le temps*) point of reference; **~ de vente** retail outlet; **~ de vue** viewpoint; (*fig*: opinion) point of view; **~ faible** weak point; **~ final** full stop, period; **~ mort** (*AUTO*): **au ~ mort** in neutral; **~s de suspension** suspension points

pointe [pwɛ̃t] *nf* point; (*fig*): **une ~ de** a hint of; **être à la ~ de** (*fig*) to be in the forefront of; **sur la ~ des pieds** on tiptoe; **en ~** *adv* (*tailler*) into a point ♦ *adj* pointed, tapered; **de ~** (*technique etc*) leading; **heures/jours de ~** peak hours/days; **~ de vitesse** burst of speed

pointer [pwɛ̃te] *vt* (*cocher*) to tick off; (*employés etc*) to check in; (*diriger*: canon, doigt): **~ vers qch** to point at sth ♦ *vi* (*employé*) to clock in

pointillé [pwɛ̃tije] *nm* (*trait*) dotted line

pointilleux, euse [pwɛ̃tijø, -øz] *adj* particular, pernickety

pointu, e [pwɛ̃ty] *adj* pointed; (*clou*) sharp; (*voix*) shrill; (*analyse*) precise

pointure [pwɛ̃tyʀ] *nf* size

point-virgule [pwɛ̃viʀgyl] *nm* semicolon

poire [pwaʀ] *nf* pear; (*fam: péj*) mug

poireau, x [pwaʀo] *nm* leek

poirier [pwaʀje] *nm* pear tree

pois [pwa] *nm* (*BOT*) pea; (*sur une étoffe*) dot, spot; **à ~** (*cravate etc*) spotted, polka-dot *cpd*

poison [pwazɔ̃] *nm* poison

poisse [pwas] *nf* rotten luck

poisseux, euse [pwasø, -øz] *adj* sticky

poisson [pwasɔ̃] *nm* fish *gén inv*; **les P~s** (*signe*) Pisces; ~ **d'avril!** April fool!; ~ **rouge** goldfish; **poissonnerie** *nf* fish-shop; **poissonnier, ière** *nm/f* fishmonger (*BRIT*), fish merchant (*US*)

poitrine [pwatrin] *nf* chest; (*seins*) bust, bosom; (*CULIN*) breast; ~ **de bœuf** brisket

poivre [pwavʀ(ə)] *nm* pepper; **poivrier** *nm* (*ustensile*) pepperpot

poivron [pwavʀɔ̃] *nm* pepper, capsicum

polar *nm* (*fam*) detective novel

pôle [pol] *nm* (*GÉO, ÉLEC*) pole

poli, e [pɔli] *adj* polite; (*lisse*) smooth; polished

police [pɔlis] *nf* police; **peine de simple** ~ *sentence given by magistrates' or police court*; ~ **d'assurance** insurance policy; ~ **des mœurs** ≈ vice squad; ~ **judiciaire** ≈ Criminal Investigation Department (*BRIT*), ≈ Federal Bureau of Investigation (*US*); ~ **secours** ≈ emergency services *pl* (*BRIT*), ≈ paramedics *pl* (*US*)

policier, ière [pɔlisje, -jɛʀ] *adj* police *cpd* ♦ *nm* policeman; (*aussi: roman* ~) detective novel

polio [pɔljɔ] *nf* polio

polir [pɔliʀ] *vt* to polish

polisson, ne [pɔlisɔ̃, -ɔn] *adj* naughty

politesse [pɔlitɛs] *nf* politeness

politicien, ne [pɔlitisjɛ̃, -ɛn] *nm/f* politician

politique [pɔlitik] *adj* political ♦ *nf* (*science, pratique, activité*) politics *sg*; (*mesures, méthode*) policies *pl*; **politiser** *vt* to politicize

pollen [pɔlɛn] *nm* pollen

pollution [pɔlysjɔ̃] *nf* pollution

polo [pɔlo] *nm* polo shirt

Pologne [pɔlɔɲ] *nf*: **la** ~ Poland; **polonais, e** *adj, nm* (*LING*) Polish; **Polonais, e** *nm/f* Pole

poltron, ne [pɔltʀɔ̃, -ɔn] *adj* cowardly

polycopier [pɔlikɔpje] *vt* to duplicate

Polynésie [pɔlinezi] *nf*: **la** ~ Polynesia

polyvalent, e [pɔlivalɑ̃, -ɑ̃t] *adj* versatile; multi-purpose

pommade [pɔmad] *nf* ointment, cream

pomme [pɔm] *nf* (*BOT*) apple; **tomber**

dans les ~s (*fam*) to pass out; ~ **d'Adam** Adam's apple; ~ **d'arrosoir** (sprinkler) rose; ~ **de pin** pine *ou* fir cone; ~ **de terre** potato

pommeau, x [pɔmo] *nm* (*boule*) knob; (*de selle*) pommel

pommette [pɔmɛt] *nf* cheekbone

pommier [pɔmje] *nm* apple tree

pompe [pɔ̃p] *nf* pump; (*faste*) pomp (and ceremony); ~ **à essence** petrol (*BRIT*) *ou* gas (*US*) pump; **~s funèbres** funeral parlour *sg*, undertaker's *sg*

pomper [pɔ̃pe] *vt* to pump; (*évacuer*) to pump out; (*aspirer*) to pump up; (*absorber*) to soak up

pompeux, euse [pɔ̃pø, -øz] *adj* pompous

pompier [pɔ̃pje] *nm* fireman

pompiste [pɔ̃pist(ə)] *nm/f* petrol (*BRIT*) *ou* gas (*US*) pump attendant

poncer [pɔ̃se] *vt* to sand (down)

ponctuation [pɔ̃ktɥasjɔ̃] *nf* punctuation

ponctuel, le [pɔ̃ktɥɛl] *adj* (*à l'heure, aussi TECH*) punctual; (*fig: opération etc*) one-off, single; (*scrupuleux*) punctilious, meticulous

ponctuer [pɔ̃ktɥe] *vt* to punctuate

pondéré, e [pɔ̃deʀe] *adj* level-headed, composed

pondre [pɔ̃dʀ(ə)] *vt* to lay; (*fig*) to produce

poney [pɔnɛ] *nm* pony

pont [pɔ̃] *nm* bridge; (*AUTO*) axle; (*NAVIG*) deck; **faire le** ~ to take the extra day off; ~ **de graissage** ramp (*in garage*); ~ **suspendu** suspension bridge; **P~s et Chaussées** highways department

pont-levis [pɔ̃lvi] *nm* drawbridge

pop [pɔp] *adj inv* pop

populace [pɔpylas] (*péj*) *nf* rabble

populaire [pɔpylɛʀ] *adj* popular; (*manifestation*) mass *cpd*; (*milieux, clientèle*) working-class

population [pɔpylasjɔ̃] *nf* population; ~ **active** *nf* working population

populeux, euse [pɔpylø, -øz] *adj* densely populated

porc [pɔʀ] *nm* (*ZOOL*) pig; (*CULIN*) pork; (*peau*) pigskin

porcelaine [pɔʀsəlɛn] *nf* porcelain, china; piece of china(ware)

porc-épic [pɔʀkepik] *nm* porcupine

porche [pɔʀʃ(ə)] *nm* porch

porcherie [pɔʀʃəʀi] *nf* pigsty

pore [pɔʀ] *nm* pore

porno [pɔʀno] *adj abr* pornographic, porno

port [pɔʀ] *nm* (*NAVIG*) harbour, port; (*ville*) port; (*de l'uniforme etc*) wearing; (*pour lettre*) postage; (*pour colis, aussi: posture*) carriage; ~ **d'arme** (*JUR*) carrying of a firearm

portable [pɔʀtabl(ə)] *nm* (*COMPUT*) laptop (computer)

portail [pɔʀtaj] *nm* gate; (*de cathédrale*) portal

portant, e [pɔʀtɑ̃, -ɑ̃t] *adj*: **bien/mal** ~ in good/poor health

portatif, ive [pɔʀtatif, -iv] *adj* portable

porte [pɔʀt(ə)] *nf* door; (*de ville, forteresse, SKI*) gate; **mettre à la** ~ to throw out; ~ **à** ~ *nm* door-to-door selling; ~ **d'entrée** front door; ~-**à-faux** *nm*: **en** ~-**à-faux** cantilevered; (*fig*) in an awkward position; ~-**avions** *nm inv* aircraft carrier; ~-**bagages** *nm inv* luggage rack; ~-**clefs** *nm inv* key ring; ~-**documents** *nm inv* attaché *ou* document case

portée [pɔʀte] *nf* (*d'une arme*) range; (*fig*) impact, import; scope, capability; (*de chatte etc*) litter; (*MUS*) stave, staff; **à/hors de** ~ (**de**) within/out of reach (of); **à** ~ **de** (**la**) **main** within (arm's) reach; **à** ~ **de voix** within earshot; **à la** ~ **de qn** (*fig*) at sb's level, within sb's capabilities

porte-: ~-**fenêtre** *nf* French window; ~-**feuille** *nm* wallet; (*POL, BOURSE*) portfolio; ~-**jarretelles** *nm inv* suspender belt; ~-**manteau, x** *nm* coat hanger; coat rack; ~-**mine** *nm* propelling (*BRIT*) *ou* mechanical (*US*) pencil; ~-**monnaie** *nm inv* purse; ~-**parole** *nm inv* spokesman

porter [pɔʀte] *vt* to carry; (*sur soi: vêtement, barbe, bague*) to wear; (*fig: responsabilité etc*) to bear, carry; (*inscription, marque, titre, patronyme: suj: arbre, fruits, fleurs*) to bear; (*apporter*):

~ **qch quelque part/à** **qn** to take sth somewhere/to sb ♦ *vi* (*voix, regard, canon*) to carry; (*coup, argument*) to hit home; **se** ~ *vi* (*se sentir*): **se** ~ **bien/mal** to be well/unwell; ~ **sur** (*peser*) to rest on; (*accent*) to fall on; (*conférence etc*) to concern; (*heurter*) to strike; **être porté à faire** to be apt *ou* inclined to do; **se faire** ~ **malade** to report sick; ~ **la main à son chapeau** to raise one's hand to one's hat; ~ **son effort sur** to direct one's efforts towards; ~ **à croire** to lead one to believe

porte-serviettes [pɔʀtsɛʀvjɛt] *nm inv* towel rail

porteur [pɔʀtœʀ] *nm* (*de bagages*) porter; (*de chèque*) bearer

porte-voix [pɔʀtəvwa] *nm inv* megaphone

portier [pɔʀtje] *nm* doorman

portière [pɔʀtjɛʀ] *nf* door

portillon [pɔʀtijɔ̃] *nm* gate

portion [pɔʀsjɔ̃] *nf* (*part*) portion, share; (*partie*) portion, section

portique [pɔʀtik] *nm* (*RAIL*) gantry

porto [pɔʀto] *nm* port (wine)

portrait [pɔʀtʀɛ] *nm* portrait; photograph; **portrait-robot** *nm* Identikit (®) *ou* photofit (®) picture

portuaire [pɔʀtɥɛʀ] *adj* port *cpd*, harbour *cpd*

portugais, e [pɔʀtygɛ, -ɛz] *adj, nm/f* Portuguese

Portugal [pɔʀtygal] *nm*: **le** ~ Portugal

pose [poz] *nf* laying; hanging; (*attitude, d'un modèle*) pose; (*PHOTO*) exposure

posé, e [poze] *adj* serious

poser [poze] *vt* (*déposer*): ~ **qch (sur)/** **qn à** to put sth down (on)/drop sb at; (*placer*): ~ **qch sur/quelque part** to put sth on/somewhere; (*installer: moquette, carrelage*) to lay; (*rideaux, papier peint*) to hang; (*question*) to ask; (*principe, conditions*) to lay *ou* set down; (*problème*) to formulate; (*difficulté*) to pose ♦ *vi* (*modèle*) to pose; **se** ~ *vi* (*oiseau, avion*) to land; (*question*) to arise

positif, ive [pozitif, -iv] *adj* positive

position [pozisjɔ̃] *nf* position; **prendre ~** *(fig)* to take a stand

posologie [pozɔlɔʒi] *nf* directions for use, dosage

posséder [posede] *vt* to own, possess; *(qualité, talent)* to have, possess; *(bien connaître: métier, langue)* to have mastered, have a thorough knowledge of; *(sexuellement, aussi: suj: colère etc)* to possess; **possession** *nf* ownership *no pl*; possession

possibilité [posibilite] *nf* possibility; **~s** *nfpl (moyens)* means; *(potentiel)* potential *sg*

possible [posibl(ə)] *adj* possible; *(projet, entreprise)* feasible ♦ *nm*: **faire son ~** to do all one can, do one's utmost; **le plus/moins de livres ~** as many/few books as possible; **le plus/moins d'eau ~** as much/little water as possible; **dès que ~** as soon as possible

postal, e, aux [postal, -o] *adj* postal

poste [pɔst(ə)] *nf (service)* post, postal service; *(administration, bureau)* post office ♦ *nm (fonction, MIL)* post; *(TÉL)* extension; *(de radio etc)* set; **mettre à la ~** to post; **P~s, Télécommunications et Télédiffusion** postal and telecommunications service; **~ d'essence** *nm* petrol *ou* filling station; **~ d'incendie** *nm* fire point; **~ de pilotage** *nm* cockpit; **~ (de police)** *nm* police station; **~ de secours** *nm* first-aid post; **~ de travail** *nm* work station; **~ restante** *nf* poste restante *(BRIT)*, general delivery *(US)*

poster¹ [poste] *vt* to post

poster² [poster] *nm* poster

postérieur, e [posterjœr] *adj (date)* later; *(partie)* back ♦ *nm (fam)* behind

posthume [postym] *adj* posthumous

postiche [postiʃ] *nm* hairpiece

postuler [postyle] *vt (emploi)* to apply for, put in for

posture [postyr] *nf* posture; position

pot [po] *nm* jar, pot; *(en plastique, carton)* carton; *(en métal)* tin; **boire** *ou* **prendre un ~** *(fam)* to have a drink; **~ catalytique** catalytic converter; **~ (de chambre)** (chamber)pot; **~ d'échappe**ment exhaust pipe; **~ de fleurs** plant pot, flowerpot; *(plante)* pot plant

potable [potabl(ə)] *adj*: **eau (non) ~** (non-)drinking water

potage [potaʒ] *nm* soup; soup course

potager, ère [potaʒe, -ɛr] *adj (plante)* edible, vegetable *cpd*; **(jardin) ~** kitchen *ou* vegetable garden

pot-au-feu [potofø] *nm inv* (beef) stew

pot-de-vin [podvɛ̃] *nm* bribe

pote [pɔt] *(fam) nm* pal

poteau, x [poto] *nm* post; **~ indicateur** signpost

potelé, e [pɔtle] *adj* plump, chubby

potence [pɔtɑ̃s] *nf* gallows *sg*

potentiel, le [potɑ̃sjɛl] *adj, nm* potential

poterie [pɔtri] *nf* pottery; piece of pottery

potier [pɔtje] *nm* potter

potins [pɔtɛ̃] *nmpl* gossip *sg*

potiron [potirɔ̃] *nm* pumpkin

pou, x [pu] *nm* louse

poubelle [pubɛl] *nf* (dust)bin

pouce [pus] *nm* thumb

poudre [pudr(ə)] *nf* powder; *(fard)* (face) powder; *(explosif)* gunpowder; **en ~: café en ~** instant coffee; **lait en ~** dried *ou* powdered milk; **poudrier** *nm* (powder) compact

pouffer [pufe] *vi*: **~ (de rire)** to snigger; to giggle

pouilleux, euse [pujø, -øz] *adj* flearidden; *(fig)* grubby; seedy

poulailler [pulaje] *nm* henhouse

poulain [pulɛ̃] *nm* foal; *(fig)* protégé

poule [pul] *nf (ZOOL)* hen; *(CULIN)* (boiling) fowl

poulet [pulɛ] *nm* chicken; *(fam)* cop

poulie [puli] *nf* pulley; block

pouls [pu] *nm* pulse; **prendre le ~ de qn** to feel sb's pulse

poumon [pumɔ̃] *nm* lung

poupe [pup] *nf* stern; **en ~** astern

poupée [pupe] *nf* doll

poupon [pupɔ̃] *nm* babe-in-arms; **pouponnière** *nf* crèche, day nursery

pour [pur] *prép* for ♦ *nm*: **le ~ et le contre** the pros and cons; **~ faire** (so as) to do, in order to do; ~ **avoir fait** for having done; ~ **que** so that, in order that; ~ **100 francs d'essence** 100 francs' worth of petrol; ~ **cent** per cent; ~ **ce qui est de** as for

pourboire [puʀbwaʀ] *nm* tip

pourcentage [puʀsɑ̃taʒ] *nm* percentage

pourchasser [puʀʃase] *vt* to pursue

pourparlers [puʀpaʀle] *nmpl* talks, negotiations

pourpre [puʀpʀ(ə)] *adj* crimson

pourquoi [puʀkwa] *adv, conj* why ♦ *nm inv*: **le ~ (de)** the reason (for)

pourrai *etc vb voir* **pouvoir**

pourri, e [puʀi] *adj* rotten

pourrir [puʀiʀ] *vi* to rot; (*fruit*) to go rotten *ou* bad ♦ *vt* to rot; (*fig*) to spoil thoroughly; **pourriture** *nf* rot

pourrons *etc vb voir* **pouvoir**

poursuite [puʀsɥit] *nf* pursuit, chase; **~s** *nfpl* (*JUR*) legal proceedings

poursuivre [puʀsɥivʀ(ə)] *vt* to pursue, chase (after); (*relancer*) to hound, harry; (*obséder*) to haunt; (*JUR*) to bring proceedings against, prosecute; (: *au civil*) to sue; (*but*) to strive towards; (*voyage, études*) to carry on with, continue ♦ *vi* to carry on, go on; **se ~** *vi* to go on, continue

pourtant [puʀtɑ̃] *adv* yet; **c'est ~ facile** (and) yet it's easy

pourtour [puʀtuʀ] *nm* perimeter

pourvoir [puʀvwaʀ] *vt*: ~ **qch/qn de** to equip sth/sb with ♦ *vi*: ~ **à** to provide for; (*emploi*) to fill; **se ~** *vi* (*JUR*): **se ~ en cassation** to take one's case to the Court of Appeal

pourvoyeur [puʀvwajœʀ] *nm* supplier

pourvu, e [puʀvy] *adj*: ~ **de** equipped with; ~ **que** (*si*) provided that, so long as; (*espérons que*) let's hope (that)

pousse [pus] *nf* growth; (*bourgeon*) shoot

poussé, e [puse] *adj* exhaustive

poussée [puse] *nf* thrust; (*coup*) push; (*MÉD*) eruption; (*fig*) upsurge

pousser [puse] *vt* to push; (*inciter*): ~ **qn à** to urge *ou* press sb to +*infin*; (*acculer*): ~ **qn à** to drive sb to; (*émettre*:

cri etc) to give; (*stimuler*) to urge on; to drive hard; (*poursuivre*) to carry on (further) ♦ *vi* to push; (*croître*) to grow; **se ~** *vi* to move over; **faire ~** (*plante*) to grow

poussette [puset] *nf* (*voiture d'enfant*) push chair (*BRIT*), stroller (*US*)

poussière [pusjeʀ] *nf* dust; (*grain*) speck of dust; **poussiéreux, euse** *adj* dusty

poussin [pusɛ̃] *nm* chick

poutre [putʀ(ə)] *nf* beam; (*en fer, ciment armé*) girder

MOT-CLÉ

pouvoir [puvwaʀ] *nm* power; (*POL: dirigeants*): **le ~** those in power; **les ~s publics** the authorities; ~ **d'achat** purchasing power

♦ *vb semi-aux* **1** (*être en état de*) can, be able to; **je ne peux pas le réparer** I can't *ou* I am not able to repair it; **déçu de ne pas ~ le faire** disappointed not to be able to do it

2 (*avoir la permission*) can, may, be allowed to; **vous pouvez aller au cinéma** you can *ou* may go to the pictures

3 (*probabilité, hypothèse*) may, might, could; **il a pu avoir un accident** he may *ou* might *ou* could have had an accident; **il aurait pu le dire!** he might *ou* could have said (so)!

♦ *vb impers* may, might, could; **il peut arriver que** it may *ou* might *ou* could happen that

♦ *vt* can, be able to; **j'ai fait tout ce que j'ai pu** I did all I could; **je n'en peux plus** (*épuisé*) I'm exhausted; (*à bout*) I can't take any more

se pouvoir *vi*: **il se peut que** it may *ou* might be that; **cela se pourrait** that's quite possible

---

prairie [pʀeʀi] *nf* meadow

praline [pʀalin] *nf* sugared almond

praticable [pʀatikabl(ə)] *adj* passable, practicable

praticien, ne [pʀatisjɛ̃, -jɛn] *nm/f* practitioner

pratique [pʀatik] *nf* practice ♦ *adj* practical

pratiquement [pʀatikmɑ̃] *adv* (*pour ainsi dire*) practically, virtually

pratiquer [pʀatike] *vt* to practise; (*SPORT etc*) to go in for; to play; (*intervention, opération*) to carry out; (*ouverture, abri*) to make

pré [pʀe] *nm* meadow

préalable [pʀealabl(ə)] *adj* preliminary; **condition ~ (de)** precondition (for), prerequisite (for); **au ~** beforehand

préambule [pʀeɑ̃byl] *nm* preamble; (*fig*) prelude; **sans ~** straight away

préavis [pʀeavi] *nm* notice; **communication avec ~** (*TÉL*) personal *ou* person to person call

précaution [pʀekosjɔ̃] *nf* precaution; **avec ~** cautiously; **par ~** as a precaution

précédemment [pʀesedamɑ̃] *adv* before, previously

précédent, e [pʀesedɑ̃, -ɑ̃t] *adj* previous ♦ *nm* precedent; **le jour ~** the day before, the previous day; **sans ~** unprecedented

précéder [pʀesede] *vt* to precede; (*marcher ou rouler devant*) to be in front of

précepteur, trice [pʀeseptœʀ, -tʀis] *nm/f* (private) tutor

prêcher [pʀeʃe] *vt* to preach

précieux, euse [pʀesjø, -øz] *adj* precious; invaluable; (*style, écrivain*) précieux, precious

précipice [pʀesipis] *nm* drop, chasm; (*fig*) abyss

précipitamment [pʀesipitamɑ̃] *adv* hurriedly, hastily

précipitation [pʀesipitasjɔ̃] *nf* (*hâte*) haste; **~s** *nfpl* (*pluie*) rain *sg*

précipité, e [pʀesipite] *adj* hurried, hasty

précipiter [pʀesipite] *vt* (*faire tomber*): **~ qn/qch du haut de** to throw *ou* hurl sb/sth off *ou* from; (*hâter: marche*) to quicken; (*: départ*) to hasten; **se ~** *vi* to speed up; **se ~ sur/vers** to rush at/towards

précis, e [pʀesi, -iz] *adj* precise; (*tir,*

mesures) accurate, precise ♦ *nm* handbook; **précisément** *adv* precisely; **préciser** *vt* (*expliquer*) to be more specific about, clarify; (*spécifier*) to state, specify; **se préciser** *vi* to become clear(er); **précision** *nf* precision; accuracy; point *ou* detail (*being or to be clarified*)

précoce [pʀekɔs] *adj* early; (*enfant*) precocious; (*calvitie*) premature

préconiser [pʀekɔnize] *vt* to advocate

prédécesseur [pʀedesesœʀ] *nm* predecessor

prédilection [pʀedilɛksjɔ̃] *nf*: **avoir une ~ pour** to be partial to; **de ~** favourite

prédire [pʀediʀ] *vt* to predict

prédominer [pʀedɔmine] *vi* to predominate; (*avis*) to prevail

préface [pʀefas] *nf* preface

préfecture [pʀefɛktyʀ] *nf* prefecture; **~ de police** police headquarters *pl*

préférable [pʀefeʀabl(ə)] *adj* preferable

préféré, e [pʀefeʀe] *adj, nm/f* favourite

préférence [pʀefeʀɑ̃s] *nf* preference; **de ~** preferably

préférer [pʀefeʀe] *vt*: **~ qn/qch (à)** to prefer sb/sth (to), like sb/sth better (than); **~ faire** to prefer to do; **je ~ais du thé** I would rather have tea, I'd prefer tea

préfet [pʀefɛ] *nm* prefect

préfixe [pʀefiks(ə)] *nm* prefix

préhistorique [pʀeistɔʀik] *adj* prehistoric

préjudice [pʀeʒydis] *nm* (*matériel*) loss; (*moral*) harm *no pl*; **porter ~ à** to harm, be detrimental to; **au ~ de** at the expense of

préjugé [pʀeʒyʒe] *nm* prejudice; **avoir un ~ contre** to be prejudiced *ou* biased against

préjuger [pʀeʒyʒe]: **~ de** *vt* to prejudge

prélasser [pʀelase]: **se ~** *vi* to lounge

prélèvement [pʀelɛvmɑ̃] *nm*: **faire un ~ de sang** to take a blood sample

prélever [pʀelve] *vt* (*échantillon*) to take; (*argent*): **~ (sur)** to deduct (from); (*: sur son compte*) to withdraw (from)

prématuré, e [pʀematyʀe] *adj* premature; (*retraite*) early ♦ *nm* premature baby

premier, ière [prəmje, -jɛr] *adj* first; (*branche, marche*) bottom; (*fig*) basic; prime; initial; **le ~ venu** the first person to come along; **P~ Ministre** Prime Minister; **première** *nf* (*THÉÂTRE*) first night; (*AUTO*) first (gear); (*AVIAT, RAIL etc*) first class; (*CINÉMA*) première; (*exploit*) first; **premièrement** *adv* firstly

prémonition [premɔnisjɔ̃] *nf* premonition

prémunir [premynir]: **se ~** *vi*: **se ~ contre** to guard against

prenant, e [prənɑ̃, -ɑ̃t] *adj* absorbing, engrossing

prénatal, e [prenatal] *adj* (*MÉD*) antenatal

prendre [prɑ̃dr(ə)] *vt* to take; (*ôter*) **~ qch à** to take sth from; (*aller chercher*) to get, fetch; (*se procurer*) to get; (*malfaiteur, poisson*) to catch; (*passager*) to pick up; (*personnel, aussi: couleur, goût*) to take on; (*locataire*) to take in; (*élève etc: traiter*) to handle; (*voix, ton*) to put on; (*coincer*) **se ~ les doigts dans** to get one's fingers caught in ♦ *vi* (*liquide, ciment*) to set; (*greffe, vaccin*) to take; (*feu: foyer*) to go; (: *incendie*) to start; (*allumette*) to light; (*se diriger*): **~ à gauche** to turn (to the) left; **à tout ~** on the whole, all in all; **se ~ pour** to think one is; **s'en ~ à** to attack; **se ~ d'amitié/d'affection pour** to befriend/ become fond of; **s'y ~** (*procéder*) to set about it

preneur [prənœr] *nm*: **être/trouver ~** to be willing to buy/find a buyer

preniez *vb voir* **prendre**

prenne *etc vb voir* **prendre**

prénom [prenɔ̃] *nm* first *ou* Christian name

prénuptial, e, aux [prenypsjal, -o] *adj* premarital

préoccupation [preɔkypasjɔ̃] *nf* (*souci*) concern; (*idée fixe*) preoccupation

préoccuper [preɔkype] *vt* to concern; to preoccupy

préparatifs [preparatif] *nmpl* preparations

préparation [preparasjɔ̃] *nf* preparation; (*SCOL*) piece of homework

préparer [prepare] *vt* to prepare; (*café*) to make; (*examen*) to prepare for; (*voyage, entreprise*) to plan; **se ~** *vi* (*orage, tragédie*) to brew, be in the air; **se ~ (à qch/faire)** to prepare (o.s.) *ou* get ready (for sth/to do); **~ qch à qn** (*surprise etc*) to have sth in store for sb

prépondérant, e [prepɔ̃derɑ̃, -ɑ̃t] *adj* major, dominating

préposé, e [prepoze] *adj*: **~ à** in charge of ♦ *nm/f* employee; official; attendant

préposition [prepozisjɔ̃] *nf* preposition

près [prɛ] *adv* near, close; **~ de** near (to), close to; (*environ*) nearly, almost; **de ~** closely; **à 5 kg ~** to within about 5 kg; **à cela ~ que** apart from the fact that

présage [preza3] *nm* omen

présager [preza3e] *vt* to foresee

presbyte [presbit] *adj* long-sighted

presbytère [presbitɛr] *nm* presbytery

prescription [preskripsjɔ̃] *nf* (*instruction*) order, instruction; (*MÉD, JUR*) prescription

prescrire [preskrir] *vt* to prescribe

préséance [preseɑ̃s] *nf* precedence *no pl*

présence [prezɑ̃s] *nf* presence; (*au bureau etc*) attendance; **~ d'esprit** presence of mind

présent, e [prezɑ̃, -ɑ̃t] *adj, nm* present; **à ~ (que)** now (that)

présentation [prezɑ̃tasjɔ̃] *nf* introduction; presentation; (*allure*) appearance

présenter [prezɑ̃te] *vt* to present; (*sympathie, condoléances*) to offer; (*soumettre*) to submit; (*invité, conférencier*): **~ qn (à)** to introduce sb (to) ♦ *vi*: **mal/bien** to have an unattractive/a pleasing appearance; **se ~** *vi* (*sur convocation*) to report, come; (*à une élection*) to stand; (*occasion*) to arise; **se ~ bien/ mal** to look good/not too good; **se ~ à** (*examen*) to sit

préservatif [prezɛrvatif] *nm* sheath, condom

préserver [prezɛrve] *vt*: **~ de** to protect

from; to save from
président [pʀezidɑ̃] *nm* (*POL*) president; (*d'une assemblée, COMM*) chairman; ~ **directeur général** chairman and managing director
présider [pʀezide] *vt* to preside over; (*dîner*) to be the guest of honour at; ~ **à** to direct; to govern
présomptueux, euse [pʀezɔ̃ptɥø, -øz] *adj* presumptuous
presque [pʀɛsk(ə)] *adv* almost, nearly; ~ **rien** hardly anything; ~ **pas** hardly (at all); ~ **pas de** hardly any
presqu'île [pʀɛskil] *nf* peninsula
pressant, e [pʀesɑ̃, -ɑ̃t] *adj* urgent; **se faire** ~ to become insistent
presse [pʀɛs] *nf* press; (*affluence*): **heures de** ~ busy times
pressé, e [pʀese] *adj* in a hurry; (*air*) hurried; (*besogne*) urgent; **orange** ~**e** fresh orange juice
pressentiment [pʀesɑ̃timɑ̃] *nm* foreboding, premonition
pressentir [pʀesɑ̃tiʀ] *vt* to sense; (*prendre contact avec*) to approach
presse-papiers [pʀɛspapje] *nm inv* paperweight
presser [pʀese] *vt* (*fruit, éponge*) to squeeze; (*bouton*) to press; (*allure, affaire*) to speed up; (*inciter*): ~ **qn de faire** to urge *ou* press sb to do ♦ *vi* to be urgent; **se** ~ *vi* (*se hâter*) to hurry (up); **se** ~ **contre qn** to squeeze up against sb; **rien ne presse** there's no hurry
pressing [pʀesiŋ] *nm* steam-pressing; (*magasin*) dry-cleaner's
pression [pʀesjɔ̃] *nf* pressure; **faire** ~ **sur** to put pressure on; ~ **artérielle** blood pressure
pressoir [pʀeswaʀ] *nm* (wine *ou* oil *etc*) press
prestance [pʀɛstɑ̃s] *nf* presence, imposing bearing
prestataire [pʀɛstatɛʀ] *nm/f* supplier
prestation [pʀɛstasjɔ̃] *nf* (*allocation*) benefit; (*d'une entreprise*) service provided; (*d'un artiste*) performance
prestidigitateur, trice [pʀɛstidiʒitatœʀ, -tʀis] *nm/f* conjurer

prestigieux, euse [pʀɛstiʒjø, -øz] *adj* prestigious
présumer [pʀezyme] *vt*: ~ **que** to presume *ou* assume that; ~ **de** to overrate
présupposer [pʀesypoze] *vt* to presuppose
prêt, e [pʀɛ, pʀɛt] *adj* ready ♦ *nm* lending *no pl*; loan; **prêt-à-porter** *nm* ready-to-wear *ou* off-the-peg (*BRIT*) clothes *pl*
prétendant [pʀetɑ̃dɑ̃] *nm* pretender; (*d'une femme*) suitor
prétendre [pʀetɑ̃dʀ(ə)] *vt* (*affirmer*): ~ **que** to claim that; (*avoir l'intention de*): ~ **faire qch** to mean *ou* intend to do sth; ~ **à** (*droit, titre*) to lay claim to; **prétendu, e** *adj* (*supposé*) so-called
prête-nom [pʀɛtnɔ̃] (*péj*) *nm* figurehead
prétentieux, euse [pʀetɑ̃sjø, -øz] *adj* pretentious
prétention [pʀetɑ̃sjɔ̃] *nf* claim; pretentiousness
prêter [pʀete] *vt* (*livres, argent*): ~ **qch (à)** to lend sth (to); (*supposer*): ~ **à qn** (*caractère, propos*) to attribute to sb ♦ *vi* (*aussi: se* ~: *tissu, cuir*) to give; **se** ~ **à** to lend o.s. (*ou* itself) to; (*manigances etc*) to go along with; ~ **à** (*commentaires etc*) to be open to, give rise to; ~ **assistance à** to give help to; ~ **attention à** to pay attention to; ~ **serment** to take the oath; ~ **l'oreille** to listen
prétexte [pʀetɛkst(ə)] *nm* pretext, excuse; **sous aucun** ~ on no account; **prétexter** *vt* to give as a pretext *ou* an excuse
prêtre [pʀɛtʀ(ə)] *nm* priest
preuve [pʀœv] *nf* proof; (*indice*) proof, evidence *no pl*; **faire** ~ **de** to show; **faire ses** ~**s** to prove o.s. (*ou* itself)
prévaloir [pʀevalwaʀ] *vi* to prevail; **se** ~ **de** *vt* to take advantage of; to pride o.s. on
prévenant, e [pʀevnɑ̃, -ɑ̃t] *adj* thoughtful, kind
prévenir [pʀevniʀ] *vt* (*avertir*): ~ **qn (de)** to warn sb (about); (*informer*): ~ **qn (de)** to tell *ou* inform sb (about); (*éviter*) to avoid, prevent; (*anticiper*) to forestall;

to anticipate

prévention [pʀevɑ̃sjɔ̃] *nf* prevention; **~ routière** road safety

prévenu, e [pʀevny] *nm/f* (*JUR*) defendant, accused

prévision [pʀevizjɔ̃] *nf*: **~s** predictions; forecast *sg*; **en ~ de** in anticipation of; **~s météorologiques** weather forecast *sg*

prévoir [pʀevwaʀ] *vt* (*deviner*) to foresee; (*s'attendre à*) to expect, reckon on; (*prévenir*) to anticipate; (*organiser*) to plan; (*préparer, réserver*) to allow; **prévu pour 10 h** scheduled for 10 o'clock

prévoyance [pʀevwajɑ̃s] *nf*: **caisse de ~** contingency fund

prévoyant, e [pʀevwajɑ̃, -ɑ̃t] *adj* gifted with (*ou* showing) foresight

prévu, e [pʀevy] *pp de* **prévoir**

prier [pʀije] *vi* to pray ♦ *vt* (*Dieu*) to pray to; (*implorer*) to beg; (*demander*): **~ qn de faire** to ask sb to do; **se faire ~** to need coaxing *ou* persuading; **je vous en prie** (*allez-y*) please do; (*de rien*) don't mention it

prière [pʀijɛʀ] *nf* prayer; **"~ de faire ..."** "please do ..."

primaire [pʀimɛʀ] *adj* primary; (*péj*) simple-minded; simplistic ♦ *nm* (*SCOL*) primary education

prime [pʀim] *nf* (*bonification*) bonus; (*subside*) premium, allowance; (*COMM: cadeau*) free gift; (*ASSURANCES, BOURSE*) premium ♦ *adj*: **de ~ abord** at first glance

primer [pʀime] *vt* (*l'emporter sur*) to prevail over; (*récompenser*) to award a prize to ♦ *vi* to dominate; to prevail

primeurs [pʀimœʀ] *nfpl* early fruits and vegetables

primevère [pʀimvɛʀ] *nf* primrose

primitif, ive [pʀimitif, -iv] *adj* primitive; (*originel*) original

prince [pʀɛ̃s] *nm* prince; **princesse** *nf* princess

principal, e, aux [pʀɛ̃sipal, -o] *adj* principal, main ♦ *nm* (*SCOL*) principal, head(master); (*essentiel*) main thing

principe [pʀɛ̃sip] *nm* principle; **pour le ~** on principle; **de ~** (*accord, hostilité*)

automatic; **par ~** on principle; **en ~** (*habituellement*) as a rule; (*théoriquement*) in principle

printemps [pʀɛ̃tɑ̃] *nm* spring

priorité [pʀijɔʀite] *nf* (*AUTO*): **avoir la ~ (sur)** to have right of way (over); **~ à droite** right of way to vehicles coming from the right

pris, e [pʀi, pʀiz] *pp de* **prendre** ♦ *adj* (*place*) taken; (*journée, mains*) full; (*billets*) sold; (*personne*) busy; **avoir le nez/la gorge ~(e)** to have a stuffy nose/a hoarse throat; **être ~ de panique** to be panic-stricken

prise [pʀiz] *nf* (*d'une ville*) capture; (*PÊCHE, CHASSE*) catch; (*point d'appui ou pour empoigner*) hold; (*ÉLEC: fiche*) plug; (*: femelle*) socket; **être aux ~s avec** to be grappling with; **~ de contact** *nf* (*rencontre*) initial meeting, first contact; **~ de courant** power point; **~ de sang** blood test; **~ de terre** earth; **~ de vue** (*photo*) shot; **~ multiple** adaptor

priser [pʀize] *vt* (*tabac, héroïne*) to take; (*estimer*) to prize, value ♦ *vi* to take snuff

prison [pʀizɔ̃] *nf* prison; **aller/être en ~** to go to/be in prison *ou* jail; **faire de la ~** to serve time; **prisonnier, ière** *nm/f* prisoner ♦ *adj* captive

prit *vb voir* **prendre**

privé, e [pʀive] *adj* private; **en ~** in private

priver [pʀive] *vt*: **~ qn de** to deprive sb of; **se ~ de** to go *ou* do without

privilège [pʀivilɛʒ] *nm* privilege

prix [pʀi] *nm* (*valeur*) price; (*récompense, SCOL*) prize; **hors de ~** exorbitantly priced; **à aucun ~** not at any price; **à tout ~** at all costs; **~ d'achat/de vente/de revient** purchasing/selling/cost price

probable [pʀɔbabl(ə)] *adj* likely, probable; **probablement** *adv* probably

probant, e [pʀɔbɑ̃, -ɑ̃t] *adj* convincing

problème [pʀɔblɛm] *nm* problem

procédé [pʀɔsede] *nm* (*méthode*) process; (*comportement*) behaviour *no pl*

procéder [pʀɔsede] *vi* to proceed; to behave; ~ **à** to carry out

procès [pʀɔsɛ] *nm* trial; (*poursuites*) proceedings *pl*; **être en ~ avec** to be involved in a lawsuit with

processus [pʀɔsesys] *nm* process

procès-verbal, aux [pʀɔsɛvɛʀbal, -o] *nm* (*constat*) statement; (*aussi: P.V.*): **avoir un ~** to get a parking ticket; to be booked; (*de réunion*) minutes *pl*

prochain, e [pʀɔʃɛ̃, -ɛn] *adj* next; (*proche*) impending; near ♦ *nm* fellow man; **la ~e fois/semaine** ~e next time/ week; **prochainement** *adv* soon, shortly

proche [pʀɔʃ] *adj* nearby; (*dans le temps*) imminent; (*parent, ami*) close; ~s *nmpl* (*parents*) close relatives; **être ~ (de)** to be near, be close (to); **de ~ en ~** gradually; **le P~ Orient** the Middle East

proclamer [pʀɔklame] *vt* to proclaim

procuration [pʀɔkyʀasjɔ̃] *nf* proxy; power of attorney

procurer [pʀɔkyʀe] *vt*: ~ **qch à qn** (*fournir*) to obtain sth for sb; (*causer: plaisir etc*) to bring sb sth; **se ~** *vt* to get

procureur [pʀɔkyʀœʀ] *nm* public prosecutor

prodige [pʀɔdiʒ] *nm* marvel, wonder; (*personne*) prodigy

prodigue [pʀɔdig] *adj* generous; extravagant; **fils ~** prodigal son

prodiguer [pʀɔdige] *vt* (*argent, biens*) to be lavish with; (*soins, attentions*): ~ **qch à qn** to give sb sth

producteur, trice [pʀɔdyktœʀ, -tʀis] *nm/f* producer

production [pʀɔdyksjɔ̃] *nf* (*gén*) production; (*rendement*) output

produire [pʀɔdɥiʀ] *vt* to produce; **se ~** *vi* (*acteur*) to perform, appear; (*événement*) to happen, occur

produit [pʀɔdɥi] *nm* (*gén*) product; ~ **d'entretien** cleaning product; ~ **national brut** gross national product; ~s **agricoles** farm produce *sg*; ~s **alimentaires** *nmpl* foodstuffs

prof [pʀɔf] (*fam*) *nm* teacher

profane [pʀɔfan] *adj* (*REL*) secular ♦ *nm/f* layman(woman)

proférer [pʀɔfeʀe] *vt* to utter

professeur [pʀɔfesœʀ] *nm* teacher; (*titulaire d'une chaire*) professor; ~ (**de faculté**) (university) lecturer

profession [pʀɔfesjɔ̃] *nf* profession; **sans ~** unemployed; **professionnel, le** *adj, nm/f* professional

profil [pʀɔfil] *nm* profile; (*d'une voiture*) line, contour; **de ~** in profile; **profiler** *vt* to streamline

profit [pʀɔfi] *nm* (*avantage*) benefit, advantage; (*COMM, FINANCE*) profit; **au ~ de** in aid of; **tirer ~ de** to profit from

profitable [pʀɔfitabl(ə)] *adj* beneficial; profitable

profiter [pʀɔfite] *vi*: ~ **de** to take advantage of; to make the most of; ~ **à** to benefit; to be profitable to

profond, e [pʀɔfɔ̃, -ɔ̃d] *adj* deep; (*méditation, mépris*) profound; **profondeur** *nf* depth

progéniture [pʀɔʒenityʀ] *nf* offspring *inv*

programme [pʀɔgʀam] *nm* programme; (*TV, RADIO*) programmes *pl*; (*SCOL*) syllabus, curriculum; (*INFORM*) program; **programmer** *vt* (*TV, RADIO*) to put on, show; (*INFORM*) to program; **programmeur, euse** *nm/f* programmer

progrès [pʀɔgʀɛ] *nm* progress *no pl*; **faire des ~** to make progress

progresser [pʀɔgʀese] *vi* to progress; (*troupes etc*) to make headway *ou* progress; **progressif, ive** *adj* progressive

prohiber [pʀɔibe] *vt* to prohibit, ban

proie [pʀwa] *nf* prey *no pl*

projecteur [pʀɔʒɛktœʀ] *nm* projector; (*de théâtre, cirque*) spotlight

projectile [pʀɔʒɛktil] *nm* missile

projection [pʀɔʒɛksjɔ̃] *nf* projection; showing; **conférence avec ~s** lecture with slides (*ou* a film)

projet [pʀɔʒɛ] *nm* plan; (*ébauche*) draft; ~ **de loi** bill

projeter [pʀɔʒte] *vt* (*envisager*) to plan; (*film, photos*) to project; (*passer*) to show; (*ombre, lueur*) to throw, cast; (*jeter*) to throw up (*ou* off *ou* out)

prolixe [pʀɔliks(ə)] *adj* verbose

prolongement [pʀɔlɔ̃ʒmɑ̃] *nm* extension; ~s *nmpl* (*fig*) repercussions, effects; **dans le ~ de** running on from

prolonger [pʀɔlɔ̃ʒe] *vt* (*débat, séjour*) to prolong; (*délai, billet, rue*) to extend; (*suj: chose*) to be a continuation *ou* an extension of; **se** ~ *vi* to go on

promenade [pʀɔmnad] *nf* walk (*ou* drive *ou* ride); **faire une ~** to go for a walk; **une ~ en voiture/à vélo** a drive/ (bicycle) ride

promener [pʀɔmne] *vt* (*chien*) to take out for a walk; (*doigts, regard*): ~ **qch sur** to run sth over; **se** ~ *vi* to go for (*ou* be out for) a walk

promesse [pʀɔmɛs] *nf* promise

promettre [pʀɔmɛtʀ(ə)] *vt* to promise ♦ *vi* to look promising; ~ **à qn de faire** to promise sb that one will do

promiscuité [pʀɔmiskɥite] *nf* crowding; lack of privacy

promontoire [pʀɔmɔ̃twaʀ] *nm* headland

promoteur, trice [pʀɔmɔtœʀ, -tʀis] *nm/f* (*instigateur*) instigator, promoter; ~ **(immobilier)** property developer (*BRIT*), real estate promoter (*US*)

promotion [pʀɔmosjɔ̃] *nf* promotion

promouvoir [pʀɔmuvwaʀ] *vt* to promote

prompt, e [pʀɔ̃, pʀɔ̃t] *adj* swift, rapid

prôner [pʀone] *vt* to advocate

pronom [pʀɔnɔ̃] *nm* pronoun

prononcer [pʀɔnɔ̃se] *vt* (*son, mot, jugement*) to pronounce; (*dire*) to utter; (*allocution*) to deliver; **se** ~ *vi* to reach a decision, give a verdict; **se** ~ **sur** to give an opinion on; **se** ~ **contre** to come down against; **prononciation** *nf* pronunciation

pronostic [pʀɔnɔstik] *nm* (*MÉD*) prognosis; (*fig: aussi*: ~s) forecast

propagande [pʀɔpagɑ̃d] *nf* propaganda

propager [pʀɔpaʒe] *vt* to spread; **se** ~ *vi* to spread

prophète [pʀɔfɛt] *nm* prophet

prophétie [pʀɔfesi] *nf* prophecy

propice [pʀɔpis] *adj* favourable

proportion [pʀɔpɔʀsjɔ̃] *nf* proportion; **toute(s) ~(s) gardée(s)** making due allowance(s)

propos [pʀɔpo] *nm* (*paroles*) talk *no pl*,

remark; (*intention*) intention, aim; (*sujet*): **à quel ~?** what about?; **à ~ de** about, regarding; **à tout ~** for no reason at all; **à ~** by the way; (*opportunément*) at the right moment

proposer [pʀɔpoze] *vt* (*suggérer*): ~ **qch (à qn)/de faire** to suggest sth (to sb)/ doing, propose sth (to sb)/to do; (*offrir*): ~ **qch à qn/de faire** to offer sb sth/to do; (*candidat*) to put forward; (*loi, motion*) to propose; **se** ~ to offer one's services; **se** ~ **de faire** to intend *ou* propose to do; **proposition** *nf* suggestion; proposal; offer; (*LING*) clause

propre [pʀɔpʀ(ə)] *adj* clean; (*net*) neat, tidy; (*possessif*) own; (*sens*) literal; (*particulier*): ~ **à** peculiar to; (*approprié*): **à** suitable for; (*de nature à*): ~ **à faire** likely to do ♦ *nm*: **recopier au** ~ to make a fair copy of; **proprement** *adv* cleanly; neatly, tidily; **le village proprement dit** the village itself; **à proprement parler** strictly speaking; **propreté** *nf* cleanliness; neatness; tidiness

propriétaire [pʀɔpʀijetɛʀ] *nm/f* owner; (*pour le locataire*) landlord(lady)

propriété [pʀɔpʀijete] *nf* (*gén*) property; (*droit*) ownership; (*objet, immeuble, terres*) property *gén no pl*

propulser [pʀɔpylse] *vt* (*missile*) to propel; (*projeter*) to hurl, fling

proroger [pʀɔʀɔʒe] *vt* to put back, defer; (*prolonger*) to extend

proscrire [pʀɔskʀiʀ] *vt* (*bannir*) to banish; (*interdire*) to ban, prohibit

prose [pʀoz] *nf* (*style*) prose

prospecter [pʀɔspɛkte] *vt* to prospect; (*COMM*) to canvass

prospectus [pʀɔspɛktys] *nm* leaflet

prospère [pʀɔspɛʀ] *adj* prosperous

prosterner [pʀɔstɛʀne]: **se** ~ *vi* to bow low, prostrate o.s.

prostituée [pʀɔstitɥe] *nf* prostitute

protecteur, trice [pʀɔtɛktœʀ, -tʀis] *adj* protective; (*air, ton: péj*) patronizing ♦ *nm/f* protector

protection [pʀɔtɛksjɔ̃] *nf* protection; (*d'un personnage influent: aide*) patronage

protéger [pʀɔteʒe] *vt* to protect; **se ~ de** *ou* **contre** to protect o.s. from

protéine [pʀɔtein] *nf* protein

protestant, e [pʀɔtestɑ̃, -ɑ̃t] *adj, nm/f* Protestant

protestation [pʀɔtestasjɔ̃] *nf* (*plainte*) protest

protester [pʀɔteste] *vi*: **~ (contre)** to protest (against *ou* about); **~ de** (*son innocence, sa loyauté*) to protest

prothèse [pʀɔtez] *nf* artificial limb, prosthesis; **~ dentaire** denture

protocole [pʀɔtɔkɔl] *nm* (*fig*) etiquette

proue [pʀu] *nf* bow(s *pl*), prow

prouesse [pʀues] *nf* feat

prouver [pʀuve] *vt* to prove

provenance [pʀɔvnɑ̃s] *nf* origin; (*de mot, coutume*) source; **avion en ~ de** plane (arriving) from

provenir [pʀɔvniʀ]: **~ de** *vt* to come from; (*résulter de*) to be the result of

proverbe [pʀɔveʀb(ə)] *nm* proverb

province [pʀɔvɛ̃s] *nf* province

proviseur [pʀɔvizœʀ] *nm* ≈ head(teacher) (*BRIT*), ≈ principal (*US*)

provision [pʀɔvizjɔ̃] *nf* (*réserve*) stock, supply; (*avance*: *à un avocat, avoué*) retainer, retaining fee; (*COMM*) funds *pl* (in account); reserve; **~s** *nfpl* (*vivres*) provisions, food *no pl*

provisoire [pʀɔvizwaʀ] *adj* temporary; (*JUR*) provisional

provoquer [pʀɔvɔke] *vt* (*inciter*): **~ qn à** to incite sb to; (*défier*) to provoke; (*causer*) to cause, bring about

proxénète [pʀɔksenet] *nm* procurer

proximité [pʀɔksimite] *nf* nearness, closeness; (*dans le temps*) imminence, closeness; **à ~** near *ou* close by; **à ~ de** near to; close to

prude [pʀyd] *adj* prudish

prudemment [pʀydamɑ̃] *adv* carefully, cautiously; wisely, sensibly

prudence [pʀydɑ̃s] *nf* carefulness; caution; **avec ~** carefully; cautiously; **par (mesure de) ~** as a precaution

prudent, e [pʀydɑ̃, -ɑ̃t] *adj* (*pas téméraire*) careful, cautious; (: *en général*) safety-conscious; (*sage, conseillé*) wise,

sensible; (*réservé*) cautious

prune [pʀyn] *nf* plum

pruneau, x [pʀyno] *nm* prune

prunelle [pʀynɛl] *nf* pupil; eye

prunier [pʀynje] *nm* plum tree

psaume [psom] *nm* psalm

pseudonyme [psødɔnim] *nm* (*gén*) fictitious name; (*d'écrivain*) pseudonym, pen name; (*de comédien*) stage name

psychiatre [psikjatʀ(ə)] *nm/f* psychiatrist

psychiatrique [psikjatʀik] *adj* psychiatric

psychique [psiʃik] *adj* psychological

psychologie [psikɔlɔʒi] *nf* psychology; **psychologique** *adj* psychological; **psychologue** *nm/f* psychologist

P.T.T. *sigle fpl* = **Postes, Télécommunications et Télédiffusion**

pu *pp de* **pouvoir**

puanteur [pɥɑ̃tœʀ] *nf* stink, stench

pub [pyb] (*fam*) *abr f* (= *publicité*): **la ~** advertising

public, ique [pyblik] *adj* public; (*école, instruction*) state *cpd* ♦ *nm* public; (*assistance*) audience; **en ~** in public

publicitaire [pyblisitɛʀ] *adj* advertising *cpd*; (*film, voiture*) publicity *cpd*

publicité [pyblisite] *nf* (*méthode, profession*) advertising; (*annonce*) advertisement; (*révélations*) publicity

publier [pyblije] *vt* to publish

publique [pyblik] *adj f voir* **public**

puce [pys] *nf* flea; (*INFORM*) chip; **~s** *nfpl* (*marché*) flea market *sg*

pudeur [pydœʀ] *nf* modesty

pudique [pydik] *adj* (*chaste*) modest; (*discret*) discreet

puer [pɥe] (*péj*) *vi* to stink

puéricultrice [pɥeʀikyltʀis] *nf* p(a)ediatric nurse

puériculture [pɥeʀikyltyʀ] *nf* p(a)ediatric nursing; infant care

puéril, e [pɥeʀil] *adj* childish

puis [pɥi] *vb voir* **pouvoir** ♦ *adv* then

puiser [pɥize] *vt*: **~ (dans)** to draw (from)

puisque [pɥisk(ə)] *conj* since

puissance [pɥisɑ̃s] *nf* power; **en ~** *adj*

potential

puissant, e [pɥisɑ̃, -ɑ̃t] *adj* powerful

puisse *etc vb voir* **pouvoir**

puits [pɥi] *nm* well; ~ **de mine** mine shaft

pull(-over) [pul(ɔvœʀ)] *nm* sweater

pulluler [pylyle] *vi* to swarm

pulpe [pylp(ə)] *nf* pulp

pulvérisateur [pylveʀizatœʀ] *nm* spray

pulvériser [pylveʀize] *vt* to pulverize; *(liquide)* to spray

punaise [pynɛz] *nf* (*ZOOL*) bug; *(clou)* drawing pin (*BRIT*), thumbtack (*US*)

punch¹ [pɔ̃ʃ] *nm* (*boisson*) punch

punch² [pœnʃ] *nm* (*BOXE, fig*) punch

punir [pyniʀ] *vt* to punish; **punition** *nf* punishment

pupille [pypij] *nf* (*ANAT*) pupil ♦ *nm/f* (*enfant*) ward; ~ **de l'État** child in care

pupitre [pypitʀ(ə)] *nm* (*SCOL*) desk; (*REL*) lectern; *(de chef d'orchestre)* rostrum

pur, e [pyʀ] *adj* pure; *(vin)* undiluted; *(whisky)* neat; **en ~e perte** to no avail

purée [pyʀe] *nf*: ~ **(de pommes de terre)** mashed potatoes *pl*; ~ **de marrons** chestnut purée

purger [pyʀʒe] *vt* *(radiateur)* to drain; *(circuit hydraulique)* to bleed; (*MÉD, POL*) to purge; (*JUR: peine*) to serve

purin [pyʀɛ̃] *nm* liquid manure

pur-sang [pyʀsɑ̃] *nm inv* thoroughbred

pusillanime [pyzilanim] *adj* fainthearted

putain [pytɛ̃] *(fam!)* *nf* whore (!)

puzzle [pœzl(ə)] *nm* jigsaw (puzzle)

P.V. *sigle m* = **procès-verbal**

pyjama [piʒama] *nm* pyjamas *pl* (*BRIT*), pajamas *pl* (*US*)

pyramide [piʀamid] *nf* pyramid

Pyrénées [piʀene] *nfpl*: **les ~** the Pyrenees

Q q

QG [kyʒe] *sigle m* (= *quartier général*) HQ

QI [kyi] *sigle m* (= *quotient intellectuel*) IQ

quadragénaire [kadʀaʒenɛʀ] *nm/f* man/woman in his/her forties

quadriller [kadʀije] *vt* (*papier*) to mark out in squares; (*POLICE*) to keep under tight control

quadruple [k(w)adʀypl(ə)] *nm*: **le ~ de** four times as much as; **quadruplés, ées** *nm/fpl* quadruplets, quads

quai [ke] *nm* (*de port*) quay; *(de gare)* platform; **être à ~** *(navire)* to be alongside; *(train)* to be in the station

qualifier [kalifje] *vt* to qualify; **se ~** *vi* to qualify; ~ **qch/qn de** to describe sth/sb as

qualité [kalite] *nf* quality; *(titre, fonction)* position

quand [kɑ̃] *conj, adv* when; ~ **je serai riche** when I'm rich; ~ **même** all the same; really; ~ **bien même** even though

quant [kɑ̃]: ~ **à** *prép* as for, as to; regarding

quant-à-soi [kɑ̃taswa] *nm*: **rester sur son ~** to remain aloof

quantité [kɑ̃tite] *nf* quantity, amount; *(SCIENCE)* quantity; *(grand nombre)*: **une ou des ~(s) de** a great deal of

quarantaine [kaʀɑ̃tɛn] *nf* (*MÉD*) quarantine; **avoir la ~** *(âge)* to be around forty; **une ~ (de)** forty or so, about forty

quarante [kaʀɑ̃t] *num* forty

quart [kaʀ] *nm* (*fraction, partie*) quarter; *(surveillance)* watch; **un ~ de beurre** a quarter kilo of butter; **un ~ de vin** a quarter litre of wine; **une livre un ~ ou et ~** one and a quarter pounds; **le ~ de** a quarter of; ~ **d'heure** quarter of an hour

quartier [kaʀtje] *nm* (*de ville*) district, area; *(de bœuf)* quarter; *(de fruit, fromage)* piece; ~**s** *nmpl* (*MIL, BLASON*) quarters; **cinéma de** ~ local cinema; **avoir ~ libre** *(fig)* to be free; ~ **général** headquarters *pl*

quartz [kwaʀts] *nm* quartz

quasi [kazi] *adv* almost, nearly; **quasiment** *adv* almost, nearly

quatorze [katɔʀz(ə)] *num* fourteen

quatre [katʀ(ə)] *num* four; **à ~ pattes** on all fours; **tiré à ~ épingles** dressed up to the nines; **faire les ~ cent coups** to get a bit wild; **se mettre en ~ pour qn** to go out of one's way for sb; **~ à ~** (*monter, descendre*) four at a time; **quatre-vingt-dix** *num* ninety; **quatre-vingts** *num* eighty; **quatrième** *num* fourth

quatuor [kwatɥɔʀ] *nm* quartet(te)

MOT-CLÉ
---

que [kə] *conj* 1 (*introduisant complétive*) that; **il sait ~ tu es là** he knows (that) you're here; **je veux ~ tu acceptes** I want you to accept; **il a dit ~ oui** he said he would (*ou* it was *etc*)
2 (*reprise d'autres conjonctions*): **quand il rentrera et qu'il aura mangé** when he gets back and (when) he has eaten; **si vous y allez ou ~ vous ...** if you go there or if you ...
3 (*en tête de phrase: hypothèse, souhait etc*): **qu'il le veuille ou non** whether he likes it or not; **qu'il fasse ce qu'il voudra!** let him do as he pleases!
4 (*après comparatif*): than; as; *voir aussi* **plus; aussi; autant** *etc*
5 (*seulement*): **ne ... ~** only; **il ne boit ~ de l'eau** he only drinks water
♦ *adv* (*exclamation*): **qu'il** *ou* **qu'est-ce qu'il est bête/court vite!** he's so silly!/he runs so fast!; **~ de livres!** what a lot of books!
♦ *pron* 1 (*relatif: personne*) whom; (*: chose*) that, which; **l'homme ~ je vois** the man (whom) I see; **le livre ~ tu vois** the book (that *ou* which) you see; **un jour ~ j'étais ...** a day when I was ...
2 (*interrogatif*) what; **~ fais-tu?, qu'est-ce ~ tu fais?** what are you doing?; **qu'est-ce ~ c'est?** what is it?, what's that?; **~ faire?** what can one do?

MOT-CLÉ
---

quel, quelle [kɛl] *adj* 1 (*interrogatif: personne*) who; (*: chose*) what; which; **~ est cet homme?** who is this man?; **~ est ce livre?** what is this book?; **~ livre/homme?** what book/man?; (*parmi un certain choix*) which book/man?; **~s ac-**

teurs **préférez-vous?** which actors do you prefer?; **dans ~s pays êtes-vous allé?** which *ou* what countries did you go to?
2 (*exclamatif*): **quelle surprise!** what a surprise!
3: **quel(le) que soit coupable** whoever is guilty; **~ que soit votre avis** whatever your opinion

quelconque [kɛlkɔ̃k] *adj* (*médiocre*) indifferent, poor; (*sans attrait*) ordinary, plain; (*indéfini*): **un ami ~** some friend or other

---
MOT-CLÉ
---

quelque [kɛlkə] *adj* 1 some; a few; (*tournure interrogative*) any; **~ espoir** some hope; **il a ~s amis** he has a few *ou* some friends; **a-t-il ~s amis?** has he any friends?; **les ~s livres qui** the few books which; **20 kg et ~(s)** a bit over 20 kg
2: **~ ... que**: **quelque livre qu'il choisisse** whatever (*ou* whichever) book he chooses
3: **~ chose** something; (*tournure interrogative*) anything; **~ chose d'autre** something else; anything else; **~ part** somewhere; anywhere; **en ~ sorte** as it were
♦ *adv* 1 (*environ*): **~ 100 mètres** some 100 metres
2: **~ peu** rather, somewhat

---

quelquefois [kɛlkəfwa] *adv* sometimes
quelques-uns, -unes [kɛlkəzœ̃, -yn] *pron* a few, some
quelqu'un [kɛlkœ̃] *pron* someone, somebody; (*+tournure interrogative*) anyone, anybody; **~ d'autre** someone *ou* somebody else; anybody else
quémander [kemɑ̃de] *vt* to beg for
qu'en dira-t-on [kɑ̃diʀatɔ̃] *nm inv*: **le ~** gossip, what people say
querelle [kəʀɛl] *nf* quarrel
quereller [kəʀele]: **se ~** *vi* to quarrel
qu'est-ce que [kɛskə] *voir* **que**
qu'est-ce qui [kɛski] *voir* **qui**
question [kɛstjɔ̃] *nf* (*gén*) question; (*fig*)

matter; issue; **il a été ~ de** we (*ou* they) spoke about; **de quoi est-il ~?** what is it about?; **il n'en est pas ~** there's no question of it; **hors de ~** out of the question; **remettre en ~** to question; **questionnaire** [kɛstjɔnɛʀ] *nm* questionnaire; **questionner** [kɛstjɔne] *vt* to question

quête [kɛt] *nf* collection; (*recherche*) quest, search; **faire la ~** (*à l'église*) to take the collection; (*artiste*) to pass the hat round; **quêter** *vi* (*à l'église*) to take the collection

quetsche [kwɛtʃə] *nf* damson

queue [kø] *nf* tail; (*fig: du classement*) bottom; (: *de poêle*) handle; (: *de fruit, feuille*) stalk; (: *de train, colonne, file*) rear; **faire la ~** to queue (up) (*BRIT*), line up (*US*); ~ **de cheval** ponytail; **queue-de-pie** *nf* (*habit*) tails *pl*, tail coat

qui [ki] *pron* (*personne*) who; (+*prép*) whom; (*chose, animal*) which, that; **qu'est-ce ~ est sur la table?** what is on the table?; ~ **est-ce ~?** who?; ~ **est-ce que?** who?; whom?; **à ~ est ce sac?** whose bag is this?; **à ~ parlais-tu?** who were you talking to?, to whom were you talking?; **amenez ~ vous voulez** bring who you like; ~ **que ce soit** whoever it may be

quiconque [kikɔ̃k] *pron* (*celui qui*) whoever, anyone who; (*personne*) anyone, anybody

quiétude [kjetyd] *nf* (*d'un lieu*) quiet, tranquillity; **en toute ~** in complete peace

quille [kij] *nf*: (**jeu de**) ~**s** skittles *sg* (*BRIT*), bowling (*US*)

quincaillerie [kɛ̃kajʀi] *nf* (*ustensiles*) hardware; (*magasin*) hardware shop; **quincaillier, ière** *nm/f* hardware dealer

quinquagénaire [kɛ̃kaʒenɛʀ] *nm/f* man/woman in his/her fifties

quintal, aux [kɛ̃tal, -o] *nm* quintal (*100 kg*)

quinte [kɛ̃t] *nf*: ~ (**de toux**) coughing fit

quintuple [kɛ̃typl(ə)] *nm*: **le ~ de** five times as much as; **quintuplés, ées** *nm/fpl* quintuplets, quins

quinzaine [kɛ̃zɛn] *nf*: **une ~ (de)** about

fifteen, fifteen or so; **une ~ (de jours)** a fortnight (*BRIT*), two weeks

quinze [kɛz] *num* fifteen; **demain en ~** a fortnight *ou* two weeks tomorrow; **dans ~ jours** in a fortnight('s time), in two weeks(' time)

quiproquo [kipʀoko] *nm* misunderstanding

quittance [kitɑ̃s] *nf* (*reçu*) receipt; (*facture*) bill

quitte [kit] *adj*: **être ~ envers qn** to be no longer in sb's debt; (*fig*) to be quits with sb; **être ~ de** (*obligation*) to be clear of; **en être ~ à bon compte** to have got off lightly; ~ **à faire** even if it means doing

quitter [kite] *vt* to leave; (*espoir, illusion*) to give up; (*vêtement*) to take off; **se ~** *vi* (*couples, interlocuteurs*) to part; **ne quittez pas** (*au téléphone*) hold the line

qui-vive [kiviv] *nm*: **être sur le ~** to be on the alert

quoi [kwa] *pron* (*interrogatif*) what; ~ **de neuf?** what's the news?; **as-tu de ~ écrire?** have you anything to write with?; **il n'a pas de ~ se l'acheter** he can't afford it; ~ **qu'il arrive** whatever happens; ~ **qu'il en soit** be that as it may; ~ **que ce soit** anything at all; "**il n'y a pas de ~**" "(please) don't mention it"; **à ~ bon?** what's the use?; **en ~ puis-je vous aider?** how can I help you?

quoique [kwak(ə)] *conj* (al)though

quolibet [kɔlibɛ] *nm* gibe, jeer

quote-part [kɔtpaʀ] *nf* share

quotidien, ne [kɔtidjɛ̃, -ɛn] *adj* daily; (*banal*) everyday ♦ *nm* (*journal*) daily (paper)

R r

r. *abr* = **route**; **rue**

rab [ʀab] (*fam*) *abr m* = **rabiot**

rabâcher [ʀabaʃe] *vt* to keep on repeating

rabais [ʀabɛ] *nm* reduction, discount

rabaisser [ʀabese] *vt* (*rabattre*) to reduce; (*dénigrer*) to belittle

rabattre [ʀabatʀ(ə)] *vt* (*couvercle, siège*) to pull down; (*gibier*) to drive; **se ~** *vi* (*bords, couvercle*) to fall shut; (*véhicule, coureur*) to cut in; **se ~ sur** to fall back on

rabbin [ʀabɛ̃] *nm* rabbi

rabiot [ʀabjo] (*fam*) *nm* extra, more

râblé, e [ʀɑble] *adj* stocky

rabot [ʀabo] *nm* plane

rabougri, e [ʀabugʀi] *adj* stunted

rabrouer [ʀabʀue] *vt* to snub

racaille [ʀakɑj] (*péj*) *nf* rabble, riffraff

raccommoder [ʀakɔmɔde] *vt* to mend, repair; (*chaussette etc*) to darn

raccompagner [ʀakɔ̃paɲe] *vt* to take *ou* see back

raccord [ʀakɔʀ] *nm* link

raccorder [ʀakɔʀde] *vt* to join (up), link up; (*suj: pont etc*) to connect, link

raccourci [ʀakuʀsi] *nm* short cut

raccourcir [ʀakuʀsiʀ] *vt* to shorten

raccrocher [ʀakʀɔʃe] *vt* (*tableau*) to hang back up; (*récepteur*) to put down ♦ *vi* (*TÉL*) to hang up, ring off; **se ~ à** *vt* to cling to, hang on to

race [ʀas] *nf* race; (*d'animaux, fig*) breed; (*ascendance*) stock, race; **de ~** purebred, pedigree

rachat [ʀaʃa] *nm* buying; buying back

racheter [ʀaʃte] *vt* (*article perdu*) to buy another; (*davantage*): **~ du lait/3 œufs** to buy more milk/another 3 eggs *ou* 3 more eggs; (*après avoir vendu*) to buy back; (*d'occasion*) to buy; (*COMM: part, firme*) to buy up; (: *pension, rente*) to redeem; **se ~** *vi* (*fig*) to make amends

racial, e, aux [ʀasjal, -o] *adj* racial

racine [ʀasin] *nf* root; **~ carrée/cubique** square/cube root

raciste [ʀasist(ə)] *adj, nm/f* raci(al)ist

racket [ʀakɛt] *nm* racketeering *no pl*

racler [ʀɑkle] *vt* (*surface*) to scrape; (*tache, boue*) to scrape off

racoler [ʀakɔle] *vt* (*attirer: suj: prostituée*) to solicit; (: *parti, marchand*) to tout for

racontars [ʀakɔ̃taʀ] *nmpl* gossip *sg*

raconter [ʀakɔ̃te] *vt*: **~ (à qn)** (*décrire*) to relate (to sb), tell (sb) about; (*dire*) to tell (sb)

racorni, e [ʀakɔʀni] *adj* hard(ened)

radar [ʀadaʀ] *nm* radar

rade [ʀad] *nf* (natural) harbour; **rester en ~** (*fig*) to be left stranded

radeau, x [ʀado] *nm* raft

radiateur [ʀadjatœʀ] *nm* radiator, heater; (*AUTO*) radiator; **~ électrique/à gaz** electric/gas heater *ou* fire

radiation [ʀadjasjɔ̃] *nf* (*voir radier*) striking off *no pl*; (*PHYSIQUE*) radiation

radical, e, aux [ʀadikal, -o] *adj* radical

radier [ʀadje] *vt* to strike off

radieux, euse [ʀadjø, -øz] *adj* radiant; brilliant, glorious

radin, e [ʀadɛ̃, -in] (*fam*) *adj* stingy

radio [ʀadjo] *nf* radio; (*MÉD*) X-ray ♦ *nm* radio operator; **à la ~** on the radio; **radioactif, ive** *adj* radioactive; **radiodiffuser** *vt* to broadcast; **radiographie** *nf* radiography; (*photo*) X-ray photograph; **radiophonique** *adj* radio *cpd*; **radioréveil** (*pl* **radios-réveils**) *nm* radio alarm clock; **radiotélévisé, e** *adj* broadcast on radio and television

radis [ʀadi] *nm* radish

radoter [ʀadɔte] *vi* to ramble on

radoucir [ʀadusiʀ]: **se ~** *vi* (*se réchauffer*) to become milder; (*se calmer*) to calm down; to soften

rafale [ʀafal] *nf* (*vent*) gust (of wind); (*tir*) burst of gunfire

raffermir [ʀafɛʀmiʀ] *vt* to firm up; (*fig*) to strengthen

raffiner [ʀafine] *vt* to refine; **raffinerie** *nf* refinery

raffoler [ʀafɔle]: **~ de** *vt* to be very keen on

rafle [ʀafl(ə)] *nf* (*de police*) raid

rafler [ʀafle] (*fam*) *vt* to swipe, nick

rafraîchir [ʀafʀeʃiʀ] *vt* (*atmosphère, température*) to cool (down); (*aussi: mettre à ~*) to chill; (*fig: rénover*) to brighten up; **se ~** *vi* to grow cooler; to freshen up; to refresh o.s.; **rafraîchissant, e** *adj* refreshing; **rafraîchissement** *nm* cooling; (*boisson*) cool drink; **rafraîchissements** *nmpl* (*boissons, fruits etc*) refreshments

rage [ʀaʒ] *nf* (*MÉD*): **la** ~ rabies; (*fureur*) rage, fury; **faire** ~ to rage; ~ **de dents** (raging) toothache

ragot [ʀago] (*fam*) *nm* malicious gossip *no pl*

ragoût [ʀagu] *nm* (*plat*) stew

raide [ʀɛd] *adj* (*tendu*) taut, tight; (*escarpé*) steep; (*droit: cheveux*) straight; (*ankylosé, dur, guindé*) stiff; (*fam*) steep, stiff; flat broke ♦ *adv* (*en pente*) steeply; ~ **mort** stone dead; **raidir** *vt* (*muscles*) to stiffen; (*câble*) to pull taut; **se raidir** *vi* to stiffen; to become taut; (*personne*) to tense up; to brace o.s.

raie [ʀɛ] *nf* (*ZOOL*) skate, ray; (*rayure*) stripe; (*des cheveux*) parting

raifort [ʀɛfɔʀ] *nm* horseradish

rail [ʀaj] *nm* rail; (*chemins de fer*) railways *pl*; **par** ~ by rail

railler [ʀaje] *vt* to scoff at, jeer at

rainure [ʀenyʀ] *nf* groove; slot

raisin [ʀezɛ̃] *nm* (*aussi: ~s*) grapes *pl*; ~**s secs** raisins

raison [ʀezɔ̃] *nf* reason; **avoir** ~ to be right; **donner** ~ **à qn** to agree with sb; to prove sb right; **se faire une** ~ to learn to live with it; **perdre la** ~ to become insane; to take leave of one's senses; ~ **de plus** all the more reason; **à plus forte** ~ all the more so; **en** ~ **de** because of; according to; in proportion to; **à** ~ **de** at the rate of; ~ **sociale** corporate name; **raisonnable** *adj* reasonable, sensible

raisonnement [ʀezɔnmɑ̃] *nm* reasoning; arguing; argument

raisonner [ʀezɔne] *vi* (*penser*) to reason; (*argumenter, discuter*) to argue ♦ *vt* (*personne*) to reason with

rajeunir [ʀaʒœniʀ] *vt* (*suj: coiffure, robe*): ~ **qn** to make sb look younger; (: *cure etc*) to rejuvenate; (*fig*) to give a new look to; to inject new blood into ♦ *vi* to become (*ou* look) younger

rajouter [ʀaʒute] *vt*: ~ **du sel/un œuf** to add some more salt/another egg

rajuster [ʀaʒyste] *vt* (*vêtement*) to straighten, tidy; (*salaires*) to adjust;

(*machine*) to readjust

ralenti [ʀalɑ̃ti] *nm*: **au** ~ (*CINÉMA*) in slow motion; (*fig*) at a slower pace; **tourner au** ~ (*AUTO*) to tick over (*AUTO*), idle

ralentir [ʀalɑ̃tiʀ] *vt* to slow down

râler [ʀɑle] *vi* to groan; (*fam*) to grouse, moan (and groan)

rallier [ʀalje] *vt* (*rassembler*) to rally; (*rejoindre*) to rejoin; (*gagner à sa cause*) to win over; **se** ~ **à** (*avis*) to come over *ou* round to

rallonge [ʀalɔ̃ʒ] *nf* (*de table*) (extra) leaf; (*argent etc*) extra *no pl*

rallonger [ʀalɔ̃ʒe] *vt* to lengthen

rallye [ʀali] *nm* rally; (*POL*) march

ramassage [ʀamasaʒ] *nm*: ~ **scolaire** school bus service

ramassé, e [ʀamase] *adj* (*trapu*) squat

ramasser [ʀamase] *vt* (*objet tombé ou par terre, fam*) to pick up; (*recueillir: récolter*) to collect; (*récolter*) to gather; **se** ~ *vi* (*sur soi-même*) to huddle up; to crouch; **ramassis** (*péj*) *nm* bunch; jumble

rambarde [ʀɑ̃baʀd] *nf* guardrail

rame [ʀam] *nf* (*aviron*) oar; (*de métro*) train; (*de papier*) ream

rameau, x [ʀamo] *nm* (small) branch; **les R~x** (*REL*) Palm Sunday *sg*

ramener [ʀamne] *vt* to bring back; (*reconduire*) to take back; (*rabattre: couverture, visière*): ~ **qch sur** to pull sth back over; ~ **qch à** (*réduire à, aussi MATH*) to reduce sth to

ramer [ʀame] *vi* to row

ramollir [ʀamɔliʀ] *vt* to soften; **se** ~ *vi* to go soft

ramoner [ʀamɔne] *vt* to sweep

rampe [ʀɑ̃p] *nf* (*d'escalier*) banister(s *pl*); (*dans un garage, d'un terrain*) ramp; (*THÉÂTRE*): **la** ~ the footlights *pl*; ~ **de lancement** launching pad

ramper [ʀɑ̃pe] *vi* to crawl

rancard [ʀɑ̃kaʀ] (*fam*) *nm* date; tip

rancart [ʀɑ̃kaʀ] *nm*: **mettre au** ~ to scrap

rance [ʀɑ̃s] *adj* rancid

rancœur [ʀɑ̃kœʀ] *nf* rancour

rançon [ʀɑ̃sɔ̃] *nf* ransom; (*fig*) price

rancune [ʀɑ̃kyn] *nf* grudge, rancour;

garder ~ **à qn (de qch)** to bear sb a grudge (for sth); **sans** ~! no hard feelings!; **rancunier, ière** *adj* vindictive, spiteful

randonnée [ʀɑ̃dɔne] *nf* ride; (*à pied*) walk, ramble; hike, hiking *no pl*

rang [ʀɑ̃] *nm* (*rangée*) row; (*grade, classement*) rank; ~**s** *nmpl* (MIL) ranks; **se mettre en** ~**s/sur un** ~ to get into *ou* form rows/a line; **au premier** ~ in the first row; (*fig*) ranking first

rangé, e [ʀɑ̃ʒe] *adj* (*sérieux*) orderly, steady

rangée [ʀɑ̃ʒe] *nf* row

ranger [ʀɑ̃ʒe] *vt* (*classer, grouper*) to order, arrange; (*mettre à sa place*) to put away; (*voiture dans la rue*) to park; (*mettre de l'ordre dans*) to tidy up; (*arranger*) to arrange; (*fig: classer*): ~ **qn/qch parmi** to rank sb/sth among; **se** ~ *vi* (*véhicule, conducteur*) to pull over *ou* in; (*piéton*) to step aside; (*s'assagir*) to settle down; **se** ~ **à** (*avis*) to come round to

ranimer [ʀanime] *vt* (*personne*) to bring round; (*forces, courage*) to restore; (*troupes etc*) to kindle new life in; (*douleur, souvenir*) to revive; (*feu*) to rekindle

rap [ʀap] *nm* rap (music)

rapace [ʀapas] *nm* bird of prey

râpe [ʀɑp] *nf* (CULIN) grater

râpé, e [ʀɑpe] *adj* (*tissu*) threadbare

râper [ʀɑpe] *vt* (CULIN) to grate

rapetisser [ʀaptise] *vt* to shorten

rapide [ʀapid] *adj* fast; (*prompt*) quick ♦ *nm* express (train); (*de cours d'eau*) rapid; **rapidement** *adv* fast; quickly

rapiécer [ʀapjese] *vt* to patch

rappel [ʀapɛl] *nm* (THÉÂTRE) curtain call; (MÉD: *vaccination*) booster; (ADMIN: *de salaire*) back pay *no pl*; (*d'une aventure, d'un nom*) reminder

rappeler [ʀaple] *vt* to call back; (*ambassadeur, MIL*) to recall; (*faire se souvenir*): ~ **qch à qn** to remind sb of sth; **se** ~ *vt* (*se souvenir de*) to remember, recall

rapport [ʀapɔʀ] *nm* (*compte rendu*) re-

port; (*profit*) yield, return; revenue; (*lien, analogie*) relationship; (MATH, TECH) ratio; ~**s** *nmpl* (*entre personnes, pays*) relations; **avoir** ~ **à** to have something to do with; **être en** ~ **avec** (*idée de corrélation*) to be related to; **être/se mettre en** ~ **avec qn** to be/get in touch with sb; **par** ~ **à** in relation to; ~ **qualité-prix** *nm* value (for money); ~**s (sexuels)** (sexual) intercourse *sg*

rapporter [ʀapɔʀte] *vt* (*rendre, ramener*) to bring back; (*apporter davantage*) to bring more; (*suj: investissement*) to yield; (: *activité*) to bring in; (*relater*) to report ♦ *vi* (*investissement*) to give a good return *ou* yield; (: *activité*) to be very profitable; **se** ~ **à** (*correspondre à*) to relate to; **s'en** ~ **à** to rely on; ~ **qch à** (*fig: rattacher*) to relate sth to; **rapporteur, euse** *nm/f* (*de procès, commission*) reporter; (*péj*) telltale ♦ *nm* (GÉOM) protractor

rapprochement [ʀapʀɔʃmɑ̃] *nm* (*de nations, familles*) reconciliation; (*analogie, rapport*) parallel

rapprocher [ʀapʀɔʃe] *vt* (*chaise d'une table*): ~ **qch (de)** to bring sth closer (to); (*deux objets*) to bring closer together; (*réunir*) to bring together; (*comparer*) to establish a parallel between; **se** ~ *vi* to draw closer *ou* nearer; **se** ~ **de** to come closer to; (*présenter une analogie avec*) to be close to

rapt [ʀapt] *nm* abduction

raquette [ʀakɛt] *nf* (*de tennis*) racket; (*de ping-pong*) bat; (*à neige*) snowshoe

rare [ʀaʀ] *adj* rare; (*main-d'œuvre, denrées*) scarce; (*cheveux, herbe*) sparse

rarement [ʀaʀmɑ̃] *adv* rarely, seldom

ras, e [ʀɑ, ʀɑz] *adj* (*tête, cheveux*) close-cropped; (*poil, herbe*) short ♦ *adv* short; **en** ~**e campagne** in open country; **à** ~ **bords** to the brim; **au** ~ **de** level with; **en avoir** ~ **le bol** (*fam*) to be fed up; ~ **du cou** *adj* (*pull, robe*) crew-neck

rasade [ʀazad] *nf* glassful

raser [ʀɑze] *vt* (*barbe, cheveux*) to shave off; (*menton, personne*) to shave; (*fam: ennuyer*) to bore; (*démolir*) to raze (to the ground); (*frôler*) to graze, skim; **se ~** *vi* to shave; (*fam*) to be bored (to tears); **rasoir** *nm* razor

rassasier [ʀasazje] *vt* to satisfy

rassemblement [ʀasɑ̃bləmɑ̃] *nm* (*groupe*) gathering, (*POL*) union

rassembler [ʀasɑ̃ble] *vt* (*réunir*) to assemble, gather; (*regrouper, amasser*) to gather together, collect; **se ~** *vi* to gather

rassis, e [ʀasi, -iz] *adj* (*pain*) stale

rassurer [ʀasyʀe] *vt* to reassure; **se ~** *vi* to be reassured; **rassure-toi** don't worry

rat [ʀa] *nm* rat

rate [ʀat] *nf* spleen

raté, e [ʀate] *adj* (*tentative*) unsuccessful, failed ♦ *nm/f* failure ♦ *nm* misfiring *no pl*

râteau, x [ʀɑto] *nm* rake

râtelier [ʀɑtəlje] *nm* rack; (*fam*) false teeth *pl*

rater [ʀate] *vi* (*affaire, projet etc*) to go wrong, fail ♦ *vt* (*cible, train, occasion*) to miss; (*démonstration, plat*) to spoil; (*examen*) to fail

ration [ʀasjɔ̃] *nf* ration; (*fig*) share

ratisser [ʀatise] *vt* (*allée*) to rake; (*feuilles*) to rake up; (*suj: armée, police*) to comb

R.A.T.P. *sigle f* (= *Régie autonome des transports parisiens*) *Paris transport authority*

rattacher [ʀataʃe] *vt* (*animal, cheveux*) to tie up again; (*incorporer*: *ADMIN etc*): **~ qch à** to join sth to; (*fig: relier*): **~ qch à** to link sth with; (: *lier*): **~ qn à** to bind *ou* tie sb to

rattraper [ʀatʀape] *vt* (*fugitif*) to recapture; (*empêcher de tomber*) to catch (hold of); (*atteindre, rejoindre*) to catch up with; (*réparer: imprudence, erreur*) to make up for; **se ~** *vi* to make good one's losses; to make up for it; **se ~ (à)** (*se raccrocher*) to stop o.s. falling (by catching hold of)

rature [ʀatyʀ] *nf* deletion, erasure

rauque [ʀok] *adj* raucous; hoarse

ravages [ʀavaʒ] *nmpl*: **faire des ~** to wreak havoc

ravaler [ʀavale] *vt* (*mur, façade*) to re-

store; (*déprécier*) to lower

ravi, e [ʀavi] *adj*: **être ~ de/que** to be delighted with/that

ravin [ʀavɛ̃] *nm* gully, ravine

ravir [ʀaviʀ] *vt* (*enchanter*) to delight; (*enlever*): **~ qch à qn** to rob sb of sth; **à ~** beautifully

raviser [ʀavize]: **se ~** *vi* to change one's mind

ravissant, e [ʀavisɑ̃, -ɑ̃t] *adj* delightful

ravisseur, euse [ʀavisœʀ, -øz] *nm/f* abductor, kidnapper

ravitailler [ʀavitaje] *vt* to resupply; (*véhicule*) to refuel; **se ~** *vi* to get fresh supplies

raviver [ʀavive] *vt* (*feu, douleur*) to revive; (*couleurs*) to brighten up

rayé, e [ʀeje] *adj* (*à rayures*) striped

rayer [ʀeje] *vt* (*érafler*) to scratch; (*barrer*) to cross out; (*d'une liste*) to cross off

rayon [ʀɛjɔ̃] *nm* (*de soleil etc*) ray; (*GÉOM*) radius; (*de roue*) spoke; (*étagère*) shelf; (*de grand magasin*) department; **dans un ~ de** within a radius of; **~ d'action** range; **~ de soleil** sunbeam; **~s X** X-rays

rayonnement [ʀɛjɔnmɑ̃] *nm* radiation; (*fig*) radiance; influence

rayonner [ʀɛjɔne] *vi* (*chaleur, énergie*) to radiate; (*fig*) to shine forth; to be radiant; (*touriste*) to go touring (*from one base*)

rayure [ʀejyʀ] *nf* (*motif*) stripe; (*éraflure*) scratch; (*rainure, d'un fusil*) groove

raz-de-marée [ʀɑdmaʀe] *nm inv* tidal wave

ré [ʀe] *nm* (*MUS*) D; (*en chantant la gamme*) re

réacteur [ʀeaktœʀ] *nm* jet engine

réaction [ʀeaksjɔ̃] *nf* reaction; **moteur à ~** jet engine

réadapter [ʀeadapte] *vt* to readjust; (*MÉD*) to rehabilitate; **se ~ (à)** to readjust (to)

réagir [ʀeaʒiʀ] *vi* to react

réalisateur, trice [ʀealizatœʀ, -tʀis] *nm/f* (*TV, CINÉMA*) director

réalisation [realizɑsjɔ̃] *nf* carrying out; realization; fulfilment; achievement; production; (*œuvre*) production; creation; work

réaliser [realize] *vt* (*projet, opération*) to carry out, realize; (*rêve, souhait*) to realize, fulfil; (*exploit*) to achieve; (*achat, vente*) to make; (*film*) to produce; (*se rendre compte de, COMM: bien, capital*) to realize; **se ~** *vi* to be realized

réaliste [realist(ə)] *adj* realistic

réalité [realite] *nf* reality; **en ~** in (actual) fact; **dans la ~** in reality; **~ virtuelle** (*COMPUT*) virtual reality

réanimation [reanimɑsjɔ̃] *nf* resuscitation; **service de ~** intensive care unit

réarmer [rearme] *vt* (*arme*) to reload ♦ *vi* (*état*) to rearm

rébarbatif, ive [rebarbatif, -iv] *adj* forbidding

rebattu, e [rəbaty] *adj* hackneyed

rebelle [rəbɛl] *nm/f* rebel ♦ *adj* (*troupes*) rebel; (*enfant*) rebellious; (*mèche etc*) unruly; **~ à** unamenable to

rebeller [rəbele]: **se ~** *vi* to rebel

rebondi, e [rəbɔ̃di] *adj* rounded; chubby

rebondir [rəbɔ̃dir] *vi* (*ballon: au sol*) to bounce; (: *contre un mur*) to rebound; (*fig*) to get moving again; **rebondissement** *nm* new development

rebord [rəbɔr] *nm* edge

rebours [rəbur]: **à ~** *adv* the wrong way

rebrousse-poil [rəbruspwal]: **à ~** *adv* the wrong way

rebrousser [rəbruse] *vt*: **~ chemin** to turn back

rebut [rəby] *nm*: **mettre au ~** to scrap;

rebuter [rəbyte] *vt* to put off

récalcitrant, e [rekalsitrɑ̃, -ɑ̃t] *adj* refractory

recaler [rəkale] *vt* (*SCOL*) to fail

récapituler [rekapityle] *vt* to recapitulate; to sum up

receler [rəsəle] *vt* (*produit d'un vol*) to receive; (*malfaiteur*) to harbour; (*fig*) to conceal; **receleur, euse** *nm/f* receiver

récemment [resamɑ̃] *adv* recently

recenser [rəsɑ̃se] *vt* (*population*) to take a census of; (*inventorier*) to list

récent, e [resɑ̃, -ɑ̃t] *adj* recent

récépissé [resepise] *nm* receipt

récepteur [reseptœr] *nm* receiver; **~ (de radio)** radio set *ou* receiver

réception [resepsjɔ̃] *nf* receiving *no pl*; (*accueil*) reception, welcome; (*bureau*) reception desk; (*réunion mondaine*) reception, party; **réceptionniste** *nm/f* receptionist

recette [rəsɛt] *nf* (*CULIN*) recipe; (*fig*) formula, recipe; (*COMM*) takings *pl*; **~s** *nfpl* (*COMM: rentrées*) receipts

receveur, euse [rəsvœr, -øz] *nm/f* (*des contributions*) tax collector; (*des postes*) postmaster(mistress); (*d'autobus*) conductor(tress)

recevoir [rəsvwar] *vt* to receive; (*client, patient*) to see ♦ *vi* to receive visitors; to give parties; to see patients *etc*; **se ~** *vi* (*athlète*) to land; **être reçu (à un examen)** to pass

rechange [rəʃɑ̃ʒ]: **de ~** *adj* (*pièces, roue*) spare; (*fig: solution*) alternative; **des vêtements de ~** a change of clothes

rechaper [rəʃape] *vt* to remould, retread

réchapper [reʃape]: **~ de** *ou* **à** *vt* (*accident, maladie*) to come through

recharge [rəʃarʒ(ə)] *nf* refill

recharger [rəʃarʒe] *vt* (*camion, fusil, appareil-photo*) to reload; (*briquet, stylo*) to refill; (*batterie*) to recharge

réchaud [reʃo] *nm* (*portable*) stove; plate-warmer

réchauffer [reʃofe] *vt* (*plat*) to reheat; (*mains, personne*) to warm; **se ~** *vi* (*température*) to get warmer

rêche [rɛʃ] *adj* rough

recherche [rəʃɛrʃ(ə)] *nf* (*action*): **la ~ de** the search for; (*raffinement*) affectedness, studied elegance; (*scientifique etc*): **la ~** research; **~s** *nfpl* (*de la police*) investigations; (*scientifiques*) research *sg*; **se mettre à la ~ de** to go in search of

recherché, e [rəʃɛrʃe] *adj* (*rare, demandé*) much sought-after; (*raffiné*) studied, affected

rechercher [rəʃɛrʃe] *vt* (*objet égaré, personne*) to look for; (*causes, nouveau* *procédé*) to try to find; (*bonheur, amitié*) to seek

rechute [rəʃyt] *nf* (*MÉD*) relapse

récidiver [residive] *vi* to commit a subsequent offence; (*fig*) to do it again

récif [resif] *nm* reef

récipient [resipjɑ̃] *nm* container

réciproque [resiprɔk] *adj* reciprocal

récit [resi] *nm* story

récital [resital] *nm* recital

réciter [resite] *vt* to recite

réclamation [reklamasjɔ̃] *nf* complaint; ~**s** *nfpl* (*bureau*) complaints department *sg*

réclame [reklam] *nf* ad, advert(isement); **article en ~** special offer

réclamer [reklame] *vt* (*aide, nourriture etc*) to ask for; (*revendiquer*) to claim, demand; (*nécessiter*) to demand, require ♦ *vi* to complain

réclusion [reklyzjɔ̃] *nf* imprisonment

recoin [rəkwɛ̃] *nm* nook, corner; (*fig*) hidden recess

reçois *etc vb voir* **recevoir**

récolte [rekɔlt(ə)] *nf* harvesting; gathering; (*produits*) harvest, crop; (*fig*) crop, collection

récolter [rekɔlte] *vt* to harvest, gather (in); (*fig*) to collect; to get

recommandé [rəkɔmɑ̃de] *nm* (*POSTES*): **en ~** by registered mail

recommander [rəkɔmɑ̃de] *vt* to recommend; (*suj: qualités etc*) to commend; (*POSTES*) to register; **se ~ de qn** to give sb's name as a reference

recommencer [rəkɔmɑ̃se] *vt* (*reprendre: lutte, séance*) to resume, start again; (*refaire: travail, explications*) to start afresh, start (over) again; (*récidiver: erreur*) to make again ♦ *vi* to start again; (*récidiver*) to do it again

récompense [rekɔ̃pɑ̃s] *nf* reward; (*prix*) award; **récompenser** *vt*: **récompenser qn (de ou pour)** to reward sb (for)

réconcilier [rekɔ̃silje] *vt* to reconcile; **se ~ (avec)** to be reconciled (with)

reconduire [rəkɔ̃dɥiʀ] *vt* (*raccompagner*) to take *ou* see back; (*JUR, POL: renouveler*) to renew

réconfort [rekɔ̃fɔʀ] *nm* comfort

réconforter [rekɔ̃fɔʀte] *vt* (*consoler*) to comfort; (*revigorer*) to fortify

reconnaissance [rəkɔnɛsɑ̃s] *nf* recognition; acknowledgement; (*gratitude*) gratitude, gratefulness; (*MIL*) reconnaissance, recce; **reconnaissant, e** [rəkɔnɛsɑ̃, -ɑ̃t] *adj* grateful

reconnaître [rəkɔnɛtʀ(ə)] *vt* to recognize; (*MIL: lieu*) to reconnoitre; (*JUR: enfant, dette, droit*) to acknowledge; ~ **que** to admit *ou* acknowledge that; ~ **qn/qch à** to recognize sb/sth by

reconnu, e [ʀ(ə)kɔny] *adj* (*indiscuté, connu*) recognized

reconstituant, e [rəkɔ̃stitɥɑ̃, -ɑ̃t] *adj* (*aliment, régime*) strength-building

reconstituer [rəkɔ̃stitɥe] *vt* (*monument ancien*) to recreate; (*fresque, vase brisé*) to piece together, reconstitute; (*événement, accident*) to reconstruct; (*fortune, patrimoine*) to rebuild

reconstruire [rəkɔ̃strɥiʀ] *vt* to rebuild

reconvertir [rəkɔ̃vɛʀtiʀ]: **se ~** *vr* (*un métier, une branche*) to go into

record [rəkɔʀ] *nm, adj* record

recoupement [rəkupmɑ̃] *nm*: **par ~** by cross-checking

recouper [rəkupe]: **se ~** *vi* (*témoignages*) to tie *ou* match up

recourbé, e [rəkuʀbe] *adj* curved; hooked; bent

recourir [rəkuʀiʀ]: ~ **à** *vt* (*ami, agence*) to turn *ou* appeal to; (*force, ruse, emprunt*) to resort to

recours [rəkuʀ] *nm* (*JUR*) appeal; **avoir ~ à** = **recourir à**; **en dernier ~** as a last resort; ~ **en grâce** plea for clemency

recouvrer [rəkuvʀe] *vt* (*vue, santé etc*) to recover, regain; (*impôts*) to collect; (*créance*) to recover

recouvrir [rəkuvʀiʀ] *vt* (*couvrir à nouveau*) to re-cover; (*couvrir entièrement, aussi fig*) to cover; (*cacher, masquer*) to conceal, hide; **se ~** *vi* (*se superposer*) to overlap

récréation [rekʀeasjɔ̃] *nf* recreation, entertainment; (*SCOL*) break

récrier [ʀekʀije]: **se ~** *vi* to exclaim

récriminations [ʀekʀiminɑsjɔ̃] *nfpl* remonstrations, complaints

recroqueviller [ʀəkʀɔkvije]: **se ~** *vi* (*feuilles*) to curl *ou* shrivel up; (*personne*) to huddle up

recrudescence [ʀəkʀydesɑ̃s] *nf* fresh outbreak

recrue [ʀəkʀy] *nf* recruit

recruter [ʀəkʀyte] *vt* to recruit

rectangle [ʀɛktɑ̃gl(ə)] *nm* rectangle; **rectangulaire** *adj* rectangular

recteur [ʀɛktœʀ] *nm* ≈ (regional) director of education (*BRIT*), ≈ state superintendent of education (*US*)

rectificatif [ʀɛktifikatif, -iv] *nm* correction

rectifier [ʀɛktifje] *vt* (*tracé, virage*) to straighten; (*calcul, adresse*) to correct; (*erreur, faute*) to rectify

rectiligne [ʀɛktiliɲ] *adj* straight; (*GÉOM*) rectilinear

reçu, e [ʀəsy] *pp de* **recevoir** ♦ *adj* (*admis, consacré*) accepted ♦ *nm* (*COMM*) receipt

recueil [ʀəkœj] *nm* collection

recueillir [ʀəkœjiʀ] *vt* to collect; (*voix, suffrages*) to win; (*accueillir: réfugiés, chat*) to take in; **se ~** *vi* to gather one's thoughts; to meditate

recul [ʀəkyl] *nm* retreat; recession; decline; (*d'arme à feu*) recoil, kick; **avoir un mouvement de ~** to recoil; **prendre du ~** to stand back

reculé, e [ʀəkyle] *adj* remote

reculer [ʀəkyle] *vi* to move back, back away; (*AUTO*) to reverse, back (up); (*fig*) to (be on the) decline; to be losing ground; (: *se dérober*) to shrink back ♦ *vt* to move back; to reverse, back (up); (*fig: possibilités, limites*) to extend; (: *date, décision*) to postpone

reculons [ʀəkylɔ̃]: **à ~** *adv* backwards

récupérer [ʀekypeʀe] *vt* to recover, get back; (*heures de travail*) to make up; (*déchets*) to salvage; (*délinquant etc*) to rehabilitate ♦ *vi* to recover

récurer [ʀekyʀe] *vt* to scour

récuser [ʀekyze] *vt* to challenge; **se ~** *vi*

to decline to give an opinion

reçut *vb voir* **recevoir**

recycler [ʀəsikle] *vt* (*SCOL*) to reorientate; (*employés*) to retrain; (*TECH*) to recycle

rédacteur, trice [ʀedaktœʀ, -tʀis] *nm/f* (*journaliste*) writer; subeditor; (*d'ouvrage de référence*) editor, compiler; **~ en chef** chief editor; **~ publicitaire** copywriter

rédaction [ʀedaksjɔ̃] *nf* writing; (*rédacteurs*) editorial staff; (*bureau*) editorial office(s); (*SCOL: devoir*) essay, composition

reddition [ʀedisjɔ̃] *nf* surrender

redemander [ʀədmɑ̃de] *vt* to ask again for; to ask for more of

redescendre [ʀədesɑ̃dʀ(ə)] *vi* to go back down ♦ *vt* (*pente etc*) to go down

redevable [ʀədvabl(ə)] *adj*: **être ~ de qch à qn** (*somme*) to owe sb sth; (*fig*) to be indebted to sb for sth

redevance [ʀədvɑ̃s] *nf* (*TÉL*) rental charge; (*TV*) licence fee

rédiger [ʀediʒe] *vt* to write; (*contrat*) to draw up

redire [ʀədiʀ] *vt* to repeat; **trouver à ~ à** to find fault with

redoublé, e [ʀəduble] *adj*: **à coups ~s** even harder, twice as hard

redoubler [ʀəduble] *vi* (*tempête, violence*) to intensify; (*SCOL*) to repeat a year; **~ de** to be twice as *+adjectif*

redoutable [ʀədutabl(ə)] *adj* formidable, fearsome

redouter [ʀədute] *vt* to fear; (*appréhender*) to dread

redresser [ʀədʀese] *vt* (*arbre, mât*) to set upright; (*pièce tordue*) to straighten out; (*situation, économie*) to put right; **se ~** *vi* (*objet penché*) to right itself; (*personne*) to sit (*ou* stand) up (straight)

réduction [ʀedyksjɔ̃] *nf* reduction

réduire [ʀeduiʀ] *vt* to reduce; (*prix, dépenses*) to cut, reduce; (*MÉD: fracture*) to set; **se ~ à** (*revenir à*) to boil down to; **se ~ en** (*se transformer en*) to be reduced to

réduit [ʀedui] *nm* tiny room; recess

rééducation [ʀeedykasjɔ̃] *nf* (*d'un*

membre) re-education; (*de délinquants, d'un blessé*) rehabilitation

réel, le [ʀeɛl] *adj* real

réellement [ʀeɛlmɑ̃] *adv* really

réévaluer [ʀeevalɥe] *vt* to revalue

réexpédier [ʀeɛkspedje] *vt* (*à l'envoyeur*) to return, send back; (*au destinataire*) to send on, forward

refaire [ʀəfɛʀ] *vt* (*faire de nouveau, recommencer*) to do again; (*réparer, restaurer*) to do up

réfection [ʀefɛksjɔ̃] *nf* repair

réfectoire [ʀefɛktwaʀ] *nm* refectory

référence [ʀefeʀɑ̃s] *nf* reference; ~s *nfpl* (*recommandations*) reference *sg*

référer [ʀefeʀe]: **se ~ à** *vt* to refer to; **en ~ à qn** to refer the matter to sb

réfléchi, e [ʀefleʃi] *adj* (*caractère*) thoughtful; (*action*) well-thought-out; (*LING*) reflexive

réfléchir [ʀefleʃiʀ] *vt* to reflect ♦ *vi* to think; ~ **à** *ou* **sur** to think about

reflet [ʀəflɛ] *nm* reflection; (*sur l'eau etc*) sheen *no pl*, glint

refléter [ʀəflete] *vt* to reflect; **se ~** *vi* to be reflected

réflexe [ʀeflɛks(ə)] *nm, adj* reflex

réflexion [ʀeflɛksjɔ̃] *nf* (*de la lumière etc, pensée*) reflection; (*fait de penser*) thought; (*remarque*) remark; ~ **faite, à la ~** on reflection

refluer [ʀəflye] *vi* to flow back; (*foule*) to surge back

reflux [ʀəfly] *nm* (*de la mer*) ebb

réforme [ʀefɔʀm(ə)] *nf* reform; (*REL*): **la R~** the Reformation

réformer [ʀefɔʀme] *vt* to reform; (*MIL*) to declare unfit for service

refouler [ʀəfule] *vt* (*envahisseurs*) to drive back; (*liquide*) to force back; (*fig*) to suppress; (*PSYCH*) to repress

réfractaire [ʀefʀaktɛʀ] *adj*: **être ~ à** to resist

refrain [ʀəfʀɛ̃] *nm* (*MUS*) refrain, chorus; (*air, fig*) tune

refréner [ʀəfʀene] *vt* to curb, check

réfréner [ʀefʀene] *vt* = **refréner**

réfrigérateur [ʀefʀiʒeʀatœʀ] *nm* refrigerator, fridge

refroidir [ʀəfʀwadiʀ] *vt* to cool ♦ *vi* to cool (down); **se ~** *vi* (*prendre froid*) to catch a chill; (*temps*) to get cooler *ou* colder; (*fig*) to cool (off); **refroidissement** *nm* (*grippe etc*) chill

refuge [ʀəfyʒ] *nm* refuge; (*pour piétons*) (traffic) island

réfugié, e [ʀefyʒje] *adj, nm/f* refugee

réfugier [ʀefyʒje]: **se ~** *vi* to take refuge

refus [ʀəfy] *nm* refusal; **ce n'est pas de ~** I won't say no, it's welcome

refuser [ʀəfyze] *vt* to refuse; (*SCOL: candidat*) to fail; ~ **qch à qn** to refuse sb sth; ~ **du monde** to have to turn people away; **se ~ à faire** to refuse to do

réfuter [ʀefyte] *vt* to refute

regagner [ʀəɡaɲe] *vt* (*argent, faveur*) to win back; (*lieu*) to get back to; ~ **le temps perdu** to make up (for) lost time

regain [ʀəɡɛ̃] *nm* (*renouveau*): **un ~ de** renewed +*nom*

régal [ʀeɡal] *nm* treat

régaler [ʀeɡale]: **se ~** *vi* to have a delicious meal; (*fig*) to enjoy o.s.

regard [ʀəɡaʀ] *nm* (*coup d'œil*) look, glance; (*expression*) look (in one's eye); **au ~ de** (*loi, morale*) from the point of view of; **en ~** (*vis à vis*) opposite; **en ~ de** in comparison with

regardant, e [ʀəɡaʀdɑ̃, -ɑ̃t] *adj*: **très/ peu ~** (**sur**) quite fussy/very free (about); (*économe*) very tight-fisted/quite generous (with)

regarder [ʀəɡaʀde] *vt* (*examiner, observer, lire*) to look at; (*film, télévision, match*) to watch; (*envisager: situation, avenir*) to view; (*considérer: son intérêt etc*) to be concerned with; (*être orienté vers*): ~ (**vers**) to face; (*concerner*) to concern ♦ *vi* to look; ~ **à** (*dépense*) to be fussy with *ou* over; ~ **qn/qch comme** to regard sb/sth as

régie [ʀeʒi] *nf* (*COMM, INDUSTRIE*) state-owned company; (*THÉÂTRE, CINÉMA*) production; (*RADIO, TV*) control room

regimber [ʀəʒɛ̃be] *vi* to balk, jib

régime [ʀeʒim] *nm* (*POL*) régime; (*ADMIN: carcéral, fiscal etc*) system; (*MÉD*) diet; (*TECH*) (engine) speed; (*fig*) rate, pace; (*de*

bananes, dattes) bunch; **se mettre au/ suivre un ~** to go on/be on a diet
régiment [ʀeʒimɑ̃] *nm* regiment; (*fig: fam*) **un ~ de** an army of
région [ʀeʒjɔ̃] *nf* region; **régional, e, aux** *adj* regional
régir [ʀeʒiʀ] *vt* to govern
régisseur [ʀeʒisœʀ] *nm* (*d'un domaine*) steward; (*CINÉMA, TV*) assistant director; (*THÉÂTRE*) stage manager
registre [ʀəʒistʀ(ə)] *nm* (*livre*) register; logbook; ledger; (*MUS, LING*) register
réglage [ʀeɡlaʒ] *nm* adjustment; tuning
règle [ʀɛɡl(ə)] *nf* (*instrument*) ruler; (*loi, prescription*) rule; **~s** *nfpl* (*PHYSIOL*) period *sg*; **en ~** (*papiers d'identité*) in order; **en ~ générale** as a (general) rule
réglé, e [ʀeɡle] *adj* well-ordered; steady; (*papier*) ruled; (*arrangé*) settled
règlement [ʀɛɡləmɑ̃] *nm* (*paiement*) settlement; (*arrêté*) regulation; (*règles, statuts*) regulations *pl*, rules *pl*; **~ de compte(s)** *nm* settling of old scores; **réglementaire** *adj* conforming to the regulations; (*tenue*) regulation *cpd*; **réglementer** [ʀɛɡləmɑ̃te] *vt* to regulate
régler [ʀeɡle] *vt* (*mécanisme, machine*) to regulate, adjust; (*moteur*) to tune; (*thermostat etc*) to set, adjust; (*conflit, facture*) to settle; (*fournisseur*) to settle up with
réglisse [ʀeɡlis] *nf* liquorice
règne [ʀɛɲ] *nm* (*d'un roi etc, fig*) reign; (*BIO*): **le ~ végétal/animal** the vegetable/animal kingdom
régner [ʀeɲe] *vi* (*roi*) to rule, reign; (*fig*) to reign
regorger [ʀəɡɔʀʒe] *vi*: **~ de** to overflow with, be bursting with
regret [ʀəɡʀɛ] *nm* regret; **à ~** with regret; **avec ~** regretfully; **être au ~ de devoir faire** to regret having to do
regrettable [ʀəɡʀɛtabl(ə)] *adj* regrettable
regretter [ʀəɡʀete] *vt* to regret; (*personne*) to miss; **je regrette** I'm sorry
regrouper [ʀəɡʀupe] *vt* (*grouper*) to group together; (*contenir*) to include, comprise; **se ~** *vi* to gather (together)

régulier, ière [ʀeɡylje, -jɛʀ] *adj* (*gén*) regular; (*vitesse, qualité*) steady; (*répartition, pression, paysage*) even; (*TRANSPORTS: ligne, service*) scheduled, regular; (*légal, réglementaire*) lawful, in order; (*fam: correct*) straight, on the level; **régulièrement** *adv* regularly; steadily; evenly; normally
rehausser [ʀəɔse] *vt* to heighten, raise
rein [ʀɛ̃] *nm* kidney; **~s** *nmpl* (*dos*) back *sg*
reine [ʀɛn] *nf* queen
reine-claude [ʀɛnklod] *nf* greengage
réintégrer [ʀeɛ̃teɡʀe] *vt* (*lieu*) to return to; (*fonctionnaire*) to reinstate
rejaillir [ʀəʒajiʀ] *vi* to splash up; **~ sur** to splash up onto; (*fig*) to rebound on; to fall upon
rejet [ʀəʒɛ] *nm* (*action, aussi MÉD*) rejection
rejeter [ʀəʒte] *vt* (*relancer*) to throw back; (*vomir*) to bring *ou* throw up; (*écarter*) to reject; (*déverser*) to throw out, discharge; **~ la responsabilité de qch sur qn** to lay the responsibility for sth at sb's door
rejoindre [ʀəʒwɛ̃dʀ(ə)] *vt* (*famille, régiment*) to rejoin, return to; (*lieu*) to get (back) to; (*suj: route etc*) to meet, join; (*rattraper*) to catch up (with); **se ~** *vi* to meet; **je te rejoins au café** I'll see *ou* meet you at the café
réjouir [ʀeʒwiʀ] *vt* to delight; **se ~** *vi* to be delighted; to rejoice; **réjouissances** *nfpl* (*joie*) rejoicing *sg*; (*fête*) festivities
relâche [ʀəlɑʃ]: **sans ~** without respite *ou* a break
relâché, e [ʀəlɑʃe] *adj* loose, lax
relâcher [ʀəlɑʃe] *vt* to release; (*étreinte*) to loosen; **se ~** *vi* to loosen; (*discipline*) to become slack *ou* lax; (*élève etc*) to slacken off
relais [ʀəlɛ] *nm* (*SPORT*): **(course de) ~** relay (race); **équipe de ~** shift team; (*SPORT*) relay team; **prendre le ~ (de)** to take over (from); **~ routier** ≈ transport café (*BRIT*), ≈ truck stop (*US*)
relancer [ʀəlɑ̃se] *vt* (*balle*) to throw back; (*moteur*) to restart; (*fig*) to boost,

revive; (*personne*): ~ **qn** to pester sb

relater [ʀəlate] *vt* to relate, recount

relatif, ive [ʀəlatif, -iv] *adj* relative

relation [ʀəlɑsjɔ̃] *nf* (*récit*) account, report; (*rapport*) relation(ship); **~s** *nfpl* (*rapports*) relations; relationship *sg*; (*connaissances*) connections; **être/entrer en ~(s) avec** to be/get in contact with

relaxer [ʀəlakse] *vt* to relax; (*JUR*) to discharge; **se** ~ *vi* to relax

relayer [ʀəleje] *vt* (*collaborateur, coureur etc*) to relieve; **se** ~ *vi* (*dans une activité*) to take it in turns

reléguer [ʀəlege] *vt* to relegate

relent(s) [ʀəlɑ̃] *nm(pl)* (foul) smell

relevé, e [ʀəlve] *adj* (*manches*) rolled-up; (*sauce*) highly-seasoned ♦ *nm* (*lecture*) reading; (*liste*) statement; list; (*facture*) account; ~ **de compte** bank statement

relève [ʀəlɛv] *nf* relief; relief team (*ou* troops *pl*); **prendre la** ~ to take over

relever [ʀəlve] *vt* (*statue, meuble*) to stand up again; (*personne tombée*) to help up; (*vitre, niveau de vie*) to raise; (*col*) to turn up; (*style, conversation*) to elevate; (*plat, sauce*) to season; (*sentinelle, équipe*) to relieve; (*fautes, points*) to pick out; (*constater: traces etc*) to find, pick up; (*répliquer à: remarque*) to react to, reply to; (: *défi*) to accept, take up; (*noter: adresse etc*) to take down, note; (: *plan*) to sketch; (: *cotes etc*) to plot; (*compteur*) to read; (*ramasser: cahiers*) to collect, take in; **se** ~ *vi* (*se remettre debout*) to get up; ~ **de** (*maladie*) to be recovering from; (*être du ressort de*) to be a matter for; (*ADMIN: dépendre de*) to come under; (*fig*) to pertain to; ~ **qn de** (*fonctions*) to relieve sb of; ~ **la tête** to look up; to hold up one's head

relief [ʀəljɛf] *nm* relief; **~s** *nmpl* (*restes*) remains; **mettre en** ~ (*fig*) to bring out, highlight

relier [ʀəlje] *vt* to link up; (*livre*) to bind; ~ **qch à** to link sth to

religieuse [ʀəliʒjøz] *nf* nun; (*gâteau*) cream bun

religieux, euse [ʀəliʒjø, -øz] *adj* religious ♦ *nm* monk

religion [ʀəliʒjɔ̃] *nf* religion; (*piété, dévotion*) faith

relire [ʀəliʀ] *vt* (*à nouveau*) to reread, read again; (*vérifier*) to read over

reliure [ʀəljyʀ] *nf* binding

reluire [ʀəlɥiʀ] *vi* to gleam

remanier [ʀəmanje] *vt* to reshape, recast; (*POL*) to reshuffle

remarquable [ʀəmaʀkabl(ə)] *adj* remarkable

remarque [ʀəmaʀk(ə)] *nf* remark; (*écrite*) note

remarquer [ʀəmaʀke] *vt* (*voir*) to notice; **se** ~ *vi* to be noticeable; **faire** ~ (**à qn**) **que** to point out (to sb) that; **faire** ~ **qch** (**à qn**) to point sth out (to sb); **remarquez, ...** mind you ...

remblai [ʀɑ̃blɛ] *nm* embankment

rembourrer [ʀɑ̃buʀe] *vt* to stuff; (*dossier, vêtement, souliers*) to pad

remboursement [ʀɑ̃buʀsəmɑ̃] *nm* repayment; **envoi contre** ~ cash on delivery; **rembourser** [ʀɑ̃buʀse] *vt* to pay back, repay

remède [ʀəmɛd] *nm* (*médicament*) medicine; (*traitement, fig*) remedy, cure

remémorer [ʀəmemɔʀe]: **se** ~ *vt* to recall, recollect

remerciements [ʀəmɛʀsimɑ̃] *nmpl* thanks

remercier [ʀəmɛʀsje] *vt* to thank; (*congédier*) to dismiss; ~ **qn de/d'avoir fait** to thank sb for/for having done

remettre [ʀəmɛtʀ(ə)] *vt* (*vêtement*): ~ **qch** to put sth back on; (*replacer*): ~ **qch quelque part** to put sth back somewhere; (*ajouter*): ~ **du sel/un sucre** to add more salt/another lump of sugar; (*ajourner*): ~ **qch (à)** to postpone sth (until); **se** ~ *vi* to get better, recover; **se** ~ **de** to recover from, get over; **s'en** ~ **à** to leave it (up) to; ~ **qch à qn** (*rendre, restituer*) to give sth back to sb; (*donner, confier: paquet, argent*) to hand over sth to sb, deliver sth to sb; (: *prix, décoration*) to present sb with sth

remise [ʀəmiz] *nf* delivery; presentation;

(*rabais*) discount; (*local*) shed; ~ **de peine** reduction of sentence; ~ **en jeu** (*FOOTBALL*) throw-in

remontant [rəmɔ̃tɑ̃] *nm* tonic, pick-me-up

remonte-pente [rəmɔ̃tpɑ̃t] *nm* ski-lift

remonter [rəmɔ̃te] *vi* to go back up; (*jupe*) to ride up ♦ *vt* (*pente*) to go up; (*fleuve*) to sail (*ou* swim *etc*) up; (*manches, pantalon*) to roll up; (*col*) to turn up; (*niveau, limite*) to raise; (*fig: personne*) to buck up; (*moteur, meuble*) to put back together, reassemble; (*montre, mécanisme*) to wind up; ~ **le moral à qn** to raise sb's spirits; ~ **à** (*dater de*) to date *ou* go back to

remontrance [rəmɔ̃trɑ̃s] *nf* reproof, reprimand

remontrer [rəmɔ̃tre] *vt* (*fig*): **en** ~ **à** to prove one's superiority over

remords [rəmɔr] *nm* remorse *no pl*; **avoir des** ~ to feel remorse

remorque [rəmɔrk(ə)] *nf* trailer; **être en** ~ to be on tow; **remorquer** *vt* to tow; **remorqueur** *nm* tug(boat)

remous [rəmu] *nm* (*d'un navire*) (back)wash *no pl*; (*de rivière*) swirl, eddy ♦ *nmpl* (*fig*) stir *sg*

remparts [rɑ̃par] *nmpl* walls, ramparts

remplaçant, e [rɑ̃plasɑ̃, -ɑ̃t] *nm/f* replacement, stand-in; (*THÉÂTRE*) understudy; (*SCOL*) supply teacher

remplacement [rɑ̃plasmɑ̃] *nm* replacement; (*job*) replacement work *no pl*

remplacer [rɑ̃plase] *vt* to replace; (*tenir lieu de*) to take the place of; ~ **qch/qn par** to replace sth/sb with

rempli, e [rɑ̃pli] *adj* (*emploi du temps*) full, busy; ~ **de** full of, filled with

remplir [rɑ̃plir] *vt* to fill (up); (*questionnaire*) to fill out *ou* up; (*obligations, fonction, condition*) to fulfil; **se** ~ *vi* to fill up

remporter [rɑ̃pɔrte] *vt* (*marchandise*) to take away; (*fig*) to win, achieve

remuant, e [rəmyɑ̃, -ɑ̃t] *adj* restless

remue-ménage [rəmymenaʒ] *nm inv* commotion

remuer [rəmye] *vt* to move; (*café,* *sauce*) to stir ♦ *vi* to move; **se** ~ *vi* to move

rémunérer [remynere] *vt* to remunerate

renard [rənar] *nm* fox

renchérir [rɑ̃ʃerir] *vi* (*fig*): ~ **(sur)** to add something (to)

rencontre [rɑ̃kɔ̃tr(ə)] *nf* meeting; (*imprévue*) encounter; **aller à la** ~ **de qn** to go and meet sb

rencontrer [rɑ̃kɔ̃tre] *vt* to meet; (*mot, expression*) to come across; (*difficultés*) to meet with; **se** ~ *vi* to meet; (*véhicules*) to collide

rendement [rɑ̃dmɑ̃] *nm* (*d'un travailleur, d'une machine*) output; (*d'une culture*) yield; (*d'un investissement*) return; **à plein** ~ at full capacity

rendez-vous [rɑ̃devu] *nm* (*rencontre*) appointment; (: *d'amoureux*) date; (*lieu*) meeting place; **donner** ~ **à qn** to arrange to meet sb; **avoir/prendre** ~ **(avec)** to have/make an appointment (with)

rendre [rɑ̃dr(ə)] *vt* (*livre, argent etc*) to give back, return; (*otages, visite etc*) to return; (*sang, aliments*) to bring up; (*exprimer, traduire*) to render; (*faire devenir*): ~ **qn célèbre/qch possible** to make sb famous/sth possible; **se** ~ *vi* (*capituler*) to surrender, give o.s. up; (*aller*): **se** ~ **quelque part** to go somewhere; **se** ~ **compte de qch** to realize sth

rênes [rɛn] *nfpl* reins

renfermé, e [rɑ̃fɛrme] *adj* (*fig*) withdrawn ♦ *nm*: **sentir le** ~ to smell stuffy

renfermer [rɑ̃fɛrme] *vt* to contain

renflement [rɑ̃fləmɑ̃] *nm* bulge

renflouer [rɑ̃flue] *vt* to refloat; (*fig*) to set back on its (*ou* his/her *etc*) feet

renfoncement [rɑ̃fɔ̃smɑ̃] *nm* recess

renforcer [rɑ̃fɔrse] *vt* to reinforce

renfort [rɑ̃fɔr]: ~**s** *nmpl* reinforcements; **à grand** ~ **de** with a great deal of

renfrogné, e [rɑ̃frɔɲe] *adj* sullen

rengaine [rɑ̃gɛn] (*péj*) *nf* old tune

renier [rənje] *vt* (*parents*) to disown, repudiate; (*foi*) to renounce

renifler [rənifle] *vi, vt* to sniff

renne [ʀɛn] *nm* reindeer *inv*
renom [ʀənɔ̃] *nm* reputation; (*célébrité*) renown; **renommé, e** *adj* celebrated, renowned; **renommée** *nf* fame
renoncer [ʀənɔ̃se]: ~ **à** *vt* to give up; ~ **à faire** to give up the idea of doing
renouer [ʀənwe] *vt*: ~ **avec** (*tradition*) to revive; (*habitude*) to take up again; ~ **avec qn** to take up with sb again
renouvelable [ʀ(ə)nuvlabl(ə)] *adj* (*énergie etc*) renewable
renouveler [ʀənuvle] *vt* to renew; (*exploit, méfait*) to repeat; **se ~** *vi* (*incident*) to recur, happen again; **renouvellement** *nm* renewal; recurrence
rénover [ʀenɔve] *vt* (*immeuble*) to renovate, do up; (*enseignement*) to reform; (*quartier*) to redevelop
renseignement [ʀɑ̃sɛɲmɑ̃] *nm* information *no pl*, piece of information; (**guichet des**) ~**s** information desk
renseigner [ʀɑ̃seɲe] *vt*: ~ **qn (sur)** to give information to sb (about); **se ~** *vi* to ask for information, make inquiries
rentabilité [ʀɑ̃tabilite] *nf* profitablity
rentable [ʀɑ̃tabl(ə)] *adj* profitable
rente [ʀɑ̃t] *nf* income; pension; government stock *ou* bond; **rentier, ière** *nm/f* person of private means
rentrée [ʀɑ̃tʀe] *nf*: ~ (**d'argent**) cash *no pl* coming in; **la ~ (des classes)** the start of the new school year
rentrer [ʀɑ̃tʀe] *vi* (*entrer de nouveau*) to go (*ou* come) back in; (*entrer*) to go (*ou* come) in; (*revenir chez soi*) to go (*ou* come) (back) home; (*air, clou: pénétrer*) to go in; (*revenu, argent*) to come in ♦ *vt* (*foins*) to bring in; (*véhicule*) to put away; (*chemise dans pantalon etc*) to tuck in; (*griffes*) to draw in; (*fig: larmes, colère etc*) to hold back; ~ **le ventre** to pull in one's stomach; ~ **dans** (*heurter*) to crash into; ~ **dans l'ordre** to be back to normal; ~ **dans ses frais** to recover one's expenses
renversant, e [ʀɑ̃vɛʀsɑ̃, -ɑ̃t] *adj* astounding
renverse [ʀɑ̃vɛʀs(ə)]: **à la ~** *adv* backwards

renverser [ʀɑ̃vɛʀse] *vt* (*faire tomber: chaise, verre*) to knock over, overturn; (*piéton*) to knock down; (*liquide, contenu*) to spill, upset; (*retourner*) to turn upside down; (*: ordre des mots etc*) to reverse; (*fig: gouvernement etc*) to overthrow; (*stupéfier*) to bowl over; **se ~** *vi* to fall over; to overturn; to spill
renvoi [ʀɑ̃vwa] *nm* (*référence*) cross-reference; (*éructation*) belch
renvoyer [ʀɑ̃vwaje] *vt* to send back; (*congédier*) to dismiss; (*lumière*) to reflect; (*son*) to echo; (*ajourner*): ~ **qch (à)** to put sth off *ou* postpone sth (until); ~ **qn à** (*fig*) to refer sb to
repaire [ʀəpɛʀ] *nm* den
répandre [ʀepɑ̃dʀ(ə)] *vt* (*renverser*) to spill; (*étaler, diffuser*) to spread; (*lumière*) to shed; (*chaleur, odeur*) to give off; **se ~** *vi* to spill; to spread; **répandu, e** *adj* (*opinion, usage*) widespread
réparation [ʀepaʀasjɔ̃] *nf* repair
réparer [ʀepaʀe] *vt* to repair; (*fig: offense*) to make up for, atone for; (*: oubli, erreur*) to put right
repartie [ʀəpaʀti] *nf* retort; **avoir de la ~** to be quick at repartee
repartir [ʀəpaʀtiʀ] *vi* to set off again; to leave again; (*fig*) to get going again; ~ **à zéro** to start from scratch (again)
répartir [ʀepaʀtiʀ] *vt* (*pour attribuer*) to share out; (*pour disperser, disposer*) to divide up; (*poids, chaleur*) to distribute; **se ~** *vt* (*travail, rôles*) to share out between themselves; **répartition** *nf* sharing out; dividing up; distribution
repas [ʀəpa] *nm* meal
repasser [ʀəpase] *vi* to come (*ou* go) back ♦ *vt* (*vêtement, tissu*) to iron; (*examen*) to retake, resit; (*film*) to show again; (*leçon, rôle: revoir*) to go over (again)
repêcher [ʀəpeʃe] *vt* (*noyé*) to recover the body of; (*candidat*) to pass (*by inflating marks*)
repentir [ʀəpɑ̃tiʀ] *nm* repentance; **se ~** *vi* to repent; **se ~ de** to repent of
répercussions [ʀepɛʀkysjɔ̃] *nfpl* (*fig*) repercussions
répercuter [ʀepɛʀkyte] *vt* (*information,*

hausse des prix) to pass on; **se ~** *vi* (*bruit*) to reverberate; (*fig*): **se ~ sur** to have repercussions on

repère [ʀəpɛʀ] *nm* mark; (*monument etc*) landmark

repérer [ʀəpeʀe] *vt* (*erreur, connaissance*) to spot; (*abri, ennemi*) to locate; **se ~** *vi* to find one's way about

répertoire [ʀepɛʀtwaʀ] *nm* (*liste*) (alphabetical) list; (*carnet*) index notebook; (*d'un artiste*) repertoire

répéter [ʀepete] *vt* to repeat; (*préparer*: *leçon*: *aussi vi*) to learn, go over; (*THÉÂTRE*) to rehearse; **se ~** *vi* (*redire*) to repeat o.s.; (*se reproduire*) to be repeated, recur

répétition [ʀepetisjɔ̃] *nf* repetition; (*THÉÂTRE*) rehearsal; **~ générale** final dress rehearsal

répit [ʀepi] *nm* respite

replet, ète [ʀəplɛ, -ɛt] *adj* chubby

replier [ʀəplije] *vt* (*rabattre*) to fold down *ou* over; **se ~** *vi* (*troupes, armée*) to withdraw, fall back

réplique [ʀeplik] *nf* (*repartie, fig*) reply; (*THÉÂTRE*) line; (*copie*) replica; **répliquer** [ʀeplike] *vi* to reply; (*riposter*) to retaliate

répondeur *nm*: **~ automatique** (*TÉL*) answering machine

répondre [ʀepɔ̃dʀ(ə)] *vi* to answer, reply; (*freins, mécanisme*) to respond; **~ à** to reply to, answer; (*affection, salut*) to return; (*provocation, suj: mécanisme etc*) to respond to; (*correspondre à: besoin*) to answer; (*: conditions*) to meet; (*: description*) to match; (*avec impertinence*): **~ à qn** to answer sb back; **~ de** to answer for

réponse [ʀepɔ̃s] *nf* answer, reply; **en ~ à** in reply to

reportage [ʀəpɔʀtaʒ] *nm* (*bref*) report; (*écrit: documentaire*) story; article; (*en direct*) commentary; (*genre, activité*): **le ~ reporting**

reporter¹ [ʀəpɔʀtɛʀ] *nm* reporter

reporter² [ʀəpɔʀte] *vt* (*total*): **~ qch sur** to carry sth forward *ou* over to; (*ajourner*): **~ qch (à)** to postpone sth

(*until*); (*transférer*): **~ qch sur** to transfer sth to; **se ~ à** (*époque*) to think back to; (*document*) to refer to

repos [ʀəpo] *nm* rest; (*fig*) peace (and quiet); peace of mind; (*MIL*): **~!** stand at ease!; **en ~** at rest; **de tout ~** safe

reposant, e [ʀəpozɑ̃, -ɑ̃t] *adj* restful

reposer [ʀəpoze] *vt* (*verre, livre*) to put down; (*délasser*) to rest; (*problème*) to reformulate ♦ *vi* (*liquide, pâte*) to settle, rest; **se ~** *vi* to rest; **se ~ sur qn** to rely on sb; **~ sur** to be built on; (*fig*) to rest on

repoussant, e [ʀəpusɑ̃, -ɑ̃t] *adj* repulsive

repousser [ʀəpuse] *vi* to grow again ♦ *vt* to repel, repulse; (*offre*) to turn down, reject; (*tiroir, personne*) to push back; (*différer*) to put back

reprendre [ʀəpʀɑ̃dʀ(ə)] *vt* (*prisonnier, ville*) to recapture; (*objet prêté, donné*) to take back; (*chercher*): **je viendrai te ~ à 4 h** I'll come and fetch you at 4; (*se resservir de*): **~ du pain/un œuf** to take (*ou* eat) more bread/another egg; (*firme, entreprise*) to take over; (*travail, promenade*) to resume; (*emprunter: argument, idée*) to take up, use; (*refaire: article etc*) to go over again; (*jupe etc*) to alter; (*émission, pièce*) to put on again; (*réprimander*) to tell off; (*corriger*) to correct ♦ *vi* (*classes, pluie*) to start (up) again; (*activités, travaux, combats*) to resume, start (up) again; (*affaires, industrie*) to pick up; (*dire*): **reprit-il** he went on; **se ~** *vi* (*se ressaisir*) to recover; **s'y ~** to make another attempt; **~ des forces** to recover one's strength; **~ courage** to take new heart; **~ la route** to set off again; **~ haleine** *ou* **son souffle** to get one's breath back

représailles [ʀəpʀezaj] *nfpl* reprisals

représentant, e [ʀəpʀezɑ̃tɑ̃, -ɑ̃t] *nm/f* representative

représentation [ʀəpʀezɑ̃tasjɔ̃] *nf* (*symbole, image*) representation; (*spectacle*) performance

représenter [ʀəpʀezɑ̃te] *vt* to represent; (*donner: pièce, opéra*) to perform; **se ~**

vt (*se figurer*) to imagine; to visualize

répression [ʀepʀesjɔ̃] *nf* (*voir réprimer*) suppression; repression

réprimer [ʀepʀime] *vt* (*émotions*) to suppress; (*peuple etc*) to repress

repris [ʀəpʀi] *nm*: ~ **de justice** ex-prisoner, ex-convict

reprise [ʀəpʀiz] *nf* (*recommencement*) resumption; recovery; (*TV*) repeat; (*CINÉMA*) rerun; (*AUTO*) acceleration *no pl*; (*COMM*) trade-in, part exchange; **à plusieurs ~s** on several occasions

repriser [ʀəpʀize] *vt* to darn; to mend

reproche [ʀəpʀɔʃ] *nm* (*remontrance*) reproach; **faire des ~s à qn** to reproach sb; **sans ~(s)** beyond reproach

reprocher [ʀəpʀɔʃe] *vt*: ~ **qch à qn** to reproach *ou* blame sb for sth; ~ **qch à** (*machine, théorie*) to have sth against

reproduction [ʀəpʀɔdyksjɔ̃] *nf* reproduction

reproduire [ʀəpʀɔdɥiʀ] *vt* to reproduce; **se** ~ *vi* (*BIO*) to reproduce; (*recommencer*) to recur, re-occur

reptile [ʀɛptil] *nm* reptile

repu, e [ʀəpy] *adj* satisfied, sated

républicain, e [ʀepyblikɛ̃, -ɛn] *adj*, *nm/f* republican

république [ʀepyblik] *nf* republic

répugnant, e [ʀepyɲɑ̃, -ɑ̃t] *adj* repulsive; loathsome

répugner [ʀepyɲe]: ~ **à** *vt* to repel *ou* disgust sb; ~ **à faire** to be loath *ou* reluctant to do

réputation [ʀepytasjɔ̃] *nf* reputation; **réputé, e** *adj* renowned

requérir [ʀəkeʀiʀ] *vt* (*nécessiter*) to require, call for; (*JUR: peine*) to call for, demand

requête [ʀəkɛt] *nf* request; (*JUR*) petition

requin [ʀəkɛ̃] *nm* shark

requis, e [ʀəki, -iz] *adj* required

R.E.R. *sigle m* (= *réseau express régional*) Greater Paris high-speed train service

rescapé, e [ʀɛskape] *nm/f* survivor

rescousse [ʀɛskus] *nf*: **aller à la** ~ **de qn** to go to sb's aid *ou* rescue

réseau, x [ʀezo] *nm* network

réservation [ʀezɛʀvɑsjɔ̃] *nf* booking, reservation

réserve [ʀezɛʀv(ə)] *nf* (*retenue*) reserve; (*entrepôt*) storeroom; (*restriction, d'Indiens*) reservation; (*de pêche, chasse*) preserve; **sous** ~ **de** subject to; **sans** ~ unreservedly; **de** ~ (*provisions etc*) in reserve

réservé, e [ʀezɛʀve] *adj* (*discret*) reserved; (*chasse, pêche*) private

réserver [ʀezɛʀve] *vt* (*gén*) to reserve; (*chambre, billet etc*) to book, reserve; (*garder*): ~ **qch pour/à** to keep *ou* save sth for; ~ **qch à qn** to reserve (*ou* book) sth for sb

réservoir [ʀezɛʀvwaʀ] *nm* tank

résidence [ʀezidɑ̃s] *nf* residence; **(en)** ~ **surveillée** (under) house arrest; ~ **secondaire** second home

résidentiel, le [ʀezidɑ̃sjɛl] *adj* residential

résider [ʀezide] *vi*: ~ **à/dans/en** to reside in; ~ **dans** (*fig*) to lie in

résidu [ʀezidy] *nm* residue *no pl*

résigner [ʀeziɲe]: **se** ~ *vi*: **se** ~ **(à qch/à faire)** to resign o.s. (to sth/to doing)

résilier [ʀezilje] *vt* to terminate

résistance [ʀezistɑ̃s] *nf* resistance; (*de réchaud, bouilloire: fil*) element

résistant, e [ʀezistɑ̃, -ɑ̃t] *adj* (*personne*) robust, tough; (*matériau*) strong, hardwearing

résister [ʀeziste] *vi* to resist; ~ **à** (*assaut, tentation*) to resist; (*effort, souffrance*) to withstand; (*désobéir à*) to stand up to, oppose

résolu, e [ʀezɔly] *pp de* **résoudre** ♦ *adj*: **être** ~ **à qch/faire** to be set upon sth/doing

résolution [ʀezɔlysjɔ̃] *nf* solving; (*fermeté, décision*) resolution

résolve *etc vb voir* **résoudre**

résonner [ʀezɔne] *vi* (*cloche, pas*) to reverberate, resound; (*salle*) to be resonant; ~ **de** to resound with

résorber [ʀezɔʀbe]: **se** ~ *vi* (*fig*) to be reduced; to be absorbed

résoudre [ʀezudʀ(ə)] *vt* to solve; **se** ~ **à faire** to bring o.s. to do

respect [Rɛspɛ] nm respect; **tenir en ~** to keep at bay

respecter [Rɛspɛkte] vt to respect

respectueux, euse [Rɛspɛktɥø, -øz] adj respectful; **~ de** respectful of

respiration [RɛspiRasjɔ̃] nf breathing no pl; **~ artificielle** artificial respiration

respirer [RɛspiRe] vi to breathe; (fig) to get one's breath; to breathe again ♦ vt to breathe (in), inhale; (manifester: santé, calme etc) to exude

resplendir [RɛsplɑdiR] vi to shine; (fig): **~ (de)** to be radiant (with)

responsabilité [Rɛspɔ̃sabilite] nf responsibility; (légale) liability

responsable [Rɛspɔ̃sabl(ə)] adj responsible ♦ nm/f (du ravitaillement etc) person in charge; (de parti, syndicat) official; **~ de** responsible for; (chargé de) in charge of, responsible for

ressaisir [RəseziR]: **se ~** vi to regain one's self-control

ressasser [Rəsase] vt to keep going over

ressemblance [Rəsɑ̃blɑ̃s] nf resemblance, similarity, likeness

ressemblant, e [Rəsɑ̃blɑ̃, -ɑ̃t] adj (portrait) lifelike, true to life

ressembler [Rəsɑ̃ble]: **~ à** vt to be like; to resemble; (visuellement) to look like; **se ~** vi to be (ou look) alike

ressemeler [Rəsəmle] vt to (re)sole

ressentiment [Rəsɑ̃timɑ̃] nm resentment

ressentir [Rəsɑ̃tiR] vt to feel; **se ~ de** to feel (ou show) the effects of

resserrer [RəseRe] vt (nœud, boulon) to tighten (up); (fig: liens) to strengthen; **se ~** vi (vallée) to narrow

resservir [RəseRviR] vi to do ou serve again ♦ vt: **~ qn (d'un plat)** to give sb a second helping (of a dish)

ressort [RəsɔR] nm (pièce) spring; (force morale) spirit; (recours): **en dernier ~** as a last resort; (compétence): **être du ~ de** to fall within the competence of

ressortir [RəsɔRtiR] vi to go (ou come) out (again); (contraster) to stand out; **~ de** to emerge from; **faire ~** (fig: souligner) to bring out

ressortissant, e [RəsɔRtisɑ̃, -ɑ̃t] nm/f national

ressource [RəsuRs(ə)] nf: **avoir la ~ de** to have the possibility of; **~s** nfpl (moyens) resources; **leur seule ~ était de** the only course open to them was to

ressusciter [Resysite] vt (fig) to revive, bring back ♦ vi to rise (from the dead)

restant, e [Rɛstɑ̃, -ɑ̃t] adj remaining ♦ nm: **le ~ (de)** the remainder (of); **un ~ de** (de trop) some left-over

restaurant [RɛstɔRɑ̃] nm restaurant

restauration [RɛstɔRasjɔ̃] nf restoration; (hôtellerie) catering; **~ rapide** fast food

restaurer [RɛstɔRe] vt to restore; **se ~** vi to have something to eat

reste [Rɛst(ə)] nm (restant): **le ~ (de)** the rest (of); (de trop): **un ~ (de)** some left-over; (vestige): **un ~ de** a remnant ou last trace of; (MATH) remainder; **~s** nmpl (nourriture) left-overs; (d'une cité etc, dépouille mortelle) remains; **du ~, au ~** besides, moreover

rester [Rɛste] vi to stay, remain; (subsister) to remain, be left; (durer) to last, live on ♦ vb impers: **il reste du pain/2 œufs** there's some bread/there are 2 eggs left (over); **il me reste assez de temps** I have enough time left; **ce qui reste à faire** what remains to be done; **restons-en là** let's leave it at that

restituer [Rɛstitɥe] vt (objet, somme): **~ qch (à qn)** to return sth (to sb); (TECH) to release; (: son) to reproduce

restoroute [RɛstɔRut] nm motorway (BRIT) ou highway (US) restaurant

restreindre [RɛstRɛ̃dR(ə)] vt to restrict, limit

restriction [RɛstRiksjɔ̃] nf restriction

résultat [Rezylta] nm result; (d'élection etc) results pl

résulter [Rezylte]: **~ de** vt to result from, be the result of

résumé [Rezyme] nm summary, résumé

résumer [Rezyme] vt (texte) to summarize; (récapituler) to sum up; **se ~ à** to come down to

résurrection [RezyRɛksjɔ̃] nf resurrection; (fig) revival

rétablir [retabliʀ] *vt* to restore, re-establish; **se ~** *vi* (*guérir*) to recover; (*silence, calme*) to return, be restored; **rétablissement** *nm* restoring; recovery; (*SPORT*) pull-up

retaper [ʀətape] *vt* (*maison, voiture etc*) to do up; (*fam: revigorer*) to buck up; (*redactylographier*) to retype

retard [ʀətaʀ] *nm* (*d'une personne attendue*) lateness *no pl*; (*sur l'horaire, un programme*) delay; (*fig: scolaire, mental etc*) backwardness; **en ~ (de 2 heures)** (2 hours) late; **avoir du ~** to be late; (*sur un programme*) to be behind (schedule); **prendre du ~** (*train, avion*) to be delayed; (*montre*) to lose (time); **sans ~** without delay

retardement [ʀətaʀdəmɑ̃]: **à ~** *adj* delayed action *cpd*; **bombe à ~** time bomb

retarder [ʀətaʀde] *vt* (*sur un horaire*): **~ qn (d'une heure)** to delay sb (an hour); (*départ, date*): **~ qch (de 2 jours)** to put sth back (2 days), delay sth (for *ou* by 2 days); (*horloge*) to put back ♦ *vi* (*montre*) to be slow; to lose (time)

retenir [ʀətniʀ] *vt* (*garder, retarder*) to keep, detain; (*maintenir: objet qui glisse, fig: colère, larmes*) to hold back; (*: objet suspendu*) to hold; (*fig: empêcher d'agir*): **~ qn (de faire)** to hold sb back (from doing); (*se rappeler*) to retain; (*réserver*) to reserve; (*accepter*) to accept; (*prélever*): **~ qch (sur)** to deduct sth (from); **se ~** *vi* (*se raccrocher*): **se ~ à** to hold onto; (*se contenir*): **se ~ de faire** to restrain o.s. from doing; **~ son souffle** to hold one's breath

retentir [ʀətɑ̃tiʀ] *vi* to ring out; (*salle*): **~ de** to ring *ou* resound with

retentissant, e [ʀətɑ̃tisɑ̃, -ɑ̃t] *adj* resounding; (*fig*) impact-making

retentissement [ʀətɑ̃tismɑ̃] *nm* repercussion; effect, impact; stir

retenu, e *adj* (*place*) reserved; (*personne: empêché*) held up

retenue [ʀətny] *nf* (*prélèvement*) deduction; (*SCOL*) detention; (*modération*) (self-)restraint; (*réserve*) reserve, reticence

réticence [ʀetisɑ̃s] *nf* hesitation, reluctance *no pl*

rétine [ʀetin] *nf* retina

retiré, e [ʀətiʀe] *adj* secluded; remote

retirer [ʀətiʀe] *vt* to withdraw; (*vêtement, lunettes*) to take off, remove; (*extraire*): **~ qch de** to take sth out of, remove sth from; (*reprendre: bagages, billets*) to collect, pick up

retombées [ʀətɔ̃be] *nfpl* (*radioactives*) fallout *sg*; (*fig*) fallout; spin-offs

retomber [ʀətɔ̃be] *vi* (*à nouveau*) to fall again; (*atterrir: après un saut etc*) to land; (*tomber, redescendre*) to fall back; (*pendre*) to fall, hang (down); (*échoir*): **~ sur qn** to fall on sb

rétorquer [ʀetɔʀke] *vt*: **~ (à qn) que** to retort (to sb) that

retors, e [ʀətɔʀ, -ɔʀs(ə)] *adj* wily

retoucher [ʀətuʃe] *vt* (*photographie*) to touch up; (*texte, vêtement*) to alter

retour [ʀətuʀ] *nm* return; **au ~** when we (*ou* they *etc*) get (*ou* got) back; (*en route*) on the way back; **être de ~ (de)** to be back (from); **par ~ du courrier** by return of post

retourner [ʀətuʀne] *vt* (*dans l'autre sens: matelas, crêpe, foin, terre*) to turn (over); (*: caisse*) to turn upside down; (*: sac, vêtement*) to turn inside out; (*émouvoir: personne*) to shake; (*renvoyer, restituer*): **~ qch à qn** to return sth to sb ♦ *vi* (*aller, revenir*): **~ quelque part/à** to go back *ou* return somewhere/to; **se ~** *vi* to turn over; (*tourner la tête*) to turn round; **~ à** (*état, activité*) to return to, go back to; **se ~ contre** (*fig*) to turn against; **savoir de quoi il retourne** to know what it is all about

retracer [ʀətʀase] *vt* to relate, recount

retrait [ʀətʀɛ] *nm* (*voir retirer*) withdrawal; collection; **en ~** set back; **~ du permis (de conduire)** disqualification from driving (*BRIT*), revocation of driver's license (*US*)

retraite [ʀətʀɛt] *nf* (*d'une armée, REL, refuge*) retreat; (*d'un employé*) retirement; (*revenu*) pension; **prendre sa ~** to retire; ~ **anticipée** early retirement; **re-traité, e** *adj* retired ♦ *nm/f* pensioner

retrancher [ʀətʀɑ̃ʃe] *vt* (*passage, détails*) to take out, remove; (*nombre, somme*) : ~ **qch de** to take *ou* deduct sth from; (*couper*) to cut off; **se ~ derrière/dans** to take refuge behind/in

retransmettre [ʀətʀɑ̃smɛtʀ(ə)] *vt* (*RADIO*) to broadcast; (*TV*) to show

rétrécir [ʀetʀesiʀ] *vt* (*vêtement*) to take in ♦ *vi* to shrink; **se ~** *vi* to narrow

rétribution [ʀetʀibysjɔ̃] *nf* payment

rétro [ʀetʀo] *adj inv*: **la mode ~** the nostalgia vogue

rétrograde [ʀetʀɔgʀad] *adj* reactionary, backward-looking

rétrograder [ʀetʀɔgʀade] *vi* (*économie*) to regress; (*AUTO*) to change down

rétroprojecteur [ʀetʀɔpʀɔʒɛktœʀ] *nm* overhead projector

rétrospective [ʀetʀɔspɛktiv] *nf* retrospective exhibition/season; **rétrospectivement** *adv* in retrospect

retrousser [ʀətʀuse] *vt* to roll up

retrouvailles [ʀətʀuvaj] *nfpl* reunion *sg*

retrouver [ʀətʀuve] *vt* (*fugitif, objet perdu*) to find; (*occasion*) to find again; (*calme, santé*) to regain; (*revoir*) to see again; (*rejoindre*) to meet (again), join; **se ~** *vi* to meet; (*s'orienter*) to find one's way; **se ~ quelque part** to find o.s. somewhere; **s'y ~** (*rentrer dans ses frais*) to break even

rétroviseur [ʀetʀɔvizœʀ] *nm* (rear-view) mirror

réunion [ʀeynjɔ̃] *nf* bringing together; joining; (*séance*) meeting

réunir [ʀeyniʀ] *vt* (*convoquer*) to call together; (*rassembler*) to gather together; (*cumuler*) to combine; (*rapprocher*) to bring together (again), reunite; (*rattacher*) to join (together); **se ~** *vi* (*se rencontrer*) to meet

réussi, e [ʀeysi] *adj* successful

réussir [ʀeysiʀ] *vi* to succeed, be successful; (*à un examen*) to pass; (*plante, culture*) to thrive, do well ♦ *vt* to make a success of; ~ **à faire** to succeed in doing; ~ **à qn** to go right for sb; (*ali-*

ment) to agree with sb

réussite [ʀeysit] *nf* success; (*CARTES*) patience

revaloir [ʀəvalwaʀ] *vt*: **je vous revaudrai cela** I'll repay you some day; (*en mal*) I'll pay you back for this

revaloriser [ʀəvalɔʀize] *vt* (*monnaie*) to revalue; (*salaires*) to raise the level of

revanche [ʀəvɑ̃ʃ] *nf* revenge; **en ~** on the other hand

rêve [ʀɛv] *nm* dream; (*activité psychique*): **le ~** dreaming

revêche [ʀəvɛʃ] *adj* surly, sour-tempered

réveil [ʀevɛj] *nm* (*d'un dormeur*) waking up *no pl*; (*fig*) awakening; (*pendule*) alarm (clock); (*MIL*) reveille; **au ~** on waking (up)

réveille-matin [ʀevɛjmatɛ̃] *nm inv* alarm clock

réveiller [ʀeveje] *vt* (*personne*) to wake up; (*fig*) to awaken, revive; **se ~** *vi* to wake up; (*fig*) to reawaken

réveillon [ʀevɛjɔ̃] *nm* Christmas Eve; (*de la Saint-Sylvestre*) New Year's Eve; **réveillonner** *vi* to celebrate Christmas Eve (*ou* New Year's Eve)

révélateur, trice [ʀevelatœʀ, -tʀis] *adj*: ~ **(de qch)** revealing (sth) ♦ *nm* (*PHOTO*) developer

révéler [ʀevele] *vt* (*gén*) to reveal; (*faire connaître au public*): ~ **qn/qch** to make sb/sth widely known, bring sb/sth to the public's notice; **se ~** *vi* to be revealed, reveal itself ♦ *vb +attrib* to prove (to be), to be revealed, reveal itself

revenant, e [ʀəvnɑ̃, -ɑ̃t] *nm/f* ghost

revendeur, euse [ʀəvɑ̃dœʀ, -øz] *nm/f* (*détaillant*) retailer; (*d'occasions*) secondhand dealer

revendication [ʀəvɑ̃dikasjɔ̃] *nf* claim, demand; **journée de ~** day of action

revendiquer [ʀəvɑ̃dike] *vt* to claim, demand; (*responsabilité*) to claim

revendre [ʀəvɑ̃dʀ(ə)] *vt* (*d'occasion*) to resell; (*détailler*) to sell; **à ~** (*en abondance*) to spare

revenir [ʀəvniʀ] *vi* to come back; (*CULIN*): **faire ~** to brown; (*coûter*): ~ **cher/à 100**

F (à qn) to cost (sb) a lot/100 F; ~ à (*études, projet*) to return to, go back to; (*équivaloir à*) to amount to; ~ à qn (*part, honneur*) to go to sb, be sb's; (*souvenir, nom*) to come back to sb; ~ de (*fig: maladie, étonnement*) to recover from; ~ sur (*question, sujet*) to go back over; (*engagement*) to go back on; ~ à la charge to return to the attack; ~ à soi to come round; n'en pas ~: je n'en reviens pas I can't get over it; ~ sur ses pas to retrace one's steps; cela revient à dire que/au même it amounts to saying that/the same thing

revenu [Rǝvny] nm income; (*de l'État*) revenue; (*d'un capital*) yield; ~s nmpl income *sg*

rêver [Reve] vi, vt to dream; ~ de/à to dream of

réverbère [ReverbeR] nm street lamp *ou* light

réverbérer [RevɛRbeRe] vt to reflect

révérence [ReveRɑ̃s] nf (*salut*) bow; (: *de femme*) curtsey

rêverie [RevRi] nf daydreaming no pl, daydream

revers [Rǝvɛʀ] nm (*de feuille, main*) back; (*d'étoffe, médaille*) back, reverse; (TENNIS, PING-PONG) backhand; (*de veston*) lapel; (*de pantalon*) turn-up; (*fig: échec*) setback

revêtement [Rǝvɛtmɑ̃] nm (*de paroi*) facing; (*des sols*) flooring; (*de chaussée*) surface; (*de tuyau etc: enduit*) coating

revêtir [RǝvetiR] vt (*habit*) to don, put on; (*fig*) to take on; ~ qn de to endow *ou* invest sb with; ~ qch de to cover sth with; (*fig*) to cloak sth in

rêveur, euse [RevœR, -øz] adj dreamy ♦ nm/f dreamer

revient [Rǝvjɛ̃] vb voir revenir

revigorer [RǝvigɔRe] vt to invigorate, brace up; to revive, buck up

revirement [RǝviRmɑ̃] nm change of mind; (*d'une situation*) reversal

réviser [Revize] vt (*texte, SCOL: matière*) to revise; (*machine, installation, moteur*) to overhaul, service; (JUR: *procès*) to review

révision [Revizjɔ̃] nf revision; auditing no pl; overhaul; servicing no pl; review; la ~ des 10 000 km (AUTO) the 10,000 km service

revivre [RǝvivR(ǝ)] vi (*reprendre des forces*) to come alive again; (*traditions*) to be revived ♦ vt (*épreuve, moment*) to relive

revoir [RǝvwaR] vt to see again; (*réviser*) to revise ♦ nm: au ~ goodbye

révoltant, e [Revɔltɑ̃, -ɑ̃t] adj revolting; appalling

révolte [Revɔlt(ǝ)] nf rebellion, revolt

révolter [Revɔlte] vt to revolt; to outrage, appal; se ~ (contre) to rebel (against)

révolu, e [Revɔly] adj past; (ADMIN): âgé de 18 ans ~s over 18 years of age; après 3 ans ~s when 3 full years have passed

révolution [Revɔlysjɔ̃] nf revolution; révolutionnaire adj, nm/f revolutionary

revolver [RevɔlvɛR] nm gun; (*à barillet*) revolver

révoquer [Revɔke] vt (*fonctionnaire*) to dismiss; (*arrêt, contrat*) to revoke

revue [Rǝvy] nf (*inventaire, examen, MIL*) review; (*périodique*) review, magazine; (*de music-hall*) variety show; passer en ~ to review; to go through

rez-de-chaussée [Redʃose] nm inv ground floor

RF *sigle* = République française

Rhin [Rɛ̃] nm: le ~ the Rhine

rhinocéros [RinɔseRɔs] nm rhinoceros

Rhône [Ron] nm: le ~ the Rhone

rhubarbe [Rybarb(ǝ)] nf rhubarb

rhum [Rɔm] nm rum

rhumatisme [Rymatism(ǝ)] nm rheumatism no pl

rhume [Rym] nm cold; ~ de cerveau head cold; le ~ des foins hay fever

ri [Ri] pp de rire

riant, e [Rjɑ̃, -ɑ̃t] adj smiling, cheerful

ricaner [Rikane] vi (*avec méchanceté*) to snigger; (*bêtement*) to giggle

riche [Riʃ] adj (*gén*) rich; (*personne, pays*) rich, wealthy; ~ en rich in; ~ de full of; rich in; richesse nf wealth; (*fig*) richness; richesses nfpl (*ressources, ar-*

gent) wealth *sg*; (*fig*: *trésors*) treasures
ricin [ʀisɛ̃] *nm*: **huile de ~** castor oil
ricocher [ʀikɔʃe] *vi*: **~ (sur)** to rebound (off); (*sur l'eau*) to bounce (on *ou* off)
ricochet [ʀikɔʃe] *nm*: **faire des ~s** to skip stones; **par ~** on the rebound; (*fig*) as an indirect result
rictus [ʀiktys] *nm* grin; (snarling) grimace
ride [ʀid] *nf* wrinkle; (*fig*) ripple
rideau, x [ʀido] *nm* curtain; (*POL*): **le ~ de fer** the Iron Curtain
rider [ʀide] *vt* to wrinkle; (*eau*) to ripple; **se ~** *vi* to become wrinkled
ridicule [ʀidikyl] *adj* ridiculous ♦ *nm*: **le ~** ridicule; **ridiculiser: se ridiculiser** *vi* to make a fool of o.s.

MOT-CLÉ
---

rien [ʀjɛ̃] *pron* 1: **(ne) ... ~** nothing; *tournure negative +* anything; **qu'est-ce que vous avez? - ~** what have you got? - nothing; **il n'a ~ dit/fait** he said/did nothing; he hasn't said/done anything; **il n'a ~** (*n'est pas blessé*) he's all right; **de ~!** not at all!
2 (*quelque chose*): **a-t-il jamais ~ fait pour nous?** has he ever done anything for us?
3: **~ de**: **~ d'intéressant** nothing interesting; **~ d'autre** nothing else; **~ du tout** nothing at all
4: **~ que** just, only; nothing but; **~ que pour lui faire plaisir** only *ou* just to please him; **~ que la vérité** nothing but the truth; **~ que cela** that alone
♦ *nm*: **un petit ~** (*cadeau*) a little something; **des ~s** trivia *pl*; **un ~ de** a hint of; **en un ~ de temps** in no time at all

rieur, euse [ʀjœʀ, -øz] *adj* cheerful
rigide [ʀiʒid] *adj* stiff; (*fig*) rigid; strict
rigole [ʀigɔl] *nf* (*conduit*) channel; (*filet d'eau*) rivulet
rigoler [ʀigɔle] *vi* (*rire*) to laugh; (*s'amuser*) to have (some) fun; (*plaisanter*) to be joking *ou* kidding
rigolo, ote [ʀigɔlo, -ɔt] (*fam*) *adj* funny ♦ *nm/f* comic; (*péj*) fraud, phoney

rigoureux, euse [ʀiguʀø, -øz] *adj* (*morale*) rigorous, strict; (*personne*) stern, strict; (*climat, châtiment*) rigorous, harsh; (*interdiction, neutralité*) strict
rigueur [ʀigœʀ] *nf* rigour; strictness; harshness; **être de ~** to be the rule; **à la ~** at a pinch; possibly; **tenir ~ à qn de qch** to hold sth against sb
rime [ʀim] *nf* rhyme
rinçage [ʀɛ̃saʒ] *nm* rinsing (out); (*opération*) rinse
rincer [ʀɛ̃se] *vt* to rinse; (*récipient*) to rinse out
ring [ʀiŋ] *nm* (boxing) ring
ringard, e [ʀɛ̃gaʀ, -aʀd(ə)] *adj* old-fashioned
rions *vb voir* **rire**
riposter [ʀipɔste] *vi* to retaliate ♦ *vt*: **~ que** to retort that; **~ à** to counter; to reply to
rire [ʀiʀ] *vi* to laugh; (*se divertir*) to have fun ♦ *nm* laugh; **le ~** laughter; **~ de** to laugh at; **pour ~** (*pas sérieusement*) for a joke *ou* a laugh
risée [ʀize] *nf*: **être la ~ de** to be the laughing stock of
risible [ʀizibl(ə)] *adj* laughable
risque [ʀisk(ə)] *nm* risk; **le ~** danger; **à ses ~s et périls** at his own risk
risqué, e [ʀiske] *adj* risky; (*plaisanterie*) risqué, daring
risquer [ʀiske] *vt* to risk; (*allusion, question*) to venture, hazard; **ça ne risque rien** it's quite safe; **~ de**: **il risque de se tuer** he could get himself killed; **ce qui risque de se produire** what might *ou* could well happen; **il ne risque pas de recommencer** there's no chance of him doing that again; **se ~ à faire** (*tenter*) to venture *ou* dare to do
rissoler [ʀisɔle] *vi, vt*: **(faire) ~** to brown
ristourne [ʀistuʀn(ə)] *nf* rebate
rite [ʀit] *nm* rite; (*fig*) ritual
rivage [ʀivaʒ] *nm* shore
rival, e, aux [ʀival, -o] *adj, nm/f* rival
rivaliser [ʀivalize] *vi*: **~ avec** to rival, vie with; (*être comparable*) to hold its own against, compare with
rivalité [ʀivalite] *nf* rivalry

rive [ʀiv] *nf* shore; (*de fleuve*) bank
river [ʀive] *vt* (*clou, pointe*) to clinch; (*plaques*) to rivet together
riverain, e [ʀivʀɛ̃, -ɛn] *nm/f* riverside (*ou* lakeside) resident; local resident
rivet [ʀivɛ] *nm* rivet
rivière [ʀivjɛʀ] *nf* river
rixe [ʀiks(ə)] *nf* brawl, scuffle
riz [ʀi] *nm* rice
RMI *sigle m* (= *revenu minimum d'insertion*) ≈ income support (*BRIT*), welfare (*US*)
R.N. *sigle f* = **route nationale**
robe [ʀɔb] *nf* dress; (*de juge, d'ecclésiastique*) robe; (*de professeur*) gown; (*pelage*) coat; ~ **de chambre** dressing gown; ~ **de grossesse** maternity dress; ~ **de soirée/de mariée** evening/wedding dress
robinet [ʀɔbinɛ] *nm* tap
robot [ʀɔbo] *nm* robot
robuste [ʀɔbyst(ə)] *adj* robust, sturdy
roc [ʀɔk] *nm* rock
rocaille [ʀɔkaj] *nf* loose stones *pl*; rocky *ou* stony ground; (*jardin*) rockery, rock garden
roche [ʀɔʃ] *nf* rock
rocher [ʀɔʃe] *nm* rock
rocheux, euse [ʀɔʃø, -øz] *adj* rocky
rodage [ʀɔdaʒ] *nm*: **en** ~ running in
roder [ʀɔde] *vt* (*AUTO*) to run in
rôder [ʀode] *vi* to roam about; (*de façon suspecte*) to lurk (about *ou* around); **rôdeur, euse** *nm/f* prowler
rogne [ʀɔɲ] *nf*: **être en** ~ to be in a temper
rogner [ʀɔɲe] *vt* to clip; ~ **sur** (*fig*) to cut down *ou* back on
rognons [ʀɔɲɔ̃] *nmpl* kidneys
roi [ʀwa] *nm* king; **le jour** *ou* **la fête des R~s, les R~s** Twelfth Night
roitelet [ʀwatlɛ] *nm* wren
rôle [ʀol] *nm* role; (*contribution*) part
romain, e [ʀɔmɛ̃, -ɛn] *adj, nm/f* Roman
roman, e [ʀɔmã, -an] *adj* (*ARCHIT*) Romanesque ♦ *nm* novel; ~ **d'espionnage** spy novel *ou* story; ~ **photo** romantic picture story
romance [ʀɔmãs] *nf* ballad

romancer [ʀɔmãse] *vt* to make into a novel; to romanticize
romancier, ière [ʀɔmãsje, -jɛʀ] *nm/f* novelist
romanesque [ʀɔmanɛsk(ə)] *adj* (*fantastique*) fantastic; storybook *cpd*; (*sentimental*) romantic
roman-feuilleton [ʀɔmãfœjtɔ̃] *nm* serialized novel
romanichel, le [ʀɔmaniʃɛl] *nm/f* gipsy
romantique [ʀɔmãtik] *adj* romantic
romarin [ʀɔmaʀɛ̃] *nm* rosemary
rompre [ʀɔ̃pʀ(ə)] *vt* to break; (*entretien, fiançailles*) to break off ♦ *vi* (*fiancés*) to break it off; **se** ~ *vi* to break; (*MÉD*) to burst, rupture
rompu, e [ʀɔ̃py] *adj*: ~ **à** with wide experience of; inured to
ronces [ʀɔ̃s] *nfpl* brambles
ronchonner [ʀɔ̃ʃɔne] (*fam*) *vi* to grouse, grouch
rond, e [ʀɔ̃, ʀɔ̃d] *adj* round; (*joues, mollets*) well-rounded; (*fam: ivre*) tight ♦ *nm* (*cercle*) ring; (*fam: sou*): **je n'ai plus un** ~ I haven't a penny left; **en** ~ (*s'asseoir, danser*) in a ring; **ronde** *nf* (*gén: de surveillance*) rounds *pl*, patrol; (*danse*) round (dance); (*MUS*) semibreve (*BRIT*), whole note (*US*); **à la ronde** (*alentour*): **à la ronde à 10 km** for 10 km round; **rondelet, te** *adj* plump
rondelle [ʀɔ̃dɛl] *nf* (*TECH*) washer; (*tranche*) slice, round
rondement [ʀɔ̃dmã] *adv* briskly; frankly
rondin [ʀɔ̃dɛ̃] *nm* log
rond-point [ʀɔ̃pwɛ̃] *nm* roundabout
ronflant, e [ʀɔ̃flã, -ãt] (*péj*) *adj* high-flown, grand
ronfler [ʀɔ̃fle] *vi* to snore; (*moteur, poêle*) to hum; to roar
ronger [ʀɔ̃ʒe] *vt* to gnaw (at); (*suj: vers, rouille*) to eat into; **se** ~ **les sangs** to worry o.s. sick; **se** ~ **les ongles** to bite one's nails; **rongeur** *nm* rodent
ronronner [ʀɔ̃ʀɔne] *vi* to purr
roquet [ʀɔkɛ] *nm* nasty little lap-dog
rosace [ʀozas] *nf* (*vitrail*) rose window
rosbif [ʀɔsbif] *nm*: **du** ~ roasting beef;

(*cuit*) roast beef; **un ~** a joint of beef

rose [ʀoz] *nf* rose ♦ *adj* pink

rosé, e [ʀoze] *adj* pinkish; **(vin)** ~ rosé

roseau, x [ʀozo] *nm* reed

rosée [ʀoze] *nf* dew

roseraie [ʀozʀɛ] *nf* rose garden

rosier [ʀozje] *nm* rosebush, rose tree

rosse [ʀɔs] *nf* (*péj: cheval*) nag ♦ *adj* nasty, vicious

rossignol [ʀɔsiɲɔl] *nm* (*ZOOL*) nightingale

rot [ʀo] *nm* belch; (*de bébé*) burp

rotatif, ive [ʀɔtatif, -iv] *adj* rotary

rotation [ʀɔtasjɔ̃] *nf* rotation; (*fig*) rotation, swap-around; turnover

roter [ʀɔte] (*fam*) *vi* to burp, belch

rôti [ʀoti] *nm*: **du ~** roasting meat; (*cuit*) roast meat; **~ de bœuf/porc** joint of beef/pork

rotin [ʀɔtɛ̃] *nm* rattan (cane); **fauteuil en ~** cane (arm)chair

rôtir [ʀotiʀ] *vi, vt* (*aussi: faire ~*) to roast; **rôtisserie** *nf* steakhouse; roast meat counter (*ou* shop); **rôtissoire** *nf* (roasting) spit

rotule [ʀɔtyl] *nf* kneecap, patella

roturier, ière [ʀɔtyʀje, -jɛʀ] *nm/f* commoner

rouage [ʀwaʒ] *nm* cog(wheel), gearwheel; (*de montre*) part; (*fig*) cog

roucouler [ʀukule] *vi* to coo

roue [ʀu] *nf* wheel; **~ dentée** cogwheel; **~ de secours** spare wheel

roué, e [ʀwe] *adj* wily

rouer [ʀwe] *vt*: **~ qn de coups** to give sb a thrashing

rouet [ʀwe] *nm* spinning wheel

rouge [ʀuʒ] *adj, nm/f* red ♦ *nm* red; (*fard*) rouge; (*vin*) ~ red wine; **sur la liste** ~ ex-directory (*BRIT*), unlisted (*US*); **passer au** ~ (*signal*) to go red; (*automobiliste*) to go through a red light; **~ (à lèvres)** lipstick; **rouge-gorge** *nm* robin (redbreast)

rougeole [ʀuʒɔl] *nf* measles *sg*

rougeoyer [ʀuʒwaje] *vi* to glow red

rouget [ʀuʒe] *nm* mullet

rougeur [ʀuʒœʀ] *nf* redness

rougir [ʀuʒiʀ] *vi* (*de honte, timidité*) to blush, flush; (*de plaisir, colère*) to flush; (*fraise, tomate*) to go *ou* turn red; (*ciel*) to redden

rouille [ʀuj] *nf* rust

rouillé, e [ʀuje] *adj* rusty

rouiller [ʀuje] *vt* to rust ♦ *vi* to rust, go rusty; **se ~** *vi* to rust

roulant, e [ʀulɑ̃, -ɑ̃t] *adj* (*meuble*) on wheels; (*surface, trottoir*) moving

rouleau, x [ʀulo] *nm* (*de papier, tissu, SPORT*) roll; (*de machine à écrire*) roller, platen; (*à mise en plis, à peinture, vague*) roller; **~ compresseur** steamroller; **~ à pâtisserie** rolling pin

roulement [ʀulmɑ̃] *nm* (*bruit*) rumbling *no pl*, rumble; (*rotation*) rotation; turnover; **par ~** on a rota (*BRIT*) *ou* rotation (*US*) basis; **~ (à billes)** ball bearings *pl*; **~ de tambour** drum roll

rouler [ʀule] *vt* to roll; (*papier, tapis*) to roll up; (*CULIN: pâte*) to roll out; (*fam*) to do, con ♦ *vi* (*bille, boule*) to roll; (*voiture, train*) to go, run; (*automobiliste*) to drive; (*cycliste*) to ride; (*bateau*) to roll; (*tonnerre*) to rumble, roll; **se ~ dans** (*boue*) to roll in; (*couverture*) to roll o.s. (up) in

roulette [ʀulɛt] *nf* (*de table, fauteuil*) castor; (*de pâtissier*) pastry wheel; (*jeu*) **la ~** roulette; **à ~s** on castors

roulis [ʀuli] *nm* roll(ing)

roulotte [ʀulɔt] *nf* caravan

Roumanie [ʀumani] *nf* Rumania

rouquin, e [ʀukɛ̃, -in] (*péj*) *nm/f* redhead

rouspéter [ʀuspete] (*fam*) *vi* to moan

rousse [ʀus] *adj voir* **roux**

roussi [ʀusi] *nm*: **ça sent le ~** there's a smell of burning; (*fig*) I can smell trouble

roussir [ʀusiʀ] *vt* to scorch ♦ *vi* (*feuilles*) to go *ou* turn brown; (*CULIN*): **faire ~** to brown

route [ʀut] *nf* road; (*fig: chemin*) way; (*itinéraire, parcours*) route; (*fig: voie*) road, path; **par (la)** ~ by road; **il y a 3 h de ~** it's a 3-hour ride *ou* journey; **en ~** on the way; **mettre en ~** to start up; **se mettre en ~** to set off; **faire ~ vers** to head towards; ~ **nationale** ≈ A road (*BRIT*), ≈ state highway (*US*); **routier, ière** *adj* road *cpd* ♦ *nm* (*camionneur*) (long-distance) lorry (*BRIT*) *ou* truck (*US*) driver; (*restaurant*) ≈ transport café (*BRIT*), ≈ truck stop (*US*); **routière** *nf* (*voiture*) touring car

routine [ʀutin] *nf* routine; **routinier, ière** (*péj*) *adj* humdrum; addicted to routine

rouvrir [ʀuvʀiʀ] *vt*, *vi* to reopen, open again; **se** ~ *vi* to reopen, open again

roux, rousse [ʀu, ʀus] *adj* red; (*personne*) red-haired ♦ *nm/f* redhead

royal, e, aux [ʀwajal, -o] *adj* royal; (*fig*) princely

royaume [ʀwajom] *nm* kingdom; (*fig*) realm; **le R~-Uni** the United Kingdom

royauté [ʀwajote] *nf* (*dignité*) kingship; (*régime*) monarchy

ruban [ʀybɑ̃] *nm* (*gén*) ribbon; (*d'acier*) strip; ~ **adhésif** adhesive tape

rubéole [ʀybeɔl] *nf* German measles *sg*, rubella

rubis [ʀybi] *nm* ruby

rubrique [ʀybʀik] *nf* (*titre, catégorie*) heading; (*PRESSE: article*) column

ruche [ʀyʃ] *nf* hive

rude [ʀyd] *adj* (*barbe, toile*) rough; (*métier, tâche*) hard, tough; (*climat*) severe, harsh; (*bourru*) harsh, rough; (*fruste*) rugged, tough; (*fam*) jolly good

rudement [ʀydmɑ̃] (*fam*) *adv* (*très*) terribly; (*beaucoup*) terribly hard

rudimentaire [ʀydimɑ̃tɛʀ] *adj* rudimentary, basic

rudoyer [ʀydwaje] *vt* to treat harshly

rue [ʀy] *nf* street

ruée [ʀɥe] *nf* rush

ruelle [ʀɥɛl] *nf* alley(-way)

ruer [ʀɥe] *vi* (*cheval*) to kick out; **se** ~ *vi*: **se** ~ **sur** to pounce on; **se** ~ **vers/dans/hors de** to rush *ou* dash towards/into/out of

rugby [ʀygbi] *nm* rugby (football)

rugir [ʀyʒiʀ] *vi* to roar

rugueux, euse [ʀygø, -øz] *adj* rough

ruine [ʀɥin] *nf* ruin; ~s *nfpl* (*de château etc*) ruins

ruiner [ʀɥine] *vt* to ruin

ruineux, euse [ʀɥinø, øz] *adj* ruinous

ruisseau, x [ʀɥiso] *nm* stream, brook

ruisseler [ʀɥisle] *vi* to stream

rumeur [ʀymœʀ] *nf* (*bruit confus*) rumbling; hubbub *no pl*; murmur(ing); (*nouvelle*) rumour

ruminer [ʀymine] *vt* (*herbe*) to ruminate; (*fig*) to ruminate on *ou* over, chew over

rupture [ʀyptyʀ] *nf* (*de câble, digue*) breaking; (*de tendon*) rupture, tearing; (*de négociations etc*) breakdown; (*de contrat*) breach; (*séparation, désunion*) break-up, split

rural, e, aux [ʀyʀal, -o] *adj* rural, country *cpd*

ruse [ʀyz] *nf*: **la** ~ cunning, craftiness; trickery; **une** ~ a trick, a ruse; **rusé, e** *adj* cunning, crafty

russe [ʀys] *adj*, *nm/f* Russian ♦ *nm* (*LING*) Russian

Russie [ʀysi] *nf*: **la** ~ Russia

rustique [ʀystik] *adj* rustic

rustre [ʀystʀ(ə)] *nm* boor

rutilant, e [ʀytilɑ̃, -ɑ̃t] *adj* gleaming

rythme [ʀitm(ə)] *nm* rhythm; (*vitesse*) rate; (*: de la vie*) pace, tempo

S s

s' [s] *pron voir* **se**

sa [sa] *dét voir* **son**[1]

S.A. *sigle* (= *société anonyme*) ≈ Ltd (*BRIT*), ≈ Inc. (*US*)

sable [sabl(ə)] *nm* sand; ~s **mouvants** quicksand(s)

sablé [sable] *nm* shortbread biscuit

sabler [sable] *vt* to sand; (*contre le verglas*) to grit; ~ **le champagne** to drink champagne

sablier [sablije] *nm* hourglass; (*de cuisine*) egg timer

sablonneux, euse [sablɔnø, -øz] *adj* sandy

saborder [sabɔʀde] *vt* (*navire*) to scuttle; (*fig*) to wind up, shut down

sabot [sabo] *nm* clog; (*de cheval, bœuf*)

hoof; ~ **de frein** brake shoe

saboter [sabɔte] *vt* to sabotage

sac [sak] *nm* bag; (*à charbon etc*) sack; **mettre à** ~ to sack; ~ **à dos** rucksack; ~ **à main** handbag; ~ **à provisions/de voyage** shopping/travelling bag; ~ **de couchage** sleeping bag

saccade [sakad] *nf* jerk

saccager [sakaʒe] *vt* (*piller*) to sack; (*dévaster*) to create havoc in

saccharine [sakaʁin] *nf* saccharin

sacerdoce [saseʁdɔs] *nm* priesthood; (*fig*) calling, vocation

sache *etc vb voir* **savoir**

sachet [saʃɛ] *nm* (small) bag; (*de lavande, poudre, shampooing*) sachet; ~ **de thé** tea bag

sacoche [sakɔʃ] *nf* (*gén*) bag; (*de bicyclette*) saddlebag

sacre [sakʁ(ə)] *nm* coronation; consecration

sacré, e [sakʁe] *adj* sacred; (*fam: satané*) blasted; (: *fameux*): **un** ~ ... a heck of a ...

sacrement [sakʁəmɑ̃] *nm* sacrament

sacrifice [sakʁifis] *nm* sacrifice

sacrifier [sakʁifje] *vt* to sacrifice; ~ **à** to conform to

sacristie [sakʁisti] *nf* sacristy; (*culte protestant*) vestry

sadique [sadik] *adj* sadistic

sage [saʒ] *adj* wise; (*enfant*) good ♦ *nm* wise man; sage

sage-femme [saʒfam] *nf* midwife

sagesse [saʒɛs] *nf* wisdom

Sagittaire [saʒitɛʁ] *nm*: **le** ~ Sagittarius

Sahara [saaʁa] *nm*: **le** ~ the Sahara (Desert)

saignant, e [sɛɲɑ̃, -ɑ̃t] *adj* (*viande*) rare

saignée [sɛɲe] *nf* (*fig*) heavy losses *pl*

saigner [sɛɲe] *vi* to bleed ♦ *vt* to bleed; (*animal*) to kill (by bleeding); ~ **du nez** to have a nosebleed

saillie [saji] *nf* (*sur un mur etc*) projection; (*trait d'esprit*) witticism

saillir [sajiʁ] *vi* to project, stick out; (*veine, muscle*) to bulge

sain, e [sɛ̃, sɛn] *adj* healthy; (*lectures*) wholesome; ~ **d'esprit** sound in mind, sane; ~ **et sauf** safe and sound, unharmed

saindoux [sɛ̃du] *nm* lard

saint, e [sɛ̃, sɛ̃t] *adj* holy; (*fig*) saintly ♦ *nm/f* saint; **le S~-Esprit** the Holy Spirit *ou* Ghost; **la S~e Vierge** the Blessed Virgin; **la S~-Sylvestre** New Year's Eve; **sainteté** *nf* holiness

sais *etc vb voir* **savoir**

saisie [sezi] *nf* seizure; ~ **(de données)** (data) capture

saisir [seziʁ] *vt* to take hold of, grab; (*fig: occasion*) to seize; (*comprendre*) to grasp; (*entendre*) to get, catch; (*données*) to capture; (*suj: émotions*) to take hold of, come over; (*CULIN*) to fry quickly; (*JUR: biens, publication*) to seize; (: *juridiction*): ~ **un tribunal d'une affaire** to submit *ou* refer a case to a court; **se** ~ **de** *vt* to seize; **saisissant, e** *adj* startling, striking

saison [sɛzɔ̃] *nf* season; **morte** ~ slack season; **saisonnier, ière** *adj* seasonal

sait *vb voir* **savoir**

salade [salad] *nf* (*BOT*) lettuce *etc*; (*CULIN*) (green) salad; (*fam*) tangle, muddle; ~ **de fruits** fruit salad; **saladier** *nm* (salad) bowl

salaire [salɛʁ] *nm* (*annuel, mensuel*) salary; (*hebdomadaire, journalier*) pay, wages *pl*; (*fig*) reward; ~ **de base** base salary (*ou* wage); ~ **minimum interprofessionnel de croissance** index-linked guaranteed minimum wage

salarié, e [salaʁje] *nm/f* salaried employee; wage-earner

salaud [salo] (*fam!*) *nm* sod (*!*), bastard (*!*)

sale [sal] *adj* dirty, filthy

salé, e [sale] *adj* (*liquide, saveur*) salty; (*CULIN*) salted; (*fig*) spicy; steep

saler [sale] *vt* to salt

saleté [salte] *nf* (*état*) dirtiness; (*crasse*) dirt, filth; (*tache etc*) dirt *no pl*; (*fig*) dirty trick; rubbish *no pl*; filth *no pl*

salière [saljɛʁ] *nf* saltcellar

salin, e [salɛ̃, -in] *adj* saline; **saline** *nf* saltworks *sg*; salt marsh

salir [salir] *vt* to (make) dirty; (*fig*) to soil the reputation of; **se ~** *vi* to get dirty; **salissant, e** *adj* (*tissu*) which shows the dirt; (*métier*) dirty, messy

salle [sal] *nf* room; (*d'hôpital*) ward; (*de restaurant*) dining room; (*d'un cinéma*) auditorium; (: *public*) audience; **faire ~ comble** to have a full house; **~ à manger** dining room; **~ commune** (*d'hôpital*) ward; **~ d'attente** waiting room; **~ de bain(s)** bathroom; **~ de classe** classroom; **~ de concert** concert hall; **~ de consultation** consulting room; **~ d'eau** shower-room; **~ d'embarquement** (*à l'aéroport*) departure lounge; **~ de jeux** games room; playroom; **~ d'opération** (*d'hôpital*) operating theatre; **~ de séjour** living room; **~ de spectacle** theatre; cinema; **~ des ventes** saleroom

salon [salɔ̃] *nm* lounge, sitting room; (*mobilier*) lounge suite; (*exposition*) exhibition, show; **~ de thé** tearoom

salopard [salɔpaʀ] (*fam!*) *nm* bastard (*!*)

salope [salɔp] (*fam!*) *nf* bitch (*!*)

saloperie [salɔpʀi] (*fam!*) *nf* filth *no pl*; dirty trick; rubbish *no pl*

salopette [salɔpɛt] *nf* dungarees *pl*; (*d'ouvrier*) overall(s)

salsifis [salsifi] *nm* salsify

salubre [salybʀ(ə)] *adj* healthy, salubrious

saluer [salɥe] *vt* (*pour dire bonjour, fig*) to greet; (*pour dire au revoir*) to take one's leave; (*MIL*) to salute

salut [saly] *nm* (*sauvegarde*) safety; (*REL*) salvation; (*geste*) wave; (*parole*) greeting; (*MIL*) salute ♦ *excl* (*fam*) hi (there)

salutations [salytasjɔ̃] *nfpl* greetings; **recevez mes ~ distinguées** *ou* **respectueuses** yours faithfully

samedi [samdi] *nm* Saturday

SAMU [samy] *sigle m* (= *service d'assistance médicale d'urgence*) ≈ ambulance (service) (*BRIT*), ≈ paramedics *pl* (*US*)

sanction [sɑ̃ksjɔ̃] *nf* sanction; (*fig*) penalty; **sanctionner** *vt* (*loi, usage*) to sanction; (*punir*) to punish

sandale [sɑ̃dal] *nf* sandal

sandwich [sɑ̃dwitʃ] *nm* sandwich

sang [sɑ̃] *nm* blood; **en ~** covered in blood; **se faire du mauvais ~** to fret, get in a state

sang-froid [sɑ̃fʀwa] *nm* calm, sangfroid; **de ~** in cold blood

sanglant, e [sɑ̃glɑ̃, -ɑ̃t] *adj* bloody, covered in blood; (*combat*) bloody

sangle [sɑ̃gl(ə)] *nf* strap

sanglier [sɑ̃glije] *nm* (wild) boar

sanglot [sɑ̃glo] *nm* sob

sangsue [sɑ̃sy] *nf* leech

sanguin, e [sɑ̃gɛ̃, -in] *adj* blood *cpd*; (*fig*) fiery; **sanguinaire** [sɑ̃ginɛʀ] *adj* bloodthirsty; bloody

Sanisette [sanizɛt] (®) *nf* (automatic) public toilet, Superloo (®: *BRIT*)

sanitaire [sanitɛʀ] *adj* health *cpd*; **~s** *nmpl* (*lieu*) bathroom *sg*

sans [sɑ̃] *prép* without; **~ qu'il s'en aperçoive** without him *ou* his noticing; **~-abri** *nmpl* homeless; **~-emploi** [sɑ̃zɑ̃plwa] *n inv* unemployed person; **les ~-emploi** the unemployed; **~-façon** *adj inv* fuss-free; free and easy; **~-gêne** *adj inv* inconsiderate; **~-logis** *nmpl* homeless

santé [sɑ̃te] *nf* health; **en bonne ~** in good health; **boire à la ~ de qn** to drink (to) sb's health; **à la ~ de** here's to; **à ta/votre ~!** cheers!

saoudien, ne [saudjɛ̃, -jɛn] *adj* Saudi Arabian ♦ *nm/f*: **S~(ne)** Saudi Arabian

saoul, e [su, sul] *adj* = **soûl**

saper [sape] *vt* to undermine, sap

sapeur-pompier [sapœʀpɔ̃pje] *nm* fireman

saphir [safiʀ] *nm* sapphire

sapin [sapɛ̃] *nm* fir (tree); (*bois*) fir; **~ de Noël** Christmas tree

sarcastique [saʀkastik] *adj* sarcastic

sarcler [saʀkle] *vt* to weed

Sardaigne [saʀdɛɲ] *nf*: **la ~** Sardinia

sardine [saʀdin] *nf* sardine

SARL *sigle f* (= *société à responsabilité limitée*) ≈ plc (*BRIT*), ≈ Inc. (*US*)

sas [sas] *nm* (*de sous-marin, d'engin spatial*) airlock; (*d'écluse*) lock

satané, e [satane] *adj* confounded
satellite [satelit] *nm* satellite
satin [satɛ̃] *nm* satin
satire [satiʀ] *nf* satire; **satirique** *adj* satirical
satisfaction [satisfaksjɔ̃] *nf* satisfaction
satisfaire [satisfɛʀ] *vt* to satisfy; ~ **à** (*engagement*) to fulfil; (*revendications, conditions*) to satisfy, meet; to comply with; **satisfaisant, e** *adj* satisfactory; (*qui fait plaisir*) satisfying; **satisfait, e** *adj* satisfied; **satisfait de** happy *ou* satisfied with
saturer [satyʀe] *vt* to saturate
sauce [sos] *nf* sauce; (*avec un rôti*) gravy; **saucière** *nf* sauceboat
saucisse [sosis] *nf* sausage
saucisson [sosisɔ̃] *nm* (slicing) sausage
sauf, sauve [sof, sov] *adj* unharmed, unhurt; (*fig: honneur*) intact, saved ♦ *prép* except; **laisser la vie sauve à qn** to spare sb's life; ~ **si** (*à moins que*) unless; ~ **erreur** if I'm not mistaken; ~ **avis contraire** unless you hear to the contrary
sauge [soʒ] *nf* sage
saugrenu, e [soɡʀəny] *adj* preposterous
saule [sol] *nm* willow (tree)
saumon [somɔ̃] *nm* salmon *inv*
saumure [somyʀ] *nf* brine
saupoudrer [sopudʀe] *vt*: ~ **qch de** to sprinkle sth with
saur [sɔʀ] *adj m*: **hareng** ~ smoked *ou* red herring, kipper
saurai *etc vb voir* **savoir**
saut [so] *nm* jump; (*discipline sportive*) jumping; **faire un** ~ **chez qn** to pop over to sb's (place); **au** ~ **du lit** on getting out of bed; ~ **à la corde** skipping; ~ **à l'élastique** bungee jumping; ~ **à la perche** pole vaulting; ~ **en hauteur/ longueur** high/long jump; ~ **périlleux** somersault
saute [sot] *nf* sudden change
saute-mouton [sotmutɔ̃] *nm*: **jouer à** ~ to play leapfrog
sauter [sote] *vi* to jump, leap; (*exploser*) to blow up, explode; (: *fusibles*) to blow; (*se rompre*) to snap, burst; (*se détacher*) to pop out (*ou* off) ♦ *vt* to jump (over), leap (over); (*fig: omettre*) to skip, miss (out); **faire** ~ to blow up; to burst open; (*CULIN*) to sauté; ~ **au cou de qn** to fly into sb's arms
sauterelle [sotʀɛl] *nf* grasshopper
sautiller [sotije] *vi* to hop; to skip
sautoir [sotwaʀ] *nm*: ~ **(de perles)** string of pearls
sauvage [sovaʒ] *adj* (*gén*) wild; (*peuplade*) savage; (*farouche*) unsociable; (*barbare*) wild, savage; (*non officiel*) unauthorized, unofficial ♦ *nm/f* savage; (*timide*) unsociable type
sauve [sov] *adj f voir* **sauf**
sauvegarde [sovɡaʀd(ə)] *nf* safeguard; **sauvegarder** *vt* to safeguard; (*INFORM: enregistrer*) to save; (: *copier*) to back up
sauve-qui-peut [sovkipø] *excl* run for your life!
sauver [sove] *vt* to save; (*porter secours à*) to rescue; (*récupérer*) to salvage, rescue; **se** ~ *vi* (*s'enfuir*) to run away; (*fam: partir*) to be off; **sauvetage** *nm* rescue; **sauveteur** *nm* rescuer; **sauvette: à la sauvette** *adv* (*vendre*) without authorization; (*se marier etc*) hastily, hurriedly; **sauveur** *nm* saviour (*BRIT*), savior (*US*)
savais *etc vb voir* **savoir**
savamment [savamɑ̃] *adv* (*avec érudition*) learnedly; (*habilement*) skilfully, cleverly
savant, e [savɑ̃, -ɑ̃t] *adj* scholarly, learned; (*calé*) clever ♦ *nm* scientist
saveur [savœʀ] *nf* flavour; (*fig*) savour
savoir [savwaʀ] *vt* to know; (*être capable de*): **il sait nager** he can swim ♦ *nm* knowledge; **se** ~ *vi* (*être connu*) to be known; **à** ~ that is, namely; **faire** ~ **qch à qn** to let sb know sth; **pas que je sache** not as far as I know
savon [savɔ̃] *nm* (*produit*) soap; (*morceau*) bar of soap; (*fam*): **passer un** ~ **à qn** to give sb a good dressing-down; **savonnette** *nf* bar of soap; **savonneux, euse** *adj* soapy
savons *vb voir* **savoir**

savourer [savure] *vt* to savour

savoureux, euse [savurø, -øz] *adj* tasty; (*fig*) spicy, juicy

saxo(phone) [saksɔ(fɔn)] *nm* sax(o-phone)

scabreux, euse [skabrø, -øz] *adj* risky; (*indécent*) improper, shocking

scandale [skɑ̃dal] *nm* scandal; (*tapage*): **faire du ~** to make a scene, create a disturbance; **faire ~** to scandalize people; **scandaleux, euse** *adj* scandalous, outrageous

scandinave [skɑ̃dinav] *adj, nm/f* Scandinavian

Scandinavie [skɑ̃dinavi] *nf* Scandinavia

scaphandre [skafɑ̃dʀ(ə)] *nm* (*de plongeur*) diving suit; (*de cosmonaute*) space-suit

scarabée [skaʀabe] *nm* beetle

sceau, x [so] *nm* seal; (*fig*) stamp, mark

scélérat, e [selera, -at] *nm/f* villain

sceller [sele] *vt* to seal

scénario [senaʀjo] *nm* (*CINÉMA*) scenario; script; (*fig*) scenario

scène [sɛn] *nf* (*gén*) scene; (*estrade, fig: théâtre*) stage; **entrer en ~** to come on stage; **mettre en ~** (*THÉÂTRE*) to stage; (*CINÉMA*) to direct; (*fig*) to present, introduce; **~ de ménage** domestic scene

sceptique [sɛptik] *adj* sceptical

schéma [ʃema] *nm* (*diagramme*) diagram, sketch; (*fig*) outline; pattern; **~tique** *adj* diagrammatic(al), schematic; (*fig*) oversimplified

sciatique [sjatik] *nf* sciatica

scie [si] *nf* saw; **~ à découper** fretsaw; **~ à métaux** hacksaw

sciemment [sjamɑ̃] *adv* knowingly

science [sjɑ̃s] *nf* science; (*savoir*) knowledge; (*savoir-faire*) art, skill; **~s naturelles** (*SCOL*) natural science *sg*, biology *sg*; **~s po** *nfpl* political science *ou* studies *pl*; **scientifique** *adj* scientific ♦ *nm/f* scientist; science student

scier [sje] *vt* to saw; (*retrancher*) to saw off; **scierie** *nf* sawmill

scinder [sɛ̃de] *vt* to split up; **se ~** *vi* to split up

scintiller [sɛ̃tije] *vi* to sparkle

scission [sisjɔ̃] *nf* split

sciure [sjyʀ] *nf*: **~ (de bois)** sawdust

sclérose [skleroz] *nf*: **~ en plaques** multiple sclerosis

scolaire [skɔlɛʀ] *adj* school *cpd*; (*péj*) schoolish; **scolariser** *vt* to provide with schooling (*ou* schools); **scolarité** *nf* schooling

scooter [skutœʀ] *nm* (motor) scooter

score [skɔʀ] *nm* score

scorpion [skɔʀpjɔ̃] *nm* (*signe*): **le S~** Scorpio

Scotch [skɔtʃ] (®) *nm* adhesive tape

scout, e [skut] *adj, nm* scout

script [skʀipt] *nm* printing; (*CINÉMA*) (shooting) script

script-girl [skʀiptgœʀl] *nf* continuity girl

scrupule [skʀypyl] *nm* scruple

scruter [skʀyte] *vt* to scrutinize; (*l'obscurité*) to peer into

scrutin [skʀytɛ̃] *nm* (*vote*) ballot; (*ensemble des opérations*) poll

sculpter [skylte] *vt* to sculpt; (*suj: érosion*) to carve; **sculpteur** *nm* sculptor

sculpture [skyltyʀ] *nf* sculpture; **~ sur bois** wood carving

S.D.F. *sigle m* (= *sans domicile fixe*) homeless person; **les ~** the homeless

---

MOT-CLÉ

se(s') [s(ə)] *pron* **1** (*emploi réfléchi*) oneself; (: *masc*) himself; (: *fém*) herself; (: *sujet non humain*) itself; (: *pl*) themselves; **se voir comme l'on est** to see o.s. as one is

2 (*réciproque*) one another, each other; **ils s'aiment** they love one another *ou* each other

3 (*passif*): **cela se répare facilement** it is easily repaired

4 (*possessif*): **se casser la jambe/laver les mains** to break one's leg/wash one's hands

---

séance [seɑ̃s] *nf* (*d'assemblée, récréative*) meeting, session; (*de tribunal*) sitting, session; (*musicale, CINÉMA, THÉÂTRE*) performance; **~ tenante** forthwith

seau, x [so] *nm* bucket, pail

sec, sèche [sɛk, sɛʃ] *adj* dry; (*raisins, figues*) dried; (*cœur, personne*: *insensible*) hard, cold ♦ *nm*: **tenir au ~** to keep in a dry place ♦ *adv* hard; **je le bois ~** I drink it straight *ou* neat; **à ~** dried up

sécateur [sekatœʀ] *nm* secateurs *pl* (*BRIT*), shears *pl*

sèche [sɛʃ] *adj f voir* **sec**

sèche-cheveux [sɛʃʃəvø] *nm inv* hairdrier

sèche-linge [sɛʃlɛ̃ʒ] *nm inv* tumble dryer

sécher [seʃe] *vt* to dry; (*dessécher*: *peau, blé*) to dry (out); (: *étang*) to dry up ♦ *vi* to dry; to dry out; to dry up; (*fam*: *candidat*) to be stumped; **se ~** (*après le bain*) to dry o.s.

sécheresse [sɛʃʀɛs] *nf* dryness; (*absence de pluie*) drought

séchoir [seʃwaʀ] *nm* drier

second, e [səɡɔ̃, -ɔ̃d] *adj* second ♦ *nm* (*assistant*) second in command; (*NAVIG*) first mate; **voyager en ~e** to travel second-class; **de ~e main** second-hand; **secondaire** *adj* secondary; **seconde** *nf* second; **seconder** *vt* to assist

secouer [səkwe] *vt* to shake; (*passagers*) to rock; (*traumatiser*) to shake (up)

secourir [səkuʀiʀ] *vt* (*aller sauver*) to (go and) rescue; (*prodiguer des soins à*) to help, assist; (*venir en aide à*) to assist, aid; **secourisme** *nm* first aid; life saving

secours [səkuʀ] *nm* help, aid, assistance ♦ *nmpl* aid *sg*; **au ~!** help!; **appeler au ~** to shout *ou* call for help; **porter ~ à qn** to give sb assistance, help sb; **les premiers ~** first aid *sg*

secousse [səkus] *nf* jolt, bump; (*électrique*) shock; (*fig*: *psychologique*) jolt, shock; **~ sismique** *ou* **tellurique** earth tremor

secret, ète [səkʀɛ, -ɛt] *adj* secret; (*fig*: *renfermé*) reticent, reserved ♦ *nm* secret; (*discrétion absolue*): **le ~** secrecy; **au ~** in solitary confinement

secrétaire [səkʀetɛʀ] *nm/f* secretary ♦ *nm* (*meuble*) writing desk; **~ de direc-**tion private *ou* personal secretary; **~ d'État** junior minister; **~ général** *nm* (*COMM*) company secretary; **secrétariat** *nm* (*profession*) secretarial work; (*bureau*) office; (: *d'organisation internationale*) secretariat

secteur [sɛktœʀ] *nm* sector; (*ADMIN*) district; (*ÉLEC*): **branché sur le ~** plugged into the mains (supply)

section [sɛksjɔ̃] *nf* section; (*de parcours d'autobus*) fare stage; (*MIL*: *unité*) platoon; **sectionner** *vt* to sever

Sécu [seky] *abr f* = **sécurité sociale**

séculaire [sekylɛʀ] *adj* secular; (*très vieux*) age-old

sécuriser [sekyʀize] *vt* to give (a feeling of) security to

sécurité [sekyʀite] *nf* safety; security; **système de ~** safety system; **être en ~** to be safe; **la ~ routière** road safety; **la ~ sociale** ≈ (the) Social Security (*BRIT*), ≈ Welfare (*US*)

sédition [sedisjɔ̃] *nf* insurrection; sedition

séduction [sedyksjɔ̃] *nf* seduction; (*charme, attrait*) appeal, charm

séduire [sedɥiʀ] *vt* to charm; (*femme*: *abuser de*) to seduce; **séduisant, e** *adj* (*femme*) seductive; (*homme, offre*) very attractive

ségrégation [seɡʀeɡasjɔ̃] *nf* segregation

seigle [sɛɡl(ə)] *nm* rye

seigneur [sɛɲœʀ] *nm* lord

sein [sɛ̃] *nm* breast; (*entrailles*) womb; **au ~ de** (*équipe, institution*) within; (*flots, bonheur*) in the midst of

séisme [seism(ə)] *nm* earthquake

seize [sɛz] *num* sixteen; **seizième** *num* sixteenth

séjour [seʒuʀ] *nm* stay; (*pièce*) living room; **séjourner** *vi* to stay

sel [sɛl] *nm* salt; (*fig*) wit; spice; **~ de cuisine/de table** cooking/table salt

sélection [seleksjɔ̃] *nf* selection; **sélectionner** *vt* to select

self-service [sɛlfsɛʀvis] *adj, nm* self-service

selle [sɛl] *nf* saddle; **~s** *nfpl* (*MÉD*) stools; **seller** *vt* to saddle

sellette [sɛlɛt] *nf*: **être sur la ~** to be on the carpet

selon [səlɔ̃] *prép* according to; (*en se conformant à*) in accordance with; **~ que** according to whether; **~ moi** as I see it

semaine [səmɛn] *nf* week; **en ~** during the week, on weekdays

semblable [sɑ̃blabl(ə)] *adj* similar; (*de ce genre*): **de ~s mésaventures** such mishaps ♦ *nm* fellow creature *ou* man; **~ à** similar to, like

semblant [sɑ̃blɑ̃] *nm*: **un ~ de vérité** a semblance of truth; **faire ~ (de faire)** to pretend (to do)

sembler [sɑ̃ble] *vb +attrib* to seem ♦ *vb impers*: **il semble (bien) que/inutile de** it (really) seems *ou* appears that/useless to; **il me semble que** it seems to me that; I think (that); **comme bon lui semble** as he sees fit

semelle [səmɛl] *nf* sole; (*intérieure*) insole, inner sole

semence [səmɑ̃s] *nf* (*graine*) seed

semer [səme] *vt* to sow; (*fig: éparpiller*) to scatter; (: *confusion*) to spread; (: *poursuivants*) to lose, shake off; **semé de** (*difficultés*) riddled with

semestre [səmɛstʀ(ə)] *nm* half-year; (*SCOL*) semester

séminaire [seminɛʀ] *nm* seminar

semi-remorque [səmiʀəmɔʀk(ə)] *nm* articulated lorry (*BRIT*), semi(trailer) (*US*)

semonce [səmɔ̃s] *nf*: **un coup de ~** a shot across the bows

semoule [səmul] *nf* semolina

sempiternel, le [sɛ̃pitɛʀnɛl] *adj* eternal, never-ending

sénat [sena] *nm* Senate; **sénateur** *nm* Senator

sens [sɑ̃s] *nm* (*PHYSIOL, instinct*) sense; (*signification*) meaning, sense; (*direction*) direction; **à mon ~** to my mind; **reprendre ses ~** to regain consciousness; **dans le ~ des aiguilles d'une montre** clockwise; **~ commun** common sense; **~ dessus dessous** upside down; **~ interdit** one-way street; **~ unique** one-way street

sensass [sɑ̃sas] (*fam*) *adj* fantastic

sensation [sɑ̃sasjɔ̃] *nf* sensation; **à ~** (*péj*) sensational

sensé, e [sɑ̃se] *adj* sensible

sensibiliser [sɑ̃sibilize] *vt*: **~ qn à** to make sb sensitive to

sensibilité [sɑ̃sibilite] *nf* sensitivity

sensible [sɑ̃sibl(ə)] *adj* sensitive; (*aux sens*) perceptible; (*appréciable: différence, progrès*) appreciable, noticeable; **sensiblement** *adv* (*notablement*) appreciably, noticeably; (*à peu près*): **ils ont sensiblement le même poids** they weigh approximately the same; **sensiblerie** *nf* sentimentality; squeamishness

sensuel, le [sɑ̃sɥɛl] *adj* sensual; sensuous

sentence [sɑ̃tɑ̃s] *nf* (*jugement*) sentence; (*adage*) maxim

sentier [sɑ̃tje] *nm* path

sentiment [sɑ̃timɑ̃] *nm* feeling; **recevez mes ~s respectueux** yours faithfully; **sentimental, e, aux** *adj* sentimental; (*vie, aventure*) love *cpd*

sentinelle [sɑ̃tinɛl] *nf* sentry

sentir [sɑ̃tiʀ] *vt* (*par l'odorat*) to smell; (*par le goût*) to taste; (*au toucher, fig*) to feel; (*répandre une odeur de*) to smell of; (: *ressemblance*) to smell like; (*avoir la saveur de*) to taste of; to taste like ♦ *vi* to smell; **~ mauvais** to smell bad; **se ~ bien** to feel good; **se ~ mal** (*être indisposé*) to feel unwell *ou* ill; **se ~ le courage/la force de faire** to feel brave/strong enough to do; **il ne peut pas le ~** (*fam*) he can't stand him

séparation [sepaʀasjɔ̃] *nf* separation; (*cloison*) division, partition; **~ de corps** legal separation

séparé, e [sepaʀe] *adj* (*appartements, pouvoirs*) separate; (*époux*) separated; **séparément** *adv* separately

séparer [sepaʀe] *vt* (*gén*) to separate; (*suj: divergences etc*) to divide; to drive apart; (*suj: différences, obstacles*) to stand between; (*détacher*): **~ qch de** to pull sth (off) from; (*diviser*): **~ qch par** to divide sth (up) with; **se ~** *vi* (*époux, amis, adversaires*) to separate, part; (*se diviser: route, tige etc*) to divide; (*se dé-*

tacher): se ~ (de) to split off (from); to come off; se ~ de (*époux*) to separate *ou* part from; (*employé, objet personnel*) to part with; ~ une pièce en deux to divide a room into two

sept [sɛt] *num* seven

septembre [sɛptɑ̃bʀ(ə)] *nm* September

septennat [sɛptena] *nm* seven year term of office (*of French President*)

septentrional, e, aux [sɛptɑ̃tʀijɔnal, -o] *adj* northern

septicémie [sɛptisemi] *nf* blood poisoning, septicaemia

septième [sɛtjɛm] *num* seventh

septique [sɛptik] *adj*: fosse ~ septic tank

sépulture [sepyltyʀ] *nf* burial; burial place, grave

séquelles [sekɛl] *nfpl* after-effects; (*fig*) aftermath *sg*; consequences

séquestrer [sekɛstʀe] *vt* (*personne*) to confine illegally; (*biens*) to impound

serai *etc vb voir* être

serein, e [səʀɛ̃, -ɛn] *adj* serene; (*jugement*) dispassionate

serez *vb voir* être

sergent [sɛʀʒɑ̃] *nm* sergeant

série [seʀi] *nf* (*de questions, d'accidents*) series *inv*; (*de clés, casseroles, outils*) set; (*catégorie: SPORT*) rank; class; en ~ in quick succession; (*COMM*) mass *cpd*; de ~ standard; hors ~ (*COMM*) custom-built; (*fig*) outstanding

sérieusement [seʀjøzmɑ̃] *adv* seriously; reliably; responsibly

sérieux, euse [seʀjø, -øz] *adj* serious; (*élève, employé*) reliable, responsible; (*client, maison*) reliable, dependable ♦ *nm* seriousness; reliability; garder son ~ to keep a straight face; prendre qch/qn au ~ to take sth/sb seriously

serin [səʀɛ̃] *nm* canary

seringue [səʀɛ̃g] *nf* syringe

serions *vb voir* être

serment [sɛʀmɑ̃] *nm* (*juré*) oath; (*promesse*) pledge, vow

sermon [sɛʀmɔ̃] *nm* sermon

séronégatif, ive [seʀo-] *adj* (*MED*) HIV negative

séropositif, ive *adj* (*MED*) HIV positive

serpent [sɛʀpɑ̃] *nm* snake

serpenter [sɛʀpɑ̃te] *vi* to wind

serpentin [sɛʀpɑ̃tɛ̃] *nm* (*tube*) coil; (*ruban*) streamer

serpillière [sɛʀpijɛʀ] *nf* floorcloth

serre [sɛʀ] *nf* (*AGR*) greenhouse; ~s *nfpl* (*griffes*) claws, talons

serré, e [seʀe] *adj* (*réseau*) dense; (*écriture*) close; (*habits*) tight; (*fig: lutte, match*) tight, close-fought; (*passagers etc*) (tightly) packed

serrer [seʀe] *vt* (*tenir*) to grip *ou* hold tight; (*comprimer, coincer*) to squeeze; (*poings, mâchoires*) to clench; (*suj: vêtement*) to be too tight for; (*to fit tightly*); (*rapprocher*) to close up, move closer together; (*ceinture, nœud, frein, vis*) to tighten ♦ *vi*: ~ à droite to keep *ou* get over to the right; se ~ *vi* (*se rapprocher*) to squeeze up; se ~ contre qn to huddle up to sb; ~ la main à qn to shake sb's hand; ~ qn dans ses bras to hug sb, clasp sb in one's arms

serrure [seʀyʀ] *nf* lock

serrurier [seʀyʀje] *nm* locksmith

sert *etc vb voir* servir

sertir [sɛʀtiʀ] *vt* (*pierre*) to set

servante [sɛʀvɑ̃t] *nf* (maid)servant

serveur, euse [sɛʀvœʀ, -øz] *nm/f* waiter(waitress)

serviable [sɛʀvjabl(ə)] *adj* obliging, willing to help

service [sɛʀvis] *nm* (*gén*) service; (*série de repas*): premier ~ first sitting; (*assortiment de vaisselle*) set, service; (*bureau: de la vente etc*) department, section; (*travail*): pendant le ~ on duty; ~s *nmpl* (*travail, ÉCON*) services; faire le ~ to serve; rendre ~ à to help; rendre un ~ à qn to do sb a favour; mettre en ~ to put into service *ou* operation; hors ~ out of order; ~ après-vente after-sales service; ~ d'ordre police (*ou* stewards) in charge of maintaining order; ~ militaire military service; ~s secrets secret service *sg*

serviette [sɛʀvjɛt] *nf* (*de table*) (table) napkin, serviette; (*de toilette*) towel;

(*porte-documents*) briefcase; ~ **hygiéni-que** sanitary towel

servir [sɛʀviʀ] *vt* (*gén*) to serve; (*au res-taurant*) to wait on; (*au magasin*) to serve, attend to; (*fig: aider*): ~ **qn** to aid sb; to serve sb's interests; (*COMM: rente*) to pay ♦ *vi* (*TENNIS*) to serve; (*CARTES*) to deal; **se** ~ *vi* (*prendre d'un plat*) to help o.s.; **se** ~ **de** (*plat*) to help o.s. to; (*voi-ture, outil, relations*) to use; **vous êtes servi?** are you being served?; ~ **à qn** (*diplôme, livre*) to be of use to sb; ~ **à qch/faire** (*outil etc*) to be used for sth/doing; **à quoi cela sert-il (de faire)?** what's the use (of doing)?; **cela ne sert à rien** it's no use; ~ **(à qn) de** to serve as (for sb); ~ **à dîner (à qn)** to serve dinner (to sb)

serviteur [sɛʀvitœʀ] *nm* servant
servitude [sɛʀvityd] *nf* servitude; (*fig*) constraint
ses [se] *dét voir* **son**[1]
seuil [sœj] *nm* doorstep; (*fig*) threshold
seul, e [sœl] *adj* (*sans compagnie*) alone; (*avec nuance affective: isolé*) lonely; (*unique*): **un** ~ **livre** only one book, a single book ♦ *adv* (*vivre*) alone, on one's own ♦ *nm, nf*: **il en reste un(e) ~(e)** there's only one left; **le** ~ **li-vre** the only book; ~ **ce livre, ce livre** ~ this book alone, only this book; **parler tout** ~ to talk to oneself; **faire qch (tout)** ~ to do sth (all) on one's own *ou* (all) by oneself; **à lui (tout)** ~ single-handed, on his own
seulement [sœlmɑ̃] *adv* only; **non** ~ ... **mais aussi** *ou* **encore** not only ... but also
sève [sɛv] *nf* sap
sévère [sevɛʀ] *adj* severe
sévices [sevis] *nmpl* (physical) cruelty *sg*, ill treatment *sg*
sévir [seviʀ] *vi* (*punir*) to use harsh measures, crack down; (*suj: fléau*) to rage, be rampant
sevrer [səvʀe] *vt* (*enfant etc*) to wean
sexe [sɛks(ə)] *nm* sex; (*organe mâle*) member
sexuel, le [sɛksɥɛl] *adj* sexual

seyant, e [sɛjɑ̃, -ɑ̃t] *adj* becoming
shampooing [ʃɑ̃pwɛ̃] *nm* shampoo; **se faire un** ~ to shampoo one's hair
short [ʃɔʀt] *nm* (pair of) shorts *pl*

MOT-CLÉ
---

si [si] *nm* (*MUS*) B; (*en chantant la gamme*) ti
♦ *adv* **1** (*oui*) yes
2 (*tellement*) so; ~ **gentil/rapidement** so kind/fast; **(tant et)** ~ **bien que** so much so that; ~ **rapide qu'il soit** how-ever fast he may be
♦ *conj* if; ~ **tu veux** if you want; **je me demande** ~ I wonder if *ou* whether; ~ **seulement** if only

Sicile [sisil] *nf*: **la** ~ Sicily
SIDA [sida] *sigle m* (= *syndrome immuno-déficitaire acquis*) AIDS *sg*
sidéré, e [sidere] *adj* staggered
sidérurgie [sideʀyʀʒi] *nf* steel industry
siècle [sjɛkl(ə)] *nm* century; (*époque*) age
siège [sjɛʒ] *nm* seat; (*d'entreprise*) head office; (*d'organisation*) headquarters *pl*; (*MIL*) siege; ~ **social** registered office
siéger [sjeʒe] *vi* to sit
sien, ne [sjɛ̃, sjɛn] *pron*: **le(la)** ~(**ne**), **les** ~(**ne**)**s** his; hers; its; **les** ~**s** (*sa fa-mille*) one's family; **faire des** ~**nes** (*fam*) to be up to one's (usual) tricks
sieste [sjɛst(ə)] *nf* (*afternoon*) snooze *ou* nap, siesta; **faire la** ~ to have a snooze *ou* nap
sifflement [sifləmɑ̃] *nm* whistle, whist-ling *no pl*; wheezing *no pl*; hissing *no pl*
siffler [sifle] *vi* (*gén*) to whistle; (*en respirant*) to wheeze; (*serpent, vapeur*) to hiss ♦ *vt* (*chanson*) to whistle; (*chien etc*) to whistle for; (*fille*) to whistle at; (*pièce, orateur*) to hiss, boo; (*faute*) to blow one's whistle at; (*fin du match, dé-part*) to blow one's whistle for; (*fam: verre*) to guzzle
sifflet [siflɛ] *nm* whistle; **coup de** ~ whistle
siffloter [siflɔte] *vi, vt* to whistle
sigle [sigl(ə)] *nm* acronym

signal, aux [siɲal, -o] *nm* (*signe convenu, appareil*) signal; (*indice, écriteau*) sign; **donner le ~ de** to give the signal for; **~ d'alarme** alarm signal; **signaux (lumineux)** (*AUTO*) traffic signals

signalement [siɲalmɑ̃] *nm* description, particulars *pl*

signaler [siɲale] *vt* to indicate; to announce; to report; (*faire remarquer*): **~ qch à qn/(à qn) que** to point out sth to sb/(to sb) that; **se ~ (par)** to distinguish o.s. (by)

signature [siɲatyʀ] *nf* signature (*action*), signing

signe [siɲ] *nm* sign; (*TYPO*) mark; **faire un ~ de la main** to give a sign with one's hand; **faire ~ à qn** (*fig*) to get in touch with sb; **faire ~ à qn d'entrer** to motion (to) sb to come in; **~s particuliers** *nmpl* distinguishing marks

signer [siɲe] *vt* to sign; **se ~** *vi* to cross o.s.

signet [siɲɛ] *nm* bookmark

significatif, ive [siɲifikatif, -iv] *adj* significant

signification [siɲifikasjɔ̃] *nf* meaning

signifier [siɲifje] *vt* (*vouloir dire*) to mean; (*faire connaître*): **~ qch (à qn)** to make sth known (to sb); (*JUR*): **~ qch à qn** to serve notice of sth on sb

silence [silɑ̃s] *nm* silence; (*MUS*) rest; **garder le ~** to keep silent, say nothing; **passer sous ~** to pass over (in silence); **silencieux, euse** *adj* quiet, silent ♦ *nm* silencer

silex [silɛks] *nm* flint

silhouette [silwɛt] *nf* outline, silhouette; (*lignes, contour*) outline; (*figure*) figure

silicium [silisjɔm] *nm* silicon; **plaquette de ~** silicon chip

sillage [sijaʒ] *nm* wake; (*fig*) trail

sillon [sijɔ̃] *nm* furrow; (*de disque*) groove; **sillonner** *vt* to criss-cross

simagrées [simagʀe] *nfpl* fuss *sg*; airs and graces

similaire [similɛʀ] *adj* similar; **similicuir** *nm* imitation leather; **similitude** *nf* similarity

simple [sɛ̃pl(ə)] *adj* (*gén*) simple; (*non multiple*) single; **~s** *nmpl* (*MÉD*) medicinal plants; **~ d'esprit** *nm/f* simpleton; **~ messieurs** *nm* (*TENNIS*) men's singles *sg*; **un ~ particulier** an ordinary citizen; **~ soldat** private

simulacre [simylakʀ(ə)] *nm* (*péj*): **un ~ de** a pretence of

simuler [simyle] *vt* to sham, simulate

simultané, e [simyltane] *adj* simultaneous

sincère [sɛ̃sɛʀ] *adj* sincere; genuine; **sincérité** *nf* sincerity

sine qua non [sinekwanɔn] *adj*: **condition ~** indispensable condition

singe [sɛ̃ʒ] *nm* monkey; (*de grande taille*) ape; **singer** [sɛ̃ʒe] *vt* to ape, mimic

singeries [sɛ̃ʒʀi] *nfpl* antics; (*simagrées*) airs and graces

singulariser [sɛ̃gylaʀize] *vt* to mark out; **se ~** *vi* to call attention to o.s.

singularité [sɛ̃gylaʀite] *nf* peculiarity

singulier, ière [sɛ̃gylje, -jɛʀ] *adj* remarkable, singular ♦ *nm* singular

sinistre [sinistʀ(ə)] *adj* sinister ♦ *nm* (*incendie*) blaze; (*catastrophe*) disaster; (*ASSURANCES*) damage (*giving rise to a claim*); **sinistré, e** *adj* disaster-stricken ♦ *nm/f* disaster victim

sinon [sinɔ̃] *conj* (*autrement, sans quoi*) otherwise, or else; (*sauf*) except, other than; (*si ce n'est*) if not

sinueux, euse [sinɥø, -øz] *adj* winding; (*fig*) tortuous

sinus [sinys] *nm* (*ANAT*) sinus; (*GÉOM*) sine; **sinusite** *nf* sinusitis

siphon [sifɔ̃] *nm* (*tube, d'eau gazeuse*) siphon; (*d'évier etc*) U-bend

sirène [siʀɛn] *nf* siren; **~ d'alarme** air-raid siren; fire alarm

sirop [siʀo] *nm* (*à diluer: de fruit etc*) syrup; (*boisson*) fruit drink; (*pharmaceutique*) syrup, mixture

siroter [siʀɔte] *vt* to sip

sismique [sismik] *adj* seismic

site [sit] *nm* (*paysage, environnement*) setting; (*d'une ville etc: emplacement*) site; **~ (pittoresque)** beauty spot; **~s touristiques** places of interest

sitôt [sito] *adv*: ~ **parti** as soon as he *etc* had left; ~ **après** straight after; **pas de** ~ not for a long time

situation [sitɥasjɔ̃] *nf* (*gén*) situation; (*d'un édifice, d'une ville*) situation, position; location; ~ **de famille** *nf* marital status

situé, e [sitɥe] *adj*: **bien** ~ well situated; ~ **à** situated at

situer [sitɥe] *vt* to site, situate; (*en pensée*) to set, place; **se** ~ *vi*: **se** ~ **à/près de** to be situated at/near

six [sis] *num* six; **sixième** *num* sixth

ski [ski] *nm* (*objet*) ski; (*sport*) skiing; **faire du** ~ to ski; ~ **de fond** cross-country skiing; ~ **nautique** water-skiing; ~ **de piste** downhill skiing; ~ **de randonnée** cross-country skiing; **skier** *vi* to ski; **skieur, euse** *nm/f* skier

slip [slip] *nm* (*sous-vêtement*) pants *pl*, briefs *pl*; (*de bain: d'homme*) trunks *pl*; (: *du bikini*) (bikini) briefs *pl*

slogan [slɔgã] *nm* slogan

S.M.I.C. [smik] *sigle m* = **salaire minimum interprofessionnel de croissance**

smicard, e [smikaʀ, -aʀd(ə)] (*fam*) *nm/f* minimum wage earner

smoking [smɔkiŋ] *nm* dinner *ou* evening suit

S.N.C.F. *sigle f* (= *Société nationale des chemins de fer français*) French railways

snob [snɔb] *adj* snobbish ♦ *nm/f* snob

sobre [sɔbʀ(ə)] *adj* temperate, abstemious; (*élégance, style*) sober; ~ **de** (*gestes, compliments*) sparing of

sobriquet [sɔbʀikɛ] *nm* nickname

social, e, aux [sɔsjal, -o] *adj* social

socialisme [sɔsjalism(ə)] *nm* socialism; **socialiste** *nm/f* socialist

société [sɔsjete] *nf* society; (*sportive*) club; (*COMM*) company; **la** ~ **d'abondance/de consommation** the affluent/consumer society; ~ **à responsabilité limitée** *type of limited liability company*; ~ **anonyme** ≈ limited (*BRIT*) *ou* incorporated (*US*) company

sociologie [sɔsjɔlɔʒi] *nf* sociology

socle [sɔkl(ə)] *nm* (*de colonne, statue*) plinth, pedestal; (*de lampe*) base

socquette [sɔkɛt] *nf* ankle sock

sœur [sœʀ] *nf* sister; (*religieuse*) nun, sister

soi [swa] *pron* oneself; **cela va de** ~ that *ou* it goes without saying; **soi-disant** *adj inv* so-called ♦ *adv* supposedly

soie [swa] *nf* silk; (*de porc, sanglier: poil*) bristle; **soierie** *nf* (*tissu*) silk

soif [swaf] *nf* thirst; **avoir** ~ to be thirsty; **donner** ~ **à qn** to make sb thirsty

soigné, e [swaɲe] *adj* (*tenue*) well-groomed, neat; (*travail*) careful, meticulous; (*fam*) whopping; stiff

soigner [swaɲe] *vt* (*malade, maladie: suj: docteur*) to treat; (*suj: infirmière, mère*) to nurse, look after; (*blessé*) to tend; (*travail, détails*) to take care over; (*jardin, chevelure, invités*) to look after

soigneux, euse [swaɲø, -øz] *adj* (*propre*) tidy, neat; (*méticuleux*) painstaking, careful; ~ **de** careful with

soi-même [swamɛm] *pron* oneself

soin [swɛ̃] *nm* (*application*) care; (*propreté, ordre*) tidiness, neatness; ~**s** *nmpl* (*à un malade, blessé*) treatment *sg*, medical attention *sg*; (*attentions, prévenance*) care and attention *sg*; (*hygiène*) care *sg*; **prendre** ~ **de** to take care of, look after; **prendre** ~ **de faire** to take care to do; **les premiers** ~**s** first aid *sg*; **aux bons** ~**s de** c/o, care of

soir [swaʀ] *nm* evening; **ce** ~ this evening, tonight; **demain** ~ tomorrow evening, tomorrow night

soirée [swaʀe] *nf* evening; (*réception*) party

soit [swa] *vb voir* **être** ♦ *conj* (*à savoir*) namely; (*ou*): ~ ... ~ either ... or ♦ *adv* so be it, very well; ~ **que** ... ~ **que** *ou* **ou que** whether ... or whether

soixantaine [swasɑ̃tɛn] *nf*: **une** ~ (**de**) sixty or so, about sixty; **avoir la** ~ (*âge*) to be around sixty

soixante [swasɑ̃t] *num* sixty; **soixante-dix** *num* seventy

soja [sɔʒa] *nm* soya; (*graines*) soya beans *pl*

sol [sɔl] *nm* ground; (*de logement*) floor; (*revêtement*) flooring *no pl*; (*territoire, AGR, GÉO*) soil; (*MUS*) G; (: *en chantant la gamme*) so(h)

solaire [sɔlɛʀ] *adj* solar, sun *cpd*

soldat [sɔlda] *nm* soldier

solde [sɔld(ə)] *nf* pay ♦ *nm* (*COMM*) balance; **~s** *nm ou f pl* sale goods; sales; **en ~** at sale price

solder [sɔlde] *vt* (*compte*) to settle; (*marchandise*) to sell at sale price, sell off; **se ~ par** (*fig*) to end in; **article soldé (à) 10 F** item reduced to 10 F

sole [sɔl] *nf* sole *inv* (*fish*)

soleil [sɔlɛj] *nm* sun; (*lumière*) sun(light); (*temps ensoleillé*) sun(shine); (*BOT*) sunflower; **il fait du ~** it's sunny; **au ~** in the sun

solennel, le [sɔlanɛl] *adj* solemn; ceremonial; **solennité** *nf* (*d'une fête*) solemnity

solfège [sɔlfɛʒ] *nm* rudiments *pl* of music; (*exercices*) ear training *no pl*

solidaire [sɔlidɛʀ] *adj* (*personnes*) who stand together, who show solidarity; (*pièces mécaniques*) interdependent; **être ~ de** (*collègues*) to stand by; **solidarité** *nf* solidarity; interdependence; **par solidarité (avec)** in sympathy (with)

solide [sɔlid] *adj* solid; (*mur, maison, meuble*) solid, sturdy; (*connaissances, argument*) sound; (*personne, estomac*) robust, sturdy ♦ *nm* solid

soliste [sɔlist(ə)] *nm/f* soloist

solitaire [sɔlitɛʀ] *adj* (*sans compagnie*) solitary, lonely; (*lieu*) lonely ♦ *nm/f* recluse; loner

solitude [sɔlityd] *nf* loneliness; (*paix*) solitude

solive [sɔliv] *nf* joist

sollicitations [sɔlisitasjɔ̃] *nfpl* entreaties, appeals; enticements; (*TECH*) stress *sg*

solliciter [sɔlisite] *vt* (*personne*) to appeal to; (*emploi, faveur*) to seek; (*suj: occupations, attractions etc*): **~ qn** to appeal to sb's curiosity *etc*; to entice sb; to make demands on sb's time

sollicitude [sɔlisityd] *nf* concern

soluble [sɔlybl(ə)] *adj* soluble

solution [sɔlysjɔ̃] *nf* solution; **~ de facilité** easy way out

solvable [sɔlvabl(ə)] *adj* solvent

sombre [sɔ̃bʀ(ə)] *adj* dark; (*fig*) gloomy

sombrer [sɔ̃bʀe] *vi* (*bateau*) to sink; **~ dans** (*misère, désespoir*) to sink into

sommaire [sɔmɛʀ] *adj* (*simple*) basic; (*expéditif*) summary ♦ *nm* summary

sommation [sɔmasjɔ̃] *nf* (*JUR*) summons *sg*; (*avant de faire feu*) warning

somme [sɔm] *nf* (*MATH*) sum; (*fig*) amount; (*argent*) sum, amount ♦ *nm*: **faire un ~** to have a (short) nap; **en ~** all in all; **~ toute** all in all

sommeil [sɔmɛj] *nm* sleep; **avoir ~** to be sleepy; **sommeiller** *vi* to doze; (*fig*) to lie dormant

sommelier [sɔmalje] *nm* wine waiter

sommer [sɔme] *vt*: **~ qn de faire** to command *ou* order sb to do; (*JUR*) to summon sb to do

sommes *vb voir* **être**

sommet [sɔmɛ] *nm* top; (*d'une montagne*) summit, top; (*fig: de la perfection, gloire*) height

sommier [sɔmje] *nm* (bed) base

sommité [sɔmite] *nf* prominent person, leading light

somnambule [sɔmnɑ̃byl] *nm/f* sleepwalker

somnifère [sɔmnifɛʀ] *nm* sleeping drug *no pl* (*ou* pill)

somnoler [sɔmnɔle] *vi* to doze

somptueux, euse [sɔ̃ptɥø, -øz] *adj* sumptuous; lavish

son¹, sa [sɔ̃, sa] (*pl* **ses**) *dét* (*antécédent humain: mâle*) his; (: *femelle*) her; (: *valeur indéfinie*) one's, his/her; (*antécédent non humain*) its

son² [sɔ̃] *nm* sound; (*de blé*) bran

sondage [sɔ̃daʒ] *nm*: **~ (d'opinion)** (opinion) poll

sonde [sɔ̃d] *nf* (*NAVIG*) lead *ou* sounding line; (*MÉD*) probe; catheter; feeding tube; (*TECH*) borer, driller; (*pour fouiller etc*) probe

sonder [sɔ̃de] *vt* (*NAVIG*) to sound; (*atmosphère, plaie, bagages etc*) to

songe [sɔ̃ʒ] *nm* dream

songer [sɔ̃ʒe] *vi*: ~ à (*penser à*) to think of; ~ que to consider that; to think that; **songeur, euse** *adj* pensive

sonnant, e [sɔnɑ̃, -ɑ̃t] *adj*: à 8 heures ~es on the stroke of 8

sonné, e [sɔne] *adj* (*fam*) cracked; **il est midi** ~ it's gone twelve

sonner [sɔne] *vi* to ring ♦ *vt* (*cloche*) to ring; (*glas, tocsin*) to sound; (*portier, infirmière*) to ring for; (*messe*) to ring the bell for; ~ **faux** (*instrument*) to sound out of tune; (*rire*) to ring false; ~ **les heures** to strike the hours

sonnerie [sɔnʀi] *nf* (*son*) ringing; (*sonnette*) bell; (*mécanisme d'horloge*) striking mechanism; ~ **d'alarme** alarm bell

sonnette [sɔnɛt] *nf* bell; ~ **d'alarme** alarm bell

sono [sɔno] *abr f* = **sonorisation**

sonore [sɔnɔʀ] *adj* (*voix*) sonorous, ringing; (*salle, métal*) resonant; (*ondes, film, signal*) sound *cpd*

sonorisation [sɔnɔʀizasjɔ̃] *nf* (*installations*) public address system, P.A. system

sonorité [sɔnɔʀite] *nf* (*de piano, violon*) tone; (*de voix, mot*) sonority; (*d'une salle*) resonance; **acoustics** *pl*

sont *vb voir* **être**

sophistiqué, e [sɔfistike] *adj* sophisticated

sorbet [sɔʀbɛ] *nm* water ice, sorbet

sorcellerie [sɔʀsɛlʀi] *nf* witchcraft *no pl*

sorcier [sɔʀsje] *nm* sorcerer; **sorcière** *nf* witch *ou* sorceress

sordide [sɔʀdid] *adj* sordid; squalid

sornettes [sɔʀnɛt] *nfpl* twaddle *sg*

sort [sɔʀ] *nm* (*fortune, destinée*) fate; (*condition, situation*) lot; (*magique*) curse, spell; **tirer au** ~ to draw lots

sorte [sɔʀt(ə)] *nf* sort, kind; **de la** ~ in that way; **de (telle)** ~ **que, en** ~ **que** so that; so much so that; **faire en** ~ **que** to see to it that

sortie [sɔʀti] *nf* (*issue*) way out, exit; (*MIL*) sortie; (*fig: verbale*) outburst; sally;

(*promenade*) outing; (*le soir: au restaurant etc*) night out; (*COMM: somme*): ~**s** items of expenditure; outgoings *sans sg*; ~ **de bain** (*vêtement*) bathrobe; ~ **de secours** emergency exit

sortilège [sɔʀtilɛʒ] *nm* (magic) spell

sortir [sɔʀtiʀ] *vi* (*gén*) to come out; (*partir, se promener, aller au spectacle*) to go out; (*numéro gagnant*) to come up ♦ *vt* (*gén*) to take out; (*produit, ouvrage, modèle*) to bring out; (*INFORM*) to output; (: *sur papier*) to print out; (*fam: expulser*) to throw out; **se** ~ **de** (*affaire, situation*) to get out of; **s'en** ~ (*malade*) to pull through; (*d'une difficulté etc*) to get through; ~ **de** (*gén*) to leave; (*endroit*) to go (*ou* come) out of, leave; (*rainure etc*) to come out of; (*cadre, compétence*) to be outside

sosie [sozi] *nm* double

sot, sotte [so, sɔt] *adj* silly, foolish ♦ *nm/f* fool; **sottise** *nf* silliness, foolishness; silly *ou* foolish thing

sou [su] *nm*: **près de ses** ~**s** tight-fisted; **sans le** ~ penniless

soubresaut [subʀəso] *nm* start; jolt

souche [suʃ] *nf* (*d'arbre*) stump; (*de carnet*) counterfoil (*BRIT*), stub; **de vieille** ~ of old stock

souci [susi] *nm* (*inquiétude*) worry; (*préoccupation*) concern; (*BOT*) marigold; **se faire du** ~ to worry

soucier [susje]: **se** ~ **de** *vt* to care about

soucieux, euse [susjø, -øz] *adj* concerned, worried

soucoupe [sukup] *nf* saucer; ~ **volante** flying saucer

soudain, e [sudɛ̃, -ɛn] *adj* (*douleur, mort*) sudden ♦ *adv* suddenly, all of a sudden

soude [sud] *nf* soda

souder [sude] *vt* (*avec fil à souder*) to solder; (*par soudure autogène*) to weld; (*fig*) to bind together

soudoyer [sudwaje] (*péj*) *vt* to bribe

soudure [sudyʀ] *nf* soldering; welding; (*joint*) soldered joint; weld

souffert, e [sufɛʀ, -ɛʀt(ə)] *pp de* **souffrir**

souffle [sufl(ə)] *nm* (*en expirant*) breath; (*en soufflant*) puff, blow; (*respiration*) breathing; (*d'explosion, de ventilateur*) blast; (*du vent*) blowing; **être à bout de ~** to be out of breath; **un ~ d'air** *ou* **de vent** a breath of air, a puff of wind

soufflé, e [sufle] *adj* (*fam: stupéfié*) staggered ♦ *nm* (*CULIN*) soufflé

souffler [sufle] *vi* (*gén*) to blow; (*haleter*) to puff (and blow) ♦ *vt* (*feu, bougie*) to blow out; (*chasser: poussière etc*) to blow away; (*TECH: verre*) to blow; (*suj: explosion*) to destroy (with its blast); (*dire*): **~ qch à qn** to whisper sth to sb; (*fam: voler*): **~ qch à qn** to pinch sth from sb

soufflet [suflɛ] *nm* (*instrument*) bellows *pl*; (*gifle*) slap (in the face)

souffleur [suflœr] *nm* (*THÉÂTRE*) prompter

souffrance [sufrɑ̃s] *nf* suffering; **en ~** (*marchandise*) awaiting delivery; (*affaire*) pending

souffrant, e [sufrɑ̃, -ɑ̃t] *adj* unwell

souffre-douleur [sufrədulœr] *nm inv* butt, underdog

souffrir [sufrir] *vi* to suffer; to be in pain ♦ *vt* to suffer, endure; (*supporter*) to bear, stand; (*admettre: exception etc*) to allow *ou* admit of; **~ de** (*maladie, froid*) to suffer from

soufre [sufr(ə)] *nm* sulphur

souhait [swɛ] *nm* wish; **tous nos ~s de** good wishes *ou* our best wishes for; **riche etc à ~** as rich etc as one could wish; **à vos ~s!** bless you!; **souhaitable** [swɛtabl(ə)] *adj* desirable

souhaiter [swete] *vt* to wish for; **~ la bonne année à qn** to wish sb a happy New Year

souiller [suje] *vt* to dirty, soil; (*fig*) to sully, tarnish

soûl, e [su, sul] *adj* drunk ♦ *nm*: **tout son ~** to one's heart's content

soulagement [sulaʒmɑ̃] *nm* relief

soulager [sulaʒe] *vt* to relieve

soûler [sule] *vt*: **~ qn** to get sb drunk; (*suj: boisson*) to make sb drunk; (*fig*) to

make sb's head spin *ou* reel; **se ~** *vi* to get drunk

soulever [sulve] *vt* to lift; (*vagues, poussière*) to send up; (*peuple*) to stir up (to revolt); (*enthousiasme*) to arouse; (*question, débat*) to raise; **se ~** *vi* (*peuple*) to rise up; (*personne couchée*) to lift o.s. up; **cela me soulève le cœur** it makes me feel sick

soulier [sulje] *nm* shoe

souligner [suliɲe] *vt* to underline; (*fig*) to emphasize; to stress

soumettre [sumɛtr(ə)] *vt* (*pays*) to subject, subjugate; (*rebelle*) to put down, subdue; **se ~ (à)** to submit (to); **~ qn/qch à** to subject sb/sth to; **~ qch à qn** (*projet etc*) to submit sth to sb

soumis, e [sumi, -iz] *adj* submissive; **revenus ~ à l'impôt** taxable income; **soumission** [sumisjɔ̃] *nf* submission; (*docilité*) submissiveness; (*COMM*) tender

soupape [supap] *nf* valve

soupçon [supsɔ̃] *nm* suspicion; (*petite quantité*): **un ~ de** a hint *ou* touch of; **soupçonner** *vt* to suspect; **soupçonneux, euse** *adj* suspicious

soupe [sup] *nf* soup; **~ au lait** *adj inv* quick-tempered

souper [supe] *vi* to have supper ♦ *nm* supper

soupeser [supəze] *vt* to weigh in one's hand(s); (*fig*) to weigh up

soupière [supjɛr] *nf* (soup) tureen

soupir [supir] *nm* sigh; (*MUS*) crotchet rest

soupirail, aux [supiraj, -o] *nm* (small) basement window

soupirer [supire] *vi* to sigh; **~ après qch** to yearn for sth

souple [supl(ə)] *adj* supple; (*fig: règlement, caractère*) flexible; (: *démarche, taille*) lithe, supple

source [surs(ə)] *nf* (*point d'eau*) spring; (*d'un cours d'eau, fig*) source; **de bonne ~** on good authority

sourcil [sursij] *nm* (eye)brow

sourciller [sursije] *vi*: **sans ~** without turning a hair *ou* batting an eyelid

sourcilleux, euse [sursijø, -øz] *adj* pernickety

sourd, e [suʀ, suʀd(ə)] *adj* deaf; (*bruit, voix*) muffled; (*douleur*) dull; (*lutte*) silent, hidden ♦ *nm/f* deaf person

sourdine [suʀdin] *nf* (*MUS*) mute; **en ~** softly, quietly

sourd-muet, sourde-muette [suʀmyɛ, suʀdmyɛt] *adj* deaf-and-dumb ♦ *nm/f* deaf-mute

souriant, e [suʀjɑ̃, -ɑ̃t] *adj* cheerful

souricière [suʀisjɛʀ] *nf* mousetrap; (*fig*) trap

sourire [suʀiʀ] *nm* smile ♦ *vi* to smile; **~ à qn** to smile at sb; (*fig*) to appeal to sb; to smile on sb; **garder le ~** to keep smiling

souris [suʀi] *nf* mouse

sournois, e [suʀnwa, -waz] *adj* deceitful, underhand

sous [su] *prép* (*gén*) under; **~ la pluie/ le soleil** in the rain/sunshine; **~ terre** underground; **~ peu** shortly, before long

sous-bois [subwa] *nm inv* undergrowth

souscrire [suskʀiʀ]: **~ à** *vt* to subscribe to

sous: **~-directeur, trice** *nm/f* assistant manager(manageress); **~-entendre** *vt* to imply, infer; **~-entendu, e** *adj* implied; (*LING*) understood ♦ *nm* innuendo, insinuation; **~-estimer** *vt* to under-estimate; **~-jacent, e** *adj* underlying; **~-louer** *vt* to sublet; **~-main** *nm inv* desk blotter; **en ~-main** secretly; **~-marin, e** *adj* (*flore, volcan*) submarine; (*navigation, pêche, explosif*) underwater ♦ *nm* submarine; **~-officier** *nm* ≈ non-commissioned officer (N.C.O.); **~-produit** *nm* by-product; (*fig: péj*) pale imitation; **~-signé, e** *adj*: **je ~signé** I the undersigned; **~-sol** *nm* basement; **~-titre** *nm* subtitle

soustraction [sustʀaksjɔ̃] *nf* subtraction

soustraire [sustʀɛʀ] *vt* to subtract, take away; (*dérober*): **~ qch à qn** to remove sth from sb; **se ~ à** (*autorité etc*) to elude, escape from; **~ qn à** (*danger*) to shield sb from

sous-traitant [sutʀɛtɑ̃] *nm* subcontractor

sous-vêtements [suvɛtmɑ̃] *nmpl* underwear *sg*

soutane [sutan] *nf* cassock, soutane

soute [sut] *nf* hold

soutènement [sutɛnmɑ̃] *nm*: **mur de ~** retaining wall

souteneur [sutnœʀ] *nm* procurer

soutenir [sutniʀ] *vt* to support; (*assaut, choc*) to stand up to, withstand; (*intérêt, effort*) to keep up; (*assurer*): **~ que** to maintain that; **~ la comparaison avec** to bear *ou* stand comparison with; **soutenu, e** *adj* (*efforts*) sustained, unflagging; (*style*) elevated

souterrain, e [sutɛʀɛ̃, -ɛn] *adj* underground ♦ *nm* underground passage

soutien [sutjɛ̃] *nm* support; **~ de famille** breadwinner; **soutien-gorge** [sutjɛ̃gɔʀʒ(ə)] *nm* bra

soutirer [sutiʀe] *vt*: **~ qch à qn** to squeeze *ou* get sth out of sb

souvenir [suvniʀ] *nm* (*réminiscence*) memory; (*objet*) souvenir ♦ *vb*: **se ~ de** *vt* to remember; **se ~ que** to remember that; **en ~ de** in memory *ou* remembrance of

souvent [suvɑ̃] *adv* often; **peu ~** seldom, infrequently

souverain, e [suvʀɛ̃, -ɛn] *adj* sovereign; (*fig: mépris*) supreme ♦ *nm/f* sovereign, monarch

soviétique [sɔvjetik] *nm/f*: **Soviétique** Soviet citizen

soyeux, euse [swajø, øz] *adj* silky

soyons *etc vb voir* **être**

spacieux, euse [spasjø, -øz] *adj* spacious; roomy

spaghettis [spageti] *nmpl* spaghetti *sg*

sparadrap [spaʀadʀa] *nm* sticking plaster (*BRIT*), bandaid (®: *US*)

spatial, e, aux [spasjal, -o] *adj* (*AVIAT*) space *cpd*

speaker, ine [spikœʀ, -kʀin] *nm/f* announcer

spécial, e, aux [spesjal, -o] *adj* special; (*bizarre*) peculiar; **spécialement** *adv* especially, particularly; (*tout exprès*) specially

spécialiser [spesjalize]: **se ~** *vi* to specialize

spécialiste [spesjalist(ə)] *nm/f* specialist
spécialité [spesjalite] *nf* speciality; (*SCOL*) special field
spécifier [spesifje] *vt* to specify, state
spécimen [spesimɛn] *nm* specimen; (*revue etc*) specimen *ou* sample copy
spectacle [spɛktakl(ə)] *nm* (*tableau, scène*) sight; (*représentation*) show; (*industrie*) show business; **spectaculaire** *adj* spectacular
spectateur, trice [spɛktatœʀ, -tʀis] *nm/f* (*CINÉMA etc*) member of the audience; (*SPORT*) spectator; (*d'un événement*) onlooker, witness
spéculer [spekyle] *vi* to speculate; ~ **sur** (*COMM*) to speculate in; (*réfléchir*) to speculate on
spéléologie [speleɔlɔʒi] *nf* potholing
sperme [spɛʀm(ə)] *nm* semen, sperm
sphère [sfɛʀ] *nf* sphere
spirale [spiʀal] *nf* spiral
spirituel, le [spiʀitɥɛl] *adj* spiritual; (*fin, piquant*) witty
spiritueux [spiʀitɥø] *nm* spirit
splendide [splɑ̃did] *adj* splendid; magnificent
spontané, e [spɔ̃tane] *adj* spontaneous
sport [spɔʀ] *nm* sport ♦ *adj inv* (*vêtement*) casual; **faire du** ~ to do sport; **~s d'hiver** winter sports; **sportif, ive** *adj* (*journal, association, épreuve*) sports *cpd*; (*allure, démarche*) athletic; (*attitude, esprit*) sporting
spot [spɔt] *nm* (*lampe*) spot(light); (*annonce*): ~ **(publicitaire)** commercial (break)
square [skwaʀ] *nm* public garden(s)
squelette [skəlɛt] *nm* skeleton; **squelettique** *adj* scrawny; (*fig*) skimpy
stabiliser [stabilize] *vt* to stabilize; (*terrain*) to consolidate
stable [stabl(ə)] *adj* stable, steady
stade [stad] *nm* (*SPORT*) stadium; (*phase, niveau*) stage
stage [staʒ] *nm* training period; training course; **stagiaire** *nm/f, adj* trainee
stalle [stal] *nf* stall, box
stand [stɑ̃d] *nm* (*d'exposition*) stand; (*de foire*) stall; ~ **de tir** (*à la foire, SPORT*)

shooting range
standard [stɑ̃daʀ] *adj inv* standard ♦ *nm* switchboard; **standardiste** *nm/f* switchboard operator
standing [stɑ̃diŋ] *nm* standing; **immeuble de grand** ~ block of luxury flats (*BRIT*), condo(minium) (*US*)
starter [staʀtɛʀ] *nm* (*AUTO*) choke
station [stasjɔ̃] *nf* station; (*de bus*) stop; (*de villégiature*) resort; (*posture*): **la** ~ **debout** standing, an upright posture; ~ **de ski** ski resort; ~ **de taxis** taxi rank (*BRIT*) *ou* stand (*US*)
stationnement [stasjɔnmɑ̃] *nm* parking; **stationner** [stasjɔne] *vi* to park
station-service [stasjɔ̃sɛʀvis] *nf* service station
statistique [statistik] *nf* (*science*) statistics *sg*; (*rapport, étude*) statistic ♦ *adj* statistical
statue [staty] *nf* statue
statuer [statɥe] *vi*: ~ **sur** to rule on, give a ruling on
statut [staty] *nm* status; ~**s** *nmpl* (*JUR, ADMIN*) statutes; **statutaire** *adj* statutory
Sté *abr* = **société**
steak [stɛk] *nm* steak
sténo(dactylo) [stenɔ(daktilo)] *nf* shorthand typist (*BRIT*), stenographer (*US*)
sténo(graphie) [stenɔ(gʀafi)] *nf* shorthand
stéréo(phonique) [steʀeɔ(fɔnik)] *adj* stereo(phonic)
stérile [steʀil] *adj* sterile; (*terre*) barren; (*fig*) fruitless, futile
stérilet [steʀilɛ] *nm* coil, loop
stériliser [steʀilize] *vt* to sterilize
stigmates [stigmat] *nmpl* scars, marks
stimulant [stimylɑ̃] *nm* (*fig*) stimulus, incentive
stimuler [stimyle] *vt* to stimulate
stipuler [stipyle] *vt* to stipulate
stock [stɔk] *nm* stock; ~ **d'or** (*FINANCE*) gold reserves *pl*; **stocker** *vt* to stock
stop [stɔp] *nm* (*AUTO: écriteau*) stop sign; (: *signal*) brake-light; **stopper** [stɔpe] *vt* to stop, halt; (*COUTURE*) to mend ♦ *vi* to stop, halt
store [stɔʀ] *nm* blind; (*de magasin*)

shade, awning

strabisme [stʀabism(ə)] *nm* squinting

strapontin [stʀapɔ̃tɛ̃] *nm* jump *ou* fold-away seat

stratégie [stʀateʒi] *nf* strategy; **stratégique** *adj* strategic

stressant, e [stʀesɑ̃, -ɑ̃t] *adj* stressful

strict, e [stʀikt(ə)] *adj* strict; (*tenue, décor*) severe, plain; **son droit le plus ~** his most basic right; **le ~ nécessaire/minimum** the bare essentials/minimum

strie [stʀi] *nf* streak

strophe [stʀɔf] *nf* verse, stanza

structure [stʀyktyʀ] *nf* structure; **~s d'accueil** reception facilities

studieux, euse [stydjø, -øz] *adj* studious; devoted to study

studio [stydjo] *nm* (*logement*) (one-roomed) flatlet (*BRIT*) *ou* apartment (*US*); (*d'artiste, TV etc*) studio

stupéfait, e [stypefɛ, -ɛt] *adj* astonished

stupéfiant [stypefjɑ̃] *nm* (*MÉD*) drug, narcotic

stupéfier [stypefje] *vt* to stupefy; (*étonner*) to stun, astonish

stupeur [stypœʀ] *nf* astonishment

stupide [stypid] *adj* stupid; **stupidité** *nf* stupidity; stupid thing (to do *ou* say)

style [stil] *nm* style; **meuble de ~** piece of period furniture

stylé, e [stile] *adj* well-trained

styliste [stilist] *nm/f* designer

stylo [stilo] *nm*: **~ (à encre)** (fountain) pen; **~ (à) bille** ball-point pen

su, e [sy] *pp de* **savoir** ♦ *nm*: **au ~ de** with the knowledge of

suave [sɥav] *adj* sweet; (*goût*) mellow

subalterne [sybaltɛʀn(ə)] *adj* (*employé, officier*) junior; (*rôle*) subordinate, subsidiary ♦ *nm/f* subordinate

subconscient [sybkɔ̃sjɑ̃] *nm* subconscious

subir [sybiʀ] *vt* (*affront, dégâts*) to suffer; (*influence, charme*) to be under; (*opération, châtiment*) to undergo

subit, e [sybi, -it] *adj* sudden; **subitement** *adv* suddenly, all of a sudden

subjectif, ive [sybʒɛktif, -iv] *adj* subjective

subjonctif [sybʒɔ̃ktif] *nm* subjunctive

submerger [sybmɛʀʒe] *vt* to submerge; (*fig*) to overwhelm

subordonné, e [sybɔʀdɔne] *adj, nm/f* subordinate; **~ à** subordinate to; subject to, depending on

subornation [sybɔʀnasjɔ̃] *nf* bribing

subrepticement [sybʀɛptismɑ̃] *adv* surreptitiously

subside [sypsid] *nm* grant

subsidiaire [sypsidjɛʀ] *adj*: **question ~** deciding question

subsister [sybziste] *vi* (*rester*) to remain, subsist; (*vivre*) to live; (*survivre*) to live on

substance [sypstɑ̃s] *nf* substance

substituer [sypstitɥe] *vt*: **~ qn/qch à** to substitute sb/sth for; **se ~ à qn** (*évincer*) to substitute o.s. for sb

substitut [sypstity] *nm* (*JUR*) deputy public prosecutor; (*succédané*) substitute

subterfuge [sybtɛʀfyʒ] *nm* subterfuge

subtil, e [syptil] *adj* subtle

subtiliser [syptilize] *vt*: **~ qch (à qn)** to spirit sth away (from sb)

subvenir [sybvəniʀ]: **~ à** *vt* to meet

subvention [sybvɑ̃sjɔ̃] *nf* subsidy, grant; **subventionner** *vt* to subsidize

suc [syk] *nm* (*BOT*) sap; (*de viande, fruit*) juice

succédané [syksedane] *nm* substitute

succéder [syksede]: **~ à** *vt* (*directeur, roi etc*) to succeed; (*venir après: dans une série*) to follow, succeed; **se ~** *vi* (*accidents, années*) to follow one another

succès [syksɛ] *nm* success; **avoir du ~** to be a success, be successful; **à ~** successful; **~ de librairie** bestseller; **~ (féminins)** conquests

succession [syksesjɔ̃] *nf* (*série, POL*) succession; (*JUR: patrimoine*) estate, inheritance

succomber [sykɔ̃be] *vi* to die, succumb; (*fig*): **~ à** to give way to, succumb to

succursale [sykyʀsal] *nf* branch

sucer [syse] *vt* to suck

sucette [sysɛt] *nf* (*bonbon*) lollipop; (*de bébé*) dummy (*BRIT*), pacifier (*US*)

sucre [sykʀ(ə)] *nm* (*substance*) sugar;

(*morceau*) lump of sugar, sugar lump *ou* cube; ~ **d'orge** barley sugar; ~ **en morceaux/cristallisé/en poudre** lump/granulated/caster sugar; **sucré, e** *adj* (*produit alimentaire*) sweetened; (*au goût*) sweet; (*péj*) sugary, honeyed; **sucrer** *vt* (*thé, café*) to sweeten, put sugar in; **sucreries** *nfpl* (*bonbons*) sweets, sweet things; **sucrier** *nm* (*récipient*) sugar bowl

sud [syd] *nm*: **le** ~ the south ♦ *adj inv* south; (*côte*) south, southern; **au** ~ (*situation*) in the south; (*direction*) to the south; **au** ~ **de** (to the) south of; **sud-africain, e** *adj, nm/f* South African; **sud-américain, e** *adj, nm/f* South American; **sud-est** [sydɛst] *nm* south-east ♦ *adj inv* south-east; **sud-ouest** [sydwɛst] *nm* south-west ♦ *adj inv* south-west

Suède [sɥɛd] *nf*: **la** ~ Sweden; **suédois, e** *adj* Swedish ♦ *nm/f*: **Suédois, e** Swede ♦ *nm* (*LING*) Swedish

suer [sɥe] *vi* to sweat; (*suinter*) to ooze

sueur [sɥœʀ] *nf* sweat; **en** ~ sweating, in a sweat

suffire [syfiʀ] *vi* (*être assez*): ~ (**à qn/pour qch/pour faire**) to be enough *ou* sufficient (for sb/for sth/to do); **cela suffit pour les irriter/qu'ils se fâchent** it's enough to annoy them/for them to get angry; **il suffit d'une négligence ...** it only takes one act of carelessness ...; **il suffit qu'on oublie pour que ...** one only needs to forget for ...

suffisamment [syfizamɑ̃] *adv* sufficiently, enough; ~ **de** sufficient, enough

suffisant, e [syfizɑ̃, -ɑ̃t] *adj* (*temps, ressources*) sufficient; (*résultats*) satisfactory; (*vaniteux*) self-important, bumptious

suffixe [syfiks(ə)] *nm* suffix

suffoquer [syfɔke] *vt* to choke, suffocate; (*stupéfier*) to stagger, astound ♦ *vi* to choke, suffocate

suffrage [syfʀaʒ] *nm* (*POL: voix*) vote; (*du public etc*) approval *no pl*

suggérer [syɡʒeʀe] *vt* to suggest; **suggestion** *nf* suggestion

suicide [sɥisid] *nm* suicide

suicider [sɥiside]: **se** ~ *vi* to commit suicide

suie [sɥi] *nf* soot

suinter [sɥɛ̃te] *vi* to ooze

suis *vb voir* **être**; **suivre**

suisse [sɥis] *adj* Swiss ♦ *nm*: **S**~ Swiss *pl inv* ♦ *nf*: **la S**~ Switzerland; **la S**~ **romande/allemande** French-speaking/German-speaking Switzerland; **Suissesse** *nf* Swiss (woman *ou* girl)

suite [sɥit] *nf* (*continuation*: *d'énumération etc*) rest, remainder; (: *de feuilleton*) continuation; (: *film etc sur le même thème*) sequel; (*série: de maisons, succès*) succession of; **une** ~ **de** a series *ou* succession of; (*MATH*) series *sg*; (*conséquence*) result; (*ordre, liaison logique*) coherence; (*appartement, MUS*) suite; (*escorte*) retinue, suite; ~**s** *nfpl* (*d'une maladie etc*) effects; **prendre la** ~ **de** (*directeur etc*) to succeed, take over from; **donner** ~ **à** (*requête, projet*) to follow up; **faire** ~ **à** to follow; (**faisant**) ~ **à votre lettre du ...** further to your letter of the ...; **de** ~ (*d'affilée*) in succession; (*immédiatement*) at once; **par la** ~ afterwards, subsequently; **à la** ~ one after the other; **à la** ~ **de** (*derrière*) behind; (*en conséquence de*) following; **par** ~ **de** owing to, as a result of

suivant, e [sɥivɑ̃, -ɑ̃t] *adj* next, following; (*ci-après*): **l'exercice** ~ the following exercise ♦ *prép* (*selon*) according to; **au** ~! next!

suivi, e [sɥivi] *adj* (*régulier*) regular; (*cohérent*) consistent; coherent; **très/peu** ~ (*cours*) well-/poorly-attended

suivre [sɥivʀ(ə)] *vt* to follow; (*SCOL: cours*) to attend; (: *programme*) to keep up with; (*COMM: article*) to continue to stock ♦ *vi* to follow; (*élève*) to attend; to keep up; **se** ~ *vi* (*accidents etc*) to follow one after the other; (*raisonnement*) to be coherent; **faire** ~ (*lettre*) to forward; ~ **son cours** (*suj: enquête etc*) to run *ou* take its course; **"à** ~**"** "to be continued"

sujet, te [syʒɛ, -ɛt] *adj*: **être** ~ **à** (*vertige etc*) to be liable *ou* subject to

♦ *nm/f* (*d'un souverain*) subject ♦ *nm* subject; **au ~ de** about; **~ à caution** questionable; **~ de conversation** topic *ou* subject of conversation; **~ d'examen** (*SCOL*) examination question; examination paper

summum [sɔmɔm] *nm*: **le ~ de** the height of

superbe [sypɛʀb(ə)] *adj* magnificent, superb

super(carburant) [sypɛʀ(kaʀbyʀɑ̃)] *nm* ≈ 4-star petrol (*BRIT*), ≈ high-octane gasoline (*US*)

supercherie [sypɛʀʃəʀi] *nf* trick

supérette [sypeʀɛt] *nf* (*COMM*) minimarket, superette (*US*)

superficie [sypɛʀfisi] *nf* (surface) area; (*fig*) surface

superficiel, le [sypɛʀfisjɛl] *adj* superficial

superflu, e [sypɛʀfly] *adj* superfluous

supérieur, e [sypeʀjœʀ] *adj* (*lèvre, étages, classes*) upper; (*plus élevé: température, niveau*): **~ (à)** higher (than); (*meilleur: qualité, produit*): **~ (à)** superior (to); (*excellent, hautain*) superior ♦ *nm, f* superior; **à l'étage ~** on the next floor up; **supériorité** *nf* superiority

superlatif [sypɛʀlatif] *nm* superlative

supermarché [sypɛʀmaʀʃe] *nm* supermarket

superposer [sypɛʀpoze] *vt* (*faire chevaucher*) to superimpose; **lits superposés** bunk beds

superproduction [sypɛʀpʀɔdyksjɔ̃] *nf* (*film*) spectacular

superpuissance [sypɛʀpɥisɑ̃s] *nf* superpower

superstitieux, euse [sypɛʀstisjø, -øz] *adj* superstitious

superviser [sypɛʀvize] *vt* to supervise

suppléant, e [sypleɑ̃, -ɑ̃t] *adj* (*juge, fonctionnaire*) deputy *cpd*; (*professeur*) supply *cpd* ♦ *nm/f* deputy; supply teacher

suppléer [syplee] *vt* (*ajouter: mot manquant etc*) to supply, provide; (*compenser: lacune*) to fill in; (: *défaut*) to make up for; (*remplacer*) to stand in for; **~ à**

to make up for; to substitute for

supplément [syplemɑ̃] *nm* supplement; (*de frites etc*) extra portion; **un ~ de travail** extra *ou* additional work; **ceci est en ~** (*au menu etc*) this is extra, there is an extra charge for this; **~aire** *adj* additional, further; (*train, bus*) relief *cpd*, extra

supplications [syplikasjɔ̃] *nfpl* pleas, entreaties

supplice [syplis] *nm* (*peine corporelle*) torture *no pl*; form of torture; (*douleur physique, morale*) torture, agony

supplier [syplije] *vt* to implore, beseech

supplique [syplik] *nf* petition

support [sypɔʀ] *nm* support; (*pour livre, outils*) stand

supportable [sypɔʀtabl(ə)] *adj* (*douleur*) bearable

supporter[1] [sypɔʀtɛʀ] *nm* supporter, fan

supporter[2] [sypɔʀte] *vt* (*poids, poussée*) to support; (*conséquences, épreuve*) to bear, endure; (*défauts, personne*) to put up with; (*suj: chose: chaleur etc*) to withstand; (: *personne: chaleur, vin*) to be able to take

supposé, e [sypoze] *adj* (*nombre*) estimated; (*auteur*) supposed

supposer [sypoze] *vt* to suppose; (*impliquer*) to presuppose; **à ~ que** supposing (that)

suppositoire [sypozitwaʀ] *nm* suppository

suppression [sypʀesjɔ̃] *nf* (*voir supprimer*) removal; deletion; cancellation; suppression

supprimer [sypʀime] *vt* (*cloison, cause, anxiété*) to remove; (*clause, mot*) to delete; (*congés, service d'autobus etc*) to cancel; (*emplois, privilèges, témoin gênant*) to do away with

supputer [sypyte] *vt* to calculate

suprême [sypʀɛm] *adj* supreme

MOT-CLÉ
---

sur *prép* **1** (*position*) on; (*pardessus*) over; (*au-dessus*) above; **pose-le ~ la table** put it on the table; **je n'ai pas d'ar-**

gent ~ **moi** I haven't any money on me **2** (*direction*) towards; **en allant ~ Paris** going towards Paris; **~ votre droite** on *ou* to your right

3 (*à propos de*) on, about; **un livre/une conférence ~ Balzac** a book/lecture on *ou* about Balzac

4 (*proportion, mesures*) out of; by; **un ~ 10** one in 10; (*SCOL*) one out of 10; **4 m ~ 2** 4 m by 2

sur ce *adv* hereupon

sûr, e [syʀ] *adj* sure, certain; (*digne de confiance*) reliable; (*sans danger*) safe; **le plus ~ est de** the safest thing is to; **~ de soi** self-confident; **~ et certain** absolutely certain

suranné, e [syʀane] *adj* outdated, outmoded

surcharge [syʀʃaʀʒ(ə)] *nf* (*de passagers, marchandises*) excess load; (*correction*) alteration

surcharger [syʀʃaʀʒe] *vt* to overload

surchoix [syʀʃwa] *adj inv* top-quality

surclasser [syʀklase] *vt* to outclass

surcroît [syʀkʀwa] *nm*: **un ~ de** additional +*nom*; **par** *ou* **de ~** moreover; **en ~** in addition

surdité [syʀdite] *nf* deafness

surélever [syʀelve] *vt* to raise, heighten

sûrement [syʀmɑ̃] *adv* reliably; safely, securely; (*certainement*) certainly

surenchère [syʀɑ̃ʃɛʀ] *nf* (*aux enchères*) higher bid; (*sur prix fixe*) overbid; (*fig*) overstatement; outbidding tactics *pl*; **surenchérir** *vi* to bid higher; (*fig*) to try and outbid each other

surent *vb voir* **savoir**

surestimer [syʀɛstime] *vt* to overestimate

sûreté [syʀte] *nf* (*voir* **sûr**) reliability; safety; (*JUR*) guaranty; surety; **mettre en ~** to put in a safe place; **pour plus de ~** as an extra precaution; to be on the safe side

surf [syʀf] *nm* surfing

surface [syʀfas] *nf* surface; (*superficie*) surface area; **faire ~** to surface; **en ~** near the surface; (*fig*) superficially

surfait, e [syʀfɛ, -ɛt] *adj* overrated

surfin, e [syʀfɛ̃, -in] *adj* superfine

surgelé, e [syʀʒəle] *adj* (deep-) frozen

surgir [syʀʒiʀ] *vi* to appear suddenly; (*jaillir*) to shoot up; (*fig: problème, conflit*) to arise

sur: **~humain, e** *adj* superhuman; **~impression** *nf* (*PHOTO*) double exposure; **en ~impression** superimposed; **~-le-champ** *adv* immediately; **~lendemain** *nm*: **le ~lendemain** two days later; **le ~lendemain (soir)** two days later (in the evening); **le ~lendemain de** two days after; **~mener** *vt* to overwork; **se ~mener** *vi* to overwork

surmonter [syʀmɔ̃te] *vt* (*suj: coupole etc*) to top; (*vaincre*) to overcome

surnager [syʀnaʒe] *vi* to float

surnaturel, le [syʀnatyʀɛl] *adj, nm* supernatural

surnom [syʀnɔ̃] *nm* nickname

surnombre [syʀnɔ̃bʀ(ə)] *nm*: **être en ~** to be too many (*ou* one too many)

surpeuplé, e [syʀpœple] *adj* overpopulated

sur-place [syʀplas] *nm*: **faire du ~** to mark time

surplomber [syʀplɔ̃be] *vi* to be overhanging ♦ *vt* to overhang; to tower above

surplus [syʀply] *nm* (*COMM*) surplus; (*reste*): **~ de bois** wood left over

surprenant, e [syʀpʀənɑ̃, -ɑ̃t] *adj* amazing

surprendre [syʀpʀɑ̃dʀ(ə)] *vt* (*étonner, prendre à l'improviste*) to surprise; (*tomber sur: intrus etc*) to catch; (*fig*) to detect; to chance upon; to overhear

surpris, e [syʀpʀi, -iz] *adj*: **~ (de/que)** surprised (at/that)

surprise [syʀpʀiz] *nf* surprise; **faire une ~ à qn** to give sb a surprise; **surprise-partie** [syʀpʀizpaʀti] *nf* party

sursaut [syʀso] *nm* start, jump; **~ de** (*énergie, indignation*) sudden fit *ou* burst of; **en ~** with a start; **sursauter** *vi* to (give a) start, jump

surseoir [syʀswaʀ]: **~ à** *vt* to defer

sursis [syʀsi] *nm* (*JUR: gén*) suspended sentence; (*à l'exécution capitale, aussi* *fig*) reprieve; (*MIL*) deferment

surtaxe [syʀtaks(ə)] *nf* surcharge

surtout [syʀtu] *adv* (*avant tout, d'abord*) above all; (*spécialement, particulièrement*) especially; ~, **ne dites rien!** whatever you do don't say anything!; ~ **pas!** certainly *ou* definitely not!; ~ **que ...** especially as ...

surveillance [syʀvɛjɑ̃s] *nf* watch; (*POLICE, MIL*) surveillance; **sous ~ médicale** under medical supervision

surveillant, e [syʀvɛjɑ̃, -ɑ̃t] *nm/f* (*de prison*) warder; (*SCOL*) monitor; (*de travaux*) supervisor, overseer

surveiller [syʀveje] *vt* (*enfant, élèves, bagages*) to watch, keep an eye on; (*malade*) to watch over; (*prisonnier, suspect*) to keep (a) watch on; (*territoire, bâtiment*) to (keep) watch over; (*travaux, cuisson*) to supervise; (*SCOL: examen*) to invigilate; **se ~** *vi* to keep a check *ou* watch on o.s.; ~ **son langage/ sa ligne** to watch one's language/figure

survenir [syʀvəniʀ] *vi* (*incident, retards*) to occur, arise; (*événement*) to take place; (*personne*) to appear, arrive

survêt(ement) [syʀvɛt(mɑ̃)] *nm* tracksuit

survie [syʀvi] *nf* survival; (*REL*) afterlife

survivant, e [syʀvivɑ̃, -ɑ̃t] *nm/f* survivor

survivre [syʀvivʀ(ə)] *vi* to survive; ~ **à** (*accident etc*) to survive; (*personne*) to outlive

survoler [syʀvɔle] *vt* to fly over; (*fig: livre*) to skim through

survolté, e [syʀvɔlte] *adj* (*fig*) worked up

sus [sy(s)]: **en ~ de** *prép* in addition to, over and above; **en ~** in addition; ~ **à:** ~ **au tyran!** at the tyrant!

susceptible [syseptibl(ə)] *adj* touchy, sensitive; ~ **d'amélioration** that can be improved, open to improvement; ~ **de faire** able to do; liable to do

susciter [sysite] *vt* (*admiration*) to arouse; (*obstacles, ennuis*): ~ (**à qn**) to create (for sb)

suspect, e [syspɛ(kt), -ɛkt(ə)] *adj* suspi-

cious; (*témoignage, opinions*) suspect ♦ *nm/f* suspect

suspecter [syspɛkte] *vt* to suspect; (*honnêteté de qn*) to question, have one's suspicions about

suspendre [syspɑ̃dʀ(ə)] *vt* (*accrocher: vêtement*): ~ **qch (à)** to hang sth up (on); (*fixer: lustre etc*): ~ **qch à** to hang sth from; (*interrompre, démettre*) to suspend; (*remettre*) to defer; **se ~ à** to hang from

suspendu, e [syspɑ̃dy] *adj* (*accroché*): ~ **à** hanging on (*ou* from); (*perché*): ~ **au-dessus de** suspended over

suspens [syspɑ̃]: **en ~** *adv* (*affaire*) in abeyance; **tenir en ~** to keep in suspense

suspense [syspɑ̃s] *nm* suspense

suspension [syspɑ̃sjɔ̃] *nf* suspension; ~ **d'audience** adjournment

sut *vb voir* **savoir**

suture [sytyʀ] *nf* (*MÉD*): **point de ~** stitch

svelte [svɛlt(ə)] *adj* slender, svelte

S.V.P. *sigle* (= *s'il vous plaît*) please

syllabe [silab] *nf* syllable

sylviculture [silvikyltyʀ] *nf* forestry

symbole [sɛ̃bɔl] *nm* symbol; **symbolique** *adj* symbolic(al); (*geste, offrande*) token *cpd*; (*salaire, dommage-intérêts*) nominal; **symboliser** *vt* to symbolize

symétrique [simetʀik] *adj* symmetrical

sympa [sɛ̃pa] *adj abr* = **sympathique**

sympathie [sɛ̃pati] *nf* (*inclination*) liking; (*affinité*) fellow feeling; (*condoléances*) sympathy; **accueillir avec ~** (*projet*) to receive favourably; **croyez à toute ma ~** you have my deepest sympathy

sympathique [sɛ̃patik] *adj* nice, friendly; likeable; pleasant

sympathisant, e [sɛ̃patizɑ̃, -ɑ̃t] *nm/f* sympathizer

sympathiser [sɛ̃patize] *vi* (*voisins etc: s'entendre*) to get on (*BRIT*) *ou* along (*US*) (well)

symphonie [sɛ̃fɔni] *nf* symphony

symptôme [sɛ̃ptom] *nm* symptom

synagogue [sinagɔg] *nf* synagogue

syncope [sɛ̃kɔp] *nf* (*MÉD*) blackout; **tomber en** ~ to faint, pass out
syndic [sɛ̃dik] *nm* managing agent
syndical, e, aux [sɛ̃dikal, -o] *adj* (trade-) union *cpd*; **syndicaliste** *nm/f* trade unionist
syndicat [sɛ̃dika] *nm* (*d'ouvriers, employés*) (trade) union; (*autre association d'intérêts*) union, association; ~ **d'initiative** tourist office
syndiqué, e [sɛ̃dike] *adj* belonging to a (trade) union; **non** ~ non-union
syndiquer [sɛ̃dike]: **se** ~ *vi* to form a trade union; (*adhérer*) to join a trade union
synonyme [sinɔnim] *adj* synonymous ♦ *nm* synonym; ~ **de** synonymous with
syntaxe [sɛ̃taks(ə)] *nf* syntax
synthèse [sɛ̃tɛz] *nf* synthesis
synthétique [sɛ̃tetik] *adj* synthetic
Syrie [siʀi] *nf*: **la** ~ Syria
systématique [sistematik] *adj* systematic
système [sistɛm] *nm* system; ~ **D** resourcefulness

T t

t' [t(ə)] *pron voir* te
ta [ta] *dét* ton[1]
tabac [taba] *nm* tobacco; tobacconist's (shop); ~ **blond/brun** light/dark tobacco
tabagie [tabaʒi] *nf*: ~ **passive** passive smoking
table [tabl(ə)] *nf* table; **à** ~! dinner *etc* is ready!; **se mettre à** ~ to sit down to eat; (*fig: fam*) to come clean; **mettre la** ~ to lay the table; **faire** ~ **rase de** to make a clean sweep of; ~ **de cuisson** *nf* (*à l'électricité*) hotplate; (*au gaz*) gas ring; ~ **de nuit** *ou* **de chevet** bedside table; ~ **des matières** (table of) contents *pl*
tableau, x [tablo] *nm* painting; (*reproduction, fig*) picture; (*panneau*) board; (*schéma*) table, chart; ~ **d'affichage** notice board; ~ **de bord** dashboard; (*AVIAT*) instrument panel; ~ **noir** blackboard
tabler [table] *vi*: ~ **sur** to bank on

tablette [tablɛt] *nf* (*planche*) shelf; ~ **de chocolat** bar of chocolate
tableur [tablœʀ] *nm* spreadsheet
tablier [tablije] *nm* apron
tabouret [tabuʀɛ] *nm* stool
tac [tak] *nm*: **du** ~ **au** ~ tit for tat
tache [taʃ] *nf* (*saleté*) stain, mark; (*ART, de couleur, lumière*) spot; splash, patch; ~ **de rousseur** freckle
tâche [tɑʃ] *nf* task; **travailler à la** ~ to do piecework
tacher [taʃe] *vt* to stain, mark; (*fig*) to sully, stain
tâcher [tɑʃe] *vi*: ~ **de faire** to try *ou* endeavour to do
tacot [tako] (*péj*) *nm* banger (*BRIT*), (old) heap
tact [takt] *nm* tact; **avoir du** ~ to be tactful
tactique [taktik] *adj* tactical ♦ *nf* (*technique*) tactics *sg*; (*plan*) tactic
taie [tɛ] *nf*: ~ **(d'oreiller)** pillowslip, pillowcase
taille [taj] *nf* cutting; pruning; (*milieu du corps*) waist; (*hauteur*) height; (*grandeur*) size; **de** ~ **à faire** capable of doing; **de** ~ sizeable
taille-crayon(s) [tajkʀɛjɔ̃] *nm* pencil sharpener
tailler [taje] *vt* (*pierre, diamant*) to cut; (*arbre, plante*) to prune; (*vêtement*) to cut out; (*crayon*) to sharpen
tailleur [tajœʀ] *nm* (*couturier*) tailor; (*vêtement*) suit; **en** ~ (*assis*) cross-legged
taillis [taji] *nm* copse
taire [tɛʀ] *vt* to keep to o.s., conceal ♦ *vi*: **faire** ~ **qn** to make sb be quiet; (*fig*) to silence sb; **se** ~ *vi* to be silent *ou* quiet
talc [talk] *nm* talc, talcum powder
talent [talɑ̃] *nm* talent
talon [talɔ̃] *nm* heel; (*de chèque, billet*) stub, counterfoil (*BRIT*); ~**s plats/ aiguilles** flat/stiletto heels
talonner [talɔne] *vt* to follow hard behind; (*fig*) to hound
talus [taly] *nm* embankment
tambour [tɑ̃buʀ] *nm* (*MUS, aussi TECH*) drum; (*musicien*) drummer; (*porte*) revolving door(s *pl*)

tamis [tami] *nm* sieve

Tamise [tamiz] *nf*: **la** ~ the Thames

tamisé, e [tamize] *adj* (*fig*) subdued, soft

tamiser [tamize] *vt* to sieve, sift

tampon [tɑ̃pɔ̃] *nm* (*de coton, d'ouate*) wad, pad; (*amortisseur*) buffer; (*bouchon*) plug, stopper; (*cachet, timbre*) stamp; (*mémoire*) ~ (*INFORM*) buffer; ~ **(hygiénique)** tampon; **tamponner** *vt* (*timbres*) to stamp; (*heurter*) to crash *ou* ram into; **tamponneuse** *adj*: **autos tamponneuses** dodgems

tandis [tɑ̃di]: ~ **que** *conj* while

tanguer [tɑ̃ge] *vi* to pitch (and toss)

tanière [tanjɛʀ] *nf* lair, den

tanné, e [tane] *adj* weather-beaten

tanner [tane] *vt* to tan

tant [tɑ̃] *adv* so much; ~ **de** (*sable, eau*) so much; (*gens, livres*) so many; ~ **que** as long as; (*comparatif*) as much as; ~ **mieux** that's great; so much the better; ~ **pis** never mind; too bad

tante [tɑ̃t] *nf* aunt

tantôt [tɑ̃to] *adv* (*parfois*): ~ ... ~ now ... now; (*cet après-midi*) this afternoon

tapage [tapaʒ] *nm* uproar, din

tapageur, euse [tapaʒœʀ, -øz] *adj* loud, flashy; noisy

tape [tap] *nf* slap

tape-à-l'œil [tapalœj] *adj inv* flashy, showy

taper [tape] *vt* (*porte*) to bang, slam; (*dactylographier*) to type (out); (*fam*: *emprunter*): ~ **qn de 10 F** to touch sb for 10 F ♦ *vi* (*soleil*) to beat down; ~ **sur qn** to thump sb; (*fig*) to run sb down; ~ **sur qch** to hit sth; to bang on sth; ~ **à** (*porte etc*) to knock on; ~ **dans** (*se servir*) to dig into; ~ **des mains/pieds** to clap one's hands/stamp one's feet; ~ **(à la machine)** to type; **se** ~ **un travail** to land o.s. with a job

tapi, e [tapi] *adj* crouching, cowering; hidden away

tapis [tapi] *nm* carpet; (*de table*) cloth; **mettre sur le** ~ (*fig*) to bring up for discussion; ~ **de sol** (*de tente*) groundsheet; ~ **roulant** conveyor belt

tapisser [tapise] *vt* (*avec du papier peint*) to paper; (*recouvrir*): ~ **qch (de)** to cover sth (with)

tapisserie [tapisʀi] *nf* (*tenture, broderie*) tapestry; (*papier peint*) wallpaper

tapissier, ière [tapisje, -jɛʀ] *nm/f*: ~ **(-décorateur)** upholsterer (and decorator)

tapoter [tapote] *vt* to pat, tap

taquiner [takine] *vt* to tease

tarabiscoté, e [taʀabiskote] *adj* overornate, fussy

tard [taʀ] *adv* late; **plus** ~ later (on); **au plus** ~ at the latest; **sur le** ~ late in life

tarder [taʀde] *vi* (*chose*) to be a long time coming; (*personne*): ~ **à faire** to delay doing; **il me tarde d'être** I am longing to be; **sans (plus)** ~ without (further) delay

tardif, ive [taʀdif, -iv] *adj* late

targuer [taʀge]: **se** ~ **de** *vt* to boast about

tarif [taʀif] *nm* (*liste*) price list; tariff; (*barème*) rates *pl*; fares *pl*; tariff; (*prix*) rate; fare

tarir [taʀiʀ] *vi* to dry up, run dry

tarte [taʀt(ə)] *nf* tart

tartine [taʀtin] *nf* slice of bread; ~ **de miel** slice of bread and honey; **tartiner** *vt* to spread; **fromage à tartiner** cheese spread

tartre [taʀtʀ(ə)] *nm* (*des dents*) tartar; (*de chaudière*) fur, scale

tas [tɑ] *nm* heap, pile; (*fig*): **un** ~ **de** heaps of, lots of; **en** ~ in a heap *ou* pile; **formé sur le** ~ trained on the job

tasse [tɑs] *nf* cup; ~ **à café** coffee cup

tassé, e [tɑse] *adj*: **bien** ~ (*café etc*) strong

tasser [tɑse] *vt* (*terre, neige*) to pack down; (*entasser*): ~ **qch dans** to cram sth into; **se** ~ *vi* (*terrain*) to settle; (*fig*) to sort itself out, settle down

tâter [tɑte] *vt* to feel; (*fig*) to try out; **se** ~ (*hésiter*) to be in two minds; ~ **de** (*prison etc*) to have a taste of

tatillon, ne [tatijɔ̃, -ɔn] *adj* pernickety

tâtonnement [tɑtɔnmɑ̃] *nm*: **par** ~**s** (*fig*) by trial and error

tâtonner [tɑtɔne] *vi* to grope one's way along

tâtons [tɑtɔ̃]: **à ~: chercher/avancer à tâtons** *adv* to grope around for/grope one's way forward

tatouer [tatwe] *vt* to tattoo

taudis [todi] *nm* hovel, slum

taule [tol] *(fam) nf* nick *(fam)*, prison

taupe [top] *nf* mole

taureau, x [tɔʀo] *nm* bull; *(signe):* **le T~** Taurus

tauromachie [tɔʀɔmaʃi] *nf* bullfighting

taux [to] *nm* rate; *(d'alcool)* level; **~ d'intérêt** interest rate

taxe [taks] *nf; (douanière)* duty; **~ à la valeur ajoutée** value added tax *(BRIT)*; **~ de séjour** tourist tax

taxer [takse] *vt (personne)* to tax; *(produit)* to put a tax on, tax; *(fig):* **~ qn de** to call sb *+attrib*; to accuse sb of, tax sb with

taxi [taksi] *nm* taxi

Tchécoslovaquie [tʃekɔslɔvaki] *nf* Czechoslovakia; **tchèque** *adj, nm/f* Czech ♦ *nm (LING)* Czech

te(t') [t(ə)] *pron* you; *(réfléchi)* yourself

technico-commercial, e, aux [teknikokɔmɛʀsjal, o] *adj:* **agent ~** sales technician

technicien, ne [teknisjɛ̃, -jɛn] *nm/f* technician

technique [teknik] *adj* technical ♦ *nf* technique; **techniquement** *adv* technically

technologie [teknɔlɔʒi] *nf* technology; **technologique** *adj* technological

teck [tɛk] *nm* teak

teignais *etc vb voir* **teindre**

teindre [tɛ̃dʀ(ə)] *vt* to dye

teint, e [tɛ̃, tɛ̃t] *adj* dyed ♦ *nm (du visage)* complexion; colour ♦ *nf* shade; **grand ~** colourfast

teinté, e [tɛ̃te] *adj:* **~ de** *(fig)* tinged with

teinter [tɛ̃te] *vt* to tint; *(bois)* to stain; **teinture** *nf* dyeing; *(substance)* dye; *(MÉD)* tincture

teinturerie [tɛ̃tyʀʀi] *nf* dry cleaner's

teinturier [tɛ̃tyʀje] *nm* dry cleaner

tel, telle [tɛl] *adj (pareil)* such; *(comme):* **~ un/des ...** like a/like ...; *(indéfini)* such-and-such a, a given; *(intensif):* **un ~/de ~s ...** such (a)/such ...; **rien de ~** nothing like it, no such thing; **~ que** like, such as; **~ quel** as it is *ou* stands *(ou* was *etc)*

télé [tele] *abr f (= télévision)* TV, telly *(BRIT); (poste)* TV (set), telly; **à la ~** on TV, on telly

télécabine [telekabin] *nf (benne)* cable car

télécarte [telekaʀt(ə)] *nf* phonecard

télé: ~commande *nf* remote control; **~copie** *nf* fax; **envoyer qch par ~copie** to fax sth; **~distribution** *nf* cable TV; **~férique** *nm =* **téléphérique; ~gramme** *nm* telegram; **~graphier** *vt* to telegraph, cable; **~guider** *vt* to operate by remote control, radio-control; **~journal** *nm TV news magazine programme;* **~matique** *nf* telematics *sg;* **~objectif** *nm* telephoto lens *sg*

téléphérique [teleferik] *nm* cable car

téléphone [telefɔn] *nm* telephone; **avoir le ~** to be on the (tele)phone; **au ~** on the phone; **~ de voiture** car phone; **téléphoner** *vi* to telephone, ring; to make a phone call; **téléphoner à** to phone, call up; **téléphonique** *adj* (tele)phone *cpd*

télescope [teleskɔp] *nm* telescope

télescoper [teleskɔpe] *vt* to smash up; **se ~** *(véhicules)* to concertina

télé: ~scripteur *nm* teleprinter; **~siège** *nm* chairlift; **~ski** *nm* ski-tow; **~spectateur, trice** *nm/f* (television) viewer; **~viseur** *nm* television set; **~vision** *nf* television; **à la ~vision** on television

télex [teleks] *nm* telex

telle [tɛl] *adj voir* **tel**

tellement [tɛlmɑ̃] *adv (tant)* so much; *(si)* so; **~ de** *(sable, eau)* so much; *(gens, livres)* so many; **il s'est endormi ~** il **était fatigué** he was so tired (that) he fell asleep; **pas ~** not (all) that much; not (all) that *+adjectif*

téméraire [temeʀɛʀ] *adj* reckless, rash; **témérité** *nf* recklessness, rashness

témoignage [temwaɲaʒ] *nm (JUR: dé-*

claration) testimony *no pl*, evidence *no pl*; (: *faits*) evidence *no pl*; (*rapport, récit*) account; (*fig: d'affection etc*) token, mark; expression

témoigner [temwaɲe] *vt* (*intérêt, gratitude*) to show ♦ *vi* (*JUR*) to testify, give evidence; ~ **de** to bear witness to, testify to

témoin [temwɛ̃] *nm* witness; (*fig*) testimony ♦ *adj* control *cpd*, test *cpd*; **appartement** ~ show flat (*BRIT*); **être** ~ **de** to witness; ~ **oculaire** eyewitness

tempe [tɑ̃p] *nf* temple

tempérament [tɑ̃peʀamɑ̃] *nm* temperament, disposition; **à** ~ (*vente*) on deferred (payment) terms; (*achat*) by instalments, hire purchase *cpd*

température [tɑ̃peʀatyʀ] *nf* temperature; **avoir** *ou* **faire de la** ~ to be running *ou* have a temperature

tempéré, e [tɑ̃peʀe] *adj* temperate

tempête [tɑ̃pɛt] *nf* storm; ~ **de sable/ neige** sand/snowstorm

temple [tɑ̃pl(ə)] *nm* temple; (*protestant*) church

temporaire [tɑ̃pɔʀɛʀ] *adj* temporary

temps [tɑ̃] *nm* (*atmosphérique*) weather; (*durée*) time; (*époque*) time, times *pl*; (*LING*) tense; (*MUS*) beat; (*TECH*) stroke; **il fait beau/mauvais** ~ the weather is fine/bad; **avoir le** ~/**tout le** ~ to have time/plenty of time; **en** ~ **de paix/ guerre** in peacetime/wartime; **en** ~ **utile** *ou* **voulu** in due time *ou* course; **de** ~ **en** ~, **de** ~ **à autre** from time to time; **à** ~ (*partir, arriver*) in time; **à** ~ **partiel** part-time; **dans le** ~ at one time; **de tout** ~ always; ~ **d'arrêt** pause, halt; ~ **mort** (*COMM*) slack period

tenable [tənabl(ə)] *adj* bearable

tenace [tənas] *adj* tenacious, persistent

tenailler [tənaje] *vt* (*fig*) to torment

tenailles [tənaj] *nfpl* pincers

tenais *etc vb voir* **tenir**

tenancier, ière [tənɑ̃sje, -jɛʀ] *nm/f* manager/manageress

tenant, e [tənɑ̃, -ɑ̃t] *nm/f* (*SPORT*): ~ **du titre** title-holder

tendance [tɑ̃dɑ̃s] *nf* (*opinions*) leanings *pl*, sympathies *pl*; (*inclination*) tendency; (*évolution*) trend; **avoir** ~ **à** to have a tendency to, tend to

tendeur [tɑ̃dœʀ] *nm* (*attache*) elastic strap

tendre [tɑ̃dʀ(ə)] *adj* tender; (*bois, roche, couleur*) soft ♦ *vt* (*élastique, peau*) to stretch, draw tight; (*muscle*) to tense; (*donner*): ~ **qch à qn** to hold sth out to sb; to offer sb sth; (*fig: piège*) to set, lay; **se** ~ *vi* (*corde*) to tighten; (*relations*) to become strained; ~ **à qch/à faire** to tend towards sth/to do; ~ **l'oreille** to prick up one's ears; ~ **la main/le bras** to hold out one's hand/stretch out one's arm; **tendrement** *adv* tenderly; **tendresse** *nf* tenderness

tendu, e [tɑ̃dy] *pp de* **tendre** ♦ *adj* tight; tensed; strained

ténèbres [tenɛbʀ(ə)] *nfpl* darkness *sg*

teneur [tənœʀ] *nf* content; (*d'une lettre*) terms *pl*, content

tenir [təniʀ] *vt* to hold; (*magasin, hôtel*) to run; (*promesse*) to keep ♦ *vi* to hold; (*neige, gel*) to last; **se** ~ *vi* (*avoir lieu*) to be held, take place; (*être: personne*) to stand; **se** ~ **droit** to stand (*ou* sit) up straight; **bien se** ~ to behave well; **se** ~ **à qch** to hold on to sth; **s'en** ~ **à qch** to confine o.s. to sth; to stick to sth; ~ **à** to be attached to; to care about; to depend on; to stem from; ~ **à faire** to want to do; ~ **de** to partake of; to take after; **ça ne tient qu'à lui** it is entirely up to him; ~ **qn pour** to take sb for; ~ **qch de qn** (*histoire*) to have heard *ou* learnt sth from sb; (*qualité, défaut*) to have inherited *ou* got sth from sb; ~ **les comptes** to keep the books; ~ **le coup** to hold out; ~ **au chaud** to keep hot; **tiens/ tenez, voilà le stylo** there's the pen!; **tiens, Alain!** look, here's Alain!; **tiens?** (*surprise*) really?

tennis [tenis] *nm* tennis; (*court*) tennis court ♦ *nm ou pl* (*aussi:* **chaussures de** ~) tennis *ou* gym shoes; ~ **de table** table tennis; **tennisman** *nm* tennis player

tension [tɑ̃sjɔ̃] *nf* tension; (*fig*) tension;

strain; (MÉD) blood pressure; **faire** *ou* **avoir de la ~** to have high blood pressure

tentation [tɑ̃tasjɔ̃] *nf* temptation

tentative [tɑ̃tativ] *nf* attempt, bid

tente [tɑ̃t] *nf* tent

tenter [tɑ̃te] *vt* (*éprouver, attirer*) to tempt; (*essayer*): **~ qch/de faire** to attempt *ou* try sth/to do; **~ sa chance** to try one's luck

tenture [tɑ̃tyr] *nf* hanging

tenu, e [tɑ̃ny] *pp de* **tenir** ♦ *adj* (*maison, comptes*): **bien ~** well-kept; (*obligé*): **~ de faire** under an obligation to do ♦ *nf* (*action de tenir*) running; keeping; holding; (*vêtements*) clothes *pl*, gear; (*allure*) dress *no pl*, appearance; (*comportement*) manners *pl*, behaviour; **en petite tenue** scantily dressed *ou* clad; **~e de route** (*AUTO*) road-holding; **~e de soirée** evening dress

ter [tɛr] *adj*: **16 ~ 16b** *ou* **B**

térébenthine [terebɑ̃tin] *nf*: **(essence de) ~** (oil of) turpentine

terme [tɛrm(ə)] *nm* term; (*fin*) end; **à court/long ~** short-/long-term *ou* -range ♦ *adv* in the short/long term; **avant ~** (*MÉD*) prematurely; **mettre un ~ à** to put an end *ou* a stop to

terminaison [tɛrminɛzɔ̃] *nf* (*LING*) ending

terminal, e, aux [tɛrminal, -o] *adj* final ♦ *nm* terminal; **terminale** *nf* (*SCOL*) ≈ sixth form *ou* year (*BRIT*), ≈ twelfth grade (*US*)

terminer [tɛrmine] *vt* to end; (*travail, repas*) to finish; **se ~** *vi* to end

terne [tɛrn(ə)] *adj* dull

ternir [tɛrnir] *vt* to dull; (*fig*) to sully, tarnish; **se ~** *vi* to become dull

terrain [tɛrɛ̃] *nm* (*sol, fig*) ground; (*COMM*) land *no pl*, plot (of land); site; **sur le ~** (*fig*) on the field; **~ d'aviation** airfield; **~ de camping** campsite; **~ de football/rugby** football/rugby pitch (*BRIT*) *ou* field (*US*); **~ de golf** golf course; **~ de jeu** games field; playground; **~ de sport** sports ground; **~ vague** waste ground *no pl*

terrasse [tɛras] *nf* terrace; **à la ~** (*café*) outside; **terrassement** [tɛrasmɑ̃] *nm* earth-moving, earthworks *pl*; embankment; **terrasser** [tɛrase] *vt* (*adversaire*) to floor; (*suj: maladie etc*) to lay low

terre [tɛr] *nf* (*gén, aussi* ÉLEC) earth; (*substance*) soil, earth; (*opposé à mer*) land *no pl*; (*contrée*) land; **~s** *nfpl* (*terrains*) lands, land *sg*; **en ~** (*pipe, poterie*) clay *cpd*; **à ~** *ou* **par ~** (*mettre, être*) on the ground (*ou* floor); (*jeter, tomber*) to the ground, down; **~ à ~** *adj inv* down-to-earth; **~ cuite** earthenware; terracotta; **la ~ ferme** dry land; **~ glaise** clay

terreau [tɛro] *nm* compost

terre-plein [tɛrplɛ̃] *nm* platform

terrer [tɛre]: **se ~** *vi* to hide away; to go to ground

terrestre [tɛrɛstr(ə)] *adj* (*surface*) earth's, of the earth; (*BOT, ZOOL, MIL*) land *cpd*; (*REL*) earthly, worldly

terreur [tɛrœr] *nf* terror *no pl*

terrible [tɛribl(ə)] *adj* terrible, dreadful; (*fam*) terrific

terrien, ne [tɛrjɛ̃, -jɛn] *adj*: **propriétaire ~** landowner ♦ *nm/f* (*non martien etc*) earthling

terrier [tɛrje] *nm* burrow, hole; (*chien*) terrier

terril [tɛril] *nm* slag heap

terrine [tɛrin] *nf* (*récipient*) terrine; (*CULIN*) pâté

territoire [tɛritwar] *nm* territory

terroir [tɛrwar] *nm* (*AGR*) soil; region

terrorisme [tɛrɔrism(ə)] *nm* terrorism; **terroriste** *nm/f* terrorist

tertiaire [tɛrsjɛr] *adj* tertiary ♦ *nm* (*ÉCON*) service industries *pl*

tertre [tɛrtr(ə)] *nm* hillock, mound

tes [te] *dét voir* **ton¹**

tesson [tɛsɔ̃] *nm*: **~ de bouteille** piece of broken bottle

test [tɛst] *nm* test

testament [tɛstamɑ̃] *nm* (*JUR*) will; (*REL*) Testament; (*fig*) legacy

tester [tɛste] *vt* to test

testicule [tɛstikyl] *nm* testicle

tétanos [tetanos] *nm* tetanus

têtard [tɛtaʀ] *nm* tadpole

tête [tɛt] *nf* head; (*cheveux*) hair *no pl*; (*visage*) face; **de ~** (*wagon etc*) front *cpd* ♦ *adv* (*calculer*) in one's head, mentally; **tenir ~ à qn** to stand up to sb; **la ~ en bas** with one's head down; **la ~ la première** (*tomber*) headfirst; **faire une ~** (*FOOTBALL*) to head the ball; **faire la ~** (*fig*) to sulk; **en ~** (*SPORT*) in the lead; at the front; **en ~ à ~** in private, alone together; **de la ~ aux pieds** from head to toe; **~ de lecture** (playback) head; **~ de liste** (*POL*) chief candidate; **~ de série** (*TENNIS*) seeded player, seed

tête-à-queue [tɛtakø] *nm inv*: **faire un ~** to spin round

téter [tete] *vt*: **~ (sa mère)** to suck at one's mother's breast, feed

tétine [tetin] *nf* teat; (*sucette*) dummy (*BRIT*), pacifier (*US*)

têtu, e [tety] *adj* stubborn, pigheaded

texte [tɛkst(ə)] *nm* text

textile [tɛkstil] *adj* textile *cpd* ♦ *nm* textile; textile industry

texture [tɛkstyʀ] *nf* texture

TGV *sigle m* (= *train à grande vitesse*) high-speed train

thé [te] *nm* tea; **prendre le ~** to have tea; **faire le ~** to make the tea

théâtral, e, aux [teatʀal, -o] *adj* theatrical

théâtre [teatʀ(ə)] *nm* theatre; (*œuvres*) plays *pl*, dramatic works *pl*; (*fig: lieu*): **le ~ de** the scene of; (*péj*) histrionics *pl*, playacting; **faire du ~** to be on the stage; to do some acting

théière [tejɛʀ] *nf* teapot

thème [tɛm] *nm* theme; (*SCOL: traduction*) prose (composition)

théologie [teɔlɔʒi] *nf* theology

théorie [teɔʀi] *nf* theory; **théorique** *adj* theoretical

thérapie [teʀapi] *nf* therapy

thermal, e, aux [tɛʀmal, -o] *adj*: **station ~e** spa; **cure ~e** water cure

thermes [tɛʀm(ə)] *nmpl* thermal baths

thermomètre [tɛʀmɔmɛtʀ(ə)] *nm* thermometer

thermos [tɛʀmos] ® *nm ou nf*: (**bou-**

teille) **~** vacuum *ou* Thermos (®) flask

thermostat [tɛʀmɔsta] *nm* thermostat

thèse [tɛz] *nf* thesis

thon [tɔ̃] *nm* tuna (fish)

thym [tɛ̃] *nm* thyme

tibia [tibja] *nm* shinbone, tibia; shin

tic [tik] *nm* tic, (nervous) twitch; (*de langage etc*) mannerism

ticket [tikɛ] *nm* ticket; **~ de caisse** *nm* receipt; **~ de quai** platform ticket

tiède [tjɛd] *adj* lukewarm; tepid; (*vent, air*) mild, warm; **tiédir** *vi* to cool; to grow warmer

tien, ne [tjɛ̃, tjɛn] *pron*: **le(la) ~(ne)**, **les ~(ne)s** yours; **à la ~ne!** cheers!

tiens [tjɛ̃] *vb, excl voir* **tenir**

tierce [tjɛʀs(ə)] *adj voir* **tiers**

tiercé [tjɛʀse] *nm* system of forecast betting giving first 3 horses

tiers, tierce [tjɛʀ, tjɛʀs(ə)] *adj* third ♦ *nm* (*JUR*) third party; (*fraction*) third; **le ~ monde** the Third World

tige [tiʒ] *nf* stem; (*baguette*) rod

tignasse [tiɲas] (*péj*) *nf* mop of hair

tigre [tigʀ(ə)] *nm* tiger

tigré, e [tigʀe] *adj* striped; spotted

tilleul [tijœl] *nm* lime (tree), linden (tree); (*boisson*) lime(-blossom) tea

timbale [tɛ̃bal] *nf* (metal) tumbler; **~s** *nfpl* (*MUS*) timpani, kettledrums

timbre [tɛ̃bʀ(ə)] *nm* (*tampon*) stamp; (*aussi: ~-poste*) (postage) stamp; (*MUS: de voix, instrument*) timbre, tone

timbré, e [tɛ̃bʀe] (*fam*) *adj* daft

timide [timid] *adj* shy; timid; (*timoré*) timid, timorous; **timidement** *adv* shyly; timidly; **timidité** *nf* shyness; timidity

tins *etc vb voir* **tenir**

tintamarre [tɛ̃tamaʀ] *nm* din, uproar

tinter [tɛ̃te] *vi* to ring, chime; (*argent, clefs*) to jingle

tir [tiʀ] *nm* (*sport*) shooting; (*fait ou manière de tirer*) firing *no pl*; (*stand*) shooting gallery; **~ à l'arc** archery; **~ au pigeon** clay pigeon shooting

tirage [tiʀaʒ] *nm* (*action*) printing; (*PHOTO*) print; (*de journal*) circulation; (*de livre*) (print-)run; edition; (*de loterie*) draw; **~ au sort** drawing lots

tirailler [tiʀaje] *vt* to pull at, tug at ♦ *vi* to fire at random

tirant [tiʀɑ̃] *nm*: ~ **d'eau** draught

tire [tiʀ] *nf*: **vol à la** ~ pickpocketing

tiré, e [tiʀe] *adj* (*traits*) drawn ♦ *nm* (*COMM*) drawee; ~ **par les cheveux** far-fetched

tire-au-flanc [tiʀoflɑ̃] (*péj*) *nm inv* skiver

tire-bouchon [tiʀbuʃɔ̃] *nm* corkscrew

tirelire [tiʀliʀ] *nf* moneybox

tirer [tiʀe] *vt* (*gén*) to pull; (*extraire*): ~ **qch de** to take *ou* pull sth out of; to get sth out of; to extract sth from; (*tracer*: *ligne, trait*) to draw, trace; (*fermer*: *rideau*) to draw, close; (*choisir*: *carte, conclusion, aussi COMM*: *chèque*) to draw; (*en faisant feu*: *balle, coup*) to fire; (: *animal*) to shoot; (*journal, livre, photo*) to print; (*FOOTBALL*: *corner etc*) to take ♦ *vi* (*faire feu*) to fire; (*faire du tir, FOOTBALL*) to shoot; (*cheminée*) to draw; **se** ~ *vi* (*fam*) to push off; **s'en** ~ to pull through, get off; ~ **sur** to pull on *ou* at; to shoot *ou* fire at; (*pipe*) to draw on; (*fig*: *avoisiner*) to verge on, border on; ~ **qn de** (*embarras etc*) to help *ou* get sb out of; ~ **à l'arc/la carabine** to shoot with a bow and arrow/with a rifle

tiret [tiʀe] *nm* dash

tireur, euse [tiʀœʀ, -øz] *nm/f* (*COMM*) drawer ♦ *nm* gunman; ~ **d'élite** marksman

tiroir [tiʀwaʀ] *nm* drawer; **tiroir-caisse** *nm* till

tisane [tizan] *nf* herb tea

tisonnier [tizɔnje] *nm* poker

tisser [tise] *vt* to weave; **tisserand** *nm* weaver

tissu [tisy] *nm* fabric, material, cloth *no pl*; (*ANAT, BIO*) tissue

tissu-éponge [tisyepɔ̃ʒ] *nm* (terry) towelling *no pl*

titre [titʀ(ə)] *nm* (*gén*) title; (*de journal*) headline; (*diplôme*) qualification; (*COMM*) security; **en** ~ (*champion*) official; **à juste** ~ with just cause, rightly; **à quel** ~? on what grounds?; **à aucun** ~ on no account; **au même** ~ (**que**) in the same

way (as); **à** ~ **d'information** for (your) information; **à** ~ **gracieux** free of charge; **à** ~ **d'essai** on a trial basis; **à** ~ **privé** in a private capacity; ~ **de propriété** title deed; ~ **de transport** ticket

tituber [titybe] *vi* to stagger (along)

titulaire [titylɛʀ] *adj* (*ADMIN*) appointed, with tenure ♦ *nm/f* incumbent; **être** ~ **de** (*poste*) to hold; (*permis*) to be the holder of

toast [tost] *nm* slice *ou* piece of toast; (*de bienvenue*) (welcoming) toast; **porter un** ~ **à qn** to propose *ou* drink a toast to sb

toboggan [tɔbɔgɑ̃] *nm* toboggan; (*jeu*) slide

tocsin [tɔksɛ̃] *nm* alarm (bell)

toge [tɔʒ] *nf* toga; (*de juge*) gown

toi [twa] *pron* you

toile [twal] *nf* (*matériau*) cloth *no pl*; (*bâche*) piece of canvas; (*tableau*) canvas; ~ **cirée** oilcloth; ~ **d'araignée** cobweb; ~ **de fond** (*fig*) backdrop

toilette [twalɛt] *nf* wash; (*habits*) outfit; dress *no pl*; ~**s** *nfpl* (*w.-c.*) toilet *sg*; **faire sa** ~ to have a wash, get washed; **articles de** ~ toiletries

toi-même [twamɛm] *pron* yourself

toiser [twaze] *vt* to eye up and down

toison [twazɔ̃] *nf* (*de mouton*) fleece; (*cheveux*) mane

toit [twa] *nm* roof; ~ **ouvrant** sunroof

toiture [twatyʀ] *nf* roof

tôle [tol] *nf* (*plaque*) steel *ou* iron sheet; ~ **ondulée** corrugated iron

tolérable [tɔleʀabl(ə)] *adj* tolerable, bearable

tolérant, e [tɔleʀɑ̃, -ɑ̃t] *adj* tolerant

tolérer [tɔleʀe] *vt* to tolerate; (*ADMIN*: *hors taxe etc*) to allow

tollé [tɔle] *nm* outcry

tomate [tɔmat] *nf* tomato

tombe [tɔ̃b] *nf* (*sépulture*) grave; (*avec monument*) tomb

tombeau, x [tɔ̃bo] *nm* tomb

tombée [tɔ̃be] *nf*: **à la** ~ **de la nuit** at the close of day, at nightfall

tomber [tɔ̃be] *vi* to fall; **laisser** ~ to drop; ~ **sur** (*rencontrer*) to come across;

(*attaquer*) to set about; ~ **de fatigue/ sommeil** to drop from exhaustion/be falling asleep on one's feet; **ça tombe bien** that's come at the right time; **il est bien tombé** he's been lucky

tome [tɔm] *nm* volume

ton¹, ta [tɔ̃, ta] (*pl* **tes**) *dét* your

ton² [tɔ̃] *nm* (*gén*) tone; (*MUS*) key; (*couleur*) shade, tone; **de bon ton** in good taste

tonalité [tɔnalite] *nf* (*au téléphone*) dialling tone; (*MUS*) key; (*fig*) tone

tondeuse [tɔ̃døz] *nf* (*à gazon*) (lawn)mower; (*du coiffeur*) clippers *pl*; (*pour la tonte*) shears *pl*

tondre [tɔ̃dʀ(ə)] *vt* (*pelouse, herbe*) to mow; (*haie*) to cut, clip; (*mouton, toison*) to shear; (*cheveux*) to crop

tonifier [tɔnifje] *vt* (*peau, organisme*) to tone up

tonique [tɔnik] *adj* fortifying ♦ *nm* tonic

tonne [tɔn] *nf* metric ton, tonne

tonneau, x [tɔno] *nm* (*à vin, cidre*) barrel; (*NAVIG*) ton; **faire des ~x** (*voiture, avion*) to roll over

tonnelle [tɔnɛl] *nf* bower, arbour

tonner [tɔne] *vi* to thunder; **il tonne** it is thundering, there's some thunder

tonnerre [tɔnɛʀ] *nm* thunder

tonus [tɔnys] *nm* dynamism

top [tɔp] *nm*: **au 3ème ~** at the 3rd stroke

topinambour [tɔpinɑ̃buʀ] *nm* Jerusalem artichoke

toque [tɔk] *nf* (*de fourrure*) fur hat; ~ **de cuisinier** chef's hat; ~ **de jockey/ juge** jockey's/judge's cap

toqué, e [tɔke] (*fam*) *adj* cracked

torche [tɔʀʃ(ə)] *nf* torch

torchon [tɔʀʃɔ̃] *nm* cloth, duster; (*à vaisselle*) tea towel *ou* cloth

tordre [tɔʀdʀ(ə)] *vt* (*chiffon*) to wring; (*barre, fig: visage*) to twist; **se ~** *vi* (*barre*) to bend; (*roue*) to twist, buckle; (*ver, serpent*) to writhe; **se ~ le pied/ bras** to twist one's foot/arm; **tordu, e** [tɔʀdy] *adj* (*fig*) warped, twisted

tornade [tɔʀnad] *nf* tornado

torpille [tɔʀpij] *nf* torpedo

torréfier [tɔʀefje] *vt* to roast

torrent [tɔʀɑ̃] *nm* torrent

torse [tɔʀs(ə)] *nm* (*ANAT*) torso; chest

torsion [tɔʀsjɔ̃] *nf* twisting; torsion

tort [tɔʀ] *nm* (*défaut*) fault; (*préjudice*) wrong *no pl*; ~**s** *nmpl* (*JUR*) fault *sg*; **avoir ~** to be wrong; **être dans son ~** to be in the wrong; **donner ~ à qn** to lay the blame on sb; (*fig*) to prove sb wrong; **causer du ~ à** to harm; to be harmful *ou* detrimental to; **à ~** wrongly; **à ~ et à travers** wildly

torticolis [tɔʀtikɔli] *nm* stiff neck

tortiller [tɔʀtije] *vt* to twist; to twiddle; **se ~** *vi* to wriggle, squirm

tortionnaire [tɔʀsjɔnɛʀ] *nm* torturer

tortue [tɔʀty] *nf* tortoise

tortueux, euse [tɔʀtɥø, -øz] *adj* (*rue*) twisting; (*fig*) tortuous

torture [tɔʀtyʀ] *nf* torture; **torturer** *vt* to torture; (*fig*) to torment

tôt [to] *adv* early; ~ **ou tard** sooner or later; **si ~** so early; (*déjà*) so soon; **au plus ~** at the earliest; **il eut ~ fait de faire** he soon did

total, e, aux [tɔtal, -o] *adj, nm* total; **au ~** in total *ou* all; **faire le ~** to work out the total, add up; **totalement** *adv* totally, completely; **totaliser** *vt* to total (up)

totalité [tɔtalite] *nf*: **la ~ de** all of, the total amount (*ou* number) of; the whole +*sg*; **en ~** entirely

toubib [tubib] (*fam*) *nm* doctor

touchant, e [tuʃɑ̃, -ɑ̃t] *adj* touching

touche [tuʃ] *nf* (*de piano, de machine à écrire*) key; (*PEINTURE etc*) stroke, touch; (*fig: de nostalgie*) touch, hint; (*FOOTBALL: aussi: remise en ~*) throw-in; (*aussi: ligne de ~*) touch-line

toucher [tuʃe] *nm* touch ♦ *vt* to touch; (*palper*) to feel; (*atteindre: d'un coup de feu etc*) to hit; (*concerner*) to concern, affect; (*contacter*) to reach, contact; (*recevoir: récompense*) to receive, get; (*: salaire*) to draw, get; (*: chèque*) to cash; **se ~** (*être en contact*) to touch; **au ~** to the touch; ~ **à** to touch; (*concerner*) to have to do with, concern; **je vais lui en ~ un mot** I'll have a word with him about it; **~ à sa fin** to be drawing to a close

touffe [tuf] *nf* tuft

touffu, e [tufy] *adj* thick, dense

toujours [tuʒuʀ] *adv* always; (*encore*) still; (*constamment*) forever; **~ plus** more and more; **pour ~** forever; **~ est-il que** the fact remains that; **essaie ~** (you can) try anyway

toupet [tupɛ] *nm* (*fam*) cheek

toupie [tupi] *nf* (spinning) top

tour [tuʀ] *nf* tower; (*immeuble*) high-rise block (*BRIT*) *ou* building (*US*); (*ÉCHECS*) castle, rook ♦ *nm* (*excursion*) stroll, walk; run, ride; trip; (*SPORT: aussi: ~ de piste*) lap; (*d'être servi ou de jouer etc*) turn; (*de roue etc*) revolution; (*circonférence*): **de 3 m de ~** 3 m round, with a circumference *ou* girth of 3 m; (*POL: aussi: ~ de scrutin*) ballot; (*ruse, de prestidigitation*) trick; (*de potier*) wheel; (*à bois, métaux*) lathe; **faire le ~ de** to go round; (*à pied*) to walk round; **c'est au ~ de Renée** it's Renée's turn; **à ~ de rôle, ~ à ~** in turn; **~ de chant** song recital; **~ de contrôle** *nf* control tower; **~ de garde** spell of duty; **~ d'horizon** (*fig*) general survey; **~ de taille/tête** waist/ head measurement

tourbe [tuʀb(ə)] *nf* peat

tourbillon [tuʀbijɔ̃] *nm* whirlwind; (*d'eau*) whirlpool; (*fig*) whirl, swirl; **tourbillonner** *vi* to whirl (round)

tourelle [tuʀɛl] *nf* turret

tourisme [tuʀism(ə)] *nm* tourism; **agence de ~** tourist agency; **faire du ~** to go sightseeing; to go touring; **touriste** *nm/f* tourist; **touristique** *adj* tourist *cpd*; (*région*) touristic

tourment [tuʀmɑ̃] *nm* torment

tourmenter [tuʀmɑ̃te] *vt* to torment; **se ~** *vi* to fret, worry o.s.

tournant [tuʀnɑ̃] *nm* (*de route*) bend; (*fig*) turning point

tournebroche [tuʀnəbʀɔʃ] *nm* roasting spit

tourne-disque [tuʀnədisk(ə)] *nm* record player

tournée [tuʀne] *nf* (*du facteur etc*) round; (*d'artiste, politicien*) tour; (*au café*) round (of drinks)

tournemain [tuʀnəmɛ̃]: **en un ~** *adv* (as) quick as a flash

tourner [tuʀne] *vt* to turn; (*sauce, mélange*) to stir; (*contourner*) to get round; (*CINÉMA*) to shoot; to make ♦ *vi* to turn; (*moteur*) to run; (*compteur*) to tick away; (*lait etc*) to turn (sour); **se ~** *vi* to turn round; **se ~ vers** to turn to; to turn towards; **bien ~** to turn out well; **~ autour de** to go round; (*péj*) to hang round; **~ à/en** to turn into; **~ le dos à** to turn one's back on; to have one's back to; **~ de l'œil** to pass out

tournesol [tuʀnəsɔl] *nm* sunflower

tournevis [tuʀnəvis] *nm* screwdriver

tourniquet [tuʀnikɛ] *nm* (*pour arroser*) sprinkler; (*portillon*) turnstile; (*présentoir*) revolving stand, spinner

tournoi [tuʀnwa] *nm* tournament

tournoyer [tuʀnwaje] *vi* to whirl round; to swirl round

tournure [tuʀnyʀ] *nf* (*LING*) turn of phrase; form; phrasing; (*évolution*): **la ~ de qch** the way sth is developing; (*aspect*): **la ~ de** the look of; **~ d'esprit** turn *ou* cast of mind; **la ~ des événements** the turn of events

tourte [tuʀt(ə)] *nf* pie

tous [*adj* tu, *pron* tus] *adj, pron voir* **tout**

Toussaint [tusɛ̃] *nf*: **la ~** All Saints' Day

tousser [tuse] *vi* to cough

MOT-CLÉ

tout, e [tu, tut] (*mpl* **tous**, *fpl* **toutes**) *adj* **1** (*avec article singulier*) all; **~ le lait** all the milk; **~e la nuit** all night, the whole night; **~ le livre** the whole book; **~ un pain** a whole loaf; **~ le temps** all the time; the whole time; **c'est ~ le contraire** it's quite the opposite

2 (*avec article pluriel*) every; all; **tous les livres** all the books; **~es les nuits** every night; **~es les fois** every time; **~es les trois/deux semaines** every third/

other *ou* second week, every three/two weeks; **tous les deux** both *ou* each of us (*ou* them *ou* you); **~es les trois** all three of us (*ou* them *ou* you)

3 (*sans article*): **à ~ âge** at any age; **pour ~e nourriture, il avait ...** his only food was ...

♦ *pron* everything, all; **il a ~ fait** he's done everything; **je les vois tous** I can see them all *ou* all of them; **nous y sommes tous allés** all of us went, we all went; **en ~ in all**; **~ ce qu'il sait** all he knows

♦ *nm* whole; **le ~** all of it (*ou* them); **le ~ est de ...** the main thing is to ...; **pas du ~** not at all

♦ *adv* **1** (*très, complètement*) very; **~ près** very near; **le ~ premier** the very first; **~ seul** all alone; **le livre ~ entier** the whole book; **~ en haut** right at the top; **~ droit** straight ahead

2: **~ en** while; **~ en travaillant** while working, as he *etc* works

3: **~ d'abord** first of all; **~ à coup** suddenly; **~ à fait** absolutely; **~ à l'heure** a short while ago; (*futur*) in a short while, shortly; **à ~ à l'heure!** see you later!; **~ de même** all the same; **~ le monde** everybody; **~ de suite** immediately, straight away; **~ terrain** *ou* **tous terrains** all-terrain

toutefois [tutfwa] *adv* however

toutes [tut] *adj, pron voir* **tout**

toux [tu] *nf* cough

toxicomane [tɔksikɔman] *nm/f* drug addict

trac [trak] *nm* nerves *pl*

tracasser [trakase] *vt* to worry, bother; to harass; **tracasseries** [trakasri] *nfpl* (*chicanes*) annoyances

trace [tras] *nf* (*empreintes*) tracks *pl*; (*marques, aussi fig*) mark; (*restes, vestige*) trace; (*indice*) sign; **~s de pas** footprints

tracé [trase] *nm* line; layout

tracer [trase] *vt* to draw; (*mot*) to trace; (*piste*) to open up

tract [trakt] *nm* tract, pamphlet

tractations [traktɑsjɔ̃] *nfpl* dealings, bargaining *sg*

tracteur [traktœr] *nm* tractor

traction [traksjɔ̃] *nf*: **~ avant/arrière** front-wheel/rear-wheel drive

tradition [tradisjɔ̃] *nf* tradition; **traditionnel, le** *adj* traditional

traducteur, trice [tradyktœr, -tris] *nm/f* translator

traduction [tradyksjɔ̃] *nf* translation

traduire [traduir] *vt* to translate; (*exprimer*) to render, convey

trafic [trafik] *nm* traffic; **~ d'armes** arms dealing; **trafiquant, e** *nm/f* trafficker; dealer; **trafiquer** (*péj*) *vt* to doctor, tamper with

tragédie [traʒedi] *nf* tragedy

tragique [traʒik] *adj* tragic

trahir [trair] *vt* to betray; (*fig*) to give away, reveal; **trahison** *nf* betrayal; (*JUR*) treason

train [trɛ̃] *nm* (*RAIL*) train; (*allure*) pace; (*fig: ensemble*) set; **mettre qch en ~** to get sth under way; **mettre qn en ~** to put sb in good spirits; **se mettre en ~** to get started; to warm up; **se sentir en ~** to feel in good form; **~ d'atterrissage** undercarriage; **~ de vie** style of living; **~ électrique** (*jouet*) (electric) train set; **~-autos-couchettes** car-sleeper train

traîne [trɛn] *nf* (*de robe*) train; **être à la ~** to be in tow; to lag behind

traîneau, x [trɛno] *nm* sleigh, sledge

traînée [trɛne] *nf* streak, trail; (*péj*) slut

traîner [trɛne] *vt* (*remorque*) to pull; (*enfant, chien*) to drag *ou* trail along ♦ *vi* (*être en désordre*) to lie around; (*marcher*) to dawdle (along); (*vagabonder*) to hang about; (*agir lentement*) to idle about; (*durer*) to drag on; **se ~** *vi* to drag o.s. along; **~ les pieds** to drag one's feet

train-train [trɛ̃trɛ̃] *nm* humdrum routine

traire [trɛr] *vt* to milk

trait [trɛ] *nm* (*ligne*) line; (*de dessin*) stroke; (*caractéristique*) feature, trait; **~s** *nmpl* (*du visage*) features; **d'un ~** (*boire*) in one gulp; **de ~** (*animal*) draught; **avoir ~ à** to concern; **~ d'union** hyphen; (*fig*) link

traitant, e [tʀɛtɑ̃, -ɑ̃t] *adj*: **votre médecin ~** your usual *ou* family doctor; **crème ~e** conditioning cream

traite [tʀɛt] *nf* (*COMM*) draft; (*AGR*) milking; **d'une ~** without stopping; **la ~ des noirs** the slave trade

traité [tʀɛte] *nm* treaty

traitement [tʀɛtmɑ̃] *nm* treatment; processing; (*salaire*) salary; **~ de données/texte** data/word processing

traiter [tʀɛte] *vt* (*gén*) to treat; (*TECH, INFORM*) to process; (*affaire*) to deal with, handle; (*qualifier*): **~ qn d'idiot** to call sb a fool ♦ *vi* to deal; **~ de** to deal with

traiteur [tʀɛtœʀ] *nm* caterer

traître, esse [tʀɛtʀ(ə), -tʀɛs] *adj* (*dangereux*) treacherous ♦ *nm* traitor

trajectoire [tʀaʒɛktwaʀ] *nf* path

trajet [tʀaʒɛ] *nm* journey; (*itinéraire*) route; (*fig*) path, course

trame [tʀam] *nf* (*de tissu*) weft; (*fig*) framework; texture

tramer [tʀame] *vt* to plot, hatch

tramway [tʀamwɛ] *nm* tram(way); tram(car) (*BRIT*), streetcar (*US*)

tranchant, e [tʀɑ̃ʃɑ̃, -ɑ̃t] *adj* sharp; (*fig*) peremptory ♦ *nm* (*d'un couteau*) cutting edge; (*de la main*) edge

tranche [tʀɑ̃ʃ] *nf* (*morceau*) slice; (*arête*) edge; (*partie*) section; (*série*) block; issue; bracket

tranché, e [tʀɑ̃ʃe] *adj* (*couleurs*) distinct, sharply contrasted; (*opinions*) clear-cut, definite; **tranchée** *nf* trench

trancher [tʀɑ̃ʃe] *vt* to cut, sever; (*fig: résoudre*) to settle ♦ *vi* to take a decision; **~ avec** to contrast sharply with

tranquille [tʀɑ̃kil] *adj* calm, quiet; (*enfant, élève*) quiet; (*rassuré*) easy in one's mind, with one's mind at rest; **se tenir ~** (*enfant*) to be quiet; **laisse-moi/laisse-ça ~** leave me/it alone; **tranquillité** *nf* quietness; peace (and quiet)

transat [tʀɑ̃zat] *nm* deckchair

transborder [tʀɑ̃sbɔʀde] *vt* to tran(s)ship

trans: ~férer *vt* to transfer; **~fert** *nm* transfer; **~figurer** *vt* to transform; **~formation** *nf* transformation; (*RUGBY*) conversion

transformer [tʀɑ̃sfɔʀme] *vt* to transform, alter; (*matière première, appartement, RUGBY*) to convert; **~ en** to transform into; to turn into; to convert into

transfusion [tʀɑ̃sfyzjɔ̃] *nf*: **~ sanguine** blood transfusion

transgresser [tʀɑ̃sgʀese] *vt* to contravene, disobey

transi, e [tʀɑ̃zi] *adj* numb (with cold), chilled to the bone

transiger [tʀɑ̃ziʒe] *vi* to compromise

transit [tʀɑ̃zit] *nm* transit; **transiter** *vi* to pass in transit

transitif, ive [tʀɑ̃zitif, -iv] *adj* transitive

transition [tʀɑ̃zisjɔ̃] *nf* transition; **transitoire** *adj* transitional; transient

translucide [tʀɑ̃slysid] *adj* translucent

transmetteur [tʀɑ̃smetœʀ] *nm* transmitter

transmettre [tʀɑ̃smetʀ(ə)] *vt* (*passer*): **~ qch à qn** to pass sth on to sb; (*TECH, TÉL, MÉD*) to transmit; (*TV, RADIO: re~*) to broadcast

trans: ~mission *nf* transmission; **~paraître** *vi* to show (through); **~parence** *nf* transparence; **par ~parence** (*regarder*) against the light; (*voir*) showing through; **~parent, e** *adj* transparent; **~percer** *vt* to go through, pierce; **~piration** *nf* perspiration; **~pirer** *vi* to perspire; **~planter** *vt* (*MÉD, BOT*) to transplant; (*personne*) to uproot; **~port** *nm* transport; **~ports en commun** public transport *sg*

transporter [tʀɑ̃spɔʀte] *vt* to carry, move; (*COMM*) to transport, convey; **transporteur** *nm* haulage contractor (*BRIT*), trucker (*US*)

transversal, e, aux [tʀɑ̃svɛʀsal, -o] *adj* transverse, cross(-); cross-country; running at right angles

trapèze [tʀapɛz] *nm* (*au cirque*) trapeze

trappe [tʀap] *nf* trap door

trapu, e [tʀapy] *adj* squat, stocky

traquenard [tʀaknaʀ] *nm* trap

traquer [tʀake] *vt* to track down; (*harce-*

ler) to hound

traumatiser [tʀomatize] *vt* to traumatize

travail, aux [tʀavaj, -o] *nm* (*gén*) work; (*tâche, métier*) work *no pl*, job; (*ÉCON, MÉD*) labour; **être sans ~** (*employé*) to be out of work *ou* unemployed; *voir aussi* **travaux**; **~ (au) noir** moonlighting

travailler [tʀavaje] *vi* to work; (*bois*) to warp ♦ *vt* (*bois, métal*) to work; (*objet d'art, discipline, fig: influencer*) to work on; **cela le travaille** it is on his mind; **~ à** to work on; (*fig: contribuer à*) to work towards; **travailleur, euse** *adj* hard-working ♦ *nm/f* worker; **travailliste** *adj* ≈ Labour (*BRIT*) *cpd*

travaux [tʀavo] *nmpl* (*de réparation, agricoles etc*) work *sg*; (*sur route*) roadworks *pl*; (*de construction*) building (work); **~ des champs** farmwork *sg*; **~ dirigés** (*SCOL*) supervised practical work *sg*; **~ forcés** hard labour *sg*; **~ manuels** (*SCOL*) handicrafts; **~ ménagers** housework *sg*

travée [tʀave] *nf* row; (*ARCHIT*) bay; span

travers [tʀavɛʀ] *nm* fault, failing; **en ~ (de)** across; **au ~ (de)** through; **de ~** askew ♦ *adv* sideways; (*fig*) the wrong way; **à ~** through; **regarder de ~** (*fig*) to look askance at

traverse [tʀavɛʀs(ə)] *nf* (*de voie ferrée*) sleeper; **chemin de ~** shortcut

traversée [tʀavɛʀse] *nf* crossing

traverser [tʀavɛʀse] *vt* (*gén*) to cross; (*ville, tunnel, aussi: percer, fig*) to go through; (*suj: ligne, trait*) to run across

traversin [tʀavɛʀsɛ̃] *nm* bolster

travestir [tʀavɛstiʀ] *vt* (*vérité*) to misrepresent; **se ~** *vi* to dress up; to dress as a woman

trébucher [tʀebyʃe] *vi*: **~ (sur)** to stumble (over), trip (against)

trèfle [tʀɛfl(ə)] *nm* (*BOT*) clover; (*CARTES: couleur*) clubs *pl*; (*: carte*) club

treille [tʀɛj] *nf* vine arbour; climbing vine

treillis [tʀeji] *nm* (*métallique*) wire-mesh

treize [tʀɛz] *num* thirteen; **treizième** *num* thirteenth

tréma [tʀema] *nm* diaeresis

tremblement [tʀɑ̃bləmɑ̃] *nm*: **~ de terre** earthquake

trembler [tʀɑ̃ble] *vi* to tremble, shake; **~ de** (*froid, fièvre*) to shiver *ou* tremble with; (*peur*) to shake *ou* tremble with; **~ pour qn** to fear for sb

trémousser [tʀemuse]: **se ~** *vi* to jig about, wriggle about

trempe [tʀɑ̃p] *nf* (*fig*): **de cette/sa ~** of this/his calibre

trempé, e [tʀɑ̃pe] *adj* soaking (wet), drenched; (*TECH*) tempered

tremper [tʀɑ̃pe] *vt* to soak, drench; (*aussi: faire ~, mettre à ~*) to soak; (*plonger*): **~ qch dans** to dip sth in(to) ♦ *vi* to soak; (*fig*): **~ dans** to be involved *ou* have a hand in; **se ~** *vi* to have a quick dip; **trempette** *nf*: **faire trempette** to go paddling

tremplin [tʀɑ̃plɛ̃] *nm* springboard; (*SKI*) ski-jump

trentaine [tʀɑ̃tɛn] *nf*: **une ~ (de)** thirty or so, about thirty; **avoir la ~** (*âge*) to be around thirty

trente [tʀɑ̃t] *num* thirty; **trentième** *num* thirtieth

trépidant, e [tʀepidɑ̃, -ɑ̃t] *adj* (*fig: rythme*) pulsating; (*: vie*) hectic

trépied [tʀepje] *nm* tripod

trépigner [tʀepiɲe] *vi* to stamp (one's feet)

très [tʀɛ] *adv* very; much +*pp*, highly +*pp*

trésor [tʀezɔʀ] *nm* treasure; (*ADMIN*) finances *pl*; funds *pl*; **T~ (public)** public revenue

trésorerie [tʀezɔʀʀi] *nf* (*gestion*) accounts *pl*; (*bureaux*) accounts department; **difficultés de ~** cash problems, shortage of cash *ou* funds

trésorier, ière [tʀezɔʀje, -jɛʀ] *nm/f* treasurer

tressaillir [tʀesajiʀ] *vi* to shiver, shudder; to quiver

tressauter [tʀesote] *vi* to start, jump

tresse [tʀɛs] *nf* braid, plait

tresser [tʀese] *vt* (*cheveux*) to braid, plait; (*fil, jonc*) to plait; (*corbeille*) to weave; (*corde*) to twist

tréteau, x [tʀeto] *nm* trestle

treuil [tʀœj] *nm* winch

trêve [tʀɛv] *nf* (*MIL, POL*) truce; (*fig*) respite; **le ~ de ...** enough of this ...

tri [tʀi] *nm* sorting out *no pl*; selection; (*POSTES*) sorting; sorting office

triangle [tʀijɑ̃gl(ə)] *nm* triangle

tribord [tʀibɔʀ] *nm*: **à ~** to starboard, on the starboard side

tribu [tʀiby] *nf* tribe

tribunal, aux [tʀibynal, -o] *nm* (*JUR*) court; (*MIL*) tribunal

tribune [tʀibyn] *nf* (*estrade*) platform, rostrum; (*débat*) forum; (*d'église, de tribunal*) gallery; (*de stade*) stand

tribut [tʀiby] *nm* tribute

tributaire [tʀibytɛʀ] *adj*: **être ~ de** to be dependent on

tricher [tʀiʃe] *vi* to cheat

tricolore [tʀikɔlɔʀ] *adj* three-coloured; (*français*) red, white and blue

tricot [tʀiko] *nm* (*technique, ouvrage*) knitting *no pl*; (*tissu*) knitted fabric; (*vêtement*) jersey, sweater

tricoter [tʀikɔte] *vt* to knit

trictrac [tʀiktʀak] *nm* backgammon

tricycle [tʀisikl(ə)] *nm* tricycle

triennal, e, aux [tʀiɛnal, -o] *adj* three-yearly; three-year

trier [tʀije] *vt* to sort out; (*POSTES, fruits*) to sort

trimestre [tʀimɛstʀ(ə)] *nm* (*SCOL*) term; (*COMM*) quarter; **trimestriel, le** *adj* quarterly; (*SCOL*) end-of-term

tringle [tʀɛ̃gl(ə)] *nf* rod

trinquer [tʀɛ̃ke] *vi* to clink glasses

triomphe [tʀijɔ̃f] *nm* triumph

triompher [tʀijɔ̃fe] *vi* to triumph, win; **~ de** to triumph over, overcome

tripes [tʀip] *nfpl* (*CULIN*) tripe *sg*

triple [tʀipl(ə)] *adj* triple; treble ♦ *nm*: **le ~ (de)** (*comparaison*) three times as much (as); **en ~ exemplaire** in triplicate; **tripler** *vi, vt* to triple, treble

triplés, ées [tʀiple] *nm/fpl* triplets

tripoter [tʀipɔte] *vt* to fiddle with

trique [tʀik] *nf* cudgel

triste [tʀist(ə)] *adj* sad; (*péj*): **~**

personnage/affaire sorry individual/ affair; **tristesse** *nf* sadness

trivial, e, aux [tʀivjal, -o] *adj* coarse, crude; (*commun*) mundane

troc [tʀɔk] *nm* barter

trognon [tʀɔɲɔ̃] *nm* (*de fruit*) core; (*de légume*) stalk

trois [tʀwa] *num* three; **troisième** *num* third; **trois-quarts** *nmpl*: **les trois-quarts de** three-quarters of

trombe [tʀɔ̃b] *nf*: **des ~s d'eau** a downpour; **en ~** like a whirlwind

trombone [tʀɔ̃bɔn] *nm* (*MUS*) trombone; (*de bureau*) paper clip

trompe [tʀɔ̃p] *nf* (*d'éléphant*) trunk; (*MUS*) trumpet, horn

tromper [tʀɔ̃pe] *vt* to deceive; (*vigilance, poursuivants*) to elude; **se ~** *vi* to make a mistake, be mistaken; **se ~ de voiture/jour** to take the wrong car/get the day wrong; **se ~ de 3 cm/20 F** to be out by 3 cm/20 F; **tromperie** *nf* deception, trickery *no pl*

trompette [tʀɔ̃pɛt] *nf* trumpet; **en ~** (*nez*) turned-up

tronc [tʀɔ̃] *nm* (*BOT, ANAT*) trunk; (*d'église*) collection box

tronçon [tʀɔ̃sɔ̃] *nm* section

tronçonner [tʀɔ̃sɔne] *vt* to saw up

trône [tʀon] *nm* throne

trop [tʀo] *adv* (+*vb*) too much; (+*adjectif, adverbe*) too; **~ (nombreux)** too many; **~ peu (nombreux)** too few; **~ (souvent)** too often; **~ (longtemps)** (for) too long; **~ de** (*nombre*) too many; (*quantité*) too much; **de ~, en ~**: **des livres en ~** a few books too many; **du lait en ~** too much milk; **3 livres/3 F de ~** 3 books too many/3 F too much

tropical, e, aux [tʀɔpikal, -o] *adj* tropical

tropique [tʀɔpik] *nm* tropic

trop-plein [tʀoplɛ̃] *nm* (*tuyau*) overflow *ou* outlet (pipe); (*liquide*) overflow

troquer [tʀɔke] *vt*: **~ qch contre** to barter *ou* trade sth for; (*fig*) to swap sth for

trot [tʀo] *nm* trot; **trotter** [tʀɔte] *vi* to trot; (*fig*) to scamper along (*ou* about)

trottiner [tʀɔtine] *vi* (*fig*) to scamper

along (*ou* about); **trottinette** [tʀɔtinɛt] *nf* (child's) scooter

trottoir [tʀɔtwaʀ] *nm* pavement; **faire le ~** (*péj*) to walk the streets; **~ roulant** moving walkway, travellator

trou [tʀu] *nm* hole; (*fig*) gap; (*COMM*) deficit; **~ d'air** air pocket; **~ d'ozone** ozone hole; **le ~ de la serrure** the keyhole; **~ de mémoire** blank, lapse of memory

trouble [tʀubl(ə)] *adj* (*liquide*) cloudy; (*image, mémoire*) indistinct, hazy; (*affaire*) shady, murky ♦ *nm* (*désarroi*) agitation; (*embarras*) confusion; (*zizanie*) unrest, discord; **~s** *nmpl* (*POL*) disturbances, troubles, unrest *sg*; (*MÉD*) trouble *sg*, disorders

troubler [tʀuble] *vt* (*embarrasser*) to confuse, disconcert; (*émouvoir*) to agitate; to disturb; (*perturber: ordre etc*) to disrupt; (*liquide*) to make cloudy; **se ~** *vi* (*personne*) to become flustered *ou* confused

trouée [tʀue] *nf* gap; (*MIL*) breach

trouer [tʀue] *vt* to make a hole (*ou* holes) in; (*fig*) to pierce

trouille [tʀuj] (*fam*) *nf*: **avoir la ~** to be scared to death

troupe [tʀup] *nf* troop; **~ (de théâtre)** (theatrical) company

troupeau, x [tʀupo] *nm* (*de moutons*) flock; (*de vaches*) herd

trousse [tʀus] *nf* case, kit; (*d'écolier*) pencil case; (*de docteur*) instrument case; **aux ~s de** (*fig*) on the heels *ou* tail of; **~ à outils** toolkit; **~ de toilette** toilet bag

trousseau, x [tʀuso] *nm* (*de mariée*) trousseau; **~ de clefs** bunch of keys

trouvaille [tʀuvaj] *nf* find

trouver [tʀuve] *vt* to find; (*rendre visite*): **aller/venir ~ qn** to go/come and see sb; **se ~** *vi* (*être*) to be; (*être soudain*) to find o.s.; **il se trouve que** it happens that, it turns out that; **se ~ bien** to feel well; **se ~ mal** to pass out; **je trouve que** I find *ou* think that; **~ à boire/critiquer** to find something to drink/criticize

truand [tʀyɑ̃] *nm* villain, crook

truander [tʀyɑ̃de] *vt* to cheat

truc [tʀyk] *nm* (*astuce*) way, device; (*de cinéma, prestidigitateur*) trick effect; (*chose*) thing, thingumajig; **avoir le ~** to have the knack

truchement [tʀyʃmɑ̃] *nm*: **par le ~ de qn** through (the intervention of) sb

truelle [tʀyɛl] *nf* trowel

truffe [tʀyf] *nf* truffle; (*nez*) nose

truffé, e [tʀyfe] *adj*: **~ de** (*fig*) peppered with; bristling with

truie [tʀɥi] *nf* sow

truite [tʀɥit] *nf* trout *inv*

truquer [tʀyke] *vt* (*élections, serrure, dés*) to fix; (*CINÉMA*) to use special effects in

T.S.V.P. *sigle* (= *tournez s.v.p.*) P.T.O.

T.T.C. *sigle* = **toutes taxes comprises**

tu¹ [ty] *pron* you

tu², e [ty] *pp de* **taire**

tuba [tyba] *nm* (*MUS*) tuba; (*SPORT*) snorkel

tube [tyb] *nm* tube; pipe; (*chanson, disque*) hit song *ou* record

tuer [tɥe] *vt* to kill; **se ~** *vi* to be killed; (*suicide*) to kill o.s.; **tuerie** *nf* slaughter *no pl*

tue-tête [tytɛt]: **à ~** *adv* at the top of one's voice

tueur [tɥœʀ] *nm* killer; **~ à gages** hired killer

tuile [tɥil] *nf* tile; (*fam*) spot of bad luck, blow

tulipe [tylip] *nf* tulip

tuméfié, e [tymefje] *adj* puffy, swollen

tumeur [tymœʀ] *nf* growth, tumour

tumulte [tymylt(ə)] *nm* commotion

tumultueux, euse [tymyltɥø, -øz] *adj* stormy, turbulent

tunique [tynik] *nf* tunic

Tunisie [tynizi] *nf*: **la ~** Tunisia; **tunisien, ne** *adj, nm/f* Tunisian

tunnel [tynɛl] *nm* tunnel

turbulences [tyʀbylɑ̃s] *nfpl* (*AVIAT*) turbulence *sg*

turbulent, e [tyʀbylɑ̃, -ɑ̃t] *adj* boisterous, unruly

turc, turque [tyʀk(ə)] *adj* Turkish ♦ *nm/f*: **T~, Turque** Turk/Turkish woman ♦ nm (LING) Turkish

turf [tyʀf] nm racing; **turfiste** nm/f racegoer

Turquie [tyʀki] nf: **la ~** Turkey

turquoise [tyʀkwaz] nf turquoise ♦ adj inv turquoise

tus etc vb voir **taire**

tutelle [tytɛl] nf (JUR) guardianship; (POL) trusteeship; **sous la ~ de** (fig) under the supervision of

tuteur [tytœʀ] nm (JUR) guardian; (de plante) stake, support

tutoyer [tytwaje] vt: **~ qn** to address sb as "tu"

tuyau, x [tɥijo] nm pipe; (flexible) tube; (fam) tip; gen no pl; **~ d'arrosage** hosepipe; **~ d'échappement** exhaust pipe; **tuyauterie** nf piping no pl

T.V.A. sigle f (= taxe à la valeur ajoutée) VAT

tympan [tɛ̃pɑ̃] nm (ANAT) eardrum

type [tip] nm type; (fam) chap, guy ♦ adj typical, standard

typé, e [tipe] adj ethnic

typhoïde [tifɔid] nf typhoid

typique [tipik] adj typical

tyran [tiʀɑ̃] nm tyrant

tzigane [dzigan] adj gypsy ♦ nm/f gypsy

U u

U.E.M. sigle f (= union économique et monétaire) EMU

ulcère [ylsɛʀ] nm ulcer; **ulcérer** [ylseʀe] vt to sicken, appal

ultérieur, e [ylteʀjœʀ] adj later, subsequent; **remis à une date ~e** postponed to a later date

ultime [yltim] adj final

ultra... [yltʀa] préfixe: **ultramoderne/ -rapide** ultra-modern/-fast

MOT-CLÉ

un, une [œ̃, yn] art indéf a ♦ art indef; (devant voyelle) an; **~ garçon/vieillard** a boy/an old man; **une fille** a girl

♦ pron one; **l'~ des meilleurs** one of the best; **l'~ ..., l'autre** (the) one ..., the other; **les ~s ..., les autres** some ..., others; **l'~ et l'autre** both (of them); **l'~ ou l'autre** either (of them); **l'~ l'autre, les ~s les autres** each other, one another; **pas ~ seul** not a single one; **~ par ~** one by one

♦ num one; **une pomme seulement** one apple only

unanime [ynanim] adj unanimous; **unanimité** nf: **à l'unanimité** unanimously

uni, e [yni] adj (ton, tissu) plain; (surface) smooth, even; (famille) close(-knit); (pays) united

unifier [ynifje] vt to unite, unify

uniforme [ynifɔʀm(ə)] adj (mouvement) regular, uniform; (surface, ton) even; (objets, maisons) uniform ♦ nm uniform; **uniformiser** vt to make uniform; (systèmes) to standardize

union [ynjɔ̃] nf union; **~ de consommateurs** consumers' association; **l'U~ soviétique** the Soviet Union

unique [ynik] adj (seul) only; (le même): **un prix/système ~** a single price/ system; (exceptionnel) unique; **fils/fille ~** only son/daughter, only child; **uniquement** adv only, solely; (juste) only, merely

unir [yniʀ] vt (nations) to unite; (éléments, couleurs) to combine; (en mariage) to unite, join together; **s'~** to unite; (en mariage) to be joined together; **~ qch à** to unite sth with; to combine sth with

unité [ynite] nf (harmonie, cohésion) unity; (COMM, MIL, de mesure, MATH) unit

univers [ynivɛʀ] nm universe

universel, le [ynivɛʀsɛl] adj universal; (esprit) all-embracing

universitaire [ynivɛʀsitɛʀ] adj university cpd; (diplôme, études) academic, university cpd ♦ nm/f academic

université [ynivɛʀsite] nf university

urbain, e [yʀbɛ̃, -ɛn] adj urban, city cpd, town cpd; (poli) urbane; **urbanisme** nm town planning

urgence [yʀʒɑ̃s] nf urgency; (MÉD etc) emergency; **d'~** emergency cpd ♦ adv as a matter of urgency

urgent, e [yʀʒã, -ãt] *adj* urgent

urine [yʀin] *nf* urine; **urinoir** *nm* (public) urinal

urne [yʀn(ə)] *nf* (*électorale*) ballot box; (*vase*) urn

urticaire [yʀtikɛʀ] *nf* nettle rash

us [ys] *nmpl*: ~ **et coutumes** (habits and) customs

USA *sigle mpl*: **les** ~ the USA

usage [yzaʒ] *nm* (*emploi, utilisation*) use; (*coutume*) custom; (*LING*): **l'**~ usage; **à l'**~ **de** (*pour*) for (use of); **en** ~ in use; **hors d'**~ out of service; wrecked; **à** ~ **interne** to be taken; **à** ~ **externe** for external use only; **usagé, e** [yzaʒe] *adj* (*usé*) worn; (*d'occasion*) used; **usager, ère** [yzaʒe, -ɛʀ] *nm/f* user

usé, e [yze] *adj* worn; (*banal*) hackneyed

user [yze] *vt* (*outil*) to wear down; (*vêtement*) to wear out; (*matière*) to wear away; (*consommer: charbon etc*) to use; **s'**~ *vi* to wear; to wear out; (*fig*) to decline; ~ **de** (*moyen, procédé*) to use, employ; (*droit*) to exercise

usine [yzin] *nf* factory; ~ **marémotrice** tidal power station

usité, e [yzite] *adj* common

ustensile [ystãsil] *nm* implement; ~ **de cuisine** kitchen utensil

usuel, le [yzɥɛl] *adj* everyday, common

usure [yzyʀ] *nf* wear; worn state

ut [yt] *nm* (*MUS*) C

utérus [yteʀys] *nm* uterus, womb

utile [ytil] *adj* useful

utilisation [ytilizasjõ] *nf* use

utiliser [ytilize] *vt* to use

utilitaire [ytilitɛʀ] *adj* utilitarian; (*objets*) practical

utilité [ytilite] *nf* usefulness *no pl*; use; **reconnu d'**~ **publique** state-approved

V v

va *vb voir* **aller**

vacance [vakãs] *nf* (*ADMIN*) vacancy; ~**s** *nfpl* holiday(s *pl*), vacation *sg*; **prendre**

des/ses ~**s** to take a holiday/one's holiday(s); **aller en** ~**s** to go on holiday; **vacancier, ière** *nm/f* holiday-maker

vacant, e [vakã, -ãt] *adj* vacant

vacarme [vakaʀm(ə)] *nm* row, din

vaccin [vaksɛ̃] *nm* vaccine; (*opération*) vaccination; **vaccination** *nf* vaccination; **vacciner** *vt* to vaccinate; (*fig*) to make immune

vache [vaʃ] *nf* (*ZOOL*) cow; (*cuir*) cowhide ♦ *adj* (*fam*) rotten, mean; ~**ment** (*fam*) *adv* damned, hellish

vaciller [vasije] *vi* to sway, wobble; (*bougie, lumière*) to flicker; (*fig*) to be failing, falter

va-et-vient [vaevjɛ̃] *nm inv* (*de personnes, véhicules*) comings and goings *pl*, to-ings and fro-ings *pl*

vagabond [vagabõ] *nm* (*rôdeur*) tramp, vagrant; (*voyageur*) wanderer; **vagabonder** [vagabõde] *vi* to roam, wander

vagin [vaʒɛ̃] *nm* vagina

vague [vag] *nf* wave ♦ *adj* vague; (*regard*) faraway; (*manteau, robe*) loose (-fitting); (*quelconque*): **un** ~ **bureau/cousin** some office/cousin or other; ~ **de fond** ground swell

vaillant, e [vajã, -ãt] *adj* (*courageux*) gallant; (*robuste*) hale and hearty

vaille *vb voir* **valoir**

vain, e [vɛ̃, vɛn] *adj* vain; **en** ~ in vain

vaincre [vɛ̃kʀ(ə)] *vt* to defeat; (*fig*) to conquer, overcome; **vaincu, e** *nm/f* defeated party; **vainqueur** *nm* victor; (*SPORT*) winner

vais *vb voir* **aller**

vaisseau, x [vɛso] *nm* (*ANAT*) vessel; (*NAVIG*) ship, vessel; ~ **spatial** spaceship

vaisselier [vɛsalje] *nm* dresser

vaisselle [vɛsɛl] *nf* (*service*) crockery; (*plats etc à laver*) (dirty) dishes *pl*; (*lavage*) washing-up (*BRIT*), dishes *pl*

val [val] (*pl* **vaux** *ou* ~**s**) *nm* valley

valable [valabl(ə)] *adj* valid; (*acceptable*) decent, worthwhile

valent *etc vb voir* **valoir**

valet [valɛ] *nm* valet; (*CARTES*) jack

valeur [valœʀ] *nf* (*gén*) value; (*mérite*) worth, merit; (*COMM: titre*) security; **met-**

tre en ~ *(terrain, région)* to develop; *(fig)* to highlight; to show off to advantage; **avoir de la ~** to be valuable; **sans ~** worthless; **prendre de la ~** to go up *ou* gain in value

valide [valid] *adj (en bonne santé)* fit; *(valable)* valid; **valider** *vt* to validate

valions *vb voir* **valoir**

valise [valiz] *nf* (suit)case

vallée [vale] *nf* valley

vallon [valɔ̃] *nm* small valley

valoir [valwaʀ] *vi (être valable)* to hold, apply ♦ *vt (prix, valeur, effort)* to be worth; *(causer):* ~ **qch à qn** to earn sb sth; **se** ~ *vi* to be of equal merit; *(péj)* to be two of a kind; **faire** ~ *(droits, prérogatives)* to assert; **faire** ~ **que** to point out that; **à** ~ **sur** to be deducted from; **vaille que vaille** somehow or other; **cela ne me dit rien qui vaille** I don't like the look of it at all; **ce climat ne me vaut rien** this climate doesn't suit me; ~ **la peine** to be worth the trouble *ou* worth it; ~ **mieux: il vaut mieux se taire** it's better to say nothing; **ça ne vaut rien** it's worthless; **que vaut ce candidat?** how good is this applicant?

valoriser [valɔʀize] *vt (ÉCON)* to develop (the economy of); *(PSYCH)* to increase the standing of

valse [vals(ə)] *nf* waltz

valu, e [valy] *pp de* **valoir**

vandalisme [vɑ̃dalism(ə)] *nm* vandalism

vanille [vanij] *nf* vanilla

vanité [vanite] *nf* vanity; **vaniteux, euse** *adj* vain, conceited

vanne [van] *nf* gate; *(fig)* joke

vannerie [vanʀi] *nf* basketwork

vantard, e [vɑ̃taʀ, -aʀd(ə)] *adj* boastful

vanter [vɑ̃te] *vt* to speak highly of, vaunt; **se** ~ *vi* to boast, brag; **se** ~ **de** to pride o.s. on; *(péj)* to boast of

vapeur [vapœʀ] *nf* steam; *(émanation)* vapour, fumes *pl;* ~**s** *nfpl (bouffées)* vapours; **à** ~ steam-powered, steam *cpd;* **cuit à la** ~ steamed

vaporeux, euse [vapɔʀø, -øz] *adj (flou)* hazy, misty; *(léger)* filmy

vaporisateur [vapɔʀizatœʀ] *nm* spray;

vaporiser [vapɔʀize] *vt (parfum etc)* to spray

varappe [vaʀap] *nf* rock climbing

vareuse [vaʀøz] *nf (blouson)* pea jacket; *(d'uniforme)* tunic

variable [vaʀjabl(ə)] *adj* variable; *(temps, humeur)* changeable; *(divers: résultats)* varied, various

varice [vaʀis] *nf* varicose vein

varicelle [vaʀisɛl] *nf* chickenpox

varié, e [vaʀje] *adj* varied; *(divers)* various

varier [vaʀje] *vi* to vary; *(temps, humeur)* to change ♦ *vt* to vary

variété [vaʀjete] *nf* variety; ~**s** *nfpl:* **spectacle/émission de ~s** variety show

variole [vaʀjɔl] *nf* smallpox

vas *vb voir* **aller**

vase [vaz] *nm* vase ♦ *nf* silt, mud

vaseux, euse [vazø, -øz] *adj* silty, muddy; *(fig: confus)* woolly, hazy; *(: fatigué)* peaky; woozy

vasistas [vazistas] *nm* fanlight

vaste [vast(ə)] *adj* vast, immense

vaudrai *etc vb voir* **valoir**

vaurien, ne [voʀjɛ̃, -ɛn] *nm/f* good-for-nothing, guttersnipe

vaut *vb voir* **valoir**

vautour [votuʀ] *nm* vulture

vautrer [votʀe]: **se** ~ *vi* to wallow in/sprawl on

vaux [vo] *nmpl de* **val** ♦ *vb voir* **valoir**

va-vite [vavit]: **à la** ~ *adv* in a rush *ou* hurry

veau, x [vo] *nm (ZOOL)* calf; *(CULIN)* veal; *(peau)* calfskin

vécu, e [veky] *pp de* **vivre**

vedette [vədɛt] *nf (artiste etc)* star; *(canot)* patrol boat; launch

végétal, e, aux [veʒetal, -o] *adj* vegetable ♦ *nm* vegetable, plant

végétarien, ne [veʒetaʀjɛ̃, -ɛn] *adj, nm/f* vegetarian

végétation [veʒetasjɔ̃] *nf* vegetation; ~**s** *nfpl (MÉD)* adenoids

véhicule [veikyl] *nm* vehicle; ~ **utilitaire** commercial vehicle

veille [vɛj] *nf (garde)* watch; *(PSYCH)* wakefulness; *(jour):* **la ~ (de)** the day before; **la ~ au soir** the previous evening; **à la ~ de** on the eve of

veillée [veje] *nf* (*soirée*) evening; (*réunion*) evening gathering; **~ (mortuaire)** watch

veiller [veje] *vi* to stay up; to be awake; to be on watch ♦ *vt* (*malade, mort*) to watch over, sit up with; **~ à** to attend to, see to; **~ à ce que** to make sure that; **~ sur** to keep a watch on; **veilleur de nuit** *nm* night watchman

veilleuse [vɛjøz] *nf* (*lampe*) night light; (*AUTO*) sidelight; (*flamme*) pilot light; **en ~** (*lampe*) dimmed

veine [vɛn] *nf* (*ANAT, du bois etc*) vein; (*filon*) seam, vein; (*fam: chance*): **avoir de la ~** to be lucky

véliplanchiste [veliplãʃist(ə)] *nm/f* windsurfer

velléités [veleite] *nfpl* vague impulses

vélo [velo] *nm* bike, cycle; **faire du ~** to go cycling; **~ tout-terrain** mountain bike

vélomoteur [velɔmɔtœʀ] *nm* moped

velours [vəluʀ] *nm* velvet; **~ côtelé** corduroy

velouté, e [vəlute] *adj* (*au toucher*) velvety; (*à la vue*) soft, mellow; (*au goût*) smooth, mellow

velu, e [vəly] *adj* hairy

venais *etc vb voir* **venir**

venaison [vənɛzɔ̃] *nf* venison

vendange [vãdãʒ] *nf* (*opération, période: aussi: ~s*) grape harvest; (*raisins*) grape crop, grapes *pl*; **vendanger** [vãdãʒe] *vi* to harvest the grapes

vendeur, euse [vãdœʀ, -øz] *nm/f* (*de magasin*) shop assistant; (*COMM*) salesman(woman) ♦ *nm* (*JUR*) vendor, seller; **~ de journaux** newspaper seller

vendre [vãdʀ(ə)] *vt* to sell; **~ qch à qn** to sell sb sth; **"à ~"** "for sale"

vendredi [vãdʀədi] *nm* Friday; **V~ saint** Good Friday

vendu, e [vãdy] *adj* (*péj: corrompu*) corrupt

vénéneux, euse [venenø, -øz] *adj* poisonous

vénérien, ne [venerjɛ̃, -ɛn] *adj* venereal

vengeance [vãʒãs] *nf* vengeance *no pl*, revenge *no pl*

venger [vãʒe] *vt* to avenge; **se ~** *vi* to avenge o.s.; **se ~ de qch** to avenge o.s. for sth; to take one's revenge for sth; **se ~ de qn** to take revenge on sb; **se ~ sur** to take revenge on; to take it out on

venimeux, euse [vənimø, -øz] *adj* poisonous, venomous; (*fig: haineux*) venomous, vicious

venin [vənɛ̃] *nm* venom, poison

venir [vəniʀ] *vi* to come; **~ de** to come from; **~ de faire: je viens d'y aller/de le voir** I've just been there/seen him; **s'il vient à pleuvoir** if it should rain; **j'en viens à croire que** I have come to believe that; **faire ~** (*docteur, plombier*) to call (out)

vent [vã] *nm* wind; **il y a du ~** it's windy; **c'est du ~** it's all hot air; **au ~** to windward; **sous le ~** to leeward; **avoir le ~ debout/arrière** to head into the wind/have the wind astern; **dans le ~** (*fam*) trendy

vente [vãt] *nf* sale; **la ~** (*activité*) selling; (*secteur*) sales *pl*; **mettre en ~** to put on sale; (*objets personnels*) to put up for sale; **~ aux enchères** auction sale; **~ de charité** jumble sale

venteux, euse [vãtø, -øz] *adj* windy

ventilateur [vãtilatœʀ] *nm* fan

ventiler [vãtile] *vt* to ventilate; (*total, statistiques*) to break down

ventouse [vãtuz] *nf* (*de caoutchouc*) suction pad; (*ZOOL*) sucker

ventre [vãtʀ(ə)] *nm* (*ANAT*) stomach; (*fig*) belly; **avoir mal au ~** to have stomach ache (*BRIT*) *ou* a stomach ache (*US*)

ventriloque [vãtʀilɔk] *nm/f* ventriloquist

venu, e [vəny] *pp de* **venir** ♦ *adj*: **être mal ~ à** *ou* **de faire** to have no grounds for doing, be in no position to do coming

ver [vɛʀ] *nm* worm; (*des fruits etc*) maggot; (*du bois*) woodworm *no pl*; *voir aussi* **vers**; **~ à soie** silkworm; **~ de terre** earthworm; **~ luisant** glow-worm; **~ solitaire** tapeworm

verbaliser [vɛʀbalize] *vi* (*POLICE*) to book

ou report an offender
verbe [vɛrb(ə)] *nm* verb
verdeur [vɛrdœr] *nf* (*vigueur*) vigour,
vitality; (*crudité*) forthrightness
verdict [vɛrdik(t)] *nm* verdict
verdir [vɛrdir] *vi, vt* to turn green
verdure [vɛrdyr] *nf* greenery
véreux, euse [verø, -øz] *adj* worm-
eaten; (*malhonnête*) shady, corrupt
verge [vɛrʒ(ə)] *nf* (*ANAT*) penis; (*baguette*) stick, cane
verger [vɛrʒe] *nm* orchard
verglacé, e [vɛrglase] *adj* icy, iced-over
verglas [vɛrgla] *nm* (black) ice
vergogne [vɛrgɔɲ]: **sans ~** *adv* shame-
lessly
véridique [veridik] *adj* truthful
vérification [verifikasjɔ̃] *nf* checking *no
pl*, check
vérifier [verifje] *vt* to check; (*corroborer*) to confirm, bear out
véritable [veritabl(ə)] *adj* real; (*ami,
amour*) true
vérité [verite] *nf* truth; (*d'un portrait
romanesque*) lifelikeness; (*sincérité*)
truthfulness, sincerity
vermeil, le [vɛrmɛj] *adj* ruby red
vermine [vɛrmin] *nf* vermin *pl*
vermoulu, e [vɛrmuly] *adj* worm-eaten,
with woodworm
verni, e [vɛrni] *adj* (*fam*) lucky; **cuir ~**
patent leather
vernir [vɛrnir] *vt* (*bois, tableau, ongles*)
to varnish; (*poterie*) to glaze
vernis [vɛrni] *nm* (*enduit*) varnish;
glaze; (*fig*) veneer; **~ à ongles** nail polish *ou* varnish; **vernissage** [vɛrnisaʒ]
nm varnishing; glazing; (*d'une exposition*) preview
vérole [verɔl] *nf* (*variole*) smallpox
verrai *etc vb voir* **voir**
verre [vɛr] *nm* glass; (*de lunettes*) lens
sg; **boire** *ou* **prendre un ~** to have a
drink; **~s de contact** contact lenses; **verrerie** [vɛrri] *nf* (*fabrique*) glassworks *sg*;
(*activité*) glass-making; (*objets*) glass-
ware; **verrière** [vɛrjɛr] *nf* (*grand vitrage*) window; (*toit vitré*) glass roof
verrons *etc vb voir* **voir**

verrou [vɛru] *nm* (*targette*) bolt; (*fig*)
constriction; **mettre qn sous les ~s** to
put sb behind bars; **verrouillage** *nm*
locking; **verrouillage centralisé** central
locking; **verrouiller** *vt* to bolt; to lock
verrue [vɛry] *nf* wart
vers [vɛr] *nm* line ♦ *nmpl* (*poésie*) verse
sg ♦ *prép* (*en direction de*) toward(s);
(*près de*) around (about); (*temporel*)
about, around
versant [vɛrsã] *nm* slopes *pl*, side
versatile [vɛrsatil] *adj* fickle, changeable
verse [vɛrs(ə)]: **à ~** *adv* it's pouring
(with rain)
Verseau [vɛrso] *nm*: **le ~** Aquarius
versement [vɛrsəmã] *nm* payment; **en
3 ~s** in 3 instalments
verser [vɛrse] *vt* (*liquide, grains*) to
pour; (*larmes, sang*) to shed; (*argent*)
to pay ♦ *vi* (*véhicule*) to overturn; (*fig*): **~
dans** to lapse into
verset [vɛrse] *nm* verse
version [vɛrsjɔ̃] *nf* version; (*SCOL*) translation (*into the mother tongue*)
verso [vɛrso] *nm* back; **voir au ~** see
over(leaf)
vert, e [vɛr, vɛrt(ə)] *adj* green; (*vin*)
young; (*vigoureux*) sprightly; (*cru*)
forthright ♦ *nm* green
vertèbre [vɛrtɛbr(ə)] *nf* vertebra
vertement [vɛrtəmã] *adv* (*réprimander*) sharply
vertical, e, aux [vɛrtikal, -o] *adj* vertical; **verticale** *nf* vertical; **à la verticale**
vertically; **verticalement** *adv* vertically
vertige [vɛrtiʒ] *nm* (*peur du vide*) vertigo; (*étourdissement*) dizzy spell; (*fig*) fever; **vertigineux, euse** *adj* breathtaking
vertu [vɛrty] *nf* virtue; **en ~ de** in accordance with; **vertueux, euse** *adj* virtuous
verve [vɛrv(ə)] *nf* witty eloquence; **être
en ~** to be in brilliant form
verveine [vɛrvɛn] *nf* (*BOT*) verbena, ver-
vain; (*infusion*) verbena tea
vésicule [vezikyl] *nf* vesicle; **~ biliaire**
gall-bladder
vessie [vesi] *nf* bladder
veste [vɛst(ə)] *nf* jacket; **~ droite/**

croisée single-/double-breasted jacket

vestiaire [vɛstjɛʀ] *nm* (*au théâtre etc*) cloakroom; (*de stade etc*) changing-room (*BRIT*), locker-room (*US*)

vestibule [vɛstibyl] *nm* hall

vestige [vɛstiʒ] *nm* relic; (*fig*) vestige; ~**s** *nmpl* remains

vestimentaire [vɛstimɑ̃tɛʀ] *adj* (*détail*) of dress; (*élégance*) sartorial; **dépenses** ~**s** spending on clothes

veston [vɛstɔ̃] *nm* jacket

vêtement [vɛtmɑ̃] *nm* garment, item of clothing; ~**s** *nmpl* clothes

vétérinaire [veteʀinɛʀ] *nm/f* vet, veterinary surgeon

vêtir [vetiʀ] *vt* to clothe, dress

veto [veto] *nm* veto; **opposer un** ~ **à** to veto

vêtu, e [vɛty] *pp de* **vêtir**

vétuste [vetyst(ə)] *adj* ancient, timeworn

veuf, veuve [vœf, vœv] *adj* widowed ♦ *nm* widower

veuille *etc vb voir* **vouloir**

veuillez *vb voir* **vouloir**

veule [vøl] *adj* spineless

veuve [vœv] *nf* widow

veux *vb voir* **vouloir**

vexations [vɛksɑsjɔ̃] *nfpl* humiliations

vexer [vɛkse] *vt* to hurt, upset; **se** ~ *vi* to be hurt, get upset

viabiliser [vjabilize] *vt* to provide with services (*water etc*)

viable [vjabl(ə)] *adj* viable; (*économie, industrie etc*) sustainable

viager, ère [vjaʒe, -ɛʀ] *adj*: **rente viagère** life annuity

viande [vjɑ̃d] *nf* meat

vibrer [vibʀe] *vi* to vibrate; (*son, voix*) to be vibrant; (*fig*) to be stirred; **faire** ~ to (cause to) vibrate; to stir, thrill

vice [vis] *nm* vice; (*défaut*) fault ♦ *préfixe*: **~ ...** vice-; ~ **de forme** legal flaw *ou* irregularity

vichy [viʃi] *nm* (*toile*) gingham

vicié, e [visje] *adj* (*air*) polluted, tainted; (*JUR*) invalidated

vicieux, euse [visjø, -øz] *adj* (*pervers*) dirty(-minded); nasty; (*fautif*) incorrect,

wrong

vicinal, e, aux [visinal, -o] *adj*: **chemin** ~ by-road, byway

victime [viktim] *nf* victim; (*d'accident*) casualty

victoire [viktwaʀ] *nf* victory

victuailles [viktɥaj] *nfpl* provisions

vidange [vidɑ̃ʒ] *nf* (*d'un fossé, réservoir*) emptying; (*AUTO*) oil change; (*de lavabo: bonde*) waste outlet; ~**s** *nfpl* (*matières*) sewage *sg*; **vidanger** *vt* to empty

vide [vid] *adj* empty ♦ *nm* (*PHYSIQUE*) vacuum; (*espace*) (empty) space, gap; (*futilité, néant*) void; **avoir peur du** ~ to be afraid of heights; **emballé sous** ~ vacuum packed; **à** ~ (*sans occupants*) empty; (*sans charge*) unladen

vidéo [video] *nf* video ♦ *adj*: **cassette** ~ video cassette

vide-ordures [vidɔʀdyʀ] *nm inv* (rubbish) chute

vide-poches [vidpɔʃ] *nm inv* tidy; (*AUTO*) glove compartment

vider [vide] *vt* to empty; (*CULIN: volaille, poisson*) to gut, clean out; **se** ~ *vi* to empty; ~ **les lieux** to quit *ou* vacate the premises; **videur** *nm* (*de boîte de nuit*) bouncer

vie [vi] *nf* life; **être en** ~ to be alive; **sans** ~ lifeless; **à** ~ for life

vieil [vjɛj] *adj m voir* **vieux**

vieillard [vjɛjaʀ] *nm* old man; **les** ~**s** old people, the elderly

vieille [vjɛj] *adj, nf voir* **vieux**

vieilleries [vjɛjʀi] *nfpl* old things

vieillesse [vjɛjɛs] *nf* old age

vieillir [vjɛjiʀ] *vi* (*prendre de l'âge*) to grow old; (*population, vin*) to age; (*doctrine, auteur*) to become dated ♦ *vt* to age; **vieillissement** *nm* growing old; ageing

Vienne [vjɛn] *nf* Vienna

viens *vb voir* **venir**

vierge [vjɛʀʒ(ə)] *adj* virgin; (*page*) clean, blank ♦ *nf* virgin; (*signe*): **la V~** Virgo; ~ **de** (*sans*) free from, unsullied by

Vietnam [vjɛtnam] *nm* = **Viêt-nam**

Viêt-nam [vjɛtnam] *nm* Vietnam

vietnamien, ne [vjɛtnamjɛ̃, -jɛn] *adj,
nm/f* Vietnamese

vieux (vieil), vieille [vjø, vjɛj] *adj* old
♦ *nm/f* old man(woman) ♦ *nmpl* old
people; **mon ~/ma vieille** (*fam*) old
man/girl; **prendre un coup de ~** to put
years on; **~ garçon** bachelor; **~ jeu** *adj
inv* old-fashioned

vif, vive [vif, viv] *adj* (*animé*) lively;
(*alerte, brusque, aigu*) sharp; (*lumière,
couleur*) brilliant; (*air*) crisp; (*vent,
émotion*) keen; (*fort: regret, déception*)
great, deep; (*vivant*): **brûlé ~** burnt
alive; **de vive voix** personally; **piquer
qn au ~** to cut sb to the quick; **à ~**
(*plaie*) open; **avoir les nerfs à ~** to be
on edge

vigie [viʒi] *nf* look-out; look-out post

vigne [viɲ] *nf* (*plante*) vine; (*plantation*) vineyard

vigneron [viɲʀɔ̃] *nm* wine grower

vignette [viɲɛt] *nf* (*motif*) vignette; (*de
marque*) manufacturer's label *ou* seal;
(*ADMIN*) ≈ (road) tax disc (*BRIT*), ≈ license
plate sticker (*US*); price label (*used for
reimbursement*)

vignoble [viɲɔbl(ə)] *nm* (*plantation*)
vineyard; (*vignes d'une région*) vine-
yards *pl*

vigoureux, euse [viguʀø, -øz] *adj* vigorous, robust

vigueur [vigœʀ] *nf* vigour; **entrer en ~**
to come into force; **en ~** current

vil, e [vil] *adj* vile, base; **à ~ prix** at a
very low price

vilain, e [vilɛ̃, -ɛn] *adj* (*laid*) ugly; (*affaire, blessure*) nasty; (*pas sage: enfant*)
naughty

villa [vila] *nf* (detached) house; **~ en
multipropriété** time-share villa

village [vilaʒ] *nm* village; **villageois, e**
adj village *cpd* ♦ *nm/f* villager

ville [vil] *nf* town; (*importante*) city; (*administration*): **la ~** ≈ the Corporation;
≈ the (town) council

villégiature [vileʒiatyʀ] *nf* holiday; (holiday) resort

vin [vɛ̃] *nm* wine; **avoir le ~ gai** to get
happy after a few drinks; **~ d'honneur**

reception (*with wine and snacks*); **~ de
pays** local wine; **~ ordinaire** table wine

vinaigre [vinɛgʀ(ə)] *nm* vinegar; **vinaigrette** *nf* vinaigrette, French dressing

vindicatif, ive [vɛ̃dikatif, -iv] *adj* vindictive

vineux, euse [vinø, -øz] *adj* win(e)y

vingt [vɛ̃, vɛ̃t] *num* twenty; **vingtaine**
nf: **une vingtaine (de)** about twenty,
twenty or so; **vingtième** *num* twentieth

vinicole [vinikɔl] *adj* wine *cpd*, wine-
growing

vins *etc vb voir* **venir**

vinyle [vinil] *nm* vinyl

viol [vjɔl] *nm* (*d'une femme*) rape; (*d'un
lieu sacré*) violation

violacé, e [vjɔlase] *adj* purplish, mauv-
ish

violemment [vjɔlamã] *adv* violently

violence [vjɔlãs] *nf* violence

violent, e [vjɔlã, -ãt] *adj* violent; (*remède*) drastic

violer [vjɔle] *vt* (*femme*) to rape; (*sépulture, loi, traité*) to violate

violet, te [vjɔlɛ, -ɛt] *adj, nm* purple,
mauve; **violette** *nf* (*fleur*) violet

violon [vjɔlɔ̃] *nm* violin; (*fam: prison*)
lock-up

violoncelle [vjɔlɔ̃sɛl] *nm* cello

violoniste [vjɔlɔnist(ə)] *nm/f* violinist

vipère [vipɛʀ] *nf* viper, adder

virage [viʀaʒ] *nm* (*d'un véhicule*) turn;
(*d'une route, piste*) bend; (*fig: POL*)
about-turn

virée [viʀe] *nf* (*courte*) run; (: *à pied*)
walk; (*longue*) trip; hike, walking tour

virement [viʀmã] *nm* (*COMM*) transfer

virent *vb voir* **voir**

virer [viʀe] *vt* (*COMM*): **~ qch (sur)** to
transfer sth (into) ♦ *vi* to turn; (*CHIMIE*)
to change colour; **~ de bord** to tack

virevolter [viʀvɔlte] *vi* to twirl around

virgule [viʀgyl] *nf* comma; (*MATH*) point

viril, e [viʀil] *adj* (*propre à l'homme*)
masculine; (*énergique, courageux*) manly, virile

virtuel, le [viʀtɥɛl] *adj* potential; (*théorique*) virtual

virtuose [viʀtɥoz] *nm/f* (*MUS*) virtuoso;

(*gén*) master

virus [viʀys] *nm* (*aussi:* COMPUT) virus

vis¹ [vi] *vb voir* **voir**; **vivre**

vis² [vis] *nf* screw

visa [viza] *nm* (*sceau*) stamp; (*validation de passeport*) visa

visage [vizaʒ] *nm* face

vis-à-vis [vizavi] *adv* face to face ♦ *nm* person opposite; house *etc* opposite; ~ **de** opposite; (*fig*) vis-à-vis; **en** ~ facing each other

viscéral, e, aux [viseʀal, -o] *adj* (*fig*) deep-seated, deep-rooted

visée [vize] : ~**s** *nfpl* (*intentions*) designs

viser [vize] *vi* to aim ♦ *vt* to aim at; (*concerner*) to be aimed *ou* directed at; (*apposer un visa sur*) to stamp, visa; ~ **à qch/faire** to aim at sth/at doing *ou* to do; **viseur** [vizœʀ] *nm* (*d'arme*) sights *pl*; (PHOTO) viewfinder

visibilité [vizibilite] *nf* visibility

visible [vizibl(ə)] *adj* visible; (*disponible*): **est-il** ~? can he see me?, will he see visitors?

visière [vizjɛʀ] *nf* (*de casquette*) peak; (*qui s'attache*) eyeshade

vision [vizjɔ̃] *nf* vision; (*sens*) (eye)sight, vision; (*fait de voir*): **la** ~ **de** the sight of

visionneuse [vizjɔnøz] *nf* viewer

visite [vizit] *nf* visit; (*visiteur*) visitor; (*médicale, à domicile*) visit, call; **la** ~ (MÉD) medical examination; **faire une** ~ **à qn** to call on sb, pay sb a visit; **rendre** ~ **à qn** to visit sb, pay sb a visit; **être en** ~ (**chez qn**) to be visiting (sb); **heures de** ~ (*hôpital, prison*) visiting hours

visiter [vizite] *vt* to visit; (*musée, ville*) to visit, go round; **visiteur, euse** *nm/f* visitor

vison [vizɔ̃] *nm* mink

visser [vise] *vt*: ~ **qch** (*fixer, serrer*) to screw sth on

visuel, le [vizɥɛl] *adj* visual

vit *vb voir* **voir**; **vivre**

vital, e, aux [vital, -o] *adj* vital

vitamine [vitamin] *nf* vitamin

vite [vit] *adv* (*rapidement*) quickly, fast; (*sans délai*) quickly; soon; **faire** ~ to act

quickly; to be quick

vitesse [vitɛs] *nf* speed; (AUTO: *dispositif*) gear; **prendre qn de** ~ to outstrip sb; to get ahead of sb; **prendre de la** ~ to pick up *ou* gather speed; **à toute** ~ at full *ou* top speed

viticole [vitikɔl] *adj* wine *cpd*, wine-growing

viticulteur [vitikyltœʀ] *nm* wine grower

vitrage [vitraʒ] *nm* glass *no pl*; (*rideau*) net curtain

vitrail, aux [vitraj, -o] *nm* stained-glass window

vitre [vitr(ə)] *nf* (window) pane; (*de portière, voiture*) window

vitré, e [vitre] *adj* glass *cpd*

vitrer [vitre] *vt* to glaze

vitreux, euse [vitrø, -øz] *adj* (*terne*) glassy

vitrine [vitrin] *nf* (*devanture*) (shop) window; (*étalage*) display; (*petite armoire*) display cabinet; ~ **publicitaire** display case, showcase

vitupérer [vitypere] *vi* to rant and rave

vivace [vivas] *adj* (*arbre, plante*) hardy; (*fig*) indestructible, inveterate

vivacité [vivasite] *nf* liveliness, vivacity, sharpness; brilliance

vivant, e [vivɑ̃, -ɑ̃t] *adj* (*qui vit*) living, alive; (*animé*) lively; (*preuve, exemple*) living ♦ *nm*: **du** ~ **de qn** in sb's lifetime

vivats [viva] *nmpl* cheers

vive [viv] *adj voir* **vif** ♦ *vb voir* **vivre** ♦ *excl*: ~ **le roi!** long live the king!; **vivement** *adv* vivaciously; sharply ♦ *excl*: **vivement les vacances!** roll on the holidays!

viveur [vivœʀ] (*péj*) *nm* high liver, pleasure-seeker

vivier [vivje] *nm* fish tank; fishpond

vivifiant, e [vivifjɑ̃, -ɑ̃t] *adj* invigorating

vivions *vb voir* **vivre**

vivoter [vivɔte] *vi* (*personne*) to scrape a living, get by; (*fig: affaire etc*) to struggle along

vivre [vivr(ə)] *vi, vt* to live; **il vit encore** he is still alive; **se laisser** ~ to take life as it comes; **ne plus** ~ (*être anxieux*) to live on one's nerves; **il a vécu** (*eu une* *vie aventureuse*) he has seen life; **être facile à ~** to be easy to get on with; **faire ~ qn** (*pourvoir à sa subsistance*) to provide (a living) for sb; **vivres** *nmpl* provisions, food supplies

vlan [vlɑ̃] *excl* wham!, bang!

vocable [vɔkabl(ə)] *nm* term

vocabulaire [vɔkabylɛʀ] *nm* vocabulary

vocation [vɔkasjɔ̃] *nf* vocation, calling

vociférer [vɔsifeʀe] *vi, vt* to scream

vœu, x [vø] *nm* wish; (*à Dieu*) vow; **faire ~ de** to take a vow of; **~x de bonne année** best wishes for the New Year

vogue [vɔg] *nf* fashion, vogue

voguer [vɔge] *vi* to sail

voici [vwasi] *prép* (*pour introduire, désigner*) here is +*sg*, here are +*pl*; **et ~ que ...** and now it (*ou* he) ...; *voir aussi* **voilà**

voie [vwa] *nf* way; (*RAIL*) track, line; (*AUTO*) lane; **être en bonne ~** to be going well; **mettre qn sur la ~** to put sb on the right track; **être en ~ d'achèvement/de rénovation** to be nearing completion/in the process of renovation; **par ~ buccale** *ou* **orale** orally; **à ~ étroite** narrow-gauge; **~ d'eau** (*NAVIG*) leak; **~ de garage** (*RAIL*) siding; **~ ferrée** railway line

voilà [vwala] *prép* (*en désignant*) there is +*sg*, there are +*pl*; **les ~** *ou* **voici** here *ou* there they are; **en ~** *ou* **voici un** here's one, there's one; **~ deux ans** two years ago; **~** *ou* **voici deux ans que** it's two years since; **et ~!** there we are!; **~ tout** that's all; **~ voici** (*en offrant etc*) there *ou* here you are

voile [vwal] *nm* veil; (*tissu léger*) net ♦ *nf* sail; (*sport*) sailing

voiler [vwale] *vt* to veil; (*fausser: roue*) to buckle; (: *bois*) to warp; **se ~** *vi* (*lune, regard*) to mist over; (*voix*) to become husky; (*roue, disque*) to buckle; (*planche*) to warp

voilier [vwalje] *nm* sailing ship; (*de plaisance*) sailing boat

voilure [vwalyʀ] *nf* (*de voilier*) sails *pl*

voir [vwaʀ] *vi, vt* to see; **se ~** *vt*: **se ~ critiquer/transformer** to be criticized/

transformed; **cela se voit** (*cela arrive*) it happens; (*c'est visible*) that's obvious, it shows; **~ venir** (*fig*) to wait and see; **faire ~ qch à qn** to show sb sth; **en faire ~ à qn** (*fig*) to give sb a hard time; **ne pas pouvoir ~ qn** not to be able to stand sb; **voyons!** let's see now; (*indignation etc*) (come along) now!; **avoir quelque chose à ~ avec** to have something to do with

voire [vwaʀ] *adv* indeed; nay; or even

voisin, e [vwazɛ̃, -in] *adj* (*proche*) neighbouring; (*contigu*) next; (*ressemblant*) connected ♦ *nm/f* neighbour; **voisinage** *nm* (*proximité*) proximity; (*environs*) vicinity; (*quartier, voisins*) neighbourhood

voiture [vwatyʀ] *nf* car; (*wagon*) coach, carriage; **~ d'enfant** pram (*BRIT*), baby carriage (*US*); **~ de sport** sports car; **~-lit** *nf* sleeper

voix [vwa] *nf* voice; (*POL*) vote; **à haute ~** aloud; **à ~ basse** in a low voice; **à 2/4 ~** (*MUS*) in 2/4 parts; **avoir ~ au chapitre** to have a say in the matter

vol [vɔl] *nm* (*mode de locomotion*) flying; (*trajet, voyage, groupe d'oiseaux*) flight; (*larcin*) theft; **à ~ d'oiseau** as the crow flies; **au ~: attraper qch au ~** to catch sth as it flies past; **en ~** in flight; **~ à main armée** armed robbery; **~ à voile** gliding; **~ libre** hanggliding

volage [vɔlaʒ] *adj* fickle

volaille [vɔlaj] *nf* (*oiseaux*) poultry *pl*; (*viande*) poultry *no pl*; (*oiseau*) fowl

volant, e [vɔlɑ̃, -ɑ̃t] *adj voir* **feuille** *etc* ♦ *nm* (*d'automobile*) (steering) wheel; (*de commande*) wheel; (*objet lancé*) shuttlecock; (*bande de tissu*) flounce

volcan [vɔlkɑ̃] *nm* volcano

volée [vɔle] *nf* (*TENNIS*) volley; **à la ~: rattraper à la ~** to catch in mid-air; **à toute ~** (*sonner les cloches*) vigorously; (*lancer un projectile*) with full force; **~ de coups/de flèches** volley of blows/arrows

voler [vɔle] *vi* (*avion, oiseau, fig*) to fly; (*voleur*) to steal ♦ *vt* (*objet*) to steal;

(*personne*) to rob; ~ **qch à qn** to steal sth from sb

volet [vɔlɛ] *nm* (*de fenêtre*) shutter; (*de feuillet, document*) section

voleur, euse [vɔlœr, -øz] *nm/f* thief ♦ *adj* thieving

volontaire [vɔlɔ̃tɛr] *adj* voluntary; (*caractère, personne: décidé*) self-willed ♦ *nm/f* volunteer

volonté [vɔlɔ̃te] *nf* (*faculté de vouloir*) will; (*énergie, fermeté*) will(power); (*souhait, désir*) wish; **à** ~ as much as one likes; **bonne** ~ goodwill, willingness; **mauvaise** ~ lack of goodwill, unwillingness

volontiers [vɔlɔ̃tje] *adv* (*de bonne grâce*) willingly; (*avec plaisir*) willingly, gladly; (*habituellement, souvent*) readily, willingly

volt [vɔlt] *nm* volt

volte-face [vɔltəfas] *nf inv* about-turn

voltige [vɔltiʒ] *nf* (ÉQUITATION) trick riding; (*au cirque*) acrobatics *sg*; **voltiger** [vɔltiʒe] *vi* to flutter (about)

volume [vɔlym] *nm* volume; (GÉOM: *solide*) solid; **volumineux, euse** *adj* voluminous, bulky

volupté [vɔlypte] *nf* sensual delight *ou* pleasure

vomir [vɔmir] *vi* to vomit, be sick ♦ *vt* to vomit, bring up; (*fig*) to belch out, spew out; (*exécrer*) to loathe, abhor

vont [vɔ̃] *vb voir* **aller**

vos [vo] *dét voir* **votre**

vote [vɔt] *nm* vote; ~ **par correspondance/procuration** postal/proxy vote

voter [vɔte] *vi* to vote ♦ *vt* (*loi, décision*) to vote for

votre [vɔtr(ə)] (*pl* **vos**) *dét* your

vôtre [votr(ə)] *pron*: **le** ~, **la** ~, **les** ~**s** yours; **les** ~**s** (*fig*) your family *ou* folks; **à la** ~ (*toast*) your (good) health!

voudrai *etc vb voir* **vouloir**

voué, e [vwe] *adj*: ~ **à** doomed to

vouer [vwe] *vt*: ~ **qch à** (*Dieu/un saint*) to dedicate sth to; ~ **sa vie à** (*étude, cause etc*) to devote one's life to; ~ **une amitié éternelle à qn** to vow undying friendship to sb

---

MOT-CLÉ

vouloir [vulwar] *nm*: **le bon** ~ **de qn** sb's goodwill; sb's pleasure

♦ *vt* **1** (*exiger, désirer*) to want; ~ **faire/que qn fasse** to want to do/sb to do; **voulez-vous du thé?** would you like *ou* do you want some tea?; **que me veut-il?** what does he want with me?; **sans le** ~ (*involontairement*) without meaning to, unintentionally; **je voudrais ceci/faire** I would *ou* I'd like this/to do

2 (*consentir*): **je veux bien** (*bonne volonté*) I'll be happy to; (*concession*) fair enough, that's fine; **oui, si on veut** (*en quelque sorte*) yes, if you like; **veuillez attendre** please wait; **veuillez agréer ...** (*formule épistolaire*) yours faithfully

3: **en** ~ **à qn** to bear sb a grudge; **s'en** ~ (**de**) to be annoyed with o.s. (for); **il en veut à mon argent** he's after my money

4: ~ **de**: **l'entreprise ne veut plus de lui** the firm doesn't want him any more; **elle ne veut pas de son aide** she doesn't want his help

5: ~ **dire** to mean

---

voulu, e [vuly] *adj* (*requis*) required, requisite; (*délibéré*) deliberate, intentional; *voir aussi* **vouloir**

vous [vu] *pron* you; (*objet indirect*) (to) you; (*réfléchi: sg*) yourself; (: *pl*) yourselves; (*réciproque*) each other; ~**-même** yourself; ~**-mêmes** yourselves

voûte [vut] *nf* vault

voûter [vute] *vt*: **se** ~ *vi* (*dos, personne*) to become stooped

vouvoyer [vuvwaje] *vt*: ~ **qn** to address sb as "vous"

voyage [vwajaʒ] *nm* journey, trip; (*fait de voyager*): **le** ~ travel(ling); **partir/être en** ~ to go off/be away on a journey *ou* trip; **faire bon** ~ to have a good journey; ~ **d'agrément/d'affaires** pleasure/business trip; ~ **de noces** honeymoon; ~ **organisé** package tour

voyager [vwajaʒe] *vi* to travel; **voyageur, euse** *nm/f* traveller; (*passager*) passenger

voyant, e [vwajɑ̃, -ɑ̃t] *adj (couleur)* loud, gaudy ♦ *nm (signal)* (warning) light.

voyante *nf* clairvoyant

voyelle [vwajɛl] *nf* vowel

voyons *etc vb voir* **voir**

voyou [vwaju] *nm* lout, hoodlum; *(enfant)* guttersnipe

vrac [vʀak]: **en ~** *adv* higgledy-piggledy; *(COMM)* in bulk

vrai, e [vʀɛ] *adj (véridique: récit, faits)* true; *(non factice, authentique)* real; **à ~ dire** to tell the truth

vraiment [vʀɛmɑ̃] *adv* really

vraisemblable [vʀɛsɑ̃blabl(ə)] *adj* likely, probable

vraisemblance [vʀɛsɑ̃blɑ̃s] *nf* likelihood; *(romanesque)* verisimilitude

vrille [vʀij] *nf (de plante)* tendril; *(outil)* gimlet; *(spirale)* spiral; *(AVIAT)* spin

vrombir [vʀɔ̃biʀ] *vi* to hum

VTT *sigle m* (= *vélo tout-terrain*) mountain bike

vu, e [vy] *pp de* **voir** ♦ *adj*: **bien/mal ~** *(fig)* well/poorly thought of; **good/bad form** ♦ *prep (en raison de)* in view of; **~ que** in view of the fact that

vue [vy] *nf (fait de voir)*: **la ~ de** the sight of; *(sens, faculté)* (eye)sight; *(panorama, image, photo)* view; **~s** *nfpl (idées)* views; *(dessein)* designs; **hors de ~** out of sight; **tirer à ~** to shoot on sight; **à ~ d'œil** visibly; **at a quick glance; en ~** *(visible)* in sight; *(COMM)* in the public eye; **en ~ de faire** with a view to doing

vulgaire [vylgɛʀ] *adj (grossier)* vulgar, coarse; *(trivial)* commonplace, mundane; *(péj: quelconque)*: **de ~s touristes** common tourists; *(BOT, ZOOL: non latin)* common; **vulgariser** *vt* to popularize

vulnérable [vylneʀabl(ə)] *adj* vulnerable

W w

wagon [vagɔ̃] *nm (de voyageurs)* carriage; *(de marchandises)* truck, wagon; **wagon-lit** *nm* sleeper, sleeping car;

wagon-restaurant *nm* restaurant *ou* dining car

wallon, ne [valɔ̃, -ɔn] *adj* Walloon

waters [watɛʀ] *nmpl* toilet *sg*

watt [wat] *nm* watt

w.-c. [vese] *nmpl* toilet *sg*, lavatory *sg*

week-end [wikɛnd] *nm* weekend

western [wɛstɛʀn] *nm* western

whisky [wiski] *(pl* **whiskies***) nm* whisky

X x

xérès [gzeʀɛs] *nm* sherry

xylophone [ksilɔfɔn] *nm* xylophone

Y y

y [i] *adv (à cet endroit)* there; *(dessus)* on it *(ou* them); *(dedans)* in it *(ou* them) ♦ *pron* (about *ou* on *ou* of) it *(d'après le verbe employé)*; **j'~ pense** I'm thinking about it; *voir aussi* **aller**; **avoir**

yacht [jɔt] *nm* yacht

yaourt [jauʀt] *nm* yoghourt

yeux [jø] *nmpl de* **œil**

yoga [jɔga] *nm* yoga

yoghourt [jɔguʀt] *nm =* **yaourt**

yougoslave [jugɔslav] *nm/f* Yugoslav(ian)

Yougoslavie [jugɔslavi] *nf* Yugoslavia

Z z

zapping [zapiŋ] *nm*: **faire du ~** to flick through the channels

zèbre [zɛbʀ(ə)] *nm (ZOOL)* zebra

zébré, e [zebʀe] *adj* striped, streaked

zèle [zɛl] *nm* zeal; **faire du ~** *(péj)* to be over-zealous

zéro [zeʀo] *nm* zero, nought *(BRIT)*; **audessous de ~** below zero (Centigrade) *ou* freezing; **partir de ~** to start from scratch; **trois (buts) à ~** 3 (goals) to nil

zeste [zɛst(ə)] *nm* peel, zest

zézayer [zezeje] *vi* to have a lisp

zigzag [zigzag] *nm* zigzag
zinc [zɛ̃g] *nm* (*CHIMIE*) zinc; (*comptoir*) bar, counter
zizanie [zizani] *nf*: **semer la** ~ to stir up ill-feeling
zodiaque [zɔdjak] *nm* zodiac
zona [zona] *nm* shingles *sg*
zone [zon] *nf* zone, area; (*quartiers*): **la** ~ the slum belt; ~ **bleue** ≈ restricted parking area; ~ **industrielle** *nf* industrial estate
zoo [zoo] *nm* zoo
zoologie [zɔɔlɔʒi] *nf* zoology; **zoologique** *adj* zoological
zut [zyt] *excl* dash (it)! (*BRIT*), nuts! (*US*)

PUZZLES AND WORDGAMES

Introduction

We are delighted that you have decided to invest in this Collins Pocket Dictionary! Whether you intend to use it in school, at home, on holiday or at work, we are sure that you will find it very useful.

In the pages which follow you will find explanations and wordgames (not too difficult!) designed to give you practice in exploring the dictionary's contents and in retrieving information for a variety of purposes. Answers are provided at the end. If you spend a little time on these pages you should be able to use your dictionary more efficiently and effectively. Have fun!

Supplement by
Roy Simon
reproduced by kind permission of
Tayside Region Education Department

WORDGAME 1

DICTIONARY ENTRIES

Complete the crossword below by looking up the English words in the list and finding the correct French translations. There is a slight catch, however! All the English words can be translated several ways into French, but only one translation will fit correctly into each part of the crossword.

1. HORN

2. THROW

3. KNOW

4. MOVE

5. LEAN

6. FORBID

7. CALF

8. PLACE

9. TRACK

10. STEEP

11. HARD

12. PLACE

WORDGAME 2

SYNONYMS

Complete the crossword by supplying SYNONYMS of the words below. You will sometimes find the synonym you are looking for in italics and bracketed at the entries for the words listed below. Sometimes you will have to turn to the English-French section for help.

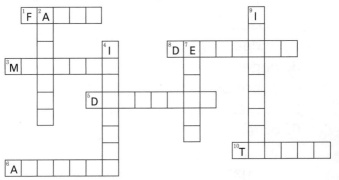

1. manière
2. se passer
3. récolte
4. feu
5. doubler

6. gentil
7. faute
8. haïr
9. défendre
10. essayer

WORDGAME 3

SPELLING

You will often use your dictionary to check spellings. The person who has compiled this list of ten French words has made <u>three</u> spelling mistakes. Find the three words which have been misspelt and write them out correctly.

1. oiseau
2. ondée
3. ongel
4. opportun
5. orage
6. ortiel
7. ouest
8. ourigan
9. ouvreuse
10. oxygène

WORDGAME 4

ANTONYMS

Complete the crossword by supplying ANTONYMS (i.e. opposites) in French of the words below. Use your dictionary to help.

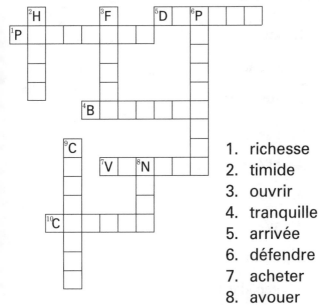

1. richesse
2. timide
3. ouvrir
4. tranquille
5. arrivée
6. défendre
7. acheter
8. avouer
9. innocent
10. révéler

PHONETIC SPELLINGS

The phonetic transcriptions of ten French words are given below. If you study pages x to xi near the front of your dictionary you should be able to work out what the words are.

1. ku

2. tɔmat

3. ʒœn

4. ɔ̃gl(ə)

5. kɛ̃z

6. mɛ̃

7. ʒy

8. ɛkskyze

9. ʀepɔ̃dʀ(ə)

10. vulwaʀ

EXPRESSIONS IN WHICH THE HEADWORD APPEARS

If you look up the headword 'coup' in the French-English section of your dictionary you will find that the word has many meanings. Study the entry carefully and translate the following sentences into English.

1. L'automobiliste a donné un coup de frein en abordant le virage.

2. Il est resté trop longtemps sur la plage et a pris un coup de soleil.

3. Ils sont arrivés sur le coup de midi.

4. On va boire un coup?

5. Il a un œil au beurre noir — quelqu'un lui a donné un coup de poing.

6. Je vais donner un coup de téléphone à mon frère.

7. Il a jeté un coup d'œil sur la liste.

8. Je vais te donner un coup de main.

9. Un coup de vent a fait chavirer le voilier.

10. Les éclairs se sont suivis coup sur coup.

WORDGAME 7

RELATED WORDS

Fill in the blanks in the pairs of sentences below. The missing words are related to the headwords on the left. Choose the correct 'relative' each time. You will find it in your dictionary near the headwords provided.

HEADWORD	RELATED WORDS
permettre	1. Il a demandé la _____ de sortir. 2. Il a son _____ de conduire.
emploi	3. Il est _____ de banque. 4. Je vais _____ tous les moyens pour réussir.
faux	5. Le _____ a été condamné à trois ans de prison. 6. Il dit qu'il a été _____ accusé de vol.
écarter	7. Le cycliste a dû faire un _____ pour éviter le poteau. 8. Ils habitent un village _____.
étudiant	9. Il fait ses _____ à la Sorbonne. 10. Le professeur a commencé à _____ le texte.
sifflement	11. Un coup de _____ a marqué le commencement du match. 12. Il s'est fait _____ par l'agent au carrefour.

8

'KEY' WORDS

Study carefully the entry **'faire'** in your dictionary and find translations for the following:

1. the weather is fine

2. to do law

3. I don't mind

4. it makes you sleep

5. to have one's eyes tested

6. it's not done

7. to do the washing

8. we must act quickly

9. to start up an engine

10. to make friends

WORDGAME 9

PARTS OF SPEECH

In each sentence below a word has been shaded. Put a tick in the appropriate box to indicate the **part of speech** each time. Remember, different parts of speech are indicated by lozenges within entries.

SENTENCE	Noun	Adj	Adv	Verb
1. Il étudie le droit à Paris.				
2. Il chante juste.				
3. Le lancer du poids est une épreuve d'athlétisme.				
4. Le dîner est prêt.				
5. Allez tout droit, puis prenez la première à gauche.				
6. Elle a le fou rire.				
7. Je vais mettre fin à cette stupidité!				
8. Nous allons dîner en ville.				
9. Il ne ferait pas de mal à une mouche.				
10. C'était un bon repas.				

NOUNS

This list contains the feminine form of some French nouns. Use your dictionary to find the **masculine** form.

Use your dictionary to find the **plural** of the following nouns.

MASCULINE	FEMININE	SINGULAR	PLURAL
	paysanne	oiseau	
	chanteuse	pneu	
	directrice	genou	
	espionne	voix	
	domestique	bail	
	lycéenne	jeu	
	épicière	bijou	
	lectrice	œil	
	cadette	lave-vaisselle	
	contractuelle	journal	

WORDGAME 11

MEANING CHANGING WITH GENDER

Some French nouns change meaning according to their gender, i.e. according to whether they are masculine or feminine. Look at the pairs of sentences below and fill in the blanks with either **'un'**, **'une'**, **'le'** or **'la'**.

1. Il a acheté _____ livre de sucre.
   Sa sœur a acheté _____ livre de cuisine.

2. Pour faire une tarte il faut _____ moule.
   Elle a trouvé _____ moule sous le rocher.

3. On va faire _____ tour en voiture.
   Ils habitent dans _____ tour de seize étages.

4. Ce bateau a _____ voile jaune.
   La mariée portait _____ voile.

5. _____ mousse est un apprenti marin.
   Tu aimes _____ mousse au chocolat?

6. Il y avait _____ poêle à bois qui chauffait la cuisine.
   Elle prépare des crêpes dans _____ poêle.

7. Il a relevé _____ manche gauche de son pull-over.
   Il tenait le couteau par _____ manche.

8. Les femmes aiment suivre _____ mode.
   _____ mode d'emploi est assez facile.

ADJECTIVES

Use your dictionary to find the **feminine singular** form of these adjectives.

MASCULINE	FEMININE
1. frais	
2. songeur	
3. épais	
4. public	
5. franc	
6. complet	
7. oisif	
8. pareil	
9. ancien	
10. mou	
11. favori	
12. doux	
13. artificiel	
14. flatteur	

WORDGAME 13

VERB TENSES

Use your dictionary to help you fill in the blanks in the table below. (Read pages 633, 634 at the back and pages 6 to 7 at the front of your dictionary.)

INFINITIVE	PRESENT TENSE	IMPERFECT	FUTURE
venir		je	
maudire	je		
voir			je
savoir		je	
avoir			j'
partir	je		
être			je
vouloir		je	
devoir	je		
permettre	je		
dormir		je	
pouvoir			je

PAST PARTICIPLES

Use the verb tables at the back of your dictionary to find the past participle of these verbs. Check that you have found the correct form by looking in the main text. Some of the verbs below have prefixes in front of them.

INFINITIVE	PAST PARTICIPLE
venir	
mourir	
couvrir	
vivre	
offrir	
servir	
connaître	
remettre	
surprendre	
pleuvoir	
renaître	
conduire	
plaire	
défaire	
sourire	

IDENTIFYING INFINITIVES

In the sentences below you will see various French verbs shaded. Use your dictionary to help you find the **infinitive** form of each verb.

1. Quand j'étais jeune je partageais une chambre avec mon frère.

2. Mes amis viennent à la discothèque.

3. Sa mère l'amène à l'école en voiture.

4. Je me lèverai à dix heures demain.

5. Ce week-end nous sortirons ensemble.

6. Ils avaient déjà vendu la maison.

7. Elle suit un régime.

8. Il est né en Espagne.

9. J'aimerais vivre aux États-Unis.

10. Ils feront une partie de tennis.

11. Il prenait un bain tous les soirs.

12. Il a repris le travail.

13. Nous voudrions visiter le château.

14. Les enfants avaient froid.

15. Quand j'essaie de réparer la voiture j'ai toujours les mains couvertes d'huile.

MORE ABOUT MEANING

In this section we will consider some of the problems associated with using a bilingual dictionary.

Overdependence on your dictionary

That the dictionary is an invaluable tool for the language learner is beyond dispute. Nevertheless, it is possible to become overdependent on your dictionary, turning to it in an almost automatic fashion every time you come up against a new French word or phrase. Tackling an unfamiliar text in this way will turn reading in French into an extremely tedious activity. If you stop to look up every new word you may actually be *hindering* your ability to read in French — you are so concerned with the individual words that you pay no attention to the text as a whole and to the context which gives them meaning. It is therefore important to develop appropriate reading skills — using clues such as titles, headlines, illustrations, etc., understanding relations within a sentence, etc. — so as to predict or infer what a text is about.

A detailed study of the development of reading skills is not within the scope of this supplement; we are concerned with knowing how to use a dictionary, which is only one of several important skills involved in reading. Nevertheless, it may be instructive to look at one example. Imagine that you see the following text in a Swiss newspaper and are interested in working out what it is about.

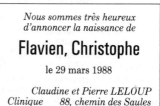

Nous sommes très heureux
d'annoncer la naissance de

Flavien, Christophe

le 29 mars 1988

Claudine et Pierre LELOUP
Clinique   88, chemin des Saules
des Etoiles   1233 Genève

Contextual clues here include the words in large type which you would probably recognise as a French name, something that looks like a date in the middle, and the name and address in the bottom right-hand corner. The French words 'annoncer' and 'clinique' closely resemble the words 'announce' and 'clinic' in English, so you would not have to look them up in your dictionary. Other 'form' words such as 'nous', 'sommes', 'très', 'la' and 'de' will be familiar to you from your general studies in French. Given that we are dealing with a newspaper, you will probably have worked out by now that this could be an announcement placed in the 'Personal Column'.

So you have used a series of cultural, contextual and word-formation clues to get you to the point where you have understood that Claudine and Pierre Leloup have placed this notice in the 'Personal Column' of the newspaper and that something happened to Christophe on 29 March 1988, something connected with a hospital. And you have reached this point *without* opening your dictionary once. Common sense and your knowledge of newspaper contents in this country might suggest that this must be an announcement of someone's birth or death. Thus 'heureux' ('happy') and 'naissance' ('birth') become the only words that you might have to look up in order to confirm that this is indeed a birth announcement.

When learning French we are helped considerably by the fact that many French and English words look and sound alike and have exactly the same meaning. Such words are called 'COGNATES'. Many words which look similar in French and English often come from a common Latin root. Other words are the same or nearly the same in both languages because the French language has borrowed a word from English or vice versa. The dictionary will often not be necessary where cognates are concerned — provided you know the English word that the French word resembles!

Words with more than one meaning

The need to examine with care *all* the information contained in a dictionary entry must be stressed. This is particularly important with the many words which have more than one meaning. For example, the French 'journal' can mean 'diary' as well as 'newspaper'. How you translated the word would depend on the context in which you found it.

Similarly, if you were trying to translate a phrase such as 'en plein visage', you would have to look through the whole entry for 'plein' to get the right translation. If you restricted your search to the first line of the entry and saw that the first meaning given is 'full', you might be tempted to assume that the phrase meant 'a full (i.e. fat) face'. But if you examined the entry closely you would see that 'en plein . . .' means 'right in the middle of . . .'. So 'en plein visage' means 'right in the middle of the face', as in the sentence 'La boule de neige l'a frappé en plein visage'.

The same need for care applies when you are using the English-French section of your dictionary to translate a word from English into French. Watch out in particular for the lozenges indicating changes in parts of speech.

18

The noun 'sink' is 'évier', while the verb is 'couler'. If you don't watch what you are doing, you could end up with ridiculous non-French e.g. 'Elle a mis la vaisselle dans le couler'!

sink [sɪŋk] (*pt* sank, *pp* sunk) *n* évier *m*
♦ *vt* (*ship*) (faire) couler, faire sombrer; (*foundations*) creuser; (*piles etc*): to ~ sth into enfoncer qch dans ♦
vi couler, sombrer; (*ground etc*) s'affaisser; ~ in *vi* s'enfoncer, pénétrer

Phrasal verbs

Another potential source of difficulty is English phrasal verbs. These consist of a common verb ('go', 'make', etc.) plus an adverb and/or a preposition to give English expressions such as 'to make out', 'to take after', etc. Entries for such verbs tend to be fairly full, therefore close examination of the contents is required. Note how these verbs appear in colour within the entry.

make [meɪk] (*pt, pp* made) *vt* faire; (*manufacture*) faire, fabriquer; (*cause to be*): to ~ sb sad *etc* rendre qn triste *etc*; (*force*): to ~ sb do sth obliger qn à faire qch, faire faire qch à qn; (*equal*): 2 and 2 ~ 4 2 et 2 font 4 ♦ *n* fabrication *f*; (*brand*) marque *f*; to ~ a fool of sb (*ridicule*) ridiculiser qn; (*trick*) avoir *or* duper qn; to ~ a profit faire un *or* des bénéfice(s); to ~ a loss essuyer une perte; to ~ it (*arrive*) arriver; (*achieve sth*) parvenir à qch; what time do you ~ it? quelle heure avez-vous?; to ~ do with se contenter de; se débrouiller avec; ~ for *vt fus* (*place*) se diriger vers; ~ out *vt* (*write out*) écrire; (:

Faux amis

Many French and English words have similar forms *and* meanings. Many French words, however, *look* like English words but have a completely *different* meaning. For example, 'le store' means 'the (window) blind'; 'les chips' means 'potato crisps'. This can easily lead to serious mistranslations.

Sometimes the meaning of the French word is **close** to the English. For example, 'la monnaie' means 'loose change' rather than 'money'; 'le surnom' means 'nickname' not 'surname'. But some French words have two meanings, one the same as the English, the other completely different! 'La figure' can mean 'face' as well as 'figure'; 'la marche' can mean 'march/walk' but also 'the step (on the stairs)'.

Such words are after referred to as 'FAUX AMIS' ('false friends'). You will have to look at the context in which they appear to arrive at the correct meaning. If they seem to fit in with the sense of the passage as a whole, you will probably not need to look them up. If they don't make sense, however, you may be dealing with 'faux amis'.

WORDGAME 16

WORDS IN CONTEXT

Study the sentences below. Translations of the shaded words are given at the bottom. Match the number of the sentence and the letter of the translation correctly each time.

1. Les vagues déferlent sur la grève.
2. La grève des cheminots a commencé hier.
3. Elle a versé le café dans une grande tasse.
4. J'ai versé la somme de 500F à titre d'arrhes.
5. L'avion a touché terre.
6. Il touche un salaire mensuel de 10 000F.
7. Beaucoup de fleurs poussent dans leur jardin.
8. Il a dû pousser la brouette.
9. Il voudrait suivre une carrière dans le commerce.
10. Il a visité une carriére où des ouvriers extrayaient des pierres.
11. Il a acheté deux pellicules pour son appareil-photo.
12. Tu as les épaules saupoudrées de pellicules – tu dois te laver les cheveux.

a. poured	e. films	i. draws
b. quarry	f. shore	j. career
c. paid	g. push	k. strike
d. grow	h. dandruff	i. touched

WORDS WITH MORE THAN ONE MEANING
UN PEU DE PUBLICITÉ

Look at the advertisements below. The words which have been shaded can
have more than one meaning. Use your dictionary to help you work out the
correct translation in the context.

1
PRÊT-À-PORTER

BENOIT

TRICOTS
LINGERIE
BAS
FOULARDS
BIJOUX

36, Rue Nationale
T O U R S
Tél. (47) 57 . 14 . 34

2
RESTAURANT 'AU PASSÉ SIMPLE'
vous accueille tous les jours sauf
dimanche midi et lundi (pendant la saison)
UNE GAMME DE 5 MENUS de 50F à 165F + carte
Fruits de mer - Poissons - Service jusqu'à 22h
- 21 bis, pl. Ch. de Gaulle AUTUN - Tél. 27.88.71.02

3
CAISSE D'ÉPARGNE
DE CHAMPIGNY
Le chéquier 'Girafe',
Complément idéal de votre livret
25, rue Maréchal-Foch   Tél. 42.38.53.55.

4
RESTAURANT LE MARAIS
Sa Cuisine du Marché, son Cadre
ses Spécialités Maison
10, rue Lesson - SEDAN
Tél 46.99.47.13

5

Le Château
PLACE DE LA GALISSONNIÈRE
VUE SUR LA PORTE DU SOLEIL
Le Self-Service pour toutes les bourses
A l'étage: le Restaurant gastronomique
LES JARDINS DU 'CHÂTEAU'
Carte de spécialités – Poissons et grillades

6

Comment vous protéger
contre le vol
adressez-vous à
SECURITAS
22, rue Levallois à Aveyron
Tél: 757.48.80

7

CHATEAUROUX D 40

l'Hostel du Roy**NN

JACQUES DE QUÉRÉ   **CUISINE SOIGNÉE**
Propriétaire   **PRIX MODÉRÉS**
                        CAVE RÉPUTÉE

8

Les produits frais...
chez HYPERFRAICHE

9

La roulotte:

Elle deviendra votre maison pendant votre
séjour. Elle est confortable et accueillante.
Prévue pour 4 personnes ou 2 adultes et 3
enfants, elle comprend:

- Le nécessaire de couchage (draps,
  couvertures);
- Vaisselle pour 5 personnes;
- Batterie de cuisine;
- 1 évier

22

WORDGAME 18

FAUX AMIS

Look at the advertisements below. The words which have been shaded resemble English words but have different meanings here. Find a correct translation for each word in the context.

1 **STAGES**
INITIATION
PERFECTIONNEMENT
48, Avenue de Baisse   Plage des Demoiselles
Tél. 61.59.27.53

2
VOYAGES LEGRAND

Cinq Cars avec toilettes   **TAXI**
Equipement lits pendant la saison d'hiver
Location de cars de 20 à 65 places assises

Voyages touristiques France et Etranger

3
PRENEZ UN CHARIOT
POUR EFFECTUER VOS
ACHATS
        MERCI!

4
Hôtel ** NN
de France
Parking important à proximité
Face à la Poste
55, rue du Docteur-Peltier
17300 BORDEAUX
Tél. : 66.89.34.00 et 66.89.33.23

23

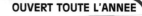
24

WORDGAME 19

MOTS CODÉS

In the boxes below, the letters of eight French words have been replaced by numbers. A number represents the same letter each time.

Try to crack the code and find the eight words. If you need help, use your dictionary.

Here is a clue: all the words you are looking for have something to do with TRANSPORT.

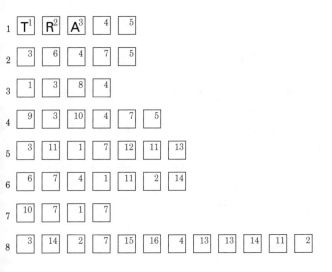

1 T¹ R² A³ 4 5

2 3 6 4 7 5

3 1 3 8 4

4 9 3 10 4 7 5

5 3 11 1 7 12 11 13

6 6 7 4 1 11 2 14

7 10 7 1 7

8 3 14 2 7 15 16 4 13 13 14 11 2

25

MOTS CROISÉS

Complete this crossword by looking up the words listed below in the English-French section of your dictionary. Remember to read through the entry carefully to find the word that will fit.

		1				2		3					4
5				6									
				7									
8													
				9									
									10		11		
	12	13											
14													15
16													
		17											
							18					
		19											

1 To dirty
2 (A piece of) news
3 Mood
4 Relationship
5 Meal
6 To record
7 Novelty
8 To fold
9 Ebony
10 Porthole
11 Heavily
12 Sad
13 To replace
14 To admire
15 To reassure
16 To start up (a car, machine)
17 Tearful
18 Width
19 To withdraw

26

MOTS COUPÉS

There are twelve French words hidden in the grid below. Each word is made up of five letters but has been split into two parts.

Find the French words. Each group of letters can only be used once.

Use your dictionary to help you.

fer	lge	at	ta	fou	re
can	ma	le	pr	su	rin
ise	bac	cre	ég	ine	por
te	ach	me	be	out	ot

WORDGAME 22

MOTS CUISINÉS

Here is a list of French words for things you will find in the kitchen. Unfortunately, they have all been jumbled up. Try to work out what each word is and put the word in the boxes on the right. You will see that there are six shaded boxes below. With the six letters in the shaded boxes make up <u>another</u> French word for an object you can find in the kitchen.

1   saset   Tu veux une ____
                 de café?

2   gfoir   Mets le beurre
                 dans le ____ !

3   telab   À ____ ! On
                 mange!

4   cpldraa   Mets les provisions
                 dans le ____ !

5   éeèirth   Elle met le thé
                 dans la ____

6   caleserso   Elle fait bouillir de
                 l'eau dans une ____

The word you are looking for is:

28

WORDGAME 23

MOTS EN CROIX

Take the four letters given each time and put them in the four empty boxes in the centre of each grid. Arrange them in such a way that you form four six letter words. Use your dictionary to check the words.

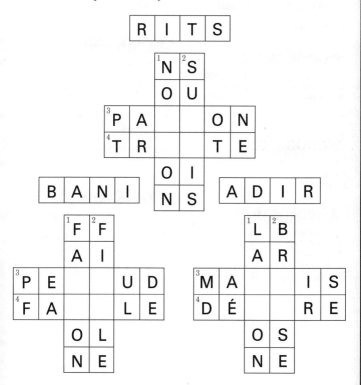

ANSWERS

WORDGAME 1

1 klaxon
2 lancer
3 connaître
4 déménager
5 pencher
6 interdire
7 mollet
8 endroit
9 piste
10 raide
11 dur
12 lieu

WORDGAME 2

1 façon
2 arriver
3 moisson
4 incendie
5 dépasser
6 aimable
7 erreur
8 détester
9 interdire
10 tenter

WORDGAME 3

1 ongle
2 orteil
3 ouragan

WORDGAME 4

1 pauvreté
2 hardi
3 fermer
4 bruyant
5 départ
6 permettre
7 vendre
8 nier
9 coupable
10 cacher

WORDGAME 5

1 cou
2 tomate
3 jeune
4 ongle
5 quinze
6 main
7 jus
8 excuser
9 répondre
10 vouloir

WORDGAME 6

1 braked
2 got sunburnt
3 on the stroke of
4 shall we have a drink?
5 punch
6 make a phone call
7 glanced
8 I'll give you a hand
9 a gust of wind
10 in quick succession

WORDGAME 7

1 permission
2 permis
3 employé
4 employer
5 faux-
   monnayeur
6 faussement
7 écart
8 écarté
9 études
10 étudier
11 sifflet
12 siffler

WORDGAME 9

1 n	6 n
2 adv	7 n
3 n	8 v
4 adj	9 n
5 adv	10 adj

WORDGAME 10

1 paysan	11 oiseaux
2 chanteur	12 pneus
3 directeur	13 genoux
4 espion	14 voix
5 domestique	15 baux
6 lycéen	16 jeux
7 épicier	17 bijoux
8 lecteur	18 yeux
9 cadet	19 lave-vaisselle
10 contractuel	20 journaux

WORDGAME 11

1 une un	5 Un la
2 un une	6 un une
3 un une	7 la le
4 une un	8 la Le

WORDGAME 12

1 fraîche	8 pareille
2 songeuse	9 ancienne
3 épaisse	10 molle
4 publique	11 favorite
5 franche	12 douce
6 complète	13 artificielle
7 oisive	14 flatteuse

WORDGAME 13

je venais	je serai
je maudis	je voulais
je verrai	je dois
je savais	je permets
j'aurai	je dormais
je pars	je pourrai

WORDGAME 14

1 venu	8 remis
2 mort	9 surpris
3 couvert	10 plu
4 vécu	11 rené
5 offert	12 conduit
6 servi	13 plu
7 connu	14 défait
	15 souri

WORDGAME 15

1 partager	9 aimer
2 venir	10 faire
3 amener	11 prendre
4 se lever	12 reprendre
5 sortir	13 vouloir
6 vendre	14 avoir
7 suivre	15 essayer
8 naître	

WORDGAME 16

1 f	5 l	9 j
2 k	6 i	10 b
3 a	7 d	11 e
4 c	8 g	12 h

WORDGAME 17

1 wear
2 except
3 bank
4 cooking; surroundings
5 purses
6 theft
7 prices
8 fresh
9 essentials; pots and pans

WORDGAME 18

1 training courses
2 coaches
3 trolley
4 large
5 cellars
6 wearing; briefs
7 accommodation
8 breeds
9 hire
10 facing; management

WORDGAME 19

1 train
2 avion
3 taxi
4 camion
5 autobus
6 voiture
7 moto
8 aéroglisseur

WORDGAME 20

1 salir
2 nouvelle
3 humeur
4 rapport
5 repas
6 enregistrer
7 nouveauté
8 plier
9 ébène
10 hublot
11 lourdement
12 triste
13 remplacer
14 admirer
15 rassurer
16 démarrer
17 larmoyant
18 largeur
19 retirer

WORDGAME 21

ferme	belge	sucre
canot	marin	foule
prise	tabac	égout
porte	achat	reine

WORDGAME 22

1 tasse
2 frigo
3 table
4 placard
5 théière
6 casserole

Missing word – **chaise**

WORDGAME 23

1 notion	1 fanion	1 lardon
2 sursis	2 fiable	2 braise
3 patron	3 penaud	3 marais
4 triste	4 faible	4 dédire

ENGLISH - FRENCH
ANGLAIS - FRANÇAIS

A a

A [eɪ] *n* (MUS) la *m*

a [eɪ, ə] (*before vowel or silent h: an*) *indef art* **1** un(e); ~ **book** un livre; **an apple** une pomme; **she's** ~ **doctor** elle est médecin

2 (*instead of the number "one"*) un(e); ~ **year ago** il y a un an; ~ **hundred/ thousand** *etc* **pounds** cent/mille *etc* livres

3 (*in expressing ratios, prices etc*): **3** ~ **day/week** 3 par jour/semaine; **10 km** ~**n hour** 10 km à l'heure; **30p** ~ **kilo** 30p le kilo

A.A. *n abbr* = **Alcoholics Anonymous;** (*BRIT:* = *Automobile Association*) ≈ TCF *m*

A.A.A. (*US*) *n abbr* (= *American Automobile Association*) ≈ TCF *m*

aback [ə'bæk] *adv:* **to be taken** ~ être stupéfait(e), être décontenancé(e)

abandon [ə'bændən] *vt* abandonner ♦ *n:* **with** ~ avec désinvolture

abate [ə'beɪt] *vi* s'apaiser, se calmer

abbey ['æbɪ] *n* abbaye *f*

abbot ['æbət] *n* père supérieur

abbreviation [əbriːvɪ'eɪʃən] *n* abréviation *f*

abdicate ['æbdɪkeɪt] *vt, vi* abdiquer

abdomen ['æbdəmən] *n* abdomen *m*

abduct [æb'dʌkt] *vt* enlever

aberration [æbə'reɪʃən] *n* anomalie *f*

abet [ə'bet] *vt see* **aid**

abeyance [ə'beɪəns] *n:* **in** ~ (*law*) tombé(e) en désuétude; (*matter*) en suspens

abide [ə'baɪd] *vt:* **I can't** ~ **it/him** je ne peux pas le souffrir *or* supporter; ~ **by** *vt fus* observer, respecter

ability [ə'bɪlɪtɪ] *n* compétence *f;* capacité *f;* (*skill*) talent *m*

abject ['æbdʒekt] *adj* (*poverty*) sordide; (*apology*) plat(e)

ablaze [ə'bleɪz] *adj* en feu, en flammes

able ['eɪbl] *adj* capable, compétent(e); **to be** ~ **to do sth** être capable de faire qch, pouvoir faire qch; ~**-bodied** *adj* robuste; **ably** ['eɪblɪ] *adv* avec compétence *or* talent, habilement

abnormal [æb'nɔːməl] *adj* anormal(e)

aboard [ə'bɔːd] *adv* à bord ♦ *prep* à bord de

abode [ə'bəud] *n* (LAW): **of no fixed** ~ sans domicile fixe

abolish [ə'bɒlɪʃ] *vt* abolir

aborigine [æbə'rɪdʒiniː] *n* aborigène *m/f*

abort [ə'bɔːt] *vt* faire avorter; ~**ion** [ə'bɔːʃən] *n* avortement *m*; **to have an** ~**ion** se faire avorter; ~**ive** *adj* manqué(e)

abound [ə'baund] *vi* abonder; **to** ~ **in** *or* **with** abonder en, regorger de

about [ə'baut] *adv* **1** (*approximately*) environ, à peu près; ~ **a hundred/ thousand** *etc* environ cent/mille *etc*, une centaine (de)/un millier (de) *etc*; **it takes** ~ **10 hours** ça prend environ *or* à peu près 10 heures; **at** ~ **2 o'clock** vers 2 heures; **I've just** ~ **finished** j'ai presque fini

2 (*referring to place*) çà et là, deci delà; **to run** ~ courir çà et là; **to walk** ~ se promener, aller et venir

3: **to be** ~ **to do sth** être sur le point de faire qch

♦ *prep* **1** (*relating to*) au sujet de, à propos de; **a book** ~ **London** un livre sur Londres; **what is it** ~? de quoi s'agit-il?;

we talked ~ **it** nous en avons parlé; **what** *or* **how** ~ **doing this?** et si nous faisions ceci?
2 (*referring to place*) dans; **to walk ~ the town** se promener dans la ville

about-face [ə'baʊt'feɪs] *n* demi-tour *m*

about-turn [ə'baʊt'tɜːn] *n* (MIL) demi-tour *m*; (*fig*) volte-face *f*

above [ə'bʌv] *adv* au-dessus ♦ *prep* au-dessus de; (*more*) plus de; **mentioned ~** mentionné ci-dessus; **~ all** par-dessus tout, surtout; **~board** *adj* franc(franche); honnête

abrasive [ə'breɪzɪv] *adj* abrasif(ive); (*fig*) caustique, agressif(ive)

abreast [ə'brest] *adv* de front; **to keep ~ of** se tenir au courant de

abridge [ə'brɪdʒ] *vt* abréger

abroad [ə'brɔːd] *adv* à l'étranger

abrupt [ə'brʌpt] *adj* (*steep, blunt*) abrupt(e); (*sudden, gruff*) brusque; **~ly** *adv* (*speak, end*) brusquement

abscess ['æbsɪs] *n* abcès *m*

abscond [əb'skɒnd] *vi* disparaître, s'enfuir

absence ['æbsəns] *n* absence *f*

absent ['æbsənt] *adj* absent(e); **~ee** [æbsən'tiː] *n* absent(e); (*habitual*) absentéiste *m/f*; **~-minded** *adj* distrait(e)

absolute ['æbsəluːt] *adj* absolu(e); **~ly** [æbsə'luːtlɪ] *adv* absolument

absolve [əb'zɒlv] *vt*: **to ~ sb (from)** (*blame, responsibility, sin*) absoudre qn (de)

absorb [əb'zɔːb] *vt* absorber; **to be ~ed in a book** être plongé(e) dans un livre; **~ent cotton** (US) *n* coton *m* hydrophile; **absorption** [əb'zɔːpʃən] *n* absorption *f*; (*fig*) concentration *f*

abstain [əb'steɪn] *vi*: **to ~ (from)** s'abstenir (de)

abstract ['æbstrækt] *adj* abstrait(e)

absurd [əb'sɜːd] *adj* absurde

abuse [*n* ə'bjuːs, *vb* ə'bjuːz] *n* abus *m*; (*insults*) insultes *fpl*, injures *fpl* ♦ *vt* abuser de; (*insult*) insulter; **abusive** [ə'bjuːsɪv] *adj* grossier(ère), injurieux(euse)

abysmal [ə'bɪzməl] *adj* exécrable; (*ignorance etc*) sans bornes

abyss [ə'bɪs] *n* abîme *m*, gouffre *m*

AC *abbr* (= *alternating current*) courant alternatif

academic [ækə'demɪk] *adj* universitaire; (*person: scholarly*) intellectuel(le); (*pej: issue*) oiseux(euse), purement théorique ♦ *n* universitaire *m/f*; **~ year** *n* année *f* universitaire

academy [ə'kædəmɪ] *n* (*learned body*) académie *f*; (*school*) collège *m*; **~ of music** conservatoire *m*

accelerate [æk'seləreɪt] *vt, vi* accélérer; **accelerator** [æk'seləreɪtə*] *n* accélérateur *m*

accent ['æksənt] *n* accent *m*

accept [ək'sept] *vt* accepter; **~able** *adj* acceptable; **~ance** *n* acceptation *f*

access ['ækses] *n* accès *m*; (JUR: *in divorce*) droit *m* de visite; **~ible** [æk'sesɪbl] *adj* accessible

accessory [æk'sesərɪ] *n* accessoire *m*; (LAW): **~ to** complice de

accident ['æksɪdənt] *n* accident *m*; (*chance*) hasard *m*; **by ~** accidentellement; par hasard; **~al** [æksɪ'dentl] *adj* accidentel(le); **~ally** [æksɪ'dentəlɪ] *adv* accidentellement; **~-prone** *adj* sujet(te) aux accidents

acclaim [ə'kleɪm] *n* acclamations *fpl* ♦ *vt* acclamer

accommodate [ə'kɒmədeɪt] *vt* loger, recevoir; (*oblige, help*) obliger; (*car etc*) contenir; **accommodating** [ə'kɒmədeɪtɪŋ] *adj* obligeant(e), arrangeant(e); **accommodation** [əkɒmə'deɪʃən] (US **accommodations**) *n* logement *m*

accompany [ə'kʌmpənɪ] *vt* accompagner

accomplice [ə'kʌmplɪs] *n* complice *m/f*

accomplish [ə'kʌmplɪʃ] *vt* accomplir; **~ment** *n* accomplissement *m*; réussite *f*; (*skill: gen pl*) talent *m*

accord [ə'kɔːd] *n* accord *m* ♦ *vt* accorder; **of his own ~** de son plein gré; **~ance** *n*: **in ~ance with** conformément à; **~ing**: **~ing to** *prep* selon; **~ingly** *adv* en conséquence

accordion [ə'kɔːdɪən] *n* accordéon *m*

accost [ə'kɒst] *vt* aborder

account [ə'kaunt] *n* (COMM) compte *m*; (*report*) compte rendu; récit *m*; ~s *npl* (COMM) comptabilité *f*, comptes; **of no ~** sans importance; **on ~** en acompte; **on no ~** en aucun cas; **on ~ of** à cause de; **to take into ~, take ~ of** tenir compte de; **~ for** *vt fus* expliquer, rendre compte de; **~able** *adj*: **~able (to)** responsable (devant); **~ancy** [ə'kauntənsɪ] *n* comptabilité *f*; **~ant** [ə'kauntənt] *n* comptable *m/f*; **~ number** *n* (*at bank etc*) numéro *m* de compte

accrued interest [əkru:d] *n* intérêt *m* cumulé

accumulate [ə'kju:mjuleɪt] *vt* accumuler, amasser ♦ *vi* s'accumuler, s'amasser

accuracy ['ækjurəsɪ] *n* exactitude *f*, précision *f*

accurate ['ækjurɪt] *adj* exact(e), précis(e); **~ly** *adv* avec précision

accusation [ækju:'zeɪʃən] *n* accusation *f*

accuse [ə'kju:z] *vt*: **to ~ sb (of sth)** accuser qn (de qch); **~d** *n*: **the ~d** l'accusé(e)

accustom [ə'kʌstəm] *vt* accoutumer, habituer; **~ed** *adj* (*usual*) habituel(le); (*in the habit*): **~ed to** habitué(e) *or* accoutumé(e) à

ace [eɪs] *n* as *m*

ache [eɪk] *n* mal *m*, douleur *f* ♦ *vi* (*yearn*): **to ~ to do sth** mourir d'envie de faire qch; **my head ~s** j'ai mal à la tête

achieve [ə'tʃi:v] *vt* (*aim*) atteindre; (*victory, success*) remporter, obtenir; **~ment** *n* exploit *m*, réussite *f*

acid ['æsɪd] *adj* acide ♦ *n* acide *m*; **~ rain** *n* pluies *fpl* acides

acknowledge [ək'nɒlɪdʒ] *vt* (*letter: also*: **~ receipt of**) accuser réception de; (*fact*) reconnaître; **~ment** *n* (*of letter*) accusé *m* de réception

acne ['æknɪ] *n* acné *m*

acorn ['eɪkɔ:n] *n* gland *m*

acoustic [ə'ku:stɪk] *adj* acoustique; **~s** *n, npl* acoustique *f*

acquaint [ə'kweɪnt] *vt*: **to ~ sb with sth** mettre qn au courant de qch; **to be ~ed with** connaître; **~ance** *n* connaissance *f*

acquiesce [ækwɪ'ɛs] *vi*: **to ~ to** acquiescer *or* consentir à

acquire [ə'kwaɪə*] *vt* acquérir

acquit [ə'kwɪt] *vt* acquitter; **to ~ o.s. well** bien se comporter, s'en tirer très honorablement

acre ['eɪkə*] *n* acre *f* (= *4047 m²*)

acrid ['ækrɪd] *adj* âcre

acrobat ['ækrəbæt] *n* acrobate *m/f*

across [ə'krɒs] *prep* (*on the other side*) de l'autre côté de; (*crosswise*) en travers de ♦ *adv* de l'autre côté; en travers; **to run/swim ~** traverser en courant/à la nage; **~ from** en face de

acrylic [ə'krɪlɪk] *adj* acrylique

act [ækt] *n* acte *m*, action *f*; (*of play*) acte; (*in music-hall etc*) numéro *m*; (LAW) loi *f* ♦ *vi* agir; (THEATRE) jouer; (*pretend*) jouer la comédie ♦ *vt* (*part*) jouer, tenir; **in the ~ of** en train de; **to ~ as** servir de; **~ing** *adj* suppléant(e), par intérim ♦ *n* (*activity*): **to do some ~ing** faire du théâtre (*or* du cinéma)

action ['ækʃən] *n* action *f*; (MIL) combat(s) *m(pl)*; (LAW) procès *m*, action en justice; **out of ~** hors de combat; (*machine*) hors d'usage; **to take ~** agir, prendre des mesures; **~ replay** *n* (TV) ralenti *m*

activate ['æktɪveɪt] *vt* (*mechanism*) actionner, faire fonctionner

active ['æktɪv] *adj* actif(ive); (*volcano*) en activité; **~ly** *adv* activement

activity [æk'tɪvɪtɪ] *n* activité *f*

actor ['æktə*] *n* acteur *m*

actress ['æktrɪs] *n* actrice *f*

actual ['æktjuəl] *adj* réel(le), véritable; **~ly** *adv* (*really*) réellement, véritablement; (*in fact*) en fait

acumen ['ækjumen] *n* perspicacité *f*

acute [ə'kju:t] *adj* aigu(ë); (*mind, observer*) pénétrant(e), perspicace

ad [æd] *n abbr* = **advertisement**

A.D. *adv abbr* (= *anno Domini*) ap. J.-C.

adamant ['ædəmənt] *adj* inflexible

adapt [ə'dæpt] *vt* adapter ♦ *vi*: **to ~ (to)** s'adapter (à); **~able** *adj* (*device*) adaptable; (*person*) qui s'adapte facilement; **~er, ~or** n (*ELEC*) adaptateur m

add [æd] vt ajouter; (*figures: also: to ~ up*) additionner ♦ vi: **to ~ to** (*increase*) ajouter à, accroître

adder ['ædə*] n vipère f

addict ['ædɪkt] n intoxiqué(e); (*fig*) fanatique m/f; **~ed** [ə'dɪktɪd] adj: **to be ~ed to** (*drugs, drink etc*) être adonné(e) à; (*fig: football etc*) être un(e) fanatique de; **~ion** [ə'dɪkʃən] n (*MED*) dépendance f; **~ive** adj qui crée une dépendance

addition [ə'dɪʃən] n addition f; (*thing added*) ajout m; **in ~** de plus; de surcroît; **in ~ to** en plus de; **~al** adj supplémentaire

additive ['ædɪtɪv] n additif m

address [ə'dres] n adresse f; (*talk*) discours m, allocution f ♦ vt adresser; (*speak to*) s'adresser à; **to ~ (o.s. to) a problem** s'attaquer à un problème

adept ['ædept] adj: **~ at** expert(e) à or en

adequate ['ædɪkwɪt] adj adéquat(e); suffisant(e)

adhere [əd'hɪə*] vi: **to ~ to** adhérer à; (*fig: rule, decision*) se tenir à

adhesive [əd'hi:zɪv] n adhésif m; **~ tape** n (*BRIT*) ruban adhésif m; (*US: MED*) sparadrap m

ad hoc [æd'hɔk] adj improvisé(e), ad hoc

adjective ['ædʒəktɪv] n adjectif m

adjoining [ə'dʒɔɪnɪŋ] adj voisin(e), adjacent(e), attenant(e)

adjourn [ə'dʒɜ:n] vt ajourner ♦ vi suspendre la séance; lever la séance; clore la session

adjust [ə'dʒʌst] vt ajuster, régler; rajuster ♦ vi: **to ~ (to)** s'adapter (à); **~able** adj réglable; **~ment** n (*PSYCH*) adaptation f; (*to machine*) ajustage m, réglage m; (*of prices, wages*) rajustement m

ad-lib [æd'lɪb] vt, vi improviser; **ad lib** adv à volonté, à loisir

administer [æd'mɪnɪstə*] vt administrer; (*justice*) rendre

administration [ədmɪnɪs'treɪʃən] n administration f

administrative [əd'mɪnɪstrətɪv] adj ad-ministratif(ive)

admiral ['ædmərəl] n amiral m; **A~ty** ['ædmərəltɪ] (*BRIT*) n (*also:* **A~ty Board**): **the A~ty** ministère m de la Marine

admire [əd'maɪə*] vt admirer

admission [əd'mɪʃən] n admission f; (*to exhibition, night club etc*) entrée f; (*confession*) aveu m

admit [əd'mɪt] vt laisser entrer; admettre; (*agree*) reconnaître, admettre; **~ to** vt fus reconnaître, avouer; **~tance** n admission f, (droit m d')entrée f; **~tedly** adv il faut en convenir

admonish [əd'mɔnɪʃ] vt donner un avertissement à; réprimander

ad nauseam [æd'nɔ:sɪæm] adv (*repeat, talk*) à n'en plus finir

ado [ə'du:] n: **without (any) more ~** sans plus de cérémonies

adolescence [ædə'lesns] n adolescence f; **adolescent** [ædə'lesnt] adj, n adolescent(e)

adopt [ə'dɔpt] vt adopter; **~ed** adj adoptif(ive), adopté(e); **~ion** [ə'dɔpʃən] n adoption f

adore [ə'dɔ:*] vt adorer

adorn [ə'dɔ:n] vt orner

Adriatic (Sea) [eɪdrɪ'ætɪk-] n Adriatique f

adrift [ə'drɪft] adv à la dérive

adult ['ædʌlt] n adulte m/f ♦ adj adulte; (*literature, education*) pour adultes

adultery [ə'dʌltərɪ] n adultère m

advance [əd'vɑ:ns] n avance f ♦ adj: **~ booking** réservation f ♦ vt avancer ♦ vi avancer, s'avancer; **~ notice** avertissement m; **to make ~s (to sb)** faire des propositions (à qn); (*amorously*) faire des avances (à qn); **in ~** à l'avance, d'avance; **~d** adj avancé(e); (*SCOL: studies*) supérieur(e)

advantage [əd'vɑ:ntɪdʒ] n (*also TENNIS*) avantage m; **to take ~ of** (*person*) exploiter

advent ['ædvent] n avènement m, venue f; **A~** Avent m

adventure [əd'ventʃə*] n aventure f

adverb ['ædvɜ:b] n adverbe m

adverse ['ædvɜ:s] adj défavorable,

contraire

advert ['ædvɜːt] (*BRIT*) *n abbr* = **advertisement**

advertise ['ædvətaɪz] *vi(vt)* faire de la publicité (pour); mettre une annonce (pour vendre); **to ~ for** (*staff, accommodation*) faire paraître une annonce pour trouver; **~ment** [əd'vɜːtɪsmənt] *n* (*COMM*) réclame *f*, publicité *f*; (*in classified ads*) annonce *f*; **~r** ['ædvətaɪzə*] *n* (*in newspaper etc*) annonceur *m*; **advertising** ['ædvətaɪzɪŋ] *n* publicité *f*

advice [əd'vaɪs] *n* conseils *mpl*; (*notification*) avis *m*; **piece of ~** conseil; **to take legal ~** consulter un avocat

advisable [əd'vaɪzəbl] *adj* conseillé(e), indiqué(e)

advise [əd'vaɪz] *vt* conseiller; **to ~ sb of sth** aviser *or* informer qn de qch; **to ~ against sth/doing sth** déconseiller qch/conseiller de ne pas faire qch; **~dly** [əd'vaɪzədlɪ] *adv* (*deliberately*) délibérément; **~r, advisor** *n* conseiller(ère); **advisory** [əd'vaɪzərɪ] *adj* consultatif(ive)

advocate [*vb* 'ædvəkeɪt, *n* 'ædvəkət] *n* (*upholder*) défenseur *m*, avocat(e), partisan(e); (*LAW*) avocat(e) ♦ *vt* recommander, prôner

aerial ['ɛərɪəl] *n* antenne *f* ♦ *adj* aérien(ne)

aerobics [ɛər'əʊbɪks] *n* aérobic *f*

aeroplane ['ɛərəpleɪn] (*BRIT*) *n* avion *m*

aerosol ['ɛərəsɒl] *n* aérosol *m*

aesthetic [ɪs'θetɪk] *adj* esthétique

afar [ə'fɑː*] *adv*: **from ~** de loin

affair [ə'fɛə*] *n* affaire *f*; (*also: love ~*) liaison *f*; aventure *f*

affect [ə'fekt] *vt* affecter; (*disease*) atteindre; **~ed** *adj* affecté(e)

affection [ə'fekʃən] *n* affection *f*; **~ate** [ə'fekʃənɪt] *adj* affectueux(euse)

affinity [ə'fɪnɪtɪ] *n* (*bond, rapport*): **to have an ~ with/for** avoir une affinité avec/pour; (*resemblance*): **to have an ~ with** avoir une ressemblance avec

afflict [ə'flɪkt] *vt* affliger

affluence ['æfluəns] *n* abondance *f*, opulence *f*

affluent ['æfluənt] *adj* (*person, family,*

surroundings) aisé(e), riche; **the ~ society** la société d'abondance

afford [ə'fɔːd] *vt* se permettre; avoir les moyens d'acheter *or* d'entretenir; (*provide*) fournir, procurer

afield [ə'fiːld] *adv*: **(from) far ~** (de) loin

afloat [ə'fləʊt] *adj, adv* à flot; **to stay ~** surnager

afoot [ə'fʊt] *adv*: **there is something ~** il se prépare quelque chose

afraid [ə'freɪd] *adj* effrayé(e); **to be ~ of** *or* **to** avoir peur de; **I am ~ that ...** je suis désolé(e), mais ...; **I am ~ so/not** hélas oui/non

afresh [ə'freʃ] *adv* de nouveau

Africa ['æfrɪkə] *n* Afrique *f*; **~n** *adj* africain(e) ♦ *n* Africain(e)

aft [ɑːft] *adv* à l'arrière, vers l'arrière

after ['ɑːftə*] *prep, adv* après ♦ *conj* après que, après avoir *or* être +*pp*; **what/who are you ~?** que/qui cherchez-vous?; **~ he left/having done** après qu'il fut parti/après avoir fait; **ask ~ him** demandez de ses nouvelles; **to name sb ~ sb** donner à qn le nom de qn; **twenty ~ eight** (*US*) huit heures vingt; **~ all** après tout; **~ you!** après vous, Monsieur (*or* Madame *etc*); **~-effects** *npl* (*of disaster, radiation, drink etc*) répercussions *fpl*; (*of illness*) séquelles *fpl*, suites *fpl*; **~math** *n* conséquences *fpl*, suites *fpl*; **~noon** *n* aprèsmidi *m or f*; **~s** (*inf*) (*dessert*) dessert *m*; **~-sales service** (*BRIT*) *n* (*for car, washing machine etc*) service *m* aprèsvente; **~-shave (lotion)** *n* after-shave *m*; **~thought** *n*: **I had an ~thought** il m'est venu une idée après coup; **~wards** (*US* **~ward**) *adv* après

again [ə'gen] *adv* de nouveau; encore (une fois); **to do sth ~** refaire qch; **not ... ~** ne ... plus; **~ and ~** à plusieurs reprises

against [ə'genst] *prep* contre; (*compared to*) par rapport à

age [eɪdʒ] *n* âge *m* ♦ *vt, vi* vieillir; **it's been ~s since** ça fait une éternité que ... ne; **he is 20 years of ~** il a 20 ans; **to come of ~** atteindre sa majorité; **~d**[1] *adj*: ~**d 10** âgé(e) de 10 ans; ~**d²** ['eɪdʒɪd] *npl*: **the** ~**d** les personnes âgées; ~ **group** *n* tranche *f* d'âge; ~ **limit** *n* limite *f* d'âge

agency ['eɪdʒənsɪ] *n* agence *f*; (*government body*) organisme *m*, office *m*

agenda [ə'dʒendə] *n* ordre *m* du jour

agent ['eɪdʒənt] *n* agent *m*, représentant *m*; (*firm*) concessionnaire *m*

aggravate ['ægrəveɪt] *vt* aggraver; (*annoy*) exaspérer

aggregate ['ægrɪgɪt] *n* ensemble *m*, total *m*

aggressive [ə'gresɪv] *adj* agressif(ive)

aggrieved [ə'griːvd] *adj* chagriné(e), affligé(e)

aghast [ə'gɑːst] *adj* consterné(e), atterré(e)

agitate ['ædʒɪteɪt] *vt* (*person*) agiter, émouvoir, troubler ♦ *vi*: **to** ~ **for/against** faire campagne pour/contre

AGM *n abbr* (= *annual general meeting*) AG *f*, assemblée générale

ago [ə'gəʊ] *adv*: **2 days** ~ il y a deux jours; **not long** ~ il n'y a pas longtemps; **how long** ~? il y a combien de temps (de cela)?

agog [ə'gɒg] *adj* en émoi

agonizing ['ægənaɪzɪŋ] *adj* angoissant(e); déchirant(e)

agony ['ægənɪ] *n* (*pain*) douleur *f* atroce; **to be in** ~ souffrir le martyre

agree [ə'griː] *vt* (*price*) convenir de ♦ *vi*: **to** ~ **with** (*person*) être d'accord avec; (*statements etc*) concorder avec; (*LING*) s'accorder avec; **to** ~ **to do** accepter de *or* consentir à faire; **to** ~ **to sth** consentir à qch; **to** ~ **that** (*admit*) convenir *or* reconnaître que; **garlic doesn't** ~ **with me** je ne supporte pas l'ail; ~**able** *adj* agréable; (*willing*) consentant(e), d'accord; ~**d** *adj* (*time, place*) convenu(e); ~**ment** *n* accord *m*; **in** ~**ment** d'accord

agricultural [ægrɪ'kʌltʃərəl] *adj* agricole

agriculture ['ægrɪkʌltʃə*] *n* agriculture *f*

aground [ə'graʊnd] *adv*: **to run** ~ échouer, s'échouer

ahead [ə'hed] *adv* (*in front: of position, place*) devant; (: *at the head*) en avant;

(*look, plan, think*) en avant; ~ **of** devant; (*fig: schedule etc*) en avance sur; ~ **of time** en avance; **go right** *or* **straight** ~ allez tout droit; **go** ~! (*fig: permission*) allez-y!

aid [eɪd] *n* aide *f*; (*device*) appareil *m* ♦ *vt* aider; **in** ~ **of** en faveur de; **to** ~ **and abet** (*LAW*) se faire le complice de; *see also* **hearing**

aide [eɪd] *n* (*person*) aide *mf*, assistant(e)

AIDS [eɪdz] *n abbr* (= *acquired immune deficiency syndrome*) SIDA *m*

ailing ['eɪlɪŋ] *adj* malade

ailment ['eɪlmənt] *n* affection *f*

aim [eɪm] *vt*: **to** ~ **sth (at)** (*gun, camera*) braquer *or* pointer qch (sur); (*missile*) lancer qch (à *or* contre *or* en direction de); (*blow*) allonger qch (à); (*remark*) destiner *or* adresser qch (à) ♦ *vi* (*also: to take* ~) viser ♦ *n* but *m*; (*skill*): **his** ~ **is bad** il vise mal; **to** ~ **at** viser; (*fig*) viser (à); **to** ~ **to do** avoir l'intention de faire; ~**less** *adj* sans but

ain't [eɪnt] (*inf*) = **am not; aren't; isn't**

air [ɛə*] *n* air *m* ♦ *vt* (*room, bed, clothes*) aérer; (*grievances, views, ideas*) exposer, faire connaître ♦ *cpd* (*currents, attack etc*) aérien(ne); **to throw sth into the** ~ jeter qch en l'air; **by** ~ (*travel*) par avion; **to be on the** ~ (*RADIO, TV: programme*) être diffusé(e); (: *station*) diffuser; ~**bed** *n* matelas *m* pneumatique; ~**borne** *adj* en vol; ~- **conditioned** *adj* climatisé(e); ~ **conditioning** *n* climatisation *f*; ~**craft** *n inv* avion *m*; ~**craft carrier** *n* porte-avions *m inv*; ~**field** *n* terrain *m* d'aviation; **A~ Force** *n* armée *f* de l'air; ~ **freshener** *n* désodorisant *m*; ~**gun** *n* fusil *m* à air comprimé; ~ **hostess** *n* (*BRIT*) hôtesse *f* de l'air; ~ **letter** *n* (*BRIT*) aérogramme *m*; ~**lift** *n* pont aérien; ~**line** *n* ligne aérienne, compagnie *f* d'aviation; ~**liner** *n* avion *m* de ligne; ~**mail** *n*: **by** ~**mail** par avion; ~**plane** *n* (*US*) avion *m*; ~**port** *n* aéroport *m*; ~ **raid** *n* attaque *or* raid aérien(ne); ~**sick** *adj*: **to be** ~**sick** avoir le mal de l'air; **air space** espace aérien;

~ **terminal** *n* aérogare *f*; ~**tight** *adj* hermétique; ~**-traffic controller** *n* aiguilleur *m* du ciel; ~**y** *adj* bien aéré(e); (*manners*) dégagé(e)

aisle [aɪl] *n* (*of church*) allée centrale; nef latérale; (*of theatre etc*) couloir *m*, passage *m*, allée

ajar [ə'dʒɑ:*] *adj* entrouvert(e)

akin [ə'kɪn] *adj*: ~ **to** (*similar*) qui tient de *or* ressemble à

alarm [ə'lɑ:m] *n* alarme *f* ♦ *vt* alarmer; ~ **call** *n* coup de fil au pour réveiller; ~ **clock** *n* réveille-matin *m inv*, réveil *m*

alas [ə'læs] *excl* hélas!

albeit [ɔ:l'bi:ɪt] *conj* (*although*) bien que +*sub*, encore que +*sub*

album ['ælbəm] *n* album *m*

alcohol ['ælkəhɒl] *n* alcool *m*; ~**ic** [ælkə'hɒlɪk] *adj* alcoolique ♦ *n* alcoolique *m/f*; A~**ics Anonymous** Alcooliques anonymes

ale [eɪl] *n* bière *f*

alert [ə'lɜ:t] *adj* alerte, vif(vive); vigilant(e) ♦ *n* alerte *f* ♦ *vt* alerter; **on the** ~ sur le qui-vive; (*MIL*) en état d'alerte

algebra ['ældʒɪbrə] *n* algèbre *m*

Algeria [æl'dʒɪərɪə] *n* Algérie *f*

alias ['eɪlɪəs] *adv* alias ♦ *n* faux nom, nom d'emprunt; (*writer*) pseudonyme *m*

alibi ['ælɪbaɪ] *n* alibi *m*

alien ['eɪlɪən] *n* étranger(ère); (*from outer space*) extraterrestre *mf* ♦ *adj*: ~ **(to)** étranger(ère) (à); ~**ate** *vt* aliéner; s'aliéner

alight [ə'laɪt] *adj*, *adv* en feu ♦ *vi* mettre pied à terre; (*passenger*) descendre; (*bird*) se poser

alike [ə'laɪk] *adj* semblable, pareil(le) ♦ *adv* de même; **to look** ~ se ressembler

alimony ['ælɪmənɪ] *n* (*payment*) pension *f* alimentaire

alive [ə'laɪv] *adj* vivant(e); (*lively*) plein(e) de vie

KEYWORD
---

all [ɔ:l] *adj* (*singular*) tout(e); (*plural*) tous(toutes); ~ **day** toute la journée; ~ **night** toute la nuit; ~ **men** tous les hommes; ~ **five** tous les cinq; ~ **the food**

toute la nourriture; ~ **the books** tous les livres; ~ **the time** tout le temps; ~ **his life** toute sa vie

♦ *pron* **1** tout; **I ate it** ~, **I ate** ~ **of it** j'ai tout mangé; ~ **of us went** nous y sommes tous allés; ~ **of the boys went** tous les garçons y sont allés

2 (*in phrases*): **above** ~ surtout, pardessus tout; **after** ~ après tout; **not at** ~ (*in answer to question*) pas du tout; (*in answer to thanks*) je vous en prie!; **I'm not at** ~ **tired** je ne suis pas du tout fatigué(e); **anything at** ~ **will do** n'importe quoi fera l'affaire; ~ **in** ~ tout bien considéré, en fin de compte

♦ *adv*: ~ **alone** tout(e) seul(e); **it's not as hard as** ~ **that** ce n'est pas si difficile que ça; ~ **the more/the better** d'autant plus/mieux; ~ **but** presque, pratiquement; **the score is 2** ~ le score est 2 partout

allay [ə'leɪ] *vt* (*fears*) apaiser, calmer

allege [ə'ledʒ] *vt* alléguer, prétendre; ~**dly** [ə'ledʒɪdlɪ] *adv* à ce que l'on prétend, paraît-il

allegiance [ə'li:dʒəns] *n* allégeance *f*, fidélité *f*, obéissance *f*

allergic [ə'lɜ:dʒɪk] *adj*: ~ **to** allergique à; **allergy** ['ælədʒɪ] *n* allergie *f*

alleviate [ə'li:vɪeɪt] *vt* soulager, adoucir

alley ['ælɪ] *n* ruelle *f*

alliance [ə'laɪəns] *n* alliance *f*

allied ['ælaɪd] *adj* allié(e)

all-in ['ɔ:lɪn] (*BRIT*) *adj* (*also adv*: *charge*) tout compris; ~ **wrestling** *n* lutte *f* libre

all-night ['ɔ:l'naɪt] *adj* ouvert(e) *or* qui dure toute la nuit

allocate ['æləkeɪt] *vt* (*share out*) répartir, distribuer; (*duties*): **to** ~ **sth to** assigner *or* attribuer qch à; (*sum, time*): **to** ~ **sth to** allouer qch à

allot [ə'lɒt] *vt*: **to** ~ **(to)** (*money*) répartir (entre), distribuer (à); (*time*) allouer (à); ~**ment** *n* (*share*) part *f*; (*garden*) lopin *m* de terre (*loué à la municipalité*)

all-out ['ɔ:l'aʊt] *adj* (*effort etc*) total(e) ♦ *adv*: **all out** à fond

allow [ə'laʊ] *vt* (*practice, behaviour*)

permettre, autoriser; (*sum to spend etc*) accorder; allouer; (*sum, time estimated*) compter, prévoir; (*claim, goal*) admettre; (*concede*): **to ~ that** convenir que; **to ~ sb to do** permettre à qn de faire, autoriser qn à faire; **he is ~ed to ...** on lui permet de ...; **~ for** *vt fus* tenir compte de; **~ance** *n* (*money received*) allocation *f*; subside *m*; indemnité *f*; (*TAX*) somme *f* déductible du revenu imposable, abattement *m*; **to make ~ances for** tenir compte de

alloy ['ælɔɪ] *n* alliage *m*

all: **~ right** *adv* (*feel, work*) bien; (*as answer*) d'accord; **~-rounder** *n*: **to be a good ~-rounder** être doué(e) en tout; **~-time** *adj* (*record*) sans précédent, absolu(e)

allude [ə'luːd] *vi*: **to ~** faire allusion à

alluring [ə'ljʊərɪŋ] *adj* séduisant(e)

ally [*n* 'ælaɪ, *vb* ə'laɪ] *n* allié *m* ♦ *vt*: **to ~ o.s. with** s'allier avec

almighty [ɔːl'maɪtɪ] *adj* tout-puissant; (*tremendous*) énorme

almond ['ɑːmənd] *n* amande *f*

almost ['ɔːlməʊst] *adv* presque

alms [ɑːmz] *npl* aumône *f*

aloft [ə'lɒft] *adv* en l'air

alone [ə'ləʊn] *adj*, *adv* seul(e); **to leave sb ~** laisser qn tranquille; **to leave sth ~** ne pas toucher à qch; **let ~ ...** sans parler de ...; encore moins ...

along [ə'lɒŋ] *prep* le long de ♦ *adv*: **is he coming ~ with us?** vient-il avec nous?; **he was hopping/limping ~** il avançait en sautillant/boitant; **~ with** (*together with: person*) en compagnie de; (: *thing*) avec, en plus de; **all ~** (*all the time*) depuis le début; **~side** *prep* le long de; à côté de ♦ *adv* bord à bord

aloof [ə'luːf] *adj* distant(e) ♦ *adv*: **to stand ~** se tenir à distance *or* à l'écart

aloud [ə'laʊd] *adv* à haute voix

alphabet ['ælfəbet] *n* alphabet *m*; **~ical** [ælfə'betɪkl] *adj* alphabétique

alpine ['ælpaɪn] *adj* alpin(e), alpestre

Alps [ælps] *npl*: **the ~** les Alpes *fpl*

already [ɔːl'redɪ] *adv* déjà

alright ['ɔːl'raɪt] (*BRIT*) *adv* = **all right**

Alsatian [æl'seɪʃən] (*BRIT*) *n* (*dog*) berger allemand

also ['ɔːlsəʊ] *adv* aussi

altar ['ɔːltə*] *n* autel *m*

alter ['ɔːltə*] *vt, vi* changer

alternate [*adj* ɒl'tɜːnɪt, *vb* 'ɒltɜːneɪt] *adj* alterné(e), alternant(e), alternatif(ive) ♦ *vi* alterner; **on ~ days** un jour sur deux, tous les deux jours; **alternating current** *n* courant alternatif

alternative [ɒl'tɜːnətɪv] *adj* (*solutions*) possible, au choix; (*plan*) autre, de rechange; (*lifestyle etc*) parallèle ♦ *n* (*choice*) alternative *f*; (*other possibility*) solution *f* de remplacement *or* de rechange, autre possibilité *f*; **~ comedian** un nouveau comique; **~ medicine** médecines *fpl* parallèles *or* douces; **~ly** *adv*: **~ly one could** une autre *or* l'autre solution serait de, on pourrait aussi

alternator ['ɒltɜːneɪtə*] *n* (*AUT*) alternateur *m*

although [ɔːl'ðəʊ] *conj* bien que +*sub*

altitude ['æltɪtjuːd] *n* altitude *f*

alto ['æltəʊ] *n* (*female*) contralto *m*; (*male*) haute-contre *f*

altogether [ɔːltə'geðə*] *adv* entièrement, tout à fait; (*on the whole*) tout compte fait; (*in all*) en tout

aluminium [ælju'mɪnɪəm] (*BRIT*), **aluminum** [ə'luːmɪnəm] (*US*) *n* aluminium *m*

always ['ɔːlweɪz] *adv* toujours

Alzheimer's (disease) [ælts'haɪməz] *n* maladie *f* d'Alzheimer

am [æm] *vb see* **be**

a.m. *adv abbr* (= *ante meridiem*) du matin

amalgamate [ə'mælgəmeɪt] *vt, vi* fusionner

amateur ['æmətə:*] *n* amateur *m*; **~ish** (*pej*) *adj* d'amateur

amaze [ə'meɪz] *vt* stupéfier; **to be ~d (at)** être stupéfait(e) (de); **~ment** *n* stupéfaction *f*, stupeur *f*; **amazing** [ə'meɪzɪŋ] *adj* étonnant(e); exceptionnel(le)

ambassador [æm'bæsədə*] *n* ambassadeur *m*

amber ['æmbə*] *n* ambre *m*; **at ~** (*BRIT, AUT*) à l'orange

ambiguous [æm'bɪgjuəs] *adj* ambigu(ë)

ambition [æm'bɪʃən] *n* ambition *f*

ambitious [æm'bɪʃəs] *adj* ambitieux(euse)

amble ['æmbl] *vi* (*also*: to ~ **along**) aller d'un pas tranquille

ambulance ['æmbjuləns] *n* ambulance *f*

ambush ['æmbuʃ] *n* embuscade *f* ♦ *vt* tendre une embuscade à

amenable [ə'miːnəbl] *adj*: ~ **to** (*advice etc*) disposé(e) à écouter

amend [ə'mend] *vt* (*law*) amender; (*text*) corriger; **to make ~s** réparer ses torts, faire amende honorable

amenities [ə'miːnɪtɪz] *npl* aménagements *mpl*, équipements *mpl*

America [ə'merɪkə] *n* Amérique *f*; **~n** *adj* américain(e) ♦ *n* Américain(e)

amiable ['eɪmɪəbl] *adj* aimable, affable

amicable ['æmɪkəbl] *adj* amical(e); (*JUR*) à l'amiable

amid(st) [ə'mɪd(st)] *prep* parmi, au milieu de

amiss [ə'mɪs] *adj, adv*: **there's something ~** il y a quelque chose qui ne va pas *or* qui cloche; **to take sth ~** prendre qch mal *or* de travers

ammonia [ə'məunɪə] *n* (*gas*) ammoniac *m*; (*liquid*) ammoniaque *f*

ammunition [æmju'nɪʃən] *n* munitions *fpl*

amok [ə'mɔk] *adv*: **to run ~** être pris(e) d'un accès de folie furieuse

among(st) [ə'mʌŋ(st)] *prep* parmi, entre

amorous ['æmərəs] *adj* amoureux(euse)

amount [ə'maunt] *n* (*sum*) somme *f*, montant *m*; (*quantity*) quantité *f*, nombre *m* ♦ *vi*: **to ~ to** (*total*) s'élever à; (*be same as*) équivaloir à, revenir à

amp(ere) ['æmp(ɛə*)] *n* ampère *m*

ample ['æmpl] *adj* ample; spacieux(euse); (*enough*): **this is ~** c'est largement suffisant; **to have ~ time/room** avoir bien assez de temps/place

amplifier ['æmplɪfaɪə*] *n* amplificateur *m*

amuse [ə'mjuːz] *vt* amuser, divertir; **~ment** *n* amusement *m*; **~ment arcade** *n* salle *f* de jeu

an [æn] *indef art see* **a**

anaemic [ə'niːmɪk] (*US* **anemic**) *adj* anémique

anaesthetic [ænɪs'θetɪk] *n* anesthésique *m*

analog(ue) ['ænəlɔg] *adj* (*watch, computer*) analogique

analyse ['ænəlaɪz] (*US* **analyze**) *vt* analyser; **analysis** [ə'nælɪsɪs] (*pl* **analyses**) *n* analyse *f*; **analyst** ['ænəlɪst] *n* (*POL etc*) spécialiste *m/f*; (*US*) psychanalyste *m/f*

analyze ['ænəlaɪz] (*US*) *vt* = **analyse**

anarchist ['ænəkɪst] *n* anarchiste *m/f*

anarchy ['ænəkɪ] *n* anarchie *f*

anatomy [ə'nætəmɪ] *n* anatomie *f*

ancestor ['ænsestə*] *n* ancêtre *m*, aïeul *m*

anchor ['æŋkə*] *n* ancre *f* ♦ *vi* (*also*: to *drop* ~) jeter l'ancre, mouiller ♦ *vt* mettre à l'ancre; (*fig*): **to ~ sth to** fixer qch à; **to weigh ~** lever l'ancre

anchovy ['æntʃəvɪ] *n* anchois *m*

ancient ['eɪnʃənt] *adj* ancien(ne), antique; (*person*) d'un âge vénérable; (*car*) antédiluvien(ne)

ancillary [æn'sɪlərɪ] *adj* auxiliaire

and [ænd] *conj* et; ~ **so on** et ainsi de suite; **try ~ come** tâchez de venir; **he talked ~ talked** il n'a pas arrêté de parler; **better ~ better** de mieux en mieux

anew [ə'njuː] *adv* à nouveau

angel ['eɪndʒəl] *n* ange *m*

anger ['æŋgə*] *n* colère *f*

angina [æn'dʒaɪnə] *n* angine *f* de poitrine

angle ['æŋgl] *n* angle *m*; **from their ~** de leur point de vue

angler ['æŋglə*] *n* pêcheur(euse) à la ligne

Anglican ['æŋglɪkən] *adj, n* anglican(e)

angling ['æŋglɪŋ] *n* pêche *f* à la ligne

Anglo- ['æŋgləu] *prefix* anglo(-)

angrily ['æŋgrɪlɪ] *adv* avec colère

angry ['æŋgrɪ] *adj* en colère, furieux(euse); (*wound*) enflammé(e); **to be ~ with sb/at sth** être furieux contre qn/de qch; **to get ~** se fâcher, se mettre en colère

anguish ['æŋgwɪʃ] *n* (*physical*) supplice

m; (*mental*) angoisse *f*

angular ['æŋgjʊlə*] *adj* anguleux(euse)

animal ['ænɪməl] *n* animal *m* ♦ *adj* animal(e)

animate [*vb* 'ænɪmeɪt, *adj* 'ænɪmət] *vt* animer ♦ *adj* animé(e), vivant(e); ~**d** *adj* animé(e)

aniseed ['ænɪsiːd] *n* anis *m*

ankle ['æŋkl] *n* cheville *f*; ~ **sock** *n* socquette *f*

annex [*n* 'æneks, *vb* ə'neks] *n* (*also*: *BRIT*: ~*e*) annexe *f* ♦ *vt* annexer

anniversary [ænɪ'vɜːsərɪ] *n* anniversaire *m*

announce [ə'naʊns] *vt* annoncer; (*birth, death*) faire part de; ~**ment** *n* annonce *f*; (*for births etc: in newspaper*) avis *m* de faire-part; (: *letter, card*) faire-part *m*; ~**r** *n* (*RADIO, TV: between programmes*) speaker(ine)

annoy [ə'nɔɪ] *vt* agacer, ennuyer, contrarier; **don't get ~ed!** ne vous fâchez pas!; ~**ance** *n* mécontentement *m*, contrariété *f*; ~**ing** *adj* agaçant(e), contrariant(e)

annual ['ænjʊəl] *adj* annuel(le) ♦ *n* (*BOT*) plante annuelle; (*children's book*) album *m*

annul [ə'nʌl] *vt* annuler

annum ['ænəm] *n* *see* **per**

anonymous [ə'nɒnɪməs] *adj* anonyme

anorak ['ænəræk] *n* anorak *m*

another [ə'nʌðə*] *adj*: ~ **book** (*one more*) un autre livre, encore un livre, un livre de plus; (*a different one*) un autre livre ♦ *pron* un(e) autre, encore un(e), un(e) de plus; *see also* **one**

answer ['ɑːnsə*] *n* réponse *f*; (*to problem*) solution *f* ♦ *vi* répondre ♦ *vt* (*reply to*) répondre à; (*problem*) résoudre; (*prayer*) exaucer; **in ~ to your letter** en réponse à votre lettre; **to ~ the phone** répondre (au téléphone); **to ~ the bell** *or* **the door** aller *or* venir ouvrir (la porte); ~ **back** *vi* répondre, répliquer; ~ **for** *vt fus* (*person*) répondre de, se porter garant de; (*crime, one's actions*) être responsable de; ~ **to** *vt fus* (*description*) répondre *or* correspondre à; ~**able** *adj*: ~**able (to sb/for sth)** responsable (de-

vant qn/de qch); ~**ing machine** *n* répondeur *m* automatique

ant [ænt] *n* fourmi *f*

antagonism [æn'tægənɪzəm] *n* antagonisme *m*

antagonize [æn'tægənaɪz] *vt* éveiller l'hostilité de, contrarier

Antarctic [ænt'ɑːktɪk] *n*: **the ~** l'Antarctique *m*

antenatal [æntɪ'neɪtl] *adj* prénatal(e); ~ **clinic** *n* service *m* de consultation prénatale

anthem ['ænθəm] *n*: **national ~** hymne national

anti- ['æntɪ]: ~**-aircraft** [æntɪ'ɛəkrɑːft] *adj* (*missile*) anti-aérien(ne); ~**biotic** ['æntɪbaɪ-'ɒtɪk] *n* antibiotique *m*; ~**body** ['æntɪ-bɒdɪ] *n* anticorps *m*

anticipate [æn'tɪsɪpeɪt] *vt* s'attendre à, prévoir; (*wishes, request*) aller au devant de, devancer

anticipation [æntɪsɪ'peɪʃən] *n* attente *f* **with ~** = impatiemment

anticlimax ['æntɪ'klaɪmæks] *n* déception *f*, douche froide (*col*)

anticlockwise ['æntɪ'klɒkwaɪz] *adj, adv* dans le sens inverse des aiguilles d'une montre

antics ['æntɪks] *npl* singeries *fpl*

antifreeze ['æntɪfriːz] *n* antigel *m*

antihistamine [æntɪ'hɪstəmiːn] *n* antihistaminique *m*

antiquated ['æntɪkweɪtɪd] *adj* vieilli(e) suranné(e), vieillot(te)

antique [æn'tiːk] *n* objet *m* d'art ancien, meuble ancien *or* d'époque, antiquité *f* ♦ *adj* ancien(ne); ~ **dealer** *n* antiquaire *m*; ~ **shop** *n* magasin *m* d'antiquités

anti-: ~**Semitism** [æntɪ'semɪtɪzəm] *n* antisémitisme *m*; ~**septic** [æntɪ'septɪk] *n* antiseptique *m* ♦ *adj*; ~**social** [æntɪ'səʊʃl] *adj* peu liant(e), sauvage, insociable; (*against society*) antisocial(e)

antlers ['æntləz] *npl* bois *mpl*, ramure *f*

anvil ['ænvɪl] *n* enclume *f*

anxiety [æŋ'zaɪətɪ] *n* anxiété *f*; (*keenness*): ~ **to do** grand désir *or* impatience *f* de faire

anxious ['æŋkʃəs] *adj* anxieux(euse), angoissé(e); (*worrying: time, situation*) inquiétant(e); (*keen*): ~ **to do/that** qui tient beaucoup à faire/à ce que; impatient(e) de faire/que

KEYWORD

any [ˈenɪ] *adj* **1** (*in questions etc: singular*) du, de l', du, de la; (*in questions etc: plural*) des; **have you ~ butter/ children/ink?** avez-vous du beurre/des enfants/de l'encre?
2 (*with negative*) de, d'; **I haven't ~ money/books** je n'ai pas d'argent/de livres
3 (*no matter which*) n'importe quel(le); **choose ~ book you like** vous pouvez choisir n'importe quel livre
4 (*in phrases*): **in ~ case** de toute façon; **~ day now** d'un jour à l'autre; **at ~ moment** à tout moment, d'un instant à l'autre; **at ~ rate** en tout cas
♦ *pron* **1** (*in questions etc*) en; **have you got ~?** est-ce que vous en avez?; **can ~ of you sing?** est-ce que parmi vous il y en a qui savent chanter?
2 (*with negative*) en; **I haven't ~ (of them)** je n'en ai pas, je n'en ai aucun
3 (*no matter which one(s)*) n'importe lequel (*or* laquelle); **take ~ of those books (you like)** vous pouvez prendre n'importe lequel de ces livres
♦ *adv* **1** (*in questions etc*): **do you want ~ more soup/sandwiches?** voulez-vous encore de la soupe/des sandwichs?; **are you feeling ~ better?** est-ce que vous vous sentez mieux?
2 (*with negative*): **I can't hear him ~ more** je ne l'entends plus; **don't wait ~ longer** n'attendez pas plus longtemps

any: ~body [ˈenɪbɒdɪ] *pron* n'importe qui; (*in interrogative sentences*) quelqu'un; (*in negative sentences*): **I don't see ~body** je ne vois personne; **~how** *adv* (*at any rate*) de toute façon, quand même; (*haphazard*) n'importe comment; **~one** [-wʌn] *pron* = **anybody**; **~thing** *pron* n'importe quoi, quelque chose, ne ... rien; **~way** *adv* de toute façon;

~where *adv* n'importe où, quelque part; **I don't see him ~where** je ne le vois nulle part

apart [əˈpɑːt] *adv* (*to one side*) à part; de côté; à l'écart; (*separately*) séparément; **10 miles ~** à 10 miles l'un de l'autre; **to take ~** démonter; **~ from** à part, excepté
apartheid [əˈpɑːteɪt] *n* apartheid *m*
apartment [əˈpɑːtmənt] *n* (*US*) appartement *m*, logement *m*; (*room*) chambre *f*; **~ building** (*US*) *n* immeuble *m*; maison divisée en appartements
ape [eɪp] *n* (grand) singe ♦ *vt* singer
apéritif [əˈpɛrɪtiːf] *n* apéritif *m*
aperture [ˈæpətjʊə*] *n* orifice *m*, ouverture *f*; (*PHOT*) ouverture (du diaphragme)
apex [ˈeɪpeks] *n* sommet *m*
apiece [əˈpiːs] *adv* chacun(e)
apologetic [əpɒləˈdʒetɪk] *adj* (*tone, letter*) d'excuse; (*person*): **to be ~** s'excuser
apologize [əˈpɒlədʒaɪz] *vi*: **to ~ (for sth to sb)** s'excuser (de qch auprès de qn), présenter des excuses (à qn pour qch)
apology [əˈpɒlədʒɪ] *n* excuses *fpl*
apostle [əˈpɒsl] *n* apôtre *m*
apostrophe [əˈpɒstrəfɪ] *n* apostrophe *f*
appal [əˈpɔːl] *vt* consterner; **~ling** [əˈpɔːlɪŋ] *adj* épouvantable; (*stupidity*) consternant(e)
apparatus [æpəˈreɪtəs] *n* appareil *m*, dispositif *m*; (*in gymnasium*) agrès *mpl*; (*of government*) appareil *m*
apparel [əˈpærəl] (*US*) *n* habillement *m*
apparent [əˈpærənt] *adj* apparent(e); **~ly** *adv* apparemment
appeal [əˈpiːl] *vi* (*LAW*) faire *or* interjeter appel ♦ *n* appel *m*; (*request*) prière *f*; appel *m*; (*charm*) attrait *m*, charme *m*; **to ~ for** lancer un appel pour; **to ~ to** (*beg*) faire appel à; (*be attractive*) plaire à; **it doesn't ~ to me** cela ne m'attire pas; **~ing** *adj* (*attractive*) attrayant(e)
appear [əˈpɪə*] *vi* apparaître, se montrer; (*LAW*) comparaître; (*publication*) paraître, sortir, être publié(e); (*seem*) paraître, sembler; **it would ~ that** il semble que; **to ~ in Hamlet** jouer dans Hamlet; **to ~ on TV** passer à la télé; **~ance** *n* apparition *f*; parution *f*; (*look,*

aspect) apparence *f*, aspect *m*

appease [ə'pi:z] *vt* apaiser, calmer

appendicitis [əpendı'saıtıs] *n* appendicite *f*; **appendix** [ə'pendıks] (*pl* **appendices**) *n* appendice *m*

appetite ['æpıtaıt] *n* appétit *m*

appetizer ['æpətaızə*] *n* amuse-gueule *m*; (*drink*) apéritif *m*

applaud [ə'plɔ:d] *vt, vi* applaudir

applause [ə'plɔ:z] *n* applaudissements *mpl*

apple ['æpl] *n* pomme *f*; ~ **tree** *n* pommier *m*

appliance [ə'plaıəns] *n* appareil *m*

applicable [ə'plıkəbl] *adj* (*revelant*): **to be ~ to** valoir pour

applicant ['æplıkənt] *n*: ~ (**for**) candidat(e) (à)

application [æplı'keıʃən] *n* application *f*; (*for a job, a grant etc*) demande *f*; candidature *f*; ~ **form** *n* formulaire *m* de demande

applied [ə'plaıd] *adj* appliqué(e)

apply [ə'plaı] *vt* (*paint, ointment*): **to ~ (to)** appliquer (sur); (*law etc*): **to ~ (to)** appliquer (à) ♦ *vi*: **to ~ to** (*be suitable for, relevant to*) s'appliquer à; (*ask*) s'adresser à; **to ~ (for)** (*permit, grant*) faire une demande (en vue d'obtenir); (*job*) poser sa candidature (pour), faire une demande d'emploi (concernant); **to ~ o.s. to** s'appliquer à

appoint [ə'pɔınt] *vt* nommer, engager; ~**ed** *adj*: **at the ~ed time** à l'heure dite; ~**ment** *n* nomination *f*; (*meeting*) rendez-vous *m*; **to make an ~ment (with)** prendre rendez-vous (avec)

appraisal [ə'preızl] *n* évaluation *f*

appreciate [ə'pri:ʃıeıt] *vt* (*like*) apprécier; (*be grateful for*) être reconnaissant(e) de; (*understand*) comprendre; se rendre compte de ♦ *vi* (*FINANCE*) prendre de la valeur

appreciation [əpri:ʃı'eıʃən] *n* appréciation *f*; (*gratitude*) reconnaissance *f*; (*COMM*) hausse *f*, valorisation *f*

appreciative [ə'pri:ʃıətıv] *adj* (*person*) sensible; (*comment*) élogieux(euse)

apprehensive [æprı'hensıv] *adj* inquiet(ète), appréhensif(ive)

apprentice [ə'prentıs] *n* apprenti *m*; ~**ship** *n* apprentissage *m*

approach [ə'prəʊtʃ] *vi* approcher ♦ *vt* (*come near*) approcher de; (*ask, apply to*) s'adresser à; (*situation, problem*) aborder ♦ *n* approche *f*; (*access*) accès *m*; ~**able** *adj* accessible

appropriate [*adj* ə'prəʊprıət, *vb* ə'prəʊprıeıt] *adj* (*moment, remark*) opportun(e); (*tool etc*) approprié(e) ♦ *vt* (*take*) s'approprier

approval [ə'pru:vəl] *n* approbation *f*; **on ~** (*COMM*) à l'examen

approve [ə'pru:v] *vt* approuver; ~ **of** *vt fus* approuver

approximate [*adj* ə'prɒksımıt, *vb* ə'prɒksımeıt] *adj* approximatif(ive) ♦ *vt* se rapprocher de, être proche de; ~**ly** *adv* approximativement

apricot ['eıprıkɒt] *n* abricot *m*

April ['eıprəl] *n* avril *m*; ~ **Fool's Day** le premier avril

apron ['eıprən] *n* tablier *m*

apt [æpt] *adj* (*suitable*) approprié(e); (*likely*): ~ **to do** susceptible de faire; qui a tendance à faire

Aquarius [ə'kwɛərıəs] *n* le Verseau

Arab ['ærəb] *adj* arabe ♦ *n* Arabe *m/f*; ~**ian** [ə'reıbıən] *adj* arabe; ~**ic** ['ærəbık] *adj* arabe ♦ *n* arabe *m*

arbitrary ['ɑ:bıtrərı] *adj* arbitraire

arbitration [ɑ:bı'treıʃən] *n* arbitrage *m*

arcade [ɑ:'keıd] *n* arcade *f*; (*passage with shops*) passage *m*, galerie marchande

arch [ɑ:tʃ] *n* arc *m*; (*of foot*) cambrure *f*, voûte *f* plantaire ♦ *vt* arquer, cambrer

archaeologist [ɑ:kı'ɒlədʒıst] *n* archéologue *m/f*; **archaeology** [ɑ:kı'ɒlədʒı] *n* archéologie *f*

archbishop ['ɑ:tʃ'bıʃəp] *n* archevêque *m*

archenemy ['ɑ:tʃ'enımı] *n* ennemi *m* toujours *or* juré

archeology *etc* (*US*) = **archaeology** *etc*

archery ['ɑ:tʃərı] *n* tir *m* à l'arc

architect ['ɑ:kıtekt] *n* architecte *m*; ~**ure** *n* architecture *f*

archives ['ɑ:kaıvz] *npl* archives *fpl*

Arctic ['ɑːktɪk] *adj* arctique ♦ *n*: **the ~** l'Arctique *m*

ardent ['ɑːdənt] *adj* fervent(e)

are [ɑː*] *vb see* **be**

area ['ɛərɪə] *n* (GEOM) superficie *f*; (*zone*) région *f*; (: *smaller*) secteur *m*, partie *f*; (*in room*) coin *m*; (*knowledge, research*) domaine *m*

aren't [ɑːnt] = **are not**

Argentina [ɑːdʒən'tiːnə] *n* Argentine *f*; **Argentinian** [ɑːdʒən'tɪnɪən] *adj* argentin(e) ♦ *n* Argentin(e)

arguably ['ɑːgjʊəblɪ] *adv*: **it is ~ ...** on peut soutenir que c'est ...

argue ['ɑːgjuː] *vi* (*quarrel*) se disputer; (*reason*) argumenter; **to ~ that** objecter *or* alléguer que

argument ['ɑːgjʊmənt] *n* (*reasons*) argument *m*; (*quarrel*) dispute *f*; **~ative** [ɑːgjʊ'mɛntətɪv] *adj* ergoteur(euse), raisonneur(euse)

Aries ['ɛəriːz] *n* le Bélier

arise [ə'raɪz] (*pt* **arose**, *pp* **arisen**) *vi* survenir, se présenter

aristocrat ['ærɪstəkræt] *n* aristocrate *m/f*

arithmetic [ə'rɪθmətɪk] *n* arithmétique *f*

ark [ɑːk] *n*: **Noah's A~** l'Arche *f* de Noé

arm [ɑːm] *n* bras *m* ♦ *vt* armer; **~s** *npl* (*weapons*, HERALDRY) armes *fpl*; **~ in ~** bras dessus bras dessous

armaments ['ɑːməmənts] *npl* armement *m*

arm: **~chair** *n* fauteuil *m*; **~ed** *adj* armé(e); **~ed robbery** *n* vol *m* à main armée

armour ['ɑːmə*] (US **armor**) *n* armure *f*; (MIL: *tanks*) blindés *mpl*; **~ed car** *n* véhicule blindé

armpit ['ɑːmpɪt] *n* aisselle *f*

armrest ['ɑːmrɛst] *n* accoudoir *m*

army ['ɑːmɪ] *n* armée *f*

aroma [ə'rəʊmə] *n* arôme *m*; **~therapy** *n* aromathérapie *f*

arose [ə'rəʊz] *pt of* **arise**

around [ə'raʊnd] *adv* autour; (*nearby*) dans les parages ♦ *prep* autour de; (*near*) près de; (*fig: about*) environ; (: *date, time*) vers

arouse [ə'raʊz] *vt* (*sleeper*) éveiller; (*curiosity, passions*) éveiller, susciter; (*anger*) exciter

arrange [ə'reɪndʒ] *vt* arranger; **to ~ to do sth** prévoir de faire qch; **~ment** *n* arrangement *m*; **~ments** *npl* (*plans etc*) arrangements *mpl*, dispositions *fpl*

array [ə'reɪ] *n*: **~ of** déploiement *m or* étalage *m* de

arrears [ə'rɪəz] *npl* arriéré *m*; **to be in ~ with one's rent** devoir un arriéré de loyer

arrest [ə'rɛst] *vt* arrêter; (*sb's attention*) retenir, attirer ♦ *n* arrestation *f*; **under ~** en état d'arrestation

arrival [ə'raɪvəl] *n* arrivée *f*; **new ~** nouveau venu, nouvelle venue; (*baby*) nouveau-né(e)

arrive [ə'raɪv] *vi* arriver

arrogant ['ærəgənt] *adj* arrogant(e)

arrow ['ærəʊ] *n* flèche *f*

arse [ɑːs] (BRIT: *inf!*) *n* cul *m* (!)

arson ['ɑːsn] *n* incendie criminel

art [ɑːt] *n* art *m*; **A~s** *npl* (SCOL) les lettres *fpl*

artery ['ɑːtərɪ] *n* artère *f*

artful ['ɑːtful] *adj* astucieux(euse), rusé(e)

art gallery *n* musée *m* d'art; (*small and private*) galerie *f* de peinture

arthritis [ɑː'θraɪtɪs] *n* arthrite *f*

artichoke ['ɑːtɪtʃəʊk] *n* (*also: globe ~*) artichaut *m*; (: *Jerusalem ~*) topinambour *m*

article ['ɑːtɪkl] *n* article *m*; **~s** *npl* (BRIT: LAW: *training*) ≈ stage *m*; **~ of clothing** vêtement *m*

articulate [*adj* ɑː'tɪkjulɪt, *vb* ɑː'tɪkjuleɪt] *adj* (*person*) qui s'exprime bien; (*speech*) bien articulé(e), prononcé(e) clairement ♦ *vt* exprimer; **~d lorry** (BRIT) *n* (camion *m*) semi-remorque *m*

artificial [ɑːtɪ'fɪʃəl] *adj* artificiel(le)

artist ['ɑːtɪst] *n* artiste *m/f*; **~ic** [ɑː'tɪstɪk] *adj* artistique; **~ry** *n* art *m*, talent *m*

art school *n* ≈ école *f* des beaux-arts

KEYWORD

as [æz] *conj* **1** (*referring to time*)

comme, alors que; à mesure que; **he came in ~ I was leaving** il est arrivé comme je partais; **~ the years went by** à mesure que les années passaient; **~ from tomorrow** à partir de demain
2 (*in comparisons*): **~ big ~** aussi grand que; **twice ~ big ~** deux fois plus grand que; **~ much** *or* **many ~** autant que; **~ much money/many books** autant d'argent/de livres que; **~ soon ~** dès que
3 (*since, because*) comme, puisque; **~ he had to be home by 10 ...** comme *or* puisqu'il devait être de retour avant 10 h ...
4 (*referring to manner, way*) comme; **do ~ you wish** faites comme vous voudrez
5 (*concerning*): **~ for** *or* **to that** quant à cela, pour ce qui est de cela
6: **~ if** *or* **though** comme si; **he looked ~ if he was ill** il avait l'air d'être malade; **see also long; such; well**
♦ *prep*: **he works ~ a driver** il travaille comme chauffeur; **~ chairman of the company, he ...** en tant que président de la société, il ...; **dressed up ~ a cowboy** déguisé en cowboy; **he gave me it ~ a present** il me l'a offert, il m'en a fait cadeau

a.s.a.p. *abbr* (= *as soon as possible*) dès que possible
asbestos [æz'bɛstəs] *n* amiante *f*
ascend [ə'sɛnd] *vt* gravir; (*throne*) monter sur
ascent [ə'sɛnt] *n* ascension *f*
ascertain [æsə'teɪn] *vt* vérifier
ascribe [ə'skraɪb] *vt*: **to ~ sth to** attribuer qch à
ash [æʃ] *n* (*dust*) cendre *f*; (*also*: ~ *tree*) frêne *m*
ashamed [ə'ʃeɪmd] *adj* honteux(euse), confus(e); **to be ~ of** avoir honte de
ashen ['æʃən] *adj* (*pale*) cendreux(euse), blême
ashore [ə'ʃɔ:*] *adv* à terre
ashtray ['æʃtreɪ] *n* cendrier *m*
Ash Wednesday *n* mercredi *m* des cendres

Asia ['eɪʃə] *n* Asie *f*; **~n** *n* Asiatique *m/f* ♦ *adj* asiatique
aside [ə'saɪd] *adv* de côté; à l'écart ♦ *n* aparté *m*
ask [ɑ:sk] *vt* demander; (*invite*) inviter; **to ~ sb sth/to do sth** demander qch à qn/à qn de faire qch; **to ~ sb about sth** questionner qn sur qch; se renseigner auprès de qn sur qch; **to ~ (sb) a question** poser une question (à qn); **to ~ sb out to dinner** inviter qn au restaurant; **~ after** *vt fus* demander des nouvelles de; **~ for** *vt fus* demander; (*trouble*) chercher
askance [əs'kɑ:ns] *adv*: **to look ~ at** regarder qn de travers *or* d'un œil désapprobateur
asking price ['ɑ:skɪŋ] *n*: **the ~** le prix de départ
asleep [ə'sli:p] *adj* endormi(e); **to fall ~** s'endormir
asparagus [əs'pærəgəs] *n* asperges *fpl*
aspect ['æspɛkt] *n* aspect *m*; (*direction in which a building etc faces*) orientation *f*, exposition *f*
aspersions [əs'pɜ:ʃənz] *npl*: **to cast ~ on** dénigrer
aspire [əs'paɪə*] *vi*: **to ~ to** aspirer à
aspirin ['æsprɪn] *n* aspirine *f*
ass [æs] *n* âne *m*; (*inf*) imbécile *m/f*; (*US: inf!*) cul *m* (!)
assailant [ə'seɪlənt] *n* agresseur *m*; assaillant *m*
assassinate [ə'sæsɪneɪt] *vt* assassiner; **assassination** [əsæsɪ'neɪʃən] *n* assassinat *m*
assault [ə'sɔ:lt] *n* (*MIL*) assaut *m*; (*gen: attack*) agression *f* ♦ *vt* attaquer; (*sexually*) violenter
assemble [ə'sɛmbl] *vt* assembler ♦ *vi* s'assembler, se rassembler
assembly [ə'sɛmblɪ] *n* assemblée *f*, réunion *f*; (*institution*) assemblée; (*construction*) assemblage *m*; **~ line** *n* chaîne *f* de montage
assent [ə'sɛnt] *n* assentiment *m*, consentement *m*
assert [ə'sɜ:t] *vt* affirmer, déclarer; (*one's authority*) faire valoir; (*one's in-*

nocence) protester de

assess [ə'ses] *vt* évaluer; (*tax, payment*) établir *or* fixer le montant de; (*property etc: for tax*) calculer la valeur imposable de; (*person*) juger la valeur de; **~ment** [ə'sesmənt] *n* évaluation *f*, fixation *f*, calcul *m* de la valeur imposable de, jugement *m*; **~or** *n* expert *m* (*impôt et assurance*)

asset ['æset] *n* avantage *m*, atout *m*; **~s** *npl* (*FINANCE*) capital *m*; avoir(s) *m(pl)*; actif *m*

assign [ə'saɪn] *vt* (*date*) fixer; (*task*) assigner à; (*resources*) affecter à; **~ment** [ə'saɪnmənt] *n* tâche *f*, mission *f*

assist [ə'sɪst] *vt* aider, assister; **~ance** *n* aide *f*, assistance *f*; **~ant** *n* assistant(e), adjoint(e); (*BRIT: also: shop ~ant*) vendeur(euse)

associate [*adj, n* ə'səʊʃɪɪt, *vb* ə'səʊʃɪeɪt] *adj, n* associé(e) ♦ *vt* associer ♦ *vi:* **to ~ with sb** fréquenter qn; **association** [əsəʊsɪ'eɪʃən] *n* association *f*

assorted [ə'sɔːtɪd] *adj* assorti(e)

assortment [ə'sɔːtmənt] *n* assortiment *m*

assume [ə'sjuːm] *vt* supposer; (*responsibilities etc*) assumer; (*attitude, name*) prendre, adopter; **~d name** *n* nom *m* d'emprunt; **assumption** [ə'sʌmpʃən] *n* supposition *f*, hypothèse *f*; (*of power*) assomption *f*, prise *f*

assurance [ə'ʃʊərəns] *n* assurance *f*

assure [ə'ʃʊə*] *vt* assurer

asthma ['æsmə] *n* asthme *m*

astonish [əs'tɒnɪʃ] *vt* étonner, stupéfier; **~ment** *n* étonnement *m*

astound [əs'taʊnd] *vt* stupéfier, sidérer

astray [əs'treɪ] *adv:* **to go ~** s'égarer; (*fig*) quitter le droit chemin; **to lead ~** détourner du droit chemin

astride [əs'traɪd] *prep* à cheval sur

astrology [əs'trɒlədʒɪ] *n* astrologie *f*

astronaut ['æstrənɔːt] *n* astronaute *m/f*

astronomy [əs'trɒnəmɪ] *n* astronomie *f*

astute [əs'tjuːt] *adj* astucieux(euse)

asylum [ə'saɪləm] *n* asile *m*

KEYWORD

at [æt] *prep* **1** (*referring to position, di-rection*) à; **~ the top** au sommet; **~ home/school** à la maison *or* chez soi/à l'école; **~ the baker's** à la boulangerie, chez le boulanger; **to look ~ sth** regarder qch

2 (*referring to time*): **~ 4 o'clock** à 4 heures; **~ Christmas** à Noël; **~ night** la nuit; **~ times** par moments, parfois

3 (*referring to rates, speed etc*) à; **~ £1 a kilo** une livre le kilo; **two ~ a time** deux à la fois; **~ 50 km/h** à 50 km/h

4 (*referring to manner*): **~ a stroke** d'un seul coup; **~ peace** en paix

5 (*referring to activity*): **to be ~ work** être au travail, travailler; **to play ~ cowboys** jouer aux cowboys; **to be good ~ sth** être bon en qch

6 (*referring to cause*): **shocked/surprised/annoyed ~ sth** choqué par/étonné de/agacé par qch; **I went ~ his suggestion** j'y suis allé sur son conseil

ate [et, eɪt] *pt of* eat

atheist ['eɪθɪɪst] *n* athée *m/f*

Athens ['æθɪnz] *n* Athènes

athlete ['æθliːt] *n* athlète *m/f*

athletic [æθ'letɪk] *adj* athlétique; **~s** *n* athlétisme *m*

Atlantic [ət'læntɪk] *adj* atlantique ♦ *n:* **the ~ (Ocean)** l'Atlantique *m*, l'océan *m* Atlantique

atlas ['ætləs] *n* atlas *m*

atmosphere ['ætməsfɪə*] *n* atmosphère *f*

atom ['ætəm] *n* atome *m*; **~ic** [ə'tɒmɪk] *adj* atomique; **~(ic) bomb** *n* bombe *f* atomique; **~izer** ['ætəmaɪzə*] *n* atomiseur *m*

atone [ə'təʊn] *vi:* **to ~ for** expier, racheter

atrocious [ə'trəʊʃəs] *adj* (*very bad*) atroce, exécrable

attach [ə'tætʃ] *vt* attacher; (*document, letter*) joindre; **to be ~ed to sb/sth** être attaché à qn/qch

attaché case [ə'tæfeɪ-] *n* mallette *f*, attaché-case *m*

attachment [ə'tætʃmənt] *n* (*tool*) accessoire *m*; (*love*): **~ (to)** affection *f* (pour), attachement *m* (à)

attack [əˈtæk] *vt* attaquer; (*task etc*) s'attaquer à ♦ *n* attaque *f*; (*also: heart ~*) crise *f* cardiaque

attain [əˈteɪn] *vt* (*also: to ~ to*) parvenir à, atteindre; (: *knowledge*) acquérir; **~ments** *npl* connaissances *fpl*, résultats *mpl*

attempt [əˈtempt] *n* tentative *f* ♦ *vt* essayer, tenter; **to make an ~ on sb's life** attenter à la vie de qn; **~ed** *adj*: **~ed murder/suicide** tentative *f* de meurtre/suicide

attend [əˈtend] *vt* (*course*) suivre; (*meeting, talk*) assister à; (*school, church*) aller à, fréquenter; (: *patient*) soigner, s'occuper de; **~ to** *vt fus* (*needs, affairs etc*) s'occuper de; (*customer, patient*) s'occuper de; **~ance** *n* (*being present*) présence *f*; (*people present*) assistance *f*; **~ant** *n* employé(e) ♦ *adj* (*dangers*) inhérent(e), concomitant(e)

attention [əˈtenʃən] *n* attention *f*; **~!** (*MIL*) garde-à-vous!; **for the ~ of** (*ADMIN*) à l'attention de

attentive [əˈtentɪv] *adj* attentif(ive); (*kind*) prévenant(e)

attest [əˈtest] *vi*: **to ~ to** (*demonstrate*) démontrer; (*confirm*) témoigner

attic [ˈætɪk] *n* grenier *m*

attitude [ˈætɪtjuːd] *n* attitude *f*; pose *f*, maintien *m*

attorney [əˈtɜːnɪ] *n* (*US: lawyer*) avoué *m*; **A~ General** *n* (*BRIT*) ≈ procureur général; (*US*) ≈ garde *m* des Sceaux, ministre *m* de la Justice

attract [əˈtrækt] *vt* attirer; **~ion** [əˈtrækʃən] *n* (*gen pl: pleasant things*) attraction *f*, attrait *m*; (*PHYSICS*) attraction *f*; (*fig: towards sb or sth*) attirance *f*; **~ive** *adj* attrayant(e); (*person*) séduisant(e)

attribute [*n* ˈætrɪbjuːt, *vb* əˈtrɪbjuːt] *n* attribut *m* ♦ *vt*: **to ~ sth to** attribuer qch à

attrition [əˈtrɪʃən] *n*: **war of ~** guerre *f* d'usure

aubergine [ˈəʊbəʒiːn] *n* aubergine *f*

auction [ˈɔːkʃən] *n* (*also: sale by ~*) vente *f* aux enchères ♦ *vt* (: *to sell by ~*) vendre aux enchères; (: *to put up for ~*) mettre aux enchères; **~eer** [ɔːkʃəˈnɪə*] *n* commissaire-priseur *m*

audience [ˈɔːdɪəns] *n* (*people*) assistance *f*; public *m*; spectateurs *mpl*; (*interview*) audience *f*

audiovisual [ˈɔːdɪəʊˈvɪzjuəl] *adj* audiovisuel(le); **~ aids** *npl* supports *or* moyens audiovisuels

audit [ˈɔːdɪt] *vt* vérifier

audition [ɔːˈdɪʃən] *n* audition *f*

auditor [ˈɔːdɪtə*] *n* vérificateur *m* des comptes

augur [ˈɔːgə*] *vi*: **it ~s well** c'est bon signe *or* de bon augure

August [ˈɔːgəst] *n* août *m*

aunt [ɑːnt] *n* tante *f*; **~ie, ~y** *n dimin of* **aunt**

au pair [ˈəʊˈpɛə*] *n* (*also: ~ girl*) jeune fille *f* au pair

auspicious [ɔːsˈpɪʃəs] *adj* de bon augure, propice

Australia [ɒsˈtreɪlɪə] *n* Australie *f*; **~n** *adj* australien(ne) ♦ *n* Australien(ne)

Austria [ˈɒstrɪə] *n* Autriche *f*; **~n** *adj* autrichien(ne) ♦ *n* Autrichien(ne)

authentic [ɔːˈθentɪk] *adj* authentique

author [ˈɔːθə*] *n* auteur *m*

authoritarian [ɔːθɒrɪˈtɛərɪən] *adj* autoritaire

authoritative [ɔːˈθɒrɪtətɪv] *adj* (*account*) digne de foi; (*study, treatise*) qui fait autorité; (*person, manner*) autoritaire

authority [ɔːˈθɒrɪtɪ] *n* autorité *f*; (*permission*) autorisation (formelle); **the authorities** *npl* (*ruling body*) les autorités *fpl*, l'administration *f*

authorize [ˈɔːθəraɪz] *vt* autoriser

auto [ˈɔːtəʊ] *n* (*US*) auto *f*, voiture *f*

auto: **~biography** [ɔːtəʊbaɪˈɒɡrəfɪ] *n* autobiographie *f*; **~graph** [ˈɔːtəɡrɑːf] *n* autographe *m* ♦ *vt* signer, dédicacer; **~mated** [ˈɔːtəmeɪtɪd] *adj* automatisé(e), automatique; **~matic** [ɔːtəˈmætɪk] *adj* automatique ♦ *n* (*gun*) automatique *m*; (*washing machine*) machine *f* à laver automatique; (*BRIT: AUT*) voiture *f* à transmission automatique; **~matically** *adv* automatiquement; **~mation** [ɔːtəˈmeɪʃən] *n* automatisation *f* (électronique); **~mobile** [ˈɔːtəməbiːl] (*US*) *n* automobile *f*; **~nomy** [ɔːˈtɒnəmɪ] *n* autonomie *f*

autumn [ˈɔːtəm] *n* automne *m*; **in ~** en automne

auxiliary [ɔːgˈzɪlɪərɪ] *adj* auxiliaire ♦ *n* auxiliaire *m/f*

avail [əˈveɪl] *vt*: **to ~ o.s. of** profiter de ♦ *n*: **to no ~** sans résultat, en vain, en pure perte

availability [əveɪləˈbɪlɪtɪ] *n* disponibilité *f*

available [əˈveɪləbl] *adj* disponible

avalanche [ˈævəlɑːnʃ] *n* avalanche *f*

Ave *abbr* = **avenue**

avenge [əˈvendʒ] *vt* venger

avenue [ˈævənjuː] *n* avenue *f*; (*fig*) moyen *m*

average [ˈævərɪdʒ] *n* moyenne *f*; (*fig*) moyen *m* ♦ *adj* moyen(ne) ♦ *vt* (*a certain figure*) atteindre *or* faire *etc* en moyenne; **on ~** en moyenne; **~ out** *vi*: **to ~ out at** représenter en moyenne, donner une moyenne de

averse [əˈvɜːs] *adj*: **to be ~ to sth/doing sth** éprouver une forte répugnance envers qch/à faire qch

avert [əˈvɜːt] *vt* prévenir, écarter; (*one's eyes*) détourner

aviary [ˈeɪvɪərɪ] *n* volière *f*

avocado [ævəˈkɑːdəʊ] *n* (*also*: *BRIT*: ~ **pear**) avocat *m*

avoid [əˈvɔɪd] *vt* éviter

await [əˈweɪt] *vt* attendre

awake [əˈweɪk] (*pt* **awoke**, *pp* **awoken**) *adj* éveillé(e) ♦ *vi* s'éveiller ♦ *vi* s'éveiller; **~ to** (*dangers, possibilities*) conscient(e) de; **to be ~** être réveillé(e); **he was still ~** il ne dormait pas encore; **~ning** *n* réveil *m*

award [əˈwɔːd] *n* récompense *f*, prix *m*; (*LAW*: *damages*) dommages-intérêts *mpl* ♦ *vt* (*prize*) décerner; (*LAW*: *damages*) accorder

aware [əˈwɛə*] *adj*: **~ (of)** (*conscious*) conscient(e) (de); (*informed*) au courant (de); **to become ~ of/that** prendre

conscience de/que; se rendre compte de/que; **~ness** *n* conscience *f*, connaissance *f*

awash [əˈwɒʃ] *adj*: **~ (with)** inondé(e) (de)

away [əˈweɪ] *adj, adv* (au) loin; absent(e); **two kilometres ~** à (une distance de) deux kilomètres, à deux kilomètres de distance; **two hours ~ by car** à deux heures de voiture *or* de route; **the holiday was two weeks ~** il restait deux semaines jusqu'aux vacances; **~ from** loin de; **he's ~ for a week** il est parti (pour) une semaine; **to pedal/work/laugh ~** être en train de pédaler/travailler/rire; **to fade ~** (*sound*) s'affaiblir; (*colour*) s'estomper; **to wither ~** (*plant*) se dessécher; **to take ~** emporter; (*subtract*) enlever; **~ game** *n* (*SPORT*) match *m* à l'extérieur

awe [ɔː] *n* respect mêlé de crainte; **~-inspiring** *adj* impressionnant(e); **~some** *adj* impressionnant(e)

awful [ˈɔːful] *adj* affreux(euse); **an ~ lot (of)** un nombre incroyable (de); **~ly** *adv* (*very*) terriblement, vraiment

awhile [əˈwaɪl] *adv* un moment, quelque temps

awkward [ˈɔːkwəd] *adj* (*clumsy*) gauche, maladroit(e); (*inconvenient*) peu pratique; (*embarrassing*) gênant(e), délicat(e)

awning [ˈɔːnɪŋ] *n* (*of tent*) auvent *m*; (*of shop*) store *m*; (*of hotel etc*) marquise *f*

awoke [əˈwəʊk] *pt of* **awake**; **~n** [əˈwəʊkən] *pp of* **awake**

awry [əˈraɪ] *adj, adv* de travers; **to go ~** mal tourner

axe [æks] (*US* **ax**) *n* hache *f* ♦ *vt* (*project etc*) abandonner; (*jobs*) supprimer

axes¹ [ˈæksɪz] *npl of* **axe**

axes² [ˈæksiːz] *npl of* **axis**

axis [ˈæksɪs] (*pl* **axes**) *n* axe *m*

axle [ˈæksl] *n* (*also*: ~-**tree**: *AUT*) essieu *m*

ay(e) [aɪ] *excl* (*yes*) oui

B b

B [bi:] *n* (*MUS*) si *m*

B.A. *abbr* = **Bachelor of Arts**

babble ['bæbl] *vi* bredouiller; (*baby, stream*) gazouiller

baby ['beɪbɪ] *n* bébé *m*; (*US: inf: darling*): **come on, ~!** viens ma belle/mon gars!; **~ carriage** (*US*) *n* voiture *f* d'enfant; **~-sit** *vi* garder les enfants; **~-sitter** *n* baby-sitter *m/f*

bachelor ['bætʃələ*] *n* célibataire *m*; **B~ of Arts/Science** ≈ licencié(e) ès *or* en lettres/sciences

back [bæk] *n* (*of person, horse, book*) dos *m*; (*of hand*) dos, revers *m*; (*of house*) derrière *m*; (*of car, train*) arrière *m*; (*of chair*) dossier *m*; (*of page*) verso *m*; (*of room, audience*) fond *m*; (*SPORT*) arrière *m* ♦ *vt* (*candidate: also*: ~ **up**) soutenir, appuyer; (*horse: at races*) parier *or* miser sur; (*car*) (faire) reculer ♦ *vi* (*also*: ~ **up**) reculer; (: *car etc*) faire marche arrière ♦ *adj* (*in compounds*) de derrière, à l'arrière ♦ *adv* (*not forward*) en arrière; (*returned*): **he's** ~ il est rentré, il est de retour; (*restitution*): **throw the ball** ~ renvoie la balle; (*again*): **he called** ~ il a rappelé; ~ **seat/wheels** (*AUT*) sièges *mpl*/roues *fpl* arrières; ~ **payments/ rent** arriéré *m* de paiements/loyer; **he ran** ~ il est revenu en courant; ~ **down** *vi* rabattre de ses prétentions; ~ **out** *vi* (*of promise*) se dédire; ~ **up** *vt* (*candidate etc*) soutenir, appuyer; (*COMPUT*) sauvegarder; **~bencher** (*BRIT*) *n* membre du parlement sans portefeuille; **~bone** *n* colonne vertébrale, épine dorsale; **~cloth** (*BRIT*) *n* toile *f* de fond; **~date** *vt* (*letter*) antidater; **~dated pay rise** augmentation *f* avec effet rétroactif; **~drop** *n* = **backcloth**; **~fire** *vi* (*AUT*) pétarader; (*plans*) mal tourner; **~ground** *n* arrière-plan *m*; (*of events*) situation *f*, conjoncture *f*; (*basic knowledge*) éléments *mpl* de base; (*experience*) formation *f*; **family**

~ground milieu familial; **~hand** *n* (*TENNIS: also*: ~*hand stroke*) revers *m*; **~hander** (*BRIT*) *n* (*bribe*) pot-de-vin *m*; **~ing** *n* (*fig*) soutien *m*, appui *m*; **~lash** *n* contre-coup *m*, répercussion *f*; **~log** *n*: **~log of work** travail *m* en retard; ~ **number** *n* (*of magazine etc*) vieux numéro; **~pack** *n* sac *m* à dos; ~ **pay** *n* rappel *m* de salaire; **~side** (*inf*) *n* derrière *m*, postérieur *m*; **~stage** *adv* derrière la scène, dans la coulisse; **~stroke** *n* dos crawlé; **~up** *adj* (*train, plane*) supplémentaire, de réserve; (*COMPUT*) de sauvegarde ♦ *n* (*support*) appui *m*, soutien *m*; (*also*: ~*up disk/file*) sauvegarde *f*; **~ward** *adj* (*movement*) en arrière; (*person, country*) arriéré(e); attardé(e); **~wards** *adv* (*move, go*) en arrière; (*read a list*) à l'envers, à rebours; (*fall*) à la renverse; (*walk*) à reculons; **~water** *n* (*fig*) coin reculé; bled perdu (*péj*); **~yard** *n* arrière-cour *f*

bacon ['beɪkən] *n* bacon *m*, lard *m*

bacteria [bæk'tɪərɪə] *npl* bactéries *fpl*

bad [bæd] *adj* mauvais(e); (*child*) vilain(e); (*mistake, accident etc*) grave; (*meat, food*) gâté(e), avarié(e); **his ~ leg** sa jambe malade; **to go** ~ (*meat, food*) se gâter

bade [bæd] *pt of* **bid**

badge [bædʒ] *n* insigne *m*; (*of policeman*) plaque *f*

badger ['bædʒə*] *n* blaireau *m*

badly ['bædlɪ] *adv* (*work, dress etc*) mal; ~ **wounded** grièvement blessé; **he needs it** ~ il en a absolument besoin; ~ **off** *adj, adv* dans la gêne

badminton ['bædmɪntən] *n* badminton *m*

bad-tempered ['bæd'tempəd] *adj* (*person: by nature*) ayant mauvais caractère; (: *on one occasion*) de mauvaise humeur

baffle ['bæfl] *vt* (*puzzle*) déconcerter

bag [bæg] *n* sac *m* ♦ *vt* (*inf: take*) empocher; s'approprier; **~s of** (*inf: lots of*) des masses de; **~gage** ['bægɪdʒ] *n* bagages *mpl*; **~gy** ['bægɪ] *adj* avachi(e), qui fait des poches; **~pipes** *npl* cornemuse *f*

bail [beɪl] n (payment) caution f; (release) mise f en liberté sous caution ♦ vt (prisoner: also: grant ~ to) mettre en liberté sous caution; (boat: also: ~ out) écoper; **on** ~ (prisoner) sous caution; see also **bale**; ~ **out** vt (prisoner) payer la caution de

bailiff ['beɪlɪf] n (BRIT) ≈ huissier m; (US) ≈ huissier-audiencier m

bait [beɪt] n appât m ♦ vt appâter; (fig: tease) tourmenter

bake [beɪk] vt (faire) cuire au four ♦ vi (bread etc) cuire (au four); (make cakes etc) faire de la pâtisserie; **~d beans** npl haricots blancs à la sauce tomate; **~r** n boulanger m; **~ry** n boulangerie f; boulangerie industrielle; **baking** n cuisson f; **baking powder** n levure f (chimique)

balance ['bæləns] n équilibre m; (COMM: sum) solde m; (remainder) reste m; (scales) balance f ♦ vt mettre or faire tenir en équilibre; (pros and cons) peser; (budget) équilibrer; (account) balancer; ~ **of trade/payments** balance commerciale/des comptes or paiements; **~d** adj (personality, diet) équilibré(e); (report) objectif(ive); ~ **sheet** n bilan m

balcony ['bælkənɪ] n balcon m; (in theatre) deuxième balcon

bald [bɔːld] adj chauve; (tyre) lisse

bale [beɪl] n balle f, ballot m; ~ **out** vi (of a plane) sauter en parachute

ball [bɔːl] n boule f; (football) ballon m; (for tennis, golf) balle f; (of wool) pelote f; (of string) bobine f; (dance) bal m; **to play** ~ **(with sb)** (fig) coopérer (avec qn)

ballast ['bæləst] n lest m

ball bearings npl roulement m à billes

ballerina [bælə'riːnə] n ballerine f

ballet ['bæleɪ] n ballet m; (art) danse f (classique); ~ **dancer** n danseur(euse) m/f de ballet

balloon [bə'luːn] n ballon m; (in comic strip) bulle f

ballot ['bælət] n scrutin m; ~ **paper** n bulletin m de vote

ballpoint (pen) ['bɔːlpɔɪnt-] n stylo m à bille

ballroom ['bɔːlrum] n salle f de bal

balm [bɑːm] n baume m

ban [bæn] n interdiction f ♦ vt interdire

banana [bə'nɑːnə] n banane f

band [bænd] n bande f; (at a dance) orchestre m; (MIL) musique f, fanfare f; ~ **together** vi se liguer

bandage ['bændɪdʒ] n bandage m, pansement m ♦ vt bander

Bandaid ['bændeɪd] (US: ®) n pansement adhésif

bandwagon ['bændwægən] n: **to jump on the** ~ (fig) monter dans or prendre le train en marche

bandy ['bændɪ] vt (jokes, insults, ideas) échanger

bandy-legged ['bændɪ'legɪd] adj aux jambes arquées

bang [bæŋ] n détonation f; (of door) claquement m; (blow) coup (violent) ♦ vt frapper (violemment); (door) claquer ♦ vi détoner; claquer ♦ excl pan!

bangs [bæŋz] (US) npl (fringe) frange f

banish ['bænɪʃ] vt bannir

banister(s) ['bænɪstə(z)] n(pl) rampe f (d'escalier)

bank [bæŋk] n banque f; (of river, lake) bord m, rive f; (of earth) talus m, remblai m ♦ vi (AVIAT) virer sur l'aile; ~ **on** vt fus miser or tabler sur; ~ **account** n compte m en banque; ~ **card** n carte f d'identité bancaire; **~er** n banquier m; **~er's card** (BRIT) n = **bank card**; ~ **holiday** (BRIT) n jour férié (les banques sont fermées); **~ing** n opérations fpl bancaires; profession f de banquier; **~note** n billet m de banque; ~ **rate** n taux m de l'escompte

bankrupt ['bæŋkrʌpt] adj en faillite; **to go** ~ faire faillite; **~cy** n faillite f

bank statement n relevé m de compte

banner ['bænə*] n bannière f

bannister(s) ['bænɪstə(z)] n(pl) = **banister(s)**

banns [bænz] npl bans mpl

baptism ['bæptɪzəm] n baptême m

bar [bɑː*] n (pub) bar m; (counter: in pub) comptoir m, bar; (rod: of metal etc) barre f; (on window etc) barreau m; (of chocolate) tablette f, plaque f; (fig) obstacle *m*; (*prohibition*) mesure *f* d'exclusion; (*MUS*) mesure *f* ♦ *vt* (*road*) barrer; (*window*) munir de barreaux; (*person*) exclure; (*activity*) interdire; ~ **of soap** savonnette *f*; **the B~** (*LAW*) le barreau; **behind ~s** (*prisoner*) sous les verrous; ~ **none** sans exception

barbaric [bɑː'bærɪk] *adj* barbare

barbecue ['bɑːbɪkjuː] *n* barbecue *m*

barbed wire ['bɑːbd-] *n* fil *m* de fer barbelé

barber ['bɑːbə*] *n* coiffeur *m* (pour hommes)

bar code *n* (*on goods*) code *m* à barres

bare [bɛə*] *adj* nu(e) ♦ *vt* mettre à nu, dénuder; (*teeth*) montrer; **the ~ necessities** le strict nécessaire; **~back** *adv* à cru, sans selle; **~faced** *adj* impudent(e), effronté(e); **~foot** *adj*, *adv* nu-pieds, (les) pieds nus; **~ly** *adv* à peine

bargain ['bɑːgɪn] *n* (*transaction*) marché *m*; (*good buy*) affaire *f*, occasion *f* ♦ *vi* (*haggle*) marchander; (*negotiate*): **to ~ (with sb)** négocier (avec qn), traiter (avec qn); **into the ~** par-dessus le marché; ~ **for** *vt fus*: **he got more than he ~ed for** il ne s'attendait pas à un coup pareil

barge [bɑːdʒ] *n* péniche *f*; ~ **in** *vi* (*walk in*) faire irruption; (*interrupt talk*) intervenir mal à propos

bark [bɑːk] *n* (*of tree*) écorce *f*; (*of dog*) aboiement *m* ♦ *vi* aboyer

barley ['bɑːlɪ] *n* orge *f*; ~ **sugar** *n* sucre *m* d'orge

barmaid ['bɑːmeɪd] *n* serveuse *f* (de bar), barmaid *f*

barman ['bɑːmən] (*irreg*) *n* serveur *m* (de bar), barman *m*

barn [bɑːn] *n* grange *f*

barometer [bə'rɒmɪtə*] *n* baromètre *m*

baron ['bærən] *n* baron *m*; **~ess** *n* baronne *f*

barracks ['bærəks] *npl* caserne *f*

barrage ['bærɑːʒ] *n* (*MIL*) tir *m* de barrage; (*dam*) barrage *m*; (*fig*) pluie *f*

barrel ['bærəl] *n* tonneau *m*; (*of oil*) baril *m*; (*of gun*) canon *m*

barren ['bærən] *adj* stérile

barricade [bærɪ'keɪd] *n* barricade *f*

barrier ['bærɪə*] *n* barrière *f*; (*fig: to progress etc*) obstacle *m*

barring ['bɑːrɪŋ] *prep* sauf

barrister ['bærɪstə*] (*BRIT*) *n* avocat (plaidant)

barrow ['bærəʊ] *n* (*wheel~*) charrette *f* à bras

bartender ['bɑːtendə*] (*US*) *n* barman *m*

barter ['bɑːtə*] *vt*: **to ~ sth for** échanger qch contre

base [beɪs] *n* base *f*; (*of tree, post*) pied *m* ♦ *vt*: **to ~ sth on** baser *or* fonder qch sur ♦ *adj* vil(e), bas(se)

baseball ['beɪsbɔːl] *n* base-ball *m*

basement ['beɪsmənt] *n* sous-sol *m*

bases[1] ['beɪsɪz] *npl of* **base**

bases[2] ['beɪsiːz] *npl of* **basis**

bash [bæʃ] (*inf*) *vt* frapper, cogner

bashful ['bæʃfʊl] *adj* timide; modeste

basic ['beɪsɪk] *adj* fondamental(e), de base; (*minimal*) rudimentaire; **~ally** *adv* fondamentalement, à la base; (*in fact*) en fait, au fond; **~s** *npl*: **the ~s** l'essentiel *m*

basil ['bæzl] *n* basilic *m*

basin ['beɪsn] *n* (*vessel, also GEO*) cuvette *f*, bassin *m*; (*also: wash~*) lavabo *m*

basis ['beɪsɪs] (*pl* **bases**) *n* base *f*; **on a trial ~** à titre d'essai; **on a part-time ~** à temps partiel

bask [bɑːsk] *vi*: **to ~ in the sun** se chauffer au soleil

basket ['bɑːskɪt] *n* corbeille *f*; (*with handle*) panier *m*; **~ball** *n* basket-ball *m*

bass [beɪs] *n* (*MUS*) basse *f*

bassoon [bə'suːn] *n* (*MUS*) basson *m*

bastard ['bɑːstəd] *n* enfant naturel(le), bâtard(e); (*inf!*) salaud *m* (!)

bat [bæt] *n* chauve-souris *f*; (*for baseball etc*) batte *f*; (*BRIT: for table tennis*) raquette *f* ♦ *vt*: **he didn't ~ an eyelid** il n'a pas sourcillé *or* bronché

batch [bætʃ] *n* (*of bread*) fournée *f*; (*of papers*) liasse *f*

bated ['beɪtɪd] *adj*: **with ~ breath** en retenant son souffle

bath [bɑːθ, *pl* bɑːðz] *n* bain *m*; (*~tub*) baignoire *f* ♦ *vt* baigner, donner un bain à; **to have a ~** prendre un bain; *see also* **baths**

bathe [beɪð] *vi* se baigner ♦ *vt* (*wound*) laver

bathing ['beɪðɪŋ] *n* baignade *f*; **~ cap** *n* bonnet *m* de bain; **~ costume** (*US* **~ suit**) *n* maillot *m* (de bain)

bath: **~robe** *n* peignoir *m* de bain; **~room** *n* salle *f* de bains; **~s** [bɑːðz] *npl* (*also: swimming ~*) piscine *f*; **~ towel** *n* serviette *f* de bain

baton ['bætən] *n* bâton *m*; (*MUS*) baguette *f*; (*club*) matraque *f*

batter ['bætə*] *vt* battre ♦ *n* pâte *f* à frire; **~ed** *adj* (*hat, pan*) cabossé(e)

battery ['bætərɪ] *n* batterie *f*; (*of torch*) pile *f*

battle ['bætl] *n* bataille *f*, combat *m* ♦ *vi* se battre, lutter; **~field** *n* champ *m* de bataille; **~ship** *n* cuirassé *m*

bawdy ['bɔːdɪ] *adj* paillard(e)

bawl [bɔːl] *vi* hurler; (*child*) brailler

bay [beɪ] *n* (*of sea*) baie *f*; **to hold sb at ~** tenir qn à distance *or* en échec; **~ leaf** *n* laurier *m*; **~ window** *n* baie vitrée

bazaar [bəˈzɑː*] *n* bazar *m*; vente *f* de charité

B & B *n abbr* = **bed and breakfast**

BBC *n abbr* (= *British Broadcasting Corporation*) *office de la radiodiffusion et télévision britannique*

B.C. *adv abbr* (= *before Christ*) av. J.-C.

KEYWORD

---

be [biː] (*pt* **was, were**, *pp* **been**) *aux vb*
1 (*with present participle: forming continuous tenses*): **what are you doing?** que faites-vous?; **they're coming tomorrow** ils viennent demain; **I've been waiting for you for 2 hours** je t'attends depuis 2 heures

2 (*with pp: forming passives*) être; **to ~ killed** être tué(e); **he was nowhere to ~ seen** on ne le voyait nulle part

3 (*in tag questions*): **it was fun, wasn't it?** c'était drôle, n'est-ce-pas?; **she's back, is she?** elle est rentrée, n'est-ce pas *or* alors?

4 (*+to +infinitive*): **the house is to ~ sold** la maison doit être vendue; **he's not to open it** il ne doit pas l'ouvrir

♦ *vb + complement* **1** (*gen*) être; **I'm English** je suis anglais(e); **I'm tired** je suis fatigué(e); **I'm hot/cold** j'ai chaud/froid; **he's a doctor** il est médecin; **2 and 2 are 4** 2 et 2 font 4

2 (*of health*) aller; **how are you?** comment allez-vous?; **he's fine now** il va bien maintenant; **he's very ill** il est très malade

3 (*of age*) avoir; **how old are you?** quel âge avez-vous?; **I'm sixteen (years old)** j'ai seize ans

4 (*cost*) coûter; **how much was the meal?** combien a coûté le repas?; **that'll ~ £5, please** ça fera 5 livres, s'il vous plaît

♦ *vi* **1** (*exist, occur etc*) être, exister; **the prettiest girl that ever was** la fille la plus jolie qui ait jamais existé; **~ that as it may** quoi qu'il en soit; **so ~ it** soit

2 (*referring to place*) être, se trouver; **I won't ~ here tomorrow** je ne serai pas là demain; **Edinburgh is in Scotland** Édimbourg est *or* se trouve en Écosse

3 (*referring to movement*) aller; **where have you been?** où êtes-vous allé(s)?

♦ *impers vb* **1** (*referring to time, distance*) être; **it's 5 o'clock** il est 5 heures; **it's the 28th of April** c'est le 28 avril; **it's 10 km to the village** le village est à 10 km

2 (*referring to the weather*) faire; **it's too hot/cold** il fait trop chaud/froid; **it's windy** il y a du vent

3 (*emphatic*): **it's me/the postman** c'est moi/le facteur

---

beach [biːtʃ] *n* plage *f* ♦ *vt* échouer

beacon ['biːkən] *n* (*lighthouse*) fanal *m*; (*marker*) balise *f*

bead [biːd] *n* perle *f*

beak [biːk] *n* bec *m*

beaker ['biːkə*] *n* gobelet *m*

beam [biːm] *n* poutre *f*; (*of light*) rayon *m* ♦ *vi* rayonner

bean [biːn] *n* haricot *m*; (*of coffee*) grain

m; **runner** ~ haricot *m* (à rames); **broad** ~ fève *f*; **~sprouts** *npl* germes *mpl* de soja

bear [bɛə*] (*pt* **bore**, *pp* **borne**) *n* ours *m* ♦ *vt* porter; (*endure*) supporter ♦ *vi*: **to** ~ **right/left** obliquer à droite/gauche, se diriger vers la droite/gauche; ~ **out** *vt* corroborer, confirmer; ~ **up** *vi* (*person*) tenir le coup

beard [bɪəd] *n* barbe *f*; **~ed** *adj* barbu(e)

bearer ['bɛərə*] *n* porteur *m*; (*of passport*) titulaire *m/f*

bearing ['bɛərɪŋ] *n* maintien *m*, allure *f*; (*connection*) rapport *m*; **~s** *npl* (*also: ball ~s*) roulement *m* (à billes); **to take a** ~ faire le point

beast [biːst] *n* bête *f*; (*inf: person*) brute *f*; **~ly** *adj* infect(e)

beat [biːt] (*pt* **beat**, *pp* **beaten**) *n* battement *m*; (*MUS*) temps *m*, mesure *f*; (*of policeman*) ronde *f* ♦ *vt*, *vi* battre; **off the** ~**en track** hors des chemins *or* sentiers battus; ~ **it!** (*inf*) fiche(-moi) le camp!; ~ **off** *vt* repousser; ~ **up** *vt* (*inf: person*) tabasser; (*eggs*) battre; **~ing** *n* raclée *f*

beautiful ['bjuːtɪful] *adj* beau(belle); **~ly** *adv* admirablement

beauty ['bjuːtɪ] *n* beauté *f*; ~ **salon** *n* institut *m* de beauté; ~ **spot** (*BRIT*) *n* (*TOURISM*) site naturel (d'une grande beauté)

beaver ['biːvə*] *n* castor *m*

became [bɪ'keɪm] *pt of* **become**

because [bɪ'kɒz] *conj* parce que; ~ **of** *prep* à cause de

beck [bek] *n*: **to be at sb's** ~ **and call** être à l'entière disposition de qn

beckon ['bekən] *vt* (*also:* ~ **to**) faire signe (de venir) à

become [bɪ'kʌm] (*irreg: like* **come**) *vi* devenir; **to** ~ **fat/thin** grossir/maigrir

becoming [bɪ'kʌmɪŋ] *adj* (*behaviour*) convenable, bienséant(e); (*clothes*) seyant(e)

bed [bed] *n* lit *m*; (*of flowers*) parterre *m*; (*of coal, clay*) couche *f*; (*of sea*) fond *m*; **to go to** ~ aller se coucher; ~ **and breakfast** *n* (*terms*) chambre et petit dé-

jeuner; (*place*) ≈ chambre *f* d'hôte; **~clothes** *npl* couvertures *fpl* et draps *mpl*; **~ding** *n* literie *f*

bedraggled [bɪ'dræɡld] *adj* (*person, clothes*) débraillé(e); (*hair: wet*) trempé(e)

bed: **~ridden** *adj* cloué(e) au lit; **~room** *n* chambre *f* (à coucher); **~side** *n*: **at sb's ~side** au chevet de qn; **~sit(ter)** (*BRIT*) *n* chambre meublée, studio *m*; **~spread** *n* couvre-lit *m*, dessus-de-lit *m inv*; **~time** *n* heure *f* du coucher

bee [biː] *n* abeille *f*

beech [biːtʃ] *n* hêtre *m*

beef [biːf] *n* boeuf *m*; **roast** ~ rosbif *m*; **~burger** *n* hamburger *m*; **~eater** *n* hallebardier de la Tour de Londres

beehive ['biːhaɪv] *n* ruche *f*

beeline ['biːlaɪn] *n*: **to make a** ~ **for** se diriger tout droit vers

been [biːn] *pp of* **be**

beer [bɪə*] *n* bière *f*

beet [biːt] *n* (*vegetable*) betterave *f*; (*US: also: red* ~) betterave (potagère)

beetle ['biːtl] *n* scarabée *m*

beetroot ['biːtruːt] (*BRIT*) *n* betterave *f*

before [bɪ'fɔː*] *prep* (*in time*) avant; (*in space*) devant ♦ *conj* avant que +*sub*; avant de ♦ *adv* avant; devant; ~ **going** avant de partir; ~ **she goes** avant qu'elle ne parte; **the week** ~ la semaine précédente *or* d'avant; **I've seen it** ~ je l'ai déjà vu; **~hand** *adv* au préalable, à l'avance

beg [beg] *vi* mendier ♦ *vt* mendier; (*forgiveness, mercy etc*) demander; (*entreat*) supplier; *see also* **pardon**

began [bɪ'ɡæn] *pt of* **begin**

beggar ['beɡə*] *n* mendiant(e)

begin [bɪ'ɡɪn] (*pt* **began**, *pp* **begun**) *vt*, *vi* commencer; **to** ~ **doing** *or* **to do sth** commencer à *or* de faire qch; **~ner** *n* débutant(e); **~ning** *n* commencement *m*, début *m*

behalf [bɪ'hɑːf] *n*: **on** ~ **of**, (*US*) **in** ~ **of** (*representing*) de la part de; (*for benefit of*) pour le compte de; **on my/his** ~ pour moi/lui

behave [bɪ'heɪv] *vi* se conduire, se

comporter; (*well: also*: ~ *o.s.*) se conduire bien *or* comme il faut
behaviour [bɪ'heɪvjə*] (*US* **behavior**) *n*
comportement *m*, conduite *f*
behead [bɪ'hed] *vt* décapiter
beheld [bɪ'held] *pt, pp of* behold
behind [bɪ'haɪnd] *prep* derrière; (*time,
progress*) en retard sur; (*work, studies*)
en retard dans ♦ *adv* derrière ♦ *n* derrière *m*; **to be** ~ **(schedule)** avoir du retard; ~ **the scenes** dans les coulisses
behold [bɪ'həʊld] (*irreg: like* hold) *vt*
apercevoir, voir
beige [beɪʒ] *adj* beige
Beijing ['beɪ'dʒɪŋ] *n* Bei-jing, Pékin
being ['bi:ɪŋ] *n* être *m*
Beirut [beɪ'ru:t] *n* Beyrouth
belated [bɪ'leɪtɪd] *adj* tardif(ive)
belch [beltʃ] *vi* avoir un renvoi, roter
♦ *vt* (*also*: ~ *out: smoke etc*) vomir, cracher
belfry ['belfrɪ] *n* beffroi *m*
Belgian ['beldʒən] *adj* belge, de Belgique
♦ *n* Belge *m/f*
Belgium ['beldʒəm] *n* Belgique *f*
belie [bɪ'laɪ] *vt* démentir
belief [bɪ'li:f] *n* (*opinion*) conviction *f*;
(*trust, faith*) foi *f*
believe [bɪ'li:v] *vt, vi* croire; **to ~ in**
(*God*) croire en; (*method, ghosts*) croire
à; **~r in** (*in idea, activity*): **~r in** parti-
san(e) de; (*REL*) croyant(e)
belittle [bɪ'lɪtl] *vt* déprécier, rabaisser
bell [bel] *n* cloche *f*; (*small*) clochette *f*,
grelot *m*; (*on door*) sonnette *f*; (*electric*)
sonnerie *f*
belligerent [bɪ'lɪdʒərənt] *adj* (*person,
attitude*) agressif(ive)
bellow ['beləʊ] *vi* (*bull*) meugler; (*person*) brailler
belly ['belɪ] *n* ventre *m*
belong [bɪ'lɒŋ] *vi*: **to ~ to** appartenir à;
(*club etc*) faire partie de; **this book ~s
here** ce livre va ici; **~ings** *npl* affaires
fpl, possessions *fpl*
beloved [bɪ'lʌvɪd] *adj* (bien-)aimé(e)
below [bɪ'ləʊ] *prep* sous, au-dessous de
♦ *adv* en dessous; **see ~** voir plus bas *or*
plus loin *or* ci-dessous

belt [belt] *n* ceinture *f*; (*of land*) région
f; (*TECH*) courroie *f* ♦ *vt* (*thrash*) donner
une raclée à; **~way** (*US*) *n* (*AUT*) route *f*
de ceinture; (: *motorway*) périphérique
m
bemused [bɪ'mju:zd] *adj* stupéfié(e)
bench [bentʃ] *n* (*gen, also BRIT: POL*)
banc *m*; (*in workshop*) établi *m*; **the B~**
(*LAW: judge*) le juge; (: *judges collective-
ly*) la magistrature, la Cour
bend [bend] (*pt, pp* bent) *vt* courber;
(*leg, arm*) plier ♦ *vi* se courber ♦ *n*
(*BRIT: in road*) virage *m*, tournant *m*; (*in
pipe, river*) coude *m*; ~ **down** *vi* se baisser; ~ **over** *vi* se pencher
beneath [bɪ'ni:θ] *prep* sous, au-dessous
de; (*unworthy of*) indigne de ♦ *adv* dessous, au-dessous, en bas
benefactor ['benɪfæktə*] *n* bienfaiteur
m
beneficial [benɪ'fɪʃl] *adj* salutaire; avan-
tageux(euse); ~ **to the health** bon(ne)
pour la santé
benefit ['benɪfɪt] *n* avantage *m*, profit *m*;
(*allowance of money*) allocation *f* ♦ *vt*
faire du bien à, profiter à ♦ *vi*: **he'll ~
from it** cela lui fera du bien, il y gagne-
ra *or* s'en trouvera bien
Benelux ['benɪlʌks] *n* Bénélux *m*
benevolent [bɪ'nevələnt] *adj* bienveil-
lant(e); (*organization*) bénévole
benign [bɪ'naɪn] *adj* (*person, smile*)
bienveillant(e), affable; (*MED*) bénin(igne)
bent [bent] *pt, pp of* bend ♦ *n* inclination *f*, penchant *m*; **to be ~ on** être réso-
lu(e) à
bequest [bɪ'kwest] *n* legs *m*
bereaved [bɪ'ri:vd] *n*: **the ~** la famille
du disparu
beret ['bereɪ] *n* béret *m*
Berlin [bə:'lɪn] *n* Berlin
berm [bɜ:m] (*US*) *n* (*AUT*) accotement *m*
berry ['berɪ] *n* baie *f*
berserk [bə'sɜ:k] *adj*: **to go ~** (*madman,
crowd*) se déchaîner
berth [bɜ:θ] *n* (*bed*) couchette *f*; (*for
ship*) poste *m* d'amarrage, mouillage *m*
♦ *vi* (*in harbour*) venir à quai; (*at anchor*) mouiller

beseech [bɪ'siːtʃ] (*pt, pp* **besought**) *vt* implorer, supplier

beset [bɪ'set] (*pt, pp* **beset**) *vt* assaillir

beside [bɪ'saɪd] *prep* à côté de; **to be ~ o.s. (with anger)** être hors de soi; **that's ~ the point** cela n'a rien à voir; **~s** [bɪ'saɪdz] *adv* en outre, de plus; (*in any case*) d'ailleurs ♦ *prep* (*as well as*) en plus de

besiege [bɪ'siːdʒ] *vt* (*town*) assiéger; (*fig*) assaillir

besought [bɪ'sɔːt] *pt, pp of* **beseech**

best [best] *adj* meilleur(e) ♦ *adv* le mieux; **the ~ part of** (*quantity*) le plus clair de, la plus grande partie de; **at ~** au mieux; **to make the ~ of sth** s'accommoder de qch (du mieux que l'on peut); **to do one's ~** faire de son mieux; **to the ~ of my knowledge** pour autant que je sache; **to the ~ of my ability** du mieux que je pourrai; **~ man** *n* garçon *m* d'honneur

bestow [bɪ'stəʊ] *vt*: **to ~ sth on sb** accorder qch à qn; (*title*) conférer qch à qn

bet [bet] (*pt, pp* **bet** *or* **betted**) *n* pari *m* ♦ *vt, vi* parier

betray [bɪ'treɪ] *vt* trahir; **~al** *n* trahison *f*

better ['betə*] *adj* meilleur(e) ♦ *adv* mieux ♦ *vt* améliorer ♦ *n*: **to get the ~ of** triompher de, l'emporter sur; **you had ~ do it** vous feriez mieux de le faire; **he thought ~ of it** il s'est ravisé; **to get ~** aller mieux; s'améliorer; **~ off** *adj* plus à l'aise financièrement; (*fig*): **you'd be ~ off this way** vous vous en trouveriez mieux ainsi

betting ['betɪŋ] *n* paris *mpl*; **~ shop** (*BRIT*) *n* bureau *m* de paris

between [bɪ'twiːn] *prep* entre ♦ *adv*: **(in) ~** au milieu; dans l'intervalle; (*in time*) dans l'intervalle

beverage ['bevərɪdʒ] *n* boisson *f* (*gén sans alcool*)

beware [bɪ'weə*] *vi*: **to ~ (of)** prendre garde (à); **"~ of the dog"** "(attention) chien méchant"

bewildered [bɪ'wɪldəd] *adj* dérouté(e), ahuri(e)

beyond [bɪ'jɔnd] *prep* (*in space, time*) au-delà de; (*exceeding*) au-dessus de ♦ *adv* au-delà; **~ doubt** hors de doute; **~ repair** irréparable

bias ['baɪəs] *n* (*prejudice*) préjugé *m*, parti pris *m*; **~(s)ed** *adj* partial(e), montrant un parti pris

bib [bɪb] *n* bavoir *m*, bavette *f*

Bible ['baɪbl] *n* Bible *f*

bicarbonate of soda [baɪ'kɑːbənɪt-] *n* bicarbonate *m* de soude

bicker ['bɪkə*] *vi* se chamailler

bicycle ['baɪsɪkl] *n* bicyclette *f*

bid [bɪd] (*pt* **bid** *or* **bade**, *pp* **bid(den)**) *n* offre *f*; (*at auction*) enchère *f*; (*attempt*) tentative *f* ♦ *vi* faire une enchère *or* offre ♦ *vt* faire une enchère *or* offre de; **to ~ sb good day** souhaiter le bonjour à qn; **~der** *n*: **the highest ~der** le plus offrant; **~ding** *n* enchères *fpl*

bide [baɪd] *vt*: **to ~ one's time** attendre son heure

bifocals [baɪ'fəʊkəlz] *npl* verres *mpl* à double foyer, lunettes bifocales

big [bɪg] *adj* grand(e); gros(se)

bigheaded ['bɪg'hedɪd] *adj* prétentieux(euse)

bigot ['bɪgət] *n* fanatique *m/f*, sectaire *m/f*; **~ed** *adj* fanatique, sectaire; **~ry** *n* fanatisme *m*, sectarisme *m*

big top *n* grand chapiteau

bike [baɪk] *n* vélo *m*, bécane *f*

bikini [bɪ'kiːnɪ] *n* bikini *m*

bilingual [baɪ'lɪŋgwəl] *adj* bilingue

bill [bɪl] *n* note *f*, facture *f*; (*POL*) projet *m* de loi; (*US: banknote*) billet *m* (de banque); (*of bird*) bec *m*; (*THEATRE*): **on the ~** à l'affiche, **"post no ~s"** "défense d'afficher"; **to fit** *or* **fill the ~** (*fig*) faire l'affaire; **~board** *n* panneau *m* d'affichage

billet ['bɪlɪt] *n* cantonnement *m* (chez l'habitant)

billfold ['bɪlfəʊld] (*US*) *n* portefeuille *m*

billiards ['bɪljədz] *n* (jeu *m* de) billard *m*

billion ['bɪljən] *n* (*BRIT*) billion *m* (*million de millions*); (*US*) milliard *m*

bimbo ['bɪmbəʊ] (*inf*) *n* ravissante idiote *f*, potiche *f*

bin [bɪn] *n* boîte *f*; (*also: dust~*) poubelle *f*; (*for coal*) coffre *m*

bind [baɪnd] (*pt, pp* **bound**) *vt* attacher; (*book*) relier; (*oblige*) obliger, contraindre ♦ *n* (*inf: nuisance*) scie *f*; **~ing** *adj* (*contract*) constituant une obligation

binge [bɪndʒ] (*inf*) *n*: **to go on a/the ~** (*inf*) aller faire la bringue

bingo ['bɪŋgəʊ] *n jeu de loto pratiqué dans des établissements publics*

binoculars [bɪ'nɒkjʊləz] *npl* jumelles *fpl*

bio... *prefix*: **~chemistry** *n* biochimie *f*; **~graphy** *n* biographie *f*; **~logical** *adj* biologique; **~logy** *n* biologie *f*

birch [bɜːtʃ] *n* bouleau *m*

bird [bɜːd] *n* oiseau *m*; (*BRIT: inf: girl*) nana *f*; **~'s-eye view** *n* vue *f* à vol d'oiseau; (*fig*) vue d'ensemble *or* générale; **~-watcher** *n* ornithologue *m/f* amateur

Biro ['baɪrəʊ] (®) *n* stylo *m* à bille

birth [bɜːθ] *n* naissance *f*; **to give ~ to** (*subj: woman*) donner naissance à; (*: animal*) mettre bas; **~ certificate** *n* acte *m* de naissance; **~ control** *n* (*policy*) limitation *f* des naissances; (*method*) méthode(s) contraceptive(s); **~day** *n* anniversaire *n* ♦ *cpd* d'anniversaire; **~place** *n* lieu *m* de naissance; (*fig*) berceau *m*; **~ rate** *n* (taux *m* de) natalité *f*

biscuit ['bɪskɪt] *n* (*BRIT*) biscuit *m*; (*US*) petit pain au lait

bisect [baɪ'sɛkt] *vt* couper *or* diviser en deux

bishop ['bɪʃəp] *n* évêque *m*; (*CHESS*) fou *m*

bit [bɪt] *pt of* **bite** ♦ *n* morceau *m*; (*of tool*) mèche *f*; (*of horse*) mors *m*; (*COMPUT*) élément *m* binaire; **a ~ of** un peu de; **a ~ mad** un peu fou; **~ by ~** petit à petit

bitch [bɪtʃ] *n* (*dog*) chienne *f*; (*inf!*) salope *f* (*!*), garce *f*

bite [baɪt] (*pt* **bit**, *pp* **bitten**) *vt, vi* mordre; (*insect*) piquer ♦ *n* (*insect ~*) piqûre *f*; (*mouthful*) bouchée *f*; **let's have a ~ (to eat)** (*inf*) mangeons un morceau; **to ~ one's nails** se ronger les ongles

bitter ['bɪtə*] *adj* amer(ère); (*weather, wind*) glacial(e); (*criticism*) cinglant(e);

(*struggle*) acharné(e) ♦ *n* (*BRIT: beer*) bière *f* (*forte*); **~ness** *n* amertume *f*; (*taste*) goût amer

blab [blæb] *vi* jaser, trop parler

black [blæk] *adj* noir(e) ♦ *n* (*colour*) noir *m*; (*person*): **B~** noir(e) ♦ *vt* (*BRIT: INDUSTRY*) boycotter; **to give sb a ~ eye** pocher l'œil à qn; **to beat sb black and blue** battre qn comme plâtre; ~ noir à qn; **~ and blue** couvert(e) de bleus; **to be in the ~** (*in credit*) être créditeur(trice); **~berry** *n* mûre *f*; **~bird** *n* merle *m*; **~board** *n* tableau noir; **~ coffee** *n* café noir; **~currant** *n* cassis *m*; **~en** *vt* noircir; **~ ice** *n* verglas *m*; **~leg** (*BRIT*) *n* briseur *m* de grève, jaune *m*; **~list** *n* liste noire; **~mail** *n* chantage *m* ♦ *vt* faire chanter, soumettre au chantage; **~ market** *n* marché noir; **~out** *n* panne *f* d'électricité; (*TV etc*) interruption *f* d'émission; (*fainting*) syncope *f*; **B~ Sea** *n*: **the B~ Sea** la mer Noire; **~sheep** *n* brebis galeuse; **~smith** *n* forgeron *m*; **~ spot** *n* (*AUT*) point noir

bladder ['blædə*] *n* vessie *f*

blade [bleɪd] *n* lame *f*; (*of propeller*) pale *f*; **~ of grass** brin *m* d'herbe

blame [bleɪm] *n* faute *f*, blâme *m* ♦ *vt*: **to ~ sb/sth for sth** attribuer à qn/qch la responsabilité de qch; reprocher qch à qn/qch; **who's to ~?** qui est le fautif *or* coupable *or* responsable?; **~less** *adj* irréprochable

bland [blænd] *adj* (*taste, food*) doux(douce), fade

blank [blæŋk] *adj* blanc(blanche); (*look*) sans expression, dénué(e) d'expression ♦ *n* espace *m* vide, blanc *m*; (*cartridge*) cartouche *f* à blanc; **his mind was a ~** il avait la tête vide; **~ cheque** *n* chèque *m* en blanc

blanket ['blæŋkɪt] *n* couverture *f*; (*of snow, cloud*) couche *f*

blare [blɛə*] *vi* beugler

blast [blɑːst] *n* souffle *m*; (*of explosive*) explosion *f* ♦ *vt* faire sauter *or* exploser; **~-off** *n* (*SPACE*) lancement *m*

blatant ['bleɪtənt] *adj* flagrant(e), criant(e)

blaze [bleɪz] *n* (*fire*) incendie *m*; (*fig*)

flamboiement *m* ♦ *vi* (*fire*) flamber; (*fig: eyes*) flamboyer; (: *guns*) crépiter ♦ *vt*: **to ~ a trail** (*fig*) montrer la voie

blazer ['bleɪzə*] *n* blazer *m*

bleach [bli:tʃ] *n* (*also: household ~*) eau *f* de Javel ♦ *vt* (*linen etc*) blanchir; **~ed** *adj* (*hair*) oxygéné(e), décoloré(e); **~ers** ['bli:tʃəz] (*US*) *npl* (*SPORT*) gradins *mpl* (en plein soleil)

bleak [bli:k] *adj* morne; (*countryside*) désolé(e)

bleary-eyed ['blɪərɪ'aɪd] *adj* aux yeux pleins de sommeil

bleat [bli:t] *vi* bêler

bleed [bli:d] (*pt, pp bled*) *vt, vi* saigner; **my nose is ~ing** je saigne du nez

bleeper ['bli:pə*] *n* (*device*) bip *m*

blemish ['blemɪʃ] *n* défaut *m*; (*on fruit, reputation*) tache *f*

blend [blend] *n* mélange *m* ♦ *vt* mélanger ♦ *vi* (*colours etc: also: ~ in*) se mélanger, se fondre

bless [bles] (*pt, pp blessed or blest*) *vt* bénir; **~ you!** (*after sneeze*) à vos souhaits!; **~ing** *n* bénédiction *f*; (*godsend*) bienfait *m*

blew [blu:] *pt of* **blow**

blight [blaɪt] *vt* (*hopes etc*) anéantir; (*life*) briser

blimey ['blaɪmɪ] (*BRIT: inf*) *excl* mince alors!

blind [blaɪnd] *adj* aveugle ♦ *n* (*for window*) store *m* ♦ *vt* aveugler; **~ alley** *n* impasse *f*; **~ corner** (*BRIT*) *n* virage *m* sans visibilité; **~fold** *n* bandeau *m* ♦ *adj, adv* les yeux bandés ♦ *vt* bander les yeux à; **~ly** *adv* aveuglément; **~ness** *n* cécité *f*; **~ spot** *n* (*AUT etc*) angle mort; **that is her ~ spot** (*fig*) elle refuse d'y voir clair sur ce point

blink [blɪŋk] *vi* cligner des yeux; (*light*) clignoter; **~ers** *npl* œillères *fpl*

bliss [blɪs] *n* félicité *f*, bonheur *m* sans mélange

blister ['blɪstə*] *n* (*on skin*) ampoule *f*, cloque *f*; (*on paintwork, rubber*) boursouflure *f* ♦ *vi* (*paint*) se boursoufler, se cloquer

blithely ['blaɪðlɪ] *adv* (*unconcernedly*)

tranquillement

blizzard ['blɪzəd] *n* blizzard *m*, tempête *f* de neige

bloated ['bləutɪd] *adj* (*face*) bouffi(e); (*stomach, person*) gonflé(e)

blob [blɔb] *n* (*drop*) goutte *f*; (*stain, spot*) tache *f*

block [blɔk] *n* bloc *m*; (*in pipes*) obstruction *f*; (*toy*) cube *m*; (*of buildings*) pâté *m* (de maisons) ♦ *vt* bloquer; (*fig*) faire obstacle à; **~ of flats** (*BRIT*) immeuble (locatif); **mental ~** trou *m* de mémoire; **~ade** *n* blocus *m*; **~age** *n* obstruction *f*; **~buster** *n* (*film, book*) grand succès; **~ letters** *npl* majuscules *fpl*

bloke [bləuk] (*BRIT: inf*) *n* type *m*

blond(e) [blɔnd] *adj, n* blond(e)

blood [blʌd] *n* sang *m*; **~ donor** *n* donneur(euse) de sang; **~ group** *n* groupe sanguin; **~hound** *n* limier *m*; **~ poisoning** *n* empoisonnement *m* du sang; **~ pressure** *n* tension *f* (artérielle); **~shed** *n* effusion *f* de sang, carnage *m*; **~shot** *adj*: **~shot eyes** yeux injectés de sang; **~stream** *n* sang *m*, système sanguin; **~ test** *n* prise *f* de sang; **~thirsty** *adj* sanguinaire; **~ vessel** *n* vaisseau sanguin; **~y** *adj* sanglant(e); (*nose*) en sang; (*BRIT: inf!*): **this ~y ...** ce foutu ... (!), ce putain de ... (!); **~y strong/good** vachement *or* sacrément fort/bon; **~y-minded** (*BRIT: inf*) *adj* contrariant(e), obstiné(e)

bloom [blu:m] *n* fleur *f* ♦ *vi* être en fleur

blossom ['blɔsəm] *n* fleur(s) *f(pl)* ♦ *vi* être en fleurs; (*fig*) s'épanouir; **to ~ into** devenir

blot [blɔt] *n* tache *f* ♦ *vt* tacher; **~ out** *vt* (*memories*) effacer; (*view*) cacher, masquer

blotchy ['blɔtʃɪ] *adj* (*complexion*) couvert(e) de marbrures

blotting paper ['blɔtɪŋ-] *n* buvard *m*

blouse [blauz] *n* chemisier *m*, corsage *m*

blow [bləu] (*pt blew, pp blown*) *n* coup *m* ♦ *vi* souffler ♦ *vt* souffler; (*fuse*) faire sauter; (*instrument*) jouer de; **to ~ one's nose** se moucher; **to ~ a whistle** siffler; **~ away** *vt* chasser, faire s'envoler; **~**

down *vt* faire tomber, renverser; ~ **off** *vt* emporter; ~ **out** *vi* (*fire, flame*) s'éteindre; ~ **over** *vi* s'apaiser; ~ **up** *vt* faire sauter; (*tyre*) gonfler; (*PHOT*) agrandir ♦ *vi* exploser, sauter; ~**-dry** *vi* brushing *m*; ~**lamp** (*BRIT*) *n* chalumeau *m*; ~**-out** *n* (*of tyre*) éclatement *m*; ~**-torch** *n* = **blowlamp**

blue [bluː] *adj* bleu(e); (*fig*) triste; ~**s** *n* (*MUS*): **the** ~**s** le blues; ~ **film/joke** film *m*/histoire *f* pornographique; **to come out of the** ~ (*fig*) être complètement inattendu; ~**bell** *n* jacinthe *f* des bois; ~**bottle** *n* mouche *f* à viande; ~**print** *n* (*fig*) projet *m*, plan directeur

bluff [blʌf] *vi* bluffer ♦ *n* bluff *m*; **to call sb's** ~ mettre qn au défi d'exécuter ses menaces

blunder ['blʌndə*] *n* gaffe *f*, bévue *f* ♦ *vi* faire une gaffe *or* une bévue

blunt [blʌnt] *adj* (*person*) brusque, ne mâchant pas ses mots; (*knife*) émoussé(e), peu tranchant(e); (*pencil*) mal taillé

blur [bləː*] *n* tache *or* masse floue *or* confuse ♦ *vt* brouiller

blurb [bləːb] *n* notice *f* publicitaire; (*for book*) texte *m* de présentation

blurt out [bləːt] *vt* (*reveal*) lâcher

blush [blʌʃ] *vi* rougir ♦ *n* rougeur *f*

blustery ['blʌstərɪ] *adj* (*weather*) à bourrasques

boar [bɔː*] *n* sanglier *m*

board [bɔːd] *n* planche *f*; (*on wall*) panneau *m*; (*for chess*) échiquier *m*; (*cardboard*) carton *m*; (*committee*) conseil *m*, comité *m*; (*in firm*) conseil d'administration; (*NAUT, AVIAT*): **on** ~ à bord ♦ *vt* (*ship*) monter à bord de; (*train*) monter dans; **full** ~ (*BRIT*) pension complète; **half** ~ demi-pension *f*; ~ **and lodging** chambre *f* avec pension; **which goes by the** ~ (*fig*) qu'on laisse tomber, qu'on abandonne; ~ **up** *vt* (*door, window*) boucher; ~**er** *n* (*SCOL*) interne *m/f*, pensionnaire; ~**ing card** *n* = **boarding pass**; ~**ing house** *n* pension *f*; ~**ing pass** *n* (*AVIAT, NAUT*) carte *f* d'embarquement; ~**ing school** *n* internat *m*, pensionnat *m*; ~

room *n* salle *f* du conseil d'administration

boast [bəʊst] *vi*: **to** ~ (**about** *or* **of**) se vanter (de)

boat [bəʊt] *n* bateau *m*; (*small*) canot *m*; barque *f*; ~**er** *n* (*hat*) canotier *m*

bob [bɒb] *vi* (*boat, cork on water: also:* ~ *up and down*) danser, se balancer

bobby ['bɒbɪ] (*BRIT: inf*) *n* ≈ agent *m* (de police)

bobsleigh ['bɒbsleɪ] *n* bob *m*

bode [bəʊd] *vi*: **to** ~ **well/ill (for)** être de bon/mauvais augure (pour)

bodily ['bɒdɪlɪ] *adj* corporel(le) ♦ *adv* dans ses bras

body ['bɒdɪ] *n* corps *m*; (*of car*) carrosserie *f*; (*of plane*) fuselage *m*; (*fig: society*) organe *m*, organisme *m*; (: *quantity*) ensemble *m*, masse *f*; (*of wine*) corps; ~**-building** *n* culturisme *m*; ~**guard** *n* garde *m* du corps; ~**work** *n* carrosserie *f*

bog [bɒg] *n* tourbière *f* ♦ *vt*: **to get** ~**ged down** (*fig*) s'enliser

boggle ['bɒgl] *vi*: **the mind** ~**s** c'est incroyable, on en reste sidéré

bogus ['bəʊgəs] *adj* bidon *inv*; fantôme

boil [bɔɪl] *vt* (faire) bouillir ♦ *vi* bouillir ♦ *n* (*MED*) furoncle *m*; **to come to the** (*BRIT*) ~ *or* **a** (*US*) ~ bouillir; ~ **down to** *vt fus* (*fig*) se réduire *or* ramener à; ~ **over** *vi* déborder; ~**ed egg** *n* œuf *m* à la coque; ~**ed potatoes** *npl* pommes *fpl* à l'anglaise *or* à l'eau; ~**er** *n* chaudière *f*; ~**ing point** *n* point *m* d'ébullition

boisterous ['bɔɪstərəs] *adj* bruyant(e), tapageur(euse)

bold [bəʊld] *adj* hardi(e), audacieux(euse); (*pej*) effronté(e); (*outline, colour*) franc(franche), tranché(e), marqué(e); (*pattern*) grand(e)

bollard ['bɒləd] (*BRIT*) *n* (*AUT*) borne lumineuse *or* de signalisation

bolster up ['bəʊlstə*] *vt* soutenir

bolt [bəʊlt] *n* (*lock*) verrou *m*; (*with nut*) boulon *m* ♦ *adv*: ~ **upright** droit(e) comme un piquet ♦ *vt* verrouiller; (*TECH: also:* ~ **on**, ~ **together**) boulonner; (*food*) engloutir ♦ *vi* (*horse*) s'emballer

bomb [bɒm] *n* bombe *f* ♦ *vt* bombarder

bombastic [bɒm'bæstɪk] *adj* pompeux(euse)

bomb: **~ disposal unit** *n* section *f* de déminage; **~er** *n* (AVIAT) bombardier *m*; **~shell** *n* (*fig*) bombe *f*

bona fide ['bəʊnə'faɪdɪ] *adj* (*traveller*) véritable

bond [bɒnd] *n* lien *m*; (*binding promise*) engagement *m*, obligation *f*; (COMM) obligation *f*; **in ~** (*of goods*) en douane

bondage ['bɒndɪdʒ] *n* esclavage *m*

bone [bəʊn] *n* os *m*; (*of fish*) arête *f* ♦ *vt* désosser; ôter les arêtes de; **~ idle** *adj* fainéant(e); **~ marrow** *n* moelle *f* osseuse

bonfire ['bɒnfaɪə*] *n* feu *m* (de joie); (*for rubbish*) feu

bonnet ['bɒnɪt] *n* bonnet *m*; (BRIT: *of car*) capot *m*

bonus ['bəʊnəs] *n* prime *f*, gratification *f*

bony ['bəʊnɪ] *adj* (*arm, face,* MED: *tissue*) osseux(euse); (*meat*) plein(e) d'os; (*fish*) plein d'arêtes

boo [bu:] *excl* hou!, peuh! ♦ *vt* huer

booby trap ['bu:bɪ-] *n* engin piégé

book [bʊk] *n* livre *m*; (*of stamps, tickets*) carnet *m* ♦ *vt* (*ticket*) prendre; (*seat, room*) réserver; (*driver*) dresser un procès-verbal à; (*football player*) prendre le nom de; **~s** *npl* (*accounts*) comptes *mpl*, comptabilité *f*; **~case** *n* bibliothèque *f* (*meuble*); **~ing office** (BRIT) *n* bureau *m* de location; **~-keeping** *n* comptabilité *f*; **~let** *n* brochure *f*; **~maker** *n* bookmaker *m*; **~seller** *n* libraire *m/f*; **~shop** *n* librairie *f*; **~store** *n* librairie *f*

boom [bu:m] *n* (*noise*) grondement *m*; (*in prices, population*) forte augmentation ♦ *vi* gronder; prospérer

boon [bu:n] *n* bénédiction *f*, grand avantage

boost [bu:st] *n* stimulant *m*, remontant *m* ♦ *vt* stimuler; **~er** *n* (MED) rappel *m*

boot [bu:t] *n* botte *f*; (*for hiking*) chaussure *f* (de marche); (*for football etc*) soulier *m*; (BRIT: *of car*) coffre *m* ♦ *vt* (COMPUT) amorcer, initialiser; **to ~** (*in addition*) par-dessus le marché

booth [bu:ð] *n* (*at fair*) baraque (foraine); (*telephone etc*) cabine *f*; (*also: voting ~*) isoloir *m*

booty ['bu:tɪ] *n* butin *m*

booze [bu:z] (*inf*) *n* boissons *fpl* alcooliques, alcool *m*

border ['bɔːdə*] *n* bordure *f*; bord *m*; (*of a country*) frontière *f* ♦ *vt* border; (*also: ~ on: country*) être limitrophe de; **B~s** (GEO): **the B~s** *la région frontière entre l'Ecosse et l'Angleterre*; **~ on** *vt fus* être voisin(e) de, toucher à; **~line** *n* (*fig*) ligne *f* de démarcation; **~line case** *n* cas *m* limite

bore [bɔː*] *pt of* **bear** ♦ *vt* (*hole*) percer; (*oil well, tunnel*) creuser; (*person*) ennuyer, raser ♦ *n* raseur(euse); (*of gun*) calibre *m*; **to be ~d** s'ennuyer; **~dom** *n* ennui *m*; **boring** *adj* ennuyeux(euse)

born [bɔːn] *adj*: **to be ~** naître; **I was ~ in 1960** je suis né en 1960

borne [bɔːn] *pp of* **bear**

borough ['bʌrə] *n* municipalité *f*

borrow ['bɒrəʊ] *vt*: **to ~ sth (from sb)** emprunter qch (à qn)

Bosnia (and) Herzegovina ['bɒznɪə (ənd) hɜːtsəɡəʊ'viːnə] *n* Bosnie-Herzégovine *f*

bosom ['bʊzəm] *n* poitrine *f*; (*fig*) sein *m*; **~ friend** *n* ami(e) intime

boss [bɒs] *n* patron(ne) ♦ *vt* (*also: ~ around/about*) commander; **~y** *adj* autoritaire

bosun ['bəʊsn] *n* maître *m* d'équipage

botany ['bɒtənɪ] *n* botanique *f*

botch [bɒtʃ] *vt* (*also: ~ up*) saboter, bâcler

both [bəʊθ] *adj* les deux, l'un(e) et l'autre ♦ *pron*: **~ (of them)** les deux, tous(toutes) (les) deux, l'un(e) et l'autre; **they sell ~ the fabric and the finished curtains** ils vendent (et) le tissu et les rideaux (finis), ils vendent à la fois le tissu et les rideaux (finis); **~ of us went, we ~ went** nous y sommes allés (tous) les deux

bother ['bɒðə*] *vt* (*worry*) tracasser; (*disturb*) déranger ♦ *vi* (*also: ~ o.s.*) se tracasser, se faire du souci ♦ *n*: **it is a ~**

to have to do c'est vraiment ennuyeux d'avoir à faire; **it's no** ~ aucun problème; **to ~ doing** prendre la peine de faire

bottle ['bɒtl] *n* bouteille *f*; (*baby's*) biberon *m* ♦ *vt* mettre en bouteille(s); ~ **up** *vt* refouler, contenir; ~ **bank** *n* conteneur *m* à verre; ~**neck** *n* étranglement *m*; ~-**opener** *n* ouvre-bouteille *m*

bottom ['bɒtəm] *n* (*of container, sea etc*) fond *m*; (*buttocks*) derrière *m*; (*of page, list*) bas *m* ♦ du fond; du bas; **the ~ of the class** le dernier de la classe; ~**less** *adj* (*funds*) inépuisable

bough [baʊ] *n* branche *f*, rameau *m*

bought [bɔːt] *pt, pp of* **buy**

boulder ['bəʊldə*] *n* gros rocher

bounce [baʊns] *vi* (*ball*) rebondir; (*cheque*) être refusé(e) (*étant sans provision*) ♦ *vt* faire rebondir ♦ *n* (*rebound*) rebond *m*; ~**r** (*inf*) *n* (*at dance, club*) videur *m*

bound [baʊnd] *pt, pp of* **bind** ♦ *n* (*gen pl*) limite *f*; (*leap*) bond *m* ♦ *vi* (*leap*) bondir ♦ *vt* (*limit*) borner ♦ *adj*: **to be ~ to do sth** (*obliged*) être obligé(e) *or* avoir obligation de faire qch; **he's ~ to fail** (*likely*) il est sûr d'échouer, son échec est inévitable *or* assuré; ~ **by** (*law, regulation*) engagé(e) par; ~ **for** à destination de; **out of** ~**s** dont l'accès est interdit

boundary ['baʊndərɪ] *n* frontière *f*

boundless ['baʊndlɪs] *adj* sans bornes

bout [baʊt] *n* période *f*; (*of malaria etc*) accès *m*, crise *f*, attaque *f*; (*BOXING etc*) combat *m*, match *m*

bow¹ [bəʊ] *n* nœud *m*; (*weapon*) arc *m*; (*MUS*) archet *m*

bow² [baʊ] *n* (*with body*) révérence *f*, inclination *f* (*du buste or corps*); (*NAUT: also*: ~**s**) proue *f* ♦ *vi* faire une révérence, s'incliner; (*yield*): **to ~ to** *or* **before** s'incliner devant, se soumettre à

bowels [baʊəlz] *npl* intestins *mpl*; (*fig*) entrailles *fpl*

bowl [bəʊl] *n* (*for eating*) bol *m*; (*ball*) boule *f* ♦ *vi* (*CRICKET, BASEBALL*) lancer (la balle)

bow-legged ['bəʊ'legɪd] *adj* aux jambes arquées

bowler ['bəʊlə*] *n* (*CRICKET, BASEBALL*) lanceur *m* (*de la balle*); (*BRIT: also*: ~ *hat*) (chapeau *m*) melon *m*

bowling ['bəʊlɪŋ] *n* (*game*) jeu *m* de boules; jeu *m* de quilles; ~ **alley** *n* bowling *m*; ~ **green** *n* terrain *m* de boules (*gazonné et carré*)

bowls [bəʊlz] *n* (*game*) (jeu *m* de) boules *fpl*

bow tie ['bəʊ-] *n* nœud *m* papillon

box [bɒks] *n* boîte *f*; (*also*: *cardboard* ~) carton *m*; (*THEATRE*) loge *f* ♦ *vt* mettre en boîte; (*SPORT*) boxer avec ♦ *vi* boxer, faire de la boxe; ~**er** *n* (*person*) boxeur *m*; ~**ing** *n* (*SPORT*) boxe *f*; **B~ing Day** (*BRIT*) *n* le lendemain de Noël; ~**ing gloves** *npl* gants *mpl* de boxe; ~**ing ring** *n* ring *m*; ~ **office** *n* bureau *m* de location; ~**room** *n* débarras *m*; chambrette *f*

boy [bɔɪ] *n* garçon *m*

boycott ['bɔɪkɒt] *n* boycottage *m* ♦ *vt* boycotter

boyfriend ['bɔɪfrend] *n* (petit) ami

boyish ['bɔɪɪʃ] *adj* (*behaviour*) de garçon; (*girl*) garçonnier(ière)

BR *abbr* = **British Rail**

bra [brɑː] *n* soutien-gorge *m*

brace [breɪs] *n* (*on teeth*) appareil *m* (dentaire); (*tool*) vilbrequin *m* ♦ *vt* (*knees, shoulders*) appuyer; ~**s** *npl* (*BRIT: for trousers*) bretelles *fpl*; **to ~ o.s.** (*lit*) s'arc-bouter; (*fig*) se préparer mentalement

bracelet ['breɪslɪt] *n* bracelet *m*

bracing ['breɪsɪŋ] *adj* tonifiant(e), tonique

bracket ['brækɪt] *n* (*TECH*) tasseau *m*, support *m*; (*group*) classe *f*, tranche *f*; (*also*: *brace* ~) accolade *f*; (: *round* ~) parenthèse *f*; (: *square* ~) crochet *m* ♦ *vt* mettre entre parenthèse(s); (*fig: also*: ~ *together*) regrouper

brag [bræg] *vi* se vanter

braid [breɪd] *n* (*trimming*) galon *m*; (*of hair*) tresse *f*

brain [breɪn] *n* cerveau *m*; ~**s** *npl* (*intellect, CULIN*) cervelle *f*; **he's got ~s** il est intelligent; **~child** *n* invention personnelle; **~wash** *vt* faire subir un lavage de cerveau à; **~wave** *n* idée géniale; **~y** *adj* intelligent(e), doué(e)

braise [breɪz] *vt* braiser

brake [breɪk] *n* (*on vehicle, also fig*) frein *m* ♦ *vi* freiner; **~ fluid** *n* liquide *m* de freins; **~ light** *n* feu *m* de stop

bran [bræn] *n* son *m*

branch [brɑːntʃ] *n* branche *f*; (*COMM*) succursale *f* ♦ *vi* bifurquer; **~ out** *vi* (*fig*): **to ~ out** into étendre ses activités à

brand [brænd] *n* marque (commerciale) ♦ *vt* (*cattle*) marquer (au fer rouge); **~new** *adj* tout(e) neuf(neuve), flambant neuf(neuve)

brandy ['brændɪ] *n* cognac *m*, fine *f*

brash [bræʃ] *adj* effronté(e)

brass [brɑːs] *n* cuivre *m* (jaune), laiton *m*; **the ~** (*MUS*) les cuivres; **~ band** *n* fanfare *f*

brassière ['bræsɪə*] *n* soutien-gorge *m*

brat [bræt] *n* (*pej*) mioche *m/f*, môme *m/f*

brave [breɪv] *adj* courageux(euse), brave ♦ *n* guerrier indien ♦ *vt* braver, affronter; **~ry** ['breɪvərɪ] *n* bravoure *f*, courage *m*

brawl [brɔːl] *n* rixe *f*, bagarre *f*

bray [breɪ] *vi* braire

brazen ['breɪzn] *adj* impudent(e), effronté(e) ♦ *vt*: **to ~ it out** payer d'effronterie, crâner

brazier ['breɪzɪə*] *n* brasero *m*

Brazil [brə'zɪl] *n* Brésil *m*

breach [briːtʃ] *vt* ouvrir une brèche dans ♦ *n* (*gap*) brèche *f*; (*breaking*): **~ of contract** rupture *f* de contrat; **~ of the peace** attentat *m* à l'ordre public

bread [brɛd] *n* pain *m*; **~ and butter** *n* tartines (beurrées); (*fig*) subsistance *f*; **~bin** (*BRIT*) *n* boîte *f* à pain; (*bigger*) huche *f* à pain; **~box** (*US*) *n* = **~bin**; **~crumbs** *npl* miettes *fpl* de pain; (*CULIN*) chapelure *f*, panure *f*; **~line** *n*: **to be on the ~line** être sans le sou *or* dans l'indigence

breadth [brɛtθ] *n* largeur *f*; (*fig*) ampleur *f*

breadwinner ['brɛdwɪnə*] *n* soutien *m* de famille

break [breɪk] (*pt* **broke**, *pp* **broken**) *vt* casser, briser; (*promise*) rompre; (*law*) violer ♦ *vi* (se) casser, se briser; (*weather*) tourner; (*story, news*) se répandre; (*day*) se lever ♦ *n* (*gap*) brèche *f*; (*fracture*) cassure *f*; (*pause, interval*) interruption *f*, arrêt *m*; (: *short*) pause *f*; (: *at school*) récréation *f*; (*chance*) chance *f*, occasion *f* favorable; **to ~ one's leg** *etc* se casser la jambe *etc*; **to ~ a record** battre un record; **to ~ the news to sb** annoncer la nouvelle à qn; **~ even** rentrer dans ses frais; **~ free** *or* **loose** se dégager, s'échapper; **~ open** (*door etc*) forcer, fracturer; **~ down** *vt* (*figures, data*) décomposer, analyser ♦ *vi* s'effondrer; (*MED*) faire une dépression (nerveuse); (*AUT*) tomber en panne; **~ in** *vt* (*horse etc*) dresser ♦ *vi* (*burglar*) entrer par effraction; (*interrupt*) interrompre; **~ into** *vt fus* (*house*) s'introduire *or* pénétrer par effraction dans; **~ off** *vi* (*speaker*) s'interrompre; (*branch*) se rompre; **~ out** *vi* éclater, se déclarer; (*prisoner*) s'évader; **to ~ out in spots** *or* **a rash** avoir une éruption de boutons; **~ up** *vi* (*ship*) se disloquer; (*crowd, meeting*) se disperser, se séparer; (*marriage*) se briser; (*SCOL*) entrer en vacances ♦ *vt* casser; (*fight etc*) interrompre, faire cesser; **~age** *n* casse *f*; **~down** *n* (*AUT*) panne *f*; (*in communications, marriage*) rupture *f*; (*MED: also:* **nervous ~down**) dépression (nerveuse); (*of statistics*) ventilation *f*; **~down van** (*BRIT*) *n* dépanneuse *f*; **~er** *n* brisant *m*

breakfast ['brɛkfəst] *n* petit déjeuner *m*

break: **~-in** *n* cambriolage *m*; **~ing and entering** *n* (*LAW*) effraction *f*; **~through** *n* percée *f*; **~water** *n* brise-lames *m inv*, digue *f*

breast [brɛst] *n* (*of woman*) sein *m*; (*chest, of meat*) poitrine *f*; **~-feed** (*irreg: like* **feed**) *vt, vi* allaiter; **~stroke** *n* brasse *f*

breath [brɛθ] *n* haleine *f*; **out of ~** à bout de souffle, essoufflé(e)

Breathalyser ['breθəlaɪzə*'] ® n Alcootest m ®

breathe [briːð] vt, vi respirer; ~ **in** vt, vi aspirer, inspirer; ~ **out** vt, vi expirer; ~**r** n moment m de repos or de répit; **breathing** ['briːðɪŋ] n respiration f; **breathing space** n (fig) (moment m de) répit m

breathless ['breθlɪs] adj essoufflé(e), haletant(e); oppressé(e)

breathtaking ['breθteɪkɪŋ] adj stupéfiant(e), à vous couper le souffle

breed [briːd] (pt, pp **bred**) vt élever, faire l'élevage de ♦ vi se reproduire ♦ n race f, variété f; ~**ing** n (upbringing) éducation f

breeze [briːz] n brise f; **breezy** ['briːzɪ] adj frais(fraîche); aéré(e); (manner etc) désinvolte, jovial(e)

brevity ['brevɪtɪ] n brièveté f

brew [bruː] vt (tea) faire infuser; (beer) brasser ♦ vi (fig) se préparer, couver; ~**ery** n brasserie f (fabrique)

bribe ['braɪb] n pot-de-vin m ♦ vt acheter; soudoyer; ~**ry** ['braɪbərɪ] n corruption f

brick [brɪk] n brique f; ~**layer** n maçon m

bridal ['braɪdl] adj nuptial(e)

bride [braɪd] n mariée f, épouse f; ~**groom** n marié m, époux m; ~**smaid** n demoiselle f d'honneur

bridge [brɪdʒ] n pont m; (NAUT) passerelle f (de commandement); (of nose) arête f; (CARDS, DENTISTRY) bridge m ♦ vt (fig: gap, gulf) combler

bridle ['braɪdl] n bride f; ~ **path** n piste or allée cavalière

brief [briːf] adj bref(brève) ♦ n (LAW) dossier m, cause f; (gen) tâche f ♦ vt mettre au courant; ~**s** npl (undergarment) slip m; ~**case** n serviette f; porte-documents m inv; ~**ly** adv brièvement

bright [braɪt] adj brillant(e); (room, weather) clair(e); (clever: person, idea) intelligent(e); (cheerful: colour, person) vif(vive)

brighten (also ~ **up**) vt (room) éclaircir, égayer; (event) égayer ♦ vi s'éclair-

cir; (person) retrouver un peu de sa gaieté; (face) s'éclairer; (prospects) s'améliorer

brilliance ['brɪljəns] n éclat m

brilliant ['brɪljənt] adj brillant(e); (sunshine, light) éclatant(e); (inf: holiday etc) super

brim [brɪm] n bord m

brine [braɪn] n (CULIN) saumure f

bring [brɪŋ] (pt, pp **brought**) vt apporter; (person) amener; ~ **about** vt provoquer, entraîner; ~ **back** vt rapporter; (restore: hanging) réinstaurer; ~ **down** vt (price) faire baisser; (enemy plane) descendre; (government) faire tomber; ~ **forward** vt avancer; ~ **off** vt (task, plan) réussir, mener à bien; ~ **out** vt (meaning) faire ressortir; (book) publier; (object) sortir; ~ **round** vt (unconscious person) ranimer; ~ **to** vt = ~ **round**; ~ **up** vt (child) élever; (carry up) monter; (question) soulever; (food: vomit) vomir, rendre

brink [brɪŋk] n bord m

brisk [brɪsk] adj vif(vive)

bristle ['brɪsl] n poil m ♦ vi se hérisser

Britain ['brɪtən] n (also: Great ~) Grande-Bretagne f

British ['brɪtɪʃ] adj britannique ♦ npl: **the** ~ les Britanniques mpl; ~ **Isles** npl: **the** ~ **Isles** les Iles fpl Britanniques; ~ **Rail** n compagnie ferroviaire britannique

Briton ['brɪtən] n Britannique m/f

Brittany ['brɪtənɪ] n Bretagne f

brittle ['brɪtl] adj cassant(e), fragile

broach [brəʊtʃ] vt (subject) aborder

broad [brɔːd] adj large; (general: outlines) grand(e); (: distinction) général(e); (accent) prononcé(e); **in** ~ **daylight** en plein jour; ~**cast** (pt, pp ~**cast**) n émission f ♦ vt radiodiffuser; téléviser ♦ vi émettre; ~**en** vt élargir ♦ vi s'élargir; **to** ~**en one's mind** élargir ses horizons; ~**ly** adv en gros, généralement; ~**minded** adj large d'esprit

broccoli ['brɒkəlɪ] n brocoli m

brochure ['brəʊʃʊə*'] n prospectus m, dépliant m

broil [brɔɪl] *vt* griller

broke [brəʊk] *pt of* **break** ♦ *adj* (*inf*) fauché(e)

broken ['brəʊkən] *pp of* **break** ♦ *adj* cassé(e), (*machine: also:* ~ **down**) fichu(e); **in ~ English/French** dans un anglais/français approximatif *or* hésitant; ~ **leg** *etc* jambe *etc* cassée; **~-hearted** *adj* (ayant) le cœur brisé

broker ['brəʊkə*] *n* courtier *m*

brolly ['brɒlɪ] (*BRIT: inf*) *n* pépin *m*, parapluie *m*

bronchitis [brɒŋ'kaɪtɪs] *n* bronchite *f*

bronze [brɒnz] *n* bronze *m*

brooch [brəʊtʃ] *n* broche *f*

brood [bru:d] *n* couvée *f* ♦ *vi* (*person*) méditer (sombrement), ruminer

broom [bru:m] *n* balai *m*; (*BOT*) genêt *m*; **~stick** *n* manche *m* à balai

Bros. *abbr* = **Brothers**

broth [brɒθ] *n* bouillon *m* de viande et de légumes

brothel ['brɒθl] *n* maison close, bordel *m*

brother ['brʌðə*] *n* frère *m*; **~-in-law** *n* beau-frère *m*

brought [brɔ:t] *pt, pp of* **bring**

brow [braʊ] *n* front *m*; (*eye~*) sourcil *m*; (*of hill*) sommet *m*

brown [braʊn] *adj* brun(e), marron *inv*; (*hair*) châtain *inv*; brun; (*eyes*) marron *inv*; (*tanned*) bronzé(e) ♦ *n* (*colour*) brun *m* ♦ *vt* (*CULIN*) faire dorer; **~ bread** *n* pain *m* bis; **B~ie** ['braʊnɪ] *n* (*also: B~ie Guide*) jeannette *f*, éclaireuse (cadette); **~ie** (*US*) *n* (*cake*) gâteau *m* au chocolat et aux noix; **~ paper** *n* papier *m* d'emballage; **~ sugar** *n* cassonade *f*

browse [braʊz] *vi* (*among books*) bouquiner, feuilleter les livres; **to ~ through a book** feuilleter un livre

bruise [bru:z] *n* bleu *m*, contusion *f* ♦ *vt* contusionner, meurtrir

brunette [bru:'net] *n* (femme) brune

brunt [brʌnt] *n*: **the ~ of** (*attack, criticism etc*) le plus gros de

brush [brʌʃ] *n* brosse *f*; (*painting*) pinceau *m*; (*shaving*) blaireau *m*; (*quarrel*) accrochage *m*, prise *f* de bec ♦ *vt* brosser; (*also:* ~ *against*) effleurer, frôler; ~

aside *vt* écarter, balayer; ~ **up** *vt* (*knowledge*) rafraîchir, réviser; **~wood** *n* broussailles *fpl*, taillis *m*

Brussels ['brʌslz] *n* Bruxelles; ~ **sprout** *n* chou de Bruxelles

brutal ['bru:tl] *adj* brutal(e)

brute [bru:t] *n* brute *f* ♦ *adj*: **by ~ force** par la force

BSc *abbr* = **Bachelor of Science**

BSE *n abbr* (= *bovine spongiform encephalopathy*) ESB *f*, BSE *f*

bubble ['bʌbl] *n* bulle *f* ♦ *vi* bouillonner, faire des bulles; (*sparkle*) pétiller; ~ **bath** *n* bain moussant; ~ **gum** *n* bubble-gum *m*

buck [bʌk] *n* mâle *m* (*d'un lapin, daim etc*); (*US: inf*) dollar *m* ♦ *vi* ruer, lancer une ruade; **to pass the ~ (to sb)** se décharger de la responsabilité (sur qn); ~ **up** *vi* (*cheer up*) reprendre du poil de la bête, se remonter

bucket ['bʌkɪt] *n* seau *m*

buckle ['bʌkl] *n* boucle *f* ♦ *vt* (*belt etc*) boucler, attacher ♦ *vi* (*warp*) tordre, gauchir; (: *wheel*) se voiler; se déformer

bud [bʌd] *n* bourgeon *m*, (*of flower*) bouton *m* ♦ *vi* bourgeonner; (*flower*) éclore

Buddhism ['bʊdɪzəm] *n* bouddhisme *m*

budding ['bʌdɪŋ] *adj* (*poet etc*) en herbe; (*passion etc*) naissant(e)

buddy ['bʌdɪ] (*US*) *n* copain *m*

budge [bʌdʒ] *vt* faire bouger; (*fig: person*) faire changer d'avis ♦ *vi* bouger; changer d'avis

budgerigar ['bʌdʒərɪgɑ:*] (*BRIT*) *n* perruche *f*

budget ['bʌdʒɪt] *n* budget *m* ♦ *vi*: **to ~ for sth** inscrire qch au budget

budgie ['bʌdʒɪ] (*BRIT*) *n* = **budgerigar**

buff [bʌf] *adj* (couleur *f*) chamois *m* ♦ *n* (*inf: enthusiast*) mordu(e); **he's a ...** c'est un mordu de ...

buffalo ['bʌfələʊ] (*pl* ~ *or* ~**es**) *n* buffle *m*; (*US*) bison *m*

buffer ['bʌfə*] *n* tampon *m*; (*COMPUT*) mémoire *f* tampon

buffet[1] ['bʌfɪt] *vt* secouer, ébranler

buffet[2] ['bufeɪ] *n* (*food, BRIT: bar*) buffet *m*; ~ **car** (*BRIT*) *n* (*RAIL*) voiture-buffet *f*

bug [bʌg] n (*insect*) punaise f; (: *gen*) insecte m, bestiole f; (*fig: germ*) virus m, microbe m; (*COMPUT*) erreur f; (*fig: spy device*) dispositif m d'écoute (électronique) ♦ vt garnir de dispositifs d'écoute; (*inf: annoy*) embêter

bugle ['bju:gl] n clairon m

build [bɪld] n (*of person*) carrure f, charpente f ♦ vt construire, bâtir; ~ **up** vt accumuler, amasser; accroître; **~er** n entrepreneur m; **~ing** n (*trade*) construction f; (*house, structure*) bâtiment m, construction; (*offices, flats*) immeuble m; **~ing society** (*BRIT*) n société f de crédit immobilier

built [bɪlt] pt, pp of **build**; **~-in** adj (*cupboard, oven*) encastré(e); (*device*) incorporé(e); intégré(e); **~-up area** n zone urbanisée

bulb [bʌlb] n (*BOT*) bulbe m, oignon m; (*ELEC*) ampoule f

bulge [bʌldʒ] n renflement m, gonflement m ♦ vi (*pocket, file etc*) être plein(e) à craquer; (*cheeks*) être gonflé(e)

bulk [bʌlk] n masse f, volume m; (*of person*) corpulence f; **in ~** (*COMM*) en vrac; **the ~ of** la plus grande or grosse partie de; **~y** adj volumineux(euse), encombrant(e)

bull [bʊl] n taureau m; (*male elephant/whale*) mâle m; **~dog** n bouledogue m

bulldozer ['bʊldəʊzə*] n bulldozer m

bullet ['bʊlɪt] n balle f (*de fusil etc*)

bulletin ['bʊlɪtɪn] n bulletin m, communiqué m; (*news ~*) (bulletin d')informations fpl

bulletproof ['bʊlɪtpru:f] adj (*car*) blindé(e); (*vest etc*) pare-balles inv

bullfight ['bʊlfaɪt] n corrida f, course f de taureaux; **~er** n torero m; **~ing** n tauromachie f

bullion ['bʊlɪən] n or m or argent m en lingots

bullock ['bʊlək] n bœuf m

bullring ['bʊlrɪŋ] n arènes fpl

bull's-eye ['bʊlzaɪ] n centre m (*de la cible*)

bully ['bʊlɪ] n brute f, tyran m ♦ vt tyranniser, rudoyer

bum [bʌm] n (*inf: backside*) derrière m; (*esp US: tramp*) vagabond(e), traîne-savates m/f inv

bumblebee ['bʌmblbi:] n bourdon m

bump [bʌmp] n (*in car: minor accident*) accrochage m; (*jolt*) cahot m; (*on road etc, on head*) bosse f ♦ vt heurter, cogner; **~ into** vt fus rentrer dans, tamponner; (*meet*) tomber sur; **~er** n pare-chocs m inv ♦ adj: **~er crop/harvest** récolte/moisson exceptionnelle

bumpy ['bʌmpɪ] adj cahoteux(euse)

bun [bʌn] n petit pain au lait; (*of hair*) chignon m

bunch [bʌntʃ] n (*of flowers*) bouquet m; (*of keys*) trousseau m; (*of bananas*) régime m; (*of people*) groupe m; **~es** npl (*in hair*) couettes fpl; **~ of grapes** grappe f de raisin

bundle ['bʌndl] n paquet m ♦ vt (*also: ~ up*) faire un paquet de; (*put*): **to ~ sth/sb into** fourrer or enfourner qch/qn dans

bungalow ['bʌŋgələʊ] n bungalow m

bungle ['bʌŋgl] vt bâcler, gâcher

bunion ['bʌnjən] n oignon m (*au pied*)

bunk [bʌŋk] n couchette f; **~ beds** npl lits superposés

bunker ['bʌŋkə*] n (*coal store*) soute f à charbon; (*MIL, GOLF*) bunker m

bunny ['bʌnɪ] n (*also: ~ rabbit*) Jeannot m lapin

bunting ['bʌntɪŋ] n pavoisement m, drapeaux mpl

buoy [bɔɪ] n bouée f; **~ up** vt faire flotter; (*fig*) soutenir, épauler; **~ant** adj capable de flotter; (*carefree*) gai(e), plein(e) d'entrain; (*economy*) ferme, actif

burden ['bɜ:dn] n fardeau m ♦ vt (*trouble*) accabler, surcharger

bureau ['bjʊərəʊ] n (pl ~x) n (*BRIT: writing desk*) bureau m, secrétaire m; (*US: chest of drawers*) commode f; (*office*) bureau, office m; **~cracy** [bjʊ'rɒkrəsɪ] n bureaucratie f

burglar ['bɜ:glə*] n cambrioleur m; **~ alarm** n sonnerie f d'alarme; **~y** n cambriolage m

Burgundy ['bɜ:gəndɪ] n Bourgogne f

burial ['berɪəl] *n* enterrement *m*
burly ['bɜːlɪ] *adj* de forte carrure, costaud(e)
Burma ['bɜːmə] *n* Birmanie *f*
burn [bɜːn] (*pt, pp* **burned** *or* **burnt**) *vt, vi* brûler ♦ *n* brûlure *f*; ~ **down** *vt* incendier, détruire par le feu; ~**er** *n* brûleur *m*; ~**ing** *adj* brûlant(e); (*house*) en flammes; (*ambition*) dévorant(e)
burrow ['bʌrəʊ] *n* terrier *m* ♦ *vt* creuser
bursary ['bɜːsərɪ] (*BRIT*) *n* bourse *f* (d'études)
burst [bɜːst] (*pt, pp* **burst**) *vt* crever; faire éclater; (*subj: river: banks etc*) rompre ♦ *vi* éclater; (*tyre*) crever ♦ *n* (*of gunfire*) rafale *f* (de tir); (*also:* ~ *pipe*) rupture *f*; fuite *f*; **a** ~ **of enthusiasm/ energy** un accès d'enthousiasme/ d'énergie; **to** ~ **into flames** s'enflammer soudainement; **to** ~ **out laughing** éclater de rire; **to** ~ **into tears** fondre en larmes; **to be** ~**ing with** être plein (à craquer) de; (*fig*) être débordant(e) de; ~ **into** *vt fus* (*room etc*) faire irruption dans
bury ['berɪ] *vt* enterrer
bus [bʌs, *pl* -ɪz] (*pl* ~**es**) *n* autobus *m*
bush [bʊʃ] *n* buisson *m*; (*scrubland*) brousse *f*; **to beat about the** ~ tourner autour du pot; ~**y** ['bʊʃɪ] *adj* broussailleux(euse), touffu(e)
busily ['bɪzɪlɪ] *adv* activement
business ['bɪznɪs] *n* (*matter, firm*) affaire *f*; (*trading*) affaires *fpl*; (*job, duty*) travail *m*; **to be away on** ~ être en déplacement d'affaires; **it's none of my** ~ cela ne me regarde pas, ce ne sont pas mes affaires; **he means** ~ il n'est pas plaisante, il est sérieux; ~**like** *adj* sérieux(euse); efficace; ~**man** (*irreg*) *n* homme *m* d'affaires; ~ **trip** *n* voyage *m* d'affaires; ~**woman** (*irreg*) *n* femme *f* d'affaires
busker ['bʌskə*] (*BRIT*) *n* musicien ambulant
bus stop *n* arrêt *m* d'autobus
bust [bʌst] *n* buste *m*; (*measurement*) tour *m* de poitrine ♦ *adj* (*inf: broken*) fichu(e), fini(e); **to go** ~ faire faillite

bustle ['bʌsl] *n* remue-ménage *m*, affairement *m* ♦ *vi* s'affairer, se démener; **bustling** *adj* (*town*) bruyant(e), affairé(e)
busy ['bɪzɪ] *adj* occupé(e); (*shop, street*) très fréquenté(e) ♦ *vt*: **to** ~ **o.s.** s'occuper; ~**body** *n* mouche *f* du coche, âme *f* charitable; ~ **signal** (*US*) *n* (*TEL*) tonalité *f* occupé *inv*

but [bʌt] *conj* mais; **I'd love to come,** ~ **I'm busy** j'aimerais venir mais je suis occupé
♦ *prep* (*apart from, except*) sauf, excepté; **we've had nothing** ~ **trouble** nous n'avons eu que des ennuis; **no-one** ~ **him can do it** lui seul peut le faire; ~ **for you/your help** sans toi/ton aide; **anything** ~ **that** tout mais pas ça
♦ *adv* (*just, only*) ne ... que; **she's** ~ **a child** elle n'est qu'une enfant; **had I** ~ **known** si seulement j'avais su; **all** ~ **finished** pratiquement terminé

butcher ['bʊtʃə*] *n* boucher *m* ♦ *vt* massacrer; (*cattle etc for meat*) tuer; ~**'s (shop)** *n* boucherie *f*
butler ['bʌtlə*] *n* maître *m* d'hôtel
butt [bʌt] *n* (*large barrel*) gros tonneau; (*of gun*) crosse *f*; (*of cigarette*) mégot *m*; (*BRIT: fig: target*) cible *f* ♦ *vt* donner un coup de tête à; ~ **in** *vi* (*interrupt*) s'immiscer dans la conversation
butter ['bʌtə*] *n* beurre *m* ♦ *vt* beurrer; ~**cup** *n* bouton d'or; ~**fly** *n* papillon *m*; (*SWIMMING: also:* ~*fly stroke*) brasse *f* papillon
buttocks ['bʌtəks] *npl* fesses *fpl*
button ['bʌtn] *n* bouton *m*; (*US: badge*) pin *m* ♦ *vt* (*also:* ~ *up*) boutonner ♦ *vi* se boutonner
buttress ['bʌtrɪs] *n* contrefort *m*
buxom ['bʌksəm] *adj* aux formes avantageuses *or* épanouies
buy [baɪ] (*pt, pp* **bought**) *vt* acheter ♦ *n* achat *m*; **to** ~ **sb sth/sth from sb** acheter qch à qn; **to** ~ **sb a drink** offrir un verre *or* à boire à qn; ~**er** *n* ache-

teur(euse)

buzz [bʌz] n bourdonnement m; (inf: phone call): **to give sb a ~** passer un coup m de fil à qn ♦ vi bourdonner; **~er** ['bʌzə*] n timbre m électrique; **~ word** (inf) n mot m à la mode

KEYWORD

by [baɪ] prep 1 (referring to cause, agent) par, de; **killed ~ lightning** tué par la foudre; **surrounded ~ a fence** entouré d'une barrière; **a painting ~ Picasso** un tableau de Picasso

2 (referring to method, manner, means): **~ bus/car** en autobus/voiture; **~ train** par le or en train; **to pay ~ cheque** payer par chèque; **~ saving hard, he ...** à force d'économiser, il ...

3 (via, through) par; **we came ~ Dover** nous sommes venus par Douvres

4 (close to, past) à côté de; **the house ~ the school** la maison à côté de l'école; **a holiday ~ the sea** des vacances au bord de la mer; **she sat ~ his bed** elle était assise à son chevet; **she went ~ me** elle est passée à côté de moi; **I go ~ the post office every day** je passe devant la poste tous les jours

5 (with time: not later than) avant; (: during): **~ daylight** à la lumière du jour; **~ night** la nuit, de nuit; **~ 4 o'clock** avant 4 heures; **~ this time tomorrow** d'ici demain à la même heure; **~ the time I got here it was too late** lorsque je suis arrivé il était déjà trop tard

6 (amount) à; **~ the kilo/metre** au kilo/au mètre; **paid ~ the hour** payé à l'heure

7 (MATH, measure): **to divide/multiply ~ 3** diviser/multiplier par 3; **a room 3 metres ~ 4** une pièce de 3 mètres sur 4; **it's broader ~ a metre** c'est plus large d'un mètre; **one ~ one** un à un; **little ~ little** petit à petit, peu à peu

8 (according to) d'après, selon; **it's 3 o'clock ~ my watch** il est 3 heures à ma montre; **it's all right ~ me** je n'ai rien contre

9: (all) **~ oneself** etc tout(e) seul(e)

10: **~ the way** au fait, à propos

♦ adv 1 see go; pass etc

2: **~ and ~** un peu plus tard, bientôt; **~ and large** dans l'ensemble

bye(-bye) ['baɪ('baɪ)] excl au revoir!, salut!

by(e)-law ['baɪlɔː] n arrêté municipal

by: **~-election** (BRIT) n élection (législative) partielle; **~gone** adj passé(e) ♦ n: **let ~gones be ~gones** passons l'éponge, oublions le passé; **~pass** n (route f de) contournement m; (MED) pontage m ♦ vt éviter; **~-product** n sous-produit m, dérivé m; (fig) conséquence f secondaire, retombée f; **~stander** ['baɪstændə*] n spectateur(trice), badaud(e)

byte [baɪt] n (COMPUT) octet m

byword ['baɪwɜːd] n: **to be a ~ for** être synonyme de (fig)

by-your-leave ['baɪjɔː'liːv] n: **without so much as a ~** sans même demander la permission

C c

C [siː] n (MUS) do m

CA abbr = chartered accountant

cab [kæb] n taxi m; (of train, truck) cabine f

cabaret ['kæbəreɪ] n (show) spectacle m de cabaret

cabbage ['kæbɪdʒ] n chou m

cabin ['kæbɪn] n (house) cabane f, hutte f; (on ship) cabine f; (on plane) compartiment m; **~ cruiser** n cruiser m

cabinet ['kæbɪnɪt] n (POL) cabinet m; (furniture) petit meuble à tiroirs et rayons; (also: display ~) vitrine f, petite armoire vitrée

cable ['keɪbl] n câble m ♦ vt câbler, télégraphier; **~-car** n téléphérique m; **~ television** n télévision f par câble

cache [kæʃ] n stock m

cackle ['kækl] vi caqueter

cactus ['kæktəs, pl-taɪ] (pl **cacti**) n cactus m

cadet [kə'det] n (MIL) élève m officier

cadge [kædʒ] (*inf*) *vt*: **to ~ (from** *or* **off)** se faire donner (par)

café ['kæfɪ] *n* ≈ café(-restaurant) *m* (*sans alcool*)

cage [keɪdʒ] *n* cage *f*

cagey ['keɪdʒɪ] (*inf*) *adj* réticent(e), méfiant(e)

cagoule [kə'guːl] *n* K-way *m* (®)

cajole [kə'dʒəʊl] *vt* couvrir de flatteries *or* de gentillesses

cake [keɪk] *n* gâteau *m*; **~ of soap** savonnette *f*; **~d** *adj*: **~d with** raidi(e) par, couvert(e) d'une croûte de

calculate ['kælkjʊleɪt] *vt* calculer; (*estimate: chances, effect*) évaluer; **calculation** [kælkjʊ'leɪʃən] *n* calcul *m*; **calculator** *n* machine *f* à calculer, calculatrice *f*; (*pocket*) calculette *f*

calendar ['kælɪndə*] *n* calendrier *m*; **~ year** *n* année civile

calf [kɑːf] (*pl* **calves**) *n* (*of cow*) veau *m*; (*of other animals*) petit *m*; (*also: ~skin*) veau *m*, vachette *f*; (*ANAT*) mollet *m*

calibre ['kælɪbə*] (*US* **caliber**) *n* calibre *m*

call [kɔːl] *vt* appeler; (*meeting*) convoquer ♦ *vi* appeler; (*visit: also:* **~ in**, **~ round**) passer ♦ *n* (*shout*) appel *m*, cri *m*; (*also: telephone ~*) coup *m* de téléphone; (*visit*) visite *f*; **she's ~ed Suzanne** elle s'appelle Suzanne; **to be on ~** être de permanence; **~ back** *vi* (*return*) repasser; (*TEL*) rappeler; **~ for** *vt fus* (*demand*) demander; (*fetch*) passer prendre; **~ off** *vt* annuler; **~ on** *vt fus* (*visit*) rendre visite à, passer voir; (*request*): **to ~ on sb to do** inviter qn à faire; **~ out** *vi* pousser un cri *or* des cris; **~ up** *vt* (*MIL*) appeler, mobiliser; (*TEL*) appeler; **~box** (*BRIT*) *n* (*TEL*) cabine *f* téléphonique; **~er** *n* (*TEL*) personne *f* qui appelle; (*visitor*) visiteur *m*; **~ girl** *n* call-girl *f*; **~-in** (*US*) *n* (*RADIO, TV*): phone-in programme *m* à ligne ouverte; **~ing** *n* vocation *f*; (*trade, occupation*) état *m*; **~ing card** (*US*) *n* carte *f* de visite

callous ['kæləs] *adj* dur(e), insensible

calm [kɑːm] *adj* calme ♦ *n* calme *m* ♦ *vt* calmer, apaiser; **~ down** *vi* se calmer ♦ *vt* calmer, apaiser

Calor gas ['kælə-] (®) *n* butane *m*, butagaz *m* (®)

calorie ['kælərɪ] *n* calorie *f*

calves [kɑːvz] *npl of* **calf**

camber ['kæmbə*] *n* (*of road*) bombement *m*

Cambodia [kæm'bəʊdjə] *n* Cambodge *m*

camcorder ['kæmkɔːdə*] *n* caméscope *m*

came [keɪm] *pt of* **come**

camel ['kæməl] *n* chameau *m*

camera ['kæmərə] *n* (*PHOT*) appareil-photo *m*; (*also: cine-~, movie ~*) caméra *f*; **in ~** à huis clos; **~man** (*irreg*) *n* caméraman *m*

camouflage ['kæməflɑːʒ] *n* camouflage *m* ♦ *vt* camoufler

camp [kæmp] *n* camp *m* ♦ *vi* camper ♦ *adj* (*man*) efféminé(e)

campaign [kæm'peɪn] *n* (*MIL, POL etc*) campagne *f* ♦ *vi* faire campagne

camp: ~bed (*BRIT*) *n* lit *m* de camp; **~er** *n* campeur(euse); (*vehicle*) camping-car *m*; **~ing** *n* camping *m*; **to go ~ing** faire du camping; **~site** ['kæmpsaɪt] *n* campement *m*, (terrain *m* de) camping *m*

campus ['kæmpəs] *n* campus *m*

can¹ [kæn] *n* (*of milk, oil, water*) bidon *m*; (*tin*) boîte *f* de conserve ♦ *vt* mettre en conserve

KEYWORD

can² [kæn] (*negative* **cannot**, **can't**; *conditional and pt* **could**) *aux vb* **1** (*be able to*) pouvoir; **you ~ do it if you try** vous pouvez le faire si vous essayez; **I ~'t hear you** je ne t'entends pas

2 (*know how to*) savoir; **I ~ swim/play tennis/drive** je sais nager/jouer au tennis/conduire; **~ you speak French?** parlez-vous français?

3 (*may*) pouvoir; **~ I use your phone?** puis-je me servir de votre téléphone?

4 (*expressing disbelief, puzzlement etc*): **it ~'t be true!** ce n'est pas possible!; **what CAN he want?** qu'est-ce qu'il peut bien vouloir?

5 (*expressing possibility, suggestion etc*): **he could be in the library** il est peut-être dans la bibliothèque; **she could have been delayed** il se peut qu'elle ait été retardée

Canada ['kænədə] *n* Canada *m*; **Canadian** [kə'neɪdɪən] *adj* canadien(ne) ♦ *n* Canadien(ne)

canal [kə'næl] *n* canal *m*

canary [kə'nɛərɪ] *n* canari *m*, serin *m*

cancel ['kænsəl] *vt* annuler; (*train*) supprimer; (*party, appointment*) décommander; (*cross out*) barrer, rayer; **~lation** [kænsə'leɪʃən] *n* annulation *f*; suppression *f*

cancer ['kænsə*] *n* (MED) cancer *m*; **C~** (ASTROLOGY) le Cancer

candid ['kændɪd] *adj* (très) franc(franche), sincère

candidate ['kændɪdeɪt] *n* candidat(e)

candle ['kændl] *n* bougie *f*; (*of tallow*) chandelle *f*; (*in church*) cierge *m*; **~light** *n*: **by ~light** à la lumière d'une bougie; (*dinner*) aux chandelles; **~stick** *n* (*also:* ~ *holder*) bougeoir *m*; (*bigger, ornate*) chandelier *m*

candour ['kændə*] (US **candor**) *n* (grande) franchise *or* sincérité

candy ['kændɪ] *n* sucre candi; (US) bonbon *m*; **~-floss** (BRIT) *n* barbe *f* à papa

cane [keɪn] *n* canne *f*; (*for furniture, baskets etc*) rotin *m* ♦ *vt* (BRIT: SCOL) administrer des coups de bâton à

canister ['kænɪstə*] *n* boîte *f*; (*of gas, pressurized substance*) bombe *f*

cannabis ['kænəbɪs] *n* (*drug*) cannabis *m*

canned [kænd] *adj* (*food*) en boîte, en conserve

cannon ['kænən] (*pl* ~ *or* ~**s**) *n* (*gun*) canon *m*

cannot ['kænɒt] = **can not**

canoe [kə'nu:] *n* pirogue *f*; (SPORT) canoë *m*

canon ['kænən] *n* (*clergyman*) chanoine *m*; (*standard*) canon *m*

can-opener [-'əʊpnə*] *n* ouvre-boîte *m*

canopy ['kænəpɪ] *n* baldaquin *m*; dais *m*

can't [kɑːnt] = **can't**

cantankerous [kæn'tæŋkərəs] *adj* querelleur(euse), acariâtre

canteen [kæn'tiːn] *n* cantine *f*; (BRIT: *of cutlery*) ménagère *f*

canter ['kæntə*] *vi* (*horse*) aller au petit galop

canvas ['kænvəs] *n* toile *f*

canvass ['kænvəs] *vi* (POL): **to ~ for** faire campagne pour ♦ *vt* (*investigate: opinions etc*) sonder

canyon ['kænjən] *n* cañon *m*, gorge (profonde)

cap [kæp] *n* casquette *f*; (*of pen*) capuchon *m*; (*of bottle*) capsule *f*; (*contraceptive: also: Dutch* ~) diaphragme *m*; (*for toy gun*) amorce *f* ♦ *vt* (*outdo*) surpasser; (*put limit on*) plafonner

capability [keɪpə'bɪlɪtɪ] *n* aptitude *f*, capacité *f*

capable ['keɪpəbl] *adj* capable

capacity [kə'pæsɪtɪ] *n* capacité *f*; (*capability*) aptitude *f*; (*of factory*) rendement *m*

cape [keɪp] *n* (*garment*) cape *f*; (GEO) cap *m*

caper ['keɪpə*] *n* (CULIN: *gen pl*) câpre *f*; (*prank*) farce *f*

capital ['kæpɪtl] *n* (*also:* ~ *city*) capitale *f*; (*money*) capital *m*; (*also:* ~ *letter*) majuscule *f*; **~ gains tax** (COMM) impôt *m* sur les plus-values; **~ism** *n* capitalisme *m*; **~ist** *adj* capitaliste ♦ *n* capitaliste *m/f*; **~ize** *vi*: **to ~ize on** tirer parti de; **~ punishment** *n* peine capitale

Capricorn ['kæprɪkɔːn] *n* (ASTROLOGY) le Capricorne

capsize [kæp'saɪz] *vt* faire chavirer ♦ *vi* chavirer

capsule ['kæpsjuːl] *n* capsule *f*

captain ['kæptɪn] *n* capitaine *m*

caption ['kæpʃən] *n* légende *f*

captive ['kæptɪv] *adj, n* captif(ive)

capture ['kæptʃə*] *vt* capturer, prendre; (*attention*) capter; (COMPUT) saisir ♦ *n* capture *f*; (*data* ~) saisie *f* de données

car [kɑː*] *n* voiture *f*, auto *f*; (RAIL) wagon *m*, voiture *f*

caramel ['kærəməl] *n* caramel *m*

caravan ['kærəvæn] *n* caravane *f*; **~ site** (BRIT) *n* camping *m* pour caravanes

carbohydrate [kɑːbəʊˈhaɪdreɪt] *n* hydrate *m* de carbone; (*food*) féculent *m*
carbon [ˈkɑːbən] *n* carbone *m*; **~ dioxide** *n* gaz *m* carbonique; **~ monoxide** *n* oxyde *m* de carbone; **~ paper** *n* papier *m* carbone
carburettor [ˈkɑːbjʊretə*] (*US* **carburetor**) *n* carburateur *m*
card [kɑːd] *n* carte *f*; (*material*) carton *m*; **~board** *n* carton *m*; **~ game** *n* jeu *m* de cartes
cardiac [ˈkɑːdɪæk] *adj* cardiaque
cardigan [ˈkɑːdɪgən] *n* cardigan *m*
cardinal [ˈkɑːdɪnl] *adj* cardinal(e) ♦ *n* cardinal *m*
card index *n* fichier *m*
care [kɛə*] *n* soin *m*, attention *f*; (*worry*) souci *m*; (*charge*) charge *f*, garde *f* ♦ *vi*: **to ~ about** se soucier de, s'intéresser à; (*person*) être attaché(e) à; **~ of** chez, aux bons soins de; **in sb's ~** à la garde de qn, confié(e) à qn; **to take ~** faire attention (à faire); **to take ~ (to do)** s'occuper de; **I don't ~** ça m'est bien égal; **I couldn't ~ less** je m'en fiche complètement (*inf*); **~ for** *vt fus* s'occuper de; (*like*) aimer
career [kəˈrɪə*] *n* carrière *f* ♦ *vi* (*also*: **~ along**) aller à toute allure; **~ woman** (*irreg*) *n* femme ambitieuse
care: **~free** [ˈkɛəfriː] *adj* sans souci, insouciant(e); **~ful** [ˈkɛəful] *adj* (*thorough*) soigneux(euse); (*cautious*) prudent(e); **(be) ~ful!** (fais) attention!; **~fully** *adv* avec soin, soigneusement; prudemment; **~less** [ˈkɛəlɪs] *adj* négligent(e); (*heedless*) insouciant(e); **~r** [kɛərə*] *n* (*MED*) aide *f*
caress [kəˈres] *n* caresse *f* ♦ *vt* caresser
caretaker [ˈkɛəteɪkə*] *n* gardien(ne), concierge *m/f*
car-ferry [ˈkɑːferɪ] *n* (*on sea*) ferry(-boat) *m*
cargo [ˈkɑːgəʊ] (*pl* **~es**) *n* cargaison *f*, chargement *m*
car hire *n* location *f* de voitures
Caribbean [kærɪˈbiːən] *adj*: **the ~ (Sea)** la mer des Antilles *or* Caraïbes
caring [ˈkɛərɪŋ] *adj* (*person*) bienveillant(e); (*society, organization*) humani-

taire
carnal [ˈkɑːnl] *adj* charnel(le)
carnation [kɑːˈneɪʃən] *n* œillet *m*
carnival [ˈkɑːnɪvəl] *n* (*public celebration*) carnaval *m*; (*US: funfair*) fête foraine
carol [ˈkærl] *n*: **(Christmas) ~** chant *m* de Noël
carp [kɑːp] *n* (*fish*) carpe *f*; **~ at** *vt fus* critiquer
car park (*BRIT*) *n* parking *m*, parc *m* de stationnement
carpenter [ˈkɑːpɪntə*] *n* charpentier *m*; **carpentry** [ˈkɑːpɪntrɪ] *n* menuiserie *f*
carpet [ˈkɑːpɪt] *n* tapis *m* ♦ *vt* recouvrir d'un tapis; **~ bombing** *n* bombardement *m* intensif; **~ slippers** *npl* pantoufles *fpl*; **~ sweeper** *n* balai *m* mécanique
car phone *n* (*TEL*) téléphone *m* de voiture
carriage [ˈkærɪdʒ] *n* voiture *f*; (*of goods*) transport *m*; (*: cost*) port *m*; **~way** (*BRIT*) *n* (*part of road*) chaussée *f*
carrier [ˈkærɪə*] *n* transporteur *m*, camionneur *m*; (*company*) entreprise *f* de transport; (*MED*) porteur(euse); **~ bag** (*BRIT*) *n* sac *m* (en papier *or* en plastique)
carrot [ˈkærət] *n* carotte *f*
carry [ˈkærɪ] *vt* (*subj: person*) porter; (*: vehicle*) transporter; (*involve: responsibilities etc*) comporter, impliquer ♦ *vi* (*sound*) porter; **to get carried away** (*fig*) s'emballer, s'enthousiasmer; **~ on** *vi*: **to ~ on with sth/doing** continuer qch/de faire ♦ *vt* poursuivre; **~ out** *vt* (*orders*) exécuter; (*investigation*) mener; **~cot** (*BRIT*) *n* porte-bébé *m*; **~-on** (*inf*) *n* (*fuss*) histoires *fpl*
cart [kɑːt] *n* charrette *f* ♦ *vt* (*inf*) transporter, trimballer (*inf*)
carton [ˈkɑːtən] *n* (*box*) carton *m*; (*of yogurt*) pot *m*; (*of cigarettes*) cartouche *f*
cartoon [kɑːˈtuːn] *n* (*PRESS*) dessin *m* (humoristique), caricature *f*; (*BRIT: comic strip*) bande dessinée; (*CINEMA*) dessin animé
cartridge [ˈkɑːtrɪdʒ] *n* cartouche *f*
carve [kɑːv] *vt* (*meat*) découper; (*wood,*

stone) tailler, sculpter; **~ up** *vt* découper; (*fig: country*) morceler; **carving** ['kɑːvɪŋ] *n* sculpture *f*; **carving knife** *n* couteau *m* à découper

car wash *n* station *f* de lavage (de voitures)

case [keɪs] *n* cas *m*; (*LAW*) affaire *f*, procès *m*; (*box*) caisse *f*, boîte *f*, étui *m*; (*BRIT: also: suit~*) valise *f*; **in ~ of** cas de; **in ~ he ...** au cas où il ...; **just in ~** à tout hasard; **in any ~** en tout cas, de toute façon

cash [kæʃ] *n* argent *m*; (*COMM*) argent liquide, espèces *fpl* ♦ *vt* encaisser; **to pay (in) ~** payer comptant; **~ on delivery** payable *or* paiement à la livraison; **~book** *n* livre *m* de caisse; **~ card** (*BRIT*) *n* carte *f* de retrait; **~ desk** (*BRIT*) *n* caisse *f*; **~ dispenser** (*BRIT*) *n* distributeur *m* automatique de billets, billeterie *f*

cashew [kæ'ʃuː] *n* (*also: ~ nut*) noix *f* de cajou

cashier [kæ'ʃɪə*] *n* caissier(ère)

cashmere ['kæʃmɪə*] *n* cachemire *m*

cash register *n* caisse (enregistreuse)

casing ['keɪsɪŋ] *n* revêtement (protecteur), enveloppe (protectrice)

casino [kə'siːnəʊ] *n* casino *m*

casket ['kɑːskɪt] *n* coffret *m*; (*US: coffin*) cercueil *m*

casserole ['kæsərəʊl] *n* (*container*) cocotte *f*; (*food*) ragoût *m* (en cocotte)

cassette [kæ'set] *n* cassette *f*, musicassette *f*; **~ player** *n* lecteur *m* de cassettes; **~ recorder** *n* magnétophone *m* à cassettes

cast [kɑːst] (*pt, pp* cast) *vt* (*throw*) jeter; (*shed*) perdre; se dépouiller de; (*statue*) mouler; (*THEATRE*): **to ~ sb as Hamlet** attribuer à qn le rôle de Hamlet ♦ *n* (*THEATRE*) distribution *f*; (*also: plaster ~*) plâtre *m*; **to ~ one's vote** voter; **~ off** *vi* (*NAUT*) larguer les amarres; (*KNITTING*) arrêter les mailles; **~ on** *vi* (*KNITTING*) monter les mailles

castaway ['kɑːstəweɪ] *n* naufragé(e)

caster sugar ['kɑːstə-] (*BRIT*) *n* sucre *m* semoule

casting vote ['kɑːstɪŋ-] (*BRIT*) *n* voix prépondérante (*pour départager*)

cast iron *n* fonte *f*

castle ['kɑːsl] *n* château (fort); (*CHESS*) tour *f*

castor ['kɑːstə*] *n* (*wheel*) roulette *f*; **~ oil** *n* huile *f* de ricin

castrate [kæs'treɪt] *vt* châtrer

casual ['kæʒjʊl] *adj* (*by chance*) de hasard, fait(e) au hasard, fortuit(e); (*irregular: work etc*) temporaire; (*unconcerned*) désinvolte; **~ly** *adv* avec désinvolture, négligemment; (*dress*) de façon décontractée

casualty ['kæʒjʊltɪ] *n* accidenté(e), blessé(e); (*dead*) victime *f*, mort(e); (*MED: department*) urgences *fpl*

casual wear *n* vêtements *mpl* décontractés

cat [kæt] *n* chat *m*

catalogue ['kætəlɒg] (*US* catalog) *n* catalogue *m* ♦ *vt* cataloguer

catalyst ['kætəlɪst] *n* catalyseur *m*

catalytic converter [kætə'lɪtɪk kən'vɜːtə*] *n* pot *m* catalytique

catapult ['kætəpʌlt] (*BRIT*) *n* (*sling*) lance-pierres *m inv*, fronde *f*

catarrh [kə'tɑː*] *n* rhume *m* chronique, catarrhe *m*

catastrophe [kə'tæstrəfɪ] *n* catastrophe *f*

catch [kætʃ] (*pt, pp* caught) *vt* attraper; (*person: by surprise*) prendre, surprendre; (*understand, hear*) saisir ♦ *vi* (*fire*) prendre; (*become trapped*) se prendre, s'accrocher ♦ *n* (*of fish*) prise *f*; (*trick*) attrape *f*; (*of lock*) loquet *m*; **to ~ sb's attention** *or* **eye** attirer l'attention de qn; **to ~ one's breath** retenir son souffle; **to ~ fire** prendre feu; **to ~ sight of** apercevoir; **~ on** *vi* saisir; (*grow popular*) prendre; **~ up** *vi* se rattraper, combler son retard ♦ *vt* (*also: ~ up with*) rattraper; **~ing** *adj* (*MED*) contagieux(euse); **~ment area** ['kætʃmənt-] (*BRIT*) *n* (*SCOL*) secteur *m* de recrutement; (*of hospital*) circonscription hospitalière; **~ phrase** *n* slogan *m*; expression *f* (à la mode); **~y** *adj* (*tune*) facile à retenir

category ['kætɪgərɪ] *n* catégorie *f*

cater ['keɪtə*] *vi* (*provide food*): **to ~ (for)** préparer des repas (pour), se charger de la restauration (pour); **~ for** (*BRIT*) *vt fus* (*needs*) satisfaire, pourvoir à; (*readers, consumers*) s'adresser à, pourvoir aux besoins de; **~er** *n* traiteur *m*; fournisseur *m*; **~ing** *n* restauration *f*; approvisionnement *m*, ravitaillement *m*

caterpillar ['kætəpɪlə*] *n* chenille *f*; **~ track** (®) *n* chenille *f*

cathedral [kə'θiːdrəl] *n* cathédrale *f*

catholic ['kæθəlɪk] *adj* (*tastes*) éclectique, varié(e); **C~** *adj* catholique ♦ *n* catholique *m/f*

Catseye ['kætsaɪ] (®: *BRIT*) *n* (*AUT*) catadioptre *m*

cattle ['kætl] *npl* bétail *m*

catty ['kætɪ] *adj* méchant(e)

caucus ['kɔːkəs] *n* (*POL: group*) comité local d'un parti politique; (*US: POL*) comité électoral (pour désigner des candidats)

caught [kɔːt] *pt, pp of* **catch**

cauliflower ['kɒlɪflaʊə*] *n* chou-fleur *m*

cause [kɔːz] *n* cause *f* ♦ *vt* causer

caution ['kɔːʃən] *n* prudence *f*; (*warning*) avertissement *m* ♦ *vt* avertir, donner un avertissement à

cautious ['kɔːʃəs] *adj* prudent(e)

cavalry ['kævəlrɪ] *n* cavalerie *f*

cave [keɪv] *n* caverne *f*, grotte *f*; **~ in** *vi* (*roof etc*) s'effondrer; **~man** (*irreg*) *n* homme *m* des cavernes

caviar(e) ['kævɪɑː*] *n* caviar *m*

cavort [kə'vɔːt] *vi* cabrioler, faire des cabrioles

CB *n abbr* (= *Citizens' Band (Radio)*) CB *f*

CBI *n abbr* (= *Confederation of British Industries*) groupement du patronat

cc *abbr* = **carbon copy**; **cubic centimetres**

CD *n abbr* (= *compact disc (player)*) CD *m*; **~-ROM** *n abbr* (= *compact disc read-only memory*) CD-ROM *m*

cease [siːs] *vt, vi* cesser; **~fire** *n* cessez-le-feu *m*; **~less** *adj* incessant(e), continuel(le)

cedar ['siːdə*] *n* cèdre *m*

ceiling ['siːlɪŋ] *n* plafond *m*

celebrate ['selɪbreɪt] *vt, vi* célébrer; **~d** *adj* célèbre; **celebration** [selɪ'breɪʃən] *n* célébration *f*

celery ['selərɪ] *n* céleri *m* (à côtes)

cell [sel] *n* cellule *f*; (*ELEC*) élément *m* (*de pile*)

cellar ['selə*] *n* cave *f*

cello ['tʃeləʊ] *n* violoncelle *m*

cellphone ['selfəʊn] *n* téléphone *m* cellulaire

Celt [kelt, selt] *n* Celte *m/f*; **~ic** ['keltɪk, 'seltɪk] *adj* celte

cement [sɪ'ment] *n* ciment *m*; **~ mixer** *n* bétonnière *f*

cemetery ['semɪtrɪ] *n* cimetière *m*

censor ['sensə*] *n* censeur *m* ♦ *vt* censurer; **~ship** *n* censure *f*

censure ['senʃə*] *vt* blâmer, critiquer

census ['sensəs] *n* recensement *m*

cent [sent] *n* (*US etc: coin*) cent *m* (= *un centième du dollar*); *see also* **per**

centenary [sen'tiːnərɪ] *n* centenaire *m*

center ['sentə*] (*US*) *n* = **centre**

centigrade ['sentɪɡreɪd] *adj* centigrade

centimetre ['sentɪmiːtə*] (*US* **centimeter**) *n* centimètre *m*

centipede ['sentɪpiːd] *n* mille-pattes *m inv*

central ['sentrəl] *adj* central(e); **C~ America** *n* Amérique centrale; **~ heating** *n* chauffage central; **~ reservation** (*BRIT*) *n* (*AUT*) terre-plein central

centre ['sentə*] (*US* **center**) *n* centre *m* ♦ *vt* centrer; **~-forward** *n* (*SPORT*) avant-centre *m*; **~-half** *n* (*SPORT*) demi-centre *m*

century ['sentjʊrɪ] *n* siècle *m*; **20th ~** XXe siècle

ceramic [sɪ'ræmɪk] *adj* céramique

cereal ['sɪərɪəl] *n* céréale *f*

ceremony ['serɪmənɪ] *n* cérémonie *f*; **to stand on ~** faire des façons

certain ['sɜːtən] *adj* certain(e); **for ~** certainement, sûrement; **~ly** *adv* certainement; **~ty** *n* certitude *f*

certificate [sə'tɪfɪkɪt] *n* certificat *m*

certified ['sɜːtɪfaɪd] *adj*: **by ~ mail** (*US*) en recommandé, avec avis de réception; **~ public accountant** (*US*) *n* expert-comptable *m*

certify ['sə'tɪfaɪ] vt certifier; (*award diploma to*) conférer un diplôme *etc* à; (*declare insane*) déclarer malade mental(e)

cervical ['sɜːvɪkl] adj: ~ **cancer** cancer m du col de l'utérus; ~ **smear** frottis vaginal

cervix ['sɜːvɪks] n col m de l'utérus

cf. abbr (= *compare*) cf., voir

CFC n abbr (= *chlorofluorocarbon*) CFC m (*gen pl*)

ch. abbr (= *chapter*) chap.

chafe [tʃeɪf] vt irriter, frotter contre

chain [tʃeɪn] n chaîne f ♦ vt (*also*: ~ *up*) enchaîner, attacher (avec une chaîne); ~ **reaction** n réaction f en chaîne; ~**smoke** vi fumer cigarette sur cigarette; ~ **store** n magasin m à succursales multiples

chair [tʃɛə*] n chaise f; (*arm~*) fauteuil m; (*of university*) chaire f; (*of meeting, committee*) présidence f ♦ vt (*meeting*) présider; ~**lift** n télésiège m; ~**man** (*irreg*) n président m

chalet ['ʃæleɪ] n chalet m

chalice ['tʃælɪs] n calice m

chalk ['tʃɔːk] n craie f

challenge ['tʃælɪndʒ] n défi m ♦ vt défier; (*statement, right*) mettre en question, contester; **to ~ sb to do** mettre qn au défi de faire; **challenging** ['tʃælɪndʒɪŋ] adj (*tone, look*) de défi, provocateur(trice); (*task, career*) qui représente un défi *or* une gageure

chamber ['tʃeɪmbə*] n chambre f; ~ **of commerce** chambre de commerce; ~**maid** n femme f de chambre; ~ **music** n musique f de chambre

champagne [ʃæm'peɪn] n champagne m

champion ['tʃæmpɪən] n champion(ne); ~**ship** n championnat m

chance [tʃɑːns] n (*opportunity*) occasion f, possibilité f; (*hope, likelihood*) chance f; (*risk*) risque m ♦ vt: **to ~ it** risquer (le coup), essayer ♦ adj fortuit(e), de hasard; **to take a ~** prendre un risque; **by ~** par hasard

chancellor ['tʃɑːnsələ*] n chancelier m; **C~ of the Exchequer** (*BRIT*) n chancelier

m de l'Échiquier, ≈ ministre m des Finances

chandelier [ʃændɪ'lɪə*] n lustre m

change [tʃeɪndʒ] vt (*alter, replace, COMM: money*) changer; (*hands, trains, clothes, one's name*) changer de; (*transform*): **to ~ sb into** changer *or* transformer qn en ♦ vi (*gen*) changer; (*one's clothes*) se changer; (*be transformed*): **to ~ into** se changer *or* transformer en ♦ n changement m; (*money*) monnaie f; **to ~ gear** (*AUT*) changer de vitesse; **to ~ one's mind** changer d'avis; **a ~ of clothes** des vêtements de rechange; **for a ~** pour changer; ~**able** adj (*weather*) variable; ~ **machine** n distributeur m de monnaie; ~**over** n (*to new system*) changement m, passage m

changing ['tʃeɪndʒɪŋ] adj changeant(e); ~ **room** (*BRIT*) n (*in shop*) salon m d'essayage; (*SPORT*) vestiaire m

channel ['tʃænl] n (*TV*) chaîne f; (*navigable passage*) chenal m; (*irrigation*) canal m ♦ vt canaliser; **the (English) C~** la Manche; **the C~ Islands** les îles de la Manche, les îles Anglo-Normandes; **the C~ Tunnel** le tunnel sous la Manche

chant [tʃɑːnt] n chant m; (*REL*) psalmodie f ♦ vt chanter, scander

chaos ['keɪɔs] n chaos m

chap [tʃæp] (*BRIT: inf*) n (*man*) type m

chapel ['tʃæpəl] n chapelle f; (*BRIT: nonconformist ~*) église f

chaplain ['tʃæplɪn] n aumônier m

chapped ['tʃæpt] adj (*skin, lips*) gercé(e)

chapter ['tʃæptə*] n chapitre m

char [tʃɑː*] vt (*burn*) carboniser

character ['kærɪktə*] n caractère m; (*in novel, film*) personnage m; (*eccentric*) numéro m, phénomène m; ~**istic** [kærɪktə'rɪstɪk] adj caractéristique ♦ n caractéristique m

charcoal ['tʃɑːkəʊl] n charbon m de bois; (*for drawing*) charbon m

charge [tʃɑːdʒ] n (*cost*) prix m (demandé); (*accusation*) accusation f; (*LAW*) inculpation f ♦ vt: **to ~ sb (with)** inculper qn (de); (*battery, enemy*) charger; (*customer, sum*) faire payer ♦ *vi* foncer; ~s *npl* (*costs*) frais *mpl*; **to reverse the ~s** (*TEL*) téléphoner en P.C.V.; **to take ~ of** se charger de; **to be in ~ of** être responsable de, s'occuper de; **how much do you ~?** combien prenez-vous?; **to ~ an expense (up) to sb** mettre une dépense sur le compte de qn; **~ card** *n* carte *f* de client

charity ['tʃærɪtɪ] *n* charité *f*; (*organization*) institution *f* charitable *or* de bienfaisance, œuvre *f* (de charité)

charm [tʃɑːm] *n* charme *m*; (*on bracelet*) breloque *f* ♦ *vt* charmer, enchanter; **~ing** *adj* charmant(e)

chart [tʃɑːt] *n* tableau *m*, diagramme *m*; graphique *m*; (*map*) carte marine ♦ *vt* dresser *or* établir la carte de; **~s** *npl* (*hit parade*) hit-parade *m*

charter ['tʃɑːtə*] *vt* (*plane*) affréter ♦ *n* (*document*) charte *f*; **~ed accountant** (*BRIT*) *n* expert-comptable *m*; **~ flight** charter *m*

chase [tʃeɪs] *vt* poursuivre, pourchasser; (*also: ~ away*) chasser ♦ *n* poursuite *f*, chasse *f*

chasm ['kæzəm] *n* gouffre *m*, abîme *m*

chat [tʃæt] *vi* (*also: have a ~*) bavarder, causer ♦ *n* conversation *f*; **~ show** (*BRIT*) *n* causerie télévisée

chatter ['tʃætə*] *vi* (*person*) bavarder; (*animal*) jacasser ♦ *n* bavardage *m*; jacassement *m*; **my teeth are ~ing** je claque des dents; **~box** (*inf*) *n* moulin *m* à paroles

chatty ['tʃætɪ] *adj* (*style*) familier(ère); (*person*) bavard(e)

chauffeur ['ʃəʊfə*] *n* chauffeur *m* (de maître)

chauvinist ['ʃəʊvɪnɪst] *n* (*male ~*) phallocrate *m*; (*nationalist*) chauvin(e)

cheap [tʃiːp] *adj* bon marché *inv*, pas cher(chère); (*joke*) facile, d'un goût douteux; (*poor quality*) bon marché, de qualité médiocre ♦ *adv* à bon marché, pour pas cher; **~er** *adj* moins cher(chère); **~ly** *adv* à bon marché, à bon compte

cheat [tʃiːt] *vi* tricher ♦ *vt* tromper, duper; (*rob*): **to ~ sb out of sth** escroquer qch à qn ♦ *n* tricheur(euse); escroc *m*

check [tʃek] *vt* vérifier; (*passport, ticket*) contrôler; (*halt*) arrêter; (*restrain*) maîtriser ♦ *n* vérification *f*; contrôle *m*; (*curb*) frein *m*; (*US: bill*) addition *f*; (*pattern: gen pl*) carreaux *mpl*; (*US*) = **cheque** ♦ *adj* (*pattern, cloth*) à carreaux; **~ in** *vi* (*in hotel*) remplir sa fiche (d'hôtel); (*at airport*) se présenter à l'enregistrement ♦ *vt* (*luggage*) (faire) enregistrer; **~ out** *vi* (*in hotel*) régler sa note; **~ up** *vi*: **to ~ up (on sth)** vérifier (qch); **to ~ up on sb** se renseigner sur le compte de qn; **~ered** (*US*) *adj* = **chequered**; **~ers** (*US*) *npl* jeu *m* de dames; **~-in (desk)** *n* enregistrement *m*; **~ing account** (*US*) *n* (*current account*) compte courant; **~mate** *n* échec et mat *m*; **~out** *n* (*in shop*) caisse *f*; **~point** *n* contrôle *m*; **~room** (*US*) *n* (*left-luggage office*) consigne *f*; **~up** *n* (*MED*) examen médical, check-up *m*

cheek [tʃiːk] *n* joue *f*; (*impudence*) toupet *m*, culot *m*; **~bone** *n* pommette *f*; **~y** *adj* effronté(e), culotté(e)

cheep [tʃiːp] *vi* piauler

cheer [tʃɪə*] *vt* acclamer, applaudir; (*gladden*) réjouir, réconforter ♦ *vi* applaudir ♦ *n* (*gen pl*) acclamations *fpl*, applaudissements *mpl*; bravos *mpl*, hourras *mpl*; **~s!** à la vôtre!; **~ up** *vi* se dérider, reprendre courage ♦ *vt* remonter le moral à *or* de, dérider; **~ful** *adj* gai(e), joyeux(euse)

cheerio ['tʃɪərɪ'əʊ] (*BRIT*) *excl* salut!, au revoir!

cheese [tʃiːz] *n* fromage *m*; **~board** *n* plateau *m* de fromages

cheetah ['tʃiːtə] *n* guépard *m*

chef [ʃef] *n* chef (cuisinier)

chemical ['kemɪkəl] *adj* chimique ♦ *n* produit *m* chimique

chemist ['kemɪst] *n* (*BRIT: pharmacist*) pharmacien(ne); (*scientist*) chimiste *m/f*; **~ry** *n* chimie *f*; **~'s (shop)** (*BRIT*) *n* pharmacie *f*

cheque [tʃek] (*BRIT*) *n* chèque *m*; **~book**

n chéquier *m*, carnet *m* de chèques; **~ card** *n* carte *f* (d'identité) bancaire

chequered ['tʃekəd] (*US* **checkered**) *adj* (*fig*) varié(e)

cherish ['tʃerɪʃ] *vt* chérir; **~ed** *adj* (*dream, memory*) cher(chère)

cherry ['tʃerɪ] *n* cerise *f*; (*also: ~ tree*) cerisier *m*

chess [tʃes] *n* échecs *mpl*; **~board** *n* échiquier *m*

chest [tʃest] *n* poitrine *f*; (*box*) coffre *m*, caisse *f*; **~ of drawers** *n* commode *f*

chestnut ['tʃesnʌt] *n* châtaigne *f*; (*also: ~ tree*) châtaignier *m*

chew [tʃuː] *vt* mâcher; **~ing gum** *n* chewing-gum *m*

chic [ʃiːk] *adj* chic *inv*, élégant(e)

chick [tʃɪk] *n* poussin *m*; (*inf*) nana *f*

chicken ['tʃɪkɪn] *n* poulet *m*; (*inf: coward*) poule mouillée; **~ out** (*inf*) *vi* se dégonfler; **~pox** ['tʃɪkɪnpɔks] *n* varicelle *f*

chicory ['tʃɪkərɪ] *n* (*for coffee*) chicorée *f*; (*salad*) endive *f*

chief [tʃiːf] *n* chef ♦ *adj* principal(e); **~ executive** (*US* **chief executive officer**) *n* directeur(trice) général(e); **~ly** *adv* principalement, surtout

chiffon ['ʃɪfɔn] *n* mousseline *f* de soie

chilblain ['tʃɪlbleɪn] *n* engelure *f*

child [tʃaɪld] (*pl* **children**) *n* enfant *m/f*; **~birth** *n* accouchement *m*; **~hood** *n* enfance *f*; **~ish** *adj* puéril(e), enfantin(e); **~like** *adj* d'enfant, innocent(e); **~ minder** (*BRIT*) *n* garde *f* d'enfants; **~ren** ['tʃɪldrən] *npl* of **child**

Chile ['tʃɪlɪ] *n* Chili *m*

chill [tʃɪl] *n* (*of water*) froid *m*; (*of air*) fraîcheur *f*; (*MED*) refroidissement *m*, coup *m* de froid ♦ *vt* (*person*) faire frissonner; (*CULIN*) mettre au frais, rafraîchir

chil(l)i ['tʃɪlɪ] *n* piment *m* (rouge)

chilly ['tʃɪlɪ] *adj* froid(e), glacé(e); (*sensitive to cold*) frileux(euse); **to feel ~** avoir froid

chime [tʃaɪm] *n* carillon *m* ♦ *vi* carillonner, sonner

chimney ['tʃɪmnɪ] *n* cheminée *f*; **~ sweep** *n* ramoneur *m*

chimpanzee [tʃɪmpæn'ziː] *n* chimpanzé *m*

chin [tʃɪn] *n* menton *m*

China ['tʃaɪnə] *n* Chine *f*

china ['tʃaɪnə] *n* porcelaine *f*; (*crockery*) (vaisselle *f* en) porcelaine

Chinese [tʃaɪ'niːz] *adj* chinois(e) ♦ *n inv* (*person*) Chinois(e); (*LING*) chinois *m*

chink [tʃɪŋk] *n* (*opening*) fente *f*, fissure *f*; (*noise*) tintement *m*

chip [tʃɪp] *n* (*gen pl: CULIN: BRIT*) frite *f*; (*: US: potato ~*) chip *m*; (*of wood*) copeau *m*; (*of glass, stone*) éclat *m*; (*also: micro~*) puce *f* ♦ *vt* (*cup, plate*) ébrécher; **~ in** *vi* mettre son grain de sel; (*contribute*) contribuer

chiropodist [kɪ'rɔpədɪst] (*BRIT*) *n* pédicure *m/f*

chirp [tʃɜːp] *vi* pépier, gazouiller

chisel ['tʃɪzl] *n* ciseau *m*

chit [tʃɪt] *n* mot *m*, note *f*

chitchat ['tʃɪttʃæt] *n* bavardage *m*

chivalry ['ʃɪvəlrɪ] *n* esprit *m* chevaleresque, galanterie *f*

chives [tʃaɪvz] *npl* ciboulette *f*, civette *f*

chock-a-block ['tʃɔkə'blɔk], **chock-full** [tʃɔk'ful] *adj* plein(e) à craquer

chocolate ['tʃɔklɪt] *n* chocolat *m*

choice [tʃɔɪs] *n* choix *m* ♦ *adj* de choix

choir ['kwaɪə*] *n* chœur *m*, chorale *f*; **~boy** *n* jeune choriste *m*

choke [tʃəuk] *vi* étouffer ♦ *vt* étrangler; étouffer ♦ *n* (*AUT*) starter *m*; **street ~d with traffic** rue engorgée *or* embouteillée

cholesterol [kə'lɛstərɔl] *n* cholestérol *m*

choose [tʃuːz] (*pt* **chose**, *pp* **chosen**) *vt* choisir; **to ~ to do** décider de faire, juger bon de faire

choosy ['tʃuːzɪ] *adj*: **(to be) ~** (faire le/la) difficile

chop [tʃɔp] *vt* (*wood*) couper (à la hache); (*CULIN: also: ~ up*) couper (fin), émincer, hacher (en morceaux) ♦ *n* (*CULIN*) côtelette *f*; **~s** *npl* (*jaws*) mâchoires *fpl*

chopper ['tʃɔpə*] *n* (*helicopter*) hélicoptère *m*, hélico *m*

choppy ['tʃɔpɪ] *adj* (*sea*) un peu agité(e)

chopsticks ['tʃɔpstɪks] *npl* baguettes *fpl*

chord [kɔːd] *n* (MUS) accord *m*

chore [tʃɔː*] *n* travail *m* de routine; **household** ~s travaux *mpl* du ménage

chortle ['tʃɔːtl] *vi* glousser

chorus ['kɔːrəs] *n* chœur *m*; (*repeated part of song: also: fig*) refrain *m*

chose [tʃəʊz] *pt of* **choose**

chosen ['tʃəʊzn] *pp of* **choose**

Christ [kraɪst] *n* Christ *m*

christen ['krɪsn] *vt* baptiser

Christian ['krɪstɪən] *adj, n* chrétien(ne); **~ity** [krɪstɪˈænɪtɪ] *n* christianisme *m*; **~ name** *n* prénom *m*

Christmas ['krɪsməs] *n* Noël *m or f*; **Happy** *or* **Merry ~!** joyeux Noël!; **~ card** *n* carte *f* de Noël; **~ Day** *n* le jour de Noël; **~ Eve** *n* la veille de Noël; la nuit de Noël; **~ tree** *n* arbre *m* de Noël

chrome [krəʊm] *n* chrome *m*

chromium ['krəʊmɪəm] *n* chrome *m*

chronic ['krɒnɪk] *adj* chronique

chronicle ['krɒnɪkl] *n* chronique *f*

chronological [krɒnəˈlɒdʒɪkəl] *adj* chronologique

chrysanthemum [krɪˈsænθəməm] *n* chrysanthème *m*

chubby ['tʃʌbɪ] *adj* potelé(e), rondelet(te)

chuck [tʃʌk] (*inf*) *vt* (*throw*) lancer, jeter; (*BRIT: also: ~ up: job*) lâcher; (: *person*) plaquer; **~ out** *vt* flanquer dehors *or* à la porte; (*rubbish*) jeter

chuckle ['tʃʌkl] *vi* glousser

chug [tʃʌg] *vi* faire teuf-teuf; (*also: ~ along*) avancer en faisant teuf-teuf

chum [tʃʌm] *n* copain(copine)

chunk [tʃʌŋk] *n* gros morceau

church [tʃɜːtʃ] *n* église *f*; **~yard** *n* cimetière *m*

churn [tʃɜːn] *n* (*for butter*) baratte *f*; (*also: milk ~*) (grand) bidon à lait; **~ out** *vt* débiter

chute [ʃuːt] *n* glissoire *f*; (*also: rubbish ~*) vide-ordures *m inv*

chutney ['tʃʌtnɪ] *n* condiment *m* à base de fruits au vinaigre

CIA (US) *n abbr* (= *Central Intelligence Agency*) CIA *f*

CID (BRIT) *n abbr* (= *Criminal Investi-*

gation Department) ≈ P.J. *f*

cider ['saɪdə*] *n* cidre *m*

cigar [sɪˈgɑː*] *n* cigare *m*

cigarette [sɪgəˈret] *n* cigarette *f*; **~ case** *n* étui *m* à cigarettes; **~ end** *n* mégot *m*

Cinderella [sɪndəˈrelə] *n* Cendrillon

cinders ['sɪndəz] *npl* cendres *fpl*

cine-camera ['sɪnɪˈkæmərə] (BRIT) *n* caméra *f*

cinema ['sɪnəmə] *n* cinéma *m*

cinnamon ['sɪnəmən] *n* cannelle *f*

circle ['sɜːkl] *n* cercle *m*; (*in cinema, theatre*) balcon *m* ♦ *vi* faire *or* décrire des cercles ♦ *vt* (*move round*) faire le tour de, tourner autour de; (*surround*) entourer, encercler

circuit ['sɜːkɪt] *n* circuit *m*; **~ous** [sɜːˈkjuːɪtəs] *adj* indirect(e), qui fait un détour

circular ['sɜːkjʊlə*] *adj* circulaire ♦ *n* circulaire *f*

circulate ['sɜːkjʊleɪt] *vi* circuler ♦ *vt* faire circuler; **circulation** [sɜːkjʊˈleɪʃən] *n* circulation *f*; (*of newspaper*) tirage *m*

circumflex ['sɜːkəmfleks] *n* (*also: ~ accent*) accent *m* circonflexe

circumstances ['sɜːkəmstənsəz] *npl* circonstances *fpl*; (*financial condition*) moyens *mpl*, situation financière

circumvent [sɜːkəmˈvent] *vt* (*rule, difficulty*) tourner

circus ['sɜːkəs] *n* cirque *m*

CIS *n abbr* (= *Commonwealth of Independent States*) CEI *f*

cistern ['sɪstən] *n* réservoir *m* (d'eau); (*in toilet*) réservoir de la chasse d'eau

citizen ['sɪtɪzn] *n* citoyen(ne); (*resident*): **the ~s of this town** les habitants de cette ville; **~ship** *n* citoyenneté *f*

citrus fruit ['sɪtrəs-] *n* agrume *m*

city ['sɪtɪ] *n* ville *f*, cité *f*; **the C~** la Cité de Londres (*centre des affaires*)

civic ['sɪvɪk] *adj* civique; (*authorities*) municipal(e); **~ centre** (BRIT) *n* centre administratif (municipal)

civil ['sɪvɪl] *adj* civil(e); (*polite*) poli(e), courtois(e); (*disobedience, defence*) passif(ive); **~ engineer** *n* ingénieur *m* des travaux publics; **~ian** [sɪˈvɪlɪən] *adj, n* ci vil(e)

civilization [sɪvɪlaɪˈzeɪʃən] *n* civilisation *f*

civilized [ˈsɪvɪlaɪzd] *adj* civilisé(e); (*fig*) où règnent les bonnes manières

civil : ~ **law** *n* code civil; (*study*) droit civil; ~ **servant** *n* fonctionnaire *m/f*; **C~ Service** *n* fonction publique, administration *f*; ~ **war** *n* guerre civile

clad [klæd] *adj*: ~ **(in)** habillé(e) (de)

claim [kleɪm] *vt* revendiquer; (*rights, inheritance*) demander, prétendre à; (*assert*) déclarer, prétendre ♦ *vi* (*for insurance*) faire une déclaration de sinistre ♦ *n* revendication *f*; demande *f*; prétention *f*, déclaration *f*; (*right*) droit *m*, titre *m*; **~ant** *n* (ADMIN, LAW) requérant(e)

clairvoyant [klɛəˈvɔɪənt] *n* voyant(e), extra-lucide *m/f*

clam [klæm] *n* palourde *f*

clamber [ˈklæmbə*] *vi* grimper, se hisser

clammy [ˈklæmɪ] *adj* humide (et froid(e)), moite

clamour [ˈklæmə*] (*US* **clamor**) *vi*: **to ~ for** réclamer à grands cris

clamp [klæmp] *n* agrafe *f*, crampon *m* ♦ *vt* serrer; (*sth to sth*) fixer; ~ **down on** *vt fus* sévir *or* prendre des mesures draconiennes contre

clan [klæn] *n* clan *m*

clang [klæŋ] *vi* émettre un bruit *or* fracas métallique

clap [klæp] *vi* applaudir; **~ping** *n* applaudissements *mpl*

claret [ˈklærɪt] *n* (vin *m* de) bordeaux *m* (rouge)

clarinet [klærɪˈnet] *n* clarinette *f*

clarity [ˈklærɪtɪ] *n* clarté *f*

clash [klæʃ] *n* choc *m*; (*fig*) conflit *m* ♦ *vi* se heurter; être *or* entrer en conflit; (*colours*) jurer; (*two events*) tomber en même temps

clasp [klɑːsp] *n* (*of necklace, bag*) fermoir *m*; (*hold, embrace*) étreinte *f* ♦ *vt* serrer, étreindre

class [klɑːs] *n* classe *f* ♦ *vt* classer, classifier

classic [ˈklæsɪk] *adj* classique ♦ *n* (*author, work*) classique *m*; **~al** *adj* classique

classified [ˈklæsɪfaɪd] *adj* (*information*) secret(ète); ~ **advertisement** *n* petite annonce

classmate [ˈklɑːsmeɪt] *n* camarade *m/f* de classe

classroom [ˈklɑːsrʊm] *n* (salle *f* de) classe *f*

clatter [ˈklætə*] *n* cliquetis *m* ♦ *vi* cliqueter

clause [klɔːz] *n* clause *f*; (LING) proposition *f*

claw [klɔː] *n* griffe *f*; (*of bird of prey*) serre *f*; (*of lobster*) pince *f*; ~ **at** *vt fus* essayer de s'agripper à *or* griffer

clay [kleɪ] *n* argile *f*

clean [kliːn] *adj* propre; (*clear, smooth*) net(te); (*record, reputation*) sans tache; (*joke, story*) correct(e) ♦ *vt* nettoyer; ~ **out** *vt* nettoyer (à fond); ~ **up** *vt* nettoyer; (*fig*) remettre de l'ordre dans; **~-cut** *adj* (*person*) net(te), soigné(e); **~er** *n* (*person*) nettoyeur(euse), femme *f* de ménage; (*product*) détachant *m*; **~er's** *n* (*also*: *dry ~er's*) teinturier *m*; **~ing** *n* nettoyage *m*; **~liness** [ˈklɛnlɪnɪs] *n* propreté *f*

cleanse [klenz] *vt* nettoyer; (*purify*) purifier; **~r** *n* (*for face*) démaquillant *m*

clean-shaven [ˈkliːnˈʃeɪvn] *adj* rasé(e) de près

cleansing department [ˈklenzɪŋ-] (BRIT) *n* service *m* de voirie

clear [ˈklɪə*] *adj* clair(e); (*glass, plastic*) transparent(e); (*road, way*) libre, dégagé(e); (*conscience*) net(te) ♦ *vt* (*room*) débarrasser; (*of people*) faire évacuer; (*cheque*) compenser; (LAW: *suspect*) innocenter; (*obstacle*) franchir *or* sauter sans heurter ♦ *vi* (*weather*) s'éclaircir; (*fog*) se dissiper ♦ *adv*: ~ **of** à distance de, à l'écart de; **to ~ the table** débarrasser la table, desservir; ~ **up** *vt* ranger, mettre en ordre; (*mystery*) éclaircir, résoudre; **~ance** [ˈklɪərns] *n* (*removal*) déblaiement *m*; (*permission*) autorisation *f*; **~-cut** *adj* clair(e), nettement défini(e); **~ing** *n* (*in forest*) clairière *f*; **~ing bank** (BRIT) *n* banque qui appartient à une chambre *de compensation;* **~ly** *adv* clairement; (*evidently*) de toute évidence; **~way** (*BRIT*) *n* route *f* à stationnement interdit

clef [klef] *n* (*MUS*) clé *f*

cleft [kleft] *n* (*in rock*) crevasse *f*, fissure *f*

clench [klentʃ] *vt* serrer

clergy [ˈkləːdʒɪ] *n* clergé *m*; **~man** (*irreg*) *n* ecclésiastique *m*

clerical [ˈklerɪkəl] *adj* de bureau, d'employé de bureau; (*REL*) clérical(e), du clergé

clerk [klɑːk, (*US*) kləːk] *n* employé(e) de bureau; (*US: salesperson*) vendeur(euse)

clever [ˈklevə*] *adj* (*mentally*) intelligent(e), (*deft, crafty*) habile, adroit(e); (*device, arrangement*) ingénieux(euse), astucieux(euse)

clew [kluː] (*US*) *n* = **clue**

click [klɪk] *vi* faire un bruit sec *or* un déclic ♦ *vt*: **to ~ one's tongue** faire claquer sa langue; **to ~ one's heels** claquer des talons

client [ˈklaɪənt] *n* client(e)

cliff [klɪf] *n* falaise *f*

climate [ˈklaɪmɪt] *n* climat *m*

climax [ˈklaɪmæks] *n* apogée *m*, point culminant; (*sexual*) orgasme *m*

climb [klaɪm] *vi* grimper, monter ♦ *vt* gravir, escalader, monter sur ♦ *n* montée *f*, escalade *f*; **~-down** *n* reculade *f*, dérobade *f*; **~er** *n* (*mountaineer*) grimpeur(euse), varappeur(euse); (*plant*) plante grimpante; **~ing** *n* (*mountaineering*) escalade *f*, varappe *f*

clinch [klɪntʃ] *vt* (*deal*) conclure, sceller

cling [klɪŋ] (*pt, pp* **clung**) *vi*: **to ~ (to)** se cramponner (à), s'accrocher (à); (*of clothes*) coller (à)

clinic [ˈklɪnɪk] *n* centre médical; **~al** *adj* clinique; (*attitude*) froid(e), détaché(e)

clink [klɪŋk] *vi* tinter, cliqueter

clip [klɪp] *n* (*for hair*) barrette *f*; (*also: paper ~*) trombone *m* ♦ *vt* (*fasten*) attacher; (*hair, nails*) couper; (*hedge*) tailler; **~pers** *npl* (*for hedge*) sécateur *m*; (*also: nail ~pers*) coupe-ongles *m inv*; **~ping** *n* (*from newspaper*) coupure *f* de journal

cloak [kləʊk] *n* grande cape ♦ *vt* (*fig*) masquer, cacher; **~room** *n* (*for coats etc*) vestiaire *m*; (*BRIT: WC*) toilettes *fpl*

clock [klɒk] *n* (*large*) horloge *f*; (*small*) pendule *f*; **~ in** (*BRIT*) *vi* pointer (en arrivant); **~ off** (*BRIT*) *vi* pointer (en partant); **~ on** (*BRIT*) *vi* = **clock in**; **~ out** (*BRIT*) *vi* = **clock off**; **~wise** *adv* dans le sens des aiguilles d'une montre; **~work** *n* rouages *mpl*, mécanisme *m*; (*of clock*) mouvement *m* (d'horlogerie) ♦ *adj* mécanique

clog [klɒg] *n* sabot *m* ♦ *vt* boucher ♦ *vi* (*also: ~ up*) se boucher

cloister [ˈklɔɪstə*] *n* cloître *m*

close1 [kləʊs] *adj* (*near*): **~ (to)** près (de), proche (de); (*contact, link*) étroit(e); (*contest*) très serré(e); (*watch*) étroit(e), strict(e); (*examination*) attentif(ive), minutieux(euse); (*weather*) lourd(e), étouffant(e) ♦ *adv* près, à proximité; **~ to** près de; **~ by** *adj* proche ♦ *adv* tout(e) près; **~ at hand** = **by**; **a ~ friend** un ami intime; **to have a ~ shave** (*fig*) l'échapper belle

close2 [kləʊz] *vt* fermer ♦ *vi* (*shop etc*) fermer; (*lid, door etc*) se fermer; (*end*) se terminer, se conclure ♦ *n* (*end*) conclusion *f*, fin *f*; **~ down** *vt, vi* fermer (*définitivement*)

closed [kləʊzd] *adj* fermé(e); **~ shop** *n* organisation *f* qui n'admet que des travailleurs syndiqués

close-knit [kləʊsˈnɪt] *adj* (*family, community*) très uni(e)

closely [ˈkləʊslɪ] *adv* (*examine, watch*) de près

closet [ˈklɒzɪt] *n* (*cupboard*) placard *m*, réduit *m*

close-up [ˈkləʊsʌp] *n* gros plan

closure [ˈkləʊʒə*] *n* fermeture *f*

clot [klɒt] *n* (*gen: blood ~*) caillot *m*; (*inf: person*) ballot *m* ♦ *vi* (*blood*) se coaguler

cloth [klɒθ] *n* (*material*) tissu *m*, étoffe *f*; (*also: tea~*) torchon *m*; lavette *f*

clothe [kləʊð] *vt* habiller, vêtir; **~s** *npl* vêtements *mpl*, habits *mpl*; **~s brush** *n* brosse *f* à habits; **~s line** *n* corde *f* (à linge); **~s peg** (*US* **~s pin**) *n* pince *f* à linge

clothing ['kləʊðɪŋ] n = **clothes**

cloud [klaʊd] n nuage m; **~burst** n grosse averse; **~y** adj nuageux(euse), couvert(e); (*liquid*) trouble

clout [klaʊt] vt flanquer une taloche à

clove [kləʊv] n (*CULIN: spice*) clou m de girofle; **~ of garlic** gousse f d'ail

clover ['kləʊvə*] n trèfle m

clown [klaʊn] n clown m ♦ vi (*also:* ~ *about*, ~ *around*) faire le clown

cloying ['klɔɪɪŋ] adj (*taste, smell*) écœurant(e)

club [klʌb] n (*society, place: also: golf* ~) club m; (*weapon*) massue f, matraque f ♦ vt matraquer ♦ vi: **to ~ together** s'associer; **~s** npl (*CARDS*) trèfle m; **~ car** n (*US*) (*RAIL*) wagon-restaurant m; **~ class** n (*AVIAT*) classe f club; **~house** n club m

cluck [klʌk] vi glousser

clue [klu:] n indice m; (*in crosswords*) définition f; **I haven't a ~** je n'en ai pas la moindre idée

clump [klʌmp] n: **~ of trees** bouquet m d'arbres; **a ~ of buildings** un ensemble de bâtiments

clumsy ['klʌmzɪ] adj gauche, maladroit(e)

clung [klʌŋ] pt, pp of **cling**

cluster ['klʌstə*] n (*of people*) (petit) groupe; (*of flowers*) grappe f; (*of stars*) amas m ♦ vi se rassembler

clutch [klʌtʃ] n (*grip, grasp*) étreinte f, prise f; (*AUT*) embrayage m ♦ vt (*grasp*) agripper; (*hold tightly*) serrer fort; (*hold on to*) se cramponner à

clutter ['klʌtə*] vt (*also:* ~ *up*) encombrer

CND n abbr (= *Campaign for Nuclear Disarmament*) mouvement pour le désarmement nucléaire

Co. abbr = **county**; **company**

c/o abbr (= *care of*) c/o, aux bons soins de

coach [kəʊtʃ] n (*bus*) autocar m; (*horse-drawn*) diligence f; (*of train*) voiture f, wagon m; (*SPORT: trainer*) entraîneur(euse); (*SCOL: tutor*) répétiteur(trice) ♦ vt entraîner; (*student*) faire

travailler; **~ trip** n excursion f en car

coal [kəʊl] n charbon m; **~ face** n front m de taille; **~field** n bassin houiller

coalition [kəʊə'lɪʃən] n coalition f

coal: ~man ['kəʊlmən] (*irreg*) n charbonnier m, marchand m de charbon; **~ merchant** n = **~man**; **~mine** ['kəʊlmaɪn] n mine f de charbon

coarse [kɔ:s] adj grossier(ère), rude

coast [kəʊst] n côte f ♦ vi (*car, cycle etc*) descendre en roue libre; **~al** adj côtier(ère); **~guard** n garde-côte m; (*service*) gendarmerie f maritime; **~line** n côte f, littoral m

coat [kəʊt] n manteau m; (*of animal*) pelage m, poil m; (*of paint*) couche f ♦ vt couvrir; **~ hanger** n cintre m; **~ing** n couche f, revêtement m; **~ of arms** n blason m, armoiries fpl

coax [kəʊks] vt persuader par des cajoleries

cob [kɒb] n see **corn**

cobbler ['kɒblə*] n cordonnier m

cobbles ['kɒblz] (*also:* **cobblestones**) npl pavés (ronds)

cobweb ['kɒbweb] n toile f d'araignée

cocaine [kə'keɪn] n cocaïne f

cock [kɒk] n (*rooster*) coq m; (*male bird*) mâle m ♦ vt (*gun*) armer; **~erel** n jeune coq m; **~-eyed** adj (*idea, method*) absurde, qui ne tient pas debout

cockle ['kɒkl] n coque f

cockney ['kɒknɪ] n cockney m, *habitant des quartiers populaires de l'East End de Londres*, ≈ faubourien(ne)

cockpit ['kɒkpɪt] n (*in aircraft*) poste m de pilotage, cockpit m

cockroach ['kɒkrəʊtʃ] n cafard m

cocktail ['kɒkteɪl] n cocktail m (*fruit ~ etc*) salade f; **~ cabinet** n (meuble-)bar m; **~ party** n cocktail m

cocoa ['kəʊkəʊ] n cacao m

coconut ['kəʊkənʌt] n noix f de coco

COD abbr = **cash on delivery**

cod [kɒd] n morue fraîche, cabillaud m

code [kəʊd] n code m

cod-liver oil ['kɒdlɪvər-] n huile f de foie de morue

coercion [kəʊ'ɜ:ʃən] n contrainte f

coffee ['kɒfɪ] *n* café *m*; ~ **bar** (BRIT) *n* café *m*; ~ **bean** *n* grain *m* de café; ~ **break** *n* pause-café *f*; ~**pot** *n* cafetière *f*; ~ **table** *n* (petite) table basse

coffin ['kɒfɪn] *n* cercueil *m*

cog [kɒg] *n* dent *f* (d'engrenage); (*wheel*) roue dentée

cogent ['kəʊdʒənt] *adj* puissant(e), convaincant(e)

coil [kɔɪl] *n* rouleau *m*, bobine *f*; (*contraceptive*) stérilet *m* ♦ *vt* enrouler

coin [kɔɪn] *n* pièce *f* de monnaie ♦ *vt* (*word*) inventer; ~**age** *n* monnaie *f*, système *m* monétaire; ~ **box** (BRIT) *n* cabine *f* téléphonique

coincide [kəʊɪn'saɪd] *vi* coïncider; ~**nce** [kəʊ'ɪnsɪdəns] *n* coïncidence *f*

Coke [kəʊk] (®) *n* coca *m*

coke [kəʊk] *n* coke *m*

colander ['kɒləndə*] *n* passoire *f*

cold [kəʊld] *adj* froid(e) ♦ *n* froid *m*; (MED) rhume *m*; **it's** ~ il fait froid; **to be** *or* **feel** ~ (*person*) avoir froid; **to catch** ~ prendre *or* attraper froid; **to catch a** ~ attraper un rhume; **in** ~ **blood** de sangfroid; ~**-shoulder** *vt* se montrer froid(e) envers, snober; ~ **sore** *n* bouton *m* de fièvre

coleslaw ['kəʊlslɔː] *n* sorte de salade de chou cru

colic ['kɒlɪk] *n* colique(s) *f(pl)*

collapse [kə'læps] *vi* s'effondrer, s'écrouler ♦ *n* effondrement *m*, écroulement *m*; **collapsible** [kə'læpsəbl] *adj* pliant(e); télescopique

collar ['kɒlə*] *n* (*of coat, shirt*) col *m*; (*for animal*) collier *m*; ~**bone** *n* clavicule *f*

collateral [kɒ'lætərəl] *n* nantissement *m*

colleague ['kɒliːg] *n* collègue *m/f*

collect [kə'lekt] *vt* rassembler; ramasser; (*as a hobby*) collectionner; (BRIT: *call and pick up*) (passer) prendre; (*mail*) faire la levée de, ramasser; (*money owed*) encaisser; (*donations, subscriptions*) recueillir ♦ *vi* (*people*) se rassembler; (*things*) s'amasser; **to call** ~ (US: TEL) téléphoner en P.C.V.; ~**ion** [kə'lekʃən] *n* collection *f*; (*of mail*) levée *f*; (*for money*) collecte *f*, quête *f*; ~**or** [kə'lektə*] *n* collectionneur *m*

college ['kɒlɪdʒ] *n* collège *m*

collide [kə'laɪd] *vi* entrer en collision

collie ['kɒlɪ] *n* (*dog*) colley *m*

colliery ['kɒlɪərɪ] (BRIT) *n* mine *f* de charbon, houillère *f*

collision [kə'lɪʒən] *n* collision *f*

colloquial [kə'ləʊkwɪəl] *adj* familier(ère)

colon ['kəʊlən] *n* (*sign*) deux-points *m inv*; (MED) côlon *m*

colonel ['kɜːnl] *n* colonel *m*

colony ['kɒlənɪ] *n* colonie *f*

colour ['kʌlə*] (US **color**) *n* couleur *f* ♦ *vt* (*paint*) peindre; (*dye*) teindre; (*news*) fausser, exagérer ♦ *vi* (*blush*) rougir; ~**s** *npl* (*of party, club*) couleurs *fpl*; ~ **in** *vt* colorier; ~ **bar** *n* discrimination raciale (*dans un établissement*); ~**blind** *adj* daltonien(ne); ~**ed** *adj* (*person*) de couleur; (*illustration*) en couleur; ~ **film** *n* (*for camera*) pellicule *f* (en) couleur; ~**ful** *adj* coloré(e), vif(vive); (*personality*) pittoresque, haut(e) en couleurs; ~**ing** *n* colorant *m*; (*complexion*) teint *m*; ~ **scheme** *n* combinaison *f* de(s) couleurs; ~ **television** *n* télévision *f* (en) couleur

colt [kəʊlt] *n* poulain *m*

column ['kɒləm] *n* colonne *f*; ~**ist** ['kɒləmnɪst] *n* chroniqueur(euse)

coma ['kəʊmə] *n* coma *m*

comb [kəʊm] *n* peigne *m* ♦ *vt* (*hair*) peigner; (*area*) ratisser, passer au peigne fin

combat ['kɒmbæt] *n* combat *m* ♦ *vt* combattre, lutter contre

combination [kɒmbɪ'neɪʃən] *n* combinaison *f*

combine [*vb* kəm'baɪn, *n* 'kɒmbaɪn] *vt*: **to** ~ **sth with sth** combiner qch avec qch; (*one quality with another*) joindre *or* allier qch à qch ♦ *vi* s'associer; (CHEM) se combiner ♦ *n* (ECON) trust *m*; ~ (**harvester**) *n* moissonneuse-batteuse(-lieuse) *f*

come [kʌm] (*pt* **came**, *pp* **come**) *vi* venir, arriver; **to** ~ **to** (*decision etc*) parvenir *or* arriver à; **to** ~ **undone/loose** se défaire/desserrer; **~ about** *vi* se produire, arriver; **~ across** *vt fus* rencontrer par hasard, tomber sur; **~ along** *vi* = **to come on**; **~ away** *vi* partir, s'en aller, se détacher; **~ back** *vi* revenir; **~ by** *vt fus* (*acquire*) obtenir, se procurer; **~ down** *vi* descendre; (*prices*) baisser; (*buildings*) s'écrouler, être démoli(e); **~ forward** *vi* s'avancer, se présenter, s'annoncer; **~ from** *vt fus* être originaire de, venir de; **~ in** *vi* entrer; **~ in for** *vi* (*criticism etc*) être l'objet de; **~ into** *vt fus* (*money*) hériter de; **~ off** *vi* (*button*) se détacher; (*stain*) s'enlever; (*attempt*) réussir; **~ on** *vi* (*pupil, work, project*) faire des progrès, s'avancer; (*lights, electricity*) s'allumer; (*central heating*) se mettre en marche; **~ on!** viens!, allons!, allez!; **~ out** *vi* sortir; (*book*) paraître; (*strike*) cesser le travail, se mettre en grève; **~ round** *vi* (*after faint, operation*) revenir à soi, reprendre connaissance; **~ to** *vi* revenir à soi; **~ up** *vi* monter; **~ up against** *vt fus* (*resistance, difficulties*) rencontrer; **~ up with** *vt fus*: **he came up with an idea** il a eu une idée, il a proposé quelque chose; **~ upon** *vt fus* tomber sur; **~back** ['kʌmbæk] *n* (THEATRE *etc*) rentrée *f*

comedian [kə'miːdɪən] *n* (*in music hall etc*) comique *m*; (THEATRE) comédien *m*

comedy ['kɒmədɪ] *n* comédie *f*

comeuppance [kʌm'ʌpəns] *n*: **to get one's ~** recevoir ce qu'on mérite

comfort ['kʌmfət] *n* confort *m*, bien-être *m*; (*relief*) soulagement *m*, réconfort *m* ♦ *vt* consoler, réconforter; **the ~s of home** les commodités *fpl* de la maison; **~able** *adj* confortable; (*person*) à l'aise; (*patient*) dont l'état est stationnaire; (*walk etc*) facile; **~ably** *adv* (*sit*) confortablement; (*live*) à l'aise; **~ station** (*US*) *n* toilettes *fpl*

comic ['kɒmɪk] *adj* (*also*: *~al*) comique ♦ *n* comique *m*; (BRIT: *magazine*) illustré *m*; **~ strip** *n* bande dessinée

coming ['kʌmɪŋ] *n* arrivée *f* ♦ *adj* prochain(e), à venir; **~(s) and going(s)** *n(pl)* va-et-vient *m inv*

comma ['kɒmə] *n* virgule *f*

command [kə'mɑːnd] *n* ordre *m*, commandement *m*; (MIL: *authority*) commandement; (*mastery*) maîtrise *f* ♦ *vt* (*troops*) commander; **to ~ sb to do** ordonner à qn de faire; **~eer** [kɒmən'dɪə*] *vt* réquisitionner; **~er** *n* (MIL) commandant *m*

commando [kə'mɑːndəʊ] *n* commando *m*; membre *m* d'un commando

commemorate [kə'meməreɪt] *vt* commémorer

commence [kə'mens] *vt*, *vi* commencer

commend [kə'mend] *vt* louer; (*recommend*) recommander

commensurate [kə'mensjʊrɪt] *adj*: **~ with** *or* **to** en proportion de, proportionné(e) à

comment ['kɒment] *n* commentaire *m* ♦ *vi*: **to ~ (on)** faire des remarques (sur); **"no ~"** "je n'ai rien à dire"; **~ary** ['kɒməntrɪ] *n* commentaire *m*; (SPORT) reportage *m* (en direct); **~ator** ['kɒməntɛɪtə*] *n* commentateur *m*; reporter *m*

commerce ['kɒmɜːs] *n* commerce *m*

commercial [kə'mɜːʃəl] *adj* commercial(e) ♦ *n* (TV, RADIO) annonce *f* publicitaire, spot *m* (publicitaire); **~ radio** *n* radio privée; **~ television** *n* télévision privée

commiserate [kə'mɪzəreɪt] *vi*: **to ~ with sb** témoigner de la sympathie pour qn

commission [kə'mɪʃən] *n* (*order for work*) commande *f*; (*committee, fee*) commission *f* ♦ *vt* (*work of art*) commander, charger un artiste de l'exécution de; **out of ~** (*not working*) hors service; **~aire** [kəmɪʃə'nɛə*] (BRIT) *n* (*at shop, cinema etc*) portier *m* (en uniforme); **~er** *n* (POLICE) préfet *m* (de police)

commit [kə'mɪt] *vt* (*act*) commettre; (*resources*) consacrer; (*to sb's care*) confier (à); **to ~ o.s. (to do)** s'engager (à faire); **to ~ suicide** se suicider; **~ment** *n* engagement *m*; (*obligation*) responsabilité(s) *f(pl)*

committee [kə'mɪtɪ] *n* comité *m*

commodity [kə'mɒdɪtɪ] *n* produit *m*,

marchandise f, article m

common ['kɒmən] *adj* commun(e); (*usual*) courant(e) ♦ *n* terrain communal; **the C~s** *npl* la chambre des Communes; **in ~** en commun; **~er** *n* roturier(ière); **~ law** *n* droit coutumier; **~ly** *adv* communément, généralement; couramment; **C~ Market** *n*: **the C~ Market** le Marché commun; **~place** *adj* banal(e), ordinaire; **~ room** *n* salle commune; **~ sense** *n* bon sens; **C~wealth** (*BRIT*) *n*: **the C~wealth** le Commonwealth

commotion [kə'məʊʃən] *n* désordre m, tumulte m

communal ['kɒmjuːnl] *adj* (*life*) communautaire; (*for common use*) commun(e)

commune [*n* 'kɒmjuːn, *vb* kə'mjuːn] *n* (*group*) communauté f ♦ *vi*: **to ~ with** communier avec

communicate [kə'mjuːnɪkeɪt] *vt, vi* communiquer

communication [kəmjuːnɪ'keɪʃən] *n* communication f; **~ cord** (*BRIT*) *n* sonnette f d'alarme

communion [kə'mjuːnɪən] *n* (*also: Holy C~*) communion f

communism ['kɒmjʊnɪzəm] *n* communisme m; **communist** ['kɒmjʊnɪst] *adj* communiste ♦ *n* communiste *m/f*

community [kə'mjuːnɪtɪ] *n* communauté f; **~ centre** *n* centre m de loisirs; **~ chest** (*US*) *n* fonds commun; **~ home** *n* (*school*) centre m d'éducation surveillée

commutation ticket [kɒmjʊ'teɪʃən-] (*US*) *n* carte f d'abonnement

commute [kə'mjuːt] *vi* faire un trajet journalier (de son domicile à son bureau) ♦ *vt* (*LAW*) commuer; **~r** *n* banlieusard(e) (qui ... *see vi*)

compact [*adj* kəm'pækt, *n* 'kɒmpækt] *adj* compact(e) ♦ *n* (*also: powder ~*) poudrier m; **~ disc** *n* disque compact; **~ disk player** *n* lecteur m de disque compact

companion [kəm'pænɪən] *n* compagnon(compagne); **~ship** *n* camaraderie f

company ['kʌmpənɪ] *n* compagnie f; **to keep sb ~** tenir compagnie à qn;

~ secretary (*BRIT*) *n* (*COMM*) secrétaire général (*d'une société*)

comparative [kəm'pærətɪv] *adj* (*study*) comparatif(ive); (*relative*) relatif(ive); **~ly** *adv* (*relatively*) relativement

compare [kəm'pɛə*] *vt*: **to ~ sth/sb with/to** comparer qch/qn avec *or* et/à ♦ *vi*: **to ~ (with)** se comparer (à); être comparable à; **comparison** [kəm'pærɪsn] *n* comparaison f

compartment [kəm'pɑːtmənt] *n* compartiment m

compass ['kʌmpəs] *n* boussole f; **~es** *npl* (*GEOM: also: pair of ~es*) compas m

compassion [kəm'pæʃən] *n* compassion f; **~ate** *adj* compatissant(e)

compatible [kəm'pætɪbl] *adj* compatible

compel [kəm'pel] *vt* contraindre, obliger; **~ling** *adj* (*fig: argument*) irrésistible

compensate ['kɒmpenseɪt] *vt* indemniser, dédommager ♦ *vi*: **to ~ for** compenser; **compensation** [kɒmpen'seɪʃn] *n* compensation f; (*money*) dédommagement m, indemnité f

compère ['kɒmpɛə*] *n* (*TV*) animateur(trice)

compete [kəm'piːt] *vi*: **to ~ (with)** rivaliser (avec), faire concurrence (à)

competent ['kɒmpɪtənt] *adj* compétent(e), capable

competition [kɒmpɪ'tɪʃən] *n* (*contest*) compétition f, concours m; (*ECON*) concurrence f

competitive [kəm'petɪtɪv] *adj* (*ECON*) concurrentiel(le); (*sport*) de compétition; (*person*) qui a l'esprit de compétition

competitor [kəm'petɪtə*] *n* concurrent(e)

complacency [kəm'pleɪsnsɪ] *n* suffisance f, vaine complaisance

complain [kəm'pleɪn] *vi*: **to ~ (about)** se plaindre (de); (*in shop etc*) réclamer (au sujet de); **to ~ of** (*pain*) se plaindre de; **~t** *n* plainte f; réclamation f; (*MED*) affection f

complement [*n* 'kɒmplɪmənt, *vb* 'kɒmplɪment] *n* complément m; (*especially of ship's crew etc*) effectif complet ♦ *vt* (*enhance*) compléter; **~ary** [kɒmplɪ'mentərɪ] *adj* complémentaire

complete [kəm'pliːt] *adj* complet(ète) ♦ *vt* achever, parachever; (*set, group*) compléter; (*a form*) remplir; **~ly** *adv* complètement; **completion** [kəm'pliːʃən] *n* achèvement *m*; (*of contract*) exécution *f*

complex ['kɒmpleks] *adj* complexe ♦ *n* complexe *m*

complexion [kəm'plekʃən] *n* (*of face*) teint *m*

compliance [kəm'plaɪəns] *n* (*submission*) docilité *f*; (*agreement*): **~ with** le fait de se conformer à; **in ~ with** en accord avec

complicate ['kɒmplɪkeɪt] *vt* compliquer; **~d** *adj* compliqué(e); **complication** [kɒmplɪ'keɪʃn] *n* complication *f*

compliment [*n* 'kɒmplɪmənt, *vb* 'kɒmplɪment] *n* compliment *m* ♦ *vt* complimenter; **~s** *npl* (*respects*) compliments *mpl*, hommages *mpl*; **to pay sb a ~** faire *or* adresser un compliment à qn; **~ary** [kɒmplɪ'mentərɪ] *adj* flatteur(euse); (*free*) (offert(e)) à titre gracieux; **~ary ticket** *n* billet *m* de faveur

comply [kəm'plaɪ] *vi*: **to ~ with** se soumettre à, se conformer à

component [kəm'pəunənt] *n* composant *m*, élément *m*

compose [kəm'pəuz] *vt* composer; (*form*): **to be ~d of** se composer de; **to ~ o.s.** se calmer, se maîtriser; prendre une contenance; **~d** *adj* calme, posé(e); **~r** *n* (*MUS*) compositeur *m*; **composition** [kɒmpə'zɪʃən] *n* composition *f*; **composure** [kəm'pəuʒə*] *n* calme *m*, maîtrise *f* de soi

compound ['kɒmpaund] *n* composé *m*; (*enclosure*) enclos *m*, enceinte *f*; **~ fracture** *n* fracture compliquée; **~ interest** *n* intérêt composé

comprehend [kɒmprɪ'hend] *vt* comprendre; **comprehension** [kɒmprɪ'henʃən] *n* compréhension *f*

comprehensive [kɒmprɪ'hensɪv] *adj* (très) complet(ète); **~ policy** *n* (*INSURANCE*) assurance *f* tous risques; **~ (school)** (*BRIT*) *n* école secondaire polyvalente, ≈

C.E.S. *m*

compress [*vb* kəm'pres, *n* 'kɒmpres] *vt* comprimer; (*text, information*) condenser ♦ *n* (*MED*) compresse *f*

comprise [kəm'praɪz] *vt* (*also: be ~d of*) comprendre; (*constitute*) constituer, représenter

compromise ['kɒmprəmaɪz] *n* compromis *m* ♦ *vt* compromettre ♦ *vi* transiger, accepter un compromis

compulsion [kəm'pʌlʃən] *n* contrainte *f*, force *f*

compulsive [kəm'pʌlsɪv] *adj* (*PSYCH*) compulsif(ive); (*book, film etc*) captivant(e)

compulsory [kəm'pʌlsərɪ] *adj* obligatoire

computer [kəm'pjuːtə*] *n* ordinateur *m*; **~ game** *n* jeu *m* vidéo; **~ize** *vt* informatiser; **~ programmer** *n* programmeur(euse); **~ programming** *n* programmation *f*; **~ science** *n* informatique *f*; **computing** *n* = **~ science**

comrade ['kɒmrɪd] *n* camarade *m/f*

con [kɒn] *vt* duper; (*cheat*) escroquer ♦ *n* escroquerie *f*

conceal [kən'siːl] *vt* cacher, dissimuler

conceit [kən'siːt] *n* vanité *f*, suffisance *f*, prétention *f*; **~ed** *adj* vaniteux(euse), suffisant(e)

conceive [kən'siːv] *vt*, *vi* concevoir

concentrate ['kɒnsəntreɪt] *vi* se concentrer ♦ *vt* concentrer

concentration [kɒnsən'treɪʃən] *n* concentration *f*; **~ camp** *n* camp *m* de concentration

concept ['kɒnsept] *n* concept *m*

concern [kən'sɜːn] *n* affaire *f*; (*COMM*) entreprise *f*, firme *f*; (*anxiety*) inquiétude *f*, souci *m* ♦ *vt* concerner; **to be ~ed (about)** s'inquiéter (de), être inquiet(e) (au sujet de); **~ing** *prep* en ce qui concerne, à propos de

concert ['kɒnsət] *n* concert *m*; **~ed** [kən'sɜːtɪd] *adj* concerté(e); **~ hall** *n* salle *f* de concert

concerto [kən'tʃɜːtəu] *n* concerto *m*

concession [kən'sɛʃən] *n* concession *f*; **tax ~** dégrèvement fiscal

conclude [kən'kluːd] *vt* conclure; **conclusion** [kən'kluːʒən] *n* conclusion *f*; **conclusive** [kən'kluːsɪv] *adj* concluant(e), définitif(ive)

concoct [kən'kɒkt] *vt* confectionner, composer; (*fig*) inventer; **~ion** [kən'kɒkʃən] *n* mélange *m*

concourse ['kɒŋkɔːs] *n* (*hall*) hall *m*, salle *f* des pas perdus

concrete ['kɒŋkriːt] *n* béton *m* ♦ *adj* concret(ète); (*floor etc*) en béton

concur [kən'kɜː*] *vi* (*agree*) être d'accord

concurrently [kən'kʌrəntlɪ] *adv* simultanément

concussion [kən'kʌʃən] *n* (*MED*) commotion (cérébrale)

condemn [kən'dem] *vt* condamner

condensation [kɒndən'seɪʃən] *n* condensation *f*

condense [kən'dens] *vi* se condenser ♦ *vt* condenser; **~d milk** *n* lait concentré (sucré)

condition [kən'dɪʃən] *n* condition *f*; (*MED*) état *m* ♦ *vt* déterminer, conditionner; **on ~ that** à condition que +*sub*, à condition de; **~al** *adj* conditionnel(le); **~er** *n* (*for hair*) baume après-shampooing *m*; (*for fabrics*) assouplissant *m*

condolences [kən'dəʊlənsɪz] *npl* condoléances *fpl*

condom ['kɒndəm] *n* préservatif *m*

condominium [kɒndə'mɪnɪəm] (*US*) *n* (*building*) immeuble *m* (en copropriété)

condone [kən'dəʊn] *vt* fermer les yeux sur, approuver (tacitement)

conducive [kən'djuːsɪv] *adj*: **~ to** favorable à, qui contribue à

conduct [*n* 'kɒndʌkt, *vb* kən'dʌkt] *n* conduite *f* ♦ *vt* conduire; (*MUS*) diriger; **to ~ o.s.** se conduire, se comporter; **~ed tour** *n* voyage organisé; (*of building*) visite guidée; **~or** [kən'dʌktə*] *n* (*of orchestra*) chef *m* d'orchestre; (*on bus*) receveur *m*; (*US: on train*) chef *m* de train; (*ELEC*) conducteur *m*; **~ress** [kən'dʌktrɪs] *n* (*on bus*) receveuse *f*

cone [kəʊn] *n* cône *m*; (*for ice-cream*) cornet *m*; (*BOT*) pomme *f* de pin, cône

confectioner [kən'fekʃənə*] *n* confiseur(euse); **~'s (shop)** *n* confiserie *f*; **~y** *n* confiserie *f*

confer [kən'fɜː*] *vt*: **to ~ sth on** conférer qch à ♦ *vi* conférer, s'entretenir

conference ['kɒnfərəns] *n* conférence *f*

confess [kən'fes] *vt* confesser, avouer ♦ *vi* se confesser; **~ion** [kən'feʃən] *n* confession *f*

confetti [kən'fetɪ] *n* confettis *mpl*

confide [kən'faɪd] *vi*: **to ~ in** se confier à

confidence ['kɒnfɪdəns] *n* confiance *f*; (*also: self-~*) assurance *f*, confiance en soi; (*secret*) confidence *f*; **in ~** (*speak, write*) en confidence, confidentiellement; **~ trick** *n* escroquerie *f*; **confident** ['kɒnfɪdənt] *adj* sûr(e), assuré(e); **confidential** [kɒnfɪ'denʃəl] *adj* confidentiel(le)

confine [kən'faɪn] *vt* limiter, borner; (*shut up*) confiner, enfermer; **~d** *adj* (*space*) restreint(e), réduit(e); **~ment** *n* emprisonnement *m*, détention *f*; **~s** ['kɒnfaɪnz] *npl* confins *mpl*, bornes *fpl*

confirm [kən'fɜːm] *vt* confirmer; (*appointment*) ratifier; **~ation** [kɒnfə'meɪʃən] *n* confirmation *f*; **~ed** *adj* invétéré(e), incorrigible

confiscate ['kɒnfɪskeɪt] *vt* confisquer

conflict [*n* 'kɒnflɪkt, *vb* kən'flɪkt] *n* conflit *m*, lutte *f* ♦ *vi* être *or* entrer en conflit; (*opinions*) s'opposer, se heurter; **~ing** [kən'flɪktɪŋ] *adj* contradictoire

conform [kən'fɔːm] *vi*: **to ~ (to)** se conformer (à)

confound [kən'faʊnd] *vt* confondre

confront [kən'frʌnt] *vt* confronter, mettre en présence; (*enemy, danger*) affronter, faire face à; **~ation** [kɒnfrən'teɪʃən] *n* confrontation *f*

confuse [kən'fjuːz] *vt* (*person*) troubler; (*situation*) embrouiller; (*one thing with another*) confondre; **~d** *adj* (*person*) dérouté(e), désorienté(e); **confusing** *adj* peu clair(e), déroutant(e); **confusion** [kən'fjuːʒən] *n* confusion *f*

congeal [kən'dʒiːl] *vi* (*blood*) se coaguler; (*oil etc*) se figer

congenial [kən'dʒi:nıəl] *adj* sympathique, agréable

congested [kən'dʒestıd] *adj* (MED) congestionné(e); (*area*) surpeuplé(e); (*road*) bloqué(e)

congestion [kən'dʒestʃən] *n* congestion *f*; (*fig*) encombrement *m*

congratulate [kən'grætjʊleıt] *vt*: **to ~ sb (on)** féliciter qn (de); **congratulations** [kəngrætjʊ'leıʃənz] *npl* félicitations *fpl*

congregate ['kɔŋgrıgeıt] *vi* se rassembler, se réunir

congregation [kɔŋgrı'geıʃən] *n* assemblée *f* (des fidèles)

congress ['kɔŋgres] *n* congrès *m*; **~man** (*irreg*: US) *n* membre *m* du Congrès

conjunction [kən'dʒʌŋkʃən] *n* (LING) conjonction *f*

conjunctivitis [kəndʒʌŋktı'vaıtıs] *n* conjonctivite *f*

conjure ['kʌndʒə*] *vi* faire des tours de passe-passe; **~ up** *vt* (*ghost, spirit*) faire apparaître; (*memories*) évoquer; **~r** *n* prestidigitateur *m*, illusionniste *m/f*

conk out [kɔŋk-] (*inf*) *vi* tomber *or* rester en panne

con man (*irreg*) *n* escroc *m*

connect [kə'nekt] *vt* joindre, relier; (ELEC) connecter; (TEL: *caller*) mettre en connection (*with* avec); (: *new subscriber*) brancher; (*fig*) établir un rapport entre, faire un rapprochement entre ♦ *vi* (*train*): **to ~ with** assurer la correspondance avec; **to be ~ed with** (*fig*) avoir un rapport avec; avoir des rapports avec, être en relation avec; **~ion** [kə'nekʃə] *n* relation *f*, lien *m*; (ELEC) connexion *f*; (*train, plane etc*) correspondance *f*; (TEL) branchement *m*, communication *f*

connive [kə'naıv] *vi*: **to ~ at** se faire le complice de

conquer ['kɔŋkə*] *vt* conquérir; (*feelings*) vaincre, surmonter

conquest ['kɔŋkwest] *n* conquête *f*

cons [kɔnz] *npl see* **convenience; pro**

conscience ['kɔnʃəns] *n* conscience *f*; **conscientious** [kɔnʃı'enʃəs] *adj* consciencieux(euse)

conscious ['kɔnʃəs] *adj* conscient(e); **~ness** *n* conscience *f*; (MED) connaissance *f*

conscript ['kɔnskrıpt] *n* conscrit *m*

consent [kən'sent] *n* consentement *m* ♦ *vi*: **to ~ (to)** consentir (à)

consequence ['kɔnsıkwəns] *n* conséquence *f*, suites *fpl*; (*significance*) importance *f*

consequently ['kɔnsıkwəntlı] *adv* par conséquent, donc

conservation [kɔnsə'veıʃən] *n* préservation *f*, protection *f*

conservative [kən'sɜ:vətıv] *adj* conservateur(trice); **at a ~ estimate** au bas mot; **C~** (BRIT) *adj, n* (POL) conservateur(trice)

conservatory [kən'sɜ:vətrı] *n* (*greenhouse*) serre *f*

conserve [kən'sɜ:v] *vt* conserver, préserver; (*supplies, energy*) économiser ♦ *n* confiture *f*

consider [kən'sıdə*] *vt* (*study*) considérer, réfléchir à; (*take into account*) penser à, prendre en considération; (*regard, judge*) considérer, estimer; **to ~ doing sth** envisager de faire qch; **~able** [kən'sıdərəbl] *adj* considérable; **~ably** *adv* nettement, bien; **~ate** [kən'sıdərıt] *adj* prévenant(e), plein(e) d'égards; **~ation** [kənsıdə'reıʃən] *n* considération *f*; **~ing** [kən'sıdərıŋ] *prep* étant donné

consign [kən'saın] *vt* expédier; (*to sb's care*) confier; (*fig*) livrer; **~ment** *n* arrivage *m*, envoi *m*

consist [kən'sıst] *vi*: **to ~ of** consister en, se composer de

consistency [kən'sıstənsı] *n* consistance *f*; (*fig*) cohérence *f*

consistent [kən'sıstənt] *adj* logique, cohérent(e)

consolation [kɔnsə'leıʃən] *n* consolation *f*

console ['kɔnsəul] *n* (COMPUT) console *f*

consonant ['kɔnsənənt] *n* consonne *f*

conspicuous [kən'spıkjuəs] *adj* voyant(e), qui attire l'attention

conspiracy [kən'spırəsı] *n* conspiration *f*, complot *m*

constable ['kʌnstəbl] (*BRIT*) *n* ≈ agent *m* de police, gendarme *m*; **chief ~** ≈ préfet *m* de police

constabulary [kən'stæbjulərɪ] (*BRIT*) *n* ≈ police *f*, gendarmerie *f*

constant ['kɒnstənt] *adj* constant(e); incessant(e); **~ly** *adv* constamment, sans cesse

constipated ['kɒnstɪpeɪtəd] *adj* constipé(e); **constipation** [kɒnstɪ'peɪʃən] *n* constipation *f*

constituency [kən'stɪtjuənsɪ] *n* circonscription électorale

constituent [kən'stɪtjuənt] *n* (*POL*) électeur(trice); (*part*) élément constitutif, composant *m*

constitution [kɒnstɪ'tjuːʃən] *n* constitution *f*; **~al** *adj* constitutionnel(le)

constraint [kən'streɪnt] *n* contrainte *f*

construct [kən'strʌkt] *vt* construire; **~ion** [kən'strʌkʃən] *n* construction *f*; **~ive** *adj* constructif(ive)

construe [kən'struː] *vt* interpréter, expliquer

consul ['kɒnsl] *n* consul *m*; **~ate** ['kɒnsjulət] *n* consulat *m*

consult [kən'sʌlt] *vt* consulter; **~ant** *n* (*MED*) médecin consultant; (*other specialist*) consultant *m*, (expert-)conseil *m*; **~ing room** (*BRIT*) *n* cabinet *m* de consultation

consume [kən'sjuːm] *vt* consommer; **~r** *n* consommateur(trice); **~r goods** *npl* biens *mpl* de consommation; **~r society** *n* société *f* de consommation

consummate ['kɒnsʌmeɪt] *vt* consommer

consumption [kən'sʌmpʃən] *n* consommation *f*

cont. *abbr* (= *continued*) suite

contact ['kɒntækt] *n* contact *m*; (*person*) connaissance *f*, relation *f* ♦ *vt* contacter, se mettre en contact or en rapport avec; **~ lenses** *npl* verres *mpl* de contact, lentilles *fpl*

contagious [kən'teɪdʒəs] *adj* contagieux(euse)

contain [kən'teɪn] *vt* contenir; **to ~ o.s.** se contenir, se maîtriser; **~er** *n* récipient *m*; (*for shipping etc*) container *m*

contaminate [kən'tæmɪneɪt] *vt* contaminer

cont'd *abbr* (= *continued*) suite

contemplate ['kɒntəmpleɪt] *vt* contempler; (*consider*) envisager

contemporary [kən'tempərərɪ] *adj* contemporain(e); (*design, wallpaper*) moderne ♦ *n* contemporain(e)

contempt [kən'tempt] *n* mépris *m*, dédain *m*; **~ of court** (*LAW*) outrage *m* à l'autorité de la justice; **~uous** *adj* dédaigneux(euse), méprisant(e)

contend [kən'tend] *vt*: **to ~ that** soutenir *or* prétendre que ♦ *vi*: **to ~ with** (*compete*) rivaliser avec; (*struggle*) lutter avec; **~er** *n* concurrent(e); (*POL*) candidat(e)

content [*adj, vb* kən'tent, *n* 'kɒntent] *adj* content(e), satisfait(e) ♦ *vt* contenter, satisfaire ♦ *n* contenu *m*; (*of fat, moisture*) teneur *f*; **~s** *npl* (*of container etc*) contenu *m*; (**table of**) **~s** table *f* des matières; **~ed** *adj* content(e), satisfait(e)

contention [kən'tenʃən] *n* dispute *f*, contestation *f*; (*argument*) assertion *f*, affirmation *f*

contest [*n* 'kɒntest, *vb* kən'test] *n* combat *m*, lutte *f*; (*competition*) concours *m* ♦ *vt* (*decision, statement*) contester, discuter; (*compete for*) disputer; **~ant** [kən'testənt] *n* concurrent(e); (*in fight*) adversaire *m/f*

context ['kɒntekst] *n* contexte *m*

continent ['kɒntɪnənt] *n* continent *m*; **the C~** (*BRIT*) l'Europe continentale; **~al** [kɒntɪ'nentl] *adj* continental(e); **~al quilt** (*BRIT*) *n* couette *f*

contingency [kən'tɪndʒənsɪ] *n* éventualité *f*, événement imprévu

continual [kən'tɪnjuəl] *adj* continuel(le)

continuation [kəntɪnju'eɪʃən] *n* continuation *f*; (*after interruption*) reprise *f*; (*of story*) suite *f*

continue [kən'tɪnjuː] *vi, vt* continuer; (*after interruption*) reprendre, poursuivre

continuity [kɒntɪ'njuːɪtɪ] *n* continuité *f*; (*TV etc*) enchaînement *m*

continuous [kən'tɪnjʊəs] *adj* continu(e); (*LING*) progressif(ive); ~ **stationery** *n* papier *m* en continu

contort [kən'tɔːt] *vt* tordre, crisper

contour ['kɒntʊə*] *n* contour *m*, profil *m*; (*on map: also:* ~ **line**) courbe *f* de niveau

contraband ['kɒntrəbænd] *n* contrebande *f*

contraceptive [kɒntrə'sɛptɪv] *adj* contraceptif(ive), anticonceptionnel(le) ♦ *n* contraceptif *m*

contract [*n* 'kɒntrækt, *vb* kən'trækt] *n* contrat *m* ♦ *vi* (*become smaller*) se contracter, se resserrer; (*COMM*): **to ~ to do sth** s'engager (par contrat) à faire qch; ~**ion** [kən'trækʃən] *n* contraction *f*; ~**or** [kən'træktə*] *n* entrepreneur *m*

contradict [kɒntrə'dɪkt] *vt* contredire

contraption [kən'træpʃən] (*pej*) *n* machin *m*, truc *m*

contrary¹ ['kɒntrərɪ] *adj* contraire, opposé(e) ♦ *n* contraire *m*; **on the ~** au contraire; **unless you hear to the ~** sauf avis contraire

contrary² [kən'trɛərɪ] *adj* (*perverse*) contrariant(e), entêté(e)

contrast [*n* 'kɒntrɑːst, *vb* kən'trɑːst] *n* contraste *m* ♦ *vt* mettre en contraste, contraster; **in ~ to** *or* **with** contrairement à

contravene [kɒntrə'viːn] *vt* enfreindre, violer, contrevenir à

contribute [kən'trɪbjuːt] *vi* contribuer ♦ *vt*: **to ~ £10/an article to** donner 10 livres/un article à; **to ~ to** contribuer à; (*newspaper*) collaborer à; **contribution** [kɒntrɪ'bjuːʃən] *n* contribution *f*; **contributor** [kən'trɪbjʊtə*] *n* (*to newspaper*) collaborateur(trice)

contrive [kən'traɪv] *vi*: **to ~ to do** s'arranger pour faire, trouver le moyen de faire

control [kən'trəʊl] *vt* maîtriser, commander; (*check*) contrôler ♦ *n* contrôle *m*, autorité *f*; maîtrise *f*; ~**s** *npl* (*of machine etc*) commandes *fpl*; (*on radio, TV*) boutons *mpl* de réglage; **everything is under ~** tout va bien, j'ai (*or* il a *etc*) la

situation en main; **to be in ~ of** être maître de, maîtriser; **the car went out of ~** j'ai (*or* il a *etc*) perdu le contrôle du véhicule; ~ **panel** *n* tableau *m* de commande; ~ **room** *n* salle *f* des commandes; ~ **tower** *n* (*AVIAT*) tour *f* de contrôle

controversial [kɒntrə'vɜːʃəl] *adj* (*topic*) discutable, controversé(e); (*person*) qui fait beaucoup parler de lui; **controversy** ['kɒntrəvɜːsɪ] *n* controverse *f*, polémique *f*

convalesce [kɒnvə'lɛs] *vi* relever de maladie, se remettre (d'une maladie)

convector [kən'vɛktə*] *n* (*heater*) radiateur *m* (à convexion)

convene [kən'viːn] *vt* convoquer, assembler ♦ *vi* se réunir, s'assembler

convenience [kən'viːnɪəns] *n* commodité *f*; **at your ~** quand *or* comme cela vous convient; **all modern ~s**, (*BRIT*) **all mod cons** avec tout le confort moderne, tout confort

convenient [kən'viːnɪənt] *adj* commode

convent ['kɒnvənt] *n* couvent *m*

convention [kən'vɛnʃən] *n* convention *f*; ~**al** *adj* conventionnel(le)

conversant [kən'vɜːsənt] *adj*: **to be ~ with** s'y connaître en; être au courant de

conversation [kɒnvə'seɪʃən] *n* conversation *f*

converse [*n* 'kɒnvɜːs, *vb* kən'vɜːs] *n* contraire *m*, inverse *m* ♦ *vi* s'entretenir; ~**ly** [kɒn'vɜːslɪ] *adv* inversement, réciproquement

convert [*vb* kən'vɜːt, *n* 'kɒnvɜːt] *vt* (*REL, COMM*) convertir; (*alter*) transformer; (*house*) aménager ♦ *n* converti(e); ~**ible** *n* (*voiture f*) décapotable *f*

convey [kən'veɪ] *vt* transporter; (*thanks*) transmettre; (*idea*) communiquer; ~**or belt** *n* convoyeur *m*, tapis roulant

convict [*vb* kən'vɪkt, *n* 'kɒnvɪkt] *vt* déclarer (*or* reconnaître) coupable ♦ *n* forçat *m*, détenu *m*; ~**ion** [kən'vɪkʃən] *n* (*LAW*) condamnation *f*; (*belief*) conviction *f*

convince [kən'vɪns] *vt* convaincre, persuader; **convincing** *adj* persuasif(ive), convaincant(e)

convoluted [kɒnvə'luːtɪd] *adj* (*argument*) compliqué(e)

convulse [kən'vʌls] *vt*: **to be ~d with laughter/pain** se tordre de rire/douleur

coo [kuː] *vi* roucouler

cook [kʊk] *vt* (faire) cuire ♦ *vi* cuire; (*person*) faire la cuisine ♦ *n* cuisinier(ière); **~book** *n* livre *m* de cuisine; **~er** *n* cuisinière *f*; **~ery** *n* cuisine *f*; **~ery book** (*BRIT*) *n* = **cookbook**; **~ie** (*US*) *n* biscuit *m*, petit gâteau sec; **~ing** *n* cuisine *f*

cool [kuːl] *adj* frais(fraîche); (*calm, unemotional*) calme; (*unfriendly*) froid(e) ♦ *vt*, *vi* rafraîchir, refroidir

coop [kuːp] *n* poulailler *m*; (*for rabbits*) clapier *m* ♦ *vt*: **to ~ up** (*fig*) cloîtrer, enfermer

cooperate [kəʊ'ɒpəreɪt] *vi* coopérer, collaborer; **cooperation** [kəʊppə'reɪʃən] *n* coopération *f*, collaboration *f*; **cooperative** [kəʊ'ɒpərətɪv] *adj* coopératif(ive) ♦ *n* coopérative *f*

coordinate [*vb* kəʊ'ɔːdɪneɪt, *n* kəʊ'ɔːdɪnət] *vt* coordonner ♦ *n* (*MATH*) coordonnée *f*; **~s** *npl* (*clothes*) ensemble *m*, coordonnés *mpl*

co-ownership [ˈkəʊˈəʊnəʃɪp] *n* copropriété *f*

cop [kɒp] (*inf*) *n* flic *m*

cope [kəʊp] *vi*: **to ~ with** faire face à; (*solve*) venir à bout de

copper [ˈkɒpə*] *n* cuivre *m*; (*BRIT*: *inf*: *policeman*) flic *m*; **~s** *npl* (*coins*) petite monnaie *f*; **~ sulphate** *n* sulfate *m* de cuivre

copy [ˈkɒpɪ] *n* copie *f*; (*of book etc*) exemplaire *m* ♦ *vt* copier; **~right** *n* droit *m* d'auteur, copyright *m*

coral [ˈkɒrəl] *n* corail *m*; **~ reef** *n* récif *m* de corail

cord [kɔːd] *n* corde *f*; (*fabric*) velours côtelé, (*ELEC*) cordon *m*, fil *m*

cordial [ˈkɔːdɪəl] *adj* cordial(e), chaleureux(euse) ♦ *n* cordial *m*

cordon [ˈkɔːdn] *n* cordon *m*; **~ off** *vt* boucler (*par cordon de police*)

corduroy [ˈkɔːdərɔɪ] *n* velours côtelé

core [kɔː*] *n* noyau *m*; (*of fruit*) trognon *m*, cœur *m*; (*of building, problem*) cœur ♦ *vt* enlever le trognon *or* le cœur de

cork [kɔːk] *n* liège *m*; (*of bottle*) bouchon *m*; **~screw** *n* tire-bouchon *m*

corn [kɔːn] *n* (*BRIT*: *wheat*) blé *m*; (*US*: *maize*) maïs *m*; (*on foot*) cor *m*; **~ on the cob** (*CULIN*) épi *m* de maïs; **~ed beef** [ˈkɔːnd-] *n* corned-beef *m*

corner [ˈkɔːnə*] *n* coin *m*; (*AUT*) tournant *m*, virage *m*; (*FOOTBALL*: *also*: **~ kick**) corner *m* ♦ *vt* acculer, mettre au pied du mur; coincer; (*COMM*: *market*) accaparer ♦ *vi* prendre un virage; **~stone** *n* pierre *f* angulaire

cornet [ˈkɔːnɪt] *n* (*MUS*) cornet *m* à pistons; (*BRIT*: *of ice-cream*) cornet (de glace)

cornflakes [ˈkɔːnfleɪks] *npl* corn-flakes *mpl*

cornflour [ˈkɔːnflaʊə*] (*BRIT*), **cornstarch** [ˈkɔːnstɑːtʃ] (*US*) *n* farine *f* de maïs, maïzena *f* (®)

Cornwall [ˈkɔːnwəl] *n* Cornouailles *f*

corny [ˈkɔːnɪ] (*inf*) *adj* rebattu(e)

coronary [ˈkɒrənərɪ] *n* (*also*: **~ thrombosis**) infarctus *m* (du myocarde), thrombose *f* coronarienne

coronation [kɒrəˈneɪʃən] *n* couronnement *m*

coroner [ˈkɒrənə*] *n* officiel chargé de déterminer les causes d'un décès

corporal [ˈkɔːpərəl] *n* caporal *m*, brigadier *m* ♦ *adj*: **~ punishment** châtiment corporel

corporate [ˈkɔːpərɪt] *adj* en commun, collectif(ive); (*COMM*) de l'entreprise

corporation [kɔːpəˈreɪʃən] *n* (*of town*) municipalité *f*, conseil municipal; (*COMM*) société *f*

corps [kɔː*, *pl* kɔːz] (*pl* **corps**) *n* corps *m*

corpse [kɔːps] *n* cadavre *m*

correct [kəˈrɛkt] *adj* (*accurate*) correct(e), exact(e); (*proper*) correct, convenable ♦ *vt* corriger; **~ion** [kəˈrɛkʃən] *n* correction *f*

correspond [kɒrɪsˈpɒnd] *vi* correspondre; **~ence** *n* correspondance *f*; **~ence course** *n* cours *m* par correspondance; **~ent** *n* correspondant(e)

corridor ['kɒrɪdɔ:*] *n* couloir *m*, corridor *m*

corrode [kə'rəʊd] *vt* corroder, ronger ♦ *vi* se corroder

corrugated ['kɒrəgeɪtɪd] *adj* plissé(e); ondulé(e); **~ iron** *n* tôle ondulée

corrupt [kə'rʌpt] *adj* corrompu(e) ♦ *vt* corrompre; **~ion** [kə'rʌpʃən] *n* corruption *f*

Corsica ['kɔ:sɪkə] *n* Corse *f*

cosmetic [kɒz'metɪk] *n* produit *m* de beauté, cosmétique *m*

cosset ['kɒsɪt] *vt* choyer, dorloter

cost [kɒst] (*pt, pp* cost) *n* coût *m* ♦ *vi* coûter ♦ *vt* établir *or* calculer le prix de revient de; **~s** *npl* (*COMM*) frais *mpl*; (*LAW*) dépens *mpl*; **it ~s £5/too much** cela coûte cinq livres/c'est trop cher; **at all ~s** coûte que coûte, à tout prix

co-star ['kəʊstɑ:*] *n* partenaire *m/f*

cost-effective ['kɒstɪ'fektɪv] *adj* rentable

costly ['kɒstlɪ] *adj* coûteux(euse)

cost-of-living ['kɒstəv'lɪvɪŋ] *adj*: **~ allowance** indemnité *f* de vie chère; **~ index** index *m* du coût de la vie

cost price (*BRIT*) *n* prix coûtant *or* de revient

costume ['kɒstju:m] *n* costume *m*; (*lady's suit*) tailleur *m*; (*BRIT*: *also*: *swimming* **~**) maillot *m* (de bain); **~ jewellery** *n* bijoux *mpl* fantaisie

cosy ['kəʊzɪ] (*US* cozy) *adj* douillet(te); (*person*) à l'aise, au chaud

cot [kɒt] *n* (*BRIT*: *child's*) lit *m* d'enfant, petit lit; (*US*: *campbed*) lit de camp

cottage ['kɒtɪdʒ] *n* petite maison (à la campagne), cottage *m*; **~ cheese** *n* fromage blanc (*maigre*)

cotton ['kɒtn] *n* coton *m*; **~ on** (*inf*) *vi*: **to ~ on to** piger; **~ candy** (*US*) *n* barbe *f* à papa; **~ wool** (*BRIT*) *n* ouate *f*, coton *m* hydrophile

couch [kaʊtʃ] *n* canapé *m*; divan *m*

couchette [ku:'ʃet] *n* couchette *f*

cough [kɒf] *vi* tousser ♦ *n* toux *f*; **~**

drop *n* pastille *f* pour *or* contre la toux

could [kʊd] *pt of* can²; **~n't** = could not

council ['kaʊnsl] *n* conseil *m*; **city** *or* **town ~** conseil municipal; **~ estate** (*BRIT*) *n* (zone *f* de) logements loués à/par la municipalité; **~ house** (*BRIT*) *n* maison *f* (à loyer modéré) louée par la municipalité; **~lor** ['kaʊnsɪlə*] *n* conseiller(ère)

counsel ['kaʊnsl] *n* (*lawyer*) avocat(e); (*advice*) conseil *m*, consultation *f*; **~lor** *n* conseiller(ère); (*US*: *lawyer*) avocat(e)

count [kaʊnt] *vt*, *vi* compter ♦ *n* compte *m*; (*nobleman*) comte *m*; **~ on** *vt fus* compter sur; **~down** *n* compte *m* à rebours

countenance ['kaʊntɪnəns] *n* expression *f* ♦ *vt* approuver

counter ['kaʊntə*] *n* comptoir *m*; (*in post office, bank*) guichet *m*; (*in game*) jeton *m* ♦ *vt* aller à l'encontre de, opposer ♦ *adv*: **~ to** contrairement à; **~act** [kaʊntə'rækt] *vt* neutraliser, contrebalancer; **~feit** ['kaʊntəfi:t] *n* faux *m*, contrefaçon *f* ♦ *vt* contrefaire ♦ *adj* faux(fausse); **~foil** ['kaʊntəfɔɪl] *n* talon *m*, souche *f*; **~mand** ['kaʊntəmɑ:nd] *vt* annuler; **~part** ['kaʊntəpɑ:t] *n* (*of person etc*) homologue *m/f*

countess ['kaʊntɪs] *n* comtesse *f*

countless ['kaʊntlɪs] *adj* innombrable

country ['kʌntrɪ] *n* pays *m*; (*native land*) patrie *f*; (*as opposed to town*) campagne *f*; (*region*) région *f*, pays; **~ dancing** (*BRIT*) *n* danse *f* folklorique; **~ house** *n* manoir *m*, (petit) château; **~man** (*irreg*) *n* (*compatriot*) compatriote *m*; (*country dweller*) habitant *m* de la campagne, campagnard *m*; **~side** *n* campagne *f*

county ['kaʊntɪ] *n* comté *m*

coup [ku:] (*pl* **~s**) *n* beau coup; (*also*: **~ d'état**) coup d'État

couple ['kʌpl] *n* couple *m*; **a ~ of** deux; (*a few*) quelques

coupon ['ku:pɒn] *n* coupon *m*, bon-prime *m*, bon-réclame *m*; (*COMM*) coupon

courage ['kʌrɪdʒ] *n* courage *m*

courier ['kʊrɪə*] *n* messager *m*, courrier *m*; (*for tourists*) accompagnateur(trice), guide *m/f*

course [kɔ:s] *n* cours *m*; (*of ship*) route *f*; (*for golf*) terrain *m*; (*part of meal*) plat *m*; **first** ~ entrée *f*; **of** ~ bien sûr; ~ **of action** parti *m*, ligne *f* de conduite; ~ **of treatment** (*MED*) traitement *m*

court [kɔ:t] *n* cour *f*; (*LAW*) cour, tribunal *m*; (*TENNIS*) court *m* ♦ *vt* (*woman*) courtiser, faire la cour à; **to take to** ~ actionner *or* poursuivre en justice

courteous [ˈkɜ:tɪəs] *adj* courtois(e), poli(e)

courtesy [ˈkɜ:təsɪ] *n* courtoisie *f*, politesse *f*; **(by)** ~ **of** avec l'aimable autorisation de

court: ~-**house** [ˈkɔ:thaʊs] (*US*) *n* palais *m* de justice; ~**ier** [ˈkɔ:tɪə*] *n* courtisan *m*, dame *f* de la cour; ~ **martial** (*pl* ~**s martial**) *n* cour martiale, conseil *m* de guerre; ~**room** [ˈkɔ:trʊm] *n* salle *f* de tribunal; ~**yard** [ˈkɔ:tjɑ:d] *n* cour *f*

cousin [ˈkʌzn] *n* cousin(e); **first** ~ cousin(e) germain(e)

cove [kəʊv] *n* petite baie, anse *f*

covenant [ˈkʌvənənt] *n* engagement *m*

cover [ˈkʌvə*] *vt* couvrir ♦ *n* couverture *f*; (*of pan*) couvercle *m*; (*over furniture*) housse *f*; (*shelter*) abri *m*; **to take** ~ se mettre à l'abri; **under** ~ à l'abri; **under** ~ **of darkness** à la faveur de la nuit; **under separate** ~ (*COMM*) sous pli séparé; **to** ~ **up for sb** couvrir qn; ~**age** *n* (*TV, PRESS*) reportage *m*; ~ **charge** *n* couvert *m* (*supplément à payer*); ~**ing** *n* couche *f*; ~**ing letter** (*US* ~ **letter**) *n* lettre explicative; ~ **note** *n* (*INSURANCE*) police *f* provisoire

covert [ˈkʌvət] *adj* (*threat*) voilé(e), caché(e); (*glance*) furtif(ive)

cover-up [ˈkʌvərʌp] *n* tentative *f* pour étouffer une affaire

covet [ˈkʌvɪt] *vt* convoiter

cow [kaʊ] *n* vache *f* ♦ *vt* effrayer, intimider

coward [ˈkaʊəd] *n* lâche *m/f*; ~**ice** [ˈkaʊədɪs] *n* lâcheté *f*; ~**ly** *adj* lâche

cowboy [ˈkaʊbɔɪ] *n* cow-boy *m*

cower [ˈkaʊə*] *vi* se recroqueviller

coy [kɔɪ] *adj* faussement effarouché(e) *or*

timide

cozy [ˈkəʊzɪ] (*US*) *adj* = **cosy**

CPA (*US*) *n abbr* = **certified public accountant**

crab [kræb] *n* crabe *m*; ~ **apple** *n* pomme *f* sauvage

crack [kræk] *n* fente *f*, fissure *f*; fêlure *f*; lézarde *f*; (*noise*) craquement *m*, coup (sec); (*drug*) crack *m* ♦ *vt* fendre, fissurer; fêler; lézarder; (*whip*) faire claquer; (*nut*) casser; (*code*) déchiffrer; (*problem*) résoudre ♦ *adj* de première classe, d'élite; ~ **down on** *vt fus* mettre un frein à; ~ **up** *vi* être au bout du rouleau, s'effondrer; ~**er** *n* (*Christmas* ~**er**) pétard *m*; (*biscuit*) biscuit (salé)

crackle [ˈkrækl] *vi* crépiter, grésiller

cradle [ˈkreɪdl] *n* berceau *m*

craft [krɑ:ft] *n* métier (artisanal); (*pl inv: boat*) embarcation *f*, barque *f*; (: *plane*) appareil *m*; ~**sman** (*irreg*) *n* artisan *m*, ouvrier (qualifié); ~**smanship** *n* travail *m*; ~**y** *adj* rusé(e), malin(igne)

crag [kræg] *n* rocher escarpé

cram [kræm] *vt* (*fill*): **to** ~ **sth with** bourrer qch de; (*put*): **to** ~ **sth into** fourrer qch dans ♦ *vi* (*for exams*) bachoter

cramp [kræmp] *n* crampe *f* ♦ *vt* gêner, entraver; ~**ed** *adj* à l'étroit, très serré(e)

cranberry [ˈkrænbərɪ] *n* canneberge *f*

crane [kreɪn] *n* grue *f*

crank [kræŋk] *n* manivelle *f*; (*person*) excentrique *m/f*; ~**shaft** *n* vilebrequin *m*

cranny [ˈkrænɪ] *n see* **nook**

crash [kræʃ] *n* fracas *m*; (*of car*) collision *f*; (*of plane*) accident *m* ♦ *vt* avoir un accident avec ♦ *vi* (*plane*) s'écraser; (*two cars*) se percuter, s'emboutir; (*COMM*) s'effondrer; **to** ~ **into** se jeter *or* se fracasser contre; ~ **course** *n* cours intensif; ~ **helmet** *n* casque (protecteur); ~ **landing** *n* atterrissage forcé *or* en catastrophe

crate [kreɪt] *n* cageot *m*; (*for bottles*) caisse *f*

cravat(e) [krəˈvæt] *n* foulard (noué autour du cou)

crave [kreɪv] *vt*, *vi*: **to** ~ (**for**) avoir un

envie irrésistible de

crawl [krɔ:l] *vi* ramper; (*vehicle*) avancer au pas ♦ *n* (SWIMMING) crawl *m*

crayfish ['kreɪfɪʃ] *n inv* (*freshwater*) écrevisse *f*; (*saltwater*) langoustine *f*

crayon ['kreɪən] *n* crayon *m* (de couleur)

craze [kreɪz] *n* engouement *m*

crazy ['kreɪzɪ] *adj* fou(folle)

creak [kri:k] *vi* grincer; craquer

cream [kri:m] *n* crème *f* ♦ *adj* (*colour*) crème *inv*; ~ **cake** *n* (petit) gâteau à la crème; ~ **cheese** *n* fromage *m* à la crème, fromage blanc; **~y** *adj* crémeux(euse)

crease [kri:s] *n* pli *m* ♦ *vt* froisser, chiffonner ♦ *vi* se froisser, se chiffonner

create [kri'eɪt] *vt* créer; **creation** [kri'eɪʃən] *n* création *f*; **creative** [kri'eɪtɪv] *adj* (*artistic*) créatif(ive); (*ingenious*) ingénieux(euse)

creature ['kri:tʃə*] *n* créature *f*

crèche [kreʃ] *n* garderie *f*, crèche *f*

credence ['kri:dəns] *n*: **to lend** *or* **give ~ to** ajouter foi à

credentials [kri'denʃəlz] *npl* (*references*) références *fpl*; (*papers of identity*) pièce *f* d'identité

credit ['kredɪt] *n* crédit *m*; (*recognition*) honneur *m* ♦ *vt* (COMM) créditer; (*believe: also*: **give ~ to**) ajouter foi à, croire; **~s** *npl* (CINEMA, TV) générique *m*; **to be in ~** (*person, bank account*) être créditeur(trice); **to ~ sb with** (*fig*) prêter *or* attribuer à qn; ~ **card** *n* carte *f* de crédit; **~or** *n* créancier(ière)

creed [kri:d] *n* croyance *f*, credo *m*

creek [kri:k] *n* crique *f*, anse *f*; (US: *stream*) ruisseau *m*, petit cours d'eau

creep [kri:p] (*pt*, *pp* **crept**) *vi* ramper; **~er** *n* plante grimpante; **~y** *adj* (*frightening*) qui fait frissonner, qui donne la chair de poule

cremate [krɪ'meɪt] *vt* incinérer

crematorium [kremə'tɔ:rɪəm] (*pl* **~ia**) *n* four *m* crématoire

crêpe [kreɪp] *n* crêpe *m*; ~ **bandage** (BRIT) *n* bande *f* Velpeau (®)

crept [krept] *pt*, *pp of* **creep**

crescent ['kresnt] *n* croissant *m*; (*street*)

rue *f* (*en arc de cercle*)

cress [kres] *n* cresson *m*

crest [krest] *n* crête *f*; **~fallen** *adj* déconfit(e), découragé(e)

crevice ['krevɪs] *n* fissure *f*, lézarde *f*, fente *f*

crew [kru:] *n* équipage *m*; (CINEMA) équipe *f*; **~-cut** *n*: **to have a ~-cut** avoir les cheveux en brosse; **~-neck** *n* col ras du cou

crib [krɪb] *n* lit *m* d'enfant; (*for baby*) berceau *m* ♦ *vt* (*inf*) copier

crick [krɪk] *n*: ~ **in the neck** torticolis *m*; ~ **in the back** tour *m* de reins

cricket ['krɪkɪt] *n* (*insect*) grillon *m*, cricri *m inv*; (*game*) cricket *m*

crime [kraɪm] *n* crime *m*; **criminal** ['krɪmɪnl] *adj*, *n* criminel(le)

crimson ['krɪmzn] *adj* cramoisi(e)

cringe [krɪndʒ] *vi* avoir un mouvement de recul

crinkle ['krɪŋkl] *vt* froisser, chiffonner

cripple ['krɪpl] *n* boiteux(euse), infirme *m/f* ♦ *vt* estropier

crisis ['kraɪsɪs] (*pl* **crises**) *n* crise *f*

crisp [krɪsp] *adj* croquant(e); (*weather*) vif(vive); (*manner etc*) brusque; **~s** (BRIT) *npl* (pommes) chips *fpl*

crisscross ['krɪskrɒs] *adj* entrecroisé(e)

criterion [kraɪ'tɪərɪən] (*pl* **~ia**) *n* critère *m*

critic ['krɪtɪk] *n* critique *m*; **~al** *adj* critique; **~ally** *adv* (*examine*) d'un œil critique; (*speak etc*) sévèrement; **~ally ill** gravement malade; **~ism** ['krɪtɪsɪzəm] *n* critique *f*; **~ize** ['krɪtɪsaɪz] *vt* critiquer

croak [krəʊk] *vi* (*frog*) coasser; (*raven*) croasser; (*person*) parler d'une voix rauque

Croatia [krəʊ'eɪʃə] *n* Croatie *f*

crochet ['krəʊʃeɪ] *n* travail *m* au crochet

crockery ['krɒkərɪ] *n* vaisselle *f*

crocodile ['krɒkədaɪl] *n* crocodile *m*

crocus ['krəʊkəs] *n* crocus *m*

croft [krɒft] (BRIT) *n* petite ferme *f*

crony ['krəʊnɪ] (*inf*: *pej*) *n* copain(copine)

crook [krʊk] *n* escroc *m*; (*of shepherd*) houlette *f*; **~ed** ['krʊkɪd] *adj* courbé(e), tordu(e); (*action*) malhonnête

crop [krɒp] *n* (*produce*) culture *f*; (*amount produced*) récolte *f*; (*riding ~*) cravache *f* ♦ *vt* (*hair*) tondre; **~ up** *vi* surgir, se présenter, survenir

cross [krɒs] *n* croix *f*; (*BIO etc*) croisement *m* ♦ *vt* (*street etc*) traverser; (*arms, legs, BIO*) croiser; (*cheque*) barrer ♦ *adj* en colère, fâché(e); **~ out** *vt* barrer, biffer; **~ over** *vi* traverser; **~bar** *n* barre (transversale); **~-country (race)** *n* cross(-country) *m*; **~-examine** *vt* (*LAW*) faire subir un examen contradictoire à; **~-eyed** *adj* qui louche; **~fire** *n* feux croisés; **~ing** *n* (*sea passage*) traversée *f*; (*also*: *pedestrian ~ing*) passage clouté; **~ing guard** (*US*) *n* contractuel(le) qui fait traverser la rue aux enfants; **~ purposes** *npl*: **to be at ~ purposes with sb** comprendre qn de travers; **~ reference** *n* renvoi *m*, référence *f*; **~roads** *n* carrefour *m*; **~ section** *n* (*of object*) coupe transversale; (*in population*) échantillon *m*; **~walk** (*US*) *n* passage clouté; **~wind** *n* vent *m* de travers; **~word** *n* mots *mpl* croisés

crotch [krɒtʃ] *n* (*ANAT, of garment*) entre-jambes *m inv*

crouch [krautʃ] *vi* s'accroupir; se tapir

crow [krəu] *n* (*bird*) corneille *f*; (*of cock*) chant *m* du coq, cocorico *m* ♦ *vi* (*cock*) chanter

crowbar ['krəuba:*] *n* levier *m*

crowd [kraud] *n* foule *f* ♦ *vt* remplir ♦ *vi* affluer, s'attrouper, s'entasser; **to ~ in** entrer en foule; **~ed** *adj* bondé(e), plein(e)

crown [kraun] *n* couronne *f*; (*of head*) sommet *m* de la tête; (*of hill*) sommet ♦ *vt* couronner; **~ jewels** *npl* joyaux *mpl* de la Couronne; **~ prince** *n* prince héritier

crow's-feet ['krəuzfi:t] *npl* pattes *fpl* d'oie

crucial ['kru:ʃəl] *adj* crucial(e), décisif(ive)

crucifix ['kru:sɪfɪks] *n* (*REL*) crucifix *m*; **~ion** [kru:sɪ'fɪkʃən] *n* (*REL*) crucifixion *f*

crude [kru:d] *adj* (*materials*) brut(e); non raffiné(e); (*fig: basic*) rudimentaire, sommaire; (: *vulgar*) cru(e), grossier(ère); **~ (oil)** *n* (pétrole) brut *m*

cruel ['kruəl] *adj* cruel(le); **~ty** *n* cruauté *f*

cruise [kru:z] *n* croisière *f* ♦ *vi* (*ship*) croiser; (*car*) rouler; **~r** *n* croiseur *m*; (*motorboat*) yacht *m* de croisière

crumb [krʌm] *n* miette *f*

crumble ['krʌmbl] *vt* émietter ♦ *vi* (*plaster etc*) s'effriter; (*land, earth*) s'ébouler; (*building*) s'écrouler, crouler; (*fig*) s'effondrer; **crumbly** ['krʌmblɪ] *adj* friable

crumpet ['krʌmpɪt] *n* petite crêpe (épaisse)

crumple ['krʌmpl] *vt* froisser, friper

crunch [krʌntʃ] *vt* croquer; (*underfoot*) faire craquer *or* crisser, écraser ♦ *n* (*fig*) instant *m or* moment *m* critique, moment de vérité; **~y** *adj* croquant(e), croustillant(e)

crusade [kru:'seɪd] *n* croisade *f*

crush [krʌʃ] *n* foule *f*, cohue *f*, (*love*): **to have a ~ on sb** avoir le béguin pour qn (*inf*); (*drink*): **lemon ~** citron pressé ♦ *vt* écraser; (*crumple*) froisser; (*fig: hopes*) anéantir

crust [krʌst] *n* croûte *f*

crutch [krʌtʃ] *n* béquille *f*

crux [krʌks] *n* point crucial

cry [kraɪ] *vi* pleurer; (*shout: also*: **~ out**) crier ♦ *n* cri *m*; **~ off** (*inf*) *vi* se dédire; se décommander

cryptic ['krɪptɪk] *adj* énigmatique

crystal ['krɪstl] *n* cristal *m*; **~-clear** *adj* clair(e) comme de l'eau de roche

cub [kʌb] *n* petit *m* (*d'un animal*); (*also*: **C~ scout**) louveteau *m*

Cuba ['kju:bə] *n* Cuba *m*

cubbyhole ['kʌbɪhəul] *n* cagibi *m*

cube [kju:b] *n* cube *m* ♦ *vt* (*MATH*) élever au cube; **cubic** ['kju:bɪk] *adj* cubique; **cubic metre** *etc* mètre *m etc* cube; **cubic capacity** *n* cylindrée *f*

cubicle ['kju:bɪkl] *n* (*in hospital*) box *m*; (*at pool*) cabine *f*

cuckoo ['kuku:] *n* coucou *m*; **~ clock** *n* (pendule *f* à) coucou *m*

cucumber ['kju:kʌmbə*] *n* concombre *m*

cuddle ['kʌdl] *vt* câliner, caresser ♦ *vi* se blottir l'un contre l'autre

cue [kju:] *n* (*snooker* ~) queue *f* de billard; (*THEATRE etc*) signal *m*

cuff [kʌf] *n* (*BRIT: of shirt, coat etc*) poignet *m*, manchette *f*; (*US: of trousers*) revers *m*; (*blow*) tape *f*; **off the ~** à l'improviste; **~ links** *npl* boutons *mpl* de manchette

cul-de-sac ['kʌldəsæk] *n* cul-de-sac *m*, impasse *f*

cull [kʌl] *vt* sélectionner ♦ *n* (*of animals*) massacre *m*

culminate ['kʌlmɪneɪt] *vi*: **to ~ in** finir *or* se terminer par; (*end in*) mener à; **culmination** [kʌlmɪ'neɪʃən] *n* point culminant

culottes [kjʊ'lɒts] *npl* jupe-culotte *f*

culprit ['kʌlprɪt] *n* coupable *m/f*

cult [kʌlt] *n* culte *m*

cultivate ['kʌltɪveɪt] *vt* cultiver; **cultivation** [kʌltɪ'veɪʃən] *n* culture *f*

cultural ['kʌltʃərəl] *adj* culturel(le)

culture ['kʌltʃə*] *n* culture *f*; **~d** *adj* (*person*) cultivé(e)

cumbersome ['kʌmbəsəm] *adj* encombrant(e), embarrassant(e)

cunning ['kʌnɪŋ] *n* ruse *f*, astuce *f* ♦ *adj* rusé(e), malin(igne); (*device, idea*) astucieux(euse)

cup [kʌp] *n* tasse *f*; (*as prize*) coupe *f*; (*of bra*) bonnet *m*

cupboard ['kʌbəd] *n* armoire *f*; (*built-in*) placard *m*

cup tie (*BRIT*) *n* match *m* de coupe

curate ['kjʊərɪt] *n* vicaire *m*

curator [kjʊ'reɪtə*] *n* conservateur *m* (*d'un musée etc*)

curb [kɜːb] *vt* refréner, mettre un frein à ♦ *n* (*fig*) frein *m*, restriction *f*; (*US: kerb*) bord *m* du trottoir

curdle ['kɜːdl] *vi* se cailler

cure [kjʊə*] *vt* guérir; (*CULIN: salt*) saler; (: *smoke*) fumer; (: *dry*) sécher ♦ *n* remède *m*

curfew ['kɜːfju:] *n* couvre-feu *m*

curio ['kjʊərɪəʊ] *n* bibelot *m*, curiosité *f*

curiosity [kjʊərɪ'ɒsɪtɪ] *n* curiosité *f*

curious ['kjʊərɪəs] *adj* curieux(euse)

curl [kɜːl] *n* boucle *f* (*de cheveux*) ♦ *vt, vi* boucler; (*tightly*) friser; **~ up** *vi* s'enrouler; se pelotonner; **~er** *n* bigoudi *m*, rouleau *m*; **~y** *adj* bouclé(e); frisé(e)

currant ['kʌrənt] *n* (*dried*) raisin *m* de Corinthe, raisin sec; (*bush*) groseiller *m*; (*fruit*) groseille *f*

currency ['kʌrənsɪ] *n* monnaie *f*; **to gain ~** (*fig*) s'accréditer

current ['kʌrənt] *n* courant *m* ♦ *adj* courant(e); **~ account** (*BRIT*) *n* compte courant; **~ affairs** *npl* (questions *fpl* d')actualité *f*; **~ly** *adv* actuellement

curriculum [kə'rɪkjʊləm] (*pl* **~s** *or* **curricula**) *n* programme *m* d'études; **~ vitae** *n* curriculum vitae *m*

curry ['kʌrɪ] *n* curry *m* ♦ *vt*: **to ~ favour with** chercher à s'attirer les bonnes grâces de

curse [kɜːs] *vi* jurer, blasphémer ♦ *vt* maudire ♦ *n* (*spell*) malédiction *f*; (*problem, scourge*) fléau *m*; (*swearword*) juron *m*

cursor ['kɜːsə*] *n* (*COMPUT*) curseur *m*

cursory ['kɜːsərɪ] *adj* superficiel(le), hâtif(ive)

curt [kɜːt] *adj* brusque, sec(sèche)

curtail [kɜː'teɪl] *vt* (*visit etc*) écourter; (*expenses, freedom etc*) réduire

curtain ['kɜːtn] *n* rideau *m*

curts(e)y ['kɜːtsɪ] *vi* faire une révérence

curve [kɜːv] *n* courbe *f*; (*in the road*) tournant *m*, virage *m* ♦ *vi* se courber; (*road*) faire une courbe

cushion ['kʊʃən] *n* coussin *m* ♦ *vt* (*fall, shock*) amortir

custard ['kʌstəd] *n* (*for pouring*) crème anglaise

custody ['kʌstədɪ] *n* (*of child*) garde *f*; **to take sb into ~** (*suspect*) placer qn en détention préventive

custom ['kʌstəm] *n* coutume *f*, usage *m*; (*COMM*) clientèle *f*; **~ary** *adj* habituel(le)

customer ['kʌstəmə*] *n* client(e)

customized ['kʌstəmaɪzd] *adj* (*car etc*) construit(e) sur commande

custom-made ['kʌstəm'meɪd] *adj* (*clothes*) fait(e) sur mesure; (*other goods*) hors série, fait(e) sur commande

customs ['kʌstəmz] *npl* douane *f*; **~ officer** *n* douanier(ière)

cut [kʌt] (*pt, pp* **cut**) *vt* couper; (*meat*) découper; (*reduce*) réduire ♦ *vi* couper ♦ *n* coupure *f*; (*of clothes*) coupe *f*; (*in salary etc*) réduction *f*; (*of meat*) morceau *m*; **to ~ one's hand** se couper la main; **to ~ a tooth** percer une dent; **~ down** *vt fus* (*tree etc*) couper, abattre; (*consumption*) réduire; **~ off** *vt* couper; (*fig*) isoler; **~ out** *vt* découper; (*stop*) arrêter; (*remove*) ôter; **~ up** *vt* (*paper, meat*) découper; **~back** *n* réduction *f*

cute [kjuːt] *adj* mignon(ne), adorable

cuticle remover ['kjuːtɪkl-] *n* (*on nail*) repousse-peaux *m inv*

cutlery ['kʌtləri] *n* couverts *mpl*

cutlet ['kʌtlɪt] *n* côtelette *f*

cut: **~out** *n* (*switch*) coupe-circuit *m inv*; (*cardboard ~out*) découpage *m*; **~-price** (*US* **~-rate**) *adj* au rabais, à prix réduit; **~throat** *n* assassin *m* ♦ *adj* acharné(e)

cutting ['kʌtɪŋ] *adj* tranchant(e), coupant(e); (*fig*) cinglant(e), mordant(e) ♦ *n* (*BRIT: from newspaper*) coupure *f* (de journal); (*from plant*) bouture *f*

CV *n abbr* = **curriculum vitae**

cwt *abbr* = **hundredweight(s)**

cyanide ['saɪənaɪd] *n* cyanure *m*

cycle ['saɪkl] *n* cycle *m*; (*bicycle*) bicyclette *f*, vélo *m* ♦ *vi* faire de la bicyclette; **cycling** ['saɪklɪŋ] *n* cyclisme *m*; **cyclist** ['saɪklɪst] *n* cycliste *m/f*

cygnet ['sɪgnɪt] *n* jeune cygne *m*

cylinder ['sɪlɪndə*] *n* cylindre *m*; **~-head gasket** *n* joint *m* de culasse

cymbals ['sɪmbəlz] *npl* cymbales *fpl*

cynic ['sɪnɪk] *n* cynique *m/f*; **~al** *adj* cynique; **~ism** ['sɪnɪsɪzəm] *n* cynisme *m*

Cypriot ['sɪprɪət] *adj* cypriote, chypriote ♦ *n* Cypriote *m/f*, Chypriote *m/f*

Cyprus ['saɪprəs] *n* Chypre *f*

cyst [sɪst] *n* kyste *m*

cystitis [sɪs'taɪtɪs] *n* cystite *f*

czar [zɑː*] *n* tsar *m*

Czech [tʃek] *adj* tchèque ♦ *n* Tchèque *m/f*; (*LING*) tchèque *m*

Czechoslovak [tʃekə'sləʊvæk] *adj, n* = **Czechoslovakian**

Czechoslovakia [tʃekəslə'vækɪə] *n* Tchécoslovaquie *f*; **~n** *adj* tchécoslovaque ♦ *n* Tchécoslovaque *m/f*

D d

D [diː] *n* (*MUS*) ré *m*

dab [dæb] *vt* (*eyes, wound*) tamponner; (*paint, cream*) appliquer (par petites touches *or* rapidement)

dabble ['dæbl] *vi*: **to ~ in** faire *or* se mêler *or* s'occuper un peu de

dad [dæd] *n* papa *m*

daddy ['dædɪ] *n* papa *m*

daffodil ['dæfədɪl] *n* jonquille *f*

daft [dɑːft] *adj* idiot(e), stupide

dagger ['dægə*] *n* poignard *m*

daily ['deɪlɪ] *adj* quotidien(ne), journalier(ère) ♦ *n* quotidien *m* ♦ *adv* tous les jours

dainty ['deɪntɪ] *adj* délicat(e), mignon(ne)

dairy ['dɛərɪ] *n* (*BRIT: shop*) crémerie *f*, laiterie *f*; (*on farm*) laiterie; **~ products** *npl* produits laitiers; **~ store** (*US*) *n* crémerie *f*, laiterie *f*

dais ['deɪɪs] *n* estrade *f*

daisy ['deɪzɪ] *n* pâquerette *f*; **~ wheel** *n* (*on printer*) marguerite *f*

dale [deɪl] *n* vallon *m*

dam [dæm] *n* barrage *m* ♦ *vt* endiguer

damage ['dæmɪdʒ] *n* dégâts *mpl*, dommages *mpl*; (*fig*) tort *m* ♦ *vt* endommager, abîmer; (*fig*) faire du tort à; **~s** *npl* (*LAW*) dommages-intérêts *mpl*

damn [dæm] *vt* condamner; (*curse*) maudire ♦ *n* (*inf*): **I don't give a ~** je m'en fous ♦ *adj* (*inf: also: ~ed*): **this ~ ...** ce sacré *or* foutu ...; **~ (it)!** zut!; **~ing** *adj* accablant(e)

damp [dæmp] *adj* humide ♦ *n* humidité *f* ♦ *vt* (*also: ~en: cloth, rag*) humecter; (*: enthusiasm*) refroidir

damson ['dæmzən] *n* prune *f* de Damas

dance [dɑːns] *n* danse *f*; (*social event*) bal *m* ♦ *vi* danser; **~ hall** *n* salle *f* de bal, dancing *m*; **~r** *n* danseur(euse); **dancing** ['dɑːnsɪŋ] *n* danse *f*

dandelion ['dændɪlaɪən] *n* pissenlit *m*

dandruff ['dændrəf] *n* pellicules *fpl*

Dane [deɪn] *n* Danois(e)

danger ['deɪndʒə*] *n* danger *m*; **there is a ~ of fire** il y a (un) risque d'incendie; **in ~** en danger; **he was in ~ of falling** il risquait de tomber; **~ous** *adj* dangereux(euse)

dangle ['dæŋgl] *vt* balancer ♦ *vi* pendre

Danish ['deɪnɪʃ] *adj* danois(e) ♦ *n* (*LING*) danois *m*

dapper ['dæpə*] *adj* pimpant(e)

dare [dɛə*] *vt*: **to ~ sb to do** défier qn de faire ♦ *vi*: **to ~ (to) do sth** oser faire qch; **I ~ say** (*I suppose*) il est probable (que); **~devil** *n* casse-cou *m inv*; **daring** ['dɛərɪŋ] *adj* hardi(e), audacieux(euse); (*dress*) osé(e) ♦ *n* audace *f*, hardiesse *f*

dark [dɑːk] *adj* (*night, room*) obscur(e), sombre; (*colour, complexion*) foncé(e), sombre ♦ *n*: **in the ~** dans le noir; **in the ~ about** (*fig*) ignorant tout de; **after ~** après la tombée de la nuit; **~en** *vt* obscurcir, assombrir ♦ *vi* s'obscurcir, s'assombrir; **~ glasses** *npl* lunettes noires; **~ness** *n* obscurité *f*; **~room** *n* chambre noire

darling ['dɑːlɪŋ] *adj* chéri(e) ♦ *n* chéri(e); (*favourite*): **to be the ~ of** être la coqueluche de

darn [dɑːn] *vt* repriser, raccommoder

dart [dɑːt] *n* fléchette *f*; (*sewing*) pince *f* ♦ *vi*: **to ~ towards** (*also: make a ~ towards*) se précipiter *or* s'élancer vers; **~s** *n* (jeu *m* de) fléchettes *fpl*; **to ~ away/along** partir/passer comme une flèche; **~board** *n* cible *f* (de jeu de fléchettes)

dash [dæʃ] *n* (*sign*) tiret *m*; (*small quantity*) goutte *f*, larme *f* ♦ *vt* (*missile*) jeter *or* lancer violemment; (*hopes*) anéantir ♦ *vi*: **to ~ towards** (*also: make a ~ towards*) se précipiter *or* se ruer vers; **~ away** *vi* partir à toute allure, filer; **~ off** *vi* = **~ away**

dashboard ['dæʃbɔːd] *n* (*AUT*) tableau *m* de bord

dashing ['dæʃɪŋ] *adj* fringant(e)

data ['deɪtə] *npl* données *fpl*; **~base** *n* (*COMPUT*) base *f* de données; **~ processing** *n* traitement *m* de données

date [deɪt] *n* date *f*; (*with sb*) rendez-vous *m*; (*fruit*) datte *f* ♦ *vt* dater; (*person*) sortir avec; **~ of birth** date de naissance; **to ~** (*until now*) à ce jour; **out of ~** (*passport*) périmé(e); (*theory etc*) dépassé(e); (*clothes etc*) démodé(e); **up to ~** moderne; (*news*) très récent; **~d** *adj* démodé(e); **~ rape** *n* viol *m* (à l'issue d'un rendez-vous galant)

daub [dɔːb] *vt* barbouiller

daughter ['dɔːtə*] *n* fille *f*; **~-in-law** *n* belle-fille *f*, bru *f*

daunting ['dɔːntɪŋ] *adj* décourageant(e)

dawdle ['dɔːdl] *vi* traîner, lambiner

dawn [dɔːn] *n* aube *f*, aurore *f* ♦ *vi* (*day*) se lever, poindre; (*fig*): **it ~ed on him that ...** il lui vint à l'esprit que ...

day [deɪ] *n* jour *m*; (*as duration*) journée *f*; (*period of time, age*) époque *f*, temps *m*; **the ~ before** la veille, le jour précédent; **the ~ after, the following ~** le lendemain, le jour suivant; **the ~ after tomorrow** après-demain; **the ~ before yesterday** avant-hier; **by ~** de jour; **~break** *n* point *m* du jour; **~dream** *vi* rêver (tout éveillé); **~light** *n* (lumière *f* du) jour *m*; **~ return** (*BRIT*) *n* billet *m* d'aller-retour (valable pour la journée); **~time** *n* jour *m*, journée *f*; **~-to-day** *adj* quotidien(ne); (*event*) journalier(ère)

daze [deɪz] *vt* (*stun*) étourdir ♦ *n*: **in a ~** étourdi(e), hébété(e)

dazzle ['dæzl] *vt* éblouir, aveugler

DC *abbr* (= *direct current*) courant continu

D-day ['diːdeɪ] *n* le jour J

dead [dɛd] *adj* mort(e); (*numb*) engourdi(e), insensible; (*battery*) à plat; (*telephone*): **the line is ~** la ligne est coupée ♦ *adv* absolument, complètement ♦ *npl*: **the ~** les morts; **he was shot ~** il a été tué d'un coup de revolver; **~ on time** à l'heure pile; **~ tired** éreinté(e), complètement fourbu(e); **to stop ~** s'arrêter pile *or* net; **~en** *vt* (*blow, sound*) amortir; (*pain*) calmer; **~ end** *n* impasse *f*; **~ heat** *n* (*SPORT*): **to finish in a ~ heat**

terminer ex æquo; **~line** *n* date *f or* heure *f* limite; **~lock** *n*: **a ~** (*fig*) impasse *f*; **~ loss** *n*: **to be a ~ loss** (*inf*: *person*) n'être bon(ne) à rien; **~ly** *adj* mortel(le); (*weapon*) meurtrier(ère); (*accuracy*) extrême; **~pan** *adj* impassible; **D~ Sea** *n*: **the D~ Sea** la mer Morte

deaf [def] *adj* sourd(e); **~en** *vt* rendre sourd; **~-mute** *n* sourd(e)-muet(te); **~ness** *n* surdité *f*

deal [diːl] (*pt, pp* **dealt**) *n* affaire *f*, marché *m* ♦ *vt* (*blow*) porter; (*cards*) donner, distribuer; **a great ~ (of)** beaucoup (de); **~ in** *vt fus* faire le commerce de; **~ with** *vt fus* (*person, problem*) s'occuper *or* se charger de; (*clear, definite*) traiter de; **~er** *n* marchand *m*; **~ings** *npl* (*COMM*) transactions *fpl*; (*relations*) relations *fpl*, rapports *mpl*

dean [diːn] *n* (*REL, BRIT: SCOL*) doyen *m*; (*US*) conseiller(ère) (principal(e)) d'éducation

dear [dɪə*] *adj* cher(chère); (*expensive*) cher, coûteux(euse) ♦ *n*: **my ~** mon cher/ma chère; **~ me!** mon Dieu!; **D~ Sir/Madam** (*in letter*) Monsieur/ Madame; **D~ Mr/Mrs X** Cher Monsieur/Chère Madame; **~ly** *adv* (*love*) tendrement; (*pay*) cher

death [deθ] *n* mort *f*; (*fatality*) mort *m*; (*ADMIN*) décès *m*; **~ certificate** *n* acte *m* de décès; **~ly** *adj* de mort; **~ penalty** *n* peine *f* de mort; **~ rate** *n* (taux *m* de) mortalité *f*; **~ toll** *n* nombre *m* de morts

debar [dɪˈbɑː*] *vt*: **to ~ sb from doing** interdire à qn de faire

debase [dɪˈbeɪs] *vt* (*value*) déprécier, dévaloriser

debatable [dɪˈbeɪtəbl] *adj* discutable

debate [dɪˈbeɪt] *n* discussion *f*, débat *m* ♦ *vt* discuter, débattre

debit [ˈdebɪt] *n* débit *m* ♦ *vt*: **to ~ a sum to sb** *or* **to sb's account** porter une somme au débit de qn, débiter qn d'une somme; *see also* **direct**

debt [det] *n* dette *f*; **to be in ~** avoir des dettes, être endetté(e); **~or** *n* débiteur(trice)

debunk [diːˈbʌŋk] *vt* (*theory, claim*)

montrer le ridicule de

decade [ˈdekeɪd] *n* décennie *f*, décade *f*

decadence [ˈdekədəns] *n* décadence *f*

decaffeinated [diːˈkæfɪneɪtɪd] *adj* décaféiné(e)

decanter [dɪˈkæntə*] *n* carafe *f*

decay [dɪˈkeɪ] *n* (*of building*) délabrement *m*; (*also*: *tooth* **~**) carie *f* (dentaire) ♦ *vi* (*rot*) se décomposer, pourrir; (: *teeth*) se carier

deceased [dɪˈsiːst] *n* défunt(e)

deceit [dɪˈsiːt] *n* tromperie *f*, supercherie *f*; **~ful** *adj* trompeur(euse); **deceive** [dɪˈsiːv] *vt* tromper

December [dɪˈsembə*] *n* décembre *m*

decent [ˈdiːsənt] *adj* décent(e), convenable; **they were very ~ about it** ils se sont montrés très chic

deception [dɪˈsepʃən] *n* tromperie *f*

deceptive [dɪˈseptɪv] *adj* trompeur(euse)

decide [dɪˈsaɪd] *vt* (*person*) décider; (*question, argument*) trancher, régler ♦ *vi* se décider, décider; **to ~ to do/that** décider de faire/que; **to ~ on** décider, se décider pour; **~d** *adj* (*resolute*) résolu(e), décidé(e); (*clear, definite*) net(te), marqué(e); **~dly** [dɪˈsaɪdɪdlɪ] *adv* résolument; (*distinctly*) incontestablement, nettement

deciduous [dɪˈsɪdjʊəs] *adj* à feuilles caduques

decimal [ˈdesɪməl] *adj* décimal(e) ♦ *n* décimale *f*; **~ point** *n* ≈ virgule *f*

decipher [dɪˈsaɪfə*] *vt* déchiffrer

decision [dɪˈsɪʒən] *n* décision *f*

decisive [dɪˈsaɪsɪv] *adj* décisif(ive); (*person*) décidé(e)

deck [dek] *n* (*NAUT*) pont *m*; (*of bus*): **top ~** impériale *f*; (*of cards*) jeu *m*; (*record* **~**) platine *f*; **~chair** *n* chaise longue

declare [dɪˈklɛə*] *vt* déclarer

decline [dɪˈklaɪn] *n* (*decay*) déclin *m*; (*lessening*) baisse *f* ♦ *vt* refuser, décliner ♦ *vi* décliner; (*business*) baisser

decoder [diːˈkəʊdə*] *n* (*TV*) décodeur *m*

decorate [ˈdekəreɪt] *vt* (*adorn, give a medal to*) décorer; (*paint and paper*) peindre et tapisser; **decoration** [dekəˈreɪʃən] *n* (*medal etc, adornment*) décoration *f*; **decorator** [ˈdekəreɪtə*] *n* peintre-décorateur *m*

decoy ['diːkɔɪ] *n* piège *m*; (*person*) compère *m*

decrease [*n* 'diːkriːs, *vb* diːˈkriːs] *n*: ~ **(in)** diminution *f* (de) ♦ *vt, vi* diminuer

decree [dɪˈkriː] *n* (*POL. REL*) décret *m*; (*LAW*) arrêt *m*, jugement *m*; ~ **nisi** [-ˈnaɪsaɪ] *n* jugement *m* provisoire de divorce

dedicate ['dedɪkeɪt] *vt* consacrer; (*book etc*) dédier; **dedication** [dedɪˈkeɪʃən] *n* (*devotion*) dévouement *m*; (*in book*) dédicace *f*

deduce [dɪˈdjuːs] *vt* déduire, conclure

deduct [dɪˈdʌkt] *vt*: **to ~ sth (from)** déduire qch (de), retrancher qch (de); ~**ion** [dɪˈdʌkʃən] *n* (*deducting, deducing*) déduction *f*; (*from wage etc*) prélèvement *m*, retenue *f*

deed [diːd] *n* action *f*, acte *m*; (*LAW*) acte notarié, contrat *m*

deem [diːm] *vt* (*formal*) juger

deep [diːp] *adj* profond(e); (*voice*) grave ♦ *adv*: **spectators stood 20 ~** il y avait 20 rangs de spectateurs; **4 metres ~** de 4 mètres de profondeur; ~**en** *vt* approfondir ♦ *vi* (*fig*) s'épaissir; ~**freeze** *n* congélateur *m*; ~**fry** *vt* faire frire (en friteuse); ~**ly** *adv* profondément; (*interested*) vivement; ~-**sea diver** *n* sous-marin(e); ~-**sea diving** *n* plongée sous-marine; ~-**sea fishing** *n* grande pêche; ~-**seated** *adj* profond(e), profondément enraciné(e)

deer [dɪə*] *n inv*: **(red) ~** cerf *m*, biche *f*; **(fallow) ~** daim *m*; **(roe) ~** chevreuil *m*; ~**skin** *n* daim

deface [dɪˈfeɪs] *vt* dégrader; (*notice, poster*) barbouiller

default [dɪˈfɔːlt] *n* (*COMPUT: also:* ~ *value*) valeur *f* par défaut; **by ~** (*LAW*) par défaut, par contumace; (*SPORT*) par forfait

defeat [dɪˈfiːt] *n* défaite *f* ♦ *vt* (*team, opponents*) battre

defect [*n* 'diːfekt, *vb* dɪˈfekt] *n* défaut *m* ♦ *vi*: **to ~ to the enemy/the West** passer à l'ennemi/à l'Ouest; ~**ive** [dɪˈfektɪv] *adj* défectueux(euse)

defence [dɪˈfens] (*US* **defense**) *n* défense

f; ~**less** *adj* sans défense

defend [dɪˈfend] *vt* défendre; ~**ant** *n* défendeur(deresse); (*in criminal case*) accusé(e), prévenu(e); ~**er** *n* défenseur *m*

defer [dɪˈfɜː*] *vt* (*postpone*) différer, ajourner

defiance [dɪˈfaɪəns] *n* défi *m*; **in ~ of** au mépris de; **defiant** [dɪˈfaɪənt] *adj* provocant(e), de défi; (*person*) rebelle, intraitable

deficiency [dɪˈfɪʃənsɪ] *n* insuffisance *f*, déficience *f*; **deficient** *adj* (*inadequate*) insuffisant(e); **to be deficient in** manquer de

deficit ['defɪsɪt] *n* déficit *m*

defile [*vb* dɪˈfaɪl, *n* 'diːfaɪl] *vt* souiller, profaner

define [dɪˈfaɪn] *vt* définir

definite ['defɪnɪt] *adj* (*fixed*) défini(e), (bien) déterminé(e); (*clear, obvious*) net(te), manifeste; (*certain*) sûr(e); **he was ~ about it** il a été catégorique; ~**ly** *adv* sans aucun doute

definition [defɪˈnɪʃən] *n* définition *f*; (*clearness*) netteté *f*

deflate [diːˈfleɪt] *vt* dégonfler

deflect [dɪˈflekt] *vt* détourner, faire dévier

deformed [dɪˈfɔːmd] *adj* difforme

defraud [dɪˈfrɔːd] *vt* frauder; **to ~ sb of sth** escroquer qch à qn

defrost [diːˈfrɒst] *vt* dégivrer; (*food*) décongeler; ~**er** (*US*) *n* (*demister*) dispositif *m* anti-buée *inv*

deft [deft] *adj* adroit(e), preste

defunct [dɪˈfʌŋkt] *adj* défunt(e)

defuse [diːˈfjuːz] *vt* désamorcer

defy [dɪˈfaɪ] *vt* défier; (*efforts etc*) résister à

degenerate [*vb* dɪˈdʒenəreɪt, *adj* dɪˈdʒenərɪt] *vi* dégénérer ♦ *adj* dégénéré(e)

degree [dɪˈɡriː] *n* degré *m*; (*SCOL*) diplôme *m* (universitaire); **a (first) ~ in maths** une licence en maths; **by ~s** (*gradually*) par degrés; **to some ~, to a certain ~** jusqu'à un certain point, dans une certaine mesure

dehydrated [diːhaɪˈdreɪtɪd] *adj* déshydraté(e); (*milk, eggs*) en poudre

de-ice [diː'aɪs] *vt* (*windscreen*) dégivrer

deign [deɪn] *vi*: **to ~ to do** daigner faire

dejected [dɪ'dʒɛktɪd] *adj* abattu(e), déprimé(e)

delay [dɪ'leɪ] *vt* retarder ♦ *vi* s'attarder ♦ *n* délai *m*, retard *m*; **to be ~ed** être en retard

delectable [dɪ'lɛktəbl] *adj* délicieux(euse)

delegate [*n* 'delɪgɪt, *vb* 'delɪgeɪt] *n* délégué(e) ♦ *vt* déléguer

delete [dɪ'liːt] *vt* rayer, supprimer

deliberate [*adj* dɪ'lɪbərɪt, *vb* dɪ'lɪbəreɪt] *adj* (*intentional*) délibéré(e); (*slow*) mesuré(e) ♦ *vi* délibérer, réfléchir; **~ly** *adv* (*on purpose*) exprès, délibérément

delicacy ['delɪkəsɪ] *n* délicatesse *f*; (*food*) mets fin *or* délicat, friandise *f*

delicate ['delɪkɪt] *adj* délicat(e)

delicatessen [delɪkə'tesn] *n* épicerie fine

delicious [dɪ'lɪʃəs] *adj* délicieux(euse)

delight [dɪ'laɪt] *n* (grande) joie, grand plaisir ♦ *vt* enchanter; **to take (a) ~ in** prendre grand plaisir à; **~ed** *adj*: **~ed (at *or* with/to do)** ravi(e) (de/de faire); **~ful** *adj* (*person*) adorable; (*meal, evening*) merveilleux(euse)

delinquent [dɪ'lɪŋkwənt] *adj, n* délinquant(e)

delirious [dɪ'lɪrɪəs] *adj*: **to be ~** délirer

deliver [dɪ'lɪvə*] *vt* (*mail*) distribuer; (*goods*) livrer; (*message*) remettre; (*speech*) prononcer; (*MED: baby*) mettre au monde; **~y** *n* distribution *f*; livraison *f*; (*of speaker*) élocution *f*; (*MED*) accouchement *m*; **to take ~y of** prendre livraison de

delude [dɪ'luːd] *vt* tromper, leurrer

delusion [dɪ'luːʒən] *n* illusion *f*

delve [delv] *vi*: **to ~ into** fouiller dans; (*subject*) approfondir

demand [dɪ'mɑːnd] *vt* réclamer, exiger ♦ *n* exigence *f*; (*claim*) revendication *f*; (*ECON*) demande *f*; **in ~** demandé(e), recherché(e); **on ~** sur demande; **~ing** *adj* (*person*) exigeant(e); (*work*) astreignant(e)

demean [dɪ'miːn] *vt*: **to ~ o.s.** s'abaisser

demeanour [dɪ'miːnə*] (*US* **demeanor**) *n* comportement *m*; maintien *m*

demented [dɪ'mentɪd] *adj* dément(e), fou(folle)

demise [dɪ'maɪz] *n* mort *f*

demister [diː'mɪstə*] (*BRIT*) *n* (*AUT*) dispositif *m* anti-buée *inv*

demo ['deməʊ] (*inf*) *n abbr* (= *demonstration*) manif *f*

democracy [dɪ'mɒkrəsɪ] *n* démocratie *f*; **democrat** ['deməkræt] *n* démocrate *m/f*; **democratic** [demə'krætɪk] *adj* démocratique

demolish [dɪ'mɒlɪʃ] *vt* démolir

demonstrate ['demənstreɪt] *vt* démontrer, prouver; (*show*) faire une démonstration de ♦ *vi*: **to ~ (for/against)** manifester (en faveur de/contre); **demonstration** [demən'streɪʃən] *n* démonstration *f*, manifestation *f*; **demonstrator** ['demənstreɪtə*] *n* (*POL*) manifestant(e)

demote [dɪ'məʊt] *vt* rétrograder

demure [dɪ'mjʊə*] *adj* sage, réservé(e)

den [den] *n* tanière *f*, antre *m*

denatured alcohol [diː'neɪtʃəd-] (*US*) *n* alcool *m* à brûler

denial [dɪ'naɪəl] *n* démenti *m*; (*refusal*) dénégation *f*

denim ['denɪm] *n* jean *m*; **~s** *npl* (*jeans*) (blue-)jean(s) *m(pl)*

Denmark ['denmɑːk] *n* Danemark *m*

denomination [dɪnɒmɪ'neɪʃən] *n* (*of money*) valeur *f*; (*REL*) confession *f*

denounce [dɪ'naʊns] *vt* dénoncer

dense [dens] *adj* dense; (*stupid*) obtus(e), bouché(e); **~ly** *adv*: **~ly populated** à forte densité de population

density ['densɪtɪ] *n* densité *f*; **double/ high-~ diskette** disquette *f* double densité/haute densité

dent [dent] *n* bosse *f* ♦ *vt* (*also*: **make a ~ in**) cabosser

dental ['dentl] *adj* dentaire; **~ surgeon** *n* (chirurgien(ne)) dentiste

dentist ['dentɪst] *n* dentiste *m/f*

dentures ['dentʃəz] *npl* dentier *m sg*

deny [dɪ'naɪ] *vt* nier; (*refuse*) refuser

deodorant [diː'əʊdərənt] *n* déodorant *m*, désodorisant *m*

depart [dɪ'pɑːt] *vi* partir; **to ~ from** (*fig: differ from*) s'écarter de

department [dɪ'pɑːtmənt] *n* (*COMM*) rayon *m*; (*SCOL*) section *f*; (*POL*) ministère *m*, département *m*; **~ store** *n* grand magasin

departure [dɪ'pɑːtʃə*] *n* départ *m*; **a new ~** une nouvelle voie; **~ lounge** *n* (*at airport*) salle *f* d'embarquement

depend [dɪ'pend] *vi*: **to ~ on** dépendre de; (*rely on*) compter sur; **it ~s** cela dépend; **~ing on the result** selon le résultat; **~able** *adj* (*person*) sérieux(euse), sûr(e); (*car, watch*) solide, fiable; **~ant** *n* personne *f* à charge; **~ent** *adj*: **to be ~ent (on)** dépendre (de) ♦ *n* = **dependant**

depict [dɪ'pɪkt] *vt* (*in picture*) représenter; (*in words*) dépeindre, décrire

depleted [dɪ'pliːtɪd] *adj* (considérablement) réduit(e) *or* diminué(e)

deport [dɪ'pɔːt] *vt* expulser

deposit [dɪ'pɔzɪt] *n* (*CHEM, COMM, GEO*) dépôt *m*; (*of ore, oil*) gisement *m*; (*part payment*) arrhes *fpl*, acompte *m*; (*on bottle etc*) consigne *f*; (*for hired goods etc*) cautionnement *m*, garantie *f* ♦ *vt* déposer; **~ account** *n* compte *m* sur livret

depot ['depəu] *n* dépôt *m*; (*US: RAIL*) gare *f*

depress [dɪ'pres] *vt* déprimer; (*press down*) appuyer sur, abaisser; (*prices, wages*) faire baisser; **~ed** *adj* (*person*) déprimé(e); (*area*) en déclin, touché(e) par le sous-emploi; **~ing** *adj* déprimant(e); **~ion** [dɪ'preʃən] *n* dépression *f*; (*hollow*) creux *m*

deprivation [deprɪ'veɪʃən] *n* privation *f*; (*loss*) perte *f*

deprive [dɪ'praɪv] *vt*: **to ~ sb of** priver qn de; **~d** *adj* déshérité(e)

depth [depθ] *n* profondeur *f*; **in the ~s of despair** au plus profond du désespoir; **to be out of one's ~** avoir perdu pied, nager

deputize ['depjutaɪz] *vi*: **to ~ for** assurer l'intérim de

deputy ['depjutɪ] *adj* adjoint(e) ♦ *n* (*second in command*) adjoint(e); (*US:*

also ~ sheriff) shérif adjoint; **~ head** directeur adjoint, sous-directeur

derail [dɪ'reɪl] *vt*: **to be ~ed** dérailler

deranged [dɪ'reɪndʒd] *adj*: **to be (mentally) ~** avoir le cerveau dérangé

derby ['dɑːbɪ] (*US*) *n* (*bowler hat*) (chapeau *m*) melon *m*

derelict ['derɪlɪkt] *adj* abandonné(e), à l'abandon

derisory [dɪ'raɪsərɪ] *adj* (*sum*) dérisoire; (*smile, person*) moqueur(euse)

derive [dɪ'raɪv] *vt*: **to ~ sth from** tirer qch de; trouver qch dans: **to ~ from** provenir de, dériver de

derogatory [dɪ'rɔɡətərɪ] *adj* désobligeant(e); péjoratif(ive)

descend [dɪ'send] *vi*, *vi* descendre; **to ~ from** descendre de, être issu(e) de; **to ~ to (doing) sth** s'abaisser à (faire) qch; **descent** [dɪ'sent] *n* descente *f*; (*origin*) origine *f*

describe [dɪs'kraɪb] *vt* décrire; **description** [dɪs'krɪpʃən] *n* description *f*; (*sort*) sorte *f*, espèce *f*

desecrate ['desɪkreɪt] *vt* profaner

desert [*n* 'dezət, *vb* dɪ'zɜːt] *n* désert *m* ♦ *vt* déserter, abandonner ♦ *vi* (*MIL*) déserter; **~s** *npl*: **to get one's just ~s** n'avoir que ce qu'on mérite; **~er** *n* déserteur *m*; **~ion** [dɪ'zɜːʃən] *n* (*MIL*) désertion *f*; (*LAW: of spouse*) abandon *m* du domicile conjugal; **~ island** *n* île déserte

deserve [dɪ'zɜːv] *vt* mériter; **deserving** [dɪ'zɜːvɪŋ] *adj* (*person*) méritant(e); (*action, cause*) méritoire

design [dɪ'zaɪn] *n* (*sketch*) plan *m*, dessin *m*; (*layout, shape*) conception *f*, ligne *f*; (*pattern*) dessin *m*, motif(s) *m(pl)*; (*COMM, art*) design *m*, stylisme *m*; (*intention*) dessein *m* ♦ *vt* dessiner; élaborer; **~er** [dɪ'zaɪnə*] *n* (*TECH*) concepteur-projeteur *m*; (*ART*) dessinateur(trice), designer *m*; (*fashion*) styliste *m/f*

desire [dɪ'zaɪə*] *n* désir *m* ♦ *vt* désirer

desk [desk] *n* (*in office*) bureau *m*; (*for pupil*) pupitre *m*; (*BRIT: in shop, restaurant*) caisse *f*; (*in hotel, at airport*) réception *f*

desolate ['desəlɪt] *adj* désolé(e); (*per-*

son) affligé(e)

despair [dɪs'pɛə*] *n* désespoir *m* ♦ *vi*: to ~ of désespérer de

despatch [dɪs'pætʃ] *n, vt* = **dispatch**

desperate ['dɛspərɪt] *adj* désespéré(e); (*criminal*) prêt(e) à tout; **to be ~ for sth/to do sth** avoir désespérément besoin de qch/de faire qch; ~**ly** ['dɛspərɪtlɪ] *adv* désespérément; (*very*) terriblement, extrêmement

desperation [dɛspə'reɪʃən] *n* désespoir *m*; **in (sheer) ~** en désespoir de cause

despicable [dɪs'pɪkəbl] *adj* méprisable

despise [dɪs'paɪz] *vt* mépriser

despite [dɪs'paɪt] *prep* malgré, en dépit de

despondent [dɪs'pɒndənt] *adj* découragé(e), abattu(e)

dessert [dɪ'zɜːt] *n* dessert *m*; ~**spoon** *n* cuiller *f* à dessert

destination [dɛstɪ'neɪʃən] *n* destination *f*

destined ['dɛstɪnd] *adj*: **to be ~ to do/ for sth** être destiné(e) à faire/à qch

destiny ['dɛstɪnɪ] *n* destinée *f*, destin *m*

destitute ['dɛstɪtjuːt] *adj* indigent(e)

destroy [dɪs'trɔɪ] *vt* détruire; (*injured horse*) abattre; (*dog*) faire piquer; ~**er** *n* (*NAUT*) contre-torpilleur *m*

destruction [dɪs'trʌkʃən] *n* destruction *f*

detach [dɪ'tætʃ] *vt* détacher; ~**ed** *adj* (*attitude, person*) détaché(e); ~**ed house** *n* pavillon *m*, maison(nette) (individuelle); ~**ment** *n* (*MIL*) détachement *m*; (*fig*) détachement, indifférence *f*

detail ['diːteɪl] *n* détail *m* ♦ *vt* raconter en détail, énumérer; **in ~** en détail; ~**ed** *adj* détaillé(e)

detain [dɪ'teɪn] *vt* retenir; (*in captivity*) détenir; (*in hospital*) hospitaliser

detect [dɪ'tɛkt] *vt* déceler, percevoir; (*MED, POLICE*) dépister; (*MIL, RADAR, TECH*) détecter; ~**ion** [dɪ'tɛkʃən] *n* découverte *f*; ~**ive** *n* agent *m* de la sûreté, policier *m*; **private ~ive** détective privé; ~**ive story** *n* roman policier

detention [dɪ'tɛnʃən] *n* détention *f*; (*SCOL*) retenue *f*, consigne *f*

deter [dɪ'tɜː*] *vt* dissuader

detergent [dɪ'tɜːdʒənt] *n* détergent *m*, détersif *m*

deteriorate [dɪ'tɪərɪəreɪt] *vi* se détériorer, se dégrader

determine [dɪ'tɜːmɪn] *vt* déterminer; **to ~ to do** résoudre de faire, se déterminer à faire; ~**d** *adj* (*person*) déterminé(e), décidé(e)

deterrent [dɪ'tɛrənt] *n* effet *m* de dissuasion; force *f* de dissuasion

detonate ['dɛtəneɪt] *vt* faire détoner *or* exploser

detour ['diːtʊə*] *n* détour *m*; (*US: AUT: diversion*) déviation *f*

detract [dɪ'trækt] *vt*: **to ~ from** (*quality, pleasure*) diminuer; (*reputation*) porter atteinte à

detriment ['dɛtrɪmənt] *n*: **to the ~ of** au détriment de, au préjudice de; ~**al** [dɛtrɪ'mɛntl] *adj*: ~**al to** préjudiciable *or* nuisible à

devaluation [dɪvæljʊ'eɪʃən] *n* dévaluation *f*

devastate ['dɛvəsteɪt] *vt* (*also fig*) dévaster; **devastating** *adj* dévastateur(trice); (*news*) accablant(e)

develop [dɪ'vɛləp] *vt* (*gen*) développer; (*disease*) commencer à souffrir de; (*resources*) mettre en valeur, exploiter ♦ *vi* se développer; (*situation, disease*: *evolve*) évoluer; (*facts, symptoms*: *appear*) se manifester, se produire; ~**ing country** pays *m* en voie de développement; **the machine has ~ed a fault** un problème s'est manifesté dans cette machine; ~**er** *n* (*also*: *property ~er*) promoteur *m*; ~**ment** *n* développement *m*; (*of affair, case*) rebondissement *m*, fait(s) nouveau(x)

device [dɪ'vaɪs] *n* (*apparatus*) engin *m*, dispositif *m*

devil ['dɛvl] *n* diable *m*; démon *m*

devious ['diːvɪəs] *adj* (*person*) sournois(e), dissimulé(e)

devise [dɪ'vaɪz] *vt* imaginer, concevoir

devoid [dɪ'vɔɪd] *adj*: ~ **of** dépourvu(e) de, dénué(e) de

devolution [diːvə'luːʃən] *n* (*POL*) décentralisation *f*

devote [dɪˈvəʊt] *vt*: **to ~ sth to** consacrer qch à; **~d** *adj* dévoué(e); **to be ~d to** (*book etc*) être consacré(e) à; (*person*) être très attaché(e) à; **~e** [devəʊˈtiː] *n* (*REL*) adepte *m/f*; (*MUS, SPORT*) fervent(e)

devotion [dɪˈvəʊʃən] *n* dévouement *m*, attachement *m*; (*REL*) dévotion *f*, piété *f*

devour [dɪˈvaʊə*] *vt* dévorer

devout [dɪˈvaʊt] *adj* pieux(euse), dévot(e)

dew [djuː] *n* rosée *f*

diabetes [daɪəˈbiːtiːz] *n* diabète *m*; **diabetic** [daɪəˈbetɪk] *adj* diabétique ♦ *n* diabétique *m/f*

diabolical [daɪəˈbɒlɪkl] (*inf*) *adj* (*weather*) atroce; (*behaviour*) infernal(e)

diagnosis [daɪəgˈnəʊsɪs, *pl* daɪəgˈnəʊsiːz] (*pl* **diagnoses**) *n* diagnostic *m*

diagonal [daɪˈægənl] *adj* diagonal(e) ♦ *n* diagonale *f*

diagram [ˈdaɪəgræm] *n* diagramme *m*, schéma *m*

dial [ˈdaɪəl] *n* cadran *m* ♦ *vt* (*number*) faire, composer; **~ code** (*US*) *n* = **dialling code**

dialect [ˈdaɪəlekt] *n* dialecte *m*

dialling code [ˈdaɪəlɪŋ-] (*BRIT*) *n* indicatif *m* (téléphonique)

dialling tone [ˈdaɪəlɪŋ-] (*BRIT*) *n* tonalité *f*

dialogue [ˈdaɪəlɒg] *n* dialogue *m*

dial tone (*US*) *n* = **dialling tone**

diameter [daɪˈæmɪtə*] *n* diamètre *m*

diamond [ˈdaɪəmənd] *n* diamant *m*; (*shape*) losange *m*; **~s** *npl* (*CARDS*) carreau *m*

diaper [ˈdaɪəpə*] (*US*) *n* couche *f*

diaphragm [ˈdaɪəfræm] *n* diaphragme *m*

diarrhoea [daɪəˈriːə] (*US* **diarrhea**) *n* diarrhée *f*

diary [ˈdaɪərɪ] *n* (*daily account*) journal *m*; (*book*) agenda *m*

dice [daɪs] *n inv* dé *m* ♦ *vt* (*CULIN*) couper en dés *or* en cubes

dictate [*vb* dɪkˈteɪt] *vt* dicter

dictation [dɪkˈteɪʃən] *n* dictée *f*

dictator [dɪkˈteɪtə*] *n* dictateur *m*; **~ship** *n* dictature *f*

dictionary [ˈdɪkʃənrɪ] *n* dictionnaire *m*

did [dɪd] *pt of* **do**; **~n't** = **did not**

die [daɪ] *vi* mourir; **to be dying for sth** avoir une envie folle de qch; **to be dying to do sth** mourir d'envie de faire qch; **~ away** *vi* s'éteindre; **~ down** *vi* se calmer, s'apaiser; **~ out** *vi* disparaître

die-hard [ˈdaɪhɑːd] *n* réactionnaire *m/f*, jusqu'au-boutiste *m/f*

diesel [ˈdiːzəl] *n* (*vehicle*) diesel *m*; (*also*: **~ oil**) carburant diesel, gas-oil *m*; **~ engine** *n* moteur *m* diesel

diet [ˈdaɪət] *n* alimentation *f*; (*restricted food*) régime *m* ♦ *vi* (*also*: **be on a ~**) suivre un régime

differ [ˈdɪfə*] *vi* (*be different*): **to ~ (from)** être différent (de); différer (de); (*disagree*): **to ~ (from sb over sth)** ne pas être d'accord (avec qn au sujet de qch); **~ence** *n* différence *f*; (*quarrel*) différend *m*, désaccord *m*; **~ent** *adj* différent(e); **~entiate** [dɪfəˈrenʃɪeɪt] *vi*: **to ~entiate (between)** faire une différence (entre)

difficult [ˈdɪfɪkəlt] *adj* difficile; **~y** *n* difficulté *f*

diffident [ˈdɪfɪdənt] *adj* qui manque de confiance *or* d'assurance

dig [dɪg] (*pt, pp* **dug**) *vt* (*hole*) creuser; (*garden*) bêcher ♦ *n* (*prod*) coup *m* de coude; (*fig*) coup de griffe *or* de patte; (*archeological*) fouilles *fpl*; **~ in** *vi* (*MIL: also*: **~ o.s. in**) se retrancher; **~ into** *vt fus* (*savings*) puiser dans; **to ~ one's nails into sth** enfoncer ses ongles dans qch; **~ up** *vt* déterrer

digest [*vb* daɪˈdʒest, *n* ˈdaɪdʒest] *vt* digérer ♦ *n* sommaire *m*, résumé *m*; **~ion** [dɪˈdʒestʃən] *n* digestion *f*

digit [ˈdɪdʒɪt] *n* (*number*) chiffre *m*; (*finger*) doigt *m*; **~al** *adj* digital(e), à affichage numérique *or* digital; **~al computer** calculateur *m* numérique

dignified [ˈdɪgnɪfaɪd] *adj* digne

dignity [ˈdɪgnɪtɪ] *n* dignité *f*

digress [daɪˈgres] *vi*: **to ~ from** s'écarter de, s'éloigner de

digs [dɪgz] (*BRIT: inf*) *npl* piaule *f*, chambre meublée

dilapidated [dɪˈlæpɪdeɪtɪd] *adj* délabré(e)

dilemma [daɪˈlemə] *n* dilemme *m*

diligent [ˈdɪlɪdʒənt] *adj* appliqué(e), assidu(e)

dilute [daɪˈluːt] *vt* diluer

dim [dɪm] *adj* (*light*) faible; (*memory, outline*) vague, indécis(e); (*figure*) vague, indistinct(e); (*room*) sombre; (*stupid*) borné(e), obtus(e) ♦ *vt* (*light*) réduire, baisser; (*US: AUT*) mettre en code

dime [daɪm] (*US*) *n* = **10 cents**

dimension [dɪˈmenʃən] *n* dimension *f*

diminish [dɪˈmɪnɪʃ] *vt, vi* diminuer

diminutive [dɪˈmɪnjʊtɪv] *adj* minuscule, tout(e) petit(e)

dimmers [ˈdɪməz] (*US*) *npl* (*AUT*) phares *mpl* code *inv*; feux *mpl* de position

dimple [ˈdɪmpl] *n* fossette *f*

din [dɪn] *n* vacarme *m*

dine [daɪn] *vi* dîner; **~r** *n* (*person*) dîneur(euse); (*US: restaurant*) petit restaurant

dinghy [ˈdɪŋgɪ] *n* youyou *m*; (*also: rubber ~*) canot *m* pneumatique; (: *sailing ~*) voilier *m*, dériveur *m*

dingy [ˈdɪndʒɪ] *adj* miteux(euse), minable

dining car [ˈdaɪnɪŋ-] (*BRIT*) *n* wagon-restaurant *m*

dining room [ˈdaɪnɪŋ-] *n* salle *f* à manger

dinner [ˈdɪnə*] *n* dîner *m*; (*lunch*) déjeuner *m*; (*public*) banquet *m*; **~ jacket** *n* smoking *m*; **~ party** *n* dîner *m*; **~ time** *n* heure *f* du dîner; (*midday*) heure du déjeuner

dint [dɪnt] *n*: **by ~ of (doing)** à force de (faire)

dip [dɪp] *n* déclivité *f*; (*in sea*) baignade *f*, bain *m*; (*CULIN*) ≈ sauce *f* ♦ *vt* tremper, plonger; (*BRIT: AUT: lights*) mettre en code, baisser ♦ *vi* plonger

diploma [dɪˈpləʊmə] *n* diplôme *m*

diplomacy [dɪˈpləʊməsɪ] *n* diplomatie *f*

diplomat [ˈdɪpləmæt] *n* diplomate *m*; **~ic** [dɪpləˈmætɪk] *adj* diplomatique

dipstick [ˈdɪpstɪk] *n* (*AUT*) jauge *f* de niveau d'huile

dipswitch [ˈdɪpswɪtʃ] (*BRIT*) *n* (*AUT*) interrupteur *m* de lumière réduite

dire [daɪə*] *adj* terrible, extrême, affreux(euse)

direct [daɪˈrekt] *adj* direct(e) ♦ *vt* diriger, orienter (*letter, remark*) adresser; (*film, programme*) réaliser; (*play*) mettre en scène; (*order*): **to ~ sb to do sth** ordonner à qn de faire qch ♦ *adv* directement; **can you ~ me to ...?** pouvez-vous m'indiquer le chemin de ...?; **~ debit** (*BRIT*) *n* prélèvement *m* automatique

direction [dɪˈrekʃən] *n* direction *f*; **~s** *npl* (*advice*) indications *fpl*; **sense of ~** sens *m* de l'orientation; **~s for use** mode *m* d'emploi

directly [dɪˈrektlɪ] *adv* (*in a straight line*) directement, tout droit; (*at once*) tout de suite, immédiatement

director [dɪˈrektə*] *n* directeur *m*; (*THEATRE*) metteur *m* en scène; (*CINEMA, TV*) réalisateur(trice)

directory [dɪˈrektərɪ] *n* annuaire *m*; (*COMPUT*) répertoire *m*

dirt [dɜːt] *n* saleté *f*; crasse *f*; (*earth*) terre *f*, boue *f*; **~-cheap** *adj* très bon marché *inv*; **~y** *adj* sale ♦ *vt* salir; **~y trick** coup tordu

disability [dɪsəˈbɪlɪtɪ] *n* invalidité *f*, infirmité *f*

disabled [dɪsˈeɪbld] *adj* infirme, invalide ♦ *npl*: **the ~** les handicapés

disadvantage [dɪsədˈvɑːntɪdʒ] *n* désavantage *m*, inconvénient *m*

disagree [dɪsəˈgriː] *vi* (*be different*) ne pas concorder; (*be against, think otherwise*): **to ~ (with)** ne pas être d'accord (avec); **~able** *adj* désagréable; **~ment** *n* désaccord *m*, différend *m*

disallow [ˈdɪsəˈlaʊ] *vt* rejeter

disappear [dɪsəˈpɪə*] *vi* disparaître; **~ance** *n* disparition *f*

disappoint [dɪsəˈpɔɪnt] *vt* décevoir; **~ed** *adj* déçu(e); **~ing** *adj* décevant(e); **~ment** *n* déception *f*

disapproval [dɪsəˈpruːvəl] *n* désapprobation *f*

disapprove [dɪsəˈpruːv] *vi*: **to ~ (of)** désapprouver

disarmament [dɪsˈɑːməmənt] *n* désarmement *m*

disarray ['dɪsə'reɪ] *n*: **in ~** (*army*) en déroute; (*organization*) en désarroi; (*hair, clothes*) en désordre

disaster [dɪ'zɑːstə*] *n* catastrophe *f*, désastre *m*

disband [dɪs'bænd] *vt* démobiliser; disperser ♦ *vi* se séparer; se disperser

disbelief ['dɪsbə'liːf] *n* incrédulité *f*

disc [dɪsk] *n* disque *m*; (*COMPUT*) = **disk**

discard ['dɪskɑːd] *vt* (*old things*) se débarrasser de; (*fig*) écarter, renoncer à

discern [dɪ'sɜːn] *vt* discerner, distinguer; **~ing** *adj* perspicace

discharge [*vb* dɪs'tʃɑːdʒ, *n* 'dɪstʃɑːdʒ] *vt* décharger; (*duties*) s'acquitter de; (*patient*) renvoyer (chez lui); (*employee*) congédier, licencier; (*soldier*) rendre à la vie civile; réformer; (*defendant*) relaxer, élargir ♦ *n* décharge *f*; (*dismissal*) renvoi *m*; licenciement *m*; élargissement *m*; (*MED*) écoulement *m*

discipline ['dɪsɪplɪn] *n* discipline *f*

disc jockey *n* disc-jockey *m*

disclaim [dɪs'kleɪm] *vt* nier

disclose [dɪs'kləʊz] *vt* révéler, divulguer; **disclosure** [dɪs'kləʊʒə*] *n* révélation *f*

disco ['dɪskəʊ] *n abbr* = **discotheque**

discomfort [dɪs'kʌmfət] *n* malaise *m*, gêne *f*; (*lack of comfort*) manque *m* de confort

disconcert [dɪskən'sɜːt] *vt* déconcerter

disconnect [dɪskə'nekt] *vt* (*ELEC, RADIO, pipe*) débrancher; (*TEL, water*) couper

discontent [dɪskən'tent] *n* mécontentement *m*; **~ed** *adj* mécontent(e)

discontinue ['dɪskən'tɪnjuː] *vt* cesser, interrompre; **"~d"** (*COMM*) "fin de série"

discord ['dɪskɔːd] *n* discorde *f*, dissension *f*; (*MUS*) dissonance *f*

discotheque ['dɪskəʊtek] *n* discothèque *f*

discount [*n* 'dɪskaʊnt, *vb* dɪs'kaʊnt] *n* remise *f*, rabais *m* ♦ *vt* (*sum*) faire une remise de; (*fig*) ne pas tenir compte de

discourage [dɪs'kʌrɪdʒ] *vt* décourager

discover [dɪs'kʌvə*] *vt* découvrir; **~y** *n* découverte *f*

discredit [dɪs'kredɪt] *vt* (*idea*) mettre en doute; (*person*) discréditer

discreet [dɪs'kriːt] *adj* discret(ète)

discrepancy [dɪs'krepənsɪ] *n* divergence *f*, contradiction *f*

discretion [dɪ'skreʃən] *n* discrétion *f*; **use your own ~** à vous de juger

discriminate [dɪs'krɪmɪneɪt] *vi*: **to ~ between** établir une distinction entre, faire la différence entre; **to ~ against** pratiquer une discrimination contre; **discriminating** *adj* qui a du discernement; **discrimination** [dɪskrɪmɪ'neɪʃən] *n* discrimination *f*; (*judgment*) discernement *m*

discuss [dɪs'kʌs] *vt* discuter de; (*debate*) discuter; **~ion** [dɪs'kʌʃən] *n* discussion *f*

disdain [dɪs'deɪn] *n* dédain *m*

disease [dɪ'ziːz] *n* maladie *f*

disembark [dɪsɪm'bɑːk] *vt, vi* débarquer

disengage [dɪsɪn'geɪdʒ] *vt*: **to ~ the clutch** (*AUT*) débrayer

disentangle [dɪsɪn'tæŋgl] *vt* (*wool, wire*) démêler, débrouiller; (*from wreckage*) dégager

disfigure [dɪs'fɪgə*] *vt* défigurer

disgrace [dɪs'greɪs] *n* honte *f*; (*disfavour*) disgrâce *f* ♦ *vt* déshonorer, couvrir de honte; **~ful** *adj* scandaleux(euse), honteux(euse)

disgruntled [dɪs'grʌntld] *adj* mécontent(e)

disguise [dɪs'gaɪz] *n* déguisement *m* ♦ *vt* déguiser; **in ~** déguisé(e)

disgust [dɪs'gʌst] *n* dégoût *m*, aversion *f* ♦ *vt* dégoûter, écœurer; **~ing** *adj* dégoûtant(e); révoltant(e)

dish [dɪʃ] *n* plat *m*; **to do** or **wash the ~es** faire la vaisselle; **~ out** *vt* servir, distribuer; **~ up** *vt* servir; **~cloth** *n* (*for washing*) lavette *f*

dishearten [dɪs'hɑːtn] *vt* décourager

dishevelled [dɪ'ʃevəld] (*US* **disheveled**) *adj* ébouriffé(e); décoiffé(e); débraillé(e)

dishonest [dɪs'ɒnɪst] *adj* malhonnête

dishonour [dɪs'ɒnə*] (*US* **dishonor**) *n* déshonneur *m*; **~able** *adj* (*behaviour*) déshonorant(e); (*person*) peu honorable

dishtowel ['dɪʃtaʊəl] (*US*) *n* torchon *m*

dishwasher ['dɪʃwɒʃə*] *n* lave-vaisselle *m*

disillusion [dɪsɪ'luːʒən] *vt* désabuser,

désillusionner

disincentive ['dɪsɪn'sentɪv] *n*: **to be a ~** être démotivant(e)

disinfect [dɪsɪn'fekt] *vt* désinfecter; **~ant** *n* désinfectant *m*

disintegrate [dɪs'ɪntɪgreɪt] *vi* se désintégrer

disinterested [dɪs'ɪntrɪstɪd] *adj* désintéressé(e)

disjointed [dɪs'dʒɔɪntɪd] *adj* décousu(e), incohérent(e)

disk [dɪsk] *n* (*COMPUT*) disque *m*; (: *floppy ~*) disquette *f*; **single-/double-sided ~** disquette simple/double face; **~ drive** *n* lecteur *m* de disquettes; **~ette** [dɪs'ket] *n* disquette *f*, disque *m* souple

dislike [dɪs'laɪk] *n* aversion *f*, antipathie *f* ♦ *vt* ne pas aimer

dislocate [ˈdɪsləʊkeɪt] *vt* disloquer; déboiter

dislodge [dɪs'lɒdʒ] *vt* déplacer, faire bouger

disloyal ['dɪs'lɔɪəl] *adj* déloyal(e)

dismal ['dɪzməl] *adj* lugubre, maussade

dismantle [dɪs'mæntl] *vt* démonter

dismay [dɪs'meɪ] *n* consternation *f*

dismiss [dɪs'mɪs] *vt* congédier, renvoyer; (*soldiers*) faire rompre les rangs à; (*idea*) écarter; (*LAW*) **to ~ a case** rendre une fin de non-recevoir; **~al** *n* renvoi *m*

dismount [dɪs'maʊnt] *vi* mettre pied à terre, descendre

disobedient [dɪsə'biːdɪənt] *adj* désobéissant(e)

disobey ['dɪsə'beɪ] *vt* désobéir à

disorder [dɪs'ɔːdə*] *n* désordre *m*; (*rioting*) désordres *mpl*; (*MED*) troubles *mpl*; **~ly** [dɪs'ɔːdəlɪ] *adj* en désordre; désordonné(e)

disorientated [dɪs'ɔːrɪənteɪtɪd] *adj* désorienté(e)

disown [dɪs'əʊn] *vt* renier

disparaging [dɪs'pærɪdʒɪŋ] *adj* désobligeant(e)

dispassionate [dɪs'pæʃnɪt] *adj* calme, froid(e); impartial(e), objectif(ive)

dispatch [dɪs'pætʃ] *vt* expédier, envoyer ♦ *n* envoi *m*, expédition *f*; (*MIL, PRESS*) dépêche *f*

dispel [dɪs'pel] *vt* dissiper, chasser

dispense [dɪs'pens] *vt* distribuer, administrer; **~ with** *vt fus* se passer de; **~r** *n* (*machine*) distributeur *m*; **dispensing chemist** (*BRIT*) *n* pharmacie *f*

disperse [dɪs'pɜːs] *vt* disperser ♦ *vi* se disperser

dispirited [dɪs'pɪrɪtɪd] *adj* découragé(e), déprimé(e)

displace [dɪs'pleɪs] *vt* déplacer

display [dɪs'pleɪ] *n* étalage *m*; déploiement *m*; affichage *m*; (*screen*) écran *m*, visuel *m*; (*of feeling*) manifestation *f* ♦ *vt* montrer; (*goods*) mettre à l'étalage, exposer; (*results, departure times*) afficher; (*pej*) faire étalage de

displease [dɪs'pliːz] *vt* mécontenter, contrarier; **~d** *adj*: **~d with** mécontent(e) de; **displeasure** [dɪs'pleʒə*] *n* mécontentement *m*

disposable [dɪs'pəʊzəbl] *adj* (*pack etc*) jetable, à jeter; (*income*) disponible; **~ nappy** (*BRIT*) *n* couche *f* à jeter, coucheculotte *f*

disposal [dɪs'pəʊzəl] *n* (*of goods for sale*) vente *f*; (*of property*) disposition *f*, cession *f*; (*of rubbish*) enlèvement *m*; destruction *f*; **at one's ~** à sa disposition

dispose [dɪs'pəʊz] *vt* disposer; **~ of** *vt fus* (*unwanted goods etc*) se débarrasser de, se défaire de; (*problem*) expédier; **~d** [dɪs'pəʊzd] *adj*: **to be ~d to do sth** être disposé(e) à faire qch; **disposition** [dɪspə'zɪʃən] *n* disposition *f*; (*temperament*) naturel *m*

disprove [dɪs'pruːv] *vt* réfuter

dispute [dɪs'pjuːt] *n* discussion *f*; (*also: industrial ~*) conflit *m* ♦ *vt* contester; (*matter*) discuter; (*victory*) disputer

disqualify [dɪs'kwɒlɪfaɪ] *vt* (*SPORT*) disqualifier; **to ~ sb for sth/from doing** rendre qn inapte à qch/à faire

disquiet [dɪs'kwaɪət] *n* inquiétude *f*, trouble *m*

disregard [dɪsrɪ'gɑːd] *vt* ne pas tenir compte de

disrepair ['dɪsrɪ'pɛə*] *n*: **to fall into ~** (*building*) tomber en ruine

disreputable [dɪs'repjʊtəbl] *adj* (*person*)

de mauvaise réputation; (*behaviour*) déshonorant(e)

disrespectful [dɪsrɪ'spɛktfʊl] *adj* irrespectueux(euse)

disrupt [dɪs'rʌpt] *vt* (*plans*) déranger; (*conversation*) interrompre

dissatisfied [dɪs'sætɪsfaɪd] *adj*: ~ **(with)** insatisfait(e) (de)

dissect [dɪ'sɛkt] *vt* disséquer

dissent [dɪ'sɛnt] *n* dissentiment *m*, différence *f* d'opinion

dissertation [dɪsə'teɪʃən] *n* mémoire *m*

disservice [dɪs'sɜːvɪs] *n*: **to do sb a ~** rendre un mauvais service à qn

dissimilar ['dɪ'sɪmɪlə*] *adj*: ~ **(to)** dissemblable (à), différent(e) (de)

dissipate ['dɪsɪpeɪt] *vt* dissiper; (*money, efforts*) disperser

dissolute ['dɪsəluːt] *adj* débauché(e), dissolu(e)

dissolve [dɪ'zɒlv] *vt* dissoudre ♦ *vi* se dissoudre, fondre; **to ~ in(to) tears** fondre en larmes

distance ['dɪstəns] *n* distance *f*; **in the ~** au loin

distant ['dɪstənt] *adj* lointain(e), éloigné(e); (*manner*) distant(e), froid(e)

distaste [dɪs'teɪst] *n* dégoût *m*; ~**ful** *adj* déplaisant(e), désagréable

distended [dɪs'tɛndɪd] *adj* (*stomach*) dilaté(e)

distil [dɪs'tɪl] *vt* distiller; ~**lery** *n* distillerie *f*

distinct [dɪs'tɪŋkt] *adj* distinct(e); (*clear*) marqué(e); **as ~ from** par opposition à, ~**ion** [dɪs'tɪŋkʃən] *n* distinction *f*; (*in exam*) mention *f* très bien; ~**ive** *adj* distinctif(ive)

distinguish [dɪs'tɪŋgwɪʃ] *vt* distinguer; ~**ed** *adj* (*eminent*) distingué(e); ~**ing** *adj* (*feature*) distinctif(ive), caractéristique

distort [dɪs'tɔːt] *vt* déformer

distract [dɪs'trækt] *vt* distraire, déranger; ~**ed** *adj* distrait(e); (*anxious*) éperdu(e), égaré(e); ~**ion** [dɪs'trækʃən] *n* distraction *f*, égarement *m*

distraught [dɪs'trɔːt] *adj* éperdu(e)

distress [dɪs'trɛs] *n* détresse *f* ♦ *vt* affliger; ~**ing** *adj* douloureux(euse), pénible

distribute [dɪs'trɪbjuːt] *vt* distribuer; **distribution** [dɪstrɪ'bjuːʃən] *n* distribution *f*; **distributor** [dɪs'trɪbjʊtə*] *n* distributeur *m*

district ['dɪstrɪkt] *n* (*of country*) région *f*; (*of town*) quartier *m*; (ADMIN) district *m*; ~ **attorney** (US) *n* ≈ procureur *m* de la République; ~ **nurse** (BRIT) *n* infirmière visiteuse

distrust [dɪs'trʌst] *n* méfiance *f* ♦ *vt* se méfier de

disturb [dɪs'tɜːb] *vt* troubler; (*inconvenience*) déranger; ~**ance** *n* dérangement *m*; (*violent event, political etc*) troubles *mpl*; ~**ed** *adj* (*worried, upset*) agité(e), troublé(e); **to be emotionally ~ed** avoir des problèmes affectifs; ~**ing** *adj* troublant(e), inquiétant(e)

disuse ['dɪs'juːs] *n*: **to fall into ~** tomber en désuétude

disused ['dɪs'juːzd] *adj* désaffecté(e)

ditch [dɪtʃ] *n* fossé *m*; (*irrigation*) rigole *f* ♦ *vt* (*inf*) abandonner; (*person*) plaquer

dither ['dɪðə*] *vi* hésiter

ditto ['dɪtəʊ] *adv* idem

dive [daɪv] *n* plongeon *m*; (*of submarine*) plongée *f* ♦ *vi* plonger; **to ~ into** (*bag, drawer etc*) plonger la main dans; (*shop, car etc*) se précipiter dans; ~**r** *n* plongeur *m*

diversion [daɪ'vɜːʃən] *n* (BRIT: AUT) déviation *f*; (*distraction, MIL*) diversion *f*

divert [daɪ'vɜːt] *vt* (*funds, BRIT: traffic*) dévier; (*river, attention*) détourner

divide [dɪ'vaɪd] *vt* diviser; (*separate*) séparer ♦ *vi* se diviser; ~**d highway** (US) *n* route *f* à quatre voies

dividend ['dɪvɪdɛnd] *n* dividende *m*

divine [dɪ'vaɪn] *adj* divin(e)

diving ['daɪvɪŋ] *n* plongée (sous-marine); ~ **board** *n* plongeoir *m*

divinity [dɪ'vɪnɪtɪ] *n* divinité *f*; (SCOL) théologie *f*

division [dɪ'vɪʒən] *n* division *f*

divorce [dɪ'vɔːs] *n* divorce *m* ♦ *vt* divorcer d'avec; (*dissociate*) séparer; ~**d** *adj* divorcé(e); ~**e** [dɪvɔː'siː] *n* divorcé(e)

D.I.Y. (BRIT) *n abbr* = **do-it-yourself**

dizzy ['dɪzɪ] *adj*: **to make sb ~** donner le

vertige à qn; **to feel ~** avoir la tête qui tourne

DJ *n abbr* = **disc jockey**

KEYWORD
---

do [du:] (*pt* **did**, *pp* **done**) *n* (*inf: party etc*) soirée *f*, fête *f*

♦ *vb* **1** (*in negative constructions*) *non traduit*; **I ~n't understand** je ne comprends pas

2 (*to form questions*) *non traduit*; **didn't you know?** vous ne le saviez pas?; **why didn't you come?** pourquoi n'êtes-vous pas venu?

3 (*for emphasis, in polite expressions*): **she does seem rather late** je trouve qu'elle est bien en retard; **~ sit down/ help yourself** asseyez-vous/servez-vous je vous en prie

4 (*used to avoid repeating vb*): **she swims better than I ~** elle nage mieux que moi; **~ you agree? - yes, I ~/no, I ~n't** vous êtes d'accord? - oui/non; **she lives in Glasgow - so ~ I** elle habite Glasgow - moi aussi; **who broke it? - I did** qui l'a cassé? - c'est moi

5 (*in question tags*): **he laughed, didn't he?** il a ri, n'est-ce pas?; **I ~n't know him, ~ I?** je ne crois pas le connaître

♦ *vt* (*gen: carry out, perform etc*) faire; **what are you ~ing tonight?** qu'est-ce que vous faites ce soir?; **to ~ the cooking/washing-up** faire la cuisine/la vaisselle; **to ~ one's teeth/hair/nails** se brosser les dents/se coiffer/se faire les ongles; **the car was ~ing 100** ≈ la voiture faisait du 160 (à l'heure)

♦ *vi* **1** (*act, behave*) faire; **~ as I ~** faites comme moi

2 (*get on, fare*) marcher; **the firm is ~ing well** l'entreprise marche bien; **how ~ you ~?** comment allez-vous?; (*on being introduced*) enchanté(e)!

3 (*suit*) aller; **will it ~?** est-ce que ça ira?

4 (*be sufficient*) suffire, aller; **will £10 ~?** est-ce que 10 livres suffiront?; **that'll ~** ça suffit, ça ira; **that'll ~!** (*in annoyance*) ça va *ou* suffit comme ça!; **to**

make ~ (with) se contenter (de)

do away *vt fus* supprimer

do up *vt* (*laces, dress*) attacher; (*buttons*) boutonner; (*zip*) fermer; (*renovate: room*) refaire; (*: house*) remettre à neuf

do with *vt fus* (*need*): **I could do with a drink/some help** quelque chose à boire/un peu d'aide ne serait pas de refus; (*be connected*): **that has nothing to ~ with you** cela ne vous concerne pas; **I won't have anything to ~ with it** je ne veux pas m'en mêler

do without *vi* s'en passer ♦ *vt fus* se passer de

---

dock [dɔk] *n* dock *m*; (*LAW*) banc *m* des accusés ♦ *vi* se mettre à quai; (*SPACE*) s'arrimer; **~er** *n* docker *m*; **~yard** *n* chantier *m* de construction navale

doctor ['dɔktə*] *n* médecin *m*, docteur *m*; (*PhD etc*) docteur ♦ *vt* (*drink*) frelater; **D~ of Philosophy** *n* (*degree*) doctorat *m* (*person*) Docteur *m* en Droit *or* Lettres *etc*, titulaire *m/f* d'un doctorat

document ['dɔkjumənt] *n* document *m*; **~ary** [dɔkju'mentəri] *adj* documentaire ♦ *n* documentaire *m*

dodge [dɔdʒ] *n* truc *m*; combine *f* ♦ *vt* esquiver, éviter

dodgems ['dɔdʒəmz] (*BRIT*) *npl* autos tamponneuses

doe [dəu] *n* (*deer*) biche *f*; (*rabbit*) lapine *f*

does [dʌz] *vb see* **do**; **~n't** = **does not**

dog [dɔg] *n* chien(ne) ♦ *vt* suivre de près; poursuivre, harceler; **~ collar** *n* collier *m* de chien; (*fig*) faux-col *m* d'ecclésiastique; **~-eared** *adj* corné(e)

dogged ['dɔgid] *adj* obstiné(e), opiniâtre

dogsbody ['dɔgzbɔdi] *n* bonne *f* à tout faire, tâcheron *m*

doings ['du:iŋz] *npl* activités *fpl*

do-it-yourself ['du:itjə'self] *n* bricolage *m*

doldrums ['dɔldrəmz] *npl*: **to be in the ~** avoir le cafard; (*business*) être dans le marasme

dole [dəul] *n* (*BRIT: payment*) allocation *f* de chômage; **on the ~** au chômage; **~**

out *vt* donner au compte-goutte
doleful ['dəʊlfʊl] *adj* plaintif(ive), lugubre
doll [dɒl] *n* poupée *f*
dollar ['dɒlə*] *n* dollar *m*
dolled up ['dɒld-] (*inf*) *adj*: (**all**) ~ sur son trente et un
dolphin ['dɒlfɪn] *n* dauphin *m*
dome [dəʊm] *n* dôme *m*
domestic [də'mestɪk] *adj* (*task, appliances*) ménager(ère); (*of country: trade, situation etc*) intérieur(e); (*animal*) domestique; **~ated** *adj* (*animal*) domestiqué(e); (*husband*) pantouflard(e)
dominate ['dɒmɪneɪt] *vt* dominer
domineering [dɒmɪ'nɪərɪŋ] *adj* dominateur(trice), autoritaire
dominion [də'mɪnɪən] *n* (*territory*) territoire *m*; **to have** ~ **over** contrôler
domino ['dɒmɪnəʊ] (*pl* ~es) *n* domino *m*; **~es** *n* (*game*) dominos *mpl*
don [dɒn] (*BRIT*) *n* professeur *m* d'université
donate [dəʊ'neɪt] *vt* faire don de, donner
done [dʌn] *pp of* **do**
donkey ['dɒŋkɪ] *n* âne *m*
donor ['dəʊnə*] *n* (*of blood etc*) donneur(euse); (*to charity*) donateur(trice)
don't [dəʊnt] *vb* = **do not**
donut (*US*) *n* = **doughnut**
doodle ['du:dl] *vi* griffonner, gribouiller
doom [du:m] *n* destin *m* ♦ *vt*: **to be ~ed (to failure)** être voué(e) à l'échec; **~sday** *n* le Jugement dernier
door [dɔ:*] *n* porte *f*; (*RAIL, car*) portière *f*; **~bell** *n* sonnette *f*; **~handle** *n* poignée *f* de la porte; (*car*) poignée de portière; **~man** (*irreg*) *n* (*in hotel*) portier *m*; **~mat** *n* paillasson *m*; **~step** *n* pas *m* de (la) porte, seuil *m*; **~way** *n* (embrasure *f* de la) porte *f*
dope [dəʊp] *n* (*inf: drug*) drogue *f*; (*: person*) andouille *f* ♦ *vt* (*horse etc*) doper
dopey ['dəʊpɪ] (*inf*) *adj* à moitié endormi(e)
dormant ['dɔ:mənt] *adj* assoupi(e), en veilleuse
dormitory ['dɔ:mɪtrɪ] *n* dortoir *m*; (*US: building*) résidence *f* universitaire

dormouse ['dɔ:maʊs, *pl* 'dɔ:maɪs] (*pl* **dormice**) *n* loir *m*
dose [dəʊs] *n* dose *f*
doss house ['dɒs-] (*BRIT*) *n* asile *m* de nuit
dot [dɒt] *n* point *m*; (*on material*) pois *m* ♦ *vt*: **~ted with** parsemé(e) de; **on the** ~ à l'heure tapante *or* pile
dote [dəʊt]: **to ~ on** *vt fus* être fou(folle) de
dot-matrix printer [dɒt'meɪtrɪks-] *n* imprimante matricielle
dotted line *n* pointillé(s) *m(pl)*
double ['dʌbl] *adj* double ♦ *adv* (*twice*): **to cost** ~ (**sth**) coûter le double (de qch) *or* deux fois plus (que qch) ♦ *n* double *m* ♦ *vt* doubler; (*fold*) plier en deux ♦ *vi* doubler; **~s** *n* (*TENNIS*) double *m*; **on** *or* (*BRIT*) **at the** ~ au pas de course; **~ bass** (*BRIT*) *n* contrebasse *f*; ~ **bed** *n* grand lit; ~ **bend** (*BRIT*) *n* virage *m* en S; **~-breasted** *adj* croisé(e); **~cross** *vt* doubler, trahir; **~-decker** *n* autobus *m* à impériale; ~ **glazing** (*BRIT*) *n* double vitrage *m*; ~ **room** *n* chambre *f* pour deux personnes; **doubly** ['dʌblɪ] *adv* doublement, deux fois plus
doubt [daʊt] *n* doute *m* ♦ *vt* douter de; **to ~ that** douter que; **~ful** *adj* douteux(euse); (*person*) incertain(e); **~less** *adv* sans doute, sûrement
dough [dəʊ] *n* pâte *f*; **~nut** (*US* **donut**) *n* beignet *m*
douse [daʊz] *vt* (*drench*) tremper, inonder; (*extinguish*) éteindre
dove [dʌv] *n* colombe *f*
Dover ['dəʊvə*] *n* Douvres
dovetail ['dʌvteɪl] *vi* (*fig*) concorder
dowdy ['daʊdɪ] *adj* démodé(e); mal fagoté(e) (*inf*)
down [daʊn] *n* (*soft feathers*) duvet *m* ♦ *adv* en bas, vers le bas; (*on the ground*) par terre ♦ *prep* en bas de; (*along*) le long de ♦ *vt* (*inf: drink, food*) s'envoyer; ~ **with X!** à bas X!; **~-and-out** *n* clochard(e); **~-at-heel** *adj* éculé(e); (*fig*) miteux(euse); **~cast** *adj* démoralisé(e); **~fall** *n* chute *f*; ruine *f*; **~hearted** *adj* découragé(e); **~hill** *adv*: **to go ~hill**

descendre; (*fig*) péricliter; ~ **payment** *n* acompte *m*; ~**pour** *n* pluie torrentielle, déluge *m*; ~**right** *adj* (*lie etc*) effronté(e); (*refusal*) catégorique

Down's syndrome [daunz-] *n* (*MED*) trisomie *f*

down: ~**stairs** *adv* au rez-de-chaussée; à l'étage inférieur; ~**stream** *adv* en aval; ~**-to-earth** *adj* terre à terre *inv*; ~**town** *adv* en ville; ~ **under** *adv* en Australie (*or* Nouvelle-Zélande); ~**ward** *adj, adv* vers le bas; ~**wards** *adv* vers le bas

dowry ['dauri] *n* dot *f*

doz. *abbr* = **dozen**

doze [dəuz] *vi* sommeiller; ~ **off** *vi* s'assoupir

dozen ['dʌzn] *n* douzaine *f*; **a ~ books** une douzaine de livres; ~**s of** des centaines de

Dr. *abbr* = **doctor; drive**

drab [dræb] *adj* terne, morne

draft [drɑːft] *n* ébauche *f*; (*of letter, essay etc*) brouillon *m*; (*COMM*) traite *f*; (*US*: *call-up*) conscription *f* ♦ *vt* faire le brouillon *or* un projet de; (*MIL*: *send*) détacher; *see also* **draught**

draftsman ['drɑːftsmən] (*irreg: US*) *n* = **draughtsman**

drag [dræg] *vt* traîner; (*river*) draguer ♦ *vi* traîner ♦ *n* (*inf*) casse-pieds *m/f*; (*women's clothing*): **in ~** (en) travesti; ~ **on** *vi* s'éterniser

dragon ['drægən] *n* dragon *m*

dragonfly ['drægənflaɪ] *n* libellule *f*

drain [dreɪn] *n* égout *m*, canalisation *f*; (*on resources*) saignée *f* ♦ *vt* (*land, marshes etc*) drainer, assécher; (*vegetables*) égoutter; (*glass*) vider ♦ *vi* (*water*) s'écouler; ~**age** *n* drainage *m*; système *m* d'égouts *or* de canalisations; ~**ing board** (*US* ~**board**) *n* égouttoir *m*; ~**pipe** *n* tuyau *m* d'écoulement

drama ['drɑːmə] *n* (*art*) théâtre *m*, art *m* dramatique; (*play*) pièce *f* (de théâtre); (*event*) drame *m*; ~**tic** [drə'mætɪk] *adj* dramatique; spectaculaire; ~**tist** ['dræmətɪst] *n* auteur *m* dramatique; ~**tize** *vt* (*events*) dramatiser; (*adapt: for TV/cinema*) adapter pour la télévision/

pour l'écran

drank [dræŋk] *pt of* **drink**

drape [dreɪp] *vt* draper; ~**s** (*US*) *npl* rideaux *mpl*

drastic ['dræstɪk] *adj* sévère; énergique; (*change*) radical(e)

draught [drɑːft] (*US* **draft**) *n* courant *m* d'air; (*NAUT*) tirant *m* d'eau; **on ~** (*beer*) à la pression; ~**board** (*BRIT*) *n* damier *m*; ~**s** (*BRIT*) *n* (jeu *m* de) dames *fpl*

draughtsman ['drɑːftsmən] (*irreg*) *n* dessinateur(trice) (industriel(le))

draw [drɔː] (*pt* **drew**, *pp* **drawn**) *vt* tirer; (*tooth*) arracher, extraire; (*attract*) attirer; (*picture*) dessiner; (*line, circle*) tracer; (*money*) retirer ♦ *vi* (*SPORT*) faire match nul ♦ *n* match nul; (*lottery*) tirage *m* au sort; loterie *f*; **to ~ near** s'approcher; approcher; ~ **out** *vi* (*lengthen*) s'allonger ♦ *vt* (*money*) retirer; ~ **up** *vi* (*stop*) s'arrêter ♦ *vt* (*chair*) approcher; (*document*) établir, dresser; ~**back** *n* inconvénient *m*, désavantage *m*; ~**bridge** *n* pont-levis *m*; ~**er** [drɔː*] *n* tiroir *m*

drawing ['drɔːɪŋ] *n* dessin *m*; ~ **board** *n* planche *f* à dessin; ~ **pin** (*BRIT*) *n* punaise *f*; ~ **room** *n* salon *m*

drawl [drɔːl] *n* accent traînant

drawn [drɔːn] *pp of* **draw**

dread [dred] *n* terreur *f*, effroi *m* ♦ *vt* redouter, appréhender; ~**ful** *adj* affreux(euse)

dream [driːm] (*pt, pp* **dreamed** *or* **dreamt**) *n* rêve *m* ♦ *vt, vi* rêver; ~**y** *adj* rêveur(euse); (*music*) langoureux(euse)

dreary ['drɪərɪ] *adj* morne, monotone

dredge [dredʒ] *vt* draguer

dregs [dregz] *npl* lie *f*

drench [drentʃ] *vt* tremper

dress [dres] *n* robe *f*; (*no pl: clothing*) habillement *m*, tenue *f* ♦ *vi* s'habiller ♦ *vt* habiller; (*wound*) panser; **to get ~ed** s'habiller; ~ **up** *vi* s'habiller; (*in fancy ~*) se déguiser; ~ **circle** (*BRIT*) *n* (*THEATRE*) premier balcon; ~ (*furniture*) vaisselier *m*; (:. *US*) coiffeuse *f*, commode *f*; ~**ing** *n* (*MED*) pansement *m*; (*CULIN*) sauce *f*, assaisonnement *m*; ~**ing**

gown (BRIT) n robe f de chambre; **~ing room** n (THEATRE) loge f; (SPORT) vestiaire m; **~ing table** n coiffeuse f; **~maker** n couturière f; **~ rehearsal** n (répétition) générale f

drew [dru:] pt of draw

dribble ['drɪbl] vi (baby) baver ♦ vt (ball) dribbler

dried [draɪd] adj (fruit, beans) sec(sèche); (eggs, milk) en poudre

drier ['draɪə*] n = dryer

drift [drɪft] n (of current etc) force f; direction f, mouvement m; (of snow) rafale f; (: on ground) congère f; (general meaning) sens (général) ♦ vi (boat) aller à la dérive, dériver; (sand, snow) s'amonceler, s'entasser; **~wood** n bois flotté

drill [drɪl] n perceuse f; (~ bit) foret m, mèche f; (of dentist) roulette f, fraise f; (MIL) exercice m ♦ vt percer; (troops) entraîner ♦ vi (for oil) faire un or des forage(s)

drink [drɪŋk] (pt **drank**, pp **drunk**) n boisson f; (alcoholic) verre m ♦ vt, vi boire; **to have a ~** boire quelque chose, boire un verre; prendre l'apéritif; **a ~ of water** un verre d'eau; **~er** n buveur(euse); **~ing water** n eau f potable

drip [drɪp] n goutte f; (MED) goutte-à-goutte m inv; perfusion f ♦ vi tomber goutte à goutte; (tap) goutter; **~-dry** adj (shirt) sans repassage; **~ping** n graisse f (de rôti)

drive [draɪv] (pt **drove**, pp **driven**) n promenade f or trajet m en voiture; (also: ~way) allée f; (energy) dynamisme m, énergie f; (push) effort (concerté), campagne f (also: disk ~) lecteur m de disquettes ♦ vt conduire; (push) chasser, pousser; (TECH: motor, wheel) faire fonctionner; entraîner; (nail, stake etc) to **sth into sth** enfoncer qch dans qch ♦ vi (AUT: at controls) conduire; (: travel) aller en voiture; **left-/right-hand ~** conduite f à gauche/droite; **to ~ sb mad** rendre qn fou(folle); **to ~ sb home/to the airport** reconduire qn chez lui/ conduire qn à l'aéroport

drivel ['drɪvl] (inf) n idioties fpl

driver ['draɪvə*] n conducteur(trice); (of taxi, bus) chauffeur m; **~'s license** (US) n permis m de conduire

driveway ['draɪvweɪ] n allée f

driving ['draɪvɪŋ] n conduite f; **~ instructor** n moniteur m d'auto-école; **~ lesson** n leçon f de conduite; **~ licence** (BRIT) n permis m de conduire; **~ school** n auto-école f; **~ test** n examen m du permis de conduire

drizzle ['drɪzl] n bruine f, crachin m

drone [drəun] n bourdonnement m; (male bee) faux bourdon

drool [dru:l] vi baver

droop [dru:p] vi (shoulders) tomber; (head) pencher; (flower) pencher la tête

drop [drɔp] n goutte f; (fall) baisse f; (also: parachute ~) saut m ♦ vt laisser tomber; (voice, eyes, price) baisser; (set down from car) déposer ♦ vi tomber; **~s** npl (MED) gouttes; **~ off** vi (sleep) s'assoupir ♦ vt (passenger) déposer; **~ out** vi (withdraw) se retirer; (student etc) abandonner, décrocher; **~out** n marginal(e); **~per** n compte-gouttes m inv; **~pings** npl crottes fpl

drought [draut] n sécheresse f

drove [drəuv] pt of drive

drown [draun] vt noyer ♦ vi se noyer

drowsy ['drauzɪ] adj somnolent(e)

drudgery ['drʌdʒərɪ] n corvée f

drug [drʌg] n médicament m; (narcotic) drogue f ♦ vt droguer; **to be on ~s** se droguer; **~ addict** n toxicomane m/f; **~gist** (US) n pharmacien(ne)-droguiste m; **~store** (US) n pharmacie-droguerie f, drugstore m

drum [drʌm] n tambour m; (for oil, petrol) bidon m; **~s** npl (kit) batterie f; **~mer** n (joueur m de) tambour m

drunk [drʌŋk] pp of drink ♦ adj ivre, soûl(e) n (also: ~ard) ivrogne m/f; **~en** adj (person) ivre, soûl(e); (rage, stupor) ivrogne, d'ivrogne

dry [draɪ] adj sec(sèche); (day) sans pluie; (humour) pince-sans-rire inv; (lake, riverbed, well) à sec ♦ vt sécher; (clothes) faire sécher ♦ vi sécher; **~ up**

vi tarir; **~-cleaner's** *n* teinturerie *f*; **~er** *n* séchoir *m*; (*spin-~er*) essoreuse *f*; **~ness** *n* sécheresse *f*; **~ rot** *n* pourriture sèche (*du bois*)

dual ['dju:əl] *adj* double; **~ carriageway** (*BRIT*) *n* route *f* à quatre voies *or* à chaussées séparées; **~ purpose** *adj* à double usage

dubbed [dʌbd] *adj* (*CINEMA*) doublé(e)

dubious ['dju:bɪəs] *adj* hésitant(e), in- certain(e); (*reputation, company*) dou- teux(euse)

duchess ['dʌtʃɪs] *n* duchesse *f*

duck [dʌk] *n* canard *m* ♦ *vi* se baisser vivement, baisser subitement la tête; **~ling** *n* caneton *m*

duct [dʌkt] *n* conduite *f*, canalisation *f*; (*ANAT*) conduit *m*

dud [dʌd] *n* (*object, tool*): **it's a ~** c'est de la camelote, ça ne marche pas ♦ *adj* **~ cheque** (*BRIT*) chèque sans provision

due [dju:] *adj* dû(due); (*expected*) atten- du(e); (*fitting*) qui convient ♦ *n*: **to give sb his** (*or* **her**) **~** être juste envers qn ♦ *adv*: **~ north** droit vers le nord; **~s** *npl* (*for club, union*) cotisation *f*; (*in harbour*) droits *mpl* (de port); **in ~ course** en temps utile *or* voulu; finale- ment; **~ to** dû(due) à; causé(e) par; **he's ~ to finish tomorrow** normalement il doit finir demain

duet [dju:'et] *n* duo *m*

duffel bag [dʌtl] *n* sac *m* marin

duffel coat *n* duffel-coat *m*

dug [dʌg] *pt, pp of* **dig**

duke [dju:k] *n* duc *m*

dull [dʌl] *adj* terne, morne; (*boring*) en- nuyeux(euse); (*sound, pain*) sourd(e); (*weather, day*) gris(e), maussade ♦ *vt* (*pain, grief*) atténuer; (*mind, senses*) en- gourdir

duly ['dju:lɪ] *adv* (*on time*) en temps voulu; (*as expected*) comme il se doit

dumb [dʌm] *adj* muet(te); (*stupid*) bête; **~founded** [dʌm'faʊndɪd] *adj* sidéré(e)

dummy ['dʌmɪ] *n* (*tailor's model*) man- nequin *m*; (*mock-up*) factice *m*, maquet- te *f*; (*BRIT: for baby*) tétine *f* ♦ *adj* faux(fausse), factice

dump [dʌmp] *n* (*also: rubbish dump*) décharge (publique); (*pej*) trou *m* ♦ *vt* (*put down*) déposer; déverser; (*get rid of*) se débarrasser de; (*COMPUT: data*) vi- der, transférer

dumpling ['dʌmplɪŋ] *n* boulette *f* (de pâte)

dumpy ['dʌmpɪ] *adj* boulot(te)

dunce [dʌns] *n* âne *m*, cancre *m*

dune [dju:n] *n* dune *f*

dung [dʌŋ] *n* fumier *m*

dungarees [dʌŋgə'ri:z] *npl* salopette *f*, bleu(s) *m(pl)*

dungeon ['dʌndʒən] *n* cachot *m*

duplex ['dju:pleks] (*US*) *n* maison jume- lée; (*apartment*) duplex *m*

duplicate [*n* 'dju:plɪkɪt, *vb* 'dju:plɪkeɪt] *n* double *m* ♦ *vt* faire un double de; (*on machine*) polycopier; photocopier; **in ~** en deux exemplaires

durable ['djʊərəbl] *adj* durable; (*clothes, metal*) résistant(e), solide

duration [djʊə'reɪʃən] *n* durée *f*

duress [djʊə'res] *n*: **under ~** sous la contrainte

during ['djʊərɪŋ] *prep* pendant, au cours de

dusk [dʌsk] *n* crépuscule *m*

dust [dʌst] *n* poussière *f* ♦ *vt* (*furniture*) épousseter, essuyer; (*cake etc*): **to ~ with** saupoudrer de; **~bin** (*BRIT*) *n* pou- belle *f*; **~er** *n* chiffon *m*; **~man** (*BRIT: irreg*) *n* boueux *m*, éboueur *m*; **~y** *adj* poussiéreux(euse)

Dutch [dʌtʃ] *adj* hollandais(e), néerlan- dais(e) ♦ *n* (*LING*) hollandais *m* ♦ *adv* (*inf*): **to go ~** partager les frais; **the ~** *npl* (*people*) les Hollandais; **~man** (*ir- reg*) *n* Hollandais; **~woman** (*irreg*) *n* Hollandaise *f*

dutiful ['dju:tɪfʊl] *adj* (*child*) respec- tueux(euse)

duty ['dju:tɪ] *n* devoir *m*; (*tax*) droit *m*, taxe *f*; **on ~** de service; (*at night etc*) de garde; **off ~** libre, pas de service *or* de garde; **~-free** *adj* exempté(e) de douane, hors taxe *inv*

duvet ['du:veɪ] (*BRIT*) *n* couette *f*

dwarf [dwɔ:f] (*pl* **dwarves**) *n* nain(e)

♦ *vt* écraser

dwell [dwel] (*pt, pp* dwelt) *vi* demeurer; **~ on** *vt fus* s'appesantir sur; **~ing** *n* habitation *f*, demeure *f*

dwindle ['dwɪndl] *vi* diminuer, décroître

dye [daɪ] *n* teinture *f* ♦ *vt* teindre

dying ['daɪɪŋ] *adj* mourant(e), agonisant(e)

dyke [daɪk] (*BRIT*) *n* digue *f*

dynamic [daɪ'næmɪk] *adj* dynamique

dynamite ['daɪnəmaɪt] *n* dynamite *f*

dynamo ['daɪnəməʊ] *n* dynamo *f*

dyslexia [dɪs'leksɪə] *n* dyslexie *f*

E e

E [iː] *n* (*MUS*) mi *m*

each [iːtʃ] *adj* chaque ♦ *pron* chacun(e); **~ other** l'un(e) l'autre; **they hate ~ other** ils se détestent (mutuellement); **you are jealous of ~ other** vous êtes jaloux l'un de l'autre; **they have 2 books ~** ils ont 2 livres chacun

eager ['iːgə*] *adj* (*keen*) avide; **to be ~ to do sth** avoir très envie de faire qch; **to be ~ for** désirer vivement, être avide de

eagle ['iːgl] *n* aigle *m*

ear [ɪə*] *n* oreille *f*; (*of corn*) épi *m*; **~ache** *n* mal *m* aux oreilles; **~drum** *n* tympan *m*

earl [ɜːl] (*BRIT*) *n* comte *m*

earlier ['ɜːlɪə*] *adj* (*date etc*) plus rapproché(e); (*edition, fashion etc*) plus ancien(ne), antérieur(e) ♦ *adv* plus tôt

early ['ɜːlɪ] *adv* tôt, de bonne heure; (*ahead of time*) en avance; (*near the beginning*) au début ♦ *adj* qui se manifeste (*or* se fait) tôt *or* de bonne heure; (*work*) de jeunesse; (*settler, Christian*) premier(ère); (*reply*) rapide; (*death*) prématuré(e); **to have an ~ night** se coucher tôt *or* de bonne heure; **in the ~ or ~ in the spring/19th century** au début du printemps/19ème siècle; **~ retirement** *n*: **to take ~ retirement** prendre sa retraite anticipée

earmark ['ɪəmɑːk] *vt*: **to ~ sth for** réserver *or* destiner qch à

earn [ɜːn] *vt* gagner; (*COMM: yield*) rapporter

earnest ['ɜːnɪst] *adj* sérieux(euse); **in ~** *adv* sérieusement

earnings ['ɜːnɪŋz] *npl* salaire *m*; (*of company*) bénéfices *mpl*

earphones ['ɪəfəʊnz] *npl* écouteurs *mpl*

earring ['ɪərɪŋ] *n* boucle *f* d'oreille

earshot ['ɪəʃɒt] *n*: **within ~** à portée de voix

earth [ɜːθ] *n* (*gen, also BRIT: ELEC*) terre *f* ♦ *vt* relier à la terre; **~enware** *n* poterie *f*; faïence *f*; **~quake** *n* tremblement *m* de terre, séisme *m*; **~y** ['ɜːθɪ] *adj* (*vulgar: humour*) truculent(e)

ease [iːz] *n* facilité *f*, aisance *f*; (*comfort*) bien-être *m* ♦ *vt* (*soothe*) calmer; (*loosen*) relâcher, détendre; **to ~ sth in/out** faire pénétrer/sortir qch délicatement *or* avec douceur; faciliter la pénétration/la sortie de qch; **at ~!** (*MIL*) repos!; **~ off** *vi* diminuer; (*slow down*) ralentir; **~ up** *vi* = **ease off**

easel ['iːzl] *n* chevalet *m*

easily ['iːzɪlɪ] *adv* facilement

east [iːst] *n* est *m* ♦ *adj* (*wind*) d'est; (*side*) est *inv* ♦ *adv* à l'est, vers l'est; **the E~** l'Orient *m*; (*POL*) les pays *mpl* de l'Est

Easter ['iːstə*] *n* Pâques *fpl*; **~ egg** *n* œuf *m* de Pâques

east: **~erly** ['iːstəlɪ] *adj* (*wind*) d'est; (*direction*) est *inv*; (*point*) à l'est; **~ern** ['iːstən] *adj* de l'est, oriental(e); **~ward(s)** ['iːstwəd(z)] *adv* vers l'est, à l'est

easy ['iːzɪ] *adj* facile; (*manner*) aisé(e) ♦ *adv*: **to take it or things ~** ne pas se fatiguer; (*not worry*) ne pas (trop) s'en faire; **~ chair** *n* fauteuil *m*; **~-going** *adj* accommodant(e), facile à vivre

eat [iːt] (*pt* ate, *pp* eaten) *vt, vi* manger; **~ away at** *vt fus* ronger, attaquer; (*savings*) entamer; **~ into** *vt fus* = **eat away at**

eaves [iːvz] *npl* avant-toit *m*

eavesdrop ['iːvzdrɒp] *vi*: **to ~ (on a conversation)** écouter (une conversation) de façon indiscrète

ebb [eb] *n* reflux *m* ♦ *vi* refluer; (*fig: also:* ~ *away*) décliner

ebony ['ebəni] *n* ébène *f*

EC *n abbr* (= *European Community*) C.E. *f*

eccentric [ik'sentrik] *adj* excentrique ♦ *n* excentrique *m/f*

echo ['ekəu] (*pl* ~es) *n* écho *m* ♦ *vt* répéter ♦ *vi* résonner, faire écho

eclipse [i'klips] *n* éclipse *f*

ecology [i'kɒlədʒi] *n* écologie *f*

economic [i:kə'nɒmik] *adj* économique; (*business etc*) rentable; **~al** *adj* économique; (*person*) économe; **~s** *n* économie *f* politique ♦ *npl* (*of project, situation*) aspect *m* financier

economize [i'kɒnəmaiz] *vi* économiser, faire des économies

economy [i'kɒnəmi] *n* économie *f*; ~ **class** *n* classe *f* touriste; ~ **size** *n* format *m* économique

ecstasy ['ekstəsi] *n* extase *f*; **ecstatic** *adj* extatique

ECU [ei:kju] *n abbr* (= *European Currency Unit*) ECU *m*

eczema ['eksimə] *n* eczéma *m*

edge [edʒ] *n* bord *m*; (*of knife etc*) tranchant *m*, fil *m* ♦ *vt* border; **on** ~ (*fig*) crispé(e), tendu(e); **to** ~ **away from** s'éloigner furtivement de; **~ways** *adv*: **he couldn't get a word in ~ways** il ne pouvait pas placer un mot

edgy ['edʒi] *adj* crispé(e), tendu(e)

edible ['edibl] *adj* comestible

edict ['i:dikt] *n* décret *m*

Edinburgh ['edinbərə] *n* Édimbourg

edit ['edit] *vt* (*text, book*) éditer; (*report*) préparer; (*film*) monter; (*broadcast*) réaliser; **~ion** [i'diʃən] *n* édition *f*; **~or** *n* (*of column*) rédacteur(trice); (*of newspaper*) rédacteur(trice) en chef; (*of sb's work*) éditeur(trice); **~orial** [edi'tɔːriəl] *adj* de la rédaction, éditorial(e) ♦ *n* éditorial *m*

educate ['edjukeit] *vt* (*teach*) instruire; (*instruct*) éduquer

education [edju'keiʃən] *n* éducation *f*; (*studies*) études *fpl*; (*teaching*) enseignement *m*, instruction *f*; **~al** *adj* (*experience, toy*) pédagogique; (*institution*) sco-

laire; (*policy*) d'éducation

eel [i:l] *n* anguille *f*

eerie ['iəri] *adj* inquiétant(e)

effect [i'fekt] *n* effet *m* ♦ *vt* effectuer; **to take** ~ (*law*) entrer en vigueur; (*drug*) agir, faire son effet; **in** ~ en fait; **~ive** *adj* efficace; (*actual*) véritable; **~ively** *adv* efficacement; (*in reality*) effectivement; **~iveness** *n* efficacité *f*

effeminate [i'feminit] *adj* efféminé(e)

effervescent [efə'vesnt] *adj* (*drink*) gazeux(euse)

efficiency [i'fiʃənsi] *n* efficacité *f*; (*of machine*) rendement *m*

efficient [i'fiʃənt] *adj* efficace; (*machine*) qui a un bon rendement

effort ['efət] *n* effort *m*; **~less** *adj* (*style*) aisé(e); (*achievement*) facile

effusive [i'fju:siv] *adj* chaleureux(euse)

e.g. *adv abbr* (= *exempli gratia*) par exemple, p. ex.

egg [eg] *n* œuf *m*; **hard-boiled/soft-boiled** ~ œuf dur/à la coque; ~ **on** *vt* pousser; **~cup** *n* coquetier *m*; **~plant** *n* (*esp US*) aubergine *f*; **~shell** *n* coquille *f* d'œuf

ego ['i:gəu] *n* (*self-esteem*) amour-propre *m*

egotism ['egəutizəm] *n* égotisme *m*

egotist ['egəutist] *n* égocentrique *m/f*

Egypt ['i:dʒipt] *n* Égypte *f*; **~ian** [i'dʒipʃən] *adj* égyptien(ne) ♦ *n* Égyptien(ne)

eiderdown ['aidədaun] *n* édredon *m*

eight [eit] *num* huit; **~een** *num* dix-huit; **eighth** [eitθ] *num* huitième; **~y** *num* quatre-vingts

Eire ['eərə] *n* République *f* d'Irlande

either ['aiðə*] *adj* l'un ou l'autre; (*both, each*) chaque ♦ *pron*: ~ (*of them*) l'un ou l'autre ♦ *adv* non plus ♦ *conj*: ~ **good or bad** ou bon ou mauvais, soit bon soit mauvais; **on** ~ **side** de chaque côté; **I don't like** ~ je n'aime ni l'un ni l'autre; **no, I don't** ~ moi non plus

eject [i'dʒekt] *vt* (*tenant etc*) expulser (*object*) éjecter

eke [i:k]: **to** ~ **out** *vt* faire durer

elaborate [*adj* i'læbərit, *vb* i'læbəreit] *adj*

compliqué(e), recherché(e) ♦ *vt* élaborer ♦ *vi*: **to ~ (on)** entrer dans les détails (de)

elapse [ɪ'læps] *vi* s'écouler, passer

elastic [ɪ'læstɪk] *adj* élastique ♦ *n* élastique *m*; **~ band** *n* élastique *m*

elated [ɪ'leɪtɪd] *adj* transporté(e) de joie

elation [ɪ'leɪʃən] *n* allégresse *f*

elbow ['elbəʊ] *n* coude *m*

elder ['eldə*] *adj* aîné(e) ♦ *n* (*tree*) sureau *m*; **one's ~s** ses aînés; **~ly** *adj* âgé(e) ♦ *npl*: **the ~ly** les personnes âgées

eldest ['eldɪst] *adj, n*: **the ~ (child)** l'aîné(e) (des enfants)

elect [ɪ'lekt] *vt* élire ♦ *adj*: **the president ~** le président désigné; **to ~ to do** choisir de faire; **~ion** [ɪ'lekʃən] *n* élection *f*; **~ioneering** [ɪlekʃə'nɪərɪŋ] *n* propagande électorale, manœuvres électorales; **~or** *n* électeur(trice); **~orate** *n* électorat *m*

electric [ɪ'lektrɪk] *adj* électrique; **~al** *adj* électrique; **~ blanket** *n* couverture chauffante; **~ fire** (*BRIT*) *n* radiateur *m* électrique; **~ian** [ɪlek'trɪʃən] *n* électricien *m*

electricity [ɪlek'trɪsɪtɪ] *n* électricité *f*

electrify [ɪ'lektrɪfaɪ] *vt* (*RAIL, fence*) électrifier; (*audience*) électriser

electronic [ɪlek'trɒnɪk] *adj* électronique; **~s** *n* électronique *f*

elegant ['elɪgənt] *adj* élégant(e)

element ['elɪmənt] *n* (*gen*) élément *m*; (*of heater, kettle etc*) résistance *f*; **~ary** [elɪ'mentərɪ] *adj* élémentaire; (*school, education*) primaire

elephant ['elɪfənt] *n* éléphant *m*

elevation [elɪ'veɪʃən] *n* (*raising, promotion*) avancement *m*, promotion *f*; (*height*) hauteur *f*

elevator ['elɪveɪtə*] *n* (*in warehouse etc*) élévateur *m*, monte-charge *m inv*; (*US: lift*) ascenseur *m*

eleven [ɪ'levn] *num* onze; **~ses** *npl* ≈ pause-café *f*; **~th** *num* onzième

elicit [ɪ'lɪsɪt] *vt*: **to ~ (from)** obtenir (de), arracher (à)

eligible ['elɪdʒəbl] *adj*: **to be ~ for** remplir les conditions requises pour; **an ~ young man/woman** un beau parti

elm [elm] *n* orme *m*

elongated ['iːlɒŋgeɪtɪd] *adj* allongé(e)

elope [ɪ'ləʊp] *vi* (*lovers*) s'enfuir (ensemble); **~ment** [ɪləʊpmənt] *n* fugue amoureuse

eloquent ['eləkwənt] *adj* éloquent(e)

else [els] *adv* d'autre; **something ~** quelque chose d'autre, autre chose; **somewhere ~** ailleurs, autre part; **everywhere ~** partout ailleurs; **nobody ~** personne d'autre; **where ~?** à quel autre endroit?; **little ~** pas grand-chose d'autre; **~where** *adv* ailleurs, autre part

elude [ɪ'luːd] *vt* échapper à

elusive [ɪ'luːsɪv] *adj* insaisissable

emaciated [ɪ'meɪsɪeɪtɪd] *adj* émacié(e), décharné(e)

emancipate [ɪ'mænsɪpeɪt] *vt* émanciper

embankment [ɪm'bæŋkmənt] *n* (*of road, railway*) remblai *m*, talus *m*; (*of river*) berge *f*, quai *m*

embark [ɪm'bɑːk] *vi* embarquer; **to ~ on** (*journey*) entreprendre; (*fig*) se lancer *or* s'embarquer dans; **~ation** [embɑː'keɪʃən] *n* embarquement *m*

embarrass [ɪm'bærəs] *vt* embarrasser, gêner; **~ed** *adj* gêné(e); **~ing** *adj* gênant(e), embarrassant(e); **~ment** *n* embarras *m*, gêne *f*

embassy ['embəsɪ] *n* ambassade *f*

embedded [ɪm'bedɪd] *adj* enfoncé(e)

embellish [ɪm'belɪʃ] *vt* orner, décorer; (*fig: account*) enjoliver

embers ['embəz] *npl* braise *f*

embezzle [ɪm'bezl] *vt* détourner

embezzlement [ɪm'bezlmənt] *n* détournement *m* de fonds

embitter [ɪm'bɪtə*] *vt* (*person*) aigrir; (*relations*) envenimer

embody [ɪm'bɒdɪ] *vt* (*features*) réunir, comprendre; (*ideas*) formuler, exprimer

embossed [ɪm'bɒst] *adj* (*metal*) estampé(e); (*leather*) frappé(e); **~ wallpaper** papier gaufré

embrace [ɪm'breɪs] *vt* embrasser, étreindre; (*include*) embrasser ♦ *vi* s'étreindre, s'embrasser ♦ *n* étreinte *f*

embroider [ɪm'brɔɪdə*] *vt* broder; **~y** *n* broderie *f*

emerald ['emərəld] *n* émeraude *f*

emerge [ı'mɜːdʒ] *vi* apparaître; (*from room, car*) surgir; (*from sleep, imprisonment*) sortir

emergency [ı'mɜːdʒənsı] *n* urgence *f*; **in an ~** en cas d'urgence; **~ cord** *n* sonnette *f* d'alarme; **~ exit** *n* sortie *f* de secours; **~ landing** *n* atterrissage forcé; **~ services** *npl*: **the ~ services** (*fire, police, ambulance*) les services *mpl* d'urgence

emergent [ı'mɜːdʒənt] *adj* (*nation*) en voie de développement; (*group*) en développement

emery board ['emərı-] *n* lime *f* à ongles (*en carton émerisé*)

emigrate ['emıgreıt] *vi* émigrer

eminent ['emınənt] *adj* éminent(e)

emissions [ı'mıʃəd] *npl* émissions *fpl*

emit [ı'mıt] *vt* émettre

emotion [ı'məʊʃən] *n* émotion *f*; **~al** *adj* (*person*) émotif(ive), très sensible; (*needs, exhaustion*) affectif(ive); (*scene*) émouvant(e); (*tone, speech*) qui fait appel aux sentiments

emotive [ı'məʊtıv] *adj* chargé(e) d'émotion; (*subject*) sensible

emperor ['empərə*] *n* empereur *m*

emphases ['emfəsiːz] *npl of* **emphasis**

emphasis ['emfəsıs] (*pl* **-ases**) *n* (*stress*) accent *m*; (*importance*) insistance *f*

emphasize ['emfəsaız] *vt* (*syllable, word, point*) appuyer or insister sur; (*feature*) souligner, accentuer

emphatic [ım'fætık] *adj* (*strong*) énergique, vigoureux(euse); (*unambiguous, clear*) catégorique; **~ally** [ım'fætıkəlı] *adv* avec vigueur or énergie; catégoriquement

empire ['empaıə*] *n* empire *m*

employ [ım'plɔı] *vt* employer; **~ee** *n* employé(e); **~er** *n* employeur(euse); **~ment** *n* emploi *m*; **~ment agency** *n* agence *f* or bureau *m* de placement

empower [ım'paʊə*] *vt*: **to ~ sb to do** autoriser or habiliter qn à faire

empress ['emprıs] *n* impératrice *f*

emptiness ['emptınəs] *n* (*of area, region*) aspect *m* désertique; (*of life*) vide *m*, vacuité *f*

empty ['emptı] *adj* vide; (*threat, promise*) en l'air, vain(e) ♦ *vt* vider ♦ *vi* se vider; (*liquid*) s'écouler; **~-handed** *adj* les mains vides

emulate ['emjʊleıt] *vt* rivaliser avec, imiter

emulsion [ı'mʌlʃən] *n* émulsion *f*; **~ (paint)** *n* peinture mate

enable [ı'neıbl] *vt*: **to ~ sb to do** permettre à qn de faire

enact [ın'ækt] *vt* (*law*) promulguer; (*play*) jouer

enamel [ı'næməl] *n* émail *m*; (*also:* **~ paint**) peinture laquée

enamoured [ın'æməd] *adj*: **to be ~ of** être entiché(e) de

encased [ın'keıst] *adj*: **~ in** enfermé(e) or enchâssé(e) dans

enchant [ın'tʃɑːnt] *vt* enchanter; **~ing** *adj* ravissant(e), enchanteur(teresse)

encl. *abbr* = **enclosed**

enclose [ın'kləʊz] *vt* (*land*) clôturer; (*space, object*) entourer; (*letter etc*): **to ~ (with)** joindre (à); **please find ~d** veuillez trouver ci-joint

enclosure [ın'kləʊʒə*] *n* enceinte *f*

encompass [ın'kʌmpəs] *vt* (*include*) contenir, inclure

encore ['ɒŋkɔː*] *excl* bis ♦ *n* bis *m*

encounter [ın'kaʊntə*] *n* rencontre *f* ♦ *vt* rencontrer

encourage [ın'kʌrıdʒ] *vt* encourager; **~ment** *n* encouragement *m*

encroach [ın'krəʊtʃ] *vi*: **to ~ (up)on** empiéter sur

encyclop(a)edia [ensaıkləʊ'piːdıə] *n* encyclopédie *f*

end [end] *n* (*gen, also: aim*) fin *f*; (*of table, street, rope etc*) bout *m*, extrémité *f* ♦ *vt* terminer; (*also:* **bring to an ~, put an ~ to**) mettre fin à ♦ *vi* se terminer, finir; **in the ~** finalement; **on ~** (*object*) debout, dressé(e); **to stand on ~** (*hair*) se dresser sur la tête; **for hours on ~** pendant des heures et des heures; **~ up** *vi*: **to ~ up in** (*condition*) finir or se terminer par; (*place*) finir or aboutir à

endanger [ın'deındʒə*] *vt* mettre en danger

endearing [ɪnˈdɪərɪŋ] *adj* attachant(e)

endeavour [ɪnˈdevə*] (*US* **endeavor**) *n* tentative *f*, effort *m* ♦ *vi*: **to ~ to do** tenter *or* s'efforcer de faire

ending [ˈendɪŋ] *n* dénouement *m*, fin *f*; (*LING*) terminaison *f*

endive [ˈendaɪv] *n* chicorée *f*; (*smooth*) endive *f*

endless [ˈendlɪs] *adj* sans fin, interminable

endorse [ɪnˈdɔːs] *vt* (*cheque*) endosser; (*approve*) appuyer, approuver, sanctionner; **~ment** *n* (*approval*) appui *m*, aval *m*; (*BRIT: on driving licence*) *contravention portée au permis de conduire*

endow [ɪnˈdaʊ] *vt*: **to ~ (with)** doter (de)

endure [ɪnˈdjʊə*] *vt* supporter, endurer ♦ *vi* durer

enemy [ˈenɪmɪ] *adj, n* ennemi(e)

energetic [enəˈdʒetɪk] *adj* énergique; (*activity*) qui fait se dépenser (physiquement)

energy [ˈenədʒɪ] *n* énergie *f*

enforce [ɪnˈfɔːs] *vt* (*LAW*) appliquer, faire respecter

engage [ɪnˈgeɪdʒ] *vt* engager; (*attention etc*) retenir ♦ *vi* (*TECH*) s'enclencher, s'engrener; **to ~ in** se lancer dans; **~d** *adj* (*BRIT: busy, in use*) occupé(e); (*betrothed*) fiancé(e); **to get ~d** se fiancer; **~d tone** *n* (*TEL*) tonalité *f* occupé *inv or* pas libre; **~ment** *n* obligation *f*, engagement *m*; rendez-vous *m inv*; (*to marry*) fiançailles *fpl*; **~ment ring** *n* bague *f* de fiançailles

engaging [ɪnˈgeɪdʒɪŋ] *adj* engageant(e), attirant(e)

engender [ɪnˈdʒendə*] *vt* produire, causer

engine [ˈendʒɪn] *n* (*AUT*) moteur *m*; (*RAIL*) locomotive *f*; **~ driver** *n* mécanicien *m*

engineer [endʒɪˈnɪə*] *n* ingénieur *m*; (*BRIT: repairer*) dépanneur *m*; (*NAVY, US RAIL*) mécanicien *m*; **~ing** [-ˈnɪərɪŋ] *n* engineering *m*, ingénierie *f*; (*of bridges, ships*) génie *m*; (*of machine*) mécanique *f*

England [ˈɪŋglənd] *n* Angleterre *f*

English [ˈɪŋglɪʃ] *adj* anglais(e) ♦ *n* (*LING*) anglais *m*; **the ~** *npl* (*people*) les Anglais; **the ~ Channel** la Manche; **~man** (*irreg*) *n* Anglais; **~woman** (*irreg*) *n* Anglaise *f*

engraving [ɪnˈgreɪvɪŋ] *n* gravure *f*

engrossed [ɪnˈgrəʊst] *adj*: **~ in** absorbé(e) par, plongé(e) dans

engulf [ɪnˈgʌlf] *vt* engloutir

enhance [ɪnˈhɑːns] *vt* rehausser, mettre en valeur

enjoy [ɪnˈdʒɔɪ] *vt* aimer, prendre plaisir à; (*have: health, fortune*) jouir de; (*: success*) connaître; **to ~ o.s.** s'amuser; **~able** *adj* agréable; **~ment** *n* plaisir *m*

enlarge [ɪnˈlɑːdʒ] *vt* accroître; (*PHOT*) agrandir ♦ *vi*: **to ~ on** (*subject*) s'étendre sur; **~ment** *n* (*PHOT*) agrandissement *m*

enlighten [ɪnˈlaɪtn] *vt* éclairer; **~ed** *adj* éclairé(e); **~ment** *n*: **the E~ment** (*HISTORY*) ≈ le Siècle des lumières

enlist [ɪnˈlɪst] *vt* recruter; (*support*) s'assurer ♦ *vi* s'engager

enmity [ˈenmɪtɪ] *n* inimitié *f*

enormous [ɪˈnɔːməs] *adj* énorme

enough [ɪˈnʌf] *adj, pron*: **~ time/books** assez *or* suffisamment de temps/livres ♦ *adv*: **big ~** assez *or* suffisamment grand; **have you got ~?** en avez-vous assez?; **he has not worked ~** il n'a pas assez *or* suffisamment travaillé; **~ to eat** assez à manger; **~!** assez!, ça suffit!; **that's ~, thanks** cela suffit *or* c'est assez, merci; **I've had ~ of him** j'en ai assez de lui; **... which, funnily** *or* **oddly ~** ... qui, chose curieuse

enquire [ɪnˈkwaɪə*] *vt, vi* = **inquire**

enrage [ɪnˈreɪdʒ] *vt* mettre en fureur *or* en rage, rendre furieux(euse)

enrol [ɪnˈrəʊl] (*US* **enroll**) *vt* inscrire ♦ *vi* s'inscrire; **~ment** (*US* **enrollment**) *n* inscription *f*

ensue [ɪnˈsjuː] *vi* s'ensuivre, résulter

ensure [ɪnˈʃʊə*] *vt* assurer; garantir; **to ~ that** s'assurer que

entail [ɪnˈteɪl] *vt* entraîner, occasionner

entangled [ɪnˈtæŋgld] *adj*: **to become ~ (in)** s'empêtrer (dans)

enter ['entə*] vt (*room*) entrer dans, pénétrer dans; (*club, army*) entrer à; (*competition*) s'inscrire à or pour; (*sb for a competition*) (faire) inscrire; (*write down*) inscrire, noter; (*COMPUT*) entrer, introduire ♦ vi entrer; **~ for** vt fus s'inscrire à, se présenter pour or à; **~ into** vt fus (*explanation*) se lancer dans; (*discussion, negotiations*) entamer; (*agreement*) conclure

enterprise ['entəpraiz] n entreprise f; (*initiative*) (esprit m d')initiative f; **free ~** libre entreprise; **private ~** entreprise privée

enterprising ['entəpraiziŋ] adj entreprenant(e), dynamique; (*scheme*) audacieux(euse)

entertain [entə'tein] vt amuser, distraire; (*invite*) recevoir (à dîner); (*idea, plan*) envisager; **~er** n artiste m/f de variétés; **~ing** adj amusant(e), distrayant(e); **~ment** n (*amusement*) divertissement m, amusement m; (*show*) spectacle m

enthralled [in'θrɔ:ld] adj captivé(e)

enthusiasm [in'θu:ziæzəm] n enthousiasme m

enthusiast [in'θu:ziæst] n enthousiaste m/f; **~ic** [inθu:zi'æstik] adj enthousiaste; **to be ~ic about** être enthousiasmé(e) par

entice [in'tais] vt attirer, séduire

entire [in'taiə*] adj (tout) entier(ère); **~ly** adv entièrement, complètement; **~ty** [in'taiərəti] n: **in its ~ty** dans sa totalité

entitle [in'taitl] vt: **to ~ sb to sth** donner droit à qch à qn; **~d** adj (*book*) intitulé(e); **to be ~d to do** avoir le droit de or être habilité à faire

entrance [n 'entrəns, vb in'tra:ns] n entrée f ♦ vt enchanter, ravir; **to gain ~ to** (*university etc*) être admis à; **~ examination** n examen m d'entrée; **~ fee** n (*to museum etc*) prix m d'entrée; (*to join club etc*) droit m d'inscription; **~ ramp** (US) n (AUT) bretelle f d'accès

entrant ['entrənt] n participant(e); concurrent(e); (BRIT: in exam) candidat(e)

entrenched [in'trentʃt] adj retranché(e),

(*ideas*) arrêté(e)

entrepreneur [ɒntrəprə'nə:*] n entrepreneur m

entrust [in'trʌst] vt: **to ~ sth to** confier qch à

entry ['entri] n entrée f; (*in register*) inscription f; **no ~** défense d'entrer, entrée interdite; (AUT) sens interdit; **~ form** n feuille f d'inscription; **~ phone** (BRIT) n interphone m

enunciate [i'nʌnsieit] vt énoncer; (*word*) articuler, prononcer

envelop [in'veləp] vt envelopper

envelope ['envələup] n enveloppe f

envious ['enviəs] adj envieux(euse)

environment [in'vaiərənmənt] n environnement m; (*social, moral*) milieu m; **~al** [invaiərən'mentl] adj écologique; du milieu; **~-friendly** adj écologique

envisage [in'vizidʒ] vt (*foresee*) prévoir

envoy ['envɔi] n (*diplomat*) ministre m plénipotentiaire

envy ['envi] n envie f ♦ vt envier; **to ~ sb sth** envier qch à qn

epic ['epik] n épopée f ♦ adj épique

epidemic [epi'demik] n épidémie f

epilepsy ['epilepsi] n épilepsie f

episode ['episəud] n épisode m

epitome [i'pitəmi] n modèle m; **epitomize** [i'pitəmaiz] vt incarner

equable ['ekwəbl] adj égal(e); de tempérament égal

equal ['i:kwl] adj égal(e) ♦ n égal(e) ♦ vt égaler; **~ to** (*task*) à la hauteur de; **~ity** [i'kwɒliti] n égalité f; **~ize** vi (SPORT) égaliser; **~ly** adv également; (*just as*) tout aussi

equanimity [ekwə'nimiti] n égalité f d'humeur

equate [i'kweit] vt: **to ~ sth with** comparer qch à; assimiler qch à; **equation** [i'kweiʒən] n (MATH) équation f

equator [i'kweitə*] n équateur m

equilibrium [i:kwi'libriəm] n équilibre m

equip [i'kwip] vt: **to ~ (with)** équiper (de); **to be well ~ped** (*office etc*) être bien équipé(e); **he is well ~ped for the job** il a les compétences requises pour ce travail; **~ment** n équipement m; (*electrical etc*) appareillage m, installation f

equities ['ekwɪtɪz] (*BRIT*) npl (*COMM*) actions cotées en Bourse

equivalent [ɪ'kwɪvələnt] adj: **~ (to)** équivalent(e) (à) ♦ n équivalent m

equivocal [ɪ'kwɪvəkəl] adj équivoque; (*open to suspicion*) douteux (euse)

era ['ɪərə] n ère f, époque f

eradicate [ɪ'rædɪkeɪt] vt éliminer

erase [ɪ'reɪz] vt effacer; **~r** n gomme f

erect [ɪ'rekt] adj droit(e) ♦ vt construire; (*monument*) ériger; élever; (*tent etc*) dresser; **~ion** [ɪ'rekʃən] n érection f

ERM n abbr (= *Exchange Rate Mechanism*) SME m

erode [ɪ'rəʊd] vt éroder; (*metal*) ronger

erotic [ɪ'rɒtɪk] adj érotique

err [ɜː*] vi (*formal: make a mistake*) se tromper

errand ['erənd] n course f, commission f

erratic [ɪ'rætɪk] adj irrégulier(ère); inconstant(e)

error ['erə*] n erreur f

erupt [ɪ'rʌpt] vi entrer en éruption; (*fig*) éclater; **~ion** [ɪ'rʌpʃən] n éruption f

escalate ['eskəleɪt] vi s'intensifier

escalator ['eskəleɪtə*] n escalier roulant

escapade [eskə'peɪd] n fredaine f; équipée f

escape [ɪs'keɪp] n fuite f; (*from prison*) évasion f ♦ vi s'échapper, fuir; (*from jail*) s'évader; (*fig*) s'en tirer; (*leak*) s'échapper ♦ vt échapper à; **to ~ from** (*person*) échapper à; (*place*) s'échapper de; (*fig*) fuir; **escapism** [-ɪzəm] n (*fig*) évasion f

escort [n 'eskɔːt, vb ɪs'kɔːt] n escorte f ♦ vt escorter

Eskimo ['eskɪməʊ] n Esquimau(de)

esophagus [iː'sɒfəgəs] (*US*) n = **oesophagus**

especially [ɪs'peʃəlɪ] adv (*particularly*) particulièrement; (*above all*) surtout

espionage ['espɪənɑːʒ] n espionnage m

Esquire [ɪs'kwaɪə*] n: **J Brown, ~** Monsieur J. Brown

essay ['eseɪ] n (*SCOL*) dissertation f; (*LITERATURE*) essai m

essence ['esəns] n essence f

essential [ɪ'senʃəl] adj essentiel(le); (*basic*) fondamental(e) ♦ n: **~s** éléments essentiels; **~ly** adv essentiellement

establish [ɪs'tæblɪʃ] vt établir; (*business*) fonder, créer; (*one's power etc*) asseoir, affermir; **~ed** adj bien établi(e); **~ment** n établissement m; (*founding*) création f; **the E~ment** les pouvoirs établis; l'ordre établi; les milieux dirigeants

estate [ɪs'teɪt] n (*land*) domaine m, propriété f; (*LAW*) biens mpl, succession f; (*BRIT: also: housing ~*) lotissement m, cité f; **~ agent** n agent immobilier; **~ car** (*BRIT*) n break m

esteem [ɪs'tiːm] n estime f

esthetic [ɪs'θetɪk] (*US*) adj = **aesthetic**

estimate [n 'estɪmət, vb 'estɪmeɪt] n estimation f; (*COMM*) devis m ♦ vt estimer; **estimation** [estɪ'meɪʃən] n opinion f; (*calculation*) estimation f

estranged [ɪ'streɪndʒd] adj séparé(e); dont on s'est séparé(e)

etc. abbr (= *et cetera*) etc

etching ['etʃɪŋ] n eau-forte f

eternal [ɪ'tɜːnl] adj éternel(le)

eternity [ɪ'tɜːnɪtɪ] n éternité f

ethical ['eθɪkəl] adj moral(e); **ethics** ['eθɪks] n éthique f ♦ npl moralité f

Ethiopia [iːθɪ'əʊpɪə] n Éthiopie f

ethnic ['eθnɪk] adj ethnique; (*music etc*) folklorique

ethos ['iːθɒs] n génie m

etiquette ['etɪket] n convenances fpl, étiquette f

Eurocheque ['jʊərəʊ'tʃek] n eurochèque m

Europe ['jʊərəp] n Europe f; **~an** [jʊərə'piːən] adj européen(ne) ♦ n Européen(ne)

evacuate [ɪ'vækjʊeɪt] vt évacuer

evade [ɪ'veɪd] vt échapper à; (*question etc*) éluder; (*duties*) se dérober à; **to ~ tax** frauder le fisc

evaporate [ɪ'væpəreɪt] vi s'évaporer; **~d milk** n lait condensé non sucré

evasion [ɪ'veɪʒən] n dérobade f; **tax ~** fraude fiscale

eve [iːv] n: **on the ~ of** à la veille de

even ['iːvən] *adj* (*level, smooth*) régulier(ère); (*equal*) égal(e); (*number*) pair(e) ♦ *adv* même; ~ **if** même si +*indic*; ~ **though** alors même que +*cond*; ~ **more** encore plus; ~ **so** quand même; **not** ~ pas même; **to get** ~ **with sb** prendre sa revanche sur qn; ~ **out** *vi* s'égaliser

evening ['iːvnɪŋ] *n* soir *m*; (*as duration, event*) soirée *f*; **in the** ~ le soir; ~ **class** *n* cours *m* du soir; ~ **dress** *n* tenue *f* de soirée

event [ɪ'vent] *n* événement *m*; (*SPORT*) épreuve *f*; **in the** ~ **of** en cas de; ~**ful** *adj* mouvementé(e)

eventual [ɪ'ventʃuəl] *adj* final(e); ~**ity** [ɪventʃu'ælɪtɪ] *n* possibilité *f*, éventualité *f*; ~**ly** *adv* finalement

ever ['evə*] *adv* jamais; (*at all times*) toujours; **the best** ~ le meilleur qu'on ait jamais vu; **have you** ~ **seen it?** l'astu déjà vu?, as-tu eu l'occasion *or* t'est-il arrivé de le voir?; **why** ~ **not?** mais enfin, pourquoi pas?; ~ **since** *adv* depuis ♦ *conj* depuis que; ~**green** *n* arbre *m* à feuilles persistantes; ~**lasting** *adj* éternel(le)

every ['evrɪ] *adj* chaque; ~ **day** tous les jours, chaque jour; ~ **other/third day** tous les deux/trois jours; ~ **other car** une voiture sur deux; ~ **now and then** de temps en temps; ~**body** *pron* tout le monde, tous *pl*; ~**day** *adj* quotidien(ne); de tous les jours; ~**one** *pron* = **everybody**; ~**thing** *pron* tout; ~**where** *adv* partout

evict [ɪ'vɪkt] *vt* expulser; ~**ion** [ɪ'vɪkʃən] *n* expulsion *f*

evidence ['evɪdəns] *n* (*proof*) preuve(s) *f(pl)*; (*of witness*) témoignage *m*; (*sign*): **to show** ~ **of** présenter des signes de; **to give** ~ témoigner, déposer

evident ['evɪdənt] *adj* évident(e); ~**ly** *adv* de toute évidence; (*apparently*) apparemment

evil ['iːvl] *adj* mauvais(e) ♦ *n* mal *m*

evoke [ɪ'vəuk] *vt* évoquer

evolution [iːvə'luːʃən] *n* évolution *f*

evolve [ɪ'vɒlv] *vt* élaborer ♦ *vi* évoluer

ewe [juː] *n* brebis *f*

ex- [eks] *prefix* ex-

exact [ɪg'zækt] *adj* exact(e) ♦ *vt*: **to** ~ **sth (from)** extorquer qch (à); exiger qch (de); ~**ing** *adj* exigeant(e); (*work*) astreignant(e); ~**ly** *adv* exactement

exaggerate [ɪg'zædʒəreɪt] *vt, vi* exagérer; **exaggeration** [ɪgzædʒə'reɪʃən] *n* exagération *f*

exalted [ɪg'zɔːltɪd] *adj* (*prominent*) élevé(e); (: *person*) haut placé(e)

exam [ɪg'zæm] *n abbr* (*SCOL*) = **examination**

examination [ɪgzæmɪ'neɪʃən] *n* (*SCOL, MED*) examen *m*

examine [ɪg'zæmɪn] *vt* (*gen*) examiner; (*SCOL: person*) interroger; ~**r** *n* examinateur(trice)

example [ɪg'zɑːmpl] *n* exemple *m*; **for** ~ par exemple

exasperate [ɪg'zɑːspəreɪt] *vt* exaspérer; **exasperation** [ɪgzɑːspə'reɪʃən] *n* exaspération *f*, irritation *f*

excavate ['ekskəveɪt] *vt* excaver; **excavation** [ekskə'veɪʃən] *n* fouilles *fpl*

exceed [ɪk'siːd] *vt* dépasser; (*one's powers*) outrepasser; ~**ingly** *adv* extrêmement

excellent ['eksələnt] *adj* excellent(e)

except [ɪk'sept] *prep* (*also*: ~ **for**, ~**ing**) sauf, excepté ♦ *vt* excepter; ~ **if/when** sauf si/quand; ~ **that** sauf que, si ce n'est que; ~**ion** [ɪk'sepʃən] *n* exception *f*; **to take** ~**ion to** s'offusquer de; ~**ional** [ɪk'sepʃənl] *adj* exceptionnel(le)

excerpt ['eksɜːpt] *n* extrait *m*

excess [ek'ses] *n* excès *m*; ~ **baggage** *n* excédent *m* de bagages; ~ **fare** (*BRIT*) *n* supplément *m*; ~**ive** *adj* excessif(ive)

exchange [ɪks'tʃeɪndʒ] *n* échange *m*; (*also: telephone* ~) central *m* ♦ *vt*: **to** ~ (**for**) échanger (contre); ~ **rate** *n* taux *m* de change

Exchequer [ɪks'tʃekə*] (*BRIT*) *n*: **the** ~ l'Échiquier *m*, ≈ le ministère des Finances

excise [*n* 'eksaɪz, *vb* ek'saɪz] *n* taxe *f* ♦ *vt* exciser

excite [ɪk'saɪt] *vt* exciter; **to get** ~**d** s'exciter; **~ment** n excitation f; **exciting** adj passionnant(e)

exclaim [ıks'kleım] vi s'exclamer; **exclamation** [eksklə'meıʃən] n exclamation f; **exclamation mark** n point m d'exclamation

exclude [ıks'klu:d] vt exclure

exclusive [ıks'klu:sıv] adj exclusif(ive); (club, district) sélect(e); (item of news) en exclusivité; **~ of VAT** TVA non comprise; **mutually ~** qui s'excluent l'un(e) l'autre

excruciating [ıks'kru:ʃıeıtıŋ] adj atroce

excursion [ıks'kə:ʃən] n excursion f

excuse n [ıks'kju:s, vb ıks'kju:z] n excuse f ♦ vt excuser; **to ~ sb from** (activity) dispenser qn de; **~ me!** excusez-moi!, pardon!; **now if you will ~ me, ...** maintenant, si vous (le) permettez ...

ex-directory ['eksdaı'rektərı] (BRIT) adj sur la liste rouge

execute ['eksıkju:t] vt exécuter

execution [eksı'kju:ʃən] n exécution f; **~er** n bourreau m

executive [ıg'zekjutıv] n (COMM) cadre m; (of organization, political party) bureau m ♦ adj exécutif(ive)

exemplify [ıg'zemplıfaı] vt illustrer; (typify) incarner

exempt [ıg'zempt] adj: **~ from** exempté(e) or dispensé(e) de ♦ vt: **to ~ sb from** exempter or dispenser qn de

exercise ['eksəsaız] n exercice m ♦ vt exercer; (patience etc) faire preuve de; (dog) promener ♦ vi prendre de l'exercice; **~ bike** n vélo m d'appartement; **~ book** n cahier m

exert [ıg'zə:t] vt exercer, employer; **to ~ o.s.** se dépenser; **~ion** [ıg'zə:ʃən] n effort m

exhale [eks'heıl] vt exhaler ♦ vi expirer

exhaust [ıg'zɔ:st] n (also: ~ fumes) gaz mpl d'échappement; (: ~ pipe) tuyau m d'échappement ♦ vt épuiser; **~ed** adj épuisé(e); **~ion** [ıg'zɔ:stʃən] n épuisement m; **nervous ~ion** fatigue nerveuse; surmenage mental; **~ive** adj très complet(ète)

exhibit [ıg'zıbıt] n (ART) pièce exposée, objet exposé; (LAW) pièce à conviction ♦ vt exposer; (courage, skill) faire preuve de; **~ion** [eksı'bıʃən] n exposition f; (of ill-temper, talent etc) démonstration f

exhilarating [ıg'zıləreıtıŋ] adj grisant(e); stimulant(e)

exile ['eksaıl] n exil m; (person) exilé(e) ♦ vt exiler

exist [ıg'zıst] vi exister; **~ence** n existence f; **~ing** adj actuel(le)

exit ['eksıt] n sortie f ♦ vi (COMPUT, THEATRE) sortir; **~ poll** n sondage m (fait à la sortie de l'isoloir); **~ ramp** n (AUT) bretelle f d'accès

exodus ['eksədəs] n exode m

exonerate [ıg'zonəreıt] vt: **to ~ from** disculper de

exotic [ıg'zotık] adj exotique

expand [ıks'pænd] vt agrandir; accroître ♦ vi (trade etc) se développer, s'accroître; (gas, metal) se dilater

expanse [ıks'pæns] n étendue f

expansion [ıks'pænʃən] n développement m, accroissement m

expect [ıks'pekt] vt (anticipate) s'attendre à, s'attendre à ce que +sub; (count on) compter sur, escompter; (require) demander, exiger; (suppose) supposer; (await, also baby) attendre ♦ vi: **to be ~ing** être enceinte; **~ancy** n (anticipation) attente f; **life ~ancy** espérance f de vie; **~ant mother** n future maman; **~ation** [ekspek'teıʃən] n attente f; espérance(s) f(pl)

expedient [ıks'pi:dıənt] adj indiqué(e), opportun(e) ♦ n expédient m

expedition [ekspı'dıʃən] n expédition f

expel [ıks'pel] vt chasser, expulser; (SCOL) renvoyer

expend [ıks'pend] vt consacrer; (money) dépenser; **~able** adj remplaçable; **~iture** [ık'spendıtʃə*] n dépense f; dépenses fpl

expense [ıks'pens] n dépense f, frais mpl; (high cost) coût m; **~s** npl (COMM) frais mpl; **at the ~ of** aux dépens de; **~ account** n (note f de) frais mpl

expensive [ıks'pensıv] adj cher(chère), coûteux(euse); **to be ~** coûter cher

experience [ıks'pıərıəns] n expérience f

♦ *vt* connaître, faire l'expérience de; (*feeling*) éprouver; **~d** *adj* expérimenté(e)

experiment [*n* ɪks'perɪmənt, *vb* ɪks'perɪment] *n* expérience *f* ♦ *vi* faire une expérience; **to ~ with** expérimenter

expert ['ekspɜːt] *adj* expert(e) ♦ *n* expert *m*; **~ise** [ekspɜː'tiːz] *n* (grande) compétence

expire [ɪks'paɪə*] *vi* expirer; **expiry** *n* expiration *f*

explain [ɪks'pleɪn] *vt* expliquer; **explanation** [eksplə'neɪʃən] *n* explication *f*; **explanatory** [ɪks'plænətərɪ] *adj* explicatif(ive)

explicit [ɪks'plɪsɪt] *adj* explicite; (*definite*) formel(le)

explode [ɪks'pləʊd] *vi* exploser

exploit [*n* 'eksplɔɪt, *vb* ɪks'plɔɪt] *n* exploit *m* ♦ *vt* exploiter; **~ation** [eksplɔɪ'teɪʃən] *n* exploitation *f*

exploratory [eks'plɒrətərɪ] *adj* (*expedition*) d'exploration; (*fig: talks*) préliminaire; **~ operation** *n* (MED) sondage *m*

explore [ɪks'plɔː*] *vt* explorer; (*possibilities*) étudier, examiner; **~r** *n* explorateur(trice)

explosion [ɪks'pləʊʒən] *n* explosion *f*; **explosive** [ɪks'pləʊzɪv] *adj* explosif(ive) ♦ *n* explosif *m*

exponent [eks'pəʊnənt] *n* (*of school of thought etc*) interprète *m*, représentant *m*

export [*vb* eks'pɔːt, *n* 'ekspɔːt] *vt* exporter ♦ *n* exportation *f* ♦ *cpd* d'exportation; **~er** *n* exportateur *m*

expose [ɪks'pəʊz] *vt* exposer; (*unmask*) démasquer, dévoiler; **~d** [ɪks'pəʊzd] *adj* (*position, house*) exposé(e)

exposure [ɪks'pəʊʒə*] *n* exposition *f*; (*publicity*) couverture *f*; (PHOT) (temps *m* de) pose *f*; (: *shot*) pose; **to die from ~** (MED) mourir de froid; **~ meter** *n* posemètre *m*

express [ɪks'pres] *adj* (*definite*) formel(le), exprès(esse); (BRIT: *letter etc*) exprès *inv* ♦ *n* (*train*) rapide *m*; (*bus*) car *m* express ♦ *vt* exprimer; **~ion** [ɪks'preʃən] *n* expression *f*; **~ly** *adv* ex-

pressément, formellement; **~way** (*US*) *n* (*urban motorway*) voie *f* express (à plusieurs files)

exquisite [eks'kwɪzɪt] *adj* exquis(e)

extend [ɪks'tend] *vt* (*visit, street*) prolonger; (*building*) agrandir; (*offer*) présenter, offrir; (*hand, arm*) tendre ♦ *vi* s'étendre

extension [ɪks'tenʃən] *n* prolongation *f*; agrandissement *m*; (*building*) annexe *f*; (*to wire, table*) rallonge *f*; (*telephone: in offices*) poste *m*; (: *in private house*) téléphone *m* supplémentaire

extensive [ɪks'tensɪv] *adj* étendu(e), vaste; (*damage, alterations*) considérable; (*inquiries*) approfondi(e); **~ly** *adv*: **he's travelled ~ly** il a beaucoup voyagé

extent [ɪks'tent] *n* étendue *f*; **to some ~** dans une certaine mesure; **to what ~?** dans quelle mesure?, jusqu'à quel point?; **to the ~ of ...** au point de ...; **to such an ~ that ...** à tel point que ...

extenuating [eks'tenjʊeɪtɪŋ] *adj*: **~ circumstances** circonstances atténuantes

exterior [eks'tɪərɪə*] *adj* extérieur(e) ♦ *n* extérieur *m*; dehors *m*

external [eks'tɜːnl] *adj* externe

extinct [ɪks'tɪŋkt] *adj* éteint(e)

extinguish [ɪks'tɪŋgwɪʃ] *vt* éteindre; **~er** *n* (*also: fire ~er*) extincteur *m*

extort [ɪks'tɔːt] *vt*: **to ~ sth (from)** extorquer qch (à); **~ionate** [ɪks'tɔːʃənɪt] *adj* exorbitant(e)

extra ['ekstrə] *adj* supplémentaire, de plus ♦ *adv* (*in addition*) en plus ♦ *n* supplément *m*; (*perk*) à-côté *m*; (THEATRE) figurant(e) ♦ *prefix* extra...

extract [*vb* ɪks'trækt, *n* 'ekstrækt] *vt* extraire; (*tooth*) arracher; (*money, promise*) soutirer ♦ *n* extrait *m*

extracurricular ['ekstrəkə'rɪkjʊlə*] *adj* parascolaire

extradite ['ekstrədaɪt] *vt* extrader

extra: **~marital** [ekstrə'mærɪtl] *adj* extra-conjugal(e); **~mural** [ekstrə'mjʊərl] *adj* hors faculté *inv*; (*lecture*) public(que); **~ordinary** [ɪks'trɔːdnrɪ] *adj* extraordinaire

extravagance [ɪks'trævəgəns] *n* prodigalités *fpl*; (*thing bought*) folie *f*, dépense excessive; **extravagant** [ɪksˈtrævəgənt] *adj* extravagant(e); (*in spending: person*) prodigue, dépensier(ère), (: *tastes*) dispendieux(euse)

extreme [ɪksˈtriːm] *adj* extrême ♦ *n* extrême *m*; ~**ly** *adv* extrêmement

extricate [ˈekstrɪkeɪt] *vt*: **to ~ sth (from)** dégager qch (de)

extrovert [ˈekstrəvɜːt] *n* extraverti(e)

eye [aɪ] *n* œil *m* (*pl* **yeux**); (*of needle*) trou *m*, chas *m* ♦ *vt* examiner; **to keep an ~ on** surveiller; ~**ball** *n* globe *m* oculaire; ~**bath** (*BRIT*) *n* œillère *f* (*pour bains d'œil*); ~**brow** *n* sourcil *m*; ~**brow pencil** *n* crayon *m* à sourcils; ~**drops** *npl* gouttes *fpl* pour les yeux; ~**lash** *n* cil *m*; ~**lid** *n* paupière *f*; ~**liner** *n* eyeliner *m*; ~-**opener** *n* révélation *f*; ~**shadow** *n* ombre *f* à paupières; ~**sight** *n* vue *f*; ~**sore** *n* horreur *f*; ~ **witness** *n* témoin *m* oculaire

F f

F [ef] *n* (*MUS*) fa *m* ♦ *abbr* = **Fahrenheit**
fable [ˈfeɪbl] *n* fable *f*
fabric [ˈfæbrɪk] *n* tissu *m*
fabrication [fæbrɪˈkeɪʃən] *n* (*lies*) invention(s) *f(pl)*, fabulation *f*; (*making*) fabrication *f*
fabulous [ˈfæbjuləs] *adj* fabuleux(euse); (*inf: super*) formidable
face [feɪs] *n* visage *m*, figure *f*; (*expression*) expression *f*; (*of clock*) cadran *m*; (*of cliff*) paroi *f*; (*of mountain*) face *f*; (*of building*) façade *f* ♦ *vt* faire face à; ~ **down** (*person*) à plat ventre; (*card*) face en dessous; **to lose/save ~** perdre/ sauver la face; **to make** *or* **pull a ~** faire une grimace; **in the ~ of** (*difficulties etc*) face à, devant; **on the ~ of it** à première vue; ~ **to ~** face à face; ~ **up to** *vt fus* faire face à, affronter; ~ **cloth** (*BRIT*) *n* gant *m* de toilette; ~ **cream** *n* crème *f* pour le visage; ~ **lift** *n* lifting *m*; (*of building etc*) ravalement *m*, retapage *m*; ~ **powder** *n* poudre *f* de riz; ~ **value** *n*

(*of coin*) valeur nominale; **to take sth at ~ value** (*fig*) prendre qch pour argent comptant

facilities [fəˈsɪlɪtɪz] *npl* installations *fpl*, équipement *m*; **credit ~** facilités *fpl* de paiement

facing [ˈfeɪsɪŋ] *prep* face à, en face de
facsimile [fækˈsɪmɪlɪ] *n* (*exact replica*) fac-similé *m*; (*fax*) télécopie *f*
fact [fækt] *n* fait *m*; **in ~** en fait
factor [ˈfæktə*] *n* facteur *m*
factory [ˈfæktərɪ] *n* usine *f*, fabrique *f*
factual [ˈfæktjuəl] *adj* basé(e) sur les faits
faculty [ˈfækəltɪ] *n* faculté *f*; (*US: teaching staff*) corps enseignant
fad [fæd] *n* (*craze*) engouement *m*
fade [feɪd] *vi* se décolorer, passer; (*light, sound*) s'affaiblir; (*flower*) se faner
fag [fæg] (*BRIT: inf*) *n* (*cigarette*) sèche *f*
fail [feɪl] *vt* (*exam*) échouer à; (*candidate*) recaler; (*subj: courage, memory*) faire défaut à ♦ *vi* échouer; (*brakes*) lâcher; (*eyesight, health, light*) baisser, s'affaiblir; **to ~ to do sth** (*neglect*) négliger de faire qch; (*be unable*) ne pas arriver *or* parvenir à faire qch; **without ~** à coup sûr; sans faute; ~**ing** *n* défaut *m* ♦ *prep* faute de; ~**ure** *n* échec *m*; (*person*) raté(e); (*mechanical etc*) défaillance *f*
faint [feɪnt] *adj* faible; (*recollection*) vague; (*mark*) à peine visible ♦ *n* évanouissement *m* ♦ *vi* s'évanouir; **to feel ~** défaillir
fair [fɛə*] *adj* équitable, juste, impartial(e); (*hair*) blond(e); (*skin, complexion*) pâle, blanc(blanche); (*weather*) beau(belle); (*good enough*) assez bon(ne); (*sizeable*) considérable ♦ *adv*: **to play ~** jouer franc-jeu ♦ *n* foire *f*; (*BRIT: fun~*) fête (foraine); ~**ly** *adv* équitablement; (*quite*) assez; ~**ness** *n* justice *f*, équité *f*, impartialité *f*
fairy [ˈfɛərɪ] *n* fée *f*; ~ **tale** *n* conte *m* de fées
faith [feɪθ] *n* foi *f*; (*trust*) confiance *f*; (*specific religion*) religion *f*; ~**ful** *adj* fidèle; ~**fully** *adv see* **yours**

fake [feɪk] n (*painting etc*) faux m; (*person*) imposteur m ♦ adj faux(fausse) ♦ vt simuler; (*painting*) faire un faux de

falcon ['fɔːlkən] n faucon m

fall [fɔːl] (*pt* fell, *pp* fallen) n chute f; (*US: autumn*) automne m ♦ vi tomber; (*price, temperature, dollar*) baisser; **~s** npl (*waterfall*) chute f d'eau, cascade f; **to ~ flat** (*on one's face*) tomber de tout son long, s'étaler; (*joke*) tomber à plat; (*plan*) échouer; **~ back** vi reculer, se retirer; **~ back on** vt fus se rabattre sur; **~ behind** vi prendre du retard; **~ down** vi (*person*) tomber; (*building*) s'effondrer, s'écrouler; **~ for** vt fus (*trick, story etc*) se laisser prendre à; (*person*) tomber amoureux de; **~ in** vi s'effondrer; (*MIL*) se mettre en rangs; **~ off** vi tomber; (*diminish*) baisser, diminuer; **~ out** vi (*hair, teeth*) tomber; (*MIL*) rompre les rangs; (*friends etc*) se brouiller; **~ through** vi (*plan, project*) tomber à l'eau

fallacy ['fæləsɪ] n erreur f, illusion f

fallout ['fɔːlaʊt] n retombées (radioactives); **~ shelter** n abri m antiatomique

fallow ['fæləʊ] adj en jachère; en friche

false [fɔːls] adj faux(fausse); **~ alarm** n fausse alerte; **~ pretences** npl: **under ~ pretences** sous un faux prétexte; **~ teeth** (*BRIT*) npl fausses dents

falter ['fɔːltə*] vi chanceler, vaciller

fame [feɪm] n renommée f, renom m

familiar [fə'mɪlɪə*] adj familier(ère); **to be ~ with** (*subject*) connaître

family ['fæmɪlɪ] n famille f ♦ cpd (*business, doctor etc*) de famille; **has he any ~?** (*children*) a-t-il des enfants?

famine ['fæmɪn] n famine f

famished ['fæmɪʃt] (*inf*) adj affamé(e)

famous ['feɪməs] adj célèbre; **~ly** adv (*get on*) fameusement, à merveille

fan [fæn] n (*folding*) éventail m; (*ELEC*) ventilateur m; (*of person*) fan m, admirateur(trice); (*of team, sport etc*) supporter m/f ♦ vt éventer; (*fire, quarrel*) attiser; **~ out** vi se déployer (en éventail)

fanatic [fə'nætɪk] n fanatique m/f

fan belt n courroie f de ventilateur

fanciful ['fænsɪfʊl] adj fantaisiste

fancy ['fænsɪ] n fantaisie f, envie f; imagination f ♦ adj (de) fantaisie inv ♦ vt (*feel like, want*) avoir envie de; (*imagine, think*) imaginer; **to take a ~ to** se prendre d'affection pour; s'enticher de; **he fancies her** (*inf*) elle lui plaît; **~ dress** n déguisement m, travesti m; **~-dress ball** n bal masqué or costumé

fang [fæŋ] n croc m; (*of snake*) crochet m

fantastic [fæn'tæstɪk] adj fantastique

fantasy ['fæntəzɪ] n imagination f, fantaisie f; (*dream*) chimère f

far [fɑː*] adj lointain(e), éloigné(e) ♦ adv loin; **~ away** or **off** au loin, dans le lointain; **at the ~ side/end** à l'autre côté/bout; **~ better** beaucoup mieux; **~ from** loin de; **by ~** de loin, de beaucoup; **go as ~ as the farm** allez jusqu'à la ferme; **as ~ as I know** pour autant que je sache; **how ~ is it to ...?** combien y a-t-il jusqu'à ...?; **how ~ have you got?** où en êtes-vous?; **~away** adj lointain(e); (*look*) distrait(e)

farce [fɑːs] n farce f

farcical ['fɑːsɪkəl] adj grotesque

fare [fɛə*] n (*on trains, buses*) prix m du billet; (*in taxi*) prix de la course; (*food*) table f, chère f; **half ~** demi-tarif; **full ~** plein tarif

Far East n: **the ~** l'Extrême-Orient m

farewell [fɛə'wel] excl adieu ♦ n adieu

farm [fɑːm] n ferme f ♦ vt cultiver; **~er** n fermier(ère); cultivateur(trice); **~hand** n ouvrier(ère) agricole; **~house** n (maison f de) ferme f; **~ing** n agriculture f; (*of animals*) élevage m; **~land** n terres cultivées; **~ worker** n = **farmhand**; **~yard** n cour f de ferme

far-reaching ['fɑː'riːtʃɪŋ] adj d'une grande portée

fart [fɑːt] (*inf!*) vi péter

farther ['fɑːðə*] adv plus loin ♦ adj plus éloigné(e), plus lointain(e)

farthest ['fɑːðɪst] superl of **far**

fascinate ['fæsɪneɪt] vt fasciner; **fascinating** adj fascinant(e)

fascism ['fæʃɪzəm] n fascisme m

fashion ['fæʃən] *n* mode *f*; (*manner*) façon *f*, manière *f* ♦ *vt* façonner; **in ~** à la mode; **out of ~** démodé(e); **~able** *adj* à la mode; **~ show** *n* défilé *m* de mannequins *or* de mode

fast [fɑːst] *adj* rapide; (*clock*): **to be ~** avancer; (*dye, colour*) grand *or* bon teint *inv* ♦ *adv* vite, rapidement; (*stuck, held*) solidement ♦ *n* jeûne *m* ♦ *vi* jeûner; **~ asleep** profondément endormi

fasten ['fɑːsn] *vt* attacher, fixer; (*coat*) attacher, fermer ♦ *vi* se fermer, s'attacher; **~er** *n* attache *f*; **~ing** *n* = **fastener**

fast food *n* fast food *m*, restauration *f* rapide

fastidious [fæs'tɪdɪəs] *adj* exigeant(e), difficile

fat [fæt] *adj* gros(se) ♦ *n* graisse *f*; (*on meat*) gras *m*; (*for cooking*) matière grasse

fatal ['feɪtl] *adj* (*injury etc*) mortel(le); (*mistake*) fatal(e); **~ity** [fə'tælɪtɪ] *n* (*road death etc*) victime *f*, décès *m*

fate [feɪt] *n* destin *m*; (*of person*) sort *m*; **~ful** *adj* fatidique

father ['fɑːðə*] *n* père *m*; **~-in-law** *n* beau-père *m*; **~ly** *adj* paternel(le)

fathom ['fæðəm] *n* brasse *f* (= *1828 mm*) ♦ *vt* (*mystery*) sonder, pénétrer

fatigue [fə'tiːg] *n* fatigue *f*

fatten ['fætn] *vt, vi* engraisser

fatty ['fætɪ] *adj* (*food*) gras(se) ♦ *n* (*inf*) gros(se)

fatuous ['fætjʊəs] *adj* stupide

faucet ['fɔːsɪt] (*US*) *n* robinet *m*

fault [fɔːlt] *n* faute *f*; (*defect*) défaut *m*; (*GEO*) faille *f* ♦ *vt* trouver des défauts à; **it's my ~** c'est de ma faute; **to find ~ with** trouver à redire *or* à critiquer à; **at ~** fautif(ive), coupable; **~y** *adj* défectueux(euse)

fauna ['fɔːnə] *n* faune *f*

faux pas ['fəʊ'pɑː] *n inv* impair *m*, bévue *f*, gaffe *f*

favour ['feɪvə*] (*US* **favor**) *n* faveur *f*; (*help*) service *m* ♦ *vt* (*proposition*) être en faveur de; (*pupil etc*) favoriser; (*team, horse*) donner gagnant; **to do sb a ~** rendre un service à qn; **to find ~**

with trouver grâce aux yeux de; **in ~ of** en faveur de; **~able** *adj* favorable; **~ite** ['feɪvərɪt] *adj, n* favori(te)

fawn [fɔːn] *n* faon *m* ♦ *adj* (*also: ~-coloured*) fauve ♦ *vi*: **to ~ (up)on** flatter servilement

fax [fæks] *n* (*document*) télécopie *f*; (*machine*) télécopieur *m* ♦ *vt* envoyer par télécopie

FBI ['efbiːˈaɪ] *n abbr* (*US*: = *Federal Bureau of Investigation*) F.B.I. *m*

fear [fɪə*] *n* crainte *f*, peur *f* ♦ *vt* craindre; **for ~ of** de peur que +*sub*, de peur de +*infin*; **~ful** *adj* craintif(ive); (*sight, noise*) affreux(euse), épouvantable; **~less** *adj* intrépide

feasible ['fiːzəbl] *adj* faisable, réalisable

feast [fiːst] *n* festin *m*, banquet *m*; (*REL: also: ~ day*) fête *f* ♦ *vi* festoyer

feat [fiːt] *n* exploit *m*, prouesse *f*

feather ['feðə*] *n* plume *f*

feature ['fiːtʃə*] *n* caractéristique *f*; (*article*) chronique *f*, rubrique *f* ♦ *vt* (*subj: film*) avoir pour vedette(s) ♦ *vi*: **to ~ in** figurer (en bonne place) dans; (*in film*) jouer dans; **~s** *npl* (*of face*) traits *mpl*; **~ film** *n* long métrage

February ['februərɪ] *n* février *m*

fed [fed] *pt, pp of* **feed**

federal ['fedərəl] *adj* fédéral(e)

fed up *adj*: **to be ~** en avoir marre, en avoir plein le dos

fee [fiː] *n* rémunération *f*; (*of doctor, lawyer*) honoraires *mpl*; (*for examination*) droits *mpl*; **school ~s** frais *mpl* de scolarité

feeble ['fiːbl] *adj* faible; (*pathetic: attempt, excuse*) pauvre; (: *joke*) piteux(euse)

feed [fiːd] (*pt, pp* **fed**) *n* (*of baby*) tétée *f*; (*of animal*) fourrage *m*; pâture *f*; (*on printer*) mécanisme *m* d'alimentation ♦ *vt* (*person*) nourrir; (*BRIT: baby*) allaiter; (: *with bottle*) donner le biberon à; (*horse etc*) donner à manger à; (*machine*) alimenter; (*data, information*): **to ~ sth into** fournir qch à; **~ on** *vt fus* se nourrir de; **~back** *n* feed-back *m inv*; **~ing bottle** (*BRIT*) *n* biberon *m*

feel [fiːl] (*pt, pp* **felt**) *n* sensation *f*; (*impression*) impression *f* ♦ *vt* toucher; (*explore*) tâter, palper; (*cold, pain*) sentir; (*grief, anger*) ressentir, éprouver; (*think, believe*) avoir; **to ~ hungry/cold** avoir faim/froid; **to ~ lonely/better** se sentir seul/mieux; **I don't ~ well** je ne me sens pas bien; **it ~s soft** c'est doux(douce) au toucher; **to ~ like** (*want*) avoir envie de; **~ about** *vi* fouiller, tâtonner; **~er** *n* (*of insect*) antenne *f*; **to put out ~ers** *or* **a ~er** tâter le terrain; **~ing** *n* (*physical*) sensation *f*; (*emotional*) sentiment *m*

feet [fiːt] *npl of* **foot**

feign [feɪn] *vt* feindre, simuler

fell [fel] *pt of* **fall** ♦ *vt* (*tree, person*) abattre

fellow ['feləʊ] *n* type *m*; (*comrade*) compagnon *m*; (*of learned society*) membre *m* ♦ *cpd*: **their ~ prisoners/students** leurs camarades prisonniers/d'étude; **~ citizen** *n* concitoyen(ne) *m/f*; **~ countryman** (*irreg*) *n* compatriote *m*; **~ men** *npl* semblables *mpl*; **~ship** *n* (*society*) association *f*; (*comradeship*) amitié *f*, camaraderie *f*; (*grant*) sorte de bourse universitaire

felony ['felənɪ] *n* crime *m*, forfait *m*

felt [felt] *pt, pp of* **feel** ♦ *n* feutre *m*; **~-tip pen** *n* stylo-feutre *m*

female ['fiːmeɪl] *n* (*ZOOL*) femelle *f*; (*pej: woman*) bonne femme ♦ *adj* (*BIO*) femelle; (*sex, character*) féminin(e); (*vote etc*) des femmes

feminine ['femɪnɪn] *adj* féminin(e)

feminist ['femɪnɪst] *n* féministe *m/f*

fence [fens] *n* barrière *f* ♦ *vt* (*also: ~ in*) clôturer ♦ *vi* faire de l'escrime; **fencing** ['fensɪŋ] *n* escrime *m*

fend [fend] *vi*: **to ~ for o.s.** se débrouiller (tout seul); **~ off** *vt* (*attack etc*) parer

fender ['fendə*] *n* garde-feu *m inv*; (*on boat*) défense *f*; (*US: of car*) aile *f*

ferment [*vb* fə'ment, *n* 'fɜːment] *vi* fermenter ♦ *n* agitation *f*, effervescence *f*

fern [fɜːn] *n* fougère *f*

ferocious [fə'rəʊʃəs] *adj* féroce

ferret ['ferɪt] *n* furet *m*

ferry ['ferɪ] *n* (*small*) bac *m*; (*large: also: ~boat*) ferry(-boat) *m* ♦ *vt* transporter

fertile ['fɜːtaɪl] *adj* fertile; (*BIO*) fécond(e); **fertilizer** ['fɜːtɪlaɪzə*] *n* engrais *m*

fester ['festə*] *vi* suppurer

festival ['festɪvəl] *n* (*REL*) fête *f*; (*ART, MUS*) festival *m*

festive ['festɪv] *adj* de fête; **the ~ season** (*BRIT: Christmas*) la période des fêtes; **festivities** [fes'tɪvɪtɪz] *npl* réjouissances *fpl*

festoon [fes'tuːn] *vt*: **to ~ with** orner de

fetch [fetʃ] *vt* aller chercher; (*sell for*) rapporter

fetching ['fetʃɪŋ] *adj* charmant(e)

fête [feɪt] *n* fête *f*, kermesse *f*

fetish ['fetɪʃ] *n*: **to make a ~ of** être obsédé(e) par

feud [fjuːd] *n* dispute *f*, dissension *f*

fever ['fiːvə*] *n* fièvre *f*; **~ish** *adj* fiévreux(euse), fébrile

few [fjuː] *adj* (*not many*) peu de; **a ~** *adj* quelques ♦ *pron* quelques-uns(unes); **~er** *adj* moins de; moins (nombreux); **~est** *adj* le moins (de)

fiancé, e [fɪ'ɑːnseɪ] *n* fiancé(e) *m/f*

fib [fɪb] *n* bobard *m*

fibre ['faɪbə*] (*US* **fiber**) *n* fibre *f*; **~glass** (*US* **Fiberglass** ®) *n* fibre de verre

fickle ['fɪkl] *adj* inconstant(e), volage, capricieux(euse)

fiction ['fɪkʃən] *n* romans *mpl*, littérature *f* romanesque; (*invention*) fiction *f*; **~al** *adj* fictif(ive)

fictitious [fɪk'tɪʃəs] *adj* fictif(ive), imaginaire

fiddle ['fɪdl] *n* (*MUS*) violon *m*; (*cheating*) combine *f*; escroquerie *f* ♦ *vt* (*BRIT: accounts*) falsifier, maquiller; **~ with** *vt fus* tripoter

fidget ['fɪdʒɪt] *vi* se trémousser, remuer

field [fiːld] *n* champ *m*; (*fig*) domaine *m*, champ *m*; (*SPORT: ground*) terrain *m*; **~ marshal** *n* maréchal *m*; **~work** *n* travaux *mpl* pratiques (sur le terrain)

fiend [fiːnd] *n* démon *m*; **~ish** *adj* diabolique, abominable

fierce [fɪəs] *adj* (*look, animal*) féroce,

sauvage; (*wind, attack, person*) (très) violent(e); (*fighting, enemy*) acharné(e)

fiery ['faɪərɪ] *adj* ardent(e), brûlant(e); (*temperament*) fougueux(euse)

fifteen [fɪf'tiːn] *num* quinze

fifth [fɪfθ] *num* cinquième

fifty ['fɪftɪ] *num* cinquante; ~-**fifty** *adj*: a ~-**fifty chance** une chance *etc* sur deux ♦ *adv* moitié-moitié

fig [fɪg] *n* figue *f*

fight [faɪt] (*pt, pp* **fought**) *n* (*MIL*) combat *m*; (*between persons*) bagarre *f*; (*against cancer etc*) lutte *f* ♦ *vt* se battre contre; (*cancer, alcoholism, emotion*) combattre, lutter contre; (*election*) se présenter à ♦ *vi* se battre; ~**er** *n* (*fig*) lutteur *m*; (*plane*) chasseur *m*; ~**ing** *n* combats *mpl* (*brawl*) bagarres *fpl*

figment ['fɪgmənt] *n*: a ~ of the imagination une invention

figurative ['fɪgərətɪv] *adj* figuré(e)

figure ['fɪgə*] *n* figure *f*; (*number, cipher*) chiffre *m*; (*body, outline*) silhouette *f*; (*shape*) ligne *f*, formes *fpl* ♦ *vt* (*think*: *esp US*) supposer ♦ *vi* (*appear*) figurer; ~ **out** *vt* (*work out*) calculer; ~**head** *n* (*NAUT*) figure *f* de proue; (*pej*) prête-nom *m*; ~ **of speech** *n* figure *f* de rhétorique

file [faɪl] *n* (*dossier*) dossier *m*; (*folder*) dossier, chemise *f*; (*: with hinges*) classeur *m*; (*COMPUT*) fichier *m*; (*row*) file *f*; (*tool*) lime *f* ♦ *vt* (*nails, wood*) limer; (*papers*) classer; (*LAW: claim*) faire enregistrer; déposer ♦ *vi*: **to** ~ **in/out** entrer/sortir l'un derrière l'autre; **to** ~ **for divorce** faire une demande en divorce; **filing cabinet** *n* classeur *m* (*meuble*)

fill [fɪl] *vt* remplir; (*need*) répondre à ♦ *n*: **to eat one's** ~ manger à sa faim; **to** ~ **with** remplir de; ~ **in** *vt* (*hole*) boucher; (*form*) remplir; ~ **up** *vt* remplir; ~ **it up, please** (*AUT*) le plein, s'il vous plaît

fillet ['fɪlɪt] *n* filet *m*; ~ **steak** *n* filet *m* de bœuf, tournedos *m*

filling ['fɪlɪŋ] *n* (*CULIN*) garniture *f*, farce *f*; (*for tooth*) plombage *m*; ~ **station** *n* station-service *f*

film [fɪlm] *n* film *m*; (*PHOT*) pellicule *f*,

film; (*of powder, liquid*) couche *f*, pellicule ♦ *vt* (*scene*) filmer ♦ *vi* tourner; ~ **star** *n* vedette *f* de cinéma

filter ['fɪltə*] *n* filtre *m* ♦ *vt* filtrer; ~ **lane** *n* (*AUT*) voie *f* de sortie; ~-**tipped** *adj* à bout filtre

filth [fɪlθ] *n* saleté *f*; ~**y** *adj* sale, dégoûtant(e); (*language*) ordurier(ère)

fin [fɪn] *n* (*of fish*) nageoire *f*

final ['faɪnl] *adj* final(e); (*definitive*) définitif(ive) ♦ *n* (*SPORT*) finale *f*; ~**s** *npl* (*SCOL*) examens *mpl* de dernière année; ~**e** [fɪ'nɑːlɪ] *n* finale *m*; ~**ize** *vt* mettre au point; ~**ly** *adv* (*eventually*) enfin, finalement; (*lastly*) en dernier lieu

finance [faɪ'næns] *n* finance *f* ♦ *vt* financer; ~**s** *npl* (*financial position*) finances *fpl*; **financial** [faɪ'nænʃəl] *adj* financier(ère)

find [faɪnd] (*pt, pp* **found**) *vt* trouver; (*lost object*) retrouver ♦ *n* trouvaille *f*, découverte *f*; **to** ~ **sb guilty** (*LAW*) déclarer qn coupable; ~ **out** *vt* (*truth, secret*) découvrir; (*person*) démasquer ♦ *vi*: **to** ~ **out about** (*make enquiries*) se renseigner; (*by chance*) apprendre; ~**ings** *npl* (*LAW*) conclusions *fpl*, verdict *m*; (*of report*) conclusions

fine [faɪn] *adj* (*excellent*) excellent(e); (*thin, not coarse, subtle*) fin(e); (*weather*) beau(belle) ♦ *adv* (*well*) très bien ♦ *n* (*LAW*) amende *f*, contravention *f* ♦ *vt* (*LAW*) condamner à une amende; donner une contravention à; **to be** ~ (*person*) aller bien; (*weather*) être beau; ~ **arts** *npl* beaux-arts *mpl*

finery ['faɪnərɪ] *n* parure *f*

finger ['fɪŋgə*] *n* doigt *m* ♦ *vt* palper, toucher; **little** ~ auriculaire *m*, petit doigt; **index** ~ index *m*; ~**nail** *n* ongle *m* (de la main); ~**print** *n* empreinte digitale; ~**tip** *n* bout *m* du doigt

finicky ['fɪnɪkɪ] *adj* tatillon(ne), méticuleux(euse); minutieux(euse)

finish ['fɪnɪʃ] *n* fin *f*; (*SPORT*) arrivée *f*; (*polish etc*) finition *f* ♦ *vt* finir, terminer ♦ *vi* finir, se terminer; **to** ~ **doing sth** finir de faire qch; **to** ~ **third** arriver *or* terminer troisième; ~ **off** *vt* finir, terminer; (*kill*) achever; **~ up** *vi*, *vt* finir; **~ing line** *n* ligne *f* d'arrivée; **~ing school** *n* institution privée (*pour jeunes filles*)

finite ['faɪnaɪt] *adj* fini(e); (*verb*) conjugué(e)

Finland ['fɪnlənd] *n* Finlande *f*

Finn [fɪn] *n* Finnois(e); Finlandais(e); **~ish** *adj* finnois(e); finlandais(e) ♦ *n* (*LING*) finnois *m*

fir [fɜ:*] *n* sapin *m*

fire [faɪə*] *n* feu *m*; (*accidental*) incendie *m*; (*heater*) radiateur *m* ♦ *vt* (*discharge*): **to ~ a gun** tirer un coup de feu; (*fig*) enflammer, animer; (*inf: dismiss*) mettre à la porte, renvoyer ♦ *vi* (*shoot*) tirer, faire feu; **on ~** en feu; **~ alarm** *n* avertisseur *m* d'incendie; **~arm** *n* arme *f* à feu; **~ brigade** *n* (sapeurs-) pompiers *mpl*; **~ department** (*US*) *n* = **fire brigade**; **~ engine** *n* (*vehicle*) voiture *f* des pompiers; **~ escape** *n* escalier *m* de secours; **~ extinguisher** *n* extincteur *m*; **~man** *n* pompier *m*; **~place** *n* cheminée *f*; **~side** *n* foyer *m*, coin *m* du feu; **~ station** *n* caserne *f* de pompiers; **~wood** *n* bois *m* de chauffage; **~works** *npl* feux *mpl* d'artifice; (*display*) feu(x) d'artifice

firing squad ['faɪərɪŋ-] *n* peloton *m* d'exécution

firm [fɜ:m] *adj* ferme ♦ *n* compagnie *f*, firme *f*

first [fɜ:st] *adj* premier(ère) ♦ *adv* (*before all others*) le premier, la première; (*before all other things*) en premier, d'abord; (*when listing reasons etc*) en premier lieu, premièrement ♦ *n* (*person: in race*) premier(ère); (*BRIT: SCOL*) mention *f* très bien; (*AUT*) première *f*; **at ~** au commencement, au début; **~ of all** tout d'abord, pour commencer; **~ aid** *n* premiers secours *or* soins *m*; **~-aid kit** *n* trousse *f* à pharmacie; **~-class** *adj* de première classe; (*excellent*) excellent(e), exceptionnel(le); **~-hand** *adj* de première main; **~ lady** (*US*) *n* femme *f* du président; **~ly** *adv* premièrement, en premier lieu; **~ name** *n* prénom *m*; **~-rate** *adj* excellent(e)

fish [fɪʃ] *n inv* poisson *m* ♦ *vt*, *vi* pêcher; **to go ~ing** aller à la pêche; **~erman** *n* pêcheur *m*; **~ farm** *n* établissement *m* piscicole; **~ fingers** (*BRIT*) *npl* bâtonnets de poisson (congelés); **~ing boat** *n* barque *f or* bateau *m* de pêche; **~ing line** *n* ligne *f* (de pêche); **~ing rod** *n* canne *f* à pêche; **~monger's (shop)** *n* poissonnerie *f*; **~ sticks** (*US*) *npl* = **fish fingers**; **~y** (*inf*) *adj* suspect(e), louche

fist [fɪst] *n* poing *m*

fit [fɪt] *adj* (*healthy*) en (bonne) forme; (*proper*) convenable; approprié(e) ♦ *vt* (*subj: clothes*) aller à; (*put in, attach*) installer, poser; adapter; (*equip*) équiper, garnir, munir; (*suit*) convenir à ♦ *vi* (*clothes*) aller; (*parts*) s'adapter; (*in space, gap*) entrer, s'adapter ♦ *n* (*MED*) accès *m*, crise *f*; (*of anger*) accès; (*of hysterics, jealousy*) crise; **~ to** en état de; **~ for** digne de; apte à; **~ of coughing** quinte *f* de toux; **a ~ of giggles** le fou rire; **this dress is a good ~** cette robe (me) va très bien; **by ~s and starts** par à-coups; **~ in** *vi* s'accorder; s'adapter; **~ful** *adj* (*sleep*) agité(e); **~ment** *n* meuble encastré, élément *m*; **~ness** *n* (*MED*) forme *f* physique; **~ted carpet** *n* moquette *f*; **~ted kitchen** (*BRIT*) *n* cuisine équipée; **~ter** *n* monteur *m*; **~ting** *adj* approprié(e) ♦ *n* (*of dress*) essayage *m*; (*of piece of equipment*) pose *f*, installation *f*; **~tings** *npl* (*in building*) installations *fpl*; **~ting room** *n* cabine *f* d'essayage

five [faɪv] *num* cinq; **~r** (*BRIT*) *n* billet *m* de cinq livres; (*US*) billet de cinq dollars

fix [fɪks] *vt* (*date, amount etc*) fixer; (*organize*) arranger; (*mend*) réparer; (*meal, drink*) préparer ♦ *n*: **to be in a ~** être dans le pétrin; **~ up** *vt* (*meeting*) arranger; **to ~ sb up with sth** faire avoir qch à qn; **~ation** [fɪk'seɪʃən] *n* (*PSYCH*) fixation *f*; (*fig*) obsession *f*; **~ed** [fɪkst] *adj* (*prices etc*) fixe; (*smile*) figé(e); **~ture** ['fɪkstʃə*] *n* installation *f* (fixe); (*SPORT*) rencontre *f* (au programme)

fizzle out ['fɪzl-] *vi* (*interest*) s'estomper;

(*strike, film*) se terminer en queue de poisson

fizzy ['fɪzɪ] *adj* pétillant(e); gazeux(euse)

flabbergasted ['flæbəgɑːstɪd] *adj* sidéré(e), ahuri(e)

flabby ['flæbɪ] *adj* mou(molle)

flag [flæg] *n* drapeau *m*; (*also:* ~*stone*) dalle *f* ♦ *vi* faiblir; fléchir; ~ **down** *vt* héler, faire signe (de s'arrêter) à; ~**pole** ['flægpəʊl] *n* mât *m*; ~**ship** *n* vaisseau *m* amiral; (*fig*) produit *m* vedette

flair [flɛə*] *n* flair *m*

flak [flæk] *n* (*MIL*) tir antiaérien; (*inf: criticism*) critiques *fpl*

flake [fleɪk] *n* (*of rust, paint*) écaille *f*; (*of snow, soap powder*) flocon *m* ♦ *vi* (*also:* ~ *off*) s'écailler

flamboyant [flæm'bɔɪənt] *adj* flamboyant(e), éclatant(e); (*person*) haut(e) en couleur

flame [fleɪm] *n* flamme *f*

flamingo [flə'mɪŋgəʊ] *n* flamant *m* (rose)

flammable ['flæməbl] *adj* inflammable

flan [flæn] (*BRIT*) *n* tarte *f*

flank [flæŋk] *n* flanc *m* ♦ *vt* flanquer

flannel ['flænl] *n* (*fabric*) flanelle *f*; (*BRIT: also: face* ~) gant *m* de toilette; ~**s** *npl* (*trousers*) pantalon *m* de flanelle

flap [flæp] *n* (*of pocket, envelope*) rabat *m* ♦ *vt* (*wings*) battre (de) ♦ *vi* (*sail, flag*) claquer; (*inf: also: be in a* ~) paniquer

flare [flɛə*] *n* (*signal*) signal lumineux; (*in skirt etc*) évasement *m*; ~ **up** *vi* s'embraser; (*fig: person*) se mettre en colère, s'emporter; (: *revolt etc*) éclater

flash [flæʃ] *n* éclair *m*; (*also: news* ~) flash *m* (d'information); (*PHOT*) flash *m* ♦ *vt* (*light*) projeter; (*send: message*) câbler; (*look*) jeter; (*smile*) lancer ♦ *vi* (*light*) clignoter; **a** ~ **of lightning** un éclair; **in a** ~ en un clin d'œil; **to** ~ **one's headlights** faire un appel de phares; **to** ~ **by** *or* **past** (*person*) passer comme un éclair (devant); ~**bulb** *n* ampoule *f* de flash; ~**cube** *n* cube-flash *m*; ~**light** *n* lampe *f* de poche

flashy ['flæʃɪ] (*pej*) *adj* tape-à-l'œil *inv*, tapageur(euse)

flask [flɑːsk] *n* flacon *m*, bouteille *f*; (*vacuum*) ~ thermos *m or f* (®)

flat [flæt] *adj* plat(e); (*tyre*) dégonflé(e), à plat; (*beer*) éventé(e); (*denial*) catégorique; (*MUS*) bémol *inv*; (: *voice*) faux(fausse); (*fee, rate*) fixe ♦ *n* (*BRIT: apartment*) appartement *m*; (*AUT*) crevaison *f*; (*MUS*) bémol *m*; **to work** ~ **out** travailler d'arrache-pied; ~**ly** *adv* catégoriquement; ~-**screen** *adj* à écran plat; ~**ten** *vt* (*also:* ~*ten out*) aplatir; (*crop*) coucher; (*building(s)*) raser

flatter ['flætə*] *vt* flatter; ~**ing** *adj* flatteur(euse); ~**y** *n* flatterie *f*

flaunt [flɔːnt] *vt* faire étalage de

flavour ['fleɪvə*] (*US* **flavor**) *n* goût *m*, saveur *f*; (*of ice cream etc*) parfum *m* ♦ *vt* parfumer; **vanilla-flavoured** à l'arôme de vanille, à la vanille; ~**ing** *n* arôme *m*

flaw [flɔː] *n* défaut *m*; ~**less** *adj* sans défaut

flax [flæks] *n* lin *m*; ~**en** *adj* blond(e)

flea [fliː] *n* puce *f*

fleck [flɛk] *n* tacheture *f*; moucheture *f*

flee [fliː] (*pt, pp* **fled**) *vt* fuir ♦ *vi* fuir, s'enfuir

fleece [fliːs] *n* toison *f* ♦ *vt* (*inf*) voler, filouter

fleet [fliːt] *n* flotte *f*; (*of lorries etc*) parc *m*, convoi *m*

fleeting ['fliːtɪŋ] *adj* fugace, fugitif(ive); (*visit*) très bref(brève)

Flemish ['flemɪʃ] *adj* flamand(e)

flesh [fleʃ] *n* chair *f*; ~ **wound** *n* blessure superficielle

flew [fluː] *pt of* **fly**

flex [flɛks] *n* fil *m or* câble *m* électrique ♦ *vt* (*knee*) fléchir; (*muscles*) tendre

flexible *adj* flexible

flick [flɪk] *n* petite tape; chiquenaude *f*; (*of duster*) petit coup *m* ♦ *vt* donner un petit coup à; (*switch*) appuyer sur; ~ **through** *vt fus* feuilleter

flicker ['flɪkə*] *vi* (*light*) vaciller; **his eyelids** ~**ed** il a cillé

flier ['flaɪə*] *n* aviateur *m*

flight [flaɪt] *n* vol *m*; (*escape*) fuite *f*; (*also:* ~ *of steps*) escalier *m*; ~ **at-**

tendant (*US*) *n* steward *m*, hôtesse *f* de l'air; **~ deck** *n* (*AVIAT*) poste *m* de pilotage; (*NAUT*) pont *m* d'envol

flimsy ['flɪmzɪ] *adj* peu solide; (*clothes*) trop léger(ère); (*excuse*) pauvre, mince

flinch [flɪntʃ] *vi* tressaillir; **to ~ from** se dérober à, reculer devant

fling [flɪŋ] (*pt, pp* **flung**) *vt* jeter, lancer

flint [flɪnt] *n* silex *m*; (*in lighter*) pierre *f* (à briquet)

flip [flɪp] *vt* (*throw*) lancer (d'une chiquenaude); **to ~ a coin** jouer à pile ou face; **to ~ sth over** retourner qch

flippant ['flɪpənt] *adj* désinvolte, irrévérencieux(euse)

flipper ['flɪpə*] *n* (*of seal etc*) nageoire *f*; (*for swimming*) palme *f*

flirt [flɜːt] *vi* flirter ♦ *n* flirteur(euse) *m/f*

flit [flɪt] *vi* voleter

float [fləʊt] *n* flotteur *m*; (*in procession*) char *m*; (*money*) réserve *f* ♦ *vi* flotter

flock [flɒk] *n* troupeau *m*; (*of birds*) vol *m*; (*REL*) ouailles *fpl* ♦ *vi*: **to ~ to** se rendre en masse à

flog [flɒg] *vt* fouetter

flood [flʌd] *n* inondation *f*; (*of letters, refugees etc*) flot *m* ♦ *vt* inonder ♦ *vi* (*people*): **to ~ into** envahir; **~ing** *n* inondation *f*; **~light** *n* projecteur *m*

floor [flɔː*] *n* sol *m*; (*storey*) étage *m*; (*of sea, valley*) fond *m* ♦ *vt* (*subj: question*) déconcenancer; (: *blow*) terrasser; **on the ~** par terre; **ground ~**, (*US*) **first ~**, de-chaussée *m inv*; **first ~**, (*US*) **second ~** premier étage; **~board** *n* planche *f* (*du plancher*); **~ show** *n* spectacle *m* de variétés

flop [flɒp] *n* fiasco *m* ♦ *vi* être un fiasco; (*fall: into chair*) s'affaler, s'effondrer

floppy ['flɒpɪ] *adj* lâche, flottant(e); **~ (disk)** *n* (*COMPUT*) disquette *f*

flora ['flɔːrə] *n* flore *f*

floral ['flɔːrəl] *adj* (*dress*) à fleurs

florid ['flɒrɪd] *adj* (*complexion*) coloré(e); (*style*) plein(e) de fioritures

florist ['flɒrɪst] *n* fleuriste *m/f*

flounce [flaʊns] *n*: **to ~ out** *vi* sortir dans un mouvement d'humeur

flounder ['flaʊndə*] *vi* patauger ♦ *n*

(*ZOOL*) flet *m*

flour ['flaʊə*] *n* farine *f*

flourish ['flʌrɪʃ] *vi* prospérer ♦ *n* (*gesture*) moulinet *m*

flout [flaʊt] *vt* se moquer de, faire fi de

flow [fləʊ] *n* (*ELEC, of river*) courant *m*; (*of blood in veins*) circulation *f*; (*of tide*) flux *m*; (*of orders, data*) flot *m* ♦ *vi* couler; (*traffic*) s'écouler; (*robes, hair*) flotter; **the ~ of traffic** l'écoulement *m* de la circulation; **~ chart** *n* organigramme *m*

flower ['flaʊə*] *n* fleur *f* ♦ *vi* fleurir; **~ bed** *n* plate-bande *f*; **~pot** *n* pot *m* (de fleurs); **~y** *adj* fleuri(e)

flown [fləʊn] *pp* of **fly**

flu [fluː] *n* grippe *f*

fluctuate ['flʌktjʊeɪt] *vi* varier, fluctuer

fluent ['fluːənt] *adj* (*speech*) coulant(e), aisé(e); **he speaks ~ French, he's ~ in French** il parle couramment le français

fluff [flʌf] *n* duvet *m*; (*on jacket, carpet*) peluche *f*; **~y** *adj* duveteux(euse); (*toy*) en peluche

fluid ['fluːɪd] *adj* fluide ♦ *n* fluide *m*

fluke [fluːk] (*inf*) *n* (*luck*) coup *m* de veine

flung [flʌŋ] *pt, pp* of **fling**

fluoride ['flʊəraɪd] *n* fluorure *f*; **~ toothpaste** *n* dentifrice *m* au fluor

flurry ['flʌrɪ] *n* (*of snow*) rafale *f*, bourrasque *f*; **~ of activity/excitement** affairement *m*/excitation *f* soudain(e)

flush [flʌʃ] *n* (*on face*) rougeur *f*; (*fig: of youth, beauty etc*) éclat *m* ♦ *vt* nettoyer à grande eau ♦ *vi* rougir ♦ *adj*: **~ with** au ras de, de niveau avec; **to ~ the toilet** tirer la chasse (d'eau); **~ out** *vt* (*game, birds*) débusquer; **~ed** *adj* (tout(e)) rouge

flustered ['flʌstəd] *adj* énervé(e)

flute [fluːt] *n* flûte *f*

flutter ['flʌtə*] *n* (*of panic, excitement*) agitation *f*; (*of wings*) battement *m* ♦ *vi* (*bird*) battre des ailes, voleter

flux [flʌks] *n*: **in a state of ~** fluctuant sans cesse

fly [flaɪ] (*pt* **flew**, *pp* **flown**) *n* (*insect*) mouche *f*; (*on trousers: also:* **flies**) braguette f ♦ vt piloter; (passengers, cargo) transporter (par avion); (distances) parcourir ♦ vi voler; (passengers) aller en avion; (escape) s'enfuir, fuir; (flag) se déployer; ~ **away** vi (bird, insect) s'envoler; ~ **off** vi = **fly away**; ~**ing** n (activity) aviation f; (action) vol m ♦ adj: a ~**ing visit** une visite éclair; **with ~ing colours** haut la main; ~**ing saucer** n soucoupe volante; ~**ing start** n: **to get off to a ~ing start** prendre un excellent départ; ~**over** (BRIT) n (bridge) saut-de-mouton m; ~**sheet** n (for tent) double toit m

foal [fəʊl] n poulain m

foam [fəʊm] n écume f; (on beer) mousse f; (also: ~ **rubber**) caoutchouc m mousse ♦ vi (liquid) écumer; (soapy water) mousser

fob [fɒb] vt: **to** ~ **sb off** se débarrasser de qn

focal point ['fəʊkəl-] n (fig) point central

focus ['fəʊkəs] (pl ~**es**) n foyer m; (of interest) centre m ♦ vt (field glasses etc) mettre au point ♦ vi: **to** ~ (**on**) (with camera) régler la mise au point (sur); (person) fixer son regard (sur); **out of/in** ~ (picture) flou(e)/net(te); (camera) pas au point/au point

fodder ['fɒdə*] n fourrage m

foe [fəʊ] n ennemi m

fog [fɒg] n brouillard m; ~**gy** adj: **it's** ~**gy** il y a du brouillard; ~ **lamp** n (AUT) phare m antibrouillard; ~ **light** (US) n = **fog lamp**

foil [fɔɪl] vt déjouer, contrecarrer ♦ n feuille f de métal; (kitchen ~) papier m d'alu(minium); (complement) repoussoir m; (FENCING) fleuret m

fold [fəʊld] n (bend, crease) pli m; (AGR) parc m à moutons; (fig) bercail m ♦ vt plier; (arms) croiser; ~ **up** vi (map, table etc) se plier; (business) fermer boutique ♦ vt (map, clothes) plier; ~**er** n (for papers) chemise f; (: with hinges) classeur m; ~**ing** adj (chair, bed) pliant(e)

foliage ['fəʊlɪdʒ] n feuillage m

folk [fəʊk] npl gens mpl ♦ cpd folklori-

que; ~**s** npl (parents) parents mpl; ~**lore** ['fəʊklɔː*] n folklore m; ~ **song** n chanson f folklorique

follow ['fɒləʊ] vt suivre ♦ vi suivre; (result) s'ensuivre; **to** ~ **suit** (fig) faire de même; ~ **up** vt (letter, offer) donner suite à; (case) suivre; ~**er** n disciple m/f, partisan(e); ~**ing** adj suivant(e) ♦ n partisans mpl, disciples mpl

folly ['fɒlɪ] n inconscience f; folie f

fond [fɒnd] adj (memory, look) tendre; (hopes, dreams) un peu fou(folle); **to be** ~ **of** aimer beaucoup

fondle ['fɒndl] vt caresser

font [fɒnt] n (in church: for baptism) fonts baptismaux; (TYP) fonte f

food [fuːd] n nourriture f; ~ **mixer** n mixer m; ~ **poisoning** n intoxication f alimentaire; ~ **processor** n robot m de cuisine; ~**stuffs** npl denrées fpl alimentaires

fool [fuːl] n idiot(e); (CULIN) mousse f de fruits ♦ vt berner, duper ♦ vi faire l'idiot or l'imbécile; ~**hardy** adj téméraire, imprudent(e); ~**ish** adj idiot(e), stupide; (rash) imprudent(e); insensé; ~**proof** adj (plan etc) infaillible

foot [fʊt] (pl **feet**) n pied m; (of animal) patte f; (measure) pied m (= 30,48 cm; 12 inches) ♦ vt (bill) payer; **on** ~ à pied; ~**age** n (CINEMA: length) ≈ métrage m; (: material) séquences fpl; ~**ball** n ballon m (de football); (sport: BRIT) football m, foot m; (: US) football américain; ~**ball player** (BRIT) n (also: footballer) joueur m de football; ~**brake** n frein m à pédale; ~**bridge** n passerelle f; ~**hills** npl contreforts mpl; ~**hold** n prise f (de pied); ~**ing** n (fig) position f; **to lose one's** ~**ing** perdre pied; ~**lights** npl rampe f; ~**man** (irreg) n valet m de pied; ~**note** n note f (en bas de page); ~**path** n sentier m; (in street) trottoir m; ~**print** n trace f (de pas); ~**step** n pas m; ~**wear** n chaussure(s) f(pl)

┌──────────────┐
│ KEYWORD │
└──────────────┘

for [fɔː*] prep **1** (indicating destination, intention, purpose) pour; **the train** ~

London le train pour *or* (à destination) de Londres; **he went ~ the paper** il est allé chercher le journal; **it's time ~ lunch** c'est l'heure du déjeuner; **what's it ~?** ça sert à quoi?; **what ~?** (*why*) pourquoi?

2 (*on behalf of, representing*) pour; **the MP ~ Hove** le député de Hove; **to work ~ sb/sth** travailler pour qn/qch; **G ~ George** G comme Georges

3 (*because of*) pour; **~ this reason** pour cette raison; **~ fear of being criticized** de peur d'être critiqué

4 (*with regard to*) pour; **it's cold ~ July** il fait froid pour juillet; **a gift ~ languages** un don pour les langues

5 (*in exchange for*): **I sold it ~ £5** je l'ai vendu 5 livres; **to pay 50 pence ~ a ticket** payer un billet 50 pence

6 (*in favour of*) pour; **are you ~ or against us?** êtes-vous pour ou contre nous?

7 (*referring to distance*) pendant, sur; **there are roadworks ~ 5 km** il y a des travaux sur *or* pendant 5 km; **we walked ~ miles** nous avons marché pendant des kilomètres

8 (*referring to time*) pendant; depuis; pour; **he was away ~ 2 years** il a été absent pendant 2 ans; **she will be away ~ a month** elle sera absente (pendant) un mois; **I have known her ~ years** je la connais depuis des années; **can you do it ~ tomorrow?** est-ce que tu peux le faire pour demain?

9 (*with infinitive clauses*): **it is not ~ me to decide** ce n'est pas à moi de décider; **it would be best ~ you to leave** le mieux serait que vous partiez; **there is still time ~ you to do it** vous avez encore le temps de le faire; **~ this to be possible ...** pour que cela soit possible ...

10 (*in spite of*): **~ all his work/efforts** malgré tout son travail/tous ses efforts; **~ all his complaints, he's very fond of her** il a beau se plaindre, il l'aime beaucoup

♦ *conj* (*since, as: rather formal*) car

forage ['fɒrɪdʒ] *vi* fourrager
foray ['fɒreɪ] *n* incursion *f*
forbid [fə'bɪd] (*pt* **forbad(e)**, *pp* **forbidden**) *vt* défendre, interdire; **to ~ sb to do** défendre *or* interdire à qn de faire; **~ding** *adj* sévère, sombre
force [fɔːs] *n* force *f* ♦ *vt* forcer; (*push*) pousser (de force); **the F~s** *npl* (*MIL*) l'armée *f*; **in ~** en vigueur; **~-feed** *vt* nourrir de force; **~ful** *adj* énergique, volontaire
forcibly ['fɔːsəblɪ] *adv* par la force, de force; (*express*) énergiquement
ford [fɔːd] *n* gué *m*
fore [fɔː*] *n*: **to come to the ~** se faire remarquer
fore: ~arm ['fɔːrɑːm] *n* avant-bras *m inv*; **~boding** [fɔː'bəʊdɪŋ] *n* pressentiment *m* (néfaste); **~cast** ['fɔːkɑːst] (*irreg: like* **cast**) *n* prévision *f* ♦ *vt* prévoir; **~court** ['fɔːkɔːt] *n* (*of garage*) devant *m*; **~fathers** ['fɔːfɑːðəz] *npl* ancêtres *mpl*; **~finger** ['fɔːfɪŋɡə*] *n* index *m*
forefront ['fɔːfrʌnt] *n*: **in the ~ of** au premier rang *or* plan de
forego [fɔː'ɡəʊ] (*irreg: like* **go**) *vt* renoncer à; **~ne** ['fɔːɡɒn] *adj*: **it's a ~ne conclusion** c'est couru d'avance
foreground ['fɔːɡraʊnd] *n* premier plan
forehead ['fɒrɪd] *n* front *m*
foreign ['fɒrɪn] *adj* étranger(ère); (*trade*) extérieur(e); **~er** *n* étranger(ère); **~ exchange** *n* change *m*; **F~ Office** (*BRIT*) *n* ministère *m* des affaires étrangères; **F~ Secretary** (*BRIT*) *n* ministre *m* des affaires étrangères
foreleg ['fɔːleɡ] *n* (*cat, dog*) patte *f* de devant; (*horse*) jambe antérieure
foreman ['fɔːmən] (*irreg*) *n* (*factory, building site*) contremaître *m*, chef *m* d'équipe
foremost ['fɔːməʊst] *adj* le(la) plus en vue; premier(ère) ♦ *adv*: **first and ~** avant tout, tout d'abord
forensic [fə'rensɪk] *adj*: **~ medicine** médecine légale; **~ scientist** médecin *m* légiste
forerunner ['fɔːrʌnə*] *n* précurseur *m*
foresee [fɔː'siː] (*irreg: like* **see**) *vt* pré-

voir; **~able** adj prévisible

foreshadow [fɔː'ʃædəʊ] vt présager, annoncer, laisser prévoir

foresight ['fɔːsaɪt] n prévoyance f

forest ['fɒrɪst] n forêt f

forestall [fɔː'stɔːl] vt devancer

forestry ['fɒrɪstrɪ] n sylviculture f

foretaste ['fɔːteɪst] n avant-goût m

foretell [fɔː'tel] (irreg: like tell) vt prédire

foretold [fɔː'təʊld] pt, pp of foretell

forever [fə'revə*] adv pour toujours; (fig) continuellement

forewent [fɔː'went] pt of forego

foreword ['fɔːwɜːd] n avant-propos m inv

forfeit ['fɔːfɪt] vt (lose) perdre

forgave [fə'geɪv] pt of forgive

forge [fɔːdʒ] n forge f ♦ vt (signature) contrefaire; (wrought iron) forger; **to ~ money** (BRIT) fabriquer de la fausse monnaie; **~ ahead** vi pousser de l'avant, prendre de l'avance; **~r** n faussaire m; **~ry** n faux m, contrefaçon f

forget [fə'get] (pt forgot, pp forgotten) vt, vi oublier; **~ful** adj distrait(e), étourdi(e); **~-me-not** n myosotis m

forgive [fə'gɪv] (pt forgave, pp forgiven) vt pardonner; **to ~ sb for sth/ for doing sth** pardonner qch à qn/à qn de faire qch; **~ness** n pardon m

forgo [fə'ɡəʊ] (pt forwent, pp forgone) vt = forego

fork [fɔːk] n (for eating) fourchette f; (for gardening) fourche f; (of roads) bifurcation f; (of railways) embranchement m ♦ vi (road) bifurquer; **~ out** vt (inf) allonger; **~-lift truck** n chariot élévateur

forlorn [fə'lɔːn] adj (deserted) abandonné(e); (attempt, hope) désespéré(e)

form [fɔːm] n forme f; (SCOL) classe f; (questionnaire) formulaire m ♦ vt former; (habit) contracter; **in top ~** en pleine forme

formal ['fɔːməl] adj (offer, receipt) en bonne et due forme; (person) cérémonieux(euse); (dinner) officiel(le); (clothes) de soirée; (garden) à la fran-

çaise; (education) à proprement parler; **~ly** adv officiellement; cérémonieusement

format ['fɔːmæt] n format m ♦ vt (COMPUT) formater

formative ['fɔːmətɪv] adj: **~ years** années fpl d'apprentissage or de formation

former ['fɔːmə*] adj ancien(ne) (before n), précédent(e); **the ~ ... the latter** le premier ... le second, celui-là ... celui-ci; **~ly** adv autrefois

formidable ['fɔːmɪdəbl] adj redoutable

formula [fɔːmjʊlə] (pl ~s or formulae) n formule f

forsake [fə'seɪk] (pt forsook, pp forsaken) vt abandonner

fort [fɔːt] n fort m

forte ['fɔːtɪ] n (point) fort m

forth [fɔːθ] adv en avant; **to go back and ~** aller et venir; **and so ~** et ainsi de suite; **~coming** adj (event) qui va avoir lieu prochainement; (character) ouvert(e), communicatif(ive); (available) disponible; **~right** adj franc(franche), direct(e); **~with** adv sur-le-champ

fortify ['fɔːtɪfaɪ] vt fortifier

fortitude ['fɔːtɪtjuːd] n courage m

fortnight ['fɔːtnaɪt] (BRIT) n quinzaine f, quinze jours mpl; **~ly** adj bimensuel(le) ♦ adv tous les quinze jours

fortunate ['fɔːtʃənɪt] adj heureux(euse); (person) chanceux (euse); **it is ~ that** c'est une chance que; **~ly** adv heureusement

fortune ['fɔːtʃən] n chance f; (wealth) fortune f; **~-teller** n diseuse f de bonne aventure

forty ['fɔːtɪ] num quarante

forward ['fɔːwəd] adj (ahead of schedule) en avance; (movement, position) en avant, vers l'avant; (not shy) direct(e); effronté(e) ♦ n (SPORT) avant m ♦ vt (letter) faire suivre; (parcel, goods) expédier; (fig) promouvoir, favoriser; **~(s)** adv en avant; **to move ~** avancer

fossil ['fɒsl] n fossile m

foster ['fɒstə*] vt encourager, favoriser; (child) élever (sans obligation d'adopter); **~ child** n enfant adoptif(ive)

fought [fɔːt] *pt, pp of* **fight**

foul [faʊl] *adj* (*weather, smell, food*) infect(e); (*language*) ordurier(ère) ♦ *n* (*SPORT*) faute *f* ♦ *vt* (*dirty*) salir, encrasser; **he's got a ~ temper** il a un caractère de chien; **~ play** *n* (*LAW*) acte criminel

found [faʊnd] *pt, pp of* **find** ♦ *vt* (*establish*) fonder; **~ation** [faʊn'deɪʃən] *n* (*act*) fondation *f*; (*base*) fondement *m*; (*also:* ~*ation cream*) fond *m* de teint; **~ations** *npl* (*of building*) fondations *fpl*

founder ['faʊndə*] *n* fondateur *m* ♦ *vi* couler, sombrer

foundry ['faʊndrɪ] *n* fonderie *f*

fountain ['faʊntɪn] *n* fontaine *f*; **~ pen** *n* stylo *m* (à encre)

four [fɔː*] *num* quatre; **on all ~s** à quatre pattes; **~-poster** *n* (*also:* ~-*poster bed*) lit *m* à baldaquin; **~some** *n* (*game*) partie *f* à quatre; (*outing*) sortie *f* à quatre

fourteen [fɔː'tiːn] *num* quatorze

fourth [fɔːθ] *num* quatrième

fowl [faʊl] *n* volaille *f*

fox [fɒks] *n* renard *m* ♦ *vt* mystifier

foyer ['fɔɪeɪ] *n* (*hotel*) hall *m*; (*THEATRE*) foyer *m*

fraction ['frækʃən] *n* fraction *f*

fracture ['fræktʃə*] *n* fracture *f*

fragile ['frædʒaɪl] *adj* fragile

fragment ['frægmənt] *n* fragment *m*

fragrant ['freɪgrənt] *adj* parfumé(e), odorant(e)

frail [freɪl] *adj* fragile, délicat(e)

frame [freɪm] *n* charpente *f*; (*of picture, bicycle*) cadre *m*; (*of door, window*) encadrement *m*, chambranle *m*; (*of spectacles: also:* ~*s*) monture *f* ♦ *vt* encadrer; **~ of mind** disposition *f* d'esprit; **~work** *n* structure *f*

France [frɑːns] *n* France *f*

franchise ['fræntʃaɪz] *n* (*POL*) droit *m* de vote; (*COMM*) franchise *f*

frank [fræŋk] *adj* franc(franche) ♦ *vt* (*letter*) affranchir; **~ly** *adv* franchement

frantic ['fræntɪk] *adj* (*hectic*) frénétique; (*distraught*) hors de soi

fraternity [frə'tɜːnɪtɪ] *n* (*spirit*) fraterni-

té *f*; (*club*) communauté *f*, confrérie *f*

fraud [frɔːd] *n* supercherie *f*, fraude *f*, tromperie *f*; (*person*) imposteur *m*

fraught [frɔːt] *adj*: **~ with** chargé(e) de, plein(e) de

fray [freɪ] *n* bagarre *f* ♦ *vi* s'effilocher; **tempers were ~ed** les gens commençaient à s'énerver

freak [friːk] *n* (*also cpd*) phénomène *m*, créature *or* événement exceptionnel(le) par sa rareté

freckle ['frekl] *n* tache *f* de rousseur

free [friː] *adj* libre; (*gratis*) gratuit(e) ♦ *vt* (*prisoner etc*) libérer; (*jammed object or person*) dégager; **~ (of charge), for ~** gratuitement; **~dom** ['friːdəm] *n* liberté *f*; **~-for-all** *n* mêlée générale; **~ gift** *n* prime *f*; **~hold** *n* propriété foncière libre; **~ kick** *n* coup franc; **~lance** *adj* indépendant(e); **~ly** *adv* librement; (*liberally*) libéralement; **F~mason** *n* francmaçon *m*; **F~post** (®) *n* port payé; **~range** *adj* (*hen, eggs*) de ferme; **~ trade** *n* libre-échange *m*; **~way** *n* (*US*) autoroute *f*; **~ will** *n* libre arbitre *m*; **of one's own ~ will** de son plein gré

freeze [friːz] (*pt* **froze**, *pp* **frozen**) *vi* geler ♦ *vt* (*food*) congeler; (*prices, salaries*) bloquer, geler ♦ *n* gel *m*; (*fig*) blocage *m*; **~-dried** *adj* lyophilisé(e); **~r** *n* congélateur *m*

freezing ['friːzɪŋ] *adj*: **~ (cold)** (*weather, water*) glacial(e) ♦ *n*: **3 degrees below ~** 3 degrés au-dessous de zéro; **~ point** *n* point *m* de congélation

freight [freɪt] *n* (*goods*) fret *m*, cargaison *f*; (*money charged*) fret, prix *m* du transport; **~ train** *n* train *m* de marchandises

French [frentʃ] *adj* français(e) ♦ *n* (*LING*) français *m*; **the ~** *npl* (*people*) les Français; **~ bean** *n* haricot vert; **~ fried (potatoes)**, **~ fries** (*US*) *npl* (pommes de terre *fpl*) frites *fpl*; **~man** (*irreg*) *n* Français *m*; **~ window** *n* porte-fenêtre *f*; **~woman** (*irreg*) *n* Française *f*

frenzy ['frenzɪ] *n* frénésie *f*

frequency ['friːkwənsɪ] *n* fréquence *f*

frequent [*adj* 'friːkwənt, *vb* friː'kwent]

adj fréquent(e) ♦ *vt* fréquenter; **~ly** *adv* fréquemment

fresh [freʃ] *adj* frais(fraîche); (*new*) nouveau(nouvelle); (*cheeky*) familier(ère), culotté(e); **~en** *vi* (*wind, air*) fraîchir; **~en up** *vi* faire un brin de toilette; **~er** (*BRIT: inf*) *n* (*SCOL*) bizuth *m*, étudiant(e) de 1ère année; **~ly** *adv* nouvellement, récemment; **~man** (*US: irreg*) *n* = **fresher**; **~ness** *n* fraîcheur *f*; **~water** *adj* (*fish*) d'eau douce

fret [fret] *vi* s'agiter, se tracasser

friar ['fraɪə*] *n* moine *m*, frère *m*

friction ['frɪkʃən] *n* friction *f*

Friday ['fraɪdeɪ] *n* vendredi *m*

fridge [frɪdʒ] (*BRIT*) *n* frigo *m*, frigidaire *m* (®)

fried [fraɪd] *adj* frit(e); **~ egg** œuf *m* sur le plat

friend [frend] *n* ami(e); **~ly** *adj* amical(e); gentil(le); (*place*) accueillant(e); **they were killed by ~ly fire** ils sont morts sous les tirs de leur propre camp; **~ship** *n* amitié *f*

frieze [friːz] *n* frise *f*

fright [fraɪt] *n* peur *f*, effroi *m*; **to take ~** prendre peur, s'effrayer; **~en** *vt* effrayer, faire peur à; **~ened** *adj*: **to be ~ened (of)** avoir peur (de); **~ening** *adj* effrayant(e); **~ful** *adj* affreux(euse)

frigid ['frɪdʒɪd] *adj* (*woman*) frigide

frill [frɪl] *n* (*of dress*) volant *m*; (*of shirt*) jabot *m*

fringe [frɪndʒ] *n* (*BRIT: of hair*) frange *f*; (*edge: of forest etc*) bordure *f*; **~ benefits** *npl* avantages sociaux *or* en nature

frisk [frɪsk] *vt* fouiller

fritter ['frɪtə*] *n* beignet *m*; **~ away** *vt* gaspiller

frivolous ['frɪvələs] *adj* frivole

frizzy ['frɪzɪ] *adj* crépu(e)

fro [frəʊ] *adv*: **to go to and ~** aller et venir

frock [frɒk] *n* robe *f*

frog [frɒg] *n* grenouille *f*; **~man** *n* homme-grenouille *m*

frolic ['frɒlɪk] *vi* folâtrer, batifoler

KEYWORD

from [frɒm] *prep* **1** (*indicating starting place, origin etc*) de; **where do you come ~?, where are you ~?** d'où venez-vous?; **~ London to Paris** de Londres à Paris; **a letter ~ my sister** une lettre de ma sœur; **to drink ~ the bottle** boire à (même) la bouteille

2 (*indicating time*) (à partir de); **~ one o'clock to** *or* **until** *or* **till two** d'une heure à deux heures; **~ January (on)** à partir de janvier

3 (*indicating distance*) de; **the hotel is one kilometre ~ the beach** l'hôtel est à un kilomètre de la plage

4 (*indicating price, number etc*) de; **the interest rate was increased ~ 9% to 10%** le taux d'intérêt est passé de 9 à 10%

5 (*indicating difference*) de; **he can't tell red ~ green** il ne peut pas distinguer le rouge du vert

6 (*because of, on the basis of*): **~ what he says** d'après ce qu'il dit; **weak ~ hunger** affaibli par la faim

---

front [frʌnt] *n* (*of house, dress*) devant *m*; (*of coach, train*) avant *m*; (*promenade: also: sea ~*) bord *m* de mer; (*MIL, METEOROLOGY*) front *m*; (*fig: appearances*) contenance *f*, façade *f* ♦ *adj* de devant; (*seat*) avant *inv*; **in ~ (of)** devant; **~age** ['frʌntɪdʒ] *n* (*of building*) façade *f*; **~ door** *n* porte *f* d'entrée; (*of car*) portière *f* avant; **~ier** ['frʌntɪə*] *n* frontière *f*; **~ page** *n* première page *f*; **~ room** (*BRIT*) *n* pièce *f* de devant, salon *m*; **~-wheel drive** *n* traction *f* avant

frost [frɒst] *n* gel *m*, gelée *f*; (*also: hoar~*) givre *m*; **~bite** *n* gelures *fpl*; **~ed** *adj* (*glass*) dépoli(e); **~y** *adj* (*weather, welcome*) glacial(e)

froth [frɒθ] *n* mousse *f*; écume *f*

frown [fraʊn] *vi* froncer les sourcils

froze [frəʊz] *pt of* **freeze**

frozen ['frəʊzn] *pp of* **freeze**

fruit [fruːt] *n inv* fruit *m*; **~erer** *n* fruitier *m*, marchand(e) de fruits; **~ful** *adj* (*fig*) fructueux(euse); **~ion** [fruː'ɪʃən] *n*: **to come to ~ion** se réaliser; **~ juice** *n* jus *m* de fruit; **~ machine** (*BRIT*) *n* machine *f* à sous; **~ salad** *n* salade *f* de fruits

frustrate [frʌs'treɪt] *vt* frustrer

fry [fraɪ] (*pt, pp* **fried**) *vt* (faire) frire; *see also* **small**; **~ing pan** *n* poêle *f* (à frire)

ft. *abbr* = **foot; feet**

fuddy-duddy ['fʌdɪdʌdɪ] (*pej*) *n* vieux schnock

fudge [fʌdʒ] *n* (*CULIN*) caramel *m*

fuel [fjʊəl] *n* (*for heating*) combustible *m*; (*for propelling*) carburant *m*; **~ oil** *n* mazout *m*; **~ tank** *n* (*in vehicle*) réservoir *m*

fugitive ['fjuːdʒɪtɪv] *n* fugitif(ive)

fulfil [fʊl'fɪl] (*US* **fulfill**) *vt* (*function, condition*) remplir; (*order*) exécuter; (*wish, desire*) satisfaire, réaliser; **~ment** (*US* **fulfillment**) *n* (*of wishes etc*) réalisation *f*; (*feeling*) contentement *m*

full [fʊl] *adj* plein(e); (*details, information*) complet(ète); (*skirt*) ample, large ♦ *adv*: **to know ~ well that** savoir fort bien que; **I'm ~ (up)** j'ai bien mangé; **a ~ two hours** deux bonnes heures; **at ~ speed** à toute vitesse; **in ~** (*reproduce, quote*) intégralement; (*write*) en toutes lettres; **~ employment** plein emploi; **to pay in ~** tout payer; **~-length** *adj* (*film*) long métrage; (*portrait, mirror*) en pied; (*coat*) long(ue); **~ moon** *n* pleine lune; **~-scale** *adj* (*attack, war*) complet(ète), total(e); (*model*) grandeur nature *inv*; **~ stop** *n* point *m*; **~-time** *adj, adv* (*work*) à temps plein; **~y** *adv* entièrement, complètement; (*at least*) au moins; **~y-fledged** *adj* (*teacher, barrister*) diplômé(e); (*citizen, member*) à part entière

fumble ['fʌmbl] *vi*: **~ with** tripoter

fume [fjuːm] *vi* rager; **~s** *npl* vapeurs *fpl*, émanations *fpl*, gaz *mpl*

fun [fʌn] *n* amusement *m*, divertissement *m*; **to have ~** s'amuser; **for ~** pour rire; **to make ~ of** se moquer de

function ['fʌŋkʃən] *n* fonction *f*; (*social occasion*) cérémonie *f*, soirée officielle ♦ *vi* fonctionner; **~al** *adj* fonctionnel(le)

fund [fʌnd] *n* caisse *f*, fonds *m*; (*source, store*) source *f*, mine *f*; **~s** *npl* (*money*) fonds *mpl*

fundamental [fʌndə'mentl] *adj* fondamental(e)

funeral ['fjuːnərəl] *n* enterrement *m*, obsèques *fpl*; **~ parlour** *n* entreprise *f* de pompes funèbres; **~ service** *n* service *m* funèbre

funfair ['fʌnfɛə*] (*BRIT*) *n* fête (foraine)

fungi ['fʌŋgaɪ] *npl of* **fungus**

fungus ['fʌŋgəs] (*pl* **fungi**) *n* champignon *m*; (*mould*) moisissure *f*

funnel ['fʌnl] *n* entonnoir *m*; (*of ship*) cheminée *f*

funny ['fʌnɪ] *adj* amusant(e), drôle; (*strange*) curieux(euse), bizarre

fur [fɜː*] *n* fourrure *f*; (*BRIT*: *in kettle etc*) (dépôt *m* de) tartre *m*; **~ coat** *n* manteau *m* de fourrure

furious ['fjʊərɪəs] *adj* furieux(euse); (*effort*) acharné(e)

furlong ['fɜːlɒŋ] *n* = 201,17 m

furlough ['fɜːləʊ] *n* permission *f*, congé *m*

furnace ['fɜːnɪs] *n* fourneau *m*

furnish ['fɜːnɪʃ] *vt* meubler; (*supply*): **to ~ sb with sth** fournir qch à qn; **~ings** *npl* mobilier *m*, ameublement *m*

furniture ['fɜːnɪtʃə*] *n* meubles *mpl*, mobilier *m*; **piece of ~** meuble *m*

furrow ['fʌrəʊ] *n* sillon *m*

furry ['fɜːrɪ] *adj* (*animal*) à fourrure; (*toy*) en peluche

further ['fɜːðə*] *adj* (*additional*) supplémentaire, autre; nouveau (nouvelle) ♦ *adv* plus loin; (*more*) davantage; (*moreover*) de plus ♦ *vt* faire avancer *or* progresser, promouvoir; **~ education** *n* enseignement *m* postscolaire; **~more** *adv* de plus, en outre

furthest ['fɜːðɪst] *superl of* **far**

fury ['fjʊərɪ] *n* fureur *f*

fuse [fjuːz] (*US* **fuze**) *n* fusible *m*; (*for bomb etc*) amorce *f*, détonateur *m* ♦ *vt, vi* (*metal*) fondre; **to ~ the lights** (*BRIT*) faire sauter les plombs; **~ box** *n* boîte *f* à fusibles

fuss [fʌs] *n (excitement)* agitation *f*; *(complaining)* histoire(s) *f(pl)*; **to make a ~** faire des histoires; **to make a ~ sb** être aux petits soins pour qn; **~y** *adj (person)* tatillon(ne), difficile; *(dress, style)* tarabiscoté(e)

future ['fjuːtʃə*] *adj* futur(e) ♦ *n* avenir *m*; *(LING)* futur *m*; **in ~** à l'avenir

fuze [fjuːz] *(US) n, vt, vi* = **fuse**

fuzzy ['fʌzɪ] *adj (PHOT)* flou(e); *(hair)* crépu(e)

G g

G [dʒiː] *n (MUS)* sol *m*

G7 *n abbr (= Group of 7)* le groupe des 7

gabble ['gæbl] *vi* bredouiller

gable ['geɪbl] *n* pignon *m*

gadget ['gædʒɪt] *n* gadget *m*

Gaelic ['geɪlɪk] *adj* gaélique ♦ *n (LING)* gaélique *m*

gag [gæg] *n (on mouth)* bâillon *m*; *(joke)* gag *m* ♦ *vt* bâillonner

gaiety ['geɪətɪ] *n* gaieté *f*

gain [geɪn] *n (improvement)* gain *m*; *(profit)* gain, profit *m*; *(increase):* **~ (in)** augmentation *f* (de) ♦ *vt* gagner ♦ *vi (watch)* avancer; **to ~ 3 lbs (in weight)** prendre 3 livres; **to ~ on sb** *(catch up)* rattraper qn; **to ~ from/by** gagner de/à

gait [geɪt] *n* démarche *f*

gal. *abbr* = **gallon**

gale [geɪl] *n* rafale *f* de vent; coup *m* de vent

gallant ['gælənt] *adj* vaillant(e), brave; *(towards ladies)* galant

gall bladder ['gɔːl-] *n* vésicule *f* biliaire

gallery ['gælərɪ] *n* galerie *f*; *(also: art ~)* musée *m*; *(: private)* galerie

galley ['gælɪ] *n (ship's kitchen)* cambuse *f*

gallon ['gælən] *n* gallon *m* (*BRIT = 4,5 l; US = 3,8 l*)

gallop ['gæləp] *n* galop *m* ♦ *vi* galoper

gallows ['gæləuz] *n* potence *f*

gallstone ['gɔːlstəun] *n* calcul *m* biliaire

galore [gə'lɔː*] *adv* en abondance, à gogo

Gambia *n*: **(The) ~** la Gambie

gambit ['gæmbɪt] *n (fig):* **(opening) ~** manœuvre *f* stratégique

gamble ['gæmbl] *n* pari *m*, risque calculé ♦ *vt, vi* jouer; **to ~ on** *(fig)* miser sur; **~r** *n* joueur *m*; **gambling** ['gæmblɪŋ] *n* jeu *m*

game [geɪm] *n* jeu *m*; *(match)* match *m*; *(strategy, scheme)* plan *m*; projet *m*; *(HUNTING)* gibier *m* ♦ *adj (willing):* **to be ~ (for)** être prêt(e) (à *or* pour); **big ~** gros gibier; **~keeper** *n* garde-chasse *m*

gammon ['gæmən] *n (bacon)* quartier *m* de lard fumé; *(ham)* jambon fumé

gamut ['gæmət] *n* gamme *f*

gang [gæŋ] *n* bande *f*; *(of workmen)* équipe *f*; **~ up** *vi*: **to ~ up on sb** se liguer contre qn; **~ster** ['gæŋstə*] *n* gangster *m*; **~way** *n* passerelle *f*; *(BRIT: of bus, plane)* couloir central; *(: in cinema)* allée centrale

gaol [dʒeɪl] *(BRIT) n* = **jail**

gap [gæp] *n* trou *m*; *(in time)* intervalle *m*; *(difference):* **~ between** écart *m* entre

gape [geɪp] *vi (person)* être *or* rester bouche bée; *(hole, shirt)* être ouvert(e); **gaping** ['geɪpɪŋ] *adj (hole)* béant(e)

garage ['gæraːʒ] *n* garage *m*

garbage ['gaːbɪdʒ] *n (US: rubbish)* ordures *fpl*, détritus *mpl*; *(inf: nonsense)* foutaises *fpl*; **~ can** *(US) n* poubelle *f*, boîte *f* à ordures

garbled ['gaːbld] *adj (account, message)* embrouillé(e)

garden ['gaːdn] *n* jardin *m*; **~s** *npl* jardin public; **~er** *n* jardinier *m*; **~ing** *n* jardinage *m*

gargle ['gaːgl] *vi* se gargariser

garish ['gɛərɪʃ] *adj* criard(e), voyant(e); *(light)* cru(e)

garland ['gaːlənd] *n* guirlande *f*; couronne *f*

garlic ['gaːlɪk] *n* ail *m*

garment ['gaːmənt] *n* vêtement *m*

garrison ['gærɪsən] *n* garnison *f*

garrulous ['gærʊləs] *adj* volubile, loquace

garter ['gɑːtə*] *n* jarretière *f*; (*US*) jarretelle *f*

gas [gæs] *n* gaz *m*; (*US: gasoline*) essence *f* ♦ *vt* asphyxier; ~ **cooker** (*BRIT*) *n* cuisinière *f* à gaz; ~ **cylinder** *n* bouteille *f* de gaz; ~ **fire** (*BRIT*) *n* radiateur *m* à gaz

gash [gæʃ] *n* entaille *f*; (*on face*) balafre *f*

gasket ['gæskɪt] *n* (*AUT*) joint *m* de culasse

gas mask *n* masque *m* à gaz

gas meter *n* compteur *m* à gaz

gasoline ['gæsəliːn] (*US*) *n* essence *f*

gasp [gɑːsp] *vi* haleter; ~ **out** *vt* (*say*) dire dans un souffle *or* d'une voix entrecoupée

gas station (*US*) *n* station-service *f*

gas tap *n* bouton *m* (de cuisinière à gaz); (*on pipe*) robinet *m* à gaz

gastric *adj* gastrique; ~ **flu** grippe *f* intestinale

gate [geɪt] *n* (*of garden*) portail *m*; (*of field*) barrière *f*; (*of building, at airport*) porte *f*; ~**crash** *vt* s'introduire sans invitation dans; ~**way** *n* porte *f*

gather ['gæðə*] *vt* (*flowers, fruit*) cueillir; (*pick up*) ramasser; (*assemble*) rassembler, réunir; recueillir; (*understand*) comprendre; (*SEWING*) froncer ♦ *vi* (*assemble*) se rassembler; **to ~ speed** prendre de la vitesse; ~**ing** *n* rassemblement *m*

gaudy ['gɔːdɪ] *adj* voyant(e)

gauge [geɪdʒ] *n* (*instrument*) jauge *f* ♦ *vt* jauger

gaunt [gɔːnt] *adj* (*thin*) décharné(e); (*grim, desolate*) désolé(e)

gauntlet ['gɔːntlɪt] *n* (*glove*) gant *m*; (*fig*): **to run the ~ through an angry crowd** se frayer un passage à travers une foule hostile; **to throw down the ~** jeter le gant

gauze [gɔːz] *n* gaze *f*

gave [geɪv] *pt of* **give**

gay [geɪ] *adj* (*homosexual*) homosexuel(le); (*cheerful*) gai(e), réjoui(e); (*colour etc*) gai, vif(vive)

gaze [geɪz] *n* regard *m* fixe ♦ *vi*: **to ~ at** fixer du regard

gazump (*BRIT*) *vi* revenir sur une promesse de vente (pour accepter une offre plus intéressante)

GB *abbr* = **Great Britain**

GCE *n abbr* (*BRIT*) = **General Certificate of Education**

GCSE *n abbr* (*BRIT*) = **General Certificate of Secondary Education**

gear [gɪə*] *n* matériel *m*, équipement *m*; attirail *m*; (*TECH*) engrenage *m*; (*AUT*) vitesse *f* ♦ *vt* (*fig: adapt*): **to ~ sth to** adapter qch à; **top** (*or US* **high**) ~ quatrième (*or* cinquième) vitesse; **low** ~ première vitesse; **in** ~ en prise; ~ **box** *n* boîte *f* de vitesses; ~ **lever** (*US* ~ **shift**) *n* levier *m* de vitesse

geese [giːs] *npl of* **goose**

gel [dʒel] *n* gel *m*

gelignite ['dʒelɪgnaɪt] *n* plastic *m*

gem [dʒem] *n* pierre précieuse

Gemini ['dʒemɪniː] *n* les Gémeaux *mpl*

gender ['dʒendə*] *n* genre *m*

general ['dʒenərəl] *n* général *m* ♦ *adj* général(e); **in** ~ en général; ~ **delivery** *n* poste restante; ~ **election** *n* élection(s) législative(s); ~**ly** *adv* généralement; ~ **practitioner** *n* généraliste *m/f*

generate ['dʒenəreɪt] *vt* engendrer; (*electricity etc*) produire

generation [dʒenə'reɪʃən] *n* génération *f*; (*of electricity etc*) production *f*

generator ['dʒenəreɪtə*] *n* générateur *m*

generosity [dʒenə'rɒsɪtɪ] *n* générosité *f*; **generous** ['dʒenərəs] *adj* généreux(euse); (*copious*) copieux(euse)

genetic [dʒɪ'netɪk] *adj*: ~ **engineering** ingénierie *f* génétique; ~ **fingerprinting** système *m* d'empreinte génétique

genetics [dʒɪ'netɪks] *n* génétique *f*

Geneva [dʒɪ'niːvə] *n* Genève

genial ['dʒiːnɪəl] *adj* cordial(e), chaleureux(euse)

genitals ['dʒenɪtlz] *npl* organes génitaux

genius ['dʒiːnɪəs] *n* génie *m*

genteel [dʒen'tiːl] *adj* de bon ton, distingué(e)

gentle ['dʒentl] *adj* doux(douce)

gentleman ['dʒentlmən] *n* monsieur *m*; (*well-bred man*) gentleman *m*

gently ['dʒentlɪ] *adv* doucement

gentry ['dʒentrɪ] *n inv*: **the ~** la petite noblesse

gents [dʒents] *n* W.-C. *mpl* (pour hommes)

genuine ['dʒenjuɪn] *adj* véritable, authentique; (*person*) sincère

geography [dʒɪ'ɒgrəfɪ] *n* géographie *f*

geology [dʒɪ'ɒlədʒɪ] *n* géologie *f*

geometric(al) [dʒɪə'metrɪk(l)] *adj* géométrique

geometry [dʒɪ'ɒmɪtrɪ] *n* géométrie *f*

geranium [dʒɪ'reɪnɪəm] *n* géranium *m*

geriatric [dʒerɪ'ætrɪk] *adj* gériatrique

germ [dʒɜːm] *n* (*MED*) microbe *m*

German ['dʒɜːmən] *adj* allemand(e) ♦ *n* Allemand(e); (*LING*) allemand *m*; **~ measles** (*BRIT*) *n* rubéole *f*

Germany ['dʒɜːmənɪ] *n* Allemagne *f*

gesture ['dʒestʃə*] *n* geste *m*

KEYWORD

get [get] (*pt, pp* got, *pp* gotten (*US*)) *vi*
1 (*become, be*) devenir; **to ~ old/tired** devenir vieux/fatigué, vieillir/se fatiguer; **to ~ drunk** s'enivrer; **to ~ killed** se faire tuer; **when do I ~ paid?** quand est-ce que je serai payé?; **it's ~ting late** il se fait tard

2 (*go*): **to ~ to/from** aller à/de; **to ~ home** rentrer chez soi; **how did you ~ here?** comment es-tu arrivé ici?

3 (*begin*) commencer *or* se mettre à; **I'm ~ting to like him** je commence à l'apprécier; **let's ~ going** *or* **started** allons-y

4 (*modal aux vb*): **you've got to do it** il faut que vous le fassiez; **I've got to tell the police** je dois le dire à la police

♦ *vt* **1**: **to ~ sth done** (*do*) faire qch; (*have done*) faire faire qch; **to ~ one's hair cut** se faire couper les cheveux; **to ~ sb to do sth** faire faire qch à qn; **to ~ sb drunk** enivrer qn

2 (*obtain: money, permission, results*) obtenir, avoir; (*find: job, flat*) trouver; (*fetch: person, doctor, object*) aller chercher; **to ~ sth for sb** procurer qch à qn; **~ me Mr Jones, please** (*on phone*)

passez-moi Mr Jones, s'il vous plaît; **can I ~ you a drink?** est-ce que je peux vous servir à boire?

3 (*receive: present, letter*) recevoir, avoir; (*acquire: reputation*) avoir; (: *prize*) obtenir; **what did you ~ for your birthday?** qu'est-ce que tu as eu pour ton anniversaire?

4 (*catch*) prendre, saisir, attraper; (*hit: target etc*) atteindre; **to ~ sb by the arm/throat** prendre *or* saisir *or* attraper qn par le bras/à la gorge; **~ him!** arrête-le!

5 (*take, move*) faire parvenir; **do you think we'll ~ it through the door?** on arrivera à le faire passer par la porte?; **I'll ~ you there somehow** je me débrouillerai pour t'y emmener

6 (*catch, take: plane, bus etc*) prendre

7 (*understand*) comprendre, saisir; (*hear*) entendre; **I've got it!** j'ai compris!; **I didn't ~ your name** je n'ai pas entendu votre nom

8 (*have, possess*): **to have got** avoir; **how many have you got?** vous en avez combien?

get about *vi* se déplacer; (*news*) se répandre

get along *vi* (*agree*) s'entendre; (*depart*) s'en aller; (*manage*) = **get by**

get at *vt fus* (*attack*) s'en prendre à; (*reach*) attraper, atteindre

get away *vi* partir, s'en aller, s'en aller; (*escape*) s'échapper

get away with *vt fus* en être quitte pour; se faire passer *or* pardonner

get back *vi* (*return*) rentrer ♦ *vt* récupérer, recouvrer

get by *vi* (*pass*) passer; (*manage*) se débrouiller

get down *vi, vt fus* descendre ♦ *vt* descendre; (*depress*) déprimer

get down to *vt fus* (*work*) se mettre à (faire)

get in *vi* rentrer; (*train*) arriver

get into *vt fus* entrer dans; (*car, train etc*) monter dans; (*clothes*) mettre, enfiler, endosser; **to get into bed/a rage** se mettre au lit/en colère

get off vi (from train etc) descendre; (depart: person, car) s'en aller; (escape) s'en tirer ♦ vt (remove: clothes, stain) enlever ♦ vt fus (train, bus) descendre de

get on vi (at exam etc) se débrouiller; (agree): **to get on (with)** s'entendre (avec) ♦ vt fus monter dans; (horse) monter sur

get out vi sortir; (of vehicle) descendre ♦ vt sortir

get out of vt fus sortir de; (duty etc) échapper à, se soustraire à

get over vt fus (illness) se remettre de

get round vt fus contourner; (fig: person) entortiller

get through vi (TEL) avoir la communication; **to get through to sb** atteindre qn

get together vi se réunir ♦ vt assembler

get up vi (rise) se lever ♦ vt fus monter

get up to vt fus (reach) arriver à; (prank etc) faire

getaway ['gɛtəweɪ] n: **to make one's ~** filer

geyser ['giːzə*] n (GEO) geyser m; (BRIT: water heater) chauffe-eau m inv

Ghana ['gɑːnə] n Ghana m

ghastly ['gɑːstlɪ] adj atroce, horrible; (pale) livide, blême

gherkin ['gɜːkɪn] n cornichon m

ghetto blaster ['gɛtəʊ-] n stéréo f portable

ghost [gəʊst] n fantôme m, revenant m

giant ['dʒaɪənt] n géant(e) ♦ adj géant(e), énorme

gibberish ['dʒɪbərɪʃ] n charabia m

giblets ['dʒɪblɪts] npl abats mpl

Gibraltar [dʒɪ'brɔːltə*] n Gibraltar

giddy ['gɪdɪ] adj (dizzy): **to be** or **feel ~** avoir le vertige

gift [gɪft] n cadeau m; (donation, ability) don m; **~ed** adj doué(e); **~ token** n chèque-cadeau m

gigantic [dʒaɪ'gæntɪk] adj gigantesque

giggle ['gɪgl] vi pouffer (de rire), rire sottement

gill [dʒɪl] n (measure) = 0.25 pints (BRIT = 0.15 l, US = 0.12 l)

gills [gɪlz] npl (of fish) ouïes fpl, branchies fpl

gilt [gɪlt] adj doré(e) ♦ n dorure f; **~-edged** adj (COMM) de premier ordre

gimmick ['gɪmɪk] n truc m

gin [dʒɪn] n (liquor) gin m

ginger ['dʒɪndʒə*] n gingembre m; **~ ale** n boisson gazeuse au gingembre; **~ beer** n = ginger ale; **~bread** n pain m d'épices

gingerly ['dʒɪndʒəlɪ] adv avec précaution

gipsy ['dʒɪpsɪ] n = gypsy

giraffe [dʒɪ'rɑːf] n girafe f

girder ['gɜːdə*] n poutrelle f

girdle ['gɜːdl] n (corset) gaine f

girl [gɜːl] n fille f, fillette f; (young unmarried woman) jeune fille; (daughter) fille; **an English ~** une jeune Anglaise; **~friend** n (of girl) amie f; (of boy) petite amie; **~ish** adj de jeune fille or de jeune fille; (for a boy) efféminé(e)

giro ['dʒaɪrəʊ] n (bank ~) virement m bancaire; (post office ~) mandat m; (BRIT: welfare cheque) mandat d'allocation chômage

girth [gɜːθ] n circonférence f; (of horse) sangle f

gist [dʒɪst] n essentiel m

give [gɪv] (pt gave, pp given) vt donner ♦ vi (break) céder; (stretch: fabric) se prêter; **to ~ sb sth, ~ sth to sb** donner qch à qn; **to ~ a cry/sigh** pousser un cri/un soupir; **~ away** vt donner; (~ free) faire cadeau de; (betray) donner, trahir; (disclose) révéler; (bride) conduire à l'autel; **~ back** vt rendre; **~ in** vi céder ♦ vt donner; **~ off** vt dégager; **~ out** vt distribuer; annoncer; **~ up** vi renoncer ♦ vt renoncer à; **to ~ up smoking** arrêter de fumer; **to ~ o.s. up** se rendre **~ way** (BRIT) vi céder; (AUT) céder la priorité

glacier ['glæsɪə*] n glacier m

glad [glæd] adj content(e); **~ly** adv volontiers

glamorous ['glæmərəs] adj (person) séduisant(e); (job) prestigieux(euse)

glamour ['glæmə*] *n* éclat *m*, prestige *m*

glance [glɑːns] *n* coup d'œil ♦ *vi*: **to ~ at** jeter un coup d'œil à; **~ off** *vt fus* (*bullet*) ricocher sur; **glancing** ['glɑːnsɪŋ] *adj* (*blow*) oblique

gland [glænd] *n* glande *f*

glare [gleə*] *n* (*of anger*) regard furieux; (*of light*) lumière éblouissante; (*of publicity*) feux *mpl* ♦ *vi* briller d'un éclat aveuglant; **to ~ at** lancer un regard furieux à; **glaring** ['gleərɪŋ] *adj* (*mistake*) criant(e), qui saute aux yeux

glass [glɑːs] *n* verre *m*; **~es** *npl* (*spectacles*) lunettes *fpl*; **~house** (*BRIT*) *n* (*for plants*) serre *f*; **~ware** *n* verrerie *f*

glaze [gleɪz] *vt* (*door, window*) vitrer; (*pottery*) vernir ♦ *n* (*on pottery*) vernis *m*; **~d** *adj* (*pottery*) verni(e); (*eyes*) vitreux(euse); **glazier** ['gleɪzɪə*] *n* vitrier *m*

gleam [gliːm] *vi* luire, briller

glean [gliːn] *vt* (*information*) glaner

glee [gliː] *n* joie *f*

glib [glɪb] *adj* (*person*) qui a du bagou; (*response*) désinvolte, facile

glide [glaɪd] *vi* glisser; (*AVIAT, birds*) planer; **~r** *n* (*AVIAT*) planeur *m*; **gliding** ['glaɪdɪŋ] *n* (*SPORT*) vol *m* à voile

glimmer ['glɪmə*] *n* lueur *f*

glimpse [glɪmps] *n* vision passagère, aperçu *m* ♦ *vt* entrevoir, apercevoir

glint [glɪnt] *vi* étinceler

glisten ['glɪsn] *vi* briller, luire

glitter ['glɪtə*] *vi* scintiller, briller

gloat [gləʊt] *vi*: **to ~ (over)** jubiler (à propos de)

global ['gləʊbl] *adj* mondial(e); **~ warming** réchauffement *m* de la planète

globe [gləʊb] *n* globe *m*

gloom [gluːm] *n* obscurité *f*; (*sadness*) tristesse *f*, mélancolie *f*; **~y** *adj* sombre, triste, lugubre

glorious ['glɔːrɪəs] *adj* glorieux(euse); splendide

glory ['glɔːrɪ] *n* gloire *f*; (*splendour*) splendeur *f*

gloss [glɒs] *n* (*shine*) brillant *m*, vernis *m*; (*also*: **~ paint**) peinture brillante *or* laquée; **~ over** *vt fus* glisser sur

glossary ['glɒsərɪ] *n* glossaire *m*

glossy ['glɒsɪ] *adj* brillant(e); **~ maga-zine** magazine *m* de luxe

glove [glʌv] *n* gant *m*; **~ compartment** *n* (*AUT*) boîte *f* à gants, vide-poches *m inv*

glow [gləʊ] *vi* rougeoyer; (*face*) rayonner; (*eyes*) briller

glower ['glaʊə*] *vi*: **to ~ (at)** lancer des regards mauvais (à)

glucose ['gluːkəʊz] *n* glucose *m*

glue [gluː] *n* colle *f* ♦ *vt* coller

glum [glʌm] *adj* sombre, morne

glut [glʌt] *n* surabondance *f*

glutton ['glʌtn] *n* glouton(ne); **a ~ for work** un bourreau de travail; **a ~ for punishment** un masochiste (*fig*)

gnarled [nɑːld] *adj* noueux(euse)

gnat [næt] *n* moucheron *m*

gnaw [nɔː] *vt* ronger

go [gəʊ] (*pt* **went**, *pp* **gone**; *pl* **~es**) *vi* aller; (*depart*) partir, s'en aller; (*work*) marcher; (*be sold*): **to ~ for £10** se vendre 10 livres; (*fit, suit*): **to ~ with** aller avec; (*become*): **to ~ pale/mouldy** pâlir/moisir; (*break etc*) céder ♦ *n*: **to have a ~ (at)** essayer (de faire); **to be on the ~** être en mouvement; **whose ~ is it?** à qui est-ce de jouer?; **he's ~ing to do** il va faire, il est sur le point de faire; **to ~ for a walk** aller se promener; **to ~ dancing** aller danser; **how did it ~?** comment est-ce que ça s'est passé?; **to ~ round the back/by the shop** passer par derrière/devant le magasin; **~ about** *vi* (*rumour*) se répandre ♦ *vt fus*: **how do I ~ about this?** comment dois-je m'y prendre (pour faire ceci)?; **~ ahead** *vi* (*make progress*) avancer; (*get going*) y aller; **~ along** *vi* aller, avancer ♦ *vt fus* longer, parcourir; **~ away** *vi* partir, s'en aller; **~ back** *vi* rentrer; revenir; (*go again*) retourner; **~ back on** *vt fus* (*promise*) revenir sur; **~ by** *vi* (*years, time*) passer, s'écouler ♦ *vt fus* s'en tenir à; en croire; **~ down** *vi* descendre; (*ship*) couler; (*sun*) se coucher ♦ *vt fus* descendre; **~ for** *vt fus* (*fetch*) aller chercher; (*like*) aimer; (*attack*) s'en prendre à, attaquer; **~ in** *vi* entrer; **~ in for** *vt fus* (*competition*) se présenter à; (*like*) aimer; **~ into** *vt fus* entrer dans; (*investigate*) étudier, examiner; (*embark on*) se lancer dans; **~ off** *vi* partir, s'en aller; (*food*) se gâter; (*explode*) sauter; (*event*) se dérouler ♦ *vt fus* ne plus aimer; **the gun went off** le coup est parti; **~ on** *vi* continuer; (*happen*) se passer; **to ~ on doing** continuer à faire; **~ out** *vi* sortir; (*fire, light*) s'éteindre; **~ over** *vt fus* (*check*) revoir, vérifier; **~ through** *vt fus* (*town etc*) traverser; **~ up** *vi* monter; (*price*) augmenter ♦ *vt fus* gravir; **~ without** *vt fus* se passer de

goad [gəʊd] *vt* aiguillonner

go-ahead ['gəʊəhed] *adj* dynamique, entreprenant(e) ♦ *n* feu vert

goal [gəʊl] *n* but *m*; **~keeper** *n* gardien *m* de but; **~post** *n* poteau *m* de but

goat [gəʊt] *n* chèvre *f*

gobble ['gɒbl] *vt* (*also:* ~ **down**, ~ **up**) engloutir

go-between ['gəʊ-] *n* intermédiaire *m/f*

god [gɒd] *n* dieu *m*; **G~** *n* Dieu *m*; **~child** *n* filleul(e); **~daughter** *n* filleule *f*; **~dess** *n* déesse *f*; **~father** *n* parrain *m*; **~forsaken** *adj* maudit(e); **~mother** *n* marraine *f*; **~send** *n* aubaine *f*; **~son** *n* filleul *m*

goggles ['gɒglz] *npl* (*for skiing etc*) lunettes protectrices

going ['gəʊɪŋ] *n* (*conditions*) état *m* du terrain ♦ *adj*: **the ~ rate** le tarif (en vigueur)

gold [gəʊld] *n* or *m* ♦ *adj* en or; (*reserves*) d'or; **~en** *adj* (*made of gold*) en or; (*gold in colour*) doré(e); **~fish** *n* poisson *m* rouge; **~-plated** *adj* plaqué(e or *inv*); **~smith** *n* orfèvre *m*

golf [gɒlf] *n* golf *m*; **~ ball** *n* balle *f* de golf; (*on typewriter*) boule *m*; **~ club** *n* club *m* de golf; (*stick*) club *m*, crosse *f* de golf; **~ course** *n* (terrain *m* de) golf *m*; **~er** *n* joueur(euse) de golf

gone [gɒn] *pp of* **go**

gong [gɒŋ] *n* gong *m*

good [gʊd] *adj* bon(ne); (*kind*) gentil(le); (*child*) sage ♦ *n* bien *m*; **~s** *npl* (COMM) marchandises *fpl*, articles *mpl*; **~!** bon!, très bien!; **to be ~ at** être bon en; **to be ~ for** être bon pour; **would you be ~ enough to ...?** auriez-vous la bonté *or* l'amabilité de ...?; **a ~ deal (of)** beaucoup (de); **a ~ many** beaucoup (de); **to make ~** *vi* (*succeed*) faire son chemin, réussir ♦ *vt* (*deficit*) combler; (*losses*) compenser; **it's no ~ complaining** cela ne sert à rien de se plaindre; **for ~** pour de bon, une fois pour toutes; **~ morning/afternoon!** bonjour!; **~ evening!** bonsoir!; **~ night!** bonsoir!; (*on going to bed*) bonne nuit!; **~bye** *excl* au revoir!; **G~ Friday** *n* Vendredi saint; **~-looking** *adj* beau(belle), bien *inv*; **~-natured** *adj* (*person*) qui a un bon naturel; **~ness** *n* (*of person*) bonté *f*; **for ~ness sake!** je vous en prie!; **~ness gracious!** mon Dieu!; **~s train** (BRIT) *n* train *m* de marchandises; **~will** *n* bonne volonté

goose [guːs] (*pl* **geese**) *n* oie *f*

gooseberry ['gʊzbəri] *n* groseille *f* à maquereau; **to play ~** (BRIT) tenir la chandelle

gooseflesh ['guːsfleʃ] *n*, **goose pimples** *npl* chair *f* de poule

gore [gɔː*] *vt* encorner ♦ *n* sang *m*

gorge [gɔːdʒ] *n* gorge *f* ♦ *vt*: **to ~ o.s. (on)** se gorger (de)

gorgeous ['gɔːdʒəs] *adj* splendide, superbe

gorilla [gə'rɪlə] *n* gorille *m*

gorse [gɔːs] *n* ajoncs *mpl*

gory ['gɔːri] *adj* sanglant(e); (*details*) horrible

go-slow ['gəʊ'sləʊ] (BRIT) *n* grève perlée

gospel ['gɒspəl] *n* évangile *m*

gossip ['gɒsɪp] *n* (*chat*) bavardages *mpl*; commérage *m*, cancans *mpl*; (*person*) commère *f* ♦ *vi* bavarder; (*maliciously*) cancaner, faire des commérages

got [gɒt] *pt, pp of* **get**

gotten ['gɒtn] (US) *pp of* **get**

gout [gaʊt] *n* goutte *f*

govern ['gʌvən] *vt* gouverner; **~ess** ['gʌvənɪs] *n* gouvernante *f*; **~ment**

['gʌvnmənt] n gouvernement m; (BRIT: *ministers*) ministère m; (*of state, bank*) gouverneur m; (*of school, hospital*) ≈ membre m/f du conseil d'établissement; (BRIT: *of prison*) directeur(trice)

gown [gaʊn] n robe f; (*of teacher*, BRIT: *of judge*) toge f

GP n abbr = **general practitioner**

grab [græb] vt saisir, empoigner ♦ vi: to ~ at essayer de saisir

grace [greɪs] n grâce f ♦ vt honorer; (*adorn*) orner; **5 days' ~** cinq jours de répit; **~ful** adj gracieux(euse), élégant(e); **gracious** ['greɪʃəs] adj bienveillant(e)

grade [greɪd] n (COMM) qualité; f (*in hierarchy*) catégorie f, grade m, échelon m; (SCOL) note f; (US: *school class*) classe f ♦ vt classer; **~ crossing** (US) n passage m à niveau; **~ school** (US) n école f primaire

gradient ['greɪdɪənt] n inclinaison f, pente f

gradual ['grædjʊəl] adj graduel(le), progressif(ive); **~ly** adv peu à peu, graduellement

graduate [n 'grædjʊɪt, vb 'grædjʊeɪt] n diplômé(e), licencié(e); (US: *of high school*) bachelier(ère) ♦ vi obtenir son diplôme; (US) obtenir son baccalauréat; **graduation** [grædʊ'eɪʃən] n (cérémonie f de) remise f des diplômes

graffiti [grə'fiːtɪ] npl graffiti mpl

graft [grɑːft] n (AGR, MED) greffe f; (*bribery*) corruption f ♦ vt greffer; **hard ~** (BRIT: inf) boulot acharné

grain [greɪn] n grain m

gram [græm] n gramme m

grammar ['græmə*] n grammaire f; **~ school** (BRIT) n ≈ lycée m; **grammatical** [grə'mætɪkl] adj grammatical(e)

gramme [græm] n = **gram**

grand [grænd] adj magnifique, splendide; (*gesture etc*) noble; **~children** npl petits-enfants mpl; **~dad** (inf) n grand-papa m; **~daughter** n petite-fille f; **~father** n grand-père m; **~ma** (inf) n grand-maman f; **~mother** n grand-mère f; **~pa** (inf) n = **~dad**; **~parents** npl grands-parents

mpl; **~ piano** n piano m à queue; **~son** n petit-fils m; **~stand** n (SPORT) tribune f

granite ['grænɪt] n granit m

granny ['grænɪ] (inf) n grand-maman f

grant [grɑːnt] vt accorder; (*admit*) concéder ♦ n (SCOL) bourse f; (ADMIN) subside m, subvention f; **to take it for ~ed that** trouver tout naturel que +*sub*; **to take sb for ~ed** considérer qn comme faisant partie du décor

granulated sugar ['grænjʊleɪtɪd-] n sucre m en poudre

grape [greɪp] n raisin m; **~fruit** ['greɪpfruːt] n pamplemousse m

graph [grɑːf] n graphique m; **~ic** ['græfɪk] adj graphique; (*account, description*) vivant(e); **~ics** n arts mpl graphiques; graphisme m ♦ npl représentations fpl graphiques

grapple ['græpl] vi: to ~ with être aux prises avec

grasp [grɑːsp] vt saisir ♦ n (*grip*) prise f; (*understanding*) compréhension f, connaissance f; **~ing** adj cupide

grass [grɑːs] n herbe f; (*lawn*) gazon m; **~hopper** n sauterelle f; **~-roots** adj de la base, du peuple

grate [greɪt] n grille f de cheminée ♦ vi grincer ♦ vt (CULIN) râper

grateful ['greɪtfʊl] adj reconnaissant(e)

grater ['greɪtə*] n râpe f

gratifying ['grætɪfaɪŋ] adj agréable

grating ['greɪtɪŋ] n (*iron bars*) grille f ♦ adj (*noise*) grinçant(e)

gratitude ['grætɪtjuːd] n gratitude f

gratuity [grə'tjuːɪtɪ] n pourboire m

grave [greɪv] n tombe f ♦ adj grave, sérieux(euse)

gravel ['grævəl] n gravier m

gravestone ['greɪvstəʊn] n pierre tombale

graveyard ['greɪvjɑːd] n cimetière m

gravity ['grævɪtɪ] n (PHYSICS) gravité f; pesanteur f; (*seriousness*) gravité

gravy ['greɪvɪ] n jus m (de viande); sauce f

gray [greɪ] (US) adj = **grey**

graze [greɪz] vi paître, brouter ♦ vt

(*touch lightly*) frôler, effleurer; (*scrape*) écorcher ♦ *n* écorchure *f*

grease [griːs] *n* (*fat*) graisse *f*; (*lubricant*) lubrifiant *m* ♦ *vt* graisser; lubrifier; **~proof paper** (*BRIT*) *n* papier sulfurisé; **greasy** ['griːsɪ] *adj* gras(se), graisseux(euse)

great [greɪt] *adj* grand(e); (*inf*) formidable; **G~ Britain** *n* Grande-Bretagne *f*; **~grandfather** *n* arrière-grand-père *m*; **~grandmother** *n* arrière-grand-mère *f*; **~ly** *adv* très, grandement; (*with verbs*) beaucoup; **~ness** *n* grandeur *f*

Greece [griːs] *n* Grèce *f*

greed [griːd] *n* (*also:* **~iness**) avidité *f*; (*for food*) gourmandise *f*, gloutonnerie *f*; **~y** *adj* avide; gourmand(e), glouton(ne)

Greek [griːk] *adj* grec(grecque) ♦ *n* Grec(Grecque) *f*; (*LING*) grec *m*

green [griːn] *adj* vert(e); (*inexperienced*) (bien) jeune, naïf(naïve); (*POL*) vert(e), écologiste; (*ecological*) écologique ♦ *n* vert *m*; (*stretch of grass*) pelouse *f*; **~s** *npl* (*vegetables*) légumes verts; (*POL*): **the G~s** les Verts *mpl*; **the G~ Party** (*BRIT: POL*) le parti écologiste; **~ belt** *n* (*round town*) ceinture verte; **~ card** *n* (*AUT*) carte verte; (*US*) permis *m* de travail; **~ery** *n* verdure *f*; **~grocer** (*BRIT*) *n* marchand *m* de fruits et légumes; **~house** *n* serre *f*; **~house effect** *n* effet *m* de serre; **~house gas** *n* gas *m* à effet de serre; **~ish** *adj* verdâtre

Greenland ['griːnlənd] *n* Groenland *m*

greet [griːt] *vt* accueillir; **~ing** *n* salutation *f*; **~ing(s) card** *n* carte *f* de vœux

gregarious [grɪ'gɛərɪəs] *adj* (*person*) sociable

grenade [grɪ'neɪd] *n* grenade *f*

grew [gruː] *pt of* **grow**

grey [greɪ] (*US* **gray**) *adj* gris(e); (*dismal*) sombre; **~-haired** *adj* grisonnant(e); **~hound** *n* lévrier *m*

grid [grɪd] *n* grille *f*; (*ELEC*) réseau *m*; **~lock** *n* (*traffic jam*) embouteillage *m*

grief [griːf] *n* chagrin *m*, douleur *f*

grievance ['griːvəns] *n* doléance *f*, grief *m*

grieve [griːv] *vi* avoir du chagrin; se désoler ♦ *vt* faire de la peine à, affliger; **to ~ for sb** (*dead person*) pleurer qn

grievous ['griːvəs] *adj* (*LAW*): **~ bodily harm** coups *mpl* et blessures *fpl*

grill [grɪl] *n* (*on cooker*) gril *m*; (*food: also mixed ~*) grillade(s) *f(pl)* ♦ *vt* (*BRIT*) griller; (*inf: question*) cuisiner

grille [grɪl] *n* grille *f*, grillage *m*; (*AUT*) calandre *f*

grim [grɪm] *adj* sinistre, lugubre; (*serious, stern*) sévère

grimace [grɪ'meɪs] *n* grimace *f* ♦ *vi* grimacer, faire une grimace

grime [graɪm] *n* crasse *f*, saleté *f*

grin [grɪn] *n* large sourire *m* ♦ *vi* sourire

grind [graɪnd] (*pt, pp* **ground**) *vt* écraser; (*coffee, pepper etc*) moudre; (*US meat*) hacher; (*make sharp*) aiguiser ♦ *n* (*work*) corvée *f*

grip [grɪp] *n* (*hold*) prise *f*, étreinte *f*; (*control*) emprise *f*; (*grasp*) connaissance *f*; (*handle*) poignée *f*; (*holdall*) sac *m* de voyage ♦ *vt* saisir, empoigner; **to come to ~s with** en venir aux prises avec; **~ping** *adj* prenant(e), palpitant(e)

grisly ['grɪzlɪ] *adj* sinistre, macabre

gristle ['grɪsl] *n* cartilage *m*

grit [grɪt] *n* gravillon *m*; (*courage*) cran *m* ♦ *vt* (*road*) sabler; **to ~ one's teeth** serrer les dents

groan [grəʊn] *n* (*of pain*) gémissement *m* ♦ *vi* gémir

grocer ['grəʊsə*] *n* épicier *m*; **~ies** *npl* provisions *fpl*; **~'s (shop)** *n* épicerie *f*

groin [grɔɪn] *n* aine *f*

groom [gruːm] *n* palefrenier *m*; (*also: bride~*) marié *m* ♦ *vt* (*horse*) panser; (*fig*): **to ~ sb for** former qn pour; **well groomed** très soigné(e)

groove [gruːv] *n* rainure *f*

grope [grəʊp] *vi*: **to ~ for** chercher à tâtons

gross [grəʊs] *adj* grossier(ère); (*COMM*) brut(e); **~ly** *adv* (*greatly*) très, grandement

grotto ['grɒtəʊ] *n* grotte *f*

grotty ['grɒtɪ] (*inf*) *adj* minable, affreux(euse)

ground [graʊnd] *pt, pp of* **grind** ♦ *n* so

m, terre *f*; (*land*) terrain *m*, terres *fpl*; (SPORT) terrain; (US: *also*: ~ *wire*) terre; (*reason: gen pl*) raison *f* ♦ *vt* (*plane*) empêcher de décoller, retenir au sol; (US: ELEC) équiper d'une prise de terre; ~s *npl* (*of coffee etc*) marc *m*; (*gardens etc*) parc *m*, domaine *m*; **on the** ~, **to the** ~ par terre; **to gain/lose** ~ gagner/perdre du terrain; ~ **cloth** (US) *n* = **ground-sheet**; ~**ing** *n* (*in education*) connaissances *fpl* de base; ~**less** *adj* sans fondement; ~**sheet** (BRIT) *n* tapis *m* de sol; ~ **staff** *n* personnel *m* au sol; ~**swell** *n* lame *f* *or* vague *f* de fond; ~**work** *n* préparation *f*

group [gru:p] *n* groupe *m* ♦ *vt* (*also*: ~ *together*) grouper ♦ *vi* se grouper

grouse [graʊs] *n inv* (*bird*) grouse *f* ♦ *vi* (*complain*) rouspéter, râler

grove [grəʊv] *n* bosquet *m*

grovel ['grɒvl] *vi* (*fig*) ramper

grow [grəʊ] (*pt* grew, *pp* grown) *vi* pousser, croître; (*person*) grandir; (*increase*) augmenter, se développer; (*become*): **to** ~ **rich/weak** s'enrichir/ s'affaiblir; (*develop*): **he's** ~**n out of his jacket** sa veste est (devenue) trop petite pour lui; **he'll** ~ **out of it!** ça lui passera! ♦ *vt* cultiver, faire pousser; (*beard*) laisser pousser; ~ **up** *vi* grandir; ~**er** *n* producteur *m*; ~**ing** *adj* (*fear, amount*) croissant(e), grandissant(e)

growl [graʊl] *vi* grogner

grown [grəʊn] *pp of* **grow**; ~-**up** *n* adulte *m/f*, grande personne

growth [grəʊθ] *n* croissance *f*, développement *m*; (*what has grown*) pousse *f*; poussée *f*; (MED) grosseur *f*, tumeur *f*

grub [grʌb] *n* larve *f*; (*inf: food*) bouffe *f*

grubby ['grʌbi] *adj* crasseux(euse)

grudge [grʌdʒ] *n* rancune *f* ♦ *vt*: **to** ~ **sb sth** (*in giving*) donner qch à qn à contre-cœur; (*resent*) reprocher qch à qn; **to bear sb a** ~ (**for**) garder rancune *or* en vouloir à qn (de)

gruelling ['grʊəlɪŋ] (US **grueling**) *adj* exténuant(e)

gruesome ['gru:səm] *adj* horrible

gruff [grʌf] *adj* bourru(e)

grumble ['grʌmbl] *vi* rouspéter, ronchonner

grumpy ['grʌmpi] *adj* grincheux(euse)

grunt [grʌnt] *vi* grogner

G-string ['dʒi:-] *n* (*garment*) cache-sexe *m inv*

guarantee [gærən'ti:] *n* garantie *f* ♦ *vt* garantir

guard [gɑ:d] *n* garde *f*; (*one man*) garde *m*; (BRIT: RAIL) chef *m* de train; (*on machine*) dispositif *m* de sûreté; (*also*: *fire*~) garde-feu *m* ♦ *vt* garder, surveiller; (*protect*): **to** ~ (**against** *or* **from**) protéger (contre); ~ **against** *vt* (*prevent*) empêcher, se protéger de; ~**ed** *adj* (*fig*) prudent(e); ~**ian** *n* gardien(ne); (*of minor*) tuteur(trice); ~'**s van** (BRIT) *n* (RAIL) fourgon *m*

guerrilla [gə'rɪlə] *n* guérillero *m*

guess [ges] *vt* deviner; (*estimate*) évaluer; (US) croire, penser ♦ *vi* deviner ♦ *n* supposition *f*, hypothèse *f*; **to take** *or* **have a** ~ essayer de deviner; ~**work** *n* hypothèse *f*

guest [gest] *n* invité(e); (*in hotel*) client(e); ~-**house** *n* pension *f*; ~ **room** *n* chambre *f* d'amis

guffaw [gʌ'fɔ:] *vi* pouffer de rire

guidance ['gaɪdəns] *n* conseils *mpl*

guide [gaɪd] *n* (*person, book etc*) guide *m*; (BRIT: *also*: *girl* ~) guide *f* ♦ *vt* guider; ~**book** *n* guide *m*; ~ **dog** *n* chien *m* d'aveugle; ~**lines** *npl* (*fig*) instructions (générales), conseils *mpl*

guild [gɪld] *n* corporation *f*; cercle *m*, association *f*

guile [gaɪl] *n* astuce *f*

guillotine ['gɪlə'ti:n] *n* guillotine *f*

guilt [gɪlt] *n* culpabilité *f*; ~**y** *adj* coupable

guinea pig ['gɪnɪ-] *n* cobaye *m*

guise [gaɪz] *n* aspect *m*, apparence *f*

guitar [gɪ'tɑ:*] *n* guitare *f*

gulf [gʌlf] *n* golfe *m*; (*abyss*) gouffre *m*

gull [gʌl] *n* mouette *f*; (*larger*) goéland *m*

gullet ['gʌlɪt] *n* gosier *m*

gullible ['gʌlɪbl] *adj* crédule

gully ['gʌlɪ] *n* ravin *m*; ravine *f*; couloir

m

gulp [gʌlp] *vi* avaler sa salive ♦ *vt* (*also*: ~ *down*) avaler

gum [gʌm] *n* (*ANAT*) gencive *f*; (*glue*) colle *f*; (*sweet: also* ~*drop*) boule *f* de gomme; (*also: chewing* ~) chewing-gum *m* ♦ *vt* coller; ~**boots** (*BRIT*) *npl* bottes *fpl* en caoutchouc

gun [gʌn] *n* (*small*) revolver *m*, pistolet *m*; (*rifle*) fusil *m*, carabine *f*; (*cannon*) canon *m*; ~**boat** *n* canonnière *f*; ~**fire** *n* fusillade *f*; ~**man** *n* bandit armé; ~**point** *n*: **at** ~**point** sous la menace du pistolet (*or* fusil); ~**powder** *n* poudre *f* à canon; ~**shot** *n* coup *m* de feu

gurgle [ˈgɜːgl] *vi* gargouiller; (*baby*) gazouiller

gush [gʌʃ] *vi* jaillir; (*fig*) se répandre en effusions

gust [gʌst] *n* (*of wind*) rafale *f*; (*of smoke*) bouffée *f*

gusto [ˈgʌstəʊ] *n* enthousiasme *m*

gut [gʌt] *n* intestin *m*, boyau *m*; ~**s** *npl* (*inf: courage*) cran *m*

gutter [ˈgʌtə*] *n* (*in street*) caniveau *m*; (*of roof*) gouttière *f*

guy [gaɪ] *n* (*inf: man*) type *m*; (*also*: ~*rope*) corde *f*; (*BRIT: figure*) effigie de Guy Fawkes (*brûlée en plein air le 5 novembre*)

guzzle [ˈgʌzl] *vt* avaler gloutonnement

gym [dʒɪm] *n* (*also*: ~*nasium*) gymnase *m*; (*also*: ~*nastics*) gym *f*; ~**nast** [ˈdʒɪmnæst] *n* gymnaste *m/f*; ~**nastics** [dʒɪmˈnæstɪks] *n*, *npl* gymnastique *f*; ~ **shoes** *npl* chaussures *fpl* de gym; ~**slip** (*BRIT*) *n* tunique *f* (d'écolière)

gynaecologist [gaɪnɪˈkɒlədʒɪst] (*US* **gynecologist**) *n* gynécologue *m/f*

gypsy [ˈdʒɪpsɪ] *n* gitan(e), bohémien(ne)

H h

haberdashery [hæbəˈdæʃərɪ] (*BRIT*) *n* mercerie *f*

habit [ˈhæbɪt] *n* habitude *f*; (*REL: costume*) habit *m*

habitual [həˈbɪtjʊəl] *adj* habituel(le);

(*drinker, liar*) invétéré(e)

hack [hæk] *vt* hacher, tailler ♦ *n* (*pej: writer*) nègre *m*; ~**er** *n* (*COMPUT*) pirate *m* (informatique); (: *enthusiast*) passionné(e) *m/f* des ordinateurs

hackneyed [ˈhæknɪd] *adj* usé(e), rebattu(e)

had [hæd] *pt, pp of* **have**

haddock [ˈhædək] (*pl* ~ *or* ~**s**) *n* églefin *m*; **smoked** ~ haddock *m*

hadn't [ˈhædnt] = **had not**

haemorrhage [ˈhemərɪdʒ] (*US* **hemorrhage**) *n* hémorragie *f*

haemorrhoids [ˈhemərɔɪdz] (*US* **hemorrhoids**) *npl* hémorroïdes *fpl*

haggle [ˈhægl] *vi* marchander

Hague [heɪg] *n*: **The** ~ La Haye

hail [heɪl] *n* grêle *f* ♦ *vt* (*call*) héler; (*acclaim*) acclamer ♦ *vi* grêler; ~**stone** *n* grêlon *m*

hair [heə*] *n* cheveux *mpl*; (*of animal*) pelage *m*; (*single hair: on head*) cheveu *m*; (: *on body; of animal*) poil *m*; **to do one's** ~ se coiffer; ~**brush** *n* brosse *f* à cheveux; ~**cut** *n* coupe *f* (de cheveux); ~**do** *n* coiffure *f*; ~**dresser** *n* coiffeur(euse); ~**dresser's** *n* salon *m* de coiffure, coiffeur *m*; ~ **dryer** *n* sèche-cheveux *m*; ~**grip** *n* pince *f* à cheveux; ~**net** *n* filet *m* à cheveux; ~**piece** *n* perruque *f*; ~**pin** *n* épingle *f* à cheveux; ~**pin bend** (*US* ~**pin curve**) *n* virage *m* en épingle à cheveux; ~**raising** *adj* à (vous) faire dresser les cheveux sur la tête; ~ **removing cream** *n* crème *f* dépilatoire; ~**spray** *n* laque *f* (pour les cheveux); ~**style** *n* coiffure *f*; ~**y** *adj* poilu(e); (*inf: fig*) effrayant(e)

hake [heɪk] (*pl* ~ *or* ~**s**) *n* colin *m*, merlu *m*

half [hɑːf] (*pl* **halves**) *n* moitié *f*; (*of beer: also*: ~ *pint*) ≈ demi *m*; (*RAIL, bus also*: ~ *fare*) demi-tarif *m* ♦ *adj* demi ♦ *adv* (à) moitié, à demi; ~ **a dozen** demi-douzaine; ~ **a pound** une demi-livre, ≈ 250 g; **two and a** ~ deux et demi; **to cut sth in** ~ couper qch en deux; ~**baked** *adj* (*plan*) qui ne tient pas debout; ~**caste** *n* métis(se); ~

hearted adj tiède, sans enthousiasme; **~-hour** n demi-heure f; **~-mast**: at **~-mast** adv (flag) en berne; **~penny** ['heipni] (BRIT) n demi-penny m; **~-price** adj, adv: (at) **~-price** à moitié prix; **~ term** (BRIT) n (SCOL) congé m de demi-trimestre; **~-time** n mi-temps f; **~way** adv à mi-chemin

hall [hɔːl] n salle f; (entrance way) hall m, entrée f

hallmark ['hɔːlmɑːk] n poinçon m; (fig) marque f

hallo [hʌˈləu] excl = **hello**

hall of residence (BRIT: pl **halls of residence**) n résidence f universitaire

Hallowe'en ['hæləuˈiːn] n veille f de la Toussaint

hallucination [həluːsɪˈneɪʃən] n hallucination f

hallway ['hɔːlweɪ] n vestibule m

halo ['heɪləu] n (of saint etc) auréole f

halt [hɔːlt] n halte f, arrêt m ♦ vt (progress etc) interrompre ♦ vi faire halte, s'arrêter

halve [hɑːv] vt (apple etc) partager or diviser en deux; (expense) réduire de moitié; **~s** [hɑːvz] npl of **half**

ham [hæm] n jambon m

hamburger ['hæmbɜːgə*] n hamburger m

hamlet ['hæmlɪt] n hameau m

hammer ['hæmə*] n marteau m ♦ vt (nail) enfoncer; (fig) démolir ♦ vi (on door) frapper à coups redoublés; **to ~ an idea into sb** faire entrer de force une idée dans la tête de qn

hammock ['hæmək] n hamac m

hamper ['hæmpə*] vt gêner ♦ n panier m (d'osier)

hamster ['hæmstə*] n hamster m

hand [hænd] n main f; (of clock) aiguille f; (handwriting) écriture f; (worker) ouvrier(ère); (at cards) jeu m ♦ vt passer, donner; **to give** or **lend sb a ~** donner un coup de main à qn; **at ~** à portée de la main; **in ~** (time) à disposition; (job, situation) en main; **to be on ~** (person) être disponible; (emergency services) se tenir prêt(e) (à intervenir); **to ~** (information etc) sous la main, à portée de la main; **on the one ~ ..., on the other ~** d'une part ..., d'autre part; **~ in** vt remettre; **~ out** vt distribuer; **~ over** vt transmettre; céder; **~bag** n sac m à main; **~book** n manuel m; **~brake** n frein m à main; **~cuffs** npl menottes fpl; **~ful** n poignée f

handicap ['hændɪkæp] n handicap m ♦ vt handicaper; **mentally/physically ~ped** handicapé(e) mentalement/physiquement

handicraft ['hændɪkrɑːft] n (travail m d')artisanat m, technique artisanale; (object) objet artisanal

handiwork ['hændɪwɜːk] n ouvrage m

handkerchief ['hæŋkətʃɪf] n mouchoir m

handle ['hændl] n (of door etc) poignée f; (of cup etc) anse f; (of knife etc) manche m; (of saucepan) queue f; (for winding) manivelle f ♦ vt toucher, manier; (deal with) s'occuper de; (treat: people) prendre; "**~ with care**" "fragile"; **to fly off the ~** s'énerver; **~bar(s)** n(pl) guidon m

hand: **~-luggage** n bagages mpl à main; **~made** adj fait(e) à la main; **~out** n (from government, parents) aide f, don m; (leaflet) documentation f, prospectus m; (summary of lecture) polycopié m; **~rail** n rampe f, main courante; **~shake** n poignée f de main

handsome ['hænsəm] adj beau (belle); (profit, return) considérable

handwriting ['hændraɪtɪŋ] n écriture f

handy ['hændɪ] adj (person) adroit(e); (close at hand) sous la main; (convenient) pratique; **~man** ['hændɪmæn] (irreg) n bricoleur m; (servant) homme m à tout faire

hang [hæŋ] (pt, pp **hung**) vt accrocher; (criminal: pt, pp: **hanged**) pendre ♦ vi pendre; (hair, drapery) tomber; **to get the ~ of (doing) sth** (inf) attraper le coup pour faire qch; **~ about** vi traîner; **~ around** vi = **hang about**; **~ on** vi (wait) attendre; **~ up** vi (TEL): **to ~ up (on sb)** raccrocher (au nez de qn) ♦ vt (coat, painting etc) accrocher, suspendre

hangar ['hæŋə*] *n* hangar *m*

hanger ['hæŋə*] *n* cintre *m*, portemanteau *m*; **~on** ['hæŋər'ɒn] *n* parasite *m*

hang: **~-gliding** ['hæŋglaidɪŋ] *n* deltaplane *m*, vol *m* libre; **~over** ['hæŋəʊvə*] *n* (*after drinking*) gueule *f* de bois; **~-up** ['hæŋʌp] *n* complexe *m*

hanker ['hæŋkə*] *vi*: **to ~ after** avoir envie de

hankie, hanky ['hæŋkɪ] *n abbr* = **handkerchief**

haphazard ['hæp'hæzəd] *adj* fait(e) au hasard, fait(e) au petit bonheur

happen ['hæpən] *vi* arriver; se passer, se produire; **it so ~s that** il se trouve que; **as it ~s** justement; **~ing** *n* événement *m*

happily ['hæpɪlɪ] *adv* heureusement; (*cheerfully*) joyeusement

happiness ['hæpɪnɪs] *n* bonheur *m*

happy ['hæpɪ] *adj* heureux(euse); **~ with** (*arrangements etc*) satisfait(e) de; **to be ~ to do** faire volontiers; **~ birthday!** bon anniversaire!; **~-go-lucky** *adj* insouciant(e)

harass ['hærəs] *vt* accabler, tourmenter; **~ment** *n* tracasseries *fpl*

harbour ['hɑ:bə*] (*US* **harbor**) *n* port *m* ♦ *vt* héberger, abriter; (*hope, fear etc*) entretenir

hard [hɑ:d] *adj* dur(e); (*question, problem*) difficile, dur(e); (*facts, evidence*) concret(ète) ♦ *adv* (*work*) dur; (*think, try*) sérieusement; **to look ~ at** regarder fixement; (*thing*) regarder de près; **no ~ feelings!** sans rancune!; **to be ~ of hearing** être dur(e) d'oreille; **to be ~ done by** être traité(e) injustement; **~back** *n* livre relié; **~ cash** *n* espèces *fpl*; **~ disk** *n* (*COMPUT*) disque dur; **~en** *vt* durcir; (*fig*) endurcir ♦ *vi* durcir; **~-headed** *adj* réaliste; décidé(e); **~ labour** *n* travaux forcés

hardly ['hɑ:dlɪ] *adv* (*scarcely, no sooner*) à peine; **~ anywhere/ever** presque nulle part/jamais

hard: **~ship** *n* épreuves *fpl*; **~ up** (*inf*) *adj* fauché(e); **~ware** *n* quincaillerie *f*; (*COMPUT, MIL*) matériel *m*; **~ware shop** *n*

quincaillerie *f*; **~-wearing** *adj* solide; **~ working** *adj* travailleur(euse)

hardy ['hɑ:dɪ] *adj* robuste; (*plant*) résistant(e) au gel

hare [hɛə*] *n* lièvre *m*; **~-brained** *ad[j]* farfelu(e)

harm [hɑ:m] *n* mal *m*; (*wrong*) tort *m* ♦ *vt* (*person*) faire du mal *or* du tort à; (*thing*) endommager; **out of ~'s way** à l'abri du danger, en lieu sûr; **~ful** *adj* nuisible; **~less** *adj* inoffensif(ive); sans méchanceté

harmony ['hɑ:mənɪ] *n* harmonie *f*

harness ['hɑ:nɪs] *n* harnais *m*; (*safety ~*) harnais de sécurité ♦ *vt* (*horse*) harnacher; (*resources*) exploiter

harp [hɑ:p] *n* harpe *f* ♦ *vi*: **to ~ on about** rabâcher

harrowing ['hærəʊɪŋ] *adj* déchirant(e), très pénible

harsh [hɑ:ʃ] *adj* (*hard*) dur(e); (*severe*) sévère; (*unpleasant: sound*) discordant(e); (: *light*) cru(e)

harvest ['hɑ:vɪst] *n* (*of corn*) moisson *f*; (*of fruit*) récolte *f*; (*of grapes*) vendange *f* ♦ *vt* moissonner; récolter; vendanger

has [hæz] *vb see* **have**

hash [hæʃ] *n* (*CULIN*) hachis *m*; (*fig: mess*) gâchis *m*

hasn't ['hæznt] = **has not**

hassle ['hæsl] *n* (*inf: bother*) histoires *fpl*, tracas *mpl*

haste [heɪst] *n* hâte *f*; précipitation *f*; **~n** ['heɪsn] *vt* hâter, accélérer ♦ *vi* se hâter s'empresser; **hastily** *adv* à la hâte; préci pitamment; **hasty** ['heɪstɪ] *adj* hâtif(ive) précipité(e)

hat [hæt] *n* chapeau *m*

hatch [hætʃ] *n* (*NAUT*: *also*: *~way*) écou tille *f*; (*also*: *service ~*) passe-plats *m in[v]* ♦ *vi* éclore

hatchback ['hætʃbæk] *n* (*AUT*) modèle *n* avec hayon arrière

hatchet ['hætʃɪt] *n* hachette *f*

hate [heɪt] *vt* haïr, détester ♦ *n* haine *f* **~ful** *adj* odieux(euse), détestable; **hatred** ['heɪtrɪd] *n* haine *f*

haughty ['hɔ:tɪ] *adj* hautain(e), arro gant(e)

haul [hɔːl] *vt* traîner, tirer ♦ *n* (*of fish*) prise *f*; (*of stolen goods etc*) butin *m*; **~age** (*of transport*) transport routier; (*costs*) frais *mpl* de transport; **~ier** (*US* **hauler**) *n* (*company*) transporteur (routier); (*driver*) camionneur *m*

haunch [hɔːntʃ] *n* hanche *f*; (*of meat*) cuissot *m*

haunt [hɔːnt] *vt* (*subj: ghost, fear*) hanter; (: *person*) fréquenter ♦ *n* repaire *m*

KEYWORD

have [hæv] (*pt, pp* had) *aux vb* **1** (*gen*) avoir; être; **to ~ arrived/gone** être arrivé(e)/allé(e); **to ~ eaten/slept** avoir mangé/dormi; **he has been promoted** il a eu une promotion

2 (*in tag questions*): **you've done it, ~n't you?** vous l'avez fait, n'est-ce pas?

3 (*in short answers and questions*): **no I ~n't/yes we ~**! mais non!/mais si!; **so I ~**! ah oui!, oui c'est vrai!; **I've been there before, ~ you?** j'y suis déjà allé, et vous?

♦ *modal aux vb* (*be obliged*): **to ~ (got) to do sth** devoir faire qch; être obligé(e) de faire qch; **she has (got) to do it** elle doit le faire, il faut qu'elle le fasse; **you ~n't to tell her** vous n'êtes pas obligé de le lui dire

♦ *vt* **1** (*possess, obtain*) avoir; **he has (got) blue eyes/dark hair** il a les yeux bleus/les cheveux bruns; **may I ~ your address?** puis-je avoir votre adresse?

2 (+*noun: take, hold etc*): **to ~ breakfast/a bath/a shower** prendre le petit déjeuner/un bain/une douche; **to ~ dinner/lunch** dîner/déjeuner; **to ~ a swim** nager; **to ~ a meeting** se réunir; **to ~ a party** organiser une fête

3: **to ~ sth done** faire faire qch; **to ~ one's hair cut** se faire couper les cheveux; **to ~ sb do sth** faire faire qch à qn

4 (*experience, suffer*) avoir; **to ~ a cold/flu** avoir un rhume/la grippe; **to ~ an operation** se faire opérer

5 (*inf: dupe*) avoir; **he's been had** il s'est fait avoir *or* rouler

have out *vt*: **to have it out with sb**

(*settle a problem etc*) s'expliquer (franchement) avec qn

haven [ˈheɪvn] *n* port *m*; (*fig*) havre *m*

haven't [ˈhævnt] = **have not**

havoc [ˈhævək] *n* ravages *mpl*

hawk [hɔːk] *n* faucon *m*

hay [heɪ] *n* foin *m*; **~ fever** *n* rhume *m* des foins; **~stack** *n* meule *f* de foin

haywire [ˈheɪwaɪə*] (*inf*) *adj*: **to go ~** (*machine*) se détraquer; (*plans*) mal tourner

hazard [ˈhæzəd] *n* (*danger*) danger *m*, risque *m* ♦ *vt* risquer, hasarder; **~ (warning) lights** *npl* (*AUT*) feux *mpl* de détresse

haze [heɪz] *n* brume *f*

hazelnut [ˈheɪzlnʌt] *n* noisette *f*

hazy [ˈheɪzɪ] *adj* brumeux(euse); (*idea*) vague

he [hiː] *pron* il; **it is ~ who ...** c'est lui qui ...

head [hed] *n* tête *f*; (*leader*) chef *m*; (*of school*) directeur(trice) ♦ *vt* (*list*) être en tête de; (*group*) être à la tête de; **~s (or tails)** pile (ou face); **~ first** la tête la première; **~ over heels in love** follement *or* éperdument amoureux(euse); **to ~ a ball** faire une tête; **~ for** *vt fus* se diriger vers; **~ache** *n* mal *m* de tête; **~dress** (*BRIT*) *n* (*of Red Indian etc*) coiffure *f*; **~ing** *n* titre *m*; **~lamp** (*BRIT*) *n* = **headlight**; **~land** *n* promontoire *m*, cap *m*; **~light** *n* phare *m*; **~line** *n* titre *m*; **~long** *adv* (*fall*) la tête la première; (*rush*) tête baissée; **~master** *n* directeur *m*; **~mistress** *n* directrice *f*; **~ office** *n* bureau central, siège *m*; **~-on** *adj* (*collision*) de plein fouet; (*confrontation*) en face à face; **~phones** *npl* casque *m* (à écouteurs); **~quarters** *npl* bureau *or* siège central; (*MIL*) quartier général; **~rest** *n* appui-tête *m*; **~room** *n* (*in car*) hauteur *f* de plafond; (*under bridge*) hauteur limite; **~scarf** *n* foulard *m*; **~strong** *adj* têtu(e), entêté(e); **~ waiter** *n* maître *m* d'hôtel; **~way** *n*: **to make ~way** avancer, faire des progrès; **~wind** *n* vent *m* contraire; (*NAUT*) vent debout; **~y** *adj* capiteux(euse); enivrant(e); (*experience*) grisant(e)

heal [hiːl] *vt, vi* guérir

health [helθ] *n* santé *f*; ~ **food** *n* aliment(s) naturel(s); ~ **food shop** *n* magasin *m* diététique; **H~ Service** (*BRIT*) *n*: **the H~ Service** ≈ la Sécurité sociale; ~**y** *adj* (*person*) en bonne santé; (*climate, food, attitude etc*) sain(e), bon(ne) pour la santé

heap [hiːp] *n* tas *m* ♦ *vt*: **to ~ (up)** entasser, amonceler; **she ~ed her plate with cakes** elle a chargé son assiette de gâteaux

hear [hɪə*] (*pt, pp* **heard**) *vt* entendre; (*news*) apprendre ♦ *vi* entendre; **to ~ about** entendre parler de; avoir des nouvelles de; **to ~ from sb** recevoir *or* avoir des nouvelles de qn; ~**ing** [ˈhɪərɪŋ] *n* (*sense*) ouïe *f*; (*of witnesses*) audition *f*; (*of a case*) audience *f*; ~**ing aid** *n* appareil *m* acoustique; ~**say** [ˈhɪəseɪ]: **by ~say** *adv* par ouï-dire *m*

hearse [həːs] *n* corbillard *m*

heart [hɑːt] *n* cœur *m*; ~**s** *npl* (*CARDS*) cœur; **to lose/take ~** perdre/prendre courage; **at ~** au fond; **by ~** (*learn, know*) par cœur; ~ **attack** *n* crise *f* cardiaque; ~**beat** *n* battement *m* du cœur; ~**breaking** *adj* déchirant(e), qui fend le cœur; ~**broken** *adj*: **to be ~broken** avoir beaucoup de chagrin *or* le cœur brisé; ~**burn** *n* brûlures *fpl* d'estomac; ~ **failure** *n* arrêt *m* du cœur; ~**felt** *adj* sincère

hearth [hɑːθ] *n* foyer *m*, cheminée *f*

heartily [ˈhɑːtɪlɪ] *adv* chaleureusement; (*laugh*) de bon cœur; (*eat*) de bon appétit; **to agree ~** être entièrement d'accord

heartland [ˈhɑːtlænd] *n* (*of country, region*) centre *m*

hearty [ˈhɑːtɪ] *adj* chaleureux(euse); (*appetite*) robuste; (*dislike*) cordial(e)

heat [hiːt] *n* chaleur *f*; (*fig*) feu *m*, agitation *f*; (*SPORT*: *also*: *qualifying ~*) éliminatoire *f* ♦ *vt* chauffer; ~ **up** *vi* (*water*) chauffer; (*room*) se réchauffer ♦ *vt* réchauffer; ~**ed** *adj* chauffé(e); (*fig*) passionné(e), échauffé(e); ~**er** *n* appareil *m*

de chauffage; radiateur *m*; (*in car*) chauffage *m*; (*water ~*) chauffe-eau *m*; ~**-seeking** *adj* guidé(e) par infrarouge

heath [hiːθ] (*BRIT*) *n* lande *f*

heather [ˈheðə*] *n* bruyère *f*

heating [ˈhiːtɪŋ] *n* chauffage *m*

heatstroke [ˈhiːtstrəʊk] *n* (*MED*) coup *m* de chaleur

heatwave *n* vague *f* de chaleur

heave [hiːv] *vt* soulever (avec effort); (*drag*) traîner ♦ *vi* se soulever; (*retch*) avoir un haut-le-cœur; **to ~ a sigh** pousser un soupir

heaven [ˈhevn] *n* ciel *m*, paradis *m*; (*fig*) paradis; ~**ly** *adj* céleste, divin(e)

heavily [ˈhevɪlɪ] *adv* lourdement; (*drink, smoke*) beaucoup; (*sleep, sigh*) profondément

heavy [ˈhevɪ] *adj* lourd(e); (*work, sea, rain, eater*) gros(se); (*snow*) beaucoup de; (*drinker, smoker*) grand(e); (*breathing*) bruyant(e); (*schedule, week*) chargé(e); ~ **goods vehicle** *n* poids lourd; ~**weight** *n* (*SPORT*) poids lourd

Hebrew [ˈhiːbruː] *adj* hébraïque ♦ *n* (*LING*) hébreu *m*

Hebrides [ˈhebrɪdiːz] *npl*: **the ~** les Hébrides *fpl*

heckle [ˈhekl] *vt* interpeller (*un orateur*)

hectic [ˈhektɪk] *adj* agité(e), trépidant(e)

he'd [hiːd] = **he would**; **he had**

hedge [hedʒ] *n* haie *f* ♦ *vi* se dérober; **to ~ one's bets** (*fig*) se couvrir

hedgehog [ˈhedʒhɒg] *n* hérisson *m*

heed [hiːd] *vt* (*also*: **take ~ of**) tenir compte de; ~**less** *adj* insouciant(e)

heel [hiːl] *n* talon *m* ♦ *vt* (*shoe*) retalonner

hefty [ˈheftɪ] *adj* (*person*) costaud(e); (*parcel*) lourd(e); (*profit*) gros(se)

heifer [ˈhefə*] *n* génisse *f*

height [haɪt] *n* (*of person*) taille *f*, grandeur *f*; (*of object*) hauteur *f*; (*of plane, mountain*) altitude *f*; (*high ground*) hauteur, éminence *f*; (*fig*: *of glory*) sommet *m*; (*of luxury, stupidity*) comble *m*; ~**en** *vt* (*fig*) augmenter

heir [εə*] *n* héritier *m*; ~**ess** [ˈεərɪs] *n* héritière *f*; ~**loom** *n* héritage *m*, meuble

m (*or* bijou *m or* tableau *m*) de famille
held [held] *pt, pp of* **hold**
helicopter ['helɪkɒptə*] *n* hélicoptère *m*
hell [hel] *n* enfer *m*; ~! (*inf!*) merde!
he'll [hi:l] = **he will; he shall**
hellish ['helɪʃ] (*inf*) *adj* infernal(e)
hello [hʌ'ləʊ] *excl* bonjour!; (*to attract attention*) hé!; (*surprise*) tiens!
helm [helm] *n* (NAUT) barre *f*
helmet ['helmɪt] *n* casque *m*
help [help] *n* aide *f*; (*cleaner*) femme *f* de ménage ♦ *vt* aider; ~! au secours!; ~ **yourself** servez-vous; **he can't ~ it** il n'y peut rien; ~**er** *n* aide *m/f*, assistant(e); ~**ful** *adj* serviable, obligeant(e); (*useful*) utile; ~**ing** *n* portion *f*; ~**less** *adj* impuissant(e); (*defenceless*) faible
hem [hem] *n* ourlet *m* ♦ *vt* ourler; ~ **in** *vt* cerner
hemorrhage ['hemərɪdʒ] (*US*) *n* = **haemorrhage**
hemorrhoids ['hemərɔɪdz] (*US*) *npl* = **haemorrhoids**
hen [hen] *n* poule *f*
hence [hens] *adv* (*therefore*) d'où, de là; **2 years** ~ d'ici 2 ans, dans 2 ans; ~**forth** *adv* dorénavant
henchman ['hentʃmən] (*pej: irreg*) *n* acolyte *m*
her [hɜ:*] *pron* (*direct*) la, l'; (*indirect*) lui; (*stressed, after prep*) elle ♦ *adj* son(sa), ses *pl*; *see also* **me; my**
herald ['herəld] *n* héraut *m* ♦ *vt* annoncer; ~**ry** ['herəldrɪ] *n* (*study*) héraldique *f*; (*coat of arms*) blason *m*
herb [hɜ:b] *n* herbe *f*
herd [hɜ:d] *n* troupeau *m*
here [hɪə*] *adv* ici; (*time*) alors ♦ *excl* tiens!, tenez!; ~! présent!; ~ **is, ~ are** voici; ~ **he/she is!** le/la voici!; ~**after** *adv* après, plus tard; ~**by** *adv* (*formal: in letter*) par la présente
hereditary [hɪ'redɪtərɪ] *adj* héréditaire
heresy ['herəsɪ] *n* hérésie *f*
heritage ['herɪtɪdʒ] *n* (*of country*) patrimoine *m*
hermit ['hɜ:mɪt] *n* ermite *m*
hernia ['hɜ:nɪə] *n* hernie *f*
hero ['hɪərəʊ] (*pl* ~**es**) *n* héros *m*

heroin ['herəʊɪn] *n* héroïne *f*
heroine ['herəʊɪn] *n* héroïne *f*
heron ['herən] *n* héron *m*
herring ['herɪŋ] *n* hareng *m*
hers [hɜ:z] *pron* le(la) sien(ne), les siens(siennes); *see also* **mine**
herself [hɜ:'self] *pron* (*reflexive*) se; (*emphatic*) elle-même; (*after prep*) elle; *see also* **oneself**
he's [hi:z] = **he is; he has**
hesitant ['hezɪtənt] *adj* hésitant(e), indécis(e)
hesitate ['hezɪteɪt] *vi* hésiter; **hesitation** [hezɪ'teɪʃən] *n* hésitation *f*
hew [hju:] (*pp* **hewed** *or* **hewn**) *vt* (*stone*) tailler; (*wood*) couper
heyday ['heɪdeɪ] *n*: **the ~ of** l'âge *m* d'or de, les beaux jours de
HGV *n abbr* = **heavy goods vehicle**
hi [haɪ] *excl* salut!; (*to attract attention*) hé!
hiatus [haɪ'eɪtəs] *n* (*gap*) lacune *f*; (*interruption*) pause *f*
hibernate ['haɪbəneɪt] *vi* hiberner
hiccough, hiccup ['hɪkʌp] *vi* hoqueter; ~**s** *npl* hoquet *m*
hide [haɪd] (*pt* **hid**, *pp* **hidden**) *n* (*skin*) peau *f* ♦ *vt* cacher ♦ *vi*: **to ~ (from sb)** se cacher (de qn); ~-**and-seek** *n* cache-cache *m*; ~-**away** *n* cachette *f*
hideous ['hɪdɪəs] *adj* hideux(euse)
hiding ['haɪdɪŋ] *n* (*beating*) correction *f*, volée *f* de coups; **to be in ~** (*concealed*) se tenir caché(e)
hierarchy ['haɪərɑ:kɪ] *n* hiérarchie *f*
hi-fi ['haɪfaɪ] *n* hi-fi *f inv* ♦ *adj* hi-fi *inv*
high [haɪ] *adj* haut(e); (*speed, respect, number*) grand(e); (*price*) élevé(e); (*wind*) fort(e), violent(e); (*voice*) aigu(aiguë) ♦ *adv* haut; **20 m** ~ haut(e) de 20 m; ~**brow** *adj*, *n* intellectuel(le); ~**chair** *n* (*child's*) chaise haute; ~**er education** *n* études supérieures; ~-**handed** *adj* très autoritaire; très cavalier(ère); ~ **jump** *n* (SPORT) saut *m* en hauteur; ~**lands** *npl*: **the H~lands** les Highlands *mpl*; ~**light** *n* (*fig: of event*) point culminant ♦ *vt* faire ressortir, souligner; ~**lights** *npl* (*in hair*) reflets *mpl*; ~**ly**

adv très, fort, hautement; **to speak/ think ~ly of sb** dire/penser beaucoup de bien de qn; **~ly paid** *adj* très bien payé(e); **~ly strung** *adj* nerveux(euse), toujours tendu(e); **~ness** *n*: Her (*or* His) H**~ness** Son Altesse *f*; **~-pitched** *adj* aigu(aiguë); **~-rise** *adj*: **~-rise block, ~-rise flats** tour *f* (d'habitation); **~ school** *n* lycée *m*; (*US*) établissement *m* d'enseignement supérieur; **~ season** (*BRIT*) *n* haute saison; **~ street** (*BRIT*) *n* grand-rue *f*; **~way** ['haɪweɪ] *n* route nationale; H**~way Code** (*BRIT*) *n* code *m* de la route
hijack ['haɪdʒæk] *vt* (*plane*) détourner; **~er** *n* pirate *m* de l'air
hike [haɪk] *vi* aller *or* faire des excursions à pied ♦ *n* excursion *f* à pied, randonnée *f*; **~r** *n* promeneur(euse), excursionniste *m/f*
hilarious [hɪ'lɛərɪəs] *adj* (*account, event*) désopilant(e)
hill [hɪl] *n* colline *f*; (*fairly high*) montagne *f*; (*on road*) côte *f*; **~side** *n* (flanc *m* de) coteau *m*; **~y** *adj* vallonné(e); montagneux(euse)
hilt [hɪlt] *n* (*of sword*) garde *f*; **to the ~** (*fig: support*) à fond
him [hɪm] *pron* (*direct*) le, l'; (*stressed, indirect, after prep*) lui; *see also* **me**; **~self** [hɪm'self] *pron* (*reflexive*) se; (*emphatic*) lui-même; (*after prep*) lui; *see also* **oneself**
hind [haɪnd] *adj* de derrière
hinder ['hɪndə*] *vt* gêner; (*delay*) retarder; **hindrance** ['hɪndrəns] *n* gêne *f*, obstacle *m*
hindsight ['haɪndsaɪt] *n*: **with ~** avec du recul, rétrospectivement
Hindu ['hɪnduː] *adj* hindou(e)
hinge [hɪndʒ] *n* charnière *f* ♦ *vi* (*fig*): **to ~ on** dépendre de
hint [hɪnt] *n* allusion *f*; (*advice*) conseil *m* ♦ *vt*: **to ~ that** insinuer que ♦ *vi*: **to ~ at** faire une allusion à
hip [hɪp] *n* hanche *f*
hippopotami [hɪpə'pɒtəmaɪ] *npl of* **hippopotamus**
hippopotamus [hɪpə'pɒtəməs] (*pl* **~es** *or* **hippopotami**) *n* hippopotame *m*

hire ['haɪə*] *vt* (*BRIT: car, equipment*) louer; (*worker*) embaucher, engager ♦ *n* location *f*; **for ~** à louer; (*taxi*) libre; **~ purchase** (*BRIT*) *n* achat *m* (*or* vente *f*) à tempérament *or* crédit
his [hɪz] *pron* le(la) sien(ne), les siens(siennes) ♦ *adj* son(sa), ses *pl*; *see also* **my**; **mine**
hiss [hɪs] *vi* siffler
historic [hɪs'tɒrɪk] *adj* historique
historical [hɪs'tɒrɪkəl] *adj* historique
history ['hɪstərɪ] *n* histoire *f*
hit [hɪt] (*pt, pp* **hit**) *vt* frapper; (*reach: target*) atteindre, toucher; (*collide with: car*) entrer en collision avec, heurter; (*fig: affect*) toucher ♦ *n* coup *m*; (*success*) succès *m*; (*: song*) tube *m*; **to ~ it off with sb** bien s'entendre avec qn; **~- and-run driver** *n* chauffard *m* (coupable du délit de fuite)
hitch [hɪtʃ] *vt* (*fasten*) accrocher, attacher; (*also: ~ up*) remonter d'une saccade ♦ *n* (*difficulty*) anicroche *f*, contretemps *m*; **to ~ a lift** faire du stop
hitchhike ['hɪtʃhaɪk] *vi* faire de l'auto-stop; **~r** *n* auto-stoppeur(euse)
hi-tech ['haɪ'tek] *adj* de pointe
hitherto ['hɪðə'tuː] *adv* jusqu'ici
HIV: **~-negative/-positive** séro-négatif (ive)/-positif(ive)
hive [haɪv] *n* ruche *f*; **~ off** (*inf*) *vt* mettre à part, séparer
HMS *abbr* = **Her (His) Majesty's Ship**
hoard [hɔːd] *n* (*of food*) provisions *fpl*, réserves *fpl*; (*of money*) trésor *m* ♦ *vt* amasser; **~ing** ['hɔːdɪŋ] (*BRIT*) *n* (*for posters*) panneau *m* d'affichage *or* publicitaire
hoarse [hɔːs] *adj* enroué(e)
hoax [həʊks] *n* canular *m*
hob [hɒb] *n* plaque (chauffante)
hobble ['hɒbl] *vi* boitiller
hobby ['hɒbɪ] *n* passe-temps favori; **~- horse** *n* (*fig*) dada *m*
hobo ['həʊbəʊ] (*US*) *n* vagabond *m*
hockey ['hɒkɪ] *n* hockey *m*
hog [hɒg] *n* porc (châtré) ♦ *vt* (*fig*) accaparer; **to go the whole ~** aller jusqu'au bout

hoist [hɔɪst] n (*apparatus*) palan m ♦ vt hisser

hold [həʊld] (*pt, pp* **held**) vt tenir; (*contain*) contenir; (*believe*) considérer; (*possess*) avoir; (*detain*) détenir ♦ vi (*withstand pressure*) tenir (bon); (*be valid*) valoir ♦ n (*also fig*) prise f; (*NAUT*) cale f; ~ **the line!** (*TEL*) ne quittez pas!; **to ~ one's own** (*fig*) (bien) se défendre; **to catch** *or* **get (a) ~ of** (*fig*) trouver; ~ **back** vt retenir; (*secret*) tenir; ~ **down** vt (*person*) maintenir à terre; (*job*) occuper; ~ **off** vt tenir à distance; ~ **on** vi tenir bon; (*wait*) attendre; ~ **on!** (*TEL*) ne quittez pas!; ~ **on to** vt *fus* se cramponner à; (*keep*) conserver, garder; ~ **out** vt offrir ♦ vi (*resist*) tenir bon; ~ **up** vt (*raise*) lever; (*support*) soutenir; (*delay*) retarder; (*rob*) braquer; **~all** (*BRIT*) n fourre-tout m *inv*; **~er** n (*of ticket, record*) détenteur(trice); (*of office, title etc*) titulaire m/f; (*container*) support m; **~ing** n (*share*) intérêts *mpl*; (*farm*) ferme f; **~-up** n (*robbery*) hold-up m; (*delay*) retard m; (*BRIT: in traffic*) bouchon m

hole [həʊl] n trou m

holiday ['hɒlədɪ] n vacances *fpl*; (*day off*) jour m de congé; (*public*) jour férié; **on ~** en congé; ~ **camp** n (*also:* ~ *centre*) camp m de vacances; **~-maker** (*BRIT*) n vacancier(ère); ~ **resort** n centre m de villégiature *or* de vacances

Holland ['hɒlənd] n Hollande f

hollow ['hɒləʊ] adj creux(euse) ♦ n creux m ♦ vt: **to ~ out** creuser, évider

holly ['hɒlɪ] n houx m

holocaust ['hɒləkɔ:st] n holocauste m

holster ['həʊlstə*] n étui m de revolver

holy ['həʊlɪ] adj saint(e); (*bread, water*) bénit(e); (*ground*) sacré(e); **H~ Ghost** n Saint-Esprit m

homage ['hɒmɪdʒ] n hommage m; **to pay ~ to** rendre hommage à

home [həʊm] n foyer m, maison f; (*country*) pays natal, patrie f; (*institution*) maison ♦ adj de famille; (*ECON, POL*) national(e), intérieur(e); (*SPORT: game*) sur leur (*or* notre) terrain; (*team*) qui reçoit ♦ adv chez soi, à la maison; au pays natal; (*right in: nail etc*) à fond; **at ~** chez soi, à la maison; **make yourself at ~** faites comme chez vous; ~ **address** n domicile permanent; **~land** n patrie f; **~less** adj sans foyer; sans abri; **~ly** adj (*plain*) simple, sans prétention; **~-made** adj fait(e) à la maison; **H~ Office** (*BRIT*) n ministère m de l'Intérieur; ~ **rule** n autonomie f; **H~ Secretary** (*BRIT*) n ministre m de l'Intérieur; **~sick** adj: **to be ~sick** avoir le mal du pays; s'ennuyer de sa famille; ~ **town** n ville natale; **~ward** adj (*journey*) du retour; **~work** n devoirs *mpl*

homogeneous [hɒmə'dʒi:nɪəs] adj homogène

homosexual ['hɒməʊ'seksjʊəl] adj, n homosexuel(le)

honest ['ɒnɪst] adj honnête; (*sincere*) franc(franche); **~ly** adv honnêtement; franchement; **~y** n honnêteté f

honey ['hʌnɪ] n miel m; **~comb** n rayon m de miel; **~moon** n lune f de miel, voyage m de noces; **~suckle** ['hʌnɪsʌkl] (*BOT*) n chèvrefeuille m

honk [hɒŋk] vi (*AUT*) klaxonner

honorary ['ɒnərərɪ] adj honoraire; (*duty, title*) honorifique

honour ['ɒnə*] (*US* honor) vt honorer ♦ n honneur m; **hono(u)rable** adj honorable; **hono(u)rs degree** n (*SCOL*) licence *avec mention*

hood [hʊd] n capuchon m; (*of cooker*) hotte f; (*AUT: BRIT*) capote f; (: *US*) capot m

hoof [hu:f] (*pl* **hooves**) n sabot m

hook [hʊk] n crochet m; (*on dress*) agrafe f; (*for fishing*) hameçon m ♦ vt accrocher; (*fish*) prendre

hooligan ['hu:lɪgən] n voyou m

hoop [hu:p] n cerceau m

hooray [hu:'reɪ] *excl* hourra

hoot [hu:t] vi (*AUT*) klaxonner; (*siren*) mugir; (*owl*) hululer; **~er** n (*BRIT: AUT*) klaxon m; (*NAUT, factory*) sirène f

Hoover ['hu:və*] (R): (*BRIT*) n aspirateur m ♦ vt: **h~** passer l'aspirateur dans *or* sur

hooves [hu:vz] *npl of* **hoof**

hop [hɒp] *vi* (*on one foot*) sauter à cloche-pied; (*bird*) sautiller

hope [həup] *vt, vi* espérer ♦ *n* espoir *m*; **I ~ so** je l'espère; **I ~ not** j'espère que non; **~ful** *adj* (*person*) plein(e) d'espoir; (*situation*) prometteur(euse), encourageant(e); **~fully** *adv* (*expectantly*) avec espoir, avec optimisme; (*one hopes*) avec un peu de chance; **~less** *adj* désespéré(e); (*useless*) nul(le)

hops [hɒps] *npl* houblon *m*

horizon [hə'raɪzn] *n* horizon *m*; **~tal** [hɒrɪ'zɒntl] *adj* horizontal(e)

horn [hɔ:n] *n* corne *f*; (*MUS: also: French* ~) cor *m*; (*AUT*) klaxon *m*

hornet ['hɔ:nɪt] *n* frelon *m*

horny ['hɔ:nɪ] (*inf*) *adj* (*aroused*) en rut, excité(e)

horoscope ['hɒrəskəup] *n* horoscope *m*

horrendous [hə'rendəs] *adj* horrible, affreux(euse)

horrible ['hɒrɪbl] *adj* horrible, affreux(euse)

horrid ['hɒrɪd] *adj* épouvantable

horrify ['hɒrɪfaɪ] *vt* horrifier

horror ['hɒrə*] *n* horreur *f*; **~ film** *n* film *m* d'épouvante

hors d'œuvre [ɔ:'də:vrə] *n* (*CULIN*) hors-d'œuvre *m inv*

horse [hɔ:s] *n* cheval *m*; **~back** *n*: **on ~back** à cheval; **~ chestnut** *n* marron *m* (d'Inde); **~man** (*irreg*) *n* cavalier *m*; **~power** *n* puissance *f* (en chevaux); **~racing** *n* courses *fpl* de chevaux; **~radish** *n* raifort *m*; **~shoe** *n* fer *m* à cheval

hose [həuz] *n* (*also*: ~*pipe*) tuyau *m*; (*: garden* ~) tuyau d'arrosage

hospitable [hɒs'pɪtəbl] *adj* hospitalier(ère)

hospital ['hɒspɪtl] *n* hôpital *m*; **in ~** à l'hôpital

hospitality [hɒspɪ'tælɪtɪ] *n* hospitalité *f*

host [həust] *n* hôte *m*; (*TV, RADIO*) animateur(trice); (*REL*) hostie *f*; (*large number*): **a ~ of** une foule de

hostage ['hɒstɪdʒ] *n* otage *m*

hostel ['hɒstəl] *n* foyer *m*; (*also: youth* ~) auberge *f* de jeunesse

hostess ['həustes] *n* hôtesse *f*; (*TV, RADIO*) animatrice *f*

hostile ['hɒstaɪl] *adj* hostile; **hostility** [hɒs'tɪlɪtɪ] *n* hostilité *f*

hot [hɒt] *adj* chaud(e); (*as opposed to only warm*) très chaud(e); (*spicy*) fort(e); (*contest etc*) acharné(e); (*temper*) passionné(e); **to be ~** (*person*) avoir chaud; (*object*) être (très) chaud(e); **it is ~** (*weather*) il fait chaud; **~bed** *n* (*fig*) foyer *m*, pépinière *f*; **~ dog** *n* hot-dog *m*

hotel [həu'tel] *n* hôtel *m*

hot: **~headed** *adj* impétueux(euse); **~house** *n* serre (chaude); **~line** *n* (*POL*) téléphone *m* rouge, ligne directe; **~ly** *adv* passionnément, violemment; **~plate** *n* (*on cooker*) plaque chauffante; **~water bottle** *n* bouillotte *f*

hound [haund] *vt* poursuivre avec acharnement ♦ *n* chien courant

hour ['auə*] *n* heure *f*; **~ly** *adj, adv* toutes les heures; (*rate*) horaire

house [*n* haus, *pl* 'hauzɪz, *vb* hauz] *n* maison *f*; (*POL*) chambre *f*; (*THEATRE*) salle *f*; auditoire *m* ♦ *vt* (*person*) loger, héberger; (*objects*) abriter; **on the ~** (*fig*) aux frais de la maison; **~ arrest** *n* assignation *f* à résidence; **~boat** *n* bateau *m* (aménagé en habitation); **~bound** *adj* confiné(e) chez soi; **~breaking** *n* cambriolage *m* (avec effraction); **~coat** *n* peignoir *m*; **~hold** *n* (*persons*) famille *f*, maisonnée *f*; (*ADMIN etc*) ménage *m*; **~keeper** *n* gouvernante *f*; **~keeping** *n* (*work*) ménage *m*; **~keeping** (*money*) argent *m* du ménage; **~warming** (*party*) *n* pendaison *f* de crémaillère; **~wife** (*irreg*) *n* ménagère *f*; femme *f* au foyer; **~work** *n* (travaux *mpl* du) ménage *m*

housing ['hauzɪŋ] *n* logement *m*; **~ development, ~ estate** *n* lotissement *m*

hovel ['hɒvəl] *n* taudis *m*

hover ['hɒvə*] *vi* planer; **~craft** *n* aéroglisseur *m*

how [hau] *adv* comment; **~ are you?** comment allez-vous?; **~ do you do?** bonjour; enchanté(e); **~ far is it to?** combine y a-t-il jusqu'à ...?; **~ long have you been here?** depuis combine de temps êtes-vous là?; ~ **lovely!** que *or* comme c'est joli!; ~ **many/much?** combien?; ~ **many people/much milk?** combien de gens/lait?; ~ **old are you?** quel âge avez-vous?

however [hau'evə*] *adv* de quelque façon *or* manière que +*subj*; (+*adj*) quelque *or* si ... que +*subj*; (*in questions*) comment ♦ *conj* pourtant, cependant

howl [haul] *vi* hurler

H.P. *abbr* = **hire purchase**

h.p. *abbr* = **horsepower**

HQ *abbr* = **headquarters**

hub [hʌb] *n* (*of wheel*) moyeu *m*; (*fig*) centre *m*, foyer *m*

hubbub ['hʌbʌb] *n* brouhaha *m*

hubcap ['hʌbkæp] *n* enjoliveur *m*

huddle ['hʌdl] *vi*: **to ~ together** se blottir les uns contre les autres

hue [hju:] *n* teinte *f*, nuance *f*; ~ **and cry** *n* tollé (général), clameur *f*

huff [hʌf] *n*: **in a ~** fâché(e)

hug [hʌg] *vt* serrer dans ses bras; (*shore, kerb*) serrer

huge [hju:dʒ] *adj* énorme, immense

hulk [hʌlk] *n* (*ship*) épave *f*; (*car, building*) carcasse *f*; (*person*) mastodonte *m*

hull [hʌl] *n* coque *f*

hullo [hʌ'ləu] *excl* = **hello**

hum [hʌm] *vt* (*tune*) fredonner ♦ *vi* fredonner; (*insect*) bourdonner; (*plane, tool*) vrombir

human ['hju:mən] *adj* humain(e) ♦ *n* ~ **(being)** être humain; **~e** [hju:'meɪn] *adj* humain(e), humanitaire; **~itarian** [hju:mænɪ'tɛərɪən] *adj* humanitaire; **~ity** [hju:'mænɪtɪ] *n* humanité *f*

humble ['hʌmbl] *adj* humble, modeste ♦ *vt* humilier

humbug ['hʌmbʌg] *n* fumisterie *f*; (*BRIT*) bonbon *m* à la menthe

humdrum ['hʌmdrʌm] *adj* monotone, banal(e)

humid ['hju:mɪd] *adj* humide

humiliate [hju:'mɪlɪeɪt] *vt* humilier; **humiliation** *n* humiliation *f*

humorous ['hju:mərəs] *adj* humoristique; (*person*) plein(e) d'humour

humour ['hju:mə*] (*US* **humor**) *n* humour *m*; (*mood*) humeur *f* ♦ *vt* (*person*) faire plaisir à; se prêter aux caprices de

hump [hʌmp] *n* bosse *f*

humpbacked ['hʌmpbækt] *adj*: ~ **bridge** pont *m* en dos d'âne

hunch [hʌntʃ] *n* (*premonition*) intuition *f*; **~back** *n* bossu(e); **~ed** *adj* voûté(e)

hundred ['hʌndrɪd] *num* cent; **~s of** des centaines de; **~weight** *n* (*BRIT*) = 50.8 *kg*; (*US*) = 45.3 *kg*

hung [hʌŋ] *pt, pp of* **hang**

Hungary ['hʌŋgərɪ] *n* Hongrie *f*

hunger ['hʌŋgə*] *n* faim *f* ♦ *vi*: **to ~ for** avoir faim de, désirer ardemment

hungry ['hʌŋgrɪ] *adj* affamé(e); (*keen*): ~ **for** avide de; **to be ~** avoir faim

hunk [hʌŋk] *n* (*of bread etc*) gros morceau

hunt [hʌnt] *vt* chasser; (*criminal*) pourchasser ♦ *vi* chasser; (*search*): **to ~ for** chercher (partout) ♦ *n* chasse *f*; **~er** *n* chasseur *m*; **~ing** *n* chasse *f*

hurdle ['hɜ:dl] *n* (*SPORT*) haie *f*; (*fig*) obstacle *m*

hurl [hɜ:l] *vt* lancer (avec violence); (*abuse, insults*) lancer

hurrah [hu'rɑ:] *excl* = **hooray**

hurray [hu'reɪ] *excl* = **hooray**

hurricane ['hʌrɪkən] *n* ouragan *m*

hurried ['hʌrɪd] *adj* pressé(e), précipité(e); (*work*) fait(e) à la hâte; **~ly** *adv* précipitamment, à la hâte

hurry ['hʌrɪ] (*vb: also:* ~ **up**) *n* hâte *f*, précipitation *f* ♦ *vi* se presser, se dépêcher ♦ *vt* (*person*) faire presser, faire se dépêcher; (*work*) presser; **to be in a ~** être pressé(e); **to do sth in a ~** faire qch en vitesse; **to ~ in/out** entrer/sortir précipitamment

hurt [hɜ:t] (*pt, pp* **hurt**) *vt* (*cause pain to*) faire mal à; (*injure, fig*) blesser ♦ *vi* faire mal ♦ *adj* blessé(e); **~ful** *adj* (*remark*) blessant(e)

hurtle ['hɜ:tl] *vi*: **to ~ past** passer en trombe; **to ~ down** dégringoler

husband ['hʌzbənd] *n* mari *m*

hush [hʌʃ] *n* calme *m*, silence *m* ♦ *vt* faire taire; ~! chut!; ~ **up** *vt* (*scandal*) étouffer

husk [hʌsk] n (of wheat) balle f; (of rice, maize) enveloppe f

husky ['hʌskɪ] adj rauque ♦ n chien m esquimau or de traîneau

hustle ['hʌsl] vt pousser, bousculer ♦ n: ~ **and bustle** tourbillon m (d'activité)

hut [hʌt] n hutte f; (shed) cabane f

hutch [hʌtʃ] n clapier m

hyacinth ['haɪəsɪnθ] n jacinthe f

hydrant ['haɪdrənt] n (also: fire ~) bouche f d'incendie

hydraulic [haɪ'drɒlɪk] adj hydraulique

hydroelectric [haɪdrəʊɪ'lektrɪk] adj hydro-électrique

hydrofoil ['haɪdrəʊfɔɪl] n hydrofoil m

hydrogen ['haɪdrɪdʒən] n hydrogène m

hyena [haɪ'iːnə] n hyène f

hygiene ['haɪdʒiːn] n hygiène f

hymn [hɪm] n hymne m; cantique m

hype [haɪp] (inf) n battage m publicitaire

hypermarket ['haɪpəˈmɑːkɪt] (BRIT) n hypermarché m

hyphen ['haɪfən] n trait m d'union

hypnotize ['hɪpnətaɪz] vt hypnotiser

hypocrisy [hɪ'pɒkrɪsɪ] n hypocrisie f; **hypocrite** ['hɪpəkrɪt] n hypocrite m/f; **hypocritical** adj hypocrite

hypothesis [haɪ'pɒθɪsɪs] (pl ~**es**) n hypothèse f

hysterical [hɪs'terɪkəl] adj hystérique; (funny) hilarant(e); ~ **laughter** fou rire m

hysterics [hɪs'terɪks] npl: **to be in/have** ~ (anger, panic) avoir une crise de nerfs; (laughter) attraper un fou rire

I i

I [aɪ] pron je; (before vowel) j'; (stressed) moi

ice [aɪs] n glace f; (on road) verglas m ♦ vt (cake) glacer ♦ vi (also: ~ over, ~ up) geler; (: window) se givrer; ~**berg** n iceberg m; ~**box** n (US) réfrigérateur m; (BRIT) compartiment m à glace; (insulated box) glacière f; ~ **cream** n glace f; ~ **cube** n glaçon m; ~**d** adj glacé(e); ~

hockey n hockey m sur glace; **I~land** ['aɪslənd] n Islande f; ~ **lolly** n (BRIT) esquimau m (glace); ~ **rink** n patinoire f; ~-**skating** n patinage m (sur glace)

icicle ['aɪsɪkl] n glaçon m (naturel)

icing ['aɪsɪŋ] n (CULIN) glace f; ~ **sugar** (BRIT) n sucre m glace

icy ['aɪsɪ] adj glacé(e); (road) verglacé(e); (weather, temperature) glacial(e)

I'd [aɪd] = **I would**; **I had**

idea [aɪ'dɪə] n idée f

ideal [aɪ'dɪəl] n idéal m ♦ adj idéal(e)

identical [aɪ'dentɪkəl] adj identique

identification [aɪdentɪfɪ'keɪʃən] n identification f; **means of** ~ pièce f d'identité

identify [aɪ'dentɪfaɪ] vt identifier

Identikit picture [aɪ'dentɪkɪt-] (®) n portrait-robot m

identity [aɪ'dentɪtɪ] n identité f; ~ **card** n carte f d'identité

ideology [aɪdɪ'ɒlədʒɪ] n idéologie f

idiom ['ɪdɪəm] n expression f idiomatique; (style) style m

idiosyncrasy [ɪdɪə'sɪŋkrəsɪ] n (of person) particularité f, petite manie

idiot ['ɪdɪət] n idiot(e), imbécile m/f; ~**ic** [ɪdɪ'ɒtɪk] adj idiot(e), bête, stupide

idle ['aɪdl] adj sans occupation, désœuvré(e); (lazy) oisif(ive), paresseux(euse); (unemployed) au chômage; (question, pleasures) vain(e), futile ♦ vi (engine) tourner au ralenti; **to lie** ~ être arrêté(e), ne pas fonctionner; ~ **away** vt: **to** ~ **away the time** passer son temps à ne rien faire

idol ['aɪdl] n idole f; ~**ize** vt idolâtrer, adorer

i.e. adv abbr (= id est) c'est-à-dire

if [ɪf] conj si; ~ **so** si c'est le cas; ~ **not** sinon; ~ **only** si seulement

ignite [ɪg'naɪt] vt mettre le feu à, enflammer ♦ vi s'enflammer

ignition [ɪg'nɪʃən] n (AUT) allumage m; ~ **switch on/off the** ~ mettre/couper le contact; ~ **key** n clé f de contact

ignorant ['ɪgnərənt] adj ignorant(e); **to be** ~ **of** (subject) ne rien connaître à; (events) ne pas être au courant de

ignore [ɪg'nɔː*] vt ne tenir aucun compte de; (*person*) faire semblant de ne pas reconnaître, ignorer; (*fact*) méconnaître

ill [ɪl] *adj* (*sick*) malade; (*bad*) mauvais(e) ♦ *n* mal *m* ♦ *adv:* **to speak/think ~ of** dire/penser du mal de; **~s** *npl* (*misfortunes*) maux *mpl*, malheurs *mpl*; **to be taken ~** tomber malade; **~-advised** *adj* (*decision*) peu judicieux(euse); (*person*) malavisé(e); **~-at-ease** *adj* mal à l'aise

I'll [aɪl] = **I will**; **I shall**

illegal [ɪ'liːɡəl] *adj* illégal(e)

illegible [ɪ'ledʒəbl] *adj* illisible

illegitimate [ɪlɪ'dʒɪtɪmət] *adj* illégitime

ill: **~-fated** [ɪl'feɪtɪd] *adj* malheureux(euse); (*day*) néfaste; **~ feeling** *n* ressentiment *m*, rancune *f*

illiterate [ɪ'lɪtərət] *adj* illettré(e); (*letter*) plein(e) de fautes

ill: **~-mannered** [ɪl'mænəd] *adj* (*child*) mal élevé(e); **~ness** ['ɪlnəs] *n* maladie *f*; **~-treat** [ɪl'triːt] *vt* maltraiter

illuminate [ɪ'luːmɪneɪt] *vt* (*room, street*) éclairer; (*for special effect*) illuminer; **illumination** [ɪluːmɪ'neɪʃən] *n* éclairage *m*; illumination *f*

illusion [ɪ'luːʒən] *n* illusion *f*

illustrate ['ɪləstreɪt] *vt* illustrer; **illustration** [ɪləs'treɪʃən] *n* illustration *f*

ill will *n* malveillance *f*

I'm [aɪm] = **I am**

image ['ɪmɪdʒ] *n* image *f*; (*public face*) image de marque; **~ry** *n* images *fpl*

imaginary [ɪ'mædʒɪnərɪ] *adj* imaginaire

imagination [ɪmædʒɪ'neɪʃən] *n* imagination *f*

imaginative [ɪ'mædʒɪnətɪv] *adj* imaginatif(ive); (*person*) plein(e) d'imagination

imagine [ɪ'mædʒɪn] *vt* imaginer, s'imaginer; (*suppose*) imaginer, supposer

imbalance [ɪm'bæləns] *n* déséquilibre *m*

imbue [ɪm'bjuː] *vt:* **to ~ sb/sth with** imprégner qn/qch de

imitate ['ɪmɪteɪt] *vt* imiter; **imitation** [ɪmɪ'teɪʃən] *n* imitation *f*

immaculate [ɪ'mækjʊlɪt] *adj* impeccable; (*REL*) immaculé(e)

immaterial [ɪmə'tɪərɪəl] *adj* sans importance, insignifiant(e)

immature [ɪmə'tjʊə*] *adj* (*fruit*) (qui n'est) pas mûr(e); (*person*) qui manque de maturité

immediate [ɪ'miːdɪət] *adj* immédiat(e); **~ly** *adv* (*at once*) immédiatement; **~ly next to** juste à côté de

immense [ɪ'mens] *adj* immense; énorme

immerse [ɪ'mɜːs] *vt* immerger, plonger; **immersion heater** [ɪ'mɜːʃən-] (*BRIT*) *n* chauffe-eau *m* électrique

immigrant ['ɪmɪɡrənt] *n* immigrant(e); immigré(e); **immigration** [ɪmɪ'ɡreɪʃən] *n* immigration *f*

imminent ['ɪmɪnənt] *adj* imminent(e)

immoral [ɪ'mɒrəl] *adj* immoral(e)

immortal [ɪ'mɔːtl] *adj, n* immortel(le)

immune [ɪ'mjuːn] *adj:* **~ (to)** immunisé(e) (contre); (*fig*) à l'abri de; **immunity** [ɪ'mjuːnɪtɪ] *n* immunité *f*

imp [ɪmp] *n* lutin *m*; (*child*) petit diable

impact ['ɪmpækt] *n* choc *m*, impact *m*; (*fig*) impact

impair [ɪm'pɛə*] *vt* détériorer, diminuer

impart [ɪm'pɑːt] *vt* communiquer, transmettre; (*flavour*) donner

impartial [ɪm'pɑːʃəl] *adj* impartial(e)

impassable [ɪm'pɑːsəbl] *adj* infranchissable; (*road*) impraticable

impassive [ɪm'pæsɪv] *adj* impassible

impatience [ɪm'peɪʃəns] *n* impatience *f*

impatient [ɪm'peɪʃənt] *adj* impatient(e); **to get** *or* **grow ~** s'impatienter

impeccable [ɪm'pekəbl] *adj* impeccable, parfait(e)

impede [ɪm'piːd] *vt* gêner

impediment [ɪm'pedɪmənt] *n* obstacle *m*; (*also: speech ~*) défaut *m* d'élocution

impending [ɪm'pendɪŋ] *adj* imminent(e)

imperative [ɪm'perətɪv] *adj* (*need*) urgent(e), pressant(e); (*tone*) impérieux(euse) ♦ *n* (*LING*) impératif *m*

imperfect [ɪm'pɜːfɪkt] *adj* imparfait(e); (*goods etc*) défectueux(euse)

imperial [ɪm'pɪərɪəl] *adj* impérial(e); (*BRIT: measure*) légal(e)

impersonal [ɪm'pɜːsnl] *adj* impersonnel(le)

impersonate [ɪm'pɜːsəneɪt] *vt* se faire passer pour; (*THEATRE*) imiter

impertinent [ɪm'pɜːtɪnənt] *adj* impertinent(e), insolent(e)

impervious [ɪmˈpɜːvɪəs] *adj* (*fig*): ~ **to** insensible à

impetuous [ɪmˈpetjʊəs] *adj* impétueux(euse), fougueux(euse)

impetus [ˈɪmpɪtəs] *n* impulsion *f*; (*of runner*) élan *m*

impinge [ɪmˈpɪndʒ]: **to ~ on** *vt fus* (*person*) affecter, toucher; (*rights*) empiéter sur

implement [*n* ˈɪmplɪmənt, *vb* ˈɪmplɪment] *n* outil *m*, instrument *m*; (*for cooking*) ustensile *m* ♦ *vt* exécuter

implicit [ɪmˈplɪsɪt] *adj* implicite; (*complete*) absolu(e), sans réserve

imply [ɪmˈplaɪ] *vt* suggérer, laisser entendre; indiquer, supposer

impolite [ɪmpəˈlaɪt] *adj* impoli(e)

import [*vb* ɪmˈpɔːt, *n* ˈɪmpɔːt] *vt* importer ♦ *n* (*COMM*) importation *f*

importance [ɪmˈpɔːtəns] *n* importance *f*

important [ɪmˈpɔːtənt] *adj* important(e)

importer [ɪmˈpɔːtə*] *n* importateur(trice)

impose [ɪmˈpəʊz] *vt* imposer ♦ *vi*: **to ~ on sb** abuser de la gentillesse de qn; **imposing** [ɪmˈpəʊzɪŋ] *adj* imposant(e), impressionnant(e); **imposition** [ɪmpəˈzɪʃən] *n* (*of tax etc*) imposition *f*; **to be an imposition on** (*person*) abuser de la gentillesse *or* la bonté de

impossible [ɪmˈpɒsəbl] *adj* impossible

impotent [ˈɪmpətənt] *adj* impuissant(e)

impound [ɪmˈpaʊnd] *vt* confisquer, saisir

impoverished [ɪmˈpɒvərɪʃt] *adj* appauvri(e), pauvre

impractical [ɪmˈpræktɪkəl] *adj* pas pratique; (*person*) qui manque d'esprit pratique

impregnable [ɪmˈpregnəbl] *adj* (*fortress*) imprenable

impress [ɪmˈpres] *vt* impressionner, faire impression sur; (*mark*) imprimer, marquer; **to ~ sth on sb** faire bien comprendre qch à qn

impression [ɪmˈpreʃən] *n* impression *f*; (*of stamp, seal*) empreinte *f*; (*imitation*) imitation *f*; **to be under the ~ that** avoir l'impression que; **~ist** *n* (*ART*) impressionniste *m/f*; (*entertainer*) imita-

teur(trice) *m/f*

impressive [ɪmˈpresɪv] *adj* impressionnant(e)

imprint [ˈɪmprɪnt] *n* (*outline*) marque *f*, empreinte *f*

imprison [ɪmˈprɪzn] *vt* emprisonner, mettre en prison

improbable [ɪmˈprɒbəbl] *adj* improbable; (*excuse*) peu plausible

improper [ɪmˈprɒpə*] *adj* (*unsuitable*) déplacé(e), de mauvais goût; indécent(e); (*dishonest*) malhonnête

improve [ɪmˈpruːv] *vt* améliorer ♦ *vi* s'améliorer; (*pupil etc*) faire des progrès; **~ment** *n* amélioration *f* (*in* de); progrès *m*

improvise [ˈɪmprəvaɪz] *vt, vi* improviser

impudent [ˈɪmpjʊdənt] *adj* impudent(e)

impulse [ˈɪmpʌls] *n* impulsion *f*; **on ~** impulsivement, sur un coup de tête; **impulsive** [ɪmˈpʌlsɪv] *adj* impulsif(ive)

KEYWORD

---

in [ɪn] *prep* **1** (*indicating place, position*) dans; ~ **the house/the fridge** dans la maison/le frigo; ~ **the garden** dans le *or* au jardin; ~ **town** en ville; ~ **the country** à la campagne; ~ **school** à l'école; ~ **here/there** ici/là

2 (*with place names: of town, region, country*): ~ **London** à Londres; ~ **England** en Angleterre; ~ **Japan** au Japon; ~ **the United States** aux États-Unis

3 (*indicating time: during*): ~ **spring** au printemps; ~ **summer** en été; ~ **May/1992** en mai/1992; ~ **the afternoon** (dans) l'après-midi; **at 4 o'clock ~ the afternoon** à 4 heures de l'après-midi

4 (*indicating time: in the space of*) en; (: *future*) dans; **I did it ~ 3 hours/days** je l'ai fait en 3 heures/jours; **I'll see you ~ 2 weeks** *or* **2 weeks' time** je te verrai dans 2 semaines

5 (*indicating manner etc*) à; ~ **a loud/soft voice** à voix haute/basse; ~ **pencil** au crayon; ~ **French** en français; **the boy ~ the blue shirt** le garçon à *or* avec la chemise bleue

6 (*indicating circumstances*): ~ **the sun**

au soleil; ~ **the shade** à l'ombre; ~ **the rain** sous la pluie

7 (*indicating mood, state*): ~ **tears** en larmes; ~ **anger** sous le coup de la colère; ~ **despair** au désespoir; ~ **good condition** en bon état; **to live** ~ **luxury** vivre dans le luxe

8 (*with ratios, numbers*): **1** ~ **10** (**households**), **1** (**household**) ~ **10 1** (ménage) sur 10; **20 pence** ~ **the pound** 20 pence par livre sterling; **they lined up** ~ **twos** ils se mirent en rangs (deux) par deux; ~ **hundreds** par centaines

9 (*referring to people, works*) chez; **the disease is common** ~ **children** c'est une maladie courante chez les enfants; ~ **(the works of) Dickens** chez Dickens, dans (l'œuvre de) Dickens

10 (*indicating profession etc*) dans; **to be** ~ **teaching** être dans l'enseignement

11 (*after superlative*) de; **the best pupil** ~ **the class** le meilleur élève de la classe

12 (*with present participle*): ~ **saying this** en disant ceci

♦ *adv*: **to be** ~ (*person: at home, work*) être là; (*train, ship, plane*) être arrivé(e); (*in fashion*) être à la mode; **to ask sb** ~ inviter qn à entrer; **to run/limp** *etc* ~ entrer en courant/boitant *etc*

♦ *n*: **the** ~**s and outs (of)** (*of proposal, situation etc*) les tenants et aboutissants (de)

in. *abbr* = **inch**

inability [ɪnəˈbɪlɪtɪ] *n* incapacité *f*

inaccurate [ɪnˈækjʊrɪt] *adj* inexact(e); (*person*) qui manque de précision

inadequate [ɪnˈædɪkwət] *adj* insuffisant(e), inadéquat(e)

inadvertently [ɪnədˈvɜːtəntlɪ] *adv* par mégarde

inadvisable [ɪnədˈvaɪzəbl] *adj* (*action*) à déconseiller

inane [ɪˈneɪn] *adj* inepte, stupide

inanimate [ɪnˈænɪmət] *adj* inanimé(e)

inappropriate [ɪnəˈprəʊprɪət] *adj* inopportun(e), mal à propos; (*word, expression*) impropre

inarticulate [ɪnɑːˈtɪkjʊlət] *adj* (*person*) qui s'exprime mal; (*speech*) indistinct(e)

inasmuch as [ɪnəzˈmʌtʃəz] *adv* (*insofar as*) dans la mesure où; (*seeing that*) attendu que

inauguration [ɪnɔːgjʊˈreɪʃən] *n* inauguration *f*; (*of president*) investiture *f*

inborn [ˈɪnbɔːn] *adj* (*quality*) inné(e)

inbred [ˈɪnbred] *adj* inné(e), naturel(le); (*family*) consanguin(e)

Inc. *abbr* = **incorporated**

incapable [ɪnˈkeɪpəbl] *adj* incapable

incapacitate [ɪnkəˈpæsɪteɪt] *vt*: **to** ~ **sb from doing** rendre qn incapable de faire

incense [*n* ˈɪnsens, *vb* ɪnˈsens] *n* encens *m* ♦ *vt* (*anger*) mettre en colère

incentive [ɪnˈsentɪv] *n* encouragement *m*, raison *f* de se donner de la peine

incessant [ɪnˈsesnt] *adj* incessant(e); ~**ly** *adv* sans cesse, constamment

inch [ɪntʃ] *n* pouce *m* (= *25 mm; 12 in a foot*); **within an** ~ **of** à deux doigts de; **he didn't give an** ~ (*fig*) il n'a pas voulu céder d'un pouce; ~ **forward** *vi* avancer petit à petit

incident [ˈɪnsɪdənt] *n* incident *m*

incidental [ɪnsɪˈdentl] *adj* (*additional*) accessoire; ~ **to** qui accompagne; ~**ly** *adv* (*by the way*) à propos

inclination [ɪnklɪˈneɪʃən] *n* (*fig*) inclination *f*

incline [*n* ˈɪnklaɪn, *vb* ɪnˈklaɪn] *n* pente *f* ♦ *vt* incliner ♦ *vi* (*surface*) s'incliner; **to be** ~**d to do** avoir tendance à faire

include [ɪnˈkluːd] *vt* inclure, comprendre; **including** [ɪnˈkluːdɪŋ] *prep* y compris

inclusive [ɪnˈkluːsɪv] *adj* inclus(e), compris(e); ~ **of tax** *etc* taxes *etc* comprises

income [ˈɪnkʌm] *n* revenu *m*; ~ **tax** *n* impôt *m* sur le revenu

incoming [ˈɪnkʌmɪŋ] *adj* qui arrive; (*president*) entrant(e); ~ **mail** courrier *m* du jour; ~ **tide** marée montante

incompetent [ɪnˈkɒmpɪtənt] *adj* incompétent(e), incapable

incomplete [ɪnkəmˈpliːt] *adj* incomplet(ète)

incongruous [ɪnˈkɒŋgrʊəs] *adj* incongru(e)

inconsiderate [ɪnkən'sɪdərɪt] *adj* (*person*) qui manque d'égards; (*action*) inconsidéré(e)

inconsistency [ɪnkən'sɪstənsɪ] *n* (*of actions etc*) inconséquence *f*; (*of work*) irrégularité *f*; (*of statement etc*) incohérence *f*

inconsistent [ɪnkən'sɪstənt] *adj* inconséquent(e); irrégulier(ère); peu cohérent(e); **~ with** incompatible avec

inconspicuous [ɪnkən'spɪkjʊəs] *adj* qui passe inaperçu(e); (*colour, dress*) discret(ète)

inconvenience [ɪnkən'viːnɪəns] *n* inconvénient *m*; (*trouble*) dérangement *m* ♦ *vt* déranger

inconvenient [ɪnkən'viːnɪənt] *adj* (*house*) malcommode; (*time, place*) mal choisi(e), qui ne convient pas; (*visitor*) importun(e)

incorporate [ɪn'kɔːpəreɪt] *vt* incorporer; (*contain*) contenir; **~d company** (*US*) *n* ≈ société *f* anonyme

incorrect [ɪnkə'rekt] *adj* incorrect(e)

increase [*n* 'ɪnkriːs, *vb* ɪn'kriːs] *n* augmentation *f* ♦ *vi, vt* augmenter; **increasing** [ɪn'kriːsɪŋ] *adj* (*number*) croissant(e); **increasingly** [ɪn'kriːsɪŋlɪ] *adv* de plus en plus

incredible [ɪn'kredəbl] *adj* incroyable

incredulous [ɪn'kredjʊləs] *adj* incrédule

incubator ['ɪnkjʊbeɪtə*] *n* (*for babies*) couveuse *f*

incumbent [ɪn'kʌmbənt] *n* (*president*) président *m* en exercice; (*REL*) titulaire *m/f* ♦ *adj*: **it is ~ on him to ...** il lui incombe *or* appartient de ...

incur [ɪn'kɜː*] *vt* (*expenses*) encourir; (*anger, risk*) s'exposer à; (*debt*) contracter; (*loss*) subir

indebted [ɪn'detɪd] *adj*: **to be ~ to sb (for)** être redevable à qn (de)

indecent [ɪn'diːsnt] *adj* indécent(e), inconvenant(e); **~ assault** (*BRIT*) *n* attentat *m* à la pudeur; **~ exposure** *n* outrage *m* (public) à la pudeur

indecisive [ɪndɪ'saɪsɪv] *adj* (*person*) indécis(e)

indeed [ɪn'diːd] *adv* vraiment; en effet; (*furthermore*) d'ailleurs; **yes ~!** certainement!

indefinitely [ɪn'defɪnɪtlɪ] *adv* (*wait*) indéfiniment

indemnity [ɪn'demnɪtɪ] *n* (*safeguard*) assurance *f*, garantie *f*; (*compensation*) indemnité *f*

independence [ɪndɪ'pendəns] *n* indépendance *f*; **independent** [ɪndɪ'pendənt] *adj* indépendant(e); (*school*) privé(e); (*radio*) libre

index ['ɪndeks] *n* (*pl*: ~**es**: *in book*) index *m*; (: *in library etc*) catalogue *m*; (*pl*: *indices*: *ratio, sign*) indice *m*; **~ card** *n* fiche *f*; **~ finger** *n* index *m*; **~-linked** *adj* indexé(e) (sur le coût de la vie *etc*)

India ['ɪndɪə] *n* Inde *f*; **~n** *adj* indien(ne) ♦ *n* Indien(ne); (**American**) **~n** Indien(ne) (d'Amérique)

indicate ['ɪndɪkeɪt] *vt* indiquer; **indication** [ɪndɪ'keɪʃən] *n* indication *f*, signe *m*; **indicative** [ɪn'dɪkətɪv] *adj*: **indicative of** symptomatique de ♦ *n* (*LING*) indicatif *m*; **indicator** ['ɪndɪkeɪtə*] *n* (*sign*) indicateur *m*; (*AUT*) clignotant *m*

indices ['ɪndɪsiːz] *npl of* index

indictment [ɪn'daɪtmənt] *n* accusation *f*

indifferent [ɪn'dɪfrənt] *adj* indifférent(e); (*poor*) médiocre, quelconque

indigenous [ɪn'dɪdʒɪnəs] *adj* indigène

indigestion [ɪndɪ'dʒestʃən] *n* indigestion *f*, mauvaise digestion

indignant [ɪn'dɪgnənt] *adj*: **~ (at sth/ with sb)** indigné(e) (de qch/contre qn)

indignity [ɪn'dɪgnɪtɪ] *n* indignité *f*, affront *m*

indirect [ɪndɪ'rekt] *adj* indirect(e)

indiscreet [ɪndɪs'kriːt] *adj* indiscret(ète); (*rash*) imprudent(e)

indiscriminate [ɪndɪs'krɪmɪnət] *adj* (*person*) qui manque de discernement; (*killings*) commis(e) au hasard

indisputable [ɪndɪs'pjuːtəbl] *adj* incontestable, indiscutable

individual [ɪndɪ'vɪdjuəl] *n* individu *m* ♦ *adj* individuel(le); (*characteristic*) particulier(ère), original(e)

indoctrination [ɪndɒktrɪ'neɪʃən] *n* endoctrinement *m*

Indonesia [ɪndəʊˈniːzɪə] *n* Indonésie *f*

indoor [ˈɪndɔː*] *adj* (*plant*) d'appartement; (*swimming pool*) couvert(e); (*sport, games*) pratiqué(e) en salle; **~s** [ɪnˈdɔːz] *adv* à l'intérieur

induce [ɪnˈdjuːs] *vt* (*persuade*) persuader; (*bring about*) provoquer; **~ment** *n* (*incentive*) récompense *f*; (*pej: bribe*) pot-de-vin *m*

indulge [ɪnˈdʌldʒ] *vt* (*whim*) céder à, satisfaire; (*child*) gâter ♦ *vi*: **to ~ in sth** (*luxury*) se permettre qch; (*fantasies etc*) se livrer à qch; **~nce** *n* fantaisie *f* (que l'on s'offre); (*leniency*) indulgence *f*; **~nt** *adj* indulgent(e)

industrial [ɪnˈdʌstrɪəl] *adj* industriel(le); (*injury*) du travail; **~ action** *n* action revendicative; **~ estate** (*BRIT*) *n* zone industrielle; **~ist** *n* industriel *m*; **~ park** (*US*) *n* = **industrial estate**

industrious [ɪnˈdʌstrɪəs] *adj* travailleur(euse)

industry [ˈɪndəstrɪ] *n* industrie *f*; (*diligence*) zèle *m*, application *f*

inebriated [ɪˈniːbrɪeɪtɪd] *adj* ivre

inedible [ɪnˈedɪbl] *adj* immangeable; (*plant etc*) non comestible

ineffective [ɪnɪˈfektɪv], **ineffectual** [ɪnɪˈfektjʊəl] *adj* inefficace

inefficient [ɪnɪˈfɪʃənt] *adj* inefficace

inequality [ɪnɪˈkwɒlɪtɪ] *n* inégalité *f*

inescapable [ɪnɪsˈkeɪpəbl] *adj* inéluctable, inévitable

inevitable [ɪnˈevɪtəbl] *adj* inévitable; **inevitably** *adv* inévitablement

inexhaustible [ɪnɪgˈzɔːstəbl] *adj* inépuisable

inexpensive [ɪnɪksˈpensɪv] *adj* bon marché *inv*

inexperienced [ɪnɪksˈpɪərɪənst] *adj* inexpérimenté(e)

infallible [ɪnˈfæləbl] *adj* infaillible

infamous [ˈɪnfəməs] *adj* infâme, abominable

infancy [ˈɪnfənsɪ] *n* petite enfance, bas âge

infant [ˈɪnfənt] *n* (*baby*) nourrisson *m*; (*young child*) petit(e) enfant; **~ school** (*BRIT*) *n* classes *fpl* préparatoires (*entre 5 et 7 ans*)

infatuated [ɪnˈfætjʊeɪtɪd] *adj*: **~ with** entiché(e) de; **infatuation** [ɪnfætjʊˈeɪʃən] *n* engouement *m*

infect [ɪnˈfekt] *vt* infecter, contaminer; **~ion** [ɪnˈfekʃən] *n* infection *f*; (*contagion*) contagion *f*; **~ious** [ɪnˈfekʃəs] *adj* infectieux(euse); (*also fig*) contagieux(euse)

infer [ɪnˈfɜː*] *vt* conclure, déduire; (*imply*) suggérer

inferior [ɪnˈfɪərɪə*] *adj* inférieur(e); (*goods*) de qualité inférieure ♦ *n* inférieur(e); (*in rank*) subalterne *m/f*; **~ity** [ɪnfɪərɪˈɒrɪtɪ] *n* infériorité *f*; **~ity complex** *n* complexe *m* d'infériorité

inferno [ɪnˈfɜːnəʊ] *n* (*blaze*) brasier *m*

infertile [ɪnˈfɜːtaɪl] *adj* stérile

infighting [ˈɪnfaɪtɪŋ] *n* querelles *fpl* internes

infinite [ˈɪnfɪnɪt] *adj* infini(e)

infinitive [ɪnˈfɪnɪtɪv] *n* infinitif *m*

infinity [ɪnˈfɪnɪtɪ] *n* infinité *f*; (*also MATH*) infini *m*

infirmary [ɪnˈfɜːmərɪ] *n* (*hospital*) hôpital *m*

inflamed [ɪnˈfleɪmd] *adj* enflammé(e)

inflammable [ɪnˈflæməbl] (*BRIT*) *adj* inflammable

inflammation [ɪnfləˈmeɪʃən] *n* inflammation *f*

inflatable [ɪnˈfleɪtəbl] *adj* gonflable

inflate [ɪnˈfleɪt] *vt* (*tyre, balloon*) gonfler; (*price*) faire monter; **inflation** [ɪnˈfleɪʃən] *n* (*ECON*) inflation *f*; **inflationary** [ɪnˈfleɪʃnərɪ] *adj* inflationniste

inflict [ɪnˈflɪkt] *vt*: **to ~ on** infliger à

influence [ˈɪnfluəns] *n* influence *f* ♦ *vt* influencer; **under the ~ of alcohol** en état d'ébriété; **influential** [ɪnflʊˈenʃəl] *adj* influent(e)

influenza [ɪnflʊˈenzə] *n* grippe *f*

influx [ˈɪnflʌks] *n* afflux *m*

inform [ɪnˈfɔːm] *vt*: **to ~ sb (of)** informer *or* avertir qn (de) ♦ *vi*: **to ~ on sb** dénoncer qn

informal [ɪnˈfɔːməl] *adj* (*person, manner, party*) simple; (*visit, discussion*) dénué(e) de formalités; (*announcement, invitation*) non officiel(le); (*colloquial*) familier(ère); **~ity** [ɪnfɔ:'mælɪtɪ] *n* simplicité *f*, absence *f* de cérémonie; caractère non officiel

informant [ɪn'fɔ:mənt] *n* informateur(trice)

information [ɪnfə'meɪʃən] *n* information *f*; renseignements *mpl*; (*knowledge*) connaissances *fpl*; **a piece of ~** un renseignement; **~ office** *n* bureau *m* de renseignements

informative [ɪn'fɔ:mətɪv] *adj* instructif(ive)

informer [ɪn'fɔ:mə*] *n* (*also*: *police* ~) indicateur(trice)

infringe [ɪn'frɪndʒ] *vt* enfreindre ♦ *vi*: **to ~ on** empiéter sur; **~ment** *n*: **~ment (of)** infraction *f* (à)

infuriating [ɪn'fjʊərɪeɪtɪŋ] *adj* exaspérant(e)

ingenious [ɪn'dʒi:nɪəs] *adj* ingénieux(euse); **ingenuity** [ɪndʒɪ'nju:ɪtɪ] *n* ingéniosité *f*

ingenuous [ɪn'dʒenjuəs] *adj* naïf(naïve), ingénu(e)

ingot ['ɪŋgət] *n* lingot *m*

ingrained [ɪn'greɪnd] *adj* enraciné(e)

ingratiate [ɪn'greɪʃɪeɪt] *vt*: **to ~ o.s. with** s'insinuer dans les bonnes grâces de, se faire bien voir de

ingredient [ɪn'gri:dɪənt] *n* ingrédient *m*; (*fig*) élément *m*

inhabit [ɪn'hæbɪt] *vt* habiter; **~ant** [ɪn'hæbɪtnt] *n* habitant(e)

inhale [ɪn'heɪl] *vt* respirer; (*smoke*) avaler ♦ *vi* aspirer; (*in smoking*) avaler la fumée

inherent [ɪn'hɪərənt] *adj*: **~ (in** *or* **to)** inhérent(e) (à)

inherit [ɪn'herɪt] *vt* hériter (de); **~ance** *n* héritage *m*

inhibit [ɪn'hɪbɪt] *vt* (*PSYCH*) inhiber; (*growth*) freiner; **~ion** [ɪnhɪ'bɪʃən] *n* inhibition *f*

inhuman [ɪn'hju:mən] *adj* inhumain(e)

initial [ɪ'nɪʃəl] *adj* initial(e) ♦ *n* initiale *f* ♦ *vt* parafer; **~s** *npl* (*letters*) initiales *fpl*; (*as signature*) parafe *m*; **~ly** *adv* initialement, au début

initiate [ɪ'nɪʃɪeɪt] *vt* (*start*) entreprendre;

amorcer; lancer; (*person*) initier; **to ~ proceedings against sb** intenter une action à qn

initiative [ɪ'nɪʃətɪv] *n* initiative *f*

inject [ɪn'dʒekt] *vt* injecter; (*person*): **to ~ sb with sth** faire une piqûre de qch à qn; **~ion** [ɪn'dʒekʃən] *n* injection *f*, piqûre *f*

injure ['ɪndʒə*] *vt* blesser; (*reputation etc*) compromettre; **~d** *adj* blessé(e); **injury** ['ɪndʒərɪ] *n* blessure *f*; **injury time** *n* (*SPORT*) arrêts *mpl* de jeu

injustice [ɪn'dʒʌstɪs] *n* injustice *f*

ink [ɪŋk] *n* encre *f*

inkling ['ɪŋklɪŋ] *n*: **to have an/no ~ of** avoir une (vague) idée de/n'avoir aucune idée de

inlaid ['ɪn'leɪd] *adj* incrusté(e); (*table etc*) marqueté(e)

inland [*adj* 'ɪnlənd, *adv* 'ɪnlænd] *adj* intérieur(e) ♦ *adv* à l'intérieur, dans les terres; **I~ Revenue** (*BRIT*) *n* fisc *m*

in-laws ['ɪnlɔ:z] *npl* beaux-parents *mpl*; belle famille

inlet ['ɪnlet] *n* (*GEO*) crique *f*

inmate ['ɪnmeɪt] *n* (*in prison*) détenu(e); (*in asylum*) interné(e)

inn [ɪn] *n* auberge *f*

innate [ɪ'neɪt] *adj* inné(e)

inner ['ɪnə*] *adj* intérieur(e); **~ city** *n* centre *m* de zone urbaine; **~ tube** *n* (*of tyre*) chambre *f* à air

innings ['ɪnɪŋz] *n* (*CRICKET*) tour *m* de batte

innocent ['ɪnəsnt] *adj* innocent(e)

innocuous [ɪ'nɒkjuəs] *adj* inoffensif(ive)

innuendo [ɪnju'endəʊ] (*pl* **~es**) *n* insinuation *f*, allusion (malveillante)

innumerable [ɪ'nju:mərəbl] *adj* innombrable

inordinately [ɪ'nɔ:dɪnɪtlɪ] *adv* démesurément

inpatient ['ɪnpeɪʃənt] *n* malade hospitalisé(e)

input ['ɪnpʊt] *n* (*resources*) ressources *fpl*; (*COMPUT*) entrée *f* (de données); (: *data*) données *fpl*

inquest ['ɪnkwest] *n* enquête *f*; **(coroner's) ~** enquête judiciaire

inquire [ɪnˈkwaɪə*] *vi* demander ♦ *vt* demander; **to ~ about** se renseigner sur; **~ into** *vt fus* faire une enquête sur; **inquiry** [ɪnˈkwaɪərɪ] *n* demande *f* de renseignements; (*investigation*) enquête *f*, investigation *f*; **inquiry office** (*BRIT*) *n* bureau *m* de renseignements

inquisitive [ɪnˈkwɪzɪtɪv] *adj* curieux(euse)

inroads [ˈɪnrəʊdz] *npl*: **to make ~ into** (*savings etc*) entamer

ins *abbr* = **inches**

insane [ɪnˈseɪn] *adj* fou(folle); (*MED*) aliéné(e); **insanity** [ɪnˈsænɪtɪ] *n* folie *f*; (*MED*) aliénation (mentale)

inscription [ɪnˈskrɪpʃən] *n* inscription *f*; (*in book*) dédicace *f*

inscrutable [ɪnˈskruːtəbl] *adj* impénétrable; (*comment*) obscur(e)

insect [ˈɪnsɛkt] *n* insecte *m*; **~icide** [ɪnˈsɛktɪsaɪd] *n* insecticide *m*

insecure [ɪnsɪˈkjʊə*] *adj* peu solide; peu sûr(e); (*person*) anxieux(euse)

insensitive [ɪnˈsɛnsɪtɪv] *adj* insensible

insert [ɪnˈsɜːt] *vt* insérer; **~ion** [ɪnˈsɜːʃən] *n* insertion *f*

in-service [ˈɪnˈsɜːvɪs] *adj* (*training*) continu(e), en cours d'emploi; (*course*) de perfectionnement; (*course*) de recyclage

inshore [ˈɪnˈʃɔː*] *adj* côtier(ère) ♦ *adv* près de la côte; (*move*) vers la côte

inside [ˈɪnˈsaɪd] *n* intérieur *m* ♦ *adj* intérieur(e) ♦ *adv* à l'intérieur, dedans ♦ *prep* à l'intérieur de; (*of time*): **~ 10 minutes** en moins de 10 minutes; **~s** *npl* (*inf*) intestins *mpl*; **~ information** *n* renseignements obtenus à la source; **~ lane** *n* (*AUT: in Britain*) voie *f* de gauche; (: *in US, Europe etc*) voie de droite; **~ out** *adv* à l'envers; (*know*) à fond

insider dealing, insider trading *n* (*St Ex*) délit *m* d'initié

insight [ˈɪnsaɪt] *n* perspicacité *f*; (*glimpse, idea*) aperçu *m*

insignificant [ɪnsɪgˈnɪfɪkənt] *adj* insignifiant(e)

insincere [ɪnsɪnˈsɪə*] *adj* hypocrite

insinuate [ɪnˈsɪnjʊeɪt] *vt* insinuer

insist [ɪnˈsɪst] *vi* insister; **to ~ on doing** insister pour faire; **to ~ on sth** exiger qch; **to ~ that** insister pour que; (*claim*) maintenir *or* soutenir que; **~ent** *adj* insistant(e), pressant(e); (*noise, action*) ininterrompu(e)

insole [ˈɪnsəʊl] *n* (*removable*) semelle intérieure

insolent [ˈɪnsələnt] *adj* insolent(e)

insolvent [ɪnˈsɒlvənt] *adj* insolvable

insomnia [ɪnˈsɒmnɪə] *n* insomnie *f*

inspect [ɪnˈspɛkt] *vt* inspecter; (*ticket*) contrôler; **~ion** [ɪnˈspɛkʃən] *n* inspection *f*; contrôle *m*; **~or** *n* inspecteur(trice); (*BRIT: on buses, trains*) contrôleur(euse)

inspire [ɪnˈspaɪə*] *vt* inspirer

install [ɪnˈstɔːl] *vt* installer; **~ation** [ɪnstəˈleɪʃən] *n* installation *f*

instalment [ɪnˈstɔːlmənt] (*US* **installment**) *n* acompte *m*, versement partiel; (*of TV serial etc*) épisode *m*; **in ~s** (*pay*) à tempérament; (*receive*) en plusieurs fois

instance [ˈɪnstəns] *n* exemple *m*; **for ~** par exemple; **in the first ~** tout d'abord, en premier lieu

instant [ˈɪnstənt] *n* instant *m* ♦ *adj* immédiat(e); (*coffee, food*) instantané(e), en poudre; **~ly** *adv* immédiatement, tout de suite

instead [ɪnˈstɛd] *adv* au lieu de cela; **~ of** au lieu de; **~ of sb** à la place de qn

instep [ˈɪnstɛp] *n* cou-de-pied *m*; (*of shoe*) cambrure *f*

instigate [ˈɪnstɪgeɪt] *vt* (*rebellion*) fomenter, provoquer; (*talks etc*) promouvoir

instil [ɪnˈstɪl] *vt*: **to ~ (into)** inculquer (à); (*courage*) insuffler (à)

instinct [ˈɪnstɪŋkt] *n* instinct *m*

institute [ˈɪnstɪtjuːt] *n* institut *m* ♦ *vt* instituer, établir; (*inquiry*) ouvrir; (*proceedings*) entamer

institution [ɪnstɪˈtjuːʃən] *n* institution *f*; (*educational*) établissement *m* (scolaire); (*mental home*) établissement (psychiatrique)

instruct [ɪnˈstrʌkt] *vt*: **to ~ sb in sth** enseigner qch à qn; **to ~ sb to do** charger qn *or* ordonner à qn de faire; **~ion**

[ɪn'strʌkʃən] *n* instruction *f*; ~**ions** *npl* (*orders*) directives *fpl*; ~**ions (for use)** mode *m* d'emploi; ~**or** *n* professeur *m*; (*for skiing, driving*) moniteur *m*

instrument ['ɪnstrʊmənt] *n* instrument *m*; ~**al** [ɪnstru'mentl] *adj*: **to be ~al in** contribuer à; ~ **panel** *n* tableau *m* de bord

insufficient [ɪnsə'fɪʃənt] *adj* insuffisant(e)

insular ['ɪnsjələ*] *adj* (*outlook*) borné(e); (*person*) aux vues étroites

insulate ['ɪnsjʊleɪt] *vt* isoler; (*against sound*) insonoriser; **insulating tape** *n* ruban isolant; **insulation** [ɪnsjʊ'leɪʃən] *n* isolation *f*; insonorisation *f*

insulin ['ɪnsjʊlɪn] *n* insuline *f*

insult [*n* 'ɪnsʌlt, *vb* ɪn'sʌlt] *n* insulte *f*, affront *m* ♦ *vt* insulter, faire affront à

insurance [ɪn'ʃʊərəns] *n* assurance *f*; **fire/life** ~ assurance-incendie/-vie; ~ **policy** *n* police *f* d'assurance

insure [ɪn'ʃʊə*] *vt* assurer; **to ~ (o.s.) against** (*fig*) parer à

intact [ɪn'tækt] *adj* intact(e)

intake ['ɪnteɪk] *n* (*of food, oxygen*) consommation *f*; (*BRIT: SCOL*): **an ~ of 200 a year** 200 admissions *fpl* par an

integral ['ɪntɪɡrəl] *adj* (*part*) intégrant(e)

integrate ['ɪntɪɡreɪt] *vt* intégrer ♦ *vi* s'intégrer

intellect ['ɪntɪlekt] *n* intelligence *f*; ~**ual** [ɪntɪ'lektjʊəl] *adj, n* intellectuel(le)

intelligence [ɪn'telɪdʒəns] *n* intelligence *f*; (*MIL etc*) informations *fpl*, renseignements *mpl*; ~ **service** *n* services secrets; **intelligent** [ɪn'telɪdʒənt] *adj* intelligent(e)

intend [ɪn'tend] *vt* (*gift etc*): **to ~ sth for** destiner qch à; **to ~ to do** avoir l'intention de faire; ~**ed** *adj* (*journey*) projeté(e); (*effect*) voulu(e); (*insult*) intentionnel(le)

intense [ɪn'tens] *adj* intense; (*person*) véhément(e); ~**ly** *adv* intensément; profondément

intensive [ɪn'tensɪv] *adj* intensif(ive); ~ **care unit** *n* service *m* de réanimation

intent [ɪn'tent] *n* intention *f* ♦ *adj* attentif(ive); (*absorbed*): ~ **(on)** absorbé(e)

(par); **to all ~s and purposes** en fait, pratiquement; **to be ~ on doing sth** être (bien) décidé à faire qch

intention [ɪn'tenʃən] *n* intention *f*; ~**al** *adj* intentionnel(le), délibéré(e)

intently [ɪn'tentlɪ] *adv* attentivement

interact [ɪntər'ækt] *vi* avoir une action réciproque; (*people*) communiquer; ~**ive** *adj* (*COMPUT*) interactif(ive)

interchange [*n* 'ɪntətʃeɪndʒ, *vb* ɪntə'tʃeɪndʒ] *n* (*exchange*) échange *m*; (*on motorway*) échangeur *m*; ~**able** [ɪntə'tʃeɪndʒəbl] *adj* interchangeable

intercom ['ɪntəkɒm] *n* interphone *m*

intercourse ['ɪntəkɔːs] *n* (*sexual*) rapports *mpl*

interest ['ɪntrest] *n* intérêt *m*; (*pastime*): **my main** ~ ce qui m'intéresse le plus; (*COMM*) intérêts *mpl* ♦ *vt* intéresser; **to be ~ed in** s'intéresser à qch; **I am ~ed in going** ça m'intéresse d'y aller; ~**ing** *adj* intéressant(e); ~ **rate** *n* taux *m* d'intérêt

interface ['ɪntəfeɪs] *n* (*COMPUT*) interface *f*

interfere [ɪntə'fɪə*] *vi*: **to ~ in** (*quarrel*) s'immiscer dans; (*other people's business*) se mêler de; **to ~ with** (*object*) toucher à; (*plans*) contrecarrer; (*duty*) être en conflit avec; ~**nce** *n* (*RADIO, TV*) parasites *mpl*

interim ['ɪntərɪm] *adj* provisoire ♦ *n*: **in the** ~ dans l'intérim, entre-temps

interior [ɪn'tɪərɪə*] *n* intérieur *m* ♦ *adj* intérieur(e); (*minister, department*) de l'Intérieur; ~ **designer** *n* styliste *m/f*

interjection [ɪntə'dʒekʃən] *n* (*interruption*) interruption *f*; (*LING*) interjection *f*

interlock [ɪntə'lɒk] *vi* s'enclencher

interlude ['ɪntəluːd] *n* intervalle *m*; (*THEATRE*) intermède *m*

intermediate [ɪntə'miːdɪət] *adj* intermédiaire; (*SCOL: course, level*) moyen(ne)

intermission [ɪntə'mɪʃən] *n* pause *f*; (*THEATRE, CINEMA*) entracte *m*

intern [*vb* ɪn'tɜːn, *n* 'ɪntɜːn] *vt* interner ♦ *n* (*US*) interne *m/f*

internal [ɪn'tɜ:nl] *adj* interne; (*politics*) intérieur(e); **~ly** *adv*: **"not to be taken ~ly"** "pour usage externe"; **I~ Revenue Service** (*US*) *n* fisc *m*

international [ɪntə'næʃnəl] *adj* international(e)

interplay ['ɪntəpleɪ] *n* effet *m* réciproque, interaction *f*

interpret [ɪn'tɜ:prɪt] *vt* interpréter ♦ *vi* servir d'interprète; **~er** *n* interprète *m/f*

interrelated [ɪntərɪ'leɪtɪd] *adj* en corrélation, en rapport étroit

interrogate [ɪn'terəgeɪt] *vt* interroger; (*suspect etc*) soumettre à un interrogatoire; **interrogation** [ɪntərə'geɪʃən] *n* interrogation *f*; interrogatoire *m*

interrupt [ɪntə'rʌpt] *vt, vi* interrompre; **~ion** *n* interruption *f*

intersect [ɪntə'sekt] *vi* (*roads*) se croiser, se couper; **~ion** *n* [ɪntə'sekʃən] *n* (*of roads*) croisement *m*

intersperse [ɪntə'spɜ:s] *vt*: **to ~ with** parsemer de

intertwine [ɪntə'twaɪn] *vi* s'entrelacer

interval ['ɪntəvəl] *n* intervalle *m*; (*BRIT: THEATRE*) entracte *m*; (*: SPORT*) mi-temps *f*; **at ~s** par intervalles

intervene [ɪntə'vi:n] *vi* (*person*) intervenir; (*event*) survenir; (*time*) s'écouler (entre-temps); **intervention** [ɪntə'venʃən] *n* intervention *f*

interview ['ɪntəvju:] *n* (*RADIO, TV etc*) interview *f*; (*for job*) entrevue *f* ♦ *vt* interviewer; avoir une entrevue avec; **~er** *n* (*RADIO, TV*) interviewer *m*

intestine [ɪn'testɪn] *n* intestin *m*

intimacy ['ɪntɪməsɪ] *n* intimité *f*

intimate [*adj* 'ɪntɪmət, *vb* 'ɪntɪmeɪt] *adj* intime; (*friendship*) profond(e); (*knowledge*) approfondi(e) ♦ *vt* (*hint*) suggérer, laisser entendre

into ['ɪntu] *prep* dans; **~ pieces/French** en morceaux/français

intolerant [ɪn'tɒlərənt] *adj*: **~ (of)** intolérant(e) (de)

intoxicated [ɪn'tɒksɪkeɪtɪd] *adj* (*drunk*) ivre; **intoxication** [ɪntɒksɪ'keɪʃən] *n* ivresse *f*

intractable [ɪn'træktəbl] *adj* (*child*) in-

docile, insoumis(e); (*problem*) insoluble

intransitive [ɪn'trænsɪtɪv] *adj* intransitif(ive)

intravenous [ɪntrə'vi:nəs] *adj* intraveineux(euse)

in-tray ['ɪntreɪ] *n* courrier *m* "arrivée"

intricate ['ɪntrɪkət] *adj* complexe, compliqué(e)

intrigue [ɪn'tri:g] *n* intrigue *f* ♦ *vt* intriguer; **intriguing** [ɪn'tri:gɪŋ] *adj* fascinant(e)

intrinsic [ɪn'trɪnsɪk] *adj* intrinsèque

introduce [ɪntrə'dju:s] *vt* introduire; (*TV show, people to each other*) présenter; **to ~ sb to** (*pastime, technique*) initier qn à; **introduction** [ɪntrə'dʌkʃən] *n* introduction *f*; (*of person*) présentation *f*; (*to new experience*) initiation *f*; **introductory** [ɪntrə'dʌktərɪ] *adj* préliminaire, d'introduction; **introductory offer** *n* (*COMM*) offre *f* de lancement

intrude [ɪn'tru:d] *vi* (*person*) être importun(e); **to ~ on** (*conversation etc*) s'immiscer dans; **~r** *n* intrus(e)

intuition [ɪntju:'ɪʃən] *n* intuition *f*

inundate ['ɪnʌndeɪt] *vt*: **to ~ with** inonder de

invade [ɪn'veɪd] *vt* envahir

invalid [*n* 'ɪnvəlɪd, *adj* ɪn'vælɪd] *n* malade *m/f*; (*with disability*) invalide *m/f* ♦ *adj* (*not valid*) non valide *or* valable

invaluable [ɪn'væljuəbl] *adj* inestimable, inappréciable

invariably [ɪn'vɛərɪəblɪ] *adv* invariablement; toujours

invent [ɪn'vent] *vt* inventer; **~ion** [ɪn'venʃən] *n* invention *f*; **~ive** *adj* inventif(ive); **~or** *n* inventeur(trice)

inventory ['ɪnvəntrɪ] *n* inventaire *m*

invert [ɪn'vɜ:t] *vt* intervertir; (*cup, object*) retourner; **~ed commas** (*BRIT*) *npl* guillemets *mpl*

invest [ɪn'vest] *vt* investir ♦ *vi*: **to ~ in sth** placer son argent dans qch; (*fig*) s'offrir qch

investigate [ɪn'vestɪgeɪt] *vt* (*crime etc*) faire une enquête sur; **investigation** [ɪnvestɪ'geɪʃən] *n* (*of crime*) enquête *f*

investment [ɪn'vestmənt] *n* investissement *m*, placement *m*

investor [ɪn'vɛstə*] *n* investisseur *m*; actionnaire *m/f*

invigilator [ɪn'vɪdʒɪleɪtə*] *n* surveillant(e)

invigorating [ɪn'vɪgəreɪtɪŋ] *adj* vivifiant(e); (*fig*) stimulant(e)

invisible [ɪn'vɪzəbl] *adj* invisible

invitation [ɪnvɪ'teɪʃən] *n* invitation *f*

invite [ɪn'vaɪt] *vt* inviter; (*opinions etc*) demander

inviting [ɪn'vaɪtɪŋ] *adj* engageant(e), attrayant(e)

invoice ['ɪnvɔɪs] *n* facture *f*

involuntary [ɪn'vɒləntərɪ] *adj* involontaire

involve [ɪn'vɒlv] *vt* (*entail*) entraîner, nécessiter; (*concern*) concerner; (*associate*): **to ~ sb (in)** impliquer qn (dans), mêler qn (à); faire participer qn (à); **~d** *adj* (*complicated*) complexe; **to be ~d in** participer à; (*engrossed*) être absorbé(e) par; **~ment** *n*: **~ment (in)** participation *f* (à); rôle *m* (dans); (*enthusiasm*) enthousiasme *m* (pour)

inward ['ɪnwəd] *adj* (*thought, feeling*) profond(e), intime; (*movement*) vers l'intérieur; **~(s)** *adv* vers l'intérieur

I/O *abbr* (*COMPUT: = input/output*) E/S

iodine ['aɪədiːn] *n* iode *m*

ioniser ['aɪənaɪzə*] *n* ioniseur *m*

iota [aɪ'əʊtə] *n* (*fig*) brin *m*, grain *m*

IOU *n abbr* (*= I owe you*) reconnaissance *f* de dette

IQ *n abbr* (*= intelligence quotient*) Q.I. *m*

IRA *n abbr* (*= Irish Republican Army*) IRA *f*

Iran [ɪ'rɑːn] *n* Iran *m*

Iraq [ɪ'rɑːk] *n* Irak *m*

irate [aɪ'reɪt] *adj* courroucé(e)

Ireland ['aɪələnd] *n* Irlande *f*

iris ['aɪrɪs] (*pl* **~es**) *n* iris *m*

Irish ['aɪrɪʃ] *adj* irlandais(e) ♦ *npl*: **the ~** les Irlandais; **~man** (*irreg*) *n* Irlandais *m*; **~ Sea** *n* mer *f* d'Irlande; **~woman** (*irreg*) *n* Irlandaise *f*

iron ['aɪən] *n* fer *m*; (*for clothes*) fer *m* à repasser ♦ *cpd* de *or* en fer; (*fig*) de fer

♦ *vt* (*clothes*) repasser; **~ out** *vt* (*fig*) aplanir; faire disparaître; **the I~ Curtain** *n* le rideau de fer

ironic(al) [aɪ'rɒnɪk(əl)] *adj* ironique

ironing ['aɪənɪŋ] *n* repassage *m*; **~ board** *n* planche *f* à repasser

ironmonger's (shop) ['aɪənmʌŋgəz-] *n* quincaillerie *f*

irony ['aɪərənɪ] *n* ironie *f*

irrational [ɪ'ræʃənl] *adj* irrationnel(le)

irregular [ɪ'regjʊlə*] *adj* irrégulier(ère); (*surface*) inégal(e)

irrelevant [ɪ'reləvənt] *adj* sans rapport, hors de propos

irresistible [ɪrɪ'zɪstəbl] *adj* irrésistible

irrespective [ɪrɪ'spektɪv]: **~ of** *prep* sans tenir compte de

irresponsible [ɪrɪ'spɒnsəbl] *adj* (*act*) irréfléchi(e); (*person*) irresponsable, inconscient(e)

irrigate ['ɪrɪgeɪt] *vt* irriguer; **irrigation** [ɪrɪ'geɪʃən] *n* irrigation *f*

irritate ['ɪrɪteɪt] *vt* irriter; **irritating** *adj* irritant(e); **irritation** [ɪrɪ'teɪʃən] *n* irritation *f*

IRS *n abbr* = **Internal Revenue Service**

is [ɪz] *vb see* **be**

Islam ['ɪzlɑːm] *n* Islam *m*

island ['aɪlənd] *n* île *f*; **~er** *n* habitant(e) d'une île, insulaire *m/f*

isle [aɪl] *n* île *f*

isn't ['ɪznt] = **is not**

isolate ['aɪsəʊleɪt] *vt* isoler; **~d** *adj* isolé(e)

isolation [aɪsəʊ'leɪʃən] *n* isolation *f*

Israel ['ɪzreɪəl] *n* Israël *m*; **~i** [ɪz'reɪlɪ] *adj* israélien(ne) ♦ *n* Israélien(ne)

issue ['ɪʃuː] *n* question *f*, problème *m*; (*of book*) publication *f*, parution *f*; (*of banknotes etc*) émission *f*; (*of newspaper etc*) numéro *m* ♦ *vt* (*rations, equipment*) distribuer; (*statement*) publier, faire; (*banknotes etc*) émettre, mettre en circulation; **at ~** en jeu, en cause; **to take ~ with sb (over)** exprimer son désaccord avec qn (sur); **to make an ~ of sth** faire une montagne de qch

it [ɪt] *pron* 1 (*specific: subject*) il(elle); (*: direct object*) le(la, l'); (*: indirect object*) lui; ~'s on the table c'est *or* il (la (*or* elle) est sur la table; **about/from/of** ~ en; I spoke to him about ~ je lui en ai parlé; **what did you learn from ~?** qu'est-ce que vous en avez retiré?; **I'm proud of** ~ j'en suis fier; **in/to** ~ y; **put the book in** ~ mettez-y le livre; **he agreed to** ~ il y a consenti; **did you go to ~?** (*party, concert etc*) est-ce que vous y êtes allé(s)?
2 (*impersonal*) il; ce; ~'s raining il pleut; ~'s Friday tomorrow demain c'est vendredi *or* nous sommes vendredi; ~'s 6 o'clock il est 6 heures; **who is ~? - ~'s me** qui est-ce? - c'est moi

Italian [ɪ'tæljən] *adj* italien(ne) ♦ *n* Italien(ne); (*LING*) italien *m*
italics [ɪ'tælɪks] *npl* italiques *fpl*
Italy ['ɪtəlɪ] *n* Italie *f*
itch [ɪtʃ] *n* démangeaison *f* ♦ *vi* (*person*) éprouver des démangeaisons; (*part of body*) démanger; ~**y** *adj* qui démange; **to be** ~**y** avoir des démangeaisons
it'd ['ɪtd] = **it would**; **it had**
item ['aɪtəm] *n* article *m*; (*on agenda*) question *f*, point *m*; (*also: news* ~) nouvelle *f*; ~**ize** *vt* détailler, faire une liste de
itinerary [aɪ'tɪnərərɪ] *n* itinéraire *m*
it'll: ~'ll ['ɪtl] = **it will**; **it shall**; ~s [ɪts] *adj* son(sa), ses *pl*; ~'s [ɪts] = **it is**; **it has**; ~**self** [ɪt'sɛlf] *pron* (*reflexive*) se; (*emphatic*) lui-même(elle-même)
ITV *n abbr* (*BRIT*: = *Independent Television*) chaîne privée
IUD *n abbr* (= *intra-uterine device*) DIU *m*, stérilet *m*
I've [aɪv] = **I have**
ivory ['aɪvərɪ] *n* ivoire *m*
ivy ['aɪvɪ] *n* lierre *m*

J j

jab [dʒæb] *vt*: **to** ~ **sth into** enfoncer *or* planter qch dans ♦ *n* (*inf: injection*) piqûre *f*
jack [dʒæk] *n* (*AUT*) cric *m*; (*CARDS*) valet *m*; ~ **up** *vt* soulever (au cric)
jackal ['dʒækəl] *n* chacal *m*
jackdaw ['dʒækdɔ:] *n* choucas *m*
jacket ['dʒækɪt] *n* veste *f*, veston *m*; (*of book*) jaquette *f*, couverture *f*
jackknife ['dʒæknaɪf] *vi*: **the lorry** ~**d** la remorque (du camion) s'est mise en travers
jack plug *n* (*ELEC*) prise jack mâle *f*
jackpot ['dʒækpɔt] *n* gros lot
jaded ['dʒeɪdɪd] *adj* éreinté(e), fatigué(e)
jagged ['dʒægɪd] *adj* dentelé(e)
jail [dʒeɪl] *n* prison *f* ♦ *vt* emprisonner, mettre en prison
jam [dʒæm] *n* confiture *f*; (*also: traffic* ~) embouteillage *m* ♦ *vt* (*passage etc*) encombrer, obstruer; (*mechanism, drawer etc*) bloquer, coincer; (*RADIO*) brouiller ♦ *vi* se coincer, se bloquer; (*gun*) s'enrayer; **to be in a** ~ (*inf*) être dans le pétrin; **to** ~ **sth into** entasser qch dans; enfoncer qch dans
jangle ['dʒæŋgl] *vi* cliqueter
janitor ['dʒænɪtə*] *n* concierge *m*
January ['dʒænjuərɪ] *n* janvier *m*
Japan [dʒə'pæn] *n* Japon *m*; ~**ese** *adj* [dʒæpə'ni:z] japonais(e) ♦ *n inv* Japonais(e); (*LING*) japonais *m*
jar [dʒɑ:*] *n* (*stone, earthenware*) pot *m*; (*glass*) bocal *m* ♦ *vi* (*sound discordant*) produire un son grinçant *or* discordant; (*colours etc*) jurer
jargon ['dʒɑ:gən] *n* jargon *m*
jaundice ['dʒɔ:ndɪs] *n* jaunisse *f*; ~**d** *adj* (*fig*) envieux(euse), désapprobateur(trice)
javelin ['dʒævlɪn] *n* javelot *m*
jaw [dʒɔ:] *n* mâchoire *f*
jay [dʒeɪ] *n* geai *m*; ~**walker** ['dʒeɪwɔ:kə*] *n* piéton indiscipliné

jazz [dʒæz] *n* jazz *m*; ~ **up** *vt* animer, égayer

jealous ['dʒeləs] *adj* jaloux(ouse); ~**y** *n* jalousie *f*

jeans [dʒiːnz] *npl* jean *m*

jeer [dʒɪə*] *vi*: **to** ~ **(at)** se moquer cruellement (de), railler

jelly ['dʒelɪ] *n* gelée *f*; ~**fish** *n* méduse *f*

jeopardy ['dʒepədɪ] *n*: **to be in** ~ être en danger *or* péril

jerk [dʒɜːk] *n* secousse *f*; saccade *f*; sursaut *m*, spasme *m*; (*inf: idiot*) pauvre type *m* ♦ *vt* (*pull*) tirer brusquement ♦ *vi* (*vehicles*) cahoter

jersey ['dʒɜːzɪ] *n* (*pullover*) tricot *m*; (*fabric*) jersey *m*

Jesus ['dʒiːzəs] *n* Jésus

jet [dʒet] *n* (*gas, liquid*) jet *m*; (*AVIAT*) avion *m* à réaction, jet *m*; ~**-black** *adj* (d'un noir) de jais; ~ **engine** *n* moteur *m* à réaction; ~ **lag** *n* (fatigue due au) décalage *m* horaire

jettison ['dʒetɪsn] *vt* jeter par-dessus bord

jetty ['dʒetɪ] *n* jetée *f*, digue *f*

Jew [dʒuː] *n* Juif *m*

jewel ['dʒuːəl] *n* bijou *m*, joyau *m*; (*in watch*) rubis *m*; ~**ler** (*US* ~**er**) *n* bijoutier(ère), joaillier *m*; ~**ler's (shop)** *n* bijouterie *f*, joaillerie *f*; ~**lery** (*US* ~**ry**) *n* bijoux *mpl*

Jewess ['dʒuːɪs] *n* Juive *f*

Jewish ['dʒuːɪʃ] *adj* juif(juive)

jibe [dʒaɪb] *n* sarcasme *m*

jiffy ['dʒɪfɪ] (*inf*) *n*: **in a** ~ en un clin d'œil

jigsaw ['dʒɪgsɔː] *n* (*also*: ~ *puzzle*) puzzle *m*

jilt [dʒɪlt] *vt* laisser tomber, plaquer

jingle ['dʒɪŋgl] *n* (*for advert*) couplet *m* publicitaire ♦ *vi* cliqueter, tinter

jinx [dʒɪŋks] (*inf*) *n* (mauvais) sort

jitters ['dʒɪtəz] (*inf*) *npl*: **to get the** ~ (*inf*) avoir la trouille *or* la frousse

job [dʒɒb] *n* (*chore, task*) travail *m*, tâche *f*; (*employment*) emploi *m*, poste *m*, place *f*; **it's a good** ~ **that** ... c'est heureux *or* c'est une chance que ...; **just the** ~! (c'est) juste *or* exactement ce qu'il faut!; ~ **centre** (*BRIT*) *n* agence *f* pour l'emploi; ~**less** *adj* sans travail, au chômage

jockey ['dʒɒkɪ] *n* jockey *m* ♦ *vi*: **to** ~ **for position** manœuvrer pour être bien placé

jocular ['dʒɒkjʊlə*] *adj* jovial(e), enjoué(e); facétieux(euse)

jog [dʒɒg] *vt* secouer ♦ *vi* (*SPORT*) faire du jogging; **to** ~ **sb's memory** rafraîchir la mémoire de qn; ~ **along** *vi* cheminer, trotter; ~**ging** *n* jogging *m*

join [dʒɔɪn] *vt* (*put together*) unir, assembler; (*become member of*) s'inscrire à; (*meet*) rejoindre, retrouver; (*queue*) se joindre à ♦ *vi* (*roads, rivers*) se rejoindre, se rencontrer ♦ *n* raccord *m*; ~ **in** *vi* se mettre de la partie, participer ♦ *vt fus* participer à, se mêler à; ~ **up** *vi* (*meet*) se rejoindre; (*MIL*) s'engager; ~**er** ['dʒɔɪnə*] (*BRIT*) *n* menuisier *m*

joint [dʒɔɪnt] *n* (*TECH*) jointure *f*; joint *m*; (*ANAT*) articulation *f*, jointure; (*BRIT: CULIN*) rôti *m*; (*inf: place*) boîte *f*; (: *of cannabis*) joint *m* ♦ *adj* commun(e); ~ **account** *n* (*with bank etc*) compte joint

joke [dʒəʊk] *n* plaisanterie *f*; (*also: practical* ~) farce *f* ♦ *vi* plaisanter; **to play a** ~ **on** jouer un tour à, faire une farce à; ~**r** *n* (*CARDS*) joker *m*

jolly ['dʒɒlɪ] *adj* gai(e), enjoué(e); (*enjoyable*) amusant(e), plaisant(e) ♦ *adv* (*BRIT: inf*) rudement, drôlement

jolt [dʒəʊlt] *n* cahot *m*, secousse *f*; (*shock*) choc *m* ♦ *vt* cahoter, secouer

Jordan ['dʒɔːdən] *n* (*country*) Jordanie *f*

jostle ['dʒɒsl] *vt* bousculer, pousser

jot [dʒɒt] *n*: **not one** ~ pas un brin; ~ **down** *vt* noter; ~**ter** (*BRIT*) *n* cahier *m* (de brouillon); (*pad*) bloc-notes *m*

journal ['dʒɜːnl] *n* journal *m*; ~**ism** *n* journalisme *m*; ~**ist** *n* journaliste *m/f*

journey ['dʒɜːnɪ] *n* voyage *m*; (*distance*

joy [dʒɔɪ] *n* joie *f*; **~ful** *adj* joyeux(euse); **~rider** *n* personne qui fait une virée dans une voiture volée; **~stick** *n* (AVIAT, COMPUT) manche *m* à balai

JP *n abbr* = **Justice of the Peace**

Jr *abbr* = **junior**

jubilant ['dʒuːbɪlənt] *adj* triomphant(e); réjoui(e)

judge [dʒʌdʒ] *n* juge *m* ♦ *vt* juger; **judg(e)ment** *n* jugement *m*

judicial [dʒuːˈdɪʃəl] *adj* judiciaire

judiciary [dʒuːˈdɪʃɪərɪ] *n* (pouvoir *m*) judiciaire *m*

judo ['dʒuːdəʊ] *n* judo *m*

jug [dʒʌg] *n* pot *m*, cruche *f*

juggernaut ['dʒʌgənɔːt] (BRIT) *n* (huge truck) énorme poids lourd

juggle ['dʒʌgl] *vi* jongler; **~r** *n* jongleur *m*

Jugoslav *etc* = **Yugoslav** *etc*

juice [dʒuːs] *n* jus *m*; **juicy** ['dʒuːsɪ] *adj* juteux(euse)

jukebox ['dʒuːkbɒks] *n* juke-box *m*

July [dʒuːˈlaɪ] *n* juillet *m*

jumble ['dʒʌmbl] *n* fouillis *m* ♦ *vt* (also: **~ up**) mélanger, brouiller; **~ sale** (BRIT) *n* vente *f* de charité

jumbo (jet) ['dʒʌmbəʊ-] *n* jumbo-jet *m*, gros porteur

jump [dʒʌmp] *vi* sauter, bondir; (start) sursauter; (increase) monter en flèche ♦ *vt* sauter, franchir ♦ *n* saut *m*, bond *m*; sursaut *m*; **to ~ the queue** (BRIT) passer avant son tour

jumper ['dʒʌmpə*] *n* (BRIT: pullover) pull-over *m*; (US: dress) robe-chasuble *f*

jumper cables (US), **jump leads** (BRIT) *npl* câbles *mpl* de démarrage

jumpy ['dʒʌmpɪ] *adj* nerveux(euse), agité(e)

Jun. *abbr* = **junior**

junction ['dʒʌŋkʃən] (BRIT) *n* (of roads) carrefour *m*; (of rails) embranchement *m*

juncture ['dʒʌŋktʃə*] *n*: **at this ~** à ce moment-là, sur ces entrefaites

June [dʒuːn] *n* juin *m*

jungle ['dʒʌŋgl] *n* jungle *f*

junior ['dʒuːnɪə*] *adj*, *n*: **he's ~ to me (by 2 years)**, **he's my ~ (by 2 years)** il est mon cadet (de 2 ans), il est plus jeune que moi (de 2 ans); **he's ~ to me** (seniority) il est en dessous de moi (dans la hiérarchie), j'ai plus d'ancienneté que lui; **~ school** (BRIT) *n* ≈ école *f* primaire

junk [dʒʌŋk] *n* (rubbish) camelote *f*; (cheap goods) bric-à-brac *m inv*; **~ bond** *n* (COMM) obligation hautement spéculative utilisée dans les OPA agressives; **~ food** *n* aliments *mpl* sans grande valeur nutritive; **~ mail** *n* prospectus *mpl* (non sollicités); **~ shop** *n* (boutique *f* de) brocanteur *m*

Junr *abbr* = **junior**

juror ['dʒʊərə*] *n* juré *m*

jury ['dʒʊərɪ] *n* jury *m*

just [dʒʌst] *adj* juste ♦ *adv*: **he's ~ done it/left** il vient de le faire/partir; **~ right/two o'clock** exactement *or* juste ce qu'il faut/deux heures; **she's ~ as clever as you** elle est tout aussi intelligente que vous; **it's ~ as well (that) ...** heureusement que ...; **~ as he was leaving** au moment *or* à l'instant précis où il partait; **~ before/enough/here** juste avant/assez/ici; **it's ~ me/rien** ce n'est que moi/(rien) qu'une erreur; **~ missed/caught** manqué/attrapé de justesse; **~ listen to this!** écoutez un peu ça!

justice ['dʒʌstɪs] *n* justice *f*; (US: judge) juge *m* de la Cour suprême; **J~ of the Peace** *n* juge *m* de paix

justify ['dʒʌstɪfaɪ] *vt* justifier

jut [dʒʌt] *vi* (also: **~ out**) dépasser, faire saillie

juvenile ['dʒuːvənaɪl] *adj* juvénile; (court, books) pour enfants ♦ *n* adolescent(e)

K k

K *abbr* (= *one thousand*) K; (= *kilobyte*) Ko

kangaroo [kæŋgə'ruː] *n* kangourou *m*

karate [kə'rɑːtɪ] *n* karaté *m*

kebab [kə'bæb] *n* kébab *m*

keel [kiːl] *n* quille *f*

keen [kiːn] *adj* (*eager*) plein(e) d'enthousiasme; (*interest, desire, competition*) vif(vive); (*eye, intelligence*) pénétrant(e); (*edge*) effilé(e); **to be ~ to do** *or* **on doing sth** désirer vivement faire qch, tenir beaucoup à faire qch; **to be ~ on sth/sb** aimer beaucoup qch/qn

keep [kiːp] (*pt, pp* **kept**) *vt* (*retain, preserve*) garder; (*detain*) retenir; (*shop, accounts, diary, promise*) tenir; (*house*) avoir; (*support*) entretenir; (*chickens, bees etc*) élever ♦ *vi* (*remain*) rester; (*food*) se conserver ♦ *n* (*of castle*) donjon *m*; (*food etc*): **enough for his ~** assez pour (assurer) sa subsistance; (*inf*): **for ~s** pour de bon, pour toujours; **to ~ doing sth** ne pas arrêter de faire qch; **to ~ sb from doing sth** empêcher qn de faire *or* que qn ne fasse; **to ~ sb happy/a place tidy** faire que qn soit content/qu'un endroit reste propre; **to ~ sth to o.s.** garder qch pour soi, tenir qch secret; **to ~ sth (back) from sb** cacher qch à qn; **to ~ time** (*clock*) être à l'heure, ne pas retarder; **well kept** bien entretenu(e); **~ on** *vi*: **to ~ on doing** continuer à faire; **don't ~ on about it!** arrête (d'en parler)!; **~ out** *vt* empêcher d'entrer; **"~ out"** "défense d'entrer"; **~ up** *vt* continuer, maintenir ♦ *vi*: **to ~ up with sb** (*in race etc*) aller aussi vite que qn; (*in work etc*) se maintenir au niveau de qn; **~er** *n* gardien(ne); **~-fit** *n* gymnastique *f* d'entretien; **~ing** *n* (*care*) garde *f*; **in ~ing with** en accord avec; **~sake** *n* souvenir *m*

kennel ['kenl] *n* niche *f*; **~s** *npl* (*boarding ~s*) chenil *m*

kerb [kəːb] (*BRIT*) *n* bordure *f* du trottoir

kernel ['kəːnl] *n* (*of nut*) amande *f*; (*fig*) noyau *m*

kettle ['ketl] *n* bouilloire *f*; **~drum** *n* timbale *f*

key [kiː] *n* (*gen, MUS*) clé *f*; (*of piano, typewriter*) touche *f* ♦ *cpd* clé ♦ *vt* (*also:* **~ in**) introduire (au clavier), saisir; **~board** *n* clavier *m*; **~ed up** *adj* (*person*) surexcité(e); **~hole** *n* trou *m* de la serrure; **~note** *n* (*of speech*) note dominante; (*MUS*) tonique *f*; **~ ring** *n* porte-clés *m*

khaki ['kɑːkɪ] *n* kaki *m*

kick [kɪk] *vt* donner un coup de pied à ♦ *vi* (*horse*) ruer ♦ *n* coup *m* de pied; (*thrill*): **he does it for ~s** il le fait parce que ça l'excite, il le fait pour le plaisir; **to ~ the habit** (*inf*) arrêter; **~ off** *vi* (*SPORT*) donner le coup d'envoi

kid [kɪd] *n* (*inf: child*) gamin(e), gosse *m/f*; (*animal, leather*) chevreau *m* ♦ *vi* (*inf*) plaisanter, blaguer

kidnap ['kɪdnæp] *vt* enlever, kidnapper; **~per** *n* ravisseur(euse); **~ping** *n* enlèvement *m*

kidney ['kɪdnɪ] *n* (*ANAT*) rein *m*; (*CULIN*) rognon *m*

kill [kɪl] *vt* tuer ♦ *n* mise *f* à mort; **~er** *n* tueur(euse); meurtrier(ère); **~ing** *n* meurtre *m*; (*of group of people*) tuerie *f*, massacre *m*; **to make a ~ing** (*inf*) réussir un beau coup (de filet); **~joy** *n* rabat-joie *m/f*

kiln [kɪln] *n* four *m*

kilo ['kiːləu] *n* kilo *m*; **~byte** *n* (*COMPUT*) kilo-octet *m*; **~gram(me)** ['kɪləugræm] *n* kilogramme *m*; **~metre** ['kɪləmiːtə*] (*US* **~meter**) *n* kilomètre *m*; **~watt** *n* kilowatt *m*

kilt [kɪlt] *n* kilt *m*

kin [kɪn] *n see* **next**; **kith**

kind [kaɪnd] *adj* gentil(le), aimable ♦ *n* sorte *f*, espèce *f*, genre *m*; **to be two of a ~** se ressembler; **in ~** (*COMM*) en nature

kindergarten ['kɪndəgɑːtn] *n* jardin *m* d'enfants

kind-hearted [kaɪnd'hɑːtɪd] *adj* bon(bonne)

kindle ['kɪndl] *vt* allumer, enflammer

kindly ['kaɪndlɪ] *adj* bienveillant(e), plein(e) de gentillesse ♦ *adv* avec bonté; **will you ~ ...!** auriez-vous la bonté *or* l'obligeance de ...?

kindness ['kaɪndnəs] *n* bonté *f*, gentillesse *f*

kindred ['kɪndrɪd] *adj:* **~ spirit** âme *f* sœur

kinetic [kɪ'netɪk] *adj* cinétique

king [kɪŋ] *n* roi *m*; **~dom** *n* royaume *m*; **~fisher** *n* martin-pêcheur *m*; **~-size bed** *n* grand lit (*de 1,95 m de large*); **~-size(d)** *adj* format géant *inv*; (*cigarettes*) long(longue)

kinky ['kɪŋkɪ] (*pej*) *adj* (*person*) excentrique; (*sexually*) aux goûts spéciaux

kiosk ['ki:ɒsk] *n* kiosque *m*; (*BRIT: TEL*) cabine *f* (téléphonique)

kipper ['kɪpə*] *n* hareng fumé et salé

kiss [kɪs] *n* baiser *m* ♦ *vt* embrasser; **to ~ (each other)** s'embrasser; **~ of life** (*BRIT*) *n* bouche à bouche *m*

kit [kɪt] *n* équipement *m*, matériel *m*; (*set of tools etc*) trousse *f*; (*for assembly*) kit *m*

kitchen ['kɪtʃɪn] *n* cuisine *f*; **~ sink** *n* évier *m*

kite [kaɪt] *n* (*toy*) cerf-volant *m*

kith [kɪθ] *n:* **~ and kin** parents et amis *mpl*

kitten ['kɪtn] *n* chaton *m*, petit chat

kitty ['kɪtɪ] *n* (*money*) cagnotte *f*

knack [næk] *n:* **to have the ~ of doing** avoir le coup pour faire

knapsack ['næpsæk] *n* musette *f*

knead [ni:d] *vt* pétrir

knee [ni:] *n* genou *m*; **~cap** *n* rotule *f*

kneel [ni:l] (*pt, pp* knelt) *vi* (*also: ~ down*) s'agenouiller

knew [nju:] *pt of* **know**

knickers ['nɪkəz] (*BRIT*) *npl* culotte *f* (de femme)

knife [naɪf] (*pl* knives) *n* couteau *m* ♦ *vt* poignarder, frapper d'un coup de couteau

knight [naɪt] *n* chevalier *m*; (*CHESS*) cavalier *m*; **~hood** (*BRIT*) *n* (*title*): **to get a ~hood** être fait chevalier

knit [nɪt] *vt* tricoter ♦ *vi* tricoter; (*broken bones*) se ressouder; **to ~ one's brows** froncer les sourcils; **~ting** *n* tricot *m*; **~ting needle** *n* aiguille *f* à tricoter; **~wear** *n* tricots *mpl*, lainages *mpl*

knives [naɪvz] *npl of* **knife**

knob [nɒb] *n* bouton *m*

knock [nɒk] *vt* frapper; (*bump into*) heurter; (*inf*) dénigrer ♦ *vi* (*at door etc*): **to ~ at** *or* **on** frapper à ♦ *n* coup *m*; **~ down** *vt* renverser; **~ off** *vi* (*inf: finish*) s'arrêter (de travailler); ♦ *vt* (*from price*) faire un rabais de; (*inf: steal*) piquer; **~ out** *vt* assommer; (*BOXING*) mettre k.-o.; (*defeat*) éliminer; **~ over** *vt* renverser, faire tomber; **~er** *n* (*on door*) heurtoir *m*; **~out** *n* (*BOXING*) knock-out *m*, K.-O. *m*; **~out competition** *n* compétition *f* avec épreuves éliminatoires

knot [nɒt] *n* (*gen*) nœud *m* ♦ *vt* nouer; **~ty** *adj* (*fig*) épineux(euse)

know [nəʊ] (*pt* knew, *pp* known) *vt* savoir; (*person, place*) connaître; **to ~ how to do** savoir (comment) faire; **to ~ how to swim** savoir nager; **to ~ about** *or* **of sth** être au courant de qch; **to ~ about** *or* **of sb** avoir entendu parler de qn; **~-all** (*pej*) *n* je-sais-tout *m/f*; **~-how** *n* savoir-faire *m*; **~ing** *adj* (*look etc*) entendu(e); **~ingly** *adv* sciemment; (*smile, look*) d'un air entendu

knowledge ['nɒlɪdʒ] *n* connaissance *f*; (*learning*) connaissances, savoir *m*; **~able** *adj* bien informé(e)

knuckle ['nʌkl] *n* articulation *f* (des doigts), jointure *f*

Koran [kɔ'rɑːn] *n* Coran *m*

Korea [kə'rɪə] *n* Corée *f*

kosher ['kəʊʃə*] *adj* kascher *inv*

L l

L *abbr* (= *lake, large*) L; (= *left*) g; (= *BRIT: AUT:* = *learner*) *signale un conducteur débutant*

lab [læb] *n abbr* (= *laboratory*) labo *m*

label ['leɪbl] *n* étiquette *f* ♦ *vt* étiqueter

labor *etc* (*US*) = **labour** *etc*

laboratory [ləˈbɒrətəri] *n* laboratoire *m*

labour [ˈleɪbə*] (*US* **labor**) *n* (*work*) travail *m*; (*workforce*) main-d'œuvre *f* ♦ *vi*: **to ~ (at)** travailler dur (à), peiner (sur) ♦ *vt*: **to ~ a point** insister sur un point; **in ~** (*MED*) en travail, en train d'accoucher; **L~, the L~ party** (*BRIT*) le parti travailliste, les travaillistes *mpl*; **~ed** *adj* (*breathing*) pénible, difficile; **~er** *n* manœuvre *m*; **farm ~er** ouvrier *m* agricole

lace [leɪs] *n* dentelle *f*; (*of shoe etc*) lacet *m* ♦ *vt* (*shoe: also:* **~ up**) lacer

lack [læk] *n* manque *m* ♦ *vt* manquer de; **through** *or* **for ~ of** faute de, par manque de; **to be ~ing** manquer, faire défaut; **to be ~ing in** manquer de

lacquer [ˈlækə*] *n* laque *f*

lad [læd] *n* garçon *m*, gars *m*

ladder [ˈlædə*] *n* échelle *f*; (*BRIT: in tights*) maille filée

laden [ˈleɪdn] *adj*: **~ (with)** chargé(e) (de)

ladle [ˈleɪdl] *n* louche *f*

lady [ˈleɪdɪ] *n* dame *f*; (*in address*): **ladies and gentlemen** Mesdames (et) Messieurs; **young ~** jeune fille *f*; (*married*) jeune femme *f*; **the ladies' (room)** les toilettes *fpl* (pour dames); **~bird** *n* coccinelle *f*; **~bug** (*US*) *n* = **ladybird**; **~like** *adj* distingué(e); **~ship** *n*: **your ~ship** Madame la comtesse (*or* la baronne *etc*)

lag [læg] *n* retard *m* ♦ *vi* (*also:* **~ behind**) rester en arrière, traîner; (*fig*) rester en traîne ♦ *vt* (*pipes*) calorifuger

lager [ˈlɑːgə*] *n* bière blonde

lagoon [ləˈguːn] *n* lagune *f*

laid [leɪd] *pt, pp of* **lay**; **~-back** (*inf*) *adj* relaxe, décontracté(e); **~ up** *adj* alité(e)

lain [leɪn] *pp of* **lie**

lake [leɪk] *n* lac *m*

lamb [læm] *n* agneau *m*; **~ chop** *n* côtelette *f* d'agneau

lame [leɪm] *adj* boiteux(euse)

lament [ləˈment] *n* lamentation *f* ♦ *vt* pleurer, se lamenter sur

laminated [ˈlæmɪneɪtɪd] *adj* laminé(e); (*windscreen*) (en verre) feuilleté

lamp [læmp] *n* lampe *f*; **~post** (*BRIT*) *n* ré-

verbère *m*; **~shade** *n* abat-jour *m inv*

lance [lɑːns] *vt* (*MED*) inciser

land [lænd] *n* (*as opposed to sea*) terre *f*; (*ferme*); (*soil*) terre; terrain *m*; (*estate*) terre(s), domaine(s) *m(pl)*; (*country*) pays *m* ♦ *vi* (*AVIAT*) atterrir; (*fig*) (re)tomber ♦ *vt* (*passengers, goods*) débarquer; **to ~ sb with sth** (*inf*) coller qch à qn; **~ up** *vi* atterrir, (finir par) se retrouver; **~fill site** *n* décharge *f*; **~ing** *n* (*AVIAT*) atterrissage *m*; (*of staircase*) palier *m*; (*of troops*) débarquement *m*; **~ing gear** *n* train *m* d'atterrissage; **~ing strip** *n* piste *f* d'atterrissage; **~lady** *n* propriétaire *f*, logeuse *f*; (*of pub*) patronne *f*; **~locked** *adj* sans littoral; **~lord** *n* propriétaire *m*, logeur *m*; (*of pub etc*) patron *m*; **~mark** *n* (point *m* de) repère *m*; **to be a ~mark** (*fig*) faire date *or* époque; **~owner** *n* propriétaire foncier *or* terrien; **~scape** [ˈlændskeɪp] *n* paysage *m*; **~scape gardener** *n* jardinier(ère) paysagiste; **~slide** [ˈlændslaɪd] *n* (*GEO*) glissement *m* (de terrain); (*fig*: *POL*) raz de-marée (électoral)

lane [leɪn] *n* (*in country*) chemin *m*; (*AUT*) voie *f*; file *f*; (*in race*) couloir *m*

language [ˈlæŋgwɪdʒ] *n* langue *f*; (*way one speaks*) langage *m*; **bad ~** grossièretés *fpl*, langage grossier; **~ laboratory** *n* laboratoire *m* de langues

lank [læŋk] *adj* (*hair*) raide et terne

lanky [ˈlæŋkɪ] *adj* grand(e) et maigre, efflanqué(e)

lantern [ˈlæntən] *n* lanterne *f*

lap [læp] *n* (*of track*) tour *m* (de piste); (*of body*): **in** *or* **on one's ~** sur les genoux ♦ *vt* (*also:* **~ up**) laper ♦ *vi* (*waves*) clapoter; **~ up** *vt* (*fig*) accepter béatement, gober

lapel [ləˈpel] *n* revers *m*

Lapland [ˈlæplænd] *n* Laponie *f*

lapse [læps] *n* défaillance *f*; (*in behaviour*) écart *m* de conduite ♦ *vi* (*LAW*) cesser d'être en vigueur; (*contract*) expirer; **to ~ into bad habits** prendre de mauvaises habitudes; **~ of time** laps *m* de temps, intervalle *m*

laptop (computer) [ˈlæptɒp-] *n* portable *m*

larceny ['lɑːsənɪ] *n* vol *m*

larch [lɑːtʃ] *n* mélèze *m*

lard [lɑːd] *n* saindoux *m*

larder ['lɑːdə*] *n* garde-manger *m inv*

large [lɑːdʒ] *adj* grand(e); (*person, animal*) gros(se); **at ~** (*free*) en liberté; (*generally*) en général; *see also* **by**; **~ly** *adv* en grande partie; (*principally*) surtout; **~-scale** *adj* (*action*) d'envergure; (*map*) à grande échelle

lark [lɑːk] *n* (*bird*) alouette *f*; (*joke*) blague *f*, farce *f*; **~ about** *vi* faire l'idiot, rigoler

laryngitis [lærɪn'dʒaɪtɪs] *n* laryngite *f*

laser ['leɪzə*] *n* laser *m*; **~ printer** *n* imprimante *f* laser

lash [læʃ] *n* coup *m* de fouet; (*also*: eye~) cil *m* ♦ *vt* fouetter; (*tie*) attacher; **~ out** *vi*: **to ~ out at** *or* **against** attaquer violemment

lass [læs] (*BRIT*) *n* (*jeune*) fille *f*

lasso [læ'suː] *n* lasso *m*

last [lɑːst] *adj* dernier(ère) ♦ *adv* en dernier; (*finally*) finalement ♦ *vi* durer; **~ week** la semaine dernière; **~ night** (*evening*) hier soir; (*night*) la nuit dernière; **at ~** enfin; **~ but one** avant-dernier(ère); **~-ditch** (*attempt*) ultime, désespéré(e); **~ing** *adj* durable; **~ly** *adv* en dernier lieu, pour finir; **~-minute** *adj* de dernière minute

latch [lætʃ] *n* loquet *m*

late [leɪt] *adj* (*not on time*) en retard; (*far on in day etc*) tardif(ive); (*edition, delivery*) dernier(ière); (*former*) ancien(ne) ♦ *adv* tard; (*behind time, schedule*) en retard; **of ~** dernièrement; **in ~ May** vers la fin (du mois) de mai, fin mai; **the ~ Mr X** feu M. X; **~comer** *n* retardataire *m/f*; **~ly** *adv* récemment; **~r** ['leɪtə*] *adj* (*date etc*) ultérieur(e); (*version etc*) plus récent(e) ♦ *adv* plus tard; **~r on** plus tard; **~st** ['leɪtɪst] *adj* tout(e) dernier(ère); **at the ~st** au plus tard

lathe [leɪð] *n* tour *m*

lather ['lɑːðə*] *n* mousse *f* (de savon) ♦ *vt* savonner

Latin ['lætɪn] *n* latin *m* ♦ *adj* latin(e); **~**

America *n* Amérique latine; **~ American** *adj* latino-américain(e)

latitude ['lætɪtjuːd] *n* latitude *f*

latter ['lætə*] *adj* deuxième, dernier(ère) ♦ *n*: **the ~** ce dernier, celui-ci; **~ly** *adv* dernièrement, récemment

laudable ['lɔːdəbl] *adj* louable

laugh [lɑːf] *n* rire *m* ♦ *vi* rire; **~ at** *vt fus* se moquer de; rire de; **~ off** *vt* écarter par une plaisanterie *or* par une boutade; **~able** *adj* risible, ridicule; **~ing stock** *n*: **the ~ing stock of** la risée de; **~ter** *n* rire *m*; rires *mpl*

launch [lɔːntʃ] *n* lancement *m*; (*motorboat*) vedette *f* ♦ *vt* lancer; **~ into** *vt fus* se lancer dans

Launderette [lɔːn'dret] (®: *BRIT*), **Laundromat** ['lɔːndrəmæt] (®: *US*) *n* laverie *f* (automatique)

laundry ['lɔːndrɪ] *n* (*clothes*) linge *m*; (*business*) blanchisserie *f*; (*room*) buanderie *f*

laureate ['lɔːrɪət] *adj see* **poet**

laurel ['lɒrəl] *n* laurier *m*

lava ['lɑːvə] *n* lave *f*

lavatory ['lævətrɪ] *n* toilettes *fpl*

lavender ['lævɪndə*] *n* lavande *f*

lavish ['lævɪʃ] *adj* (*amount*) copieux(euse); (*person*): **~ with** prodigue de ♦ *vt*: **to ~ sth on sb** prodiguer qch à qn; (*money*) dépenser qch sans compter pour qn/qch

law [lɔː] *n* loi *f*; (*science*) droit *m*; **~-abiding** *adj* respectueux(euse) des lois; **~ and order** *n* l'ordre public; **~ court** *n* tribunal *m*, cour *f* de justice; **~ful** *adj* légal(e); **~less** *adj* (*action*) illégal(e)

lawn [lɔːn] *n* pelouse *f*; **~mower** *n* tondeuse *f* à gazon; **~ tennis** *n* tennis *m*

law school (*US*) *n* faculté *f* de droit

lawsuit ['lɔːsuːt] *n* procès *m*

lawyer ['lɔːjə*] *n* (*consultant, with company*) juriste *m*; (*for sales, wills etc*) notaire *m*; (*partner, in court*) avocat *m*

lax [læks] *adj* relâché(e)

laxative ['læksətɪv] *n* laxatif *m*

lay [leɪ] (*pt, pp* laid) *pt of* **lie** ♦ *adj* laïque; (*not expert*) profane ♦ *vt* poser, mettre; (*eggs*) pondre; **to ~ the table** mettre la table; **~ aside** *vt* mettre de côté; **~ by** *vt* = **lay aside**; **~ down** *vt* poser; **to ~ down the law** faire la loi; **to ~ down one's life** sacrifier sa vie; **~ off** *vt* (*workers*) licencier; **~ on** *vt* (*provide*) fournir; **~ out** *vt* (*display*) disposer, étaler; **~about** (*inf*) *n* fainéant(e); **~by** (*BRIT*) *n* aire *f* de stationnement (sur le bas-côté)

layer ['leɪə*] *n* couche *f*

layman ['leɪmən] (*irreg*) *n* profane *m*

layout ['leɪaʊt] *n* disposition *f*, plan *m*, agencement *m*; (*PRESS*) mise *f* en page

laze [leɪz] *vi* (*also*: *~ about*) paresser

lazy ['leɪzɪ] *adj* paresseux(euse)

lb *abbr* = **pound** (*weight*)

lead[1] [li:d] (*pt, pp* **led**) *n* (*distance, time ahead*) avance *f*; (*clue*) piste *f*; (*THEATRE*) rôle principal; (*ELEC*) fil *m*; (*for dog*) laisse *f* ♦ *vt* mener, conduire; (*be leader of*) être à la tête de ♦ *vi* (*street etc*) mener, conduire; (*SPORT*) mener, être en tête; **in the ~** en tête; **to ~ the way** montrer le chemin; **~ away** *vt* emmener; **~ back** *vt*: **to ~ back to** ramener à; **~ on** *vt* (*tease*) faire marcher; **~ to** *vt fus* mener à; conduire à; **~ up to** *vt fus* conduire à

lead[2] [led] *n* (*metal*) plomb *m*; (*in pencil*) mine *f*; **~en** ['lɛdn] *adj* (*sky, sea*) de plomb

leader ['li:də*] *n* chef *m*; dirigeant(e), leader *m*; (*SPORT: in league*) leader; (: *in race*) coureur *m* de tête; **~ship** *n* direction *f*; (*quality*) qualités *fpl* de chef

lead-free ['led'fri:] *adj* (*petrol*) sans plomb

leading ['li:dɪŋ] *adj* principal(e); de premier plan; (*in race*) de tête; **~ lady** *n* (*THEATRE*) vedette (féminine); **~ light** *n* (*person*) vedette *f*, sommité *f*; **~ man** (*irreg*) *n* vedette (masculine)

lead singer [li:d-] *n* (*in pop group*) (chanteur *m*) vedette *f*

leaf [li:f] (*pl* **leaves**) *n* feuille *f* ♦ *vi*: **to ~ through** feuilleter; **to turn over a new ~** changer de conduite *or* d'existence

leaflet ['li:flɪt] *n* prospectus *m*, brochure *f*; (*POL, REL*) tract *m*

league [li:g] *n* ligue *f*; (*FOOTBALL*) championnat *m*; **to be in ~ with** avoir partie liée avec, être de mèche avec

leak [li:k] *n* fuite *f* ♦ *vi* (*pipe, liquid etc*) fuir; (*shoes*) prendre l'eau; (*ship*) faire eau ♦ *vt* (*information*) divulguer

lean [li:n] (*pt, pp* **leaned** *or* **leant**) *adj* maigre ♦ *vt*: **to ~ sth on sth** appuyer qch sur qch ♦ *vi* (*slope*) pencher; (*rest*): **to ~ against** s'appuyer contre; être appuyé(e) contre; **to ~ on** s'appuyer sur; **to ~ back/forward** se pencher en arrière/ avant; **~ out** *vi* se pencher au dehors; **~ over** *vi* se pencher; **~ing** *n*: **~ing (towards)** tendance *f* (à), penchant *m* (pour); **leant** [lent] *pt, pp of* **lean**

leap [li:p] (*pt, pp* **leaped** *or* **leapt**) *n* bond *m*, saut *m* ♦ *vi* bondir, sauter; **~frog** *n* saute-mouton *m*; **leapt** [lept] *pt, pp of* **leap**; **~ year** *n* année *f* bissextile

learn [lɜ:n] (*pt, pp* **~ed** *or* **learnt**) *vt, vi* apprendre; **to ~ to do sth** apprendre à faire qch; **to ~ about** *or* **of sth** (*hear, read*) apprendre qch; **~ed** ['lɜ:nɪd] *adj* érudit(e), savant(e); **~er** (*BRIT*) *n* (*also:* **~er driver**) (conducteur(trice)) débutant(e); **~ing** *n* (*knowledge*) savoir *m*; **learnt** [lɜ:nt] *pl, pp of* **learn**

lease [li:s] *n* bail *m* ♦ *vt* louer à bail

leash [li:ʃ] *n* laisse *f*

least [li:st] *adj*: **the ~** (+*noun*) le(la) plus petit(e), le(la) moindre; (: *smallest amount of*) le moins de ♦ *adv* (+*verb*) le moins; (+*adj*): **the ~** le(la) moins; **at ~** au moins; (*or rather*) du moins; **not in the ~** pas le moins du monde

leather ['lɛðə*] *n* cuir *m*

leave [li:v] (*pt, pp* **left**) *vt* laisser; (*go away from*) quitter; (*forget*) oublier ♦ *vi* partir, s'en aller ♦ *n* (*time off*) congé *m*, (*MIL also: consent*) permission *f*; **to be left** rester; **there's some milk left over** il reste du lait; **on ~** en permission; **~ behind** *vt* (*person, object*) laisser; (*forget*) oublier; **~ out** *vt* oublier, omettre; **~ of absence** *n* congé exceptionnel; (*MIL*) permission spéciale

leaves [li:vz] *npl of* **leaf**

Lebanon ['lɛbənən] *n* Liban *m*

lecherous ['letʃərəs] (*pej*) *adj* lubrique
lecture ['lektʃə*] *n* conférence *f*; (*SCOL*) cours *m* ♦ *vi* donner des cours; enseigner ♦ *vt* (*scold*) sermonner, réprimander; **to give a ~ on** faire une conférence sur; donner un cours sur; **~r** ['lektʃərə*] (*BRIT*) *n* (*at university*) professeur *m* (d'université)
led [led] *pt, pp of* **lead**
ledge [ledʒ] *n* (*of window, on wall*) rebord *m*; (*of mountain*) saillie *f*, corniche *f*
ledger ['ledʒə*] *n* (*COMM*) registre *m*, grand livre
leech [liːtʃ] *n* (*also fig*) sangsue *f*
leek [liːk] *n* poireau *m*
leer [lɪə*] *vi*: **to ~ at sb** regarder qn d'un air mauvais *or* concupiscent
leeway ['liːweɪ] *n* (*fig*): **to have some ~** avoir une certaine liberté d'action
left [left] *pt, pp of* **leave** ♦ *adj* (*not right*) gauche ♦ *n* gauche *f* ♦ *adv* à gauche; **on the ~, to the ~** à gauche; **the L~** (*POL*) la gauche; **~-handed** *adj* gaucher(ère); **~-hand side** *n* gauche *f*, côté *m* gauche; **~-luggage (office)** (*BRIT*) *n* consigne *f*; **~overs** *npl* restes *mpl*; **~wing** *adj* (*POL*) de gauche
leg [leg] *n* jambe *f*; (*of animal*) patte *f*; (*of furniture*) pied *m*; (*CULIN*: *of chicken, pork*) cuisse *f*; (: *of lamb*) gigot *m*; (*of journey*) étape *f*; **1st/2nd ~** (*SPORT*) match *m* aller/retour
legacy ['legəsɪ] *n* héritage *m*, legs *m*
legal ['liːgəl] *adj* légal(e); **~ holiday** (*US*) *n* jour férié; **~ tender** *n* monnaie légale
legend ['ledʒənd] *n* légende *f*
legible ['ledʒəbl] *adj* lisible
legislation [ledʒɪs'leɪʃən] *n* législation *f*; **legislature** ['ledʒɪsleɪtʃə*] *n* (*corps*) *m* législatif
legitimate [lɪ'dʒɪtɪmət] *adj* légitime
leg-room ['legrʊm] *n* place *f* pour les jambes
leisure ['leʒə*] *n* loisir *m*, temps *m* libre; loisirs *mpl*; **at ~** (*tout*) à loisir; à tête reposée; **~ centre** *n* centre *m* de loisirs; **~ly** *adj* tranquille; fait(e) sans se presser

lemon ['lemən] *n* citron *m*; **~ade** [lemə'neɪd] *n* limonade *f*; **~ tea** *n* thé *m* au citron
lend [lend] (*pt, pp* lent) *vt*: **to ~ sth (to sb)** prêter qch (à qn)
length [leŋθ] *n* longueur *f*; (*section*: *of road, pipe etc*) morceau *m*, bout *m*; (*of time*) durée *f*; **at ~** (*at last*) enfin, à la fin; (*lengthily*) longuement; **~en** *vt* allonger, prolonger ♦ *vi* s'allonger; **~ways** *adv* dans le sens de la longueur, en long; **~y** (*très*) long(longue)
lenient ['liːnɪənt] *adj* indulgent(e), clément(e)
lens [lenz] *n* lentille *f*; (*of spectacles*) verre *m*; (*of camera*) objectif *m*
Lent [lent] *n* Carême *m*
lent [lent] *pt, pp of* **lend**
lentil ['lentl] *n* lentille *f*
Leo ['liːəʊ] *n* le Lion
leotard ['liːətɑːd] *n* maillot *m* (*de danseur etc*), collant *m*
leprosy ['leprəsɪ] *n* lèpre *f*
lesbian ['lezbɪən] *n* lesbienne *f*
less [les] *adj* moins de ♦ *pron, adv* moins ♦ *prep* moins; **~ than that/you** moins que cela/vous; **~ than half** moins de la moitié; **~ than ever** moins que jamais; **~ and ~** de moins en moins; **the ~ he works ...** moins il travaille ...
lessen ['lesn] *vi* diminuer, s'atténuer ♦ *vt* diminuer, réduire, atténuer
lesser ['lesə*] *adj* moindre; **to a ~ extent** à un degré moindre
lesson ['lesn] *n* leçon *f*; **to teach sb a ~** (*fig*) donner une bonne leçon à qn
lest [lest] *conj* de peur que +*sub*
let [let] (*pt, pp* let) *vt* laisser; (*BRIT*: *lease*) louer; **to ~ sb do sth** laisser qn faire qch; **to ~ sb know sth** faire savoir qch à qn, prévenir qn de qch; **~'s go** allons-y; **~ him come** qu'il vienne; **"to ~"** "à louer"; **~ down** *vt* (*tyre*) dégonfler; (*person*) décevoir, faire faux bond à; **~ go** *vi* lâcher prise ♦ *vt* lâcher; **~ in** *vt* laisser entrer; (*visitor etc*) faire entrer; **~ off** *vt* (*culprit*) ne pas punir; (*firework etc*) faire partir; **~ on** (*inf*) *vi* dire; **~ out** *vt* laisser sortir; (*scream*) laisser échapper;

~ up *vi* diminuer; (*cease*) s'arrêter

lethal ['liːθəl] *adj* mortel(le), fatal(e)

letter ['letə*] *n* lettre *f*; **~ bomb** *n* lettre piégée; **~box** (*BRIT*) *n* boîte *f* aux *or* à lettres; **~ing** *n* lettres *fpl*; caractères *mpl*

lettuce ['letɪs] *n* laitue *f*, salade *f*

let-up ['letʌp] *n* répit *m*, arrêt *m*

leukaemia [luːˈkiːmɪə] (*US* **leukemia**) *n* leucémie *f*

level ['levl] *adj* plat(e), plan(e), uni(e); horizontal(e) ♦ *n* niveau *m* ♦ *vt* niveler, aplanir; **to be ~ with** être au même niveau que; **to draw ~ with** (*person, vehicle*) arriver à la hauteur de; **"A" ~s** (*BRIT*) ≈ baccalauréat *m*; **"O" ~s** (*BRIT*) ≈ B.E.P.C.; **on the ~** (*fig: honest*) régulier(ère); **~ off** *vi* (*prices etc*) se stabiliser; **~ out** *vi* = **level off**; **~ crossing** (*BRIT*) *n* passage *m* à niveau; **~-headed** *adj* équilibré(e)

lever ['liːvə*] *n* levier *m*; **~age** *n*: **~age (on** *or* **with)** prise *f* (sur)

levity ['levɪtɪ] *n* légèreté *f*

levy ['levɪ] *n* taxe *f*, impôt *m* ♦ *vt* prélever, imposer; percevoir

lewd [luːd] *adj* obscène, lubrique

liability [laɪəˈbɪlɪtɪ] *n* responsabilité *f*; (*handicap*) handicap *m*; **liabilities** *npl* (*on balance sheet*) passif *m*

liable ['laɪəbl] *adj* (*subject*): **~ to** sujet(te) à; passible de; (*responsible*): **~ (for)** responsable (de); (*likely*): **~ to do** susceptible de faire

liaise [lɪˈeɪz] *vi*: **to ~ with** assurer la liaison avec; **liaison** [liːˈeɪzɒn] *n* liaison *f*

liar ['laɪə*] *n* menteur(euse)

libel ['laɪbəl] *n* diffamation *f*; (*document*) écrit *m* diffamatoire ♦ *vt* diffamer

liberal ['lɪbərəl] *adj* libéral(e); (*generous*): **~ with** prodigue de, généreux(euse) avec; **the L~ Democrats** (*BRIT*) le parti libéral-démocrate

liberation [lɪbəˈreɪʃən] *n* libération *f*

liberty ['lɪbətɪ] *n* liberté *f*; **to be at ~ to do** être libre de faire

Libra ['liːbrə] *n* la Balance

librarian [laɪˈbrɛərɪən] *n* bibliothécaire *m/f*

library ['laɪbrərɪ] *n* bibliothèque *f*

libretto [lɪˈbretəʊ] *n* livret *m*

Libya ['lɪbɪə] *n* Libye *f*

lice [laɪs] *npl of* **louse**

licence ['laɪsəns] (*US* **license**) *n* autorisation *f*, permis *m*; (*RADIO, TV*) redevance *f*; **driving ~**, (*US*) **driver's license** permis *m* (de conduire); **~ number** *n* numéro *m* d'immatriculation; **~ plate** *n* plaque *f* minéralogique

license ['laɪsəns] *n* (*US*) = **licence** ♦ *vt* donner une licence à; **~d** *adj* (*car*) muni(e) de la vignette; (*to sell alcohol*) patenté(e) pour la vente des spiritueux, qui a une licence de débit de boissons

lick [lɪk] *vt* lécher; (*inf: defeat*) écraser; **to ~ one's lips** (*fig*) se frotter les mains

licorice ['lɪkərɪs] (*US*) *n* = **liquorice**

lid [lɪd] *n* couvercle *m*; (*eye~*) paupière *f*

lie [laɪ] (*pt* **lay**, *pp* **lain**) *vi* (*rest*) être étendu(e) *or* allongé(e) *or* couché(e); (*in grave*) être enterré(e), reposer; (*be situated*) se trouver, être; (*be untruthful: pt, pp* **lied**) mentir ♦ *n* mensonge *m*; **to ~ low** (*fig*) se cacher; **~ about** *vi* traîner; **~ around** *vi* = **lie about**; **~-down** (*BRIT*) *n*: **to have a ~-down** s'allonger, se reposer; **~-in** (*BRIT*) *n*: **to have a ~-in** faire la grasse matinée

lieutenant [lefˈtenənt, (*US*) luːˈtenənt] *n* lieutenant *m*

life [laɪf] (*pl* **lives**) *n* vie *f*; **to come to ~** (*fig*) s'animer; (*BRIT*) *n* = **life insurance**; **~ assurance** (*BRIT*) *n* = **life insurance**; **~belt** (*BRIT*) *n* bouée *f* de sauvetage; **~boat** *n* canot *m or* chaloupe *f* de sauvetage; **~buoy** *n* bouée *f* de sauvetage; **~guard** *n* surveillant *m* de baignade; **~ insurance** *n* assurance-vie *f*; **~ jacket** *n* gilet *m or* ceinture *f* de sauvetage; **~less** *adj* sans vie, inanimé(e); (*dull*) qui manque de vie *or* de vigueur; **~like** *adj* qui semble vrai(e) *or* vivant(e); (*painting*) réaliste; **~line** *n*: **it was his ~line** ça l'a sauvé; **~long** *adj* de toute une vie, de toujours; **~ preserver** (*US*) *n* = **lifebelt** *or* **life jacket**; **~ sentence** *n* condamnation *f* à perpétuité; **~-size(d)** *adj* grandeur nature *inv*; **~ span** *n* (durée *f* de) vie *f*; **~ style** *n* style *m or* mode *m* de vie; **~-support system** *n*

(*MED*) respirateur artificiel; **~time** *n* vie *f*; **in his ~time** de son vivant

lift [lɪft] *vt* soulever, lever; (*end*) supprimer, lever ♦ *vi* (*fog*) se lever ♦ *n* (*BRIT: elevator*) ascenseur *m*; **to give sb a ~** (*BRIT: AUT*) emmener *or* prendre qn en voiture; **~-off** *n* décollage *m*

light [laɪt] (*pt, pp* lit) *n* lumière *f*; (*lamp*) lampe *f*; (*AUT: rear ~*) feu *m*; (: *head~*) phare *m*; (*for cigarette etc*) **have you got a ~?** avez-vous du feu? ♦ *vt* (*candle, cigarette, fire*) allumer; (*room*) éclairer ♦ *adj* (*room, colour*) clair(e); (*not heavy*) léger(ère); (*not strenuous*) peu fatigant(e); **~s** *npl* (*AUT: traffic ~s*) feux *mpl*; **to come to ~** être dévoilé(e) *or* découvert(e); **~ up** *vi* (*face*) s'éclairer ♦ *vt* (*illuminate*) éclairer, illuminer; **~ bulb** *n* ampoule *f*; **~en** *vt* (*make less heavy*) alléger; **~er** *n* (*also: cigarette ~er*) briquet *m*; **~-headed** *adj* étourdi(e); (*excited*) grisé(e); **~-hearted** *adj* gai(e), joyeux(euse), enjoué(e); **~house** *n* phare *m*; **~ing** *n* (*on road*) éclairage *m*; (*in theatre*) éclairages; **~ly** *adv* légèrement; **to get off ~ly** s'en tirer à bon compte; **~ness** *n* (*in weight*) légèreté *f*

lightning [ˈlaɪtnɪŋ] *n* éclair *m*, foudre *f*; **~ conductor** *n* paratonnerre *m*; **~ rod** (*US*) *n* = **lightning conductor**

light pen *n* crayon *m* optique

lightweight [ˈlaɪtweɪt] *adj* (*suit*) léger(ère) ♦ *n* (*BOXING*) poids léger

like [laɪk] *vt* aimer (bien) ♦ *prep* comme ♦ *adj* semblable, pareil(le) ♦ *n*: **and the ~** et d'autres du même genre; **his ~s and dislikes** ses goûts *mpl or* préférences *fpl*; **I would ~, I'd ~** je voudrais, j'aimerais; **would you ~ a coffee?** voulez-vous du café?; **to be/look ~ sb/sth** ressembler à qn/qch; **what does it look ~?** de quoi est-ce que ça a l'air?; **what does it taste ~?** quel goût est-ce que ça a?; **that's just ~ him** c'est bien de lui, ça lui ressemble; **do it ~ this** fais-le comme ceci; **it's nothing ~ ...** ce n'est pas du tout comme ...; **~able** *adj* sympathique, agréable

likelihood [ˈlaɪklɪhʊd] *n* probabilité *f*

likely [ˈlaɪklɪ] *adj* probable; plausible; **he's ~ to leave** il va sûrement partir, il risque fort de partir; **not ~!** (*inf*) pas de danger!

likeness [ˈlaɪknɪs] *n* ressemblance *f*; **that's a good ~** c'est très ressemblant

likewise [ˈlaɪkwaɪz] *adv* de même, pareillement

liking [ˈlaɪkɪŋ] *n* (*for person*) affection *f*; (*for thing*) penchant *m*, goût *m*

lilac [ˈlaɪlək] *n* lilas *m*

lily [ˈlɪlɪ] *n* lis *m*; **~ of the valley** *n* muguet *m*

limb [lɪm] *n* membre *m*

limber up [ˈlɪmbə*-] *vi* se dégourdir, faire des exercices d'assouplissement

limbo [ˈlɪmbəʊ] *n*: **to be in ~** (*fig*) être tombé(e) dans l'oubli

lime [laɪm] *n* (*tree*) tilleul *m*; (*fruit*) lime *f*, citron vert; (*GEO*) chaux *f*

limelight [ˈlaɪmlaɪt] *n*: **in the ~** (*fig*) en vedette, au premier plan

limerick [ˈlɪmərɪk] *n* poème *m* humoristique (de 5 vers)

limestone [ˈlaɪmstəʊn] *n* pierre *f* à chaux; (*GEO*) calcaire *m*

limit [ˈlɪmɪt] *n* limite *f* ♦ *vt* limiter; **~ed** *adj* limité(e), restreint(e); **to be ~ed to** se limiter à, ne concerner que; **~ed (liability) company** (*BRIT*) *n* ≈ société *f* anonyme

limp [lɪmp] *n*: **to have a ~** boiter ♦ *vi* boiter ♦ *adj* mou(molle)

limpet [ˈlɪmpɪt] *n* patelle *f*

line [laɪn] *n* ligne *f*; (*stroke*) trait *m*; (*wrinkle*) ride *f*; (*rope*) corde *f*; (*wire*) fil *m*; (*of poem*) vers *m*; (*row, series*) rangée *f*; (*of people*) file *f*, queue *f*; (*railway track*) voie *f*; (*COMM: series of goods*) article(s) *m(pl)*; (*work*) métier *m*, type *m* d'activité; (*attitude, policy*) position *f* ♦ *vt*: **to ~ (with)** (*clothes*) doubler (de); (*box*) garnir *or* tapisser (de); (*subj: trees, crowd*) border; **in a ~** aligné(e); **in his ~ of business** dans sa partie, dans son rayon; **in ~ with** en accord avec; **~ up** *vi* s'aligner, se mettre en rang(s) ♦ *vt* aligner; (*event*) prévoir, préparer

lined [laɪnd] *adj* (*face*) ridé(e), marqué(e); (*paper*) réglé(e)

linen ['lɪnɪn] *n* linge *m* (de maison); (*cloth*) lin *m*

liner ['laɪnə*] *n* paquebot *m* (de ligne); (*for bin*) sac *m* à poubelle

linesman ['laɪnzmən] (*irreg*) *n* juge *m* de touche; (*TENNIS*) juge *m* de ligne

line-up ['laɪnʌp] *n* (*US*: *queue*) file *f*; (*SPORT*) composition *f* de l'équipe *f*

linger ['lɪŋgə*] *vi* s'attarder; traîner; (*smell, tradition*) persister

lingo ['lɪŋgəʊ] (*inf pej: pl* ~es) *n* jargon *m*

linguist ['lɪŋgwɪst] *n*: **to be a good** ~ être doué(e) par les langues

linguistics [lɪŋ'gwɪstɪks] *n* linguistique *f*

lining ['laɪnɪŋ] *n* doublure *f*

link [lɪŋk] *n* lien *m*, rapport *m*; (*of a chain*) maillon *m* ♦ *vt* relier, lier, unir; ~**s** *npl* (*GOLF*) (terrain *m* de) golf *m*; ~ **up** *vt* relier ♦ *vi* se rejoindre; s'associer

lino ['laɪnəʊ] *n* = **linoleum**

linoleum [lɪ'nəʊlɪəm] *n* linoléum *m*

lion ['laɪən] *n* lion *m*; ~**ess** *n* lionne *f*

lip [lɪp] *n* lèvre *f*

liposuction ['lɪpəʊsʌkʃən] *n* liposuccion *f*

lip: ~**-read** *vi* lire sur les lèvres; ~ **salve** *n* pommade *f* rosat *or* pour les lèvres; ~ **service** *n*: **to pay** ~ **service to sth** ne reconnaître le mérite de qch que pour la forme; ~**stick** *n* rouge *m* à lèvres

liqueur [lɪ'kjʊə*] *n* liqueur *f*

liquid ['lɪkwɪd] *adj* liquide ♦ *n* liquide *m*; ~**ize** ['lɪkwɪdaɪz] *vt* (*CULIN*) passer au mixer; ~**izer** *n* mixer *m*

liquor ['lɪkə*] (*US*) *n* spiritueux *m*, alcool *m*

liquorice ['lɪkərɪs] (*BRIT*) *n* réglisse *f*

liquor store (*US*) *n* magasin *m* de vins et spiritueux

lisp [lɪsp] *vi* zézayer

list [lɪst] *n* liste *f* ♦ *vt* (*write down*) faire une *or* la liste de; (*mention*) énumérer; ~**ed building** (*BRIT*) *n* monument classé

listen ['lɪsn] *vi* écouter; **to** ~ **to** écouter; ~**er** *n* auditeur(trice)

listless ['lɪstləs] *adj* indolent(e), apathi-

que

lit [lɪt] *pt, pp of* **light**

liter ['liːtə*] (*US*) *n* = **litre**

literacy ['lɪtərəsɪ] *n* degré *m* d'alphabéti-sation, fait *m* de savoir lire et écrire

literal ['lɪtərəl] *adj* littéral(e); ~**ly** *adv* lit-téralement; (*really*) réellement

literary ['lɪtərərɪ] *adj* littéraire

literate ['lɪtərət] *adj* qui sait lire et écri-re, instruit(e)

literature ['lɪtrɪtʃə*] *n* littérature *f*; (*brochures etc*) documentation *f*

lithe [laɪð] *adj* agile, souple

litigation [lɪtɪ'geɪʃən] *n* litige *m*; conten-tieux *m*

litre ['liːtə*] (*US* **liter**) *n* litre *m*

litter ['lɪtə*] *n* (*rubbish*) détritus *mpl* ordures *fpl*; (*young animals*) portée *f*; ~ **bin** (*BRIT*) *n* boîte *f* à ordures, poubelle *f* ~**ed** *adj*: ~**ed with** jonché(e) de, cou-vert(e) de

little ['lɪtl] *adj* (*small*) petit(e) ♦ *adv* peu; ~ **milk/time** peu de lait/temps; **a** ~ un peu (de); **a** ~ **bit** un peu; ~ **by** ~ peti-à petit, peu à peu

live¹ [laɪv] *adj* (*animal*) vivant(e), en vie (*wire*) sous tension; (*bullet, bomb*) non explosé(e); (*broadcast*) en direct; (*per-formance*) en public

live² [lɪv] *vi* vivre; (*reside*) vivre, habiter ~ **down** *vt* faire oublier (avec le temps) ~ **on** *vt fus* (*food, salary*) vivre de; ~ **together** *vi* vivre ensemble, cohabiter; ~ **up to** *vt fus* se montrer à la hauteur de

livelihood ['laɪvlɪhʊd] *n* moyens *mp* d'existence

lively ['laɪvlɪ] *adj* vif(vive), plein(e) d'en train; (*place, book*) vivant(e)

liven up ['laɪvn-] *vt* animer ♦ *vi* s'ani mer

liver ['lɪvə*] *n* foie *m*

lives [laɪvz] *npl of* **life**

livestock ['laɪvstɒk] *n* bétail *m*, chepte *m*

livid ['lɪvɪd] *adj* livide, blafard(e); (*inf furious*) furieux(euse), furibond(e)

living ['lɪvɪŋ] *adj* vivant(e), en vie ♦ *n* **to earn** *or* **make a** ~ gagner sa vie; ~ **conditions** *npl* conditions *fpl* de vie; ~

room *n* salle *f* de séjour; ~ **standards** *npl* niveau *m* de vie; ~ **wage** *n* salaire *m* permettant de vivre (décemment)

lizard ['lɪzəd] *n* lézard *m*

load [ləʊd] *n* (*weight*) poids *m*; (*thing carried*) chargement *m*, charge *f* ♦ *vt* (*also*: ~ *up*): **to ~ (with)** charger (de); (*gun, camera*) charger (avec); (*COMPUT*) charger; **a ~ of, ~s of** (*fig*) un *or* des tas de, des masses de; **to talk a ~ of rubbish** dire des bêtises; ~**ed** *adj* (*question*) insidieux(euse); (*inf: rich*) bourré(e) de fric

loaf [ləʊf] (*pl* **loaves**) *n* pain *m*, miche *f*

loan [ləʊn] *n* prêt *m* ♦ *vt* prêter; **on ~** prêté(e), en prêt

loath [ləʊθ] *adj*: **to be ~ to do** répugner à faire

loathe [ləʊð] *vt* détester, avoir en horreur

loaves [ləʊvz] *npl of* **loaf**

lobby ['lɒbɪ] *n* hall *m*, entrée *f*; (*POL*) groupe *m* de pression, lobby *m* ♦ *vt* faire pression sur

lobster ['lɒbstə*] *n* homard *m*

local ['ləʊkəl] *adj* local(e) ♦ *n* (*BRIT: pub*) pub *m or* café *m* du coin; **the ~s** *npl* (*inhabitants*) les gens *mpl* du pays *or* du coin; ~ **anaesthetic** *n* anesthésie locale; ~ **call** *n* communication urbaine; ~ **government** *n* administration locale *or* municipale; ~**ity** [ləʊ'kælɪtɪ] *n* région *f*, environs *mpl*; (*position*) lieu *m*

locate [ləʊ'keɪt] *vt* (*find*) trouver, repérer; (*situate*): **to be ~d in** être situé(e) à *or* en

location [ləʊ'keɪʃən] *n* emplacement *m*; **on ~** (*CINEMA*) en extérieur

loch [lɒx] *n* lac *m*, loch *m*

lock [lɒk] *n* (*of door, box*) serrure *f*; (*of canal*) écluse *f*; (*of hair*) mèche *f*, boucle *f* ♦ *vt* (*with key*) fermer à clé ♦ *vi* (*door etc*) fermer à clé; (*wheels*) se bloquer; ~ **in** *vt* enfermer; ~ **out** *vt* enfermer dehors; (*deliberately*) mettre à la porte; ~ **up** *vt* (*person*) enfermer; (*house*) fermer à clé ♦ *vi* tout fermer (à clé)

locker ['lɒkə*] *n* casier *m*; (*in station*) consigne *f* automatique

locket ['lɒkɪt] *n* médaillon *m*

locksmith ['lɒksmɪθ] *n* serrurier *m*

lockup ['lɒkʌp] *n* (*prison*) prison *f*

locum ['ləʊkəm] *n* (*MED*) suppléant(e) (de médecin)

lodge [lɒdʒ] *n* pavillon *m* (de gardien); (*hunting* ~) pavillon de chasse ♦ *vi* (*person*): **to ~ (with)** être logé(e) (chez), être en pension (chez); (*bullet*) se loger ♦ *vt*: **to ~ a complaint** porter plainte; ~**r** *n* locataire *m/f*; (*with meals*) pensionnaire *m/f*; **lodgings** ['lɒdʒɪŋz] *npl* chambre *f*; meublé *m*

loft [lɒft] *n* grenier *m*

lofty ['lɒftɪ] *adj* (*noble*) noble, élevé(e); (*haughty*) hautain(e)

log [lɒg] *n* (*of wood*) bûche *f*; (*book*) = **logbook** ♦ *vt* (*record*) noter

logbook ['lɒgbʊk] *n* (*NAUT*) livre *m or* journal *m* de bord; (*AVIAT*) carnet *m* de vol; (*of car*) ≈ carte grise

loggerheads ['lɒgəhedz] *npl*: **at ~ (with)** à couteaux tirés (avec)

logic ['lɒdʒɪk] *n* logique *f*; ~**al** *adj* logique

loin [lɔɪn] *n* (*CULIN*) filet *m*, longe *f*

loiter ['lɔɪtə*] *vi* traîner

loll [lɒl] *vi* (*also*: ~ *about*) se prélasser, fainéanter

lollipop ['lɒlɪpɒp] *n* sucette *f*; ~ **man/lady** (*BRIT: irreg*) *n* contractuel(le) qui fait traverser la rue aux enfants

London ['lʌndən] *n* Londres *m*; ~**er** *n* Londonien(ne)

lone [ləʊn] *adj* solitaire

loneliness ['ləʊnlɪnəs] *n* solitude *f*, isolement *m*; **lonely** ['ləʊnlɪ] *adj* seul(e); solitaire, isolé(e)

long [lɒŋ] *adj* long(longue) ♦ *adv* longtemps ♦ *vi*: **to ~ for sth** avoir très envie de qch; attendre qch avec impatience; **so** *or* **as ~ as** pourvu que; **don't be ~!** dépêchez-vous!; **how ~ is this river/course?** quelle est la longueur de ce fleuve/la durée de ce cours?; **6 metres ~** (long) de 6 mètres; **6 months ~** qui dure 6 mois, de 6 mois; **all night ~** toute la nuit; **he no ~er comes** il ne vient plus; ~ **before/after** longtemps avant/après;

before ~ (+*future*) avant peu, dans peu de temps; (+*past*) peu (de temps) après; **at** ~ **last** enfin; **~-distance** *adj* (*call*) interurbain(e); **~hand** *n* écriture normale *or* courante; **~ing** *n* désir *m*, envie *f*, nostalgie *f*

longitude [ˈlɒŋgɪtjuːd] *n* longitude *f*

long: ~ **jump** *n* saut *m* en longueur; **~-life** *adj* longue durée *inv*; (*milk*) upérisé(e); **~-lost** *adj* (*person*) perdu(e) de vue depuis longtemps; **~-playing record** *n* (disque *m*) 33 tours *inv*; **~-range** *adj* à longue portée; **~-sighted** *adj* (*MED*) presbyte; **~-standing** *adj* de longue date; **~-suffering** *adj* empreint(e) d'une patience résignée; extrêmement patient(e); **~-term** *adj* à long terme; ~ **wave** *n* grandes ondes; **~-winded** *adj* intarissable, interminable

loo [luː] (*BRIT: inf*) *n* W.-C. *mpl*, petit coin

look [lʊk] *vi* regarder; (*seem*) sembler, paraître, avoir l'air; (*building etc*): **to ~ south/(out) onto the sea** donner au sud/sur la mer ♦ *n* regard *m*; (*appearance*) air *m*, allure *f*, aspect *m*; **~s** *npl* (*good ~s*) physique *m*, beauté *f*; **to have a ~** regarder; **~!** regardez!; **~ (here)!** (*annoyance*) écoutez!; ~ **after** *vt fus* (*care for, deal with*) s'occuper de; ~ **at** *vt fus*, regarder (*problem etc*) examiner; ~ **back** *vi*: **to ~ back on** (*event etc*) évoquer, repenser à; ~ **down on** *vt fus* (*fig*) regarder de haut, dédaigner; ~ **for** *vt fus* chercher; ~ **forward to** *vt fus* attendre avec impatience; **we ~ forward to hearing from you** (*in letter*) dans l'attente de vous lire; ~ **into** *vt fus* examiner, étudier; ~ **on** *vi* regarder (en spectateur); ~ **out** *vi* (*beware*): **to ~ out (for)** prendre garde (à), faire attention (à); ~ **out for** *vt fus* être à la recherche de; guetter; ~ **round** *vi* se tourner derrière soi, se retourner; ~ **to** *vt fus* (*rely on*) compter sur; ~ **up** *vi* lever les yeux; (*improve*) s'améliorer ♦ *vt* (*word, name*) chercher; ~ **up to** *vt fus* avoir du respect pour; **~out** *n* poste *m* de guet; (*person*) guetteur *m*; **to be on the ~out**

(for) guetter

loom [luːm] *vi* (*also*: ~ **up**) surgir; (*approach: event etc*) être imminent(e), (*threaten*) menacer ♦ *n* (*for weaving*) métier *m* à tisser

loony [ˈluːnɪ] (*inf*) *adj*, *n* timbré(e), cinglé(e)

loop [luːp] *n* boucle *f*; **~hole** *n* (*fig*) porte *f* de sortie; échappatoire *f*

loose [luːs] *adj* (*knot, screw*) desserré(e); (*clothes*) ample, lâche; (*hair*) dénoué(e), épars(e); (*not firmly fixed*) pas solide; (*morals, discipline*) relâché(e), ♦ *n*: **on the ~** en liberté; ~ **change** *n* petite monnaie; ~ **chippings** *npl* (*on road*) gravillons *mpl*; ~ **end** *n*: **to be at a ~ end** *or* (*US*) **at ~ ends** ne pas trop savoir quoi faire; **~ly** *adv* sans serrer; (*imprecisely*) approximativement; **~n** *vt* desserrer

loot [luːt] *n* (*inf: money*) pognon *m*, fric *m* ♦ *vt* piller

lopsided [ˈlɒpˈsaɪdɪd] *adj* de travers, asymétrique

lord [lɔːd] *n* seigneur *m*; **L~ Smith** lord Smith; **the L~** le Seigneur; **good L~!** mon Dieu!; **the (House of) L~s** (*BRIT*) la Chambre des lords; **my L~** = **your Lordship**; **L~ship** *n*: **your L~ship** Monsieur le comte (*or* le baron *or* le juge) (*to bishop*) Monseigneur

lore [lɔː*] *n* tradition(s) *f(pl)*

lorry [ˈlɒrɪ] (*BRIT*) *n* camion *m*; ~ **driver** (*BRIT*) *n* camionneur *m*, routier *m*

lose [luːz] (*pt, pp* **lost**) *vt, vi* perdre; **to ~ (time)** (*clock*) retarder; **to get lost** *vi* se perdre; **~r** *n* perdant(e)

loss [lɒs] *n* perte *f*; **to be at a ~** être perplexe *or* embarrassé(e)

lost [lɒst] *pt, pp of* **lose** ♦ *adj* perdu(e) ~ **and found** (*US*), ~ **property** *n* objets trouvés

lot [lɒt] *n* (*set*) lot *m*; **the ~** le tout; **a ~ (of)** beaucoup (de); **~s of** des tas de; **to draw ~s (for sth)** tirer (qch) au sort

lotion [ˈləʊʃən] *n* lotion *f*

lottery [ˈlɒtərɪ] *n* loterie *f*

loud [laʊd] *adj* bruyant(e), sonore (*voice*) fort(e); (*support, condemnation*) vigoureux(euse); (*gaudy*) voyant(e), tapageur(euse) ♦ *adv* (*speak etc*) fort; **out ~** tout haut; **~-hailer** (*BRIT*) *n* porte-voix *m inv*; **~ly** *adv* fort, bruyamment; **~speaker** *n* haut-parleur *m*

lounge [laundʒ] *n* salon *m*; (*at airport*) salle *f*; (*BRIT: also*: ~ **bar**) (salle de) café *m or* bar *m* ♦ *vi* (*also*: ~ **about or around**) se prélasser, paresser; **~ suit** (*BRIT*) *n* complet *m*; (*on invitation*) "tenue de ville"

louse [laus] (*pl* **lice**) *n* pou *m*

lousy ['lauzɪ] (*inf*) *adj* infect(e), moche; **I feel ~** je suis mal fichu(e)

lout [laut] *n* rustre *m*, butor *m*

lovable ['lʌvəbl] *adj* adorable; très sympathique

love [lʌv] *n* amour *m* ♦ *vt* aimer; (*caringly, kindly*) aimer beaucoup; **"~ (from) Anne"** "affectueusement, Anne"; **I ~ chocolate** j'adore le chocolat; **to be/ fall in ~ with** être/tomber amoureux(euse) de; **to make ~** faire l'amour; **"15 ~"** (*TENNIS*) "15 à rien *or* zéro"; **~ affair** *n* liaison (amoureuse); **~ life** *n* vie sentimentale

lovely ['lʌvlɪ] *adj* (très) joli(e), ravissant(e); (*delightful: person*) charmant(e); (*holiday etc*) très agréable

lover ['lʌvə*] *n* amant *m*; (*person in love*) amoureux(euse); (*amateur*): **a ~ of** un amateur de; un(e) amoureux(euse) de

loving ['lʌvɪŋ] *adj* affectueux(euse), tendre

low [ləu] *adj* bas(basse); (*quality*) mauvais(e), inférieur(e); (*person: depressed*) déprimé(e); (*: ill*) bas(basse), affaibli(e) ♦ *adv* bas ♦ *n* (*METEOROLOGY*) dépression *f*; **to be ~ on** être à court de; **to feel ~** se sentir déprimé(e); **to reach an all-time ~** être au plus bas; **~-alcohol** *adj* peu alcoolisé(e); **~-cut** *adj* (*dress*) décolleté(e)

lower ['ləuə*] *adj* inférieur(e) ♦ *vt* abaisser, baisser

low: ~-fat *adj* maigre; **~lands** *npl* (*GEO*) plaines *fpl*; **~ly** *adj* humble, modeste

loyalty ['lɔɪəltɪ] *n* loyauté *f*, fidélité *f*

lozenge ['lɔzɪndʒ] *n* (*MED*) pastille *f*

LP *n abbr* = **long-playing record**

L-plates ['elpleɪts] (*BRIT*) *npl* plaques *fpl* d'apprenti conducteur

Ltd *abbr* (= *limited*) ≈ S.A.

lubricant ['lu:brɪkənt] *n* lubrifiant *m*

lubricate ['lu:brɪkeɪt] *vt* lubrifier, graisser

luck [lʌk] *n* chance *f*; **bad ~** malchance *f*, malheur *m*; **bad *or* hard ~!** pas de chance!; **good ~!** bonne chance!; **~ily** *adv* heureusement, par bonheur; **~y** *adj* (*person*) qui a de la chance; (*coincidence, event*) heureux(euse); (*object*) porte-bonheur *inv*

ludicrous ['lu:dɪkrəs] *adj* ridicule, absurde

lug [lʌg] (*inf*) *vt* traîner, tirer

luggage ['lʌgɪdʒ] *n* bagages *mpl*; **~ rack** *n* (*on car*) galerie *f*

lukewarm ['lu:kwɔ:m] *adj* tiède

lull [lʌl] *n* accalmie *f*; (*in conversation*) pause *f* ♦ *vt*: **to ~ sb to sleep** bercer qn pour qu'il s'endorme; **to be ~ed into a false sense of security** s'endormir dans une fausse sécurité

lullaby ['lʌləbaɪ] *n* berceuse *f*

lumbago [lʌm'beɪgəu] *n* lumbago *m*

lumber ['lʌmbə*] *n* (*wood*) bois *m* de charpente; (*junk*) bric-à-brac *m inv* ♦ *vt*: **to be ~ed with** (*inf*) se farcir; **~jack** *n* bûcheron *m*

luminous ['lu:mɪnəs] *adj* lumineux(euse)

lump [lʌmp] *n* morceau *m*; (*swelling*) grosseur *f* ♦ *vt*: **to ~ together** réunir, mettre en tas; **~ sum** *n* somme globale *or* forfaitaire; **~y** *adj* (*sauce*) avec des grumeaux; (*bed*) défoncé(e), peu confortable

lunar ['lu:nə*] *adj* lunaire

lunatic ['lu:nətɪk] *adj* fou(folle), cinglé(e) (*inf*)

lunch [lʌntʃ] *n* déjeuner *m*

luncheon ['lʌntʃən] *n* déjeuner *m* (chic); **~ meat** *n* *sorte de mortadelle*; **~ voucher** (*BRIT*) *n* chèque-repas *m*

lung [lʌŋ] *n* poumon *m*

lunge [lʌndʒ] *vi* (*also*: ~ **forward**) faire un mouvement brusque en avant; **to ~ at** envoyer *or* assener un coup à

lurch [lɜ:tʃ] *vi* vaciller, tituber ♦ *n* écart *m* brusque; **to leave sb in the ~** laisser qn se débrouiller *or* se dépêtrer tout(e) seul(e)

lure [ljʊə*] *n* (*attraction*) attrait *m*, charme *m* ♦ *vt* attirer *or* persuader par la ruse

lurid ['ljʊərɪd] *adj* affreux(euse), atroce; (*pej: colour, dress*) criard(e)

lurk [lɜ:k] *vi* se tapir, se cacher

luscious ['lʌʃəs] *adj* succulent(e); appétissant(e)

lush [lʌʃ] *adj* luxuriant(e)

lust [lʌst] *n* (*sexual*) luxure *f*; lubricité *f*; désir *m*; (*fig*): **~ for** soif *f* de; **~ after, ~ for** *vt fus* (*sexually*) convoiter, désirer; **~y** ['lʌstɪ] *adj* vigoureux(euse), robuste

Luxembourg ['lʌksəmbɜ:g] *n* Luxembourg *m*

luxurious [lʌg'zjʊərɪəs] *adj* luxueux(euse); **luxury** ['lʌkʃərɪ] *n* luxe *m* ♦ *cpd* de luxe

lying ['laɪɪŋ] *n* mensonge(s) *m(pl)* ♦ *vb see* lie

lyrical *adj* lyrique

lyrics ['lɪrɪks] *npl* (*of song*) paroles *fpl*

M m

m. *abbr* = metre; mile; million

M.A. *abbr* = Master of Arts

mac [mæk] (*BRIT*) *n* imper(méable) *m*

macaroni [mækə'rəʊnɪ] *n* macaroni *mpl*

machine [mə'ʃi:n] *n* machine *f* ♦ *vt* (*TECH*) façonner à la machine; (*dress etc*) coudre à la machine; **~ gun** *n* mitrailleuse *f*; **~ language** *n* (*COMPUT*) langage-machine *m*; **~ry** [mə'ʃi:nərɪ] *n* machinerie *f*, machines *fpl*; (*fig*) mécanisme(s) *m(pl)*

mackerel ['mækrəl] *n inv* maquereau *m*

mackintosh ['mækɪntɒʃ] (*BRIT*) *n* imperméable *m*

mad [mæd] *adj* fou(folle); (*foolish*) insensé(e); (*angry*) furieux(euse); (*keen*): **to be ~ about** fou(folle) de

madam ['mædəm] *n* madame *f*

madden ['mædn] *vt* exaspérer

made [meɪd] *pt, pp of* make

Madeira [mə'dɪərə] *n* (*GEO*) Madère *f*; (*wine*) madère *m*

made-to-measure ['meɪdtə'meʒə*] (*BRIT*) *adj* fait(e) sur mesure

madly ['mædlɪ] *adv* follement; **~ in love** éperdument amoureux(euse)

madman ['mædmən] (*irreg*) *n* fou *m*

madness ['mædnəs] *n* folie *f*

magazine ['mægəzi:n] *n* (*PRESS*) magazine *m*, revue *f*; (*RADIO, TV: also:* **~ programme**) magazine

maggot ['mægət] *n* ver *m*, asticot *m*

magic ['mædʒɪk] *n* magie *f* ♦ *adj* magique; **~al** *adj* magique; (*experience, evening*) merveilleux(euse); **~ian** [mə'dʒɪʃən] *n* magicien(ne); (*conjurer*) prestidigitateur *m*

magistrate ['mædʒɪstreɪt] *n* magistrat *m*; juge *m*

magnet ['mægnɪt] *n* aimant *m*; **~ic** [mæg'netɪk] *adj* magnétique

magnificent [mæg'nɪfɪsənt] *adj* superbe, magnifique; (*splendid: robe, building*) somptueux(euse), magnifique

magnify ['mægnɪfaɪ] *vt* grossir; (*sound*) amplifier; **~ing glass** *n* loupe *f*

magnitude ['mægnɪtju:d] *n* ampleur *f*

magpie ['mægpaɪ] *n* pie *f*

mahogany [mə'hɒgənɪ] *n* acajou *m*

maid [meɪd] *n* bonne *f*; **old ~** (*pej*) vieille fille

maiden ['meɪdn] *n* jeune fille *f* ♦ *adj* (*aunt etc*) non mariée; (*speech, voyage*) inaugural(e); **~ name** *n* nom *m* de jeune fille

mail [meɪl] *n* poste *f*; (*letters*) courrier *m* ♦ *vt* envoyer (par la poste); **~box** (*US*) *n* boîte *f* aux lettres; **~ing list** *n* liste *f* d'adresses; **~-order** *n* vente *f or* achat *m* par correspondance

maim [meɪm] *vt* mutiler

main [meɪn] *adj* principal(e) ♦ *n*: **the ~(s)** *n(pl)* (*gas, water*) conduite principale, canalisation *f*; **the ~s** *npl* (*ELEC*) le secteur; **in the ~** dans l'ensemble; **~frame** *n* (*COMPUT*) (gros) ordinateur unité centrale; **~land** *n* continent *m*; **~ly** *adv* principalement, surtout; **~ road** *n* grand-route *f*; **~stay** *n* (*fig*) pilier *m*

~**stream** *n* courant principal

maintain [meɪn'teɪn] *vt* entretenir; (*continue*) maintenir; (*affirm*) soutenir; **maintenance** ['meɪntənəns] *n* entretien *m*; (*alimony*) pension *f* alimentaire

maize [meɪz] *n* maïs *m*

majestic [mə'dʒestɪk] *adj* majestueux(euse)

majesty ['mædʒɪstɪ] *n* majesté *f*

major ['meɪdʒə*] *n* (*MIL*) commandant *m* ♦ *adj* (*important*) important(e); (*most important*) principal(e); (*MUS*) majeur(e)

Majorca [mə'jɔːkə] *n* Majorque *f*

majority [mə'dʒɒrɪtɪ] *n* majorité *f*

make [meɪk] (*pt, pp* **made**) *vt* faire; (*manufacture*) faire, fabriquer; (*earn*) gagner; (*cause to be*): **to ~ sb sad** *etc* rendre qn triste *etc*; (*force*): **to ~ sb do sth** obliger qn à faire qch, faire faire qch à qn; (*equal*): **2 and 2 ~ 4** 2 et 2 font 4 ♦ *n* fabrication *f*; (*brand*) marque *f*; **to ~ a fool of sb** (*ridicule*) ridiculiser qn; (*trick*) duper qn; **to ~ a profit** faire *or* des bénéfice(s); **to ~ a loss** essuyer une perte; **to ~ it** (*arrive*) arriver; (*achieve sth*) parvenir à qch, réussir; **what time do you ~ it?** quelle heure avez-vous?; **to ~ do with** se contenter de; **~ for** *vt fus* se diriger vers; **~ out** *vt* (*write out: cheque*) faire; (*decipher*) déchiffrer; (*understand*) comprendre; (*see*) distinguer; **~ up** *vt* (*constitute*) constituer; (*invent*) inventer, imaginer; (*parcel, bed*) faire ♦ *vi* se réconcilier; (*with cosmetics*) se maquiller; **~ up for** *vt fus* compenser; **~-believe** *n*: **it's just ~-believe** (*game*) c'est pour faire semblant; (*invention*) c'est de l'invention pure; **~r** *n* fabricant *m*; **~shift** *adj* provisoire, improvisé(e); **~-up** *n* maquillage *m*; **~-up remover** *n* démaquillant *m*

making ['meɪkɪŋ] *n* (*fig*): **in the ~** en formation *or* gestation; **to have the ~s of** (*actor, athlete etc*) avoir l'étoffe de

malaria [mə'lɛərɪə] *n* malaria *f*

Malaysia [mə'leɪzɪə] *n* Malaisie *f*

male [meɪl] *n* (*BIO*) mâle *m* ♦ *adj* mâle; (*sex, attitude*) masculin(e); (*child etc*) du sexe masculin

malevolent [mə'levələnt] *adj* malveillant(e)

malfunction [mæl'fʌŋkʃən] *n* fonctionnement défectueux

malice ['mælɪs] *n* méchanceté *f*, malveillance *f*; **malicious** [mə'lɪʃəs] *adj* méchant(e), malveillant(e)

malign [mə'laɪn] *vt* diffamer, calomnier

malignant [mə'lɪgnənt] *adj* (*MED*) malin(igne)

mall [mɔːl] *n* (*also: shopping ~*) centre commercial

mallet ['mælɪt] *n* maillet *m*

malpractice ['mæl'præktɪs] *n* faute professionnelle; négligence *f*

malt [mɔːlt] *n* malt *m* ♦ *cpd* (*also: ~ whisky*) pur malt

Malta ['mɔːltə] *n* Malte *f*

mammal ['mæməl] *n* mammifère *m*

mammoth ['mæməθ] *n* mammouth *m* ♦ *adj* géant(e), monstre

man [mæn] (*pl* **men**) *n* homme *m* ♦ *vt* (*NAUT: ship*) garnir d'hommes; (*MIL: gun*) servir; (: *post*) être de service à; (*machine*) assurer le fonctionnement de; **an old ~** un vieillard; **~ and wife** mari et femme

manage ['mænɪdʒ] *vi* se débrouiller ♦ *vt* (*be in charge of*) s'occuper de; (: *business etc*) gérer; (*control: ship*) manier, manœuvrer; (: *person*) savoir s'y prendre avec; **to ~ to do** réussir à faire; **~able** *adj* (*task*) faisable; (*number*) raisonnable; **~ment** *n* gestion *f*, administration *f*, direction *f*; **~r** *n* directeur *m*; administrateur *m*; (*SPORT*) manager *m*; (*of artist*) impresario *m*; **~ress** [mænɪdʒə'rəs] *n* directrice *f*; gérante *f*; **~rial** [mænə'dʒɪərɪəl] *adj* directorial(e); (*skills*) de cadre, de gestion; **managing director** ['mænɪdʒɪŋ] *n* directeur général

mandarin ['mændərɪn] *n* (*also: ~ orange*) mandarine *f*; (*person*) mandarin *m*

mandatory ['mændətərɪ] *adj* obligatoire

mane [meɪn] *n* crinière *f*

maneuver (*US*) *vt, vi, n* = **manoeuvre**

manfully ['mænfʊlɪ] *adv* vaillamment

mangle ['mæŋgl] *vt* déchiqueter; mutiler

mango ['mæŋgəʊ] (*pl* ~es) *n* mangue *f*

mangy ['meɪndʒɪ] *adj* galeux(euse)

manhandle ['mænhændl] *vt* malmener

man: ~**hole** ['mænhəʊl] *n* trou *m* d'homme; ~**hood** ['mænhʊd] *n* âge *m* d'homme; virilité *f*; ~**-hour** ['mæn'aʊə*] *n* heure *f* de main-d'œuvre; ~**hunt** ['mænhʌnt] *n* (*POLICE*) chasse *f* à l'homme

mania ['meɪnɪə] *n* manie *f*; ~**c** ['meɪnɪæk] *n* maniaque *m/f*; (*fig*) fou(folle) *m/f*; **manic** ['mænɪk] *adj* maniaque

manicure ['mænɪkjʊə*] *n* manucure *f*; ~ **set** *n* trousse *f* à ongles

manifest ['mænɪfest] *vt* manifester ♦ *adj* manifeste, évident(e)

manifesto [mænɪ'festəʊ] *n* manifeste *m*

manipulate [mə'nɪpjʊleɪt] *vt* manipuler; (*system, situation*) exploiter

man: ~**kind** [mæn'kaɪnd] *n* humanité *f*, genre humain; ~**ly** ['mænlɪ] *adj* viril(le); ~**-made** ['mæn'meɪd] *adj* artificiel(le); (*fibre*) synthétique

manner ['mænə*] *n* manière *f*, façon *f*; (*behaviour*) attitude *f*, comportement *m*; (*sort*): **all** ~ **of** toutes sortes de; ~**s** *npl* (*behaviour*) manières; ~**ism** *n* particularité *f* de langage (*or* de comportement), tic *m*

manoeuvre [mə'nu:və*] (*US* **maneuver**) *vt* (*move*) manœuvrer; (*manipulate: person*) manipuler; (: *situation*) exploiter ♦ *vi* manœuvrer ♦ *n* manœuvre *f*

manor ['mænə*] *n* (*also*: ~ *house*) manoir *m*

manpower ['mænpaʊə*] *n* main-d'œuvre *f*

mansion ['mænʃən] *n* château *m*, manoir *m*

manslaughter ['mænslɔ:tə*] *n* homicide *m* involontaire

mantelpiece ['mæntlpi:s] *n* cheminée *f*

manual ['mænjʊəl] *adj* manuel(le) ♦ *n* manuel *m*

manufacture [mænjʊ'fæktʃə*] *vt* fabriquer ♦ *n* fabrication *f*; ~**r** *n* fabricant *m*

manure [mə'njʊə*] *n* fumier *m*

manuscript ['mænjʊskrɪpt] *n* manuscrit *m*

many ['menɪ] *adj* beaucoup de, de nom-

breux(euses) ♦ *pron* beaucoup, un grand nombre; **a great** ~ un grand nombre (de); ~ **a ...** bien des ..., plus d'un(e) ...

map [mæp] *n* carte *f*; (*of town*) plan *m*; ~ **out** *vt* tracer; (*task*) planifier

maple ['meɪpl] *n* érable *m*

mar [mɑ:*] *vt* gâcher, gâter

marathon ['mærəθən] *n* marathon *m*

marble ['mɑ:bl] *n* marbre *m*; (*toy*) bille *f*

March [mɑ:tʃ] *n* mars *m*

march [mɑ:tʃ] *vi* marcher au pas; (*fig: protesters*) défiler ♦ *n* marche *f*; (*demonstration*) manifestation *f*

mare [mɛə*] *n* jument *f*

margarine [mɑ:dʒə'ri:n] *n* margarine *f*

margin ['mɑ:dʒɪn] *n* marge *f*; ~**al (seat)** *n* (*POL*) siège disputé

marigold ['mærɪgəʊld] *n* souci *m*

marijuana [mærɪ'wɑ:nə] *n* marijuana *f*

marina [mə'ri:nə] *n* (*harbour*) marina *f*

marine [mə'ri:n] *adj* marin(e) ♦ *n* fusilier marin; (*US*) marine *m*; ~ **engineer** *n* ingénieur *m* en génie maritime

marital ['mærɪtl] *adj* matrimonial(e); ~ **status** situation *f* de famille

marjoram ['mɑ:dʒərəm] *n* marjolaine *f*

mark [mɑ:k] *n* marque *f*; (*of skid etc*) trace *f*; (*BRIT: SCOL*) note *f*; (*currency*) mark *m* ♦ *vt* marquer; (*stain*) tacher; (*BRIT: SCOL*) noter; corriger; **to** ~ **time** marquer le pas; ~**er** *n* (*sign*) jalon *m*; (*bookmark*) signet *m*

market ['mɑ:kɪt] *n* marché *m* ♦ *vt* (*COMM*) commercialiser; ~ **garden** (*BRIT*) *n* jardin maraîcher; ~**ing** *n* marketing *m*; ~**place** *n* place *f* du marché; (*COMM*) marché *m*; ~ **research** *n* étude *f* de marché

marksman ['mɑ:ksmən] (*irreg*) *n* tireur *m* d'élite

marmalade ['mɑ:məleɪd] *n* confiture *f* d'oranges

maroon [mə'ru:n] *vt*: **to be** ~**ed** être abandonné(e); (*fig*) être bloqué(e) ♦ *adj* bordeaux *inv*

marquee [mɑ:'ki:] *n* chapiteau *m*

marriage ['mærɪdʒ] *n* mariage *m*; ~ **bureau** *n* agence matrimoniale; ~ **certificate** *n* extrait *m* d'acte de mariage

married ['mærɪd] *adj* marié(e); (*life, love*) conjugal(e)

marrow ['mærəʊ] *n* moelle *f*; (*vegetable*) courge *f*

marry ['mærɪ] *vt* épouser, se marier avec; (*subj: father, priest etc*) marier ♦ *vi* (*also: get married*) se marier

Mars [mɑːz] *n* (*planet*) Mars *f*

marsh [mɑːʃ] *n* marais *m*, marécage *m*

marshal ['mɑːʃəl] *n* maréchal *m*; (*US: fire, police*) ≈ capitaine *m*; (*SPORT*) membre *m* du service d'ordre ♦ *vt* rassembler

marshy ['mɑːʃɪ] *adj* marécageux(euse)

martyr ['mɑːtə*] *n* martyr(e); **~dom** *n* martyre *m*

marvel ['mɑːvəl] *n* merveille *f* ♦ *vi*: **to ~ (at)** s'émerveiller (de); **~lous** (*US* **~ous**) *adj* merveilleux(euse)

Marxist ['mɑːksɪst] *adj* marxiste ♦ *n* marxiste *m/f*

marzipan [mɑːzɪˈpæn] *n* pâte *f* d'amandes

mascara [mæsˈkɑːrə] *n* mascara *m*

masculine ['mæskjʊlɪn] *adj* masculin(e)

mash [mæʃ] *vt* écraser, réduire en purée; **~ed potatoes** *npl* purée *f* de pommes de terre

mask [mɑːsk] *n* masque *m* ♦ *vt* masquer

mason ['meɪsn] *n* (*also: stone~*) maçon *m*; (: *free~*) franc-maçon *m*; **~ry** *n* maçonnerie *f*

masquerade [mæskəˈreɪd] *vi*: **to ~ as** se faire passer pour

mass [mæs] *n* multitude *f*, masse *f*; (*PHYSICS*) masse; (*REL*) messe *f* ♦ *cpd* (*communication*) de masse; (*unemployment*) massif(ive) ♦ *vi* se masser; **the ~es** les masses; **~es of** des tas de

massacre ['mæsəkə*] *n* massacre *m*

massage ['mæsɑːʒ] *n* massage *m* ♦ *vt* masser

massive ['mæsɪv] *adj* énorme, massif(ive)

mass media *n inv* mass-media *mpl*

mass production *n* fabrication *f* en série

mast [mɑːst] *n* mât *m*; (*RADIO*) pylône *m*

master ['mɑːstə*] *n* maître *m*; (*in sec-ondary school*) professeur *m*; (*title for boys*): **M~ X** Monsieur X ♦ *vt* maîtriser; (*learn*) apprendre à fond; **~ly** *adj* magistral(e); **~mind** *n* esprit supérieur ♦ *vt* diriger, être le cerveau de; **M~ of Arts/ Science** *n* ≈ maîtrise *f* (en lettres/ sciences); **~piece** *n* chef-d'œuvre *m*; **~plan** *n* stratégie *f* d'ensemble; **~y** *n* maîtrise *f*; connaissance parfaite

mat [mæt] *n* petit tapis; (*also: door~*) paillasson *m*; (: *table~*) napperon *m* ♦ *adj* = **matt**

match [mætʃ] *n* allumette *f*; (*game*) match *m*, partie *f*; (*fig*) égal(e) ♦ *vt* (*also: ~ up*) assortir; (*go well with*) aller bien avec, s'assortir à; (*equal*) égaler, valoir ♦ *vi* être assorti(e); **to be a good ~** être bien assorti(e); **~box** *n* boîte *f* d'allumettes; **~ing** *adj* assorti(e)

mate [meɪt] *n* (*inf*) copain(copine); (*animal*) partenaire *m/f*, mâle/femelle; (*in merchant navy*) second *m* ♦ *vi* s'accoupler

material [məˈtɪərɪəl] *n* (*substance*) matière *f*, matériau *m*; (*cloth*) tissu *m*, étoffe *f*; (*information, data*) données *fpl* ♦ *adj* matériel(le); (*relevant: evidence*) pertinent(e); **~s** *npl* (*equipment*) matériaux *mpl*

maternal [məˈtɜːnl] *adj* maternel(le)

maternity [məˈtɜːnɪtɪ] *n* maternité *f*; **~ dress** *n* robe *f* de grossesse; **~ hospital** *n* maternité *f*

mathematical [mæθəˈmætɪkl] *adj* mathématique; **mathematics** [mæθəˈmætɪks] *n* mathématiques *fpl*

maths [mæθs] (*US* **math**) *n* math(s) *fpl*

matinée ['mætɪneɪ] *n* matinée *f*

mating call ['meɪtɪŋ-] *n* appel *m* du mâle

matrices ['meɪtrɪsiːz] *npl of* **matrix**

matriculation [mətrɪkjʊˈleɪʃən] *n* inscription *f*

matrimonial [mætrɪˈməʊnɪəl] *adj* matrimonial(e), conjugal(e)

matrimony ['mætrɪmənɪ] *n* mariage *m*

matrix ['meɪtrɪks] (*pl* **matrices**) *n* matrice *f*

matron ['meɪtrən] *n* (*in hospital*)

infirmière-chef *f*; (*in school*) infirmière
gre

mat(t) [mæt] *adj* mat(e)

matted ['mætɪd] *adj* emmêlé(e)

matter ['mætə*] *n* question *f*; (PHYSICS) matière *f*; (*content*) contenu *m*, fond *m*; (MED: *pus*) pus *m* ♦ *vi* importer; ~**s** *npl* (*affairs, situation*) la situation; **it doesn't** ~ cela n'a pas d'importance; (*I don't mind*) cela ne fait rien; **what's the** ~? qu'est-ce qu'il y a?, qu'est-ce qui ne va pas?; **no** ~ **what** quoiqu'il arrive; **as a** ~ **of course** tout naturellement; **as a** ~ **of fact** en fait; ~**-of-fact** *adj* terre à terre; (*voice*) neutre

mattress ['mætrəs] *n* matelas *m*

mature [mə'tjuə*] *adj* mûr(e); (*cheese*) fait(e); (*wine*) arrivé(e) à maturité ♦ *vi* (*person*) mûrir; (*wine, cheese*) se faire

maul [mɔːl] *vt* lacérer

mausoleum [mɔːsə'lɪəm] *n* mausolée *m*

mauve [məʊv] *adj* mauve

maverick ['mævərɪk] *n* (*fig*) nonconformiste *m/f*

maximum ['mæksɪməm] (*pl* **maxima**) *adj* maximum ♦ *n* maximum *m*

May [meɪ] *n* mai *m*; ~ **Day** *n* le Premier Mai; *see also* **mayday**

may [meɪ] (*conditional* **might**) *vi* (*indicating possibility*): **he** ~ **come** il se peut qu'il vienne; (*be allowed to*): ~ **I smoke?** puis-je fumer?; (*wishes*): ~ **God bless you!** (que) Dieu vous bénisse!; **you** ~ **as well go** à votre place, je partirais

maybe ['meɪbiː] *adv* peut-être; ~ **he'll ...** peut-être qu'il ...

mayday ['meɪdeɪ] *n* SOS *m*

mayhem ['meɪhem] *n* grabuge *m*

mayonnaise [meɪə'neɪz] *n* mayonnaise *f*

mayor [mɛə*] *n* maire *m*; ~**ess** *n* épouse *f* du maire

maze [meɪz] *n* labyrinthe *m*, dédale *m*

MD *n abbr* (= Doctor of Medicine) titre universitaire; = **managing director**

me [miː] *pron* me, m' +*vowel*; (*stressed, after prep*) moi; **he heard** ~ il m'a entendu(e); **give** ~ **a book** donnez-moi un livre; **after** ~ après moi

meadow ['medəʊ] *n* prairie *f*, pré *m*

meagre ['miːgə*] (*US* **meager**) *adj* maigre

meal [miːl] *n* repas *m*; (*flour*) farine *f*; ~**time** *n* l'heure *f* du repas

mean [miːn] (*pt, pp* **meant**) *adj* (*with money*) avare, radin(e); (*unkind*) méchant(e); (*shabby*) misérable; (*average*) moyen(ne) ♦ *vt* signifier, vouloir dire; (*refer to*) faire allusion à, parler de; (*intend*): **to** ~ **to do** avoir l'intention de faire ♦ *n* moyenne *f*; ~**s** *npl* (*way, money*) moyens *mpl*; **by** ~**s of** par l'intermédiaire de; **au moyen de; by all** ~**s!** je vous en prie!; **to be** ~**t for sb/sth** être destiné(e) à qn/qch; **do you** ~ **it?** vous êtes sérieux?; **what do you** ~? que voulez-vous dire?

meander [mɪ'ændə*] *vi* faire des méandres

meaning ['miːnɪŋ] *n* signification *f*, sens *m*; ~**ful** *adj* significatif(ive); (*relationship, occasion*) important(e); ~**less** *adj* dénué(e) de sens

meanness ['miːnnɪs] *n* (*with money*) avarice *f*; (*unkindness*) méchanceté *f*; (*shabbiness*) médiocrité *f*

meant [ment] *pt, pp of* **mean**

meantime ['miːntaɪm] *adv* (*also*: **in the** ~) pendant ce temps

meanwhile ['miːnwaɪl] *adv* = **meantime**

measles ['miːzlz] *n* rougeole *f*

measly ['miːzlɪ] (*inf*) *adj* minable

measure ['meʒə*] *vt, vi* mesurer ♦ *n* mesure *f*; (*ruler*) règle (graduée); ~**ments** *npl* mesures *fpl*; **chest/hip(s) ~ment** tour *m* de poitrine/hanches

meat [miːt] *n* viande *f*; ~**ball** *n* boulette *f* de viande

Mecca ['mekə] *n* la Mecque

mechanic [mɪ'kænɪk] *n* mécanicien *m*; ~**al** *adj* mécanique; ~**s** *n* (PHYSICS) mécanique *f* ♦ *npl* (*of reading, government etc*) mécanisme *m*

mechanism ['mekənɪzəm] *n* mécanisme *m*

medal ['medl] *n* médaille *f*; ~**lion** [mɪ'dælɪən] *n* médaillon *m*; ~**list** (*US* ~**ist**) *n* (SPORT) médaillé(e)

meddle ['medl] *vi*: **to** ~ **in** se mêler de,

s'occuper de; **to ~ with** toucher à
media ['miːdɪə] *npl* media *mpl*
mediaeval [medɪ'iːvəl] *adj* = **medieval**
median ['miːdɪən] (*US*) *n* (*also:* **~ strip**) bande médiane
mediate ['miːdɪeɪt] *vi* servir d'intermédiaire
Medicaid ['medɪkeɪd] (®: *US*) *n* assistance médicale aux indigents
medical ['medɪkəl] *adj* médical(e) ♦ *n* visite médicale
Medicare ['medɪkɛə*] (®: *US*) *n* assistance médicale aux personnes âgées
medication [medɪ'keɪʃən] *n* (*drugs*) médicaments *mpl*
medicine ['medsɪn] *n* médecine *f*; (*drug*) médicament *m*
medieval [medɪ'iːvəl] *adj* médiéval(e)
mediocre [miːdɪ'əʊkə*] *adj* médiocre
meditate ['medɪteɪt] *vi* méditer
Mediterranean [medɪtə'reɪnɪən] *adj* méditerranéen(ne); **the ~ (Sea)** la (mer) Méditerranée
medium ['miːdɪəm] (*pl* **media**) *adj* moyen(ne) ♦ *n* (*means*) moyen *m*; (*pl* **mediums:** *person*) médium *m*; **the happy ~** le juste milieu; **~ wave** *n* ondes moyennes
medley ['medlɪ] *n* mélange *m*; (*MUS*) potpourri *m*
meek [miːk] *adj* doux(douce), humble
meet [miːt] (*pt, pp* **met**) *vt* rencontrer; (*by arrangement*) retrouver, rejoindre; (*for the first time*) faire la connaissance de; (*go and fetch*): **I'll ~ you at the station** j'irai te chercher à la gare; (*opponent, danger*) faire face à; (*obligations*) satisfaire à ♦ *vi* (*friends*) se rencontrer, se retrouver; (*in session*) se réunir; (*join: lines, roads*) se rejoindre; **~ with** *vt fus* rencontrer; **~ing** *n* rencontre *f*; (*session: of club etc*) réunion *f*; (*POL*) meeting *m*; **she's at a ~ing** (*COMM*) elle est en conférence
megabyte ['megəbaɪt] *n* (*COMPUT*) mégaoctet *m*
megaphone ['megəfəʊn] *n* porte-voix *m inv*
melancholy ['melənkəlɪ] *n* mélancolie *f*
♦ *adj* mélancolique
mellow ['meləʊ] *adj* velouté(e); doux(douce); (*sound*) mélodieux(euse)
♦ *vi* (*person*) s'adoucir
melody ['melədɪ] *n* mélodie *f*
melon ['melən] *n* melon *m*
melt [melt] *vi* fondre ♦ *vt* faire fondre; (*metal*) fondre; **~ away** *vi* fondre complètement; **~ down** *vt* fondre; **~down** *n* fusion *f* (du cœur d'un réacteur nucléaire); **~ing pot** *n* (*fig*) creuset *m*
member ['membə*] *n* membre *m*; **M~ of Parliament** (*BRIT*) député *m*; **M~ of the European Parliament** Eurodéputé *m*; **~ship** *n* adhésion *f*; statut *m* de membre; (*members*) membres *mpl*, adhérents *mpl*; **~ship card** *n* carte *f* de membre
memento [mə'mentəʊ] *n* souvenir *m*
memo ['meməʊ] *n* note *f* (de service)
memoirs ['memwɑːz] *npl* mémoires *mpl*
memorandum [memə'rændəm] (*pl* **memoranda**) *n* note *f* (de service)
memorial [mɪ'mɔːrɪəl] *n* mémorial *m*
♦ *adj* commémoratif(ive)
memorize ['meməraɪz] *vt* apprendre par cœur; retenir
memory ['memərɪ] *n* mémoire *f*; (*recollection*) souvenir *m*
men [men] *npl of* **man**
menace ['menɪs] *n* menace *f*; (*nuisance*) plaie *f* ♦ *vt* menacer; **menacing** *adj* menaçant(e)
mend [mend] *vt* réparer; (*darn*) raccommoder, repriser ♦ *n*: **on the ~** en voie de guérison; **to ~ one's ways** s'amender; **~ing** *n* réparation *f*; (*clothes*) raccommodage *m*
menial ['miːnɪəl] *adj* subalterne
meningitis [menɪn'dʒaɪtɪs] *n* méningite *f*
menopause ['menəʊpɔːz] *n* ménopause *f*
menstruation [menstrʊ'eɪʃən] *n* menstruation *f*
mental ['mentl] *adj* mental(e); **~ity** [men'tælɪtɪ] *n* mentalité *f*
mention ['menʃən] *n* mention *f* ♦ *vt* mentionner, faire mention de; **don't ~ it!** je vous en prie, il n'y a pas de quoi!
menu ['menjuː] *n* (*set ~, COMPUT*) menu

m; (*list of dishes*) carte *f*

MEP *n abbr* = **Member of the European Parliament**

mercenary ['mɜːsɪnərɪ] *adj* intéressé(e), mercenaire ♦ *n* mercenaire *m*

merchandise ['mɜːtʃəndaɪz] *n* marchandises *fpl*

merchant ['mɜːtʃənt] *n* négociant *m*, marchand *m*; **~ bank** (BRIT) *n* banque *f* d'affaires; **~ navy** (US **~ marine**) *n* marine marchande

merciful ['mɜːsɪfʊl] *adj* miséricordieux(euse), clément(e); **a ~ release** une délivrance

merciless ['mɜːsɪləs] *adj* impitoyable, sans pitié

mercury ['mɜːkjʊrɪ] *n* mercure *m*

mercy ['mɜːsɪ] *n* pitié *f*, indulgence *f*; (REL) miséricorde *f*; **at the ~ of** à la merci de

mere [mɪə*] *adj* simple; (*chance*) pur(e); **a ~ two hours** seulement deux heures; **~ly** *adv* simplement, purement

merge [mɜːdʒ] *vt* unir ♦ *vi* (*colours, shapes, sounds*) se mêler; (*roads*) se joindre; (COMM) fusionner; **~r** *n* (COMM) fusion *f*

meringue [mə'ræŋ] *n* meringue *f*

merit ['merɪt] *n* mérite *m*, valeur *f*

mermaid ['mɜːmeɪd] *n* sirène *f*

merry ['merɪ] *adj* gai(e); **M~ Christmas!** Joyeux Noël!; **~-go-round** *n* manège *m*

mesh [meʃ] *n* maille *f*

mesmerize ['mezməraɪz] *vt* hypnotiser; fasciner

mess [mes] *n* désordre *m*, fouillis *m*, pagaille *f*; (*muddle: of situation*) gâchis *m*; (*dirt*) saleté *f*; (MIL) mess *m*, cantine *f*; **~ about** (*inf*) *vi* perdre son temps; **~ about with** (*inf*) *vt fus* tripoter; **~ around** (*inf*) *vi* = **mess about**; **~ around with** *vt fus* = **mess about with**; **~ up** *vt* (*dirty*) salir; (*spoil*) gâcher

message ['mesɪdʒ] *n* message *m*

messenger ['mesɪndʒə*] *n* messager *m*

Messrs ['mesəz] *abbr* (*on letters*) MM

messy ['mesɪ] *adj* sale; en désordre

met [met] *pt, pp of* **meet**

metal ['metl] *n* métal *m*; **~lic** [me'tælɪk] *adj* métallique

meteorology [miːtɪə'rɒlədʒɪ] *n* météorologie *f*

mete out [miːt-] *vt* infliger; (*justice*) rendre

meter ['miːtə*] *n* (*instrument*) compteur *m*; (*also: parking ~*) parcomètre *m*; (US: *unit*) = **metre**

method ['meθəd] *n* méthode *f*; **~ical** [mɪ'θɒdɪkl] *adj* méthodique; **M~ist** ['meθədɪst] *n* méthodiste *m/f*

meths [meθs] (BRIT), **methylated spirit** ['meθɪleɪtɪd-] (BRIT) *n* alcool *m* à brûler

metre ['miːtə*] (US **meter**) *n* mètre *m*

metric ['metrɪk] *adj* métrique

metropolitan [metrə'pɒlɪtən] *adj* métropolitain(e); **the M~ Police** (BRIT) la police londonienne

mettle ['metl] *n*: **to be on one's ~** être d'attaque

mew [mjuː] *vi* (*cat*) miauler

mews [mjuːz] (BRIT) *n*: **~ cottage** cottage aménagé dans une ancienne écurie

Mexico ['meksɪkəʊ] *n* Mexique *m*

miaow [miː'aʊ] *vi* miauler

mice [maɪs] *npl of* **mouse**

micro ['maɪkrəʊ] *n* (*also: ~computer*) micro-ordinateur *m*

microchip ['maɪkrəʊtʃɪp] *n* puce *f*

microphone ['maɪkrəfəʊn] *n* microphone *m*

microscope ['maɪkrəskəʊp] *n* microscope *m*

microwave ['maɪkrəʊweɪv] *n* (*also: ~ oven*) four *m* à micro-ondes

mid [mɪd] *adj*: **in ~ May** à la mi-mai; **~ afternoon** le milieu de l'après-midi; **in ~ air** en plein ciel; **~day** *n* midi *m*

middle ['mɪdl] *n* milieu *m*; (*waist*) taille *f* ♦ *adj* du milieu; (*average*) moyen(ne); **in the ~ of the night** au milieu de la nuit; **~-aged** *adj* d'un certain âge; **M~ Ages** *npl*: **the M~ Ages** le moyen âge; **~-class** *adj* ≈ bourgeois(e); **~ class(es)** *n(pl)*: **the ~ class(es)** ≈ les classes moyennes; **M~ East** *n* Proche-Orient *m*, Moyen-Orient *m*; **~man** (*irreg*) *n* intermédiaire *m*; **~ name** *n* deuxième nom m; **~-of-the-road** adj (*politician*) modéré(e); (*music*) neutre; **~weight** n (*BOXING*) poids moyen; **middling** ['mɪdlɪŋ] adj moyen(ne)

midge [mɪdʒ] n moucheron m

midget ['mɪdʒɪt] n nain(e)

Midlands ['mɪdləndz] npl comtés du centre de l'Angleterre

midnight ['mɪdnaɪt] n minuit m

midriff ['mɪdrɪf] n estomac m, taille f

midst [mɪdst] n: **in the ~ of** au milieu de

midsummer ['mɪd'sʌmə*] n milieu m de l'été

midway ['mɪd'weɪ] adj, adv: **~ (between)** à mi-chemin (entre); **~ through** ... au milieu de ..., en plein(e) ...

midweek ['mɪd'wiːk] n milieu m de la semaine

midwife ['mɪdwaɪf] (pl **midwives**) n sage-femme f

midwinter ['mɪd'wɪntə*] n: **in ~** en plein hiver

might [maɪt] vb see **may** ♦ n puissance f, force f; **~y** adj puissant(e)

migraine ['miːɡreɪn] n migraine f

migrant ['maɪɡrənt] adj (*bird*) migrateur(trice); (*worker*) saisonnier(ère)

migrate [maɪ'ɡreɪt] vi émigrer

mike [maɪk] n abbr (= *microphone*) micro m

mild [maɪld] adj doux(douce), (*reproach, infection*) léger(ère); (*illness*) bénin(igne); (*interest*) modéré(e); (*taste*) peu relevé(e)

mildly ['maɪldlɪ] adv doucement; légèrement; **to put it ~** c'est le moins qu'on puisse dire

mile [maɪl] n mil(l)e m (= *1609 m*); **~age** n distance f en milles, ≈ kilométrage m; **~ometer** [maɪ'lɒmɪtə*] n compteur m (kilométrique); **~stone** n borne f; (*fig*) jalon m

militant ['mɪlɪtnt] adj militant(e)

military ['mɪlɪtərɪ] adj militaire

militate ['mɪlɪteɪt] vi: **to ~ against** (*prevent*) empêcher

militia [mɪ'lɪʃə] n milice(s) f(pl)

milk [mɪlk] n lait m ♦ vt (*cow*) traire;

(*fig: person*) dépouiller, plumer; (: *situation*) exploiter à fond; **~ chocolate** n chocolat m au lait; **~man** (*irreg*) n laitier m; **~ shake** n milk-shake m; **~y** adj (*drink*) au lait; (*colour*) laiteux(euse); **M~y Way** n voie lactée

mill [mɪl] n moulin m; (*steel ~*) aciérie f; (*spinning ~*) filature f; (*flour ~*) minoterie f ♦ vt moudre, broyer ♦ vi (*also: ~ about*) grouiller; **~er** n meunier m

milligram(me) ['mɪlɪɡræm] n milligramme m

millimetre ['mɪlɪmiːtə*] (*US* **millimeter**) n millimètre m

millinery ['mɪlɪnərɪ] n chapellerie f

million ['mɪljən] n million m; **~aire** [mɪljə'nɛə*] n millionnaire m

milometer [maɪ'lɒmɪtə*] n ≈ compteur m kilométrique

mime [maɪm] n mime m ♦ vt, vi mimer

mimic ['mɪmɪk] n imitateur(trice) ♦ vt imiter, contrefaire

min. abbr = **minute(s)**; **minimum**

mince [mɪns] vt hacher ♦ vi (*in walking*) marcher à petits pas maniérés ♦ n (*BRIT: CULIN*) viande hachée, hachis m; **~meat** n (*fruit*) hachis de fruits secs utilisé en pâtisserie; (*US: meat*) viande hachée, hachis; **~ pie** n (*sweet*) sorte de tarte aux fruits secs; **~r** n hachoir m

mind [maɪnd] n esprit m ♦ vt (*attend to, look after*) s'occuper de; (*be careful*) faire attention à; (*object to*): **I don't ~ the noise** le bruit ne me dérange pas; **I don't ~ cela** ne me dérange pas; **it is on my ~ cela** me préoccupe; **to my ~** à mon avis or sens; **to be out of one's ~** ne plus avoir toute sa raison; **to keep or bear sth in ~** tenir compte de qch; **to make up one's ~** se décider; **~ you, ...** remarquez ...; **never ~** ça ne fait rien; (*don't worry*) ne vous en faites pas; **"~ the step"** "attention à la marche"; **~er** n (*child-~er*) gardienne f; (*inf: bodyguard*) ange gardien (*fig*); **~ful** adj: **~ful of** attentif(ive) à, soucieux(euse) de; **~less** adj irréfléchi(e); (*boring: job*) idiot(e)

mine¹ [maɪn] pron le(la) mien(ne), les miens(miennes) ♦ adj: **this book is**

~ livre est à moi

mine² [maɪn] *n* mine *f* ♦ *vt* (*coal*) extraire; (*ship, beach*) miner; **~field** *n* champ *m* de mines; (*fig*) situation (très délicate); **~r** *n* mineur *m*

mineral ['mɪnərəl] *adj* minéral(e) ♦ *n* minéral *m*; **~s** *npl* (*BRIT: soft drinks*) boissons gazeuses; **~ water** *n* eau minérale

mingle ['mɪŋgl] *vi*: **to ~ with** se mêler à

miniature ['mɪnɪtʃə*] *adj* (en) miniature ♦ *n* miniature *f*

minibus ['mɪnɪbʌs] *n* minibus *m*

minim ['mɪnɪm] *n* (*MUS*) blanche *f*

minimal ['mɪnɪməl] *adj* minime

minimize ['mɪnɪmaɪz] *vt* (*reduce*) réduire au minimum; (*play down*) minimiser

minimum ['mɪnɪməm] (*pl* **minima**) *adj, n* minimum *m*

mining ['maɪnɪŋ] *n* exploitation minière

miniskirt ['mɪnɪskɜːt] *n* mini-jupe *f*

minister ['mɪnɪstə*] *n* (*BRIT: POL*) ministre *m*; (*REL*) pasteur *m* ♦ *vi*: **to ~ to sb('s needs)** pourvoir aux besoins de qn; **~ial** [mɪnɪs'tɪərɪəl] (*BRIT*) *adj* (*POL*) ministériel(le)

ministry ['mɪnɪstrɪ] *n* (*BRIT: POL*) ministère *m*; (*REL*): **to go into the ~** devenir pasteur

mink [mɪŋk] *n* vison *m*

minor ['maɪnə*] *adj* petit(e), de peu d'importance; (*MUS, poet, problem*) mineur(e) ♦ *n* (*LAW*) mineur(e)

minority [maɪ'nɒrɪtɪ] *n* minorité *f*

mint [mɪnt] *n* (*plant*) menthe *f*; (*sweet*) bonbon *m* à la menthe ♦ *vt* (*coins*) battre; **the (Royal) M~**, (*US*) **the (US) M~** ≈ l'Hôtel *m* de la Monnaie; **in ~ condition** à l'état de neuf

minus ['maɪnəs] *n* (*also*: **~ sign**) signe *m* moins ♦ *prep* moins

minute¹ [maɪ'njuːt] *adj* minuscule; (*detail, search*) minutieux(euse)

minute² ['mɪnɪt] *n* minute *f*; **~s** *npl* (*official record*) procès-verbal, compte rendu

miracle ['mɪrəkl] *n* miracle *m*

mirage ['mɪrɑːʒ] *n* mirage *m*

mirror ['mɪrə*] *n* miroir *m*, glace *f*; (*in car*) rétroviseur *m*

mirth [mɜːθ] *n* gaieté *f*

misadventure [mɪsəd'ventʃə*] *n* mésaventure *f*

misapprehension ['mɪsæprɪ'henʃən] *n* malentendu *m*, méprise *f*

misappropriate [mɪsə'prəuprɪeɪt] *vt* détourner

misbehave ['mɪsbɪ'heɪv] *vi* se conduire mal

miscalculate ['mɪs'kælkjuleɪt] *vt* mal calculer

miscarriage ['mɪskærɪdʒ] *n* (*MED*) fausse couche; **~ of justice** erreur *f* judiciaire

miscellaneous [mɪsɪ'leɪnɪəs] *adj* (*items*) divers(es); (*selection*) variée(e)

mischief ['mɪstʃɪf] *n* (*naughtiness*) sottises *fpl*; (*fun*) farce *f*; (*playfulness*) espièglerie *f*; (*maliciousness*) méchanceté *f*; **mischievous** ['mɪstʃɪvəs] *adj* (*playful, naughty*) coquin(e), espiègle

misconception ['mɪskən'sepʃən] *n* idée fausse

misconduct [mɪs'kɒndʌkt] *n* inconduite *f*; **professional ~** faute professionnelle

misdemeanour [mɪsdɪ'miːnə*] (*US* **misdemeanor**) *n* écart *m* de conduite; infraction *f*

miser ['maɪzə*] *n* avare *m/f*

miserable ['mɪzərəbl] *adj* (*person, expression*) malheureux(euse); (*conditions*) misérable; (*weather*) maussade; (*offer, donation*) minable; (*failure*) pitoyable

miserly ['maɪzəlɪ] *adj* avare

misery ['mɪzərɪ] *n* (*unhappiness*) tristesse *f*; (*pain*) souffrances *fpl*; (*wretchedness*) misère *f*

misfire ['mɪs'faɪə*] *vi* rater

misfit ['mɪsfɪt] *n* (*person*) inadapté(e)

misfortune [mɪs'fɔːtʃən] *n* malchance *f*, malheur *m*

misgiving [mɪs'gɪvɪŋ] *n* (*apprehension*) craintes *fpl*; **to have ~s about** avoir des doutes quant à

misguided ['mɪs'gaɪdɪd] *adj* malavisé(e)

mishandle ['mɪs'hændl] *vt* (*mismanage*) mal s'y prendre pour faire *or* résoudre *etc*

mishap ['mɪshæp] *n* mésaventure *f*

misinform [mɪsɪn'fɔːm] *vt* mal renseigner

misinterpret ['mɪsɪn'tɜːprɪt] *vt* mal interpréter

misjudge ['mɪs'dʒʌdʒ] *vt* méjuger

mislay [mɪs'leɪ] (*irreg: like* lay) *vt* égarer

mislead [mɪs'liːd] (*irreg: like* lead) *vt* induire en erreur; **~ing** *adj* trompeur(euse)

mismanage [mɪs'mænɪdʒ] *vt* mal gérer

misnomer ['mɪs'nəʊmə*] *n* terme *or* qualificatif trompeur *or* peu approprié

misplace ['mɪs'pleɪs] *vt* égarer

misprint ['mɪsprɪnt] *n* faute *f* d'impression

Miss [mɪs] *n* Mademoiselle

miss [mɪs] *vt* (*fail to get, attend or see*) manquer, rater; (*regret the absence of*): **I ~ him/it** il/cela me manque ♦ *vi* manquer ♦ *n* (*shot*) coup manqué; **~ out** (*BRIT*) *vt* oublier

misshapen ['mɪs'ʃeɪpən] *adj* difforme

missile ['mɪsaɪl] *n* (*MIL*) missile *m*; (*object thrown*) projectile *m*

missing ['mɪsɪŋ] *adj* manquant(e); (*after escape, disaster: person*) disparu(e); **to go ~** disparaître; **to be ~** avoir disparu

mission ['mɪʃən] *n* mission *f*; **~ary** *n* missionnaire *m/f*

misspent ['mɪs'spent] *adj*: **his ~ youth** sa folle jeunesse

mist [mɪst] *n* (*light*) brume *f*; (*heavy*) brouillard *m* ♦ *vi* (*also: ~ over: eyes*) s'embuer; (*windows etc*) s'embuer; **~ over** *vi* (*windows etc*) s'embuer; **~ up** *vi* = **mist over**

mistake [mɪs'teɪk] (*irreg: like* take) *n* erreur *f*, faute *f* ♦ *vt* (*meaning, remark*) mal comprendre; se méprendre sur; **to make a ~** se tromper, faire une erreur; **by ~** par erreur, par inadvertance; **to ~ for** prendre pour; **~n** *pp of* **mistake** ♦ *adj* (*idea etc*) erroné(e); **to be ~n** faire erreur, se tromper

mister ['mɪstə*] *n* (*inf*) Monsieur *m*; *see also* **Mr**

mistletoe ['mɪsltəʊ] *n* gui *m*

mistook [mɪs'tʊk] *pt of* **mistake**

mistress ['mɪstrɪs] *n* maîtresse *f*; (*BRIT: in primary school*) institutrice *f*; (: *in secondary school*) professeur *m*

mistrust ['mɪs'trʌst] *vt* se méfier de

misty ['mɪstɪ] *adj* brumeux(euse); (*glasses, window*) embué(e)

misunderstand ['mɪsʌndə'stænd] (*irreg*) *vt*, *vi* mal comprendre; **~ing** *n* méprise *f*, malentendu *m*

misuse [*n* 'mɪs'juːs, *vb* 'mɪs'juːz] *n* mauvais emploi; (*of power*) abus *m* ♦ *vt* mal employer; abuser de; **~ of funds** détournement *m* de fonds

mitigate ['mɪtɪgeɪt] *vt* atténuer

mitt(en) ['mɪt(n)] *n* mitaine *f*; moufle *f*

mix [mɪks] *vt* mélanger; (*sauce, drink etc*) préparer ♦ *vi* se mélanger; (*socialize*): **he doesn't ~ well** il est peu sociable ♦ *n* mélange *m*; **to ~ with** (*people*) fréquenter; **~ up** *vt* mélanger; (*confuse*) confondre; **~ed** *adj* (*feelings, reactions*) contradictoire; (*salad*) mélangé(e); (*school, marriage*) mixte; **~ed grill** *n* assortiment *m* de grillades; **~ed-up** *adj* (*confused*) désorienté(e), embrouillé(e); **~er** *n* (*for food*) batteur *m*, mixer *m*; (*person*): **he is a good ~er** il est très liant; **~ture** *n* assortiment *m*, mélange *m*; (*MED*) préparation *f*; **~-up** *n* confusion *f*

mm *abbr* (= *millimeter*) mm

moan [məʊn] *n* gémissement *m* ♦ *vi* gémir; (*inf: complain*): **to ~ (about)** se plaindre (de)

moat [məʊt] *n* fossé *m*, douves *fpl*

mob [mɒb] *n* foule *f*; (*disorderly*) cohue *f* ♦ *vt* assaillir

mobile ['məʊbaɪl] *adj* mobile ♦ *n* mobile *m*; **~ home** *n* (grande) caravane; **~ phone** *n* téléphone portatif

mock [mɒk] *vt* ridiculiser; (*laugh at*) se moquer de ♦ *adj* faux(fausse); **~ exam** examen blanc; **~ery** *n* moquerie *f*, raillerie *f*; **to make a ~ery of** tourner en dérision; **~-up** *n* maquette *f*

mod [mɒd] *adj see* **convenience**

mode [məʊd] *n* mode *m*

model ['mɒdl] *n* modèle *m*; (*person: for fashion*) mannequin *m*; (: *for artist*) modèle ♦ *vt* (*with clay etc*) modeler ♦ *vi* travailler comme mannequin ♦ *adj* (*railway: toy*) modèle réduit *inv*; (*child, fac-*

tory) modèle; **to ~ clothes** présenter des vêtements; **to ~ o.s. on** imiter

modem ['məʊdem] (*COMPUT*) *n* modem *m*

moderate [*adj* 'mɒdərət, *vb* 'mɒdəreɪt] *adj* modéré(e); (*amount*, *change*) peu important(e) ♦ *vi* se calmer ♦ *vt* modérer

modern ['mɒdən] *adj* moderne; **~ize** *vt* moderniser

modest ['mɒdɪst] *adj* modeste; **~y** *n* modestie *f*

modicum ['mɒdɪkəm] *n*: **a ~ of** un minimum de

modify ['mɒdɪfaɪ] *vt* modifier

mogul ['məʊgəl] *n* (*fig*) nabab *m*

mohair ['məʊhɛə*] *n* mohair *m*

moist [mɔɪst] *adj* humide, moite; **~en** ['mɔɪsən] *vt* humecter, mouiller légèrement; **~ure** ['mɔɪstʃə*] *n* humidité *f*; **~urizer** ['mɔɪstʃəraɪzə*] *n* produit hydratant

molar ['məʊlə*] *n* molaire *f*

molasses [mə'læsɪz] *n* mélasse *f*

mold [məʊld] *n*, *vt* = **mould**

mole [məʊl] *n* (*animal*, *fig*: *spy*) taupe *f*; (*spot*) grain *m* de beauté

molest [mə'lest] *vt* (*harass*) molester; (*JUR*: *sexually*) attenter à la pudeur de

mollycoddle ['mɒlɪkɒdl] *vt* chouchouter, couver

molt [məʊlt] (*US*) *vi* = **moult**

molten ['məʊltən] *adj* fondu(e); (*rock*) en fusion

mom [mɒm] (*US*) *n* = **mum**

moment ['məʊmənt] *n* moment *m*, instant *m*; **at the ~** en ce moment; **at that ~** à ce moment-là; **~ary** *adj* momentané(e), passager(ère); **~ous** [məʊ'mentəs] *adj* important(e), capital(e)

momentum [məʊ'mentəm] *n* élan *m*, vitesse acquise; (*fig*) dynamique *f*; **to gather ~** prendre de la vitesse

mommy ['mɒmɪ] (*US*) *n* maman *f*

Monaco ['mɒnəkəʊ] *n* Monaco *m*

monarch ['mɒnək] *n* monarque *m*; **~y** *n* monarchie *f*

monastery ['mɒnəstrɪ] *n* monastère *m*

Monday ['mʌndeɪ] *n* lundi *m*

monetary ['mʌnɪtərɪ] *adj* monétaire

money ['mʌnɪ] *n* argent *m*; **to make ~** gagner de l'argent; **~ order** *n* mandat *m*; **~-spinner** (*inf*) *n* mine *f* d'or (*fig*)

mongrel ['mʌŋgrəl] *n* (*dog*) bâtard *m*

monitor ['mɒnɪtə*] *n* (*TV*, *COMPUT*) moniteur *m* ♦ *vt* contrôler; (*broadcast*) être à l'écoute de; (*progress*) suivre (de près)

monk [mʌŋk] *n* moine *m*

monkey ['mʌŋkɪ] *n* singe *m*; **~ nut** (*BRIT*) *n* cacahuète *f*; **~ wrench** *n* clé *f* à molette

monopoly [mə'nɒpəlɪ] *n* monopole *m*

monotone ['mɒnətəʊn] *n* ton *m* (*or* voix *f*) monocorde

monotonous [mə'nɒtənəs] *adj* monotone

monsoon [mɒn'su:n] *n* mousson *f*

monster ['mɒnstə*] *n* monstre *m*

monstrous ['mɒnstrəs] *adj* monstrueux(euse); (*huge*) gigantesque

month [mʌnθ] *n* mois *m*; **~ly** *adj* mensuel(le) ♦ *adv* mensuellement

monument ['mɒnjʊmənt] *n* monument *m*

moo [mu:] *vi* meugler, beugler

mood [mu:d] *n* humeur *f*, disposition *f*; **to be in a good/bad ~** être de bonne/mauvaise humeur; **~y** *adj* (*variable*) d'humeur changeante, lunatique; (*sullen*) morose, maussade

moon [mu:n] *n* lune *f*; **~light** *n* clair *m* de lune; **~lighting** *n* travail *m* au noir; **~lit** *adj*: **a ~lit night** une nuit de lune

moor [mʊə*] *n* lande *f* ♦ *vt* (*ship*) amarrer ♦ *vi* mouiller; **~land** ['mʊələnd] *n* lande *f*

moose [mu:s] *n inv* élan *m*

mop [mɒp] *n* balai *m* à laver; (*for dishes*) lavette *f* (à vaisselle) ♦ *vt* essuyer; **~ of hair** tignasse *f*; **~ up** *vt* éponger

mope [məʊp] *vi* avoir le cafard, se morfondre

moped ['məʊped] *n* cyclomoteur *m*

moral ['mɒrəl] *adj* moral(e) ♦ *n* morale *f*; **~s** *npl* (*attitude*, *behaviour*) moralité *f*

morale [mɒ'rɑ:l] *n* moral *m*

morality [mə'rælɪtɪ] *n* moralité *f*

morass [mə'ræs] *n* marais *m*, marécage

m

| KEYWORD |

more [mɔ:*] *adj* **1** (*greater in number etc*) plus (de), davantage; ~ **people/work (than)** plus de gens/de travail (que) **2** (*additional*) encore (de); **do you want (some) ~ tea?** voulez-vous encore du thé?; **I have no** *or* **I don't have any ~ money** je n'ai plus d'argent; **it'll take a few ~ weeks** ça prendra encore quelques semaines

♦ *pron* plus, davantage; ~ **than 10** plus de 10; **it cost ~ than we expected** cela a coûté plus que prévu; **I want ~** j'en veux plus *or* davantage; **is there any ~?** est-ce qu'il en reste?; **there's no ~** il n'y en a plus; **a little ~** un peu plus; **many/much ~** beaucoup plus, bien davantage

♦ *adv*: ~ **dangerous/easily (than)** plus dangereux/facilement (que); ~ **and ~ expensive** de plus en plus cher; ~ **or less** plus ou moins; ~ **than ever** plus que jamais

moreover [mɔ:'rəʊvə*] *adv* de plus
morning ['mɔ:nɪŋ] *n* matin *m*; matinée *f* ♦ *cpd* matinal(e); (*paper*) du matin; **in the ~** le matin; **7 o'clock in the ~** 7 heures du matin; ~ **sickness** *n* nausées matinales
Morocco [mə'rɒkəʊ] *n* Maroc *m*
moron ['mɔ:rɒn] (*inf*) *n* idiot(e)
Morse [mɔ:s] *n*: ~ (**code**) morse *m*
morsel ['mɔ:sl] *n* bouchée *f*
mortar ['mɔ:tə*] *n* mortier *m*
mortgage ['mɔ:gɪdʒ] *n* hypothèque *f*; (*loan*) prêt *m* (*or* crédit *m*) hypothécaire ♦ *vt* hypothéquer; ~ **company** (*US*) *n* société *f* de crédit immobilier
mortuary ['mɔ:tjʊərɪ] *n* morgue *f*
mosaic [məʊ'zeɪk] *n* mosaïque *f*
Moscow ['mɒskəʊ] *n* Moscou
Moslem ['mɒzləm] *adj, n* = **Muslim**
mosque [mɒsk] *n* mosquée *f*
mosquito [mɒs'ki:təʊ] (*pl* ~**es**) *n* moustique *m*
moss [mɒs] *n* mousse *f*

most [məʊst] *adj* la plupart de; le plus de ♦ *pron* la plupart ♦ *adv* le plus; (*very*) très, extrêmement; **the ~** (*also*: + *adjective*) le plus; ~ **of** la plus grande partie de; ~ **of them** la plupart d'entre eux; **I saw (the) ~** j'en ai vu la plupart; c'est moi qui en ai vu le plus; **at the (very) ~** au plus; **to make the ~ of** profiter au maximum de; ~**ly** *adv* (*chiefly*) surtout; (*usually*) généralement
MOT *n abbr* (*BRIT*: = *Ministry of Transport*): **the ~ (test)** la visite technique (annuelle) obligatoire des véhicules à moteur
motel [məʊ'tel] *n* motel *m*
moth [mɒθ] *n* papillon *m* de nuit; (*in clothes*) mite *f*; ~**ball** *n* boule *f* de naphtaline
mother ['mʌðə*] *n* mère *f* ♦ *vt* (*act as mother to*) servir de mère à; (*pamper, protect*) materner; ~ **country** mère patrie; ~**hood** *n* maternité *f*; ~**-in-law** *n* belle-mère *f*; ~**ly** *adj* maternel(le); ~**-of-pearl** *n* nacre *f*; ~**-to-be** *n* future maman; ~ **tongue** *n* langue maternelle
motion ['məʊʃən] *n* mouvement *m*; (*gesture*) geste *m*; (*at meeting*) motion *f* ♦ *vt, vi*: **to ~ (to) sb to do** faire signe à qn de faire; ~**less** *adj* immobile, sans mouvement; ~ **picture** *n* film *m*
motivated ['məʊtɪveɪtɪd] *adj* motivé(e)
motive ['məʊtɪv] *n* motif *m*, mobile *m*
motley ['mɒtlɪ] *adj* hétéroclite
motor ['məʊtə*] *n* moteur *m*; (*BRIT*: *inf*: *vehicle*) auto *f* ♦ *cpd* (*industry, vehicle*) automobile; ~**bike** *n* moto *f*; ~**boat** *n* bateau *m* à moteur; ~**car** (*BRIT*) *n* automobile *f*; ~**cycle** *n* vélomoteur *m*; ~**cycle racing** *n* course *f* de motos; ~**cyclist** *n* motocycliste *m/f*; ~**ing** (*BRIT*) *n* tourisme *m* automobile; ~**ist** ['məʊtərɪst] *n* automobiliste *m/f*; ~ **mechanic** *n* mécanicien *m* garagiste; ~**racing** (*BRIT*) *n* course *f* automobile; ~ **trade** *n* secteur *m* de l'automobile; ~**way** (*BRIT*) *n* autoroute *f*
mottled ['mɒtld] *adj* tacheté(e), marbré(e)
motto ['mɒtəʊ] (*pl* ~**es**) *n* devise *f*
mould [məʊld] (*US* **mold**) *n* moule *m*;

(*mildew*) moisissure *f* ♦ *vt* mouler, modeler; (*fig*) façonner; **mo(u)ldy** *adj* moisi(e); (*smell*) de moisi

moult [məʊlt] (*US* **molt**) *vi* muer

mound [maʊnd] *n* monticule *m*, tertre *m*; (*heap*) monceau *m*, tas *m*

mount [maʊnt] *n* mont *m*, montagne *f* ♦ *vt* monter ♦ *vi* (*inflation, tension*) augmenter; (*also*: ~ **up**: *problems etc*) s'accumuler; ~ **up** *vi* (*bills, costs, savings*) s'accumuler

mountain ['maʊntɪn] *n* montagne *f* ♦ *cpd* de montagne; ~ **bike** *n* VTT *m*, vélo tout-terrain; **~eer** [maʊntɪ'nɪə*] *n* alpiniste *m/f*; **~eering** *n* alpinisme *m*; **~ous** *adj* montagneux(euse); ~ **rescue team** *n* équipe de secours en montagne; **~side** *n* flanc *m* or versant *m* de la montagne

mourn [mɔːn] *vt* pleurer ♦ *vi*: **to** ~ **(for)** (*person*) pleurer (la mort de); **~er** *n* parent(e) or ami(e) du défunt; personne *f* en deuil; **~ful** *adj* triste, lugubre; **~ing** *n* deuil *m*; **in ~ing** en deuil

mouse [maʊs] (*pl* **mice**) *n* (*also* COMPUT) souris *f*; **~trap** *n* souricière *f*

mousse [muːs] *n* mousse *f*

moustache [məs'tɑːʃ] (*US* **mustache**) *n* moustache(s) *f(pl)*

mousy ['maʊsɪ] *adj* (*hair*) d'un châtain terne

mouth [maʊθ, *pl* maʊðz] (*pl* **~s**) *n* bouche *f*; (*of dog, cat*) gueule *f*; (*of river*) embouchure *f*; (*of hole, cave*) ouverture *f*; **~ful** *n* bouchée *f*; ~ **organ** *n* harmonica *m*; **~piece** *n* (*of musical instrument*) embouchure *f*; (*spokesman*) porte-parole *m inv*; **~wash** *n* eau *f* dentifrice; **~watering** *adj* qui met l'eau à la bouche

movable ['muːvəbl] *adj* mobile

move [muːv] *n* (*movement*) mouvement *m*; (*in game*) coup *m*; (*: turn to play*) tour *m*; (*change: of house*) déménagement *m*; (*: of job*) changement *m* d'emploi ♦ *vt* déplacer, bouger; (*emotionally*) émouvoir; (POL: *resolution etc*) proposer; (*in game*) jouer ♦ *vi* (*gen*) bouger, remuer; (*traffic*) circuler; (*also*: ~ *house*) déménager; (*situation*) progresser; **that was a good ~** bien joué!; **to ~ sb to do**

sth pousser or inciter qn à faire qch; **to get a ~ on** se dépêcher, se remuer; ~ **about** *vi* (*fidget*) remuer; (*travel*) voyager, se déplacer; (*change residence, job*) ne pas rester au même endroit; ~ **along** *vi* se pousser; ~ **around** *vi* = **move about**; ~ **away** *vi* s'en aller; ~ **back** *vi* revenir, retourner; ~ **forward** *vi* avancer; ~ **in** *vi* (*to a house*) emménager; (*police, soldiers*) intervenir; ~ **on** *vi* se remettre en route; ~ **out** *vi* (*of house*) déménager; ~ **over** *vi* se pousser, se déplacer; ~ **up** *vi* (*pupil*) passer dans la classe supérieure; (*employee*) avoir de l'avancement; **~able** *adj* = **movable**

movement ['muːvmənt] *n* mouvement *m*

movie ['muːvɪ] *n* film *m*; **the ~s** le cinéma; ~ **camera** *n* caméra *f*

moving ['muːvɪŋ] *adj* en mouvement; (*emotional*) émouvant(e)

mow [məʊ] (*pt* **mowed**, *pp* **mowed** or **mown**) *vt* faucher; (*lawn*) tondre; ~ **down** *vt* faucher; **~er** *n* (*also*: *lawnmower*) tondeuse *f* à gazon

MP *n abbr* = **Member of Parliament**

mph *abbr* = **miles per hour**

Mr ['mɪstə*] (*US* **Mr.**) *n*: ~ **Smith** Monsieur **Smith**, M. **Smith**

Mrs ['mɪsɪz] (*US* **Mrs.**) *n*: ~ **Smith** Madame **Smith**, Mme **Smith**

Ms [mɪz] (*US* **Ms.**) *n* (= **Miss** or **Mrs**): ~ **Smith** ≈ Madame **Smith**, Mme **Smith**

MSc *abbr* = **Master of Science**

much [mʌtʃ] *adj* beaucoup de ♦ *adv, n, pron* beaucoup; **how ~ is it?** combien est-ce que ça coûte?; **too ~** trop de; **as ~ as** autant de

muck [mʌk] *n* (*dirt*) saleté *f*; ~ **about** or **around** (*inf*) *vi* faire l'imbécile; ~ **up** (*inf*) *vt* (*exam, interview*) se planter à (*fam*); **~y** *adj* (très) sale; (*book, film*) cochon(ne)

mud [mʌd] *n* boue *f*

muddle ['mʌdl] *n* (*mess*) pagaille *f*, désordre *m*; (*mix-up*) confusion *f* ♦ *vt* (*also*: ~ **up**) embrouiller; ~ **through** *vi* se débrouiller

muddy ['mʌdɪ] *adj* boueux(euse); **mud-**

guard ['mʌdgɑːd] *n* garde-boue *m inv*

muffin ['mʌfɪn] *n* muffin *m*

muffle ['mʌfl] *vt* (*sound*) assourdir, étouffer; (*against cold*) emmitoufler; **~d** *adj* (*sound*) étouffé(e); (*person*) emmitouflé(e); **~r** (*US*) *n* (*AUT*) silencieux *m*

mug [mʌg] *n* (*cup*) grande tasse (*sans soucoupe*); (: *for beer*) chope *f*; (*inf*: *face*) bouille *f*; (: *fool*) poire *f* ♦ *vt* (*assault*) agresser; **~ging** *n* agression *f*

muggy ['mʌgɪ] *adj* lourd(e), moite

mule [mjuːl] *n* mule *f*

mull over [mʌl-] *vt* réfléchir à

multi-level ['mʌltɪlevl] (*US*) *adj* = **multistorey**

multiple ['mʌltɪpl] *adj* multiple ♦ *n* multiple *m*; **~ sclerosis** *n* sclérose *f* en plaques

multiplication [mʌltɪplɪ'keɪʃən] *n* multiplication *f*; **multiply** ['mʌltɪplaɪ] *vt* multiplier ♦ *vi* se multiplier

multistorey ['mʌltɪ'stɔːrɪ] (*BRIT*) *adj* (*building*) à étages; (*car park*) à étages *or* niveaux multiples

mum [mʌm] (*BRIT*: *inf*) *n* maman *f* ♦ *adj*: **to keep ~** ne pas souffler mot

mumble ['mʌmbl] *vt, vi* marmotter, marmonner

mummy ['mʌmɪ] *n* (*BRIT*: *mother*) maman *f*; (*embalmed*) momie *f*

mumps [mʌmps] *n* oreillons *mpl*

munch [mʌntʃ] *vt, vi* mâcher

mundane [mʌn'deɪn] *adj* banal(e), terre à terre *inv*

municipal [mjuː'nɪsɪpəl] *adj* municipal(e)

murder ['mɜːdə*] *n* meurtre *m*, assassinat *m* ♦ *vt* assassiner; **~er** *n* meurtrier *m*, assassin *m*; **~ous** *adj* meurtrier(ère)

murky ['mɜːkɪ] *adj* sombre, ténébreux(euse); (*water*) trouble

murmur ['mɜːmə*] *n* murmure *m* ♦ *vt, vi* murmurer

muscle ['mʌsl] *n* muscle *m*; (*fig*) force *f*; **~ in** *vi* (*on territory*) envahir; (*on success*) exploiter

muscular ['mʌskjʊlə*] *adj* musculaire; (*person, arm*) musclé(e)

muse [mjuːz] *vi* méditer, songer

museum [mjuː'zɪəm] *n* musée *m*

mushroom ['mʌʃruːm] *n* champignon *m* ♦ *vi* pousser comme un champignon

music ['mjuːzɪk] *n* musique *f*; **~al** *adj* musical(e); (*person*) musicien(ne) ♦ *n* (*show*) comédie musicale; **~al instrument** *n* instrument *m* de musique; **~ian** [mjuː'zɪʃən] *n* musicien(ne)

Muslim ['mʌzlɪm] *adj, n* musulman(e)

muslin ['mʌzlɪn] *n* mousseline *f*

mussel ['mʌsl] *n* moule *f*

must [mʌst] *aux vb* (*obligation*): **I ~ do it** je dois le faire, il faut que je le fasse; (*probability*): **he ~ be there by now** il doit y être maintenant, il y est probablement maintenant; (*suggestion, invitation*): **you ~ come and see me** il faut que vous veniez me voir; (*indicating sth unwelcome*): **why ~ he behave so badly?** qu'est-ce qui le pousse à se conduire si mal? ♦ *n* nécessité *f*, impératif *m*; **it's a ~** c'est indispensable

mustache (*US*) *n* = **moustache**

mustard ['mʌstəd] *n* moutarde *f*

muster ['mʌstə*] *vt* rassembler

mustn't ['mʌsnt] = **must not**

mute [mjuːt] *adj* muet(te)

muted ['mjuːtɪd] *adj* (*colour*) sourd(e); (*reaction*) voilé(e)

mutiny ['mjuːtɪnɪ] *n* mutinerie *f* ♦ *vi* se mutiner

mutter ['mʌtə*] *vt, vi* marmonner, marmotter

mutton ['mʌtn] *n* mouton *m*

mutual ['mjuːtjʊəl] *adj* mutuel(le), réciproque; (*benefit, interest*) commun(e); **~ly** *adv* mutuellement

muzzle ['mʌzl] *n* museau *m*; (*protective device*) muselière *f*; (*of gun*) gueule *f* ♦ *vt* museler

my [maɪ] *adj* mon(ma), mes *pl*; **~ house/car/gloves** ma maison/mon auto/mes gants; **I've washed ~ hair/cut ~ finger** je me suis lavé les cheveux/ coupé le doigt; **~self** [maɪ'self] *pron* (*reflexive*) me; (*emphatic*) moi-même; (*after prep*) moi; *see also* **oneself**

mysterious [mɪs'tɪərɪəs] *adj* mystérieux(euse)

mystery ['mɪstərɪ] *n* mystère *m*
mystify ['mɪstɪfaɪ] *vt* mystifier; (*puzzle*) ébahir
myth [mɪθ] *n* mythe *m*; **~ology** [mɪ'θɒlədʒɪ] *n* mythologie *f*

N n

n/a *abbr* = **not applicable**
nag [næg] *vt* (*scold*) être toujours après, reprendre sans arrêt; **~ging** *adj* (*doubt, pain*) persistant(e)
nail [neɪl] *n* (*human*) ongle *m*; (*metal*) clou *m* ♦ *vt* clouer; **to ~ sb down to a date/price** contraindre qn à accepter *or* donner une date/un prix; **~brush** *n* brosse *f* à ongles; **~file** *n* lime *f* à ongles; **~ polish** *n* vernis *m* à ongles; **~ polish remover** *n* dissolvant *m*; **~ scissors** *npl* ciseaux *mpl* à ongles; **~ varnish** (*BRIT*) *n* = **nail polish**
naïve [naɪ'iːv] *adj* naïf(ïve)
naked ['neɪkɪd] *adj* nu(e)
name [neɪm] *n* nom *m*; (*reputation*) réputation *f* ♦ *vt* nommer; (*identify: accomplice etc*) citer; (*price, date*) fixer, donner; **by ~** par son nom; **in the ~ of** au nom de; **what's your ~?** comment vous appelez-vous?; **~less** *adj* sans nom; (*witness, contributor*) anonyme; **~ly** *adv* à savoir; **~sake** *n* homonyme *m*
nanny ['nænɪ] *n* bonne *f* d'enfants
nap [næp] *n* (*sleep*) (petit) somme ♦ *vi*: **to be caught ~ping** être pris à l'improviste *or* en défaut
nape [neɪp] *n*: **~ of the neck** nuque *f*
napkin ['næpkɪn] *n* serviette *f* (de table)
nappy ['næpɪ] (*BRIT*) *n* couche *f* (*gen pl*); **~ rash** *n*: **to have ~ rash** avoir les fesses rouges
narcissus [nɑː'sɪsəs, *pl* nɑː'sɪsaɪ] (*pl* **narcissi**) *n* narcisse *m*
narcotic [nɑː'kɒtɪk] *n* (*drug*) stupéfiant *m*; (*MED*) narcotique *m*
narrative ['nærətɪv] *n* récit *m*
narrow ['nærəʊ] *adj* étroit(e); (*fig*) restreint(e), limité(e) ♦ *vi* (*road*) devenir plus étroit, se rétrécir; (*gap, difference*) se réduire; **to have a ~ escape** l'échapper belle; **to ~ sth down to** réduire qch à; **~ly** *adv*: **he ~ly missed injury/the tree** il a failli se blesser/rentrer dans l'arbre; **~-minded** *adj* à l'esprit étroit, borné(e); (*attitude*) borné
nasty ['nɑːstɪ] *adj* (*person: malicious*) méchant(e); (: *rude*) très désagréable; (*smell*) dégoûtant(e); (*wound, situation, disease*) mauvais(e)
nation ['neɪʃən] *n* nation *f*
national ['næʃənl] *adj* national(e) ♦ *n* (*abroad*) ressortissant(e); (*when home*) national(e); **~ dress** *n* costume national; **N~ Health Service** (*BRIT*) *n* service national de santé, ≈ Sécurité Sociale; **N~ Insurance** (*BRIT*) *n* ≈ Sécurité Sociale; **~ism** *n* ['næʃnəlɪzəm] *n* nationalisme *m*; **~ist** ['næʃnəlɪst] *adj* nationaliste *m/f*; **~ity** [næʃə'nælɪtɪ] *n* nationalité *f*; **~ize** *vt* nationaliser; **~ly** *adv* (*as a nation*) du point de vue national; (*nationwide*) dans le pays entier
nationwide ['neɪʃənwaɪd] *adj* s'étendant à l'ensemble du pays; (*problem*) à l'échelle du pays entier ♦ *adv* à travers *or* dans tout le pays
native ['neɪtɪv] *n* autochtone *m/f*, habitant(e) du pays ♦ *adj* du pays, indigène; (*country*) natal(e); (*ability*) inné(e); **a ~ of Russia** une personne originaire de Russie; **a ~ speaker of French** une personne de langue maternelle française; **N~ American** *n* Indien(ne) d'Amérique; **~ language** *n* langue maternelle
NATO ['neɪtəʊ] *n abbr* (= *North Atlantic Treaty Organization*) OTAN *f*
natural ['nætʃrəl] *adj* naturel(le); **~ gas** *n* gaz naturel; **~ize** *vt* naturaliser; (*plant*) acclimater; **to become ~ized** (*person*) se faire naturaliser; **~ly** *adv* naturellement
nature ['neɪtʃə*] *n* nature *f*; **by ~** par tempérament, de nature
naught [nɔːt] *n* = **nought**
naughty ['nɔːtɪ] *adj* (*child*) vilain(e), pas sage
nausea ['nɔːsɪə] *n* nausée *f*; **~te** ['nɔːsɪeɪt] *vt* écœurer, donner la nausée à

naval ['neɪvəl] *adj* naval(e); ~ **officer** *n* officier *m* de marine

nave [neɪv] *n* nef *f*

navel ['neɪvl] *n* nombril *m*

navigate ['nævɪgeɪt] *vt* (*steer*) diriger; (*plot course*) naviguer ♦ *vi* naviguer; **navigation** [nævɪ'geɪʃən] *n* navigation *f*

navvy ['nævɪ] (*BRIT*) *n* terrassier *m*

navy ['neɪvɪ] *n* marine *f*; ~**(-blue)** *adj* bleu marine *inv*

Nazi ['nɑːtsɪ] *n* Nazi(e)

NB *abbr* (= *nota bene*) NB

near [nɪə*] *adj* proche ♦ *adv* près ♦ *prep* (*also:* ~ **to**) près de ♦ *vt* approcher de; ~**by** *adj* proche ♦ *adv* tout près, à proximité; ~**ly** *adv* presque; **I** ~**ly fell** j'ai failli tomber; ~ **miss** *n* (*AVIAT*) quasi-collision *f*; **that was a** ~ **miss** (*gen*) il s'en est fallu de peu; (*of shot*) c'est passé très près; ~**side** *n* (*AUT: in Britain*) côté *m* gauche; (: *in US, Europe etc*) côté droit; ~**-sighted** *adj* myope

neat [niːt] *adj* (*person, work*) soigné(e); (*room etc*) bien tenu(e) *or* rangé(e); (*skilful*) habile; (: *spirits*) pur(e); ~**ly** *adv* avec soin *or* ordre; habilement

necessarily ['nesɪsərɪlɪ] *adv* nécessairement

necessary ['nesɪsərɪ] *adj* nécessaire

necessity [nɪ'sesɪtɪ] *n* nécessité *f*; (*thing needed*) chose nécessaire *or* essentielle; **necessities** *npl* nécessaire *m*

neck [nek] *n* cou *m*; (*of animal, garment*) encolure *f*; (*of bottle*) goulot *m* ♦ *vi* (*inf*) se peloter; ~ **and** ~ à égalité; ~**lace** ['neklɪs] *n* collier *m*; ~**line** *n* encolure *f*; ~**tie** *n* cravate *f*

need [niːd] *n* besoin *m* ♦ *vt* avoir besoin de; **to** ~ **to do** devoir faire; avoir besoin de faire; **you don't** ~ **to go** vous n'avez pas besoin *or* vous n'êtes pas obligé de partir

needle ['niːdl] *n* aiguille *f* ♦ *vt* asticoter, tourmenter

needless ['niːdlɪs] *adj* inutile

needlework ['niːdlwɜːk] *n* (*activity*) travaux *mpl* d'aiguille; (*object(s)*) ouvrage *m*

needn't ['niːdnt] = **need not**

needy ['niːdɪ] *adj* nécessiteux(euse)

negative ['negətɪv] *n* (*PHOT, ELEC*) négatif *m*; (*LING*) terme *m* de négation ♦ *adj* négatif(ive)

neglect [nɪ'glekt] *vt* négliger ♦ *n* (*of person, duty, garden*) le fait de négliger; (*state*) abandon *m*

negligee ['neglɪʒeɪ] *n* déshabillé *m*

negotiate [nɪ'gəʊʃɪeɪt] *vi, vt* négocier; **negotiation** [nɪgəʊʃɪ'eɪʃən] *n* négociation *f*, pourparlers *mpl*

Negro ['niːgrəʊ] (*inf!; pl* ~**es**) *n* Noir(e)

neigh [neɪ] *vi* hennir

neighbour ['neɪbə*] (*US* **neighbor**) *n* voisin(e); ~**hood** *n* (*place*) quartier *m*; (*people*) voisinage *m*; ~**ing** *adj* voisin(e), avoisinant(e); ~**ly** *adj* obligeant(e); (*action etc*) amical(e)

neither ['naɪðə*] *adj, pron* aucun(e) (des deux), ni l'un(e) ni l'autre ♦ *conj*: **I didn't move and** ~ **did Claude** je n'ai pas bougé, (et) Claude non plus; ..., ~ **did I refuse** ..., (et *or* mais) je n'ai pas non plus refusé ... ♦ *adv*: ~ **good nor bad** ni bon ni mauvais

neon ['niːɒn] *n* néon *m*; ~ **light** *n* lampe *f* au néon

nephew ['nefjuː] *n* neveu *m*

nerve [nɜːv] *n* nerf *m*; (*fig: courage*) sang-froid *m*, courage *m*; (: *impudence*) aplomb *m*, toupet *m*; **to have a fit of** ~**s** avoir le trac; ~**-racking** *adj* angoissant(e)

nervous ['nɜːvəs] *adj* nerveux(euse); (*anxious*) inquiet(ète), plein(e) d'appréhension; (*timid*) intimidé(e); ~ **breakdown** *n* dépression nerveuse

nest [nest] *n* nid *m* ♦ *vi* (se) nicher, faire son nid; ~ **egg** *n* (*fig*) bas *m* de laine, magot *m*

nestle ['nesl] *vi* se blottir

net [net] *n* filet *m* ♦ *adj* net(te) ♦ *vt* (*fish etc*) prendre au filet; (*profit*) rapporter; ~**ball** *n* netball *m*; ~ **curtains** *npl* voilages *mpl*

Netherlands ['neðələndz] *npl*: **the** ~ les Pays-Bas *mpl*

nett [net] *adj* = **net**

netting ['netɪŋ] *n* (*for fence etc*) treillis

m, grillage *m*

nettle ['nɛtl] *n* ortie *f*

network ['nɛtwɜ:k] *n* réseau *m*

neurotic [njʊə'rɒtɪk] *adj*, *n* névrosé(e)

neuter ['nju:tə*] *adj* neutre ♦ *vt* (*cat etc*) châtrer, couper

neutral ['nju:trəl] *adj* neutre ♦ *n* (*AUT*) point mort; ~**ize** *vt* neutraliser

never ['nɛvə*] *adv* (ne ...) jamais; ~ **again** plus jamais; ~ **in my life** jamais de ma vie; *see also* **mind**; ~**-ending** *adj* interminable; ~**theless** [nɛvəðə'lɛs] *adv* néanmoins, malgré tout

new [nju:] *adj* nouveau(nouvelle); (*brand new*) neuf(neuve); **N~ Age** *n* New Age *m*; ~**born** *adj* nouveau-né(e); ~**comer** ['nju:kʌmə*] *n* nouveau venu/ nouvelle venue; ~**fangled** (*pej*) *adj* ultramoderne (et farfelu(e)); ~**found** *adj* (*enthusiasm*) de fraîche date; (*friend*) nouveau(nouvelle); ~**ly** *adv* nouvellement, récemment; ~**ly-weds** *npl* jeunes mariés *mpl*

news [nju:z] *n* nouvelle(s) *f(pl)*; (*RADIO, TV*) informations *fpl*, actualités *fpl*; **a piece of** ~ une nouvelle; ~ **agency** *n* agence *f* de presse; ~**agent** (*BRIT*) *n* marchand *m* de journaux; ~**caster** *n* présentateur(trice); ~**dealer** (*US*) *n* = **newsagent**; ~ **flash** *n* flash *m* d'information; ~**letter** *n* bulletin *m*; ~**paper** *n* journal *m*; ~**print** *n* papier *m* (de) journal; ~**reader** *n* = **newscaster**; ~**reel** *n* actualités (filmées); ~ **stand** *n* kiosque *m* à journaux

newt [nju:t] *n* triton *m*

New Year *n* Nouvel An; ~**'s Day** *n* le jour de l'An; ~**'s Eve** *n* la Saint-Sylvestre

New Zealand [-'zi:lənd] *n* la Nouvelle-Zélande; ~**er** *n* Néo-zélandais(e)

next [nɛkst] *adj* (*seat, room*) voisin(e), d'à côté; (*meeting, bus stop*) suivant(e); (*in time*) prochain(e) ♦ *adv* (*place*) à côté; (*time*) la fois suivante, la prochaine fois; (*afterwards*) ensuite; **the ~ day** le lendemain, le jour suivant *or* d'après; ~ **year** l'année prochaine; ~ **time** la prochaine fois; ~ **to** à côté de; ~ **to nothing**

presque rien; ~, **please!** (*at doctor's etc*) au suivant!; ~ **door** *adv* à côté ♦ *adj* d'à côté; ~**-of-kin** *n* parent *m* le plus proche

NHS *n abbr* = **National Health Service**

nib [nɪb] *n* (bec *m* de) plume *f*

nibble ['nɪbl] *vt* grignoter

nice [naɪs] *adj* (*pleasant, likeable*) agréable; (*pretty*) joli(e); (*kind*) gentil(le); ~**ly** *adv* agréablement; joliment; gentiment

niceties ['naɪsɪtɪz] *npl* subtilités *fpl*

nick [nɪk] *n* (*indentation*) encoche *f*; (*wound*) entaille *f* ♦ *vt* (*BRIT*: *inf*) faucher, piquer; **in the ~ of time** juste à temps

nickel ['nɪkl] *n* nickel *m*; (*US*) pièce *f* de 5 cents

nickname ['nɪkneɪm] *n* surnom *m* ♦ *vt* surnommer

niece [ni:s] *n* nièce *f*

Nigeria [naɪ'dʒɪərɪə] *n* Nigéria *m or f*

niggling ['nɪɡlɪŋ] *adj* (*person*) tatillon(ne); (*detail*) insignifiant(e); (*doubts, injury*) persistant(e)

night [naɪt] *n* nuit *f*; (*evening*) soir *m*; **at** ~ la nuit; **by** ~ de nuit; **the ~ before last** avant-hier soir; ~**cap** *n* boisson prise avant le coucher; ~ **club** *n* boîte *f* de nuit; ~**dress** *n* chemise *f* de nuit; ~**fall** *n* tombée *f* de la nuit; ~**gown** *n* chemise *f* de nuit; ~**ie** ['naɪtɪ] *n* chemise *f* de nuit; ~**ingale** ['naɪtɪŋɡeɪl] *n* rossignol *m*; ~**life** ['naɪtlaɪf] *n* vie *f* nocturne; ~**ly** ['naɪtlɪ] *adj* de chaque nuit *or* soir; (*by night*) nocturne ♦ *adv* chaque nuit *or* soir; ~**mare** ['naɪtmɛə*] *n* cauchemar *m*; ~ **porter** *n* gardien *m* de nuit, concierge *m* de service la nuit; ~ **school** *n* cours *mpl* du soir; ~ **shift** *n* équipe *f* de nuit; ~**time** *n* nuit *f*; ~ **watchman** *n* veilleur *m or* gardien *m* de nuit

nil [nɪl] *n* rien *m*; (*BRIT*: *SPORT*) zéro *m*

Nile [naɪl] *n*: **the** ~ le Nil

nimble ['nɪmbl] *adj* agile

nine [naɪn] *num* neuf; ~**teen** *num* dix-neuf; ~**ty** *num* quatre-vingt-dix

ninth [naɪnθ] *num* neuvième

nip [nɪp] *vt* pincer

nipple ['nɪpl] n (ANAT) mamelon m, bout m du sein

nitrogen ['naɪtrədʒən] n azote m

KEYWORD
---

no [nəʊ] (pl ~es) adv (opposite of "yes") non; **are you coming? - ~ (I'm not)** est-ce que vous venez? - non; **would you like some more? - ~ thank you** vous en voulez encore? - non merci

♦ adj (not any) pas de, aucun(e) (used with "ne"); **I have ~ money/books** je n'ai pas d'argent/de livres; **~ student would have done it** aucun étudiant ne l'aurait fait; **"~ smoking"** "défense de fumer"; **"~ dogs"** "les chiens ne sont pas admis"

♦ n non m

---

nobility [nəʊ'bɪlɪtɪ] n noblesse f

noble ['nəʊbl] adj noble

nobody ['nəʊbədɪ] pron personne

nod [nɒd] vi faire un signe de tête (affirmatif ou amical); (sleep) somnoler ♦ vt: **to ~ one's head** faire un signe de (la) tête; (in agreement) faire signe que oui ♦ n signe de (la) tête; **~ off** vi s'assoupir

noise [nɔɪz] n bruit m; **noisy** ['nɔɪzɪ] adj bruyant(e)

nominal ['nɒmɪnl] adj (rent, leader) symbolique

nominate ['nɒmɪneɪt] vt (propose) proposer; (appoint) nommer; **nominee** [nɒmɪ'niː] n candidat agréé; personne nommée

non... prefix non-; **~-alcoholic** adj non-alcoolisé(e); **~-committal** adj évasif(ive)

nondescript ['nɒndɪskrɪpt] adj quelconque, indéfinissable

none [nʌn] pron aucun(e); **~ of you** aucun d'entre vous, personne parmi vous; **I've ~ left** je n'en ai plus; **he's ~ the worse for it** il ne s'en porte pas plus mal

nonentity [nɒ'nentɪtɪ] n personne insignifiante

nonetheless [nʌnðə'les] adv néanmoins

non-existent [nɒnɪg'zɪstənt] adj inexistant(e)

non-fiction [nɒn'fɪkʃən] n littérature f non-romanesque

nonplussed ['nɒn'plʌst] adj perplexe

nonsense ['nɒnsəns] n absurdités fpl, idioties fpl; **~!** ne dites pas d'idioties!

non: **~-smoker** n non-fumeur m; **~-stick** adj qui n'attache pas; **~-stop** adj direct(e), sans arrêt (or escale) ♦ adv sans arrêt

noodles ['nuːdlz] npl nouilles fpl

nook [nʊk] n: **~s and crannies** recoins mpl

noon [nuːn] n midi m

no one ['nəʊwʌn] pron = **nobody**

noose [nuːs] n nœud coulant; (hangman's) corde f

nor [nɔː*] conj = **neither** ♦ adv see **neither**

norm [nɔːm] n norme f

normal ['nɔːməl] adj normal(e); **~ly** adv normalement

Normandy ['nɔːməndɪ] n Normandie f

north [nɔːθ] n nord m ♦ adj du nord, nord inv ♦ adv au or vers le nord; **N~ America** n Amérique f du Nord; **~-east** n nord-est m; **~erly** ['nɔːðəlɪ] adj du nord; **~ern** ['nɔːðən] adj du nord, septentrional(e); **N~ern Ireland** n Irlande f du Nord; **N~ Pole** n pôle m Nord; **N~ Sea** n mer f du Nord; **~ward(s)** ['nɔːθwəd(z)] adv vers le nord; **~-west** n nord-ouest m

Norway ['nɔːweɪ] n Norvège f

Norwegian [nɔː'wiːdʒən] adj norvégien(ne) ♦ n Norvégien(ne); (LING) norvégien m

nose [nəʊz] n nez m; **~ about, around** vi fouiner or fureter (partout); **~bleed** n saignement m du nez; **~-dive** n (descente f en) piqué m; **~y** (inf) adj = **nosy**

nostalgia [nɒs'tældʒɪə] n nostalgie f

nostril ['nɒstrɪl] n narine f; (of horse) naseau m

nosy ['nəʊzɪ] (inf) adj curieux(euse)

not [nɒt] adv (ne ...) pas; **he is ~ or isn't here** il n'est pas ici; **you must ~ or you mustn't do that** tu ne dois pas faire ça; **it's too late, isn't it or is it ~?** c'est trop tard, n'est-ce pas?; ~ **yet/now** pas encore/actuellement; *see also* **all; only**

notably ['nəʊtəblɪ] *adv (particularly)* en particulier; *(markedly)* spécialement

notary ['nəʊtərɪ] *n* notaire *m*

notch [nɒtʃ] *n* encoche *f*

note [nəʊt] *n* note *f*; *(letter)* mot *m*; *(banknote)* billet *m* ♦ *vt (also:* ~ **down)** noter; *(observe)* constater; ~**book** *n* carnet *m*; ~**d** ['nəʊtɪd] *adj* réputé(e); ~**pad** *n* bloc-notes *m*; ~**paper** *n* papier *m* à lettres

nothing ['nʌθɪŋ] *n* rien *m*; **he does** ~ il ne fait rien; ~ **new** rien de nouveau; **for** ~ pour rien

notice ['nəʊtɪs] *n (announcement, warning)* avis *m*; *(period of time)* délai *m*; *(resignation)* démission *f*; *(dismissal)* congé *m* ♦ *vt* remarquer, s'apercevoir de; **to take** ~ **of** prêter attention à; **to bring sth to sb's** ~ porter qch à la connaissance de qn; **at short** ~ dans un délai très court; **until further** ~ jusqu'à nouvel ordre; **to hand in one's** ~ donner sa démission, démissionner; ~**able** *adj* visible; ~ **board** *(BRIT)* *n* panneau *m* d'affichage

notify ['nəʊtɪfaɪ] *vt:* **to** ~ **sth to sb** notifier qch à qn; **to** ~ **sb (of sth)** avertir qn (de qch)

notion ['nəʊʃən] *n* idée *f*; *(concept)* notion *f*

notorious [nəʊ'tɔːrɪəs] *adj* notoire *(souvent en mal)*

notwithstanding [nɒtwɪθ'stændɪŋ] *adv* néanmoins ♦ *prep* en dépit de

nought [nɔːt] *n* zéro *m*

noun [naʊn] *n* nom *m*

nourish ['nʌrɪʃ] *vt* nourrir; ~**ing** *adj* nourrissant(e); ~**ment** *n* nourriture *f*

novel ['nɒvəl] *n* roman *m* ♦ *adj* nouveau(nouvelle), original(e); ~**ist** *n* romancier *m*; ~**ty** *n* nouveauté *f*

November [nəʊ'vɛmbə*] *n* novembre *m*

now [naʊ] *adv* maintenant ♦ *conj:* ~ **(that)** maintenant que; **right** ~ tout de suite; **by** ~ à l'heure qu'il est; **just** ~: **that's the fashion just** ~ c'est la mode en ce moment; ~ **and then,** ~ **and again** de temps en temps; **from** ~ **on** dorénavant; ~**adays** ['naʊədeɪz] *adv* de nos jours

nowhere ['nəʊwɛə*] *adv* nulle part

nozzle ['nɒzl] *n (of hose etc)* ajutage *m*; *(of vacuum cleaner)* suceur *m*

nuclear ['njuːklɪə*] *adj* nucléaire

nucleus ['njuːklɪəs, *pl* 'njuːklɪaɪ] *(pl* **nuclei)** *n* noyau *m*

nude [njuːd] *adj* nu(e) ♦ *n* nu *m*; **in the** ~ (tout(e)) nu(e)

nudge [nʌdʒ] *vt* donner un (petit) coup de coude à

nudist ['njuːdɪst] *n* nudiste *m/f*

nuisance ['njuːsns] *n:* **it's a** ~ c'est (très) embêtant; **he's a** ~ il est assommant *or* casse-pieds; **what a** ~! quelle barbe!

null [nʌl] *adj:* ~ **and void** nul(le) et non avenu(e)

numb [nʌm] *adj* engourdi(e); *(with fear)* paralysé(e)

number ['nʌmbə*] *n* nombre *m*; *(numeral)* chiffre *m*; *(of house, bank account etc)* numéro *m* ♦ *vt* numéroter; *(amount to)* compter; **a** ~ **of** un certain nombre de; **to be** ~**ed among** compter parmi; **they were seven in** ~ ils étaient (au nombre de) sept; ~ **plate** *n (AUT)* plaque *f* minéralogique *or* d'immatriculation

numeral ['njuːmərəl] *n* chiffre *m*

numerate ['njuːmərɪt] *(BRIT) adj:* **to be** ~ avoir des notions d'arithmétique

numerical [njuː'mɛrɪkəl] *adj* numérique

numerous ['njuːmərəs] *adj* nombreux(euse)

nun [nʌn] *n* religieuse *f*, sœur *f*

nurse [nɜːs] *n* infirmière *f* ♦ *vt (patient, cold)* soigner

nursery ['nɜːsərɪ] *n (room)* nursery *f*; *(institution)* crèche *f*; *(for plants)* pépinière *f*; ~ **rhyme** *n* comptine *f*, chansonnette *f* pour enfants; ~ **school** *n* école maternelle; ~ **slope** *n (SKI)* piste *f* pour débutants

nursing ['nɜːsɪŋ] *n (profession)* profession *f* d'infirmière; *(care)* soins *mpl;* ~ **home** *n* clinique *f*; maison *f* de convalescence; ~ **mother** *n* mère *f* qui allaite

nut [nʌt] *n* (*of metal*) écrou *m*; (*fruit*) noix *f*; noisette *f*; cacahuète *f*; **~crackers** ['nʌtkrækəz] *npl* casse-noix *m inv*, casse-noisette(s) *m*

nutmeg ['nʌtmeg] *n* (noix *f*) muscade *f*

nutritious [njuː'trɪʃəs] *adj* nutritif(ive), nourrissant(e)

nuts (*inf*) *adj* dingue

nutshell ['nʌtʃel] *n*: **in a ~** en un mot

nylon ['naɪlɒn] *n* nylon *m* ♦ *adj* de *or* en nylon

O o

oak [əuk] *n* chêne *m* ♦ *adj* de *or* en (bois de) chêne

OAP (*BRIT*) *n abbr* = **old age pensioner**

oar [ɔː*] *n* aviron *m*, rame *f*

oasis [əu'eɪsɪs, *pl* əu'eɪsiːz] (*pl* **oases**) *n* oasis *f*

oath [əuθ] *n* serment *m*; (*swear word*) juron *m*; **under ~**, (*BRIT*) **on ~** sous serment

oatmeal ['əutmiːl] *n* flocons *mpl* d'avoine

oats [əuts] *n* avoine *f*

obedience [ə'biːdɪəns] *n* obéissance *f*; **obedient** [ə'biːdɪənt] *adj* obéissant(e)

obey [ə'beɪ] *vt* obéir à; (*instructions*) se conformer à

obituary [ə'bɪtjuərɪ] *n* nécrologie *f*

object [*n* 'ɒbdʒɪkt, *vb* əb'dʒekt] *n* objet *m*; (*purpose*) but *m*, objet; (*LING*) complément *m* d'objet ♦ *vi*: **to ~ to** (*attitude*) désapprouver; (*proposal*) protester contre; **expense is no ~** l'argent n'est pas un problème; **he ~ed that ...** il a fait valoir *or* a objecté que ...; **I ~!** je proteste!; **~ion** [əb'dʒekʃən] *n* objection *f*; **~ionable** [əb'dʒekʃnəbl] *adj* très désagréable; (*language*) choquant(e); **~ive** [əb'dʒektɪv] *n* objectif *m* ♦ *adj* objectif(ive)

obligation [ɒblɪ'geɪʃən] *n* obligation *f*, devoir *m*; **without ~** sans engagement

oblige [ə'blaɪdʒ] *vt* (*force*): **to ~ sb to do** obliger *or* forcer qn à faire; (*do a favour*) rendre service à, obliger; **to be ~d to sb for sth** être obligé(e) à qn de qch;

obliging [ə'blaɪdʒɪŋ] *adj* obligeant(e), serviable

oblique [ə'bliːk] *adj* oblique; (*allusion*) indirect(e)

obliterate [ə'blɪtəreɪt] *vt* effacer

oblivion [ə'blɪvɪən] *n* oubli *m*; **oblivious** [ə'blɪvɪəs] *adj*: **oblivious of** oublieux(euse) de

oblong ['ɒblɒŋ] *adj* oblong(ue) ♦ *n* rectangle *m*

obnoxious [əb'nɒkʃəs] *adj* odieux (euse); (*smell*) nauséabond(e)

oboe ['əubəu] *n* hautbois *m*

obscene [əb'siːn] *adj* obscène

obscure [əb'skjuə*] *adj* obscur(e) ♦ *vt* obscurcir; (*hide*: *sun*) cacher

observant [əb'zɜːvənt] *adj* observateur(trice)

observation [ɒbzə'veɪʃən] *n* (*remark*) observation *f*; (*watching*) surveillance *f*; **observatory** [əb'zɜːvətrɪ] *n* observatoire *m*

observe [əb'zɜːv] *vt* observer; (*remark*) faire observer *or* remarquer; **~r** *n* observateur(trice)

obsess [əb'ses] *vt* obséder; **~ive** *adj* obsédant(e)

obsolescence [ɒbsə'lesns] *n* vieillissement *m*

obsolete ['ɒbsəliːt] *adj* dépassé(e); démodé(e)

obstacle ['ɒbstəkl] *n* obstacle *m*; **~ race** *n* course *f* d'obstacles

obstinate ['ɒbstɪnət] *adj* obstiné(e)

obstruct [əb'strʌkt] *vt* (*block*) boucher, obstruer; (*hinder*) entraver

obtain [əb'teɪn] *vt* obtenir; **~able** *adj* qu'on peut obtenir

obvious ['ɒbvɪəs] *adj* évident(e), manifeste; **~ly** *adv* manifestement; **~ly not!** bien sûr que non!

occasion [ə'keɪʒən] *n* occasion *f*; (*event*) événement *m*; **~al** *adj* pris(e) *or* fait(e) *etc* de temps en temps; occasionnel(le); **~ally** *adv* de temps en temps, quelquefois

occupation [ɒkju'peɪʃən] *n* occupation *f*; (*job*) métier *m*, profession *f*; **~al hazard** *n* risque *m* du métier

occupier [ˈɒkjupaɪə*] *n* occupant(e)
occupy [ˈɒkjupaɪ] *vt* occuper; **to ~ o.s.
in** *or* **with doing** s'occuper à faire
occur [əˈkɜː*] *vi* (*event*) se produire;
(*phenomenon, error*) se rencontrer; **to ~
to sb** venir à l'esprit de qn; **~rence** *n*
(*existence*) présence *f*, existence *f*;
(*event*) cas *m*, fait *m*
ocean [ˈəuʃən] *n* océan *m*; **~-going** *adj*
de haute mer
o'clock [əˈklɒk] *adv*: **it is 5 ~** il est 5
heures
OCR *n abbr* = **optical character reader; optical character recognition**
October [ɒkˈtəubə*] *n* octobre *m*
octopus [ˈɒktəpəs] *n* pieuvre *f*
odd [ɒd] *adj* (*strange*) bizarre, cu-
rieux(euse); (*number*) impair(e); (*not of
a set*) dépareillé(e); **60-odd** 60 et quelques; **at ~ times** de temps en temps; **the
~ one out** l'exception *f*; **~ity** *n* (*person*)
excentrique *m/f*; (*thing*) curiosité *f*; **~-
job man** *n* homme *m* à tout faire; **~
jobs** *npl* petits travaux divers; **~ly** *adv*
bizarrement, curieusement; **~ments** *npl*
(*COMM*) fins *fpl* de série; **~s** *npl* (*in betting*) cote *f*; **it makes no ~s** cela n'a pas
d'importance; **at ~s** en désaccord; **~s
and ends** de petites choses
odour [ˈəudə*] (*US* **odor**) *n* odeur *f*

<hr>

KEYWORD

of [ɒv, əv] *prep* **1** (*gen*) de; **a friend ~
ours** un de nos amis; **a boy ~ 10** un
garçon de 10 ans; **that was kind ~ you**
c'était gentil de votre part
2 (*expressing quantity, amount, dates
etc*) de; **a kilo ~ flour** un kilo de farine;
how much ~ this do you need?
combien vous en faut-il?; **there were 3
~ them** (*people*) ils étaient 3; (*objects*) il
y en avait 3; **3 ~ us went** 3 d'entre nous
y sont allé(e)s; **the 5th ~ July** le 5 juillet
3 (*from, out of*) en, de; **a statue ~ marble** une statue de *or* en marbre; **made ~
wood** (fait) en bois

off [ɒf] *adj, adv* (*engine*) coupé(e); (*tap*)
fermé(e); (*BRIT: food: bad*) mauvais(e);

(: *milk*) tourné(e); (*absent*) absent(e);
(*cancelled*) annulé(e) ♦ *prep* de; sur; **to
be ~** (*to leave*) partir, s'en aller; **to be ~
sick** être absent pour cause de maladie;
a day ~ un jour de congé; **to have an ~
day** n'être pas en forme; **he had his
coat ~** il avait enlevé son manteau; **10%
~** (*COMM*) 10% de rabais; **~ the coast** au
large de la côte; **I'm ~ meat** je ne mange
plus de viande, je n'aime plus la viande;
on the ~ chance à tout hasard
offal [ˈɒfəl] *n* (*CULIN*) abats *mpl*
off-colour [ˈɒfˈkʌlə*] (*BRIT*) *adj* (*ill*) malade, mal fichu(e)
offence [əˈfens] (*US* **offense**) *n* (*crime*)
délit *m*, infraction *f*; **to take ~ at** se
vexer de, s'offenser de
offend [əˈfend] *vt* (*person*) offenser, blesser; **~er** *n* délinquant(e)
offense [əˈfens] (*US*) *n* = **offence**
offensive [əˈfensɪv] *adj* offensant(e), cho-
quant(e); (*smell etc*) très déplaisant(e);
(*weapon*) offensif(ive) ♦ *n* (*MIL*) offensive
f
offer [ˈɒfə*] *n* offre *f*, proposition *f* ♦ *vt*
offrir, proposer; **"on ~"** (*COMM*) "en promotion"; **~ing** *n* offrande *f*
offhand [ˈɒfˈhænd] *adj* désinvolte ♦ *adv*
spontanément
office [ˈɒfɪs] *n* (*place, room*) bureau *m*;
(*position*) charge *f*, fonction *f*; **doctor's
~** (*US*) cabinet (médical); **to take ~** entrer en fonctions; **~ automation** *n* bureautique *f*; **~ block** (*US* **~ building**) *n*
immeuble *m* de bureaux; **~ hours** *npl*
heures *fpl* de bureau; (*US: MED*) heures de
consultation
officer [ˈɒfɪsə*] *n* (*MIL etc*) officier *m*;
(*also: police ~*) agent *m* (de police); (*of
organization*) membre *m* du bureau directeur
office worker *n* employé(e) de bureau
official [əˈfɪʃəl] *adj* officiel(le) ♦ *n* officiel
m; (*civil servant*) fonctionnaire *m/f*; em-
ployé(e); **~dom** *n* administration *f*, bureaucratie *f*
officiate [əˈfɪʃɪeɪt] *vi* (*REL*) officier; **to ~
at a marriage** célébrer un mariage
officious [əˈfɪʃəs] *adj* trop empressé(e)

offing ['ɒfɪŋ] *n*: **in the** ~ (*fig*) en perspective

off: ~**-licence** (*BRIT*) *n* (*shop*) débit *m* de vins et de spiritueux; ~**-line** *adj, adv* (*COMPUT*) (en mode) autonome; (: *switched off*) non connecté(e); ~**-peak** *adj* aux heures creuses; (*electricity, heating, ticket*) au tarif heures creuses; ~**-putting** (*BRIT*) *adj* (*remark*) rébarbatif(ive); (*person*) rebutant(e), peu engageant(e); ~**-season** *adj, adv* hors-saison *inv*

offset ['ɒfset] (*irreg*) *vt* (*counteract*) contrebalancer, compenser

offshoot ['ɒfʃuːt] *n* (*fig*) ramification *f*, antenne *f*

offshore ['ɒf'ʃɔː*] *adj* (*breeze*) de terre; (*fishing*) côtier(ère)

offside ['ɒf'saɪd] *adj* (*SPORT*) hors jeu; (*AUT: in Britain*) de droite; (: *in US, Europe etc*) de gauche

offspring ['ɒfsprɪŋ] *n inv* progéniture *f*

off: ~**stage** *adv* dans les coulisses; ~**the-peg** (*US* ~**-the-rack**) *adv* en prêt-à-porter; ~**-white** *adj* blanc cassé *inv*

often ['ɒfən] *adv* souvent; **how** ~ **do you go?** vous y allez tous les combien?; **how** ~ **have you gone there?** vous y êtes allé combien de fois?

ogle ['əʊgl] *vt* lorgner

oh [əʊ] *excl* ô!, oh!, ah!

oil [ɔɪl] *n* huile *f*; (*petroleum*) pétrole *m*; (*for central heating*) mazout *m* ♦ *vt* (*machine*) graisser; ~**can** *n* burette *f* de graissage; (*for storing*) bidon *m* à huile; ~**field** *n* gisement *m* de pétrole; ~ **filter** *n* (*AUT*) filtre *m* à huile; ~ **painting** *n* peinture *f* à l'huile; ~ **refinery** *n* raffinerie *f*; ~ **rig** *n* derrick *m*; (*at sea*) plate-forme pétrolière; ~**skins** *npl* ciré *m*; ~ **tanker** *n* (*ship*) pétrolier *m*; (*truck*) camion-citerne *m*; ~ **well** *n* puits *m* de pétrole; ~**y** *adj* huileux(euse); (*food*) gras(se)

ointment ['ɔɪntmənt] *n* onguent *m*

O.K., okay ['əʊ'keɪ] *excl* d'accord! ♦ *adj* (*average*) pas mal ♦ *vt* approuver, donner son accord à; **is it** ~?, **are you** ~? ça va?

old [əʊld] *adj* vieux(vieille); (*person*) vieux,

âgé(e); (*former*) ancien(ne), vieux; **how** ~ **are you?** quel âge avez-vous?; **he's 10 years** ~ il a 10 ans, il est âgé de 10 ans; ~**er brother/sister** frère/sœur aîné(e); ~ **age** *n* vieillesse *f*; ~ **age pensioner** (*BRIT*) *n* retraité(e); ~**-fashioned** *adj* démodé(e); (*person*) vieux jeu *inv*

olive ['ɒlɪv] *n* (*fruit*) olive *f*; (*tree*) olivier *m* ♦ *adj* (*also:* ~**-green**) (vert) olive *inv*; ~ **oil** *n* huile *f* d'olive

Olympic [əʊ'lɪmpɪk] *adj* olympique; **the** ~ **Games, the** ~**s** les Jeux *mpl* olympiques

omelet(te) ['ɒmlət] *n* omelette *f*

omen ['əʊmən] *n* présage *m*

ominous ['ɒmɪnəs] *adj* menaçant(e), inquiétant(e); (*event*) de mauvais augure

omit [əʊ'mɪt] *vt* omettre; **to** ~ **to do** omettre de faire

---

KEYWORD

---

on [ɒn] *prep* **1** (*indicating position*) sur; ~ **the table** sur la table; ~ **the wall** sur le *or* au mur; ~ **the left** à gauche

2 (*indicating means, method, condition etc*): ~ **foot** à pied; ~ **the train/plane** (*be*) dans le train/l'avion; (*go*) en train/ avion; ~ **the telephone/radio/television** au téléphone/à la radio/à la télévision; **to be** ~ **drugs** se droguer; ~ **holiday** en vacances

3 (*referring to time*): ~ **Friday** vendredi; ~ **Fridays** le vendredi; ~ **June 20th** le 20 juin; **a week** ~ **Friday** vendredi en huit; ~ **arrival** à l'arrivée; ~ **seeing this** en voyant cela

4 (*about, concerning*) sur, de; **a book** ~ **Balzac/physics** un livre sur Balzac/de physique

♦ *adv* **1** (*referring to dress, covering*): **to have one's coat** ~ avoir (mis) son manteau; **to put one's coat** ~ mettre son manteau; **what's she got** ~? qu'est-ce qu'elle porte?; **screw the lid** ~ **tightly** vissez bien le couvercle

2 (*further, continuously*): **to walk** *etc* ~ continuer à marcher *etc*; ~ **and off** de temps à autre

♦ *adj* **1** (*in operation: machine*) en marche; (: *radio*, *TV*, *light*) allumé(e); (: *tap*, *gas*) ouvert(e); (: *brakes*) mis(e); **is the meeting still ~?** (*not cancelled*) est-ce que la réunion a bien lieu?; (*in progress*) la réunion dure-t-elle encore?; **when is this film ~?** quand passe ce film?

2 (*inf*): **that's not ~!** (*not acceptable*) cela ne se fait pas!; (*not possible*) pas question!

once [wʌns] *adv* une fois; (*formerly*) autrefois ♦ *conj* une fois que; **~ he had left/it was done** une fois qu'il fut parti/que ce fut terminé; **at ~** tout de suite, immédiatement; (*simultaneously*) à la fois; **~ a week** une fois par semaine; **~ more** encore une fois; **~ and for all** une fois pour toutes; **~ upon a time** il y avait une fois, il était une fois

oncoming [ˈɒnkʌmɪŋ] *adj* (*traffic*) venant en sens inverse

⎡ *KEYWORD* ⎤

one [wʌn] *num* un(e); **~ hundred and fifty** cent cinquante; **~ day** un jour
♦ *adj* **1** (*sole*) seul(e), unique; **the ~ book which** l'unique *or* le seul livre qui; **the ~ man who** le seul (homme) qui
2 (*same*) même; **they came in the ~ car** ils sont venus dans la même voiture
♦ *pron* **1**: **this ~** celui-ci(celle-ci); **that ~** celui-là(celle-là); **I've already got ~/a red ~** j'en ai déjà un(e)/un(e) rouge; **~ by ~** un(e) à *or* par une
2: **~ another** l'un(e) l'autre; **to look at ~ another** se regarder
3 (*impersonal*) on; **~ never knows** on ne sait jamais; **to cut ~'s finger** se couper le doigt

one: **~-day excursion** (*US*) *n* billet *m* d'aller-retour (valable pour la journée); **~-man** *adj* (*business*) dirigé(e) *etc* par un seul homme; **~-man band** *n* homme-orchestre *m*; **~-off** (*BRIT: inf*) *n* exemplaire *m* unique

oneself [wʌnˈself] *pron* (*reflexive*) se;

(*after prep*) soi(-même); (*emphatic*) soi-même; **to hurt ~** se faire mal; **to keep sth for ~** garder qch pour soi; **to talk to ~** se parler à soi-même

one: **~-sided** *adj* (*argument*) unilatéral; **~-to-~** *adj* (*relationship*) univoque; **~-upmanship** *n*: **the art of ~-upmanship** l'art de faire mieux que les autres; **~-way** *adj* (*street*, *traffic*) à sens unique

ongoing [ˈɒngəʊɪŋ] *adj* en cours; (*relationship*) suivi(e)

onion [ˈʌnjən] *n* oignon *m*

on-line [ˈɒnlaɪn] *adj*, *adv* (*COMPUT*) en ligne; (: *switched on*) connecté(e)

onlooker [ˈɒnlʊkə*] *n* spectateur (trice)

only [ˈəʊnlɪ] *adv* seulement ♦ *adj* seul(e), unique ♦ *conj* seulement, mais; **an ~ child** un enfant unique; **not ~ ... but also** non seulement ... mais aussi

onset [ˈɒnset] *n* début *m*; (*of winter*, *old age*) approche *f*

onshore [ˈɒnʃɔː*] *adj* (*wind*) du large

onslaught [ˈɒnslɔːt] *n* attaque *f*, assaut *m*

onto [ˈɒntʊ] *prep* = **on to**

onus [ˈəʊnəs] *n* responsabilité *f*

onward(s) [ˈɒnwəd(z)] *adv* (*move*) en avant; **from that time ~** à partir de ce moment

ooze [uːz] *vi* suinter

opaque [əʊˈpeɪk] *adj* opaque

OPEC [ˈəʊpɛk] *n abbr* (= *Organization of Petroleum Exporting Countries*) O.P.E.P. *f*

open [ˈəʊpən] *adj* ouvert(e); (*car*) découvert(e); (*road*, *view*) dégagé(e); (*meeting*) public(ique); (*admiration*) manifeste ♦ *vt* ouvrir ♦ *vi* (*flower*, *eyes*, *door*, *debate*) s'ouvrir; (*shop*, *bank*, *museum*) ouvrir; (*book etc*: *commence*) commencer, débuter; **in the ~ (air)** en plein air; **~ on to** *vt fus* (*subj*: *room*, *door*) donner sur; **~ up** *vt* ouvrir; (*blocked road*) dégager ♦ *vi* s'ouvrir; **~ing** *n* ouverture *f*; (*opportunity*) occasion *f* ♦ *adj* (*remarks*) préliminaire; **~ learning centre** *n* centre ouvert à tous où l'on dispense un enseignement général à temps partiel; **~ly** *adv* ouvertement; **~-minded** *adj* à l'esprit ouvert; **~-necked** adj à col ouvert; **~-plan** adj sans cloisons

opera ['ɒpərə] n opéra m; **~ singer** n chanteur(euse) d'opéra

operate ['ɒpəreɪt] vt (machine) faire marcher, faire fonctionner ♦ vi fonctionner; (MED): **to ~ (on sb)** opérer (qn)

operatic [ɒpə'rætɪk] adj d'opéra

operating ['ɒpəreɪtɪŋ]: **~-table** n table f d'opération; **~ theatre** n salle f d'opération

operation [ɒpə'reɪʃən] n opération f; (of machine) fonctionnement m; **to be in ~** (system, law) être en vigueur; **to have an ~** (MED) se faire opérer

operative ['ɒpərətɪv] adj (measure) en vigueur

operator ['ɒpəreɪtə*] n (of machine) opérateur(trice); (TEL) téléphoniste m/f

opinion [ə'pɪnjən] n opinion f, avis m; **in my ~** à mon avis; **~ated** adj aux idées bien arrêtées; **~ poll** n sondage m (d'opinion)

opponent [ə'pəʊnənt] n adversaire m/f

opportunity [ɒpə'tju:nɪtɪ] n occasion f; **to take the ~ of doing** profiter de l'occasion pour faire; en profiter pour faire

oppose [ə'pəʊz] vt s'opposer à; **~d to** opposé(e) à; **as ~d to** par opposition à; **opposing** [ə'pəʊzɪŋ] adj (side) opposé(e)

opposite ['ɒpəzɪt] adj opposé(e); (house etc) d'en face ♦ adv en face ♦ prep en face de ♦ n opposé m, contraire m; **the ~ sex** l'autre sexe, le sexe opposé

opposition [ɒpə'zɪʃən] n opposition f

oppress [ə'pres] vt opprimer

oppressive adj (political regime) oppressif(ive); (weather) lourd(e); (heat) accablant(e)

opt [ɒpt] vi: **to ~ for** opter pour; **to ~ to do** choisir de faire; **~ out** vi: **to ~ out of** choisir de ne pas participer à or de ne pas faire

optical ['ɒptɪkəl] adj optique; (instrument) d'optique; **~ character recognition/reader** n lecture f/lecteur m optique

optician [ɒp'tɪʃən] n opticien(ne)

optimist ['ɒptɪmɪst] n optimiste m/f; **~ic** adj optimiste

option ['ɒpʃən] n choix m, option f; (SCOL) matière f à option; (COMM) option; **~al** adj facultatif(ive); (COMM) en option

or [ɔ:*] conj ou; (with negative): **he hasn't seen ~ heard anything** il n'a rien vu ni entendu; **~ else** sinon; ou bien

oral ['ɔ:rəl] adj oral(e) ♦ n oral m

orange ['ɒrɪndʒ] n (fruit) orange f ♦ adj orange inv

orator ['ɒrətə*] n orateur(trice)

orbit ['ɔ:bɪt] n orbite f ♦ vt graviter autour de

orchard ['ɔ:tʃəd] n verger m

orchestra ['ɔ:kɪstrə] n orchestre m; (US: seating) (fauteuils mpl d')orchestre

orchid ['ɔ:kɪd] n orchidée f

ordain [ɔ:'deɪn] vt (REL) ordonner

ordeal [ɔ:'di:l] n épreuve f

order ['ɔ:də*] n ordre m; (COMM) commande f ♦ vt ordonner; (COMM) commander; **in ~** en ordre; (document) en règle; **in (working) ~** en état de marche; **out of ~** (not in correct order) en désordre; (not working) en dérangement; **in ~ to do/that** pour faire/que +sub; **on ~** (COMM) en commande; **to ~ sb to do** ordonner à qn de faire; **~ form** n bon m de commande; **~ly** n (MIL) ordonnance f; (MED) garçon m de salle ♦ adj (room) en ordre; (person) qui a de l'ordre

ordinary ['ɔ:dnrɪ] adj ordinaire, normal(e); (pej) ordinaire, quelconque; **out of the ~** exceptionnel(le)

Ordnance Survey map n ≈ carte f d'Etat-Major

ore [ɔ:*] n minerai m

organ ['ɔ:gən] n organe m; (MUS) orgue m, orgues fpl; **~ic** [ɔ:'gænɪk] adj organique

organization [ɔ:gənaɪ'zeɪʃən] n organisation f

organize ['ɔ:gənaɪz] vt organiser; **~r** n organisateur(trice)

orgasm ['ɔ:gæzəm] n orgasme m

Orient ['ɔ:rɪənt] n: **the ~** l'Orient m; **o~al** [ɔ:rɪ'entəl] adj oriental(e)

origin ['ɒrɪdʒɪn] n origine f

original [əˈrɪdʒɪnl] *adj* original(e); (*earliest*) originel(le) ♦ *n* original *m*; **~ly** *adv* (*at first*) à l'origine

originate [əˈrɪdʒɪneɪt] *vi*: **to ~ from** (*person*) être originaire de; (*suggestion*) provenir de; **to ~ in** prendre naissance dans; avoir son origine dans

Orkneys [ˈɔːknɪz] *npl*: **the ~** (*also: the Orkney Islands*) les Orcades *fpl*

ornament [ˈɔːnəmənt] *n* ornement *m*; (*trinket*) bibelot *m*; **~al** [ɔːnəˈmentl] *adj* décoratif(ive); (*garden*) d'agrément

ornate [ɔːˈneɪt] *adj* très orné(e)

orphan [ˈɔːfən] *n* orphelin(e); **~age** *n* orphelinat *m*

orthopaedic [ɔːθəʊˈpiːdɪk] (*US* **orthopedic**) *adj* orthopédique

ostensibly [ɒsˈtensəblɪ] *adv* en apparence

ostentatious [ɒstenˈteɪʃəs] *adj* prétentieux(euse)

ostracize [ˈɒstrəsaɪz] *vt* frapper d'ostracisme

ostrich [ˈɒstrɪtʃ] *n* autruche *f*

other [ˈʌðə*] *adj* autre ♦ *pron*: **the ~ (one)** l'autre; **~s** (*~ people*) d'autres; **than** autrement que; à part; **~wise** *adv*, *conj* autrement

otter [ˈɒtə*] *n* loutre *f*

ouch [aʊtʃ] *excl* aïe!

ought [ɔːt] (*pt* **ought**) *aux vb*: **I ~ to do it** je devrais le faire, il faudrait que je le fasse; **this ~ to have been corrected** cela aurait dû être corrigé; **he ~ to win** il devrait gagner

ounce [aʊns] *n* once *f* (= *28.35g; 16 in a pound*)

our [aʊə*] *adj* notre, nos *pl; see also* **my; ~s** *pron* le(la) nôtre, les nôtres; *see also* **mine; ~selves** *pron pl* (*reflexive, after preposition*) nous; (*emphatic*) nous-mêmes; *see also* **oneself**

oust [aʊst] *vt* évincer

out [aʊt] *adv* dehors; (*published, not at home etc*) sorti(e); (*light, fire*) éteint(e); **~ here** ici; **~ there** là-bas; **he's ~** (*absent*) il est sorti; (*unconscious*) il est sans connaissance; **to be ~ in one's calculations** s'être trompé dans ses calculs;

to run/back *etc* **~** sortir en courant/en reculant *etc*; **~ loud** à haute voix; **~ of** (*outside*) en dehors de; (*because of: anger etc*) par; (*from among*): **~ of 10** sur 10; **~ of**; (*without*): **~ of petrol** sans essence, à court d'essence; **~ of order** (*machine*) en panne; (*TEL: line*) en dérangement; **~-and-out** *adj* (*liar, thief etc*) véritable

outback [ˈaʊtbæk] *n* (*in Australia*): **the ~** l'intérieur *m*

outboard [ˈaʊtbɔːd] *n* (*also: ~ motor*) (moteur *m*) hors-bord *m*;

out: ~break [ˈaʊtbreɪk] *n* (*of war, disease*) début *m*; (*of violence*) éruption *f*; **~burst** [ˈaʊtbɜːst] *n* explosion *f*, accès *m*; **~cast** [ˈaʊtkɑːst] *n* exilé(e); (*socially*) paria *m*; **~come** [ˈaʊtkʌm] *n* issue *f*, résultat *m*; **~crop** [ˈaʊtkrɒp] *n* (*of rock*) affleurement *m*; **~cry** [ˈaʊtkraɪ] *n* tollé (général); **~dated** [aʊtˈdeɪtɪd] *adj* démodé(e); **~do** [aʊtˈduː] (*irreg*) *vt* surpasser

outdoor [aʊtˈdɔː*] *adj* de *or* en plein air; **~s** *adv* dehors; au grand air

outer [ˈaʊtə*] *adj* extérieur(e); **~ space** *n* espace *m* cosmique

outfit [ˈaʊtfɪt] *n* (*clothes*) tenue *f*

outgoing [ˈaʊtɡəʊɪŋ] *adj* (*character*) ouvert(e), extraverti(e); (*retiring*) sortant(e); **~s** (*BRIT*) *npl* (*expenses*) dépenses *fpl*

outgrow [aʊtˈɡrəʊ] (*irreg*) *vt* (*clothes*) devenir trop grand(e) pour

outhouse [ˈaʊthaʊs] *n* appentis *m*, remise *f*

outing [ˈaʊtɪŋ] *n* sortie *f*; excursion *f*

outlandish [aʊtˈlændɪʃ] *adj* étrange

outlaw [ˈaʊtlɔː] *n* hors-la-loi *m inv* ♦ *vt* mettre hors-la-loi

outlay [ˈaʊtleɪ] *n* dépenses *fpl*; (*investment*) mise *f* de fonds

outlet [ˈaʊtlet] *n* (*for liquid etc*) issue *f*, sortie *f*; (*US: ELEC*) prise *f* de courant; (*also: retail ~*) point *m* de vente

outline [ˈaʊtlaɪn] *n* (*shape*) contour *m*; (*summary*) esquisse *f*, grandes lignes ♦ *vt* (*fig: theory, plan*) exposer à grands traits

out: ~live [aʊtˈlɪv] *vt* survivre à; **~look**

['aʊtlʊk] n perspective f; **~lying** ['aʊtlaɪɪŋ] adj écarté(e); **~moded** [aʊt'məʊdɪd] adj démodé(e); dépassé(e); **~number** [aʊt'nʌmbə*] vt surpasser en nombre

out-of-date [aʊtəv'deɪt] adj (passport) périmé(e); (theory etc) dépassé(e); (clothes etc) démodé(e)

out-of-the-way [aʊtəvðə'weɪ] adj (place) loin de tout

outpatient ['aʊtpeɪʃənt] n malade m/f en consultation externe

outpost ['aʊtpəʊst] n avant-poste m

output ['aʊtpʊt] n rendement m, production f; (COMPUT) sortie f

outrage ['aʊtreɪdʒ] n (anger) indignation f; (violent act) atrocité f; (scandal) scandale m ♦ vt outrager; **~ous** [aʊt'reɪdʒəs] adj atroce; scandaleux(euse)

outright [adv 'aʊtraɪt, adj aʊt'raɪt] adv complètement; (deny, refuse) catégoriquement; (ask) carrément; (kill) sur le coup ♦ adj complet(ète); catégorique

outset ['aʊtset] n début m

outside ['aʊt'saɪd] n extérieur m ♦ adj extérieur(e) ♦ adv (au) dehors, à l'extérieur ♦ prep hors de, à l'extérieur de; **at the ~** (fig) au plus or maximum; **~ lane** n (AUT: in Britain) voie f de droite; (: in US, Europe) voie de gauche; **~ line** n (TEL) ligne extérieure; **~r** n (stranger) étranger(ère)

out: **~size** ['aʊtsaɪz] adj énorme; (clothes) grande taille inv; **~skirts** ['aʊtskɜːts] npl faubourgs mpl; **~spoken** [aʊt'spəʊkən] adj très franc(franche)

outstanding [aʊt'stændɪŋ] adj remarquable, exceptionnel(le); (unfinished) en suspens; (debt) impayé(e); (problem) non réglé(e)

outstay [aʊt'steɪ] vt: **to ~ one's welcome** abuser de l'hospitalité de son hôte

out: **~stretched** ['aʊtstretʃt] adj (hand) tendu(e); **~strip** [aʊt'strɪp] vt (competitors, demand) dépasser; **~ tray** n courrier m "départ"

outward ['aʊtwəd] adj (sign, appearances) extérieur(e); (journey) (d')aller; **~ly** adv extérieurement; en apparence

outweigh [aʊt'weɪ] vt l'emporter sur

outwit [aʊt'wɪt] vt se montrer plus malin que

oval ['əʊvəl] adj ovale ♦ n ovale m

ovary ['əʊvərɪ] n ovaire m

oven ['ʌvn] n four m; **~proof** adj allant au four

over ['əʊvə*] adv (par-)dessus ♦ adj (finished) fini(e), terminé(e); (too much) en plus ♦ prep sur; par-dessus; (above) au-dessus de; (on the other side of) de l'autre côté de; (more than) plus de; (during) pendant; **~ here** ici; **~ there** là-bas; **all ~** (everywhere) partout; (finished) fini(e); **~ and ~ (again)** à plusieurs reprises; **~ and above** en plus de; **to ask sb ~** inviter qn (à passer)

overall [adj, n 'əʊvərɔːl, adv əʊvər'ɔːl] adj (length, cost etc) total(e); (study) d'ensemble ♦ n (BRIT) blouse f ♦ adv dans l'ensemble, en général; **~s** npl bleus mpl (de travail)

overawe [əʊvər'ɔː] vt impressionner

over: **~balance** [əʊvə'bæləns] vi basculer; **~bearing** [əʊvə'beərɪŋ] adj impérieux(euse), autoritaire; **~board** ['əʊvəbɔːd] adv (NAUT) par-dessus bord; **~book** [əʊvə'bʊk] vt faire du surbooking; **~cast** ['əʊvəkɑːst] adj couvert(e)

overcharge ['əʊvə'tʃɑːdʒ] vt: **to ~ sb for sth** faire payer qch trop cher à qn

overcoat ['əʊvəkəʊt] n pardessus m

overcome [əʊvə'kʌm] (irreg) vt (defeat) triompher de; (difficulty) surmonter

overcrowded [əʊvə'kraʊdɪd] adj bondé(e)

overdo [əʊvə'duː] (irreg) vt exagérer; (overcook) trop cuire; **to ~ it** (work etc) se surmener

overdose ['əʊvədəʊs] n dose excessive

overdraft ['əʊvədrɑːft] n découvert m;

overdrawn [əʊvə'drɔːn] adj (account) à découvert; (person) dont le compte est à découvert

overdue ['əʊvə'djuː] adj en retard; (change, reform) qui tarde

overestimate [əʊvər'estɪmeɪt] vt surestimer

overexcited [əʊvərɪk'saɪtɪd] adj surexcité(e)

overflow [vb əʊvə'fləʊ, n 'əʊvəfləʊ] vi déborder ♦ n (also: ~ pipe) tuyau m d'écoulement, trop-plein m

overgrown ['əʊvə'grəʊn] adj (garden) envahi(e) par la végétation

overhaul [vb əʊvə'hɔːl, n 'əʊvəhɔːl] vt réviser ♦ n révision f

overhead [adv əʊvə'hed, adj, n 'əʊvəhed] adv au-dessus ♦ adj aérien(ne); (lighting) vertical(e) ♦ n (US) = ~s; ~s npl (expenses) frais généraux

overhear [əʊvə'hɪə*] (irreg) vt entendre (par hasard)

overheat [əʊvə'hiːt] vi (engine) chauffer

overjoyed [əʊvə'dʒɔɪd] adj: ~ (at) ravi(e) (de), enchanté(e) (de)

overkill ['əʊvəkɪl] n: that would be ~ ce serait trop

overland adj, adv par voie de terre

overlap [vb əʊvə'læp, n 'əʊvəlæp] vi se chevaucher

overleaf [əʊvə'liːf] adv au verso

overload ['əʊvə'ləʊd] vt surcharger

overlook [əʊvə'lʊk] vt (have view of) donner sur; (miss: by mistake) oublier; (forgive) fermer les yeux sur

overnight [adv 'əʊvə'naɪt, adj 'əʊvənaɪt] adv (happen) durant la nuit; (fig) soudain ♦ adj d'une (or de) nuit; **he stayed there ~** il y a passé la nuit

overpass n pont autoroutier

overpower [əʊvə'paʊə*] vt vaincre; (fig) accabler; **~ing** adj (heat, stench) suffocant(e)

overrate ['əʊvə'reɪt] vt surestimer

override [əʊvə'raɪd] (irreg: like **ride**) vt (order, objection) passer outre à; **overriding** [əʊvə'raɪdɪŋ] adj prépondérant(e)

overrule [əʊvə'ruːl] vt (decision) annuler; (claim) rejeter; (person) rejeter l'avis de

overrun [əʊvə'rʌn] (irreg: like **run**) vt (country) occuper; (time limit) dépasser

overseas ['əʊvə'siːz] adv outre-mer; (abroad) à l'étranger ♦ adj (trade) extérieur(e); (visitor) étranger(ère)

overshadow [əʊvə'ʃædəʊ] vt (fig) éclipser

oversight ['əʊvəsaɪt] n omission f, oubli m

oversleep ['əʊvə'sliːp] (irreg) vi se réveiller (trop) tard

overstate vt exagérer

overstep ['əʊvə'step] vt: **to ~ the mark** dépasser la mesure

overt [əʊ'vɜːt] adj non dissimulé(e)

overtake [əʊvə'teɪk] (irreg) vt (AUT) dépasser, doubler

overthrow [əʊvə'θrəʊ] (irreg) vt (government) renverser

overtime ['əʊvətaɪm] n heures fpl supplémentaires

overtone ['əʊvətəʊn] n (also: ~s) note f, sous-entendus mpl

overture ['əʊvətʃʊə*] n (MUS, fig) ouverture f

overturn [əʊvə'tɜːn] vt renverser ♦ vi se retourner

overweight ['əʊvə'weɪt] adj (person) trop gros(se)

overwhelm [əʊvə'welm] vt (subj: emotion) accabler; (enemy, opponent) écraser; **~ing** adj (victory, defeat) écrasant(e); (desire) irrésistible

overwork ['əʊvə'wɜːk] n surmenage m

overwrought ['əʊvə'rɔːt] adj excédé(e)

owe [əʊ] vt: **to ~ sb sth, to ~ sth to sb** devoir qch à qn; **owing to** ['əʊɪŋ-] prep à cause de, en raison de

owl [aʊl] n hibou m

own [əʊn] vt posséder ♦ adj propre; **a room of my ~** une chambre à moi, ma propre chambre; **to get one's ~ back** prendre sa revanche; **on one's ~** tout(e) seul(e); **~ up** vi avouer; **~er** n propriétaire m/f, **~ership** n possession f

ox [ɒks] (pl **oxen**) n bœuf m

oxtail ['ɒksteɪl] n: **~ soup** soupe f à la queue de bœuf

oxygen ['ɒksɪdʒən] n oxygène m; **~ mask** n masque m à oxygène

oyster ['ɔɪstə*] n huître f

oz. abbr = **ounce(s)**

ozone hole n trou m d'ozone

ozone layer n couche f d'ozone

P p

p [piː] abbr = **penny**; **pence**
PA n abbr = **personal assistant**; **public address system**
pa [pɑː] (inf) n papa m
p.a. abbr = **per annum**
pace [peɪs] n pas m; (speed) allure f; vitesse f ♦ vi: **to ~ up and down** faire les cent pas; **to keep ~ with** aller à la même vitesse que; **~maker** n (MED) stimulateur m cardiaque; (SPORT: also: pacesetter) meneur(euse) de train
Pacific n: **the ~ (Ocean)** le Pacifique, l'océan m Pacifique
pack [pæk] n (packet; US: of cigarettes) paquet m; (of hounds) meute f; (of thieves etc) bande f; (back pack) sac m à dos; (of cards) jeu m ♦ vt (goods) empaqueter, emballer; (box) remplir; (cram) entasser; **to ~ one's suitcase** faire sa valise; **to ~ (one's bags)** faire ses bagages; **to ~ sb off** to expédier qn à; **~ it in!** laisse tomber!, écrase!
package ['pækɪdʒ] n paquet m; (also: ~ deal) forfait m; **~ tour** (BRIT) n voyage organisé
packed lunch ['pækt-] (BRIT) n repas froid
packet ['pækɪt] n paquet m
packing ['pækɪŋ] n emballage m; **~ case** n caisse f (d'emballage)
pact [pækt] n pacte m; traité m
pad [pæd] n bloc(-notes) m; (to prevent friction) tampon m; (inf: home) piaule f ♦ vt rembourrer; **~ding** n rembourrage m
paddle ['pædl] n (oar) pagaie f; (US: for table tennis) raquette f de ping-pong ♦ vt: **to ~ a canoe** etc pagayer ♦ vi barboter, faire trempette; **~ steamer** n bateau m à aubes; **paddling pool** (BRIT) n petit bassin
paddock ['pædək] n enclos m; (RACING) paddock m
paddy field ['pædɪ-] n rizière f
padlock ['pædlɒk] n cadenas m

paediatrics [piːdɪ'ætrɪks] (US **pediatrics**) n pédiatrie f
pagan ['peɪgən] adj, n païen(ne)
page [peɪdʒ] n (of book) page f; (also: ~ boy) groom m, chasseur m; (at wedding) garçon m d'honneur♦ vt (in hotel etc) (faire) appeler
pageant ['pædʒənt] n spectacle m historique; **~ry** n apparat m, pompe f
pager ['peɪdʒə*], **paging device** ['peɪdʒɪŋ-] n (TEL) récepteur m d'appels
paid [peɪd] pt, pp of **pay** ♦ adj (work, official) rémunéré(e); (holiday) payé(e); **to put ~ to** (BRIT) mettre fin à, régler; **~ gunman** n tueur m à gages
pail [peɪl] n seau m
pain [peɪn] n douleur f; **to be in ~** souffrir, avoir mal; **to take ~s to do** se donner du mal pour faire; **~ed** adj peiné(e), chagrin(e); **~ful** adj douloureux(euse); (fig) difficile, pénible; **~fully** adv (fig: very) terriblement; **~killer** n analgésique m; **~less** adj indolore
painstaking ['peɪnzteɪkɪŋ] adj (person) soigneux(euse); (work) soigné(e)
paint [peɪnt] n peinture f ♦ vt peindre; **to ~ the door blue** peindre la porte en bleu; **~brush** n pinceau m; **~er** n peintre m; **~ing** n peinture f; (picture) tableau m; **~work** n peinture f
pair [peə*] n (of shoes, gloves etc) paire f; (of people) couple m; **~ of scissors** (paire de) ciseaux mpl; **~ of trousers** pantalon m
pajamas [pə'dʒɑːməz] (US) npl pyjama(s) m(pl)
Pakistan [pɑːkɪ'stɑːn] n Pakistan m; **~i** adj pakistanais(e) ♦ n Pakistanais(e)
pal [pæl] (inf) n copain(copine)
palace ['pæləs] n palais m
palatable ['pælətəbl] adj bon(bonne), agréable au goût
palate ['pælɪt] n palais m (ANAT)
pale [peɪl] adj pâle ♦ n: **beyond the ~** (behaviour) inacceptable; **to grow ~** pâlir
Palestine ['pælɪstaɪn] n Palestine f; **Palestinian** [pæləs'tɪnɪən] adj palestinien(ne) ♦ n Palestinien(ne)

palette ['pælɪt] *n* palette *f*

pall [pɔ:l] *n* (*of smoke*) voile *m* ♦ *vi* devenir lassant(e)

pallet ['pælɪt] *n* (*for goods*) palette *f*

pallid ['pælɪd] *adj* blême

palm [pɑ:m] *n* (*of hand*) paume *f*; (*also*: ~ *tree*) palmier *m* ♦ *vt*: **to ~ sth off on sb** (*inf*) refiler qch à qn; **P~ Sunday** *n* le dimanche des Rameaux

palpable ['pælpəbl] *adj* évident(e), manifeste

paltry ['pɔ:ltrɪ] *adj* dérisoire

pamper ['pæmpə*] *vt* gâter, dorloter

pamphlet ['pæmflət] *n* brochure *f*

pan [pæn] *n* (*also*: *sauce~*) casserole *f*; (: *frying ~*) poêle *f*

pancake ['pænkeɪk] *n* crêpe *f*

panda ['pændə] *n* panda *m*; ~ **car** (*BRIT*) *n* ≈ voiture *f* pie *inv* (*de police*)

pandemonium [pændɪ'məunɪəm] *n* tohu-bohu *m*

pander ['pændə*] *vi*: **to ~ to** flatter bassement; obéir servilement à

pane [peɪn] *n* carreau *m*, vitre *f*

panel ['pænl] *n* (*of wood, cloth etc*) panneau *m*; (*RADIO, TV*) experts *mpl*; (*for interview, exams*) jury *m*; **~ling** (*US* **~ing**) *n* boiseries *fpl*

pang [pæŋ] *n*: **~s of remorse/jealousy** affres *mpl* du remords/de la jalousie; **~s of hunger/conscience** tiraillements *mpl* d'estomac/de la conscience

panic ['pænɪk] *n* panique *f*, affolement *m* ♦ *vi* s'affoler, paniquer; **~ky** *adj* (*person*) qui panique *or* s'affole facilement; **~-stricken** *adj* affolé(e)

pansy ['pænzɪ] *n* (*BOT*) pensée *f*; (*inf*: *pej*) tapette *f*, pédé *m*

pant [pænt] *vi* haleter

panther ['pænθə*] *n* panthère *f*

panties ['pæntɪz] *npl* slip *m*

pantomime ['pæntəmaɪm] (*BRIT*) *n* spectacle *m* de Noël

pantry ['pæntrɪ] *n* garde-manger *m inv*

pants [pænts] *npl* (*BRIT*: *woman's*) slip *m*; (: *man's*) slip, caleçon *m*; (*US*: *trousers*) pantalon *m*

pantyhose ['pæntɪhəʊz] (*US*) *npl* collant *m*

paper ['peɪpə*] *n* papier *m*; (*also*: *wall~*) papier peint; (: *news~*) journal *m*; (*academic essay*) article *m*; (*exam*) épreuve écrite ♦ *adj* en *or* de papier ♦ *vt* tapisser (de papier peint); **~s** *npl* (*also*: *identity ~s*) papiers (d'identité); **~back** *n* livre *m* de poche; livre broché *or* non relié; **~ bag** *n* sac *m* en papier; **~ clip** *n* trombone *m*; **~ hankie** *n* mouchoir *m* en papier; **~weight** *n* presse-papiers *m inv*; **~work** *n* papiers *mpl*; (*pej*) paperasserie *f*

par [pɑ:*] *n* pair *m*; (*GOLF*) normale *f* du parcours; **on a ~ with** à égalité avec, au même niveau que

parable ['pærəbl] *n* parabole *f* (*REL*)

parachute ['pærəʃu:t] *n* parachute *m*

parade [pə'reɪd] *n* défilé *m* ♦ *vt* (*fig*) faire étalage de ♦ *vi* défiler

paradise ['pærədaɪs] *n* paradis *m*

paradox ['pærədɔks] *n* paradoxe *m*; **~ically** [pærə'dɔksɪkəlɪ] *adv* paradoxalement

paraffin ['pærəfɪn] (*BRIT*) *n* (*also*: ~ *oil*) pétrole (lampant)

paragon ['pærəgən] *n* modèle *m*

paragraph ['pærəgrɑ:f] *n* paragraphe *m*

parallel ['pærəlel] *adj* parallèle; (*fig*) semblable ♦ *n* (*line*) parallèle *f*; (*fig*, *GEO*) parallèle *m*

paralyse ['pærəlaɪz] (*BRIT*) *vt* paralyser

paralysis [pə'ræləsɪs] *n* paralysie *f*

paralyze ['pærəlaɪz] (*US*) *vt* = **paralyse**

paramount ['pærəmaʊnt] *adj*: **of ~ importance** de la plus haute *or* grande importance

paranoid ['pærənɔɪd] *adj* (*PSYCH*) paranoïaque

paraphernalia ['pærəfə'neɪlɪə] *n* attirail *m*

parasol ['pærəsɔl] *n* ombrelle *f*; (*over table*) parasol *m*

paratrooper ['pærətru:pə*] *n* parachutiste *m* (*soldat*)

parcel ['pɑ:sl] *n* paquet *m*, colis *m* ♦ *vt* (*also*: ~ *up*) empaqueter

parch [pɑ:tʃ] *vt* dessécher; **~ed** *adj* (*person*) assoiffé(e)

parchment ['pɑ:tʃmənt] *n* parchemin *m*

pardon ['pɑːdn] *n* pardon *m*; grâce *f* ♦ *vt* pardonner à; ~ **me!, I beg your** ~! pardon!, je suis désolé!; **(I beg your)** ~?, (*US*) ~ **me?** pardon?

parent ['pɛərənt] *n* père *m or* mère *f*; ~**s** *npl* parents *mpl*

Paris ['pærɪs] *n* Paris

parish ['pærɪʃ] *n* paroisse *f*; (*BRIT*: *civil*) ≈ commune *f*

Parisian [pə'rɪzɪən] *adj* parisien(ne) ♦ *n* Parisien(ne)

park [pɑːk] *n* parc *m*, jardin public ♦ *vt* garer ♦ *vi* se garer

parking ['pɑːkɪŋ] *n* stationnement *m*; **"no** ~**"** "stationnement interdit"; ~ **lot** (*US*) *n* parking *m*, parc *m* de stationnement; ~ **meter** *n* parcomètre *m*; ~ **ticket** *n* P.V. *m*

parlance ['pɑːləns] *n* langage *m*

parliament ['pɑːləmənt] *n* parlement *m*; ~**ary** [pɑːlə'mɛntərɪ] *adj* parlementaire

parlour ['pɑːlə*] (*US* **parlor**) *n* salon *m*

parochial [pə'rəʊkɪəl] (*pej*) *adj* à l'esprit de clocher

parody ['pærədɪ] *n* parodie *f*

parole [pə'rəʊl] *n*: **on** ~ en liberté conditionnelle

parrot ['pærət] *n* perroquet *m*

parry ['pærɪ] *vt* (*blow*) esquiver

parsley ['pɑːslɪ] *n* persil *m*

parsnip ['pɑːsnɪp] *n* panais *m*

parson ['pɑːsn] *n* ecclésiastique *m*; (*Church of England*) pasteur *m*

part [pɑːt] *n* partie *f*; (*of machine*) pièce *f*; (*THEATRE etc*) rôle *m*; (*of serial*) épisode *m*; (*US*: *in hair*) raie *f* ♦ *adv* = **partly** ♦ *vt* séparer ♦ *vi* (*people*) se séparer; (*crowd*) s'ouvrir; **to take** ~ **in** participer à, prendre part à; **to take sth in good** ~ prendre qch du bon côté; **to take sb's** ~ prendre le parti de qn, prendre parti pour qn; **for my** ~ en ce qui me concerne; **for the most** ~ dans la plupart des cas; ~ **with** *vt fus* se séparer de; ~ **exchange** (*BRIT*) *n*: **in** ~ **exchange** en reprise

partial ['pɑːʃəl] *adj* (*not complete*) partiel(le); **to be** ~ **to** avoir un faible pour

participate [pɑː'tɪsɪpeɪt] *vi*: **to** ~ (**in**)

participer (à), prendre part (à); **participation** [pɑːtɪsɪ'peɪʃən] *n* participation *f*

participle ['pɑːtɪsɪpl] *n* participe *m*

particle ['pɑːtɪkl] *n* particule *f*

particular [pə'tɪkjʊlə*] *adj* particulier(ère); (*special*) spécial(e); (*fussy*) difficile; méticuleux(euse); ~**s** *npl* (*details*) détails *mpl*; (*personal*) nom, adresse *etc*; **in** ~ en particulier; ~**ly** *adv* particulièrement

parting ['pɑːtɪŋ] *n* séparation *f*; (*BRIT*: *in hair*) raie *f* ♦ *adj* d'adieu

partisan [pɑːtɪ'zæn] *n* partisan(e) ♦ *adj* partisan(e); de parti

partition [pɑː'tɪʃən] *n* (*wall*) cloison *f*; (*POL*) partition *f*, division *f*

partly ['pɑːtlɪ] *adv* en partie, partiellement

partner ['pɑːtnə*] *n* partenaire *m/f*; (*in marriage*) conjoint(e); (*boyfriend, girlfriend*) ami(e); (*COMM*) associé(e); (*at dance*) cavalier(ère); ~**ship** *n* association *f*

partridge ['pɑːtrɪdʒ] *n* perdrix *f*

part-time ['pɑːt'taɪm] *adj, adv* à mi-temps, à temps partiel

party ['pɑːtɪ] *n* (*POL*) parti *m*; (*group*) groupe *m*; (*LAW*) partie *f*; (*celebration*) réception *f*, soirée *f*; fête *f* ♦ *cpd* (*POL*) de *or* du parti; ~ **dress** *n* robe habillée; ~ **line** *n* (*TEL*) ligne partagée

pass [pɑːs] *vt* passer; (*place*) passer devant; (*friend*) croiser; (*overtake*) dépasser; (*exam*) être reçu(e) à, réussir; (*approve*) approuver, accepter ♦ *vi* passer; (*SCOL*) être reçu(e) *or* admis(e), réussir ♦ *n* (*permit*) laissez-passer *m inv*; carte *f* d'accès *or* d'abonnement; (*in mountains*) col *m*; (*SPORT*) passe *f*; (*SCOL*: *also*: ~ **mark**): **to get a** ~ être reçu(e) (sans mention); **to make a** ~ **at sb** (*inf*) faire des avances à qn; ~ **away** *vi* mourir; ~ **by** *vi* passer ♦ *vt* négliger; ~ **on** *vt* (*news, object*) transmettre; (*illness*) passer; ~ **out** *vi* s'évanouir; ~ **up** *vt* (*opportunity*) laisser passer; ~**able** *adj* (*road*) praticable; (*work*) acceptable

passage ['pæsɪdʒ] *n* (*also*: ~**way**) couloir *m*; (*gen, in book*) passage *m*; (*by*

boat) traversée *f*
passbook ['pɑːsbʊk] *n* livret *m*
passenger ['pæsɪndʒə*] *n* passager(ère)
passer-by ['pɑːsə'baɪ] (*pl* **~s-by**) *n* passant(e)
passing ['pɑːsɪŋ] *adj* (*fig*) passager(ère); **in ~** en passant
passing place *n* (*AUT*) aire *f* de croisement
passion ['pæʃən] *n* passion *f*; **~ate** *adj* passionné(e)
passive ['pæsɪv] *adj* (*also LING*) passif(ive); **~ smoking** *n* tabagisme *m* passif
Passover ['pɑːsəʊvə*] *n* Pâque *f* (*juive*)
passport ['pɑːspɔːt] *n* passeport *m*; **~ control** *n* contrôle *m* des passeports
password ['pɑːswɜːd] *n* mot *m* de passe
past [pɑːst] *prep* (*in front of*) devant; (*further than*) au delà de, plus loin que; après; (*later than*) après ♦ *adj* passé(e); (*president etc*) ancien(ne) ♦ *n* passé *m*; **he's ~ forty** il a dépassé la quarantaine, il a plus de *or* passé quarante ans; **for the ~ few/3 days** depuis quelques/3 jours; ces derniers/3 derniers jours; **ten/quarter ~ eight** huit heures dix/un *or* et quart
pasta ['pæstə] *n* pâtes *fpl*
paste [peɪst] *n* pâte *f*; (*meat ~*) pâté *m* (à tartiner); (*tomato ~*) purée *f*, concentré *m*; (*glue*) colle *f* (de pâte) ♦ *vt* coller
pasteurized ['pæstəraɪzd] *adj* pasteurisé(e)
pastille ['pæstl] *n* pastille *f*
pastime ['pɑːstaɪm] *n* passe-temps *m inv*
pastry ['peɪstrɪ] *n* pâte *f*; (*cake*) pâtisserie *f*
pasture ['pɑːstʃə*] *n* pâturage *m*
pasty [*n* 'pæstɪ, *adj* 'peɪstɪ] *n* petit pâté (en croûte) ♦ *adj* (*complexion*) terreux(euse)
pat [pæt] *vt* tapoter; (*dog*) caresser
patch [pætʃ] *n* (*of material*) pièce *f*; (*eye ~*) cache *m*; (*spot*) tache *f*; (*on tyre*) rustine *f* ♦ *vt* (*clothes*) rapiécer; (**to go through**) **a bad ~** (passer par) une période difficile; **~ up** *vt* réparer (grossièrement); **to ~ up a quarrel** se rac-

commoder; **~y** *adj* inégal(e); (*incomplete*) fragmentaire
pâté ['pætei] *n* pâté *m*, terrine *f*
patent ['peɪtənt] *n* brevet *m* (d'invention) ♦ *vt* faire breveter ♦ *adj* patent(e), manifeste; **~ leather** *n* cuir verni
paternal [pə'tɜːnl] *adj* paternel(le)
path [pɑːθ] *n* chemin *m*, sentier *m*; (*in garden*) allée *f*; (*trajectory*) trajectoire *f*
pathetic [pə'θetɪk] *adj* (*pitiful*) pitoyable; (*very bad*) lamentable, minable
pathological [pæθə'lɒdʒɪkl] *adj* pathologique
pathos ['peɪθɒs] *n* pathétique *m*
pathway ['pɑːθwei] *n* sentier *m*, passage *m*
patience ['peɪʃəns] *n* patience *f*; (*BRIT: CARDS*) réussite *f*
patient ['peɪʃənt] *n* patient(e); malade *m/f* ♦ *adj* patient(e)
patriotic [pætrɪ'ɒtɪk] *adj* patriotique; (*person*) patriote
patrol [pə'trəʊl] *n* patrouille *f* ♦ *vt* patrouiller dans; **~ car** *n* voiture *f* de police; **~man** (*irreg*: *US*) *n* agent *m* de police
patron ['peɪtrən] *n* (*in shop*) client(e); (*of charity*) patron(ne); **~ of the arts** mécène *m*; **~ize** *vt* (*pej*) traiter avec condescendance; (*shop, club*) être (un) client *or* un habitué de
patter ['pætə*] *n* crépitement *m*, tapotement *m*; (*sales talk*) boniment *m*
pattern ['pætən] *n* (*design*) motif *m*; (*SEWING*) patron *m*
paunch [pɔːntʃ] *n* gros ventre, bedaine *f*
pauper ['pɔːpə*] *n* indigent(e)
pause [pɔːz] *n* pause *f*, arrêt *m* ♦ *vi* faire une pause, s'arrêter
pave [peɪv] *vt* paver, daller; **to ~ the way for** ouvrir la voie à; **~ment** ['peɪvmənt] (*BRIT*) *n* trottoir *m*
pavilion [pə'vɪlɪən] *n* pavillon *m*; tente *f*
paving ['peɪvɪŋ] *n* (*material*) pavé *m*, dalle *f*; **~ stone** *n* pavé *m*
paw [pɔː] *n* patte *f*
pawn [pɔːn] *n* (*CHESS, also fig*) pion *m* ♦ *vt* mettre en gage; **~broker** *n* prêteur *m* sur gages; **~shop** *n* mont-de-piété *m*

pay [peɪ] (*pt, pp* **paid**) *n* salaire *m*; paie *f* ♦ *vt* payer ♦ *vi* payer; (*be profitable*) être rentable; **to ~ attention (to)** prêter attention (à); **to ~ sb a visit** rendre visite à qn; **to ~ one's respects to sb** présenter ses respects à qn; **~ back** *vt* rembourser; **~ for** *vt fus* payer; **~ in** *vt* verser; **~ off** *vt* régler, acquitter; (*person*) rembourser ♦ *vi* (*scheme, decision*) se révéler payant(e); **~ up** *vt* (*money*) payer; **~able** *adj*: **~able to sb** (*cheque*) à l'ordre de qn; **~ee** [peɪˈiː] *n* bénéficiaire *m/f*; **~ envelope** (*US*) *n* = **pay packet**; **~ment** *n* paiement *m*; règlement *m*; **monthly ~ment** mensualité *f*; **~ packet** (*BRIT*) *n* paie *f*; **~ phone** *n* cabine *f* téléphonique, téléphone public; **~roll** *n* registre *m* du personnel; **~ slip** (*BRIT*) *n* bulletin *m* de paie; **~ television** *n* chaînes *fpl* payantes

PC *n abbr* = **personal computer**

p.c. *abbr* = **per cent**

pea [piː] *n* (petit) pois

peace [piːs] *n* paix *f*; (*calm*) calme *m*, tranquillité *f*; **~ful** *adj* paisible, calme

peach [piːtʃ] *n* pêche *f*

peacock [ˈpiːkɒk] *n* paon *m*

peak [piːk] *n* (*mountain*) pic *m*, cime *f*; (*of cap*) visière *f*; (*fig: highest level*) maximum *m*; (: *of career, fame*) apogée *m*; **~ hours** *npl* heures *fpl* de pointe

peal [piːl] *n* (*of bells*) carillon *m*; **~ of laughter** éclat *m* de rire

peanut [ˈpiːnʌt] *n* arachide *f*, cacahuète *f*

pear [pɛə*] *n* poire *f*

pearl [pɜːl] *n* perle *f*

peasant [ˈpezənt] *n* paysan(ne)

peat [piːt] *n* tourbe *f*

pebble [ˈpebl] *n* caillou *m*, galet *m*

peck [pek] *vt* (*also*: **~ at**) donner un coup de bec à ♦ *n* coup de bec; (*kiss*) bise *f*; **~ing order** *n* ordre *m* des préséances; **~ish** (*BRIT: inf*) *adj*: **I feel ~ish** je mangerais bien quelque chose

peculiar [pɪˈkjuːlɪə*] *adj* étrange, bizarre, curieux(euse); **~ to** particulier(ère) à

pedal [ˈpedl] *n* pédale *f* ♦ *vi* pédaler

pedantic [pɪˈdæntɪk] *adj* pédant(e)

peddler [ˈpedlə*] *n* (*of drugs*) revendeur(euse)

pedestal [ˈpedɪstl] *n* piédestal *m*

pedestrian [pɪˈdestrɪən] *n* piéton *m*; **~ crossing** (*BRIT*) *n* passage clouté

pediatrics [piːdɪˈætrɪks] (*US*) *n* = **paediatrics**

pedigree [ˈpedɪɡriː] *n* ascendance *f*; (*of animal*) pedigree *m* ♦ *cpd* (*animal*) de race

pee [piː] (*inf*) *vi* faire pipi, pisser

peek [piːk] *vi* jeter un coup d'œil (furtif)

peel [piːl] *n* pelure *f*, épluchure *f*; (*of orange, lemon*) écorce *f* ♦ *vt* peler, éplucher ♦ *vi* (*paint etc*) s'écailler; (*wallpaper*) se décoller; (*skin*) peler

peep [piːp] *n* (*BRIT: look*) coup d'œil furtif; (*sound*) pépiement *m* ♦ *vi* (*BRIT*) jeter un coup d'œil (furtif); **~ out** (*BRIT*) *vi* se montrer (furtivement); **~hole** *n* judas *m*

peer [pɪə*] *vi*: **to ~ at** regarder attentivement, scruter ♦ *n* (*noble*) pair *m*; (*equal*) pair, égal(e); **~age** *n* pairie *f*

peeved [piːvd] *adj* irrité(e), fâché(e)

peg [peg] *n* (*for coat etc*) patère *f*; (*BRIT: also: clothes ~*) pince *f* à linge

Peking [piːˈkɪŋ] *n* Pékin; **Peking(g)ese** [piːkɪˈniːz] *n* (*dog*) pékinois *m*

pelican [ˈpelɪkən] *n* pélican *m*; **~ crossing** (*BRIT*) *n* (*AUT*) feu *m* à commande manuelle

pellet [ˈpelɪt] *n* boulette *f*; (*of lead*) plomb *m*

pelt [pelt] *vt*: **to ~ sb (with)** bombarder qn (de) ♦ *vi* (*rain*) tomber à seaux; (*inf: run*) courir à toutes jambes ♦ *n* peau *f*

pelvis [ˈpelvɪs] *n* bassin *m*

pen [pen] *n* (*for writing*) stylo *m*; (*for sheep*) parc *m*

penal [ˈpiːnl] *adj* pénal(e); (*system, colony*) pénitentiaire; **~ize** *vt* pénaliser

penalty [ˈpenəltɪ] *n* pénalité *f*; sanction *f*; (*fine*) amende *f*; (*SPORT*) pénalisation *f*; (*FOOTBALL*) penalty *m*; (*RUGBY*) pénalité *f*

penance [ˈpenəns] *n* pénitence *f*

pence [pens] (*BRIT*) *npl of* **penny**

pencil [ˈpensl] *n* crayon *m*; **~ case** *n* trousse *f* (d'écolier); **~ sharpener** *n* taille-crayon(s) *m inv*

pendant ['pendənt] *n* pendentif *m*

pending ['pendɪŋ] *prep* en attendant ♦ *adj* en suspens

pendulum ['pendjʊləm] *n* (*of clock*) balancier *m*

penetrate ['penɪtreɪt] *vt* pénétrer dans; pénétrer

penfriend ['penfrend] (*BRIT*) *n* correspondant(e)

penguin ['peŋgwɪn] *n* pingouin *m*

penicillin [penɪ'sɪlɪn] *n* pénicilline *f*

peninsula [pɪ'nɪnsjʊlə] *n* péninsule *f*

penis ['piːnɪs] *n* pénis *m*, verge *f*

penitentiary [penɪ'tenʃərɪ] *n* prison *f*

penknife ['pennaɪf] *n* canif *m*

pen name *n* nom *m* de plume, pseudonyme *m*

penniless ['penɪləs] *adj* sans le sou

penny ['penɪ] (*pl* **pennies** *or* (*BRIT*) **pence**) *n* penny *m*; (*US*) = **cent**

penpal ['penpæl] *n* correspondant(e)

pension ['penʃən] *n* pension *f*, (*from company*) retraite *f*; ~**er** (*BRIT*) *n* retraité(e); ~ **fund** *n* caisse *f* de pension

Pentecost ['pentɪkɒst] *n* Pentecôte *f*

penthouse ['penthaʊs] *n* appartement *m* (de luxe) (en attique)

pent-up ['pentʌp] *adj* (*feelings*) refoulé(e)

penultimate [pɪ'nʌltɪmɪt] *adj* avant-dernier(ère)

people ['piːpl] *npl* gens *mpl*; personnes *fpl*; (*inhabitants*) population *f*; (*POL*) peuple *m* ♦ *n* (*nation, race*) peuple *m*; **several** ~ **came** plusieurs personnes sont venues; ~ **say that ...** on dit que ...

pep [pep] (*inf*) *n* entrain *m*, dynamisme *m*; ~ **up** *vt* remonter

pepper ['pepə*] *n* poivre *m*; (*vegetable*) poivron *m* ♦ *vt* (*fig*): **to ~ with** bombarder de; ~**mint** *n* (*sweet*) pastille *f* de menthe

peptalk ['peptɔːk] (*inf*) *n* (petit) discours d'encouragement

per [pɜː*] *prep* par; ~ **hour** (*miles etc*) à l'heure; (*fee*) (de) l'heure; ~ **kilo** *etc* le kilo *etc*; ~ **annum** *adv* par an; ~ **capita** *adj, adv* par personne, par habitant

perceive [pə'siːv] *vt* percevoir; (*notice*) remarquer, s'apercevoir de

per cent [pə'sent] *adv* pour cent

percentage [pə'sentɪdʒ] *n* pourcentage *m*

perception [pə'sepʃən] *n* perception *f*; (*insight*) perspicacité *f*

perceptive [pə'septɪv] *adj* pénétrant(e); (*person*) perspicace

perch [pɜːtʃ] *n* (*fish*) perche *f*; (*for bird*) perchoir *m* ♦ *vi*: **to ~ on** se percher sur

percolator ['pɜːkəleɪtə*] *n* cafetière *f* (électrique)

perennial [pə'renɪəl] *adj* perpétuel(le); (*BOT*) vivace

perfect [*adj, n* 'pɜːfɪkt, *vb* pə'fekt] *adj* parfait(e) ♦ *n* (*also*: ~ *tense*) parfait *m* ♦ *vt* parfaire; mettre au point; ~**ly** *adv* parfaitement

perforate ['pɜːfəreɪt] *vt* perforer, percer; **perforation** [pɜːfə'reɪʃən] *n* perforation *f*

perform [pə'fɔːm] *vt* (*carry out*) exécuter; (*concert etc*) jouer, donner ♦ *vi* jouer; ~**ance** *n* représentation *f*, spectacle *m*; (*of an artist*) interprétation *f*; (*SPORT*) performance *f*, (*of car, engine*) fonctionnement *m*; (*of company, economy*) résultats *mpl*; ~**er** *n* artiste *m/f*, interprète *m/f*

perfume ['pɜːfjuːm] *n* parfum *m*

perfunctory [pə'fʌŋktərɪ] *adj* négligent(e), pour la forme

perhaps [pə'hæps] *adv* peut-être

peril ['perɪl] *n* péril *m*

perimeter [pə'rɪmɪtə*] *n* périmètre *m*

period ['pɪərɪəd] *n* période *f*; (*HISTORY*) époque *f*; (*SCOL*) cours *m*; (*full stop*) point *m*; (*MED*) règles *fpl* ♦ *adj* (*costume, furniture*) d'époque; ~**ic(al)** [pɪərɪ'ɒdɪk(əl)] *adj* périodique; ~**ical** *n* périodique *m*

peripheral [pə'rɪfərəl] *adj* périphérique ♦ *n* (*COMPUT*) périphérique *m*

perish ['perɪʃ] *vi* périr; (*decay*) se détériorer; ~**able** *adj* périssable

perjury ['pɜːdʒərɪ] *n* parjure *m*, faux serment

perk [pɜːk] *n* avantage *m*; accessoire, à-côté *m*; ~ **up** *vi* (*cheer up*) se ragaillardir; ~**y** *adj* (*cheerful*) guilleret(te)

perm [pɜːm] *n* (*for hair*) permanente *f*

permanent ['pɜːmənənt] *adj* permanent(e)

permeate ['pɜːmɪeɪt] *vi* s'infiltrer ♦ *vt* s'infiltrer dans; pénétrer

permissible [pəˈmɪsəbl] *adj* permis(e), acceptable

permission [pəˈmɪʃən] *n* permission *f*, autorisation *f*

permissive [pəˈmɪsɪv] *adj* tolérant(e), permissif(ive)

permit [*n* 'pɜːmɪt, *vb* pəˈmɪt] *n* permis *m* ♦ *vt* permettre

perpendicular [pɜːpənˈdɪkjʊlə*] *adj* perpendiculaire

perplex [pəˈpleks] *vt* (*person*) rendre perplexe

persecute ['pɜːsɪkjuːt] *vt* persécuter

persevere [pɜːsɪˈvɪə*] *vi* persévérer

Persian ['pɜːʃən] *adj* persan(e) ♦ *n* (*LING*) persan *m*; **the ~ Gulf** le golfe Persique

persist [pəˈsɪst] *vi*: **to ~ (in doing)** persister *or* s'obstiner (à faire); **~ent** *adj* persistant(e), tenace

person ['pɜːsn] *n* personne *f*; **in ~** en personne; **~al** *adj* personnel(le); **~al assistant** *n* secrétaire privé(e); **~al call** *n* communication privée; **~al column** *n* annonces personnelles; **~al computer** *n* ordinateur personnel; **~ality** [pɜːsəˈnælɪtɪ] *n* personnalité *f*; **~ally** *adv* personnellement; **to take sth ~ally** se sentir visé(e) (par qch); **~al organizer** *n* filofax *m* (®); **~al stereo** *n* Walkman *m* (®), baladeur *m*

personnel [pɜːsəˈnel] *n* personnel *m*

perspective [pəˈspektɪv] *n* perspective *f*; **to get things into ~** faire la part des choses

Perspex ['pɜːspeks] (®) *n* plexiglas *m* (®)

perspiration [pɜːspəˈreɪʃən] *n* transpiration *f*

persuade [pəˈsweɪd] *vt*: **to ~ sb to do sth** persuader qn de faire qch

persuasion [pəˈsweɪʒən] *n* persuasion *f*; (*creed*) réligion *f*

pertaining [pɜːˈteɪnɪŋ]: **~ to** *prep* relatif(ive) à

peruse [pəˈruːz] *vt* lire (attentivement)

pervade [pɜːˈveɪd] *vt* se répandre dans, envahir

perverse [pəˈvɜːs] *adj* pervers(e); (*contrary*) contrariant(e); **pervert** [*n* 'pɜːvɜːt, *vb* pəˈvɜːt] *n* perverti(e) ♦ *vt* pervertir; (*words*) déformer

pessimist ['pesɪmɪst] *n* pessimiste *m/f*; **~ic** [pesɪˈmɪstɪk] *adj* pessimiste

pest [pest] *n* animal *m* (*or* insecte *m*) nuisible; (*fig*) fléau *m*

pester ['pestə*] *vt* importuner, harceler

pet [pet] *n* animal familier ♦ *cpd* (*favourite*) favori(te) ♦ *vt* (*stroke*) caresser, câliner ♦ *vi* (*inf*) se peloter; **teacher's ~** chouchou *m* du professeur; **~ hate** bête noire

petal ['petl] *n* pétale *m*

peter out ['piːtə-] *vi* (*stream, conversation*) tarir; (*meeting*) tourner court; (*road*) se perdre

petite [pəˈtiːt] *adj* menu(e)

petition [pəˈtɪʃən] *n* pétition *f*

petrified ['petrɪfaɪd] *adj* (*fig*) mort(e) de peur

petrol ['petrəl] (*BRIT*) *n* essence *f*; **two-star ~** essence *f* ordinaire; **four-star ~** super *m*; **~ can** *n* bidon *m* à essence

petroleum [pɪˈtrəʊlɪəm] *n* pétrole *m*

petrol: **~ pump** (*BRIT*) *n* pompe *f* à essence; **~ station** (*BRIT*) *n* station-service *f*; **~ tank** (*BRIT*) *n* réservoir *m* (d'essence)

petticoat ['petɪkəʊt] *n* combinaison *f*

petty ['petɪ] *adj* (*mean*) mesquin(e); (*unimportant*) insignifiant(e), sans importance; **~ cash** *n* caisse *f* des dépenses courantes; **~ officer** *n* second-maître *m*

petulant ['petjʊlənt] *adj* boudeur(euse), irritable

pew [pjuː] *n* banc *m* (d'église)

pewter ['pjuːtə*] *n* étain *m*

phantom ['fæntəm] *n* fantôme *m*

pharmacy ['fɑːməsɪ] *n* pharmacie *f*

phase [feɪz] *n* phase *f* ♦ *vt*: **to ~ sth in/out** introduire/supprimer qch progressivement

PhD *abbr* = **Doctor of Philosophy** *n* (*title*) ≈ docteur *m* (en droit *or* lettres *etc*) ≈ doctorat *m*; titulaire *m/f* d'un doctorat

pheasant ['feznt] *n* faisan *m*

phenomenon [fi'nɒmɪnən] (*pl* **phenomena**) *n* phénomène *m*

philosophical [fɪlə'sɒfɪkl] *adj* philosophique

philosophy [fɪ'lɒsəfɪ] *n* philosophie *f*

phobia ['fəʊbjə] *n* phobie *f*

phone [fəʊn] *n* téléphone *m* ♦ *vt* téléphoner; **to be on the ~** avoir le téléphone; (*be calling*) être au téléphone; **~ back** *vt*, *vi* rappeler; **~ up** *vt* téléphoner à ♦ *vi* téléphoner; **~ book** *n* annuaire *m*; **~ booth** *n* = **phone box**; **~ box** (*BRIT*) *n* cabine *f* téléphonique; **~ call** *n* coup *m* de fil *or* de téléphone; **~ card** *n* carte *f* de téléphone; **~-in** (*BRIT*) *n* (*RADIO, TV*) programme *m* à ligne ouverte

phonetics [fə'netɪks] *n* phonétique *f*

phoney ['fəʊnɪ] *adj* faux(fausse), factice; (*person*) pas franc(he), poseur(euse)

photo ['fəʊtəʊ] *n* photo *f*

photo...: ~copier [-kɒpɪə*] *n* photocopieuse *f*; **~copy** [-kɒpɪ] *n* photocopie *f* ♦ *vt* photocopier; **~graph** [-grɑːf] *n* photographie *f* ♦ *vt* photographier; **~grapher** [fə'tɒgrəfə*] *n* photographe *m/f*; **~graphy** [fə'tɒgrəfɪ] *n* photographie *f*

phrase [freɪz] *n* expression *f*; (*LING*) locution *f* ♦ *vt* exprimer; **~ book** *n* recueil *m* d'expressions (pour touristes)

physical ['fɪzɪkəl] *adj* physique; **~ education** *n* éducation *f* physique; **~ly** *adv* physiquement

physician [fɪ'zɪʃən] *n* médecin *m*

physicist ['fɪzɪsɪst] *n* physicien(ne)

physics ['fɪzɪks] *n* physique *f*

physiotherapy [fɪzɪə'θerəpɪ] *n* kinésithérapie *f*

physique [fɪ'ziːk] *n* physique *m*; constitution *f*

pianist ['pɪənɪst] *n* pianiste *m/f*

piano [pɪ'ænəʊ] *n* piano *m*

pick [pɪk] *n* (*tool: also: ~axe*) pic *m*, pioche *f* ♦ *vt* choisir; (*fruit etc*) cueillir; (*remove*) prendre; (*lock*) forcer; **take your ~** faites votre choix; **the ~ of** le(la) meilleur(e) de; **to ~ one's nose** se mettre les doigts dans le nez; **to ~ one's teeth** se curer les dents; **to ~ a quarrel with sb** chercher noise à qn; **~ at** *vt fus*: **to ~ at one's food** manger du bout des dents, chipoter; **~ on** *vt fus* (*person*) harceler; **~ out** *vt* choisir; (*distinguish*) distinguer; **~ up** *vi* (*improve*) s'améliorer ♦ *vt* ramasser; (*collect*) passer prendre; (*AUT: give lift to*) prendre, emmener; (*learn*) apprendre; (*RADIO*) capter; **to ~ up speed** prendre de la vitesse; **to ~ o.s. up** se relever

picket ['pɪkɪt] *n* (*in strike*) piquet *m* de grève ♦ *vt* mettre un piquet de grève devant

pickle ['pɪkl] *n* (*also: ~s: as condiment*) pickles *mpl*, petits légumes macérés dans du vinaigre ♦ *vt* conserver dans du vinaigre *or* dans de la saumure; **to be in a ~** (*mess*) être dans le pétrin

pickpocket ['pɪkpɒkɪt] *n* pickpocket *m*

pick-up ['pɪkʌp] *n* (*small truck*) pick-up *m inv*

picnic ['pɪknɪk] *n* pique-nique *m*

picture ['pɪktʃə*] *n* image *f*; (*painting*) peinture *f*, tableau *m*; (*etching*) gravure *f*; (*photograph*) photo(graphie) *f*; (*drawing*) dessin *m*; (*film*) film *m*; (*fig*) description *f*; tableau *m* ♦ *vt* se représenter; **the ~s** (*BRIT: inf*) le cinéma; **~ book** *n* livre *m* d'images

picturesque [pɪktʃə'resk] *adj* pittoresque

pie [paɪ] *n* tourte *f*; (*of fruit*) tarte *f*; (*of meat*) pâté *m* en croûte

piece [piːs] *n* morceau *m*; (*item*): **a ~ of furniture/advice** un meuble/conseil ♦ *vt*: **to ~ together** rassembler; **to take to ~s** démonter; **~meal** *adv* (*irregularly*) au coup par coup; (*bit by bit*) par bouts; **~ work** *n* travail *m* aux pièces

pie chart *n* graphique *m* circulaire, camembert *m*

pier [pɪə*] *n* jetée *f*

pierce [pɪəs] *vt* percer, transpercer

pig [pɪg] *n* cochon *m*, porc *m*

pigeon ['pɪdʒən] *n* pigeon *m*; **~hole** *n* casier *m*

piggy bank ['pɪgɪ-] *n* tirelire *f*

pig: ~headed [-'hedɪd] *adj* entêté(e), têtu(e); **~let** *n* porcelet *m*, petit cochon;

~skin [-skɪn] n peau m de porc; **~sty** [-staɪ] n porcherie f; **~tail** [-teɪl] n natte f, tresse f

pike [paɪk] n (*fish*) brochet m

pilchard ['pɪltʃəd] n pilchard m (*sorte de sardine*)

pile [paɪl] n (*pillar, of books*) pile f; (*heap*) tas m; (*of carpet*) poils mpl ♦ vt (*also*: ~ *up*) empiler, entasser ♦ vi (*also*: ~up) s'entasser, s'accumuler; **to ~ into** (*car*) s'entasser dans

piles [paɪlz] npl hémorroïdes fpl

pile-up ['paɪlʌp] n (AUT) télescopage m, collision f en série

pilfering ['pɪlfərɪŋ] n chapardage m

pilgrim ['pɪlgrɪm] n pèlerin m

pill [pɪl] n pilule f

pillage ['pɪlɪdʒ] vt piller

pillar ['pɪlə*] n pilier m; **~ box** (BRIT) n boîte f aux lettres (*publique*)

pillion ['pɪljən] n: **to ride ~** (*on motorcycle*) monter derrière

pillow ['pɪləʊ] n oreiller m; **~case** n taie f d'oreiller

pilot ['paɪlət] n pilote m ♦ cpd (*scheme etc*) pilote, expérimental(e) ♦ vt piloter; **~ light** n veilleuse f

pimp [pɪmp] n souteneur m, maquereau m

pimple ['pɪmpl] n bouton m

pin [pɪn] n épingle f; (TECH) cheville f ♦ vt épingler; **~s and needles** fourmis fpl; **to ~ sb down** (*fig*) obliger qn à répondre; **to ~ sth on sb** (*fig*) mettre qch sur le dos de qn

pinafore ['pɪnəfɔː*] n tablier m

pinball ['pɪnbɔːl] n flipper m

pincers ['pɪnsəz] npl tenailles fpl; (*of crab etc*) pinces fpl

pinch [pɪntʃ] n (*of salt etc*) pincée f ♦ vt pincer; (*inf: steal*) piquer, chiper; **at a ~** à la rigueur

pincushion ['pɪnkʊʃən] n pelote f à épingles

pine [paɪn] n (*also*: ~ *tree*) pin m ♦ vi: **to ~ for** s'ennuyer de, désirer ardemment; **~ away** vi dépérir

pineapple ['paɪnæpl] n ananas m

ping [pɪŋ] n (*noise*) tintement m; **~-pong**

(®) n ping-pong m (®)

pink [pɪŋk] adj rose ♦ n (*colour*) rose m; (BOT) œillet m, mignardise f

PIN (number) n code m confidentiel

pinpoint ['pɪnpɔɪnt] vt indiquer or localiser (*avec précision*); (*problem*) mettre le doigt sur

pint [paɪnt] n pinte f (BRIT = 0.57l; US = 0.47l); (BRIT: inf) ≈ demi m

pioneer [paɪə'nɪə*] n pionnier m

pious ['paɪəs] adj pieux(euse)

pip [pɪp] n (*seed*) pépin m; **the ~s** npl (BRIT: *time signal on radio*) le(s) top(s) sonore(s)

pipe [paɪp] n tuyau m, conduite f; (*for smoking*) pipe f ♦ vt amener par tuyau; **~s** npl (*also*: *bag~s*) cornemuse f; **~ down** (*inf*) vi se taire; **~ cleaner** n cure-pipe m; **~ dream** n chimère f, château m en Espagne; **~line** n pipe-line m; **~r** n joueur(euse) de cornemuse

piping ['paɪpɪŋ] adv: **~ hot** très chaud(e)

pique [piːk] n dépit m

pirate ['paɪərɪt] n pirate m

Pisces ['paɪsiːz] n les Poissons mpl

piss [pɪs] (*inf!*) vi pisser; **~ed** (*inf!*) adj (*drunk*) bourré(e)

pistol ['pɪstl] n pistolet m

piston ['pɪstən] n piston m

pit [pɪt] n trou m, fosse f; (*also*: *coal ~*) puits m de mine; (*quarry*) carrière f ♦ vt: **to ~ one's wits against sb** se mesurer à qn; **~s** npl (AUT) aire f de service

pitch [pɪtʃ] n (MUS) ton m; (BRIT: SPORT) terrain m; (*tar*) poix f; (*fig*) degré m; point m ♦ vt (*throw*) lancer ♦ vi (*fall*) tomber; **to ~ a tent** dresser une tente; **~-black** adj noir(e) (comme du cirage); **~ed battle** n bataille rangée

piteous ['pɪtɪəs] adj pitoyable

pitfall ['pɪtfɔːl] n piège m

pith [pɪθ] n (*of orange etc*) intérieur m de l'écorce

pithy ['pɪθɪ] adj piquant(e)

pitiful ['pɪtɪfʊl] adj (*touching*) pitoyable

pitiless ['pɪtɪləs] adj impitoyable

pittance ['pɪtəns] n salaire m de misère

pity ['pɪtɪ] n pitié f ♦ vt plaindre; **what a ~!** quel dommage!

pizza ['piːtsə] *n* pizza *f*
placard ['plækɑːd] *n* affiche *f*; (*in march*) pancarte *f*
placate [plə'keɪt] *vt* apaiser, calmer
place [pleɪs] *n* endroit *m*, lieu *m*; (*proper position, job, rank, seat*) place *f*; (*home*): **at/to his ~** chez lui ♦ *vt* (*object*) placer, mettre; (*identify*) situer; reconnaître; **to take ~** avoir lieu; **out of ~** (*not suitable*) déplacé(e), inopportun(e); **to change ~s with sb** changer de place avec qn; **in the first ~** d'abord, en premier
plague [pleɪg] *n* fléau *m*; (MED) peste *f* ♦ *vt* (*fig*) tourmenter
plaice [pleɪs] *n inv* carrelet *m*
plaid [plæd] *n* tissu écossais
plain [pleɪn] *adj* (*in one colour*) uni(e); (*simple*) simple; (*clear*) clair(e), évident(e); (*not handsome*) quelconque, ordinaire ♦ *adv* franchement, carrément ♦ *n* plaine *f*; **~ chocolate** *n* chocolat *m* à croquer; **~ clothes** *adj* (*police officer*) en civil; **~ly** *adv* clairement, (*frankly*) carrément, sans détours
plaintiff ['pleɪntɪf] *n* plaignant(e)
plait [plæt] *n* tresse *f*, natte *f*
plan [plæn] *n* plan *m*; (*scheme*) projet *m* ♦ *vt* (*think in advance*) projeter; (*prepare*) organiser; (*house*) dresser les plans de, concevoir ♦ *vi* faire des projets; **to ~ to do** prévoir de faire
plane [pleɪn] *n* (AVIAT) avion *m*; (ART, MATH *etc*) plan *m*; (*fig*) niveau *m*, plan; (*tool*) rabot *m*; (*also*: *~ tree*) platane *m* ♦ *vt* raboter
planet ['plænɪt] *n* planète *f*
plank [plæŋk] *n* planche *f*
planner ['plænə*] *n* planificateur(trice); (*town ~*) urbaniste *m/f*
planning ['plænɪŋ] *n* planification *f*; **family ~** planning familial; **~ permission** *n* permis *m* de construire
plant [plɑːnt] *n* plante *f*; (*machinery*) matériel *m*; (*factory*) usine *f* ♦ *vt* planter; (*bomb*) poser; (*microphone, incriminating evidence*) cacher
plaster ['plɑːstə*] *n* plâtre *m*; (*also*: *~ of Paris*) plâtre à mouler; (BRIT: *also*:

sticking ~) pansement adhésif ♦ *vt* plâtrer; (*cover*): **to ~ with** couvrir de; **~ed** (*inf*) *adj* soûl(e)
plastic ['plæstɪk] *n* plastique *m* ♦ *adj* (*made of ~*) en plastique; **~ bag** *n* sac *m* en plastique
Plasticine ['plæstɪsiːn] (®) *n* pâte *f* à modeler
plastic surgery *n* chirurgie *f* esthétique
plate [pleɪt] *n* (*dish*) assiette *f*; (*in book*) gravure *f*, planche *f*; (*dental ~*) dentier *m*
plateau ['plætəʊ] (*pl* **~s** *or* **~x**) *n* plateau *m*
plate glass *n* verre *m* (de vitrine)
platform ['plætfɔːm] *n* plate-forme *f*; (*at meeting*) tribune *f*; (*stage*) estrade *f*; (RAIL) quai *m*
platinum ['plætɪnəm] *n* platine *m*
platter ['plætə*] *n* plat *m*
plausible ['plɔːzɪbl] *adj* plausible; (*person*) convaincant(e)
play [pleɪ] *n* (THEATRE) pièce *f* (de théâtre) ♦ *vt* (*game*) jouer à; (*team, opponent*) jouer contre; (*instrument*) jouer de; (*part, piece of music, note*) jouer; (*record etc*) passer ♦ *vi* jouer; **to ~ safe** ne prendre aucun risque; **~ down** *vt* minimiser; **~ up** *vi* (*cause trouble*) faire des siennes; **~boy** *n* playboy *m*; **~er** *n* joueur(euse); (THEATRE) acteur(trice); (MUS) musicien(ne); **~ful** *adj* enjoué(e); **~ground** *n* cour *f* de récréation; (*in park*) aire *f* de jeux; **~group** *n* garderie *f*; **~ing card** *n* carte *f* à jouer; **~ing field** *n* terrain *m* de sport; **~mate** *n* camarade *m/f*, copain(copine) *f*; **~-off** *n* (SPORT) belle *f*; **~pen** *n* parc *m* (pour bébé); **~thing** *n* jouet *m*; **~time** *n* récréation *f*; **~wright** *n* dramaturge *m*
plc *abbr* (= *public limited company*) ≈ SARL *f*
plea [pliː] *n* (*request*) appel *m*; (LAW) défense *f*; **~ bargaining** *n* (LAW) négociations entre le procureur et l'avocat de la défense, incluant parfois le juge, pour réduire la gravité des charges
plead [pliːd] *vt* plaider; (*give as excuse*

invoquer ♦ *vi* (*LAW*) plaider; (*beg*): **to ~ with sb** implorer qn

pleasant ['plɛznt] *adj* agréable; **~ries** *npl* (*polite remarks*) civilités *fpl*

please [pli:z] *excl* s'il te (*or* vous) plaît ♦ *vt* plaire à ♦ *vi* plaire; (*think fit*): **do as you ~** faites comme il vous plaira; **~ yourself!** à ta (*or* votre) guise!; **~d** *adj*: **~d (with)** content(e) (de); **~d to meet you** enchanté (de faire votre connaissance); **pleasing** ['pli:zɪŋ] *adj* plaisant(e), qui fait plaisir

pleasure ['plɛʒə*] *n* plaisir *m*; **"it's a ~"** "je vous en prie"; **~ boat** *n* bateau *m* de plaisance

pleat [pli:t] *n* pli *m*

pledge [plɛdʒ] *n* (*promise*) promesse *f* ♦ *vt* engager; promettre

plentiful ['plɛntɪful] *adj* abondant(e), copieux(euse)

plenty ['plɛntɪ] *n*: **~ of** beaucoup de; (*bien*) assez de

pliable ['plaɪəbl] *adj* flexible; (*person*) malléable

pliers ['plaɪəz] *npl* pinces *fpl*

plight [plaɪt] *n* situation *f* critique

plimsolls ['plɪmsəlz] (*BRIT*) *npl* chaussures *fpl* de tennis, tennis *mpl*

plinth [plɪnθ] *n* (*of statue*) socle *m*

PLO *n abbr* (= *Palestine Liberation Organization*) OLP *f*

plod [plɒd] *vi* avancer péniblement; (*fig*) peiner

plonk [plɒŋk] (*inf*) *n* (*BRIT: wine*) pinard *m*, piquette *f* ♦ *vt*: **to ~ sth down** poser brusquement qch

plot [plɒt] *n* complot *m*, conspiration *f*; (*of story, play*) intrigue *f*; (*of land*) lot *m* de terrain, lopin *m* ♦ *vt* (*sb's downfall*) comploter; (*mark out*) pointer; relever, déterminer ♦ *vi* comploter

plough [plaʊ] (*US* **plow**) *n* charrue *f* ♦ *vt* (*earth*) labourer; **to ~ money into** investir dans; **~ through** *vt fus* (*snow etc*) avancer péniblement dans; **~man's lunch** (*BRIT*) *n* assiette froide avec du pain, du fromage et des pickles

ploy [plɔɪ] *n* stratagème *m*

pluck [plʌk] *vt* (*fruit*) cueillir; (*musical instrument*) pincer; (*bird*) plumer; (*eyebrow*) épiler ♦ *n* courage *m*, cran *m*; **to ~ up courage** prendre son courage à deux mains

plug [plʌg] *n* (*ELEC*) prise *f* de courant; (*stopper*) bouchon *m*, bonde *f*; (*AUT: also*: **spark(ing) ~**) bougie *f* ♦ *vt* (*hole*) boucher; (*inf: advertise*) faire du battage pour; **~ in** *vt* (*ELEC*) brancher

plum [plʌm] *n* (*fruit*) prune *f* ♦ *cpd*: **~ job** (*inf*) travail *m* en or

plumb [plʌm] *vt*: **to ~ the depths** (*fig*) toucher le fond (du désespoir)

plumber ['plʌmə*] *n* plombier *m*

plumbing ['plʌmɪŋ] *n* (*trade*) plomberie *f*; (*piping*) tuyauterie *f*

plummet ['plʌmɪt] *vi*: **to ~ (down)** plonger, dégringoler

plump [plʌmp] *adj* rondelet(te), dodu(e), bien en chair ♦ *vi*: **to ~ for** (*col: choose*) se décider pour

plunder ['plʌndə*] *n* pillage *m* (*loot*) butin *m* ♦ *vt* piller

plunge [plʌndʒ] *n* plongeon *m*; (*fig*) chute *f* ♦ *vt* plonger ♦ *vi* (*dive*) plonger (*fall*) tomber, dégringoler; **to take the ~** se jeter à l'eau; **~r** (*for drain*) (débouchoir *m* à) ventouse *f*; **plunging** *adj*: **plunging neckline** décolleté plongeant

pluperfect [plu:'pə:fɪkt] *n* plus-que-parfait *m*

plural ['pluərəl] *adj* pluriel(le) ♦ *n* pluriel *m*

plus [plʌs] *n* (*also*: **~ sign**) signe *m* plus ♦ *prep* plus; **ten/twenty ~** plus de dix/vingt

plush [plʌʃ] *adj* somptueux(euse)

ply [plaɪ] *vt* (*a trade*) exercer ♦ *vi* (*ship*) faire la navette ♦ *n* (*of wool, rope*) fil *m*, brin *m*; **to ~ sb with drink** donner continuellement à boire à qn; **to ~ sb with questions** presser qn de questions; **~wood** *n* contre-plaqué *m*

PM *abbr* = **Prime Minister**

p.m. *adv abbr* (= *post meridiem*) de l'après-midi

pneumatic drill [nju:'mætɪk-] *n* marteau-piqueur *m*

pneumonia [nju:'məʊnɪə] *n* pneumonie *f*

poach [pəʊtʃ] *vt* (*cook*) pocher; (*steal*) pêcher (*or* chasser) sans permis ♦ *vi* braconner; **~ed egg** *n* œuf poché; **~er** *n* braconnier *m*

P.O. box *n abbr* = **post office box**

pocket ['pɒkɪt] *n* poche *f* ♦ *vt* empocher; **to be out of ~** (*BRIT*) en être de sa poche; **~book** (*US*) *n* (*wallet*) portefeuille *m*; **~ knife** *n* canif *m*; **~ money** *n* argent *m* de poche

pod [pɒd] *n* cosse *f*

podgy ['pɒdʒɪ] *adj* rondelet(te)

podiatrist [pɒ'diːətrɪst] (*US*) *n* pédicure *m/f*, podologue *m/f*

poem ['pəʊəm] *n* poème *m*

poet ['pəʊɪt] *n* poète *m*; **~ic** [pəʊ'ɛtɪk] *adj* poétique; **~ laureate** *n* poète lauréat (*nommé par la Cour royal*); **~ry** *n* poésie *f*

poignant ['pɔɪnjənt] *adj* poignant(e); (*sharp*) vif(vive)

point [pɔɪnt] *n* point *m*; (*tip*) pointe *f*; (*in time*) moment *m*; (*in space*) endroit *m*; (*subject, idea*) point, sujet *m*; (*purpose*) sens *m*; (*ELEC*) prise *f*; (*also: decimal* ~): **2 ~ 3** (2.3) 2 virgule 3 (2,3) ♦ *vt* (*show*) indiquer; (*gun etc*): **to ~ sth at** braquer *or* diriger qch sur ♦ *vi*: **to ~ at** montrer du doigt; **~s** *npl* (*AUT*) vis platinées; (*RAIL*) aiguillage *m*; **to be on the ~ of doing sth** être sur le point de faire qch; **to make a ~ of doing** ne pas manquer de faire; **to get the ~** comprendre, saisir; **to miss the ~** ne pas comprendre; **to come to the ~** en venir au fait; **there's no ~ (in doing)** cela ne sert à rien (de faire); **~ out** *vt* faire remarquer, souligner; **~ to** *vt fus* (*fig*) indiquer; **~-blank** *adv* (*fig*) catégoriquement; (*also: at ~-blank range*) à bout portant; **~ed** *adj* (*shape*) pointu(e); (*remark*) plein(e) de sous-entendus; **~er** *n* (*needle*) aiguille *f*; (*piece of advice*) conseil *m*; (*clue*) indice *m*; **~less** *adj* inutile, vain(e); **~ of view** *n* point *m* de vue

poise [pɔɪz] *n* (*composure*) calme *m*

poison ['pɔɪzn] *n* poison *m* ♦ *vt* empoisonner; **~ous** *adj* (*snake*) venimeux(euse); (*plant*) vénéneux(euse);

(*fumes etc*) toxique

poke [pəʊk] *vt* (*fire*) tisonner; (*jab with finger, stick etc*) piquer; pousser du doigt; (*put*): **to ~ sth in(to)** fourrer *or* enfoncer qch dans; **~ about** *vi* fureter

poker ['pəʊkə*] *n* tisonnier *m*; (*CARDS*) poker *m*

poky ['pəʊkɪ] *adj* exigu(ë)

Poland ['pəʊlənd] *n* Pologne *f*

polar ['pəʊlə*] *adj* polaire; **~ bear** *n* ours blanc

Pole [pəʊl] *n* Polonais(e)

pole [pəʊl] *n* poteau *m*; (*of wood*) mât *m*, perche *f*; (*GEO*) pôle *m*; **~ bean** (*US*) *n* haricot *m* (à rames); **~ vault** *n* saut *m* à la perche

police [pə'liːs] *npl* police *f* ♦ *vt* maintenir l'ordre dans; **~ car** *n* voiture *f* de police; **~man** (*irreg*) *n* agent *m* de police, policier *m*; **~ station** *n* commissariat *m* de police; **~woman** (*irreg*) *n* femme-agent *f*

policy ['pɒlɪsɪ] *n* politique *f*; (*also: insurance* ~) police *f* (d'assurance)

polio ['pəʊlɪəʊ] *n* polio *f*

Polish ['pəʊlɪʃ] *adj* polonais(e) ♦ *n* (*LING*) polonais *m*

polish ['pɒlɪʃ] *n* (*for shoes*) cirage *m*; (*for floor*) cire *f*, encaustique *f*; (*shine*) éclat *m*, poli *m*; (*fig: refinement*) raffinement *m* ♦ *vt* (*put polish on shoes, wood*) cirer; (*make shiny*) astiquer, faire briller; **~ off** *vt* (*work*) expédier; (*food*) liquider; **~ed** *adj* (*fig*) raffiné(e)

polite [pə'laɪt] *adj* poli(e); **in ~ society** dans la bonne société; **~ness** *n* politesse *f*

political [pə'lɪtɪkəl] *adj* politique

politician [pɒlɪ'tɪʃən] *n* homme *m* politique, politicien *m*

politics ['pɒlɪtɪks] *npl* politique *f*

poll [pəʊl] *n* scrutin *m*, vote *m*; (*also: opinion* ~) sondage *m* (d'opinion) ♦ *vt* obtenir

pollen ['pɒlən] *n* pollen *m*

polling day ['pəʊlɪŋ-] (*BRIT*) *n* jour *m* des élections

polling station (*BRIT*) *n* bureau *m* de vote

pollute [pə'luːt] *vt* polluer; **pollution** *n* pollution *f*

polo ['pəʊləʊ] *n* polo *m*; **~-necked** *adj* à col roulé; **~ shirt** *n* polo *m*

poltergeist ['pɔltəgaɪst] *n* esprit frappeur

polyester [pɔlɪ'estə*] *n* polyester *m*

polytechnic [pɔlɪ'teknɪk] (*BRIT*) *n* (*college*) I.U.T. *m*, Institut *m* Universitaire de Technologie

polythene ['pɔlɪθiːn] *n* polyéthylène *m*; **~ bag** *n* sac *m* en plastique

pomegranate ['pɔmɪgrænɪt] *n* grenade *f*

pomp [pɔmp] *n* pompe *f*, faste *f*, apparat *m*; **~ous** ['pɔmpəs] *adj* pompeux(euse)

pond [pɔnd] *n* étang *m*; mare *f*

ponder ['pɔndə*] *vt* considérer, peser; **~ous** *adj* pesant(e), lourd(e)

pong [pɔŋ] (*BRIT*: *inf*) *n* puanteur *f*

pony ['pəʊnɪ] *n* poney *m*; **~tail** *n* queue *f* de cheval; **~ trekking** (*BRIT*) *n* randonnée *f* à cheval

poodle ['puːdl] *n* caniche *m*

pool [puːl] *n* (*of rain*) flaque *f*; (*pond*) mare *f*; (*also*: *swimming ~*) piscine *f*; (*billiards*) poule *f* ♦ *vt* mettre en commun; **~s** *npl* (*football pools*) ≈ loto sportif

poor [pʊə*] *adj* pauvre; (*mediocre*) médiocre, faible, mauvais(e) ♦ *npl*: **the ~** les pauvres *mpl*; **~ly** *adj* souffrant(e), malade ♦ *adv* mal; médiocrement

pop [pɔp] *n* (*MUS*) musique *f* pop; (*drink*) boisson gazeuse; (*US*: *inf*: *father*) papa *m*; (*noise*) bruit sec ♦ *vt* (*put*) mettre (rapidement) ♦ *vi* éclater; (*cork*) sauter; **~ in** *vi* entrer en passant; **~ out** *vi* sortir (brièvement); **~ up** *vi* apparaître, surgir

pope [pəʊp] *n* pape *m*

poplar ['pɔplə*] *n* peuplier *m*

popper ['pɔpə*] (*BRIT*: *inf*) *n* bouton-pression *m*

poppy ['pɔpɪ] *n* coquelicot *m*; pavot *m*

Popsicle ['pɔpsɪkl] (®: *US*) *n* esquimau *m* (*glace*)

popular ['pɔpjʊlə*] *adj* populaire; (*fashionable*) à la mode

population [pɔpjʊ'leɪʃən] *n* population *f*

porcelain ['pɔːslɪn] *n* porcelaine *f*

porch [pɔːtʃ] *n* porche *m*; (*US*) véranda *f*

porcupine ['pɔːkjʊpaɪn] *n* porc-épic *m*

pore [pɔː*] *n* pore *m* ♦ *vi*: **to ~ over** s'absorber dans, être plongé(e) dans

pork [pɔːk] *n* porc *m*

pornography [pɔː'nɔɡrəfɪ] *n* pornographie *f*

porpoise ['pɔːpəs] *n* marsouin *m*

porridge ['pɔrɪdʒ] *n* porridge *m*

port [pɔːt] *n* (*harbour*) port *m*; (*NAUT*: *left side*) bâbord *m*; (*wine*) porto *m*; **~ of call** escale *f*

portable ['pɔːtəbl] *adj* portatif(ive)

porter ['pɔːtə*] *n* (*for luggage*) porteur *m*; (*doorkeeper*) gardien(ne); portier *m*

portfolio [pɔːt'fəʊlɪəʊ] *n* portefeuille *m*; (*of artist*) portfolio *m*

porthole ['pɔːthəʊl] *n* hublot *m*

portion ['pɔːʃən] *n* portion *f*, part *f*

portly ['pɔːtlɪ] *adj* corpulent(e)

portrait ['pɔːtrɪt] *n* portrait *m*

portray [pɔː'treɪ] *vt* faire le portrait de; (*in writing*) dépeindre, représenter; (*subj*: *actor*) jouer; **~al** *n* portrait *m*, représentation *f*

Portugal ['pɔːtjʊɡəl] *n* Portugal *m*

Portuguese [pɔːtjʊ'ɡiːz] *adj* portugais(e) ♦ *n inv* Portugais(e); (*LING*) portugais *m*

pose [pəʊz] *n* pose *f* ♦ *vi* (*pretend*): **to ~ as** se poser en ♦ *vt* poser; (*problem*) créer

posh [pɔʃ] (*inf*) *adj* chic *inv*

position [pə'zɪʃən] *n* position *f*; (*job*) situation *f* ♦ *vt* placer

positive ['pɔzɪtɪv] *adj* positif(ive); (*certain*) sûr(e), certain(e); (*definite*) formel(le), catégorique

posse ['pɔsɪ] (*US*) *n* détachement *m*

possess [pə'zes] *vt* posséder; **~ion** [pə'zeʃən] *n* possession *f*

possibility [pɔsə'bɪlɪtɪ] *n* possibilité *f*; éventualité *f*

possible ['pɔsəbl] *adj* possible; **as big as ~** aussi gros que possible

possibly ['pɔsəblɪ] *adv* (*perhaps*) peut-être; **if you ~ can** si cela vous est possible; **I cannot ~ come** il m'est impossible de venir

post [pəʊst] *n* poste *f*; (*BRIT*: *letters, de-*

livery) courrier *m*; (*job, situation*, MIL) poste *m*; (*pole*) poteau *m* ♦ *vt* (BRIT: *send by* ~) poster; (: *appoint*): **to** ~ **to** affecter à; ~**age** *n* tarifs *mpl* d'affranchissement; ~**al order** *n* mandat(-poste) *m*; ~**box** (BRIT) *n* boîte *f* aux lettres; ~**card** *n* carte postale; ~**code** (BRIT) *n* code postal

poster ['pəʊstə*] *n* affiche *f*

poste restante ['pəʊst'restãːnt] (BRIT) *n* poste restante

postgraduate ['pəʊst'grædjuɪt] *n* ≈ étudiant(e) de troisième cycle

posthumous ['pɒstjʊməs] *adj* posthume

postman ['pəʊstmən] (*irreg*) *n* facteur *m*

postmark ['pəʊstmɑːk] *n* cachet *m* (de la poste)

postmortem ['pəʊst'mɔːtəm] *n* autopsie *f*

post office *n* (*building*) poste *f*; (*organization*): **the Post Office** les Postes; **post office box** *n* boîte postale

postpone [pə'spəʊn] *vt* remettre (à plus tard)

posture ['pɒstʃə*] *n* posture *f*; (*fig*) attitude *f*

postwar ['pəʊst'wɔː*] *adj* d'après-guerre

posy ['pəʊzɪ] *n* petit bouquet

pot [pɒt] *n* pot *m*; (*for cooking*) marmite *f*, casserole *f*; (*tea*~) théière *f*; (*coffee*~) cafetière *f*; (*inf: marijuana*) herbe *f* ♦ *vt* (*plant*) mettre en pot; **to go to** ~ (*inf: work, performance*) aller à vau-l'eau

potato [pə'teɪtəʊ] (*pl* ~**es**) *n* pomme *f* de terre; ~ **peeler** *n* épluche-légumes *m inv*

potent ['pəʊtənt] *adj* puissant(e); (*drink*) fort(e), très alcoolisé(e); (*man*) viril

potential [pəʊ'tenʃəl] *adj* potentiel(le) ♦ *n* potentiel *m*

pothole ['pɒthəʊl] *n* (*in road*) nid *m* de poule; (BRIT: *underground*) gouffre *m*, caverne *f*; **potholing** ['pɒthəʊlɪŋ] (BRIT) *n*: **to go potholing** faire de la spéléologie

potluck ['pɒt'lʌk] *n*: **to take** ~ tenter sa chance

potted ['pɒtɪd] *adj* (*food*) en conserve; (*plant*) en pot; (*abbreviated*) abrégé(e)

potter ['pɒtə*] *n* potier *m* ♦ *vi*: **to** ~ **around**, ~ **about** (BRIT) bricoler; ~**y** *n*

poterie *f*

potty ['pɒtɪ] *adj* (*inf: mad*) dingue ♦ *n* (*child's*) pot *m*

pouch [paʊtʃ] *n* (ZOOL) poche *f*; (*for tobacco*) blague *f*; (*for money*) bourse *f*

poultry ['pəʊltrɪ] *n* volaille *f*

pounce [paʊns] *vi*: **to** ~ (**on**) bondir (sur), sauter (sur)

pound [paʊnd] *n* (*unit of money*) livre *f*; (*unit of weight*) livre ♦ *vt* (*beat*) bourrer de coups, marteler; (*crush*) piler, pulvériser ♦ *vi* (*heart*) battre violemment, taper

pour [pɔː*] *vt* verser ♦ *vi* couler à flots; **to** ~ (**with rain**) pleuvoir à verse; **to** ~ **sb a drink** verser *or* servir à boire à qn; ~ **away** *vt* vider; ~ **in** *vi* (*people*) affluer, se précipiter; (*news, letters etc*) arriver en masse; ~ **off** *vt* = **pour away**; ~ **out** *vi* (*people*) sortir en masse ♦ *vt* vider; (*fig*) déverser; (*serve: a drink*) verser; ~**ing** *adj*: ~**ing rain** pluie torrentielle

pout [paʊt] *vi* faire la moue

poverty ['pɒvətɪ] *n* pauvreté *f*, misère *f*; ~-**stricken** *adj* pauvre, déshérité(e)

powder ['paʊdə*] *n* poudre *f* ♦ *vt*: **to** ~ **one's face** se poudrer; ~ **compact** *n* poudrier *m*; ~**ed milk** *n* lait *m* en poudre; ~ **puff** *n* houppette *f*; ~ **room** *n* toilettes *fpl* (pour dames)

power ['paʊə*] *n* (*strength*) puissance *f*, force *f*; (*ability, authority*) pouvoir *m*; (*of speech, thought*) faculté *f*; (ELEC) courant *m*; **to be in** ~ (POL etc) être au pouvoir; ~ **cut** (BRIT) *n* coupure *f* de courant; ~**ed** *adj*: ~**ed by** actionné(e) par, fonctionnant à; ~ **failure** *n* panne *f* de courant; ~**ful** *adj* puissant(e); ~**less** *adj* impuissant(e); ~ **point** (BRIT) *n* prise *f* de courant; ~ **station** *n* centrale *f* électrique

p.p. *abbr* (= *per procurationem*): ~ **J. Smith** pour M. J. Smith

PR *n abbr* = **public relations**

practical ['præktɪkəl] *adj* pratique; ~**ities** [præktɪ'kælɪtɪz] *npl* (*of situation*) aspect *m* pratique; ~**ity** (*no pl*) *n* (*of person*) sens *m* pratique; ~ **joke** *n* farce *f*; ~**ly**

adv (*almost*) pratiquement

practice ['præktɪs] *n* pratique *f*; (*of profession*) exercice *m*; (*at football etc*) entraînement *m*; (*business*) cabinet *m* ♦ *vt, vi* (*US*) = **practise**; **in ~** (*in reality*) en pratique; **out of ~** rouillé(e)

practise ['præktɪs] (*US* **practice**) *vt* (*musical instrument*) travailler; (*train for: sport*) s'entraîner à; (*a sport, religion*) pratiquer; (*profession*) exercer ♦ *vi* s'exercer, travailler; (*train*) s'entraîner; (*lawyer, doctor*) exercer; **practising** ['præktɪsɪŋ] *adj* (*Christian etc*) pratiquant(e); (*lawyer*) en exercice

practitioner [præk'tɪʃənə*] *n* praticien(ne)

prairie ['prɛərɪ] *n* steppe *f*, prairie *f*

praise [preɪz] *n* éloge(s) *m(pl)*, louange(s) *f(pl)* ♦ *vt* louer, faire l'éloge de; **~worthy** *adj* digne d'éloges

pram [præm] (*BRIT*) *n* landau *m*, voiture *f* d'enfant

prance [prɑːns] *vi* (*also: to ~ about: person*) se pavaner

prank [præŋk] *n* farce *f*

prawn [prɔːn] *n* crevette *f* (rose)

pray [preɪ] *vi* prier; **~er** [prɛə*] *n* prière *f*

preach [priːtʃ] *vt, vi* prêcher

precaution [prɪ'kɔːʃən] *n* précaution *f*

precede [prɪ'siːd] *vt* précéder

precedent ['presɪdənt] *n* précédent *m*

precinct ['priːsɪŋkt] *n* (*US*) circonscription *f*, arrondissement *m*; **~s** *npl* (*neighbourhood*) alentours *mpl*, environs *mpl*; **pedestrian ~** (*BRIT*) zone piétonnière; **shopping ~** (*BRIT*) centre commercial

precious ['preʃəs] *adj* précieux(euse)

precipitate [*vb* prɪ'sɪpɪteɪt] *vt* précipiter

precise [prɪ'saɪs] *adj* précis(e); **~ly** *adv* précisément

preclude [prɪ'kluːd] *vt* exclure

precocious [prɪ'kəʊʃəs] *adj* précoce

precondition ['priːkən'dɪʃən] *n* condition *f* nécessaire

predecessor ['priːdɪsesə*] *n* prédécesseur *m*

predicament [prɪ'dɪkəmənt] *n* situation *f* difficile

predict [prɪ'dɪkt] *vt* prédire; **~able** *adj*

prévisible

predominantly [prɪ'dɒmɪnəntlɪ] *adv* en majeure partie; surtout

preempt *vt* anticiper, devancer

preen [priːn] *vt*: **to ~ itself** (*bird*) se lisser les plumes; **to ~ o.s.** s'admirer

prefab ['priːfæb] *n* bâtiment préfabriqué

preface ['prefɪs] *n* préface *f*

prefect ['priːfekt] (*BRIT*) *n* (*in school*) élève chargé(e) de certaines fonctions de discipline

prefer [prɪ'fɜː*] *vt* préférer; **~ably** ['prefərəblɪ] *adv* de préférence; **~ence** ['prefərəns] *n* préférence *f*; **~ential** [prefə'renʃəl] *adj*: **~ential treatment** traitement *m* de faveur *or* préférentiel

prefix ['priːfɪks] *n* préfixe *m*

pregnancy ['pregnənsɪ] *n* grossesse *f*

pregnant ['pregnənt] *adj* enceinte; (*animal*) pleine

prehistoric ['priːhɪs'tɔrɪk] *adj* préhistorique

prejudice ['predʒʊdɪs] *n* préjugé *m*; **~d** *adj* (*person*) plein(e) de préjugés; (*in a matter*) partial(e)

premarital ['priː'mærɪtl] *adj* avant le mariage

premature ['premətʃʊə*] *adj* prématuré(e)

premier ['premɪə*] *adj* premier(ère), principal(e) ♦ *n* (*POL*) Premier ministre

première [premɪ'ɛə*] *n* première *f*

premise ['premɪs] *n* prémisse *f*; **~s** *npl* (*building*) locaux *mpl*; **on the ~s** sur les lieux; sur place

premium ['priːmɪəm] *n* prime *f*; **to be at a ~** faire prime; **~ bond** (*BRIT*) *n* bon *m* à lot, obligation *f* à prime

premonition [premə'nɪʃən] *n* prémonition *f*

preoccupied [priː'ɒkjʊpaɪd] *adj* préoccupé(e)

prep [prep] *n* (*SCOL: study*) étude *f*

prepaid ['priː'peɪd] *adj* payé(e) d'avance

preparation [prepə'reɪʃən] *n* préparation *f*; **~s** *npl* (*for trip, war*) préparatifs *mpl*

preparatory [prɪ'pærətərɪ] *adj* préliminaire; **~ school** (*BRIT*) *n* école primaire privée

prepare [prɪ'pεə*] *vt* préparer ♦ *vi*: **to ~ for** se préparer à; **~d to** prêt(e) à

preposition [prepə'zɪʃən] *n* préposition *f*

preposterous [prɪ'pɒstərəs] *adj* absurde

prep school *n* = **preparatory school**

prerequisite ['priː'rekwɪzɪt] *n* condition *f* préalable

prescribe [prɪs'kraɪb] *vt* prescrire

prescription [prɪs'krɪpʃən] *n* (MED) ordonnance *f*; (: *medicine*) médicament (obtenu sur ordonnance)

presence ['prezns] *n* présence *f*; **~ of mind** présence d'esprit

present [*adj, n* 'preznt, *vb* prɪ'zent] *adj* présent(e) ♦ *n* (*gift*) cadeau *m*; (*actuality*) présent *m* ♦ *vt* présenter; (*prize, medal*) remettre; (*give*): **to ~ sb with sth** or **sth to sb** offrir qch à qn; **to give sb a ~** offrir un cadeau à qn; **at ~** en ce moment; **~ation** *n* présentation *f*; (*ceremony*) remise *f* du cadeau (or de la médaille *etc*); **~-day** *adj* contemporain(e), actuel(le); **~er** *n* (RADIO, TV) présentateur(trice); **~ly** *adv* (*with verb in past*) peu après; (*soon*) tout à l'heure, bientôt; (*at present*) en ce moment

preservative [prɪ'zɜːvətɪv] *n* agent *m* de conservation

preserve [prɪ'zɜːv] *vt* (*keep safe*) préserver, protéger; (*maintain*) conserver, garder; (*food*) mettre en conserve ♦ *n* (*often pl*: *jam*) confiture *f*

president ['prezɪdənt] *n* président(e); **~ial** *adj* présidentiel(le)

press [pres] *n* presse *f*; (*for wine*) pressoir *m* ♦ *vt* (*squeeze*) presser, serrer; (*push*) appuyer sur; (*clothes: iron*) repasser; (*put pressure on*) faire pression sur; (*insist*): **to ~ sth on sb** presser qn d'accepter qch ♦ *vi* appuyer, peser; **to ~ for sth** faire pression pour obtenir qch; **we are ~ed for time/money** le temps/l'argent nous manque; **~ on** *vi* continuer; **~ conference** *n* conférence *f* de presse; **~ing** *adj* urgent(e), pressant(e); **~ stud** (BRIT) *n* bouton-pression *m*; **~-up** (BRIT) *n* traction *f*

pressure ['preʃə*] *n* pression *f*; (*stress*) tension *f*; **to put ~ on sb (to do)** faire pression sur qn (pour qu'il/elle fasse); **~ cooker** *n* cocotte-minute *f*; **~ gauge** *n* manomètre *m*; **~ group** *n* groupe *m* de pression

prestige [pres'tiːʒ] *n* prestige *m*

presumably [prɪ'zjuːməblɪ] *adv* vraisemblablement

presume [prɪ'zjuːm] *vt* présumer, supposer

pretence [prɪ'tens] (US **pretense**) *n* (*claim*) prétention *f*; **under false ~s** sous des prétextes fallacieux

pretend [prɪ'tend] *vt* (*feign*) feindre, simuler ♦ *vi* faire semblant

pretext ['priːtekst] *n* prétexte *m*

pretty ['prɪtɪ] *adj* joli(e) ♦ *adv* assez

prevail [prɪ'veɪl] *vi* (*be usual*) avoir cours; (*win*) l'emporter, prévaloir; **~ing** *adj* dominant(e)

prevalent ['prevələnt] *adj* répandu(e), courant(e)

prevent [prɪ'vent] *vt*: **to ~ (from doing)** empêcher (de faire); **~ative** *adj* = **preventive**; **~ive** *adj* préventif(ive)

preview ['priːvjuː] *n* (*of film etc*) avant-première *f*

previous ['priːvɪəs] *adj* précédent(e), antérieur(e); **~ly** *adv* précédemment, auparavant

prewar ['priː'wɔː*] *adj* d'avant-guerre

prey [preɪ] *n* proie *f* ♦ *vi*: **to ~ on** s'attaquer à; **it was ~ing on his mind** cela le travaillait

price [praɪs] *n* prix *m* ♦ *vt* (*goods*) fixer le prix de; **~less** *adj* sans prix, inestimable; **~ list** *n* liste *f* des prix, tarif *m*

prick [prɪk] *n* piqûre *f* ♦ *vt* piquer; **to ~ up one's ears** dresser or tendre l'oreille

prickle ['prɪkl] *n* (*of plant*) épine *f*; (*sensation*) picotement *m*; **prickly** ['prɪklɪ] *adj* piquant(e), épineux(euse); **prickly heat** *n* fièvre *f* miliaire

pride [praɪd] *n* orgueil *m*; fierté *f* ♦ *vt*: **to ~ o.s. on** se flatter de; s'enorgueillir de

priest [priːst] *n* prêtre *m*; **~hood** *n* prêtrise *f*, sacerdoce *m*

prim [prɪm] *adj* collet monté *inv*, guindé(e)

primarily ['praɪmərɪlɪ] *adv* principalement, essentiellement

primary ['praɪmərɪ] *adj* (*first in importance*) premier(ère), primordial(e), principal(e) ♦ *n* (*US: election*) (élection *f*) primaire *f*; ~ **school** (*BRIT*) *n* école primaire *f*

prime [praɪm] *adj* primordial(e), fondamental(e); (*excellent*) excellent(e) ♦ *n*: **in the ~ of life** dans la fleur de l'âge ♦ *vt* (*wood*) apprêter; (*fig*) mettre au courant; **P~ Minister** *n* Premier ministre *m*

primeval [praɪ'miːvəl] *adj* primitif(ive); ~ **forest** forêt *f* vierge

primitive ['prɪmɪtɪv] *adj* primitif(ive)

primrose ['prɪmrəʊz] *n* primevère *f*

Primus (stove) ['praɪməs-] (®: *BRIT*) *n* réchaud *m* de camping

prince [prɪns] *n* prince *m*

princess [prɪn'ses] *n* princesse *f*

principal ['prɪnsɪpəl] *adj* principal(e) ♦ *n* (*headmaster*) directeur(trice), principal *m*

principle ['prɪnsɪpəl] *n* principe *m*; **in/on ~** en/par principe

print [prɪnt] *n* (*mark*) empreinte *f*; (*letters*) caractères *mpl*; (*ART*) gravure *f*, estampe *f*; (: *photograph*) photo *f* ♦ *vt* imprimer; (*publish*) publier; (*write in block letters*) écrire en caractères d'imprimerie; **out of ~** épuisé(e); ~**ed matter** *n* imprimé(s) *m(pl)*; ~**er** *n* imprimeur *m*; (*machine*) imprimante *f*; ~**ing** *n* impression *f*; ~**-out** *n* copie *f* papier

prior ['praɪə*] *adj* antérieur(e), précédent(e); (*more important*) prioritaire ♦ *adv*: ~ **to doing** avant de faire

priority [praɪ'ɒrɪtɪ] *n* priorité *f*

prise [praɪz] *vt*: **to ~ open** forcer

prison ['prɪzn] *n* prison *f* ♦ *cpd* pénitentiaire; ~**er** *n* prisonnier(ère)

pristine ['prɪstiːn] *adj* parfait(e)

privacy ['prɪvəsɪ] *n* intimité *f*, solitude *f*

private ['praɪvɪt] *adj* privé(e); (*personal*) personnel(le); (*house, lesson*) particulier(ère); (*quiet: place*) tranquille; (*reserved: person*) secret(ète) ♦ *n* soldat *m* de deuxième classe; "**~**" (*on envelope*) "personnelle"; **in ~** en privé; ~ **enter-**prise *n* l'entreprise privée; ~ **eye** *n* détective privé; ~ **property** *n* propriété privée; **privatize** *vt* privatiser

privet ['prɪvɪt] *n* troène *m*

privilege ['prɪvɪlɪdʒ] *n* privilège *m*

privy ['prɪvɪ] *adj*: **to be ~ to** être au courant de

prize [praɪz] *n* prix *m* ♦ *adj* (*example, idiot*) parfait(e); (*bull, novel*) primé(e) ♦ *vt* priser, faire grand cas de; ~**-giving** *n* distribution *f* des prix; ~**winner** *n* gagnant(e)

pro [prəʊ] *n* (*SPORT*) professionnel(le); **the ~s and cons** le pour et le contre

probability [prɒbə'bɪlɪtɪ] *n* probabilité *f*; **probable** ['prɒbəbl] *adj* probable; **probably** *adv* probablement

probation [prə'beɪʃən] *n*: **on ~** (*LAW*) en liberté surveillée, en sursis; (*employee*) à l'essai

probe [prəʊb] *n* (*MED, SPACE*) sonde *f*; (*enquiry*) enquête *f*, investigation *f* ♦ *vt* sonder, explorer

problem ['prɒbləm] *n* problème *m*

procedure [prə'siːdʒə*] *n* (*ADMIN, LAW*) procédure *f*; (*method*) marche *f* à suivre, façon *f* de procéder

proceed [prə'siːd] *vi* continuer; (*go forward*) avancer; **to ~ (with)** continuer, poursuivre; **to ~ to do** se mettre à faire; ~**ings** *npl* (*LAW*) poursuites *fpl*; (*meeting*) réunion *f*, séance *f*; ~**s** ['prəʊsiːdz] *npl* produit *m*, recette *f*

process ['prəʊses] *n* processus *m*; (*method*) procédé *m* ♦ *vt* traiter; ~**ing** *n* (*PHOT*) développement *m*; ~**ion** [prə'seʃən] *n* défilé *m*, cortège *m*; (*REL*) procession *f*; **funeral** ~**ion** (*on foot*) cortège *m* funèbre; (*in cars*) convoi *m* mortuaire

pro-choice [prəʊ'tʃɔɪs] *adj* en faveur de l'avortement

proclaim [prə'kleɪm] *vt* déclarer, proclamer

procrastinate [prəʊ'kræstɪneɪt] *vi* faire traîner les choses, vouloir tout remettre au lendemain

procure [prə'kjʊə*] *vt* obtenir

prod [prɒd] *vt* pousser

prodigal ['prɒdɪgəl] *adj* prodigue

prodigy ['prɒdɪdʒɪ] *n* prodige *m*

produce [*n* 'prɒdjuːs, *vb* prə'djuːs] *n* (*AGR*) produits *mpl* ♦ *vt* produire; (*to show*) présenter; (*cause*) provoquer, causer; (*THEATRE*) monter, mettre en scène; **~r** *n* producteur *m*; (*THEATRE*) metteur *m* en scène

product ['prɒdʌkt] *n* produit *m*

production [prə'dʌkʃən] *n* production *f*; (*THEATRE*) mise *f* en scène; **~ line** *n* chaîne *f* (de fabrication)

productivity [prɒdʌk'tɪvɪtɪ] *n* productivité *f*

profession [prə'feʃən] *n* profession *f*; **~al** *n* professionnel(le) ♦ *adj* professionnel(le); (*work*) de professionnel

professor [prə'fesə*] *n* professeur *m* (*titulaire d'une chaire*)

proficiency [prə'fɪʃənsɪ] *n* compétence *f*, aptitude *f*

profile ['prəʊfaɪl] *n* profil *m*

profit ['prɒfɪt] *n* bénéfice *m*; profit *m* ♦ *vi*: **to ~ (by *or* from)** profiter (de); **~able** *adj* lucratif(ive), rentable

profound [prə'faʊnd] *adj* profond(e)

profusely [prə'fjuːslɪ] *adv* abondamment; avec effusion

prognosis [prɒg'nəʊsɪs] (*pl* **prognoses**) *n* pronostic *m*

programme ['prəʊgræm] (*US* **program**) *n* programme *m*; (*RADIO, TV*) émission *f* ♦ *vt* programmer; **~r** (*US* **programer**) *n* programmeur(euse)

progress [*n* 'prəʊgres, *vb* prə'gres] *n* progrès *m(pl)* ♦ *vi* progresser, avancer; **in ~** en cours; **~ive** *adj* progressif(ive); (*person*) progressiste

prohibit [prə'hɪbɪt] *vt* interdire, défendre

project [*n* 'prɒdʒekt, *vb* prə'dʒekt] *n* (*plan*) projet *m*, plan *m*; (*venture*) opération *f*, entreprise *f*; (*research*) étude *f*, dossier *m* ♦ *vt* projeter ♦ *vi* (*stick out*) faire saillie, s'avancer; **~ion** [prə'dʒekʃən] *n* projection *f*; (*overhang*) saillie *f*; **~or** [prə'dʒektə*] *n* projecteur *m*

pro-life [prəʊ'laɪf] *adj* contre l'avortement

prolong [prə'lɒŋ] *vt* prolonger

prom [prɒm] *n abbr* = **promenade**; (*US:*

ball) bal *m* d'étudiants

promenade [prɒmɪ'nɑːd] *n* (*by sea*) esplanade *f*, promenade *f*; **~ concert** (*BRIT*) *n* concert *m* populaire (de musique classique)

prominent ['prɒmɪnənt] *adj* (*standing out*) proéminent(e); (*important*) important(e)

promiscuous [prə'mɪskjʊəs] *adj* (*sexually*) de mœurs légères

promise ['prɒmɪs] *n* promesse *f* ♦ *vt, vi* promettre; **promising** ['prɒmɪsɪŋ] *adj* prometteur(euse)

promote [prə'məʊt] *vt* promouvoir; (*new product*) faire la promotion de; **~r** *n* (*of event*) organisateur(trice); (*of cause, idea*) promoteur(trice); **promotion** [prə'məʊʃən] *n* promotion *f*

prompt [prɒmpt] *adj* rapide ♦ *adv* (*punctually*) à l'heure ♦ *n* (*COMPUT*) message *m* (de guidage) ♦ *vt* provoquer; (*person*) inciter, pousser; (*THEATRE*) souffler (son rôle *or* ses répliques) à; **~ly** *adv* rapidement, sans délai; ponctuellement

prone [prəʊn] *adj* (*lying*) couché(e) (face contre terre); **~ to** enclin(e) à

prong [prɒŋ] *n* (*of fork*) dent *f*

pronoun ['prəʊnaʊn] *n* pronom *m*

pronounce [prə'naʊns] *vt* prononcer

pronunciation [prənʌnsɪ'eɪʃən] *n* prononciation *f*

proof [pruːf] *n* preuve *f*; (*TYP*) épreuve *f* ♦ *adj*: **~ against** à l'épreuve de

prop [prɒp] *n* support *m*, étai *m*; (*fig*) soutien *m* ♦ *vt* (*also: ~ up*) étayer, soutenir; (*lean*): **to ~ sth against** appuyer qch contre *or* à

propaganda [prɒpə'gændə] *n* propagande *f*

propel [prə'pel] *vt* propulser, faire avancer; **~ler** *n* hélice *f*

propensity [prə'pensɪtɪ] *n*: **a ~ for** *or* **to/to do** une propension à/à faire

proper ['prɒpə*] *adj* (*suited, right*) approprié(e), bon(bonne); (*seemly*) correct(e), convenable; (*authentic*) vrai(e), véritable; (*referring to place*): **the village ~** le village proprement dit; **~ly** *adv* correctement, convenablement; **~ noun** *n* nom *m* propre

property ['propəti] *n* propriété *f*; (*things owned*) biens *mpl*; propriété(s) *f(pl)*; (*land*) terres *fpl*

prophecy ['profisi] *n* prophétie *f*

prophesy ['profisai] *vt* prédire

prophet ['profit] *n* prophète *m*

proportion [prə'pɔ:ʃən] *n* proportion *f*; (*share*) part *f*, partie *f*; **~al, ~ate** *adj* proportionnel(le)

proposal [prə'pəuzl] *n* proposition *f*, offre *f*; (*plan*) projet *m*; (*of marriage*) demande *f* en mariage

propose [prə'pəuz] *vt* proposer, suggérer ♦ *vi* faire sa demande en mariage; **to ~ to do** avoir l'intention de faire; **proposition** [propə'zɪʃən] *n* proposition *f*

propriety [prə'praɪətɪ] *n* (*seemliness*) bienséance *f*, convenance *f*

prose [prəuz] *n* (*not poetry*) prose *f*

prosecute ['prɒsɪkjuːt] *vt* poursuivre; **prosecution** [prɒsɪ'kjuːʃen] *n* poursuites *fpl* judiciaires; (*accusing side*) partie plaignante; **prosecutor** ['prɒsɪkjuːtə*] *n* (*US: plaintiff*) plaignant(e); (*also: public ~*) procureur *m*, ministère public

prospect [*n* 'prɒspekt, *vb* prə'spekt] *n* perspective *f* ♦ *vt, vi* prospecter; **~s** *npl* (*for work etc*) possibilités *fpl* d'avenir, débouchés *mpl*; **~ing** *n* (*for gold, oil etc*) prospection *f*; **~ive** *adj* (*possible*) éventuel(le); (*future*) futur(e)

prospectus [prə'spektəs] *n* prospectus *m*

prosperity [prɒ'spɛrɪtɪ] *n* prospérité *f*

prostitute ['prɒstɪtjuːt] *n* prostitué(e)

protect [prə'tɛkt] *vt* protéger; **~ion** *n* protection *f*; **~ive** *adj* protecteur(trice); (*clothing*) de protection

protein ['prəutiːn] *n* protéine *f*

protest [*n* 'prəutest, *vb* prə'test] *n* protestation *f* ♦ *vi, vt*: **to ~ (that)** protester (que)

Protestant ['prɒtɪstənt] *adj, n* protestant(e)

protester [prə'testə*] *n* manifestant(e)

protracted [prə'træktɪd] *adj* prolongé(e)

protrude [prə'truːd] *vi* avancer, dépasser

proud [praud] *adj* fier(ère); (*pej*) orgueil-

leux(euse)

prove [pruːv] *vt* prouver, démontrer ♦ *vi*: **to ~ (to be) correct** *etc* s'avérer juste *etc*; **to ~ o.s.** montrer ce dont on est capable

proverb ['prɒvɜːb] *n* proverbe *m*

provide [prə'vaid] *vt* fournir; **to ~ sb with sth** fournir qch à qn; **~ for** *vt fus* (*person*) subvenir aux besoins de; (*future event*) prévoir; **~d (that)** *conj* à condition que *+sub*; **providing** [prə'vaidɪŋ] *conj*: **providing (that)** à condition que *+sub*

province ['prɒvɪns] *n* province *f*; (*fig*) domaine *m*; **provincial** [prə'vɪnʃəl] *adj* provincial(e)

provision [prə'vɪʒən] *n* (*supplying*) fourniture *f*; approvisionnement *m*; (*stipulation*) disposition *f*; **~s** *npl* (*food*) provisions *fpl*; **~al** *adj* provisoire

proviso [prə'vaizəu] *n* condition *f*

provocative [prə'vɒkətɪv] *adj* provocateur(trice), provocant(e)

provoke [prə'vəuk] *vt* provoquer

prow [prau] *n* proue *f*

prowess ['praues] *n* prouesse *f*

prowl [praul] *vi* (*also: ~ about, ~ around*) rôder ♦ *n*: **on the ~** à l'affût; **~er** *n* rôdeur/euse

proxy ['prɒksɪ] *n* procuration *f*

prudent ['pruːdənt] *adj* prudent(e)

prune [pruːn] *n* pruneau *m* ♦ *vt* élaguer

pry [praɪ] *vi*: **to ~ into** fourrer son nez dans

PS *n abbr* (= *postscript*) p.s.

psalm [sɑːm] *n* psaume *m*

pseudo- ['sjuːdəu] *prefix* pseudo-; **~nym** ['sjuːdənɪm] *n* pseudonyme *m*

psyche ['saɪkɪ] *n* psychisme *m*

psychiatrist [saɪ'kaɪətrɪst] *n* psychiatre *m/f*

psychic ['saɪkɪk] *adj* (*also: ~al*) (méta)psychique; (*person*) doué(e) d'un sixième sens

psychoanalyst [saɪkəu'ænəlɪst] *n* psychanalyste *m/f*

psychological [saɪkə'lɒdʒɪkəl] *adj* psychologique; **psychologist** [saɪ'kɒlədʒɪst] *n* psychologue *m/f*; **psychology** [saɪ'kɒl-

ədʒɪ] *n* psychologie *f*
PTO *abbr* (= *please turn over*) T.S.V.P.
pub [pʌb] *n* (= *public house*) pub *m*
public ['pʌblɪk] *adj* public(ique) ♦ *n* public *m*; **in** ~ en public; **to make** ~ rendre public; ~ **address system** *n* (système *m* de) sonorisation *f*; hautsparleurs *mpl*
publican ['pʌblɪkən] *n* patron *m* de pub
public: ~ **company** *n* société *f* anonyme (*cotée en Bourse*); ~ **convenience** (*BRIT*) *n* toilettes *fpl*; ~ **holiday** *n* jour férié; ~ **house** (*BRIT*) *n* pub *m*
publicity [pʌb'lɪsɪtɪ] *n* publicité *f*
publicize ['pʌblɪsaɪz] *vt* faire connaître, rendre public(ique)
public: ~ **opinion** *n* opinion publique; ~ **relations** *n* relations publiques; ~ **school** (*BRIT*) école (secondaire) privée; (*US*) école publique; ~**-spirited** *adj* qui fait preuve de civisme; ~ **transport** *n* transports *mpl* en commun
publish ['pʌblɪʃ] *vt* publier; ~**er** *n* éditeur *m*; ~**ing** *n* édition *f*
pucker ['pʌkə*] *vt* plisser
pudding ['pʊdɪŋ] *n* pudding *m*; (*BRIT*: *sweet*) dessert *m*, entremets *m*; **black** ~, (*US*) **blood** ~ boudin (noir)
puddle ['pʌdl] *n* flaque *f* (d'eau)
puff [pʌf] *n* bouffée *f* ♦ *vt*: **to** ~ **one's pipe** tirer sur sa pipe ♦ *vi* (*pant*) haleter; ~ **out** *vt* (*fill with air*) gonfler; ~**ed** (**out**) (*inf*) *adj* (*out of breath*) tout(e) essoufflé(e); ~ **pastry** (*US*: ~ **paste**) *n* pâte feuilletée; ~**y** *adj* bouffi(e), boursouflé(e)
pull [pʊl] *n* (*tug*): **to give sth a** ~ tirer sur qch ♦ *vt* tirer; (*trigger*) presser ♦ *vi* tirer; **to** ~ **to pieces** mettre en morceaux; **to** ~ **one's punches** ménager son adversaire; **to** ~ **one's weight** faire sa part (du travail); **to** ~ **o.s. together** se ressaisir; **to** ~ **sb's leg** (*fig*) faire marcher qn; ~ **apart** *vt* (*break*) mettre en pièces, démantibuler; ~ **down** *vt* (*house*) démolir; ~ **in** *vi* (*AUT*) entrer; (*RAIL*) entrer en gare; ~ **off** *vt* enlever, ôter; (*deal etc*) mener à bien, conclure; ~ **out** *vi* démarrer, partir ♦ *vt* sortir; arracher; ~ **over** *vi* (*AUT*) se ranger; ~ **through** *vi*

s'en sortir; ~ **up** *vi* (*stop*) s'arrêter ♦ *vt* remonter; (*uproot*) déraciner, arracher
pulley ['pʊlɪ] *n* poulie *f*
pullover ['pʊləʊvə*] *n* pull(-over) *m*, tricot *m*
pulp [pʌlp] *n* (*of fruit*) pulpe *f*
pulpit ['pʊlpɪt] *n* chaire *f*
pulsate [pʌl'seɪt] *vi* battre, palpiter; (*music*) vibrer
pulse [pʌls] *n* (*of blood*) pouls *m*; (*of heart*) battement *m*; (*of music, engine*) vibrations *fpl*; (*BOT, CULIN*) légume sec
pump [pʌmp] *n* pompe *f*; (*shoe*) escarpin *m* ♦ *vt* pomper; ~ **up** *vt* gonfler
pumpkin ['pʌmpkɪn] *n* potiron *m*, citrouille *f*
pun [pʌn] *n* jeu *m* de mots, calembour *m*
punch [pʌntʃ] *n* (*blow*) coup *m* de poing; (*tool*) poinçon *m*; (*drink*) punch *m* ♦ *vt* (*hit*): **to** ~ **sb/sth** donner un coup de poing à qn/sur qch; ~**line** *n* (*of joke*) conclusion *f*; ~**-up** (*inf*) *n* bagarre *f*
punctual ['pʌŋktjʊəl] *adj* ponctuel(le)
punctuation [pʌŋktjʊ'eɪʃən] *n* ponctuation *f*
puncture ['pʌŋktʃə*] *n* crevaison *f*
pundit ['pʌndɪt] *n* individu *m* qui pontifie, pontife *m*
pungent ['pʌndʒənt] *adj* piquant(e), âcre
punish ['pʌnɪʃ] *vt* punir; ~**ment** *n* punition *f*, châtiment *m*
punk [pʌŋk] *n* (*also*: ~ *rocker*) punk *m/f*; (: ~ *rock*) le punk rock; (*US*: *inf*: *hoodlum*) voyou *m*
punt [pʌnt] *n* (*boat*) bachot *m*
punter ['pʌntə*] *n* (*BRIT*) *n* (*gambler*) parieur(euse); (*inf*): **the** ~**s** le public
puny ['pjuːnɪ] *adj* chétif(ive); (*effort*) piteux(euse)
pup [pʌp] *n* chiot *m*
pupil ['pjuːpl] *n* (*SCOL*) élève *m/f*; (*of eye*) pupille *f*
puppet ['pʌpɪt] *n* marionnette *f*, pantin *m*
puppy ['pʌpɪ] *n* chiot *m*, jeune chien(ne)
purchase ['pɜːtʃɪs] *n* achat *m* ♦ *vt* acheter; ~**r** *n* acheteur(euse)
pure [pjʊə*] *adj* pur(e); ~**ly** ['pjʊəlɪ] *adv* purement

purge [pɜːdʒ] n purge f
purple ['pɜːpl] adj violet(te); (face) cramoisi(e)
purport [pɜː'pɔːt] vi: **to ~ to be/do** prétendre être/faire
purpose ['pɜːpəs] n intention f, but m; **on ~** exprès; **~ful** adj déterminé(e), résolu(e)
purr [pɜː*] vi ronronner
purse [pɜːs] n (BRIT: for money) portemonnaie m inv; (US: handbag) sac m à main ♦ vt serrer, pincer
purser ['pɜːsə*] n (NAUT) commissaire m du bord
pursue [pə'sjuː] vt poursuivre
pursuit [pə'sjuːt] n poursuite f; (occupation) occupation f, activité f
push [puʃ] n poussée f ♦ vt pousser; (button) appuyer sur; (thrust): **to ~ sth (into)** enfoncer qch (dans); (product) faire de la publicité pour ♦ vi pousser; (demand): **to ~ for** exiger, demander avec insistance; **~ aside** vt écarter; **~ off** (inf) vi filer, ficher le camp; **~ on** vi (continue) continuer; **~ through** vi se frayer un chemin ♦ vt (measure) faire accepter; **~ up** vt (total, prices) faire monter; **~chair** (BRIT) n poussette f; **~er** n (drug ~er) revendeur(euse) (de drogue), ravitailleur(euse) (en drogue); **~over** (inf) n: **it's a ~over** c'est un jeu d'enfant; **~up** (US) n traction f; **~y** (pej) adj arriviste
puss [pus] (inf) n minet m
pussy (cat) ['pusi (kæt)] (inf) n minet m
put [put] (pt, pp put) vt mettre, poser, placer; (say) dire, exprimer; (a question) poser; (case, view) exposer, présenter; (estimate) estimer; **~ about** vt (rumour) faire courir; **~ across** vt (ideas etc) communiquer; **~ away** vt (store) ranger; **~ back** vt (replace) remettre, replacer; (postpone) remettre; (delay) retarder; **~ by** vt (money) mettre de côté, économiser; **~ down** vt (parcel etc) poser, déposer; (in writing) mettre par écrit, inscrire; (suppress: revolt etc) réprimer, faire cesser; (animal) abattre; (dog, cat) faire piquer; (attribute) attribuer; **~ forward** vt (ideas) avancer; **~ in** vt (gas, elec-

tricity) installer; (application, complaint) soumettre; (time, effort) consacrer; **~ off** vt (light etc) éteindre; (postpone) remettre à plus tard, ajourner; (discourage) dissuader; **~ on** vt (clothes, lipstick, record) mettre; (light etc) allumer; (play etc) monter; (food: cook) mettre à cuire or à chauffer; (gain): **to ~ on weight** prendre du poids, grossir; **to ~ the brakes on** freiner; **to ~ the kettle on** mettre l'eau à chauffer; **~ out** vt (take out) mettre dehors; (one's hand) tendre; (light etc) éteindre; (person: inconvenience) déranger, gêner; **~ through** vt (TEL: call) passer; (: person) mettre en communication; (plan) faire accepter; (pin up) afficher; (hang) accrocher; (build) construire, ériger; (tent) monter; (umbrella) ouvrir; (increase) augmenter; (accommodate) loger; **~ up** **with** vt fus supporter
putt [pʌt] n coup roulé; **~ing green** n green m
putty ['pʌtɪ] n mastic m
put-up ['putʌp] (BRIT) adj: **~ job** coup monté
puzzle ['pʌzl] n énigme f, mystère m; (jigsaw) puzzle m ♦ vt intriguer, rendre perplexe ♦ vi se creuser la tête; **puzzling** adj déconcertant(e)
pyjamas [pɪ'dʒɑːməz] (BRIT) npl pyjama(s) m(pl)
pyramid ['pɪrəmɪd] n pyramide f
Pyrenees [pɪrɪ'niːz] npl: **the ~** les Pyrénées fpl

Q q

quack [kwæk] n (of duck) coin-coin m inv; (pej: doctor) charlatan m
quad [kwɒd] n abbr = **quadrangle**; **quadruplet**
quadrangle ['kwɒdræŋgl] n (courtyard) cour f
quadruple [kwɒ'druːpl] vt, vi quadrupler; **~ts** [kwɒ'druːpləts] npl quadruplés

quagmire ['kwægmaɪə*] *n* bourbier *m*
quail [kweɪl] *n* (ZOOL) caille *f* ♦ *vi*: **to ~ at** *or* **before** reculer devant
quaint [kweɪnt] *adj* bizarre; (*house, village*) au charme vieillot, pittoresque
quake [kweɪk] *vi* trembler
qualification [kwɒlɪfɪ'keɪʃən] *n* (*often pl: degree etc*) diplôme *m*; (: *training*) qualification(s) *f(pl)*, expérience *f*; (*ability*) compétence(s) *f(pl)*; (*limitation*) réserve *f*, restriction *f*
qualified ['kwɒlɪfaɪd] *adj* (*trained*) qualifié(e); (*professionally*) diplômé(e); (*fit, competent*) compétent(e), qualifié(e); (*limited*) conditionnel(le)
qualify ['kwɒlɪfaɪ] *vt* qualifier; (*modify*) atténuer, nuancer ♦ *vi*: **to ~ (as)** obtenir son diplôme (de); **to ~ (for)** remplir les conditions requises (pour); (SPORT) se qualifier (pour)
quality ['kwɒlɪtɪ] *n* qualité *f*
qualm [kwɑːm] *n* doute *m*; scrupule *m*
quandary ['kwɒndərɪ] *n*: **in a ~** devant un dilemme, dans l'embarras
quantity ['kwɒntɪtɪ] *n* quantité *f*; **~ surveyor** *n* métreur *m* vérificateur
quarantine ['kwɒrəntiːn] *n* quarantaine *f*
quarrel ['kwɒrəl] *n* querelle *f*, dispute *f* ♦ *vi* se disputer, se quereller; **~some** *adj* querelleur(euse)
quarry ['kwɒrɪ] *n* (*for stone*) carrière *f*; (*animal*) proie *f*, gibier *m*
quart [kwɔːt] *n* ≈ litre *m*
quarter ['kwɔːtə*] *n* quart *m*; (US: coin: 25 cents) quart de dollar; (*of year*) trimestre *m*; (*district*) quartier *m* ♦ *vt* (*divide*) partager en quartiers *or* en quatre; **~s** *npl* (*living ~*) logement *m*; (MIL) quartiers *mpl*, cantonnement *m*; **a ~ of an hour** un quart d'heure; **~ final** *n* quart *m* de finale; **~ly** *adj* trimestriel(le) ♦ *adv* tous les trois mois
quartet(te) [kwɔː'tet] *n* quatuor *m*; (*jazz players*) quartette *m*
quartz [kwɔːts] *n* quartz *m*
quash [kwɒʃ] *vt* (*verdict*) annuler
quaver ['kweɪvə*] *n* (BRIT: MUS) croche *f* ♦ *vi* trembler
quay [kiː] *n* (*also*: ~side) quai *m*

queasy ['kwiːzɪ] *adj*: **to feel ~** avoir mal au cœur
queen [kwiːn] *n* reine *f*; (CARDS etc) dame *f*; **~ mother** *n* reine mère *f*
queer [kwɪə*] *adj* étrange, curieux(euse); (*suspicious*) louche ♦ *n* (*inf!*) homosexuel *m*
quell [kwel] *vt* réprimer, étouffer
quench [kwentʃ] *vt*: **to ~ one's thirst** se désaltérer
querulous ['kwerʊləs] *adj* (*person*) récriminateur(trice); (*voice*) plaintif(ive)
query ['kwɪərɪ] *n* question *f* ♦ *vt* remettre en question, mettre en doute
quest [kwest] *n* recherche *f*, quête *f*
question ['kwestʃən] *n* question *f* ♦ *vt* (*person*) interroger; (*plan, idea*) remettre en question, mettre en doute; **beyond ~** sans aucun doute; **out of the ~** hors de question; **~able** *adj* discutable; **~ mark** *n* point *m* d'interrogation; **~naire** [kwestʃə'nɛə*] *n* questionnaire *m*
queue [kjuː] *n* (BRIT) queue *f*, file *f* ♦ *vi* (*also*: ~ **up**) faire la queue
quibble ['kwɪbl] *vi*: **to ~ (about)** *or* **(over)** *or* **(with sth)** ergoter (sur qch)
quick [kwɪk] *adj* rapide; (*agile*) agile, vif(vive) ♦ *n*: **cut to the ~** (*fig*) touché(e) au vif; **be ~!** dépêche-toi!; **~en** *vt* accélérer, presser ♦ *vi* s'accélérer, devenir plus rapide; **~ly** *adv* vite, rapidement; **~sand** *n* sables mouvants; **~-witted** *adj* à l'esprit vif
quid [kwɪd] (BRIT: *inf*) *n*, *pl inv* livre *f*
quiet ['kwaɪət] *adj* tranquille, calme; (*voice*) bas(se); (*ceremony, colour*) discret(ète) ♦ *n* tranquillité *f*, calme *m*; (*silence*) silence *m* ♦ *vt*, *vi* (US) = **quieten**; **keep ~!** tais-toi!; **~en** *vi* (*also*: ~ *down*) se calmer, s'apaiser ♦ *vt* calmer, apaiser; **~ly** *adv* tranquillement, calmement; (*silently*) silencieusement; **~ness** *n* tranquillité *f*, calme *m*; (*silence*) silence *m*
quilt [kwɪlt] *n* édredon *m*; (*continental ~*) couette *f*
quin [kwɪn] *n abbr* = **quintuplet**
quintuplets [kwɪn'tjuːpləts] *npl* quintuplé(e)s
quip [kwɪp] *n* remarque piquante *or* spi-

rituelle, pointe *f*

quirk [kwɜːk] *n* bizarrerie *f*

quit [kwɪt] (*pt, pp* ~ *or* ~ted) *vt* quitter; (*smoking, grumbling*) arrêter de ♦ *vi* (*give up*) abandonner, renoncer; (*resign*) démissionner

quite [kwaɪt] *adv* (*rather*) assez, plutôt; (*entirely*) complètement, tout à fait; (*following a negative = almost*): **that's not ~ big enough** ce n'est pas tout à fait assez grand; **I ~ understand** je comprends très bien; **~ a few of them** un assez grand nombre d'entre eux; **~ (so)!** exactement!

quits [kwɪts] *adj*: **~ (with)** quitte (envers); **let's call it ~** restons-en là

quiver ['kwɪvə*] *vi* trembler, frémir

quiz [kwɪz] *n* (*game*) jeu-concours *m* ♦ *vt* interroger; **~zical** *adj* narquois(e)

quota ['kwəʊtə] *n* quota *m*

quotation [kwəʊ'teɪʃən] *n* citation *f*; (*estimate*) devis *m*; **~ marks** *npl* guillemets *mpl*

quote [kwəʊt] *n* citation *f*; (*estimate*) devis *m* ♦ *vt* citer; (*price*) indiquer; **~s** *npl* guillemets *mpl*

R r

rabbi ['ræbaɪ] *n* rabbin *m*

rabbit ['ræbɪt] *n* lapin *m*; **~ hutch** *n* clapier *m*

rabble ['ræbl] (*pej*) *n* populace *f*

rabies ['reɪbiːz] *n* rage *f*

RAC *n abbr* (*BRIT*) = **Royal Automobile Club**

rac(c)oon [rə'kuːn] *n* raton laveur

race [reɪs] *n* (*species*) race *f*; (*competition, rush*) course *f* ♦ *vt* (*horse*) faire courir ♦ *vi* (*compete*) faire la course, courir; (*hurry*) aller à toute vitesse, courir; (*engine*) s'emballer; (*pulse*) augmenter; **~ car** (*US*) *n* = **racing car**; **~ car driver** (*US*) *n* = **racing driver**; **~course** *n* champ *m* de courses; **~horse** *n* cheval *m* de course; **~track** *n* piste *f*

racial ['reɪʃəl] *adj* racial(e)

racing ['reɪsɪŋ] *n* courses *fpl*; **~ car** (*BRIT*)

n voiture *f* de course; **~ driver** (*BRIT*) *n* pilote *m* de course

racism ['reɪsɪzəm] *n* racisme *m*; **racist** *adj* raciste ♦ *n* raciste *m/f*

rack [ræk] *n* (*for guns, tools*) râtelier *m*; (*also: luggage ~*) porte-bagages *m inv*, filet *m* à bagages; (: *roof ~*) galerie *f*; (*dish ~*) égouttoir *m* ♦ *vt* tourmenter; **to ~ one's brains** se creuser la cervelle

racket ['rækɪt] *n* (*for tennis*) raquette *f*; (*noise*) tapage *m*; vacarme *m*; (*swindle*) escroquerie *f*

racquet ['rækɪt] *n* raquette *f*

racy ['reɪsɪ] *adj* plein(e) de verve; (*slightly indecent*) osé(e)

radar ['reɪdɑː*] *n* radar *m*

radial ['reɪdɪəl] *adj* (*also: ~-ply*) à carcasse radiale

radiant ['reɪdɪənt] *adj* rayonnant(e)

radiate ['reɪdɪeɪt] *vt* (*heat*) émettre, dégager; (*emotion*) rayonner de ♦ *vi* (*lines*) rayonner

radiation [reɪdɪ'eɪʃən] *n* rayonnement *m*; (*radioactive*) radiation *f*

radiator ['reɪdɪeɪtə*] *n* radiateur *m*

radical ['rædɪkəl] *adj* radical(e)

radii ['reɪdɪaɪ] *npl of* **radius**

radio ['reɪdɪəʊ] *n* radio *f* ♦ *vt* appeler par radio; **on the ~** à la radio; **~active** [reɪdɪəʊ'æktɪv] *adj* radioactif(ive); **~ station** *n* station *f* de radio

radish ['rædɪʃ] *n* radis *m*

radius ['reɪdɪəs] (*pl* **radii**) *n* rayon *m*

RAF *n abbr* = **Royal Air Force**

raffle ['ræfl] *n* tombola *f*

raft [rɑːft] *n* (*craft; also: life ~*) radeau *m*

rafter ['rɑːftə*] *n* chevron *m*

rag [ræg] *n* chiffon *m*; (*pej: newspaper*) feuille *f* de chou, torchon *m*; (*student ~*) *attractions organisées au profit d'œuvres de charité*; **~s** *npl* (*torn clothes etc*) haillons *mpl*; **~ doll** *n* poupée *f* de chiffon

rage [reɪdʒ] *n* (*fury*) rage *f*, fureur *f* ♦ *vi* (*person*) être fou(folle) de rage; (*storm*) faire rage, être déchaîné(e); **it's all the ~** cela fait fureur

ragged ['rægɪd] *adj* (*edge*) inégal(e);

(*clothes*) en loques; (*appearance*) dégue-nillé(e)

raid [reɪd] *n* (*attack, also:* MIL) raid *m*; (*criminal*) hold-up *m inv*; (*by police*) descente *f*, rafle *f* ♦ *vt* faire un raid sur *or* un hold-up *or* une descente dans

rail [reɪl] *n* (*on stairs*) rampe *f*; (*on bridge, balcony*) balustrade *f*; (*of ship*) bastingage *m*; **~s** *npl* (*track*) rails *mpl*, voie ferrée; **by ~** par chemin de fer, en train; **~ing(s)** *n(pl)* grille *f*; **~road** (US), **~way** (BRIT) *n* (*track*) chemin *m* de fer; **~way line** (BRIT) *n* ligne *f* de chemin de fer; **~way-man** (BRIT: *irreg*) *n* cheminot *m*; **~way station** (BRIT) *n* gare *f*

rain [reɪn] *n* pluie *f* ♦ *vi* pleuvoir; **in the ~** sous la pluie; **it's ~ing** il pleut; **~bow** *n* arc-en-ciel *m*; **~coat** *n* imperméable *m*; **~drop** *n* goutte *f* de pluie; **~fall** *n* chute *f* de pluie; (*measurement*) hauteur *f* des précipitations; **~forest** *n* forêt *f* tropicale humide; **~y** *adj* pluvieux(euse)

raise [reɪz] *n* augmentation *f* ♦ *vt* (*lift*) lever; hausser; (*increase*) augmenter; (*morale*) remonter; (*standards*) améliorer; (*question, doubt*) provoquer, soulever; (*cattle, family*) élever; (*crop*) faire pousser; (*funds*) rassembler; (*loan*) obtenir; (*army*) lever; **to ~ one's voice** élever la voix

raisin [ˈreɪzən] *n* raisin sec

rake [reɪk] *n* (*tool*) râteau *m* ♦ *vt* (*garden, leaves*) ratisser; (*with machine gun*) balayer

rally [ˈrælɪ] *n* (POL *etc*) meeting *m*, rassemblement *m*; (AUT) rallye *m*; (TENNIS) échange *m* ♦ *vt* (*support*) gagner ♦ *vi* (*sick person*) aller mieux; (*Stock Exchange*) reprendre; **~ round** *vt fus* venir en aide à

RAM [ræm] *n abbr* (= *random access memory*) mémoire vive

ram [ræm] *n* bélier *m* ♦ *vt* enfoncer; (*crash into*) emboutir; percuter

ramble [ˈræmbl] *n* randonnée *f* ♦ *vi* (*walk*) se promener, faire une randonnée; (*talk: also:* ~ **on**) discourir, pérorer; **~r** *n* promeneur(euse), randonneur(euse); (BOT) rosier

grimpant; **rambling** [ˈræmblɪŋ] *adj* (*speech*) décousu(e); (*house*) plein(e) de coins et de recoins; (BOT) grimpant(e)

ramp [ræmp] *n* (*incline*) rampe *f*; dénivellation *f*; **on ~, off ~** (US: AUT) bretelle *f* d'accès

rampage [ræmˈpeɪdʒ] *n*: **to be on the ~** se déchaîner

rampant [ˈræmpənt] *adj* (*disease etc*) qui sévit

ram raiding *n* pillage d'un magasin en enfonçant la vitrine avec une voiture

ramshackle [ˈræmʃækl] *adj* (*house*) délabré(e); (*car etc*) déglingué(e)

ran [ræn] *pt of* **run**

ranch [rɑːntʃ] *n* ranch *m*; **~er** *n* propriétaire *m* de ranch

rancid [ˈrænsɪd] *adj* rance

rancour [ˈræŋkə*] (US **rancor**) *n* rancune *f*

random [ˈrændəm] *adj* fait(e) *or* établi(e) au hasard; (MATH) aléatoire ♦ *n*: **at ~** au hasard; **~ access** *n* (COMPUT) accès sélectif

randy [ˈrændɪ] (BRIT: *inf*) *adj* excité(e); lubrique

rang [ræŋ] *pt of* **ring**

range [reɪndʒ] *n* (*of mountains*) chaîne *f*; (*of missile, voice*) portée *f*; (*of products*) choix *m*, gamme *f*; (MIL: *also: shooting* ~) champ *m* de tir; (*indoor*) stand *m* de tir; (*also: kitchen* ~) fourneau *m* (de cuisine) ♦ *vt* (*place in a line*) mettre en rang, ranger ♦ *vi*: **to ~ over** (*extend*) couvrir; **to ~ from ... to** aller de ... à; **a ~ of** (*series: of proposals etc*) divers(e)

ranger [ˈreɪndʒə*] *n* garde forestier

rank [ræŋk] *n* rang *m*; (MIL) grade *m*; (BRIT: *also: taxi* ~) station *f* de taxis ♦ *vi*: **to ~ among** compter *or* se classer parmi ♦ *adj* (*stinking*) fétide, puant(e); **the ~ and file** (*fig*) la masse, la base

rankle [ˈræŋkl] *vi* (*insult*) rester sur le cœur

ransack [ˈrænsæk] *vt* fouiller (à fond); (*plunder*) piller

ransom [ˈrænsəm] *n* rançon *f*; **to hold to**

~ (*fig*) exercer un chantage sur

rant [rænt] *vi* fulminer

rap [ræp] *vt* frapper sur *or* à; taper sur; *n*: ~ (*music*) rap *m*

rape [reɪp] *n* viol *m*; (*BOT*) colza *m* ♦ *vt* violer; ~(**seed**) **oil** *n* huile *f* de colza

rapid ['ræpɪd] *adj* rapide; ~s *npl* (*GEO*) rapides *mpl*

rapist ['reɪpɪst] *n* violeur *m*

rapport [ræ'pɔ:*] *n* entente *f*

rapture ['ræptʃə*] *n* extase *f*, ravissement *m*; **rapturous** ['ræptʃərəs] *adj* enthousiaste, frénétique

rare [rɛə*] *adj* rare; (*CULIN*: *steak*) saignant(e)

raring ['rɛərɪŋ] *adj*: ~ **to go** (*inf*) très impatient(e) de commencer

rascal ['rɑ:skəl] *n* vaurien *m*

rash [ræʃ] *adj* imprudent(e), irréfléchi(e) ♦ *n* (*MED*) rougeur *f*, éruption *f*; (*spate: of events*) série (noire)

rasher ['ræʃə*] *n* fine tranche (de lard)

raspberry ['rɑ:zbərɪ] *n* framboise *f*; ~ **bush** *n* framboisier *m*

rasping ['rɑ:spɪŋ] *adj*: ~ **noise** grincement *m*

rat [ræt] *n* rat *m*

rate [reɪt] *n* taux *m*; (*speed*) vitesse *f*, rythme *m*; (*price*) tarif *m* ♦ *vt* classer; évaluer; ~s *npl* (*BRIT*: *tax*) impôts locaux; (*fees*) tarifs *mpl*; **to** ~ **sb/sth as** considérer qn/qch comme; ~**able value** (*BRIT*) *n* valeur locative imposable; ~**payer** (*BRIT*) *n* contribuable *m/f* (*payant les impôts locaux*)

rather ['rɑ:ðə*] *adv* plutôt; **it's** ~ **expensive** c'est assez cher; (*too much*) c'est un peu cher; **there's** ~ **a lot** il y en a beaucoup; **I would** *or* **I'd** ~ **go** j'aimerais mieux *or* je préférerais partir

rating ['reɪtɪŋ] *n* (*assessment*) évaluation *f*; (*score*) classement *m*; (*NAUT*: *BRIT*: *sailor*) matelot *m*; ~**s** *npl* (*RADIO, TV*) indice *m* d'écoute

ratio ['reɪʃɪəʊ] *n* proportion *f*

ration ['ræʃən] *n* (*gen pl*) ration(s) *f(pl)*

rational ['ræʃənl] *adj* raisonnable, sensé(e); (*solution, reasoning*) logique; ~**e** [ræʃə'nɑ:l] *n* raisonnement *m*; ~**ize** ['ræʃnəlaɪz] *vt* rationaliser; (*conduct*) essayer d'expliquer *or* de motiver

rat race *n* foire *f* d'empoigne

rattle ['rætl] *n* (*of door, window*) battement *m*; (*of coins, chain*) cliquetis *m*; (*of train, engine*) bruit *m* de ferraille; (*object: for baby*) hochet *m* ♦ *vi* cliqueter; (*car, bus*): **to** ~ **along** rouler dans un bruit de ferraille ♦ *vt* agiter (bruyamment); (*unnerve*) décontenancer; ~**snake** *n* serpent *m* à sonnettes

raucous ['rɔ:kəs] *adj* rauque; (*noisy*) bruyant(e), tapageur(euse)

rave [reɪv] *vi* (*in anger*) s'emporter; (*with enthusiasm*) s'extasier; (*MED*) délirer

raven ['reɪvn] *n* corbeau *m*

ravenous ['rævənəs] *adj* affamé(e)

ravine [rə'vi:n] *n* ravin *m*

raving ['reɪvɪŋ] *adj*: ~ **lunatic** *n* fou(folle) furieux(euse)

ravishing ['rævɪʃɪŋ] *adj* enchanteur(eresse)

raw [rɔ:] *adj* (*uncooked*) cru(e); (*not processed*) brut(e); (*sore*) à vif, irrité(e); (*inexperienced*) inexpérimenté(e); (*weather, day*) froid(e) et humide; ~ **deal** (*inf*) *n* sale coup *m*; ~ **material** *n* matière première

ray [reɪ] *n* rayon *m*; ~ **of hope** lueur *f* d'espoir

raze [reɪz] *vt* (*also*: ~ **to the ground**) raser, détruire

razor ['reɪzə*] *n* rasoir *m*; ~ **blade** *n* lame *f* de rasoir

Rd *abbr* = **road**

re [ri:] *prep* concernant

reach [ri:tʃ] *n* portée *f*, atteinte *f*; (*of river etc*) étendue *f* ♦ *vt* atteindre; (*conclusion, decision*) parvenir à ♦ *vi* s'étendre, étendre le bras; **out of/within** ~ **s** hors de/à portée; **within** ~ **of the shops** pas trop loin des *or* à proximité des magasins; ~ **out** *vt* tendre ♦ *vi*: **to** ~ **out (for)** allonger le bras (pour prendre)

react [ri:'ækt] *vi* réagir; ~**ion** [ri:'ækʃən] *n* réaction *f*

reactor [ri:'æktə*] *n* réacteur *m*

read[1] [ri:d] (*pt, pp* **read**) *vi* lire ♦ *vt* lire;

(*understand*) comprendre, interpréter; (*study*) étudier; (*meter*) relever; **~ out** *vt* lire à haute voix; **~able** *adj* facile or agréable à lire; (*writing*) lisible; **~er** *n* lecteur(trice); (*book*) livre *m* de lecture; (*BRIT: at university*) chargé(e) d'enseignement; **~ership** *n* (*of paper etc*) (nombre *m* de) lecteurs *mpl*

read² [red] *pt, pp of* **read¹**

readily ['redɪlɪ] *adv* volontiers, avec empressement; (*easily*) facilement

readiness ['redɪnəs] *n* empressement *m*; **in ~** (*prepared*) prêt(e)

reading ['riːdɪŋ] *n* lecture *f*; (*understanding*) interprétation *f*; (*on instrument*) indications *fpl*

ready ['redɪ] *adj* prêt(e); (*willing*) prêt, disposé(e); (*available*) disponible ♦ *n*: **at the ~** (*MIL*) prêt à faire feu; **to get ~** se préparer ♦ *vt* préparer; **~-made** *adj* tout(e) fait(e); **~ money** *n* (argent *m*) liquide *m*; **~-to-wear** *adj* prêt(e) à porter

real [rɪəl] *adj* véritable; réel(le); **in ~ terms** dans la réalité; **~ estate** *n* biens fonciers or immobiliers; **~istic** [rɪə'lɪstɪk] *adj* réaliste; **~ity** [rɪː'ælɪtɪ] *n* réalité *f*

realization [rɪəlaɪ'zeɪʃən] *n* (*awareness*) prise *f* de conscience; (*fulfilment; also: of asset*) réalisation *f*

realize ['rɪəlaɪz] *vt* (*understand*) se rendre compte de; (*a project, COMM: asset*) réaliser

really ['rɪəlɪ] *adv* vraiment; **~?** vraiment?, c'est vrai?

realm [relm] *n* royaume *m*; (*fig*) domaine *m*

realtor ['rɪəltɔː*] (® *US*) *n* agent immobilier

reap [riːp] *vt* moissonner; (*fig*) récolter

reappear ['riːə'pɪə*] *vi* réapparaître, reparaître

rear [rɪə*] *adj* de derrière, arrière *inv*; (*AUT: wheel etc*) arrière ♦ *n* arrière *m* ♦ *vt* (*cattle, family*) élever ♦ *vi* (*also: ~ up*: *animal*) se cabrer; **~guard** *n* (*MIL*) arrière-garde *f*

rear-view mirror ['rɪəvjuː-] *n* (*AUT*) rétroviseur *m*

reason ['riːzn] *n* raison *f* ♦ *vi*: **to ~ with**

sb raisonner qn, faire entendre raison à qn; **to have ~ to think** avoir lieu de penser; **it stands to ~ that** il va sans dire que; **~able** *adj* raisonnable; (*not bad*) acceptable; **~ably** *adv* raisonnablement; **~ing** *n* raisonnement *m*

reassurance ['riːə'ʃuərəns] *n* réconfort *m*; (*factual*) assurance *f*, garantie *f*; **reassure** ['riːə'ʃuə*] *vt* rassurer

rebate ['riːbeɪt] *n* (*on tax etc*) dégrèvement *m*

rebel [*n* 'rebl, *vb* rɪ'bel] *n* rebelle *m/f* ♦ *vi* se rebeller, se révolter; **~lious** *adj* rebelle

rebound [*vb* rɪ'baund, *n* 'riːbaund] *vi* (*ball*) rebondir ♦ *n* rebond *m*; **to marry on the ~** se marier immédiatement après une déception amoureuse

rebuff [rɪ'bʌf] *n* rebuffade *f*

rebuke [rɪ'bjuːk] *vt* réprimander

rebut [rɪ'bʌt] *vt* réfuter

recall [rɪ'kɔːl] *vt* rappeler; (*remember*) se rappeler, se souvenir de ♦ *n* rappel *m*; (*ability to remember*) mémoire *f*

recant [rɪ'kænt] *vi* se rétracter; (*REL*) abjurer

recap ['riːkæp], **recapitulate** [riːkə'pɪtjuleɪt] *vt, vi* récapituler

rec'd *abbr* = **received**

recede [rɪ'siːd] *vi* (*tide*) descendre; (*disappear*) disparaître peu à peu; (*memory, hope*) s'estomper; **receding** [rɪ'siːdɪŋ] *adj* (*chin*) fuyant(e); **receding hairline** front dégarni

receipt [rɪ'siːt] *n* (*document*) reçu *m*; (*for parcel etc*) accusé *m* de réception; (*act of receiving*) réception *f*; **~s** *npl* (*COMM*) recettes *fpl*

receive [rɪ'siːv] *vt* recevoir

receiver [rɪ'siːvə*] *n* (*TEL*) récepteur *m*, combiné *m*; (*RADIO*) récepteur *m*; (*of stolen goods*) receleur *m*; (*LAW*) administrateur *m* judiciaire

recent ['riːsnt] *adj* récent(e); **~ly** *adv* récemment

receptacle [rɪ'septəkl] *n* récipient *m*

reception [rɪ'sepʃən] *n* réception *f*; (*welcome*) accueil *m*, réception; **~ desk** *n* réception *f*; **~ist** *n* réceptionniste *m/f*

recess [rɪˈsɛs] *n* (*in room*) renfoncement *m*, alcôve *f*; (*secret place*) recoin *m*; (*POL etc : holiday*) vacances *fpl*
recession [rɪˈsɛʃən] *n* récession *f*
recipe [ˈrɛsɪpɪ] *n* recette *f*
recipient [rɪˈsɪpɪənt] *n* (*of payment*) bénéficiaire *m/f*; (*of letter*) destinataire *m/f*
recital [rɪˈsaɪtl] *n* récital *m*
recite [rɪˈsaɪt] *vt* (*poem*) réciter
reckless [ˈrɛkləs] *adj* (*driver etc*) imprudent(e)
reckon [ˈrɛkən] *vt* (*count*) calculer, compter; (*think*): **I ~ that ...** je pense que ...; **~ on** *vt fus* compter sur, s'attendre à; **~ing** *n* compte *m*, calcul *m*; estimation *f*
reclaim [rɪˈkleɪm] *vt* (*demand back*) réclamer (le remboursement *or* la restitution de); (*land: from sea*) assécher; (*waste materials*) récupérer
recline [rɪˈklaɪn] *vi* être allongé(e) *or* étendu(e); **reclining** [rɪˈklaɪnɪŋ] *adj* (*seat*) à dossier réglable
recluse [rɪˈkluːs] *n* reclus(e), ermite *m*
recognition [rɛkəgˈnɪʃən] *n* reconnaissance *f*; **to gain ~** être reconnu(e); **transformed beyond ~** méconnaissable
recognize [ˈrɛkəgnaɪz] *vt*: **to ~ (by/as)** reconnaître (à/comme étant)
recoil [rɪˈkɔɪl] *vi* (*person*): **to ~ (from sth/doing sth)** reculer (devant qch/ l'idée de faire qch) ♦ *n* (*of gun*) recul *m*
recollect [rɛkəˈlɛkt] *vt* se rappeler, se souvenir de; **~ion** [rɛkəˈlɛkʃən] *n* souvenir *m*
recommend [rɛkəˈmɛnd] *vt* recommander
reconcile [ˈrɛkənsaɪl] *vt* (*two people*) réconcilier; (*two facts*) concilier, accorder; **to ~ o.s. to** se résigner à
recondition [ˈriːkənˈdɪʃən] *vt* remettre à neuf, réviser entièrement
reconnoitre [rɛkəˈnɔɪtər] (*US* **reconnoiter**) *vt* (*MIL*) reconnaître
reconstruct [ˈriːkənˈstrʌkt] *vt* (*building*) reconstruire; (*crime, policy, system*) reconstituer
record [*n* ˈrɛkɔːd, *vb* rɪˈkɔːd] *n* rapport *m*, récit *m*; (*of meeting etc*) procès-verbal *m*; (*register*) registre *m*; (*file*) dossier *m*; (*also: criminal ~*) casier *m* judiciaire; (*MUS: disc*) disque *m*; (*SPORT*) record *m*; (*COMPUT*) article *m* ♦ *vt* (*set down*) noter; (*MUS: song etc*) enregistrer; **in ~ time** un temps record *inv*; **off the ~** *adj* officieux(euse) ♦ *adv* officieusement; **~ card** *n* (*in file*) fiche *f*; **~ed delivery** [rɪˈkɔːdɪd-] *n* (*BRIT: POST*): **~ed delivery letter** *etc* lettre *etc* recommandée; **~er** [rɪˈkɔːdər] *n* (*MUS*) flûte *f* à bec; **~ holder** *n* (*SPORT*) détenteur(trice) du record; **~ing** [rɪˈkɔːdɪŋ] *n* (*MUS*) enregistrement *m*; **~ player** *n* tourne-disque *m*
recount [rɪˈkaunt] *vt* raconter
re-count [ˈriːkaunt] *n* (*POL: of votes*) deuxième compte *m* ♦ *vt* recompter
recoup [rɪˈkuːp] *vt*: **to ~ one's losses** récupérer ce qu'on a perdu, se refaire
recourse [rɪˈkɔːs] *n*: **to have ~ to** avoir recours à
recover [rɪˈkʌvər] *vt* récupérer ♦ *vi*: **to ~ (from)** (*illness*) se rétablir (de); (*from shock*) se remettre (de); **~y** [rɪˈkʌvərɪ] *n* récupération *f*; rétablissement *m*; (*ECON*) redressement *m*
recreation [rɛkrɪˈeɪʃən] *n* récréation *f*, détente *f*; **~al** *adj* pour la détente, récréatif(ive); **~al drug** drogue que l'on prend pour le plaisir et non pour des raisons médicales ou par dépendance
recruit [rɪˈkruːt] *n* recrue *f* ♦ *vt* recruter
rectangle [ˈrɛktæŋgl] *n* rectangle *m*; **rectangular** [rɛkˈtæŋgjulər] *adj* rectangulaire
rectify [ˈrɛktɪfaɪ] *vt* (*error*) rectifier, corriger
rector [ˈrɛktər] *n* (*REL*) pasteur *m*
recuperate [rɪˈkuːpəreɪt] *vi* récupérer; (*from illness*) se rétablir
recur [rɪˈkɜːr] *vi* se reproduire; (*symptoms*) réapparaître; **~rence** *n* répétition *f*; réapparition *f*; **~rent** *adj* périodique, fréquent(e)
recycle [riːˈsaɪkl] *vt* recycler
red [rɛd] *n* rouge *m*; (*POL: pej*) rouge *m/f* ♦ *adj* rouge; (*hair*) roux(rousse); **in the ~** (*account*) à découvert; (*business*) en

déficit; ~ **carpet treatment** n réception f en grande pompe; **R~ Cross** n Croix-Rouge f; **~currant** n groseille f (rouge); **~den** vt, vi rougir; **~dish** adj rougeâtre; (hair) qui tirent sur le roux

redeem [rɪ'diːm] vt (debt) rembourser; (sth in pawn) dégager; (fig, also REL) racheter; **~ing** adj (feature) qui sauve, qui rachète (le reste)

redeploy ['riːdɪ'plɔɪ] vt (resources) réorganiser

redevelopment [riːdɪ'velǝpmǝnt] n rénovation f, reconstruction f

red: **~-haired** ['hɛǝd] adj roux(rousse); **~-handed** [-'hændɪd] adj: **to be caught ~-handed** être pris(e) en flagrant délit or la main dans le sac; **~head** [-'hed] n roux(rousse); **~ herring** n (fig) diversion f, fausse piste; **~-hot** [-'hɒt] adj chauffé(e) au rouge, brûlant(e)

redirect ['riːdaɪ'rekt] vt (mail) faire suivre

red light n: **to go through a ~** (AUT) brûler un feu rouge; **red-light district** n quartier m des prostituées

redo ['riː'duː] (irreg) vt refaire

redolent ['redǝlǝnt] adj: **~ of** qui sent; (fig) qui évoque

redress [rɪ'dres] n réparation f ♦ vt redresser

Red Sea n: **the ~** la mer Rouge

redskin ['redskɪn] n Peau-Rouge m/f

red tape n (fig) paperasserie (administrative)

reduce [rɪ'djuːs] vt réduire; (lower) abaisser; **"~ speed now"** (AUT) "ralentir"; **reduction** [rɪ'dʌkʃǝn] n réduction f; (discount) rabais m

redundancy [rɪ'dʌndǝnsɪ] (BRIT) n licenciement m, mise f au chômage

redundant [rɪ'dʌndǝnt] adj (BRIT: worker) mis(e) au chômage, licencié(e); (detail, object) superflu(e); **to be made ~** être licencié(e), être mis(e) au chômage

reed [riːd] n (BOT) roseau m; (MUS: of clarinet etc) anche f

reef [riːf] n (at sea) récif m, écueil m

reek [riːk] vi: **to ~ (of)** puer, empester

reel [riːl] n bobine f; (FISHING) moulinet m; (CINEMA) bande f; (dance) quadrille écossais ♦ vi (sway) chanceler; **~ in** vt (fish, line) ramener

ref [ref] (inf) n abbr (= referee) arbitre m

refectory [rɪ'fektǝrɪ] n réfectoire m

refer [rɪ'fɜː*] vt: **to ~ sb to** (inquirer: for information, patient: to specialist) adresser qn à; (reader: to text) renvoyer qn à; (dispute, decision): **to ~ sth to** soumettre qch à ♦ vi: **~ to** (allude to) parler de, faire allusion à; (consult) se reporter à

referee [refǝ'riː] n arbitre m; (TENNIS) juge-arbitre m; (BRIT: for job application) répondant(e)

reference ['refrǝns] n référence f, renvoi m; (mention) allusion f, mention f; (for job application: letter) références fpl, lettre f de recommandation; **with ~ to** (COMM: in letter) me référant à, suite à; **~ book** n ouvrage m de référence

refill [vb riː'fɪl, n 'riːfɪl] vt remplir à nouveau; (pen, lighter etc) recharger ♦ n (for pen etc) recharge f

refine [rɪ'faɪn] vt (sugar, oil) raffiner; (taste) affiner; (theory, idea) fignoler (inf); **~d** adj (person, taste) raffiné(e)

reflect [rɪ'flekt] vt (light, image) réfléchir, refléter; (fig) refléter ♦ vi (think) réfléchir, méditer; **it ~s badly on him** cela le discrédite; **it ~s well on him** c'est tout à son honneur; **~ion** [rɪ'flekʃǝn] n réflexion f; (image) reflet m; (criticism): **~ion on** critique f de; atteinte f à; **on ~ion** réflexion faite

reflex ['riːfleks] adj réflexe ♦ n réflexe m; **~ive** [rɪfleksɪv] adj (LING) réfléchi(e)

reform [rɪ'fɔːm] n réforme f ♦ vt réformer; **R~ation** [refǝ'meɪʃǝn] n: **the R~ation** la Réforme; **~atory** (US) n ≈ centre m d'éducation surveillée

refrain [rɪ'freɪn] vi: **to ~ from doing** s'abstenir de faire ♦ n refrain m

refresh [rɪ'freʃ] vt rafraîchir; (subj: sleep) reposer; **~er course** (BRIT) n cours m de recyclage; **~ing** adj (drink) rafraîchissant(e); (sleep) réparateur(trice); **~ments** npl rafraîchissements mpl

refrigerator [rɪ'frɪdʒəreɪtə*] *n* réfrigérateur *m*, frigidaire *m* (®)

refuel ['riː'fjʊəl] *vi* se ravitailler en carburant

refuge ['refjuːdʒ] *n* refuge *m*; **to take ~ in** se réfugier dans

refugee [refjʊ'dʒiː] *n* réfugié(e)

refund [*n* 'riːfʌnd, *vb* rɪ'fʌnd] *n* remboursement *m* ♦ *vt* rembourser

refurbish ['riː'fɜːbɪʃ] *vt* remettre à neuf

refusal [rɪ'fjuːzəl] *n* refus *m*; **to have first ~ on** avoir droit de préemption sur

refuse¹ [rɪ'fjuːz] *vt, vi* refuser

refuse² ['refjuːs] *n* ordures *fpl*, détritus *mpl*; **~ collection** *n* ramassage *m* d'ordures

regain [rɪ'geɪn] *vt* regagner; retrouver

regal ['riːgəl] *adj* royal(e)

regard [rɪ'gɑːd] *n* respect *m*, estime *f*, considération *f* ♦ *vt* considérer; **to give one's ~s to** faire ses amitiés à; **"with kindest ~s"** "bien amicalement"; **as ~s, with ~ to = regarding; ~ing** *prep* en ce qui concerne; **~less** *adv* quand même; **~less of** sans se soucier de

régime [reɪ'ʒiːm] *n* régime *m*

regiment [*n* 'redʒɪmənt, *vb* 'redʒɪment] *n* régiment *m*; **~al** [redʒɪ'mentl] *adj* d'un or du régiment

region ['riːdʒən] *n* région *f*; **in the ~ of** (*fig*) aux alentours de; **~al** *adj* régional(e)

register ['redʒɪstə*] *n* registre *m*; (*also: electoral ~*) liste électorale ♦ *vt* enregistrer; (*birth, death*) déclarer; (*vehicle*) immatriculer; (*POST: letter*) envoyer en recommandé; (*subj: instrument*) marquer ♦ *vi* s'inscrire; (*at hotel*) signer le registre; (*make impression*) être (bien) compris(e); **~ed** *adj* (*letter, parcel*) recommandé(e); **~ed trademark** *n* marque déposée; **registrar** ['redʒɪs'trɑː*] *n* officier *m* de l'état civil; **registration** [redʒɪs'treɪʃən] *n* enregistrement *m*; (*BRIT AUT: also: ~ number*) numéro *m* d'immatriculation

registry ['redʒɪstrɪ] *n* bureau *m* de l'enregistrement; **~ office** (*BRIT*) *n* bureau *m* de l'état civil; **to get married in a ~ office** ≈ se marier à la mairie

regret [rɪ'gret] *n* regret *m* ♦ *vt* regretter; **~fully** *adv* à *or* avec regret

regular ['regjʊlə*] *adj* régulier(ère); (*usual*) habituel(le); (*soldier*) de métier ♦ *n* (*client etc*) habitué(e); **~ly** *adv* régulièrement

regulate ['regjʊleɪt] *vt* régler; **regulation** [regjʊ'leɪʃən] *n* (*rule*) règlement *m*; (*adjustment*) réglage *m*

rehabilitation ['riːhəbɪlɪ'teɪʃən] *n* (*of offender*) réinsertion *f*; (*of addict*) réadaptation *f*

rehearsal [rɪ'hɜːsəl] *n* répétition *f*

rehearse [rɪ'hɜːs] *vt* répéter

reign [reɪn] *n* règne *m* ♦ *vi* régner

reimburse [riːɪm'bɜːs] *vt* rembourser

rein [reɪn] *n* (*for horse*) rêne *f*

reindeer ['reɪndɪə*] *n, pl inv* renne *m*

reinforce [riːɪn'fɔːs] *vt* renforcer; **~d concrete** *n* béton armé; **~ments** *npl* (*MIL*) renfort(s) *m(pl)*

reinstate ['riːɪn'steɪt] *vt* rétablir, réintégrer

reject [*n* 'riːdʒekt, *vb* rɪ'dʒekt] *n* (*COMM*) article *m* de rebut ♦ *vt* refuser; (*idea*) rejeter; **~ion** [rɪ'dʒekʃən] *n* rejet *m*, refus *m*

rejoice [rɪ'dʒɔɪs] *vi*: **to ~ (at or over)** se réjouir (de)

rejuvenate [rɪ'dʒuːvɪneɪt] *vt* rajeunir

relapse [rɪ'læps] *n* (*MED*) rechute *f*

relate [rɪ'leɪt] *vt* (*tell*) raconter; (*connect*) établir un rapport entre ♦ *vi*: **this ~s to** cela se rapporte à; **to ~ to sb** entretenir des rapports avec qn; **~d** *adj* apparenté(e); **relating to** *prep* concernant

relation [rɪ'leɪʃən] *n* (*person*) parent(e); (*link*) rapport *m*, lien *m*; **~ship** *n* rapport *m*, lien *m*; (*personal ties*) relations *fpl*, rapports; (*also: family ~ship*) lien de parenté

relative ['relətɪv] *n* parent(e) ♦ *adj* relatif(ive); **all her ~s** toute sa famille; **~ly** *adv* relativement

relax [rɪ'læks] *vi* (*muscle*) se relâcher; (*person: unwind*) se détendre ♦ *vt* relâcher; (*mind, person*) détendre; **~ation** [riːlæk'seɪʃən] *n* relâchement *m*; (*of* *mind*) détente *f*, relaxation *f*; (*recreation*) détente, délassement *m*; ~ed *adj* détendu(e); ~ing *adj* délassant(e)

relay ['riːleɪ] *n* (*SPORT*) course *f* de relais ♦ *vt* (*message*) retransmettre, relayer

release [rɪ'liːs] *n* (*from prison, obligation*) libération *f*; (*of gas etc*) émission *f*; (*of film etc*) sortie *f*; (*new recording*) disque *m* ♦ *vt* (*prisoner*) libérer; (*gas etc*) émettre, dégager; (*free: from wreckage etc*) dégager; (*TECH: catch, spring etc*) faire jouer; (*book, film*) sortir; (*report, news*) rendre public, publier

relegate ['relɪgeɪt] *vt* reléguer; (*BRIT: SPORT*): **to be ~d** descendre dans une division inférieure

relent [rɪ'lent] *vi* se laisser fléchir; ~less *adj* implacable; (*unceasing*) continuel(le)

relevant ['relɪvənt] *adj* (*question*) pertinent(e); (*fact*) significatif(ive); (*information*) utile; ~ **to** ayant rapport à, approprié à

reliable [rɪ'laɪəbl] *adj* (*person, firm*) sérieux(euse), fiable; (*method, machine*) fiable; (*news, information*) sûr(e); **reliably** *adv*: **to be reliably informed** savoir de source sûre

reliance [rɪ'laɪəns] *n*: ~ **(on)** (*person*) confiance *f* (en); (*drugs, promises*) besoin *m* (de), dépendance *f* (de)

relic ['relɪk] *n* (*REL*) relique *f*; (*of the past*) vestige *m*

relief [rɪ'liːf] *n* (*from pain, anxiety etc*) soulagement *m*; (*help, supplies*) secours *m(pl)*; (*ART, GEO*) relief *m*

relieve [rɪ'liːv] *vt* (*pain, patient*) soulager; (*fear, worry*) dissiper; (*bring help*) secourir; (*take over from: gen*) relayer; (*: guard*) relever; **to ~ sb of sth** débarrasser qn de qch; **to ~ o.s.** se soulager

religion [rɪ'lɪdʒən] *n* religion *f*; **religious** [rɪ'lɪdʒəs] *adj* religieux(euse); (*book*) de piété

relinquish [rɪ'lɪŋkwɪʃ] *vt* abandonner; (*plan, habit*) renoncer à

relish ['relɪʃ] *n* (*CULIN*) condiment *m*; (*enjoyment*) délectation *f* ♦ *vt* (*food etc*) savourer; **to ~ doing** se délecter à faire

relocate ['riːləʊ'keɪt] *vt* installer ailleurs ♦ *vi* déménager, s'installer ailleurs

reluctance [rɪ'lʌktəns] *n* répugnance *f*

reluctant [rɪ'lʌktənt] *adj* peu disposé(e), qui hésite; ~**ly** *adv* à contrecœur

rely on [rɪlaɪ] *vt fus* (*be dependent*) dépendre de; (*trust*) compter sur

remain [rɪ'meɪn] *vi* rester; ~**der** *n* reste *m*; ~**ing** *adj* qui reste; ~**s** *npl* restes *mpl*

remand [rɪ'mɑːnd] *n*: **on** ~ en détention préventive ♦ *vt*: **to be ~ed in custody** être placé(e) en détention préventive; ~ **home** (*BRIT*) *n* maison *f* d'arrêt

remark [rɪ'mɑːk] *n* remarque *f*, observation *f* ♦ *vt* (*faire*) remarquer, dire; ~**able** *adj* remarquable

remedial [rɪ'miːdɪəl] *adj* (*tuition, classes*) de rattrapage; ~ **exercises** gymnastique corrective

remedy ['remədɪ] *n*: ~ **(for)** remède *m* (contre *or* à) ♦ *vt* remédier à

remember [rɪ'membə*] *vt* se rappeler, se souvenir de; (*send greetings*): ~ **me to him** saluez-le de ma part; **remembrance** [rɪ'membrəns] *n* souvenir *m*; mémoire *f*

remind [rɪ'maɪnd] *vt*: **to ~ sb of** rappeler à qn; **to ~ sb to do** faire penser à qn à faire, rappeler à qn qu'il doit faire; ~**er** *n* (*souvenir*) souvenir *m*; (*letter*) rappel *m*

réminisce [remɪ'nɪs] *vi*: **to ~ (about)** évoquer ses souvenirs (de)

reminiscent [remɪ'nɪsnt] *adj*: **to be ~ of** rappeler, faire penser à

remiss [rɪ'mɪs] *adj* négligent(e)

remission [rɪ'mɪʃən] *n* (*of illness, sins*) rémission *f*; (*of debt, prison sentence*) remise *f*

remit [rɪ'mɪt] *vt* (*send: money*) envoyer; ~**tance** *n* paiement *m*

remnant ['remnənt] *n* reste *m*, restant *m*; (*of cloth*) coupon *m*; ~**s** *npl* (*COMM*) fins *fpl* de série

remorse [rɪ'mɔːs] *n* remords *m*; ~**ful** *adj* plein(e) de remords; ~**less** *adj* (*fig*) impitoyable

remote [rɪ'məʊt] *adj* éloigné(e), lointain(e); (*person*) distant(e); (*possibility*) vague; ~ **control** *n* télécommande *f*; ~**ly**

adv au loin; (*slightly*) très vaguement
remould ['riːməʊld] (*BRIT*) *n* (*tyre*) pneu rechapé
removable [rɪ'muːvəbl] *adj* (*detachable*) amovible
removal [rɪ'muːvəl] *n* (*taking away*) enlèvement *m*; suppression *f*; (*BRIT: from house*) déménagement *m*; (*from office: dismissal*) renvoi *m*; (*of stain*) nettoyage *m*; (*MED*) ablation *f*; ~ **van** (*BRIT*) *n* camion *m* de déménagement
remove [rɪ'muːv] *vt* enlever, retirer; (*employee*) renvoyer; (*stain*) faire partir; (*abuse*) supprimer; (*doubt*) chasser
render ['rendə*] *vt* rendre; ~**ing** *n* (*MUS etc*) interprétation *f*
rendezvous *n* rendez-vous *m inv*
renew [rɪ'njuː] *vt* renouveler; (*negotiations*) reprendre; (*acquaintance*) renouer; ~**able** *adj* (*energy*) renouvelable; ~**al** *n* renouvellement *m*; reprise *f*
renounce [rɪ'naʊns] *vt* renoncer à
renovate ['renəveɪt] *vt* rénover; (*art work*) restaurer
renown [rɪ'naʊn] *n* renommée *f*; ~**ed** *adj* renommé(e)
rent [rent] *n* loyer *m* ♦ *vt* louer; ~**al** *n* (*for television, car*) (prix *m* de) location *f*
rep [rep] *n abbr* = **representative**; = **repertory**
repair [rɪ'peə*] *n* réparation *f* ♦ *vt* réparer; **in good/bad** ~ en bon/mauvais état; ~ **kit** *n* trousse *f* de réparation
repatriate [riː'pætrɪeɪt] *vt* rapatrier
repay [riː'peɪ] (*irreg*) *vt* (*money, creditor*) rembourser; (*sb's efforts*) récompenser; ~**ment** *n* remboursement *m*
repeal [rɪ'piːl] *n* (*of law*) abrogation *f* ♦ *vt* (*law*) abroger
repeat [rɪ'piːt] *n* (*RADIO, TV*) reprise *f* ♦ *vt* répéter; (*COMM: order*) renouveler; (*SCOL: a class*) redoubler ♦ *vi* répéter; ~**edly** *adv* souvent, à plusieurs reprises
repel [rɪ'pel] *vt* repousser; ~**lent** *adj* repoussante(e) ♦ *n*: **insect** ~**lent** insectifuge *m*
repent [rɪ'pent] *vi*: **to** ~ (**of**) se repentir (de); ~**ance** *n* repentir *m*

repertory ['repətərɪ] *n* (*also*: ~ *theatre*) théâtre *m* de répertoire
repetition [repɪ'tɪʃən] *n* répétition *f*
repetitive [rɪ'petɪtɪv] *adj* (*movement, work*) répétitif(ive); (*speech*) plein(e) de redites
replace [rɪ'pleɪs] *vt* (*put back*) remettre, replacer; (*take the place of*) remplacer; ~**ment** *n* (*substitution*) remplacement *m*; (*person*) remplaçant(e)
replay ['riːpleɪ] *n* (*of match*) match rejoué; (*of tape, film*) répétition *f*
replenish [rɪ'plenɪʃ] *vt* (*glass*) remplir (de nouveau); (*stock etc*) réapprovisionner
replica ['replɪkə] *n* réplique *f*, copie exacte
reply [rɪ'plaɪ] *n* réponse *f* ♦ *vi* répondre; ~ **coupon** *n* coupon-réponse *m*
report [rɪ'pɔːt] *n* rapport *m*; (*PRESS etc*) reportage *m*; (*BRIT: also: school* ~) bulletin *m* (scolaire); (*of gun*) détonation *f* ♦ *vt* rapporter, faire un compte rendu de; (*PRESS etc*) faire un reportage sur; (*bring to notice: occurrence*) signaler ♦ *vi* (*make a* ~) faire un rapport (*or* un reportage); (*present o.s.*): **to** ~ (**to sb**) se présenter (chez qn); (*be responsible to*): **to** ~ **to sb** être sous les ordres de qn; ~ **card** (*US, SCOTTISH*) *n* bulletin *m* scolaire; ~**edly** *adv*: **she is** ~**edly living in ...** elle habiterait ...; **he** ~**edly told them to ...** il leur aurait ordonné de ...; ~**er** *n* reporter *m*
repose [rɪ'pəʊz] *n*: **in** ~ en *or* au repos
represent [reprɪ'zent] *vt* représenter; (*view, belief*) présenter, expliquer; (*describe*): **to** ~ **sth as** présenter *or* décrire qch comme; ~**ation** [reprɪzen'teɪʃən] *n* représentation *f*; ~**ations** *npl* (*protest*) démarche *f*; ~**ative** *n* représentant(e); (*US: POL*) député *m* ♦ *adj* représentatif(ive), caractéristique
repress [rɪ'pres] *vt* réprimer; ~**ion** [rɪ'preʃən] *n* répression *f*
reprieve [rɪ'priːv] *n* (*LAW*) grâce *f*; (*fig*) sursis *m*, délai *m*
reprisal [rɪ'praɪzəl] *n*: ~**s** *npl* représailles *fpl*

reproach [rɪ'prəʊtʃ] vt: **to ~ sb with sth** reprocher qch à qn; **~ful** adj de reproche

reproduce [ri:prə'dju:s] vt reproduire ♦ vi se reproduire; **reproduction** [ri:prə'dʌkʃən] n reproduction f

reproof [rɪ'pru:f] n reproche m

reptile ['reptaɪl] n reptile m

republic [rɪ'pʌblɪk] n république f; **~an** adj républicain(e)

repudiate [rɪ'pju:dɪeɪt] vt répudier, rejeter

repulsive [rɪ'pʌlsɪv] adj repoussant(e), répulsif(ive)

reputable ['repjʊtəbl] adj de bonne réputation; (occupation) honorable

reputation [repjʊ'teɪʃən] n réputation f

reputed [rɪ'pju:tɪd] adj (supposed) supposé(e); **~ly** adv d'après ce qu'on dit

request [rɪ'kwest] n demande f; (formal) requête f ♦ vt: **to ~ (of or from sb)** demander (à qn); **~ stop** (BRIT) n (for bus) arrêt facultatif

require [rɪ'kwaɪə*] vt (need: subj: person) avoir besoin de; (: thing, situation) demander; (want) exiger; (order): **to ~ sb to do sth/sth of sb** exiger que qn fasse qch/qch de qn; **~ment** n exigence f; besoin m; condition requise

requisite ['rekwɪzɪt] n chose f nécessaire ♦ adj requis(e), nécessaire; **toilet ~s** accessoires mpl de toilette

requisition [rekwɪ'zɪʃən] n: **~ (for)** demande f (de) ♦ vt (MIL) réquisitionner

rescue ['reskju:] n (from accident) sauvetage m; (help) secours mpl ♦ vt sauver; **~ party** n équipe f de sauvetage; **~r** n sauveteur m

research [rɪ'sɜ:tʃ] n recherche(s) f(pl) ♦ vt faire des recherches sur

resemblance [rɪ'zembləns] n ressemblance f

resemble [rɪ'zembl] vt ressembler à

resent [rɪ'zent] vt être contrarié(e) par; **~ful** adj irrité(e), plein(e) de ressentiment; **~ment** n ressentiment m

reservation [rezə'veɪʃən] n (booking) réservation f; (doubt) réserve f; (for tribe) réserve; **to make a ~ (in a hotel/a restaurant/on a plane)** réserver or retenir une chambre/une table/une place

reserve [rɪ'zɜ:v] n réserve f; (SPORT) remplaçant(e) ♦ vt (seats etc) réserver, retenir; **~s** npl (MIL) réservistes mpl; **in ~** en réserve; **~d** adj réservé(e)

reshuffle ['ri:'ʃʌfl] n: **Cabinet ~** (POL) remaniement ministériel

residence ['rezɪdəns] n résidence f; **~ permit** (BRIT) n permis m de séjour

resident ['rezɪdənt] n résident(e) ♦ adj résidant(e); **~ial** [rezɪ'denʃəl] adj (area) résidentiel(le); (course) avec hébergement sur place; **~ial school** n internat m

residue ['rezɪdju:] n reste m; (CHEM, PHYSICS) résidu m

resign [rɪ'zaɪn] vt (one's post) démissionner de ♦ vi démissionner; **to ~ o.s. to** résigner à; **~ation** [rezɪg'neɪʃən] n (of post) démission f; (state of mind) résignation f; **~ed** adj résigné(e)

resilient [rɪ'zɪlɪənt] adj (material) élastique; (person) qui réagit, qui a du ressort

resist [rɪ'zɪst] vt résister à; **~ance** n résistance f

resolution [rezə'lu:ʃən] n résolution f

resolve [rɪ'zɒlv] n résolution f ♦ vt (problem) résoudre ♦ vi: **to ~ to do** résoudre or décider de faire

resort [rɪ'zɔ:t] n (town) station f; (recourse) recours m ♦ vi: **to ~ to** avoir recours à; **in the last ~** en dernier ressort

resound [rɪ'zaʊnd] vi: **to ~ (with)** retentir or résonner (de); **~ing** [rɪ'zaʊndɪŋ] adj retentissant(e)

resource [rɪ'sɔ:s] n ressource f; **~s** npl (supplies, wealth etc) ressources; **~ful** adj ingénieux(euse), débrouillard(e)

respect [rɪs'pekt] n respect m ♦ vt respecter; **~s** npl (compliments) respects hommages mpl; **with ~ to** en ce qui concerne; **in this ~** à cet égard; **~able** adj respectable; **~ful** adj respectueux(euse)

respite ['respaɪt] n répit m

resplendent [rɪs'plendənt] adj resplendissant(e)

respond [rɪs'pɒnd] vi répondre; (react)

réagir; **response** [rɪs'pɒns] *n* réponse *f*; réaction *f*

responsibility [rɪspɒnsə'bɪlɪtɪ] *n* responsabilité *f*

responsible [rɪs'pɒnsəbl] *adj* (*liable*): ~ **(for)** responsable (de); (*person*) digne de confiance; (*job*) qui comporte des responsabilités

responsive [rɪs'pɒnsɪv] *adj* qui réagit; (*person*) qui n'est pas réservé(e) *or* indifférent(e)

rest [rest] *n* repos *m*; (*stop*) arrêt *m*, pause *f*; (*MUS*) silence *m*; (*support*) support *m*, appui *m*; (*remainder*) reste *m*, restant *m* ♦ *vi* se reposer; (*be supported*): **to ~ on** appuyer *or* reposer sur; (*remain*) rester ♦ *vt* (*lean*): **to ~ sth on/against** appuyer qch sur/contre; **the ~ of them** les autres; **it ~s with him to ...** c'est à lui de ...

restaurant ['restərɒŋ] *n* restaurant *m*; ~ **car** (*BRIT*) *n* wagon-restaurant *m*

restful ['restful] *adj* reposant(e)

restive ['restɪv] *adj* agité(e), impatient(e); (*horse*) rétif(ive)

restless ['restləs] *adj* agité(e)

restoration [restə'reɪʃən] *n* restauration *f*; restitution *f*; rétablissement *m*

restore [rɪ'stɔː*] *vt* (*building*) restaurer; (*sth stolen*) restituer; (*peace, health*) rétablir; **to ~ to** (*former state*) ramener à

restrain [rɪs'treɪn] *vt* contenir; (*person*): **to ~ (from doing)** retenir (de faire); ~**ed** *adj* (*style*) sobre; (*manner*) mesuré(e); ~**t** *n* (*restriction*) contrainte *f*; (*moderation*) retenue *f*

restrict [rɪs'trɪkt] *vt* restreindre, limiter; ~**ion** [rɪs'trɪkʃən] *n* restriction *f*, limitation *f*

rest room (*US*) *n* toilettes *fpl*

result [rɪ'zʌlt] *n* résultat *m* ♦ *vi*: **to ~ in** aboutir à, se terminer par; **as a ~ of** à la suite de

resume [rɪ'zjuːm] *vt, vi* (*work, journey*) reprendre

résumé ['reɪzjuːmeɪ] *n* résumé *m*; (*US*) curriculum vitae *m*

resumption [rɪ'zʌmpʃən] *n* reprise *f*

resurgence [rɪ'sɜːdʒəns] *n* (*of energy,* *activity*) regain *m*

resurrection [rezə'rekʃən] *n* résurrection *f*

resuscitate [rɪ'sʌsɪteɪt] *vt* (*MED*) réanimer

retail [*n, adj* 'riːteɪl, *vb* 'riːteɪl] *adj* de *or* au détail ♦ *adv* au détail; ~**er** ['riːteɪlə*] *n* détaillant(e); ~ **price** *n* prix *m* de détail

retain [rɪ'teɪn] *vt* (*keep*) garder, conserver; ~**er** *n* (*fee*) acompte *m*, provision *f*

retaliate [rɪ'tælɪeɪt] *vi*: **to ~ (against)** se venger (de); **retaliation** [rɪtælɪ'eɪʃən] *n* représailles *fpl*, vengeance *f*

retarded [rɪ'tɑːdɪd] *adj* retardé(e)

retch [retʃ] *vi* avoir des haut-le-cœur

retentive [rɪ'tentɪv] *adj*: ~ **memory** excellente mémoire

retina ['retɪnə] *n* rétine *f*

retire [rɪ'taɪə*] *vi* (*give up work*) prendre sa retraite; (*withdraw*) se retirer, partir; (*go to bed*) aller se coucher; ~**d** *adj* (*person*) retraité(e); ~**ment** *n* retraite *f*; **retiring** [rɪ'taɪərɪŋ] *adj* (*shy*) réservé(e); (*leaving*) sortant(e)

retort [rɪ'tɔːt] *vi* riposter

retrace [rɪ'treɪs] *vt*: **to ~ one's steps** revenir sur ses pas

retract [rɪ'trækt] *vt* (*statement, claws*) rétracter; (*undercarriage, aerial*) rentrer, escamoter

retrain [riː'treɪn] *vt* (*worker*) recycler

retread ['riːtred] *n* (*tyre*) pneu rechapé

retreat [rɪ'triːt] *n* retraite *f* ♦ *vi* battre en retraite

retribution [retrɪ'bjuːʃən] *n* châtiment *m*

retrieval [rɪ'triːvəl] *n* (*see vb*) récupération *f*, réparation *f*

retrieve [rɪ'triːv] *vt* (*sth lost*) récupérer; (*situation, honour*) sauver; (*error, loss*) réparer; ~**r** *n* chien *m* d'arrêt

retrospect ['retrəuspekt] *n*: **in ~** rétrospectivement, après coup; ~**ive** [retrəu-'spektɪv] *adj* rétrospectif(ive); (*law*) rétroactif(ive)

return [rɪ'tɜːn] *n* (*going or coming* *back*) retour *m*; (*of sth stolen etc*) restitution *f*; (*FINANCE: from land, shares*) rendement *m*, rapport *m* ♦ *cpd* (*jour-*

ney) de retour; (*BRIT: ticket*) aller et retour; (*match*) retour ♦ *vi* (*come back*) revenir; (*go back*) retourner ♦ *vt* rendre; (*bring back*) rapporter; (*send back; also: ball*) renvoyer; (*put back*) remettre; (*POL: candidate*) élire; **~s** *npl* (*COMM*) recettes *fpl*; (*FINANCE*) bénéfices *mpl*; **in ~ (for)** en échange (de); **by ~ (of post)** par retour (du courrier); **many happy ~s (of the day)!** bon anniversaire!

reunion [riːˈjuːnjən] *n* réunion *f*

reunite [ˈriːjuːˈnaɪt] *vt* réunir

rev [rev] *n abbr* (*AUT*: = *revolution*) tour *m* ♦ *vt* (*also:* ~ **up**) emballer

revamp [ˈriːˈvæmp] *vt* (*firm, system etc*) réorganiser

reveal [rɪˈviːl] *vt* (*make known*) révéler; (*display*) laisser voir; **~ing** *adj* révélateur(trice); (*dress*) au décolleté généreux *or* suggestif

revel [ˈrevl] *vi*: **to ~ in sth/in doing** se délecter de qch/à faire

revelry [ˈrevlrɪ] *n* festivités *fpl*

revenge [rɪˈvendʒ] *n* vengeance *f*; **to take ~ on** (*enemy*) se venger sur

revenue [ˈrevənjuː] *n* revenu *m*

reverberate [rɪˈvɜːbəreɪt] *vi* (*sound*) retentir, se répercuter; (*fig: shock etc*) se propager

reverence [ˈrevərəns] *n* vénération *f*, révérence *f*

Reverend [ˈrevərənd] *adj* (*in titles*): **the ~ John Smith** (*Anglican*) le révérend John Smith; (*Catholic*) l'abbé (John) Smith; (*Protestant*) le pasteur (John) Smith

reversal [rɪˈvɜːsəl] *n* (*of opinion*) revirement *m*; (*of order*) renversement *m*; (*of direction*) changement *m*

reverse [rɪˈvɜːs] *n* contraire *m*, opposé *m*; (*back*) dos *m*, envers *m*; (*of paper*) verso *m*; (*of coin; also: setback*) revers *m*; (*AUT: also:* ~ **gear**) marche *f* arrière ♦ *adj* (*order, direction*) opposé(e), inverse ♦ *vt* (*order, position*) changer, inverser; (*direction, policy*) changer complètement de; (*decision*) annuler; (*roles*) renverser; (*car*) faire marche arrière avec ♦ *vi* (*BRIT: AUT*) faire marche arrière; **he**

~d (the car) into a wall il a embout un mur en marche arrière; **~d charg call** (*BRIT*) *n* (*TEL*) communication *f* e PCV; **reversing lights** (*BRIT*) *npl* (*AUT* feux *mpl* de marche arrière *or* de recul

revert [rɪˈvɜːt] *vi*: **to ~ to** revenir à, re tourner à

review [rɪˈvjuː] *n* revue *f*; (*of book film*) critique *f*, compte rendu; (*of situa tion, policy*) examen *m*, bilan *m* ♦ *v* passer en revue; faire la critique de; exa miner; **~er** *n* critique *m*

revile [rɪˈvaɪl] *vt* injurier

revise [rɪˈvaɪz] *vt* réviser, modifier (*manuscript*) revoir, corriger ♦ *vi* (*stu dy*) réviser; **revision** [rɪˈvɪʒən] *n* révisio *f*

revival [rɪˈvaɪvəl] *n* reprise *f*; (*recovery* rétablissement *m*; (*of faith*) renouvea *m*

revive [rɪˈvaɪv] *vt* (*person*) ranimer; (*cus tom*) rétablir; (*economy*) relancer; (*hope courage*) raviver, faire renaître; (*play* reprendre ♦ *vi* (*person*) reprendr connaissance; (: *from ill health*) se réta blir; (*hope etc*) renaître; (*activity*) re prendre

revoke [rɪˈvəuk] *vt* révoquer; (*law*) abro ger

revolt [rɪˈvəult] *n* révolte *f* ♦ *vi* se révo ter, se rebeller ♦ *vt* révolter, dégoûter **~ing** *adj* dégoûtant(e)

revolution [revəˈluːʃən] *n* révolution *j* (*of wheel etc*) tour *m*, révolution; **~ar** *adj* révolutionnaire ♦ *n* révolutionnair *m/f*

revolve [rɪˈvɒlv] *vi* tourner

revolver [rɪˈvɒlvə*] *n* revolver *m*

revolving [rɪˈvɒlvɪŋ] *adj* tournant(e (*chair*) pivotant(e); **~ door** *n* (porte *f* à tambour *m*

revulsion [rɪˈvʌlʃən] *n* dégoût *m*, répu gnance *f*

reward [rɪˈwɔːd] *n* récompense *f* ♦ *vt*: **t ~ (for)** récompenser (de); **~ing** *adj* (*fig* qui (en) vaut la peine, gratifiant(e)

rewind [ˈriːˈwaɪnd] (*irreg*) *vt* (*tape*) ren bobiner

rewire [ˈriːˈwaɪə*] *vt* (*house*) refaire l'in

tallation électrique de

rheumatism ['ru:mətɪzəm] *n* rhumatisme *m*

Rhine [raɪn] *n*: the ~ le Rhin

rhinoceros [raɪ'nɒsərəs] *n* rhinocéros *m*

Rhone [rəʊn] *n*: the ~ le Rhône

rhubarb ['ru:bɑ:b] *n* rhubarbe *f*

rhyme [raɪm] *n* rime *f*; (*verse*) vers *mpl*

rhythm ['rɪðəm] *n* rythme *m*

rib [rɪb] *n* (*ANAT*) côte *f*

ribbon ['rɪbən] *n* ruban *m*; **in ~s** (*torn*) en lambeaux

rice [raɪs] *n* riz *m*; ~ **pudding** *n* riz au lait

rich [rɪtʃ] *adj* riche; (*gift, clothes*) somptueux(euse) ♦ *npl*: **the ~** les riches *mpl*; **~es** *npl* richesses *fpl*; **~ly** *adv* richement; (*deserved, earned*) largement

rickets ['rɪkɪts] *n* rachitisme *m*

rickety ['rɪkɪtɪ] *adj* branlant(e)

rickshaw ['rɪkʃɔ:] *n* pousse-pousse *m inv*

rid [rɪd] (*pt, pp* rid) *vt*: **to ~ sb of** débarrasser qn de; **to get ~ of** se débarrasser de

riddle ['rɪdl] *n* (*puzzle*) énigme *f* ♦ *vt*: **to be ~d with** être criblé(e) de; (*fig: guilt, corruption, doubts*) être en proie à

ride [raɪd] (*pt* rode, *pp* ridden) *n* promenade *f*, tour *m*; (*distance covered*) trajet *m* ♦ *vi* (*as sport*) monter (à cheval), faire du cheval; (*go somewhere: on horse, bicycle*) aller (à cheval *or* bicyclette *etc*); (*journey: on bicycle, motorcycle, bus*) rouler ♦ *vt* (*a certain horse*) monter; (*distance*) parcourir, faire; **to take sb for a ~** (*fig*) faire marcher qn; **to ~ a horse/bicycle** monter à cheval/à bicyclette; **~r** *n* cavalier(ère); (*in race*) jockey *m*; (*on bicycle*) cycliste *m/f*; (*on motorcycle*) motocycliste *m/f*

ridge [rɪdʒ] *n* (*of roof, mountain*) arête *f*; (*of hill*) faîte *m*; (*on object*) strie *f*

ridicule ['rɪdɪkju:l] *n* ridicule *m*; dérision *f*

ridiculous [rɪ'dɪkjʊləs] *adj* ridicule

riding ['raɪdɪŋ] *n* équitation *f*; ~ **school** *n* manège *m*, école *f* d'équitation

rife [raɪf] *adj* répandu(e); ~ **with** abon-

dant(e) en, plein(e) de

riffraff ['rɪfræf] *n* racaille *f*

rifle ['raɪfl] *n* fusil *m* (à canon rayé) ♦ *vt* vider, dévaliser; ~ **through** *vt* (*belongings*) fouiller; (*papers*) feuilleter; ~ **range** *n* champ *m* de tir; (*at fair*) stand *m* de tir

rift [rɪft] *n* fente *f*, fissure *f*; (*fig: disagreement*) désaccord *m*

rig [rɪg] *n* (*also:* oil ~: at sea) plateforme pétrolière ♦ *vt* (*election etc*) truquer; ~ **out** (*BRIT*) *vt*: **to ~ out as/in** habiller en/de; ~ **up** *vt* arranger, faire avec des moyens de fortune; **~ging** *n* (*NAUT*) gréement *m*

right [raɪt] *adj* (*correctly chosen: answer, road etc*) bon(bonne); (*true*) juste, exact(e); (*suitable*) approprié(e), convenable; (*just*) juste, équitable; (*morally good*) bien *inv*; (*not left*) droit(e) ♦ *n* (*what is morally right*) bien *m*; (*title, claim*) droit *m*; (*not left*) droite *f* ♦ *adv* (*answer*) correctement, juste; (*treat*) bien, comme il faut; (*not on the left*) à droite ♦ *vt* redresser ♦ *excl* bon!; **to be ~** (*person*) avoir raison; (*answer*) être juste *or* correct(e); (*clock*) à l'heure (juste); **by ~s** en toute justice; **on the ~** à droite; **to be in the ~** avoir raison; ~ **now** en ce moment même; tout de suite; ~ **in the middle** en plein milieu; ~ **away** immédiatement; ~ **angle** *n* (*MATH*) angle droit; **~eous** ['raɪtʃəs] *adj* droit(e), vertueux(euse); (*anger*) justifié(e); **~ful** *adj* légitime; **~-handed** *adj* (*person*) droitier(ère); **~-hand man** *n* bras droit (*fig*); **~-hand side** *n* côté droit; **~ly** *adv* (*with reason*) à juste titre; ~ **of way** *n* droit *m* de passage; (*AUT*) priorité *f*; **~-wing** *adj* (*POL*) de droite

rigid ['rɪdʒɪd] *adj* rigide; (*principle, control*) strict(e)

rigmarole ['rɪgmərəʊl] *n* comédie *f*

rigorous ['rɪgərəs] *adj* rigoureux(euse)

rile [raɪl] *vt* agacer

rim [rɪm] *n* bord *m*; (*of spectacles*) monture *f*; (*of wheel*) jante *f*

rind [raɪnd] *n* (*of bacon*) couenne *f*; (*of lemon etc*) écorce *f*, zeste *m*; (*of cheese*) croûte *f*

ring [rɪŋ] (*pt* **rang**, *pp* **rung**) *n* anneau *m*; (*on finger*) bague *f*; (*also: wedding* ~) alliance *f*; (*of people, objects*) cercle *m*; (*of spies*) réseau *m*; (*of smoke etc*) rond *m*; (*arena*) piste *f*, arène *f*; (*for boxing*) ring *m*; (*sound of bell*) sonnerie *f* ♦ *vi* (*telephone, bell*) sonner; (*person: by telephone*) téléphoner; (*also: ~ out: voice, words*) retentir; (*ears*) bourdonner ♦ *vt* (*BRIT: TEL: also: ~ up*) téléphoner à, appeler; (*bell*) faire sonner; **to ~ the bell** sonner; **to give sb a ~** (*BRIT: TEL*) appeler qn; **~ back** (*BRIT*) *vt, vi* (*TEL*) rappeler; **~ off** (*BRIT*) *vi* (*TEL*) raccrocher; **~ up** (*BRIT*) *vt* (*TEL*) appeler; **~ing** *n* (*of telephone*) sonnerie *f*; (*of bell*) tintement *m*; (*in ears*) bourdonnement *m*; **~ing tone** *n* (*TEL*) sonnerie *f*; **~leader** *n* (*of gang*) chef *m*, meneur *m*

ringlets ['rɪŋlɪts] *npl* anglaises *fpl*

ring road: (*BRIT*) *n* route *f* de ceinture; (*motorway*) périphérique *m*

rink [rɪŋk] *n* (*also: ice* ~) patinoire *f*

rinse [rɪns] *vt* rincer

riot ['raɪət] *n* émeute *f*; (*of flowers, colour*) profusion *f* ♦ *vi* faire une émeute, manifester avec violence; **to run ~** se déchaîner; **~ous** *adj* (*mob, assembly*) séditieux(euse), déchaîné(e); (*living, behaviour*) débauché(e); (*party*) très animé(e); (*welcome*) délirant(e)

rip [rɪp] *n* déchirure *f* ♦ *vt* déchirer ♦ *vi* se déchirer; **~cord** ['rɪpkɔːd] *n* poignée *f* d'ouverture

ripe [raɪp] *adj* (*fruit*) mûr(e); (*cheese*) fait(e); **~n** *vt* mûrir ♦ *vi* mûrir

ripple ['rɪpl] *n* ondulation *f*; (*of applause, laughter*) cascade *f* ♦ *vi* onduler

rise [raɪz] (*pt* **rose**, *pp* **risen**) *n* (*slope*) côte *f*, pente *f*; (*hill*) hauteur *f*; (*increase: in wages: BRIT*) augmentation *f*; (: *in prices, temperature*) hausse *f*, augmentation *f*; (*fig: to power etc*) ascension *f* ♦ *vi* s'élever, monter; (*prices, numbers*) augmenter; (*waters*) monter; (*sun; person: from chair, bed*) se lever; (*also: ~ up: tower, building*) s'élever; (: *rebel*) se révolter; se rebeller; (*in rank*) s'éle-

ver; **to give ~ to** donner lieu à; **to ~ to the occasion** se montrer à la hauteur; **rising** *adj* (*increasing: number, prices*) en hausse; (*tide*) montant(e); (*sun, moon*) levant(e)

risk [rɪsk] *n* risque *m* ♦ *vt* risquer; **at ~** en danger; **at one's own ~** à ses risques et périls; **~y** *adj* risqué(e)

rissole ['rɪsəʊl] *n* croquette *f*

rite [raɪt] *n* rite *m*; **last ~s** derniers sacrements; **ritual** ['rɪtjʊəl] *adj* rituel(le) ♦ *n* rituel *m*

rival ['raɪvl] *adj, n* rival(e); (*in business*) concurrent(e) ♦ *vt* (*match*) égaler; **~ry** *n* rivalité *f*, concurrence *f*

river ['rɪvə*] *n* rivière *f*; (*major, also fig*) fleuve *m* ♦ *cpd* (*port, traffic*) fluvial(e); **up/down ~** en amont/aval; **~bank** *n* rive *f*, berge *f*

rivet ['rɪvɪt] *n* rivet *m* ♦ *vt* (*fig*) river, fixer

Riviera [rɪvɪ'ɛərə] *n*: **the (French) ~** la Côte d'Azur; **the Italian ~** la Riviera (italienne)

road [rəʊd] *n* route *f*; (*in town*) rue *f*; (*fig*) chemin, voie *f*; **major/minor ~** route principale *or* à priorité/voie secondaire; **~ accident** *n* accident *m* de la circulation; **~block** *n* barrage routier; **~hog** *n* chauffard *m*; **~ map** *n* carte routière; **~ safety** *n* sécurité routière; **~side** *n* bord *m* de la route, bas-côté *m*; **~sign** *n* panneau *m* de signalisation; **~way** *n* chaussée *f*; **~ works** *npl* travaux *mpl* (de réfection des routes); **~worthy** *adj* en bon état de marche

roam [rəʊm] *vi* errer, vagabonder

roar [rɔː*] *n* rugissement *m*; (*of crowd*) hurlements *mpl*; (*of vehicle, thunder, storm*) grondement *m* ♦ *vi* rugir; hurler; gronder; **to ~ with laughter** éclater de rire; **to do a ~ing trade** faire des affaires d'or

roast [rəʊst] *n* rôti *m* ♦ *vt* (faire) rôtir; (*coffee*) griller, torréfier; **~ beef** *n* rôti *m* de bœuf, rosbif *m*

rob [rɒb] *vt* (*person*) voler; (*bank*) dévaliser; **to ~ sb of sth** voler *or* dérober qch à qn; (*fig: deprive*) priver qn de qch;

~**ber** n bandit m, voleur m; ~**bery** n vol m

robe [rəʊb] n (*for ceremony etc*) robe f; (*also: bath~*) peignoir m; (*US*) couverture f

robin ['rɒbɪn] n rouge-gorge m

robust [rəʊ'bʌst] adj robuste; (*material, appetite*) solide

rock [rɒk] n (*substance*) roche f, roc m; (*boulder*) rocher m; (*US: small stone*) caillou m; (*BRIT: sweet*) ≈ sucre m d'orge ♦ vt (*swing gently: cradle*) balancer; (*: child*) bercer; (*shake*) ébranler, secouer ♦ vi (se) balancer; être ébranlé(e) or secoué(e); **on the ~s** (*drink*) avec des glaçons; (*marriage etc*) en train de craquer; ~ **and roll** n rock (and roll) m, rock'n'roll m; ~**-bottom** adj (*fig: prices*) sacrifié(e); ~**ery** n (jardin m de) rocaille f

rocket ['rɒkɪt] n fusée f; (*MIL*) fusée, roquette f

rocking chair ['rɒkɪŋ-] n fauteuil m à bascule

rocking horse n cheval m à bascule

rocky ['rɒkɪ] adj (*hill*) rocheux(euse); (*path*) rocailleux(euse)

rod [rɒd] n (*wooden*) baguette f; (*metallic*) tringle f; (*TECH*) tige f; (*also: fishing ~*) canne f à pêche

rode [rəʊd] pt of **ride**

rodent ['rəʊdənt] n rongeur m

rodeo ['rəʊdɪəʊ] (*US*) n rodéo m

roe [rəʊ] n (*species: also: ~ deer*) chevreuil m; (*of fish, also: hard ~*) œufs mpl de poisson; **soft ~** laitance f

rogue [rəʊg] n coquin(e)

role [rəʊl] n rôle m

roll [rəʊl] n rouleau m; (*of banknotes*) liasse f; (*also: bread ~*) petit pain; (*register*) liste f; (*sound: of drums etc*) roulement m ♦ vt rouler; (*also: ~ up: string*) enrouler; (*: sleeves*) retrousser; (*: ~ out: pastry*) étendre au rouleau, abaisser ♦ vi rouler; ~ **about** vi rouler çà et là; (*person*) se rouler par terre; ~ **around** vi = **roll about**; ~ **by** vi (*time*) s'écouler, passer; ~ **in** vi (*mail, cash*) affluer; ~ **over** vi se retourner; ~ **up** vi

(*inf: arrive*) arriver, s'amener ♦ vt rouler; ~ **call** n appel m; ~**er** n rouleau m; (*wheel*) roulette f; (*for road*) rouleau compresseur; ~**er coaster** n montagnes fpl russes; ~**er skates** npl patins mpl à roulettes; ~**ing** ['rəʊlɪŋ] adj (*landscape*) onduleux(euse); ~**ing pin** n rouleau m à pâtisserie; ~**ing stock** n (*RAIL*) matériel roulant

ROM [rɒm] n abbr (= *read only memory*) mémoire morte

Roman ['rəʊmən] adj romain(e); ~ **Catholic** adj, n catholique (m/f)

romance [rəʊ'mæns] n (*love affair*) idylle f; (*charm*) poésie f; (*novel*) roman m à l'eau de rose

Romania [rəʊ'meɪnɪə] n Roumanie f; ~**n** adj roumain(e) ♦ n Roumain(e); (*LING*) roumain m

Roman numeral n chiffre romain

romantic [rəʊ'mæntɪk] adj romantique; sentimental(e)

Rome [rəʊm] n Rome

romp [rɒmp] n jeux bruyants ♦ vi (*also: ~ about*) s'ébattre, jouer bruyamment; ~**ers** ['rɒmpəz] npl barboteuse f

roof [ru:f] (*pl ~s*) n toit m ♦ vt couvrir (d'un toit); **the ~ of the mouth** la voûte du palais; ~**ing** n toiture f; ~ **rack** n (*AUT*) galerie f

rook [rʊk] n (*bird*) freux m; (*CHESS*) tour f

room [rum] n (*in house*) pièce f; (*also: bed~*) chambre f (à coucher); (*in school etc*) salle f; (*space*) place f; ~**s** npl (*lodging*) meublé m; "**~s to let**" (*BRIT*), "**~s for rent**" (*US*) "chambres à louer"; **single/double ~** chambre pour une personne/deux personnes; **there is ~ for improvement** cela laisse à désirer; ~**ing house** (*US*) n maison f or immeuble m de rapport; ~**mate** n camarade m/f de chambre; ~ **service** n service m des chambres (*dans un hôtel*); ~**y** adj spacieux(euse); (*garment*) ample

roost [ru:st] vi se jucher

rooster ['ru:stə*] n (*esp US*) coq m

root [ru:t] n (*BOT, MATH*) racine f; (*fig: of problem*) origine f, fond m ♦ vi (*plant*)

s'enraciner; ~ **about** *vi* (*fig*) fouiller; ~
for *vt fus* encourager, applaudir; ~ **out**
vt (*find*) dénicher

rope [rəʊp] *n* corde *f*; (*NAUT*) cordage *m*
♦ *vt* (*tie up or together*) attacher;
(*climbers: also:* ~ *together*) encorder;
(*area:* ~ *off*) interdire l'accès de; (: *di-*
vide off) séparer; **to know the ~s** (*fig*)
être au courant, connaître les ficelles; ~
in *vt* (*fig: person*) embringuer

rosary [ˈrəʊzərɪ] *n* chapelet *m*

rose [rəʊz] *pt of* **rise** ♦ *n* rose *f*; (*also:*
~*bush*) rosier *m*; (*on watering can*)
pomme *f*

rosé [ˈrəʊzeɪ] *n* rosé *m*

rosebud [ˈrəʊzbʌd] *n* bouton *m* de rose

rosemary [ˈrəʊzmərɪ] *n* romarin *m*

roster [ˈrɒstə*] *n*: **duty** ~ tableau *m* de
service

rostrum [ˈrɒstrəm] *n* tribune *f* (*pour un*
orateur etc)

rosy [ˈrəʊzɪ] *adj* rose; **a** ~ **future** un bel
avenir

rot [rɒt] *n* (*decay*) pourriture *f*; (*fig: pej*)
idioties *fpl* ♦ *vt*, *vi* pourrir

rota [ˈrəʊtə] *n* liste *f*, tableau *m* de service; **on a** ~ **basis** par roulement

rotary [ˈrəʊtərɪ] *adj* rotatif(ive)

rotate [rəʊˈteɪt] *vt* (*revolve*) faire tourner; (*change round: jobs*) faire à tour
de rôle ♦ *vi* (*revolve*) tourner; **rotating**
adj (*movement*) tournant(e)

rote [rəʊt] *n*: **by** ~ machinalement, par
cœur

rotten [ˈrɒtn] *adj* (*decayed*) pourri(e);
(*dishonest*) corrompu(e); (*inf: bad*) mau-
vais(e), moche; **to feel** ~ (*ill*) être mal
fichu(e)

rotund [rəʊˈtʌnd] *adj* (*person*) ronde-
let(te)

rough [rʌf] *adj* (*cloth, skin*) rêche, ru-
gueux(euse); (*terrain*) accidenté(e);
(*path*) rocailleux(euse); (*voice*) rauque,
rude; (*person, manner: coarse*) rude,
fruste; (: *violent*) brutal(e); (*district,*
weather) mauvais(e); (*sea*) hou-
leux(euse); (*plan etc*) ébauché(e); (*guess*)
approximatif(ive) ♦ *n* (*GOLF*) rough *m*; **to**
~ **it** vivre à la dure; **to sleep** ~ (*BRIT*)

coucher à la dure; ~**age** *n* fibres *fpl* alimentaires; ~-**and-ready** *adj* rudimentaire; ~ **copy**, ~**draft** *n* brouillon *m*; ~**ly**
adv (*handle*) rudement, brutalement;
(*speak*) avec brusquerie; (*make*) grossièrement; (*approximately*) à peu près,
en gros

roulette [ruːˈlet] *n* roulette *f*

Roumania [ruːˈmeɪnɪə] *n* = **Romania**

round [raʊnd] *adj* rond(e) ♦ *n* (*BRIT:*
toast) tranche *f*; (*duty: of policeman,*
milkman etc) tournée *f*; (: *of doctor*) visites *fpl*; (*game: of cards, in competi-*
tion) partie *f*; (*BOXING*) round *m*; (*of*
talks) série *f* ♦ *vt* (*corner*) tourner
♦ *prep* autour de ♦ *adv*: **all** ~ tout
autour; **the long way** ~ (par) le chemin
le plus long; **all the year** ~ toute l'année; **it's just** ~ **the corner** (*fig*) c'est
tout près; ~ **the clock** 24 heures sur 24;
to go ~ **to sb's (house)** aller chez qn; **go**
~ **the back** passez par derrière; **to go** ~
a house visiter une maison, faire le tour
d'une maison; **enough to go** ~ assez
pour tout le monde; ~ **of applause** ban *m*, applaudissements *mpl*; ~ **of drinks** tournée *f*; ~ **of sandwiches** sandwich *m*; ~
off *vt* (*speech etc*) terminer; ~ **up** *vt* rassembler; (*criminals*) effectuer une rafle
de; (*price, figure*) arrondir (au chiffre
supérieur); ~**about** *n* (*BRIT: AUT*) rond-
point *m* (à sens giratoire); (: *at fair*) manège *m* (de chevaux de bois) ♦ *adj* (*rou-*
te, means) détourné(e); ~**ers** *n* (*game*)
sorte de baseball; ~**ly** *adv* (*fig*) tout net,
carrément; ~-**shouldered** *adj* au dos
rond; ~ **trip** *n* (voyage *m*) aller et retour
m; ~**up** *n* rassemblement *m*; (*of crimi-*
nals) rafle *f*

rouse [raʊz] *vt* (*wake up*) réveiller; (*stir*
up) susciter; provoquer; éveiller.

rousing [ˈraʊzɪŋ] *adj* (*welcome*) enthousiaste

rout [raʊt] *n* (*MIL*) déroute *f*

route [ruːt] *n* itinéraire *m*; (*of bus*) parcours *m*; (*of trade, shipping*) route *f*; ~
map (*BRIT*) *n* (*for journey*) croquis *m*
d'itinéraire

routine [ruːˈtiːn] *adj* (*work*) ordinaire, courant(e); (*procedure*) d'usage ♦ *n* (*habits*) habitudes *fpl*; (*pej*) train-train *m*; (*THEATRE*) numéro *m*

rove [rəʊv] *vt* (*area, streets*) errer dans

row¹ [rəʊ] *n* (*line*) rangée *f*; (*of people, seats, KNITTING*) rang *m*; (*behind one another: of cars, people*) file *f* ♦ *vi* (*in boat*) ramer; (*as sport*) faire de l'aviron ♦ *vt* (*boat*) faire aller à la rame *or* à l'aviron; **in a ~** (*fig*) d'affilée

row² [raʊ] *n* (*noise*) vacarme *m*; (*dispute*) dispute *f*, querelle *f*; (*scolding*) réprimande *f*, savon *m* ♦ *vi* se disputer, se quereller

rowboat [ˈrəʊbəʊt] (*US*) *n* canot *m* (à rames)

rowdy [ˈraʊdɪ] *adj* chahuteur(euse); (*occasion*) tapageur(euse)

rowing [ˈrəʊɪŋ] *n* canotage *m*; (*as sport*) aviron *m*; **~ boat** (*BRIT*) *n* canot *m* (à rames)

royal [ˈrɔɪəl] *adj* royal(e); **R~ Air Force** (*BRIT*) *n* armée de l'air britannique

royalty [ˈrɔɪəltɪ] *n* (*royal persons*) (membres *mpl* de la) famille royale; (*payment: to author*) droits *mpl* d'auteur; (*: to inventor*) royalties *fpl*

rpm *abbr* (*AUT:* = *revs per minute*) tr/mn

RSVP *abbr* (= *répondez s'il vous plaît*) R.S.V.P.

Rt Hon. *abbr* (*BRIT:* = *Right Honourable*) *titre donné aux députés de la Chambre des communes*

rub [rʌb] *vt* frotter; frictionner; (*hands*) se frotter ♦ *n* (*with cloth*) coup *m* chiffon *or* de torchon; **to give sth a ~** donner un coup de chiffon *or* de torchon à; **to ~ sb up** (*BRIT*) *or* **to ~ sb** (*US*) **the wrong way** prendre qn à rebrousse-poil; **~ off** *vi* partir; **~ off on** *vt fus* déteindre sur; **~ out** *vt* effacer

rubber [ˈrʌbə*] *n* caoutchouc *m*; (*BRIT: eraser*) gomme *f* (à effacer); **~ band** *n* élastique *m*; **~ plant** *n* caoutchouc *m* (*plante verte*)

rubbish [ˈrʌbɪʃ] *n* (*from household*) ordures *fpl*; (*fig: pej*) camelote *f*; (*: non-*

sense) bêtises *fpl*, idioties *fpl*; **~ bin** (*BRIT*) *n* poubelle *f*; **~ dump** *n* décharge publique, dépotoir *m*

rubble [ˈrʌbl] *n* décombres *mpl*; (*smaller*) gravats *mpl*; (*CONSTR*) blocage *m*

ruby [ˈruːbɪ] *n* rubis *m*

rucksack [ˈrʌksæk] *n* sac *m* à dos

rudder [ˈrʌdə*] *n* gouvernail *m*

ruddy [ˈrʌdɪ] *adj* (*face*) coloré(e); (*inf: damned*) sacré(e), fichu(e)

rude [ruːd] *adj* (*impolite*) impoli(e); (*coarse*) grossier(ère); (*shocking*) indécent(e), inconvenant(e)

ruffian [ˈrʌfɪən] *n* brute *f*, voyou *m*

ruffle [ˈrʌfl] *vt* (*hair*) ébouriffer; (*clothes*) chiffonner; (*fig: person*): **to get ~d** s'énerver

rug [rʌg] *n* petit tapis; (*BRIT: blanket*) couverture *f*

rugby [ˈrʌgbɪ] *n* (*also:* **~ football**) rugby *m*

rugged [ˈrʌgɪd] *adj* (*landscape*) accidenté(e); (*features, character*) rude

rugger [ˈrʌgə*] (*BRIT: inf*) *n* rugby *m*

ruin [ˈruːɪn] *n* ruine *f* ♦ *vt* ruiner; (*spoil, clothes*) abîmer; (*event*) gâcher; **~s** *npl* (*of building*) ruine(s)

rule [ruːl] *n* règle *f*; (*regulation*) règlement *m*; (*government*) autorité *f*, gouvernement *m* ♦ *vt* (*country*) gouverner; (*person*) dominer ♦ *vi* commander; (*LAW*) statuer; **as a ~** normalement, en règle générale; **~ out** *vt* exclure; **~d** *adj* (*paper*) réglé(e); **~r** *n* (*sovereign*) souverain(e); (*for measuring*) règle *f*; **ruling** *adj* (*party*) au pouvoir; (*class*) dirigeant(e) ♦ *n* (*LAW*) décision *f*

rum [rʌm] *n* rhum *m*

Rumania [ruːˈmeɪnɪə] *n* = **Romania**

rumble [ˈrʌmbl] *vi* gronder; (*stomach, pipe*) gargouiller

rummage [ˈrʌmɪdʒ] *vi* fouiller

rumour [ˈruːmə*] (*US* **rumor**) *n* rumeur *f*, bruit *m* (qui court) ♦ *vt*: **it is ~ed that** le bruit court que

rump [rʌmp] *n* (*of animal*) croupe *f*; (*inf: of person*) postérieur *m*; **~ steak** *n* rumsteck *m*

rumpus [ˈrʌmpəs] (*inf*) *n* tapage *m*, chahut *m*

run [rʌn] (*pt* **ran**, *pp* **run**) *n* (*fast pace*) (pas *m* de) course *f*; (*outing*) tour *m or* promenade *f* (en voiture); (*distance travelled*) parcours *m*, trajet *m*; (*series*) suite *f*, série *f*; (*THEATRE*) série de représentations; (*SKI*) piste *f*; (*CRICKET, BASEBALL*) point *m*; (*in tights, stockings*) maille filée, échelle *f* ♦ *vt* (*operate*: *business*) diriger; (: *competition, course*) organiser; (: *hotel, house*) tenir; (*race*) participer à; (*COMPUT*) exécuter; (*to pass*: *hand, finger*) passer; (*water, bath*) faire couler; (*PRESS*: *feature*) publier ♦ *vi* courir; (*flee*) s'enfuir; (*work*: *machine, factory*) marcher; (*bus, train*) circuler; (*continue*: *play*) se jouer; (: *contract*) être valide; (*flow*: *river, bath; nose*) couler; (*colours, washing*) déteindre; (*in election*) être candidat, se présenter; **to go for a ~** faire un peu de course à pied; **there was a ~ on ...** (*meat, tickets*) les gens se sont rués sur ...; **in the long ~** à longue échéance; à la longue; en fin de compte; **on the ~** en fuite; **I'll ~ you to the station** je vais vous emmener *or* conduire à la gare; **to ~ a risk** courir un risque; **~ about** *vi* (*children*) courir çà et là; **~ across** *vt fus* (*find*) trouver par hasard; **~ around** *vi* = **run about**; **~ down** *vt* (*production*) réduire progressivement; (*factory*) réduire progressivement la production de; (*AUT*) renverser; (*criticize*) critiquer, dénigrer; **to be ~ down** (*person*: *tired*) être fatigué(e) *or* à plat; **~ in** (*BRIT*) *vt* (*car*) roder; **~ into** *vt fus* (*meet*: *person*) rencontrer par hasard; (: *trouble*) se heurter à; (*collide with*) heurter; **~ off** *vi* s'enfuir ♦ *vt* (*water*) laisser s'écouler; (*copies*) tirer; **~ out** *vi* (*person*) sortir en courant; (*liquid*) couler; (*lease*) expirer; (*money*) être épuisé(e); **~ out of** *vt fus* se trouver à court de; **~ over** *vt* (*AUT*) écraser ♦ *vt fus* (*revise*) revoir, reprendre; **~ through** *vt fus* (*recapitulate*) reprendre; (*play*) répéter; **~ up** *vt*: **to ~ up against** (*difficulties*) se heurter à; **to ~ up a debt** s'endetter; **~away** *adj* (*horse*) emballé(e); (*truck*) fou(folle); (*person*) fugitif(ive); (*teenager*) fugueur(euse)

rung [rʌŋ] *pp of* **ring** ♦ *n* (*of ladder*) barreau *m*

runner ['rʌnə*] *n* (*in race*: *person*) coureur(euse); (: *horse*) partant *m*; (*on sledge*) patin *m*; (*for drawer etc*) coulisseau *m*; **~ bean** (*BRIT*) *n* haricot *m* (à rames); **~-up** *n* second(e)

running ['rʌnɪŋ] *n* course *f*; (*of business, organization*) gestion *f*, direction *f* ♦ *adj* (*water*) courant(e); **to be in/out of the ~ for sth** être/ne pas être sur les rangs pour qch; **6 days ~** 6 jours de suite; **~ commentary** *n* commentaire détaillé; **~ costs** *npl* frais *mpl* d'exploitation

runny ['rʌnɪ] *adj* qui coule

run-of-the-mill ['rʌnəvðə'mɪl] *adj* ordinaire, banal(e)

runt [rʌnt] (*also pej*) *n* avorton *m*

run-up ['rʌnʌp] *n*: **~ to sth** (*election etc*) période *f* précédant qch

runway ['rʌnweɪ] *n* (*AVIAT*) piste *f*

rupee [ruː'piː] *n* roupie *f*

rupture ['rʌptʃə*] *n* (*MED*) hernie *f*

rural ['ruərəl] *adj* rural(e)

rush [rʌʃ] *n* (*hurry*) hâte *f*, précipitation *f*; (*of crowd*; *COMM*: *sudden demand*) ruée *f*; (*current*) flot *m*; (*of emotion*) vague *f*; (*BOT*) jonc *m* ♦ *vt* (*hurry*) transporter *or* envoyer d'urgence ♦ *vi* se précipiter; **~ hour** *n* heures *fpl* de pointe

rusk [rʌsk] *n* biscotte *f*

Russia ['rʌʃə] *n* Russie *f*; **~n** *adj* russe ♦ *n* Russe *m/f*; (*LING*) russe *m*

rust [rʌst] *n* rouille *f* ♦ *vi* rouiller

rustic ['rʌstɪk] *adj* rustique

rustle ['rʌsl] *vi* bruire, produire un bruissement ♦ *vt* (*paper*) froisser; (*US*: *cattle*) voler

rustproof ['rʌstpruːf] *adj* inoxydable

rusty ['rʌstɪ] *adj* rouillé(e)

rut [rʌt] *n* ornière *f*; (*ZOOL*) rut *m*; **to be in a ~** suivre l'ornière, s'encroûter

ruthless ['ruːθləs] *adj* sans pitié, impitoyable

rye [raɪ] *n* seigle *m*; **~ bread** *n* pain de seigle

S s

Sabbath ['sæbəθ] *n* (*Jewish*) sabbat *m*; (*Christian*) dimanche *m*

sabotage ['sæbətɑːʒ] *n* sabotage *m* ♦ *vt* saboter

saccharin(e) ['sækərɪn] *n* saccharine *f*

sachet ['sæʃeɪ] *n* sachet *m*

sack [sæk] *n* (*bag*) sac *m* ♦ *vt* (*dismiss*) renvoyer, mettre à la porte; (*plunder*) piller, mettre à sac; **to get the ~** être renvoyé(e), être mis(e) à la porte; **~ing** *n* (*material*) toile *f* à sac; (*dismissal*) renvoi *m*

sacrament ['sækrəmənt] *n* sacrement *m*

sacred ['seɪkrɪd] *adj* sacré(e)

sacrifice ['sækrɪfaɪs] *n* sacrifice *m* ♦ *vt* sacrifier

sad [sæd] *adj* triste; (*deplorable*) triste, fâcheux(euse)

saddle ['sædl] *n* selle *f* ♦ *vt* (*horse*) seller; **to be ~d with sth** (*inf*) avoir qch sur les bras; **~bag** *n* sacoche *f*

sadistic [sə'dɪstɪk] *adj* sadique

sadly *adv* tristement; (*unfortunately*) malheureusement; (*seriously*) fort

sadness ['sædnəs] *n* tristesse *f*

s.a.e. *n abbr* = **stamped addressed envelope**

safe [seɪf] *adj* (*out of danger*) hors de danger, en sécurité; (*not dangerous*) sans danger; (*unharmed*): **~ journey!** bon voyage!; (*cautious*) prudent(e); (*sure: bet etc*) assuré(e) ♦ *n* coffre-fort *m*; **~ from** à l'abri de; **~ and sound** sain(e) et sauf(sauve); **(just) to be on the ~ side** pour plus de sûreté, par précaution; **~-conduct** *n* sauf-conduit *m*; **~-deposit** *n* (*vault*) dépôt *m* de coffres-forts; (*box*) coffre-fort *m*; **~guard** *n* sauvegarde *f*, protection *f* ♦ *vt* sauvegarder, protéger; **~keeping** *n* bonne garde; **~ly** *adv* (*assume, say*) sans risque d'erreur; (*drive, arrive*) sans accident; **~ sex** *n* rapports *mpl* sexuels sans risque

safety ['seɪftɪ] *n* sécurité *f*; **~ belt** *n* ceinture *f* de sécurité; **~ pin** *n* épingle *f* de sûreté *or* de nourrice; **~ valve** *n* soupape *f* de sûreté

sag [sæg] *vi* s'affaisser; (*hem, breasts*) pendre

sage [seɪdʒ] *n* (*herb*) sauge *f*; (*person*) sage *m*

Sagittarius [sædʒɪ'tɛərɪəs] *n* le Sagittaire

Sahara [sə'hɑːrə] *n*: **the ~ (Desert)** le (désert du) Sahara

said [sed] *pt, pp of* **say**

sail [seɪl] *n* (*on boat*) voile *f*; (*trip*): **to go for a ~** faire un tour en bateau ♦ *vt* (*boat*) manœuvrer, piloter ♦ *vi* (*travel: ship*) avancer, naviguer; (*set off*) partir, prendre la mer; (*SPORT*) faire de la voile; **they ~ed into Le Havre** ils sont entrés dans le port du Havre; **~ through** *vi, vt fus* (*fig*) réussir haut la main; **~boat** (*US*) *n* bateau *m* à voiles, voilier *m*; **~ing** *n* (*SPORT*) voile *f*; **to go ~ing** faire de la voile; **~ing boat** *n* bateau *m* à voiles, voilier *m*; **~ing ship** *n* grand voilier; **~or** *n* marin *m*, matelot *m*

saint [seɪnt] *n* saint(e)

sake [seɪk] *n*: **for the ~ of** pour (l'amour de), dans l'intérêt de; par égard pour

salad ['sæləd] *n* salade *f*; **~ bowl** *n* saladier *m*; **~ cream** (*BRIT*) *n* (sorte *f* de) mayonnaise *f*; **~ dressing** *n* vinaigrette *f*

salary ['sælərɪ] *n* salaire *m*

sale [seɪl] *n* vente *f*; (*at reduced prices*) soldes *mpl*; **"for ~"** "à vendre"; **on ~** en vente; **on ~ or return** vendu(e) avec faculté de retour; **~room** *n* salle *f* des ventes; **~s assistant** *n* vendeur(euse); **~s clerk** (*US*) *n* vendeur(euse); **~sman** (*irreg*) *n* vendeur *m*; (*representative*) représentant *m* de commerce; **~swoman** (*irreg*) *n* vendeuse *f*; (*representative*) représentante *f* de commerce

sallow ['sæləu] *adj* cireux(euse)

salmon ['sæmən] *n inv* saumon *m*

saloon [sə'luːn] *n* (*US*) bar *m*; (*BRIT: AUT*) berline *f*; (*ship's lounge*) salon *m*

salt [sɔːlt] *n* sel *m* ♦ *vt* saler; **~ cellar** *n* salière *f*; **~water** *adj* de mer; **~y** *adj* salé(e)

salute [sə'luːt] *n* salut *m* ♦ *vt* saluer

salvage ['sælvɪdʒ] *n* (*saving*) sauvetage *m*; (*things saved*) biens sauvés *or* récupérés ♦ *vt* sauver, récupérer

salvation [sæl'veɪʃən] *n* salut *m*; S~ Army *n* armée *f* du Salut

same [seɪm] *adj* même ♦ *pron*: **the ~** le(la) même, les mêmes; **the ~ book as** le même livre que; **at the ~ time** en même temps; **all *or* just the ~** tout de même, quand même; **to do the ~** faire de même, en faire autant; **to do the ~ as sb** faire comme qn; **the ~ to you!** à vous de même!; (*after insult*) toi-même!

sample ['sɑːmpl] *n* échantillon *m*; (*blood*) prélèvement *m* ♦ *vt* (*food, wine*) goûter

sanctimonious [sæŋktɪ'məʊnɪəs] *adj* moralisateur(trice)

sanction ['sæŋkʃən] *n* approbation *f*, sanction *f*

sanctity ['sæŋktɪtɪ] *n* sainteté *f*, caractère sacré

sanctuary ['sæŋktjʊərɪ] *n* (*holy place*) sanctuaire *m*; (*refuge*) asile *m*; (*for wild life*) réserve *f*

sand [sænd] *n* sable *m* ♦ *vt* (*furniture: also*: ~ **down**) poncer

sandal ['sændl] *n* sandale *f*

sand: ~**box** (*US*) *n* tas *m* de sable; ~**castle** *n* château *m* de sable; ~**paper** *n* papier *m* de verre; ~**pit** (*BRIT*) *n* (*for children*) tas *m* de sable; ~**stone** *n* grès *m*

sandwich ['sænwɪdʒ] *n* sandwich *m*; **cheese/ham ~** sandwich au fromage/jambon; **~ course** (*BRIT*) *n* cours *m* de formation professionnelle

sandy ['sændɪ] *adj* sablonneux(euse); (*colour*) sable *inv*, blond roux *inv*

sane [seɪn] *adj* (*person*) sain(e) d'esprit; (*outlook*) sensé(e), sain(e)

sang [sæŋ] *pt of* **sing**

sanitary ['sænɪtərɪ] *adj* (*system, arrangements*) sanitaire; (*clean*) hygiénique; **~ towel** (*US* **~ napkin**) *n* serviette *f* hygiénique

sanitation [sænɪ'teɪʃən] *n* (*in house*) installations *fpl* sanitaires; (*in town*) système *m* sanitaire; **~ department** (*US*) *n*

service *m* de voirie

sanity ['sænɪtɪ] *n* santé mentale; (*common sense*) bon sens

sank [sæŋk] *pt of* **sink**

Santa Claus [sæntə'klɔːz] *n* le père Noël

sap [sæp] *n* (*of plants*) sève *f* ♦ *vt* (*strength*) saper, miner

sapling ['sæplɪŋ] *n* jeune arbre *m*

sapphire ['sæfaɪə*] *n* saphir *m*

sarcasm ['sɑːkæzəm] *n* sarcasme *m* raillerie *f*

sardine [sɑː'diːn] *n* sardine *f*

Sardinia [sɑː'dɪnɪə] *n* Sardaigne *f*

sash [sæʃ] *n* écharpe *f*

sat [sæt] *pt, pp of* **sit**

satchel ['sætʃəl] *n* cartable *m*

satellite ['sætəlaɪt] *n* satellite *m*; ~ **dish** *n* antenne *f* parabolique; ~ **television** *n* télévision *f* par câble

satin ['sætɪn] *n* satin *m* ♦ *adj* en *or* de satin, satiné(e)

satisfaction [sætɪs'fækʃən] *n* satisfaction *f*; **satisfactory** [sætɪs'fæktərɪ] *adj* satisfaisant(e)

satisfy ['sætɪsfaɪ] *vt* satisfaire, contenter (*convince*) convaincre, persuader; ~**ing** *adj* satisfaisant(e)

Saturday ['sætədeɪ] *n* samedi *m*

sauce [sɔːs] *n* sauce *f*; ~**pan** *n* casserole *f*

saucer ['sɔːsə*] *n* soucoupe *f*

saucy ['sɔːsɪ] *adj* impertinent(e)

Saudi ['saʊdɪ]: ~ **Arabia** *n* Arabie Saoudite; ~ **(Arabian)** *adj* saoudien(ne)

sauna ['sɔːnə] *n* sauna *m*

saunter ['sɔːntə*] *vi*: **to ~ along/in/out** *etc* marcher/entrer/sortir *etc* d'un pas nonchalant

sausage ['sɒsɪdʒ] *n* saucisse *f*; (*cold meat*) saucisson *m*; ~ **roll** *n* ≈ friand *m*

savage ['sævɪdʒ] *adj* (*cruel, fierce*) brutal(e), féroce; (*primitive*) primitif(ive) ♦ sauvage *m/f*

save [seɪv] *vt* (*person, belongings*) sauver; (*money*) mettre de côté, économiser (*time*) (faire) gagner; (*keep*) garder (*COMPUT*) sauvegarder; (*SPORT: stop*) arrêter; (*avoid: trouble*) éviter ♦ *vi* (*also*: ~ **up**) mettre de l'argent de côté

(*SPORT*) arrêt *m* (du ballon) ♦ *prep* sauf, à l'exception de

saving ['seɪvɪŋ] *n* économie *f* ♦ *adj*: **the ~ grace of sth** ce qui rachète qch; **~s** *npl* (*money saved*) économies *fpl*; **~s account** *n* compte *m* d'épargne; **~s bank** *n* caisse *f* d'épargne

saviour ['seɪvjə*] (*US* **savior**) *n* sauveur *m*

savour ['seɪvə*] (*US* **savor**) *vt* savourer; **~y** (*US* **savory**) *adj* (*dish: not sweet*) salé(e)

saw [sɔː] (*pt* ~**ed**, *pp* ~**ed** *or* **sawn**) *vt* scier ♦ *n* (*tool*) scie *f* ♦ *pt of* **see**; **~dust** *n* sciure *f*; **~mill** *n* scierie *f*; **~-off** *adj*: **~-off shotgun** carabine *f* à canon scié

saxophone ['sæksəfəʊn] *n* saxophone *m*

say [seɪ] (*pt, pp* **said**) *n*: **to have one's ~** dire ce qu'on a à dire ♦ *vt* dire; **to have a** *or* **some ~ in sth** avoir voix au chapitre; **could you ~ that again?** pourriez-vous répéter ce que vous venez de dire?; **that goes without ~ing** cela va sans dire, cela va de soi; **~ing** *n* dicton *m*, proverbe *m*

scab [skæb] *n* croûte *f*; (*pej*) jaune *m*

scaffold ['skæfəʊld] *n* échafaud *m*; **~ing** *n* échafaudage *m*

scald [skɔːld] *n* brûlure *f* ♦ *vt* ébouillanter

scale [skeɪl] *n* (*of fish*) écaille *f*; (*MUS*) gamme *f*; (*of ruler, thermometer etc*) graduation *f*, échelle (graduée); (*of salaries, fees etc*) barème *m*; (*of map, also size, extent*) échelle *f* ♦ *vt* (*mountain*) escalader; **~s** *npl* (*for weighing*) balance *f*; (*also*: **bathroom ~**) pèse-personne *m inv*; **on a large ~** sur une grande échelle, en grand; **~ of charges** tableau *m* des tarifs; **~ down** *vt* réduire

scallop ['skɒləp] *n* coquille *f* Saint-Jacques; (*SEWING*) feston *m*

scalp [skælp] *n* cuir chevelu ♦ *vt* scalper

scamper ['skæmpə*] *vi*: **to ~ away** *or* **off** détaler

scampi ['skæmpɪ] *npl* langoustines (frites), scampi *mpl*

scan [skæn] *vt* scruter, examiner; (*glance at quickly*) parcourir; (*TV, RADAR*) ba-

layer ♦ *n* (*MED*) scanographie *f*

scandal ['skændl] *n* scandale *m*; (*gossip*) ragots *mpl*

Scandinavian [skændɪ'neɪvɪən] *adj* scandinave

scant [skænt] *adj* insuffisant(e); **~y** *adj* peu abondant(e), insuffisant(e); (*underwear*) minuscule

scapegoat ['skeɪpgəʊt] *n* bouc *m* émissaire

scar [skɑː*] *n* cicatrice *f* ♦ *vt* marquer (d'une cicatrice)

scarce ['skɛəs] *adj* rare, peu abondant(e); **to make o.s. ~** (*inf*) se sauver; **~ly** *adv* à peine; **scarcity** *n* manque *m*, pénurie *f*

scare ['skɛə*] *n* peur *f*, panique *f* ♦ *vt* effrayer, faire peur à; **to ~ sb stiff** faire une peur bleue à qn; **bomb ~** alerte *f* à la bombe; **~ away** *vt* faire fuir; **~ off** *vt* = **scare away**; **~crow** *n* épouvantail *m*; **~d** *adj*: **to be ~d** avoir peur

scarf [skɑːf] (*pl* **~s** *or* **scarves**) *n* (*long*) écharpe *f*; (*square*) foulard *m*

scarlet ['skɑːlət] *adj* écarlate; **~ fever** *n* scarlatine *f*

scary ['skɛərɪ] (*inf*) *adj* effrayant(e)

scathing ['skeɪðɪŋ] *adj* cinglant(e), acerbe

scatter ['skætə*] *vt* éparpiller, répandre; (*crowd*) disperser ♦ *vi* se disperser; **~brained** *adj* écervelé(e), étourdi(e)

scavenger ['skævɪndʒə*] *n* (*person: in bins etc*) pilleur *m* de poubelles

scene [siːn] *n* scène *f*; (*of crime, accident*) lieu(x) *m(pl)*; (*sight, view*) spectacle *m*, vue *f*; **~ry** ['siːnərɪ] *n* (*THEATRE*) décor(s) *m(pl)*; (*landscape*) paysage *m*; **scenic** ['siːnɪk] *adj* (*picturesque*) offrant de beaux paysages *or* panoramas

scent [sɛnt] *n* parfum *m*, odeur *f*; (*track*) piste *f*

sceptical ['skɛptɪkəl] (*US* **skeptical**) *adj* sceptique

schedule ['ʃɛdjuːl, (*US*) 'skɛdjuːl] *n* programme *m*, plan *m*; (*of trains*) horaire *m*; (*of prices etc*) barème *m*, tarif *m* ♦ *vt* prévoir; **on ~** à l'heure (prévue); à la date prévue; **to be ahead of/behind ~**

avoir de l'avance/du retard; ~d flight *n* vol régulier

scheme [skiːm] *n* plan *m*, projet *m*; (*dishonest plan, plot*) complot *m*, combine *f*; (*arrangement*) arrangement *m*, classification *f*; (*pension* ~ *etc*) régime *m* ♦ *vi* comploter, manigancer; **scheming** ['skiːmɪŋ] *adj* rusé(e), intrigant(e) ♦ *n* manigances *fpl*, intrigues *fpl*

scholar ['skɔlə*] *n* érudit(e); (*pupil*) boursier(ière); ~**ly** *adj* érudit(e), savant(e); ~**ship** *n* (*knowledge*) érudition *f*; (*grant*) bourse *f* (d'études)

school [skuːl] *n* école *f*; (*secondary* ~) collège *m*, lycée *m*; (*US: university*) université *f*; (*in university*) faculté *f* ♦ *cpd* scolaire; ~**book** *n* livre *m* scolaire *or* de classe; ~**boy** *n* écolier *m*; collégien *m*, lycéen *m*; ~**children** *npl* écoliers *mpl*; collégiens *mpl*, lycéens *mpl*; ~**days** *npl* années *fpl* de scolarité; ~**girl** *n* écolière *f*; collégienne *f*, lycéenne *f*; ~**ing** *n* instruction *f*, études *fpl*; ~**master** *n* (*primary*) instituteur *m*; (*secondary*) professeur *m*; ~**mistress** *n* institutrice *f*; professeur *m*; ~**teacher** *n* instituteur(trice); professeur *m*

sciatica [saɪ'ætɪkə] *n* sciatique *f*

science ['saɪəns] *n* science *f*; ~ **fiction** *n* science-fiction *f*; **scientific** [saɪən'tɪfɪk] *adj* scientifique; **scientist** ['saɪəntɪst] *n* scientifique *m/f*; (*eminent*) savant *m*

scissors ['sɪzəz] *npl* ciseaux *mpl*

scoff [skɔf] *vt* (*BRIT: inf: eat*) avaler, bouffer ♦ *vi*: **to** ~ (**at**) (*mock*) se moquer (de)

scold [skəuld] *vt* gronder

scone [skɔn] *n* sorte de petit pain rond au lait

scoop [skuːp] *n* pelle *f* (à main); (*for ice cream*) boule *f* à glace; (*PRESS*) scoop *m*; ~ **out** *vt* évider, creuser; ~ **up** *vt* ramasser

scooter ['skuːtə*] *n* (*also: motor* ~) scooter *m*; (*toy*) trottinette *f*

scope [skəup] *n* (*capacity: of plan, undertaking*) portée *f*, envergure *f*; (: *of person*) compétence *f*, capacités *fpl*; (*opportunity*) possibilités *fpl*; **within the** ~

of dans les limites de

scorch [skɔːtʃ] *vt* (*clothes*) brûler (légèrement), roussir; (*earth, grass*) dessécher, brûler

score [skɔː*] *n* score *m*, décompte *m* des points; (*MUS*) partition *f*; (*twenty*) vingt ♦ *vt* (*goal, point*) marquer; (*success*) remporter ♦ *vi* marquer des points; (*FOOTBALL*) marquer un but; (*keep* ~) compter les points; ~**s of** (*very many*) beaucoup de, un tas de (*fam*); **on that** ~ sur ce chapitre, à cet égard; **to** ~ **6 out of 10** obtenir 6 sur 10; ~ **out** *vt* rayer, barrer, biffer; ~**board** *n* tableau *m*

scorn ['skɔːn] *n* mépris *m*, dédain *m*

Scorpio ['skɔːpɪəu] *n* le Scorpion

Scot [skɔt] *n* Écossais(e)

Scotch [skɔtʃ] *n* whisky *m*, scotch *m*

scotch *vt* (*plan*) faire échouer; (*rumour*) étouffer

scot-free ['skɔt'friː] *adv*: **to get off** ~ s'en tirer sans être puni(e)

Scotland ['skɔtlənd] *n* Écosse *f*

Scots [skɔts] *adj* écossais(e); ~**man** (*irreg*) *n* Écossais; ~**woman** (*irreg*) *n* Écossaise *f*

Scottish ['skɔtɪʃ] *adj* écossais(e)

scoundrel ['skaundrəl] *n* vaurien *m*

scour ['skauə*] *vt* (*search*) battre, parcourir

scourge [skɜːdʒ] *n* fléau *m*

scout [skaut] *n* (*MIL*) éclaireur *m*; (*also: boy* ~) scout *m*; **girl** ~ (*US*) guide *f*; ~ **around** *vi* explorer, chercher

scowl [skaul] *vi* se renfrogner, avoir l'air maussade; **to** ~ **at** regarder de travers

scrabble ['skræbl] *vi* (*also:* ~ *around/search*) chercher à tâtons; (*claw*): **to** ~ (**at**) gratter ♦ *n*: **S~** ® Scrabble *m* ®

scram [skræm] (*inf*) *vi* ficher le camp

scramble ['skræmbl] *n* (*rush*) bousculade *f*, ruée *f* ♦ *vi*: **to** ~ **up/down** grimper/descendre tant bien que mal; **to** ~ **out** sortir *or* descendre à toute vitesse; **to** ~ **through** se frayer un passage (à travers); **to** ~ **for** se bousculer *or* se disputer pour (avoir); ~**d eggs** *npl* œufs brouillés

scrap [skræp] *n* bout *m*, morceau *m*; (*fight*) bagarre *f*; (*also*: ~ *iron*) ferraille *f* ♦ *vt* jeter, mettre au rebut; (*fig*) abandonner, laisser tomber ♦ *vi* (*fight*) se bagarrer; **~s** *npl* (*waste*) déchets *mpl*; **~book** *n* album *m*; **~ dealer** *n* marchand *m* de ferraille

scrape [skreɪp] *vt, vi* gratter, racler ♦ *n*: **to get into a ~** s'attirer des ennuis; **to ~ through** réussir de justesse; **~ together** *vt* (*money*) racler ses fonds de tiroir pour réunir

scrap: **~ heap** *n* (*fig*) au rancart *or* rebut; **~ merchant** (*BRIT*) *n* marchand *m* de ferraille; **~ paper** *n* papier *m* brouillon; **~py** *adj* décousu(e)

scratch [skrætʃ] *n* égratignure *f*, rayure *f*; éraflure *f*; (*from claw*) coup *m* de griffe *f* ♦ *cpd*: **~ team** équipe de fortune *or* improvisée ♦ *vt* (*rub*) (se) gratter; (*record*) rayer; (*paint etc*) érafler; (*with claw, nail*) griffer ♦ *vi* (se) gratter; **to start from ~** partir de zéro; **to be up to ~** être à la hauteur

scrawl [skrɔːl] *vi* gribouiller

scrawny [ˈskrɔːnɪ] *adj* décharné(e)

scream [skriːm] *n* cri perçant, hurlement *m* ♦ *vi* crier, hurler

screech [skriːtʃ] *vi* hurler; (*tyres*) crisser; (*brakes*) grincer

screen [skriːn] *n* écran *m*; (*in room*) paravent *m*; (*fig*) écran, rideau *m* ♦ *vt* (*conceal*) masquer, cacher; (*from the wind etc*) abriter, protéger; (*film*) projeter; (*candidates etc*) filtrer; **~ing** *n* (*MED*) test *m* (*or* tests) de dépistage; **~play** *n* scénario *m*

screw [skruː] *n* vis *f* ♦ *vt* (*also*: ~ *in*) visser; **~ up** *vt* (*paper etc*) froisser; **to ~ up one's eyes** plisser les yeux; **~driver** *n* tournevis *m*

scribble [ˈskrɪbl] *vt, vi* gribouiller, griffonner

script [skrɪpt] *n* (*CINEMA etc*) scénario *m*, texte *m*; (*system of writing*) (écriture *f*) script *m*

Scripture(s) [ˈskrɪptʃə*(z)] *n(pl)* (*Christian*) Écriture sainte; (*other religions*) écritures saintes

scroll [skrəʊl] *n* rouleau *m*

scrounge [skraʊndʒ] (*inf*) *vt*: **to ~ sth off** *or* **from sb** taper qn de qch; **~r** (*inf*) *n* parasite *m*

scrub [skrʌb] *n* (*land*) broussailles *fpl* ♦ *vt* (*floor*) nettoyer à la brosse; (*pan*) récurer; (*washing*) frotter; (*inf: cancel*) annuler

scruff [skrʌf] *n*: **by the ~ of the neck** par la peau du cou

scruffy [ˈskrʌfɪ] *adj* débraillé(e)

scrum(mage) [ˈskrʌm(ɪdʒ)] *n* (*RUGBY*) mêlée *f*

scruple [ˈskruːpl] *n* scrupule *m*

scrutiny [ˈskruːtɪnɪ] *n* examen minutieux

scuff [skʌf] *vt* érafler

scuffle [ˈskʌfl] *n* échauffourée *f*, rixe *f*

sculptor [ˈskʌlptə*] *n* sculpteur *m*

sculpture [ˈskʌlptʃə*] *n* sculpture *f*

scum [skʌm] *n* écume *f*, mousse *f*; (*pej: people*) rebut *m*, lie *f*

scurrilous [ˈskʌrɪləs] *adj* calomnieux(euse)

scurry [ˈskʌrɪ] *vi* filer à toute allure; **to ~ off** détaler, se sauver

scuttle [ˈskʌtl] *n* (*also: coal ~*) seau *m* (à charbon) ♦ *vt* (*ship*) saborder ♦ *vi* (*scamper*): **to ~ away** *or* **off** détaler

scythe [saɪð] *n* faux *f*

sea [siː] *n* mer *f* ♦ *cpd* marin(e), de (la) mer; **by ~** (*travel*) par mer, en bateau; **on the ~** (*boat*) en mer; (*town*) au bord de la mer; **to be all at ~** (*fig*) nager complètement; **out to ~** au large; (**out**) **at ~** en mer; **~board** *n* côte *f*; **~food** *n* fruits *mpl* de mer; **~front** *n* bord *m* de mer; **~going** *adj* (*ship*) de mer; **~gull** *n* mouette *f*

seal [siːl] *n* (*animal*) phoque *m*; (*stamp*) sceau *m*, cachet *m* ♦ *vt* sceller; (*envelope*) coller; (: *with seal*) cacheter; **~ off** *vt* (*forbid entry to*) interdire l'accès de

sea level *n* niveau *m* de la mer

sea lion *n* otarie *f*

seam [siːm] *n* couture *f*; (*of coal*) veine *f*, filon *m*

seaman [ˈsiːmən] (*irreg*) *n* marin *m*

seance [ˈseɪɑ̃ns] *n* séance *f* de spiritisme

seaplane ['si:pleɪn] *n* hydravion *m*

search [sɜ:tʃ] *n* (*for person, thing,* COMPUT) recherche(s) *f(pl)*; (LAW: *at sb's home*) perquisition *f* ♦ *vt* fouiller; (*examine*) examiner minutieusement; scruter ♦ *vi*: **to ~ for** chercher; **in ~ of** à la recherche de; **~ through** *vt fus* fouiller; **~ing** *adj* pénétrant(e); **~light** *n* projecteur *m*; **~ party** expédition *f* de secours; **~ warrant** *n* mandat *m* de perquisition

sea: **~shore** ['si:ʃɔ:*] *n* rivage *m*, plage *f*, bord *m* de (la) mer; **~sick** ['si:sɪk] *adj*: **to be ~sick** avoir le mal de mer; **~side** ['si:saɪd] *n* bord *m* de la mer; **~side resort** *n* station *f* balnéaire

season ['si:zn] *n* saison *f* ♦ *vt* assaisonner, relever; **to be in/out of ~** être/ne pas être de saison; **~al** *adj* (*work*) saisonnier(ère); **~ed** *adj* (*fig*) expérimenté(e); **~ ticket** *n* carte *f* d'abonnement

seat [si:t] *n* siège *m*; (*in bus, train: place*) place *f*; (*buttocks*) postérieur *m*; (*of trousers*) fond *m* ♦ *vt* faire asseoir, placer; (*have room for*) avoir des places assises pour, pouvoir accueillir; **~ belt** *n* ceinture *f* de sécurité

sea: **~ water** *n* eau *f* de mer; **~weed** ['si:wi:d] *n* algues *fpl*; **~worthy** ['si:wɜ:ðɪ] *adj* en état de naviguer

sec. *abbr* = **second(s)**

secluded [sɪ'klu:dɪd] *adj* retiré(e), à l'écart

seclusion [sɪ'klu:ʒən] *n* solitude *f*

second[1] [sɪ'kɒnd] (BRIT) *vt* (*employee*) affecter provisoirement

second[2] ['sekənd] *adj* deuxième, second(e) ♦ *adv* (*in race etc*) en seconde position ♦ *n* (*unit of time*) seconde *f*; (AUT: **~ gear**) seconde *f*; (COMM: *imperfect*) article *m* de second choix; (BRIT: UNIV) licence *f* avec mention ♦ *vt* (*motion*) appuyer; **~ary** *adj* secondaire; **~ary school** *n* collège *m*, lycée *m*; **~-class** *adj* de deuxième classe; (RAIL) de seconde (classe) (POST) au tarif réduit (*pej*) de qualité inférieure ♦ *adv* (RAIL) en seconde; (POST) au tarif réduit; **~hand** *adj* d'occasion; de seconde main; **~ hand** *n* (*on clock*) trot-

teuse *f*; **~ly** *adv* deuxièmement; **~ment** [sɪ'kɒndmənt] (BRIT) *n* détachement *m*; **~rate** *adj* de deuxième ordre, de qualité inférieure; **~ thoughts** *npl* doutes *mpl*; **on ~ thoughts** *or* (US) **thought** à la réflexion

secrecy ['si:krəsɪ] *n* secret *m*

secret ['si:krət] *adj* secret(ète) ♦ *n* secret *m*; **in ~** en secret, secrètement, en cachette

secretary ['sekrətrɪ] *n* secrétaire *m/f*; (COMM) secrétaire général; **S~ of State (for)** (BRIT: POL) ministre *m* (de)

secretive ['si:krətɪv] *adj* dissimulé

sectarian [sek'tɛərɪən] *adj* sectaire

section ['sekʃən] *n* section *f*; (*of document*) section, article *m*, paragraphe *m*; (*cut*) coupe *f*

sector ['sektə*] *n* secteur *m*

secular ['sekjulə*] *adj* profane; laïque; séculier(ère)

secure [sɪ'kjuə*] *adj* (*free from anxiety*) sans inquiétude, sécurisé(e); (*firmly fixed*) solide, bien attaché(e) (*or* fermé(e) *etc*); (*in safe place*) en lieu sûr, en sûreté ♦ *vt* (*fix*) fixer, attacher; (*get*) obtenir, se procurer

security [sɪ'kjuərɪtɪ] *n* sécurité *f*, mesures *fpl* de sécurité; (*for loan*) caution *f*, garantie *f*

sedan [sɪ'dæn] (US) *n* (AUT) berline *f*

sedate [sɪ'deɪt] *adj* calme; posé(e) ♦ *vt* (MED) donner des sédatifs à

sedative ['sedətɪv] *n* calmant *m*, sédatif *m*

seduce [sɪ'dju:s] *vt* séduire; **seduction** [sɪ'dʌkʃən] *n* séduction *f*; **seductive** [sɪ'dʌktɪv] *adj* séduisant(e); (*smile*) séducteur(trice); (*fig: offer*) alléchant(e)

see [si:] (*pt* saw, *pp* seen) *vt* voir; (*accompany*): **to ~ sb to the door** reconduire *or* raccompagner qn jusqu'à la porte ♦ *vi* voir ♦ *n* évêché *m*; **to ~ that** (*ensure*) veiller à ce que +*sub*, faire en sorte que; s'assurer que; **~ you soon!** à bientôt!; **~ about** *vt fus* s'occuper de; **~ off** *vt* accompagner (à la gare *or* à l'aéroport *etc*); **~ through** *vt* mener à bonne fin ♦ *vt fus* voir clair dans; **~ to** *vt fus* s'occuper de, se charger de

seed [siːd] *n* graine *f*; (*sperm*) semence *f*; (*fig*) germe *m*; (TENNIS) tête *f* de série; **to go to ~** monter en graine; (*fig*) se laisser aller; **~ling** *n* jeune plant *m*, semis *m*; **~y** *adj* (*shabby*) minable, miteux(euse)

seeing ['siːɪŋ] *conj*: **~ (that)** vu que, étant donné que

seek [siːk] (*pt, pp* **sought**) *vt* chercher, rechercher

seem [siːm] *vi* sembler, paraître; **there ~s to be ...** il semble qu'il y a ...; on dirait qu'il y a ...; **~ingly** *adv* apparemment

seen [siːn] *pp of* **see**

seep [siːp] *vi* suinter, filtrer

seesaw ['siːsɔː] *n* (jeu *m* de) bascule *f*

seethe [siːð] *vi* être en effervescence; **to ~ with anger** bouillir de colère

see-through ['siːθruː] *adj* transparent(e)

segment *n* segment *m*; (*of orange*) quartier *m*

segregate ['sɛgrɪgeɪt] *vt* séparer, isoler

seize [siːz] *vt* saisir, attraper; (*take possession of*) s'emparer de; (*opportunity*) saisir; **~ up** *vi* (TECH) se gripper; **~ (up)on** *vt fus* saisir, sauter sur

seizure ['siːʒə*] *n* (MED) crise *f*, attaque *f*; (*of power*) prise *f*

seldom ['sɛldəm] *adv* rarement

select [sɪ'lɛkt] *adj* choisi(e), d'élite ♦ *vt* sélectionner, choisir; **~ion** [sɪ'lɛkʃən] *n* sélection *f*, choix *m*

self [sɛlf] (*pl* **selves**) *n*: **the ~** le moi *inv* ♦ *prefix* auto-; **~-assured** *adj* sûr(e) de soi; **~-catering** (BRIT) *adj* avec cuisine, où l'on peut faire sa cuisine; **~-centred** (US **~-centered**) *adj* égocentrique; **~-confidence** *n* confiance *f* en soi; **~-conscious** *adj* timide, qui manque d'assurance; **~-contained** (BRIT) *adj* (*flat*) avec entrée particulière, indépendant(e); **~-control** *n* maîtrise *f* de soi; **~-defence** (US **~-defense**) *n* autodéfense *f*; (LAW) légitime défense *f*; **~-discipline** *n* discipline personnelle; **~-employed** *adj* qui travaille à son compte; **~-evident** *adj*: **to be ~-evident** être évident(e), aller de soi; **~-governing** *adj* autonome; **~-indulgent** *adj* qui ne se refuse rien; **~-interest** *n* intérêt personnel; **~ish** *adj* égoïste; **~ishness** *n* égoïsme *m*; **~less** *adj* désintéressé(e); **~-pity** *n* apitoiement *m* sur soi-même; **~-possessed** *adj* assuré(e); **~-preservation** *n* instinct *m* de conservation; **~-respect** *n* respect *m* de soi, amour-propre *m*; **~-righteous** *adj* suffisant(e); **~-sacrifice** *n* abnégation *f*; **~-satisfied** *adj* content(e) de soi, suffisant(e); **~-service** *adj* libre-service, self-service; **~-sufficient** *adj* autosuffisant(e); (*person: independent*) indépendant(e); **~-taught** *adj* (*artist, pianist*) qui a appris par lui-même

sell [sɛl] (*pt, pp* **sold**) *vt* vendre ♦ *vi* se vendre; **to ~ at** *or* **for 10 F** se vendre 10 F; **~ off** *vt* liquider; **~ out** *vi*: **to ~ out (of sth)** (*use up stock*) vendre tout son stock (de qch); **the tickets are all sold out** il ne reste plus de billets; **~-by date** *n* date *f* limite de vente; **~er** *n* vendeur(euse), marchand(e); **~ing price** *n* prix *m* de vente

Sellotape ['sɛləʊteɪp] (®: BRIT) *n* papier *m* collant, scotch *m* (®)

selves [sɛlvz] *npl of* **self**

semblance ['sɛmbləns] *n* semblant *m*

semen ['siːmən] *n* sperme *m*

semester [sɪ'mɛstə*] (*esp* US) *n* semestre *m*

semi ['sɛmɪ] *prefix* semi-, demi-; à demi, à moitié; **~circle** *n* demi-cercle *m*; **~colon** *n* point-virgule *m*; **~detached (house)** (BRIT) *n* maison jumelée *or* jumelle; **~final** *n* demi-finale *f*

seminar ['sɛmɪnɑː*] *n* séminaire *m*

seminary ['sɛmɪnərɪ] *n* (REL: *for priests*) séminaire *m*

semiskilled ['sɛmɪ'skɪld] *adj*: **~ worker** ouvrier(ère) spécialisé(e)

semi-skimmed milk ['sɛmɪ'skɪmd-] *n* lait demi-écrémé

senate ['sɛnɪt] *n* sénat *m*; **senator** *n* sénateur *m*

send [sɛnd] (*pt, pp* **sent**) *vt* envoyer; **~ away** *vt* (*letter, goods*) envoyer, expédier; (*unwelcome visitor*) renvoyer; **~**

away for *vt fus* commander par correspondance, se faire envoyer; **~ back** *vt* renvoyer; **~ for** *vt fus* envoyer chercher; faire venir; **~ off** *vt* (*goods*) envoyer, expédier; (*BRIT: SPORT: player*) expulser *or* renvoyer du terrain; **~ out** *vt* (*invitation*) envoyer (par la poste); (*light, heat, signal*) émettre; **~ up** *vt* faire monter; (*BRIT: parody*) mettre en boîte, parodier; **~er** *n* expéditeur(trice); **~-off** *n*: **a good ~-off** des adieux chaleureux

senior ['si:nɪə*] *adj* (*high-ranking*) de haut niveau; (*of higher rank*): **to be ~ to sb** être le supérieur de qn ♦ *n* (*older*): **she is 15 years his ~** elle est son aînée de 15 ans, elle est plus âgée que lui de 15 ans; **~ citizen** *n* personne âgée; **~ity** [si:nɪ'ɒrɪtɪ] *n* (*in service*) ancienneté *f*

sensation [sen'seɪʃən] *n* sensation *f*; **~al** *adj* qui fait sensation; (*marvellous*) sensationnel(le)

sense [sens] *n* sens *m*; (*feeling*) sentiment *m*; (*meaning*) sens, signification *f*; (*wisdom*) bon sens ♦ *vt* sentir, pressentir; **it makes ~** c'est logique; **~less** *adj* insensé(e), stupide; (*unconscious*) sans connaissance

sensible ['sensəbl] *adj* sensé(e), raisonnable; sage

sensitive ['sensɪtɪv] *adj* sensible

sensual ['sensjʊəl] *adj* sensuel(le)

sensuous ['sensjʊəs] *adj* voluptueux(euse), sensuel(le)

sent [sent] *pt, pp of* **send**

sentence ['sentəns] *n* (*LING*) phrase *f*; (*LAW: judgment*) condamnation *f*, sentence *f*; (: *punishment*) peine *f* ♦ *vt*: **to ~ sb to death/to 5 years in prison** condamner qn à mort/à 5 ans de prison

sentiment ['sentɪmənt] *n* sentiment *m*; (*opinion*) opinion *f*, avis *m*; **~al** [sentɪ'mentl] *adj* sentimental(e)

sentry ['sentrɪ] *n* sentinelle *f*

separate [*adj* 'seprət, *vb* 'sepəreɪt] *adj* séparé(e), indépendant(e), différent(e) ♦ *vt* (*make a distinction between*) distinguer ♦ *vi* se séparer; **~ly** *adv* séparément; **~s** *npl* (*clothes*) coordonnés *mpl*; **separation** [sepə'reɪʃən] *n*

séparation *f*

September [sep'tembə*] *n* septembre *m*

septic ['septɪk] *adj* (*wound*) infecté(e); **~ tank** *n* fosse *f* septique

sequel ['si:kwl] *n* conséquence *f*; séquelles *fpl*; (*of story*) suite *f*

sequence ['si:kwəns] *n* ordre *m*, suite *f*; (*film ~*) séquence *f*; (*dance ~*) numéro *m*

sequin ['si:kwɪn] *n* paillette *f*

serene [sə'ri:n] *adj* serein(e), calme, paisible

sergeant ['sɑ:dʒənt] *n* sergent *m*; (*POLICE*) brigadier *m*

serial ['sɪərɪəl] *n* feuilleton *m*; **~ killer** *n* meurtrier *m* tuant en série; **~ number** *n* numéro *m* de série

series ['sɪərɪz] *n inv* série *f*; (*PUBLISHING*) collection *f*

serious ['sɪərɪəs] *adj* sérieux(euse); (*illness*) grave; **~ly** *adv* sérieusement; (*hurt*) gravement

sermon ['sɜ:mən] *n* sermon *m*

serrated [se'reɪtɪd] *adj* en dents de scie

servant ['sɜ:vənt] *n* domestique *m/f*; (*fig*) serviteur/servante

serve [sɜ:v] *vt* (*employer etc*) servir, être au service de; (*purpose*) servir à; (*customer, food, meal*) servir; (*subj: train*) desservir; (*apprenticeship*) faire, accomplir; (*prison term*) purger ♦ *vi* servir; (*be useful*): **to ~ as/for/to do** servir de/à/à faire ♦ *n* (*TENNIS*) service *m*; **it ~s him right** c'est bien fait pour lui; **~ out**, **~ up** *vt* (*food*) servir

service ['sɜ:vɪs] *n* service *m*; (*AUT: maintenance*) révision *f* ♦ *vt* (*car, washing machine*) réviser; **the S~s** les forces armées; **to be of ~ to sb** rendre service à qn; **~able** *adj* pratique, commode; **~ charge** (*BRIT*) *n* service *m*; **~man** (*irreg*) *n* militaire *m*; **~ station** *n* station-service *f*

serviette [sɜ:vɪ'et] (*BRIT*) *n* serviette *f* (de table)

session ['seʃən] *n* séance *f*

set [set] (*pt, pp* **set**) *n* série *f*, assortiment *m*; (*of tools etc*) jeu *m*; (*RADIO, TV*) poste *m*; (*TENNIS*) set *m*; (*group of peo-*

ple) cercle *m*, milieu *m*; (THEATRE: *stage*) scène *f*; (: *scenery*) décor *m*; (HAIRDRESSING) mise *f* en plis ♦ *adj* (*fixed*) fixe, déterminé(e); (*ready*) prêt(e) ♦ *vt* (*place*) poser, placer; (*fix, establish*) fixer; (: *record*) établir; (*adjust*) régler; (*decide: rules etc*) fixer, choisir; (*task*) donner; (*exam*) composer ♦ *vi* (*sun*) se coucher; (*jam, jelly, concrete*) prendre; (*bone*) se ressouder; **to be ~ on doing** être résolu à faire; **to ~ the table** mettre la table; **to ~ (to music)** mettre en musique; **to ~ on fire** mettre le feu à; **to ~ free** libérer; **to ~ sth going** déclencher qch; **to ~ sail** prendre la mer; **~ about** *vt fus* (*task*) entreprendre, se mettre à; **~ aside** *vt* mettre de côté; (*time*) garder; **~ back** *vt* (*in time*): **to ~ back (by)** retarder (de); (*cost*): **to ~ sb back £5** coûter 5 livres à qn; **~ off** *vi* se mettre en route, partir ♦ *vt* (*bomb*) faire exploser; (*cause to start*) déclencher; (*show up well*) mettre en valeur, faire valoir; **~ out** *vi* se mettre en route, partir ♦ *vt* (*arrange*) disposer; (*arguments*) présenter, exposer; **to ~ out to do** entreprendre de faire, avoir pour but *or* intention de faire; **~ up** *vt* (*organization*) fonder, créer; **~back** *n* (*hitch*) revers *m*, contretemps *m*; **~ menu** *n* menu *m*
settee [se'ti:] *n* canapé *m*
setting ['setɪŋ] *n* cadre *m*; (*of jewel*) monture *f*; (*position of controls*) réglage *m*
settle ['setl] *vt* (*argument, matter, account*) régler; (*problem*) résoudre; (MED: *calm*) calmer ♦ *vi* (*bird, dust etc*) se poser; (*also*: **~ down**) s'installer, se fixer; (*calm down*) se calmer; **to ~ for sth** accepter qch, se contenter de qch; **to ~ on sth** opter *or* se décider pour qch; **~ in** *vi* s'installer; **~ up** *vi*: **to ~ up with sb** régler (ce que l'on doit à) qn; **~ment** *n* (*payment*) règlement *m*; (*agreement*) accord *m*; (*village etc*) établissement *m*; hameau *m*; **~ r** *n* colon *m*
setup ['setʌp] *n* (*arrangement*) manière *f* dont les choses sont organisées; (*situation*) situation *f*

seven ['sevn] *num* sept; **~teen** *num* dix-sept; **~th** *num* septième; **~ty** *num* soixante-dix
sever ['sevə*] *vt* couper, trancher; (*relations*) rompre
several ['sevrəl] *adj, pron* plusieurs *m/fpl*; **~ of us** plusieurs d'entre nous
severance ['sevərəns] *n* (*of relations*) rupture *f*, **~ pay** *n* indemnité *f* de licenciement
severe [sɪ'vɪə*] *adj* (*stern*) sévère, strict(e); (*serious*) grave, sérieux(euse); (*plain*) sévère, austère; **severity** [sɪ'verɪtɪ] *n* sévérité *f*; gravité *f*; rigueur *f*
sew [səu] (*pt* **sewed**, *pp* **sewn**) *vt, vi* coudre; **~ up** *vt* (re)coudre
sewage ['sju:ɪdʒ] *n* vidange(s) *f(pl)*
sewer ['sjuə*] *n* égout *m*
sewing ['səuɪŋ] *n* couture *f*; (*item(s)*) ouvrage *m*; **~ machine** *n* machine *f* à coudre
sewn [səun] *pp of* **sew**
sex [seks] *n* sexe *m*; **to have ~ with** avoir des rapports (sexuels) avec; **~ist** *adj* sexiste; **~ual** ['seksjuəl] *adj* sexuel(le); **~y** ['seksɪ] *adj* sexy *inv*
shabby ['ʃæbɪ] *adj* miteux(euse); (*behaviour*) mesquin(e), méprisable
shack [ʃæk] *n* cabane *f*, hutte *f*
shackles ['ʃæklz] *npl* chaînes *fpl*, entraves *fpl*
shade [ʃeɪd] *n* ombre *f*; (*for lamp*) abat-jour *m inv*; (*of colour*) nuance *f*, ton *m* ♦ *vt* abriter du soleil, ombrager; **in the ~** à l'ombre; **a ~ too large/more** un tout petit peu trop grand(e)/plus
shadow ['ʃædəu] *n* ombre *f* ♦ *vt* (*follow*) filer; **~ cabinet** (BRIT) *n* (POL) *cabinet parallèle formé par l'Opposition*; **~y** *adj* ombragé(e); (*dim*) vague, indistinct(e)
shady ['ʃeɪdɪ] *adj* ombragé(e); (*fig: dishonest*) louche, véreux(euse)
shaft [ʃɑ:ft] *n* (*of arrow, spear*) hampe *f*; (AUT, TECH) arbre *m*; (*of mine*) puits *m*; (*of lift*) cage *f*; (*of light*) rayon *m*, trait *m*
shaggy ['ʃægɪ] *adj* hirsute; en broussaille
shake [ʃeɪk] (*pt* **shook**, *pp* **shaken**) *vt*

secouer; (*bottle, cocktail*) agiter; (*house, confidence*) ébranler ♦ *vi* trembler; **to ~ one's head** (*in refusal*) dire *or* faire non de la tête; (*in dismay*) secouer la tête; **to ~ hands with sb** serrer la main à qn; **~ off** *vt* secouer; (*pursuer*) se débarrasser de; **~ up** *vt* secouer; **~n** [ʃeɪkn] *pp of* **shake**; **shaky** [ʃeɪkɪ] *adj* (*hand, voice*) tremblant(e); (*building*) branlant(e), peu solide

shall [ʃæl] *aux vb*: **I ~ go** j'irai; **~ I open the door?** j'ouvre la porte?; **I'll get the coffee, ~ I?** je vais chercher le café, d'accord?

shallow [ʃæləʊ] *adj* peu profond(e); (*fig*) superficiel(le)

sham [ʃæm] *n* frime *f* ♦ *vt* simuler

shambles [ʃæmblz] *n* (*muddle*) confusion *f*, pagaïe *f*, fouillis *m*

shame [ʃeɪm] *n* honte *f* ♦ *vt* faire honte à; **it is a ~ (that/to do)** c'est dommage (que +*sub*/de faire); **what a ~!** quel dommage!; **~faced** *adj* honteux(euse), penaud(e); **~ful** *adj* honteux(euse), scandaleux(euse); **~less** *adj* éhonté(e), effronté(e)

shampoo [ʃæmˈpuː] *n* shampooing *m* ♦ *vt* faire un shampooing à; **~ and set** *n* shampooing et mise *f* en plis

shamrock [ʃæmrɒk] *n* trèfle *m* (*emblème de l'Irlande*)

shandy [ʃændɪ] *n* bière panachée

shan't [ʃɑːnt] = **shall not**

shanty town [ʃæntɪ-] *n* bidonville *m*

shape [ʃeɪp] *n* forme *f* ♦ *vt* façonner, modeler; (*sb's ideas*) former; (*sb's life*) déterminer ♦ *vi* (*also*: **~ up**: *events*) prendre tournure; (: *person*) faire des progrès, s'en sortir; **to take ~** prendre forme *or* tournure; **-shaped** *suffix*: **heart-shaped** en forme de cœur; **~less** *adj* informe, sans forme; **~ly** *adj* bien proportionné(e), beau(belle)

share [ʃɛə*] *n* part *f*; (*COMM*) action *f* ♦ *vt* partager; (*have in common*) avoir en commun; **~ out** *vi* partager; **~holder** *n* actionnaire *m/f*

shark [ʃɑːk] *n* requin *m*

sharp [ʃɑːp] *adj* (*razor, knife*) tranchant(e), bien aiguisé(e); (*point, voice*) aigu(guë); (*nose, chin*) pointu(e); (*outline, increase*) net(te); (*cold, pain*) vif(vive); (*taste*) piquant(e), âcre; (*MUS*) dièse; (*person: quick-witted*) vif(vive), éveillé(e); (: *unscrupulous*) malhonnête ♦ *n* (*MUS*) dièse *m* ♦ *adv* (*precisely*): **at 2 o'clock ~** à 2 heures pile *or* précises; **~en** *vt* aiguiser; (*pencil*) tailler; **~ener** *n* (*also*: **pencil ~ener**) taille-crayon(s) *m inv*; **~-eyed** *adj* à qui rien n'échappe; **~ly** *adv* (*turn, stop*) brusquement; (*stand out*) nettement; (*criticize, retort*) sèchement, vertement

shatter [ʃætə*] *vt* briser; (*fig: upset*) bouleverser; (: *ruin*) briser, ruiner ♦ *vi* voler en éclats, se briser

shave [ʃeɪv] *vt* raser ♦ *vi* se raser ♦ *n*: **to have a ~** se raser; **~r** *n* (*also: electric ~r*) rasoir *m* électrique

shaving [ʃeɪvɪŋ] *n* (*action*) rasage *m*; **~s** *npl* (*of wood etc*) copeaux *mpl*; **~ brush** *n* blaireau *m*; **~ cream** *n* crème *f* à raser; **~ foam** *n* mousse *f* à raser

shawl [ʃɔːl] *n* châle *m*

she [ʃiː] *pron* elle ♦ *prefix*: **~-cat** chatte *f*; **~-elephant** éléphant *m* femelle

sheaf [ʃiːf] (*pl* **sheaves**) *n* gerbe *f*; (*of papers*) liasse *f*

shear [ʃɪə*] (*pt* **~ed**, *pp* **shorn**) *vt* (*sheep*) tondre; **~ off** *vi* (*branch*) partir, se détacher; **~s** *npl* (*for hedge*) cisaille(s) *f(pl)*

sheath [ʃiːθ] *n* gaine *f*, fourreau *m*, étui *m*; (*contraceptive*) préservatif *m*

shed [ʃed] (*pt, pp* **shed**) *n* remise *f*, resserre *f* ♦ *vt* perdre; (*tears*) verser, répandre; (*workers*) congédier

she'd [ʃiːd] = **she had; she would**

sheen [ʃiːn] *n* lustre *m*

sheep [ʃiːp] *n inv* mouton *m*; **~dog** *n* chien *m* de berger; **~ish** *adj* penaud(e); **~skin** *n* peau *f* de mouton

sheer [ʃɪə*] *adj* (*utter*) pur(e), pur et simple; (*steep*) à pic, abrupt(e); (*almost transparent*) extrêmement fin(e) ♦ *adv* à pic, abruptement

sheet [ʃiːt] *n* (*on bed*) drap *m*; (*of paper*) feuille *f*; (*of glass, metal etc*) feuille, plaque *f*

sheik(h) [ʃeɪk] *n* cheik *m*

shelf [ʃelf] (*pl* **shelves**) *n* étagère *f*, rayon *m*

shell [ʃel] *n* (*on beach*) coquillage *m*; (*of egg, nut etc*) coquille *f*; (*explosive*) obus *m*; (*of building*) carcasse *f* ♦ *vt* (*peas*) écosser; (*MIL*) bombarder (d'obus)

she'll [ʃiːl] = **she will; she shall**

shellfish [ˈʃelfɪʃ] *n inv* (*crab etc*) crustacé *m*; (*scallop etc*) coquillage *m* ♦ *npl* (*as food*) fruits *mpl* de mer

shell suit *n* survêtement *m* (*en synthétique froissé*)

shelter [ˈʃeltə*] *n* abri *m*, refuge *m* ♦ *vt* abriter, protéger; (*give lodging to*) donner asile à ♦ *vi* s'abriter, se mettre à l'abri; **~ed housing** *n* foyers *mpl* (*pour personnes âgées ou handicapées*)

shelve [ʃelv] *vt* (*fig*) mettre en suspens *or* en sommeil; **~s** *npl* *of* **shelf**

shepherd [ˈʃepəd] *n* berger *m* ♦ *vt* (*guide*) guider, escorter; **~'s pie** (*BRIT*) *n* ≈ hachis *m* Parmentier

sheriff [ˈʃerɪf] (*US*) *n* shérif *m*

sherry [ˈʃerɪ] *n* xérès *m*, sherry *m*

she's [ʃiːz] = **she is; she has**

Shetland [ˈʃetlənd] *n* (*also*: **the ~s, the ~ Islands**) les îles *fpl* Shetland

shield [ʃiːld] *n* bouclier *m*; (*protection*) écran *m* de protection ♦ *vt*: **to ~ (from)** protéger (de *or* contre)

shift [ʃɪft] *n* (*change*) changement *m*; (*work period*) période *f* de travail; (*of workers*) équipe *f*, poste *m* ♦ *vt* déplacer, changer de place; (*remove*) enlever ♦ *vi* changer de place, bouger; **~less** *adj* (*person*) fainéant(e); **~ work** *n* travail *m* en équipe *or* par relais *or* par roulement; **~y** *adj* sournois(e); (*eyes*) fuyant(e)

shilly-shally [ˈʃɪlɪʃælɪ] *vi* tergiverser, atermoyer

shimmer [ˈʃɪmə*] *vi* miroiter, chatoyer

shin [ʃɪn] *n* tibia *m*

shine [ʃaɪn] (*pt, pp* **shone**) *n* éclat *m*, brillant *m* ♦ *vi* briller ♦ *vt* (*torch etc*): **to ~ on** braquer sur; (*polish*: *pt, pp* **~d**) faire briller *or* reluire

shingle [ˈʃɪŋgl] *n* (*on beach*) galets *mpl*; **~s** *n* (*MED*) zona *m*

shiny [ˈʃaɪnɪ] *adj* brillant(e)

ship [ʃɪp] *n* bateau *m*; (*large*) navire *m* ♦ *vt* transporter (par mer); (*send*) expédier (par mer); **~building** *n* construction navale; **~ment** *n* cargaison *f*; **~per** *n* affréteur *m*; **~ping** *n* (*ships*) navires *mpl*; (*the industry*) industrie navale; (*transport*) transport *m*; **~wreck** *n* (*ship*) épave *f*; (*event*) naufrage *m* ♦ *vt*: **to be ~wrecked** faire naufrage; **~yard** *n* chantier naval

shire [ˈʃaɪə*] (*BRIT*) *n* comté *m*

shirk [ʃɜːk] *vt* esquiver, se dérober à

shirt [ʃɜːt] *n* (*man's*) chemise *f*; (*woman's*) chemisier *m*; **in (one's) ~ sleeves** en bras de chemise

shit [ʃɪt] (*inf!*) *n, excl* merde *f* (!)

shiver [ˈʃɪvə*] *n* frisson *m* ♦ *vi* frissonner

shoal [ʃəʊl] *n* (*of fish*) banc *m*; (*fig*: *also*: **~s**) masse *f*, foule *f*

shock [ʃɒk] *n* choc *m*; (*ELEC*) secousse *f*; (*MED*) commotion *f*, choc ♦ *vt* (*offend*) choquer, scandaliser; (*upset*) bouleverser; **~ absorber** *n* amortisseur *m*; **~ing** *adj* (*scandalizing*) choquant(e), scandaleux(euse); (*appalling*) épouvantable

shod [ʃɒd] *pt, pp* of **shoe**

shoddy [ˈʃɒdɪ] *adj* de mauvaise qualité, mal fait(e)

shoe [ʃuː] (*pt, pp* **shod**) *n* chaussure *f*, soulier *m*; (*also*: **horse~**) fer *m* à cheval ♦ *vt* (*horse*) ferrer; **~lace** *n* lacet *m* (*de soulier*); **~ polish** *n* cirage *m*; **~ shop** *n* magasin *m* de chaussures; **~string** *n* (*fig*): **on a ~string** avec un budget dérisoire

shone [ʃɒn] *pt, pp* of **shine**

shoo [ʃuː] *excl* ouste!

shook [ʃʊk] *pt* of **shake**

shoot [ʃuːt] (*pt, pp* **shot**) *n* (*on branch, seedling*) pousse *f* ♦ *vt* (*game*) chasser; tirer; abattre; (*person*) blesser (*or* tuer) d'un coup de fusil (*or* de revolver); (*execute*) fusiller; (*arrow*) tirer; (*gun*) tirer un coup de; (*film*) tourner ♦ *vi* (*with gun, bow*): **to ~ (at)** tirer (sur); (*FOOT-*

BALL) shooter, tirer; ~ **down** *vt* (*plane*) abattre; ~ **in** *vi* entrer comme une flèche; ~ **out** *vi* sortir comme une flèche; ~ **up** *vi* (*fig*) monter en flèche; ~**ing** *n* (*shots*) coups *mpl* de feu, fusillade *f*; (*HUNTING*) chasse *f*; ~**ing star** *n* étoile filante

shop [ʃɒp] *n* magasin *m*; (*workshop*) atelier *m* ♦ *vi* (*also: go ~ping*) faire ses courses *or* ses achats; ~ **assistant** (*BRIT*) *n* vendeur(euse); ~ **floor** (*BRIT*) *n* (*INDUSTRY: fig*) ouvriers *mpl*; ~**keeper** *n* commerçant(e); ~**lifting** *n* vol *m* à l'étalage; ~**per** *n* personne *f* qui fait ses courses, acheteur(euse); ~**ping** *n* (*goods*) achats *mpl*, provisions *fpl*; ~**ping bag** *n* sac *m* (à provisions); ~**ping centre** (*US* ~**ping center**) *n* centre commercial; ~**soiled** *adj* défraîchi(e), qui a fait la vitrine; ~ **steward** (*BRIT*) *n* (*INDUSTRY*) délégué(e) syndical(e); ~ **window** *n* vitrine *f*

shore [ʃɔː*] *n* (*of sea, lake*) rivage *m*, rive *f* ♦ *vt*: **to ~ (up)** étayer; **on ~** à terre

shorn [ʃɔːn] *pp of* **shear**

short [ʃɔːt] *adj* (*not long*) court(e); (*soon finished*) court, bref(brève); (*person, step*) petit(e); (*curt*) brusque, sec(sèche); (*insufficient*) insuffisant(e); **to be/run ~ of sth** être à court de *or* manquer de qch; **in ~** bref; en bref; ~ **of doing** ... à moins de faire ...; **everything ~ of** tout sauf; **it is ~ for** c'est l'abréviation *or* le diminutif de; **to cut ~** (*speech, visit*) abréger, écourter; **to fall ~ of** ne pas être à la hauteur de; **to run ~ of** arriver à court de, venir à manquer de; **to stop ~** s'arrêter net; **to stop ~ of** ne pas aller jusqu'à; ~**age** *n* manque *m*, pénurie *f*; ~**bread** *n* ≈ sablé *m*; ~**change** *vt* ne pas rendre assez à; ~**circuit** *n* court-circuit *m*; ~**coming** *n* défaut *m*; ~(**crust**) **pastry** (*BRIT*) *n* pâte brisée; ~**cut** *n* raccourci *m*; ~**en** *vt* raccourcir; (*text, visit*) abréger; ~**fall** *n* déficit *m*; ~**hand** (*BRIT*) *n* sténo(graphie) *f*; ~**hand typist** (*BRIT*) *n* sténodactylo *m/f*; ~**list** (*BRIT*) *n* (*for job*) liste *f* des candidats sélectionnés; ~**lived** *adj* de courte durée; ~**ly** *adv* bientôt,

sous peu; ~**s** *npl*: (**a pair of**) ~**s** un short; ~**sighted** *adj* (*BRIT*) myope; (*fig*) qui manque de clairvoyance; ~**staffed** *adj* à court de personnel; ~ **story** *n* nouvelle *f*; ~**tempered** *adj* qui s'emporte facilement; ~**term** *adj* (*effect*) à court terme; ~ **wave** *n* (*RADIO*) ondes courtes

shot [ʃɒt] *pt, pp of* **shoot** ♦ *n* coup *m* (de feu); (*try*) coup, essai *m*; (*injection*) piqûre *f*; (*PHOT*) photo *f*; **he's a good/poor** ~ il tire bien/mal; **like a** ~ comme une flèche; (*very readily*) sans hésiter; ~**gun** *n* fusil *m* de chasse

should [ʃʊd] *aux vb*: **I** ~ **go now** je devrais partir maintenant; **he** ~ **be there now** il devrait être arrivé maintenant; **I** ~ **go if I were you** si j'étais vous, j'irais; **I** ~ **like to** j'aimerais bien, volontiers

shoulder ['ʃəʊldə*] *n* épaule *f* ♦ *vt* (*fig*) endosser, se charger de; ~ **bag** *n* sac *m* à bandoulière; ~ **blade** *n* omoplate *f*; ~ **strap** *n* bretelle *f*

shouldn't ['ʃʊdnt] = **should not**

shout [ʃaʊt] *n* cri *m* ♦ *vt* crier ♦ *vi* (*also:* ~ **out**) crier, pousser des cris; ~ **down** *vt* huer; ~**ing** *n* cris *mpl*

shove [ʃʌv] *vt* pousser; (*inf: put*): **to ~ sth in** fourrer *or* ficher qch dans; ~ **off** (*inf*) *vi* ficher le camp

shovel ['ʃʌvl] *n* pelle *f*

show [ʃəʊ] *pt* ~**ed**, *pp* **shown**) *n* (*of emotion*) manifestation *f*, démonstration *f*; (*semblance*) semblant *m*, apparence *f*; (*exhibition*) exposition *f*, salon *m*; (*THEATRE, TV*) spectacle *m* ♦ *vt* montrer; (*film*) donner; (*courage etc*) faire preuve de, manifester; (*exhibit*) exposer ♦ *vi* se voir, être visible; **for ~** pour l'effet; **on ~** (*exhibits etc*) exposé(es); ~ **in** *vt* (*person*) faire entrer; ~ **off** *vi* (*pej*) crâner ♦ *vt* (*display*) faire valoir; ~ **out** *vt* (*person*) reconduire (jusqu'à la porte); ~ **up** *vi* (*stand out*) ressortir; (*inf: turn up*) se montrer ♦ *vt* (*flaw*) faire ressortir; ~ **business** *n* le monde du spectacle; ~**down** *n* épreuve *f* de force

shower ['ʃaʊə*] *n* (*rain*) averse *f*; (*of stones etc*) pluie *f*, grêle *f*; (*also:* ~**bath**) douche *f* ♦ *vi* prendre une douche, se doucher ♦ *vt*: **to ~ sb with** (*gifts etc*) combler qn de; **to have** *or* **take a ~** prendre une douche; **~proof** *adj* imperméabilisé(e)

showing ['ʃəʊɪŋ] *n* (*of film*) projection *f*

show jumping *n* concours *m* hippique

shown [ʃəʊn] *pp of* **show**

show: **~-off** ['ʃəʊf] (*inf*) *n* (*person*) crâneur(euse), m'as-tu-vu(e); **~piece** *n* (*of exhibition*) trésor *m*; **~room** ['ʃəʊrʊm] *n* magasin *m or* salle *f* d'exposition

shrank [ʃræŋk] *pt of* **shrink**

shrapnel ['ʃræpnl] *n* éclats *mpl* d'obus

shred [ʃred] *n* (*gen pl*) lambeau *m*, petit morceau ♦ *vt* mettre en lambeaux, déchirer; (*CULIN*) râper; couper en lanières; **~der** *n* (*for vegetables*) râpeur *m*; (*for documents*) déchiqueteuse *f*

shrewd [ʃru:d] *adj* astucieux(euse), perspicace; (*businessman*) habile

shriek [ʃri:k] *vi* hurler, crier

shrill [ʃrɪl] *adj* perçant(e), aigu(guë), strident(e)

shrimp [ʃrɪmp] *n* crevette *f*

shrine [ʃraɪn] *n* (*place*) lieu *m* de pèlerinage

shrink [ʃrɪŋk] (*pt* **shrank**, *pp* **shrunk**) *vi* rétrécir; (*fig*) se réduire, diminuer; (*move*: *also*: **~ away**) reculer ♦ *vt* (*wool*) faire rétrécir ♦ *n* (*inf: pej*) psychiatre *m/f*, psy *mf*; **to ~ from (doing) sth** reculer devant (la pensée de faire) qch; **~age** *n* rétrécissement *m*; **~wrap** *vt* emballer sous film plastique

shrivel ['ʃrɪvl] *vt* (*also*: **~ up**) ratatiner, flétrir ♦ *vi* se ratatiner, se flétrir

shroud [ʃraʊd] *n* linceul *m* ♦ *vt*: **~ed in mystery** enveloppé(e) de mystère

Shrove Tuesday ['ʃrəʊv-] *n* (le) Mardi gras

shrub [ʃrʌb] *n* arbuste *m*; **~bery** *n* massif *m* d'arbustes

shrug [ʃrʌg] *vt*, *vi*: **to ~ (one's shoulders)** hausser les épaules; **~ off** *vt* faire fi de

shrunk [ʃrʌŋk] *pp of* **shrink**

shudder ['ʃʌdə*] *vi* frissonner, frémir

shuffle ['ʃʌfl] *vt* (*cards*) battre ♦ *vt*, *vi*: **to ~ (one's feet)** traîner les pieds

shun [ʃʌn] *vt* éviter, fuir

shunt [ʃʌnt] *vt* (*RAIL*) aiguiller

shut [ʃʌt] (*pt*, *pp* **shut**) *vt* fermer ♦ *vi* (se) fermer; **~ down** *vt*, *vi* fermer définitivement; **~ off** *vt* couper, arrêter; **~ up** *vi* (*inf*: *keep quiet*) se taire ♦ *vt* (*close*) fermer; (*silence*) faire taire; **~ter** *n* volet *m*; (*PHOT*) obturateur *m*

shuttle ['ʃʌtl] *n* navette *f*; (*also*: **~ service**) (service *m* de) navette *f*; **~cock** *n* volant *m* (*de badminton*); **~ diplomacy** *n* navettes *fpl* diplomatiques

shy [ʃaɪ] *adj* timide

sibling ['sɪblɪŋ] *n*: **~s** enfants *mpl* de mêmes parents

Sicily ['sɪsɪlɪ] *n* Sicile *f*

sick [sɪk] *adj* (*ill*) malade; (*vomiting*): **to be ~** vomir; (*humour*) noir(e), macabre; **to feel ~** avoir envie de vomir, avoir mal au cœur; **to be ~ of** (*fig*) en avoir assez de; **~ bay** *n* infirmerie *f*; **~en** *vt* écœurer; (*silence*) faire taire; **~ening** *adj* (*fig*) écœurant(e), dégoûtant(e)

sickle ['sɪkl] *n* faucille *f*

sick: **~ leave** *n* congé *m* de maladie; **~ly** *adj* maladif(ive), souffreteux(euse); (*causing nausea*) écœurant(e); **~ness** *n* maladie *f*; (*vomiting*) vomissement(s) *m(pl)*; **~ pay** *n* indemnité *f* de maladie

side [saɪd] *n* côté *m*; (*of lake, road*) bord *m*; (*team*) camp *m*, équipe *f* ♦ *adj* (*door, entrance*) latéral(e) ♦ *vi*: **to ~ with sb** prendre le parti de qn, se ranger du côté de qn; **by the ~ of** au bord de; **~ by ~** côte à côte; **from ~ to ~** d'un côté à l'autre; **to take ~s (with)** prendre parti (pour); **~board** *n* buffet *m*; **~boards** (*BRIT*), **~burns** *npl* (*whiskers*) pattes *fpl*; **~ drum** *n* tambour plat; **~ effect** *n* effet *m* secondaire; **~light** *n* (*AUT*) veilleuse *f*; **~line** *n* (*SPORT*) (ligne *f* de) touche *f*; (*fig*) travail *m* secondaire; **~long** *adj* oblique; **~-saddle** *adv* en amazone; **~show** *n* attraction *f*; **~step** *vt* (*fig*) éluder; éviter; **~ street** *n* (petite) rue transversale; **~track** *vt* (*fig*) faire dévier de son sujet; **~walk** (*US*) *n* trottoir *m*; **~ways** *adv* de côté

siding ['saɪdɪŋ] *n* (RAIL) voie *f* de garage

sidle ['saɪdl] *vi*: **to ~ up (to)** s'approcher furtivement (de)

siege [siːdʒ] *n* siège *m*

sieve [sɪv] *n* tamis *m*, passoire *f*

sift [sɪft] *vt* (fig: also: ~ *through*) passer en revue; (lit: *flour etc*) passer au tamis

sigh [saɪ] *n* soupir *m* ♦ *vi* soupirer, pousser un soupir

sight [saɪt] *n* (*faculty*) vue *f*; (*spectacle*) spectacle *m*; (*on gun*) mire *f* ♦ *vt* apercevoir; **in ~** visible; **out of ~** hors de vue; **~seeing** *n* tourisme *m*; **to go ~seeing** faire du tourisme

sign [saɪn] *n* signe *m*; (*with hand etc*) signe, geste *m*; (*notice*) panneau *m*, écriteau *m* ♦ *vt* signer; **~ on** *vi* (MIL) s'engager; (*as unemployed*) s'inscrire au chômage; (*for course*) s'inscrire ♦ *vt* (MIL) engager; (*employee*) embaucher; **~ over** *vt*: **to ~ sth over to sb** céder qch par écrit à qn; **~ up** *vt* engager ♦ *vi* (MIL) s'engager; (*for course*) s'inscrire

signal ['sɪɡnl] *n* signal *m* ♦ *vi* (AUT) mettre son clignotant ♦ *vt* (*person*) faire signe à; (*message*) communiquer par signaux; **~man** (*irreg*) *n* (RAIL) aiguilleur *m*

signature ['sɪɡnətʃə*] *n* signature *f*; **~ tune** *n* indicatif musical

signet ring ['sɪɡnət-] *n* chevalière *f*

significance [sɪɡ'nɪfɪkəns] *n* signification *f*; importance *f*; **significant** [sɪɡ'nɪfɪkənt] *adj* significatif(ive); (*important*) important(e), considérable

signpost ['saɪnpəʊst] *n* poteau indicateur

silence ['saɪləns] *n* silence *m* ♦ *vt* faire taire, réduire au silence; **~r** *n* (*on gun*, BRIT: AUT) silencieux *m*

silent ['saɪlənt] *adj* silencieux(euse); (*film*) muet(te); **to remain ~** garder le silence, ne rien dire; **~ partner** *n* (COMM) bailleur *m* de fonds, commanditaire *m*

silhouette [sɪluː'et] *n* silhouette *f*

silicon chip ['sɪlɪkən-] *n* puce *f* électronique

silk [sɪlk] *n* soie *f* ♦ *cpd* de or en soie; **~y** *adj* soyeux(euse)

silly ['sɪlɪ] *adj* stupide, sot(te), bête

silt [sɪlt] *n* vase *f*; limon *m*

silver ['sɪlvə*] *n* argent *m*; (*money*) monnaie *f* (en pièces d'argent); (*also*: **~ware**) argenterie *f* ♦ *adj* d'argent, en argent; **~ paper** (BRIT) *n* papier *m* d'argent *or* d'étain; **~-plated** *adj* plaqué(e) argent; **~smith** *n* orfèvre *m/f*; **~y** *adj* argenté(e)

similar ['sɪmɪlə*] *adj*: **~ (to)** semblable (à); **~ly** *adv* de la même façon, de même

simile ['sɪmɪlɪ] *n* comparaison *f*

simmer ['sɪmə*] *vi* cuire à feu doux, mijoter

simple ['sɪmpl] *adj* simple; **simplicity** [sɪm'plɪsɪtɪ] *n* simplicité *f*; **simply** *adv* (*without fuss*) avec simplicité

simultaneous [sɪməl'teɪnɪəs] *adj* simultané(e)

sin [sɪn] *n* péché *m* ♦ *vi* pécher

since [sɪns] *adv*, *prep* depuis ♦ *conj* (*time*) depuis que; (*because*) puisque, étant donné que, comme; **~ then, ever ~** depuis ce moment-là

sincere [sɪn'sɪə*] *adj* sincère; **~ly** *adv* **see yours; sincerity** [sɪn'serɪtɪ] *n* sincérité *f*

sinew ['sɪnjuː] *n* tendon *m*

sinful ['sɪnful] *adj* coupable; (*person*) pécheur(eresse)

sing [sɪŋ] (*pt* **sang**, *pp* **sung**) *vt*, *vi* chanter

singe [sɪndʒ] *vt* brûler légèrement; (*clothes*) roussir

singer ['sɪŋə*] *n* chanteur(euse)

singing ['sɪŋɪŋ] *n* chant *m*

single ['sɪŋɡl] *adj* seul(e), unique; (*unmarried*) célibataire; (*not double*) simple ♦ *n* (BRIT: *also*: **~ ticket**) aller *m* (simple); (*record*) 45 tours *m*; **~ out** *vt* choisir; (*distinguish*) distinguer; **~-breasted** *adj* droit(e); **~ file** *n*: **in ~ file** en file indienne; **~-handed** *adv* tout(e) seul(e), sans (aucune) aide; **~-minded** *adj* résolu(e), tenace; **~ room** *n* chambre *f* à un lit *or* pour une personne; **~s** *n* (TENNIS) simple *m*; **singly** *adv* séparément

singular ['sɪŋɡjulə*] *adj* singulier(ère), étrange; (*outstanding*) remarquable;

(*LING*) (au) singulier, du singulier ♦ *n* singulier *m*

sinister ['sınıstə*] *adj* sinistre

sink [sıŋk] (*pt* **sank**, *pp* **sunk**) *n* évier *m* ♦ *vt* (*ship*) (faire) couler, faire sombrer; (*foundations*) creuser ♦ *vi* couler, sombrer; (*ground etc*) s'affaisser; (*also:* ~ *back*, ~ *down*) s'affaisser, se laisser retomber; **to** ~ **sth into** enfoncer qch dans; **my heart sank** j'ai complètement perdu courage; ~ **in** *vi* (*fig*) pénétrer, être compris(e)

sinner ['sınə*] *n* pécheur(eresse)

sinus ['saınəs] *n* sinus *m inv*

sip [sıp] *n* gorgée *f* ♦ *vt* boire à petites gorgées

siphon ['saıfən] *n* siphon *m*; ~ **off** *vt* siphonner; (*money: illegally*) détourner

sir [sɜ:*] *n* monsieur *m*; **S~ John Smith** sir John Smith; **yes** ~ oui, Monsieur

siren ['saıərən] *n* sirène *f*

sirloin ['sɜ:lɔın] *n* (*also:* ~ *steak*) aloyau *m*

sissy ['sısı] (*inf*) *n* (*coward*) poule mouillée

sister ['sıstə*] *n* sœur *f*; (*nun*) religieuse *f*, sœur; (*BRIT: nurse*) infirmière *f* en chef; ~**-in-law** *n* belle-sœur *f*

sit [sıt] (*pt, pp* **sat**) *vi* s'asseoir; (*be sitting*) être assis(e); (*assembly*) être en séance, siéger; (*for painter*) poser ♦ *vt* (*exam*) passer, se présenter à; ~ **down** *vi* s'asseoir; ~ **in on** *vt fus* assister à; ~ **up** *vi* s'asseoir; (*straight*) se redresser; (*not go to bed*) rester debout, ne pas se coucher

sitcom ['sıtkɒm] *n abbr* (= *situation comedy*) comédie *f* de situation

site [saıt] *n* emplacement *m*, site *m*; (*also: building* ~) chantier *m* ♦ *vt* placer

sit-in ['sıtın] *n* (*demonstration*) sit-in *m inv*, occupation *f* (de locaux)

sitting ['sıtıŋ] *n* (*of assembly etc*) séance *f*; (*in canteen*) service *m*; ~ **room** *n* salon *m*

situated ['sıtjueıtıd] *adj* situé(e)

situation [sıtju'eıʃən] *n* situation *f*; **"~s vacant"** (*BRIT*) "offres d'emploi"

six [sıks] *num* six; ~**teen** *num* seize; ~**th** *num* sixième; ~**ty** *num* soixante

size [saız] *n* taille *f*; dimensions *fpl*; (*of clothing*) taille; (*of shoes*) pointure *f*; (*fig*) ampleur *f*; (*glue*) colle *f*; ~ **up** *vt* juger, jauger; ~**able** *adj* assez grand(e); assez important(e)

sizzle ['sızl] *vi* grésiller

skate [skeıt] *n* patin *m*; (*fish: pl inv*) raie *f* ♦ *vi* patiner; ~**board** *n* skateboard *m*, planche *f* à roulettes; ~**r** *n* patineur(euse); **skating** ['skeıtıŋ] *n* patinage *m*; **skating rink** *n* patinoire *f*

skeleton ['skelıtn] *n* squelette *m*; (*outline*) schéma *m*; ~ **staff** *n* effectifs réduits

skeptical ['skeptıkl] (*US*) *adj* = **sceptical**

sketch [sketʃ] *n* (*drawing*) croquis *m*, esquisse *f*; (*THEATRE*) sketch *m*, saynète *f* ♦ *vt* esquisser, faire un croquis *or* une esquisse de; ~ **book** *n* carnet *m* à dessin; ~**y** *adj* incomplet(ète), fragmentaire

skewer ['skjuə*] *n* brochette *f*

ski [ski:] *n* ski *m* ♦ *vi* skier, faire du ski; ~ **boot** *n* chaussure *f* de ski

skid [skıd] *vi* déraper

ski: ~**er** ['ski:ə*] *n* skieur(euse); ~**ing** ['ski:ıŋ] *n* ski *m*; ~ **jump** *n* saut *m* à skis

skilful ['skılful] (*US* **skillful**) *adj* habile, adroit(e)

ski lift *n* remonte-pente *m inv*

skill [skıl] *n* habileté *f*, adresse *f*, talent *m*; (*requiring training: gen pl*) compétences *fpl*; ~**ed** *adj* habile, adroit(e); (*worker*) qualifié(e)

skim [skım] *vt* (*milk*) écrémer; (*glide over*) raser, effleurer ♦ *vi*: **to** ~ **through** (*fig*) parcourir; ~**med milk** *n* lait écrémé

skimp [skımp] *vt* (*also:* ~ *on: work*) bâcler, faire à la va-vite; (: *cloth etc*) lésiner sur; ~**y** *adj* maigre; (*skirt*) étriqué(e)

skin [skın] *n* peau *f* ♦ *vt* (*fruit etc*) éplucher; (*animal*) écorcher; ~ **cancer** *n* cancer *m* de la peau; ~**-deep** *adj* superficiel(le); ~**-diving** *n* plongée sous-marine; ~**ny** *adj* maigre, maigrichon(ne); ~**tight** *adj* (*jeans etc*) collant(e), ajusté(e)

skip [skıp] *n* petit bond *or* saut; (*BRIT:*

container) benne *f* ♦ *vi* gambader, sautiller; (*with rope*) sauter à la corde ♦ *vt* sauter

ski pants *npl* fuseau *m* (de ski)

ski pole *n* bâton *m* de ski

skipper ['skɪpə*] *n* capitaine *m*; (*in race*) skipper *m*

skipping rope ['skɪpɪŋ-] (BRIT) *n* corde *f* à sauter

skirmish ['skɜːmɪʃ] *n* escarmouche *f*, accrochage *m*

skirt [skɜːt] *n* jupe *f* ♦ *vt* longer, contourner; **~ing board** (BRIT) *n* plinthe *f*

ski slope *n* piste *f* de ski

ski suit *n* combinaison *f* (de ski)

skittle ['skɪtl] *n* quille *f*; **skittles** (*game*) (jeu *m* de) quilles *fpl*

skive [skaɪv] (BRIT: *inf*) *vi* tirer au flanc

skulk [skʌlk] *vi* rôder furtivement

skull [skʌl] *n* crâne *m*

skunk [skʌŋk] *n* mouffette *f*

sky [skaɪ] *n* ciel *m*; **~light** *n* lucarne *f*; **~scraper** *n* gratte-ciel *m inv*

slab [slæb] *n* (*of stone*) dalle *f*; (*of food*) grosse tranche

slack [slæk] *adj* (*loose*) lâche, desserré(e); (*slow*) stagnant(e); (*careless*) négligent(e), peu sérieux(euse) *or* consciencieux(euse); **~s** *npl* (*trousers*) pantalon *m*; **~en** *vi* ralentir, diminuer ♦ *vt* (*speed*) réduire; (*grip*) relâcher; (*clothing*) desserrer

slag heap [slæg-] *n* crassier *m*

slag off (BRIT: *inf*) *vt* dire du mal de

slain [sleɪn] *pp of* **slay**

slam [slæm] *vt* (*door*) (faire) claquer; (*throw*) jeter violemment, flanquer (*fam*); (*criticize*) démolir ♦ *vi* claquer

slander ['slɑːndə*] *n* calomnie *f*; diffamation *f*

slang [slæŋ] *n* argot *m*

slant [slɑːnt] *n* inclinaison *f*; (*fig*) angle *m*, point *m* de vue; **~ed** *adj* = **slanting**; **~ing** *adj* en pente, incliné(e); **~ing eyes** yeux bridés

slap [slæp] *n* claque *f*, gifle *f*; tape *f* ♦ *vt* donner une claque *or* une gifle *or* une tape à; (*paint*) appliquer rapidement ♦ *adv* (*directly*) tout droit, en plein;

~dash *adj* fait(e) sans soin *or* à la va-vite; (*person*) insouciant(e), négligent(e); **~stick** *n* (*comedy*) grosse farce, style *m* tarte à la crème; **~-up** (BRIT) *adj*: **a ~-up meal** un repas extra *or* fameux

slash [slæʃ] *vt* entailler, taillader; (*fig*: *prices*) casser

slat [slæt] *n* latte *f*, lame *f*

slate [sleɪt] *n* ardoise *f* ♦ *vt* (*fig*: *criticize*) éreinter, démolir

slaughter ['slɔːtə*] *n* carnage *m*, massacre *m* ♦ *vt* (*animal*) abattre; (*people*) massacrer; **~house** *n* abattoir *m*

slave [sleɪv] *n* esclave *m/f* ♦ *vi* (*also*: ~ *away*) trimer, travailler comme un forçat; **~ry** *n* esclavage *m*; **slavish** *adj* servile

slay [sleɪ] (*pt* **slew**, *pp* **slain**) *vt* tuer

sleazy ['sliːzɪ] *adj* miteux(euse), minable

sledge [sledʒ] *n* luge *f*

sledgehammer *n* marteau *m* de forgeron

sleek [sliːk] *adj* (*hair*, *fur* etc) brillant(e), lisse; (*car*, *boat* etc) aux lignes pures *or* élégantes

sleep [sliːp] (*pt*, *pp* **slept**) *n* sommeil *m* ♦ *vi* dormir; (*spend night*) dormir, coucher; **to go to ~** s'endormir; **~ around** *vi* coucher à droite et à gauche; **~ in** *vi* (*over~*) se réveiller trop tard; **~er** (BRIT) *n* (RAIL: *train*) train-couchettes *m*; (: *berth*) couchette *f*; **~ing bag** *n* sac *m* de couchage; **~ing car** *n* (RAIL) wagon-lit *m*, voiture-lit *f*; **~ing partner** (BRIT) *n* associé *m* commanditaire; **~ing pill** *n* somnifère *m*; **~less** *adj*: **a ~less night** une nuit blanche; **~walker** *n* somnambule *m/f*; **~y** *adj* qui a sommeil; (*fig*) endormi(e)

sleet [sliːt] *n* neige fondue

sleeve [sliːv] *n* manche *f*; (*of record*) pochette *f*

sleigh [sleɪ] *n* traîneau *m*

sleight [slaɪt] *n*: **~ of hand** tour *m* de passe-passe

slender ['slendə*] *adj* svelte, mince; (*fig*) faible, ténu(e)

slept [slept] *pt*, *pp of* **sleep**

slew [sluː] *vi* (*also*: ~ *around*) virer, pivoter ♦ *pt of* **slay**

slice [slaɪs] *n* tranche *f*; (*round*) rondelle *f*; (*utensil*) spatule *f*, truelle *f* ♦ *vt* couper en tranches (*or* en rondelles)

slick [slɪk] *adj* (*skilful*) brillant(e) (*an apparence*); (*salesman*) qui a du bagout ♦ *n* (*also: oil* ~) nappe *f* de pétrole, marée noire

slide [slaɪd] (*pt, pp* **slid**) *n* (*in playground*) toboggan *m*; (*PHOT*) diapositive *f*; (*BRIT: also: hair* ~) barrette *f*; (*in prices*) chute *f*, baisse *f* ♦ *vt* (faire) glisser ♦ *vi* glisser; **sliding** [ˈslaɪdɪŋ] *adj* (*door*) coulissant(e); **sliding scale** *n* échelle *f* mobile

slight [slaɪt] *adj* (*slim*) mince, menu(e); (*frail*) frêle; (*trivial*) faible, insignifiant(e); (*small*) petit(e), léger(ère) (*before n*) *n* offense *f*, affront *m*; **not in the ~est** pas le moins du monde, pas du tout; **~ly** *adv* légèrement, un peu

slim [slɪm] *adj* mince ♦ *vi* maigrir; (*diet*) suivre un régime amaigrissant

slime [slaɪm] *n* (*mud*) vase *f*; (*other substance*) substance visqueuse

slimming [ˈslɪmɪŋ] *adj* (*diet, pills*) amaigrissant(e); (*foodstuff*) qui ne fait pas grossir

sling [slɪŋ] (*pt, pp* **slung**) *n* (*MED*) écharpe *f*; (*for baby*) porte-bébé *m*; (*weapon*) fronde *f*, lance-pierre *m* ♦ *vt* lancer, jeter

slip [slɪp] *n* faux pas; (*mistake*) erreur *f*; étourderie *f*; bévue *f*; (*underskirt*) combinaison *f*; (*of paper*) petite feuille, fiche *f* ♦ *vt* (*slide*) glisser ♦ *vi* glisser; (*decline*) baisser; (*move smoothly*): **to ~ into/out of** se glisser *or* se faufiler dans/hors de; **to ~ sth on/off** enfiler/enlever qch; **to give sb the ~** fausser compagnie à qn; **a ~ of the tongue** un lapsus; **~ away** *vi* s'esquiver; **~ in** *vt* glisser ♦ *vi* (*errors*) s'y glisser; **~ out** *vi* sortir; **~ up** *vi* faire une erreur, gaffer; **~ped disc** *n* déplacement *m* de vertèbre

slipper [ˈslɪpə*] *n* pantoufle *f*

slippery [ˈslɪpərɪ] *adj* glissant(e)

slip road (*BRIT*) *n* (*to motorway*) bretelle *f* d'accès

slipshod [ˈslɪpʃɒd] *adj* négligé(e), peu soigné(e)

slip-up [ˈslɪpʌp] *n* bévue *f*

slipway [ˈslɪpweɪ] *n* cale *f* (de construction *or* de lancement)

slit [slɪt] (*pt, pp* **slit**) *n* fente *f*; (*cut*) incision *f* ♦ *vt* fendre; couper; inciser

slither [ˈslɪðə*] *vi* glisser; (*snake*) onduler

sliver [ˈslɪvə*] *n* (*of glass, wood*) éclat *m*; (*of cheese etc*) petit morceau, fine tranche

slob [slɒb] (*inf*) *n* rustaud(e)

slog [slɒg] (*BRIT*) *vi* travailler très dur ♦ *n* gros effort; tâche fastidieuse

slogan [ˈsləʊgən] *n* slogan *m*

slop [slɒp] *vi* (*also:* ~ *over*) se renverser; déborder ♦ *vt* répandre; renverser

slope [sləʊp] *n* pente *f*, côte *f*; (*side of mountain*) versant *m*; (*slant*) inclinaison *f* ♦ *vi*: **to ~ down** être *or* descendre en pente; **to ~ up** monter; **sloping** *adj* en pente; (*writing*) penché(e)

sloppy [ˈslɒpɪ] *adj* (*work*) peu soigné(e), bâclé(e); (*appearance*) négligé(e), débraillé(e)

slot [slɒt] *n* fente *f* ♦ *vt*: **to ~ sth into** encastrer *or* insérer qch dans

sloth [sləʊθ] *n* (*laziness*) paresse *f*

slot machine *n* (*BRIT: vending machine*) distributeur *m* (automatique); (*for gambling*) machine *f* à sous

slouch [slaʊtʃ] *vi* avoir le dos rond, être voûté(e)

slovenly [ˈslʌvnlɪ] *adj* sale, débraillé(e); (*work*) négligé(e)

slow [sləʊ] *adj* lent(e); (*watch*): **to be ~** retarder ♦ *adv* lentement ♦ *vt, vi* (*also:* ~ *down,* ~ *up*) ralentir; **"~"** (*road sign*) "ralentir"; **~ly** *adv* lentement; ~ **motion** *n*: **in ~ motion** au ralenti

sludge [slʌdʒ] *n* boue *f*

slue [sluː] (*US*) *vi* = **slew**

slug [slʌg] *n* limace *f*; (*bullet*) balle *f*

sluggish [ˈslʌgɪʃ] *adj* (*person*) mou(molle), lent(e); (*stream, engine, trading*) lent

sluice [sluːs] *n* (*also:* ~ *gate*) vanne *f*

slum [slʌm] *n* (*house*) taudis *m*

slump [slʌmp] *n* baisse soudaine, effondrement *m*; (ECON) crise *f* ♦ *vi* s'effondrer, s'affaisser

slung [slʌŋ] *pt, pp of* **sling**

slur [slɜː*] *n* (*fig: smear*): ~ **(on)** atteinte *f* (à); insinuation *f* (contre) ♦ *vt* mal articuler

slush [slʌʃ] *n* neige fondue; ~ **fund** *n* caisse noire, fonds secrets

slut [slʌt] (*pej*) *n* souillon *f*

sly [slaɪ] *adj* (*person*) rusé(e); (*smile, expression, remark*) sournois(e)

smack [smæk] *n* (*slap*) tape *f*; (*on face*) gifle *f* ♦ *vt* donner une tape à; (*on face*) gifler; (*on bottom*) donner la fessée à ♦ *vi*: **to ~ of** avoir des relents de, sentir

small [smɔːl] *adj* petit(e); ~ **ads** (BRIT) *npl* petites annonces; ~ **change** *n* petite *or* menue monnaie; ~ **fry** *n* (*fig*) menu fretin; **~holder** (BRIT) *n* petit cultivateur; ~ **hours** *npl*: **in the ~ hours** au petit matin; **~pox** *n* variole *f*; ~ **talk** *n* menus propos

smart [smɑːt] *adj* (*neat, fashionable*) élégant(e), chic *inv*; (*clever*) intelligent(e), astucieux(euse), futé(e); (*quick*) rapide, vif(vive), prompt(e) ♦ *vi* faire mal, brûler; (*fig*) être piqué(e) au vif; **~en up** *vi* devenir plus élégant(e), se faire beau(belle) ♦ *vt* rendre plus élégant(e)

smash [smæʃ] *n* (*also*: ~-*up*) collision *f*, accident *m*; (: ~ *hit*) succès foudroyant ♦ *vt* casser, briser, fracasser; (*opponent*) écraser; (SPORT: *record*) pulvériser ♦ *vi* se briser, se fracasser; s'écraser; **~ing** (*inf*) *adj* formidable

smattering ['smætərɪŋ] *n*: **a ~ of** quelques notions de

smear [smɪə*] *n* tache *f*, salissure *f*; trace *f*; (MED) frottis *m* ♦ *vt* enduire; (*make dirty*) salir; ~ **campaign** *n* campagne *f* de diffamation

smell [smel] (*pt, pp* **smelt** *or* **smelled**) *n* odeur *f*; (*sense*) odorat *m* ♦ *vt* sentir ♦ *vi* (*food etc*): **to ~ (of)** sentir (de); (*pej*) sentir mauvais

smelly ['smelɪ] *adj* qui sent mauvais, malodorant(e)

smile [smaɪl] *n* sourire *m* ♦ *vi* sourire

smirk [smɜːk] *n* petit sourire suffisant *or* affecté

smock [smɒk] *n* blouse *f*

smog [smɒg] *n* brouillard mêlé de fumée, smog *m*

smoke [sməʊk] *n* fumée *f* ♦ *vt, vi* fumer; **~d** *adj* (*bacon, glass*) fumé(e); **~r** *n* (*person*) fumeur(euse); (RAIL) wagon *m* fumeurs; ~ **screen** *n* rideau *or* écran *m* de fumée; (*fig*) paravent *m*; **smoking** ['sməʊkɪŋ] *n* tabagisme *m*; **"no smoking"** (*sign*) "défense de fumer"; **to give up smoking** arrêter de fumer; **smoky** ['sməʊkɪ] *adj* enfumé(e); (*taste*) fumé(e)

smolder ['sməʊldə*] (US) *vi* = **smoulder**

smooth [smuːð] *adj* lisse; (*sauce*) onctueux(euse); (*flavour, whisky*) moelleux(euse); (*movement*) régulier(ère), sans à-coups *or* heurts; (*pej: person*) doucereux(euse), mielleux(euse) ♦ *vt* (*also*: ~ *out: skirt, paper*) lisser, défroisser; (: *creases, difficulties*) faire disparaître

smother ['smʌðə*] *vt* étouffer

smoulder ['sməʊldə*] (US **smolder**) *vi* couver

smudge [smʌdʒ] *n* tache *f*, bavure *f* ♦ *vt* salir, maculer

smug [smʌg] *adj* suffisant(e)

smuggle ['smʌgl] *vt* passer en contrebande *or* en fraude; **~r** *n* contrebandier(ère); **smuggling** ['smʌglɪŋ] *n* contrebande *f*

smutty ['smʌtɪ] *adj* (*fig*) grossier(ère), obscène

snack [snæk] *n* casse-croûte *m inv*; ~ **bar** *n* snack(-bar) *m*

snag [snæg] *n* inconvénient *m*, difficulté *f*

snail [sneɪl] *n* escargot *m*

snake [sneɪk] *n* serpent *m*

snap [snæp] *n* (*sound*) claquement *m*, bruit sec; (*photograph*) photo *f*, instantané *m* ♦ *adj* subit(e); fait(e) sans réflechir ♦ *vt* (*break*) casser net; (*fingers*) faire claquer ♦ *vi* se casser net *or* avec un bruit sec; (*speak sharply*) parler d'un ton brusque; **to ~ shut** se refermer brusquement; ~ **at** *vt fus* (*subj: dog*) essayer de mordre; ~ **off** *vi* (*break*) casser net; ~ **up** *vt* sauter sur, saisir; ~**py** (*inf*) *adj* prompt(e); (*slogan*) qui a du punch; **make it ~py!** grouille-toi!, et que ça saute!; ~**shot** *n* photo *f*, instantané *m*

snare [snɛə*] *n* piège *m*

snarl [snɑ:l] *vi* gronder

snatch [snætʃ] *n* (*small amount*): ~**es of** des fragments *mpl* or bribes *fpl* de ♦ *vt* saisir (*d'un geste vif*); (*steal*) voler

sneak [sni:k] (*pt* (*US*) *also* **snuck**) *vi*: **to ~ in/out** entrer/sortir furtivement *or* à la dérobée ♦ *n* (*inf, pej: informer*) faux jeton; **to ~ up on sb** s'approcher de qn sans faire de bruit; ~**ers** [ˈsni:kəz] *npl* tennis *mpl*, baskets *mpl*

sneer [snɪə*] *vi* ricaner; **to ~ at** traiter avec mépris

sneeze [sni:z] *vi* éternuer

sniff [snɪf] *vi* renifler ♦ *vt* renifler, flairer; (*glue, drugs*) sniffer, respirer

snigger [ˈsnɪgə*] *vi* ricaner; pouffer de rire

snip [snɪp] *n* (*cut*) petit coup; (*BRIT: inf: bargain*) (bonne) occasion *or* affaire ♦ *vt* couper

sniper [ˈsnaɪpə*] *n* tireur embusqué

snippet [ˈsnɪpɪt] *n* bribe(s) *f(pl)*

snivelling [ˈsnɪvlɪŋ] *adj* larmoyant(e), pleurnicheur(euse)

snob [snɔb] *n* snob *m/f*; ~**bish** *adj* snob *inv*

snooker [ˈsnu:kə*] *n* sorte de jeu de billard

snoop [snu:p] *vi*: **to ~ about** fureter

snooty [ˈsnu:tɪ] *adj* snob *inv*

snooze [snu:z] *n* petit somme ♦ *vi* faire un petit somme

snore [snɔ:*] *vi* ronfler

snorkel [ˈsnɔ:kl] *n* tuba *m*

snort [snɔ:t] *vi* grogner; (*horse*) renâcler

snout [snaut] *n* museau *m*

snow [snəu] *n* neige *f* ♦ *vi* neiger; ~**ball** *n* boule *f* de neige; ~**bound** *adj* enneigé(e), bloqué(e) par la neige; ~**drift** *n* congère *f* or amoncellement *m* de neige; ~**drop** *n* perce-neige *m or f*; ~**fall** *n* chute *f* de neige; ~**flake** *n* flocon *m* de neige; ~**man** (*irreg*) *n* bonhomme *m* de neige; ~**plough** (*US* ~**plow**) *n*

chasse-neige *m inv*; ~**shoe** *n* raquette *f* (*pour la neige*); ~**storm** *n* tempête *f* de neige

snub [snʌb] *vt* repousser, snober ♦ *n* rebuffade *f*; ~**-nosed** *adj* au nez retroussé

snuff [snʌf] *n* tabac *m* à priser

snug [snʌg] *adj* douillet(te), confortable; (*person*) bien au chaud

snuggle [ˈsnʌgl] *vi*: **to ~ up to sb** se serrer *or* se blottir contre qn

so [səu] *adv* **1** (*thus, likewise*) ainsi; **if ~** si oui; ~ **do** *or* **have I** moi aussi; **it's 5 o'clock - ~ it is!** il est 5 heures - en effet! *or* c'est vrai!; **I hope/think ~** je l'espère/le crois; **~ far** jusqu'ici, jusqu'à maintenant; (*in past*) jusque-là

2 (*in comparisons etc: to such a degree*) si, tellement; **~ big (that)** si *or* tellement grand (que); **she's not ~ clever as her brother** elle n'est pas aussi intelligente que son frère

3: ~ **much** *adj, adv* tant (de); **I've got ~ much work** j'ai tant de travail; **I love you ~ much** je vous aime tant; ~ **many** tant (de)

4 (*phrases*): **10 or ~** à peu près *or* environ 10; **~ long!** (*inf: goodbye*) au revoir!, à un de ces jours!

♦ *conj* **1** (*expressing purpose*): ~ **as to do** pour, afin de faire; ~ **(that)** pour que *or* afin que +*sub*

2 (*expressing result*) donc, par conséquent; ~ **that** si bien que, de (telle) sorte que

soak [səuk] *vt* faire tremper; (*drench*) tremper ♦ *vi* tremper; ~ **in** *vi* être absorbé(e); ~ **up** *vt* absorber

soap [səup] *n* savon *m*; ~**flakes** *npl* paillettes *fpl* de savon; ~ **opera** *n* feuilleton télévisé; ~ **powder** *n* lessive *f*; ~**y** *adj* savonneux(euse)

soar [sɔ:*] *vi* monter (en flèche), s'élancer; (*building*) s'élancer

sob [sɔb] *n* sanglot *m* ♦ *vi* sangloter

sober [ˈsəubə*] *adj* qui n'est pas (*or* plus) ivre; (*serious*) sérieux(euse), sensé(e); (*colour, style*) sobre, discret(ète); ~ **up** *vt* dessoûler (*inf*) ♦ *vi* dessoûler (*inf*)

so-called ['sɔu'kɔːld] *adj* soi-disant *inv*

soccer ['sɔkə*] *n* football *m*

social ['sɔuʃəl] *adj* social(e); (*sociable*) sociable ♦ *n* (petite) fête; ~ **club** *n* amicale *f*, foyer *m*; ~**ism** *n* socialisme *m*; ~**ist** *adj* socialiste ♦ *n* socialiste *m/f*; ~**ize** *vi*: **to ~ize (with)** lier connaissance (avec); parler (avec); ~ **security** (*BRIT*) *n* aide sociale; ~ **work** *n* assistance sociale, travail social; ~ **worker** *n* assistant(e) social(e)

society [sə'saɪətɪ] *n* société *f*; (*club*) société, association *f*; (*also*: **high ~**) (haute) société, grand monde

sociology [sɔusɪ'ɔlədʒɪ] *n* sociologie *f*

sock [sɔk] *n* chaussette *f*

socket ['sɔkɪt] *n* cavité *f*; (*BRIT*: *ELEC*: *also*: **wall ~**) prise *f* de courant

sod [sɔd] *n* (*of earth*) motte *f*; (*BRIT*: *inf!*) con *m* (*!*); salaud *m* (*!*)

soda ['sɔudə] *n* (*CHEM*) soude *f*; (*also*: ~ **water**) eau *f* de Seltz; (*US*: *also*: ~ **pop**) soda *m*

sodden ['sɔdn] *adj* trempé(e); détrempé(e)

sofa ['sɔufə] *n* sofa *m*, canapé *m*

soft [sɔft] *adj* (*not rough*) doux(douce); (*not hard*) doux; mou(molle); (*not loud*) doux, léger(ère); (*kind*) doux, gentil(le); ~ **drink** *n* boisson non alcoolisée; ~**en** ['sɔfn] *vt* (r)amollir; (*fig*) adoucir; atténuer ♦ *vi* se ramollir; s'adoucir; s'atténuer; ~**ly** *adv* doucement; gentiment; ~**ness** *n* douceur *f*; ~ **spot** *n*: **to have a ~ spot for sb** avoir un faible pour qn; ~**ware** ['sɔftwɛə*] *n* (*COMPUT*) logiciel *m*, software *m*

soggy ['sɔgɪ] *adj* trempé(e); détrempé(e)

soil [sɔɪl] *n* (*earth*) sol *m*, terre *f* ♦ *vt* salir; (*fig*) souiller

solace ['sɔləs] *n* consolation *f*

solar ['sɔulə*] *adj* solaire; ~ **panel** *n* panneau *m* solaire; ~ **power** *n* énergie *f* solaire

sold [sɔuld] *pt*, *pp* *of* **sell**

solder ['sɔuldə*] *vt* souder (*au fil à souder*) ♦ *n* soudure *f*

soldier ['sɔuldʒə*] *n* soldat *m*, militaire *m*

sole [sɔul] *n* (*of foot*) plante *f*; (*of shoe*) semelle *f*; (*fish*: *pl inv*) sole *f* ♦ *adj* seul(e), unique

solemn ['sɔləm] *adj* solennel(le); (*person*) sérieux(euse), grave

sole trader *n* (*COMM*) chef *m* d'entreprise individuelle

solicit [sə'lɪsɪt] *vt* (*request*) solliciter ♦ *vi* (*prostitute*) racoler

solicitor [sə'lɪsɪtə*] *n* (*for wills etc*) ≈ notaire *m*; (*in court*) ≈ avocat *m*

solid ['sɔlɪd] *adj* solide; (*not hollow*) plein(e), compact(e), massif(ive); (*entire*): **3 ~ hours** 3 heures entières ♦ *n* solide *m*

solidarity [sɔlɪ'dærɪtɪ] *n* solidarité *f*

solitary ['sɔlɪtərɪ] *adj* solitaire; ~ **confinement** *n* (*LAW*) isolement *m*

solo ['sɔuləu] *n* solo *m* ♦ *adv* (*fly*) en solitaire; ~**ist** *n* soliste *m/f*

soluble ['sɔljubl] *adj* soluble

solution [sə'luːʃən] *n* solution *f*

solve [sɔlv] *vt* résoudre

solvent ['sɔlvənt] *adj* (*COMM*) solvable ♦ *n* (*CHEM*) (dis)solvant *m*

KEYWORD

some [sʌm] *adj* **1** (*a certain amount or number of*): ~ **tea/water/ice cream** du thé/de l'eau/de la glace; ~ **children/apples** des enfants/pommes

2 (*certain: in contrasts*): ~ **people say that ...** il y a des gens qui disent que ...; ~ **films were excellent, but most ...** certains films étaient excellents, mais la plupart ...

3 (*unspecified*): ~ **woman was asking for you** il y avait une dame qui vous demandait; **he was asking for ~ book (or other)** il demandait un livre quelconque; ~ **day** un de ces jours; ~ **day next week** un jour la semaine prochaine

♦ *pron* **1** (*a certain number*) quelques-un(e)s, certain(e)s; **I've got ~** (*books etc*) j'en ai (quelques-uns); ~ **(of them) have been sold** certains ont été vendus

2 (*a certain amount*) un peu; **I've got ~**

(*money, milk*) j'en ai (un peu)
♦ *adv*: ~ **10 people** quelque 10 personnes, 10 personnes environ

some: ~**body** ['sʌmbədɪ] *pron* = **someone**; ~**how** ['sʌmhau] *adv* d'une façon ou d'une autre; (*for some reason*) pour une raison ou une autre; ~**one** ['sʌmwʌn] *pron* = **somebody**; ~**place** ['sʌmpleɪs] (*US*) *adv* = **somewhere**

somersault ['sʌməsɔːlt] *n* culbute *f*, saut périlleux ♦ *vi* faire la culbute *or* un saut périlleux; (*car*) faire un tonneau

something ['sʌmθɪŋ] *pron* quelque chose; ~ **interesting** quelque chose d'intéressant

sometime ['sʌmtaɪm] *adv* (*in future*) un de ces jours, un jour ou l'autre; (*in past*): ~ **last month** au cours du mois dernier

some: ~**times** ['sʌmtaɪmz] *adv* quelquefois, parfois; ~**what** ['sʌmwɒt] *adv* quelque peu, un peu; ~**where** ['sʌmwɛə*] *adv* quelque part

son [sʌn] *n* fils *m*

song [sɒŋ] *n* chanson *f*; (*of bird*) chant *m*

son-in-law ['sʌnɪnlɔː] *n* gendre *m*, beau-fils *m*

sonny ['sʌnɪ] (*inf*) *n* fiston *m*

soon [suːn] *adv* bientôt; (*early*) tôt; ~ **afterwards** peu après; **as ~ as possible** dès que possible, aussitôt possible; *see also* **as**; ~**er** *adv* (*time*) plus tôt; (*preference*): **I would ~er do** j'aimerais autant *or* je préférerais faire; ~**er or later** tôt ou tard

soot [sut] *n* suie *f*

soothe [suːð] *vt* calmer, apaiser

sophisticated [sə'fɪstɪkeɪtɪd] *adj* raffiné(e); sophistiqué(e); (*machinery*) hautement perfectionné(e), très complexe

sophomore ['sɒfəmɔː*] (*US*) *n* étudiant(e) de seconde année

sopping ['sɒpɪŋ] *adj* (*also*: ~ **wet**) complètement trempé(e)

soppy ['sɒpɪ] (*pej*) *adj* sentimental(e)

soprano [sə'prɑːnəu] *n* (*singer*) soprano *m/f*

sorcerer ['sɔːsərə*] *n* sorcier *m*

sore [sɔː*] *adj* (*painful*) douloureux(euse), sensible ♦ *n* plaie *f*; ~**ly** *adv* (*tempted*) fortement

sorrow ['sɒrəu] *n* peine *f*, chagrin *m*

sorry ['sɒrɪ] *adj* désolé(e); (*condition, excuse*) triste, déplorable; ~! pardon!, excusez-moi!; ~? pardon?; **to feel ~ for sb** plaindre qn

sort [sɔːt] *n* genre *m*, espèce *f*, sorte *f* ♦ *vt* (*also*: ~ *out*) trier; classer; ranger; (: *problems*) résoudre, régler; ~**ing office** *n* bureau *m* de tri

SOS *n abbr* (= *save our souls*) S.O.S. *m*

so-so ['səu'səu] *adv* comme ci comme ça

sought [sɔːt] *pt, pp of* **seek**

soul [səul] *n* âme *f*; ~-**destroying** *adj* démoralisant(e); ~**ful** *adj* sentimental(e); (*eyes*) expressif(ive)

sound [saund] *adj* (*healthy*) en bonne santé, sain(e); (*safe, not damaged*) solide, en bon état; (*reliable, not superficial*) sérieux(euse), solide; (*sensible*) sensé(e) ♦ *adv*: ~ **asleep** profondément endormi(e) ♦ *n* son *m*; bruit *m*; (*GEO*) détroit *m*, bras *m* de mer ♦ *vt* (*alarm*) sonner ♦ *vi* sonner, retentir; (*fig*: *seem*) sembler (être); **to ~ like** ressembler à; ~ **out** *vt* sonder; ~ **barrier** *n* mur *m* du son; ~ **bite** *n* phrase *f* toute faite (*pour être citée dans les médias*); ~ **effects** *npl* bruitage *m*; ~**ly** *adv* (*sleep*) profondément; (*beat*) complètement, à plate couture; ~**proof** *adj* insonorisé(e); ~**track** *n* (*of film*) bande *f* sonore

soup [suːp] *n* soupe *f*, potage *m*; **in the ~** (*fig*) dans le pétrin; ~ **plate** *n* assiette creuse *or* à soupe; ~**spoon** *n* cuiller *f* à soupe

sour ['sauə*] *adj* aigre; **it's ~ grapes** (*fig*) c'est du dépit

source [sɔːs] *n* source *f*

south [sauθ] *n* sud *m* ♦ *adj* sud *inv*, du sud ♦ *adv* au sud, vers le sud; **S~ Africa** *n* Afrique *f* du Sud; **S~ African** *adj* sud-africain(e) ♦ *n* Sud-Africain(e); **S~ America** *n* Amérique *f* du Sud; **S~ American** *adj* sud-américain(e) ♦ *n*

Sud-Américain(e); **~-east** *n* sud-est *m*; **~erly** ['sʌðəlɪ] *adj* du sud; au sud; **~ern** ['sʌðən] *adj* (du) sud; méridional(e); **S~ Pole** *n* Pôle *m* Sud; **~ward(s)** *adv* vers le sud; **~-west** *n* sud-ouest *m*

souvenir [suːvə'nɪə*] *n* (*objet*) souvenir *m*

sovereign ['sɒvrɪn] *n* souverain(e)

soviet ['səʊvɪət] *adj* soviétique; **the S~ Union** l'Union *f* soviétique

sow[1] [saʊ] *n* truie *f*

sow[2] [səʊ] (*pt* ~**ed**, *pp* **sown**) *vt* semer; **~n** [səʊn] *pp of* **sow**[2]

soya ['sɔɪə] (*US* **soy**) *n*: ~ **bean** graine *f* de soja; ~ **sauce** sauce *f* de soja

spa [spaː] *n* (*town*) station thermale; (*US: also: health* ~) établissement *m* de cure de rajeunissement *etc*

space [speɪs] *n* espace *m*; (*room*) place *f*; espace; (*length of time*) laps *m* de temps ♦ *cpd* spatial(e) ♦ *vt* (*also:* ~ **out**) espacer; **~craft** *n* engin spatial; **~man** (*irreg*) *n* astronaute *m*, cosmonaute *m*; **~ship** *n* = **spacecraft**; **~woman** (*irreg*) *n* astronaute *f*, cosmonaute *f*; **spacing** *n* espacement *m*

spade [speɪd] *n* (*tool*) bêche *f*, pelle *f*; (*child's*) pelle; **~s** *npl* (*CARDS*) pique *m*

Spain [speɪn] *n* Espagne *f*

span [spæn] *n* (*of bird, plane*) envergure *f*; (*of arch*) portée *f*; (*in time*) espace *m* de temps, durée *f* ♦ *vt* enjamber, franchir; (*fig*) couvrir, embrasser

Spaniard ['spænjəd] *n* Espagnol(e)

spaniel ['spænjəl] *n* épagneul *m*

Spanish ['spænɪʃ] *adj* espagnol(e) ♦ *n* (*LING*) espagnol *m*; **the** ~ *npl* les Espagnols *mpl*

spank [spæŋk] *vt* donner une fessée à

spanner ['spænə*] (*BRIT*) *n* clé *f* (de mécanicien)

spar [spaː*] *n* espar *m* ♦ *vi* (*BOXING*) s'entraîner

spare [speə*] *adj* de réserve, de rechange; (*surplus*) de *or* en trop, de reste ♦ *n* (*part*) pièce *f* de rechange, pièce détachée ♦ *vt* (*do without*) se passer de; (*afford to give*) donner, accorder; (*refrain from hurting*) épargner; **to** ~ (*surplus*)

en surplus, de trop; ~ **part** *n* pièce *f* de rechange, pièce détachée; ~ **time** *n* moments *mpl* de loisir, temps *m* libre; ~ **wheel** *n* (*AUT*) roue *f* de secours; **sparing** ['speərɪŋ] *adj*: **to be sparing with** ménager; **sparingly** *adv* avec modération

spark [spaːk] *n* étincelle *f*; **~(ing) plug** *n* bougie *f*

sparkle ['spaːkl] *n* scintillement *m*, éclat *m* ♦ *vi* étinceler, scintiller; **sparkling** ['spaːklɪŋ] *adj* (*wine*) mousseux(euse), pétillant(e); (*water*) pétillant(e); (*fig: conversation, performance*) étincelant(e), pétillant(e)

sparrow ['spærəʊ] *n* moineau *m*

sparse [spaːs] *adj* clairsemé(e)

spartan ['spaːtən] *adj* (*fig*) spartiate

spasm ['spæzəm] *n* (*MED*) spasme *m*; **~odic** [spæz'mɒdɪk] *adj* (*fig*) intermittent(e)

spastic ['spæstɪk] *n* handicapé(e) moteur

spat [spæt] *pt, pp of* **spit**

spate [speɪt] *n* (*fig*): **a** ~ **of** une avalanche *or* un torrent de

spatter ['spætə*] *vt* éclabousser

spawn [spɔːn] *vi* frayer ♦ *n* frai *m*

speak [spiːk] (*pt* **spoke**, *pp* **spoken**) *vt* parler; (*truth*) dire ♦ *vi* parler; (*make a speech*) prendre la parole; **to** ~ **to sb/of** *or* **about sth** parler à qn/de qch; ~ **up!** parle plus fort!; **~er** *n* (*in public*) orateur *m*; (*also: loud~er*) haut-parleur *m*; **the S~er** (*BRIT POL*) le président de la chambre des Communes; (*US POL*) le président de la chambre des Représentants

spear [spɪə*] *n* lance *f* ♦ *vt* transpercer; **~head** *vt* (*attack etc*) mener

spec [spek] (*inf*) *n*: **on** ~ à tout hasard

special ['speʃəl] *adj* spécial(e); **~ist** *n* spécialiste *m/f*; **~ity** [speʃɪ'ælɪtɪ] *n* spécialité *f*; **~ize** *vi*: **to ~ize (in)** se spécialiser (dans); **~ly** *adv* spécialement, particulièrement; **~ty** (*esp US*) *n* = **speciality**

species ['spiːʃiːz] *n inv* espèce *f*

specific [spə'sɪfɪk] *adj* précis(e); particulier(ère); (*BOT, CHEM etc*) spécifique; **~ally** *adv* expressément, explicitement; **~ation** *n* (*TECH*) spécification *f*; (*require-*

ment) stipulation f

specimen ['spesɪmɪn] n spécimen m, échantillon m; *(of blood)* prélèvement m

speck [spek] n petite tache, petit point; *(particle)* grain m; **~led** ['spekld] adj tacheté(e), moucheté(e)

specs [speks] *(inf)* npl lunettes fpl

spectacle ['spektəkl] n spectacle m; **~s** npl *(glasses)* lunettes fpl

spectacular [spek'tækjulə*] adj spectaculaire

spectator [spek'teɪtə*] n spectateur(trice)

spectrum ['spektrəm] *(pl* **spectra)** n spectre m

speculation [spekjʊ'leɪʃən] n spéculation f

speech [spiːtʃ] n *(faculty)* parole f; *(talk)* discours m, allocution f; *(manner of speaking)* façon f de parler, langage m; *(enunciation)* élocution f; **~less** adj muet(te)

speed [spiːd] n vitesse f; *(promptness)* rapidité f ♦ vi: **to ~ along/past** etc aller/passer etc à toute vitesse; **at full** or **top ~** à toute vitesse or allure; **~ up** vi aller plus vite, accélérer ♦ vt accélérer; **~boat** n vedette f, hors-bord m inv; **~ily** adv rapidement, promptement; **~ing** n *(AUT)* excès m de vitesse; **~ limit** n limitation f de vitesse, vitesse maximale permise; **~ometer** [spɪ'dɒmɪtə*] n compteur m *(de vitesse);* **~way** n *(SPORT: also:* **~way racing)** épreuve(s) f(pl) de vitesse de motos; **~y** adj rapide, prompt(e)

spell [spel] *(pt, pp* **spelt** *(BRIT)* or **~ed)** n *(also: magic ~)* sortilège m, charme m; *(period of time)* (courte) période f ♦ vt *(in writing)* écrire, orthographier; *(aloud)* épeler; *(fig)* signifier; **to cast a ~ on sb** jeter un sort à qn; **he can't ~** il fait des fautes d'orthographe; **~bound** adj envoûté(e), subjugué(e); **~ing** n orthographe f

spend [spend] *(pt, pp* **spent)** vt *(money)* dépenser; *(time, life)* passer; consacrer; **~thrift** n dépensier(ère)

sperm [spɜːm] n sperme m

spew [spjuː] vt *(also: ~ out)* vomir

sphere [sfɪə*] n sphère f

spice [spaɪs] n épice f

spick-and-span ['spɪkən'spæn] adj impeccable

spicy ['spaɪsɪ] adj épicé(e), relevé(e); *(fig)* piquant(e)

spider ['spaɪdə*] n araignée f

spike [spaɪk] n pointe f; *(BOT)* épi m

spill [spɪl] *(pt, pp* **spilt** or **~ed)** vt renverser; répandre ♦ vi se répandre; **~ over** vi déborder

spin [spɪn] *(pt* **spun** or **span,** *pp* **spun)** n *(revolution of wheel)* tour m; *(AVIAT)* (chute f en) vrille f; *(trip in car)* petit tour, balade f ♦ vt *(wool etc)* filer; *(wheel)* faire tourner ♦ vi filer; *(turn)* tourner, tournoyer; **~ out** vt faire durer

spinach ['spɪnɪtʃ] n épinard m; *(as food)* épinards

spinal ['spaɪnl] adj vertébral(e), spinal(e); **~ cord** n moelle épinière

spindly ['spɪndlɪ] adj grêle, filiforme

spin doctor n personne employée pour présenter un parti politique sous un jour favorable

spin-dryer ['spɪn'draɪə*] n *(BRIT)* essoreuse f

spine [spaɪn] n colonne vertébrale; *(thorn)* épine f; **~less** adj *(fig)* mou(molle)

spinning ['spɪnɪŋ] n *(of thread)* filature f; **~ top** n toupie f; **~ wheel** n rouet m

spin-off ['spɪnɒf] n avantage inattendu; sous-produit m

spinster ['spɪnstə*] n célibataire f; vieille fille *(péj)*

spiral ['spaɪərl] n spirale f ♦ vi *(fig)* monter en flèche; **~ staircase** n escalier m en colimaçon

spire [spaɪə*] n flèche f, aiguille f

spirit ['spɪrɪt] n esprit m; *(mood)* état m d'esprit; *(courage)* courage m, énergie f; **~s** npl *(drink)* spiritueux mpl, alcool m; **in good ~s** de bonne humeur; **~ed** adj vif(vive), fougueux(euse), plein(e) d'allant; **~ual** ['spɪrɪtjʊəl] adj spirituel(le); *(religious)* religieux(euse)

spit [spɪt] *(pt, pp* **spat)** n *(for roasting)* broche f; *(saliva)* salive f ♦ vi cracher;

(*sound*) crépiter

spite [spaɪt] *n* rancune *f*, dépit *m* ♦ *vt* contrarier, vexer; **in ~ of** en dépit de, malgré; **~ful** *adj* méchant(e), malveillant(e)

spittle ['spɪtl] *n* salive *f*; (*of animal*) bave *f*; (*spat out*) crachat *m*

splash [splæʃ] *n* (*sound*) plouf *m*; (*of colour*) tache *f* ♦ *vt* éclabousser ♦ *vi* (*also: ~ about*) barboter, patauger

spleen [spli:n] *n* (*ANAT*) rate *f*

splendid ['splendɪd] *adj* splendide, superbe, magnifique

splint [splɪnt] *n* attelle *f*, éclisse *f*

splinter ['splɪntə*] *n* (*wood*) écharde *f*; (*glass*) éclat *m* ♦ *vi* se briser, se fendre

split [splɪt] (*pt, pp* **split**) *n* fente *f*, déchirure *f*; (*fig: POL*) scission *f* ♦ *vt* diviser; (*work, profits*) partager, répartir ♦ *vi* (*divide*) se diviser; **~ up** *vi* (*couple*) se séparer, rompre; (*meeting*) se disperser

splutter ['splʌtə*] *vi* bafouiller; (*spit*) postillonner

spoil [spɔɪl] (*pt, pp* **spoilt** *or* **~ed**) *vt* (*damage*) abîmer; (*mar*) gâcher; (*child*) gâter; **~s** *npl* butin *m*; (*fig: profits*) bénéfices *npl*; **~sport** *n* trouble-fête *m*, rabat-joie *m*

spoke [spəʊk] *pt* **speak** ♦ *n* (*of wheel*) rayon *m*; **~n** ['spəʊkn] *pp* of **speak**; **~sman** ['spəʊksmən] (*irreg*) *n* porte-parole *m inv*; **~swoman** ['spəʊkswʊmən] (*irreg*) *n* porte-parole *m inv*

sponge [spʌndʒ] *n* éponge *f*; (*also: ~ cake*) ≈ biscuit *m* de Savoie ♦ *vt* éponger ♦ *vi*: **to ~ off** *or* **on** vivre aux crochets de; **~ bag** (*BRIT*) *n* trousse *f* de toilette

sponsor ['spɒnsə*] *n* (*RADIO, TV, SPORT*) sponsor *m*; (*for application*) parrain *m*, marraine *f*; (*BRIT: for fund-raising event*) donateur(trice) ♦ *vt* sponsoriser, parrainer; faire un don à; **~ship** *n* sponsoring *m*; parrainage *m*; dons *mpl*

spontaneous [spɒn'teɪnɪəs] *adj* spontané(e)

spooky ['spu:kɪ] (*inf*) *adj* qui donne la chair de poule

spool [spu:l] *n* bobine *f*

spoon [spu:n] *n* cuiller *f*; **~-feed** *vt* nourrir à la cuiller; (*fig*) mâcher le travail à; **~ful** *n* cuillerée *f*

sport [spɔ:t] *n* sport *m*; (*person*) chic type(fille) ♦ *vt* arborer; **~ing** *adj* sportif(ive); **to give sb a ~ing chance** donner sa chance à qn; **~ jacket** (*US*) *n* = **sports jacket**; **~s car** *n* voiture *f* de sport; **~s jacket** (*BRIT*) *n* veste *f* de sport; **~sman** (*irreg*) *n* sportif *m*; **~smanship** *n* esprit sportif, sportivité *f*; **~swear** *n* vêtements *mpl* de sport; **~swoman** (*irreg*) *n* sportive *f*; **~y** *adj* sportif(ive)

spot [spɒt] *n* tache *f*; (*dot: on pattern*) pois *m*; (*pimple*) bouton *m*; (*place*) endroit *m*, coin *m*; (*RADIO, TV*: *in programme: for person*) numéro *m*; (*: for activity*) rubrique *f*; (*small amount*): **a ~ of** un peu de ♦ *vt* (*notice*) apercevoir, repérer; **on the ~** sur place, sur les lieux; (*immediately*) sur-le-champ; (*in difficulty*) dans l'embarras; **~ check** *n* sondage *m*, vérification ponctuelle; **~less** *adj* immaculé(e); **~light** *n* projecteur *m*; **~ted** *adj* (*fabric*) à pois; **~ty** *adj* (*face, person*) boutonneux(euse)

spouse [spaʊz] *n* époux(épouse)

spout [spaʊt] *n* (*of jug*) bec *m*; (*of pipe*) orifice *m* ♦ *vi* jaillir

sprain [spreɪn] *n* entorse *f*, foulure *f* ♦ *vt*: **to ~ one's ankle** *etc* se fouler *or* se tordre la cheville *etc*

sprang [spræŋ] *pt* of **spring**

sprawl [sprɔ:l] *vi* s'étaler

spray [spreɪ] *n* jet *m* (en fines gouttelettes); (*from sea*) embruns *mpl*; (*container*) vaporisateur *m*; (*for garden*) pulvérisateur *m*; (*aerosol*) bombe *f*; (*of flowers*) petit bouquet ♦ *vt* vaporiser, pulvériser; (*crops*) traiter

spread [spred] (*pt, pp* **spread**) *n* (*distribution*) répartition *f*; (*CULIN*) pâte *f* à tartiner; (*inf: meal*) festin *m* ♦ *vt* étendre, étaler; répandre; (*wealth, workload*) distribuer ♦ *vi* (*disease, news*) se propager; (*also: ~ out: stain*) s'étaler; **~ out** *vi* (*people*) se disperser; **~-eagled** ['spredi:gld] *adj* étendu(e) bras et jambes écartés; **~sheet** *n* (*COMPUT*) tableur *m*

spree [spri:] *n*: **to go on a** ~ faire la fête

sprightly ['spraɪtlɪ] *adj* alerte

spring [sprɪŋ] (*pt* **sprang**, *pp* **sprung**) *n* (*leap*) bond *m*, saut *m*; (*coiled metal*) ressort *m*; (*season*) printemps *m*; (*of water*) source *f* ♦ *vi* (*leap*) bondir, sauter; **in** ~ au printemps; **to** ~ **from** provenir de; ~ **up** *vi* (*problem*) se présenter, surgir; (*plant, buildings*) surgir de terre; ~**board** *n* tremplin *m*; ~**-clean(ing)** *n* grand nettoyage de printemps; ~**time** *n* printemps *m*

sprinkle ['sprɪŋkl] *vt*: **to** ~ **water etc on,** ~ **with water etc** asperger d'eau *etc*; **to** ~ **sugar etc on,** ~ **with sugar etc** saupoudrer de sucre *etc*; ~**r** ['sprɪŋklə*] *n* (*for lawn*) arroseur *m*; (*to put out fire*) diffuseur *m* d'extincteur automatique d'incendie

sprint [sprɪnt] *n* sprint *m* ♦ *vi* courir à toute vitesse; (*SPORT*) sprinter

sprout [spraʊt] *vi* germer, pousser; ~**s** *npl* (*also*: **Brussels** ~**s**) choux *mpl* de Bruxelles

spruce [spru:s] *n inv* épicéa *m* ♦ *adj* net(te), pimpant(e)

sprung [sprʌŋ] *pp of* **spring**

spry [spraɪ] *adj* alerte, vif(vive)

spun [spʌn] *pt*, *pp of* **spin**

spur [spə:*] *n* éperon *m*; (*fig*) aiguillon *m* ♦ *vt* (*also*: ~ **on**) éperonner; aiguillonner; **on the** ~ **of the moment** sous l'impulsion du moment

spurious ['spjʊərɪəs] *adj* faux(fausse)

spurn [spə:n] *vt* repousser avec mépris

spurt [spə:t] *n* (*of blood*) jaillissement *m*; (*of energy*) regain *m*, sursaut *m* ♦ *vi* jaillir, gicler

spy [spaɪ] *n* espion(ne) ♦ *vi*: **to** ~ **on** espionner, épier; (*see*) apercevoir; ~**ing** *n* espionnage *m*

sq. *abbr* = **square**

squabble ['skwɒbl] *vi* se chamailler

squad [skwɒd] *n* (*MIL, POLICE*) escouade *f*, groupe *m*; (*FOOTBALL*) contingent *m*

squadron ['skwɒdrən] *n* (*MIL*) escadron *m*; (*AVIAT, NAUT*) escadrille *f*

squalid ['skwɒlɪd] *adj* sordide

squall [skwɔ:l] *n* rafale *f*, bourrasque *f*

squalor ['skwɒlə*] *n* conditions *fpl* sordides

squander ['skwɒndə*] *vt* gaspiller, dilapider

square [skwɛə*] *n* carré *m*; (*in town*) place *f* ♦ *adj* carré(e); (*inf: ideas, tastes*) vieux jeu *inv* ♦ *vt* (*arrange*) régler; arranger; (*MATH*) élever au carré ♦ *vi* (*reconcile*) concilier; **all** ~ quitte; à égalité; **a** ~ **meal** un repas convenable; **2 metres** ~ (de) 2 mètres sur 2; **2** ~ **metres** 2 mètres carrés; ~**ly** *adv* carrément

squash [skwɒʃ] *n* (*BRIT: drink*): **lemon/orange** ~ citronnade *f*/orangeade *f*; (*US: marrow*) courge *f*; (*SPORT*) squash *m* ♦ *vt* écraser

squat [skwɒt] *adj* petit(e) et épais(se), ramassé(e) ♦ *vi* (*also*: ~ **down**) s'accroupir; ~**ter** *n* squatter *m*

squawk [skwɔ:k] *vi* pousser un *or* des gloussement(s)

squeak [skwi:k] *vi* grincer, crier; (*mouse*) pousser un petit cri

squeal [skwi:l] *vi* pousser un *or* des cri(s) aigu(s) *or* perçant(s); (*brakes*) grincer

squeamish ['skwi:mɪʃ] *adj* facilement dégoûté(e)

squeeze [skwi:z] *n* pression *f*; (*ECON*) restrictions *fpl* de crédit ♦ *vt* presser; (*hand, arm*) serrer; ~ **out** *vt* exprimer

squelch [skweltʃ] *vi* faire un bruit de succion

squid [skwɪd] *n* calmar *m*

squiggle ['skwɪgl] *n* gribouillis *m*

squint [skwɪnt] *vi* loucher ♦ *n*: **he has a** ~ il louche, il souffre de strabisme

squirm [skwə:m] *vi* se tortiller

squirrel ['skwɪrəl] *n* écureuil *m*

squirt [skwə:t] *vi* jaillir, gicler

Sr *abbr* = **senior**

St *abbr* = **saint; street**

stab [stæb] *n* (*with knife etc*) coup *m* (de couteau *etc*); (*of pain*) lancée *f*; (*inf: try*): **to have a** ~ **at (doing) sth** s'essayer à (faire) qch ♦ *vt* poignarder

stable ['steɪbl] *n* écurie *f* ♦ *adj* stable

stack [stæk] *n* tas *m*, pile *f* ♦ *vt* (*also*: ~ **up**) empiler, entasser

stadium ['steɪdɪəm] (*pl* **stadia** *or* ~**s**) *n* stade *m*

staff [stɑːf] *n* (*workforce*) personnel *m*; (*BRIT: SCOL*) professeurs *mpl* ♦ *vt* pourvoir en personnel

stag [stæg] *n* cerf *m*

stage [steɪdʒ] *n* scène *f*; (*platform*) estrade *f* ♦ *n*; (*profession*): **the** ~ le théâtre; (*point*) étape *f*, stade *m* ♦ *vt* (*play*) monter, mettre en scène; (*demonstration*) organiser; **in** ~**s** par étapes, par degrés; ~ **coach** *n* diligence *f*; ~ **manager** *n* régisseur *m*

stagger ['stægə*] *vi* chanceler, tituber ♦ *vt* (*person: amaze*) stupéfier; (*hours, holidays*) étaler, échelonner; ~**ing** *adj* (*amazing*) stupéfant(e), renversant(e)

stagnate ['stægneɪt] *vi* stagner, croupir

stag party *n* enterrement *m* de vie de garçon

staid [steɪd] *adj* posé(e), rassis(e)

stain [steɪn] *n* tache *f*; (*colouring*) colorant *m* ♦ *vt* tacher; (*wood*) teindre; ~**ed glass window** *n* vitrail *m*; ~**less steel** *n* acier *m* inoxydable, inox *m*; ~ **remover** *n* détachant *m*

stair [stɛə*] *n* (*step*) marche *f*; ~**s** *npl* (*flight of steps*) escalier *m*; ~**case** *n* escalier *m*; ~**way** *n* = **staircase**

stake [steɪk] *n* pieu *m*, poteau *m*; (*BETTING*) enjeu *m*; (*COMM: interest*) intérêts *mpl* ♦ *vt* risquer, jouer; **to be at** ~ être en jeu; **to** ~ **one's claim (to)** revendiquer

stale [steɪl] *adj* (*bread*) rassis(e); (*food*) pas frais(fraîche); (*beer*) éventé(e); (*smell*) de renfermé; (*air*) confiné(e)

stalemate ['steɪlmeɪt] *n* (*CHESS*) pat *m*; (*fig*) impasse *f*

stalk [stɔːk] *n* tige *f* ♦ *vt* traquer ♦ *vi*: **to** ~ **out/off** sortir/partir d'un air digne

stall [stɔːl] *n* (*BRIT: in street, market etc*) éventaire *m*, étal *m*; (*in stable*) stalle *f* ♦ *vt* (*AUT*) caler; (*delay*) retarder ♦ *vi* (*AUT*) caler; (*fig*) essayer de gagner du temps; ~**s** *npl* (*BRIT: in cinema, theatre*) orchestre *m*

stallion ['stælɪən] *n* étalon *m* (*cheval*)

stalwart ['stɔːlwət] *adj* dévoué(e); fidèle

stamina ['stæmɪnə] *n* résistance *f*, endurance *f*

stammer ['stæmə*] *n* bégaiement *m* ♦ *vi* bégayer

stamp [stæmp] *n* timbre *m*; (*rubber* ~) tampon *m*; (*mark, also fig*) empreinte *f* ♦ *vi* (*also*: ~ **one's foot**) taper du pied ♦ *vt* (*letter*) timbrer; (*with rubber* ~) tamponner; ~ **album** *n* album *m* de timbres(-poste); ~ **collecting** *n* philatélie *f*

stampede [stæm'piːd] *n* ruée *f*

stance [stæns] *n* position *f*

stand [stænd] (*pt, pp* **stood**) *n* (*position*) position *f*; (*for taxis*) station *f* (de taxis); (*music* ~) pupitre *m* à musique; (*COMM*) étalage *m*, stand *m*; (*SPORT*) tribune *f* ♦ *vi* être *or* se tenir (debout); (*rise*) se lever, se mettre debout; (*be placed*) se trouver; (*remain: offer etc*) rester valable; (*BRIT: in election*) être candidat(e), se présenter ♦ *vt* (*place*) mettre, poser; (*tolerate, withstand*) supporter; (*treat, invite to*) offrir (*treat, invite*), payer; **to make** *or* **take a** ~ prendre position; **to** ~ **at** (*score, value etc*) être de; **to** ~ **for parliament** (*BRIT*) se présenter aux élections législatives; ~ **by** *vi* (*be ready*) se tenir prêt(e) ♦ *vt fus* (*opinion*) s'en tenir à; (*person*) ne pas abandonner, soutenir; ~ **down** *vi* (*withdraw*) se retirer; ~ **for** *vt fus* (*signify*) représenter, signifier; (*tolerate*) supporter, tolérer; ~ **in for** *vt fus* remplacer; ~ **out** *vi* (*be prominent*) ressortir; ~ **up** *vi* (*rise*) se lever, se mettre debout; ~ **up for** *vt fus* défendre; ~ **up to** *vt fus* tenir tête à, résister à

standard ['stændəd] *n* (*level*) niveau (voulu); (*norm*) norme *f*, étalon *m*; (*criterion*) critère *m*; (*flag*) étendard *m* ♦ *adj* (*size etc*) ordinaire, normal(e); courant(e); (*text*) de base; ~**s** *npl* (*morals*) morale *f*, principes *mpl*; ~ **lamp** *n* (*BRIT*) lampadaire *m*; ~ **of living** *n* niveau *m* de vie

stand-by ['stændbaɪ] *n* remplaçant(e); **to be on** ~ se tenir prêt(e) (à intervenir); être de garde; ~ **ticket** *n* (*AVIAT*) billet *m* stand-by

stand-in ['stændɪn] *n* remplaçant(e)

standing ['stændɪŋ] *adj* debout *inv*; (*permanent*) permanent(e) ♦ *n* réputation *f*, rang *m*, standing *m*; **of many years' ~** qui dure *or* existe depuis longtemps; **~ joke** *n* vieux sujet de plaisanterie; **~ order** (*BRIT*) *n* (*at bank*) virement *m* automatique, prélèvement *m* bancaire; **~ room** *n* places *fpl* debout

standoffish [-'ɒfɪʃ] *adj* distant(e), froid(e)

standpoint ['stændpɔɪnt] *n* point *m* de vue

standstill ['stændstɪl] *n*: **at a ~** paralysé(e); **to come to a ~** s'immobiliser, s'arrêter

stank [stæŋk] *pt of* **stink**

staple ['steɪpl] *n* (*for papers*) agrafe *f* ♦ *adj* (*food etc*) de base ♦ *vt* agrafer; **~r** *n* agrafeuse *f*

star [stɑː*] *n* étoile *f*; (*celebrity*) vedette *f* ♦ *vi*: **to ~ (in)** être la vedette (de) ♦ *vt* (*CINEMA etc*) avoir pour vedette; **the ~s** *npl* l'horoscope *m*

starboard ['stɑːbəd] *n* tribord *m*

starch [stɑːtʃ] *n* amidon *m*; (*in food*) fécule *f*

stardom ['stɑːdəm] *n* célébrité *f*

stare [steə*] *n* regard *m* fixe ♦ *vi*: **to ~ at** regarder fixement

starfish ['stɑːfɪʃ] *n* étoile *f* de mer

stark [stɑːk] *adj* (*bleak*) désolé(e), morne ♦ *adv*: **~ naked** complètement nu(e)

starling ['stɑːlɪŋ] *n* étourneau *m*

starry ['stɑːrɪ] *adj* étoilé(e); **~-eyed** *adj* (*innocent*) ingénu(e)

start [stɑːt] *n* commencement *m*, début *m*; (*of race*) départ *m*; (*sudden movement*) sursaut *m*; (*advantage*) avance *f*, avantage *m* ♦ *vt* commencer; (*found*) créer; (*engine*) mettre en marche ♦ *vi* partir, se mettre en route; (*jump*) sursauter; **to ~ doing** *or* **to do sth** se mettre à faire qch; **~ off** *vi* commencer; (*leave*) partir; **~ up** *vi* commencer; (*car*) démarrer ♦ *vt* (*business*) créer; (*car*) mettre en marche; **~er** *n* (*AUT*) démarreur *m*; (*SPORT: official*) starter *m*; (*BRIT: CULIN*) entrée *f*; **~ing point** *n* point *m* de départ

startle ['stɑːtl] *vt* faire sursauter; donner un choc à; **startling** *adj* (*news*) surprenant(e)

starvation [stɑː'veɪʃən] *n* faim *f*, famine *f*; **starve** [stɑːv] *vi* mourir de faim; être affamé(e) ♦ *vt* affamer

state [steɪt] *n* état *m*; (*POL*) État ♦ *vt* déclarer, affirmer; **the S~s** *npl* (*America*) les États-Unis *mpl*; **to be in a ~** être dans tous ses états; **~ly** *adj* majestueux(euse), imposant(e); **~ment** *n* déclaration *f*; **~sman** (*irreg*) *n* homme *m* d'État

static ['stætɪk] *n* (*RADIO, TV*) parasites *mpl* ♦ *adj* statique

station ['steɪʃən] *n* gare *f*; (*police ~*) poste *m* de police ♦ *vt* placer, poster

stationary ['steɪʃənərɪ] *adj* à l'arrêt, immobile

stationer ['steɪʃənə*] *n* papetier(ère); **~'s (shop)** *n* papeterie *f*; **~y** *n* papier *m* à lettres, petit matériel de bureau

stationmaster ['steɪʃənmɑːstə*] *n* (*RAIL*) chef *m* de gare

station wagon (*US*) *n* break *m*

statistic [stə'tɪstɪk] *n* statistique *f*; **~s** *n* (*science*) statistique *f*

statue ['stætjuː] *n* statue *f*

status ['steɪtəs] *n* position *f*, situation *f*; (*official*) statut *m*; (*prestige*) prestige *m*; **~ symbol** *n* signe extérieur de richesse

statute ['stætjuːt] *n* loi *f*, statut *m*; **statutory** *adj* statutaire, prévu(e) par un article de loi

staunch [stɔːntʃ] *adj* sûr(e), loyal(e)

stave off [steɪv] *vt* (*attack*) parer; (*threat*) conjurer

stay [steɪ] *n* (*period of time*) séjour *m* ♦ *vi* rester; (*reside*) loger; (*spend some time*) séjourner; **to ~ put** ne pas bouger; **to ~ with friends** loger chez des amis; **to ~ the night** passer la nuit; **~ behind** *vi* rester en arrière; **~ in** *vi* (*at home*) rester à la maison; **~ on** *vi* rester; **~ out** *vi* (*of house*) ne pas rentrer; **~ up** *vi* (*at night*) ne pas se coucher; **~ing power** *n* endurance *f*

stead [sted] *n*: **in sb's ~** à la place de

qn; **to stand sb in good** ~ être très utile à qn

steadfast ['stedfəst] *adj* ferme, résolu(e)

steadily ['stedɪlɪ] *adv* (*regularly*) progressivement; (*firmly*) fermement; (: *walk*) d'un pas ferme; (*fixedly*: *look*) sans détourner les yeux

steady ['stedɪ] *adj* stable, solide, ferme; (*regular*) constant(e), régulier(ère); (*person*) calme, pondéré(e) ♦ *vt* stabiliser; (*nerves*) calmer; **a** ~ **boyfriend** un petit ami

steak [steɪk] *n* (*beef*) bifteck *m*, steak *m*; (*fish, pork*) tranche *f*

steal [stiːl] (*pt* **stole**, *pp* **stolen**) *vt* voler ♦ *vi* voler; (*move secretly*) se faufiler, se déplacer furtivement

stealth [stelθ] *n*: **by** ~ furtivement

steam [stiːm] *n* vapeur *f* ♦ *vt* (*CULIN*) cuire à la vapeur ♦ *vi* fumer; ~ **engine** *n* locomotive *f* à vapeur; ~**er** *n* (bateau *m* à) vapeur *m*; ~**ship** *n* = **steamer**; ~**y** *adj* embué(e), humide

steel [stiːl] *n* acier *m* ♦ *adj* d'acier; ~**works** *n* aciérie *f*

steep [stiːp] *adj* raide, escarpé(e); (*price*) excessif(ive)

steeple ['stiːpl] *n* clocher *m*

steer [stɪə*] *vt* diriger; (*boat*) gouverner; (*person*) guider, conduire ♦ *vi* tenir le gouvernail; ~**ing** *n* (*AUT*) conduite *f*; ~**ing wheel** *n* volant *m*

stem [stem] *n* (*of plant*) tige *f*; (*of glass*) pied *m* ♦ *vt* contenir, arrêter, juguler; ~ **from** *vt fus* provenir de, découler de

stench [stentʃ] *n* puanteur *f*

stencil ['stensl] *n* stencil *m*; (*pattern used*) pochoir *m* ♦ *vt* polycopier

stenographer [ste'nɒɡrəfə*] (*US*) *n* sténographe *m/f*

step [step] *n* pas *m*; (*stair*) marche *f*; (*action*) mesure *f*, disposition *f* ♦ *vi*: **to** ~ **forward/back** faire un pas en avant/ arrière, avancer/reculer; ~**s** *npl* (*BRIT*) = **stepladder**; **to be in/out of** ~ (**with**) (*fig*) aller dans le sens (de)/être déphasé(e) (par rapport à); ~ **down** *vi* (*fig*) se retirer, se désister; ~ **up** *vt* augmenter; intensifier; ~**brother** *n* demi-frère *m*;

~**daughter** *n* belle-fille *f*; ~**father** *n* beau-père *m*; ~**ladder** (*BRIT*) *n* escabeau *m*; ~**mother** *n* belle-mère *f*; ~**ping stone** *n* pierre *f* de gué; (*fig*) tremplin *m*; ~**sister** *n* demi-sœur *f*; ~**son** *n* beau-fils *m*

stereo ['sterɪəʊ] *n* (*sound*) stéréo *f*; (*hifi*) chaîne *f* stéréo *inv* ♦ *adj* (*also*: ~**phonic**) stéréo(phonique)

sterile ['steraɪl] *adj* stérile; **sterilize** ['sterɪlaɪz] *vt* stériliser

sterling ['stɜːlɪŋ] *adj* (*silver*) de bon aloi, fin(e) ♦ *n* (*ECON*) livres *fpl* sterling *inv*; **a pound** ~ une livre sterling

stern [stɜːn] *adj* sévère ♦ *n* (*NAUT*) arrière *m*, poupe *f*

stew [stjuː] *n* ragoût *m* ♦ *vt, vi* cuire (à la casserole)

steward ['stjuːəd] *n* (*on ship, plane, train*) steward *m*; ~**ess** *n* hôtesse *f* (de l'air)

stick [stɪk] (*pt, pp* **stuck**) *n* bâton *m*; (*walking* ~) canne *f* ♦ *vt* (*glue*) coller; (*inf: put*) mettre, fourrer; (: *tolerate*) supporter; (*thrust*): **to** ~ **sth into** planter *or* enfoncer qch dans ♦ *vi* (*become attached*) rester collé(e) *or* fixé(e); (*be unmoveable: wheels etc*) se bloquer; (*remain*) rester; ~ **out** *vi* dépasser, sortir; ~ **up** *vi* = **stick out**; ~ **up for** *vt fus* défendre; ~**er** *n* auto-collant *m*; ~**ing plaster** *n* sparadrap *m*, pansement adhésif

stickler ['stɪklə*] *n*: **to be a** ~ **for** être pointilleux(euse) sur

stick-up ['stɪkʌp] (*inf*) *n* braquage *m*, hold-up *m inv*

sticky ['stɪkɪ] *adj* poisseux(euse); (*label*) adhésif(ive); (*situation*) délicat(e)

stiff [stɪf] *adj* raide; rigide; dur(e); (*difficult*) difficile, ardu(e); (*cold*) froid(e), distant(e); (*strong, high*) fort(e), élevé(e) ♦ *adv*: **to be bored/scared/frozen** ~ s'ennuyer à mort/être mort(e) de peur/ froid; ~**en** *vi* se raidir; ~ **neck** *n* torticolis *m*

stifle ['staɪfl] *vt* étouffer, réprimer

stigma ['stɪɡmə] *n* stigmate *m*

stile [staɪl] *n* échalier *m*

stiletto [stɪ'letəʊ] (*BRIT*) *n* (*also*: ~ *heel*)

talon *m* aiguille
still [stɪl] *adj* immobile ♦ *adv* (*up to this time*) encore, toujours; (*even*) encore; (*nonetheless*) quand même, tout de même; **~born** *adj* mort-né(e); **~ life** *n* nature morte
stilt [stɪlt] *n* (*for walking on*) échasse *f*; (*pile*) pilotis *m*
stilted ['stɪltɪd] *adj* guindé(e), emprunté(e)
stimulate ['stɪmjʊleɪt] *vt* stimuler
stimuli ['stɪmjʊlaɪ] *npl of* **stimulus**
stimulus ['stɪmjʊləs] (*pl* **stimuli**) *n* stimulant *m*; (*BIOL, PSYCH*) stimulus *m*
sting [stɪŋ] (*pt, pp* **stung**) *n* piqûre *f*; (*organ*) dard *m* ♦ *vt, vi* piquer
stingy ['stɪndʒɪ] *adj* avare, pingre
stink [stɪŋk] (*pt* **stank**, *pp* **stunk**) *n* puanteur *f* ♦ *vi* puer, empester; **~ing** (*inf*) *adj* (*fig*) infect(e), vache; **a ~ing ...** un(e) foutu(e) ...
stint [stɪnt] *n* part *f* de travail ♦ *vi*: **to ~ on** lésiner sur, être chiche de
stir [stɜ:*] *n* agitation *f*, sensation *f* ♦ *vt* remuer ♦ *vi* remuer, bouger; **~ up** *vt* (*trouble*) fomenter, provoquer
stirrup ['stɪrəp] *n* étrier *m*
stitch [stɪtʃ] *n* (*in SEWING*) point *m*; (*KNITTING*) maille *f*; (*MED*) point de suture; (*pain*) point de côté ♦ *vt* coudre, piquer; (*MED*) suturer
stoat [stəʊt] *n* hermine *f* (*avec son pelage d'été*)
stock [stɒk] *n* réserve *f*, provision *f*; (*COMM*) stock *m*; (*AGR*) cheptel *m*, bétail *m*; (*CULIN*) bouillon *m*; (*descent, origin*) souche *f*; (*FINANCE*) valeurs *fpl*, titres *mpl* ♦ *adj* (*fig: reply etc*) classique ♦ *vt* (*have in*) avoir, vendre; **~s and shares** valeurs (mobilières), titres; **in/out of ~** en stock *or* en magasin/épuisé(e); **to take ~ of** (*fig*) faire le point de; **~ up** *vi*: **to ~ up (with)** s'approvisionner (en); **~broker** ['stɒkbrəʊkə*] *n* agent *m* de change; **~ cube** *n* bouillon-cube *m*; **~ exchange** *n* Bourse *f*
stocking ['stɒkɪŋ] *n* bas *m*
stock: **~ market** *n* Bourse *f*, marché financier; **~ phrase** *n* cliché *m*; **~pile** *n*

stock *m*, réserve *f* ♦ *vt* stocker, accumuler; **~taking** (*BRIT*) *n* (*COMM*) inventaire *m*
stocky ['stɒkɪ] *adj* trapu(e), râblé(e)
stodgy ['stɒdʒɪ] *adj* bourratif(ive), lourd(e)
stoke [stəʊk] *vt* (*fire*) garnir, entretenir; (*boiler*) chauffer
stole [stəʊl] *pt of* **steal** ♦ *n* étole *f*
stolen ['stəʊlən] *pp of* **steal**
stolid ['stɒlɪd] *adj* impassible, flegmatique
stomach ['stʌmək] *n* estomac *m*; (*abdomen*) ventre *m* ♦ *vt* digérer, supporter; **~ache** *n* mal *m* à l'estomac *or* au ventre
stone [stəʊn] *n* pierre *f*; (*pebble*) caillou *m*, galet *m*; (*in fruit*) noyau *m*; (*MED*) calcul *m*; (*BRIT: weight*) = 6,348 kg ♦ *adj* de *or* en pierre ♦ *vt* (*person*) lancer des pierres sur, lapider; **~-cold** *adj* complètement froid(e); **~-deaf** *adj* sourd(e) comme un pot; **~work** *n* maçonnerie *f*
stood [stʊd] *pt, pp of* **stand**
stool [stu:l] *n* tabouret *m*
stoop [stu:p] *vi* (*also: have a ~*) être voûté(e); (: **~ down: bend**) se baisser
stop [stɒp] *n* arrêt *m*; halte *f*; (*in punctuation: also: full ~*) point *m* ♦ *vt* arrêter, bloquer; (*break off*) interrompre; (*also: put a ~ to*) mettre fin à ♦ *vi* s'arrêter; (*rain, noise etc*) cesser, s'arrêter; **to ~ doing sth** cesser *or* arrêter de faire qch; **~ dead** *vi* s'arrêter net; **~ off** *vi* faire une courte halte; **~ up** *vt* (*hole*) boucher; **~gap** *n* (*person*) bouche-trou *m*; (*measure*) mesure *f* intérimaire; **~over** *n* halte *f*, (*AVIAT*) escale *f*; **~page** ['stɒpɪdʒ] *n* (*strike*) arrêt de travail; (*blockage*) obstruction *f*; **~per** ['stɒpə*] *n* bouchon *m*; **~ press** *n* nouvelles *fpl* de dernière heure; **~watch** ['stɒpwɒtʃ] *n* chronomètre *m*
storage ['stɔ:rɪdʒ] *n* entreposage *m*; **~ heater** *n* radiateur *m* électrique par accumulation
store [stɔ:*] *n* (*stock*) provision *f*, réserve *f*; (*depot*) entrepôt *m*; (*BRIT: large shop*) grand magasin; (*US*) magasin *m* ♦ *vt* emmagasiner; (*information*) enre-

gistrer; ~s *npl* (*food*) provisions; **in ~** en réserve; **~ up** *vt* mettre en réserve; accumuler; **~room** *n* réserve *f*, magasin *m*
storey ['stɔːrɪ] (*US* **story**) *n* étage *m*
stork [stɔːk] *n* cigogne *f*
storm [stɔːm] *n* tempête *f*; (*thunder~*) orage *m* ♦ *vi* (*fig*) fulminer ♦ *vt* prendre d'assaut; **~y** *adj* orageux(euse)
story ['stɔːrɪ] *n* histoire *f*; récit *m*; (*US*) = **storey**; **~book** *n* livre *m* d'histoires *or* de contes
stout [staʊt] *adj* solide; (*fat*) gros(se), corpulent(e) ♦ *n* bière brune
stove [stəʊv] *n* (*for cooking*) fourneau *m*; (: *small*) réchaud *m*; (*for heating*) poêle *m*
stow [stəʊ] *vt* (*also*: ~ *away*) ranger; **~away** *n* passager(ère) clandestin(e)
straddle ['strædl] *vt* enjamber, être à cheval sur
straggle ['strægl] *vi* être (*or* marcher) en désordre; (*houses*) être disséminé(e)
straight [streɪt] *adj* droit(e); (*hair*) raide; (*frank*) honnête, franc(franche); (*simple*) simple ♦ *adv* (tout) droit; (*drink*) sec, sans eau; **to put** *or* **get ~** (*fig*) mettre au clair; **~ away**, **~ off** (*at once*) tout de suite; **~en** *vt* ajuster; (*bed*) arranger; **~en out** *vt* (*fig*) débrouiller; **~-faced** *adj* impassible; **~forward** *adj* simple; (*honest*) honnête, direct(e)
strain [streɪn] *n* tension *f*; pression *f*; (*physical*) effort *m*; (*mental*) tension (nerveuse); (*breed*) race *f* ♦ *vt* (*stretch: resources etc*) mettre à rude épreuve, grever; (*hurt: back etc*) se faire mal à; (*vegetables*) égoutter; **~s** *npl* (*MUS*) accords *mpl*, accents *mpl*; **back ~** tour *m* de rein; **~ed** *adj* (*muscle*) froissé(e); (*laugh etc*) forcé(e), contraint(e); (*relations*) tendu(e); **~er** *n* passoire *f*
strait [streɪt] *n* (*GEO*) détroit *m*; **~s** *npl*: **to be in dire ~s** avoir de sérieux ennuis (d'argent); **~jacket** *n* camisole *f* de force; **~-laced** *adj* collet monté *inv*
strand [strænd] *n* (*of thread*) fil *m*, brin *m*; (*of rope*) toron *m*; (*of hair*) mèche *f*; **~ed** *adj* en rade, en plan
strange [streɪndʒ] *adj* (*not known*) in-

connu(e); (*odd*) étrange, bizarre; **~ly** *adv* étrangement, bizarrement; *see also* **enough**; **~r** *n* inconnu(e); (*from another area*) étranger(ère)
strangle ['stræŋgl] *vt* étrangler; **~hold** *n* (*fig*) emprise totale, mainmise *f*
strap [stræp] *n* lanière *f*, courroie *f*, sangle *f*; (*of slip, dress*) bretelle *f*
strapping ['stræpɪŋ] *adj* costaud(e)
strategic [strə'tiːdʒɪk] *adj* stratégique.
strategy ['strætədʒɪ] *n* stratégie *f*
straw [strɔː] *n* paille *f*; **that's the last ~!** ça, c'est le comble!
strawberry ['strɔːbərɪ] *n* fraise *f*
stray [streɪ] *adj* (*animal*) perdu(e), errant(e); (*scattered*) isolé(e) ♦ *vi* s'égarer; **~ bullet** *n* balle perdue
streak ['striːk] *n* bande *f*, filet *m*; (*in hair*) raie *f* ♦ *vt* zébrer, strier ♦ *vi*: **to ~ past** passer à toute allure
stream [striːm] *n* ruisseau *m*; courant *m*, flot *m*; (*of people*) défilé ininterrompu, flot ♦ *vt* (*SCOL*) répartir par niveau ♦ *vi* ruisseler; **to ~ in/out** entrer/sortir à flots; **~er** ['striːmə*] *n* serpentin *m*; (*banner*) banderole *f*; **~lined** ['striːmlaɪnd] *adj* aérodynamique; (*fig*) rationalisé(e)
street [striːt] *n* rue *f*; **~car** (*US*) *n* tramway *m*; **~ lamp** *n* réverbère *m*; **~ plan** *n* plan *m* (des rues); **~wise** (*inf*) *adj* futé(e), réaliste
strength [streŋθ] *n* force *f*; (*of girder, knot etc*) solidité *f*; **~en** *vt* fortifier; renforcer; consolider
strenuous ['strenjʊəs] *adj* vigoureux(euse), énergique
stress [stres] *n* (*force, pressure*) pression *f*; (*mental strain*) tension (nerveuse), stress *m*; (*accent*) accent *m* ♦ *vt* insister sur, souligner
stretch [stretʃ] *n* (*of sand etc*) étendue *f* ♦ *vi* s'étirer; (*extend*): **to ~ to** *or* **as far as** s'étendre jusqu'à ♦ *vt* tendre, étirer; (*fig*) pousser (au maximum); **~ out** *vi* s'étendre ♦ *vt* (*arm etc*) allonger, tendre; (*spread*) étendre
stretcher ['stretʃə*] *n* brancard *m*, civière *f*
strewn [struːn] *adj*: **~ with** jonché(e) de

stricken ['strɪkən] *adj* (*person*) très éprouvé(e); (*city, industry etc*) dévasté(e); ~ **with** (*disease etc*) frappé(e) or atteint(e) de

strict [strɪkt] *adj* strict(e)

stride [straɪd] (*pt* strode, *pp* stridden) *n* grand pas, enjambée *f* ♦ *vi* marcher à grands pas

strife [straɪf] *n* conflit *m*, dissensions *fpl*

strike [straɪk] (*pt, pp* struck) *n* grève *f*; (*of oil etc*) découverte *f*; (*attack*) raid *m* ♦ *vt* frapper; (*oil etc*) trouver, découvrir; (*deal*) conclure ♦ *vi* faire grève; (*attack*) attaquer; (*clock*) sonner; **on** ~ (*workers*) en grève; **to** ~ **a match** frotter une allumette; ~ **down** *vt* terrasser; ~ **up** *vt* (*MUS*) se mettre à jouer; **to** ~ **up a friendship with** se lier d'amitié avec; **to** ~ **up a conversation (with)** engager une conversation (avec); ~**r** *n* gréviste *m/f*; (*SPORT*) buteur *m*; **striking** ['straɪkɪŋ] *adj* frappant(e), saisissant(e); (*attractive*) éblouissant(e)

string [strɪŋ] (*pt, pp* strung) *n* ficelle *f*; (*row: of beads*) rang *m*; (: *of onions*) chapelet *m*; (*MUS*) corde *f* ♦ *vt*: **to** ~ **out** échelonner; **the** ~**s** *npl* (*MUS*) les instruments *mpl* à cordes; **to** ~ **together** enchaîner; **to pull** ~**s** (*fig*) faire jouer le piston; ~ **bean** *n* haricot vert; ~**(ed) instrument** *n* (*MUS*) instrument *m* à cordes

stringent ['strɪndʒənt] *adj* rigoureux(euse)

strip [strɪp] *n* bande *f* ♦ *vt* (*undress*) déshabiller; (*paint*) décaper; (*also:* ~ *down: machine*) démonter ♦ *vi* se déshabiller; ~ **cartoon** *n* bande dessinée

stripe [straɪp] *n* raie *f*, rayure *f*; (*MIL*) galon *m*; ~**d** *adj* rayé(e), à rayures

strip lighting (*BRIT*) *n* éclairage *m* au néon or fluorescent

stripper ['strɪpə*] *n* strip-teaseur(euse) *f*

strive [straɪv] (*pt* strove, *pp* striven) *vi*: **to** ~ **to do/for sth** s'efforcer de faire/d'obtenir qch

strode [strəʊd] *pt of* stride

stroke [strəʊk] *n* coup *m*; (*SWIMMING*) nage *f*; (*MED*) attaque *f* ♦ *vt* caresser; **at a** ~ d'un (seul) coup

stroll [strəʊl] *n* petite promenade ♦ *vi* flâner, se promener nonchalamment; ~**er** (*US*) *n* (*pushchair*) poussette *f*

strong [strɒŋ] *adj* fort(e); vigoureux(euse); (*heart, nerves*) solide; **they are 50** ~ ils sont au nombre de 50; ~**hold** *n* bastion *m*; ~**ly** *adv* fortement, avec force; vigoureusement; solidement; ~**room** *n* chambre forte

strove [strəʊv] *pt of* strive

struck [strʌk] *pt, pp of* strike

structural ['strʌktʃərəl] *adj* structural(e); (*CONSTR: defect*) de construction; (*damage*) affectant les parties portantes

structure ['strʌktʃə*] *n* structure *f*; (*building*) construction *f*

struggle ['strʌgl] *n* lutte *f* ♦ *vi* lutter, se battre

strum [strʌm] *vt* (*guitar*) jouer (en sourdine) de

strung [strʌŋ] *pt, pp of* string

strut [strʌt] *n* étai *m*, support *m* ♦ *vi* se pavaner

stub [stʌb] *n* (*of cigarette*) bout *m*, mégot *m*; (*of cheque etc*) talon *m* ♦ *vt*: **to** ~ **one's toe** se cogner le doigt de pied; ~ **out** *vt* écraser

stubble ['stʌbl] *n* chaume *m*; (*on chin*) barbe *f* de plusieurs jours

stubborn ['stʌbən] *adj* têtu(e), obstiné(e), opiniâtre

stuck [stʌk] *pt, pp of* stick ♦ *adj* (*jammed*) bloqué(e), coincé(e); ~-**up** (*inf*) *adj* prétentieux(euse)

stud [stʌd] *n* (*on boots etc*) clou *m*; (*on collar*) bouton *m* de col; (*earring*) petite boucle d'oreille; (*of horses: also:* ~ *farm*) écurie *f*, haras *m*; (*also:* ~ *horse*) étalon *m* ♦ *vt* (*fig*): ~**ded with** parsemé(e) or criblé(e) de

student ['stjuːdənt] *n* étudiant(e) ♦ *adj* estudiantin(e); d'étudiant; ~ **driver** (*US*) *n* (conducteur(trice)) débutant(e)

studio ['stjuːdɪəʊ] *n* studio *m*, atelier *m*; (*TV etc*) studio

studious ['stjuːdɪəs] *adj* studieux(euse), appliqué(e); (*attention*) soutenu(e); ~**ly** *adv* (*carefully*) soigneusement

study ['stʌdɪ] *n* étude *f*; (*room*) bureau *m* ♦ *vt* étudier; (*examine*) examiner ♦ *vi* étudier, faire ses études

stuff [stʌf] *n* chose(s) *f(pl)*; affaires *fpl*, trucs *mpl*; (*substance*) substance *f* ♦ *vt* rembourrer; (*CULIN*) farcir; (*inf: push*) fourrer; **~ing** *n* bourre *f*, rembourrage *m*; (*CULIN*) farce *f*; **~y** *adj* (*room*) mal ventilé(e) *or* aéré(e); (*ideas*) vieux jeu *inv*

stumble ['stʌmbl] *vi* trébucher; **to ~ across** *or* **on** (*fig*) tomber sur; **stumbling block** *n* pierre *f* d'achoppement

stump [stʌmp] *n* souche *f*; (*of limb*) moignon *m* ♦ *vt*: **to be ~ed** sécher, ne pas savoir que répondre

stun [stʌn] *vt* étourdir; abasourdir

stung [stʌŋ] *pt, pp of* **sting**

stunk [stʌŋk] *pp of* **stink**

stunning *adj* (*news etc*) stupéfiant(e); (*girl etc*) éblouissant(e)

stunt [stʌnt] *n* (*in film*) cascade *f*, acrobatie *f*; (*publicity ~*) truc *m* publicitaire ♦ *vt* retarder, arrêter(r) **~ed** *adj* rabougri(e); (*growth*) retardé(e); **~man** (*irreg*) *n* cascadeur *m*

stupendous [stjʊ'pɛndəs] *adj* prodigieux(euse), fantastique

stupid ['stjuːpɪd] *adj* stupide, bête; **~ity** [stjuː'pɪdɪtɪ] *n* stupidité *f*, bêtise *f*

sturdy ['stɜːdɪ] *adj* robuste; solide

stutter ['stʌtə*] *vi* bégayer

sty [staɪ] *n* (*for pigs*) porcherie *f*

stye [staɪ] *n* (*MED*) orgelet *m*

style [staɪl] *n* style *m*; (*distinction*) allure *f*, cachet *m*, style; **stylish** ['staɪlɪʃ] *adj* élégant(e), chic *inv*

stylus ['staɪləs] (*pl* **styli** *or* **~es**) *n* (*of record player*) pointe *f* de lecture

suave [swɑːv] *adj* doucereux(euse), onctueux(euse)

sub... [sʌb] *prefix* sub..., sous-; **~conscious** *adj* subconscient(e); **~contract** *vt* sous-traiter

subdue [səb'djuː] *vt* subjuguer, soumettre; **~d** *adj* (*light*) tamisé(e); (*person*) qui a perdu de son entrain

subject [*n* 'sʌbdʒɪkt, *vb* səb'dʒɛkt] *n* sujet *m*; (*SCOL*) matière *f* ♦ *vt*: **to ~** soumet-

tre à; exposer à; **to be ~ to** (*law*) être soumis(e) à; (*disease*) être sujet(te) à; **~ive** [səb'dʒɛktɪv] *adj* subjectif(ive); **~ matter** *n* (*content*) contenu *m*

sublet ['sʌb'lɛt] *vt* sous-louer

submarine [sʌbmə'riːn] *n* sous-marin *m*

submerge [səb'mɜːdʒ] *vt* submerger ♦ *vi* plonger

submission [səb'mɪʃən] *n* soumission *f*; **submissive** [səb'mɪsɪv] *adj* soumis(e)

submit [səb'mɪt] *vt* soumettre ♦ *vi* se soumettre

subnormal ['sʌb'nɔːməl] *adj* au-dessous de la normale

subordinate [sə'bɔːdɪnət] *adj* subalterne ♦ *n* subordonné(e)

subpoena [sə'piːnə] *n* (*LAW*) citation *f*, assignation *f*

subscribe [səb'skraɪb] *vi* cotiser; **to ~ to** (*opinion, fund*) souscrire à; (*newspaper*) s'abonner à; être abonné(e) à; **~r** *n* (*to periodical, telephone*) abonné(e); **subscription** [səb'skrɪpʃən] *n* (*to magazine etc*) abonnement *m*

subsequent ['sʌbsɪkwənt] *adj* ultérieur(e), suivant(e); consécutif(ive); **~ly** *adv* par la suite

subside [səb'saɪd] *vi* (*flood*) baisser; (*wind, feelings*) tomber; **~nce** [sʌb'saɪdəns] *n* affaissement *m*

subsidiarity [səbsɪdɪ'ærɪtɪ] *n* (*POL*) subsidiarité *f*

subsidiary [səb'sɪdɪərɪ] *adj* subsidiaire; accessoire ♦ *n* (*also*: **~ company**) filiale *f*

subsidize ['sʌbsɪdaɪz] *vt* subventionner; **subsidy** ['sʌbsɪdɪ] *n* subvention *f*

substance ['sʌbstəns] *n* substance *f*

substantial [səb'stænʃəl] *adj* substantiel(le); (*fig*) important(e); **~ly** *adv* considérablement; (*in essence*) en grande partie

substantiate [səb'stænʃɪeɪt] *vt* étayer, fournir des preuves à l'appui de

substitute ['sʌbstɪtjuːt] *n* (*person*) remplaçant(e); (*thing*) succédané *m* ♦ *vt*: **to ~ sth/sb for** substituer qch/qn à, remplacer par qch/qn

subterranean [sʌbtə'reɪnɪən] *adj* souterrain(e)

subtitle ['sʌbtaɪtl] n (CINEMA) sous-titre m

subtle ['sʌtl] adj subtil(e)

subtotal [sʌb'təʊtl] n total partiel

subtract [səb'trækt] vt soustraire, retrancher; **~ion** n soustraction f

suburb ['sʌbəːb] n faubourg m; **the ~s** npl la banlieue; **~an** [sə'bəːbən] adj de banlieue, suburbain(e); **~ia** [sə'bəːbɪə] n la banlieue

subway ['sʌbweɪ] n (US: railway) métro m; (BRIT: underpass) passage souterrain

succeed [sək'siːd] vi réussir ♦ vt succéder à; **to ~ in doing** réussir à faire; **~ing** adj (following) suivant(e)

success [sək'ses] n succès m; réussite f; **~ful** adj (venture) couronné(e) de succès; **to be ~ful (in doing)** réussir (à faire); **~fully** adv avec succès

succession [sək'seʃən] n succession f; **3 days in ~** 3 jours de suite

successive [sək'sesɪv] adj successif(ive); consécutif(ive)

such [sʌtʃ] adj tel(telle); (of that kind): **~ a book** un livre de ce genre, un livre pareil, un tel livre; (so much): **~ courage** un tel courage ♦ adv si; **~ books** des livres de ce genre, des livres pareils, de tels livres; **~ a long trip** un si long voyage; **~ a lot of** tellement or tant de; **~ as** (like) tel que, comme; **as ~** en tant que tel, à proprement parler; **~-and-such** adj tel ou tel

suck [sʌk] vt sucer; (breast, bottle) téter; **~er** n ventouse f; (inf) poire f

suction ['sʌkʃən] n succion f

sudden ['sʌdn] adj soudain(e), subit(e); **all of a ~** soudain, tout à coup; **~ly** adv brusquement, tout à coup, soudain

suds [sʌdz] npl eau savonneuse

sue [suː] vt poursuivre en justice, intenter un procès à

suede [sweɪd] n daim m

suet [suɪt] n graisse f de rognon

suffer ['sʌfə*] vt subir, subir; (bear) tolérer, supporter ♦ vi souffrir; **~er** n (MED) malade m/f; **~ing** n souffrance(s) f(pl)

sufficient [sə'fɪʃənt] adj suffisant(e); **~ money** suffisamment d'argent; **~ly** adv suffisamment, assez

suffocate ['sʌfəkeɪt] vi suffoquer; étouffer

sugar ['ʃʊgə*] n sucre m ♦ vt sucrer; **~ beet** n betterave sucrière; **~ cane** n canne f à sucre

suggest [sə'dʒest] vt suggérer, proposer; (indicate) dénoter; **~ion** n suggestion f

suicide ['sʊɪsaɪd] n suicide m; see also **commit**

suit [suːt] n (man's) costume m, complet m; (woman's) tailleur m, ensemble m; (LAW) poursuite(s) procès m; (CARDS) couleur f ♦ vt aller à; convenir à; (adapt): **to ~ sth to** adapter or approprier qch à; **well ~ed** (couple) faits l'un pour l'autre, très bien assortis; **~able** adj qui convient; approprié(e); **~ably** adv comme il se doit (or se devait etc), convenablement

suitcase ['suːtkeɪs] n valise f

suite [swiːt] n (of rooms, also MUS) suite f; (furniture): **bedroom/dining room ~** (ensemble m de) chambre f à coucher/salle f à manger

suitor ['suːtə*] n soupirant m, prétendant m

sulfur ['sʌlfə*] (US) n = **sulphur**

sulk [sʌlk] vi bouder; **~y** adj boudeur(euse), maussade

sullen ['sʌlən] adj renfrogné(e), maussade

sulphur ['sʌlfə*] (US **sulfur**) n soufre m

sultana [sʌl'tɑːnə] n (CULIN) raisin (sec) de Smyrne

sultry ['sʌltrɪ] adj étouffant(e)

sum [sʌm] n somme f; (SCOL etc) calcul m; **~ up** vt, vi résumer

summarize ['sʌməraɪz] vt résumer

summary ['sʌmərɪ] n résumé m

summer ['sʌmə*] n été m ♦ adj d'été, estival(e); **~house** n (in garden) pavillon m; **~time** n été m; **~ time** n (by clock) heure f d'été

summit ['sʌmɪt] n sommet m

summon ['sʌmən] vt appeler, convoquer; **~ up** vt rassembler, faire appel à;

~s *n* citation *f*, assignation *f*

sump [sʌmp] (*BRIT*) *n* (*AUT*) carter *m*

sun [sʌn] *n* soleil *m*; **in the ~** au soleil; **~bathe** *vi* prendre un bain de soleil; **~burn** *n* coup *m* de soleil; **~burned** *adj* = **sunburnt**; **~burnt** *adj* (*tanned*) bronzé(e)

Sunday ['sʌndeɪ] *n* dimanche *m*; **~ school** *n* ≈ catéchisme *m*

sundial ['sʌndaɪəl] *n* cadran *m* solaire

sundown ['sʌndaʊn] *n* coucher *m* du (*or* de) soleil

sundries ['sʌndrɪz] *npl* articles divers

sundry ['sʌndrɪ] *adj* divers(e), différent(e) ♦ *n*: **all and ~** tout le monde, n'importe qui

sunflower ['sʌnflaʊə*] *n* tournesol *m*

sung [sʌŋ] *pp of* **sing**

sunglasses ['sʌnglɑːsɪz] *npl* lunettes *fpl* de soleil

sunk [sʌŋk] *pp of* **sink**

sun: **~light** ['sʌnlaɪt] *n* (lumière *f* du) soleil *m*; **~lit** *adj* ensoleillé(e); **~ny** *adj* ensoleillé(e); **~rise** *n* lever *m* du (*or* de) soleil; **~ roof** *n* (*AUT*) toit ouvrant; **~set** *n* coucher *m* du (*or* de) soleil; **~shade** *n* (*over table*) parasol *m*; **~shine** *n* (lumière *f* du) soleil *m*; **~stroke** *n* insolation *f*; **~tan** *n* bronzage *m*; **~tan lotion** *n* lotion *f* *or* lait *m* solaire; **~tan oil** *n* huile *f* solaire

super ['suːpə*] (*inf*) *adj* formidable

superannuation ['suːpərænjʊ'eɪʃən] *n* (*contribution*) cotisations *fpl* pour la pension

superb [suː'pɜːb] *adj* superbe, magnifique

supercilious [suːpə'sɪlɪəs] *adj* hautain(e), dédaigneux(euse)

superficial [suːpə'fɪʃəl] *adj* superficiel(le)

superimpose [suːpərɪm'pəʊz] *vt* superposer

superintendent [suːpərɪn'tendənt] *n* directeur(trice); (*POLICE*) ≈ commissaire *m*

superior [su'pɪərɪə*] *adj* supérieur(e); **~ity** [supɪərɪ'ɒrɪtɪ] *n* supériorité *f*

superlative [suː'pɜːlətɪv] *n* (*LING*) superlatif *m*

superman ['suːpəmæn] (*irreg*) *n* surhomme *m*

supermarket ['suːpəmɑːkɪt] *n* supermarché *m*

supernatural [suːpə'nætʃərəl] *adj* surnaturel(le)

superpower ['suːpəpaʊə*] *n* (*POL*) superpuissance *f*

supersede [suːpə'siːd] *vt* remplacer, supplanter

superstitious [suːpə'stɪʃəs] *adj* superstitieux(euse)

supervise ['suːpəvaɪz] *vt* surveiller; diriger; **supervision** [suːpə'vɪʒən] *n* surveillance *f*; contrôle *m*; **supervisor** ['suːpəvaɪzə*] *n* surveillant(e); (*in shop*) chef *m* de rayon

supine ['suːpaɪn] *adj* couché(e) *or* étendu(e) sur le dos

supper ['sʌpə*] *n* dîner *m*; (*late*) souper *m*

supple ['sʌpl] *adj* souple

supplement [*n* 'sʌplɪmənt, *vb* sʌplɪ'ment] *n* supplément *m* ♦ *vt* compléter; **~ary** *adj* supplémentaire; **~ary benefit** (*BRIT*) *n* allocation *f* (supplémentaire) d'aide sociale

supplier [sə'plaɪə*] *n* fournisseur *m*

supply [sə'plaɪ] *vt* (*provide*) fournir; (*equip*): **to ~ (with)** approvisionner *or* ravitailler (en); fournir (en) provision *f*, réserve *f*; (*~ing*) approvisionnement *m*; **supplies** *npl* (*food*) vivres *mpl*; (*MIL*) subsistances *fpl*; **~ teacher** (*BRIT*) *n* suppléant(e)

support [sə'pɔːt] *n* (*moral, financial etc*) soutien *m*, appui *m*; (*TECH*) support *m*, soutien ♦ *vt* soutenir, supporter; (*financially*) subvenir aux besoins de; (*uphold*) être pour, être partisan de, appuyer; **~er** *n* (*POL etc*) partisan(e); (*SPORT*) supporter *m*

suppose [sə'pəʊz] *vt* supposer; imaginer; **to be ~d to do** être censé(e) faire; **~dly** [sə'pəʊzɪdlɪ] *adv* soi-disant; **supposing** [sə'pəʊzɪŋ] *conj* si, à supposer que +*sub*

suppress [sə'pres] *vt* (*revolt*) réprimer; (*information*) supprimer; (*yawn*) étouffer; (*feelings*) refouler

supreme [suˈpriːm] *adj* suprême

surcharge [ˈsɜːtʃɑːdʒ] *n* surcharge *f*

sure [ʃʊə*] *adj* sûr(e); (*definite, convinced*) sûr, certain(e); **~!** (*of course*) bien sûr!; **~ enough** effectivement; **to make ~ of sth** s'assurer de *or* vérifier qch; **to make ~ that** s'assurer *or* vérifier que; **~ly** *adv* sûrement; certainement

surety [ˈʃʊərətɪ] *n* caution *f*

surf [sɜːf] *n* (*waves*) ressac *m*

surface [ˈsɜːfɪs] *n* surface *f* ♦ *vt* (*road*) poser un revêtement sur ♦ *vi* remonter à la surface; faire surface; **~ mail** *n* courrier *m* par voie de terre (*or* maritime)

surfboard [ˈsɜːfbɔːd] *n* planche *f* de surf

surfeit [ˈsɜːfɪt] *n*: **a ~ of** un excès de; une indigestion de

surfing [ˈsɜːfɪŋ] *n* surf *m*

surge [sɜːdʒ] *n* vague *f*, montée *f* ♦ *vi* déferler

surgeon [ˈsɜːdʒən] *n* chirurgien *m*

surgery [ˈsɜːdʒərɪ] *n* chirurgie *f*; (*BRIT: room*) cabinet *m* (de consultation); (: *also:* **~ hours**) heures *fpl* de consultation

surgical [ˈsɜːdʒɪkəl] *adj* chirurgical(e); **~ spirit** (*BRIT*) *n* alcool *m* à 90°

surly [ˈsɜːlɪ] *adj* revêche, maussade

surname [ˈsɜːneɪm] *n* nom *m* de famille

surplus [ˈsɜːpləs] *n* surplus *m*, excédent *m* ♦ *adj* en surplus, de trop; (*COMM*) excédentaire

surprise [səˈpraɪz] *n* surprise *f*; (*astonishment*) étonnement *m* ♦ *vt* surprendre; (*astonish*) étonner; **surprising** [səˈpraɪzɪŋ] *adj* surprenant(e), étonnant(e); **surprisingly** *adv* (*easy, helpful*) étonnamment

surrender [səˈrendə*] *n* reddition *f*, capitulation *f* ♦ *vi* se rendre, capituler

surreptitious [sʌrəpˈtɪʃəs] *adj* subreptice, furtif(ive)

surrogate [ˈsʌrəgɪt] *n* substitut *m*; **~ mother** *n* mère porteuse *or* de substitution

surround [səˈraʊnd] *vt* entourer; (*MIL etc*) encercler; **~ing** *adj* environnant(e); **~ings** *npl* environs *mpl*, alentours *mpl*

surveillance [sɜːˈveɪləns] *n* surveillance *f*

survey [*n* ˈsɜːveɪ, *vb* sɜːˈveɪ] *n* enquête *f*, étude *f*; (*in housebuying etc*) inspection *f*, (rapport *m* d')expertise *f*; (*of land*) levé *m* ♦ *vt* enquêter sur; inspecter; (*look at*) embrasser du regard; **~or** [səˈveɪə*] *n* (*of house*) expert *m*; (*of land*) (arpenteur *m*) géomètre *m*

survival [səˈvaɪvəl] *n* survie *f*; (*relic*) vestige *m*

survive [səˈvaɪv] *vi* survivre; (*custom etc*) subsister ♦ *vt* survivre à; **survivor** [səˈvaɪvə*] *n* survivant(e); (*fig*) battant(e)

susceptible [səˈseptəbl] *adj*: **~ (to)** sensible (à); (*disease*) prédisposé(e) (à)

suspect [*n, adj* ˈsʌspekt, *vb* səsˈpekt] *adj, n* suspect(e) ♦ *vt* soupçonner, suspecter

suspend [səsˈpend] *vt* suspendre; **~ed sentence** *n* condamnation *f* avec sursis; **~er belt** *n* porte-jarretelles *m inv*; **~ers** *npl* (*BRIT*) jarretelles *fpl*; (*US*) bretelles *fpl*

suspense [səsˈpens] *n* attente *f*, incertitude *f*; (*in film etc*) suspense *m*

suspension [səsˈpenʃən] *n* suspension *f*; (*of driving licence*) retrait *m* provisoire; **~ bridge** *n* pont suspendu

suspicion [səsˈpɪʃən] *n* soupçon(s) *m(pl)*

suspicious [səsˈpɪʃəs] *adj* (*suspecting*) soupçonneux(euse), méfiant(e); (*causing suspicion*) suspect(e)

sustain [səsˈteɪn] *vt* soutenir; (*food etc*) nourrir, donner des forces à; (*suffer*) subir; recevoir; **~able** *adj* (*development, growth etc*) viable; **~ed** *adj* (*effort*) soutenu(e), prolongé(e)

sustenance [ˈsʌstɪnəns] *n* nourriture *f*; (*money*) moyens *mpl* de subsistance

swab [swɒb] *n* (*MED*) tampon *m*

swagger [ˈswægə*] *vi* plastronner

swallow [ˈswɒləʊ] *n* (*bird*) hirondelle *f* ♦ *vt* avaler; **~ up** *vt* engloutir

swam [swæm] *pt of* **swim**

swamp [swɒmp] *n* marais *m*, marécage *m* ♦ *vt* submerger

swan [swɒn] *n* cygne *m*

swap [swɒp] *vt*: **to ~ (for)** échanger (contre), troquer (contre)

swarm [swɔːm] *n* essaim *m* ♦ *vi* fourmiller, grouiller

swarthy ['swɔ:ðɪ] *adj* basané(e), bis-tré(e)

swastika ['swɒstɪkə] *n* croix gammée

swat [swɒt] *vt* écraser

sway [sweɪ] *vi* se balancer, osciller ♦ *vt* (*influence*) influencer

swear [swɛə*] (*pt* **swore**, *pp* **sworn**) *vt, vi* jurer; **~word** *n* juron *m*, gros mot

sweat [swet] *n* sueur *f*, transpiration *f* ♦ *vi* suer

sweater ['swetə*] *n* tricot *m*, pull *m*

sweaty ['swetɪ] *adj* en sueur, moite *or* mouillé(e) de sueur

Swede [swi:d] *n* Suédois(e)

swede [swi:d] (*BRIT*) *n* rutabaga *m*

Sweden ['swi:dn] *n* Suède *f*; **Swedish** ['swi:dɪʃ] *adj* suédois(e) ♦ *n* (*LING*) sué-dois *m*

sweep [swi:p] (*pt, pp* **swept**) *n* coup *m* de balai; (*also: chimney ~*) ramoneur *m* ♦ *vt* balayer; (*subj: current*) emporter ♦ *vi* (*hand, arm*) faire un mouvement; (*wind*) souffler; **~ away** *vt* balayer; en-traîner; emporter; **~ past** *vi* passer ma-jestueusement *or* rapidement; **~ up** *vt, vi* balayer; **~ing** *adj* (*gesture*) large; cir-culaire; **a ~ing statement** une générali-sation hâtive

sweet [swi:t] *n* (*candy*) bonbon *m*; (*BRIT*: *pudding*) dessert *m* ♦ *adj* doux(douce); (*not savoury*) sucré(e); (*fig: kind*) gen-til(le); (*baby*) mignon(ne); **~corn** *n* maïs *m*; **~en** *vt* adoucir; (*with sugar*) sucrer; **~heart** *n* amoureux(euse); **~ness** *n* goût sucré; douceur *f*; **~pea** *n* pois *m* de sen-teur

swell [swel] (*pt* **~ed**, *pp* **swollen** *or* **~ed**) *n* (*of sea*) houle *f* ♦ *adj* (*US: inf: excel-lent*) chouette ♦ *vi* grossir, augmenter; (*sound*) s'enfler; (*MED*) enfler; **~ing** *n* (*MED*) enflure *f*; (*lump*) grosseur *f*

sweltering ['sweltərɪŋ] *adj* étouffant(e), oppressant(e)

swept [swept] *pt, pp of* **sweep**

swerve [swɜ:v] *vi* faire une embardée *or* un écart; dévier

swift [swɪft] *n* (*bird*) martinet *m* ♦ *adj* rapide, prompt(e)

swig [swɪg] (*inf*) *n* (*drink*) lampée *f*

swill [swɪl] *vt* (*also: ~ out, ~ down*) la-ver à grande eau

swim [swɪm] (*pt* **swam**, *pp* **swum**) *n*: t[o] **go for a ~** aller nager *or* se baigner ♦ *v[i]* nager; (*SPORT*) faire de la natation; (*head[room]*) tourner ♦ *vt* traverser (à la nage); (*a length*) faire (à la nage); **~mer** *n* na[geur(euse)]; **~ming** *n* natation *f*; **~ming cap** *n* bonnet *m* de bain; **~ming cos[tume]**; **~ming cos-tume** (*BRIT*) *n* maillot *m* (de bain); **~ming pool** *n* piscine *f*; **~ming trunk[s]** *npl* caleçon *m* ou slip *m* de bain; **~sui[t]** *n* maillot *m* (de bain)

swindle ['swɪndl] *n* escroquerie *f*

swine [swaɪn] (*inf!*) *n inv* salaud *m* (!)

swing [swɪŋ] (*pt, pp* **swung**) *n* balan[çoire] *f*; (*movement*) balancement *m*, os[cillations *fpl*; (*MUS: also rhythm*) rythme] *m*; (*change: in opinion etc*) revireme[nt] *m* ♦ *vt* balancer, faire osciller; (*also: ~ round*) tourner, faire virer ♦ *vi* se ba[lancer, osciller; (*also: ~ round*) vire[r]] tourner; **to be in full ~** battre son plein[;] **~ bridge** *n* pont tournant; **~ door** (*U[S]*: **~ing door**) *n* porte battante

swingeing ['swɪndʒɪŋ] (*BRIT*) *adj* écra[sant(e); (*cuts etc*) considérable

swipe [swaɪp] (*inf*) *vt* (*steal*) piquer

swirl [swɜ:l] *vi* tourbillonner, tournoyer

swish [swɪʃ] *vi* (*tail*) remuer; (*clothes*[)] froufrouter

Swiss [swɪs] *adj* suisse ♦ *n inv* Suisse[*m/f*

switch [swɪtʃ] *n* (*for light, radio etc*[)] bouton *m*; (*change*) changement *m*, revi[rement *m* ♦ *vt* changer; **~ off** *vt* étein[dre; (*engine*) arrêter; **~ on** *vt* allumer[;] (*engine, machine*) mettre en marche[;] **~board** *n* (*TEL*) standard *m*

Switzerland ['swɪtsələnd] *n* Suisse *f*

swivel ['swɪvl] *vi* (*also: ~ round*) pivo[ter, tourner

swollen ['swəʊlən] *pp of* **swell**

swoon [swu:n] *vi* se pâmer

swoop [swu:p] *n* (*by police*) descente[*f*] ♦ *vi* (*also: ~ down*) descendre en piqué[;] piquer

swop [swɒp] *vt = swap*

sword [sɔ:d] *n* épée *f*; **~fish** *n* espadon *m*

swore [swɔ:*] *pt of* **swear**

sworn [swɔ:n] *pp of* **swear** ♦ *adj (statement, evidence)* donné(e) sous serment

swot [swɒt] *vi* bûcher, potasser

swum [swʌm] *pp of* **swim**

swung [swʌŋ] *pt, pp of* **swing**

syllable ['sɪləbl] *n* syllabe *f*

syllabus ['sɪləbəs] *n* programme *m*

symbol ['sɪmbəl] *n* symbole *m*

symmetry ['sɪmɪtrɪ] *n* symétrie *f*

sympathetic [sɪmpə'θetɪk] *adj* compatissant(e); bienveillant(e), compréhensif(ive); *(likeable)* sympathique; **~ towards** bien disposé(e) envers

sympathize ['sɪmpəθaɪz] *vi*: **to ~ with sb** plaindre qn; *(in grief)* s'associer à la douleur de qn; **to ~ with sth** comprendre qch; **~r** *n* (POL) sympathisant(e)

sympathy ['sɪmpəθɪ] *n (pity)* compassion *f*; **sympathies** *npl (support)* soutien *m*; **left-wing** *etc* **sympathies** penchants *mpl* à gauche *etc*; **in ~ with** *(strike)* en *or* par solidarité avec; **with our deepest ~** en vous priant d'accepter nos sincères condoléances

symphony ['sɪmfənɪ] *n* symphonie *f*

symptom ['sɪmptəm] *n* symptôme *m*; indice *m*

syndicate ['sɪndɪkət] *n* syndicat *m*, coopérative *f*

synonym ['sɪnənɪm] *n* synonyme *m*

synopsis [sɪ'nɒpsɪs, *pl* -siːz] *(pl* **synopses)** *n* résumé *m*

syntax ['sɪntæks] *n* syntaxe *f*

synthetic [sɪn'θetɪk] *adj* synthétique

syphon ['saɪfən] *n, vb* = **siphon**

Syria ['sɪrɪə] *n* Syrie *f*

syringe [sɪ'rɪndʒ] *n* seringue *f*

syrup ['sɪrəp] *n* sirop *m*; *(also: golden ~)* mélasse raffinée

system ['sɪstəm] *n* système *m*; (ANAT) organisme *m*; **~atic** [sɪstə'mætɪk] *adj* systématique; méthodique; **~ disk** *n* (COMPUT) disque *m* système; **~s analyst** *n* analyste fonctionnel(le)

T t

ta [tɑ:] *(BRIT: inf)* excl merci!

tab [tæb] *n (label)* étiquette *f*; *(on drinks can etc)* languette *f*; **to keep ~s on** *(fig)* surveiller

tabby ['tæbɪ] *n (also: ~ cat)* chat(te) tigré(e)

table ['teɪbl] *n* table *f* ♦ *vt* (BRIT: *motion etc)* présenter; **to lay** *or* **set the ~** mettre le couvert *or* la table; **~cloth** *n* nappe *f*; **~ d'hôte** ['tɑ:bl'dəut] *adj (meal)* à prix fixe; **~ lamp** *n* lampe *f* de table; **~mat** *n (for plate)* napperon *m*, set *m*; *(for hot dish)* dessous-de-plat *m inv*; **~ of contents** *n* table *f* des matières; **~spoon** *n* cuiller *f* de service; *(also: ~spoonful: as measurement)* cuillerée *f* à soupe

tablet ['tæblət] *n* (MED) comprimé *m*; *(of stone)* plaque *f*

table tennis *n* ping-pong *m* (®), tennis *m* de table

table wine *n* vin *m* de table

tabloid ['tæblɔɪd] *n* quotidien *m* populaire

tabulate ['tæbjuleɪt] *vt (data, figures)* présenter sous forme de table(s)

tack [tæk] *n (nail)* petit clou ♦ *vt* clouer; *(fig)* direction *f*; (BRIT: *stitch)* faufiler ♦ *vi* tirer un *or* des bord(s)

tackle ['tækl] *n* matériel *m*, équipement *m*; *(for lifting)* appareil *m* de levage; (RUGBY) plaquage *m* ♦ *vt (difficulty, animal, burglar etc)* s'attaquer à; *(person: challenge)* s'expliquer avec; (RUGBY) plaquer

tacky ['tækɪ] *adj* collant(e); *(pej: of poor quality)* miteux(euse)

tact [tækt] *n* tact *m*; **~ful** *adj* plein(e) de tact

tactical ['tæktɪkəl] *adj* tactique

tactics ['tæktɪks] *npl* tactique *f*

tactless ['tæktləs] *adj* qui manque de tact

tadpole ['tædpəul] *n* têtard *m*

taffy ['tæfɪ] *(US)* *n* (bonbon *m* au) caramel *m*

tag [tæg] *n* étiquette *f*; ~ **along** *vi* suivre

tail [teɪl] *n* queue *f*; (*of shirt*) pan *m* ♦ *vt* (*follow*) suivre, filer; ~**s** *npl* habit *m*; ~ **away**, ~ **off** *vi* (*in size, quality etc*) baisser peu à peu; ~**back** (*BRIT*) *n* (*AUT*) bouchon *m*; ~ **end** *n* bout *m*, fin *f*; ~**gate** *n* (*AUT*) hayon *m* arrière

tailor ['teɪlə*] *n* tailleur *m*; ~**ing** *n* (*cut*) coupe *f*; ~-**made** *adj* fait(e) sur mesure; (*fig*) conçu(e) spécialement

tailwind ['teɪlwɪnd] *n* vent *m* arrière *inv*

tainted ['teɪntɪd] *adj* (*food*) gâté(e); (*water, air*) infecté(e); (*fig*) souillé(e)

take [teɪk] (*pt* **took**, *pp* **taken**) *vt* prendre; (*gain: prize*) remporter; (*require: effort, courage*) demander; (*tolerate*) accepter, supporter; (*hold: passengers etc*) contenir; (*accompany*) emmener, accompagner; (*bring, carry*) apporter, emporter; (*exam*) passer, se présenter à; **to** ~ **sth from** (*drawer etc*) prendre qch dans; (*person*) prendre qch à; **I** ~ **it that** ... je suppose que ...; ~ **after** *vt fus* ressembler à; ~ **apart** *vt* démonter; ~ **away** *vt* enlever; (*carry off*) emporter; ~ **back** *vt* (*return*) rendre, rapporter; (*one's words*) retirer; ~ **down** *vt* (*building*) démolir; (*letter etc*) prendre, écrire; ~ **in** *vt* (*deceive*) tromper, rouler; (*understand*) comprendre, saisir; (*include*) comprendre, inclure; (*lodger*) prendre; ~ **off** *vi* (*AVIAT*) décoller ♦ *vt* (*go away*) s'en aller; (*remove*) enlever; ~ **on** *vt* (*work*) accepter, se charger de; (*employee*) prendre, embaucher; (*opponent*) accepter de se battre contre; ~ **out** *vt* (*invite*) emmener, sortir; (*remove*) enlever; **to** ~ **sth out of sth** (*drawer, pocket etc*) prendre qch dans qch; ~ **over** *vt* (*business*) reprendre ♦ *vi*: **to** ~ **over from sb** prendre la relève de qn; ~ **to** *vt fus* (*person*) se prendre d'amitié pour; (*thing*) prendre goût à; ~ **up** *vt* (*activity*) se mettre à; (*dress*) raccourcir; (*occupy: time, space*) prendre, occuper; **to** ~ **sb up on an offer** accepter la proposition de qn; ~**away** (*BRIT*) *adj* (*food*) à emporter ♦ *n* (*shop, restaurant*) qui vend

de plats à emporter; ~**off** *n* (*AVIAT*) décollage *m*; ~**over** *n* (*COMM*) rachat *m*; **takings** ['teɪkɪŋz] *npl* (*COMM*) recette *f*

talc [tælk] *n* (*also:* ~**um powder**) talc *m*

tale [teɪl] *n* (*story*) conte *m*, histoire *f*; (*account*) récit *m*; **to tell** ~**s** (*fig*) rapporter

talent ['tælənt] *n* talent *m*, don *m*; ~**ed** *adj* doué(e), plein(e) de talent

talk [tɔːk] *n* (*a speech*) causerie *f*, exposé *m*; (*conversation*) discussion *f*, entretien *m*; (*gossip*) racontars *mpl* ♦ *vi* parler; ~**s** *npl* (*POL etc*) entretiens *mpl*; **to ~ about** parler de; **to ~ sb into/out of doing** persuader qn de faire/ne pas faire; **to ~ shop** parler métier *or* affaires; ~ **over** *vt* discuter (de); ~**ative** ['tɔːkətɪv] *adj* bavard(e); ~ **show** *n* causerie (télévisée *or* radiodiffusée)

tall [tɔːl] *adj* (*person*) grand(e); (*building, tree*) haut(e); **to be 6 feet** ~ ≈ mesurer 1 mètre 80; ~ **story** *n* histoire *f* invraisemblable

tally ['tælɪ] *n* compte *m* ♦ *vi*: **to ~ (with)** correspondre (à)

talon ['tælən] *n* griffe *f*; (*of eagle*) serre *f*

tame [teɪm] *adj* apprivoisé(e); (*fig: story, style*) insipide

tamper ['tæmpə*] *vi*: **to ~ with** toucher à

tampon ['tæmpən] *n* tampon *m* (hygiénique *or* périodique)

tan [tæn] *n* (*also:* **sun~**) bronzage *m* ♦ *vt, vi* bronzer ♦ *adj* (*colour*) brun roux *inv*

tang [tæŋ] *n* odeur (*or* saveur) piquante

tangent ['tændʒənt] *n* (*MATH*) tangente *f*; **to go off at a ~** (*fig*) changer de sujet

tangerine [tændʒəˈriːn] *n* mandarine *f*

tangle ['tæŋgl] *n* enchevêtrement *m*; **to get in(to) a ~** s'embrouiller

tank [tæŋk] *n* (*water* ~) réservoir *m*; (*for fish*) aquarium *m*; (*MIL*) char *m* d'assaut, tank *m*

tanker ['tæŋkə*] *n* (*ship*) pétrolier *m*, tanker *m*; (*truck*) camion-citerne *m*

tantalizing ['tæntəlaɪzɪŋ] *adj* (*smell*) extrêmement appétissant(e); (*offer*) terriblement tentant(e)

tantamount [ˈtæntəmaʊnt] *adj*: ~ **to** qui équivaut à

tantrum [ˈtæntrəm] *n* accès *m* de colère

tap [tæp] *n* (*on sink etc*) robinet *m*; (*gentle blow*) petite tape ♦ *vt* frapper *or* taper légèrement; (*resources*) exploiter, utiliser; (*telephone*) mettre sur écoute; **on** ~ (*fig*: *resources*) disponible; ~-**dancing** [ˈtæpdɑːnsɪŋ] *n* claquettes *fpl*

tape [teɪp] *n* ruban *m*; (*also: magnetic* ~) bande *f* (magnétique); (*cassette*) cassette *f*; (*sticky*) scotch *m* ♦ *vt* (*record*) enregistrer; (*stick with* ~) coller avec du scotch; ~ **deck** *n* platine *f* d'enregistrement; ~ **measure** *n* mètre *m* à ruban

taper [ˈteɪpə*] *n* cierge *m* ♦ *vi* s'effiler

tape recorder *n* magnétophone *m*

tapestry [ˈtæpɪstrɪ] *n* tapisserie *f*

tar [tɑː*] *n* goudron *m*

target [ˈtɑːgɪt] *n* cible *f*; (*fig*) objectif *m*

tariff [ˈtærɪf] *n* (*COMM*) tarif *m*; (*taxes*) tarif douanier

tarmac [ˈtɑːmæk] *n* (*BRIT*: *on road*) macadam *m*; (*AVIAT*) piste *f*

tarnish [ˈtɑːnɪʃ] *vt* ternir

tarpaulin [tɑːˈpɔːlɪn] *n* bâche (goudronnée)

tarragon [ˈtærəgən] *n* estragon *m*

tart [tɑːt] *n* (*CULIN*) tarte *f*; (*BRIT*: *inf*: *prostitute*) putain *f* ♦ *adj* (*flavour*) âpre, aigrelet(te); ~ **up** (*BRIT*: *inf*) *vt* (*object*) retaper; **to** ~ **o.s. up** se faire beau(belle), s'attifer (*pej*)

tartan [ˈtɑːtən] *n* tartan *m* ♦ *adj* écossais(e)

tartar [ˈtɑːtə*] *n* (*on teeth*) tartre *m*; ~(**e**) **sauce** *n* sauce *f* tartare

task [tɑːsk] *n* tâche *f*; **to take sb to** ~ prendre qn à partie; ~ **force** *n* (*MIL*, *PO-LICE*) détachement spécial

tassel [ˈtæsəl] *n* gland *m*; pompon *m*

taste [teɪst] *n* goût *m*; (*fig*: *glimpse, idea*) idée *f*, aperçu *m* ♦ *vt* goûter ♦ *vi*: **to** ~ **of** *or* **like** (*fish etc*) avoir le *or* un goût de; **you can** ~ **the garlic (in it)** on sent bien l'ail; **can I have a** ~ **of this wine?** puis-je goûter un peu de ce vin?; **in good/bad** ~ de bon/mauvais goût; ~**ful** *adj* de bon goût; ~**less** *adj* (*food*) fade; (*remark*) de mauvais goût; **tasty** [ˈteɪstɪ] *adj* savoureux(euse), délicieux(euse)

tatters [ˈtætəz] *npl*: **in** ~ en lambeaux

tattoo [təˈtuː] *n* tatouage *m*; (*spectacle*) parade *f* militaire ♦ *vt* tatouer

tatty (*BRIT*: *inf*) *adj* (*clothes*) frippé(e); (*shop, area*) délabré(e)

taught [tɔːt] *pt, pp of* **teach**

taunt [tɔːnt] *n* raillerie *f* ♦ *vt* railler

Taurus [ˈtɔːrəs] *n* le Taureau

taut [tɔːt] *adj* tendu(e)

tax [tæks] *n* (*on goods etc*) taxe *f*; (*on income*) impôts *mpl*, contributions *fpl* ♦ *vt* taxer; imposer; (*fig*: *patience etc*) mettre à l'épreuve; ~**able** *adj* (*income*) imposable; ~**ation** [tækˈseɪʃən] *n* taxation *f*; impôts *mpl*, contributions *fpl*; ~ **avoidance** *n* dégrèvement fiscal; ~ **disc** (*BRIT*) *n* (*AUT*) vignette *f* (automobile); ~ **evasion** *n* fraude fiscale; ~-**free** *adj* exempt(e) d'impôts

taxi [ˈtæksɪ] *n* taxi *m* ♦ *vi* (*AVIAT*) rouler (lentement) au sol; ~ **driver** *n* chauffeur *m* de taxi; ~ **rank** (*BRIT*) *n* station *f* de taxis; ~ **stand** *n* = **taxi rank**

tax: ~ **payer** *n* contribuable *m/f*; ~ **relief** *n* dégrèvement fiscal; ~ **return** *n* déclaration *f* d'impôts *or de* revenus

TB *n abbr* = **tuberculosis**

tea [tiː] *n* thé *m*; (*BRIT*: *snack: for children*) goûter *m*; **high** ~ *collation combinant goûter et dîner*; ~ **bag** *n* sachet *m* de thé; ~ **break** (*BRIT*) *n* pause-thé *f*

teach [tiːtʃ] (*pt, pp* **taught**) *vt*: **to** ~ **sb sth**, ~ **sth to sb** apprendre qch à qn; (*in school etc*) enseigner qch à qn enseigner; ~**er** *n* (*in secondary school*) professeur *m*; (*in primary school*) instituteur(trice); ~**ing** *n* enseignement *m*

tea cosy *n* cloche *f* à thé

teacup [ˈtiːkʌp] *n* tasse *f* à thé

teak [tiːk] *n* teck *m*

team [tiːm] *n* équipe *f*; (*of animals*) attelage *m*; ~**work** *n* travail *m* d'équipe

teapot [ˈtiːpɒt] *n* théière *f*

tear[1] [tɛə*] (*pt* **tore**, *pp* **torn**) *n* déchiure *f* ♦ *vt* déchirer ♦ *vi* se déchirer; ~ **along** *vi* (*rush*) aller à toute vitesse; ~

up *vt* (*sheet of paper etc*) déchirer, mettre en morceaux *or* pièces

tear² [tɪə*] *n* larme *f*; **in ~s** en larmes; **~ful** *adj* larmoyant(e); **~ gas** *n* gaz *m* lacrymogène

tearoom ['tiːrʊm] *n* salon *m* de thé

tease [tiːz] *vt* taquiner; (*unkindly*) tourmenter

tea set *n* service *m* à thé

teaspoon ['tiːspuːn] *n* petite cuiller; (*also: ~ful: as measurement*) ≈ cuillerée *f* à café

teat [tiːt] *n* tétine *f*

teatime ['tiːtaɪm] *n* l'heure *f* du thé

tea towel (*BRIT*) *n* torchon *m* (à vaisselle)

technical ['teknɪkəl] *adj* technique; **~ity** [teknɪ'kælɪtɪ] *n* (*detail*) détail *m* technique; (*point of law*) vice *m* de forme; **~ly** *adv* techniquement; (*strictly speaking*) en théorie

technician [tek'nɪʃən] *n* technicien(ne)

technique [tek'niːk] *n* technique *f*

technological [teknə'lɒdʒɪkəl] *adj* technologique; **technology** [tek'nɒlədʒɪ] *n* technologie *f*

teddy (bear) ['tedɪ-] *n* ours *m* en peluche

tedious ['tiːdɪəs] *adj* fastidieux(euse)

tee [tiː] *n* (*GOLF*) tee *m*

teem [tiːm] *vi*: **to ~ (with)** grouiller (de); **it is ~ing (with rain)** il pleut à torrents

teenage ['tiːneɪdʒ] *adj* (*fashions etc*) pour jeunes, pour adolescents; (*children*) adolescent(e); **~r** *n* adolescent(e)

teens [tiːnz] *npl*: **to be in one's ~** être adolescent(e)

tee-shirt ['tiːʃɜːt] *n* = T-shirt

teeter ['tiːtə*] *vi* chanceler, vaciller

teeth [tiːθ] *npl of* **tooth**

teethe [tiːð] *vi* percer ses dents

teething ring ['tiːðɪŋ-] *n* anneau pour bébé qui perce ses dents

teething troubles *npl* (*fig*) difficultés initiales

teetotal ['tiː'təʊtl] *adj* (*person*) qui ne boit jamais d'alcool

telegram ['telɪɡræm] *n* télégramme *m*

telegraph ['telɪɡrɑːf] *n* télégraphe *m*; **~**

pole *n* poteau *m* télégraphique

telephone ['telɪfəʊn] *n* téléphone *m* ♦ *vt* (*person*) téléphoner à; (*message*) téléphoner; **on the ~** au téléphone; **to be on the ~** (*BRIT: have a ~*) avoir le téléphone; **~ booth** (*BRIT*) *n* = **telephone box**; **~ box** *n* cabine *f* téléphonique; **~ call** *n* coup *m* de téléphone, appel *m* téléphonique; **~ directory** *n* annuaire *m* (du téléphone); **~ number** *n* numéro *m* de téléphone; **telephonist** [tə'lefənɪst] (*BRIT*) *n* téléphoniste *m/f*

telescope ['telɪskəʊp] *n* télescope *m*

television ['telɪvɪʒən] *n* télévision *f*; **on ~** à la télévision; **~ set** *n* (poste *f* de) télévision *m*

telex ['teleks] *n* télex *m*

tell [tel] (*pt, pp* **told**) *vt* dire; (*relate: story*) raconter; (*distinguish*): **to ~ sth from** distinguer qch de ♦ *vi* (*talk*): **to ~ (of)** parler (de); (*have effect*) se faire sentir, se voir; **to ~ sb to do** dire à qn de faire; **~ off** *vt* réprimander, gronder; **~er** *n* (*in bank*) caissier(ère); **~ing** *adj* (*remark, detail*) révélateur(trice); **~tale** *adj* (*sign*) éloquent(e), révélateur(trice)

telly ['telɪ] (*BRIT: inf*) *n abbr* (= *television*) télé *f*

temp [temp] *n abbr* (= *temporary*) (secrétaire *f*) intérimaire *f*

temper ['tempə*] *n* (*nature*) caractère *m*; (*mood*) humeur *f*; (*fit of anger*) colère *f* ♦ *vt* (*moderate*) tempérer, adoucir; **to be in a ~** être en colère; **to lose one's ~** se mettre en colère

temperament ['temprəmənt] *n* (*nature*) tempérament *m*; **~al** [temprə'mentl] *adj* capricieux(euse)

temperate ['tempərət] *adj* (*climate, country*) tempérée(e)

temperature ['temprɪtʃə*] *n* température *f*; **to have** *or* **run a ~** avoir de la fièvre

temple ['templ] *n* (*building*) temple *m*; (*ANAT*) tempe *f*

temporary ['tempərərɪ] *adj* temporaire, provisoire; (*job, worker*) temporaire

tempt [tempt] *vt* tenter; **to ~ sb into doing** persuader qn de faire; **~ation**

[temp'teɪʃən] n tentation f
ten [ten] num dix
tenacity [tə'næsɪtɪ] n ténacité f
tenancy ['tenənsɪ] n location f; état m de locataire
tenant ['tenənt] n locataire m/f
tend [tend] vt s'occuper de ♦ vi: **to ~ to do** avoir tendance à faire
tendency ['tendənsɪ] n tendance f
tender ['tendə*] adj tendre; (delicate) délicat(e); (sore) sensible ♦ n (COMM: offer) soumission f ♦ vt offrir
tenement ['tenəmənt] n immeuble m
tenet ['tenət] n principe m
tennis ['tenɪs] n tennis m; ~ **ball** n balle f de tennis; ~ **court** n (court m de) tennis; ~ **player** n joueur(euse) de tennis; ~ **racket** n raquette f de tennis; ~ **shoes** npl (chaussures fpl de) tennis mpl
tenor ['tenə*] n (MUS) ténor m
tenpin bowling (BRIT) n bowling m (à dix quilles)
tense [tens] adj tendu(e) ♦ n (LING) temps m
tension ['tenʃən] n tension f
tent [tent] n tente f
tentative ['tentətɪv] adj timide, hésitant(e); (conclusion) provisoire
tenterhooks ['tentəhʊks] npl: **on ~** sur des charbons ardents
tenth [tenθ] num dixième
tent peg n piquet m de tente
tent pole n montant m de tente
tenuous ['tenjʊəs] adj ténu(e)
tenure ['tenjʊə*] n (of property) bail m; (of job) période f de jouissance
tepid ['tepɪd] adj tiède
term [tɜːm] n terme m; (SCOL) trimestre m ♦ vt appeler; ~**s** npl (conditions) conditions fpl; (COMM) tarif m; **in the short/long ~** à court/long terme; **to come to ~s with** (problem) faire face à
terminal ['tɜːmɪnl] adj (disease) dans sa phase terminale; (patient) incurable ♦ n (ELEC) borne f; (for oil, ore etc, COMPUT) terminal m; (also: air ~) aérogare f; (BRIT: also: coach ~) gare routière
terminate ['tɜːmɪneɪt] vt mettre fin à; (pregnancy) interrompre

termini ['tɜːmɪnaɪ] npl of **terminus**
terminus ['tɜːmɪnəs] (pl **termini**) n terminus m inv
terrace ['terəs] n terrasse f; (BRIT: row of houses) rangée f de maisons (attenantes); **the ~s** npl (BRIT: SPORT) les gradins mpl; ~**d** adj (garden) en terrasses
terracotta ['terə'kɔtə] n terre cuite
terrain [te'reɪn] n terrain m (sol)
terrible ['terɪbl] adj terrible, atroce; (weather, conditions) affreux(euse), épouvantable; **terribly** ['terɪblɪ] adv terriblement; (very badly) affreusement mal
terrier ['terɪə*] n terrier m (chien)
terrific [tə'rɪfɪk] adj fantastique, incroyable, terrible; (wonderful) formidable, sensationnel(le)
terrify ['terɪfaɪ] vt terrifier
territory ['terɪtərɪ] n territoire m
terror ['terə*] n terreur f; ~**ism** n terrorisme m; ~**ist** n terroriste m/f
terse [tɜːs] adj (style) concis(e); (reply) sec(sèche)
Terylene ['terɪliːn] (®) n tergal m (®)
test [test] n (trial, check) essai m; (of courage etc) épreuve f; (MED) examen m; (CHEM) analyse f; (SCOL) interrogation f; (also: driving ~) (examen du) permis m de conduire ♦ vt essayer; mettre à l'épreuve; examiner; analyser; faire subir une interrogation à
testament ['testəmənt] n testament m; **the Old/New T~** l'Ancien/le Nouveau Testament
testicle ['testɪkl] n testicule m
testify ['testɪfaɪ] vi (LAW) témoigner, déposer; **to ~ to sth** attester qch
testimony ['testɪmənɪ] n témoignage m; (clear proof): **to be (a) ~** to être la preuve de
test: ~ **match** n (CRICKET, RUGBY) match international; ~ **pilot** n teste m d'essai; ~ **tube** n éprouvette f
tetanus ['tetənəs] n tétanos m
tether ['teðə*] vt attacher ♦ n: **at the end of one's ~** à bout (de patience)
text [tekst] n texte m; ~**book** n manuel m
textile n textile m

texture ['tɛkstʃə*] *n* texture *f*; (*of skin, paper etc*) grain *m*

Thames [tɛmz] *n*: **the ~** la Tamise

than [ðæn, ðən] *conj* que; (*with numerals*): **more ~ 10/once** plus de 10/d'une fois; **I have more/less ~ you** j'en ai plus/moins que toi; **she has more apples ~ pears** elle a plus de pommes que de poires

thank [θæŋk] *vt* remercier, dire merci à; **~s** *npl* (*gratitude*) remerciements *mpl* ♦ *excl* merci!; **~ you (very much)** merci (beaucoup); **~s to** grâce à; **~ God!** Dieu merci!; **~ful** *adj*: **~ful (for)** reconnaissant(e) (de); **~less** *adj* ingrat(e); **T~sgiving (Day)** *n* jour *m* d'action de grâce (*fête américaine*)

KEYWORD

that [ðæt] *adj* (*demonstrative*: *pl* **those**) ce, cet +*vowel or h mute*, *f* cette; **~ man/woman/book** cet homme/cette femme/ce livre; (*not this*) cet homme-là/cette femme-là/ce livre-là; **~ one** celui-là(celle-là)

♦ *pron* **1** (*demonstrative*: *pl* **those**) ce; (*not this one*) cela, ça; **who's ~?** qui est-ce?; **what's ~?** qu'est-ce que c'est?; **is ~ you?** c'est toi?; **I prefer this to ~** je préfère ceci à cela *or* ça; **~'s what he said** c'est *or* voilà ce qu'il a dit; **~ is (to say)** c'est-à-dire, à savoir

2 (*relative*: *subject*) qui; (: *object*) que; (: *indirect*) lequel(laquelle), lesquels (lesquelles) *pl*; **the book ~ I read** le livre que j'ai lu; **the books ~ are in the library** les livres qui sont dans la bibliothèque; **all ~ I have** tout ce que j'ai; **the box ~ I put it in** la boîte dans laquelle je l'ai mis; **the people ~ I spoke to** les gens auxquels *or* à qui j'ai parlé

3 (*relative*: *of time*) où; **the day ~ he came** le jour où il est venu

♦ *conj* que; **he thought ~ I was ill** il pensait que j'étais malade

♦ *adv* (*demonstrative*): **I can't work ~ much** je ne peux pas travailler autant que cela; **I didn't know it was ~ bad** je ne savais pas que c'était si *or* aussi

mauvais; **it's about ~ high** c'est à peu près de cette hauteur

thatched [θætʃt] *adj* (*roof*) de chaume; **~ cottage** chaumière *f*

thaw [θɔː] *n* dégel *m* ♦ *vi* (*ice*) fondre; (*food*) dégeler ♦ *vt* (*food*: *also*: **~ out**) (faire) dégeler

KEYWORD

the [ðiː, ðə] *def art* **1** (*gen*) le, la *f*, l' +*vowel or h mute*, les *pl*; **~ boy/girl/ink** le garçon/la fille/l'encre; **~ children** les enfants; **~ history of the world** l'histoire du monde; **give it to ~ postman** donne-le au facteur; **to play ~ piano/flute** jouer du piano/de la flûte; **~ rich and ~ poor** les riches et les pauvres

2 (*in titles*): **Elizabeth ~ First** Elisabeth première; **Peter ~ Great** Pierre le Grand

3 (*in comparisons*): **~ more he works, ~ more he earns** plus il travaille, plus il gagne de l'argent

theatre ['θɪətə*] *n* théâtre *m*; (*also*: *lecture* **~**) amphi(théâtre) *m*; (*MED*: *also*: *operating* **~**) salle *f* d'opération; **~-goer** *n* habitué(e) du théâtre; **theatrical** [θɪˈætrɪkəl] *adj* théâtral(e)

theft [θɛft] *n* vol *m* (*larcin*)

their [ðɛə*] *adj* leur; (*pl*) leurs; *see also* **my**; **~s** *pron* le(la) leur; (*pl*) les leurs; *see also* **mine**

them [ðɛm, ðəm] *pron* (*direct*) les; (*indirect*) leur; (*stressed*, *after prep*) eux(elles); *see also* **me**

theme [θiːm] *n* thème *m*; **~ park** *n* parc *m* (d'attraction) à thème; **~ song** *n* chanson principale

themselves [ðəmˈsɛlvz] *pl pron* (*reflexive*) se; (*emphatic*, *after prep*) eux-mêmes(elles-mêmes); *see also* **oneself**

then [ðɛn] *adv* (*at that time*) alors, à ce moment-là; (*next*) puis, ensuite; (*and also*) et puis ♦ *conj* (*therefore*) alors, dans ce cas ♦ *adj*: **the ~ president** le président d'alors *or* de l'époque; **by ~**

(*past*) à ce moment-là; (*future*) d'ici là; **from ~ on** dès lors

theology [θɪˈɒlədʒɪ] *n* théologie *f*

theoretical [θɪəˈretɪkəl] *adj* théorique

theorize [ˈθɪəraɪz] *vi* faire des théories

theory [ˈθɪərɪ] *n* théorie *f*

therapy [ˈθerəpɪ] *n* thérapie *f*

KEYWORD
---

there [ðɛə*] *adv* **1**: **~ is, ~ are** il y a; **~ are 3 of them** (*people, things*) il y en a 3; **~ has been an accident** il y a eu un accident

2 (*referring to place*) là, là-bas; **it's ~** c'est là(-bas); **in/on/up/down ~** là-dedans/là-dessus/là-haut/en bas; **he went ~ on Friday** il y est allé vendredi; **I want that book ~** je veux ce livre-là; **~ he is!** le voilà!

3: **~, ~** (*esp to child*) allons, allons!

---

thereabouts [ðɛərəˈbaʊts] *adv* (*place*) par là, près de là; (*amount*) environ, à peu près

thereafter [ðɛərˈɑːftə*] *adv* par la suite

thereby [ðɛəˈbaɪ] *adv* ainsi

therefore [ˈðɛəfɔː*] *adv* donc, par conséquent

there's [ˈðɛəz] = **there is; there has**

thermal [ˈθəːml] *adj* (*springs*) thermal(e); (*underwear*) en thermolactyl (®); (COMPUT: *paper*) thermosensible; (: *printer*) thermique

thermometer [θəˈmɒmɪtə*] *n* thermomètre *m*

Thermos [ˈθəːməs] (®) *n* (*also*: **~ flask**) thermos *m or f inv* (®)

thermostat [ˈθəːməʊstæt] *n* thermostat *m*

thesaurus [θɪˈsɔːrəs] *n* dictionnaire *m* des synonymes

these [ðiːz] *pl adj* ces; (*not "those"*): **~ books** ces livres-ci ♦ *pl pron* ceux-ci(celles-ci)

thesis [ˈθiːsɪs] (*pl* **theses**) *n* thèse *f*

they [ðeɪ] *pl pron* ils(elles); (*stressed*) eux(elles); **~ say that ...** (*it is said that*) on dit que ...; **~'d** = **~ had; ~ would; ~'ll** = **~ shall; ~ will; ~'re** = **~ are;**

~'ve = **~ have**

thick [θɪk] *adj* épais(se); (*stupid*) bête, borné(e) ♦ *n*: **in the ~ of** au beau milieu de, en plein cœur de; **it's 20 cm ~** il/elle a 20 cm d'épaisseur; **~en** *vi* s'épaissir ♦ *vt* (*sauce etc*) épaissir; **~ness** *n* épaisseur *f*; **~set** *adj* trapu(e), costaud(e); **~skinned** *adj* (*fig*) peu sensible

thief [θiːf] (*pl* **thieves**) *n* voleur(euse)

thigh [θaɪ] *n* cuisse *f*

thimble [ˈθɪmbl] *n* dé *m* (à coudre)

thin [θɪn] *adj* mince; (*skinny*) maigre; (*soup, sauce*) peu épais(se), clair(e); (*hair, crowd*) clairsemé(e) ♦ *vt*: **to ~ (down)** (*sauce, paint*) délayer

thing [θɪŋ] *n* chose *f*; (*object*) objet *m*; (*contraption*) truc *m*; (*mania*): **to have a ~ about** être obsédé(e) par; **~s** *npl* (*belongings*) affaires *fpl*; **poor ~!** le(la) pauvre!; **the best ~ would be to** le mieux serait de; **how are ~s?** comment ça va?

think [θɪŋk] (*pt, pp* **thought**) *vi* penser, réfléchir; (*believe*) penser ♦ *vt* (*imagine*) imaginer; **what did you ~ of them?** qu'avez-vous pensé d'eux?; **to ~ about sth/sb** penser à qch/qn; **I'll ~ about it** je vais y réfléchir; **to ~ of doing** avoir l'idée de faire; **I ~ so/not** je crois *or* pense que oui/non; **to ~ well of** avoir une haute opinion de; **~ over** *vt* bien réfléchir à; **~ up** *vt* inventer, trouver; **~ tank** *n* groupe *m* de réflexion

thinly *adv* (*cut*) en fines tranches; (*spread*) en une couche mince

third [θəːd] *num* troisième ♦ *n* (*fraction*) tiers *m*; (AUT) troisième (vitesse) *f*; (BRIT: SCOL: *degree*) ≈ licence *f* sans mention; **~ly** *adv* troisièmement; **~ party insurance** (BRIT) *n* assurance *f* au tiers; **~-rate** *adj* de qualité médiocre; **the T~ World** *n* le tiers monde

thirst [θəːst] *n* soif *f*; **~y** *adj* (*person*) qui a soif, assoiffé(e); (*work*) qui donne soif; **to be ~y** avoir soif

thirteen [ˈθəːˈtiːn] *num* treize

thirty [ˈθəːtɪ] *num* trente

KEYWORD
---

this [ðɪs] *adj* (*demonstrative: pl* **these**)

ce, cet +*vowel or h mute*, cette *f*; ~ **man/woman/book** cet homme/cette femme/ce livre; (*not that*) cet homme-ci/cette femme-ci/ce livre-ci; ~ **one** celui-ci(celle-ci)

♦ *pron* (*demonstrative*: *pl these*) ce; (*not that one*) celui-ci(celle-ci), ceci; **who's** ~? qui est-ce?; **what's** ~? qu'est-ce que c'est?; **I prefer** ~ **to that** je préfère ceci à cela; ~ **is what he said** voici ce qu'il a dit; ~ **is Mr Brown** (*in introductions*) je vous présente Mr Brown; (*in photo*) c'est Mr Brown; (*on telephone*) ici Mr Brown

♦ *adv* (*demonstrative*): **it was about** ~ **big** c'était à peu près de cette grandeur *or* grand comme ça; **I didn't know it was** ~ **bad** je ne savais pas que c'était si *or* aussi mauvais

thistle ['θɪsl] *n* chardon *m*
thorn [θɔːn] *n* épine *f*
thorough ['θʌrə] *adj* (*search*) minutieux(euse); (*knowledge, research*) approfondi(e); (*work, person*) consciencieux(euse); (*cleaning*) à fond; **~bred** *n* (*horse*) pur-sang *m inv*; **~fare** *n* route *f*; **"no ~fare"** "passage interdit"; **~ly** *adv* minutieusement; en profondeur; à fond; (*very*) tout à fait
those [ðəuz] *pl adj* ces; (*not "these"*): ~ **books** ces livres-là ♦ *pl pron* ceux-là(celles-là)
though [ðəu] *conj* bien que +*sub*, quoique +*sub* ♦ *adv* pourtant
thought [θɔːt] *pt, pp of* think ♦ *n* pensée *f*; (*idea*) idée *f*; (*opinion*) avis *m*; **~ful** *adj* (*deep in thought*) pensif(ive); (*serious*) réfléchi(e); (*considerate*) prévenant(e); **~less** *adj* étourdi(e); qui manque de considération
thousand ['θauzənd] *num* mille; **two** ~ deux mille; **~s of** des milliers de; **~th** *num* millième
thrash [θræʃ] *vt* rouer de coups; donner une correction à; (*defeat*) battre à plate couture; ~ **about**, ~ **around** *vi* se débattre; ~ **out** *vt* débattre de
thread [θred] *n* fil *m*; (*of screw*) pas *m*,

filetage *m* ♦ *vt* (*needle*) enfiler; **~bare** *adj* râpé(e), élimé(e)
threat [θret] *n* menace *f*; **~en** *vi* menacer ♦ *vt*: **to ~en sb with sth/to do** menacer qn de qch/de faire
three [θriː] *num* trois; **~-dimensional** *adj* à trois dimensions; **~-piece suit** *n* complet *m* (avec gilet); **~-piece suite** *n* salon *m* comprenant un canapé et deux fauteuils assortis; **~-ply** *adj* (*wool*) trois fils *inv*
thresh [θreʃ] *vt* (*AGR*) battre
threshold ['θreʃhəuld] *n* seuil *m*
threw [θruː] *pt of* throw
thrift [θrɪft] *n* économie *f*; **~y** *adj* économe
thrill [θrɪl] *n* (*excitement*) émotion *f*, sensation forte; (*shudder*) frisson *m* ♦ *vt* (*audience*) électriser; **to be ~ed** (*with gift etc*) être ravi(e); **~er** *n* film *m* (*or* roman *m or* pièce *f*) à suspense; **~ing** *adj* saisissant(e), palpitant(e)
thrive [θraɪv] (*pt* **~d**, throve, *pp* **~d**) *vi* pousser, se développer; (*business*) prospérer; **he ~s on it** cela lui réussit; **thriving** ['θraɪvɪŋ] *adj* (*business, community*) prospère
throat [θrəut] *n* gorge *f*; **to have a sore** ~ avoir mal à la gorge
throb [θrɒb] *vi* (*heart*) palpiter; (*engine*) vibrer; **my head is ~bing** j'ai des élancements dans la tête
throes [θrəuz] *npl*: **in the** ~ **of** au beau milieu de
throne [θrəun] *n* trône *m*
throng [θrɒŋ] *n* foule *f* ♦ *vt* se presser dans
throttle ['θrɒtl] *n* (*AUT*) accélérateur *m* ♦ *vt* étrangler
through [θruː] *prep* à travers; (*time*) pendant, durant; (*by means of*) par, par l'intermédiaire de; (*owing to*) à cause de ♦ *adj* (*ticket, train, passage*) direct(e) ♦ *adv* à travers; **to put sb** ~ **to sb** (*BRIT: TEL*) passer qn à qn; **to be** ~ (*esp US: have finished*) avoir fini; **to be** ~ **with sb** (*relationship*) avoir rompu avec qn; **"no** ~ **road"** (*BRIT*) "impasse"; **~out** [θruː'aut] *prep*

(*place*) partout dans; (*time*) durant tout(e) le(la) ♦ *adv* partout

throve [θrəʊv] *pt of* **thrive**

throw [θrəʊ] (*pt* **threw**, *pp* **thrown**) *n* jet *m*; (*SPORT*) lancer *m* ♦ *vt* lancer, jeter; (*SPORT*) lancer; (*rider*) désarçonner; (*fig*) décontenancer; **to ~ a party** donner une réception; **~ away** *vt* jeter; **~ off** *vt* se débarrasser de; **~ out** *vt* jeter; (*reject*) rejeter; (*person*) mettre à la porte; **~ up** *vi* vomir; **~away** *adj* à jeter; (*remark*) fait(e) en passant; **~-in** *n* (*SPORT*) remise *f* en jeu

thru [θru:] (*US*) = **through**

thrush [θrʌʃ] *n* (*bird*) grive *f*

thrust [θrʌst] (*pt, pp* **thrust**) *n* (*TECH*) poussée *f* ♦ *vt* pousser brusquement; (*push in*) enfoncer

thud [θʌd] *n* bruit sourd

thug [θʌg] *n* voyou *m*

thumb [θʌm] *n* (*ANAT*) pouce *m*, arrêter une voiture; **to ~ a lift** faire de l'auto-stop; **~ through** *vt* (*book*) feuilleter; **~tack** (*US*) *n* punaise *f* (*clou*)

thump [θʌmp] *n* grand coup; (*sound*) bruit sourd ♦ *vt* cogner sur ♦ *vi* cogner, battre fort

thunder [ˈθʌndə*] *n* tonnerre *m* ♦ *vi* tonner; (*train etc*): **to ~ past** passer dans un grondement *or* un bruit de tonnerre; **~bolt** *n* foudre *f*; **~clap** *n* coup *m* de tonnerre; **~storm** *n* orage *m*; **~y** *adj* orageux(euse)

Thursday [ˈθɜːzdeɪ] *n* jeudi *m*

thus [ðʌs] *adv* ainsi

thwart [θwɔːt] *vt* contrecarrer

thyme [taɪm] *n* thym *m*

tiara [tɪˈɑːrə] *n* (*woman's*) diadème *m*

tick [tɪk] *n* (*sound: of clock*) tic-tac *m*; (*mark*) coche *f*; (*ZOOL*) tique *f*; (*BRIT: inf*): **in a ~** dans une seconde ♦ *vi* faire tic-tac ♦ *vt* (*item on list*) cocher; **~ off** *vt* (*item on list*) cocher; (*person*) réprimander, attraper; **~ over** *vi* (*engine*) tourner au ralenti; (*fig*) aller *or* marcher doucettement

ticket [ˈtɪkɪt] *n* billet *m*; (*for bus, tube*) ticket *m*; (*in shop: on goods*) étiquette *f*; (*for library*) carte *f*; (*parking* ~) papillon *m*, p.-v. *m*; **~ collector** *n* contrôleur(euse); **~ office** *n* guichet *m*, bureau *m* de vente des billets

tickle [ˈtɪkl] *vt, vi* chatouiller; **ticklish** *adj* (*person*) chatouilleux(euse); (*problem*) épineux(euse)

tidal [ˈtaɪdl] *adj* (*force*) de la marée; (*estuary*) à marée; **~ wave** *n* raz-de-marée *m inv*

tidbit [ˈtɪdbɪt] (*US*) *n* = **titbit**

tiddlywinks [ˈtɪdlɪwɪŋks] *n* jeu *m* de puce

tide [taɪd] *n* marée *f*; (*fig: of events*) cours *m* ♦ *vt*: **to ~ sb over** dépanner qn; **high/low ~** marée haute/basse

tidy [ˈtaɪdɪ] *adj* (*room*) bien rangé(e); (*dress, work*) net(te), soigné(e); (*person*) ordonné(e), qui a de l'ordre ♦ *vt* (*also: ~ up*) ranger

tie [taɪ] *n* (*string etc*) cordon *m*; (*BRIT: also: neck~*) cravate *f*; (*fig: link*) lien *m*; (*SPORT: draw*) égalité *f* de points; match nul ♦ *vt* (*parcel*) attacher; (*ribbon, shoelaces*) nouer ♦ *vi* (*SPORT*) faire match nul; finir à égalité de points; **to ~ sth in a bow** faire un nœud à *or* avec qch; **to ~ a knot in sth** faire un nœud à qch; **~ down** *vt* (*fig*): **to ~ sb down (to)** contraindre qn (à accepter); **to be ~d down** (*by relationship*) se fixer; **~ up** *vt* (*parcel*) ficeler; (*dog, boat*) attacher; (*prisoner*) ligoter; (*arrangements*) conclure; **to be ~d up** (*busy*) être pris(e) *or* occupé(e)

tier [tɪə*] *n* gradin *m*; (*of cake*) étage *m*

tiger [ˈtaɪgə*] *n* tigre *m*

tight [taɪt] *adj* (*rope*) tendu(e), raide; (*clothes*) étroit(e), très juste; (*budget, programme, bend*) serré(e); (*control*) strict(e), sévère; (*inf: drunk*) ivre, rond(e) ♦ *adv* (*squeeze*) très fort; (*shut*) hermétiquement, bien; **~en** *vt* (*rope*) tendre; (*screw*) resserrer; (*control*) renforcer ♦ *vi* se tendre, se resserrer; **~fisted** *adj* avare; **~ly** *adv* (*grasp*) bien, très fort; **~rope** *n* corde *f* raide; **~s** (*BRIT*) *npl* collant *m*

tile [taɪl] *n* (*on roof*) tuile *f*; (*on wall or floor*) carreau *m*; **~d** *adj* en tuiles; carrelé(e)

till [tɪl] *n* caisse (enregistreuse) ♦ *vt* (*land*) cultiver ♦ *prep, conj* = **until**

tiller ['tɪlə*] *n* (*NAUT*) barre *f* (du gouvernail)

tilt [tɪlt] *vt* pencher, incliner ♦ *vi* pencher, être incliné(e)

timber ['tɪmbə*] *n* (*material*) bois *m* (de construction); (*trees*) arbres *mpl*

time [taɪm] *n* temps *m*; (*epoch: often pl*) époque *f*, temps; (*by clock*) heure *f*; (*moment*) moment *m*; (*occasion, also MATH*) fois *f*; (*MUS*) mesure *f* ♦ *vt* (*race*) chronométrer; (*programme*) minuter; (*visit*) fixer; (*remark etc*) choisir le moment de; **a long** ~ un long moment, longtemps; **for the ~ being** pour le moment; **4 at a** ~ 4 à la fois; **from ~ to ~** de temps en temps; **at** ~**s** parfois; **in ~** (*soon enough*) à temps; (*after some ~*) avec le temps, à la longue; (*MUS*) en mesure; **in a week's** ~ dans une semaine; **in no ~** en un rien de temps; **any ~** n'importe quand; **on** ~ à l'heure; **5** ~**s 5** 5 fois 5; **what ~ is it?** quelle heure est-il?; **to have a good** ~ bien s'amuser; ~ **bomb** *n* bombe *f* à retardement; ~ **lag** (*BRIT*) *n* décalage *m*; (*in travel*) décalage horaire; ~**less** *adj* éternel(le); ~**ly** *adj* opportun(e); ~ **off** *n* temps *m* libre; ~**r** *n* (*TECH*) minuteur *m*; (*in kitchen*) compte-minutes *m inv*; ~**scale** *n* délais *mpl*; ~**share** *n* maison *f* (*or* appartement *m*) en multipropriété; ~ **switch** (*BRIT*) *n* minuteur *m*; (*for lighting*) minuterie *f*; ~**table** (*RAIL*) (indicateur *m*) horaire *m*; (*SCOL*) emploi *m* du temps; ~ **zone** *n* fuseau *m* horaire

timid ['tɪmɪd] *adj* timide; (*easily scared*) peureux(euse)

timing ['taɪmɪŋ] *n* minutage *m*; chronométrage *m*; **the** ~ **of his resignation** le moment choisi pour sa démission

timpani ['tɪmpənɪ] *npl* timbales *fpl*

tin [tɪn] *n* étain *m*; (*also:* ~ **plate**) fer-blanc *m*; (*BRIT: can*) boîte *f* (de conserve); (*for storage*) boîte *f*; ~**foil** *n* papier *m* d'étain *or* aluminium

tinge [tɪndʒ] *n* nuance *f* ♦ *vt*: ~**d with**

tingle ['tɪŋgl] *vi* picoter; (*person*) avoir des picotements

tinker ['tɪŋkə*] *n* (*gipsy*) romanichel *m*; ~ **with** *vt fus* bricoler, rafistoler

tinkle ['tɪŋkl] *vi* tinter

tinned [tɪnd] (*BRIT*) *adj* (*food*) en boîte, en conserve

tin opener [-'əupnə*] (*BRIT*) *n* ouvre-boîte(s) *m*

tinsel ['tɪnsəl] *n* guirlandes *fpl* de Noël (*argentées*)

tint [tɪnt] *n* teinte *f*; (*for hair*) shampooing colorant; ~**ed** *adj* (*hair*) teint(e); (*spectacles, glass*) teinté(e)

tiny ['taɪnɪ] *adj* minuscule

tip [tɪp] *n* (*end*) bout *m*; (*gratuity*) pourboire *m*; (*BRIT: for rubbish*) décharge *f*; (*advice*) tuyau *m* ♦ *vt* (*waiter*) donner un pourboire à; (*tilt*) incliner; (*overturn: also:* ~ **over**) renverser; (*empty:* ~ **out**) déverser; ~**off** *n* (*hint*) tuyau *m*; ~**ped** (*BRIT*) *adj* (*cigarette*) (à bout) filtre *inv*

tipsy ['tɪpsɪ] (*inf*) *adj* un peu ivre, éméché(e)

tiptoe ['tɪptəu] *n*: **on** ~ sur la pointe des pieds

tiptop ['tɪp'tɒp] *adj*: **in** ~ **condition** en excellent état

tire ['taɪə*] *n* (*US*) = **tyre** ♦ *vt* fatiguer ♦ *vi* se fatiguer; ~**d** *adj* fatigué(e); **to be** ~**d of** en avoir assez de, être las(lasse) de; ~**less** *adj* (*person*) infatigable; (*efforts*) inlassable; ~**some** *adj* ennuyeux(euse); **tiring** ['taɪərɪŋ] *adj* fatigant(e)

tissue ['tɪʃuː] *n* tissu *m*; (*paper handkerchief*) mouchoir *m* en papier, kleenex *m* (®); ~ **paper** *n* papier *m* de soie

tit [tɪt] *n* (*bird*) mésange *f*; **to give** ~ **for tat** rendre la pareille

titbit ['tɪtbɪt] *n* (*food*) friandise *f*; (*news*) potin *m*

title ['taɪtl] *n* titre *m*; ~ **deed** *n* (*LAW*) titre (constitutif) de propriété; ~ **role** *n* rôle principal

titter ['tɪtə*] *vi* rire (bêtement)

TM *abbr* = **trademark**

---

to [tu:, tə] *prep* **1** (*direction*) à; **to go ~ France/Portugal/London/school** aller en France/au Portugal/à Londres/à l'école; **to go ~ Claude's/the doctor's** aller chez Claude/le docteur; **the road ~ Edinburgh** la route d'Édimbourg

2 (*as far as*) (jusqu')à; **to count ~ 10** compter jusqu'à 10; **from 40 ~ 50 people** de 40 à 50 personnes

3 (*with expressions of time*): **a quarter ~ 5** 5 heures moins le quart; **it's twenty ~ 3** il est 3 heures moins vingt

4 (*for, of*) de; **the key ~ the front door** la clé de la porte d'entrée; **a letter ~ his wife** une lettre (adressée) à sa femme

5 (*expressing indirect object*) à; **to give sth ~ sb** donner qch à qn; **to talk ~ sb** parler à qn

6 (*in relation to*) à; **3 goals ~ 2** 3 (buts) à 2; **30 miles ~ the gallon** ≈ 9,4 litres aux cent (km)

7 (*purpose, result*): **to come ~ sb's aid** venir au secours de qn, porter secours à qn; **to sentence sb ~ death** condamner qn à mort; **~ my surprise** à ma grande surprise

♦ *with vb* **1** (*simple infinitive*): **~ go/ eat** aller/manger

2 (*following another vb*): **want/try/ start ~ do** vouloir/essayer de/ commencer à faire

3 (*with vb omitted*): **I don't want ~** je ne veux pas

4 (*purpose, result*) pour; **I did it ~ help you** je l'ai fait pour vous aider

5 (*equivalent to relative clause*): **I have things ~ do** j'ai des choses à faire; **the main thing is ~ try** l'important est d'essayer

6 (*after adjective etc*): **ready ~ go** prêt(e) à partir; **too old/young ~ ...** trop vieux/jeune pour ...

♦ *adv*: **push/pull the door ~** tirez/ poussez la porte

---

toad [təʊd] *n* crapaud *m*

toadstool *n* champignon (vénéneux)

toast [təʊst] *n* (*CULIN*) pain grillé, toast *m*; (*drink, speech*) toast ♦ *vt* (*CULIN*) faire griller; (*drink to*) porter un toast à; **~er** *n* grille-pain *m inv*

tobacco [tə'bækəʊ] *n* tabac *m*; **~nist** [tə'bækənɪst] *n* marchand(e) de tabac; **~nist's (shop)** *n* (bureau *m* de) tabac *m*

toboggan [tə'bɒgən] *n* toboggan *m*; (*child's*) luge *f*

today [tə'deɪ] *adv* (*also fig*) aujourd'hui ♦ *n* aujourd'hui *m*

toddler ['tɒdlə*] *n* enfant *m/f* qui commence à marcher, bambin *m*

to-do [tə'du:] *n* (*fuss*) histoire *f*, affaire *f*

toe [təʊ] *n* doigt *m* de pied, orteil *m*; (*of shoe*) bout *m* ♦ *vt*: **to ~ the line** (*fig*) obéir, se conformer; **~nail** *n* ongle *m* du pied

toffee ['tɒfɪ] *n* caramel *m*; **~ apple** (*BRIT*) *n* pomme caramélisée

toga ['təʊgə] *n* toge *f*

together [tə'geðə*] *adv* ensemble; (*at same time*) en même temps; **~ with** avec

toil [tɔɪl] *n* dur travail, labeur *m* ♦ *vi* peiner

toilet ['tɔɪlət] *n* (*BRIT: lavatory*) toilettes *fpl* ♦ *cpd* (*accessories etc*) de toilette; **~ paper** *n* papier *m* hygiénique; **~ries** ['tɔɪlətrɪz] *npl* articles *mpl* de toilette; **~ roll** *n* rouleau *m* de papier hygiénique; **~ water** *n* eau *f* de toilette

token ['təʊkən] *n* (*sign*) marque *f*, témoignage *m*; (*metal disc*) jeton *m* ♦ *adj* (*strike, payment etc*) symbolique; **book/record ~** (*BRIT*) chèque-livre/ -disque *m*; **gift ~** bon-cadeau *m*

told [təʊld] *pt, pp of* **tell**

tolerable ['tɒlərəbl] *adj* (*bearable*) tolérable; (*fairly good*) passable

tolerant ['tɒlərnt] *adj*: **~ (of)** tolérant(e) (à l'égard de)

tolerate ['tɒləreɪt] *vt* supporter, tolérer

toll [təʊl] *n* (*tax, charge*) péage *m* ♦ *vi* (*bell*) sonner; **the accident ~ on the roads** le nombre des victimes de la route

tomato [tə'mɑ:təʊ] (*pl* **~es**) *n* tomate *f*

tomb [tu:m] *n* tombe *f*

tomboy ['tɒmbɔɪ] *n* garçon manqué

tombstone → *touch*

262

ENGLISH–FRENCH

tombstone ['tuːmstəun] *n* pierre tombale

tomcat ['tɒmkæt] *n* matou *m*

tomorrow [tə'mɒrəu] *adv* (*also fig*) demain ♦ *n* demain *m*; **the day after ~** après-demain; **~ morning** demain matin

ton [tʌn] *n* tonne *f* (*BRIT* = 1016kg; *US* = 907kg); (*metric*) tonne (= 1000 kg); **~s** of (*inf*) des tas de

tone [təun] *n* ton *m* ♦ *vi* (*also*: **~ in**) s'harmoniser; **~ down** *vt* (*colour, criticism*) adoucir; (*sound*) baisser; **~ up** *vt* (*muscles*) tonifier; **~-deaf** *adj* qui n'a pas d'oreille

tongs [tɒŋz] *npl* (*for coal*) pincettes *fpl*; (*for hair*) fer *m* à friser

tongue [tʌŋ] *n* langue *f*; **~ in cheek** ironiquement; **~-tied** *adj* (*fig*) muet(te); **~ twister** *n* phrase *f* très difficile à prononcer

tonic ['tɒnɪk] *n* (*MED*) tonique *m*; (*also*: **~ water**) tonic *m*, Schweppes *m* (®)

tonight [tə'naɪt] *adv, n* cette nuit; (*this evening*) ce soir

tonsil ['tɒnsl] *n* amygdale *f*; **~litis** [tɒnsɪ'laɪtɪs] *n* angine *f*

too [tuː] *adv* (*excessively*) trop; (*also*) aussi; **~ much** *adv* trop de ♦ *adj* trop; **~ many** trop de; **~ bad!** tant pis!

took [tuk] *pt of* **take**

tool [tuːl] *n* outil *m*; **~ box** *n* boîte *f* à outils

toot [tuːt] *n* (*of car horn*) coup *m* de klaxon; (*of whistle*) coup de sifflet ♦ *vi* (*with car horn*) klaxonner

tooth [tuːθ] (*pl* **teeth**) *n* (*ANAT, TECH*) dent *f*; **~ache** *n* mal *m* de dents; **~brush** *n* brosse *f* à dents; **~paste** *n* (pâte *f*) dentifrice *m*; **~pick** *n* cure-dent *m*

top [tɒp] *n* (*of mountain, head*) sommet *m*; (*of page, ladder, garment*) haut *m*; (*of box, cupboard, table*) dessus *m*; (*lid: of box, jar*) couvercle *m*; (: *of bottle*) bouchon *m*; (*toy*) toupie *f* ♦ *adj* du haut; (*in rank*) premier(ère); (*best*) meilleur(e) ♦ *vt* (*exceed*) dépasser; (*be first in*) être en tête de; **on ~ of** sur; (*in addition to*) en plus de; **from ~ to bottom** de fond en comble; **~ up** (*US* **~ off**) *vt* (*bottle*)

remplir; (*salary*) compléter; **~ floor** *n* dernier étage; **~ hat** *n* haut-de-forme *m*; **~-heavy** *adj* (*object*) trop lourd(e) du haut

topic ['tɒpɪk] *n* sujet *m*, thème *m*; **~al** *adj* d'actualité

top: **~less** ['tɒpləs] *adj* (*bather etc*) aux seins nus; **~-level** ['tɒp'levl] *adj* (*talks*) au plus haut niveau; **~most** ['tɒpməust] *adj* le(la) plus haut(e)

topple ['tɒpl] *vt* renverser, faire tomber ♦ *vi* basculer; tomber

top-secret ['tɒp'siːkrət] *adj* top secret(ète)

topsy-turvy ['tɒpsɪ'tɜːvɪ] *adj, adv* sens dessus dessous

torch [tɔːtʃ] *n* torche *f*; (*BRIT: electric*) lampe *f* de poche

tore [tɔː*] *pt of* **tear**[1]

torment [*n* 'tɔːment, *vb* tɔː'ment] *n* tourment *m* ♦ *vt* tourmenter; (*fig: annoy*) harceler

torn [tɔːn] *pp of* **tear**[1]

tornado [tɔː'neɪdəu] (*pl* **~es**) *n* tornade *f*

torpedo [tɔː'piːdəu] (*pl* **~es**) *n* torpille *f*

torrent ['tɒrənt] *n* torrent *m*

tortoise ['tɔːtəs] *n* tortue *f*; **~shell** *adj* en écaille

torture ['tɔːtʃə*] *n* torture *f* ♦ *vt* torturer

Tory ['tɔːrɪ] (*BRIT POL*) *adj* tory, conservateur(trice) ♦ *n* tory *m/f*, conservateur(trice)

toss [tɒs] *vt* lancer, jeter; (*pancake*) faire sauter; (*head*) rejeter en arrière; **to ~ a coin** jouer à pile ou face; **to ~ up for sth** jouer qch à pile ou face; **to ~ and turn** (*in bed*) se tourner et se retourner

tot [tɒt] *n* (*BRIT: drink*) petit verre; (*child*) bambin *m*

total ['təutl] *adj* total(e) ♦ *n* total *m* ♦ *vt* (*add up*) faire le total de, additionner; (*amount to*) s'élever à; **~ly** ['təutəlɪ] *adv* totalement

totter ['tɒtə*] *vi* chanceler

touch [tʌtʃ] *n* contact *m*, toucher *m*; (*sense, also skill: of pianist etc*) toucher ♦ *vt* toucher; (*tamper with*) toucher à; **a ~ of** (*fig*) un petit peu de; une touche de;

to get in ~ with prendre contact avec; **to lose ~** (friends) se perdre de vue; **~ on** vt fus (topic) effleurer, aborder; **~ up** vt (paint) retoucher; **~-and-go** adj incertain(e); **~down** n atterrissage m; (on sea) amerrissage m; (US: FOOTBALL) touché-en-but m; **~ed** adj (moved) touché(e); **~ing** adj touchant(e), attendrissant(e); **~line** n (SPORT) (ligne f de) touche f; **~y** adj (person) susceptible

tough [tʌf] adj dur(e); (resistant) résistant(e), solide; (meat) dur, coriace; (firm) inflexible; (task) dur, pénible; **~en** vt (character) endurcir; (glass etc) renforcer

toupee ['tuːpeɪ] n postiche m

tour ['tʊə*] n voyage m; (also: package ~) voyage organisé; (of town, museum) tour m, visite f; (by artist) tournée f ♦ vt visiter

tourism ['tʊərɪzm] n tourisme m

tourist ['tʊərɪst] n touriste m/f ♦ cpd touristique; **~ office** n syndicat m d'initiative

tournament ['tʊənəmənt] n tournoi m

tousled ['taʊzld] adj (hair) ébouriffé(e)

tout [taut] vi: **to ~ for** essayer de raccrocher, racoler (also: ticket ~) revendeur m de billets

tow [təu] vt remorquer; (caravan, trailer) tracter; **"on** (BRIT) **or in** (US) **~"** (AUT) "véhicule en remorque"

toward(s) [tə'wɔːd(z)] prep vers; (of attitude) envers, à l'égard de; (of purpose) pour

towel ['tauəl] n serviette f (de toilette); **~ling** n (fabric) tissu éponge m; **~ rail** (US **~ rack**) n porte-serviettes m inv

tower ['tauə*] n tour f; **~ block** (BRIT) n tour f (d'habitation); **~ing** adj très haut(e), imposant(e)

town [taun] n ville f; **to go to ~** aller en ville; (fig) y mettre le paquet; **~ centre** n centre m de la ville, centre-ville m; **~ council** n conseil municipal; **~ hall** n ≈ mairie f; **~ plan** n plan m de ville; **~ planning** n urbanisme m

towrope ['təurəup] n (câble m de) remorque f

tow truck (US) n dépanneuse f

toy [tɔɪ] n jouet m; **~ with** vt fus jouer avec; (idea) caresser

trace [treɪs] n trace f ♦ vt (draw) tracer, dessiner; (follow) suivre la trace de; (locate) retrouver; **tracing paper** n papier-calque m

track [træk] n (mark) trace f; (path: gen) chemin m, piste f; (: of bullet etc) trajectoire f; (: of suspect, animal) piste f; (RAIL) voie ferrée, rails mpl; (on tape, SPORT) piste f; (on record) plage f ♦ vt suivre la trace or la piste de; **to keep ~ of** suivre; **~ down** vt (prey) trouver et capturer; (sth lost) finir par retrouver; **~suit** n survêtement m

tract [trækt] n (GEO) étendue f, zone f; (pamphlet) tract m

traction ['trækʃən] n traction f; (MED): **in ~** en extension

tractor ['træktə*] n tracteur m

trade [treɪd] n commerce m; (skill, job) métier m ♦ vi faire du commerce ♦ vt (exchange): **to ~ sth (for sth)** échanger qch (contre qch); **~ in** vt (old car etc) faire reprendre; **~ fair** n foire(-exposition) commerciale; **~-in price** n prix m à la reprise; **~mark** n marque f de fabrique; **~ name** n nom m de marque; **~r** n commerçant(e), négociant(e); **~sman** (irreg) n (shopkeeper) commerçant; **~ union** n syndicat m; **~ unionist** n syndicaliste m/f

tradition [trə'dɪʃən] n tradition f; **~al** adj traditionnel(le)

traffic ['træfɪk] n trafic m; (cars) circulation f ♦ vi: **to ~ in** (pej: liquor, drugs) faire le trafic de; **~ circle** (US) n rond-point m; **~ jam** n embouteillage m; **~ lights** npl feux mpl (de signalisation); **~ warden** n contractuel(le)

tragedy ['trædʒədɪ] n tragédie f

tragic ['trædʒɪk] adj tragique

trail [treɪl] n (tracks) trace f, piste f; (path) chemin m, piste f; (of smoke etc) traînée f ♦ vt traîner, tirer; (follow) suivre ♦ vi traîner; (in game, contest) être en retard; **~ behind** vi traîner, être à la traîne; **~er** n (AUT) remorque f; (US) caravane f; (CINEMA) bande-annonce f; **~er**

truck (US) *n* (camion *m*) semi-remorque *m*

train [treɪn] *n* train *m*; (*in underground*) rame *f*; (*of dress*) traîne *f* ♦ *vt* (*apprentice, doctor etc*) former; (*sportsman*) entraîner; (*dog*) dresser; (*memory*) exercer; (*point: gun etc*): **to ~ sth on** braquer qch sur ♦ *vi* suivre un formation; (*SPORT*) s'entraîner; **one's ~ of thought** le fil de sa pensée; **~ed** *adj* qualifié(e), qui a reçu une formation; (*animal*) dressé(e); **~ee** [treɪ'niː] *n* stagiaire *m/f*; (*in trade*) apprenti(e); **~er** *n* (*SPORT: coach*) entraîneur(euse); (: *shoe*) chaussure *f* de sport; (*of dogs etc*) dresseur(euse); **~ing** *n* formation *f*; entraînement *m*; **in ~ing** (*SPORT*) à l'entraînement; (*fit*) en forme; **~ing college** *n* école professionnelle; (*for teachers*) ≈ école normale; **~ing shoes** *npl* chaussures *fpl* de sport

traipse [treɪps] *vi*: **to ~ in/out** entrer/sortir d'un pas traînant

trait [treɪ(t)] *n* trait *m* (de caractère)

traitor ['treɪtə*] *n* traître *m*

tram ['træm] (BRIT) *n* (*also*: *~car*) tram(way) *m*

tramp [træmp] *n* (*person*) vagabond(e), clochard(e); (*inf: pej: woman*): **to be a ~** être coureuse ♦ *vi* marcher d'un pas lourd

trample ['træmpl] *vt*: **to ~ (underfoot)** piétiner

trampoline ['træmpəliːn] *n* trampoline *m*

tranquil ['træŋkwɪl] *adj* tranquille; **~lizer** (US **~izer**) *n* (MED) tranquillisant *m*

transact [træn'zækt] *vt* (*business*) traiter; **~ion** *n* transaction *f*

transatlantic ['trænzət'læntɪk] *adj* transatlantique

transfer [*n* 'trænsfə*, *vt* træns'fɜː*] *n* (*gen, also SPORT*) transfert *m*; (POL: *of power*) passation *f*; (*picture, design*) décalcomanie *f*; (: *stick-on*) autocollant *m* ♦ *vt* transférer; passer; **to ~ the charges** (BRIT: TEL) téléphoner en P.C.V.

transform [træns'fɔːm] *vt* transformer

transfusion [træns'fjuːʒən] *n* transfusion *f*

transient ['trænzɪənt] *adj* transitoire, éphémère

transistor [træn'zɪstə*] *n* (ELEC, *also*: *~ radio*) transistor *m*

transit ['trænzɪt] *n*: **in ~** en transit

transitive ['trænzɪtɪv] *adj* (LING) transitif(ive)

transit lounge *n* salle *f* de transit

translate [trænz'leɪt] *vt* traduire; **translation** [trænz'leɪʃən] *n* traduction *f*; **translator** [trænz'leɪtə*] *n* traducteur(trice)

transmission [trænz'mɪʃən] *n* transmission *f*

transmit [trænz'mɪt] *vt* transmettre; (RADIO, TV) émettre

transparency [træns'pærənsɪ] *n* (*of glass etc*) transparence *f*; (BRIT: PHOT) diapositive *f*; **transparent** [træns'pærənt] *adj* transparent(e)

transpire [træns'paɪə*] *vi* (*turn out*): **it ~d that ...** on a appris que ...; (*happen*) arriver

transplant [*vb* træns'plɑːnt, *n* 'trænsplɑːnt] *vt* transplanter; (*seedlings*) repiquer ♦ *n* (MED) transplantation *f*

transport [*n* 'trænspɔːt, *vb* træns'pɔːt] *n* transport *m*; (*car*) moyen *m* de transport, voiture *f* ♦ *vt* transporter; **~ation** [trænspɔː'teɪʃən] *n* transport *m*; (*means of ~*) moyen *m* de transport; **~ café** (BRIT) *n* ≈ restaurant *m* de routiers

trap [træp] *n* (*snare, trick*) piège *m*; (*carriage*) cabriolet *m* ♦ *vt* prendre au piège; (*confine*) coincer; **~ door** *n* trappe *f*

trapeze [trə'piːz] *n* trapèze *m*

trappings ['træpɪŋz] *npl* ornements *mpl*; attributs *mpl*

trash [træʃ] (*pej*) *n* (*goods*) camelote *f*; (*nonsense*) sottises *fpl*; **~ can** (US) *n* poubelle *f*

trauma ['trɔːmə] *n* traumatisme *m*; **~tic** [trɔː'mætɪk] *adj* traumatisant(e)

travel ['trævl] *n* voyage(s) *m(pl)* ♦ *vi* voyager; (*news, sound*) circuler, se propager ♦ *vt* (*distance*) parcourir; **~ agency** *n* agence *f* de voyages; **~ agent**

n agent *m* de voyages; ~ler (*US* ~er) *n* voyageur(euse); ~ler's cheque (*US* ~er's check) *n* chèque *m* de voyage; ~ling (*US* ~ing) *n* voyage(s) *m(pl)*; ~ sickness *n* mal *m* de la route (*or* de mer *or* de l'air)

travesty ['trævəstɪ] *n* parodie *f*

trawler ['trɔːlə*] *n* chalutier *m*

tray [treɪ] *n* (*for carrying*) plateau *m*; (*on desk*) corbeille *f*

treacherous *adj* (*person, look*) traître(esse); (*ground, tide*) dont il faut se méfier

treachery ['tretʃərɪ] *n* traîtrise *f*

treacle ['triːkl] *n* mélasse *f*

tread [tred] (*pt* **trod**, *pp* **trodden**) *n* pas *m*; (*sound*) bruit *m* de pas; (*of tyre*) chape *f*, bande *f* de roulement ♦ *vi* marcher; ~ on *vt fus* marcher sur

treason ['triːzn] *n* trahison *f*

treasure ['treʒə*] *n* trésor *m* ♦ *vt* (*value*) tenir beaucoup à

treasurer ['treʒərə*] *n* trésorier(ère)

treasury ['treʒərɪ] *n*: **the T~**, (*US*) **the T~ Department** le ministère des Finances

treat [triːt] *n* petit cadeau, petite surprise ♦ *vt* traiter; **to ~ sb to sth** offrir qch à qn

treatment ['triːtmənt] *n* traitement *m*

treaty ['triːtɪ] *n* traité *m*

treble ['trebl] *adj* triple ♦ *vt, vi* tripler; ~ **clef** *n* (*MUS*) clé *f* de sol

tree [triː] *n* arbre *m*

trek [trek] *n* (*long*) voyage *m*; (*on foot*) (longue) marche, tirée *f*

tremble ['trembl] *vi* trembler

tremendous [trə'mendəs] *adj* (*enormous*) énorme, fantastique; (*excellent*) formidable

tremor ['tremə*] *n* tremblement *m*; (*also*: *earth* ~) secousse *f* sismique

trench [trentʃ] *n* tranchée *f*

trend [trend] *n* (*tendency*) tendance *f*; (*of events*) cours *m*; (*fashion*) mode *f*; ~**y** *adj* (*idea, person*) dans le vent; (*clothes*) dernier cri *inv*

trepidation [trepɪ'deɪʃən] *n* vive agitation *or* inquiétude *f*

trespass ['trespəs] *vi*: **to ~ on** s'introduire sans permission dans; **"no ~ing"**

"propriété privée", "défense d'entrer"

trestle ['tresl] *n* tréteau *m*

trial ['traɪəl] *n* (*LAW*) procès *m*, jugement *m*; (*test: of machine etc*) essai *m*; ~s *npl* (*unpleasant experiences*) épreuves *fpl*; **to be on ~** (*LAW*) passer en jugement; **by ~ and error** par tâtonnements; ~ **period** *n* période *f* d'essai

triangle ['traɪæŋgl] *n* (*MATH, MUS*) triangle *m*

tribe [traɪb] *n* tribu *f*; ~**sman** (*irreg*) *n* membre *m* d'une tribu

tribunal [traɪ'bjuːnl] *n* tribunal *m*

tributary ['trɪbjutərɪ] *n* (*river*) affluent *m*

tribute ['trɪbjuːt] *n* tribut *m*, hommage *m*; **to pay ~ to** rendre hommage à

trice [traɪs] *n*: **in a ~** en un clin d'œil

trick [trɪk] *n* (*magic ~*) tour *m*; (*joke, prank*) tour, farce *f*; (*skill, knack*) astuce *f*, truc *m*; (*CARDS*) levée *f* ♦ *vt* attraper, rouler; **to play a ~ on sb** jouer un tour à qn; **that should do the ~** ça devrait faire l'affaire; ~**ery** *n* ruse *f*

trickle ['trɪkl] *n* (*of water etc*) filet *m* ♦ *vi* couler en un filet *or* goutte à goutte

tricky ['trɪkɪ] *adj* difficile, délicat(e)

tricycle ['traɪsɪkl] *n* tricycle *m*

trifle ['traɪfl] *n* bagatelle *f*; (*CULIN*) ≈ diplomate *m* ♦ *adv*: **a ~ long** un peu long

trifling ['traɪflɪŋ] *adj* insignifiant(e)

trigger ['trɪgə*] *n* (*of gun*) gâchette *f*; ~ **off** *vt* déclencher

trim [trɪm] *adj* (*house, garden*) bien tenu(e); (*figure*) svelte ♦ *n* (*haircut etc*) légère coupe; (*on car*) garnitures *fpl* ♦ *vt* (*cut*) couper légèrement; (*NAUT*: *a sail*) gréer; (*decorate*): **to ~ (with)** décorer (de); ~**mings** *npl* (*CULIN*) garniture *f*

trinket ['trɪŋkɪt] *n* bibelot *m*; (*piece of jewellery*) colifichet *m*

trip [trɪp] *n* voyage *m*; (*excursion*) excursion *f*; (*stumble*) faux pas ♦ *vi* faire un faux pas, trébucher; (*go lightly*) marcher d'un pas léger; **on a ~** en voyage; ~ **up** *vi* trébucher ♦ *vt* faire un croc-en-jambe à

tripe [traɪp] *n* (*CULIN*) tripes *fpl*; (*pej*: *rubbish*) idioties *fpl*

triple ['trɪpl] *adj* triple

triplets ['trɪplɪts] *npl* triplés(ées)

triplicate ['trɪplɪkɪt] *n*: **in** ~ en trois exemplaires

tripod ['traɪpɒd] *n* trépied *m*

trite [traɪt] (*pej*) *adj* banal(e)

triumph ['traɪʌmf] *n* triomphe *m* ♦ *vi*: **to** ~ **(over)** triompher (de)

trivia ['trɪvɪə] (*pej*) *npl* futilités *fpl*

trivial ['trɪvɪəl] *adj* insignifiant(e); (*commonplace*) banal(e)

trod [trɒd] *pt of* **tread**

trodden ['trɒdn] *pp of* **tread**

trolley ['trɒlɪ] *n* chariot *m*

trombone [trɒm'bəʊn] *n* trombone *m*

troop [tru:p] *n* bande *f*, groupe *m* ♦ *vi*: ~ **in/out** entrer/sortir en groupe; ~**s** *npl* (*MIL*) troupes *fpl*; (: *men*) hommes *mpl*, soldats *mpl*; ~**ing the colour** (*BRIT*) *n* (*ceremony*) le salut au drapeau

trophy ['trəʊfɪ] *n* trophée *m*

tropic ['trɒpɪk] *n* tropique *m*; ~**al** *adj* tropical(e)

trot [trɒt] *n* trot *m* ♦ *vi* trotter; **on the** ~ (*BRIT*: *fig*) d'affilée

trouble ['trʌbl] *n* difficulté(s) *f(pl)*, problème(s) *m(pl)*; (*worry*) ennuis *mpl*, soucis *mpl*; (*bother*, *effort*) peine *f*; (*POL*) troubles *mpl*; (*MED*): **stomach** *etc* ~ troubles gastriques *etc* ♦ *vt* (*disturb*) déranger, gêner; (*worry*) inquiéter ♦ *vi*: **to** ~ **to do** prendre la peine de faire; ~**s** *npl* (*POL etc*) troubles *mpl*; (*personal*) ennuis, soucis; **to be in** ~ avoir des ennuis; (*ship*, *climber etc*) être en difficulté; **what's the** ~? qu'est-ce qui ne va pas?; ~**d** *adj* (*person*) inquiet(ète); (*epoch*, *life*) agitée(e); ~**maker** *n* élément perturbateur, fauteur *m* de troubles; ~**shooter** *n* (*in conflict*) médiateur *m*; ~**some** *adj* (*child*) fatigant(e), difficile; (*cough etc*) gênant(e)

trough [trɒf] *n* (*also*: *drinking* ~) abreuvoir *m*; (: *feeding* ~) auge *f*; (*depression*) creux *m*

trousers ['traʊzəz] *npl* pantalon *m*; **short** ~ culottes courtes

trout [traʊt] *n inv* truite *f*

trowel ['traʊəl] *n* truelle *f*; (*garden tool*) déplantoir *m*

truant ['trʊənt] (*BRIT*) *n*: **to play** ~ faire l'école buissonnière

truce [tru:s] *n* trêve *f*

truck [trʌk] *n* camion *m*; (*RAIL*) wagon *m* à plate-forme; ~ **driver** *n* camionneur *m*; ~ **farm** (*US*) *n* jardin maraîcher

trudge [trʌdʒ] *vi* marcher lourdement, se traîner

true [tru:] *adj* vrai(e); (*accurate*) exact(e); (*genuine*) vrai, véritable; (*faithful*) fidèle; **to come** ~ se réaliser

truffle ['trʌfl] *n* truffe *f*

truly ['tru:lɪ] *adv* vraiment, réellement; (*truthfully*) sans mentir; *see also* **yours**

trump [trʌmp] *n* (*also*: ~ *card*) atout *m*; ~**ed up** *adj* inventé(e) (de toutes pièces)

trumpet ['trʌmpɪt] *n* trompette *f*

truncheon ['trʌntʃən] (*BRIT*) *n* bâton *m* (d'agent de police); matraque *f*

trundle ['trʌndl] *vt*, *vi*: **to** ~ **along** rouler lentement (et bruyamment)

trunk [trʌŋk] *n* (*of tree*, *person*) tronc *m*; (*of elephant*) trompe *f*; (*case*) malle *f*; (*US*: *AUT*) coffre *m*; ~**s** *npl* (*also*: *swimming* ~**s**) maillot *m* or slip *m* de bain

truss [trʌs] *n* (*MED*) bandage *m* herniaire ♦ *vt*: **to** ~ **(up)** (*CULIN*) brider, trousser

trust [trʌst] *n* confiance *f*; (*responsibility*) charge *f*; (*LAW*) fidéicommis *m* ♦ *vt* (*rely on*) avoir confiance en; (*hope*) espérer; (*entrust*): **to** ~ **sth to sb** confier qch à qn; **to take sth on** ~ accepter qch les yeux fermés; ~**ed** *adj* en qui l'on a confiance; ~**ee** *n* (*LAW*) fidéicommissaire *m/f*; (*of school etc*) administrateur(trice); ~**ful**, ~**ing** *adj* confiant(e); ~**worthy** *adj* digne de confiance

truth [tru:θ, *pl* tru:ðz] *n* vérité *f*; ~**ful** *adj* (*person*) qui dit la vérité; (*answer*) sincère

try [traɪ] *n* essai *m*, tentative *f*; (*RUGBY*) essai ♦ *vt* (*attempt*) essayer, tenter; (*test*: *sth new*: *also*: ~ *out*) essayer, tester; (*LAW*: *person*) juger; (*strain*) éprouver ♦ *vi* essayer; **to have a** ~ essayer; **to do** essayer de faire; (*seek*) chercher à faire; ~ **on** *vt* (*clothes*) essayer; ~**ing** *adj* pénible

T-shirt ['tiːʃɜːt] *n* tee-shirt *m*
T-square ['tiːskwɛə*] *n* équerre *f* en T, té *m*
tub [tʌb] *n* cuve *f*; (*for washing clothes*) baquet *m*; (*bath*) baignoire *f*
tubby ['tʌbɪ] *adj* rondelet(te)
tube [tjuːb] *n* tube *m*; (BRIT: *underground*) métro *m*; (*for tyre*) chambre *f* à air
TUC *n abbr* (BRIT: = *Trades Union Congress*) confédération *f* des syndicats britanniques
tuck [tʌk] *vt* (*put*) mettre; ~ **away** *vt* cacher, ranger; ~ **in** *vt* rentrer; (*child*) border ♦ *vi* (*eat*) manger (de bon appétit); ~ **up** *vt* (*child*) border; ~ **shop** (BRIT) *n* boutique *f* à provisions (*dans une école*)
Tuesday ['tjuːzdeɪ] *n* mardi *m*
tuft [tʌft] *n* touffe *f*
tug [tʌg] *n* (*ship*) remorqueur *m* ♦ *vt* tirer (sur); ~-**of-war** *n* lutte *f* à la corde; (*fig*) lutte acharnée
tuition [tjuːˈɪʃən] *n* (BRIT) leçons *fpl*; (: *private* ~) cours particuliers; (US: *school fees*) frais *mpl* de scolarité
tulip ['tjuːlɪp] *n* tulipe *f*
tumble ['tʌmbl] *n* (*fall*) chute *f*, culbute *f* ♦ *vi* tomber, dégringoler; **to** ~ **to sth** (*inf*) réaliser qch; ~**down** *adj* délabré(e); ~ **dryer** (BRIT) *n* séchoir *m* à air chaud
tumbler ['tʌmblə*] *n* (*glass*) verre (droit), gobelet *m*
tummy ['tʌmɪ] (*inf*) *n* ventre *m*
tumour ['tjuːmə*] (US **tumor**) *n* tumeur *f*
tuna ['tjuːnə] *n inv* (*also:* ~ *fish*) thon *m*
tune [tjuːn] *n* (*melody*) air *m* ♦ *vt* (MUS) accorder; (RADIO, TV, AUT) régler; **to be in/out of** ~ (*instrument*) être accordé/désaccordé; (*singer*) chanter juste/faux; **to be in/out of** ~ **with** (*fig*) être en accord/désaccord avec; ~ **in** *vi* (RADIO, TV): **to** ~ **in (to)** se mettre à l'écoute (de); ~ **up** *vi* (*musician*) accorder son instrument; ~**ful** *adj* mélodieux(euse); ~**r** *n*: **piano** ~**r** accordeur *m* (de pianos)
tunic ['tjuːnɪk] *n* tunique *f*
Tunisia [tjuːˈnɪzɪə] *n* Tunisie *f*
tunnel ['tʌnl] *n* tunnel *m*; (*in mine*) galerie *f* ♦ *vi* percer un tunnel

turbulence ['tɜːbjʊləns] *n* (AVIAT) turbulence *f*
tureen [tjʊˈriːn] *n* (*for soup*) soupière *f*; (*for vegetables*) légumier *m*
turf [tɜːf] *n* gazon *m*; (*clod*) motte *f* (de gazon) ♦ *vt* gazonner; ~ **out** (*inf*) *vt* (*person*) jeter dehors
turgid ['tɜːdʒɪd] *adj* (*speech*) pompeux(euse)
Turk [tɜːk] *n* Turc(Turque) *m(f)*
Turkey ['tɜːkɪ] *n* Turquie *f*
turkey ['tɜːkɪ] *n* dindon *m*, dinde *f*
Turkish ['tɜːkɪʃ] *adj* turc(turque) ♦ *n* (LING) turc *m*
turmoil ['tɜːmɔɪl] *n* trouble *m*, bouleversement *m*; **in** ~ en émoi, en effervescence
turn [tɜːn] *n* tour *m*; (*in road*) tournant *m*; (*of mind, events*) tournure *f*; (*performance*) numéro *m*; (MED) crise *f*, attaque *f* ♦ *vt* tourner; (*collar, steak*) retourner; (*change*): **to** ~ **sth into** changer qch en ♦ *vi* (*object, wind, milk*) tourner; (*person: look back*) se (re)tourner; (*reverse direction*) faire demi-tour; (*become*) devenir; (*age*) atteindre; **to** ~ **into** se changer en; **a good** ~ un service; **it gave me quite a** ~ ça m'a fait un coup; **"no left** ~" (AUT) "défense de tourner à gauche"; **it's your** ~ c'est (à) votre tour; **in** ~ à son tour; à tour de rôle; **to take** ~**s (at)** se relayer (pour *or* à); ~ **away** *vi* se détourner ♦ *vt* (*applicants*) refuser; ~ **back** *vi* revenir, faire demi-tour ♦ *vt* (*person, vehicle*) faire faire demi-tour à; (*clock*) reculer; ~ **down** *vt* (*refuse*) rejeter, refuser; (*reduce*) baisser; (*fold*) rabattre; ~ **in** *vi* (*inf*: *go to bed*) aller se coucher ♦ *vt* (*fold*) rentrer; ~ **off** *vi* (*from road*) tourner ♦ *vt* (*light, radio etc*) éteindre; (*tap*) fermer; (*engine*) arrêter; ~ **on** *vt* (*light, radio etc*) allumer; (*tap*) ouvrir; (*engine*) mettre en marche; ~ **out** *vt* (*light, gas*) éteindre; (*produce*) produire ♦ *vi* (*voters, troops etc*) se présenter; **to** ~ **out to be ...** s'avérer ..., se révéler ...; ~ **over** *vi* (*person*) se retourner ♦ *vt* (*object*) retourner; (*page*) tourner; ~ **round** *vi* faire demi-tour; (*rotate*)

tourner; **~ up** *vi* (*person*) arriver, se pointer (*inf*); (*lost object*) être retrouvé(e) ♦ *vt* (*collar*) remonter; (*radio*, *heater*) mettre plus fort; **~ing** *n* (*in road*) tournant *m*; **~ing point** *n* (*fig*) tournant *m*, moment décisif

turnip ['tɜːnɪp] *n* navet *m*

turnout ['tɜːnaʊt] *n* (*of voters*) taux *m* de participation

turnover ['tɜːnəʊvə*] *n* (COMM: *amount of money*) chiffre *m* d'affaires; (: *of goods*) roulement *m*; (*of staff*) renouvellement *m*, changement *m*

turnpike ['tɜːnpaɪk] (US) *n* autoroute *f* à péage

turnstile ['tɜːnstaɪl] *n* tourniquet *m* (*d'entrée*)

turntable ['tɜːnteɪbl] *n* (*on record player*) platine *f*

turn-up ['tɜːnʌp] (BRIT) *n* (*on trousers*) revers *m*

turpentine ['tɜːpəntaɪn] *n* (*also*: *turps*) (*essence f de*) térébenthine *f*

turquoise ['tɜːkwɔɪz] *n* (*stone*) turquoise *f* ♦ *adj* turquoise *inv*

turret ['tʌrɪt] *n* tourelle *f*

turtle ['tɜːtl] *n* tortue marine *or* d'eau douce; **~neck (sweater)** *n* (BRIT) pullover *m* à col montant; (US) pullover à col roulé

tusk [tʌsk] *n* défense *f*

tussle ['tʌsl] *n* bagarre *f*, mêlée *f*

tutor ['tjuːtə*] *n* (*in college*) directeur(trice) d'études; (*private teacher*) précepteur(trice); **~ial** [tjuːˈtɔːrɪəl] *n* (SCOL) (séance *f* de) travaux *mpl* pratiques

tuxedo [tʌkˈsiːdəʊ] (US) *n* smoking *m*

TV ['tiːˈviː] *n abbr* (= *television*) télé *f*

twang [twæŋ] *n* (*of instrument*) son vibrant; (*of voice*) ton nasillard

tweed [twiːd] *n* tweed *m*

tweezers ['twiːzəz] *npl* pince *f* à épiler

twelfth [twelfθ] *num* douzième

twelve [twelv] *num* douze; **at ~ (o'clock)** à midi; (*midnight*) à minuit

twentieth ['twentɪθ] *num* vingtième

twenty ['twentɪ] *num* vingt

twice [twaɪs] *adv* deux fois; **~ as much** deux fois plus

twiddle ['twɪdl] *vt, vi*: **to ~ (with) sth** tripoter qch; **to ~ one's thumbs** (*fig*) se tourner les pouces

twig [twɪg] *n* brindille *f* ♦ *vi* (*inf*) piger

twilight ['twaɪlaɪt] *n* crépuscule *m*

twin [twɪn] *adj, n* jumeau(elle) ♦ *vt* jumeler; **~(-bedded) room** *n* chambre *f* à deux lits

twine [twaɪn] *n* ficelle *f* ♦ *vi* (*plant*) s'enrouler

twinge [twɪndʒ] *n* (*of pain*) élancement *m*; **a ~ of conscience** un certain remords; **a ~ of regret** un pincement au cœur

twinkle ['twɪŋkl] *vi* scintiller; (*eyes*) pétiller

twirl [twɜːl] *vt* faire tournoyer ♦ *vi* tournoyer

twist [twɪst] *n* torsion *f*, tour *m*; (*in road*) virage *m*; (*in wire, flex*) tortillon *m*; (*in story*) coup *m* de théâtre ♦ *vt* tordre; (*weave*) entortiller; (*roll around*) enrouler; (*fig*) déformer ♦ *vi* (*road, river*) serpenter

twit [twɪt] (*inf*) *n* crétin(e)

twitch [twɪtʃ] *n* (*pull*) coup sec, saccade *f*; (*nervous*) tic *m* ♦ *vi* se convulser; avoir un tic

two [tuː] *num* deux; **to put ~ and ~ together** (*fig*) faire le rapprochement; **~door** (AUT) *adj* à deux portes; **~-faced** (*pej*) *adj* (*person*) faux(fausse); **~fold** *adv*: **to increase ~fold** doubler; **~-piece (suit)** *n* (*man's*) costume *m* (deux pièces); (*woman's*) (tailleur *m*) deux pièces *m inv*; **~-piece (swimsuit)** *n* (maillot *m* de bain) deux-pièces *m inv*; **~some** *n* (*people*) couple *m*; **~-way** *adj*: (*traffic*) dans les deux sens

tycoon [taɪˈkuːn] *n*: **(business) ~** gros homme d'affaires

type [taɪp] *n* (*category*) type *m*, genre *m*, espèce *f*; (*model, example*) type *m*, modèle *m*; (TYP) type, caractère *m* ♦ *vt* (*letter etc*) taper (à la machine); **~-cast** *adj* (*actor*) condamné(e) à toujours jouer le même rôle; **~face** *n* (TYP) œil *m* de caractère; **~script** *n* texte dactylographié

~**writer** *n* machine *f* à écrire; ~**written** *adj* dactylographié(e)

typhoid ['taɪfɔɪd] *n* typhoïde *f*

typical ['tɪpɪkəl] *adj* typique, caractéristique

typing ['taɪpɪŋ] *n* dactylo(graphie) *f*

typist ['taɪpɪst] *n* dactylo *m/f*

tyrant ['taɪərnt] *n* tyran *m*

tyre [taɪə*] (*US* tire) *n* pneu *m*; ~ **pressure** *n* pression *f* (de gonflage)

U u

U-bend ['juːˈbend] *n* (*in pipe*) coude *m*

ubiquitous *adj* omniprésent(e)

udder ['ʌdə*] *n* pis *m*, mamelle *f*

UFO ['juːfəʊ] *n abbr* (= *unidentified flying object*) ovni *m*

Uganda [juːˈgændə] *n* Ouganda *m*

ugh [ɜːh] *excl* pouah!

ugly ['ʌglɪ] *adj* laid(e), vilain(e), (*situation*) inquiétant(e)

UK *n abbr* = **United Kingdom**

ulcer ['ʌlsə*] *n* ulcère *m*; (*also: mouth* ~) aphte *f*

Ulster ['ʌlstə*] *n* Ulster *m*; (*inf: Northern Ireland*) Irlande *f* du Nord

ulterior [ʌlˈtɪərɪə*] *adj*: ~ **motive** arrière-pensée *f*

ultimate ['ʌltɪmət] *adj* ultime, final(e); (*authority*) suprême; ~**ly** *adv* en fin de compte; finalement

ultrasound ['ʌltrəˈsaʊnd] *n* ultrason *m*

umbilical cord [ʌmˈbɪlɪkl-] *n* cordon ombilical

umbrella [ʌmˈbrelə] *n* parapluie *m*; (*for sun*) parasol *m*

umpire ['ʌmpaɪə*] *n* arbitre *m*; (*TENNIS*) juge *m* de chaise

umpteen ['ʌmptiːn] *adj* je ne sais combien de; ~**th** *adj*: **for the** ~**th time** pour la nième fois

UN *n abbr* = **United Nations**

unable ['ʌnˈeɪbl] *adj*: **to be** ~ **to** ne pas pouvoir, être dans l'impossibilité de; (*incapable*) être incapable de

unaccompanied ['ʌnəˈkʌmpənɪd] *adj* (*child, lady*) non accompagné(e); (*song*) sans accompagnement

unaccountably ['ʌnəˈkaʊntəblɪ] *adv* inexplicablement

unaccustomed ['ʌnəˈkʌstəmd] *adj*: **to be** ~ **to sth** ne pas avoir l'habitude de qch

unanimous [juːˈnænɪməs] *adj* unanime; ~**ly** *adv* à l'unanimité

unarmed [ʌnˈɑːmd] *adj* (*without a weapon*) non armé(e); (*combat*) sans armes

unashamed [ʌnəˈʃeɪmd] *adj* effronté(e), impudent(e)

unassuming [ʌnəˈsjuːmɪŋ] *adj* modeste, sans prétentions

unattached ['ʌnəˈtætʃt] *adj* libre, sans attaches; (*part*) non attaché(e), indépendant(e)

unattended ['ʌnəˈtendɪd] *adj* (*car, child, luggage*) sans surveillance

unattractive [ʌnəˈtræktɪv] *adj* peu attrayant(e); (*character*) peu sympathique

unauthorized ['ʌnˈɔːθəraɪzd] *adj* non autorisé(e), sans autorisation

unavoidable [ʌnəˈvɔɪdəbl] *adj* inévitable

unaware [ʌnəˈwɛə*] *adj*: **to be** ~ **of** ignorer, être inconscient(e) de; ~**s** *adv* à l'improviste, au dépourvu

unbalanced [ʌnˈbælənst] *adj* déséquilibré(e); (*report*) peu objectif(ive)

unbearable [ʌnˈbɛərəbl] *adj* insupportable

unbeatable [ʌnˈbiːtəbl] *adj* imbattable

unbeknown(st) ['ʌnbɪˈnəʊn(st)] *adv*: ~ **to me/Peter** à mon insu/l'insu de Peter

unbelievable [ʌnbɪˈliːvəbl] *adj* incroyable

unbend [ʌnˈbend] (*irreg*) *vi* se détendre ♦ *vt* (*wire*) redresser, détordre

unbiased [ʌnˈbaɪəst] *adj* impartial(e)

unborn [ʌnˈbɔːn] *adj* à naître, qui n'est pas encore né(e)

unbreakable ['ʌnˈbreɪkəbl] *adj* incassable

unbroken ['ʌnˈbrəʊkən] *adj* intact(e); (*fig*) continu(e), ininterrompu(e)

unbutton ['ʌnˈbʌtn] *vt* déboutonner

uncalled-for [ʌnˈkɔːldfɔː*] *adj* déplacé(e), injustifié(e)

uncanny [ʌnˈkænɪ] *adj* étrange, troublant(e)

unceasing [ʌnˈsiːsɪŋ] *adj* incessant(e), continu(e)

unceremonious [ˈʌnserɪˈməʊnɪəs] *adj* (*abrupt, rude*) brusque

uncertain [ʌnˈsɜːtn] *adj* incertain(e); (*hesitant*) hésitant(e); **in no ~ terms** sans équivoque possible; **~ty** *n* incertitude *f*, doute(s) *m(pl)*

unchecked [ˈʌntʃekt] *adv* sans contrôle *or* opposition

uncivilized [ʌnˈsɪvɪlaɪzd] *adj* (*gen*) non civilisé(e); (*fig: behaviour etc*) barbare; (*hour*) indu(e)

uncle [ˈʌŋkl] *n* oncle *m*

uncomfortable [ʌnˈkʌmfətəbl] *adj* inconfortable, peu confortable; (*uneasy*) mal à l'aise, gêné(e); (*situation*) désagréable

uncommon [ʌnˈkɒmən] *adj* rare, singulier(ère), peu commun(e)

uncompromising [ʌnˈkɒmprəmaɪzɪŋ] *adj* intransigeant(e), inflexible

unconcerned [ʌnkənˈsɜːnd] *adj*: **to be ~ (about)** ne pas s'inquiéter (de)

unconditional [ˈʌnkənˈdɪʃənl] *adj* sans conditions

unconscious [ʌnˈkɒnʃəs] *adj* sans connaissance, évanoui(e); (*unaware*): **~ of** inconscient(e) de ♦ *n*: **the ~** l'inconscient *m*; **~ly** *adv* inconsciemment

uncontrollable [ʌnkənˈtrəʊləbl] *adj* indiscipliné(e); (*temper, laughter*) irrépressible

unconventional [ʌnkənˈvenʃənl] *adj* peu conventionnel(le)

uncouth [ʌnˈkuːθ] *adj* grossier(ère), fruste

uncover [ʌnˈkʌvə*] *vt* découvrir

undecided [ˈʌndɪˈsaɪdɪd] *adj* indécis(e), irrésolu(e)

under [ˈʌndə*] *prep* sous; (*less than*) (de) moins de; au-dessous de; (*according to*) selon, en vertu de ♦ *adv* au-dessous; en dessous; **~ there** là-dessous; **~ repair** en (cours de) réparation

under: **~age** *adj* (*person*) qui n'a pas l'âge réglementaire; **~carriage** *n* (*AVIAT*)

train *m* d'atterrissage; **~charge** *vt* ne pas faire payer assez à; **~coat** *n* (*paint*) couche *f* de fond; **~cover** *adj* secret(ète), clandestin(e); **~current** *n* courant *or* sentiment sous-jacent; **~cut** *vt* (*irreg*) *vt* vendre moins cher que; **~dog** *n* opprimé *m*; **~done** *adj* (*CULIN*) saignant(e); (*pej*) pas assez cuit(e); **~estimate** *vt* sous-estimer; **~fed** *adj* sous-alimenté(e); **~foot** *adv* sous les pieds; **~go** (*irreg*) *vt* subir (*treatment*) suivre; **~graduate** *n* étudiant(e) (qui prépare la licence); **~ground** *n* (*BRIT: railway*) métro *m* (*POL*) clandestinité *f* ♦ *adj* souterrain(e) (*fig*) clandestin(e) ♦ *adv* dans la clandestinité, clandestinement; **~growth** *n* broussailles *fpl*, sous-bois *m*; **~hand(ed)** *adj* (*fig: behaviour, method etc*) en dessous; **~lie** (*irreg*) *vt* être à la base de; **~line** *vt* souligner; **~ling** (*pej*) *n* sousfifre *m*, subalterne *m*; **~mine** *vt* saper, miner; **~neath** [ʌndəˈniːθ] *adv* (en) dessous ♦ *prep* sous, au-dessous de; **~paid** *adj* sous-payé(e); **~pants** *npl* caleçon *m*, slip *m*; **~pass** (*BRIT*) *n* passage souterrain; (*on motorway*) passage inférieur; **~privileged** [ˈʌndəˈprɪvɪlɪdʒd] *adj* défavorisé(e), économiquement faible; **~rate** *vt* sous-estimer; **~shirt** (*US*) *n* tricot *m* de corps; **~shorts** (*US*) *npl* caleçon *m*, slip *m*; **~side** *n* dessous *m*; **~skirt** (*BRIT*) *n* jupon *m*

understand [ʌndəˈstænd] (*irreg: like* **stand**) *vt, vi* comprendre; **I ~ that ...** j me suis laissé dire que ...; je crois comprendre que ...; **~able** *adj* compréhensible; **~ing** *adj* compréhensif(ive) ♦ *n* compréhension *f*; (*agreement*) accord *m*

understatement [ˈʌndəsteɪtmənt] *n* **that's an ~** c'est (bien) peu dire, le terme est faible

understood [ʌndəˈstʊd] *pt, pp* of **understand** ♦ *adj* entendu(e); (*implied*) sous-entendu(e)

understudy [ˈʌndəstʌdɪ] *n* doublure *f*

undertake [ʌndəˈteɪk] (*irreg*) *vt* entreprendre; se charger de; **to ~ to do st** s'engager à faire qch

undertaker [ˈʌndəteɪkə*] *n* entrepreneu

m des pompes funèbres, croque-mort *m*

undertaking [ʌndə'teɪkɪŋ] *n* entreprise *f*; (*promise*) promesse *f*

undertone ['ʌndətəʊn] *n*: **in an ~** à mi-voix

under: ~water ['ʌndə'wɔːtə*] *adv* sous l'eau ♦ *adj* sous-marin(e); **~wear** ['ʌndəwɛə*] *n* sous-vêtements *mpl*; (*women's only*) dessous *mpl*; **~world** ['ʌndəwɜːld] *n* (*of crime*) milieu *m*, pègre *f*; **~writer** ['ʌndəraɪtə*] *n* (INSURANCE) assureur *m*

undies ['ʌndɪz] (*inf*) *npl* dessous *mpl*, lingerie *f*

undiplomatic [ʌndɪplə'mætɪk] *adj* peu diplomatique

undo ['ʌn'duː] (*irreg*) *vt* défaire; **~ing** *n* ruine *f*, perte *f*

undoubted [ʌn'daʊtɪd] *adj* indubitable, certain(e); **~ly** *adv* sans aucun doute

undress ['ʌn'dres] *vi* se déshabiller

undue ['ʌndjuː] *adj* indu(e), excessif(ive)

undulating ['ʌndjʊleɪtɪŋ] *adj* ondoyant(e), onduleux(euse)

unduly ['ʌn'djuːlɪ] *adv* trop, excessivement

unearth ['ʌn'ɜːθ] *vt* déterrer; (*fig*) dénicher

unearthly [ʌn'ɜːθlɪ] *adj* (*hour*) indu(e), impossible

uneasy [ʌn'iːzɪ] *adj* mal à l'aise, gêné(e); (*worried*) inquiet(ète); (*feeling*) désagréable; (*peace, truce*) fragile

uneconomic(al) [ʌniːkə'nɒmɪk(l)] *adj* peu économique

uneducated [ʌn'edjukeɪtɪd] *adj* (*person*) sans instruction

unemployed ['ʌnɪm'plɔɪd] *adj* sans travail, en *or* au chômage ♦ *n*: **the ~** les chômeurs *mpl*; **unemployment** ['ʌnɪm-'plɔɪmənt] *n* chômage *m*

unending [ʌn'endɪŋ] *adj* interminable, sans fin

unerring ['ʌn'ɜːrɪŋ] *adj* infaillible, sûr(e)

uneven ['ʌn'iːvən] *adj* inégal(e); irrégulier(ère)

unexpected [ʌnɪk'spektɪd] *adj* inattendu(e), imprévu(e); **~ly** *adv* (*arrive*) à l'improviste; (*succeed*) contre toute at-

tente

unfailing [ʌn'feɪlɪŋ] *adj* inépuisable; infaillible

unfair [ʌn'fɛə*] *adj*: **~ (to)** injuste (envers)

unfaithful [ʌn'feɪθful] *adj* infidèle

unfamiliar [ʌnfə'mɪlɪə*] *adj* étrange, inconnu(e); **to be ~ with** mal connaître

unfashionable [ʌn'fæʃnəbl] *adj* (*clothes*) démodé(e); (*place*) peu chic *inv*

unfasten ['ʌn'fɑːsn] *vt* défaire; détacher; (*open*) ouvrir

unfavourable ['ʌn'feɪvərəbl] (*US* **unfavorable**) *adj* défavorable

unfeeling [ʌn'fiːlɪŋ] *adj* insensible, dur(e)

unfinished [ʌn'fɪnɪʃt] *adj* inachevé(e)

unfit ['ʌn'fɪt] *adj* en mauvaise santé; pas en forme; (*incompetent*): **~ (for)** impropre (à); (*work, service*) inapte (à)

unfold [ʌn'fəʊld] *vt* déplier ♦ *vi* se dérouler

unforeseen ['ʌnfɔː'siːn] *adj* imprévu(e)

unforgettable [ʌnfə'getəbl] *adj* inoubliable

unfortunate [ʌn'fɔːtʃnət] *adj* malheureux(euse); (*event, remark*) malencontreux(euse); **~ly** *adv* malheureusement

unfounded ['ʌn'faʊndɪd] *adj* sans fondement

unfriendly ['ʌn'frendlɪ] *adj* inamical(e), peu aimable

ungainly [ʌn'geɪnlɪ] *adj* gauche, dégingandé(e)

ungodly [ʌn'gɒdlɪ] *adj* (*hour*) indu(e)

ungrateful [ʌn'greɪtful] *adj* ingrat(e)

unhappiness [ʌn'hæpɪnəs] *n* tristesse *f*, peine *f*

unhappy [ʌn'hæpɪ] *adj* triste, malheureux(euse); **~ about** *or* **with** (*arrangements etc*) mécontent(e) de, peu satisfait(e) de

unharmed ['ʌn'hɑːmd] *adj* indemne, sain(e) et sauf(sauve)

unhealthy [ʌn'helθɪ] *adj* malsain(e); (*person*) maladif(ive)

unheard-of [ʌn'hɜːdɒv] *adj* inouï(e), sans précédent

unhurt [ʌn'hɜːt] *adj* indemne

unidentified [ʌnaɪ'dentɪfaɪd] *adj* non identifié(e); *see also* **UFO**

uniform ['juːnɪfɔːm] *n* uniforme *m* ♦ *adj* uniforme

uninhabited [ʌnɪn'hæbɪtɪd] *adj* inhabité(e)

unintentional [ʌnɪn'tenʃənəl] *adj* involontaire

union ['juːnjən] *n* union *f*; (*also: trade* ~) syndicat *m* ♦ *cpd* du syndicat, syndical(e); **U~ Jack** *n* drapeau *du Royaume-Uni*

unique [juː'niːk] *adj* unique

unison ['juːnɪsn] *n*: **in** ~ (*sing*) à l'unisson; (*say*) en chœur

unit ['juːnɪt] *n* unité *f*; (*section: of furniture etc*) élément *m*, bloc *m*; **kitchen** ~ élément de cuisine

unite [juː'naɪt] *vt* unir ♦ *vi* s'unir; ~d *adj* uni(e); unifié(e); (*effort*) conjuguée(e); **U~d Kingdom** *n* Royaume-Uni *m*; **U~d Nations (Organization)** *n* (Organisation *f* des) Nations unies; **U~d States (of America)** *n* États-Unis *mpl*

unit trust (*BRIT*) *n* fonds commun de placement

unity ['juːnɪtɪ] *n* unité *f*

universal [juːnɪ'vɜːsəl] *adj* universel(le)

universe ['juːnɪvɜːs] *n* univers *m*

university [juːnɪ'vɜːsɪtɪ] *n* université *f*

unjust ['ʌn'dʒʌst] *adj* injuste

unkempt ['ʌn'kempt] *adj* négligé(e), débraillé(e); (*hair*) mal peigné(e)

unkind [ʌn'kaɪnd] *adj* peu gentil(le), méchant(e)

unknown ['ʌn'nəun] *adj* inconnu(e)

unlawful [ʌn'lɔːful] *adj* illégal(e)

unleaded [ʌn'ledɪd] *adj* (*petrol, fuel*) sans plomb

unleash ['ʌn'liːʃ] *vt* (*fig*) déchaîner, déclencher

unless [ən'les] *conj*: ~ **he leaves** à moins qu'il ne parte

unlike ['ʌn'laɪk] *adj* dissemblable, différent(e) ♦ *prep* contrairement à

unlikely [ʌn'laɪklɪ] *adj* improbable; invraisemblable

unlimited [ʌn'lɪmɪtɪd] *adj* illimité(e)

unlisted [ʌn'lɪstɪd] (*US*) *adj* (*TEL*) sur la liste rouge

unload ['ʌn'ləud] *vt* décharger

unlock ['ʌn'lɒk] *vt* ouvrir

unlucky [ʌn'lʌkɪ] *adj* (*person*) malchanceux(euse); (*object, number*) qui porte malheur; **to be** ~ (*person*) ne pas avoir de chance

unmarried ['ʌn'mærɪd] *adj* célibataire

unmistak(e)able [ʌnmɪs'teɪkəbl] *adj* indubitable; qu'on ne peut pas ne pas reconnaître

unmitigated [ʌn'mɪtɪgeɪtɪd] *adj* non mitigé(e), absolu(e), pur(e)

unnatural [ʌn'nætʃrəl] *adj* non naturel(le); (*habit*) contre nature

unnecessary ['ʌn'nesəsərɪ] *adj* inutile, superflu(e)

unnoticed [ʌn'nəutɪst] *adj*: (**to go** or **pass**) ~ (passer) inaperçu(e)

UNO ['juːnəu] *n abbr* = **United Nations Organization**

unobtainable ['ʌnəb'teɪnəbl] *adj* impossible à obtenir

unobtrusive [ʌnəb'truːsɪv] *adj* discret(ète)

unofficial [ʌnə'fɪʃl] *adj* (*news*) officieux(euse); (*strike*) sauvage

unorthodox [ʌn'ɔːθədɒks] *adj* peu orthodoxe; (*REL*) hétérodoxe

unpack ['ʌn'pæk] *vi* défaire sa valise ♦ *vt* (*suitcase*) défaire; (*belongings*) déballer

unpalatable [ʌn'pælətəbl] *adj* (*meal*) mauvais(e); (*truth*) désagréable (à entendre)

unparalleled [ʌn'pærəleld] *adj* incomparable, sans égal

unpleasant [ʌn'pleznt] *adj* déplaisant(e), désagréable

unplug ['ʌn'plʌg] *vt* débrancher

unpopular [ʌn'pɒpjulə*] *adj* impopulaire

unprecedented [ʌn'presɪdəntɪd] *adj* sans précédent

unpredictable [ʌnprɪ'dɪktəbl] *adj* imprévisible

unprofessional [ʌnprə'feʃənl] *adj*: ~ **conduct** manquement *m* aux devoirs de la profession

unqualified [ˈʌnˈkwɒlɪfaɪd] *adj* (*teacher*) non diplômé(e), sans titres; (*success, disaster*) sans réserve, total(e)

unquestionably [ʌnˈkwestʃənəblɪ] *adv* incontestablement

unravel [ʌnˈrævəl] *vt* démêler

unreal [ˈʌnˈrɪəl] *adj* irréel(le); (*extraordinary*) incroyable; **~istic** [ʌnrɪəˈlɪstɪk] *adj* irréaliste; peu réaliste

unreasonable [ʌnˈriːznəbl] *adj* qui n'est pas raisonnable

unrelated [ʌnrɪˈleɪtɪd] *adj* sans rapport; sans lien de parenté

unrelenting [ʌnrɪˈlentɪŋ] *adj* implacable

unreliable [ʌnrɪˈlaɪəbl] *adj* sur qui (*or* quoi) on ne peut pas compter, peu fiable

unremitting [ʌnrɪˈmɪtɪŋ] *adj* inlassable, infatigable, acharné(e)

unreservedly [ʌnrɪˈzɜːvɪdlɪ] *adv* sans réserve

unrest [ʌnˈrest] *n* agitation *f*, troubles *mpl*

unroll [ˈʌnˈrəul] *vt* dérouler

unruly [ʌnˈruːlɪ] *adj* indiscipliné(e)

unsafe [ˈʌnˈseɪf] *adj* (*in danger*) en danger; (*journey, car*) dangereux(euse)

unsaid [ˈʌnˈsed] *adj*: **to leave sth ~** passer qch sous silence

unsatisfactory [ˈʌnsætɪsˈfæktərɪ] *adj* peu satisfaisant(e)

unsavoury [ˈʌnˈseɪvərɪ] (*US* **unsavory**) *adj* (*fig*) peu recommandable

unscathed [ʌnˈskeɪðd] *adj* indemne

unscrew [ˈʌnˈskruː] *vt* dévisser

unscrupulous [ʌnˈskruːpjuləs] *adj* sans scrupules

unsettled [ˈʌnˈsetld] *adj* perturbé(e); instable

unshaven [ˈʌnˈʃeɪvn] *adj* non *or* mal rasé(e)

unsightly [ʌnˈsaɪtlɪ] *adj* disgracieux(euse), laid(e)

unskilled [ˈʌnˈskɪld] *adj*: **~ worker** manœuvre *m*

unspeakable [ʌnˈspiːkəbl] *adj* indicible; (*awful*) innommable

unstable [ʌnˈsteɪbl] *adj* instable

unsteady [ʌnˈstedɪ] *adj* mal assuré(e), chancelant(e), instable

unstuck [ˈʌnˈstʌk] *adj*: **to come ~** se décoller; (*plan*) tomber à l'eau

unsuccessful [ˈʌnsəkˈsesful] *adj* (*attempt*) infructueux(euse), vain(e); (*writer, proposal*) qui n'a pas de succès; **to be ~** (*in attempting sth*) ne pas réussir; ne pas avoir de succès; (*application*) ne pas être retenu(e)

unsuitable [ʌnˈsuːtəbl] *adj* qui ne convient pas, peu approprié(e); inopportun(e)

unsure [ʌnˈʃuə*] *adj* pas sûr(e); **to be ~ of o.s.** manquer de confiance en soi

unsuspecting [ʌnsəˈspektɪŋ] *adj* qui ne se doute de rien

unsympathetic [ˈʌnsɪmpəˈθetɪk] *adj* (*person*) antipathique; (*attitude*) peu compatissant(e)

untapped [ˈʌnˈtæpt] *adj* (*resources*) inexploité(e)

unthinkable [ʌnˈθɪŋkəbl] *adj* impensable, inconcevable

untidy [ʌnˈtaɪdɪ] *adj* (*room*) en désordre; (*appearance, person*) débraillé(e); (*person: in character*) sans ordre, désordonné

untie [ˈʌnˈtaɪ] *vt* (*knot, parcel*) défaire; (*prisoner, dog*) détacher

until [ənˈtɪl] *prep* jusqu'à; (*after negative*) avant ♦ *conj* jusqu'à ce que +*sub*; (*in past, after negative*) avant que +*sub*; **~ he comes** jusqu'à ce qu'il vienne, jusqu'à son arrivée; **~ now** jusqu'à présent, jusqu'ici; **~ then** jusque-là

untimely [ʌnˈtaɪmlɪ] *adj* inopportun(e); (*death*) prématuré(e)

untold [ˈʌnˈtəuld] *adj* (*story*) jamais raconté(e); (*wealth*) incalculable; (*joy, suffering*) indescriptible

untoward [ʌntəˈwɔːd] *adj* fâcheux(euse), malencontreux(euse)

unused¹ [ʌnˈjuːzd] *adj* (*clothes*) neuf(neuve)

unused² [ʌnˈjuːst] *adj*: **to be ~ to sth/to doing sth** ne pas avoir l'habitude de qch/de faire qch

unusual [ʌnˈjuːʒuəl] *adj* insolite, exceptionnel(le), rare

unveil [ʌnˈveɪl] *vt* dévoiler

unwanted [ʌn'wɒntɪd] *adj* (*child, pregnancy*) non désiré(e); (*clothes etc*) à donner

unwelcome [ʌn'welkəm] *adj* importun(e); (*news*) fâcheux(euse)

unwell ['ʌn'wel] *adj* souffrant(e); **to feel** ~ ne pas se sentir bien

unwieldy [ʌn'wiːldɪ] *adj* (*object*) difficile à manier; (*system*) lourd(e)

unwilling ['ʌn'wɪlɪŋ] *adj*: **to be** ~ **to do** ne pas vouloir faire; **~ly** *adv* à contre-cœur, contre son gré

unwind ['ʌn'waɪnd] (*irreg*) *vt* dérouler ♦ *vi* (*relax*) se détendre

unwise [ʌn'waɪz] *adj* irréfléchi(e), imprudent(e)

unwitting [ʌn'wɪtɪŋ] *adj* involontaire

unworkable [ʌn'wɜːkəbl] *adj* (*plan*) impraticable

unworthy [ʌn'wɜːðɪ] *adj* indigne

unwrap ['ʌn'ræp] *vt* défaire; ouvrir

unwritten ['ʌn'rɪtn] *adj* (*agreement*) tacite

KEYWORD

---

up [ʌp] *prep*: **he went** ~ **the stairs/the hill** il a monté l'escalier/la colline; **the cat was** ~ **a tree** le chat était dans un arbre; **they live further** ~ **the street** ils habitent plus haut dans la rue
♦ *adv* **1** (*upwards, higher*): ~ **in the sky/the mountains** (là-haut) dans le ciel/les montagnes; **put it a bit higher** ~ mettez-le un peu plus haut; ~ **there** là-haut; ~ **above** au-dessus
2: **to be** ~ (*out of bed*) être levé(e); (*prices*) avoir augmenté *or* monté
3: ~ **to** (*as far as*) jusqu'à; ~ **to now** jusqu'à présent
4: **to be** ~ **to** (*depending on*): **it's** ~ **to you** c'est à vous de décider; (*equal to*): **he's not** ~ **to it** (*job, task etc*) il n'en est pas capable; (*inf: be doing*): **what is he** ~ **to?** qu'est-ce qu'il peut bien faire?
♦ *n*: **~s and downs** hauts et bas *mpl*

---

up-and-coming [ʌpənd'kʌmɪŋ] *adj* plein(e) d'avenir *or* de promesses

upbringing ['ʌpbrɪŋɪŋ] *n* éducation *f*

update [ʌp'deɪt] *vt* mettre à jour

upgrade *vt* (*house*) moderniser; (*job*) revaloriser; (*employee*) promouvoir

upheaval [ʌp'hiːvəl] *n* bouleversement *m*; branle-bas *m*; crise *f*

uphill ['ʌp'hɪl] *adj* qui monte; (*fig: task*) difficile, pénible ♦ *adv* (*face, look*) en amont; **to go** ~ monter

uphold [ʌp'həʊld] (*irreg*) *vt* (*law, decision*) maintenir

upholstery [ʌp'həʊlstərɪ] *n* rembourrage *m*; (*cover*) tissu *m* d'ameublement; (*of car*) garniture *f*

upkeep ['ʌpkiːp] *n* entretien *m*

upon [ə'pɒn] *prep* sur

upper ['ʌpə*] *adj* supérieur(e); du dessus ♦ *n* (*of shoe*) empeigne *f*; **~-class** *adj* de la haute société, aristocratique; ~ **hand** *n*: **to have the** ~ **hand** avoir le dessus; **~most** *adj* le(la) plus haut(e); **what was ~most in my mind** ce à quoi je pensais surtout

upright ['ʌpraɪt] *adj* droit(e); vertical(e); (*fig*) droit, honnête

uprising ['ʌp'raɪzɪŋ] *n* soulèvement *m*, insurrection *f*

uproar ['ʌprɔː*] *n* tumulte *m*; (*protests*) tempête *f* de protestations

uproot [ʌp'ruːt] *vt* déraciner

upset [*n* 'ʌpset, *vb, adj* ʌp'set] (*irreg: like* set) *n* bouleversement *m*; (*stomach* ~) indigestion *f* ♦ *vt* (*glass etc*) renverser; (*plan*) déranger; (*person: offend*) contrarier; (: *grieve*) faire de la peine à; bouleverser ♦ *adj* contrarié(e); peiné(e); (*stomach*) dérangé(e)

upshot ['ʌpʃɒt] *n* résultat *m*

upside-down ['ʌpsaɪd'daʊn] *adv* à l'envers; **to turn** ~ mettre sens dessus dessous

upstairs ['ʌp'stɛəz] *adv* en haut ♦ *adj* (*room*) du dessus, d'en haut ♦ *n*: **the** ~ l'étage *m*

upstart ['ʌpstɑːt] (*pej*) *n* parvenu(e)

upstream ['ʌp'striːm] *adv* en amont

uptake ['ʌpteɪk] *n*: **to be quick/slow on the** ~ comprendre vite/être lent à comprendre

uptight ['ʌp'taɪt] (*inf*) *adj* très tendu(e),

crispé(e)

up-to-date [ˈʌptəˈdeɪt] *adj* moderne; (*information*) très récent(e)

upturn [ˈʌptɜːn] *n* (*in luck*) retournement *m*; (*COMM: in market*) hausse *f*

upward [ˈʌpwəd] *adj* ascendant(e); vers le haut; **~(s)** *adv* vers le haut; **~(s) of 200** 200 et plus

urban [ˈɜːbən] *adj* urbain(e)

urbane [ɜːˈbeɪn] *adj* urbain(e), courtois(e)

urchin [ˈɜːtʃɪn] *n* polisson *m*

urge [ɜːdʒ] *n* besoin *m*; envie *f*; forte envie, désir *m* ♦ *vt*: **to ~ sb to do** exhorter qn à faire, pousser qn à faire; recommander vivement à qn de faire

urgency [ˈɜːdʒənsɪ] *n* urgence *f*; (*of tone*) insistance *f*

urgent [ˈɜːdʒənt] *adj* urgent(e); (*tone*) insistant(e), pressant(e)

urinal *n* urinoir *m*; (*vessel*) urinal *m*

urine [ˈjʊərɪn] *n* urine *f*

urn [ɜːn] *n* urne *f*; (*also: tea ~*) fontaine *f* à thé

US *n abbr* = **United States**

us [ʌs] *pron* **nous**; *see also* **me**

USA *n abbr* = **United States of America**

use [*n* juːs, *vb* juːz] *n* emploi *m*, utilisation *f*; usage *m*; (*usefulness*) utilité *f* ♦ *vt* se servir de, utiliser, employer; **in ~** en usage; **out of ~** hors d'usage; **to be of ~** servir, être utile; **it's no ~** ça ne sert à rien; **she ~d to do it** elle le faisait (autrefois), elle avait coutume de le faire; **~d to: to be ~d to** avoir l'habitude de, être habitué(e) à; **~ up** *vt* finir, épuiser; consommer; **~d** *adj* (*car*) d'occasion; **~ful** *adj* utile; **~fulness** *n* utilité *f*; **~less** *adj* inutile; (*person: hopeless*) nul(le); **~r** *n* utilisateur(trice), usager *m*; **~r-friendly** *adj* (*computer*) convivial(e), facile d'emploi

usher [ˈʌʃə*] *n* (*at wedding ceremony*) placeur *m*; **~ette** [ʌʃəˈrɛt] *n* (*in cinema*) ouvreuse *f*

usual [ˈjuːʒuəl] *adj* habituel(le); **as ~** comme d'habitude; **~ly** *adv* d'habitude, d'ordinaire

utensil [juːˈtɛnsl] *n* ustensile *m*

uterus [ˈjuːtərəs] *n* utérus *m*

utility [juːˈtɪlɪtɪ] *n* utilité *f*; (*also: public ~*) service public; **~ room** *n* buanderie *f*

utmost [ˈʌtməʊst] *adj* extrême, le(la) plus grand(e) ♦ *n*: **to do one's ~** faire tout son possible

utter [ˈʌtə*] *adj* total(e), complet(ète) ♦ *vt* (*words*) prononcer, proférer; (*sounds*) émettre; **~ance** *n* paroles *fpl*; **~ly** *adv* complètement, totalement

U-turn [ˈjuːˈtɜːn] *n* demi-tour *m*

V v

v. *abbr* = **verse; versus; volt;** (= *vide*) **voir**

vacancy [ˈveɪkənsɪ] *n* (*BRIT: job*) poste vacant; (*room*) chambre *f* disponible

vacant [ˈveɪkənt] *adj* (*seat etc*) libre, disponible; (*expression*) distrait(e); **~ lot** (*US*) *n* terrain inoccupé; (*for sale*) terrain à vendre

vacate [vəˈkeɪt] *vt* quitter

vacation [vəˈkeɪʃən] *n* vacances *fpl*

vaccinate [ˈvæksɪneɪt] *vt* vacciner

vacuum [ˈvækjʊm] *n* vide *m*; **~ cleaner** *n* aspirateur *m*; **~-packed** *adj* emballé(e) sous vide

vagina [vəˈdʒaɪnə] *n* vagin *m*

vagrant [ˈveɪgrənt] *n* vagabond *m*

vague [veɪg] *adj* vague, imprécis(e); (*blurred: photo, outline*) flou(e); **~ly** *adv* vaguement

vain [veɪn] *adj* (*useless*) vain(e); (*conceited*) vaniteux(euse); **in ~** en vain

valentine [ˈvæləntaɪn] *n* (*also: ~ card*) carte *f* de la Saint-Valentin; (*person*) bien-aimé(e) (*le jour de la Sainte-Valentin*)

valiant [ˈvæliənt] *adj* vaillant(e)

valid [ˈvælɪd] *adj* valable; (*document*) valable, valide

valley [ˈvælɪ] *n* vallée *f*

valour [ˈvælə*] (*US* **valor**) *n* courage *m*

valuable [ˈvæljʊəbl] *adj* (*jewel*) de valeur; (*time, help*) précieux(euse); **~s** *npl* objets *mpl* de valeur

valuation [ˌvæljʊˈeɪʃən] *n* (*price*) estimation *f*; (*quality*) appréciation *f*
value [ˈvæljuː] *n* valeur *f* ♦ *vt* (*fix price*) évaluer, expertiser; (*appreciate*) apprécier; **~ added tax** (*BRIT*) *n* taxe *f* à la valeur ajoutée; **~d** *adj* (*person*) estimé(e); (*advice*) précieux(euse)
valve [vælv] *n* (*in machine*) soupape *f*, valve *f*; (*MED*) valve, valvule *f*
van [væn] *n* (*AUT*) camionnette *f*
vandal [ˈvændl] *n* vandale *m/f*; **~ism** *n* vandalisme *m*; **~ize** [ˈvændəlaɪz] *vt* saccager
vanguard [ˈvænɡɑːd] *n* (*fig*): **in the ~ of** à l'avant-garde de
vanilla [vəˈnɪlə] *n* vanille *f*
vanish [ˈvænɪʃ] *vi* disparaître
vanity [ˈvænɪtɪ] *n* vanité *f*
vantage point [ˈvɑːntɪdʒ-] *n* bonne position
vapour [ˈveɪpə*] (*US* **vapor**) *n* vapeur *f*; (*on window*) buée *f*
variable [ˈvɛərɪəbl] *adj* variable; (*mood*) changeant(e)
variance [ˈvɛərɪəns] *n*: **to be at ~ (with)** être en désaccord (avec); (*facts*) être en contradiction (avec)
varicose [ˈværɪkəʊs] *adj*: **~ veins** varices *fpl*
varied [ˈvɛərɪd] *adj* varié(e), divers(e)
variety [vəˈraɪətɪ] *n* variété *f*; (*quantity*) nombre *m*, quantité *f*; **~ show** *n* (*spectacle m de*) variétés *fpl*
various [ˈvɛərɪəs] *adj* divers(e), différent(e); (*several*) plusieurs
varnish [ˈvɑːnɪʃ] *n* vernis *m* ♦ *vt* vernir
vary [ˈvɛərɪ] *vt, vi* varier, changer
vase [vɑːz] *n* vase *m*
Vaseline [ˈvæsɪliːn] ® *n* vaseline *f*
vast [vɑːst] *adj* vaste, immense; (*amount, success*) énorme
VAT [væt] *n abbr* (= *value added tax*) TVA *f*
vat [væt] *n* cuve *f*
vault [vɔːlt] *n* (*of roof*) voûte *f*; (*tomb*) caveau *m*; (*in bank*) salle *f* des coffres; chambre forte ♦ *vt* (*also*: **~ over**) sauter (d'un bond)
vaunted [ˈvɔːntɪd] *adj*: **much-~** tant

vanté(e)
VCR *n abbr* = **video cassette recorder**
VD *n abbr* = **venereal disease**
VDU *n abbr* = **visual display unit**
veal [viːl] *n* veau *m*
veer [vɪə*] *vi* tourner; virer
vegeburger [ˈvedʒɪbɜːɡə*] *n* burger végétarien
vegetable [ˈvedʒətəbl] *n* légume *m* ♦ *adj* végétal(e)
vegetarian [vedʒɪˈtɛərɪən] *adj, n* végétarien(ne)
vehement [ˈviːɪmənt] *adj* violent(e), impétueux(euse); (*impassioned*) ardent(e)
vehicle [ˈviːɪkl] *n* véhicule *m*
veil [veɪl] *n* voile *m*
vein [veɪn] *n* veine *f*; (*on leaf*) nervure *f*
velocity [vɪˈlɒsɪtɪ] *n* vitesse *f*
velvet [ˈvelvɪt] *n* velours *m*
vending machine [ˈvendɪŋ-] *n* distributeur *m* automatique
veneer [vəˈnɪə*] *n* (*on furniture*) placage *m*; (*fig*) vernis *m*
venereal [vɪˈnɪərɪəl] *adj*: **~ disease** maladie vénérienne
Venetian blind [vɪˈniːʃən-] *n* store vénitien
vengeance [ˈvendʒəns] *n* vengeance *f*; **with a ~** (*fig*) vraiment, pour de bon
venison [ˈvenɪsn] *n* venaison *f*
venom [ˈvenəm] *n* venin *m*
vent [vent] *n* conduit *m* d'aération; (*in dress, jacket*) fente *f* ♦ *vt* (*fig: one's feelings*) donner libre cours à
ventilator [ˈventɪleɪtə*] *n* ventilateur *m*
ventriloquist [venˈtrɪləkwɪst] *n* ventriloque *m/f*
venture [ˈventʃə*] *n* entreprise *f* ♦ *vt* risquer, hasarder ♦ *vi* s'aventurer, se risquer
venue [ˈvenjuː] *n* lieu *m*
verb [vɜːb] *n* verbe *m*; **~al** *adj* verbal(e); (*translation*) littéral(e)
verbatim [vɜːˈbeɪtɪm] *adj, adv* mot pour mot
verdict [ˈvɜːdɪkt] *n* verdict *m*
verge [vɜːdʒ] *n* (*BRIT*) bord *m*, bas-côté *m*; **"soft ~s"** (*BRIT: AUT*) "accotement non stabilisé"; **on the ~ of doing** sur le

point de faire; **~ on** *vt fus* approcher de

verify ['verɪfaɪ] *vt* vérifier; (*confirm*) confirmer

vermin ['vɜːmɪn] *npl* animaux *mpl* nuisibles; (*insects*) vermine *f*

vermouth ['vɜːməθ] *n* vermouth *m*

versatile ['vɜːsətaɪl] *adj* polyvalent(e)

verse [vɜːs] *n* (*poetry*) vers *mpl*; (*stanza*) strophe *f*; (*in Bible*) verset *m*

version ['vɜːʃən] *n* version *f*

versus ['vɜːsəs] *prep* contre

vertical ['vɜːtɪkəl] *adj* vertical(e) ♦ *n* verticale *f*

vertigo ['vɜːtɪgəu] *n* vertige *m*

verve [vɜːv] *n* brio *m*; enthousiasme *m*

very ['verɪ] *adv* très ♦ *adj*: **the ~ book which** le livre même que; **the ~ last** le tout dernier; **at the ~ least** tout au moins; **~ much** beaucoup

vessel ['vesl] *n* (*ANAT, NAUT*) vaisseau *m*; (*container*) récipient *m*

vest [vest] *n* (*BRIT*) tricot *m* de corps; (*US*: *waistcoat*) gilet *m*

vested interest ['vestɪd-] *n* (*COMM*) droits acquis

vet [vet] *n abbr* (*BRIT*: = *veterinary surgeon*) vétérinaire *m/f* ♦ *vt* examiner soigneusement

veteran ['vetərn] *n* vétéran *m*; (*also*: *war ~*) ancien combattant

veterinarian [vetrə'neərɪən] (*US*) *n* = **veterinary surgeon**

veterinary surgeon ['vetrɪnərɪ-] (*BRIT*) *n* vétérinaire *m/f*

veto ['viːtəu] (*pl* **~es**) *n* veto *m* ♦ *vt* opposer son veto à

vex [veks] *vt* fâcher, contrarier; **~ed** *adj* (*question*) controversé(e)

via ['vaɪə] *prep* par, via

viable ['vaɪəbl] *adj* viable

vibrate [vaɪ'breɪt] *vi* vibrer

vicar ['vɪkə*] *n* pasteur *m* (*de l'Église anglicane*); **~age** *n* presbytère *m*

vicarious [vɪ'keərɪəs] *adj* indirect(e)

vice [vaɪs] *n* (*evil*) vice *m*; (*TECH*) étau *m*

vice- *prefix* vice-

vice squad *n* ≈ brigade mondaine

vice versa ['vaɪsɪ'vɜːsə] *adv* vice versa

vicinity [vɪ'sɪnɪtɪ] *n* environs *mpl*, alen-

tours *mpl*

vicious ['vɪʃəs] *adj* (*remark*) cruel(le), méchant(e); (*blow*) brutal(e); (*dog*) méchant(e), dangereux(euse); (*horse*) vicieux(euse); **~ circle** *n* cercle vicieux

victim ['vɪktɪm] *n* victime *f*

victor ['vɪktə*] *n* vainqueur *m*

Victorian [vɪk'tɔːrɪən] *adj* victorien(ne)

victory ['vɪktərɪ] *n* victoire *f*

video ['vɪdɪəu] *cpd* vidéo *inv* ♦ *n* (~ *film*) vidéo *f*; (*also*: ~ *cassette*) vidéocassette *f*; (: ~ *cassette recorder*) magnétoscope *m*; **~ tape** *n* bande *f* vidéo *inv*; (*cassette*) vidéocassette *f*

vie [vaɪ] *vi*: **to ~ with** rivaliser avec

Vienna [vɪ'enə] *n* Vienne

Vietnam [vjet'næm] *n* Viêt-nam *m*, Vietnam *m*; **~ese** [vjetnə'miːz] *adj* vietnamien(ne) ♦ *n inv* Vietnamien(ne); (*LING*) vietnamien *m*

view [vjuː] *n* vue *f*; (*opinion*) avis *m*, vue ♦ *vt* voir, regarder; (*situation*) considérer; (*house*) visiter; **in full ~ of** sous les yeux de; **in ~ of the weather/ the fact that** étant donné le temps/que; **in my ~** à mon avis; **~er** *n* (*TV*) téléspectateur(trice); **~finder** *n* viseur *m*; **~point** *n* point *m* de vue

vigorous ['vɪgərəs] *adj* vigoureux(euse)

vile [vaɪl] *adj* (*action*) vil(e); (*smell, food*) abominable; (*temper*) massacrant(e)

villa ['vɪlə] *n* villa *f*

village ['vɪlɪdʒ] *n* village *m*; **~r** *n* villageois(e)

villain ['vɪlən] *n* (*scoundrel*) scélérat *m*; (*BRIT*: *criminal*) bandit *m*; (*in novel etc*) traître *m*

vindicate ['vɪndɪkeɪt] *vt* (*person*) innocenter; (*action*) justifier

vindictive [vɪn'dɪktɪv] *adj* vindicatif(ive), rancunier(ère)

vine [vaɪn] *n* vigne *f*; (*climbing plant*) plante grimpante

vinegar ['vɪnɪgə*] *n* vinaigre *m*

vineyard ['vɪnjəd] *n* vignoble *m*

vintage ['vɪntɪdʒ] *n* (*year*) année *f*, millésime *m*; **~ car** *n* voiture *f* d'époque; **~ wine** *n* vin *m* de grand cru

viola [vɪˈəʊlə] *n* (MUS) alto *m*

violate [ˈvaɪəleɪt] *vt* violer

violence [ˈvaɪələns] *n* violence *f*

violent [ˈvaɪələnt] *adj* violent(e)

violet [ˈvaɪələt] *adj* violet(te) ♦ *n* (colour) violet *m*; (plant) violette *f*

violin [vaɪəˈlɪn] *n* violon *m*; **~ist** *n* violoniste *m/f*

VIP *n abbr* (= *very important person*) V.I.P. *m*

virgin [ˈvɜːdʒɪn] *n* vierge *f* ♦ *adj* vierge

Virgo [ˈvɜːgəʊ] *n* la Vierge

virile [ˈvɪraɪl] *adj* viril(e)

virtually [ˈvɜːtjʊəlɪ] *adv* (almost) pratiquement

virtual reality *n* (COMPUT) réalité virtuelle

virtue [ˈvɜːtjuː] *n* vertu *f*; (advantage) mérite *m*, avantage *m*; **by ~ of** en vertu *or* en raison de; **virtuous** [ˈvɜːtjʊəs] *adj* vertueux(euse)

virus [ˈvaɪərəs] *n* (also COMPUT) virus *m*

visa [ˈviːzə] *n* visa *m*

visibility [vɪzɪˈbɪlɪtɪ] *n* visibilité *f*

visible [ˈvɪzəbl] *adj* visible

vision [ˈvɪʒən] *n* (sight) vue *f*, vision *f*; (foresight, in dream) vision

visit [ˈvɪzɪt] *n* visite *f*; (stay) séjour *m* ♦ *vt* (person) rendre visite à; (place) visiter; **~ing hours** *npl* (in hospital etc) heures *fpl* de visite; **~or** *n* visiteur(euse); (to one's house) visite *f*, invité(e)

visor [ˈvaɪzə*] *n* visière *f*

vista [ˈvɪstə] *n* vue *f*

visual [ˈvɪzjʊəl] *adj* visuel(le); **~ aid** *n* support visuel; **~ display unit** *n* console *f* de visualisation, visuel *m*; **~ize** [ˈvɪzjʊəlaɪz] *vt* se représenter, s'imaginer

vital [ˈvaɪtl] *adj* vital(e); (person) plein(e) d'entrain; **~ly** *adv* (important) absolument; **~ statistics** *npl* (fig) mensurations *fpl*

vitamin [ˈvɪtəmɪn] *n* vitamine *f*

vivacious [vɪˈveɪʃəs] *adj* animé(e), qui a de la vivacité

vivid [ˈvɪvɪd] *adj* (account) vivant(e); (light, imagination) vif(vive); **~ly** *adv* (describe) d'une manière vivante; (re-

member) de façon précise

V-neck [ˈviːˈnek] *n* décolleté *m* en V

vocabulary [vəʊˈkæbjʊlərɪ] *n* vocabulaire *m*

vocal [ˈvəʊkəl] *adj* vocal(e); (articulate) qui sait s'exprimer; **~ cords** *npl* cordes vocales

vocation [vəʊˈkeɪʃən] *n* vocation *f*; **~al** *adj* professionnel(le)

vociferous [vəʊˈsɪfərəs] *adj* bruyant(e)

vodka [ˈvɒdkə] *n* vodka *f*

vogue [vəʊg] *n*: **in ~** en vogue *f*

voice [vɔɪs] *n* voix *f* ♦ *vt* (opinion) exprimer, formuler

void [vɔɪd] *n* vide *m* ♦ *adj* nul(le); **~ of** vide de, dépourvu(e) de

volatile [ˈvɒlətaɪl] *adj* volatil(e); (person) versatile; (situation) explosif(ive)

volcano [vɒlˈkeɪnəʊ] (*pl* **~es**) *n* volcan *m*

volition [vəˈlɪʃən] *n*: **of one's own ~** de son propre gré

volley [ˈvɒlɪ] *n* (of gunfire) salve *f*; (of stones etc) grêle *f*, volée *f*; (of questions) multitude *f*, série *f*; (TENNIS etc) volée *f*; **~ball** *n* volley(-ball) *m*

volt [vəʊlt] *n* volt *m*; **~age** *n* tension *f*, voltage *m*

volume [ˈvɒljuːm] *n* volume *m*

voluntarily *adv* volontairement

voluntary [ˈvɒləntərɪ] *adj* volontaire; (unpaid) bénévole

volunteer [vɒlənˈtɪə*] *n* volontaire *m/f* ♦ *vt* (information) fournir (spontanément) ♦ *vi* (MIL) s'engager comme volontaire; **to ~ to do** se proposer pour faire

vomit [ˈvɒmɪt] *vt*, *vi* vomir

vote [vəʊt] *n* vote *m*, suffrage *m*; (cast) voix *f*, vote; (franchise) droit *m* de vote ♦ *vt* (elect): **to be ~d chairman** etc être élu président etc; (propose): **to ~ that** proposer que ♦ *vi* voter; **~ of thanks** discours *m* de remerciement; **~r** *n* électeur(trice); **voting** [ˈvəʊtɪŋ] *n* scrutin *m*, vote *m*

voucher [ˈvaʊtʃə*] *n* (for meal, petrol, gift) bon *m*

vouch for [vaʊtʃ] *vt fus* se porter garant de

vow [vaʊ] *n* vœu *m*, serment *m* ♦ *vi* jurer

vowel ['vauəl] n voyelle f

voyage ['vɔɪdʒ] n voyage m par mer, traversée f; (by spacecraft) voyage m

vulgar ['vʌlgə*] adj vulgaire

vulnerable ['vʌlnərəbl] adj vulnérable

vulture ['vʌltʃə*] n vautour m

W w

wad [wɒd] n (of cotton wool, paper) tampon m; (of banknotes etc) liasse f

waddle ['wɒdl] vi se dandiner

wade [weɪd] vi: **to ~ through** marcher dans, patauger dans; (fig: book) s'évertuer à lire

wafer ['weɪfə*] n (CULIN) gaufrette f

waffle ['wɒfl] n (CULIN) gaufre f; (inf) verbiage m, remplissage m ♦ vi parler pour ne rien dire, faire du remplissage

waft [wɑ:ft] vt porter ♦ vi flotter

wag [wæg] vt agiter, remuer ♦ vi remuer

wage [weɪdʒ] n (also: ~s) salaire m, paye f ♦ vt: **to ~ war** faire la guerre; **~ earner** n salarié(e); **~ packet** n (enveloppe f de) paye f

wager ['weɪdʒə*] n pari m

waggle ['wægl] vt, vi remuer

wag(g)on ['wægən] n (horse-drawn) chariot m; (BRIT: RAIL) wagon m (de marchandises)

wail [weɪl] vi gémir; (siren) hurler

waist [weɪst] n taille f; **~coat** (BRIT) n gilet m; **~line** n (tour m de) taille f

wait [weɪt] n attente f ♦ vi attendre; **to keep sb ~ing** faire attendre qn; **to ~ for** attendre; **I can't ~ to ...** (fig) je meurs d'envie de ...; **~ behind** vi rester (à attendre); **~ on** vt fus servir; **~er** n garçon m (de café), serveur m; **~ing** n: **"no ~ing"** (BRIT: AUT) "stationnement interdit"; **~ing list** n liste f d'attente; **~ing room** n salle f d'attente; **~ress** n serveuse f

waive [weɪv] vt renoncer à, abandonner

wake [weɪk] (pt **woke**, **~d**, pp **woken**, **~d**) vt (also: ~ **up**) réveiller ♦ vi (also: ~ **up**) se réveiller ♦ n (for dead person) veillée f mortuaire; (NAUT) sillage m

Wales [weɪlz] n pays m de Galles; **the Prince of ~** le prince de Galles

walk [wɔ:k] n promenade f; (short) petit tour; (gait) démarche f; (path) chemin m; (in park etc) allée f ♦ vi marcher; (for pleasure, exercise) se promener ♦ vt (distance) faire à pied; (dog) promener; **10 minutes' ~ from** à 10 minutes à pied de; **from all ~s of life** de toutes conditions sociales; **~ out** vi (audience) sortir, quitter la salle; (workers) se mettre en grève; **~ out on** (inf) vt fus quitter, plaquer; **~er** n (person) marcheur(euse); **~ie-talkie** n talkie-walkie m; **~ing** n marche f à pied; **~ing shoes** npl chaussures fpl de marche; **~ing stick** n canne f; **~out** n (of workers) grève-surprise f; **~over** (inf) n victoire f or examen m etc facile; **~way** n promenade f, cheminement m piéton

wall [wɔ:l] n mur m; (of tunnel, cave etc) paroi m; **~ed** adj (city) fortifié(e); (garden) entouré(e) d'un mur, clos(e)

wallet ['wɒlɪt] n portefeuille m

wallflower ['wɔ:lflauə*] n giroflée f; **to be a ~** (fig) faire tapisserie

wallop ['wɒləp] (BRIT: inf) vt donner un grand coup à

wallow ['wɒləu] vi se vautrer

wallpaper ['wɔ:lpeɪpə*] n papier peint ♦ vt tapisser

walnut ['wɔ:lnʌt] n noix f; (tree, wood) noyer m

walrus ['wɔ:lrəs] (pl ~ or ~es) n morse m

waltz [wɔ:lts] n valse f ♦ vi valser

wan [wɒn] adj pâle; triste

wand [wɒnd] n (also: magic ~) baguette f (magique)

wander ['wɒndə*] vi (person) errer; (thoughts) vagabonder, errer ♦ vt errer dans

wane [weɪn] vi (moon) décroître; (reputation) décliner

wangle ['wæŋgl] (BRIT: inf) vt se débrouiller pour avoir; carotter

want [wɒnt] vt vouloir; (need) avoir besoin de ♦ *n*: **for ~ of** par manque de, faute de; **~s** *npl* (*needs*) besoins *mpl*; **to ~ to do** vouloir faire; **to ~ sb to do** vouloir que qn fasse; **~ed** *adj* (*criminal*) recherché(e) par la police; **"cook ~ed"** "on recherche un cuisinier"; **~ing** *adj*: **to be found ~ing** ne pas être à la hauteur

wanton ['wɒntən] *adj* (*gratuitous*) gratuit(e); (*promiscuous*) dévergondé(e)

war [wɔ:*] *n* guerre *f*; **to make ~ (on)** faire la guerre (à)

ward [wɔ:d] *n* (*in hospital*) salle *f*, (POL) canton *m*; (LAW: *child*) pupille *m/f*; **~ off** *vt* (*attack, enemy*) repousser, éviter

warden ['wɔ:dən] *n* gardien(ne); (BRIT: *of institution*) directeur(trice); (: *also: traffic ~*) contractuel(le); (*of youth hostel*) père *m or* mère *f* aubergiste

warder ['wɔ:də*] *n* (BRIT) gardien *m* de prison

wardrobe ['wɔ:drəub] *n* (*cupboard*) armoire *f*; (*clothes*) garde-robe *f*; (THEATRE) costumes *mpl*

warehouse ['wɛəhaus] *n* entrepôt *m*

wares [wɛəz] *npl* marchandises *fpl*

warfare ['wɔ:fɛə*] *n* guerre *f*

warhead ['wɔ:hed] *n* (MIL) ogive *f*

warily ['wɛərɪlɪ] *adv* avec prudence

warm [wɔ:m] *adj* chaud(e); (*thanks, welcome, applause, person*) chaleureux(euse); **it's ~** il fait chaud; **I'm ~** j'ai chaud; **~ up** *vi* (*person, room*) se réchauffer; (*water*) chauffer; (*athlete*) s'échauffer ♦ *vt* (*food*) (faire) réchauffer, (faire) chauffer; (*engine*) faire chauffer; **~-hearted** *adj* affectueux(euse); **~ly** *adv* chaudement; chaleureusement; **~th** *n* chaleur *f*

warn [wɔ:n] *vt* avertir, prévenir; **to ~ sb (not) to do** conseiller à qn de (ne pas) faire; **~ing** *n* avertissement *m*; (*notice*) avis *m*; (*signal*) avertisseur *m*; **~ing light** *n* avertisseur lumineux; **~ing triangle** *n* (AUT) triangle *m* de présignalisation

warp [wɔ:p] *vi* (*wood*) travailler, se déformer ♦ *vt* (*fig: character*) pervertir

warrant ['wɒrənt] *n* (*guarantee*) garantie *f*; (LAW: *to arrest*) mandat *m* d'arrêt;

(: *to search*) mandat de perquisition

warranty ['wɒrəntɪ] *n* garantie *f*

warren ['wɒrən] *n* (*of rabbits*) terrier *m*; (*fig: of streets etc*) dédale *m*

warrior ['wɒrɪə*] *n* guerrier(ère)

Warsaw ['wɔ:sɔ:] *n* Varsovie

warship ['wɔ:ʃɪp] *n* navire *m* de guerre

wart [wɔ:t] *n* verrue *f*

wartime ['wɔ:taɪm] *n*: **in ~** en temps de guerre

wary ['wɛərɪ] *adj* prudent(e)

was [wɒz, wəz] *pt of* **be**

wash [wɒʃ] *vt* laver ♦ *vi* se laver; (*sea*): **to ~ over/against sth** inonder/baigner qch ♦ *n* (*clothes*) lessive *f*; (*~ing programme*) lavage *m*; (*of ship*) sillage *m*; **to have a ~** se laver, faire sa toilette; **to give sth a ~** laver qch; **~ away** *vt* (*stain*) enlever au lavage; (*subj: river etc*) emporter; **~ off** *vi* partir au lavage; **~ up** *vi* (BRIT) faire la vaisselle; (US) se débarbouiller; **~able** *adj* lavable; **~basin** (US **~bowl**) *n* lavabo *m*; **~cloth** (US) *n* gant *m* de toilette; **~er** *n* (TECH) rondelle *f*, joint *m*; **~ing** *n* (*dirty*) linge *m*; (*clean*) lessive *f*; **~ing machine** *n* machine *f* à laver; **~ing powder** *n* (BRIT) lessive *f* (en poudre); **~ing-up** *n* vaisselle *f*; **~ing-up liquid** *n* produit *m* pour la vaisselle; **~-out** (*inf*) *n* désastre *m*; **~room** (US) *n* toilettes *fpl*

wasn't ['wɒznt] = **was not**

wasp [wɒsp] *n* guêpe *f*

wastage ['weɪstɪdʒ] *n* gaspillage *m*; (*in manufacturing, transport etc*) pertes *fpl*, déchets *mpl*; **natural ~** départs naturels

waste [weɪst] *n* gaspillage *m*; (*of time*) perte *f*; (*rubbish*) déchets *mpl*; (*also: household ~*) ordures *fpl* ♦ *adj* (*leftover*): **~ material** déchets *mpl*; (*land, ground: in city*) à l'abandon ♦ *vt* gaspiller; (*time, opportunity*) perdre; **~s** *npl* (*area*) étendue *f* désertique; **~ away** *vi* dépérir; **~ disposal unit** (BRIT) *n* broyeur *m* d'ordures; **~ful** *adj* gaspilleur(euse); (*process*) peu économique; **~ ground** (BRIT) *n* terrain *m* vague; **~paper basket** *n* corbeille *f* à papier; **~ pipe**

(tuyau *m* de) vidange *f*

watch [wɒtʃ] *n* montre *f*; (*act of ~ing*) surveillance *f*; guet *m*; (*MIL: guards*) garde *f*; (*NAUT: guards, spell of duty*) quart *m* ♦ *vt* (*look at*) observer; (*: match, programme, TV*) regarder; (*spy on, guard*) surveiller; (*be careful of*) faire attention à ♦ *vi* regarder; (*keep guard*) monter la garde; ~ **out** *vi* faire attention; ~**dog** *n* chien *m* de garde; (*fig*) gardien(ne); ~**ful** *adj* attentif(ive), vigilant(e); ~**maker** *n* horloger(ère); ~**man** (*irreg*) *n* see **night**; ~**strap** *n* bracelet *m* de montre

water ['wɔːtə*] *n* eau *f* ♦ *vt* (*plant, garden*) arroser ♦ *vi* (*eyes*) larmoyer; (*mouth*): **it makes my mouth ~** j'en ai l'eau à la bouche; **in British ~s** dans les eaux territoriales britanniques; (*: down vt* (*milk*) couper d'eau; (*fig: story*) édulcorer; ~**colour** (*US* ~**color**) *n* aquarelle *f*; ~**cress** *n* cresson *m* (de fontaine); ~**fall** *n* chute *f* d'eau; ~ **heater** *n* chauffe-eau *m*; ~**ing can** *n* arrosoir *m*; ~ **lily** *n* nénuphar *m*; ~**line** *n* (*NAUT*) ligne *f* de flottaison; ~**logged** *adj* (*ground*) détrempé(e); ~ **main** *n* canalisation *f* d'eau; ~**melon** *n* pastèque *f*; ~**proof** *adj* imperméable; ~**shed** *n* (*GEO*) ligne *f* de partage des eaux; (*fig*) moment *m* critique, point décisif; ~**skiing** *n* ski *m* nautique; ~**tight** *adj* étanche; ~**way** *n* cours *m* d'eau navigable; ~**works** *npl* (*building*) station *f* hydraulique; ~**y** *adj* (*coffee, soup*) trop faible; (*eyes*) humide, larmoyant(e)

watt [wɒt] *n* watt *m*

wave [weɪv] *n* vague *f*; (*of hand*) geste *m*, signe *m*; (*RADIO*) onde *f*; (*in hair*) ondulation *f* ♦ *vi* faire signe de la main; (*flag*) flotter au vent; (*grass*) ondoyer ♦ *vt* (*handkerchief*) agiter; (*stick*) brandir; ~**length** *n* longueur *f* d'ondes

waver ['weɪvə*] *vi* vaciller; (*voice*) trembler; (*person*) hésiter

wavy ['weɪvɪ] *adj* ondulé(e); onduleux(euse)

wax [wæks] *n* cire *f*; (*for skis*) fart *m* ♦ *vt* cirer; (*car*) lustrer; (*skis*) farter ♦ *vi* (*moon*) croître; ~**works** *npl* personnages *mpl* de cire ♦ *n* musée *m* de cire

way [weɪ] *n* chemin *m*, voie *f*; (*distance*) distance *f*; (*direction*) chemin, direction *f*; (*manner*) façon *f*, manière *f*; (*habit*) habitude *f*, façon; **which ~? - this ~** par où? - par ici; **on the ~** (*en route*) en route; **to be on one's ~** être en route; **to go out of one's ~ to do** (*fig*) se donner du mal pour faire; **to be in the ~** bloquer le passage; (*fig*) gêner; **to lose one's ~** perdre son chemin; **under ~** en cours; **in a ~** dans un sens; **in some ~s** à certains égards; **no ~!** (*inf*) pas question!; **by the ~ ...** à propos ...; **"~ in"** (*BRIT*) "entrée"; **"~ out"** (*BRIT*) "sortie"; **the ~ back** le chemin du retour; **"give ~"** (*BRIT: AUT*) "cédez le passage"; ~**lay** [weɪ'leɪ] (*irreg*) *vt* attaquer

wayward ['weɪwəd] *adj* capricieux(euse), entêté(e)

we [wiː] *pl pron* nous

weak [wiːk] *adj* faible; (*health*) fragile; (*beam etc*) peu solide; ~**en** *vi* faiblir, décliner ♦ *vt* affaiblir; ~**ling** *n* (*physically*) gringalet *m*; (*morally etc*) faible *m/f*; ~**ness** *n* faiblesse *f*; (*fault*) point *m* faible; **to have a ~ness for** avoir un faible pour

wealth [welθ] *n* (*money, resources*) richesse(s) *f(pl)*; (*of details*) profusion *f*; ~**y** *adj* riche

wean [wiːn] *vt* sevrer

weapon ['wepən] *n* arme *f*

wear [wɛə*] (*pt* **wore**, *pp* **worn**) *n* (*use*) usage *m*; (*deterioration through use*) usure *f*; (*clothing*): **sports/baby~** vêtements *mpl* de sport/pour bébés ♦ *vt* (*clothes*) porter; (*put on*) mettre; (*damage: through use*) user ♦ *vi* (*last*) faire de l'usage; (*rub etc through*) s'user; **town/evening ~** tenue *f* de ville/soirée; ~ **away** *vt* user, ronger ♦ *vi* (*inscription*) s'effacer; ~ **down** *vt* user; (*strength, person*) épuiser; ~ **off** *vi* disparaître; ~ **out** *vt* user; (*person, strength*) épuiser; ~ **and tear** *n* usure *f*

weary ['wɪərɪ] *adj* (*tired*) épuisé(e); (*dispirited*) las(lasse); abattu(e) ♦ *vi*: **to ~ of** se lasser de

weasel ['wiːzl] *n* (*ZOOL*) belette *f*

weather ['weðə*] *n* temps *m* ♦ *vt* (*tempest, crisis*) essuyer, réchapper à, survivre à; **under the ~** (*fig: ill*) mal fichu(e); **~-beaten** *adj* (*person*) hâlé(e); (*building*) dégradé(e) par les intempéries; **~cock** *n* girouette *f*; **~ forecast** *n* prévisions *fpl* météorologiques, météo *f*; **~ man** (*irreg: inf*) *n* météorologue *m*; **~ vane** *n* = **~cock**

weave [wi:v] (*pt* **wove**, *pp* **woven**) *vt* (*cloth*) tisser; (*basket*) tresser; **~r** *n* tisserand(e)

web [web] *n* (*of spider*) toile *f*; (*on foot*) palmure *f*; (*fabric, also fig*) tissu *m*

wed [wed] (*pt, pp* **wedded**) *vt* épouser ♦ *vi* se marier

we'd [wi:d] = **we had; we would**

wedding ['wedɪŋ] *n* mariage *m*; **silver/ golden ~ (anniversary)** noces *fpl* d'argent/d'or; **~ day** *n* jour *m* du mariage; **~ dress** *n* robe *f* de mariée; **~ ring** *n* alliance *f*

wedge [wedʒ] *n* (*of wood etc*) coin *m*, cale *f*; (*of cake*) part *f* ♦ *vt* (*fix*) caler; (*pack tightly*) enfoncer

Wednesday ['wenzdeɪ] *n* mercredi *m*

wee [wi:] *adj* (*SCOTTISH*) petit(e); tout(e) petit(e)

weed [wi:d] *n* mauvaise herbe ♦ *vt* désherber; **~killer** *n* désherbant *m*; **~y** *adj* (*man*) gringalet

week [wi:k] *n* semaine *f*; **a ~ today/on Friday** aujourd'hui/vendredi en huit; **~day** *n* jour *m* de semaine; (*COMM*) jour ouvrable; **~end** *n* week-end *m*; **~ly** *adv* une fois par semaine, chaque semaine ♦ *adj* hebdomadaire ♦ *n* hebdomadaire *m*

weep [wi:p] (*pt, pp* **wept**) *vi* (*person*) pleurer; **~ing willow** *n* saule pleureur

weigh [weɪ] *vt, vi* peser; **to ~ anchor** lever l'ancre; **~ down** *vt* (*person, animal*) écraser; (*fig: with worry*) accabler; **~ up** *vt* examiner

weight [weɪt] *n* poids *m*; **to lose/put on ~** maigrir/grossir; **~ing** *n* (*allowance*) indemnité *f*, allocation *f*; **~lifter** *n* haltérophile *m*; **~y** *adj* lourd(e); (*important*) de poids, important(e)

weir [wɪə*] *n* barrage *m*

weird [wɪəd] *adj* bizarre

welcome ['welkəm] *adj* bienvenu(e) ♦ *n* accueil *m* ♦ *vt* accueillir; (*also: bid ~*) souhaiter la bienvenue à; (*be glad of*) se réjouir de; **thank you - you're ~!** merci - de rien *or* il n'y a pas de quoi!

weld [weld] *vt* souder; **~er** *n* soudeur(euse)

welfare ['welfɛə*] *n* (*well-being*) bien-être *m*; (*social aid*) assistance sociale; **~ state** *n* État-providence *m*; **~ work** *n* travail social

well [wel] *n* puits *m* ♦ *adv* bien ♦ *adj*: **to be ~** aller bien ♦ *excl* eh bien!; bon!, enfin!; **as ~** aussi, également; **as ~ as** (*in addition to*) en plus de; **~ done!** bravo!; **get ~ soon** remets-toi vite!; **to do ~** bien réussir; (*business*) prospérer; **~ up** *vi* monter

we'll [wi:l] = **we will; we shall**

well: **~-behaved** ['welbɪ'heɪvd] *adj* sage obéissant(e); **~-being** ['welbi:ŋ] *n* bien-être *m*; **~-built** ['wel'bɪlt] *adj* (*person*) bien bâti(e); **~-deserved** *adj* (*bien*) mérité(e); **~-dressed** *adj* bien habillé(e); **~- heeled** (*inf*) *adj* (*wealthy*) nanti(e)

wellingtons ['welɪŋtənz] *npl* (*also:* **wellington boots**) bottes *fpl* de caoutchouc

well: **~-known** ['wel'nəʊn] *adj* (*person*) bien connu(e); **~-mannered** ['wel'mænəd] *adj* bien élevé(e); **~-meaning** ['wel'mi:nɪŋ] *adj* bien intentionné(e); **~- off** ['wel'ɒf] *adj* aisé(e); **~-read** ['wel'red] *adj* cultivé(e); **~-to-do** ['weltə'du:] *adj* aisé(e); **~-wishers** ['welwɪʃəz] *npl* amis *mpl* et admirateurs *mpl*; (*friends*) amis *mpl*

Welsh [welʃ] *adj* gallois(e) ♦ *n* (*LING*) gallois *m*; **the ~** *npl* (*people*) les Gallois *mpl*; **~man** (*irreg*) *n* Gallois *m*; **~ rarebit** *n* toast *m* au fromage; **~woman** (*irreg*) *n* Galloise *f*

went [went] *pt of* **go**

wept [wept] *pt, pp of* **weep**

were [wɜ:*] *pt of* **be**

we're [wɪə*] = **we are**

weren't [wɜ:nt] = **were not**

west [west] *n* ouest *m* ♦ *adj* ouest *inv*

de *or* à l'ouest ♦ *adv* à *or* vers l'ouest; **the W~** *n* l'Occident *m*, l'Ouest; **the W~ Country** (*BRIT*) *n* le sud-ouest de l'Angleterre; **~erly** *adj* (*wind*) d'ouest; (*point*) à l'ouest; **~ern** *adj* occidental(e), de *or* à l'ouest ♦ *n* (*CINEMA*) western *m*; **W~ Indian** *adj* antillais(e) ♦ *n* Antillais(e); **W~ Indies** *npl* Antilles *fpl*; **~ward(s)** *adv* vers l'ouest

wet [wɛt] *adj* mouillé(e); (*damp*) humide; (*soaked*) trempé(e); (*rainy*) pluvieux(euse) ♦ *n* (*BRIT: POL*) modéré *m* du parti conservateur; **to get ~** se mouiller; **"~ paint"** "attention peinture fraîche"; **~ blanket** *n* (*fig*) rabat-joie *m inv*; **~ suit** *n* combinaison *f* de plongée

we've [wi:v] = **we have**

whack [wæk] *vt* donner un grand coup à

whale [weɪl] *n* (*ZOOL*) baleine *f*

wharf [wɔ:f] (*pl* **wharves**) *n* quai *m*

what [wɔt] *adj* quel(le); **~ size is he?** quelle taille fait-il?; **~ colour is it?** de quelle couleur est-ce?; **~ books do you need?** quels livres vous faut-il?; **~ a mess!** quel désordre!

♦ *pron* **1** (*interrogative*) que, *prep* +quoi; **~ are you doing?** que faites-vous?, qu'est-ce que vous faites?; **~ is happening?** qu'est-ce qui se passe?, que se passe-t-il?; **~ are you talking about?** de quoi parlez-vous?; **~ is it called?** comment est-ce que ça s'appelle?; **~ about me?** et moi?; **~ about doing ...?** et si on faisait ...?

2 (*relative: subject*) ce qui; (: *direct object*) ce que; (: *indirect object*) ce *+prep* +quoi, ce dont; **I saw ~ you did/was on the table** j'ai vu ce que vous avez fait/ce qui était sur la table; **tell me ~ you remember** dites-moi ce dont vous vous souvenez

♦ *excl* (*disbelieving*) quoi!, comment!

whatever [wɔt'ɛvə*] *adj*: **~ book** quel que soit le livre que (*or* qui) *+sub*; n'importe quel livre ♦ *pron*: **do ~ is necessary** faites (tout) ce qui est nécessaire; **~**

happens quoi qu'il arrive; **no reason ~** pas la moindre raison; **nothing ~** rien du tout

whatsoever [wɔt'səuɛvə*] *adj* = **whatever**

wheat [wi:t] *n* blé *m*, froment *m*

wheedle [wi:dl] *vt*: **to ~ sb into doing sth** cajoler *or* enjôler qn pour qu'il fasse qch; **to ~ sth out of sb** obtenir qch de qn par des cajoleries

wheel [wi:l] *n* roue *f*; (*also: steering ~*) volant *m*; (*NAUT*) gouvernail *m* ♦ *vt* (*pram etc*) pousser ♦ *vi* (*birds*) tournoyer; (*also: ~ round: person*) virevolter; **~barrow** *n* brouette *f*; **~chair** *n* fauteuil roulant; **~ clamp** *n* (*AUT*) sabot *m* (de Denver)

wheeze [wi:z] *vi* respirer bruyamment

when [wɛn] *adv* quand; **~ did he go?** quand est-ce qu'il est parti?

♦ *conj* **1** (*at, during, after the time that*) quand, lorsque; **she was reading ~ I came in** elle lisait quand *or* lorsque je suis entré

2 (*on, at which*): **on the day ~ I met him** le jour où je l'ai rencontré

3 (*whereas*) alors que; **I thought I was wrong ~ in fact I was right** j'ai cru que j'avais tort alors qu'en fait j'avais raison

whenever [wɛn'ɛvə*] *adv* quand donc ♦ *conj* quand; (*every time that*) chaque fois que

where [wɛə*] *adv, conj* où; **this is ~** c'est là que; **~abouts** [wɛərə'baʊts] *adv* où donc ♦ *n*: **nobody knows his ~abouts** personne ne sait où il se trouve; **~as** [wɛər'æz] *conj* alors que; **~by** *adv* par lequel (*or* laquelle *etc*); **~upon** *adv* sur quoi

wherever [wɛər'ɛvə*] *adv* où donc ♦ *conj* où que *+sub*

wherewithal [wɛəwɪðɔ:l] *n* moyens *mpl*

whet [wɛt] *vt* aiguiser

whether [wɛðə*] *conj* si; **I don't know**

~ **to accept or not** je ne sais pas si je dois accepter ou non; **it's doubtful** ~ il est peu probable que +*sub*; ~ **you go or not** que vous y alliez ou non

---
KEYWORD
---

which [wɪtʃ] *adj* **1** (*interrogative: direct, indirect*) quel(le); ~ **picture do you want?** quel tableau voulez-vous?; ~ **one?** lequel(laquelle)?

2: in ~ **case** auquel cas

♦ **1** *pron* (*interrogative*) lequel(laquelle), lesquels(lesquelles) *pl*; **I don't mind** ~ peu importe lequel; ~ (**of these) are yours?** lesquels sont à vous?; **tell me** ~ **you want** dites-moi lesquels *or* ceux que vous voulez

2 (*relative: subject*) qui; (: *object*) que, *prep* +lequel(laquelle); **the apple** ~ **you ate/**~ **is on the table** la pomme que vous avez mangée/qui est sur la table; **the chair on** ~ **you are sitting** la chaise sur laquelle vous êtes assis; **the book of** ~ **you spoke** le livre dont vous avez parlé; **he knew,** ~ **is true/I feared** il le savait, ce qui est vrai/ce que je craignais; **after** ~ après quoi

---

whichever [wɪtʃ'evə*] *adj*: **take** ~ **book you prefer** prenez le livre que vous préférez, peu importe lequel; ~ **book you take** quel que soit le livre que vous preniez

whiff [wɪf] *n* bouffée *f*

while [waɪl] *n* moment *m* ♦ *conj* pendant que; (*as long as*) tant que; (*whereas*) alors que; bien que +*sub*; **for a** ~ pendant quelque temps; ~ **away** *vt* (*time*) (faire) passer

whim [wɪm] *n* caprice *m*

whimper ['wɪmpə*] *vi* geindre

whimsical ['wɪmzɪkəl] *adj* (*person*) capricieux(euse); (*look, story*) étrange

whine [waɪn] *vi* gémir, geindre

whip [wɪp] *n* fouet *m*; (*for riding*) cravache *f*; (*POL: person*) chef de file assurant la discipline dans son groupe parlementaire ♦ *vt* fouetter; (*eggs*) battre; (*move quickly*) enlever (*or* sortir)

brusquement; ~**ped cream** *n* crème fouettée; ~**-round** (*BRIT*) *n* collecte *f*

whirl [wɜ:l] *vt* faire tourbillonner; faire tournoyer ♦ *vi* tourbillonner; (*dancers*) tournoyer; ~**pool** *n* tourbillon *m*; ~**wind** *n* tornade *f*

whirr [wɜ:*] *vi* (*motor etc*) ronronner; (: *louder*) vrombir

whisk [wɪsk] *n* (*CULIN*) fouet *m* ♦ *vt* fouetter; (*eggs*) battre; **to** ~ **sb away** *or* **off** emmener qn rapidement

whiskers ['wɪskəz] *npl* (*of animal*) moustaches *fpl*; (*of man*) favoris *mpl*

whisky ['wɪskɪ] (*IRELAND, US* **whiskey**) *n* whisky *m*

whisper ['wɪspə*] *vt, vi* chuchoter

whistle ['wɪsl] *n* (*sound*) sifflement *m*; (*object*) sifflet *m* ♦ *vi* siffler

white [waɪt] *adj* blanc(blanche); (*with fear*) blême ♦ *n* blanc *m*; (*person*) blanc(blanche); ~ **coffee** (*BRIT*) *n* café *m* au lait, (*café*) crème *m*; ~**-collar worker** *n* employé(e) de bureau; ~ **elephant** *n* (*fig*) objet dispendieux et superflu; ~ **lie** *n* pieux mensonge; ~ **paper** *n* (*POL*) livre blanc; ~**wash** *vt* blanchir à la chaux; (*fig*) blanchir ♦ *n* (*paint*) blanc *m* de chaux

whiting ['waɪtɪŋ] *n inv* (*fish*) merlan *m*

Whitsun ['wɪtsn] *n* la Pentecôte

whittle ['wɪtl] *vt*: **to** ~ **away,** ~ **down** (*costs*) réduire

whizz [wɪz] *vi*: **to** ~ **past** *or* **by** passer à toute vitesse; ~ **kid** (*inf*) *n* petit prodige

who [hu:] *pron* qui; ~**dunit** [hu:'dʌnɪt] (*inf*) *n* roman policier

whoever [hu:'evə*] *pron*: ~ **finds it** celui(celle) qui le trouve(, qui que ce soit), quiconque le trouve; **ask** ~ **you like** demandez à qui vous voulez; ~ **he marries** quelle que soit la personne qu'il épouse; ~ **told you that?** qui a bien pu vous dire ça?

whole [həʊl] *adj* (*complete*) entier(ère), tout(e); (*not broken*) intact(e), complet(ète) ♦ *n* (*all*): **the** ~ **of** la totalité de, tout(e) le(la); (*entire unit*) tout *m*; **the** ~ **of the town** la ville tout entière; **on the** ~, **as a** ~ dans l'ensemble; ~**food(s)**

n(pl) aliments complets; **~hearted** *adj* sans réserve(s); **~meal** (*BRIT*) *adj* (*bread, flour*) complet(ète); **~sale** *n* (vente *f* en) gros *m* ♦ *adj* (*price*) de gros; (*destruction*) systématique ♦ *adv* en gros; **~saler** *n* grossiste *m/f*; **~some** *adj* sain(e); **~wheat** *adj* = **~meal**; **wholly** ['həʊlɪ] *adv* entièrement, tout à fait

whom [huːm] *pron* **1** (*interrogative*) qui; **~ did you see?** qui avez-vous vu?; **to ~ did you give it?** à qui l'avez-vous donné?
2 (*relative*) que, *prep* + qui; **the man ~ I saw/to ~ I spoke** l'homme que j'ai vu/à qui j'ai parlé

whooping cough ['huːpɪŋ-] *n* coqueluche *f*
whore ['hɔː*] (*inf: pej*) *n* putain *f*

whose [huːz] *adj* **1** (*possessive: interrogative*): **~ book is this?** à qui est ce livre?; **~ pencil have you taken?** à qui est le crayon que vous avez pris?; **~ daughter are you?** de qui êtes-vous la fille?
2 (*possessive: relative*): **the man ~ son you rescued** l'homme dont *or* de qui vous avez sauvé le fils; **the girl ~ sister you were speaking to** la fille à la sœur de qui *or* de laquelle vous parliez; **the woman ~ car was stolen** la femme dont la voiture a été volée
♦ *pron* à qui; **~ is this?** à qui est ceci?; **I know ~ it is** je sais à qui c'est

why [waɪ] *adv* pourquoi ♦ *excl* eh bien!, tiens!; **the reason ~** la raison pour laquelle; **tell me ~** dites-moi pourquoi; **~ not?** pourquoi pas?; **~ever** *adv* pourquoi donc, mais pourquoi
wicked ['wɪkɪd] *adj* mauvais(e), méchant(e); (*crime*) pervers(e); (*mischievous*) malicieux(euse)
wicket ['wɪkɪt] *n* (*CRICKET*) guichet *m*
wide [waɪd] *adj* large; (*area, knowledge*)

vaste, très étendu(e); (*choice*) grand(e) ♦ *adv*: **to open ~** ouvrir tout grand; **to shoot ~** tirer à côté; **~-angle lens** *n* objectif *m* grand angle; **~-awake** *adj* bien éveillé(e); **~ly** *adv* (*differing*) radicalement; (*spaced*) sur une grande étendue; (*believed*) généralement; (*travel*) beaucoup; **~n** *vt* élargir ♦ *vi* s'élargir; **~ open** *adj* grand(e) ouvert(e); **~spread** *adj* (*belief etc*) très répandu(e)

widow ['wɪdəu] *n* veuve *f*; **~ed** *adj* veuf(veuve); **~er** *n* veuf *m*
width [wɪdθ] *n* largeur *f*
wield [wiːld] *vt* (*sword*) manier; (*power*) exercer
wife [waɪf] (*pl* **wives**) *n* femme *f*, épouse *f*
wig [wɪg] *n* perruque *f*
wiggle ['wɪgl] *vt* agiter, remuer
wild [waɪld] *adj* sauvage; (*sea*) déchaîné(e); (*idea, life*) fou(folle); (*behaviour*) extravagant(e), déchaîné(e); **~s** *npl* (*remote area*) régions *fpl* sauvages; **to make a ~ guess** émettre une hypothèse à tout hasard; **~erness** ['wɪldənəs] *n* désert *m*, région *f* sauvage; **~-goose chase** *n* (*fig*) fausse piste; **~life** *n* (*animals*) faune *f*; **~ly** *adv* (*behave*) de manière déchaînée; (*applaud*) frénétiquement; (*hit, guess*) au hasard; (*happy*) follement
wilful ['wɪlful] (*US* **willful**) *adj* (*person*) obstiné(e); (*action*) délibéré(e)

will [wɪl] (*vt: pt, pp* **willed**) *aux vb* **1** (*forming future tense*): **I ~ finish it tomorrow** je le finirai demain; **I ~ have finished it by tomorrow** je l'aurai fini d'ici demain; **~ you do it? - yes I ~/no I won't** le ferez-vous? - oui/non
2 (*in conjectures, predictions*): **he ~ or he'll be there by now** il doit être arrivé à l'heure qu'il est; **that ~ be the postman** ça doit être le facteur
3 (*in commands, requests, offers*): **~ you be quiet!** voulez-vous bien vous taire!; **~ you help me?** est-ce que vous pouvez m'aider?; **~ you have a cup of tea?**

voulez-vous une tasse de thé?; **I won't put up with it!** je ne le tolérerai pas!
♦ *vt*: **to ~ sb to do** souhaiter ardemment que qn fasse; **he ~ed himself to go on** par un suprême effort de volonté, il continua
♦ *n* volonté *f*; testament *m*

willing ['wɪlɪŋ] *adj* de bonne volonté, serviable; **he's ~ to do it** il est disposé à le faire,, il veut bien le faire; **~ly** *adv* volontiers; **~ness** *n* bonne volonté
willow ['wɪləʊ] *n* saule *m*
willpower ['wɪl'paʊə*] *n* volonté *f*
willy-nilly ['wɪlɪ'nɪlɪ] *adv* bon gré mal gré
wilt [wɪlt] *vi* dépérir; *(flower)* se faner
wily ['waɪlɪ] *adj* rusé(e)
win [wɪn] *(pt, pp* **won)** *n (in sports etc)* victoire *f* ♦ *vt* gagner; *(prize)* remporter; *(popularity)* acquérir ♦ *vi* gagner; **~ over** *vt* convaincre; **~ round** *(BRIT) vt =* **~ over**
wince [wɪns] *vi* tressaillir
winch [wɪntʃ] *n* treuil *m*
wind[1] [wɪnd] *n (also MED)* vent *m*; *(breath)* souffle *m*
wind[2] [waɪnd] *(pt, pp* **wound)** *vt* enrouler; *(wrap)* envelopper; *(clock, toy)* remonter ♦ *vi (road, river)* serpenter; **~ up** *vt (clock)* remonter; *(debate)* terminer, clôturer
windfall ['wɪndfɔːl] *n* coup *m* de chance
winding ['waɪndɪŋ] *adj (road)* sinueux(euse); *(staircase)* tournant(e)
wind instrument *n (MUS)* instrument *m* à vent
windmill ['wɪndmɪl] *n* moulin *m* à vent
window ['wɪndəʊ] *n* fenêtre *f*; *(in car, train, also:* **~ pane)** vitre *f*; *(in shop etc)* vitrine *f*; **~ box** *n* jardinière *f*; **~ cleaner** *n (person)* laveur(euse) de vitres; **~ ledge** *n* rebord de la fenêtre; **~ pane** *n* vitre *f*, carreau *m*; **~-shopping** *n*: **to go ~-shopping** faire du lèche-vitrines; **~sill** *n (inside)* appui de la fenêtre; *(outside)* rebord *m* de la fenêtre
windpipe ['wɪndpaɪp] *n* trachée *f*
wind power *n* énergie éolienne

windscreen ['wɪndskriːn] *n* pare-brise *m inv*; **~ washer** *n* lave-glace *m inv*; **~ wiper** *n* essuie-glace *m inv*
windshield ['wɪndʃiːld] *(US) n =* **windscreen**
windswept ['wɪndswept] *adj* balayé(e) par le vent; *(person)* ébouriffé(e)
windy ['wɪndɪ] *adj* venteux(euse); **it's ~** il y a du vent
wine [waɪn] *n* vin *m*; **~ bar** *n* bar *m* à vin; **~ cellar** *n* cave *f* à vin; **~ glass** *n* verre *m* à vin; **~ list** *n* carte *f* des vins; **~ waiter** *n* sommelier *m*
wing [wɪŋ] *n* aile *f*; **~s** *npl (THEATRE)* coulisses *fpl*; **~er** *n (SPORT)* ailier *m*
wink [wɪŋk] *n* clin *m* d'œil ♦ *vi* faire un clin d'œil; *(blink)* cligner des yeux
winner ['wɪnə*] *n* gagnant(e)
winning ['wɪnɪŋ] *adj (team)* gagnant(e); *(goal)* décisif(ive); **~s** *npl* gains *mpl*
winter ['wɪntə*] *n* hiver *m*; **in ~** en hiver; **~ sports** *npl* sports *mpl* d'hiver; **wintry** ['wɪntrɪ] *adj* hivernal(e)
wipe [waɪp] *n*: **to give sth a ~** donner un coup de torchon *(or* de chiffon *or* d'éponge) à qch ♦ *vt* essuyer; *(erase: tape)* effacer; **~ off** *vt* enlever; **~ out** *vt (debt)* éteindre, amortir; *(memory)* effacer; *(destroy)* anéantir; **~ up** *vt* essuyer
wire ['waɪə*] *n* fil *m* (de fer); *(ELEC)* fil électrique; *(TEL)* télégramme *m* ♦ *vt (house)* faire l'installation électrique de; *(also:* **~ up)** brancher; *(person: send telegram to)* télégraphier à; **~less** ['waɪəlɪs] *(BRIT) n* poste *m* de radio; **wiring** ['waɪərɪŋ] *n* installation *f* électrique
wiry ['waɪərɪ] *adj* noueux(euse), nerveux(euse); *(hair)* dru(e)
wisdom ['wɪzdəm] *n* sagesse *f*; *(of action)* prudence *f*; **~ tooth** *n* dent *f* de sagesse
wise [waɪz] *adj* sage, prudent(e); *(remark)* judicieux(euse) ♦ *suffix*: **...wise**: **timewise** *etc* en ce qui concerne le temps *etc*; **~crack** *n* remarque *f* ironique
wish [wɪʃ] *n (desire)* désir *m*; *(specific desire)* souhait *m*, vœu *m* ♦ *vt* souhaiter, désirer, vouloir; **best ~es** *(on birthday etc)* meilleurs vœux; **with best ~es**

(*in letter*) bien amicalement; **to ~ sb goodbye** dire au revoir à qn; **he ~ed me well** il m'a souhaité bonne chance; **to ~ to do/sb to do** désirer *or* vouloir faire/que qn fasse; **to ~ for** souhaiter; ~**ful** *adj*: **it's ~ful thinking** c'est prendre ses désirs pour des réalités

wistful ['wɪstful] *adj* mélancolique

wit [wɪt] *n* (*gen pl*) intelligence *f*, esprit *m*; (*presence of mind*) présence *f* d'esprit; (*wittiness*) esprit; (*person*) homme/femme d'esprit

witch [wɪtʃ] *n* sorcière *f*; ~**craft** *n* sorcellerie *f*

KEYWORD
---

with [wɪð, wɪθ] *prep* **1** (*in the company of*) avec; (*at the home of*) chez; **we stayed ~ friends** nous avons logé chez des amis; **I'll be ~ you in a minute** je suis à vous dans un instant

2 (*descriptive*): **a room ~ a view** une chambre avec vue; **the man ~ the grey hat/blue eyes** l'homme au chapeau gris/aux yeux bleus

3 (*indicating manner, means, cause*): ~ **tears in her eyes** les larmes aux yeux; **to walk ~ a stick** marcher avec une canne; **red ~ anger** rouge de colère; **to fill sth ~ water** remplir qch d'eau

4: **I'm ~ you** (*I understand*) je vous suis; **to be ~ it** (*inf*: *up-to-date*) être dans le vent

---

withdraw [wɪθ'drɔː] (*irreg*) *vt* retirer ♦ *vi* se retirer; ~**al** *n* retrait *m*; ~**n** *adj* (*person*) renfermé(e)

wither ['wɪðə*] *vi* (*plant*) se faner

withhold [wɪθ'həʊld] (*irreg*) *vt* (*money*) retenir; **to ~ (from)** (*information*) cacher (à); (*permission*) refuser (à)

within [wɪð'ɪn] *prep* à l'intérieur de ♦ *adv* à l'intérieur; ~ **his reach** à sa portée; ~ **sight of** en vue de; ~ **a kilometre of** à moins d'un kilomètre de; ~ **the week** avant la fin de la semaine

without [wɪð'aʊt] *prep* sans; ~ **a coat** sans manteau; ~ **speaking** sans parler; **to go ~ sth** se passer de qch

withstand [wɪθ'stænd] (*irreg*) *vt* résister à

witness ['wɪtnəs] *n* (*person*) témoin *m* ♦ *vt* (*event*) être témoin de; (*document*) attester l'authenticité de; **to bear ~ (to)** (*fig*) attester; ~ **box** *n* barre *f* des témoins; ~ **stand** (*US*) *n* = ~ **box**

witticism ['wɪtɪsɪzəm] *n* mot *m* d'esprit; **witty** ['wɪtɪ] *adj* spirituel(le), plein(e) d'esprit

wives [waɪvz] *npl of* **wife**

wizard ['wɪzəd] *n* magicien *m*

wk *abbr* = **week**

wobble ['wɒbl] *vi* trembler; (*chair*) branler

woe [wəʊ] *n* malheur *m*

woke [wəʊk] *pt of* **wake**

woken ['wəʊkən] *pp of* **wake**

wolf [wʊlf, *pl* wʊlvz] (*pl* **wolves**) *n* loup *m*

woman ['wʊmən] (*pl* **women**) *n* femme *f*; ~ **doctor** *n* femme *f* médecin; ~**ly** *adj* féminin(e)

womb [wuːm] *n* (*ANAT*) utérus *m*

women ['wɪmɪn] *npl of* **woman**; ~**'s lib** (*inf*) *n* MLF *m*; **W~'s (Liberation) Movement** *n* mouvement *m* de libération de la femme

won [wʌn] *pt, pp of* **win**

wonder ['wʌndə*] *n* merveille *f*, miracle *m*; (*feeling*) émerveillement *m* ♦ *vi*: **to ~ whether/why** se demander si/pourquoi; **to ~ at** (*marvel*) s'émerveiller de; **to ~ about** songer à; **it's no ~ (that)** il n'est pas étonnant (que +*sub*); ~**ful** *adj* merveilleux(euse)

won't [wəʊnt] = **will not**

wood [wʊd] *n* (*timber, forest*) bois *m*; ~ **carving** *n* sculpture *f* en *or* sur bois; ~**ed** *adj* boisé(e); ~**en** *adj* en bois; (*fig*) raide; inexpressif(ive); ~**pecker** *n* pic *m* (*oiseau*); ~**wind** *n* (*MUS*): **the ~wind** les bois *mpl*; ~**work** *n* menuiserie *f*; ~**worm** *n* ver *m* du bois

wool [wʊl] *n* laine *f*; **to pull the ~ over sb's eyes** (*fig*) en faire accroire à qn; ~**len** (*US* ~**en**) *adj* de *or* en laine; (*industry*) lainier(ère); ~**lens** *npl* (*clothes*) lainages *mpl*; ~**ly** (*US* ~**y**) *adj* laineux(euse);

(fig: ideas) confus(e)

word [wɜːd] *n* mot *m*; *(promise)* parole *f*; *(news)* nouvelles *fpl* ♦ *vt* rédiger, formuler; **in other ~s** en d'autres termes; **to break/keep one's ~** manquer à sa parole/tenir parole; **~ing** *n* termes *mpl*; libellé *m*; **~ processing** *n* traitement *m* de texte; **~ processor** *n* machine *f* de traitement de texte

wore [wɔː*] *pt of* **wear**

work [wɜːk] *n* travail *m*; *(ART, LITERATURE)* œuvre *f* ♦ *vi* travailler; *(mechanism)* marcher, fonctionner; *(plan etc)* marcher; *(medicine)* agir ♦ *vt* *(clay, wood etc)* travailler; *(mine etc)* exploiter; *(machine)* faire marcher *or* fonctionner; *(miracles, wonders etc)* faire; **to be out of ~** être sans emploi; **to ~ loose** se défaire, se desserrer; **~ on** *vt fus* travailler à; *(principle)* se baser sur; *(person)* (essayer d')influencer; **~ out** *vi* *(plans etc)* marcher ♦ *vt* *(problem)* résoudre; *(plan)* élaborer; **it ~s out at £100** ça fait 100 livres; **~ up** *vt*: **to get ~ed up** se mettre dans tous ses états; **~able** *adj* *(solution)* réalisable; **~aholic** [wɜːkəˈhɒlɪk] *n* bourreau *m* de travail; **~er** *n* travailleur(euse), ouvrier(ère); **~force** *n* main-d'œuvre *f*; **~ing-class** *n* classe ouvrière; **~ing-class** *adj* ouvrier(ère); **~ing order** *n*: **in ~ing order** en état de marche; **~man** *(irreg)* *n* ouvrier *m*; **~manship** *n* *(skill)* métier *m*, habileté *f*; **~s** *n* *(BRIT: factory)* usine *f* ♦ *npl* *(of clock, etc)* mécanisme *m*; **~ sheet** *n* *(COMPUT)* feuille *f* de programmation; **~shop** *n* atelier *m*; **~ station** *n* poste *m* de travail; **~-to-rule** *(BRIT)* *n* grève *f* du zèle

world [wɜːld] *n* monde *m* ♦ *cpd* *(champion)* du monde; *(power, war)* mondial(e); **to think the ~ of sb** *(fig)* ne jurer que par qn; **~ly** *adj* de ce monde; *(knowledgeable)* qui a l'expérience du monde; **~wide** *adj* universel(le)

worm [wɜːm] *n* ver *m*

worn [wɔːn] *pp of* **wear** ♦ *adj* usé(e); **~-out** *adj* *(object)* complètement usé(e); *(person)* épuisé(e)

worried [ˈwʌrɪd] *adj* inquiet(ète)

worry [ˈwʌrɪ] *n* souci *m* ♦ *vt* inquiéter ♦ *vi* s'inquiéter, se faire du souci

worse [wɜːs] *adj* pire, plus mauvais(e) ♦ *adv* plus mal ♦ *n* pire *m*; **a change for the ~** une détérioration; **~n** *vt, vi* empirer; **~ off** *adj* moins à l'aise financièrement

worship [ˈwɜːʃɪp] *n* culte *m* ♦ *vt* *(God)* rendre un culte à; *(person)* adorer; **Your W~** *(BRIT: to mayor)* Monsieur le maire; *(: to judge)* Monsieur le juge

worst [wɜːst] *adj* le(la) pire, le(la) plus mauvais(e) ♦ *adv* le plus mal ♦ *n* pire *m*; **at ~** au pis aller

worth [wɜːθ] *n* valeur *f* ♦ *adj*: **to be ~** valoir; **it's ~ it** cela en vaut la peine; **it is ~ one's while (to do)** on gagne à (faire); **~less** *adj* qui ne vaut rien; **~while** *adj* *(activity, cause)* utile, louable

worthy [ˈwɜːðɪ] *adj* *(person)* digne; *(motive)* louable; **~ of** digne de

---
KEYWORD
---

would [wʊd] *aux vb* **1** *(conditional tense)*: **if you asked him he ~ do it** si vous le lui demandiez, il le ferait; **if you had asked him he ~ have done it** si vous le lui aviez demandé, il l'aurait fait **2** *(in offers, invitations, requests)*: **~ you like a biscuit?** voulez-vous un biscuit?; **~ you close the door please?** voulez-vous fermer la porte, s'il vous plaît? **3** *(in indirect speech)*: **I said I ~ do it** j'ai dit que je le ferais **4** *(emphatic)*: **it WOULD have to snow today!** naturellement il neige aujourd'hui!, il fallait qu'il neige aujourd'hui! **5** *(insistence)*: **she ~n't do it** elle n'a pas voulu *or* elle a refusé de le faire **6** *(conjecture)*: **it ~ have been midnight** il devait être minuit **7** *(indicating habit)*: **he ~ go there on Mondays** il y allait le lundi

would-be [ˈwʊdbiː] *(pej)* *adj* soi-disant
wouldn't [ˈwʊdnt] = **would not**
wound¹ [wuːnd] *n* blessure *f* ♦ *vt* blesser

wound² [waʊnd] *pt, pp of* **wind²**

wove [wəʊv] *pt of* **weave**

woven ['wəʊvən] *pp of* **weave**

wrap [ræp] *vt* (*also:* ~ *up*) envelopper, emballer; (*wind*) enrouler; **~per** *n* (*BRIT: of book*) couverture *f*; (*on chocolate*) papier *m*; **~ping paper** *n* papier *m* d'emballage; (*for gift*) papier cadeau

wrath [rɒθ] *n* courroux *m*

wreak [riːk] *vt:* **to ~ havoc (on)** avoir un effet désastreux (sur)

wreath [riːθ, *pl* riːðz] *n* couronne *f*

wreck [rɛk] *n* (*ship*) épave *f*; (*vehicle*) véhicule accidenté; (*pej: person*) loque humaine ♦ *vt* démolir; (*fig*) briser, ruiner; **~age** *n* débris *mpl*; (*of building*) décombres *mpl*; (*of ship*) épave *f*

wren [rɛn] *n* (*ZOOL*) roitelet *m*

wrench [rɛntʃ] *n* (*TECH*) clé *f* (à écrous); (*tug*) violent mouvement de torsion; (*fig*) déchirement *m* ♦ *vt* tirer violemment sur; **to ~ sth from** arracher qch à *or* de

wrestle ['rɛsl] *vi:* **to ~ (with sb)** lutter (avec qn); **~r** *n* lutteur(euse); **wrestling** *n* lutte *f*; (*also: all-in wrestling*) catch *m*

wretched ['rɛtʃɪd] *adj* misérable; (*inf*) maudit(e)

wriggle ['rɪgl] *vi* (*also:* ~ *about*) se tortiller

wring [rɪŋ] (*pt, pp* **wrung**) *vt* tordre; (*wet clothes*) essorer; (*fig*): **to ~ sth out of sb** arracher qch à qn

wrinkle ['rɪŋkl] *n* (*on skin*) ride *f*; (*on paper etc*) pli *m* ♦ *vt* plisser ♦ *vi* se plisser

wrist [rɪst] *n* poignet *m*; **~watch** *n* montre-bracelet *f*

writ [rɪt] *n* acte *m* judiciaire

write [raɪt] (*pt* **wrote**, *pp* **written**) *vt, vi* écrire; (*prescription*) rédiger; **~ down** *vt* noter; (*put in writing*) mettre par écrit; **~ off** *vt* (*debt*) passer aux profits et pertes; (*project*) mettre une croix sur; **~ out** *vt* écrire; **~ up** *vt* rédiger; **~-off** *n* perte totale; **~r** *n* auteur *m*, écrivain *m*

writhe [raɪð] *vi* se tordre

writing ['raɪtɪŋ] *n* écriture *f*; (*of author*) œuvres *fpl*; **in** ~ par écrit; ~ **paper** *n* papier *m* à lettres

wrong [rɒŋ] *adj* (*incorrect: answer, information*) faux(fausse); (*inappropriate: choice, action etc*) mauvais(e); (*wicked*) mal; (*unfair*) injuste ♦ *adv* mal ♦ *n* tort *m* ♦ *vt* faire du tort à, léser; **you are ~ to do it** tu as tort de le faire; **you are ~ about that, you've got it ~** tu te trompes; **what's ~?** qu'est-ce qui ne va pas?; **to go ~** (*person*) se tromper; (*plan*) mal tourner; (*machine*) tomber en panne; **to be in the ~** avoir tort; **~ful** *adj* injustifié(e); **~ly** *adv* mal, incorrectement; ~ **side** *n* (*of material*) envers *m*

wrote [rəʊt] *pt of* **write**

wrought [rɔːt] *adj:* ~ **iron** fer forgé

wrung [rʌŋ] *pt, pp of* **wring**

wry [raɪ] *adj* désabusé(e)

wt. *abbr* = **weight**

X Y Z

Xmas ['ɛksməs] *n abbr* = **Christmas**

X-ray ['ɛks'reɪ] *n* (*ray*) rayon *m* X; (*photo*) radio(graphie) *f*

xylophone ['zaɪləfəʊn] *n* xylophone *m*

yacht [jɒt] *n* yacht *m*; voilier *m*; **~ing** *n* yachting *m*, navigation *f* de plaisance; **~sman** (*irreg*) *n* plaisancier *m*

Yank(ee) [jæŋk(ɪ)] (*pej*) *n* Amerloque *m/f*

yap [jæp] *vi* (*dog*) japper

yard [jɑːd] *n* (*of house etc*) cour *f*; (*measure*) yard *m* (= 91,4 cm); **~stick** *n* (*fig*) mesure *f*, critères *mpl*

yarn [jɑːn] *n* fil *m*; (*tale*) longue histoire

yawn [jɔːn] *n* bâillement *m* ♦ *vi* bâiller; **~ing** *adj* (*gap*) béant(e)

yd. *abbr* = **yard(s)**

yeah [jɛə] (*inf*) *adv* ouais

year [jɪə*] *n* an *m*, année *f*; **to be 8 ~s old** avoir 8 ans; **an eight-~-old child** un enfant de huit ans; **~ly** *adj* annuel(le) ♦ *adv* annuellement

yearn [jɜːn] *vi:* **to ~ for sth** aspirer à qch, languir après qch; **to ~ to do** aspirer à faire

yeast [jiːst] *n* levure *f*

yell [jel] *vi* hurler

yellow ['jeləu] *adj* jaune

yelp [jelp] *vi* japper; glapir

yeoman ['jəumən] (*irreg*) *n*: ~ **of the guard** hallebardier *m* de la garde royale

yes [jes] *adv* oui; (*answering negative question*) si ♦ *n* oui *m*

yesterday ['jestədeı] *adv* hier ♦ *n* hier *m*; ~ **morning/evening** hier matin/soir; **all day** ~ toute la journée d'hier

yet [jet] *adv* encore; déjà ♦ *conj* pourtant, néanmoins; **it is not finished** ~ ce n'est pas encore fini *or* toujours pas fini; **the best** ~ le meilleur jusqu'ici *or* jusque-là; **as** ~ jusqu'ici, encore

yew [ju:] *n* if *m*

yield [ji:ld] *n* production *f*, rendement *m*; rapport *m* ♦ *vt* produire, rendre, rapporter; (*surrender*) céder ♦ *vi* céder; (*US*: *AUT*) céder la priorité

YMCA *n abbr* (= *Young Men's Christian Association*) YMCA *m*

yoghourt, yog(h)urt ['jɒgət] *n* yaourt *m*

yoke [jəuk] *n* joug *m*

yolk [jəuk] *n* jaune *m* (d'œuf)

KEYWORD
---

you [ju:] *pron* **1** (*subject*) tu; (*polite form*) vous; (*plural*) vous; ~ **French enjoy your food** vous autres Français, vous aimez bien manger; ~ **and I will go** toi et moi/vous et moi, nous irons

2 (*object: direct, indirect*) te, t' +*vowel*; vous; **I know** ~ je te/vous connais; **I gave it to** ~ je vous l'ai donné, je te l'ai donné

3 (*stressed*) toi; vous; **I told YOU to do it** c'est à toi/vous que j'ai dit de le faire

4 (*after prep, in comparisons*) toi; vous; **it's for** ~ c'est pour toi/vous; **she's younger than** ~ elle est plus jeune que toi/vous

5 (*impersonal: one*) on; **fresh air does** ~ **good** l'air frais fait du bien; ~ **never know** on ne sait jamais

you'd [ju:d] = **you had; you would**

you'll [ju:l] = **you will; you shall**

young [jʌŋ] *adj* jeune ♦ *npl* (*of animal*) petits *mpl*; (*people*): **the** ~ les jeunes, la jeunesse; ~**er** *adj* (*brother etc*) cadet(te);

~**ster** *n* jeune *m* (garçon *m*); (*child*) enfant *m/f*

your ['jɔ:*] *adj* ton(ta), tes *pl*; (*polite form, pl*) votre, vos *pl*; *see also* **my**

you're ['juə*] = **you are**

yours [jɔ:z] *pron* le(la) tien(ne), les tiens(tiennes); (*polite form, pl*) le(la) vôtre, les vôtres; ~ **sincerely/faithfully/truly** veuillez agréer l'expression de mes sentiments les meilleurs; *see also* **mine**[1]

yourself [jɔ:'self] *pron* (*reflexive*) te; (: *polite form*) vous; (*after prep*) toi; vous; (*emphatic*) toi-même; vous-même; *see also* **oneself**; **yourselves** *pl pron* vous; (*emphatic*) vous-mêmes

youth [ju:θ, *pl* ju:ðz] *n* jeunesse *f*; (*young man: pl youths*) jeune homme *m*; ~ **club** *n* centre *m* de jeunes; ~**ful** *adj* jeune; (*enthusiasm*) de jeunesse, juvénile; ~ **hostel** *n* auberge *f* de jeunesse

you've [ju:v] = **you have**

YTS (*BRIT*) *n abbr* (= *Youth Training Scheme*) ≈ TUC *m*

Yugoslav *adj* yougoslave ♦ *n* Yougoslave *m/f*; ~**ia** *n* Yougoslavie *f*

yuppie ['jʌpɪ] (*inf*) *n* yuppie *m/f*

YWCA *n abbr* (= *Young Women's Christian Association*) YWCA *m*

zap [zæp] *vt* (*COMPUT*) effacer

zeal [zi:l] *n* zèle *m*, ferveur *f*; empressement *m*

zebra ['zi:brə] *n* zèbre *m*; ~ **crossing** (*BRIT*) *n* passage clouté *or* pour piétons

zero ['zɪərəu] *n* zéro *m*

zest [zest] *n* entrain *m*, élan *m*; (*of orange*) zeste *m*

Zimbabwe [zɪm'bɑ:bwɪ] *n* Zimbabwe *m*

zip [zɪp] *n* (*also*: ~ *fastener*) fermeture *f* éclair (®) ♦ *vt* (*also*: ~ *up*) fermer avec une fermeture éclair (®); ~ **code** (*US*) *n* code postal; ~**per** (*US*) *n* = **zip**

zodiac ['zəudɪæk] *n* zodiaque *m*

zone [zəun] *n* zone *f*

zoo [zu:] *n* zoo *m*

zoom [zu:m] *vi*: **to** ~ **past** passer en trombe; ~ **lens** *n* zoom *m*

zucchini [zu:'ki:nɪ] *n(pl)* courgette(s) *f(pl)*

LE DICTIONNAIRE ET LA GRAMMAIRE

Bien qu'un dictionnaire ne puisse jamais remplacer une grammaire détaillée, il fournit néanmoins un grand nombre de renseignements grammaticaux. Le Robert & Collins Mini présente les indications grammaticales de la façon suivante:

Les catégories grammaticales

Elles sont données en italique immédiatement après la transcription phonétique des entrées. La liste des abréviations se trouve pages viii et ix.

Les changements de catégorie grammaticale au sein d'un article – par exemple, d'adjectif à adverbe, ou de nom à verbe intransitif à verbe transitif – sont indiqués au moyen de losanges – comme pour le mot français "large" et l'anglais "act".

Les adverbes

La règle générale pour former les adverbes en anglais est d'ajouter "-ly" à l'adjectif ou à sa racine. Ainsi:

bad > badly

gentle > gently

La terminaison en "-ly" est souvent l'équivalent du français "-ment":

slowly – lentement

slyly – sournoisement

Il faut toutefois faire attention car certains mots en "-ly" sont des adjectifs et non des adverbes. Par exemple: "friendly", "likely", "ugly", "silly". Ces mots ne peuvent pas être utilisés en tant qu'adverbes. Il faut donc bien vérifier la catégorie grammaticale du mot que vous voulez utiliser.

Les adverbes figurent soit dans les articles des adjectifs correspondants s'ils suivent ces adjectifs dans l'ordre alphabétique ("fortunately"), soit comme entrées à part entière s'ils précèdent alphabétiquement l'adjectif ("happily"). Si leur usage est moins fréquent, ils n'apparaissent pas du tout. Vous pouvez cependant les traduire facilement en français d'après la traduction de l'adjectif correspondant.

Le pluriel des noms en anglais

Normalement, on forme le pluriel des noms anglais en ajoutant un "-s" au singulier.

cat > cats

Le pluriel des noms qui finissent en "-o" est formé en ajoutant "-es" au singulier.

Tous les pluriels irréguliers sont donnés entre parenthèses et en caractères gras immédiatement après la transcription phonétique (v. "tomato").

Certains noms ont un pluriel irrégulier, comme "knife" et "man" en regard. Ces pluriels irréguliers apparaissent également en tant qu'entrées à part entière dans le texte et renvoient au singulier (v. "knives" et "men").

Les verbes irréguliers

Les verbes irréguliers sont clairement signalés dans ce dictionnaire: les formes du prétérit (*pt*) et du participe passé (*pp*) sont données en caractères gras entre parenthèses immédiatement après la transcription phonétique de l'entrée. Voir les verbes "to teach" et "to swim".

Par ailleurs les formes du prétérit et du participe passé des verbes irréguliers apparaissent elles-mêmes comme des entrées à part entière dans le dictionnaire et renvoient à l'infinitif du verbe. Voir "taught", "swam" et "swum".

De plus, vous avez la possibilité de vous référer rapidement à la liste des verbes irréguliers anglais pages 635 et 636 vers la fin de votre dictionnaire.

Enfin, pour ce qui est des verbes réguliers, vous remarquerez que leur prétérit et leur participe passé ne sont pas donnés. Ceci est dû au fait que ces formes ne présentent aucun problème puisqu'on ajoute toujours "-ed" à l'infinitif pour les obtenir (ou bien "-d" si l'infinitif se termine par la voyelle "-e").

		prétérit		**participe passé**
exemples:	to help	– helped	–	helped
	to love	– loved	–	loved

THE DICTIONARY AND GRAMMAR

While it is true that a dictionary can never be a substitute for a detailed grammar it nevertheless provides a great deal of grammatical information. If you know how to extract this information you will be able to use French more accurately both in speech and in writing.

The Collins Pocket Dictionary presents grammatical information as follows.

Parts of speech

Parts of speech are given in italics immediately after the phonetic spellings of headwords. Abbreviated forms are used. Abbreviations can be checked on pages viii and ix.

Changes in parts of speech within an entry – for example, from adjective to adverb to noun, or from noun to intransitive verb to transitive verb – are indicated by means of lozenges - ♦ - as with the French 'large' and the English 'act'.

Genders of French nouns

The gender of each noun in the French-English section of the dictionary is indicated in the following way:

> *nm* = nom masculin
>
> *nf* = nom féminin

You will occasionally see *nm/f* beside an entry. This indicates that a noun – 'concierge', for example – can be either masculine or feminine.

Feminine and *irregular* plural forms of nouns are shown, as with 'chercheur' and 'cheval': the ending which follows the entry is substituted, so that 'chercheur' becomes 'chercheuse' in the feminine, and 'cheval' becomes 'chevaux' in the plural.

In the English-French section of the dictionary, the gender immediately follows the noun translation, as with 'grass'. Where a noun can be either masculine or feminine, this is shown by '*m/f*' if the form of the noun does not change, or by the bracketed feminine ending if it does change, as with 'graduate'.

So many things depend on your knowing the correct gender of a French noun – whether you use 'il' or 'elle' to translate 'it'; the way you spell and pronounce certain adjectives; the changes you make to past participles, etc. If you are in any doubt as to the gender of a noun, it is always best to check it in your dictionary.

Adjectives

Adjectives are given in both their masculine and feminine forms, where these are different. The usual rule is to add an '-e' to the masculine form to make an adjective feminine, as with 'noir'.

In the English-French section, an adjective's feminine form or ending appears immediately after it in brackets, as with 'soft'.

Some adjectives have identical masculine and feminine forms. Where this occurs, there is no 'e' beside the basic masculine form.

Many French adjectives, however, do not follow the regular pattern. Where an adjective has an irregular feminine or plural form, this information is clearly provided in your dictionary, usually with the irregular form being given in full. Consider the entries for 'net' and 'sec'.

Adverbs

The normal 'rule' for forming adverbs in French is to add '-ment' to the feminine form of the adjective. Thus:

lent > lente > lentement

The '-ment' ending is often the equivalent of the English '-ly':

lentement   – slowly
sournoisement – slyly

Adjectives ending in '-ant' and '-ent' are slightly different:

courant   >   couramment
prudent   >   prudemment

In your dictionary some adverbs appear as a separate entry; others appear as subentries of adjective headwords; while others do not feature in the dictionary at all. Compare 'heureusement', 'froidement' and 'sournoisement'.

Where an adverb does not appear, this is usually because it is not a particularly common one. However, you should be able to work out a translation from the adjective once you have found that in the dictionary.

Information about verbs

A major problem facing language learners is that the form of a verb will change according to the subject and/or the tense being used. A typical French verb can take many different forms – too many to list in a dictionary entry.

Yet, although verbs are listed in your dictionary in their infinitive forms only, this does not mean that the dictionary is of limited value when it comes to handling the verb system of the French language. On the contrary, it contains much valuable information.

First of all, your dictionary will help you with the meanings of unfamiliar verbs. If you came across the word 'remplit' in a text and looked it up in your dictionary you wouldn't find it. You must deduce that it is part of a verb and look for the infinitive form. Thus you will see that 'remplit' is a form of the verb 'remplir'. You now have the basic meaning of the word you are concerned with – something to do with the English verb 'fill' – and this should be enough to help you understand the text you are reading.

It is usually an easy task to make the connection between the form of a verb and the infinitive. For example, 'remplissent', 'remplira', 'remplissons' and 'rempli' are all recognisable as parts of the infinitive 'remplir'. However, sometimes it is less obvious – for example, 'voyons', 'verrai' and 'vu' are all parts of 'voir'. The only real solution to this problem is to learn the various forms of the main French regular and irregular verbs.

And this is the second source of help offered by your dictionary. The verb tables on pages 633 to 634 of the Collins Pocket Dictionary provide a summary of some of the main forms of the main tenses of regular and irregular verbs. Consider the verb 'voir' below where the following information is given:

1	voyant	–	Present Participle
2	vu	–	Past Participle
3	vois, voyons, voient	–	Present Tense forms
4	voyais	–	1st Person Singular of the Imperfect Tense
5	verrai	–	1st Person Singular of the Future Tense
7	voie	–	1st Person Singular of the Present Subjunctive

The regular '-er' verb 'parler' is presented in greater detail. The main tenses and the different endings are given in full. This information can be transferred and applied to all verbs in the list. In addition, the main parts of the most common irregular verbs are listed in the body of the dictionary.

PARLER

1 parlant
2 parlé
3 parle, parles, parle, parlons, parlez, parlent
4 parlais, parlais, parlait, parlions, parliez, parlaient
5 parlerai, parleras, parlera, parlerons, parlerez, parleront
6 parlerais, parlerais, parlerait, parlerions, parleriez, parleraient
7 parle, parles, parle, parlions, parliez, parlent *impératif* parle!, parlez!

In order to make maximum use of the information contained in these pages, a good working knowledge of the various rules affecting French verbs is required. You will acquire this in the course of your French studies and your Collins dictionary will serve as a useful 'aide-mémoire'. If you happen to forget how to form the second person singular form of the Future Tense of 'voir' there will be no need to panic — your dictionary contains the information!

FRENCH VERB FORMS

1 Participe présent *2* Participe passé *3* Présent *4* Imparfait *5* Futur *6* Conditionnel *7* Subjonctif présent

acquérir *1* acquérant *2* acquis *3* acquiers, acquérons, acquièrent *4* acquérais *5* acquerrai *7* acquière

ALLER *1* allant *2* allé *3* vais, vas, va, allons, allez, vont *4* allais *5* irai *6* irais *7* aille

asseoir *1* asseyant *2* assis *3* assieds, asseyons, asseyez, asseyent *4* asseyais *5* assiérai *7* asseye

atteindre *1* atteignant *2* atteint *3* atteins, atteignons *4* atteignais *7* atteigne

AVOIR *1* ayant *2* eu *3* ai, as, a, avons, avez, ont *4* avais *5* aurai *6* aurais *7* aie, aies, ait, ayons, ayez, aient

battre *1* battant *2* battu *3* bats, bat, battons *4* battais *7* batte

boire *1* buvant *2* bu *3* bois, buvons, boivent *4* buvais *7* boive

bouillir *1* bouillant *2* bouilli *3* bous, bouillons *4* bouillais *7* bouille

conclure *1* concluant *2* conclu *3* conclus, concluons *4* concluais *7* conclue

conduire *1* conduisant *2* conduit *3* conduis, conduisons *4* conduisais *7* conduise

connaître *1* connaissant *2* connu *3* connais, connaît, connaissons *4* connaissais *7* connaisse

coudre *1* cousant *2* cousu *3* couds, cousons, cousez, cousent *4* cousais *7* couse

courir *1* courant *2* couru *3* cours, courons *4* courais *5* courrai *7* coure

couvrir *1* couvrant *2* couvert *3* couvre, couvrons *4* couvrais *7* couvre

craindre *1* craignant *2* craint *3* crains, craignons *4* craignais *7* craigne

croire *1* croyant *2* cru *3* crois, croyons, croient *4* croyais *7* croie

croître *1* croissant *2* crû, crue, crus, crues *3* croîs, croissons *4* croissais *7* croisse

cueillir *1* cueillant *2* cueilli *3* cueille, cueillons *4* cueillais *5* cueillerai *7* cueille

devoir *1* devant *2* dû, due, dus, dues *3* dois, devons, doivent *4* devais *5* devrai *7* doive

dire *1* disant *2* dit *3* dis, disons, dites, disent *4* disais *7* dise

dormir *1* dormant *2* dormi *3* dors, dormons *4* dormais *7* dorme

écrire *1* écrivant *2* écrit *3* écris, écrivons *4* écrivais *7* écrive

ÊTRE *1* étant *2* été *3* suis, es, est, sommes, êtes, sont *4* étais *5* serai *6* serais *7* sois, sois, soit, soyons, soyez, soient

FAIRE *1* faisant *2* fait *3* fais, fais, fait, faisons, faites, font *4* faisais *5* ferai *6* ferais *7* fasse

falloir *2* fallu *3* faut *4* fallait *5* faudra *7* faille

FINIR *1* finissant *2* fini *3* finis, finis, finit, finissons, finissez, finissent *4* finissais *5* finirai *6* finirais *7* finisse

fuir *1* fuyant *2* fui *3* fuis, fuyons, fuient *4* fuyais *7* fuie

joindre *1* joignant *2* joint *3* joins, joignons *4* joignais *7* joigne

lire *1* lisant *2* lu *3* lis, lisons *4* lisais *7* lise

luire *1* luisant *2* lui *3* luis, luisons *4* luisais *7* luise

maudire *1* maudissant *2* maudit *3* maudis, maudissons *4* maudissait *7* maudisse

mentir *1* mentant *2* menti *3* mens, mentons *4* mentais *7* mente

mettre *1* mettant *2* mis *3* mets, mettons *4* mettais *7* mette

mourir *1* mourant *2* mort *3* meurs, mourons, meurent *4* mourais *5* mourrai *7* meure

naître *1* naissant *2* né *3* nais, naît, naissons *4* naissais *7* naisse

offrir *1* offrant *2* offert *3* offre, offrons *4* offrais *7* offre

PARLER *1* parlant *2* parlé *3* parle, parles, parle, parlons, parlez, parlent *4* parlais, parlais, parlait, parlions, parliez, parlaient *5* parlerai, parleras, parlera, parlerons, parlerez, parleront *6* parlerais, parlerais, parlerait, parlerions, parleriez, parleraient *7* parle, parles, parle, parlions, parliez, parlent *impératif* parle, parlez

partir *1* partant *2* parti *3* pars, partons *4* partais *7* parte

plaire *1* plaisant *2* plu *3* plais, plaît, plaisons *4* plaisais *7* plaise

pleuvoir *1* pleuvant *2* plu *3* pleut, pleuvent *4* pleuvait *5* pleuvra *7* pleuve

pourvoir *1* pourvoyant *2* pourvu *3* pourvois, pourvoyons, pourvoient *4* pourvoyais *7* pourvoie

pouvoir *1* pouvant *2* pu *3* peux, peut, pouvons, peuvent *4* pouvais *5* pourrai *7* puisse

prendre *1* prenant *2* pris *3* prends, prenons, prennent *4* prenais *7* prenne

prévoir *comme voir* *5* prévoirai

RECEVOIR *1* recevant *2* reçu *3* reçois, reçois,

reçoit, recevons, recevez, reçoivent *4* recevais *5* recevrai *6* recevrais *7* reçoive

RENDRE *1* rendant *2* rendu *3* rends, rends, rend, rendons, rendez, rendent *4* rendais *5* rendrai *6* rendrais *7* rende

résoudre *1* résolvant *2* résolu *3* résous, résout, résolvons *4* résolvais *7* résolve

rire *1* riant *2* ri *3* ris, rions *4* riais *7* rie

savoir *1* sachant *2* su *3* sais, savons, savent *4* savais *5* saurai *7* sache *impératif* sache, sachons, sachez

servir *1* servant *2* servi *3* sers, servons *4* servais *7* serve

sortir *1* sortant *2* sorti *3* sors, sortons *4* sortais *7* sorte

souffrir *1* souffrant *2* souffert *3* souffre, souffrons *4* souffrais *7* souffre

suffire *1* suffisant *2* suffi *3* suffis, suffisons *4* suffisais *7* suffise

suivre *1* suivant *2* suivi *3* suis, suivons *4* suivais *7* suive

taire *1* taisant *2* tu *3* tais, taisons *4* taisais *7* taise

tenir *1* tenant *2* tenu *3* tiens, tenons, tiennent *4* tenais *5* tiendrai *7* tienne

vaincre *1* vainquant *2* vaincu *3* vaincs, vainc, vainquons *4* vainquais *7* vainque

valoir *1* valant *2* valu *3* vaux, vaut, valons *4* valais *5* vaudrai *7* vaille

venir *1* venant *2* venu *3* viens, venons, viennent *4* venais *5* viendrai *7* vienne

vivre *1* vivant *2* vécu *3* vis, vivons *4* vivais *7* vive

voir *1* voyant *2* vu *3* vois, voyons, voient *4* voyais *5* verrai *7* voie

vouloir *1* voulant *2* voulu *3* veux, veut, voulons, veulent *4* voulais *5* voudrai *7* veuille *impératif* veuillez

LE VERBE ANGLAIS

present	pt	pp	present	pt	pp
arise	arose	arisen	fall	fell	fallen
awake	awoke	awoken	feed	fed	fed
be (am, is, are; being)	was, were	been	feel	felt	felt
			fight	fought	fought
bear	bore	born(e)	find	found	found
beat	beat	beaten	flee	fled	fled
become	became	become	fling	flung	flung
begin	began	begun	fly (flies)	flew	flown
behold	beheld	beheld	forbid	forbade	forbidden
bend	bent	bent	forecast	forecast	forecast
beseech	besought	besought	forego	forewent	foregone
beset	beset	beset	foresee	foresaw	foreseen
bet	bet, betted	bet, betted	foretell	foretold	foretold
bid	bid, bade	bid, bidden	forget	forgot	forgotten
bind	bound	bound	forgive	forgave	forgiven
bite	bit	bitten	forsake	forsook	forsaken
bleed	bled	bled	freeze	froze	frozen
blow	blew	blown	get	got	got, (US) gotten
break	broke	broken			
breed	bred	bred	give	gave	given
bring	brought	brought	go (goes)	went	gone
build	built	built	grind	ground	ground
burn	burnt, burned	burnt, burned	grow	grew	grown
			hang	hung, hanged	hung, hanged
burst	burst	burst			
buy	bought	bought	have (has; having)	had	had
can	could	(been able)			
cast	cast	cast	hear	heard	heard
catch	caught	caught	hide	hid	hidden
choose	chose	chosen	hit	hit	hit
cling	clung	clung	hold	held	held
come	came	come	hurt	hurt	hurt
cost	cost	cost	keep	kept	kept
creep	crept	crept	kneel	knelt, kneeled	knelt, kneeled
cut	cut	cut			
deal	dealt	dealt	know	knew	known
dig	dug	dug	lay	laid	laid
do (3rd person: he/she/it does)	did	done	lead	led	led
			lean	leant, leaned	leant, leaned
draw	drew	drawn			
dream	dreamed, dreamt	dreamed, dreamt	leap	leapt, leaped	leapt, leaped
			learn	learnt, learned	learnt, learned
drink	drank	drunk			
drive	drove	driven	leave	left	left
dwell	dwelt	dwelt	lend	lent	lent
eat	ate	eaten	let	let	let

present	pt	pp	present	pt	pp
lie (lying)	lay	lain	speed	sped, speeded	sped, speeded
light	lit, lighted	lit, lighted			
lose	lost	lost	spell	spelt, spelled	spelt, spelled
make	made	made			
may	might	—	spend	spent	spent
mean	meant	meant	spill	spilt, spilled	spilt, spilled
meet	met	met			
mistake	mistook	mistaken	spin	spun	spun
mow	mowed	mown, mowed	spit	spat	spat
must	(had to)	(had to)	split	split	split
pay	paid	paid	spoil	spoiled, spoilt	spoiled, spoilt
put	put	put			
quit	quit, quitted	quit, quitted	spread	spread	spread
			spring	sprang	sprung
read	read	read	stand	stood	stood
rid	rid	rid	steal	stole	stolen
ride	rode	ridden	stick	stuck	stuck
ring	rang	rung	sting	stung	stung
rise	rose	risen	stink	stank	stunk
run	ran	run	stride	strode	stridden
saw	sawed	sawn	strike	struck	struck, stricken
say	said	said			
see	saw	seen	strive	strove	striven
seek	sought	sought	swear	swore	sworn
sell	sold	sold	sweep	swept	swept
send	sent	sent	swell	swelled	swollen, swelled
set	set	set			
shake	shook	shaken	swim	swam	swum
shall	should	—	swing	swung	swung
shear	sheared	shorn, sheared	take	took	taken
shed	shed	shed	teach	taught	taught
shine	shone	shone	tear	tore	torn
shoot	shot	shot	tell	told	told
show	showed	shown	think	thought	thought
shrink	shrank	shrunk	throw	threw	thrown
shut	shut	shut	thrust	thrust	thrust
sing	sang	sung	tread	trod	trodden
sink	sank	sunk	wake	woke	woken
sit	sat	sat	waylay	waylaid	waylaid
slay	slew	slain	wear	wore	worn
sleep	slept	slept	weave	wove, weaved	woven, weaved
slide	slid	slid			
sling	slung	slung	wed	wedded, wed	wedded, wed
slit	slit	slit			
smell	smelt, smelled	smelt, smelled	weep	wept	wept
			win	won	won
sow	sowed	sown, sowed	wind	wound	wound
speak	spoke	spoken	wring	wrung	wrung
			write	wrote	written

LES NOMBRES

NUMBERS

un(une)	1	one
deux	2	two
trois	3	three
quatre	4	four
cinq	5	five
six	6	six
sept	7	seven
huit	8	eight
neuf	9	nine
dix	10	ten
onze	11	eleven
douze	12	twelve
treize	13	thirteen
quatorze	14	fourteen
quinze	15	fifteen
seize	16	sixteen
dix-sept	17	seventeen
dix-huit	18	eighteen
dix-neuf	19	nineteen
vingt	20	twenty
vingt et un(une)	21	twenty-one
vingt-deux	22	twenty-two
trente	30	thirty
quarante	40	forty
cinquante	50	fifty
soixante	60	sixty
soixante-dix	70	seventy
soixante et onze	71	seventy-one
soixante-douze	72	seventy-two
quatre-vingts	80	eighty
quatre-vingt-un(-une)	81	eighty-one
quatre-vingt-dix	90	ninety
quatre-vingt-onze	91	ninety-one
cent	100	a hundred
cent un(une)	101	a hundred and one
trois cents	300	three hundred
trois cent un(une)	301	three hundred and one
mille	1 000	a thousand
un million	1 000 000	a million

premier (première), 1er	first, 1st
deuxième, 2e *or* 2ème	second, 2nd
troisième, 3e *or* 3ème	third, 3rd
quatrième	fourth, 4th
cinquième	fifth, 5th
sixième	sixth, 6th
septième	seventh

LES NOMBRES

NUMBERS

huitième	eighth
neuvième	ninth
dixième	tenth
onzième	eleventh
douzième	twelfth
treizième	thirteenth
quatorzième	fourteenth
quinzième	fifteenth
seizième	sixteenth
dix-septième	seventeenth
dix-huitième	eighteenth
dix-neuvième	nineteenth
vingtième	twentieth
vingt-et-unième	twenty-first
vingt-deuxième	twenty-second
trentième	thirtieth
centième	hundredth
cent-unième	hundred-and-first
millième	thousandth

Les Fractions etc

Fractions etc

un demi	a half
un tiers	a third
deux tiers	two thirds
un quart	a quarter
un cinquième	a fifth
zéro virgule cinq, 0,5	(nought) point five, 0.5
trois virgule quatre, 3,4	three point four, 3.4
dix pour cent	ten per cent
cent pour cent	a hundred per cent

Exemples

Examples

il habite au dix	he lives at number 10
c'est au chapitre sept	it's in chapter 7
à la page sept	on page 7
il habite au septième (étage)	he lives on the 7th floor
il est arrivé (le) septième	he came in 7th
une part d'un septième	a share of one seventh
échelle au vingt-cinq millième	scale one to twenty-five thousand

THE TIME

heure est-il?   *what time is it?*

...   *it's ...*

it   midnight, twelve p.m.
eure (du matin)   one o'clock (in the morning), one (a.m.)
eure cinq   five past one
eure dix   ten past one
eure et quart   a quarter past one, one fifteen
eure vingt-cinq   twenty-five past one, one twenty-five
eure et demie, une heure trente   half past one, one thirty
eure trente-cinq, deux heures ins vingt-cinq   twenty-five to two, one thirty-five
heures moins vingt, une heure rante   twenty to two, one forty
heures moins le quart, une heure rante-cinq   a quarter to two, one forty-five
heures moins dix, une heure quante   ten to two, one fifty

     twelve o'clock, midday, noon
heures (de l'après-midi)   two o'clock (in the afternoon), two (p.m.)
heures (du soir)   seven o'clock (in the evening), seven (p.m.)

lle heure?   *at what time?*

uit   at midnight
t heures   at seven o'clock

vingt minutes   in twenty minutes
quinze minutes   fifteen minutes ago

L'HEURE	THE TIME
quelle heure est-il?	*what time is it?*
il est ...	*it's ...*
minuit	midnight, twelve p.m.
une heure (du matin)	one o'clock (in the morning), one (a.m.)
une heure cinq	five past one
une heure dix	ten past one
une heure et quart	a quarter past one, one fifteen
une heure vingt-cinq	twenty-five past one, one twenty-five
une heure et demie, une heure trente	half past one, one thirty
une heure trente-cinq, deux heures moins vingt-cinq	twenty-five to two, one thirty-five
deux heures moins vingt, une heure quarante	twenty to two, one forty
deux heures moins le quart, une heure quarante-cinq	a quarter to two, one forty-five
deux heures moins dix, une heure cinquante	ten to two, one fifty
midi	twelve o'clock, midday, noon
deux heures (de l'après-midi)	two o'clock (in the afternoon), two (p.m.)
sept heures (du soir)	seven o'clock (in the evening), seven (p.m.)
à quelle heure?	*at what time?*
à minuit	at midnight
à sept heures	at seven o'clock
dans vingt minutes	in twenty minutes
il y a quinze minutes	fifteen minutes ago

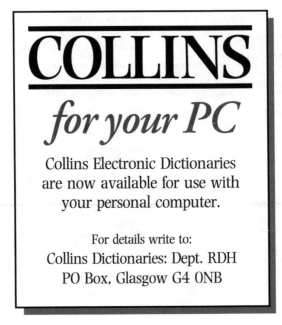